Pro Football Prospectus 2007

THE ESSENTIAL GUIDE TO THE 2007 PRO FOOTBALL SEASON

Aaron Schatz

with

Ben Alamar · Jim Armstrong · Bill Barnwell · Maury Brown
Alex Carnevale · Will Carroll · Doug Farrar · Vin Gauri
Tim Gerheim · Shawn Krest · Russell Levine · David Lewin
Ned Macey · Jason McKinley · Bill Moore · Michael David Smith
Mike Tanier · Ryan Wilson

A PLUME BOOK

PLUME
Published by Penguin Group
Penguin Group (USA) Inc., 375 Hudson Street, New York, New York 10014, U.S.A.
Penguin Group (Canada), 90 Eglinton Avenue East, Suite 700, Toronto, Ontario, Canada M4P 2Y3 (a division of Pearson Penguin Canada Inc.)
Penguin Books Ltd., 80 Strand, London WC2R 0RL, England
Penguin Ireland, 25 St. Stephen's Green, Dublin 2, Ireland (a division of Penguin Books Ltd.)
Penguin Group (Australia), 250 Camberwell Road, Camberwell, Victoria 3124, Australia (a division of Pearson Australia Group Pty. Ltd.)
Penguin Books India Pvt. Ltd., 11 Community Centre, Panchsheel Park, New Delhi – 110 017, India
Penguin Group (NZ), 67 Apollo Drive, Mairangi Bay, Auckland 1311, New Zealand (a division of Pearson New Zealand Ltd.)
Penguin Books (South Africa) (Pty.) Ltd., 24 Sturdee Avenue, Rosebank, Johannesburg 2196, South Africa

Penguin Books Ltd., Registered Offices: 80 Strand, London WC2R 0RL, England

First published by Plume, a member of Penguin Group (USA) Inc.

First Printing (2007 edition), July 2007
10 9 8 7 6 5 4 3 2 1

 REGISTERED TRADEMARK—MARCA REGISTRADA

Library of congress cataloging-in-publication data is available.

Printed in the United States of America
Set in Utopia and Univers Condensed
Designed by Pen & Palette Unlimited

Contents

Teams — National Football Conference

Skill Players

Fantasy Football

Introduction

Aaron Schatz

31. 155. 4.38. 100.

Over the past 25 years, advanced statistical analysis has spread throughout the world of baseball, all the way from the fans to the front offices. It's starting to happen in basketball as well, spreading from grassroots websites such as 82games.com and into management with stat-oriented executives such as Daryl Morey, of Houston.

According to conventional wisdom, football is not like baseball or basketball. No one football player can control the game the way a dominant player can in basketball or a dominant pitcher can in baseball. The 11 men on the field work in tandem, and their complex interactions cannot be measured with numbers. Advanced statistical analysis in football? The predominant belief is that, when it comes to the NFL, numbers won't make your argument.

Is that true? Each of the numbers above has meaning, and each one was part of an important football decision. LaDainian Tomlinson's record-setting total of 31 touchdowns made him the overwhelming choice for the Most Valuable Player of 2006. DeMeco Ryans was second in the NFL with 155 tackles, a big reason why he won Defensive Rookie of the Year. Ted Ginn was drafted ahead of bigger receivers with better pass-catching skills because he posted a 4.38 time in the 40-yard dash during a private workout for NFL scouts. Finally, 100 is the golden number of running yardage, the magical break point after which, according to sportswriters and television analysts, a running back suddenly gives his team a much bigger chance of winning the game.

Everybody who likes to talk about the NFL uses both stats and scouting to make a point. That includes sportswriters, general managers, head coaches, agents, color commentators, and the fans drinking beer at the sports bar down the street.

There's a stereotype that sportswriters who use advanced statistics are trying to replace scouting by boiling everything down to emotionless numbers. This is, of course, ridiculous. Like everyone else, the writers of this book analyze the NFL with both our eyes and our stats. The only difference is that we've worked hard to dramatically improve the "stats" side of that equation, both on our website, FootballOutsiders.com, and in three editions of *Pro Football Prospectus*, the latest of which you hold in your hands.

Football statistics are heavily dependent on context. Down and distance, field position, the current score, time left on the clock, the quality of the opponent—all of these elements influence the objective of the play and/or its outcome. Yet, conventional statistics will add together all yardage gained by a specific team or player without considering the impact of that particular yardage on wins and losses.

Many of our statistics attempt to tease out these context-dependent effects. If all teams are compared on a level playing field, we can get as close as possible to figuring out which teams are most likely to win games in the future. We also attempt to filter out the effects of luck and random chance. A close football game can turn on a single bounce of the ball. In a season of only 16 games, those effects can have a huge impact on a team's win-loss record, thus obscuring the team's true talent level, which is a better indicator of how well the team will play for the rest of the season or even in the following season.

If we want to know how to build a Super Bowl champion and which teams are going to win the most games next season, we also have to figure out a way to evaluate the players at positions that aren't measured by standard statistics. That's why we created our game charting project, which, for two years now, has used a crew of volunteers to track things that the league's official statisticians do not: pass coverage by defensive backs, blown blocks by offensive linemen, yards after catch, and performance when using various strategies such as blitzing or play-action.

We've used these resulting stats to forecast the NFL with more accuracy than anyone else in print or on the Web. King Kaufman of Salon.com tracks the picks of every preseason magazine, every ESPN and *Sports Illustrated* commentator, and many websites, and over the past three years, no group or person has correctly forecast more playoff teams than the writers of this book, first on our website and then in the first two editions of *Pro Football Prospectus*.

Despite our work to gather more information, we still must deal with the fact that not everything on a football field is accurately measured. Some people will argue that if we can't measure everything, there's no point in measuring anything. We disagree. The motto of Football Outsiders has always been that the best is the enemy of the better. The fact that we cannot develop perfect analysis is not a reason to give up on better analysis. When there are holes in our numbers, we fill them in with the knowledge we gather with our eyes, just like everyone else who writes about the NFL.

Critics argue that it is impossible to make forecasts based on a limited sample size of 16 games. Certainly, our powers of prediction have been tested by two straight Super Bowl runs without precedent. The 2005 Pittsburgh Steelers are the only sixth seed ever to advance to the Super Bowl, much less win it. The 2006 Indianapolis Colts are the only team ever to finish last in the league in run defense and advance to the Super Bowl, much less win it.

Of course, in every sport, using the past to predict the future will result in failure when something unprecedented takes place. Before the 2004 Boston Red Sox, no team in baseball history had come back from a 3–0 deficit to win a seven-game playoff series. Before the 2006–2007 Golden State Warriors, no eighth seed in NBA history had ever won a seven-game playoff series after a full 82-game season.

The general feel of our work will be familiar to those who also read our partners at Baseball Prospectus. For new readers, we've included an essay called "Pregame Show," which introduces the most important research that we've done in our first two books and our first three years online. In "Statistical Toolbox," we present our new statistics, what they mean, and how they are derived. We also have an essay on the greatest running back seasons in NFL history, inspired by the great numbers LaDainian Tomlinson put up a year ago. Consider that an appetizer before we get into the main course of 32 team chapters.

Each team chapter features an essay that covers what happened in 2006 and what that team's prospects are for the upcoming season. Are there reasons to believe that the team was actually better or worse than its record last year? What did the team do in the offseason, and what does that mean for the team's chances to win in 2007? Many chapters also include a second essay that features primary research on a subject related to the team. Then come statistics for each team's weekly performance in 2006, the statistical record for the past five years, and individual offensive and defensive numbers. New for this year are pass coverage statistics for linebackers as well as hits and hurries, expanding our knowledge of pass-rushers past the use of just sacks (those new numbers are explained further near the end of the book, in an essay called "Beyond Sacks").

We also present some unique numbers that examine team strategies. How often does this team run or pass? How often does the offense like to run play-action or use specific formations? How aggressive is the pass rush, and how aggressive is the head coach on fourth down? This year, for the first time, we've supplemented these numbers with comments that shed light on each team's tendencies, strengths, and weaknesses. The team chapters end with commentary on each of the major units of the team: offensive line, defensive

front seven, defensive secondary, special teams, and coaching staff.

You'll notice the phrase "skill players" missing from that paragraph. That is because skill players get their own section in the back of the book. We list the major players at each position alphabetically, along with commentary and a 2007 KUBIAK projection that will help you win your fantasy football league. Finally, there is a series of longer research essays on various topics in the back of the book. We explore play-action and two-point conversion strategies, update last year's groundbreaking system for projecting college quarterbacks, and review league-wide issues such as concussive brain trauma and the decisions of the competition committee. We finish up with our first-ever Top 25 Prospects list, made up not of the best college players, but of the best young players sitting on NFL benches, waiting to explode into stardom.

Of course, we couldn't call ourselves Prospectus if we didn't also offer a website that provides nonstop coverage as the drama of the 2007 season unfolds. If you enjoy this book, we invite you to visit FootballOutsiders.com. Each week, you'll find updated DVOA and DPAR ratings as well as regular columns on a variety of subjects, including game-tape analysis, fantasy football advice, an in-depth breakdown of the upset of the week, and commentary on college football—an area into which we are hoping to expand in 2007. All of these columns will continue to be free of charge, and each one features a discussion thread with the kind of intelligent conversation about the game that you won't find at a site where readers spell *rules* with five *z*'s at the end.

Speaking of expansion, 2007 will also introduce the Football Outsiders premium stat database, giving our readers a chance to see 11 years of DVOA ratings split in numerous ways: by year, by quarter, or by down, for example. We've made improvements to our downloadable spreadsheet of KUBIAK fantasy football projections, which are customizable to your league's rules and updated constantly based on preseason news, and we've also made game charting data from both 2005 and 2006 available to anyone who wants to research their favorite team.

Whether you randomly picked up *Pro Football Prospectus* in your local bookstore, had it recommended to you by a friend, or have been reading Football Outsiders since the days of dual scrolling windows and the "Homage to TMQ" contest, we hope you enjoy the next 500 pages as much as we enjoyed writing and researching them. If you learn more about your favorite team, gain a new appreciation for the game, and win your fantasy football league, we've done our job. Bring on the opening kickoff.

Aaron Schatz
Framingham, MA
May 31, 2007

Pregame Show

Aaron Schatz

This is the third edition of *Pro Football Prospectus*, and our website, FootballOutsiders.com, has been online for four seasons. During that time, we've done a lot of primary research on the National Football League, and we reference that research in many of the articles and comments in *Pro Football Prospectus 2007*.

New readers may come across an offhand comment in a team chapter about, for example, the idea that fumble recovery is not a skill, and wonder what in the heck we are talking about. We can't repeat all our research in every new edition of the book, so we wanted to start this year's *Pro Football Prospectus* with a basic look at some of the most important precepts that have emerged during four years of Football Outsiders research. You will see these issues come up again and again throughout the book.

You can also find this introduction online at http://www.footballoutsiders.com/pregame.php, along with links to the original research in the cases in which that research appeared online instead of (or as well as) in print.

You run when you win, not win when you run.

If we could share only one piece of anti-conventional wisdom with you before you read the rest of our book, this would be it. The first article ever written for Football Outsiders was devoted to debunking the myth of "establishing the run." There is no correlation whatsoever between giving your running backs a lot of carries early in the game and winning the game. Just running the ball is not going to help a team score; it has to run successfully.

There are two reasons why nearly every beat writer and television analyst still repeats the tired old-school mantra that "establishing the run" is the secret to winning football games. The first problem is confusing cause and effect. There are exceptions—usually involving the Indianapolis Colts without Bob Sanders—but, in general, winning teams have a lot of carries because their running backs are running out the clock at the end of wins, not because they are running wild early in games.

The second problem is history. Most of the current crop of NFL analysts came of age or actually played the game during the 1970s. They believe that the run-heavy game of that decade is how football is meant to be, and today's pass-first game is an aberration. As we addressed in an essay in last year's book on the history of NFL stats, it was actually the game of the 1970s that was the aberration. The seventies were far more slanted toward the run than any era since the arrival of Paul Brown, Otto Graham, and the Cleveland Browns in 1946. Optimal strategies from 1974 are not optimal strategies for 2007.

A sister statement to "you have to establish the run" is "team X is 5–1 when running back John Doe runs for at least 100 yards." Unless John Doe is ripping off six-yard gains LaDainian Tomlinson–style, the team isn't winning because of his 100-yard games. He's putting up 100-yard games because his team is winning.

A great defense against the run is nothing without a good pass defense.

This is a corollary to the absurdity of "establish the run." If you don't believe us, meet our good friends the 2006 Minnesota Vikings. With rare exceptions, teams win or lose with the passing game more than the running game—and by stopping the passing game more than the running game. The reason why teams need a strong run defense in the playoffs is not to shut the run down early, it's to keep the other team from icing the clock if they get a lead. You can't mount a comeback if you can't stop the run.

One person who is willing to buck conventional wisdom when it comes to the primacy of the passing game is the new analyst for *Monday Night Football*, Ron Jaworski. As he often says, "the pass gives you the lead, and the run solidifies it."

Note that "good pass defense" may mean "good pass rush" rather than "good defensive backs."

Running on 3rd-and-short is more likely to convert than passing on 3rd-and-short.

On average, passing will always gain more yardage than running, with one very important exception: when a team is just one or two yards away from a new set of downs or the goal line. On 3rd-and-1, a run will convert for a new set of downs 36 percent more often than a pass. Expand that to all third or fourth downs with 1–2 yards to go, and the run is successful 40 percent more often. With these percentages, the possibility of a long gain with a pass is not worth the tradeoff of an incomplete that kills a drive.

This is one reason why teams have to be able to both run and pass. The offense also has to keep some semblance of balance so they can use their play-action fakes, and so the defense doesn't just run their nickel-and-dime packages all game. Balance also means that teams do need to pass occasionally in short-yardage situations; they just need to do it less than they do now. Teams pass roughly 60 percent of the time on 3rd-and-2 even though runs in that situation convert 20 percent more often than passes. They pass 68 percent of the time on 4th-and-2 even though runs in that situation convert twice as often as passes.

Standard team rankings based on total yardage are inherently flawed.

When you open your newspaper on Sunday morning, you'll see that the little agate-type previews of each game list team rankings by total yardage. That is still how the NFL "officially" ranks teams, but these rankings rarely match up with common sense. That is because total team yardage may be the most context-dependent number in football.

It starts with the basic concept that rate stats are generally more valuable than cumulative stats. Yards per carry says more about a running back's quality than total yardage; completion percentage says more than just a quarterback's total number of completions. The same thing is true for teams; in fact, it is even more important because of the way football strategy influences the number of runs and passes in the game plan. Poor teams will give up fewer passing yards and more rushing yards because opponents will stop passing once they have a late-game lead and will run out the clock instead. For winning teams, the opposite is true. Did Detroit really have a better passing game than San Diego or New England last year, or did the Lions have more passing yards because they went 3–13 and thus threw the ball more than any team except for Green Bay, while the Chargers and Patriots were a combined 26–6 and spent a lot of time killing the clock with the running game?

Total yardage rankings are also skewed because some teams play at a faster pace than other teams. New Orleans had nearly 200 more passing yards than Indianapolis last year, but were the Saints really a better offense than the Colts? The Saints ran 183 offensive drives, while the Colts had just 148. No other team in the league had fewer than 160 offensive drives. If you gave Peyton Manning another 35 drives, he would probably rack up more than 200 passing yards.

A team will score more when playing a bad defense and will give up more points when playing a good offense.

This sounds absurdly basic, but when people consider team and player stats without looking at strength of schedule, they are ignoring this. In 2004, Carson Palmer and Byron Leftwich had very similar numbers, but Palmer faced a much tougher schedule than Leftwich did. Palmer was better that year and better in the long run. Last year,

Travis Henry had four games of 120 rushing yards or more, and all four came against defenses that ranked 24th or worse in yards per carry allowed.

The 2007 Sugar Bowl was also a good example of conventional wisdom ignoring the importance of opponent quality. Most observers came out of that game saying that JaMarcus Russell was a better pro prospect than Brady Quinn, ignoring the fact that the LSU defense (5.2 passing yards per attempt in 2006) was far superior to the Notre Dame defense (7.8 passing yards per attempt in 2006).

Because players and teams don't give the exact same performance every week, this is more of a general law, and it doesn't necessarily apply in the short term. Sometimes the short term lasts 16 games, which is an issue addressed in the Jacksonville chapter.

If their overall yards per carry are equal, a running back who consistently gains yardage on every play is more valuable than a boom-and-bust running back who is frequently stuffed at the line but occasionally breaks a long highlight-worthy run.

Our brethren at Baseball Prospectus believe that the most precious commodity in baseball is outs. Teams only get 27 of them per game, and you can't afford to give one up for very little return. So imagine if there was a new rule in baseball that gave a team a way to earn another three outs in the middle of the inning. That would be pretty useful, right?

That's the way football works. You may start a drive 80 yards away from scoring, but as long as you can earn ten yards in four chances, you get another four chances. Long gains have plenty of value, but if those long gains are mixed with a lot of short gains, you are going to put the quarterback in a lot of difficult 3rd-and-long situations. That means more punts and more giving the ball back to the other team rather than moving the chains and giving the offense four more plays to work with.

The running back who gains consistent yardage is also going to do a lot more for you late in the game, when the goal of running the ball is not just to gain yardage but to eat clock time. If you are a Carolina Panthers fan watching your team with a late lead, you don't want to see three straight DeShaun Foster stuffs at the line followed by a punt. You want to see a game-icing first down.

A common historical misconception is that our preference for consistent running backs means that "Football Outsiders believes that Barry Sanders was overrated." Sanders wasn't just any boom-and-bust running back, though; he was the greatest boom-and-bust runner of all time, with bigger booms and fewer busts. Our DVOA stats only go back to 1996, but Sanders led the league in rushing DPAR for 1996 and was second behind Terrell Davis in 1997. Sanders also figures quite prominently in the chapter "The Greatest Running Back Seasons of All Time."

Rushing is more dependent on the offensive line than people realize, but pass protection is more dependent on the quarterback himself than people realize.

The first half of this sentence is easily summed up by eight words: Edgerrin James, Arizona Cardinals, three yards per carry.

Some readers complain that this idea contradicts the previous one. Aren't those consistent running backs just the product of good offensive lines? The truth is somewhere in between. There are certainly good running backs, such as James in 2006, who suffer because their offensive lines cannot create consistent holes. Most boom-and-bust running backs, however, contribute to their own problems by hesitating behind the line whenever the hole is unclear, looking for the home run instead of charging forward for the four-yard gain that keeps the offense moving.

As for pass protection, some quarterbacks have better instincts for the rush than others and are thus better at getting out of trouble by moving around in the pocket or throwing the ball away. Others will hesitate, hold on to the ball too long, and lose yardage over and over.

Note that "moving around in the pocket" does not necessarily mean "scrambling." In fact, a scrambling quarterback will often take more sacks than a pocket quarterback, because while he's running around trying to make something happen, a defensive lineman will catch up with him.

The 2006 Dallas Cowboys embodied this precept, both in terms of pass protection and in terms of run blocking. The Cowboys started the same offensive line in all 16 games of the regular season. Drew Bledsoe was sacked once every 11.6 dropbacks, while the more mobile Tony Romo was sacked once every 17.0 dropbacks. Boom-or-bust starting running back Julius Jones had a 45 percent success rate, 30th in the NFL, while the more consistent Marion Barber had a 56 percent success rate, which ranked fourth.

A running back with 370 or more carries during the regular season will usually suffer either a major injury or a loss of effectiveness the following year, unless he is named Eric Dickerson.

Terrell Davis, Jamal Anderson, and Edgerrin James all blew out their knees. Earl Campbell, Jamal Lewis, and Eddie George went from legendary powerhouses to plodding, replacement-level players. Shaun Alexander struggled with foot injuries, and Curtis Martin had to retire. This is what happens when a running back is overworked to the point of having at least 370 carries during the regular season.

The "Curse of 370" was expanded last year and now includes seasons with 390 or more carries in the regular season and postseason combined. Research in last year's book showed that receptions don't cause a problem, only workload on the ground.

Plenty of running backs get injured without hitting 370 carries in a season, but there is a clear difference. On average, running backs with 300 to 369 carries and no postseason appearance will see their total rushing yardage decline by 15 percent the following year and their yards per carry decline by two percent. The average running back with 370 or more regular-season carries, or 390 including the postseason, will see their rushing yardage decline by 35 percent and their yards per carry decline by eight percent.

Wide receivers must be judged on both complete and incomplete passes.

We don't yet know enough to precisely parse the blame for incomplete passes, but we know that wide receiver catch rates are as consistent from year to year as quarterback completion percentages. From 2001 to 2005, Hines Ward caught more than 60 percent of intended passes every year, whether from Kordell Stewart, Tommy Maddox, or Ben Roethlisberger. Plaxico Burress, playing with the same quarterbacks as well as Eli Manning, has never caught more than 60 percent of intended passes.

The total quality of an NFL team is three parts offense, three parts defense, and one part special teams.

There are three units on a football team, but they are not of equal importance. Our DVOA ratings provide good evidence for this. The special teams ratings are turned into DVOA by looking at how often field position on special teams leads to scoring compared to field position and first downs on offense. After figuring out these numbers, the top ratings for special teams are roughly one-third as high as the top ratings for offense or defense.

Offense is more consistent from year to year than defense, and offensive performance is easier to project than defensive performance. Special teams is less consistent than either.

Nobody in the NFL understands this concept better than Indianapolis Colts general manager Bill Polian. Both the Super Bowl champion Colts and the four-time AFC champion Buffalo Bills of the early 1990s were built around the idea that if you put together an offense that can dominate the league year after year, eventually you will luck into a year in which good health and a few smart decisions will give you a defense good enough to win a championship. (As the Colts learned a few months ago, you don't even need a year, just four weeks.) Even the New England Patriots, who are led by a defense-first head coach in Bill Belichick, have been more consistent on offense than on defense since they began their run of success in 2001.

Recovery of a fumble, despite being the product of hard work, is almost entirely random.

Stripping the ball is a skill. Holding on to the ball is a skill. Pouncing on the ball as it is bouncing all over the place is not a skill. There is no correlation whatsoever between the percentage of fumbles recovered by a team in one year and the percentage they recover in the next year. The odds of recovery are based solely on the type of play involved, not the teams or any of their players.

Fans like to insist that specific coaches can teach their teams to recover more fumbles by swarming to the ball. Chicago's Lovie Smith, in particular, is supposed to have this ability. The NFC Champion Bears forced 24 fumbles on defense and recovered 16 of them, one of the highest percentages in the league.

But where were Smith's powers a year earlier, when the Bears forced 21 fumbles on defense and recovered just seven, the worst percentage in the league? The 2004 Bears recovered 13 of 17 fumbles on defense, meaning that in three years, their recovery rate went from a league-best 76 percent to a league-worst 33 percent and then back to 67 percent.

Fumble recovery is equally erratic on offense. The 2005 Oakland Raiders fumbled 20 times but recovered 13 of them, the best percentage in the league. The 2006 Raiders fumbled 30 times and recovered just nine of them, one of the worst percentages in the league.

Fumble recovery is a major reason why the general public overestimates or underestimates certain teams. Fumbles are huge, turning-point plays that dramatically impact wins and losses in the past, while fumble recovery percentage says absolutely nothing about a team's chances of winning games in the future. With this in mind, Football Outsiders stats treat all fumbles as equal, penalizing them based on the likelihood of each type of fumble (run, pass, sack, etc.) being recovered by the defense.

Other plays that qualify as "non-predictive events" include blocked kicks and touchdowns during turnover returns. These plays are not "lucky," per se, but they have no value whatsoever for predicting future performance.

Field position is fluid.

As discussed in the Statistical Toolbox, every yard line on the field has a value based on how likely a team is to score from that location on the field as opposed to from a yard farther back. The change in value from one yard to the next is the same whether the team has the ball or not. The goal of a defense is not just to prevent scoring, but to hold the opposition so that the offense can get the ball back in the best possible field position. A bad offense will score as many points as a good offense if it starts each drive five yards closer to the goal line.

Last year, San Diego and St. Louis both averaged 32.2 yards per drive on offense. They ran roughly the same number of drives, excluding kneeldowns (181 for St. Louis, 179 for San Diego). How did the Chargers score 125 more points than the Rams? With far superior defense and special teams, the Chargers began their average drive on the 31.6-yard line. The Rams began their average drive on the 28.1-yard line.

A corollary to this precept: The most underrated aspect of an NFL team's performance is the field position gained or lost on kickoffs and punts.

Teams that are strong on first and second down but weak on third down, will tend to improve the following year. Teams that are weak on first and second down but strong on third down will tend to decline the following year.

We discovered this when creating our first team projection system in 2004. It said that the lowly San Diego Chargers would have one of the best offenses in the league, which seemed a little ridiculous. But looking closer, our projection system treated the previous year's performance on different downs as different variables, and the 2003 Chargers were actually good on first and second down but terrible on third.

Teams get fewer opportunities on third down, so third-down performance is more volatile—but it's also a bigger part of a team's overall performance than first or second down, because the result is usually either very good (four more downs) or very bad (losing the ball to the other team with a punt). Over time, a team will play as well in those situations as it does in other situations, which will bring the overall offense or defense in line with the offense and defense on first and second down.

This trend is even stronger between seasons. Struggles on third down are a pretty obvious problem, and teams will generally target their offseason moves at improving their third-down performance . . . which often leads to an improvement in third-down performance.

The third-down issue is particularly important this year, because it is the main driver behind our surprisingly positive projection for the Washington Redskins. In the 11 years for which we have DVOA numbers, only the 2000 Vikings had a worse defense on third down, and no team had a worse pass defense on third down. Only one thing can keep this team from a dramatic rebound. . . .

By and large, a team built on depth is better than a team built on stars and scrubs.

The Redskins went into last year with a Super Bowl–quality starting lineup and finished 5–11 because they had no depth. You cannot concentrate your salaries on a handful of star players, because there is no such thing as avoiding injuries in the NFL. Every team will suffer injuries; the only question is how many. The game is too fast and the players too strong to build a team based around the idea that "if we can avoid all injuries this year, we'll win."

Running backs usually decline after age 28, tight ends after age 29, wide receivers after age 30, and quarterbacks after age 32.

This research was originally done by Doug Drinen of foot-ballguys.com in 2000. In recent years, a few players have had huge seasons above these general age limits (for example, Tiki Barber, Tony Gonzalez, and Corey Dillon), but the peak ages Drinen found a few years ago still apply to the majority of players.

This summer, *ESPN The Magazine* asked us to research when players decline at "non-skill" positions. This research was not as rigorous as our usual work and needs a little more attention before we're ready to stand by it. For the curious, however, the preliminary results said that defensive ends and defensive backs generally begin to decline after age 29, linebackers and offensive linemen after age 30, and defensive tackles after age 31.

Championship teams are generally defined by their ability to dominate inferior opponents, not their ability to win close games.

Football games are often decided by just one or two plays— a missed field goal, a bouncing fumble, the subjective spot of an official on 4th-and-1. One missed assignment by a cornerback, or one slightly askew pass that bounces off a receiver's hands and into those of a defensive back five yards away, and the game could be over. In a blowout, however, one lucky bounce isn't going to change things.

Championship teams beat their good opponents convincingly and destroy the cupcakes on the schedule. Certainly there are exceptions to this rule, including the 2006 Colts. The fact that the most recent Super Bowl champion is an exception to the rule, however, does not mean the rule will no longer exist.

Statistical Toolbox

Aaron Schatz

Two years ago, *Pro Football Prospectus* introduced a number of new statistics unlike any that had been used to measure the National Football League in the past. Over the past two years we've improved the accuracy of those statistics and introduced some new ones, in particular a number of metrics that would not be possible without the Football Outsiders game charting project, which is explained later in this introduction. Our statistical palette contains a wide variety of colors with which to paint a picture of the NFL. What follows is an explanation of all the statistics you'll find in this book: how we calculate them, what the numbers mean, and what they tell us about why teams win or lose football games. We've done our best to present these numbers in a way that makes them easy to understand. This explanation is long, so feel free to read some of it, flip around the rest of the book, and then come back. It will still be here.

Veteran readers of FootballOutsiders.com and *Pro Football Prospectus* will be familiar with most of these stats but should make note of the following: the introduction of the "fantasy risk" factor, the rearrangement and expansion of the individual defensive player tables, and some small changes that have been made to the special teams and strategic tendencies tables.

Defense-Adjusted Value Over Average (DVOA)

One running back runs for three yards. Another running back runs for three yards. Which is the better run?

This sounds like a stupid question, but it isn't. In fact, this question is at the heart of nearly all of the analysis in this book.

Several factors can differentiate one three-yard run from another. What is the down and distance? Is it 3rd-and-2 or 2nd-and-15? Where on the field is the ball? Does the player get only three yards because he hits the goal line and scores? Is the player's team up by two touchdowns in the fourth quarter and thus running out the clock, or down by two touchdowns and thus facing a defense that is playing purely against the pass? Is the running back playing against the porous defense of the Jets or the stalwart defense of the Giants?

Conventional NFL statistics value plays based solely on their net yardage. The NFL determines the best players by adding up all their yards no matter what situations they came in or how many plays it took to get them. Now, why would they do that? Football has one objective—to get to the end zone—and two ways to achieve that, by gaining yards and achieving first downs. These two goals need to be balanced to determine a player's value or a team's performance. All the yards in the world won't help a team win if they all come in eight-yard chunks on 3rd-and-10.

The popularity of fantasy football only exacerbates the problem. Fans have gotten used to judging players based on how much they help fantasy teams win and lose, not how much they help *real* teams win and lose. Typical fantasy scoring further skews things by counting the yard between the one and the goal line as 61 times more important than all the other yards on the field (each yard worth 0.1 points, a touchdown worth 6). Let's say Anquan Boldin catches a pass on 3rd-and-15 and goes 50 yards but gets tackled two yards from the goal line, and then Edgerrin James takes the ball on 1st-and-goal from the two-yard line and plunges in for the score. Has Edgerrin James done something special? Not really. When an offense gets the ball on 1st-and-goal at the two-yard line, they are going to score a touchdown five out of six times. Edge is getting credit for the work done by the passing game.

Doing a better job of distributing credit for scoring points and winning games is the goal of **DVOA,** or Defense-adjusted Value Over Average. DVOA breaks down every single play of the NFL season, assigning each play a value based on both total yards and yards toward a first down, based on work done by Pete Palmer, Bob Carroll, and John Thorn in their seminal book, *The Hidden Game of Football.* On first down, a play is considered a success if it gains 45 percent of needed yards; on second down, a play needs to gain 60 percent of needed yards; on third or fourth down, only gaining a new first down is considered a success.

We then expand upon that basic idea with a more complicated system of "success points," improved over the past four years with a lot of mathematics and a bit of trial and error. A successful play is worth one point; an unsuccessful play, zero points with fractional points in between (for example, eight yards on 3rd-and-10 is worth 0.54 "success points"). Extra points are awarded for big plays, gradually increasing to three points for ten yards (assuming those yards result in a first down), four points for 20 yards, and five points for 40 yards or more. Losing three or more yards is –1 point, an interception is –8 points, and a fumble is worth anywhere from –2.15 to –6.54 points depending on how often a fumble in that situation is lost to the defense—no matter who actually recovers the fumble. Red zone plays are worth 20 percent more, and there is a bonus given for a touchdown acknowledging that the goal line is significantly more difficult to cross than the previous 99 yards (this bonus is nowhere near as large as the one used in fantasy football).

(Our system is a bit more complex than the one in *Hidden Game* thanks to our subsequent research, which added a larger penalty for turnovers, the fractional points, and a slightly higher baseline for success on first down. The reason why all fumbles are counted, whether they are recovered by the offense or defense, is that fumble recovery is random, as explained in the essay "Pregame Show.")

Every single play run in the NFL gets a "success value" based on this system, and then that number gets compared with the average success values of plays in similar situations for all players, adjusted for a number of variables. These include down and distance, field location, time remaining in game, and the team's lead or deficit in the game score. Teams are always compared with the overall offensive average, as the team made its own choice whether to pass or rush. When it comes to individual players, however, rushing plays are compared with other rushing plays, passing plays with other passing plays, tight ends with tight ends, and wideouts with wideouts.

Going back to our example of the three-yard rush, if Player A gains three yards under a set of circumstances in which the average NFL running back gains only one yard, then Player A has a certain amount of value above others at his position. Likewise, if Player B gains three yards on a play on which, under similar circumstances, an average NFL back gains four yards, that Player B has negative value relative to others at his position. Once we make all our adjustments, we can evaluate the difference between this player's rate of success and the expected success rate of an average running back in the same situation (or between the opposing defense and the average defense in the same situation, etc.). Add up every play by a certain team or player, divide by the total of the various baselines for success in all those situations, and you get VOA, or Value Over Average.

Of course, the biggest variable in football is the fact that each team plays a different schedule against teams of disparate quality. By adjusting each play based on the opposing defense's average success in stopping that type of play over the course of a season, we get DVOA. Rushing and passing plays are adjusted based on down and location on the field; passing plays are also adjusted based on how the defense performs against passes to running backs, tight ends, or wide receivers. Defenses are adjusted based on the average success of the *offenses* they are facing. (Yes, technically the defensive stats are actually "offense-adjusted." If it seems weird, think of the "D" in "DVOA" as standing for "opponent-Dependent" or something.)

The biggest advantage of DVOA is the ability to break teams and players down to find strengths and weaknesses in a variety of situations. In the aggregate, DVOA may not be quite as accurate as some of the other, similar "power ratings" formulas based on comparing drives rather than individual plays, but unlike those other ratings, DVOA can be separated not only by player but also by down, by week, or by distance needed for a first down. This can give us a better idea of not just which team is better, but why, and what a team has to do in order to improve itself in the future. You will find DVOA used in this book in a lot of different ways—because it takes every single play into account, it can be used to measure a player or a team's performance in any situation. All Minnesota third downs can be compared with how an average team does on third down. Byron Leftwich and David Garrard can each be compared with how an average quarterback performs in the red zone, or with a lead, or in the second half of the game.

Since DVOA compares each play only with plays with similar circumstances, it gives a more accurate picture of how much better a team really is compared with the league as a whole. The list of top DVOA offenses on third down, for example, is more accurate than the conventional NFL conversion statistic because it takes into account that converting 3rd-and-long is more difficult than converting 3rd-and-short, and that a turnover is worse than an incomplete pass because it eliminates the opportunity to move the other team back with a punt on fourth down.

One of the hardest parts of understanding a new statistic is interpreting its scale, or what numbers represent good performance or bad performance. We've made that easy with DVOA. In all cases, 0% represents league average. A positive DVOA represents a situation that favors the offense, while a negative DVOA represents a situation that favors the defense. This is why the best offenses have positive DVOA ratings (Indianapolis: +33.8%) and the best defenses have negative DVOA ratings (Baltimore: –25.6%). For both teams and starting players, the best and worst ratings tend to be around +/–30%. Because league average is determined across multiple years, no single year will average exactly 0%. This gives DVOA the added benefit of being able to show us how the scoring environment has fluctuated from year to year. Last year was the "most average" season in the last decade, with a league average of 0.2%. The NFL's offensive level was higher in 2002 and 2004, and lower in 2003 and 2005.

Team DVOA totals combine offense and defense by subtracting the latter from the former because the better defenses will have negative DVOAs. (Special teams performance is also added, as described later in this essay.)

Does it work? Using correlation coefficients, we can show that only actual points scored are better than DVOA at indicating how many games a team has won (table 1), and DVOA does a better job of predicting wins in the coming season than either wins or points scored in the previous season (table 2).

Table 1. Correlation of Various Stats to Wins, 2000–2006

Stat	Offense	Defense	Total
Points Scored/Allowed	.72	−.68	.92
DVOA	.66	−.53	.86
Yards Gained/Allowed	.51	−.41	.65
Yards Gained/Allowed per Play	.48	−.32	.66

Table 2. Correlation of Various Stats to Wins Following Year, 2000–2005

Stat	Correlation
DVOA	.32
Point Differential	.27
Yards per Play Differential	.26
Wins	.25
Yardage Differential	.22

(Correlation coefficient is a statistical tool that measures how two variables are related by using a number between 1 and −1. The closer to −1 or 1, the stronger the relationship, but the closer to 0, the weaker the relationship.)

Defense-Adjusted Points Above Replacement (DPAR)

After using DVOA for a few months, we came across a strange phenomenon: Well-regarded players, particularly those known for their durability, had DVOA ratings that came out around average. The reason is that DVOA, by virtue of being a percentage or rate statistic, doesn't take into account the cumulative value of having a player producing at a league-average level over the course of an above-average number of plays. By definition, an average level of performance is better than that provided by half of

the league, and the ability to maintain that level of performance while carrying a heavy workload is very valuable indeed. In addition, a player who is involved in a high number of plays can draw the defense's attention away from other parts of the offense, and if that player is a running back, he can take time off the clock with repeated runs.

Let's say you have a running back who carries the ball 300 times in a season. What would happen if you were to remove this player from his team's offense? What would happen to those 300 plays? Those plays don't disappear with the player, though some might be lost to the defense because of the associated loss of first downs. Rather, those plays would have to be distributed among the remaining players in the offense, with the bulk of them being given to a replacement running back. This is where we arrive at the concept of replacement level, borrowed from our partners at Baseball Prospectus. When a player is removed from an offense, he is usually not replaced by a player of similar ability. Nearly every starting player in the NFL is a starter because he is better than the alternative. Those 300 plays will typically be given to a significantly worse player, someone who is the backup because he doesn't have as much experience and/or talent. A player's true value can then be measured by the level of performance he provides above that replacement-level baseline.

Using a scale similar to the one Baseball Prospectus uses to determine baseball's replacement level, we've determined that a replacement-level offensive player has a DVOA of roughly −13.3%. Thus, instead of determining value by comparing each play's "success value" with the average, as in DVOA, DPAR compares each play with a number roughly 13.3% below the average success value of similar plays. That gives us value over a replacement-level player, a better representation of a player's total contribution to his team on all his plays.

We say "roughly" −13.3% because replacement level is actually different for each position depending on whether we are measuring passing, rushing, or receiving. Of course, the *real* replacement player is different for each team in the NFL. The second-string running back in Dallas (Marion Barber) had a much higher DVOA than the first-string back (Julius Jones). Damon Huard sat on the bench behind Trent Green for years, but when he finally entered the lineup, he put up the second-highest passing DVOA in the NFL. On other teams, the drop from the starter to the backup can be even greater than the general drop to replacement level. Imagine if Peyton Manning broke his leg, for example. The choice to start an inferior player or to employ a sub-replacement level backup, however, falls to the team, not the starter being evaluated. Thus we generalize replacement level for the league as a whole, as the ultimate goal is to evaluate players independent of the quality of their teammates.

Once again, the challenge of any new stat is to present it on a scale that's meaningful to those attempting to use it. Saying that Carson Palmer was worth 108.2 success value points over replacement in 2006 has very little value without a context to tell us if 108.2 is good total or a bad one. What we've done to fix this problem is translate those success value points into a number that represents actual points scored. After working through statistics from the past five seasons, our best approximation is that a team made up entirely of replacement-level players would be outscored 407 to 260 and finish with a 4–12 record. Conveniently, this is close to the average record of the last four expansion teams. What's missing is that part of the reason this team gives up so many more points than it scores is that it has replacement-level special teams. Those replacement-level special teams are worth −27 points. If we divide those points evenly between the offense and the defense, we establish a 274-point baseline for determining offensive value, and a 394-point baseline for defensive value.

With a bit of math, it works out that each success value point over replacement level is worth about .48 actual points above this offensive baseline, a number that is further adjusted for the strength of the opponents each player has faced. The end result is that we can say that Peyton Manning was worth 175 points more than a replacement-level quarterback in 2006, or 175.0 DPAR. By comparison, Tom Brady was worth 75.9 DPAR, Jason Campbell was worth 14.8 DPAR, and so on.

Problems with DVOA and DPAR

Football is a game in which nearly every action requires the work of two or more teammates—in fact, usually 11 teammates all working in unison. Unfortunately, when it comes to individual player ratings, we are still far from the point at which we can determine the value of a player independent of the performance of his teammates. That means that when we say, "In 2006, Edgerrin James had a DVOA of −11.4%," what we are really saying is "In 2006, Edgerrin James, playing in the Arizona offensive system with the Arizona offensive line blocking for him and Matt Leinart selling the fake when necessary, had a DVOA of −11.4%." James is the best example of the fact that DVOA cannot filter out team context. In 2005, playing in the Indianapolis offensive system with the Indianapolis offensive line blocking for him, he had a DVOA of 16.0%.

DVOA is limited by what's included in the official NFL play-by-play or tracked by the Football Outsiders game charting project (introduced below). Because we need to have the entire play-by-play of a season in order to compute DVOA and DPAR, these metrics are not yet ready to compare players of today with players throughout the league's history. As of this writing, we have processed 11 seasons, 1996 to 2006. (The first year for NFL play-by-play on the Internet was 1996, so going back further will require massive amounts of research and mind-numbing data entry. We hope to do it anyway.)

Special Teams

The problem with a system based on measuring both yardage and yardage toward a first down is what to do with plays that don't have the possibility of a first down. Special teams are an important part of football and we needed a way to add that performance to the team DVOA rankings. Our special teams metric includes five separate measurements: field goals and extra points, net punting, punt returns, net kickoffs, and kick returns.

The foundation of most of these special teams ratings is the concept that each yard line has a different value based on the likelihood of scoring from that position on the field. In *Hidden Game*, the authors suggested that each additional yard for the offense had equal value, with a team's own goal line being worth −2 points, the 50-yard line 2 points, and the opposing goal line 6 points. (−2 points is not only the value of a safety but also reflects the fact that when a team is backed up in its own territory, it is likely that its drive will stall, forcing a punt that will give the ball to the other team in good field position. Thus, the negative point value reflects the fact that the defense is more likely to score next.)

Our studies have updated this concept to reflect the actual likelihood that the offense or defense will have the next score from a given position on the field based on actual results from the past four seasons. The line that represents the value of field position is not straight, but curved, with the value of each yard increasing as teams approach either goal line (figure 1).

Figure 1. Value of Field Position 2002–2006

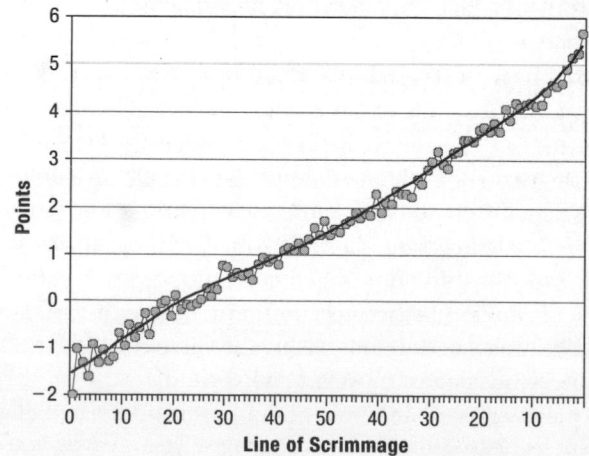

Our special teams ratings compare each kick or punt with league average based on the point value of the position of the kick, catch, and return. We've determined a league average for how far a kick goes based on the line of scrimmage for each kick (almost always the 30-yard line for kickoffs, variable for punts) and a league average for how far a return goes based on both the yard line where the ball is caught and the distance that it traveled in the air.

The kicking or punting team is rated based on net points compared with average, taking into account both the kick and the return if there is one. Because the average return is always positive, punts that are not returnable (touchbacks, out of bounds, fair catches, and punts downed by the coverage unit) will rate higher than punts of the same distance that are returnable. (This is also true of touchbacks on kickoffs.) There are also separate individual ratings for kickers and punters that are based on distance and whether the kick is returnable, assuming an average return in order to judge the kicker separate from the coverage.

For the return team, the rating is based on how many points the return is worth compared with average, based on the location of the catch and the distance the ball traveled in the air. Return teams are not judged on the distance of kicks, nor are they judged on kicks that cannot be returned. As explained below, blocked kicks are so rare as to be statistically insignificant as predictors for future performance and are thus ignored. For the kicking team they simply count as missed field goals; for the defense they are gathered with their opponents' other missed field goals in Hidden value (also explained below).

Field goal kicking is measured differently. Measuring kickers by field goal percentage is a bit absurd, as it assumes that all field goals are of equal difficulty. In our metric, each field goal is compared with the average number of points scored on all field goal attempts from that distance over the past decade, with adjustments for rule changes such as the introduction of the special-teams-use-only "k-ball" in 1999. The value of a field goal increases as distance from the goal line increases. Kickoffs, punts, and field goals are then adjusted based on weather and altitude. It will surprise no one to learn that it is easier to kick the ball in Denver or a dome than it is to kick the ball in Buffalo in December. Because we do not yet have enough data to tailor our adjustments specifically to each stadium, each one is assigned to one of four categories: Cold, Warm, Dome, and Denver. There is also an additional adjustment dropping the value of field goals in Florida (because the warm temperatures allow the ball to carry better) and raising the value of punts in San Francisco (because of those infamous winds).

Once we've totaled how many points above or below average can be attributed to special teams, we translate those points into DVOA so the ratings can be added to offense and defense to get total team DVOA.

There are three aspects of special teams that have an impact on wins and losses but don't show up in the standard special teams rating, because a team has little or no influence on them. The first is the length of kickoffs by the opposing team. The other two are field goals against your team and punt distance against your team. Research shows no indication that teams can influence the accuracy or strength of field-goal kickers and punters, except for blocks. As mentioned above, although blocked field goals and punts are definitely skillful plays, they are so rare that they have no correlation to how well teams have played in the past or will play in the future; thus they are included here as if they were any other missed field goal or botched punt, giving the defense no additional credit for their efforts. In a new addition to our special teams tables this year, the value of these three elements is listed separately as "Hidden" value.

Special teams ratings also do not include two-point conversions or onside kick attempts, both of which, like blocks, are so infrequent as to be statistically insignificant in judging future performance.

Pythagorean Projection

The Pythagorean projection is an approximation of each team's wins based solely on their points scored and allowed. This basic concept was introduced by baseball analyst Bill James, who discovered that the record of a baseball team could be very closely approximated by taking the square of team runs scored and dividing it by the sum of the squares of team runs scored and allowed. Statistician Daryl Morey later extended this theorem to professional football, refining the exponent to 2.37 rather than 2.

Pythagorean projections have done a remarkable job of projecting Super Bowl champions. Of the 19 Super Bowls played since the 1987 strike season, 11 were won by the team that led the NFL in Pythagorean wins, but only seven were won by the team with the most actual victories. Super Bowl champions that led the league in Pythagorean wins but not actual wins include the 2004 Patriots, 2000 Ravens, 1999 Rams, and 1997 Broncos. Last year was an exception to this general trend; in fact, the 2006 Indianapolis Colts had fewer Pythagorean wins (9.6) than any Super Bowl champion in history, which we discuss in further detail in the Indianapolis chapter.

Teams that win a minimum of one full game more than their Pythagorean projection tend to regress the following year; teams that win a minimum of one full game less than their Pythagorean projection tend to improve the following year, particularly if they were at or above .500

despite their underachieving. The 2005 San Diego Chargers, for example, went 9–7 with 10.7 Pythagorean wins, then improved to 14–2 the next year. In the upcoming season, this trend favors Pittsburgh, Cincinnati, and Jacksonville, all of whom went 8–8 with at least 9.0 Pythagorean wins in 2006. Jacksonville fans have particular cause for optimism as the 1989 Cincinnati Bengals were the only .500 team in NFL history to have more Pythagorean wins than the 2006 Jaguars.

Adjusted Line Yards

One of the most difficult goals of statistical analysis in football is isolating the degree to which each of the 22 men on the field is responsible for the result of a given play. Nowhere is this as significant as in the running game, in which one player runs while up to nine other players—including wideouts, tight ends, and a fullback—block in different directions. None of the statistics we use for measuring rushing—yards, touchdowns, yards per carry—differentiate between the contribution of the running back and the contribution of the offensive line. Neither do our advanced metrics DVOA and DPAR.

We do, however, have enough play-by-play data amassed that we can try to separate the effect that the running back has on a particular play from the effects of the offensive line (and other offensive blockers) and the opposing defense. A team might have two running backs in its stable: RB A, who averages 3.0 yards per carry, and RB B, who averages 3.5 yards per carry. Who is the better back? Imagine that RB A doesn't just average 3.0 yards per carry, but gets exactly 3 yards on every single carry, while RB B has a highly variable yardage output: sometimes 5 yards, sometimes –2 yards, sometimes 20 yards. The difference in variability between the runners can be exploited to determine not only the difference between the runners, but the effect the offensive line has on every running play.

At some point in every long running play, the running back passes all of his offensive line blocks as well as additional blocking backs or receivers. From there on, the rest of the play is dependent on the runner's own speed and elusiveness and the speed and tackling ability of the opposing defense. If Frank Gore breaks through the line for 50 yards, avoiding tackles all the way to the goal line, his offensive line has done a great job—but they aren't responsible for the majority of the yards gained. The trick is figuring out exactly how much they *are* responsible for.

For each running back carry, we calculated the probability that the back involved would run for the specific yardage on that play based on that back's average yardage per carry and the variability of their yardage from play to play. We also calculated the probability that the offense would get the yardage based on the team's rushing average and variability using all backs *other* than the one involved in the given play, and the probability that the defense would give up the specific amount of yardage based on its average rushing yards allowed per carry and variability. For example, based on his rushing average and variability, the probability in 2004 that Tiki Barber would have a positive carry was 80 percent, while the probability that the Giants would have a positive carry without Barber running was only 73 percent.

A regression analysis breaks the value for rushing yardage into the following categories: losses, 0–4 yards, 5–10 yards, and 11+ yards. In general, the offensive line is 20 percent more responsible for lost yardage than it is for positive gains up to four yards, but it's 50 percent less responsible for additional yardage gained between five and ten yards, and not at all responsible for additional yardage past ten yards.

By applying those percentages to every running back carry, we were able to create **Adjusted Line Yards,** a statistic that measured offensive line performance. (We don't include carries by receivers, which are usually based on deception rather than straight blocking, or carries by quarterbacks, which are almost always busted passing plays unless they involve Michael Vick or Vince Young.) Those numbers are then adjusted based on down, distance, and situation, as well as opponent (similar to DVOA), and then normalized so that the league average for Adjusted Line Yards per carry is the same as the league average for RB yards per carry (in 2006, 4.19 yards).

The NFL distinguishes between runs made to seven different locations on the line: left/right end, left/right tackle, left/right guard, and middle. Further research showed no statistically significant difference between how well a team performed on runs listed as having gone up the middle or past a guard, so we separated runs into just five different directions (left/right end, left/right tackle, and middle). Note that there may not be a statistically significant difference between right tackle and middle/guard either, but pending further research (and for the sake of symmetry) we still list runs behind the right tackle separately. These splits allow us to evaluate subsections of a team's offensive line, but not necessarily individual linesmen, as we can't account for blocking assignments or guards who pull toward the opposite side of the line after the snap.

Success Rate

Success rate is a statistic for running backs that measures how consistently they achieve the yardage necessary for a play to be deemed successful. Some running backs will mix a few long runs with a lot of failed runs of one or two yards, while others with similar yards-per-carry averages will consistently gain five yards on first down, or as many yards as necessary on third down. This statistic helps us differentiate between the two.

Since Success Rate compares rush attempts with other rush attempts without consideration of passing, the standard for success on first down is slightly lower than those described above for DVOA. In addition, the standard for success changes slightly in the fourth quarter when running backs are used to run out the clock. A team with the lead is satisfied with a shorter run as long as it stays in bounds. Conversely, for a team down by a couple of touchdowns in the fourth quarter, four yards on first down isn't going to be a big help.

The formula for Success Rate is as follows:

- A successful play must gain 40 percent of needed yards on first down, 60 percent of needed yards on second down, and 100 percent of needed yards on third or fourth down.

- If the offense is behind by more than a touchdown in the fourth quarter, the benchmarks switch to 50%/65%/100%.

- If the offense is ahead by any amount in the fourth quarter, the benchmarks switch to 30%/50%/100%.

The league-average Success Rate in 2006 was 45.7 percent. Success Rate is not adjusted based on defenses faced. Success Rates are not calculated for quarterbacks and wide receivers who occasionally carry the ball.

Similarity Scores

Similarity scores were first introduced by Bill James to compare baseball players with other baseball players from the past. It was only natural that the idea would spread to other sports as statistical analysis spread to other sports. NBA analyst John Hollinger has created his own version to compare basketball players, and we have created our own version to compare football players.

Similarity scores have a lot of uses, and we aren't the only football analysts who use them. Doug Drinen, of the website Footballguys.com, has his own system that is specific to comparing fantasy football performances. The major goal of our similarity scores is to compare career progressions to try to determine when players have a higher chance of a breakout, a decline, or—due to age or usage—an injury (much like Baseball Prospectus's PECOTA player projection system). Therefore we compare not only numbers such as attempts, yards, and touchdowns but also age and experience. We often are looking not for players who had similar seasons, but for players who had similar two- or three-year spans in their careers.

Similarity scores have some important weaknesses. The database for player comparison begins in 1978, the year the 16-game season began and passing rules were liberalized (a reasonable starting point to measure the "modern" NFL); thus the method only compares standard statistics such as yards and attempts, which are of course subject to all kinds of biases from strength of schedule to quality of receiver corps. For our comparisons, we project full-season statistics for the strike years of 1982 and 1987, although we cannot correct for players who crossed the 1987 picket line to play more than 12 games.

If you are interested in the specific computations behind our similarity scores system, we have listed the standards for each position online at www.footballout siders.com/stats/similarity.php.

KUBIAK Projection System

Most "skill position" players whom we expect to play a role this season receive a projection of their standard 2007 NFL statistics using the KUBIAK projection system. KUBIAK takes into account a number of different factors including expected role, performance over the past two seasons, age, height, weight, historical comparables, and projected team performance on offense and defense. When we named our system KUBIAK, it was a play on the PECOTA system used by our partners at Baseball Prospectus—if they were going to name their system after a long-time eighties backup, we would name our system after a long-time eighties backup. Little did we know that Gary Kubiak would finally get a head coaching job the very next season. After some debate, we decided to keep the name, although discussing projections for Houston players can be a bit awkward.

To clear up a common misconception among our readers, KUBIAK projects individual player performances only, not team performances.

2007 Win Projection System

In this book, each of the 32 NFL teams receives a **2007 Mean Projection** at the beginning of its chapter. These projections stem from three equations that forecast 2007 DVOA for offense, defense, and special teams based on a number of different factors including the previous two years of DVOA in various situations, improvement in the second half of 2006, recent draft history, coaching experience, and the combined tenure of the offensive line. This year's improvements to the projection system include variables based on penalties and injuries during the previous season, offensive and defensive pace (game clock seconds per play), and specific coaching styles. A new variable based on the number of home games helps to correct for the 2005 New Orleans Saints (and penalizes the 2007

Miami Dolphins, who only play seven games at home because of their midseason "home" game in London). Compared with last year's model, the standard error is now 10 percent smaller on offense, 15 percent smaller on defense, and seven percent smaller on special teams.

These three equations produce precise numbers representing the most likely outcome, and they also produce a range of possibilities. This is particularly important when projecting football teams, because with only 16 games in a season, a team's performance may vary wildly from its actual talent level due to a couple of random bounces of the ball or badly timed injuries. In addition, the economic structure of the NFL allows teams to make sudden jumps or drops in overall ability more often than in other sports.

Right now, we're projecting the New England Patriots to have the best offense in football, but there are a number of scenarios in which the Patriots' offense is average or even worse. Tom Brady could be injured. Laurence Maroney's shoulder injury could prove to be worse than anyone thought. Randy Moss could poison team chemistry. The Patriots might have bad luck on third-down conversions. The range of possibilities produced by the equations can be used to determine the probability of each possible offensive, defensive, and special teams DVOA for each team.

To project wins, Dr. Benjamin Alamar created a simulation that plays out the entire schedule for each team using random draws of DVOA for each team's offense, defense, and special teams to calculate a final score for each game in each season. The values and frequencies of these DVOA ratings are based on the projection equations described above. This game-by-game simulation also accounts for home-field advantage, warm-weather or dome-stadium teams playing in the cold after November 1, and several other variables that can affect the outcome of each game. We ran the simulation 10,000 times, producing 10,000 unique seasons representing the full range of possibilities for each team in 2007. We then compared the results to the historical probability that a certain win total would be achieved in a 16-game NFL season, adjusting the simulation to produce a more realistic number of 16, 15, 1 and 0-win seasons, as these are historically very low probability.

The resulting possible win totals are then separated into five categories:

- The Brohm Closet (0–4 wins)
- Bad Team (5–6 wins)
- Mediocre (7–8 wins)
- Playoff Contender (9–10 wins)
- Super Bowl Contender (11+ wins)

In previous two years, the 0–4 win category was called "Leinart Land" and "Quest for Quinn." Here's hoping we've done a better job of naming it after the actual number-one pick this year; if not, we've doomed the Louisville Cardinals.

From 2000 to 2006, the projection system explains roughly 56 percent of the change in each team's win total between seasons. That percentage does shift from year to year, because 32 teams isn't a particularly large sample size. Last year was a particularly tough year to project, with the system explaining only 40 percent of the variance in win totals. In 2005, it explained 61 percent of the variance in win totals.

Unlike last year, the 2007 projection system forecasts some major changes in the NFL standings. Washington, Pittsburgh, and Jacksonville are among the teams projected to improve significantly this year. Kansas City and Super Bowl runner-up Chicago are among the teams projected to decline. On first glance, it also looks as though we are projecting a decline for the Super Bowl champion Colts, but as the Colts' chapter explains, that's not quite true. We're actually projecting Indianapolis to be the exact same team they were in the 2006 regular season—as opposed to the team they were in January and February 2007.

The percentage given for each category is dependent not only on how good we project the team to be in 2007, but on the level of variation possible in that projection, and the expected performance of the teams on the schedule. Each variable has a different impact on the variability of the projection. For example, offenses that were better through the air in 2006 have more variation in their 2007 projections than offenses that were better on the ground. Defensive improvement in the second half of last season leads to less variation in this year's projection, while a rookie kicker or punter leads to more variation.

In response to reader requests, we also list the mean projection for each team. We do not expect any teams to win the exact number of games in their mean projection, however—particularly since no team can win 0.8 of a game. (Unfortunately, Herman Edwards believes he can win 0.8 of a game—*if we would just let him run Larry Johnson another ten times!*)

Drive Stats

In a statistical appendix at the back of the book you'll find drive stats for the last three years, compiled by Jim Armstrong. These are occasionally referred to throughout the book. Drive stats are computed from NFL Drive Charts and are not adjusted for strength of schedule or situation. Take-a-knee drives at the end of a half are discarded.

These stats are generally self-explanatory, giving each team's total number of drives as well as average yards per drive, points per drive, touchdowns per drive, punts per drive, plays per drive, and turnovers per drive. **LOS/Drive** represents average starting field position (line of scrimmage) per drive from the offensive point of view. Drive stats are given for offense and defense, with **NET** representing simply offense minus defense.

Football Outsiders Game Charting Project

Each of the formulas listed above relies primarily on the play-by-play data published by the NFL. When we began to analyze the NFL, that was all that we had to work with. Just as a television broadcast has a color commentator who gives more detail to the facts related by the play-by-play announcer, so too we need some color commentary to provide contextual information that breathes life into these plain lines of numbers and text. The Football Outsiders Game Charting Project is our attempt to provide color for the simple play-by-play.

Providing color to 512 hours of football is a daunting task. To put it into perspective, there were more than 54,000 lines of play-by-play information in the 2006 NFL season and our goal is to add several layers of detail to nearly all of them. We recruited more than 50 volunteers to collectively chart each week's NFL games. Unfortunately, we do not have access to the coaches' film the NFL provides to the 32 teams. That tape includes sideline and end zone perspectives for each play and shows all 22 players at all times. Only NFL teams and NFL Films are allowed to have access to the film, and the only place it is ever shown to the public is on NFL Network or ESPN's *NFL Matchup*. Anyone who has watched *Matchup* knows the benefit of watching coaches' film. It is easy to see the type of coverage being run and the cause and effect of certain actions taken on the field; the end zone perspective enables the identification of individual linemen.

Without access to coaches' film, we had to chart games using regular broadcast footage. Broadcast footage is not as definitive, but it served our purposes. In the end, we have data on nearly every play from the past two NFL seasons.[1] A handful of plays is missing due to technical difficulties—for example, many games were charted using Direct TV Short Cuts, which would occasionally skip a play to fit the 30-minute window.

Through trial and error during the first few weeks of charting in 2005, we have narrowed our focus to things both traceable and definitive. We are limited by the camera angles on standard television broadcasts and the time constraints of our volunteers. Charting a game and rewinding to make sure mistakes are minimized can take two to three hours. More than a couple of these per week can be hazardous to one's marriage. Our goal was to provide comprehensive information while understanding that our charters were doing this on a volunteer basis.

We want to emphasize that all data from the charting project is unofficial. (For this reason, we will usually mention the charting project when using this data in comments later in the book.) Other sources for football statistics may keep their own measurements of yards after catch or how teams perform against the blitz. Our data will not necessarily match theirs. However, any other group that is publicly tracking this data is also working off the same television broadcast footage and thus will run into the same issues of difficulty. No one outside the league can get official game film from the NFL.

The Football Outsiders game charting project tracks the following information:

Formation

For each play, charters recorded the number of running backs, wide receivers, and tight ends. The formation was recorded in the moment prior to the snap. Therefore, it does not include any pre-snap motion. Formations have become more fluid in recent years, so these numbers should not be considered gospel. Because television cameras do not always show player numbers, we told our game charters to mark formations based on appearance, not personnel. It can be hard to tell where to draw the distinction between an H-back and an offset fullback, or between a flex tight end and a slot receiver. We did not want a hard and fast rule that any tight end standing up off the line becomes a slot receiver, because that's not the way defensive coordinators think when they send in their personnel in response.

Rushers and Blockers

Blitz is a rather ubiquitous word in football, and a standard definition is difficult to nail down. Rather than asking charters to determine when a team was blitzing, we asked them to record the number of blockers and rushers on passing plays. Counting rushers was easy, but counting blockers proved to be an art as much as a science. Offenses base their blocking schemes on how many rushers they expect. A running back's or tight end's assignment may depend on

---

1. Unlike in 2005, charting data for 2006 includes Week 17. However, due to taping errors, a handful of games is still missing from our data: the first half of Dallas at Carolina from Week 8, most of Minnesota at Green Bay from Week 16, the second half of the Giants at Washington from Week 17, and all of Jacksonville–Kansas City and Carolina–New Orleans from Week 17. If you can provide tape for one of these games, please e-mail charting@footballoutsiders.com.

how many pass-rushers cross the line at the snap. Therefore, an offensive player was deemed to be a blocker if he engaged in an actual block, or if there was some hesitation before running a route. A running back that immediately heads out into the flat is not a blocker, but one that waits to verify that the blocking scheme is working and then goes out to the flat would, in fact, be considered a blocker.

Quarterback Action

In passing situations, the charters recorded the movement of the quarterback. This consisted of three items:

- Marking plays that began with a play-action fake.
- Marking when the quarterback left the pocket. Charters marked rollouts and bootlegs. (A rollout has the quarterback moving behind his blockers, while a bootleg has the quarterback moving one way and his blockers the other, usually in connection with a play-action fake.) Charters also marked when a quarterback run past the line of scrimmage was a sneak, a draw, or a scramble. We asked the charters to differentiate between designed runs and plays on which the quarterback originally intended to pass, although this is often a judgment call.
- Marking a defender with a "hurry" if he clearly caused the quarterback to rush his motion or leave the pocket after originally setting up in the pocket to throw. If the quarterback stood tall and delivered the pass with defenders in his face, this was not a hurry. Charters were allowed to list two names if necessary and could also attribute a hurry to Overall Pressure or list a play as a Coverage Scramble when the quarterback wasn't under pressure but ran because there were no open receivers. Hurries are discussed further at the end of the book, in an essay called "Beyond Sacks."

Pass Details

We divided all pass yardage into two numbers: distance in the air and yards after catch. You will see much of this information throughout the team chapters and in each of the individual player tables. Distance in the air was based on the distance from the line of scrimmage to the place where the receiver either caught or was supposed to catch the pass. We did not count how far the quarterback was behind the line or horizontal yardage if the quarterback threw across the field. All touchdowns were counted to the goal line, so that distance in the air added to yards after catch always equals the official yardage total kept by the league. Charters also tracked whether a pass went in one of five directions: left or right sideline (from the sideline to the numbers), left or right (from the numbers to the hash marks), or middle (within the hash marks).

Charters also marked screen passes and tried to differentiate between passes to running backs that were standard pass routes, swing passes, or dumpoffs.

Defenders

The NFL play-by-play lists tackles and, occasionally, tipped balls, but it does not definitively list the defender on the play. Charters were asked to determine which defender was primarily responsible for covering either the receiver at the time of the throw or the location to which the pass was thrown, regardless of whether the pass was complete.

Every defense in the league plays zone coverage—some more than others, which leaves us with the question of how to handle plays without a clear man assigned to that receiver. We gave charters three alternatives:

- In 2006, for the first time, we asked charters to mark passes that found the holes in zone coverage as Hole in Zone, rather than straining to assign that pass to an individual defender. We asked the charter also to note the player who appeared to be responsible for that zone, and these defenders are assigned half credit for those passes. Some holes were so large that no defender could be listed along with the Hole in Zone designation.
- Another change from our first year of charting was to allow charters to list two defenders instead of one. This could be used for actual double coverage, or for zone coverage in which the receiver was right between two close defenders rather than sitting in a gaping hole. When two defenders are listed, ratings assign each with half credit.
- Screen passes and dumpoffs are marked as Uncovered unless a defender (normally a linebacker) is obviously shadowing that specific receiver on the other side of the line of scrimmage.

Since we began the charting project two years ago, nothing has changed our analysis more than this information on pass coverage. However, we want to be up-front: It was often the most difficult information to chart. Broadcast camera angles often do not show the setup of the secondary, making it impossible to identify before the play if there is man coverage. On passes longer than a few yards, the camera won't show the receiver until the pass is in the air. The sideline view of network cameras makes seeing the specific numbers on some jerseys difficult. (At this point, we would like to give a big shout-out to all the defensive backs with dreadlocks that come out of their helmets, making them easier to identify.) Zone coverage makes things twice as difficult. That being said, reviewing tape kept mistakes to a minimum, and if two cornerbacks might have been confused for one other once or twice, such mistakes tend to cancel out.

Incomplete Passes

Quarterbacks are evaluated based on their ability to complete passes. However, not all incompletes should have the same weight. Throwing a ball away to avoid a sack is actually a valuable incomplete, and a receiver dropping an otherwise quality pass is hardly a reflection on the quarterback. Therefore, our charters marked the reason for every incomplete pass. Possible entries included Overthrown, Underthrown, Thrown Away, Tipped/Batted at Line, Hit in Motion (indicating the quarterback was hit as his arm was coming forward to make a pass), Defensed, Dropped, and a few others. Defensed was listed when the pass was incomplete as the direct result of actions by the defender. That action can include balls tipped or batted in coverage or hard hits that jar a ball loose.

(Our count of passes defensed will be different from the unofficial totals kept by the league, as explained later in the section on Defensive Secondary tables.)

Additional Details

Charters marked each quarterback sack with one of the following terms: Blown Block, Coverage Sack, QB Fault, or Blitz/Overall Pressure. Blown Blocks were listed with the name of a specific offensive player who allowed the defender to come through. Coverage Sack denotes when the quarterback has plenty of time to throw but cannot find an open receiver. QB Fault was sometimes a subjective call (for example, plays on which the quarterback gave up on the pass and looked to run without a running lane) and sometimes an objective one (quarterbacks going back to pass, only to find the ball slip out of their hands with no pass-rusher nearby).

All draw plays were marked, whether by halfbacks or quarterbacks.

An additional column called Extra Comment allowed the charters to add any description they wanted to the play. These comments might be good blitz pickup by a running back, a missed tackle, a great hit, a description of a pass route, an angry tirade about the poor camera angles of network broadcasts, or a number of other possibilities.

Finally, we asked the game charters to mark when a mistake was made in the official play-by-play. The most common mistake was for an official scorer not to mark a quarterback hit, since that was being tracked in the official play-by-play for the first time in 2006. Last year the official play-by-play also began to differentiate between quarterback scrambles and other runs, but·many times the "scramble" designation was missing. Other mistakes included incorrect names on tackles, penalties, or intended receivers. Thanks to the diligence of our volunteers and a friendly contact at the league office, the NFL corrected more than 150 mistakes in the official play-by-play based on the data collected by our game charters.

Acknowledgments

None of this would have been possible without the time spent by all the volunteer game charters. There are some specific acknowledgments at the end of the book, but we want to give a general thank you here to everyone who has helped collect data over the last two seasons. Without your unpaid time, the task of gathering all this information would have been too time-consuming to yield anything useful.

If you are interested in participating in next year's charting project, please e-mail your contact information to charting@footballoutsiders.com. Please make sure to mention where you live, what team you follow, and whether you have the Sunday Ticket package.

How to Read the Prospectus Box

Here is a rundown of all the tables and stats that appear in the 32 team chapters. On the first page of each team chapter there is a centered box that gives a summary of our statistics for that team, as follows:

2006 Record gives each team's actual win-loss record.

DVOA Estimated Wins estimates how many games a team would have been expected to win based on 2006 performance in specific situations, normalized to eliminate luck (fumble recoveries, opponents' missed field goals, etc.) and assume an average schedule strength. The formula emphasizes consistency and overall DVOA as well as DVOA in the most important specific situations: red zone defense, first quarter offense, and performance in the second half when the score is close. Rank is given in parentheses. This is not the number of wins we estimate the team will have in the upcoming season. That comes later.

Pythagorean Wins gives the approximate number of wins expected last year based on this team's raw totals of points scored and allowed, along with their NFL rank.

DVOA gives the team's total DVOA rating, with rank. We also give each team's **weighted DVOA,** based on a formula that gives more emphasis to performance in games later in the season. This gives a more accurate picture of where each team stood at the end of the regular season and is a useful indicator for which teams may improve or decline in 2007 (particularly on defense).

Offense, Defense, and **Special Teams** list the team's DVOA rating in each category, along with NFL rank. Remember that good offenses and special teams have positive DVOA numbers, while a negative DVOA means better defense, so the lowest defensive DVOA is ranked number one (Baltimore).

Variance measures a team's consistency over the 2006 season. Teams are ranked from least consistent (the completely ridiculous, off-the-charts Jacksonville Jaguars) to most consistent (32nd-ranked Minnesota).

2007 Mean Projection gives the average number of wins for this team based on the 2007 Win Projection System described earlier in this chapter. The next few lines give the team's chances of finishing in the five different win categories.

Projected Average Opponent gives the team's strength of schedule for 2007 based not on last year's record but on the median projected DVOA for each opponent. A positive schedule is harder, a negative schedule easier. Teams are ranked from the hardest projected schedule (top-ranked Buffalo) to the easiest (32nd-ranked San Francisco). This strength of schedule projection does not take into account which games are home and which are away, or the timing of the bye week.

After the Prospectus Box, each team then gets an essay discussing its 2006 season and prospects for 2007, followed in some chapters by a research essay connected to a particular issue related to that team. You'll also find a table with the team's 2007 schedule placed within each chapter. Then come statistical tables and comments related to that team and its specific units.

The first table gives a quick look at the team's week-to-week performance in 2006. This includes the playoffs for those teams that made the postseason, with the four weeks of playoffs numbered 18 (wild card) through 21 (Super Bowl). All other tables in the team chapters represent regular-season performance only unless otherwise noted.

Looking at the first week for the Atlanta Falcons in table 3, the first five columns are fairly obvious: The Falcons

beat Carolina on the road in Week 1, 20–6. **YDF** and **YDA** are net yards on offense and net yards against the defense. These numbers do not include penalty yardage or special teams yardage. **TO** represents the turnover margin. Unlike other parts of the book in which we consider all fumbles as equal, this only represents actual turnovers: fumbles lost and interceptions. The Falcons forced two more turnovers than they had themselves in Week 1 but turned the ball over two more times than their opponent in Week 9.

Finally, you'll see **DVOA** ratings for this game: Total DVOA first, then offense (**Off**), defense (**Def**), and special teams (**ST**). Note that these are DVOA ratings, adjusted for opponent. A good example of this is Atlanta's 17–6 win over Tampa Bay in Week 14. Although the Falcons won that game, they are listed with a total DVOA of −22.1% while Tampa Bay had a DVOA of −10.1% that day. This is because Tampa Bay was one of the league's worst teams. The Falcons actually played below-average football that day despite winning the game, while Tampa Bay can be said to have played better than the Falcons because of the opponent adjustments.

Next to this table is a graph representing each team's weekly performance throughout the season, based on total DVOA. Opponent and week are listed on the x-axis; the breaks in the line represent the bye week (or, for the top two playoff seeds in each conference, bye weeks). The curved line that runs through the graph represents the trend of the team's performance as the season progressed. (For you math types, this curve is the closest-fit third-order

Table 3. Weekly Performance

Falcons 2006 Stats by Week

Wk	vs.	W–L	PF	PA	YDF	YDA	TO	Total	Off	Def	ST
								DVOA			
1	@CAR	W	20	6	385	215	+2	64.0%	28.3%	-38.2%	-2.5%
2	TB	W	14	3	382	351	+1	-19.9%	5.8%	-0.5%	-26.1%
3	@NO	L	3	23	112	326	0	-94.5%	-58.0%	11.0%	-25.6%
4	ARI	W	32	10	405	187	+3	86.7%	-3.7%	-71.3%	19.1%
5	BYE										
6	NYG	L	14	27	377	439	0	-48.5%	-38.4%	13.0%	2.9%
7	PIT	W	41	38	399	473	+1	-12.0%	12.9%	34.5%	9.7%
8	@CIN	W	29	27	420	331	+1	20.0%	34.9%	9.3%	-5.6%
9	@DET	L	14	30	319	435	-2	-48.5%	-11.6%	28.0%	-8.9%
10	CLE	L	13	17	343	236	-1	-29.6%	-33.8%	-0.9%	3.3%
11	@BAL	L	10	24	186	328	+1	-18.6%	12.8%	16.7%	-14.8%
12	NO	L	13	31	333	427	0	-45.0%	-24.0%	25.7%	4.7%
13	@WAS	W	24	14	369	381	+2	25.1%	21.7%	-9.4%	-5.9%
14	@TB	W	17	6	280	282	+1	-22.1%	-9.3%	-1.8%	-14.6%
15	DAL	L	28	38	376	352	-1	13.0%	16.3%	9.1%	5.8%
16	CAR	L	3	10	177	194	-2	-14.5%	-19.5%	-10.9%	-5.9%
17	@PHI	L	17	24	378	393	0	-2.6%	25.9%	28.9%	0.3%

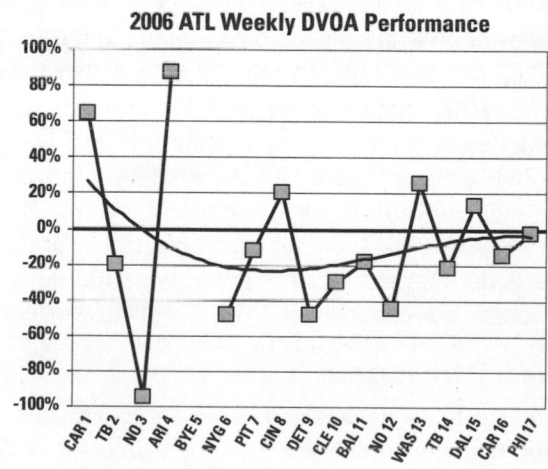

2006 ATL Weekly DVOA Performance

polynomial equation. For you non-math types, that means it bends twice.)

Trends and Splits

This section gives DVOA split into different portions of a team's performance, for both offense and defense. Each split is listed with the team's rank among the 32 NFL teams. These numbers represent regular-season performance only.

Total DVOA gives total offensive and defensive DVOA in all situations. **Unadjusted VOA** represents the breakdown of play-by-play considering situation but not opponent. A team whose offensive DVOA is higher than its offensive VOA played a harder-than-average schedule of opposing defenses; a team with a lower defensive DVOA than defensive VOA player a harder-than-average schedule of opposing offenses.

Weighted Trend lowers the importance of earlier games to give a better idea of how the team was playing at the end of the regular season. The final four weeks of the season are full strength; moving backward through the season, each week is given less and less weight until the first three weeks of the season, which are not included at all. **Variance** is the same as noted above, with a higher percentage representing less consistency. This is true for both offense and defense: Denver, for example, had one of the league's *least* consistent offenses (10.1% variance, ranked third) and one of the *most* consistent defenses (5.1% variance, ranked 28th).

Passing and **Rushing** are fairly self-explanatory. Note that rushing includes all rushes, not just those by running backs, including quarterback scrambles that may have begun as pass plays.

The next three lines split out DVOA on **First Down, Second Down,** and **Third Down.** Third Down here includes fourth downs on which a team runs a regular offensive play instead of punting or attempting a field goal. Next comes DVOA in the **Red Zone,** which is any offensive play starting from the defense's 20-yard line through the goal line. The final split is **Late and Close,** which includes any play in the second half or overtime when the teams are within eight points of each other in either direction. (Eight points, of course, is the biggest deficit that can be made up with a single score—a touchdown and two-point conversion.)

Five-Year Performance

This table gives each team's performance over the past five seasons. It includes win-loss record, Pythagorean Wins, Estimated Wins, and Total DVOA, along with DVOA for offense, defense, and special teams. The four DVOA ratings are listed with the team's rank among that season's 32 NFL teams.

Individual Offensive Statistics

Each team chapter contains a table giving passing and receiving numbers for any player who either threw five passes or was thrown five passes, along with rushing numbers for any players who carried the ball at least three times. These numbers also appear in the player comments at the end of the book (except for wide receiver rushing attempts). By putting them together in the team chapters we hope we make it easier to compare the performances of different players on the same team.

Players who are no longer on the team are marked with an asterisk. New players who were on a different team in 2006 are in italics. Rookies are not included.

All players are listed with DPAR and DVOA. Passing statistics (table 4) list total pass plays (**Plys**), net yardage (**NtYds**), and net yards per pass (**Avg**). These numbers include not just passes (and the positive yardage from them) but aborted snaps and sacks (and the negative yardage from them). Then comes average yards after catch (**YAC**) as determined by the game charting project. This average is based on charted receptions, not total pass attempts. The final three numbers are completion percentage (**C%**), which does not include aborted snaps or sacks, passing touchdowns (**TD**), and interceptions (**Int**).

Table 4. Sample Passing Table

Player	DPAR	DVOA	Plys	NtYds	Avg	YAC	C%	TD	Int
Michael Vick	-6.5	-16.7%	388	2164	5.6	4.1	52.6%	20	11
Matt Schaub*	5.9	40.7%	27	200	7.4	3.8	66.7%	1	1
Joey Harrington	5.7	-9.9%	386	2122	5.5	4.0	57.8%	12	15

Rushing statistics (table 5) start with DPAR and DVOA, then list rushing plays and net yards along with average yards per carry and rushing touchdowns. The final two columns are fumbles (**Fum**)—both those lost to the defense and those recovered by the offense—and Success Rate (**Suc**), explained earlier in this chapter.

Table 5. Sample Rushing Table

Player	DPAR	DVOA	Plys	Yds	Avg	TD	Fum	Suc
Warrick Dunn	12.6	-3.9%	286	1140	4.0	4	1	39%
Michael Vick	32.4	27.6%	119	1038	8.7	2	9	—
Jerious Norwood	21.3	35.8%	99	633	6.4	2	0	53%

Receiving statistics (table 6) start with DPAR and DVOA and then list the number of passes thrown to this receiver (**Plys**), the number of passes caught (**Ctch**), and the total receiving yards (**Yds**). Yards per catch (**Y/C**) includes total yardage per reception, based on standard play-by-play, while yards after catch (**YAC**) is based on information from our game charting project. Finally we list total receiving touchdowns, and catch percentage (**C%**), which is the percentage of passes intended for this receiver that were caught.

Table 6. Sample Receiving Table

Player	DPAR	DVOA	Plys	Ctch	Yds	Y/C	YAC	TD	C%
Michael Jenkins	-1.4	-17.7%	83	39	436	11.2	2.4	7	47%
Ashley Lelie*	-1.4	-18.0%	68	28	430	15.4	2.3	1	41%
Roddy White	-0.5	-16.4%	64	30	509	17.0	2.6	0	47%
Joe Horn	*19.7*	*31.7%*	*61*	*37*	*679*	*18.4*	*4.4*	*4*	*59%*

AN IMPORTANT NOTE: Individual numbers in the team tables will differ from individual numbers in the player comments. The team tables feature our numbers, which are edited to remove plays such as kneeldowns, Hail Marys, and clock-stopping spikes, and include aborted snaps as passes rather than rush attempts. The tables in the player comment chapters at the end of the book contain the official NFL totals.

Strategic Tendencies

The Strategic Tendencies table (table 7) presents a mix of information garnered from both the standard play-by-play and the Football Outsiders game charting project. It gives you an idea of what kind of plays teams run in what situations and with what personnel. Each category is given a league-wide **Rank** from most often (1) to least often (32) except as noted below. The sample table shown here lists the NFL average in each category for 2006.

The first column gives the frequency with which each team ran different **Formations,** as tracked by our game charters.

3+WR/4+WR: Plays with 3 or more wide receivers and plays with 4 or more wide receivers.

2+ TE: Plays with multiple tight ends, including "H-backs."

Single back/Empty back: Plays with one running back/no running backs, no matter the mixture of tight ends and wide receivers.

Max protect: The percentage of this team's passing plays (including quarterback scrambles) on which blockers outnumber pass-rushers by at least two, with a minimum of seven blockers.

The second column of strategic tendencies comes from standard play-by-play, not game charting, and lists how often teams ran in different situations. The first three are self-evident: **Runs** on **all plays,** in the **first half,** and on **first down.**

Runs, power situations is the percentage of runs on third or fourth down with 1–2 yards to go, or at the goal line with 1–2 yards to go.

Runs, behind 2H tells you how often teams ran when they were behind in the second half, generally a passing situation. **Pass, ahead 2H** tells you how often teams passed when they had the lead in the second half, generally a running situation.

In each case, you can determine the percentage of plays that were passes by subtracting the run percentage from 100 (the reverse being true for Pass, ahead 2H, of course).

The third column shows strategies used by the **Defense.**

Sacks by LB/Sacks by DB: The percentage of this team's sacks that came from linebackers and defensive backs. To figure out the percentage of sacks from defensive linemen, simply subtract the sum of these numbers from 100%.

Rush 6+/Rush 7+/Rush 3: The percentage of pass plays (including quarterback scrambles) on which our game charters recorded this team rushing the passer with six or more defenders, seven or more defenders, and three or fewer defenders. These percentages do not include goal-line plays on the one- or two-yard line.

CB1 on WR1: The percentage of passes targeting the team's number-one cornerback that were thrown with the offense's number-one receiver as the intended target. Obviously, both of these designations are subjective, but this gives a good idea of how often a defensive coordinator assigned his top corner to shadow a specific receiver. In two years of game charting, we've learned that each team's best cornerback does not necessarily match up against the opponent's best receiver. Most cornerbacks play a particular side of the field and in fact cover a wider range of receivers than we assumed before we saw the charting data.

The cornerback used in this rating is always ranked first in the individual defensive back stats table (described later

Table 7. Sample Strategic Tendencies Table

Formations		Rank	Run/Pass		Rank	Defense		Rank	Other		Rank
3+ WR	48%	16	Runs, all plays	44%	16	Sacks by LB	30%	16	Run with 2+ RB	58%	16
4+ WR	11%	16	Runs, first half	45%	16	Sacks by DB	8%	16	Run with 2+ TE	35%	16
2+ TE	25%	16	Runs, first down	53%	16	Rush 6+	9%	16	Play action	19%	16
Single back	54%	16	Runs, power sit.	64%	16	Rush 7+	1.8%	16	Go for it on 4th	1.00	16
Empty back	2.6%	16	Runs, behind 2H	32%	16	Rush 3	5%	16	Offensive Pace	30.6	16
Max protect	12%	16	Pass, ahead 2H	42%	16	CB1 on WR1	44%	16	Defensive Pace	30.6	16

in this chapter). In some cases, however, different corner-backs were used for different weeks depending on injuries.

The fourth column has data on pace, coach aggressiveness, and run strategies.

Run with 2+RB: The percentage of running plays that involved two or more running backs. This usually means a halfback and a fullback, but not necessarily.

Run with 2+TE: The percentage of running plays that involved multiple tight ends/H-backs.

Play action: The percentage of pass plays (including quarterback scrambles) that began with a play-action fake to the running back. This percentage does not include fake end-arounds unless there was also a fake handoff.

Go for it on 4th: This is the Aggressiveness Index (AI) introduced by Jim Armstrong in *Pro Football Prospectus 2006*, which measures how often a team goes for a first down in various fourth down situations compared with the league average. A coach over 1.00 is more aggressive, and one below 1.00 is less aggressive. Coaches are ranked from most aggressive to least aggressive.

Offensive Pace: Situation-neutral pace represents the seconds of game clock per offensive play, with the following restrictions: No drives are included if they start in the fourth quarter or final five minutes of the first half, and drives are only included if the score is within six points or less. Teams are ranked from quickest pace (Chicago, 28.0 seconds) to slowest pace (Jacksonville, 34.0 seconds).

Defensive Pace: Situation-neutral pace based on seconds of game clock per defensive play. This is a representation of how a defense was approached by its opponents, not the strategy of the defense itself (an issue discussed in last year's Indianapolis chapter). Teams are ranked from quickest pace (Minnesota, 28.5 seconds) to slowest pace (Indianapolis, 33.3 seconds).

Following each strategic tendencies table, you'll find a series of comments highlighting interesting data from that team's charting numbers. These comments are primarily written by Bill Moore, coordinator of the game charting project. For the first time, we are able to give DVOA ratings based on formations, blitzes, or play-action passing. Please note that all DVOA ratings given in these comments are standard DVOA with no adjustments for the specific situation being analyzed, and the average DVOA for a specific situation will not necessarily be 0%. For example, the average DVOA on play-action passes in 2006 was 12.7%.

How to Read the Offensive Line Tables

The offensive line tables (table 8) list the last three years of Adjusted Line Yards and other statistics for each team.

The first column gives standard yards per carry by each team's running backs (**Yards**). The next two columns give Adjusted Line Yards (**ALY**) followed by rank among the 32 teams.

Then come three other rushing statistics. **Power** gives the percentage of runs in "power situations" that achieved a first down or touchdown. Those situations include any third or fourth down with one or two yards to go, and any runs in goal-to-go situations from the two-yard line or closer. Unlike the other rushing numbers on the Offensive Line table, Power includes quarterbacks.

10+ Yds gives the percentage of a team's rushing yards that came more than 10 yards past the line of scrimmage. A team with a high ranking in Adjusted Line Yards but a low ranking in 10+ Yards is heavily dependent on its offensive line to make the running game work. A team with a low ranking in Adjusted Line Yards but a high ranking in 10+ Yards is heavily dependent on its running back breaking long runs to make the running game work, and therefore tends to have a less consistent running attack.

Stuff gives the percentage of runs that are stuffed based on the following parameters:

- On first down, zero or negative gain.
- On other downs, less than one-fourth the yards needed for another first down.

Since being stuffed is bad, teams are ranked from stuffed least often (1) to most often (32).

The final two numbers on the first part of the table are Adjusted Sack Rate (**ASR**) and its rank among the 32 teams. Some teams allow a lot of sacks because they throw a lot of passes; Adjusted Sack Rate accounts for this by dividing sacks and intentional grounding by total pass plays. It is

Table 8. Sample Offensive Line Tables

Year	Yards	ALY	Rank	Power	Rank	10+ Yds	Rank	Stuff	Rank	Sack	ASR	Rank
2004	4.36	4.52	6	72%	5	16%	22	18%	1	49	11.6%	31
2005	4.49	4.46	7	65%	14	20%	12	24%	13	39	8.0%	25
2006	4.64	4.30	13	59%	23	23%	4	25%	24	47	10.4%	31

Year	LE	Rank	LT	Rank	Mid	Rank	RT	Rank	RE	Rank
2004	4.49	12	4.78	7	4.59	9	4.57	11	3.50	22
2005	5.17	4	4.75	4	3.93	21	4.74	5	5.05	2
2006	4.53	10	3.71	28	4.50	11	4.27	12	4.67	9

also adjusted for situation (sacks are much more common on third down, particularly 3rd-and-long) and opponent, all of which makes it a better measurement than raw sacks totals. Remember that quarterbacks share responsibility for sacks, and two different quarterbacks behind the same line can have very different Adjusted Sack Rates. Particularly if one is named Rob Johnson. (The addition of intentional grounding to Adjusted Sack Rate is new for 2007. Intentional grounding and sacks have the same cause, pass pressure, and the same effect, lost yardage.)

The second part of the Offensive Line table gives Adjusted Line Yards in each of the five directions with rank among the 32 teams. Note that the league average is higher on the left than on the right. Specifically in 2006, the league average was 4.12 on left end runs (**LE**), 4.36 on left tackle runs (**LT**), 4.32 on runs up the middle (**Mid**), 4.21 on right tackle runs (**RT**), and 4.08 on right end runs (**RE**).

How to Read the Defensive Front Seven Tables

Defensive players make plays. Plays aren't just tackles—interceptions and pass deflections change the course of the game, and so does the act of forcing a fumble or beating the offensive players to a fumbled ball. While some plays stop a team on third down and force a punt, others merely stop a receiver after he's caught a 30-yard pass. We still cannot measure each player's opportunities to make a tackle. For the last two years, however, we can measure a linebacker's opportunities in pass coverage, thanks to the Football Outsiders game charting project.

Defensive Linemen

Defensive linemen are listed in the team chapters if they made at least 15 plays during the 2006 season. Players are listed with the following numbers (table 9):

Age: The player's age, listed simply as the difference between birth year and 2007. Players born in January and December of the same year will have the same listed age.

Position (Pos): The player's position on the line.

Plays (Plys): The total defensive plays including tackles, pass deflections, interceptions, fumbles forced, and fumble recoveries. This number comes from the official NFL gamebooks and therefore does not include plays on which the player is listed by the Football Outsiders game charting project as in coverage, but does not appear in the standard play-by-play. Special teams tackles are also not included.

Percentage of Team Plays (**TmPct**): The percentage of total team plays involving this defender. The sum of the percentages of team plays for all defenders on a given team will exceed 100 percent, primarily due to shared tackles. New to this year's book, this number is adjusted based on games played, so an injured player may be fifth on his team in plays but third in **TmPct**.

Stops (**Stop**): The total number of plays that prevent a "success" by the offense (45 percent of needed yards on first down, 60 percent on second down, 100 percent on third or fourth down).

Defeats (**Dfts**): The total number of plays that stop the offense from gaining first down yardage on third or fourth down, stop the offense behind the line of scrimmage, or result in a fumble (regardless of which team recovers) or interception.

Stop Rate (**StpRt**): The percentage of all Plays that are Stops.

Average Yards (**AvYd**): The average number of yards gained by the offense when this player is credited with making the play. Note that passes defensed count as zero yards.

Sack: Standard NFL sack totals.

Hit: A new element added to the official NFL play-by-play this year. To qualify as a quarterback hit, the defender must knock the quarterback to the ground in the act of throwing or after the pass is thrown. We have listed hits on all plays, including those canceled by penalties.

Hurries (**Hur**): The number of quarterback hurries recorded by the Football Outsiders game charting project.

Hits and hurries are discussed further later in the book, in an essay called "Beyond Sacks."

Finally, we split our stats for defensive linemen into **Run** plays and **Pass** plays. Pass plays include sacks, tackles after completions, and pass deflections. We list separate Stop Rate for passes (**PaStp**) and runs (**RuStp**) as well as separate average yards for passes (**PaYd**) and runs (**RuYd**).

Defensive linemen are ranked by percentage of team plays, Stop Rate, and average yards. The lowest number of average yards earns the top rank (negative numbers indicate the average play ending behind the line of scrimmage). Except for pass-rush specialists, most linemen do not have enough pass plays to make separate rankings of pass and run statistics viable. Defensive linemen are

Table 9. Sample Defensive Line Table

Defensive Line	Age	Pos	Plys	TmPct	Rk	Stop	Dfts	StpRt	Rk	AvYd	Rk	Sack	Hit	Hur	Runs	RuStp	RuYd	Pass	PaStp	PaYd
Tommy Kelly	29	DE	68	8.3%	13	56	19	82%	20	1.8	53	3.5	3	4	60	80%	2.3	8	100%	-2.0
Derrick Burgess	29	DE	50	6.1%	38	41	17	82%	23	1.0	22	11	4	12	34	76%	3.2	16	94%	-3.6
Warren Sapp	35	DT	47	5.8%	26	45	19	96%	1	0.2	3	10	9	11	33	97%	2.0	14	93%	-4.1

Table 10. Sample Linebackers Table

Linebackers	Age	Pos	Plys	TmPct	Rk	Stop	Dfts	StpRt	AvYd	Sack	Hit	Hur	Runs	RuStp	Rk	RuYd	Rk	Tgts	Suc%	Rk	PaYd	Rk
Kirk Morrison	25	ILB	128	15.7%	19	82	33	64%	3.5	1	0	0	101	63%	53	3.1	29	29	67%	6	3.5	7
Thomas Howard	24	OLB	108	13.3%	39	56	19	52%	4.9	0	1	1	71	56%	78	4.1	81	28	59%	22	4.4	10

ranked if they have 25 or more plays during 2006. There are 76 defensive ends who qualify, and 70 defensive tackles. Each position is ranked separately.

Linebackers

Linebackers are listed in team chapters if they made at least 15 plays during the season. Most of the stats for linebackers are the same as those for defensive linemen (table 10). The listings of both total plays and percentage of team plays are based on standard play-by-play. Average yards, on the left side of the table, is also based on standard play-by-play, and gives us a good indication of which linebackers play closer to the line of scrimmage and which players drop into coverage.

Linebackers are ranked in percentage of team plays and in Stop Rate and average yards for running plays specifically. Linebackers are ranked if they have at least 50 plays during the 2006 season. Inside and outside linebackers are all ranked together, with 99 players ranked in total.

The final five columns in the linebacker stats come from the Football Outsiders game charting project. Last year, we only listed these stats for defensive backs, listing linebackers in an appendix. This year, by giving charters the choice of marking plays with two defenders or "Hole in Zone," we feel that the linebacker coverage stats are as accurate as those for defensive backs.

Targets (**Tgts**): The number of pass plays on which our game charters listed this player in coverage.

Success Rate (**Suc%**): The percentage of plays targeting this player on which the offense did not have a successful play. This means not only incomplete passes and interceptions but also short completions that do not meet our baselines for success (45 percent of needed yards on first down, 60 percent on second down, 100 percent on third or fourth down). Note: Last year, we called this number Stop Rate. We have changed the name in order to avoid confusion between one metric based on conventional play-by-play (Stop Rate), and another metric based on game charting (Success Rate).

Average Yards per Pass (**PaYd**): The average number of yards gained on plays on which this defender was the listed target.

These stats are explained in more detail below, in the section on secondary tables. Plays listed with two defenders or as "Hole in Zone" with this defender as the closest player count only for half credit in computing both Success

Rate and Average Yards per Pass. Ninety-eight linebackers are ranked in the charting stats, with a minimum of 16 charted passes. As a result of the different thresholds, some linebackers are ranked in standard stats but not charting stats, or vice versa.

Further Details

Just as we did in the offensive tables, players who are no longer on the team are marked with asterisks, and players who were on other teams last year are in italics. However, unlike our offensive metrics, these defensive player statistics are not adjusted for situation or opponent. Numbers for defensive linemen and linebackers unfortunately do not reflect all of the opportunities a player had to make a play, but they do show us which players were most active on the field. A large number of plays could mean a strong defensive performance, or it could mean that the linebacker in question plays behind a poor part of the line.

In general, defensive numbers should be taken as information that tells us what happened on the field in 2006, but not as a strict, unassailable judgment of which players are better than others.

After the individual statistics for linemen and linebackers, the Defensive Front Seven section contains a table that looks exactly like the table in the Offensive Line section. The difference is that the numbers here are for all opposing running backs against this team's defensive front. As we're on the opposite side of the ball, teams are now ranked in the opposite order, so the number-one Defensive Front Seven is the one that allows the fewest adjusted line yards, has the lowest percentage in Power situations, and has the highest Adjusted Sack Rate. Directions for Adjusted Line Yards are given from the offense's perspective, so runs left end and left tackle are aimed at the right defensive end and (assuming the tight end is on the other side) weak-side linebacker.

How to Read the Secondary Tables

The first few columns in the secondary tables (table 11) are based on standard play-by-play, not game charting. Age, Total Plays, Percentage of Team Plays, Stops, and Defeats are computed the same way they are for other defensive players so that the secondary can be compared with the defensive line and linebackers. That means that Total Plays here includes passes defensed, sacks, tackles after recep-

Table 11. Sample of Individual Statistics for Defensive Secondary

Secondary	Age	Pos	Plys	TmPct	Rk	Stop	Dfts	RuYd	Rk	RuStp	Rk	Tgts	Tgt%	Rk	Dist	Suc%	Rk	PaYd	Rk	PD	Int
Asante Samuel	26	CB	88	12.6%	7	40	20	8.4	57	38%	51	101	23%	8	12.9	60%	11	5.9	9	10	26
Ellis Hobbs	24	CB	52	7.5%	54	17	8	14.0	80	14%	78	78	18%	48	14.6	55%	24	7.7	46	2	9
Rodney Harrison	35	SS	53	11.4%	23	22	6	5.6	24	45%	34	27	9%	24	7.6	65%	8	5.3	6	1	2

tions, tipped passes, and interceptions, but not pass plays on which this player was in coverage but was not given a tackle or passed defense by the NFL's official scorer. Because of the odd habits of the official scorer at Lincoln Financial Field, as discussed in last year's Philadelphia chapter, all passes defensed in Philadelphia home games count as only half a play.

The middle four columns address each defensive back's role in stopping the run. Average Yardage and Stop Rate for running plays is computed in the same manner as for defensive linemen and linebackers.

The third section of statistics represents data from the game charting project:

Targets (**Tgts**): The number of pass plays on which our game charters listed this player in coverage. This number gives full credit to all passes, including those on which two defenders are listed and those listed as "Hole in Zone" with this player as the closest zone defender (both of those count as half credit in the other stats below). We do not count pass plays on which this player was in coverage but the incomplete was listed as Thrown Away, Tipped at Line, or Hit in Motion.

Target Percentage (**Tgt%**): The number of plays on which this player was targeted divided by the total number of charted passes against his defense, not including plays listed as Uncovered. (Last year, Target Percentage was percentage of passes charted against the secondary only; this year, it is the percentage of all charted passes.) Like Percentage of Team Plays, this metric is adjusted based on number of games played.

Distance (**Dist**): The average distance in the air beyond the line of scrimmage of all passes targeted at this defender. It does not include yards after catch, and it is useful for seeing which defenders were covering receivers deeper or shorter.

Success Rate (**Suc%**): The percentage of plays targeting this player on which the offense did not have a successful play. This means not only incomplete passes and interceptions but also short completions that do not meet our baselines for success (45 percent of needed yards on first down, 60 percent on second down, 100 percent on third or fourth down).

Average Yards per Pass (**PaYd**): The average number of yards gained on plays on which this defender was the listed target.

Passes Defensed (**PD**): This is our count of passes defensed, and it will differ from the total found in NFL gamebooks. Our count includes:

- All passes listed by our charters as Defensed.
- All interceptions or tipped passes leading to interceptions.
- All passes defensed listed in the NFL game books for games that remain uncharted.
- Any pass on which the defender is given a pass defensed by the official scorer and the game charter listed a reason for incomplete that can be hard to differentiate from a pass defensed, including: Dropped, Miscommunication, Alligator Arms, and Catch Out of Bounds.

Our count of passes defensed does not include passes marked as defensed in the official game books but listed by our charters as Overthrown, Underthrown, or Thrown Away. It also does not include passes tipped in the act of rushing the passer.

Interceptions (**Int**): Standard NFL interception total.

These pass coverage numbers differ from last year's as follows:

- All 17 weeks of the season are included.
- Defensive pass interference is counted as a failure by the defender, and he is held responsible for the penalty yardage as if it were a completion.
- Any play on which a teammate is listed in coverage but the defender in question makes an interception or pass defensed is counted as a successful play by this defender.
- Last year, we measured the percentage of targets compared with other defensive backs. This year, we are measuring the percentage of all pass targets against a given defense.

Cornerbacks need 45 charted passes to be ranked in the defensive stats, with 81 cornerbacks ranked in total. Safeties are ranked in charting stats if they played a minimum of eight games and have either 16 charted passes or 20 running plays, but they are only ranked in the conventional metrics if they have 20 running plays. Eighty safeties are ranked in charting stats, and 71 safeties are ranked in the stats based on standard play-by-play.

Table 12. Sample of Team Statistics for Defensive Secondary

Year	Pass D Rank	DVOA vs. #1 WR	Rank	DVOA vs. #2 WR	Rank	DVOA vs. Other WR	Rank	DVOA vs. TE	Rank	DVOA vs. RB	Rank
2004	18	26.0%	17	53.2%	28	-8.9%	7	10.9%	15	-4.2%	14
2005	3	-7.4%	9	-14.4%	3	-22.3%	3	-13.6%	9	6.1%	19
2006	6	-13.6%	4	-4.6%	15	-9.5%	9	-7.6%	12	20.2%	30

Just like the front seven, the secondary has a table of team statistics following the individual numbers. This table (table 12) gives DVOA figured against different types of receivers. Each offense's wide receivers have had one receiver designated as number one, and another as number two. (Occasionally this is difficult, due to injury or a constantly changing offense such as that of last year's Raiders, but it's usually pretty obvious.) The other receivers form a third category, with tight ends and running backs as fourth and fifth categories. The defense is then judged on the performance of each receiver based on the standard DVOA method, with each rating adjusted based on strength of schedule. (Opponents with Lee Evans and Chad Johnson as top receivers, for example, are tougher than opponents with Reche Caldwell and Michael Jenkins as top receivers.) **Pass D Rank** is the total ranking of the pass defense, as seen before in the Trends and Splits table, and combines all five categories plus sacks and passes with no intended target.

The defensive secondary table should be used to analyze the defense as a whole rather than individual players. The ratings against types of receivers are generally based on defensive schemes, not specific cornerbacks, and the ratings against tight ends and running backs are in large part due to the performance of linebackers.

How to Read the Special Teams Tables

The special teams tables (table 13) list the last three years of kick, punt, and return numbers for each team.

The first two columns list total special teams DVOA and rank among the 32 teams. The next two columns list the value in actual points of field goals and extra points (**FG/XP**) when compared with how a league-average kicker would do from the same distances (adjusted for weather and altitude) and rank among the 32 teams. Next, we list the estimated value in actual points of field position over or under the league average based on net punting (**Net**

Punt) and rank that value among the 32 teams. That is followed by the estimated point values of field position for punt returns (**Punt Ret**), net kickoffs (**Net Kick**), and kick returns (**Kick Ret**), and their respective ranks.

The final two columns are new to the book this year and represent the value of **"Hidden"** special teams, plays based solely on the performance of opponents without this team being able to control the outcome. We combine the opposing team's value on field goals, kickoff distance, and punt distance, adjusted for weather and altitude, and then switch the sign to represent that good special teams by the opponent will cost the listed team points, and bad special teams will effectively hand them points. Teams are ranked from the most hidden value gained (New Orleans, 12.8 points) to the most value lost (Philadelphia, −15.2 points).

Individual statistics for kicks, punts, and returns can be found online at www.footballoutsiders.com/stats/indst.php. In previous years, kickers had their own section of player comments, but this year they are discussed along with the rest of the special teams in each team chapter.

Administrative Minutiae

Receiving statistics include all passes intended for the receiver in question, including those that are incomplete or intercepted. The word *passes* refers to both complete and incomplete pass attempts. When rating receivers, interceptions are treated as incomplete passes with no penalty.

For the computation of DVOA and DPAR, passing statistics include sacks as well as fumbles on aborted snaps. We do not include kneeldown plays or spikes for the purpose of stopping the clock. Some interceptions that we have determined to be "Hail Mary" plays that end the first half or the game are counted as regular incomplete passes, not turnovers.

Table 13. Special Teams Sample

Year	DVOA	Rank	FG/XP	Rank	Net Punt	Rank	Punt Ret	Rank	Net Kick	Rank	Kick Ret	Rank	Hidden	Rank
2004	5.7%	3	1.9	13	11.7	3	4.8	7	4.2	11	10.9	5	2.7	10
2005	-2.0%	23	-6.7	25	10.0	3	-0.6	15	0.1	18	-14.5	32	-7.0	25
2006	0.7%	14	2.7	10	6.3	9	-1.9	19	0.4	17	-3.3	19	12.8	1

All mentions of yards after catch, hurries, hits, blitzes, and screens come from the Football Outsiders game charting project and may be different from totals compiled by other sources.

Unless we say otherwise, when we refer to third-down performance in this book we are referring to a combination of third down and the handful of rushing and passing plays that take place on fourth down (primarily 4th-and-1).

Thank you to Dr. Benjamin Alamar for help with the calculation of both the improved Adjusted Line Yards formula and the 2006 Win Projection System, as well as the explanations for each. Additional thanks to Roland Beech of 82Games.com and TwoMinuteWarning.com, who first developed these individual defensive statistics and has allowed us to use them and develop them further.

The Greatest Running Back Seasons of All Time

Aaron Schatz

In 2006, LaDainian Tomlinson broke the all-time NFL record for single-season touchdowns with three games to spare. Even before he broke the record, sportswriters and TV commentators around the country were already asking the question: Was this the greatest season by any running back in NFL history?

If the question sounds familiar, it's because the same question was asked the year before, when Shaun Alexander broke the all-time record for single-season touchdowns. It was also asked when Priest Holmes broke the record in 2003, and when Marshall Faulk broke the record in 2000.

Peyton Manning broke the single-season record for passing touchdowns two years ago, but that accomplishment was different from Tomlinson's. On one hand, the 2004 season was the most passing-friendly season in NFL history, while the league-wide rushing numbers in 2006 weren't anything out of the ordinary. On the other hand, Manning broke a record that had stood for 20 years. Since the AFL-NFL merger in 1970, the record for passing touchdowns has only been broken twice, by Dan Marino in 1984 and Manning in 2004. The record for rushing and receiving touchdowns was broken seven times in the same time period, four of those coming in the last seven seasons.

Clearly, running back usage patterns have changed in recent years. There's also nothing to say that the season with the most touchdowns is the best season overall. Tomlinson is better than other backs when he gets near the goal line, but he also gets more opportunities near the goal line. Tomlinson had 38 carries in goal-to-go situations last year. Larry Johnson had 40, but nobody else had more than 28.

How can we figure out who truly had the greatest running back season of all time? The best method would be to break down 50 years of NFL play-by-play to create DVOA and DPAR statistics, but that's impossible. Right now we only have DVOA stats going back to 1996, and who knows if accurate play-by-play even exists for Jim Brown's greatest seasons?

We faced this same dilemma two years ago in *Pro Football Prospectus 2005* when we asked if Manning's 2004 campaign was the greatest quarterback season in history. Since we couldn't break down the actual play-by-play, we created an equation to give an approximation of our PAR (Points Above Replacement) numbers, based on the standard available NFL statistics. We translated every quarterback season to the 2004 offensive environment, put them all through the equation, and added in an adjustment for strength of schedule. Voila: The greatest quarterback seasons of all time. (For those wondering, the winner was Bert Jones in 1976, followed by Manning in 2004 and Marino in 1984.) With Tomlinson's spectacular season coming on the heels of Alexander's spectacular season, it makes sense to do the same type of study.

We quickly learned that comparing running backs across different eras is much more complicated than comparing quarterbacks. Our first problem was that running backs have fewer standard stats, making the lack of play-by-play a bigger problem. DPAR gives significant value to running backs who gain yardage on a consistent basis. That means not only converting third downs to keep the chains moving but also gaining four to six yards on first downs to put the offense in an advantageous 2nd-and-short position. Without play-by-play, we don't have the number of passes thrown to each running back, only the number of passes that were actually caught. We also don't know when a running back averages eight yards per catch because he's a useful part of the passing game, and when a running back averages eight yards per catch because he's constantly getting dumpoffs behind the line of scrimmage on 3rd-and-long.

The second problem had to do with the translation of past stats. Today's offensive environment is not just different from the past because teams pass more often or gain more yards per carry. It's also different because running backs are used in a completely different way than they were 30 or 40 years ago.

This was not an issue with quarterbacks. No matter how much the ratio of passing to running changes, only a few teams in modern NFL history have tried any kind of job-sharing arrangement at the quarterback position. Running back usage patterns, however, have been in a constant state of flux for 50 years.

Thirty years ago, teams would split carries between two or three running backs. Until 1980, only two running backs were given more than 60 percent of their team's carries in a single season: Jim Brown, of the NFL Browns, and Jim Nance, of the AFL Patriots. Earl Campbell had 65 percent of Houston's carries in 1980, setting a new NFL record. Last year, ten different running backs had a higher percentage of team carries than Campbell had in 1980. Steven Jackson, Larry Johnson, and Edgerrin James were all over 80 percent.

The workload changes involve not just number of carries, but type of carries. Once upon a time, halfbacks and fullbacks shared the load. After O. J. Simpson and Earl Campbell and the arrival of workhorse halfbacks, fullback carries started to slip until they approached zero. Many of those carries became pass attempts as the league became more pass oriented. The rest, five or six per game, went to the feature halfbacks. These were primarily short-yardage carries, so giving them to halfbacks had two effects: It lowered the average yards per carry of the top halfbacks without necessarily lowering the average yards per carry for the entire league, and it raised the number of touchdowns for the halfback without a change in his actual level of performance.

To show just how much workload and offensive environment have both changed over the years, table 1 has the average numbers for each team and for the top 50 percent of starting running backs during four record-setting seasons: 1963 (Jim Brown's best season), 1973 (O. J. Simpson and the first 2,000-yard season), 1984 (Eric Dickerson sets the all-time high for rushing yardage), and 2006 (LaDainian Tomlinson sets the all-time high for rushing touchdowns). The 1963 and 1973 seasons are prorated to 16 games for easier comparison with the current numbers.

We adjusted for both issues (our methodology is explained at the end of this essay) as well as strength of schedule, but we still ended up with a list that was topped entirely by running backs from either the 21st century or the Cleveland Browns of the sixties. No matter how much we tried to correct for the change in workloads, certain teams in certain years just used their running backs more than the rest of the league. So our final step was to grade

each player using a statistical method known as "Z-scores." Z-scores measure how many standard deviations a player's value is above the mean for running backs that season. The best Z-scores will come from players having great seasons in years in which running back workloads were fairly consistent across all teams.

Having settled on a system, the question became: How far back should we consider players for our list? If we went too far back, we'd have no running backs to consider. The early statistical record prior only lists "backs" and "ends." The AFL began in 1960, so that provides a clear line of demarcation, but it also means leaving out the first three seasons from the greatest running back who ever lived. Instead, our list begins in Jim Brown's rookie year of 1957.

The resulting list is not perfect. Fumbles are included, but special teams are not, so the list undervalues players such as Herschel Walker. Even the intricate play-by-play analysis we do with DVOA isn't perfect, because it doesn't perfectly correct for all the changes in workload and style, or who had the better offensive linemen. Still, we think the list we came up with is fairly accurate, as it consists primarily of well-known players having their greatest seasons, with a few surprise entries.

Our choice for the greatest running back season ever is the same season we chose last year as the greatest fantasy football season ever. We only wish we could celebrate a better human being.

1. O. J. Simpson   1975 Buffalo Bills

	Rush	RuYd	TD	Avg	Rec	RecYd	TD	Fum
Actual:	329	1817	16	5.52	28	426	7	7
Adjusted:	337	1841	21	5.46	33	427	4	4

What marks O. J. Simpson's 1975 season is not just great numbers, but how far those numbers were ahead of the rest of the league. Simpson's league-leading rushing yardage was almost 50 percent higher than the second-highest total (Franco Harris, with 1,246 yards). He also led in combined rushing and receiving yardage by nearly 500 yards over Chuck Foreman. Simpson had 23 total touchdowns, Foreman, 22, and nobody else had more than 16.

Table 1. The Evolution of the NFL Offense

Year	Team Average							Top 50% of Starting RB						
	P/R Ratio*	Runs	Yards	Avg	TD	RB Rec	RB RecYd	Runs	Yards	Avg	TD	Rec	RecYd	FUM
1963	0.89	499	2022	4.05	15.5	78	859	248	1103	4.45	7.0	30	341	7.1
1973	0.68	569	2310	4.03	14.5	83	725	285	1189	4.17	6.6	39	345	7.5
1984	1.04	493	1982	4.01	14.6	90	754	301	1251	4.16	8.9	44	362	7.1
2006	1.13	451	1877	4.16	13.3	79	606	310	1321	4.26	9.3	44	347	3.5

* Average team's ratio of passes to runs. 1963 and 1973 are prorated to 16 games.

2.   Marshall Faulk   1999 St. Louis Rams

	Rush	RuYd	TD	Avg	Rec	RecYd	TD	Fum
Actual:	253	1381	7	5.46	87	1048	5	2
Adjusted:	265	1498	8	5.65	90	1005	3	2

Would you trade a second-round pick for the second-greatest running back season of all time? Faulk was only the second back in history to combine 1,000 yards rushing and 1,000 yards receiving, and he set a single-season record for yards from scrimmage that still stands. This is a good example of why you can't judge a running back on touchdown totals. Twelve players had more rushing touchdowns than Faulk in 1999, including players such as Leroy Hoard, Mario Bates, and Steve McNair, who isn't even a running back, but nobody can say that Faulk was not helping the Rams score points. His 1999 season is even more impressive because he put up these numbers right before rushing numbers league-wide took two leaps forward, first in 2000 and then again in 2002.

Faulk would have the number-one season overall if we didn't consider schedule strength, but as great as the 1999 Rams were, they may have played the easiest schedule in NFL history. The average Rams opponent had a DVOA of −14.3%. In the 11 years of DVOA, only two other teams have ever had opponents with an average DVOA below −10.0%: the 2000 Eagles (−10.3%) and the 2005 Seahawks (−10.1%).

The Colts can't feel too bad about trading Faulk away, because they drafted Edgerrin James to replace him, and James's first two seasons rank 59th and 66th on our list.

3.   Barry Sanders   1997 Detroit Lions

	Rush	RuYd	TD	Avg	Rec	RecYd	TD	Fum
Actual:	335	2053	11	6.13	33	305	3	3
Adjusted:	345	2134	13	6.19	43	394	2	3

Next time a star running back starts the season off slowly, consider Barry Sanders's 1997 season. Over his first two games, Sanders had just 25 carries for 53 yards. Over the next 14 weeks, he averaged more than 140 yards per game and 6.45 yards per carry. Sanders finishes third because he didn't score as much as Simpson, and he wasn't as far ahead of the league (Terrell Davis had 1,750 yards that year, with a season that ranks 44th).

4.   Earl Campbell   1980 Houston Oilers

	Rush	RuYd	TD	Avg	Rec	RecYd	TD	Fum
Actual:	373	1934	13	5.18	11	47	0	4
Adjusted:	396	2194	19	5.54	11	40	0	2

The Tyler Rose had his best season in 1980. It was his only season with more than five yards per carry, and the only season during his prime (1978 to 1981) in which he had fewer than eight fumbles. As noted earlier, Campbell represented a big milestone in the transition from shared running back workloads to teams using a single feature back. Because he was the first workhorse after the move to a 16-game season, Campbell also was the first running back to face the Curse of 370. In 1981, he dropped below four yards per carry, and 1983 was his only other above-average season.

5.   Thurman Thomas   1991 Buffalo Bills

	Rush	RuYd	TD	Avg	Rec	RecYd	TD	Fum
Actual:	288	1407	7	4.89	62	631	5	5
Adjusted:	347	1766	8	5.09	73	734	5	5

This was Thomas's MVP season, and the normalized numbers get a big boost because the workload for average top halfbacks rose significantly one year later. Unfortunately, this was also the year in which Thomas couldn't find his helmet before the Super Bowl, and when he did get in, he managed only 13 yards on ten carries.

6.   Leroy Kelly   1968 Cleveland Browns

	Rush	RuYd	TD	Avg	Rec	RecYd	TD	Fum
Actual:	248	1239	16	5.00	22	297	4	6
Adjusted:	335	1717	24	5.13	32	349	3	5

Kelly was an eighth-round pick out of Morgan State in 1964, and after Jim Brown retired, he took over and was almost as valuable. Kelly's best season actually comes out ahead of Jim Brown's best season, because we are using Z-scores rather than simply adjusted value. The starting running backs of 1968 had more value than they did during Brown's career, and those values were grouped closer together, making Kelly's dominance more impressive. Kelly led the league in rushing by 272 yards. He led the league in rushing touchdowns by five and in combined rushing and receiving touchdowns by six. He led the league by 21 carries, but that's not much compared with Brown's prime years, and Kelly actually did not lead the league in percentage of his team's total workload. Kelly had 55 percent of Cleveland's carries, but Tom Woodeshick had 59 percent of Philadelphia's carries, and Paul Robinson had 57 percent of the carries for the AFL's expansion Cincinnati Bengals.

Kelly's first three seasons as the featured back are in the top 100, and his fourth season ranks in the top 150, but Brown still had the better career. If we ranked the top five seasons for the pre-merger Cleveland Browns, Kelly's 1968 would rank number one, but Brown would have the next four.

7.   Barry Sanders   1994 Detroit Lions

	Rush	RuYd	TD	Avg	Rec	RecYd	TD	Fum
Actual:	331	1883	7	5.69	44	283	1	0
Adjusted:	372	2298	9	6.17	49	303	1	0

Sanders is the only running back with two seasons in the top ten and the only running back with three seasons in the top 20. His 1994 season stands out because it was a terrible year for running backs overall. Sanders's average per carry was more than a yard higher than any other starting running back's, and the 1994 league average of 3.73 yards per carry was the lowest in NFL history. Sanders also touched the ball 375 times without fumbling even once.

8.   Terrell Davis   1998 Denver Broncos

	Rush	RuYd	TD	Avg	Rec	RecYd	TD	Fum
Actual:	392	2008	21	5.12	25	217	2	2
Adjusted:	365	1975	22	5.41	29	219	1	2

Conventional wisdom says you could stick a Denver Broncos helmet on any running back and he would gain 1,000 yards. As we've written in the past, just because any running back could gain 1,000 yards in the Denver system, that does not mean that all running backs could have equal success in the Denver system. In his three best seasons, Davis comes in eighth, 44th, and 63rd. The only other Denver running back to make our top 100 under the current coaching staff was Clinton Portis in 2002 (91st). The second-best Denver season ever doesn't even belong to a runner during the Shanahan years. It belongs to the somewhat obscure Otis Armstrong, whose 1974 season ranks 23rd overall.

9.   Jim Brown   1963 Cleveland Browns

	Rush	RuYd	TD	Avg	Rec	RecYd	TD	Fum
Actual:	291	1863	12	6.40	24	268	3	7
Adjusted:	368	2358	19	6.41	39	298	1	5

It took until number nine, but here's our first season by the man considered by most to be the greatest running back in history. Brown's 1963 season produces the most adjusted rushing yardage of any season in the study, but it only comes in at number nine because the 1963 Browns' running game (primarily Brown) didn't move the chains as much as most of the other seasons in the top 20, and he doesn't have much value as a receiver.

Sanders has more top-20 seasons than Brown. Both have six seasons in the top 100. So why is Jim Brown considered the greatest running back of all time instead of Sanders? Every single one of Jim Brown's nine seasons ranks in the top 400, while three of Sanders's ten seasons don't finish in the top 500: 1992, 1993, and 1998. Brown and Walter Payton are the only backs with more than seven seasons in the top 500.

10. Larry Csonka   1971 Miami Dolphins

	Rush	RuYd	TD	Avg	Rec	RecYd	TD	Fum
Actual:	195	1051	7	5.39	13	113	1	0
Adjusted:	246	1361	12	5.52	21	162	1	0

Larry Csonka is a great example of how much running back usage has changed in the last 35 years. First of all, he was a fullback, not a halfback. Mack Strong led all fullbacks in

carries last year... with 33. (Mike Alstott is usually playing halfback when he carries the ball.) Unlike the fullbacks of today, Csonka carried the ball in all situations, but he also had a much smaller workload than the starting halfbacks of today, racking up just 40 percent of Miami's carries. Thus, our adjusted numbers increase his number of carries even though today's offenses run much less than the 1971 Dolphins did.

On top of everything else, Csonka played against an above-average schedule and didn't put the ball on the ground once. However, this is the only Miami Dolphins season in the top 100. Csonka's season for the perfect 1972 Dolphins comes in 156th because Csonka averaged fewer yards per carry against a far easier schedule.

11. O. J. Simpson   1973 Buffalo Bills

	Rush	RuYd	TD	Avg	Rec	RecYd	TD	Fum
Actual:	332	2003	12	6.03	6	70	0	7
Adjusted:	310	1811	18	5.84	8	77	0	6

Simpson's 1973 season would probably rank higher if we could go back and count the average defensive men in the box faced by each of these running backs. Simpson set a new all-time rushing record even though Joe Ferguson had one of the ten worst quarterback seasons in history according to our study from two years ago. Ferguson completed fewer than 45 percent of his passes, with ten interceptions and only four touchdowns. Eight in the box? Simpson was facing 11 in the box on every down.

12. Larry Johnson   2005 Kansas City Chiefs

	Rush	RuYd	TD	Avg	Rec	RecYd	TD	Fum
Actual:	336	1750	20	5.21	33	343	1	5
Adjusted:	338	1829	19	5.41	40	430	1	6

What if Larry Johnson had been the starting Kansas City running back right from the beginning of the season, instead of coming off the bench to spell Priest Holmes until Week 9? We tried to find out by removing the five weeks when Johnson had fewer than ten carries (Weeks 1 to 4 and Week 8) and replacing those five games with his average game from the other 11 weeks of the year. The resulting season would have shattered NFL records with 432 carries and 2,177 yards. However, it also would end up ranked in the exact same place in our list of the top running back seasons of all time, because if you take away the weeks when Johnson came off the bench, you have to take away his nine carries, 110 yards, and two touchdowns against the Jets in Week 1.

13. William Andrews   1983 Atlanta Falcons

	Rush	RuYd	TD	Avg	Rec	RecYd	TD	Fum
Actual:	331	1567	7	4.73	59	609	4	6
Adjusted:	313	1497	8	4.79	61	529	2	4

William Andrews *(continued)*

So far we've got a bunch of Hall of Famers, one borderline Hall of Famer, and one hot young back. Here's our first name that will be unfamiliar to most fans of today's game. Andrews was one of the last of the running fullbacks, and, unlike Csonka, he got the majority of his team's carries. Early in Andrews's career, the Falcons' halfback was Lynn Cain. In 1983, the Falcons hired Washington assistant head coach Dan Henning as their new head coach. Henning installed a Redskins-style, one-back offense, and Andrews flourished with huge numbers in everything but touchdowns. At the goal line, the Falcons often switched to their first-round pick from the 1982 draft, Gerald Riggs, who had 100 carries playing behind Andrews but led the team with eight touchdowns.

The next year, Andrews blew out his knee in training camp, and Riggs became the starter and one of the league's top backs. Riggs gained at least 1,300 yards for three straight years, and his 1985 season ranks 71st in our top 100. Andrews, unfortunately, lost two years to his knee injury, then retired after 52 substandard carries in 1986.

Fans today may not know about Andrews, but they know his legacy. Andrews was the first great Auburn running back in the NFL, the beginning of a line that includes men such as James Brooks, Bo Jackson, Stephen Davis, Rudi Johnson, and now Ronnie Brown and Cadillac Williams.

14. Jim Brown — 1965 Cleveland Browns

	Rush	RuYd	TD	Avg	Rec	RecYd	TD	Fum
Actual:	289	1544	17	5.34	34	328	4	6
Adjusted:	384	2154	27	5.61	47	319	2	4

The two greatest final seasons in the history of American sports ended within nine months of each other: Jim Brown retired at the top of his game after the 1965 season, and Dodgers pitcher Sandy Koufax called it quits nine months later.

15. Emmitt Smith — 1995 Dallas Cowboys

	Rush	RuYd	TD	Avg	Rec	RecYd	TD	Fum
Actual:	377	1773	25	4.70	62	375	0	7
Adjusted:	382	1843	23	4.82	64	384	0	6

When the day finally comes when we can analyze play-by-play from the glory years of the Dallas Cowboys, it will be interesting to see just how much value Smith's touchdowns really represent. The Cowboys gave the ball to Emmitt as soon as they crossed into the red zone, so a lot of his scores represent drives that were heavily fueled by passing. On the other hand, Troy Aikman wouldn't have completed as many passes if Smith wasn't putting him in 2nd-and-5 so often.

16. James Brooks — 1986 Cincinnati Bengals

	Rush	RuYd	TD	Avg	Rec	RecYd	TD	Fum
Actual:	205	1087	5	5.30	54	686	4	2
Adjusted:	222	1257	6	5.66	62	711	3	1

From *The New York Times*, May 30, 1984:

> The Cincinnati Bengals traded the disgruntled fullback Pete Johnson, their leading rusher the last seven seasons, to the San Diego Chargers yesterday for another top back, James Brooks. The deal ended what had become a stormy relationship between the Bengals' leadership and Johnson, whose 70 touchdowns are the most in the team's history.
>
> Part of the cause was Johnson's tendency to put on weight, a problem that was evident when he reported to the team last year after having been suspended by the National Football League the first month of the season because of cocaine use. Then, after the season, he demanded that his contract be renegotiated, and in recent weeks he had insisted that Cincinnati trade him or he would jump to the United States Football League.

If you like eighties nostalgia, you can't beat cocaine and the USFL in one paragraph. Johnson gained 46 yards for the Chargers on 19 carries before he was traded a second time, to Miami. He never played again after 1984, not even in the USFL. Brooks made the Pro Bowl for Cincinnati four times and played in a Super Bowl, and his best seasons rank 16th, 68th (1989), and 104th (1988) on our all-time list.

It was not a good trade for San Diego.

17. Jim Taylor — 1962 Green Bay Packers

	Rush	RuYd	TD	Avg	Rec	RecYd	TD	Fum
Actual:	272	1474	19	5.42	22	106	0	5
Adjusted:	342	1841	18	5.39	31	109	0	3

Vince Lombardi's power sweep dominated football during the sixties, and Jim Taylor was the man most often running behind it. Because running backs lose their speed quicker than they lose their jobs, Taylor was one of a number of players who has seasons in both the top *and* bottom 100 all-time. After nine great years in Green Bay, his final season came with the expansion New Orleans Saints in 1967. Taylor ran for 390 yards on 130 carries and scored just two touchdowns. It comes out as the 19th worst running back season ever. Abner Haynes, Chuck Foreman, and Ron Johnson also have seasons in both the top 100 and bottom 40.

18. Barry Sanders — 1995 Detroit Lions

	Rush	RuYd	TD	Avg	Rec	RecYd	TD	Fum
Actual:	314	1500	11	4.78	48	398	1	3
Adjusted:	339	1729	12	5.10	49	407	1	3

Here's our third Barry Sanders season. What would Sanders have done if the Lions had given him teammates?

19. Billy Sims   1981 Detroit Lions

	Rush	RuYd	TD	Avg	Rec	RecYd	TD	Fum
Actual:	296	1437	13	4.85	28	451	2	9
Adjusted:	264	1345	13	5.10	26	354	1	5

Billy Sims was the number-one overall pick in 1980 and had one of the greatest seasons ever just one year later. He was Barry Sanders before Barry Sanders: a spectacularly talented running back stuck on a Detroit Lions team that couldn't put any talent around him. Sims put up these numbers despite missing two games with injuries. There are two other seasons that might have made the top 20 if the running backs in question had not missed two games with injuries: Marshall Faulk in 2000 (22) and Priest Holmes in 2002 (25). And speaking of Mr. Holmes . . .

20. Priest Holmes   2003 Kansas City Chiefs

	Rush	RuYd	TD	Avg	Rec	RecYd	TD	Fum
Actual:	320	1420	27	4.44	74	690	0	1
Adjusted:	302	1302	25	4.31	69	675	0	1

Unfortunately, as much as we tried to approximate our DPAR stats with standard play-by-play from the past, the numbers are not exact. The top two running back seasons in DPAR (which dates back to 1996) are Priest Holmes in 2002 and Priest Holmes in 2003. In this study, those seasons come out 25th and 20th, respectively. Faulk's 1999 season and Johnson's 2005 season both finish above them, while Faulk's 2000 season finishes between them.

Oddly, while Holmes set a new all-time rushing touchdown record in 2003—since broken, of course—he was also one of just four players in NFL history to have more than 74 receptions in a single season without a receiving touchdown.

Other Seasons of Note

28. Clem Daniels   1963 Oakland Raiders

	Rush	RuYd	TD	Avg	Rec	RecYd	TD	Fum
Actual:	215	1099	3	5.11	30	685	5	8
Adjusted:	276	1425	5	5.17	49	763	2	5

This is the best running back season in AFL history, and one of three Raiders seasons in the top five for receiving value. Faulk's 1999 is the best running back receiving season ever, but Charlie Garner is second (41st overall), Marcus Allen is third (50th overall), and Daniels is fifth. Daniels was a product of Prairie View A&M, which won five national black college football titles back in the days of segregation but is now better known for its 80-game losing streak between 1989 and 1998.

30. Roger Craig   1985 San Francisco 49ers

	Rush	RuYd	TD	Avg	Rec	RecYd	TD	Fum
Actual:	214	1050	9	4.91	92	1016	6	5
Adjusted:	214	1055	11	4.93	93	866	4	3

Craig was the first running back ever to gain more than 1,000 yards both rushing and receiving in the same season. With our adjusted numbers, however, only Marshall Faulk's 1999 season hits 1,000 yards in both categories. Compared to the present, the average team in 1985 threw to the running back 14 percent more often with 20 percent more yards per reception.

33. LaDainian Tomlinson   2006 San Diego Chargers

	Rush	RuYd	TD	Avg	Rec	RecYd	TD	Fum
Actual:	348	1815	28	5.22	56	508	3	2
Adjusted:	334	1719	28	5.14	54	486	5	3

Tomlinson may not have had one of the best running back seasons ever, but he certainly is the touchdown king. His adjusted numbers actually include two extra touchdowns, because receiving touchdowns for running backs were significantly down last year across the league. No other running back has a season with more than 30 combined touchdowns, even after projecting everyone into a 21st century offense. Jim Brown's 1965 is the only season within five touchdowns of Tomlinson's 2006 campaign. All those touchdowns also make this the second-best fantasy football season in history, behind Simpson's 1975 campaign.

Tomlinson is the only player who makes the top 100 from 2006. Four other running backs from last year make the top 250: Larry Johnson (113), Steven Jackson (167), Brian Westbrook (202), and Joseph Addai (246).

NA. Bo Jackson   1989 Los Angeles Raiders

	Rush	RuYd	TD	Avg	Rec	RecYd	TD	Fum
Actual:	173	950	4	5.49	9	69	0	1
Adjusted:	190	1092	4	5.75	11	72	0	1
What If:	280	1618	8	5.75	16	104	0	1

What if Bo Jackson didn't play baseball? We took Jackson's best year in the NFL and prorated his stats to a full season, as if he spent September with the Raiders instead of the Kansas City Royals. The resulting Z-score would put Jackson right below Tomlinson on our all-time list of the greatest running back seasons. If we count just the 11 games that Jackson actually played, this season doesn't even make the top 600.

48. Eric Dickerson   1988 Indianapolis Colts

	Rush	RuYd	TD	Avg	Rec	RecYd	TD	Fum
Actual:	388	1659	14	4.28	36	377	1	5
Adjusted:	402	1762	16	4.38	41	397	1	3

85. Eric Dickerson   1984 Los Angeles Rams

	Rush	RuYd	TD	Avg	Rec	RecYd	TD	Fum
Actual:	379	2105	14	5.55	21	139	0	14
Adjusted:	366	2014	14	5.51	21	128	0	8

Eric Dickerson (continued)

Eric Dickerson is the grand exception to the Curse of 370, the only running back to carry high workloads year after year without falling apart. He had a Hall of Fame career, but only two of his seasons show up in the top 100. We judge 84 seasons as better than the year in which Dickerson set the all-time rushing yardage record. Where's the love for everyone's favorite former sideline announcer?

Dickerson's problem was an acute case of fumblitis. His 1988 season in Indianapolis ranks highest on our list because it only has five fumbles. In his first four seasons, Dickerson fumbled a total of 49 times. Even in the eighties, when running backs fumbled more often, this was a huge problem. Since 1978, the only running back with more fumbles in a season than Dickerson's 14 in 1984 was Joe Cribbs with 16 in 1990.

82. Shaun Alexander   2005 Seattle Seahawks

	Rush	RuYd	TD	Avg	Rec	RecYd	TD	Fum
Actual:	370	1880	27	5.08	15	78	1	5
Adjusted:	369	1866	24	5.06	18	98	1	6

Here's the touchdown total that stood as an NFL record for less than 12 months. Tomlinson's normalized numbers include more touchdowns than he actually had, but normalization and accounting for schedule strength takes three touchdowns away from Alexander.

229. Jamal Lewis   2003 Baltimore Ravens

	Rush	RuYd	TD	Avg	Rec	RecYd	TD	Fum
Actual:	387	2066	14	5.34	26	205	0	8
Adjusted:	370	1921	13	5.18	24	201	0	7

How does the second-highest rushing total in NFL history not make a list of the top 100 running back seasons of all time? Belying his reputation as an up-the-middle battering ram, Lewis had a classic boom-and-bust year in 2003. Sanders is known as the greatest boom-and-bust runner ever, but when he gained 2,053 yards in 1997, the Lions had 120 rushing first downs. In 2003, the Ravens had only 115 rushing first downs, even though Lewis had 56 more carries than Sanders, and the Ravens as a team had 106 more carries than the 1997 Lions. The Ravens' running game—consisting mostly of Lewis—had 4.8 runs for every rushing first down. No player in our top 50 was on a team that needed more than 4.5 runs for every rushing first down.

NA. Herschel Walker   1985 New Jersey Generals

	Rush	RuYd	TD	Avg	Rec	RecYd	TD	Fum
Actual:	438	2411	21	5.50	37	467	1	NA

We didn't bother trying to do any kind of adjustment, but we figured it was worth mentioning the best running season that isn't in the NFL record books. The USFL had an 18-game sea-

son, but still, these numbers are completely absurd. Four hundred thiry-eight carries? He certainly didn't face NFL-level defenses, but Walker had more yards per game than Dickerson had when he set the NFL record for rushing yardage in 1984.

A full list of the top 100 seasons can be found in an appendix at the end of this book.

Most Seasons in the Top 100

Jim Brown: 6 (1958, 1960–61, 1963–65)
Barry Sanders: 6 (1989–90, 1994–97)
Walter Payton: 5 (1977–1979, 1983–84)
Jim Taylor: 4 (1960–62, 1964)

Most Seasons in the Top 500

Jim Brown: 9 (1958–65)
Walter Payton: 9 (1976–80, 1983–86)
Barry Sanders: 7 (1989–91, 1994–97)
Emmitt Smith: 7 (1991–95, 1998–99)
James Brooks: 6 (1982, 1985–86, 1988–90)
Earnest Byner: 6 (1987, 1989–92, 1996)
Marshall Faulk: 6 (1994, 1997–2001)
Curtis Martin: 6 (1995–96, 1999–2001, 2004)
Lenny Moore: 6 (1957–1961, 1964)

Franchises with the Most Seasons in the Top 100

Cleveland Browns: 9 (Jim Brown 6, Leroy Kelly 3)
Baltimore/Indianapolis Colts: 9 (Lenny Moore 3, Edgerrin James 3, Albert Bentley 1, Eric Dickerson 1, Tom Matte 1)
Detroit Lions: 8 (Barry Sanders 6, Steve Owens 1, Billy Sims 1)
Chicago Bears: 8 (Walter Payton 5, Gale Sayers 2, Neal Anderson 1)
Kansas City Chiefs: 7 (Priest Holmes 3, Abner Haynes 2, Larry Johnson 1, Tony Reed 1)

Franchise Highs

Here are the top seasons for each franchise, unless mentioned above:

Chicago Bears: Walter Payton, 1977 (21)
Baltimore/Indianapolis Colts: Tom Matte, 1969 (24)
San Francisco 49ers: Garrison Hearst, 1998 (29)
Philadelphia Eagles: Wilbert Montgomery, 1981 (34)
New York Giants: Joe Morrison, 1969 (42)
New York Jets: Freeman McNeil, 1982 (46)
Minnesota Vikings: Chuck Foreman, 1976 (57)
Chicago/St. Louis/Arizona Cardinals: MacArthur Lane, 1970 (64)
Seattle Seahawks: Curt Warner, 1986 (77)
Washington Redskins: Larry Brown, 1970 (79)
New England Patriots: Corey Dillon, 2004 (95)

Pittsburgh Steelers: Rocky Bleier, 1976 (106)

New Orleans Saints: Chuck Muncie, 1979 (135)

Jacksonville Jaguars: Fred Taylor, 1998 (175)

Tampa Bay Buccaneers: Ricky Bell, 1979 (302)

Houston Texans: Domanick Davis, 2004 (375)

Carolina Panthers: Stephen Davis, 2003 (422)

Morrison was often split out as a receiver; the best Giants season by a more conventional running back belongs to Tiki Barber in 2005 (54th overall). The best non-strike year for the New York Jets is Curtis Martin in 2004 (52nd).

The most shocking omission from the top 100 is not any particular player, but rather a specific team. The Steelers may be identified with the running game more than any other NFL franchise, yet no running back from Pittsburgh has ever had a really phenomenal season.

By conventional stats, that's not true. Barry Foster ran for 1,690 yards in 1992, and Jerome Bettis for 1,665 yards in 1997. Unfortunately, Bettis needed 375 carries, which works out to 4.4 yards per carry. Foster needed 390 carries, which works out to 4.3 yards per carry. Normalized, Foster's 1992 season comes out as 1,932 yards on 429 carries, which is the highest number of carries in the study. Both players also suffered from fumblitis and didn't score as much as you might expect. Bettis had six fumbles and seven rushing touchdowns. Foster had nine fumbles and 11 rushing touchdowns. As a result, Foster's 1992 season comes in at number 173, and Bettis's 1997 season comes in at number 237.

As for Carolina, there are 772 seasons with a positive Z score, and only two of them are by members of the Carolina Panthers: Anthony Johnson in 1996, and Davis in 2003.

Universities with the Most Alumni Seasons in the Top 100

Oklahoma State: 9 (Barry Sanders 6, Thurman Thomas 3)

Syracuse: 7 (Jim Brown 6, Larry Csonka 1)

Georgia: 6 (Terrell Davis 3, Herschel Walker 2, Garrison Hearst 1)

Miami: 6 (Edgerrin James 3, Albert Bentley 1, Chuck Foreman 1, Clinton Portis 1)

Auburn: 5 (William Andrews 2, James Brooks 2, Stephen Davis 1)

Jackson State: 5 (Walter Payton)

Penn State: 5 (Lenny Moore 3, Larry Johnson 1, Curt Warner 1)

Texas: 5 (Priest Holmes 3, Earl Campbell 2)

Best Rookie Running Backs

1. Gale Sayers, 1965 Chicago Bears (43)
2. Edgerrin James, 1999 Indianapolis Colts (59)
3. Tony Dorsett, 1977 Dallas Cowboys (81)
4. Barry Sanders, 1989 Detroit Lions (89)
5. Clinton Portis, 2002 Denver Broncos (90)

How much easier is the transition from college to the NFL for running backs, compared to quarterbacks? Five rookie running backs rank in the top 100. When we did our list of the top quarterback seasons two years ago, only two rookies even made the top 300: Greg Cook and Ben Roethlisberger.

The Worst Running Back Season of All Time

Melvin Carver   1983 Tampa Bay Buccaneers

	Rush	RuYd	TD	Avg	Rec	RecYd	TD	Fum
Actual:	114	348	0	3.05	32	262	1	6
Adjusted:	106	322	0	3.02	33	227	1	4

Not only did Carver barely make it over three yards per carry, he struggled against an easy schedule. Normalized to current conditions, the 1983 Tampa Bay Bucs had less than four rushing first downs per game.

Methodology

This study began with a regression analysis on all starting running backs between 2002 and 2006. This created an equation that took standard stats and turned them into an approximation of our DPAR numbers. Since we couldn't use play-by-play to figure out which running backs were consistent on the ground or useful in the passing game, we tested a number of team stats in our equation, trying to find indicators that would help us separate the low-DPAR seasons from high-DPAR seasons with similar standard numbers.

We don't have access to individual first downs, but we do have access to team first downs, split into rushing and passing. That allowed us to give credit to running backs for having a higher percentage of their team's first downs come on the ground, but also for total first downs, since consistent running on first downs usually leads to more conversions in the passing game on second and third down. We also looked at what percentage of a team's total carries resulted in a first down.

The regression showed that a high interception total from the quarterback indicated a lower DPAR from the running back, because a bad running game puts the quarterback in a bad position, and that makes interceptions more likely. The more a team outscored its opponents, the higher the running back's DPAR in the passing game—until the team scored 105 points more than its opponents, at which point outscoring opponents became less favorable.

It also turned out that better performance from the backup running backs meant less DPAR for the starter. The smaller the gap between the starting running back and his backups, the more likely it was that we were giving the starter too much credit for all the team stats we were using in the equation. However, we didn't want to give the number-one overall slot to someone just because the other backs on the team happened to average only two yards per carry, so we made the minimum for "other team running backs" equal replacement level—which, as it is for DPAR, was 13.3 percent below that season's league-average performance.

Our regression analysis included one last important number that we didn't have for our quarterback study two years ago: fumbles. Even better, the fumble totals represent actual fumbles, not just fumbles recovered by the running back's own team.

To solve the problem of running back workloads, we based our adjustments on two different averages. The first set consisted of the basic numbers from each season: yards per carry, rushing touchdowns per team, etc. The second set represented the average performance of the running backs with the biggest workloads in the league each year. We called this group "average top-half backs" because the number of running backs measured always equaled half the number of teams that year. For today's game, we used the top 16 backs; for the NFL in the sixties, we used seven. The baseline for adjusting stats came from the past five years, rather than just 2006.

Strength of schedule was the final step, adjusting numbers based on the yards per carry, rushing touchdowns, total carries, and overall yards per play for the average defense faced by the running back in that season.

Running backs who did not cross picket lines in 1987 were adjusted based on a 12-game season, not a 15-game season.

Baltimore Ravens

Brian Billick long ago made peace with the fact that defense rules the roost in Baltimore, allowing his reputation as an offensive genius to get a little dustier each year as his record-setting 1998 Vikings unit fades into the rearview mirror. Billick has stifled his aerial instincts as the Ravens' head coach, understanding that the job of the Baltimore offense during his tenure has been to capitalize on the good field position provided by the defense and salt away games with a smashmouth rushing attack led by Jamal Lewis and a short passing game.

As expected, veteran quarterback Steve McNair, a late offseason acquisition from Tennessee, proved to be the right type of passer for this system in 2006. McNair helped the offense hold up its end of the bargain in a way that Kyle Boller and a host of other Baltimore quarterbacks failed to in years past. McNair understood his—and the offense's—role in Baltimore's winning formula. He rarely took ill-advised chances, and though he threw 12 interceptions, few of them were killers. At this point in his career, McNair is leaning on his considerable football IQ as much as his physical skills. He's no longer a scrambler but can still use his legs to step out of a sack or pick up a key first down. His strength on his feet and his pocket awareness allowed him to avoid countless sacks last year. He deserves much of the credit for his offensive line's league-leading Adjusted Sack Rate.

McNair was interception-free in seven of Baltimore's final ten regular-season games, content to throw short crossing routes and dumpoffs and to watch Lewis bludgeon teams into submission in the fourth quarter. It wasn't always pretty, but the net results were impressive. The Ravens improved from 27th in offensive DVOA in 2005 to 14th in 2006. Moreover, most of the improvement came in

---

RAVENS PROSPECTUS

2006 Record: 13-3

DVOA Estimated Wins: 12.0 (2nd)

Pythagorean Wins: 12.7 (1st)

DVOA: 31.8% total (1st), 36.0% weighted (1st)

Offense: 2.6% DVOA (15th)

Defense: −25.8% DVOA (1st)

Special Teams: 3.5% DVOA (4th)

Variance: 17.0% (12th)

2006: Defense still carried the day, but the offense tried to do its part.

2007: Brian Billick will attempt to earn his offensive "genius" stripes again.

2007 Mean Projection: 9.0 wins

The Brohm Closet (0–4): 3%

Bad Team (5–6): 9%

Mediocre (7–8): 30%

Playoff Contender (9–10): 32%

Super Bowl Contender (11+): 26%

Projected Average Opponent: 1.0% DVOA (12th in NFL)

---

the passing game, where Baltimore went from 25th in 2005 to 11th with McNair at the controls. The running game was only slightly better than the year before (improving from 31st to 24th). The Ravens' offense ranked even higher (11th) in our weighted DVOA metric, which discounts early season results to show how a team is playing at the end of the year. For a team whose offensive approach for years has been simply to find a way to score 17 points, the improvement was marked.

If there's one thing the Ravens need from their offense, it is consistency. With a defense strong enough to win games on its own, an inconsistent offense could have cost Baltimore several wins. But here, too, the even-handed play of McNair proved effective. Baltimore's offensive variance went from 11th in 2005 to 29th in 2006, indicating a unit whose play varied little from week to week.

The Ravens began the season playing offense the way they always have—relying on Lewis and a bevy of slants and short passes. A growing comfort with McNair led to a more aggressive approach in the second half—coinciding roughly with the dismissal of Jim Fassel as offensive coordinator and the assumption of the play-calling duties by Billick. The head coach seemed to have a knack for calling the deep ball at precisely the right time, and Baltimore scored a number of long touchdowns on plays on which receivers were completely uncovered down the field.

The formula worked to perfection in the regular season, but Baltimore's season ended with a meek offensive display in a 15–6 home loss to Indianapolis in the divisional round. McNair threw two costly interceptions and the Ravens turned the ball over twice more on fumbles. Whatever gains the offense had made during the season were lost as the Ravens managed just three drives of more than five plays.

2007 Ravens Schedule

Week	Opp	Week	Opp	Week	Opp
1	at CIN (Mon.)	7	at BUF	13	NE (Mon.)
2	NYJ	8	BYE	14	IND
3	ARI	9	at PIT (Mon.)	15	at MIA
4	at CLE	10	CIN	16	at SEA
5	at SF	11	CLE	17	PIT
6	STL	12	at SD		

Perhaps it was that performance—losing a home play-off game despite not allowing a touchdown—that convinced Billick and general manager Ozzie Newsome of the need to create a more explosive offense to better complement the team's defense. The Ravens entered the offseason with a tight salary cap, but for the second straight year they managed to make an impact acquisition on offense. Baltimore said good-bye to Lewis and replaced him with Willis McGahee, acquired via an offseason trade with Buffalo. On the surface, this is a simple upgrade. Though McGahee has yet to show the consistent production that would place him among the league's elite backs, he represents an improvement over the aging Lewis.

McGahee's presence in the Baltimore backfield could also lead to a change in offensive philosophy for the Ravens. With Lewis in 2006, Baltimore ran between the tackles at an abnormally high rate. Play-by-play data shows that 67 percent of Baltimore's running plays were up the middle or over the guard—tied with Jacksonville for the league lead—as compared with the league average of 49 percent. Just 10 percent of Baltimore's carries were around the ends, less than half the league average of 22 percent.

We aren't the only observers who noticed this stunning lack of variety in the Baltimore running game. Opponents who studied film of the Ravens saw this trend flashing like a neon sign and stacked defenses to prepare for it. The approach certainly didn't help Baltimore's offensive line, which, despite its first overall ranking in Adjusted Sack Rate (the statistic we use to measure pass protection), ranked just 19th in Adjusted Line Yards.

The Ravens displayed slightly more variety in the run game in 2005—when 55 percent of their attempts were up the middle—but with even worse results. Perhaps Billick just decided last year to play to Lewis's remaining strength—his power. Billick may have come to peace with the fact that Lewis has lost a step or three but could still be somewhat effective when deployed as a battering ram.

That strategy will change with McGahee, a more dynamic back than Lewis was even in his prime. Despite running behind a worse offensive line (Buffalo was 26th in Adjusted Line Yards) and on a team with a worse offense

overall (24th vs. 14th for Baltimore), McGahee outperformed Lewis last season, finishing 21st in DPAR compared with 40th for Lewis.

Billick and the Ravens got a firsthand view of the possibilities McGahee presents to their offense when the Bills visited Baltimore in Week 17 last season. Buffalo's first two offensive snaps in that game were a screen pass to McGahee, which he turned into a big gain (called back by penalty), and a handoff to McGahee on an outside run—two plays that last year's Baltimore offense rarely executed.

If McGahee is successful in making the Baltimore running game more dynamic, the Ravens may finally have an offense that can win a few games on its own. Though Rick Neuheisel nominally takes over as the offensive coordinator in 2007, Billick will maintain play-calling duties and control over the direction of the offense. With McGahee in the picture, Billick might be wise to start leaning on his improving offense a little more.

It can be difficult to see past the Ravens' defense, however. Baltimore's defense was the NFL's dominant unit in 2006—ranking first in both DVOA and total yardage allowed. The Ravens led the league with 37 takeaways, as their brand of ultra-aggressive, shifting defense confused and harried opposing quarterbacks into mistakes. Defensive coordinator Rex Ryan developed this scheme, which mirrors the approach of his father, the legendary defensive strategist Buddy Ryan, and seems perfectly suited to the personality of his club.

Baltimore's defensive leader remains Ray Lewis, who is not nearly the player he was four or five years ago, but who still sets the emotional tone for his fellow defenders to follow. It seems at times that when players put on a Ravens uniform, they all adopt Lewis's fiery persona. Indeed, the Ravens can look lost without Lewis on the field. The defense was completely discombobulated when Lewis missed a game in Nashville against the Titans. Tennessee piled up big plays and early points before McNair led the Ravens to a late rally.

Baltimore blitzes from everywhere, gets everyone involved in rushing the passer, and ball-hawks like no other team. When the Ravens do get a turnover, all 11 players instantly begin devising a path to the end zone.

All that aggression comes with a price—the Ravens are vulnerable to pump-fakes and double moves and give up plenty of big plays. While Baltimore's offense rode a more consistent attack to improvement in 2006, the opposite was true for the defense. As the Ravens improved from fifth to first in overall DVOA, their defensive variance rose to 14th in the league from 28th. Such is the price of the big-play approach.

If the Ravens are to build on the successes of 2006 and contend for a Super Bowl berth this fall, they'll have to overcome some key personnel losses—none bigger than pass-rushing outside linebacker Adalius Thomas, who signed as a free agent with New England. The Ravens hope that Jarret Johnson, a fourth-round pick in 2003, develops into the same kind of threat off the edge. Still, even if Johnson proves a decent stand-in for Thomas, Baltimore is thin at the position.

The offense must also replace some key contributors. Longtime starting guard Edwin Mulitalo was released, and starting right tackle Tony Pashos signed with Jacksonville. The Ravens feel good about Adam Terry replacing Pashos on the right side, but the club is thin at tackle beyond Terry and Jonathan Ogden, and it took the veteran All-Pro Ogden a good chunk of the offseason to decide to return for a 12th season.

Also lost to free agency was starting fullback Ovie Mughelli, who signed a lucrative deal with the Falcons. The Ravens will replace him with either Justin Green, who is coming off an ACL tear, or 2007 draftee Le'Ron McClain. The Ravens like to use their fullbacks in the passing game and as short-yardage rushers, and Green did display decent hands in limited action last season.

The draft also brought help for the offensive line in the form of Auburn guard Ben Grubbs, selected with the 29th pick, and third-round guard/tackle Marshall Yanda. Grubbs should compete for a starting spot in camp, while Yanda will be counted on to back up both positions.

Aside from personnel changes, our statistical models hint at several factors working against Baltimore heading into the 2007 season. Our research shows that teams that pile up a lot of sacks tend to suffer a drop-off the following season; Baltimore was second in the NFL with 60 sacks last year, a big increase over their 2005 total of 42.

Perhaps the biggest factor suggesting a tougher season for the Ravens was their offensive performance on third down in 2006. As ranked by DVOA, Baltimore's offense was 17th in the NFL on first down, 22nd on second down, but 6th on third down. When an offense performs significantly better on third down than overall, it suggests that a regression to the mean may be forthcoming.

Baltimore also benefited from some friendly bounces on both sides of the ball. During one three-game, midseason stretch, Baltimore scored five touchdowns on deflected balls, three of them on offense. That type of outright luck is unlikely to carry over from season to season—or, in the Ravens' case, from season to postseason. Against the Colts, Baltimore saw a field goal bounce in off the crossbar, lost two interceptions when teammates collided with one another, and lost a fumble on a replay-reversal.

Still, even if their luck evens out a bit, Baltimore will contend for another AFC North title. Maybe these will be the same old Ravens—too stout on defense to fail, too empty of offense to contend. But the tea leaves suggest the balance could shift a bit this season—which might be exactly what Baltimore needs to get over the hump and return to the Super Bowl.

Russell Levine

Do Certain Backs Improve with Consecutive Carries?

Willis McGahee's arrival in Baltimore means that Brian Billick is about to get dumber. Up and down the dial, from "Sportsline" on WBAL to "SportsTalk 1570," get ready for all the callers pleading for the Ravens coach to "commit to the run."

The public wants to know: Why won't anyone just give Willis the ball? McGahee played for two regimes in Buffalo, and both showed a reluctance to let him pound it four straight times on 1st-and-goal. Late-game leads were rare, but rarer still was a steady diet of McGahee to wear down the defense and kill the clock.

Why the history of frustrating play calling? After all, it isn't as if all of McGahee's coaches have been pass happy tricksters more concerned with looking smart than succeeding (although we'll give you Mike Mularkey).

Part of the problem is that McGahee seems to wear down faster than the defenses he's supposed to be pounding. And he's not alone. While McGahee may benefit from rest more than other backs, the trend is league-wide. The returns on back-to-back carries don't just diminish, they shrivel. On a second straight carry, yardage declines by an average of more than five percent; on the third straight carry, it drops by nine percent. This trend has been relatively consistent over the past five years (table 1).

An obvious explanation for this trend would be that teams don't need as many yards on the second and third carry. For instance, after gains of five and four yards, a one-yard run on third down would be considered a success, even though it pulls down the consecutive yardage numbers.

Table 1. Average Gain on Consecutive Carries, 2002–2006

Year	Rested	Carry 2	Carry 3	Carry 4+
2006	4.28	4.05	3.69	3.15
2005	4.12	4.06	3.61	3.31
2004	4.30	3.99	3.62	3.18
2003	4.27	4.06	3.92	2.75
2002	4.27	3.97	3.21	3.72

NOTE: "Rested" indicates a carry following a play in which the player did not carry the ball; it does not necessarily mean he was not on the field for the previous play.

Removing all plays with just one yard to go, we see that while the fullback dives and over-the-top goal line plays are skewing the numbers slightly, the decline on consecutive carries doesn't go away (table 2).

Table 2. Average Gain on Consecutive Carries, 2+ Yards to Go, 2006

Year	Rested	Carry 2	Carry 3	Carry 4+
2006	4.39	4.10	4.04	3.46
2005	4.19	4.18	3.69	3.53
2004	4.37	4.11	3.91	3.37
2003	4.38	4.11	4.06	3.03
2002	4.35	4.07	3.15	4.08

Looking for the true battering rams? The guys who beat a defense into submission, taking a little more each time they hit a defense? Think Barry Sanders, not Ironhead Heyward. A look at the seven backs from 2006 who increased their rushing average on repeated carries shows that it's harder to swat a fly three times in a row than it is to stop a locomotive (table 3).

Table 3. RB with Increased Rushing Average on Successive Carries, 2006

Player	Rested	Carry 2	Carry 3
Frank Gore	5.20	5.93	6.06
Jamal Lewis	3.47	3.94	4.36
Tiki Barber	4.90	5.34	8.00
Corey Dillon	3.91	4.23	7.43
Shaun Alexander	3.45	3.76	4.91
Warrick Dunn	3.95	4.18	4.43
Ronnie Brown	4.03	4.25	5.44

Improvement on successive carries is rare and inconsistent. None of the seven backs on the battering ram list for 2006 repeated the achievement in a prior year. In fact, Lewis, Dunn, and Brown were on the opposite list in 2005—backs whose average fell on each successive carry. That's an easier list to make, as there have been about twice as many falling backs as improving backs each of the last three years.

Aggregate data over the last five seasons shows how rare it is to get stronger on three successive carries. Only six backs improved on their second and third carries over that time period (table 4), and only two of them continued their improvement on a fourth carry. Of the two that could be considered full-time backs, one (Westbrook) is often split out and hardly a banger. The other (Williams) has just two years of history.

It's easier for a running back to keep a spot on the steady decline list. Three of the 11 backs who showed

Table 4. Backs with Increased Rushing Average on Successive Carries, 2002–2006

Player	Rested	Carry 2	Carry 3
Artose Pinner	2.88	3.24	5.17
Cadillac Williams	3.47	4.61	6.12
Jonathan Wells *	3.00	3.46	3.78
Michael Pittman *	4.09	4.55	5.91
Brian Westbrook	4.61	4.86	6.93
Mike Anderson	4.20	4.41	4.73

* Also increased rushing average on fourth straight carry.

decline on carries two and three were repeats from 2005 (table 5). Fred Taylor and Kevin Jones fell just shy of the minimum number of carries to qualify last season, or they too would have repeated from 2005. Edgerrin James, Tatum Bell, McGahee, and Chester Taylor all made the 2004 list as well.

Table 5. RB with Decreased Rushing Average on Successive Carries, 2006

Player	Rested	Carry 2	Carry 3
Edgerrin James	**3.56**	**3.55**	**1.53**
Willis McGahee	**4.03**	**3.74**	**3.00**
Ladell Betts	**5.32**	**3.48**	**2.93**
Maurice Jones-Drew	6.07	5.75	2.45
Chester Taylor	4.34	3.87	2.00
Rudi Johnson	4.04	3.53	3.18
LaDainian Tomlinson	5.47	4.92	2.64
Larry Johnson	4.60	3.78	3.28
Tatum Bell	4.83	3.98	1.55
Steven Jackson	4.87	3.03	2.54
Mike Bell	4.94	3.03	2.20

NOTE: Bold indicates repeat performance from 2005.

Over the last five years, 36 backs saw their averages drop on each of three successive carries. Fourteen of them continued the decline on carry four. Just like with movies, the running back sequel is rarely as good as the original.

It's no coincidence that Denver's running backs-by-committee and Jacksonville's tandem of Jones-Drew and Taylor are all regulars on the steady-decline list. As the league trends toward time-shares in the backfield, one benefit is a more potent attack on repeated runs. When we look at teams running the ball on consecutive downs, regardless of whether the same back gets the ball, the decline is less steep (table 6).

When the Bills used Anthony Thomas to give Willis a breather, McGahee's numbers went up significantly. Buffalo's performance on back-to-back rushes was almost flat—3.92 on the first carry, 3.91 on the second.

Table 6. Consecutive Runs, Team vs. Player, 2006

	Rested	Carry 2	Carry 3
Same back	4.28	4.05	3.69
Team carries	4.28	4.13	3.83

Teams didn't need equal time at running back in order to be able to hammer a defense. A back that could step in for a breather was sufficient. Among the teams that had virtually no drop-off from carry to carry were Carolina (Foster and Williams), Tampa (Williams, Alstott, and Pittman), Chicago (Jones and Benson), and Indianapolis (Rhodes and Addai).

Baltimore, on the strength of a battering ram season from the since-departed Jamal Lewis, was the only team to improve from carry to carry last year. That sets up unreachable expectations for the Ravens' running game in 2007. Whether Brian Billick and company heed the evidence above or learn the same lesson on their own, Ravens fans are far less likely to witness McGahee wearing down opposing lines than they are to clog the sports-radio phone lines with outraged cries of "Get Willis the ball!"

Shawn Krest

Ravens 2006 Stats by Week

Wk	vs.	W–L	PF	PA	YDF	YDA	TO	Total	Off	Def	ST
1	@TB	W	27	0	271	142	+3	38.6%	-13.6%	-52.7%	-0.5%
2	OAK	W	28	6	264	162	+5	67.2%	6.1%	-55.0%	6.1%
3	@CLE	W	15	14	340	288	+2	2.7%	-5.1%	3.3%	11.1%
4	SD	W	16	13	207	284	-2	17.1%	-31.5%	-43.1%	5.4%
5	@DEN	L	3	13	257	222	-1	-37.1%	-38.2%	-13.1%	-11.9%
6	CAR	L	21	23	292	414	0	0.3%	-12.3%	-5.0%	7.7%
7	BYE										
8	@NO	W	35	22	293	403	+4	71.4%	17.7%	-53.1%	0.6%
9	CIN	W	26	20	374	275	+3	50.0%	23.4%	-7.0%	19.6%
10	@TEN	W	27	26	421	367	-1	-12.8%	-2.8%	13.1%	3.1%
11	ATL	W	24	10	328	186	-1	35.0%	15.4%	-8.9%	10.7%
12	PIT	W	27	0	275	172	+3	112.7%	34.9%	-70.5%	7.3%
13	@CIN	L	7	13	316	294	-1	-29.8%	-3.6%	9.3%	-16.9%
14	@KC	W	20	10	376	276	+2	52.6%	16.9%	-30.4%	5.3%
15	CLE	W	27	17	373	276	-1	2.3%	-9.1%	-12.1%	-0.7%
16	@PIT	W	31	7	359	251	0	77.3%	24.0%	-45.3%	8.0%
17	BUF	W	19	7	327	253	+2	56.7%	6.8%	-46.3%	3.6%
18	BYE										
19	IND	L	6	15	244	261	-2	10.0%	-55.6%	-52.8%	12.8%

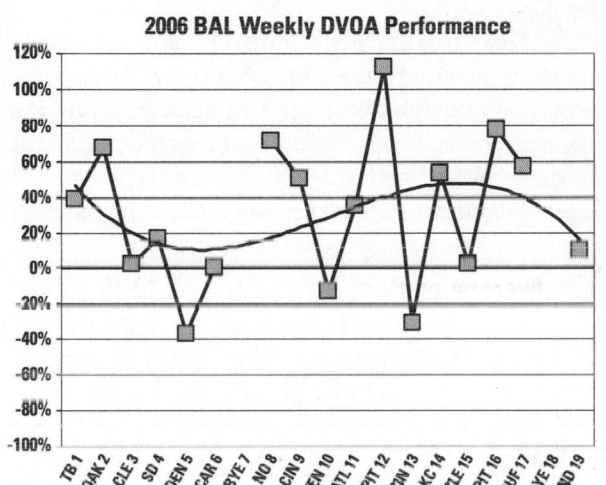

2006 BAL Weekly DVOA Performance

Trends and Splits

	Offense	Rank	Defense	Rank
Total DVOA	2.6%	15	-25.8%	1
Unadjusted VOA	3.7%	13	-28.6%	1
Weighted Trend	8.9%	11	-23.6%	1
Variance	3.8%	29	6.9%	14
Passing	13.8%	11	-25.1%	1
Rushing	-9.7%	24	-26.7%	2
First Down	-1.3%	17	-20.8%	3
Second Down	-5.5%	22	-26.4%	2
Third Down	20.7%	6	-34.2%	3
Red Zone	11.9%	10	-46.4%	1
Late and Close	-0.2%	15	-26.8%	2

Five-Year Performance

	2006	2005	2004	2003	2002
W-L	13-3	6-10	9-7	10-6	7-9
Pythagorean Wins	12.7	6.9	9.6	11.0	6.9
Estimated Wins	0.0	7.3	10.0	10.2	8.5
Total DVOA	31.8%	-5.2%	16.8%	18.5%	-1.5%
Rank	1	19	9	6	17
Offense	2.6%	-16.7%	-5.4%	-12.7%	-5.4%
Rank	15	27	20	26	24
Defense	-25.8%	-11.1%	-19.3%	-28.4%	-6.5%
Rank	1	5	2	1	6
Special Teams	3.5%	0.4%	3.0%	2.8%	-2.6%
Rank	4	13	8	6	23

Strategic Tendencies

Formations		Rank	Run/Pass		Rank	Defense		Rank	Other		Rank
3+ WR	33%	32	Runs, all plays	45%	15	Sacks by LB	61%	4	Run with 2+ RB	73%	5
4+ WR	8%	20	Runs, first half	45%	17	Sacks by DB	11%	10	Run with 2+ TE	48%	4
2+ TE	36%	3	Runs, first down	58%	11	Rush 6+	9.8%	13	Play action	24%	6
Single back	39%	29	Runs, power sit.	59%	24	Rush 7+	1.6%	14	Go for it on 4th	0.94	14
Empty back	4.8%	5	Runs, behind 2H	32%	19	Rush 3	5.8%	7	Offensive Pace	32.1	28
Max protect	16%	5	Pass, ahead 2H	45%	12	CB1 on WR1	32%	31	Defensive Pace	30.7	18

Baltimore opponents only ran 62 play-action fakes, the lowest total in the league, and gained just 4.7 net yards per pass attempt on play-action. The Jets and Patriots were the only teams with a better defensive DVOA against play-action passes, and the Jets were the only other team to allow fewer than five yards per play-action pass.... The Ravens posted their best DVOA (50.4%) with four-wide receiver sets (which includes plays with tight end Todd Heap as a slot receiver), well in excess of their other formations.... The passing attack was more efficient with two wide receivers (20.1% DVOA) than with three wide receivers (0.4% DVOA).... Only Tampa Bay lined up more often with both two running backs *and* two tight ends.... In formations with only one wide receiver, the Ravens threw to the tight end 50 percent of the time (compared with a league average of 35 percent). Two-thirds of these throws were in long-yardage situations (7+ yards).... Derrick Mason was the most common Baltimore target on third down.... The Ravens' offense ran the second-lowest number of draw plays and the third-lowest number of screens yet ranked fifth in DVOA on draws and second in DVOA on screens.... Baltimore never used a screen pass on third down and never ran a draw play on first down.... Ravens opponents used screen passes 66 percent less often than the league average, and with good reason. Only Arizona and Seattle had a better defensive DVOA against screen passes.... Brian Billick was ultra-conservative in his first three seasons, with an Aggressiveness Index of .29. Since 2002, the Ravens have gone for it on fourth down at a league-average rate.

Passing

Player	DPAR	DVOA	Plys	NtYds	Avg	YAC	C%	TD	Int
Steve McNair	47.9	10.9%	461	2945	6.4	4.3	64.0%	16	12
Kyle Boller	7.7	17.6%	55	457	8.3	6.2	60.0%	5	2

Rushing

Player	DPAR	DVOA	Plys	Yds	Avg	TD	Fum	Suc
Jamal Lewis*	3.7	-9.9%	314	1130	3.6	9	4	42%
Mike Anderson	5.9	18.0%	39	183	4.7	1	0	30%
Musa Smith	1.7	-6.0%	36	153	4.3	0	1	33%
Steve McNair	6.7	34.5%	21	135	6.4	1	7	—
Ovie Mughelli*	2.3	26.5%	12	50	4.2	0	0	41%
Kyle Boller	-2.2	-53.5%	11	43	3.9	0	3	—
Mark Clayton	-5.5	-149.7%	7	-30	-4.3	0	1	—
Willis McGahee	*13.8*	*-1.7%*	*259*	*996*	*3.8*	*6*	*4*	*45%*

Receiving

Player	DPAR	DVOA	Plys	Ctch	Yds	Y/C	YAC	TD	C%
WR									
Mark Clayton	12.7	1.9%	112	67	938	14.0	5.4	5	60%
Derrick Mason	9.9	-1.8%	112	68	750	11.0	2.0	2	61%
Demetrius Williams	5.4	3.3%	45	22	396	18.0	5.4	2	49%
Clarence Moore	-1.8	-63.0%	6	2	1	0.5	0.0	1	33%
TE									
Todd Heap	14.4	6.9%	116	73	765	10.5	3.5	6	63%
Daniel Wilcox	-0.6	-16.9%	27	20	166	8.3	3.6	3	74%
RB									
Jamal Lewis*	-0.4	-13.3%	26	18	115	6.4	7.4	0	69%
Ovie Mughelli*	4.0	21.5%	24	21	182	8.7	6.6	2	88%
Musa Smith	0.6	-3.6%	23	20	128	6.4	7.2	0	87%
Mike Anderson	-1.6	-35.6%	14	9	54	6.0	7.0	0	64%
Willis McGahee	*-1.7*	*-21.4%*	*28*	*18*	*156*	*8.7*	*10.7*	*0*	*64%*

Offensive Line

Year	Yards	ALY	Rank	Power	Rank	10+ Yds	Rank	Stuff	Rank	Sack	ASR	Rank
2004	4.34	4.35	11	59%	19	18%	8	22%	8	35	6.5%	12
2005	3.57	3.71	28	76%	4	13%	24	24%	12	42	7.4%	20
2006	3.78	4.22	19	59%	24	14%	24	23%	10	17	3.6%	2

Year	LE	Rank	LT	Rank	Mid	Rank	RT	Rank	RE	Rank
2004	4.13	20	4.77	8	4.67	4	3.76	24	3.26	24
2005	4.50	8	3.72	25	3.75	27	2.69	31	4.94	5
2006	3.09	26	4.69	9	4.33	20	4.12	19	4.02	17

Baltimore will begin the year with at least two new starters on the offensive line after the departures of guard Edwin Muli-talo and tackle Tony Pashos, but the Ravens are in better shape than most teams to handle such position turnover because of a forward-thinking draft strategy. The team has spent four of its last nine first-day draft selections on linemen, including two this April on Auburn guard Ben Grubbs in the first round and Iowa guard/tackle Marshall Yanda in the third. Grubbs is Baltimore's highest-drafted lineman since Jonathan Ogden in 1996 and he could challenge Keydrick Vincent for a starting spot in camp. Yanda will take a year or two to develop, much as previous first-day picks Adam Terry and Chris Chester have. Though the Ravens are no doubt pleased to be in good position to undergo a youth movement up front, they are also thrilled that future Hall of Fame left tackle Ogden opted not to retire and can be counted upon to protect Steve McNair's blind side for another year.

Grubbs and Yanda continue Baltimore's trend of selecting versatile, athletic linemen. Indeed, the line the Ravens put on the field in 2007 should be more mobile than last season's unit—which is a good thing now that straight-ahead masher Jamal Lewis has been replaced by Willis McGahee in the backfield. To open holes for McGahee, the linemen will have to do more than just maul the man directly in front. Ogden, whose decision to return was said to hinge on his opinion of the club's direction, must be happy with the new personnel. He certainly has to be pleased to block for Steve McNair, a quarterback who knows when and how to get rid of the ball. McNair's footwork and decision making had a lot to do with Baltimore's dramatic improvement in Adjusted Sack Rate last year.

Defensive Front Seven

Defensive Line	Age	Pos	Plys	TmPct	Rk	Stop	Dfts	StpRt	Rk	AvYd	Rk	Sack	Hit	Hur	Runs	RuStp	RuYd	Pass	PaStp	PaYd
Trevor Pryce	32	DE	50	6.6%	31	41	18	82%	21	-0.7	2	12.5	10	16	31	74%	2.3	19	95%	-5.5
Kelly Gregg	31	DT	66	8.7%	4	54	17	82%	25	1.6	29	3.5	2	4	56	79%	2.4	10	100%	-3.4
Haloti Ngata	23	DT	33	4.3%	56	28	4	85%	18	1.9	39	1	2	1	29	83%	2.0	4	100%	1.3
Aubrayo Franklin*	27	DT	18	2.7%	—	13	2	72%	—	2.9	—	0	1	1	14	79%	2.6	4	50%	4.3
Justin Bannan	28	DT	15	2.9%	—	9	1	60%	—	1.9	—	0	1	1	15	60%	1.9	0	0%	0.0

Linebackers	Age	Pos	Plys	TmPct	Rk	Stop	Dfts	StpRt	AvYd	Sack	Hit	Hur	Runs	RuStp	Rk	RuYd	Rk	Tgts	Suc%	Rk	PaYd	Rk
Ray Lewis	32	ILB	111	16.7%	15	68	28	61%	3.6	5	2	3	70	67%	37	3.4	44	31	41%	78	7.1	74
Bart Scott	27	OLB	112	14.8%	25	81	28	72%	2.6	9.5	11	15	72	76%	6	2.6	11	36	53%	41	5.4	21
Adalius Thomas*	30	OLB	91	12.0%	54	60	28	66%	3.9	10.5	10	13	36	72%	20	4.4	90	35	61%	16	4.6	13
Terrell Suggs	25	OLB	73	9.6%	74	51	25	70%	1.5	9.5	8	14	43	70%	29	2.2	3	12	71%	—	4.8	—
Jarret Johnson	26	OLB	21	2.8%	—	15	8	71%	1.8	2	3	3	11	82%	—	2.4	—	5	40%	—	4.2	—

Year	Yards	ALY	Rank	Power	Rank	10+ Yds	Rank	Stuff	Rank	Sack	ASR	Rank
2004	3.62	4.01	7	65%	20	9%	4	26%	9	39	7.7%	11
2005	3.91	3.91	12	50%	2	19%	22	24%	21	42	7.2%	16
2006	3.26	3.42	2	56%	8	14%	9	25%	12	60	9.3%	2

Year	LE	Rank	LT	Rank	Mid	Rank	RT	Rank	RE	Rank
2004	4.13	20	4.77	8	4.67	4	3.76	24	3.26	24
2005	4.50	8	3.72	25	3.75	27	2.69	31	4.94	5
2006	3.09	26	4.69	9	4.33	20	4.12	19	4.02	17

Baltimore's defense should see the return of 10 of 11 starters from last year's league-leading unit, but the one departure was a big one: do-everything outside linebacker Adalius Thomas, who signed with the Patriots as a free-agent. Thomas's 10.5 sacks and run-stuffing ability probably can't be replaced by a single player, but Baltimore expects good things from Thomas's presumed replacement, Jarret Johnson. The Ravens have developed many play-making defenders and are hoping Jarret, a fourth-round selection in 2003, will blossom as did Thomas, who was himself a sixth-round pick. Baltimore used a fourth-round pick on Antwan Barnes, who set a school record at Florida International with 23 sacks. He's an interesting prospect who could be deployed as a pass-rushing linebacker/end as he learns to play the at the NFL level.

The loss of Thomas will hurt, but he wasn't the most productive player in the front seven last year. That was fellow outside linebacker Bart Scott, who was in on a team-leading 112 plays. Defenders with diverse skills are key to Balitmore's attack, and Scott is the rare breed of linebacker who can both stuff a run up near the line and cover a tight end 35 yards down the middle of the field. In the middle, age and injuries have taken a toll on Ray Lewis, but the Ravens still count on him to get everyone in the right position and to raise the defense's collective intensity. Lewis's weaknesses can be hidden with schemes, as the Ravens are only nominally a 3-4 team. Rex Ryan uses movement and shifting fronts to keep Lewis from having to deal with offensive guards as he sifts to find the ballcarrier. The defensive line is also getting a little long in the tooth with Trevor Pryce and Kelly Gregg both on the wrong side of 30, but second-year tackle Haloti Ngata is already established as Baltimore's huge run-stuffing tackle of the next several years.

Defensive Secondary

Secondary	Age	Pos	Plys	TmPct	Rk	Stop	Dfts	RuYd	Rk	RuStp	Rk	Tgts	Tgt%	Rk	Dist	Suc%	Rk	PaYd	Rk	PD	Int
Chris McAlister	30	CB	70	9.2%	37	41	24	9.0	61	50%	29	90	22%	17	13.2	60%	8	7.2	34	20	6
Samari Rolle	29	CB	62	8.2%	47	22	11	5.8	28	67%	4	88	21%	22	12.7	39%	78	11.0	81	9	3
Dawan Landry	25	SS	78	10.3%	38	38	21	6.1	31	60%	5	37	9%	23	12.2	49%	50	8.5	46	9	5
Ed Reed	29	FS	69	9.1%	51	25	14	6.9	46	52%	20	33	7%	39	15.2	43%	65	11.7	71	8	5
Corey Ivy	30	CB	20	3.2%	—	14	9	3.6	—	100%	—	22	7%	—	9.5	45%	—	9.1	—	5	1
Evan Oglesby	26	CB	10	1.3%	—	4	2	3.0	—	100%	—	16	4%	—	16.1	56%	—	4.4	—	0	2
Ronnie Prude	25	CB	8	1.1%	—	7	4	6.0	—	100%	—	16	4%	—	11.9	81%	—	4.2	—	2	3

Year	Pass D Rank	DVOA vs. #1 WR	Rank	DVOA vs. #2 WR	Rank	DVOA vs. Other WR	Rank	DVOA vs. TE	Rank	DVOA vs. RB	Rank
2004	2	4.1%	15	-5.4%	8	-21.4%	4	1.7%	16	-49.5%	2
2005	10	1.2%	13	-8.6%	11	0.5%	18	-3.8%	16	-9.6%	9
2006	1	-4.6%	12	-24.7%	4	-6.1%	15	-24.0%	5	-43.7%	1

In safety Ed Reed and cornerback Chris McAlister, the Ravens have two of the best players at their positions in the entire NFL. Throw those two in with a couple of undrafted free agents and Baltimore would still have an above-average secondary. Strong safety Dawan Landry—the older brother of Redskins rookie LaRon—is better than that. He was a great find as a fifth-round pick a year ago and won the job as a rookie in training camp. The problem lies with the other corner, Samari Rolle, a one-time standout who has faded badly the over the last two seasons. Given that there are 32 teams and 64 starting corners in the league, ranking 78th in Success Rate is not good. Ranking dead last in average yards allowed per pass is even worse.

So why is Rolle still on the field? Because the third corner is Corey Ivy, whose contributions would be limited to special teams in just about any other NFL club. (Ivy might be a better pass-rusher than pass-defender, as he was the only cornerback in the league with five quarterback hurries in 2006.) Baltimore could only spend so much money on the defense, so an upgrade through free agency wasn't possible, and the club opted not to draft a corner. The good news is Rolle doesn't have to perform at a Pro Bowl level for the Ravens to be successful—the team's outstanding pass rush lessens the importance of its corners' coverage ability. It may also be that coordinator Rex Ryan feels that, with Reed patrolling the middle, he can compensate for whatever coverage skills Rolle has lost. Baltimore's frequent blitzing also means that no matter how well the secondary plays, the unit will surrender some big plays. All its members—Reed and McAlister included—fall victim to double moves or pump-fakes at times. That might be one of the reasons why McAlister led all NFL players with 18 penalties and seven pass interference calls in 2006, but as noted in the St. Louis chapter, defensive penalties often indicate a good defense, not a bad one.

Special Teams

Year	DVOA	Rank	FG/XP	Rank	Net Punt	Rank	Punt Ret	Rank	Net Kick	Rank	Kick Ret	Rank	Hidden	Rank
2004	3.0%	8	8.8	4	5.9	10	9.5	5	-3.0	22	-3.6	19	0.1	13
2005	0.4%	14	4.3	8	-8.0	29	8.4	2	1.1	15	-3.4	20	-11.2	31
2006	3.5%	4	9.0	2	5.3	10	-2.1	20	4.6	12	3.6	8	-4.8	23

The same ultra-aggressive approach that gives the Ravens' defense its bite is a liability on the coverage units. Kick coverage requires discipline, as players must stay in their lanes and exercise proper technique in bringing down ballcarriers. Having 11 men fly to the ball is great for a defense, but the same approach can spell disaster for special teams. Despite having overall excellent special teams, Baltimore regularly surrendered big kick and punt returns in 2006.

The Ravens' own return units weren't as effective after the explosive B. J. Sams went down with an injury. Sams's off-the-field troubles have made him a question mark, so Baltimore used a third-round pick on diminutive return specialist Yamon Figurs, of Kansas State, the fastest player at this year's scouting combine. Ageless kicker Matt Stover remains one of the NFL's steadiest performers even as he nears 40, while rookie punter Sam Koch showed an explosive leg last year but needs to improve his consistency. He's also a bit slow getting the ball off, which could lead to blocked punts if not addressed.

Coaching Staff

The success of 2006 solidified Brian Billick's future in Baltimore after several years of disappointing results had all but used up the security he earned by winning Super Bowl XXXV. Billick was awarded a contract extension in the offseason. The biggest change to the staff from the start of last season is the departure of offensive coordinator Jim Fassel, who was dismissed in October. Fassel and Billick were great friends off the field but never clicked on it, and the Baltimore offense improved after Fassel was let go and Billick assumed the play-calling duties.

The new offensive coordinator is Rick Neuheisel, a former college head coach at Colorado and Washington. Neuheisel will have as little input as any coordinator in the league, as Billick will continue to call plays. Neuheisel was once a hot name in coaching circles, but his career came crashing down amid allegations of improper gambling while at Washington. He's an innovative offensive mind but is no threat to Billick as he continues to rehabilitate his coaching reputation. Defensive coordinator Rex Ryan's personality and approach make him the perfect fit for Baltimore's defense, but he's not going to be around much longer. Baltimore lured him back for another year with a contract extension, but he's a viable head coaching candidate who drew interest from San Diego during the offseason and will be hired somewhere very soon.

Buffalo Bills

The date was January 8, 2000. The business world was filled with rumors that AOL and Time Warner were discussing a merger. The number-one movie in America was *Stuart Little*. Elvis fans gathered at Graceland to celebrate what would have been the King's 65th birthday. On the other side of the state, Steve Christie kicked an apparent game-winning field goal for the Buffalo Bills in their wild-card playoff game against the Tennessee Titans.

Every football fan knows what came next. Lorenzo Neal fielded the kickoff that would close the game and handed it to Frank Wycheck, who flipped it to Kevin Dyson, who ran it back all the way for a touchdown and a 22–16 Titans victory. The shocked Bills players walked solemnly off the field and out of the playoffs . . . and they haven't been back since.

Since 2001, every other AFC team has been in the playoffs at least once, except for the expansion Texans. Buffalo, the team that once made four straight Super Bowls, hasn't made the postseason for seven years running.

Last year, the Bills decided that the head coach who brought them to all those Super Bowls was the general manager who could bring January football back to Buffalo. Most observers disagreed. He hadn't been running a bed and breakfast or anything, but Marv Levy had been out of the league for close to a decade and had no experience running a franchise. That Levy appeared with team owner and fellow octogenarian Ralph Wilson in a series of rambling media appearances did nothing to instill confidence in Bills fans, who had watched the team's management make bad decision after bad decision in the seven years since the Music City Miracle.

In a league in which Bill Belichick's single-minded obsession with winning is not just praised but considered a necessity, Levy came out of the box sounding like a relic

from a gentler era. It was easy to write off the phrases being thrown around by Buffalo's personnel department such as "character first" and "internal improvement" as bad motivational speaking. Sure enough, come April, NFL analysts—including last year's *PFP*—all agreed that Buffalo reached in the 2006 draft, overvaluing character and not getting enough value with their first-day selections.

Levy's suspect decision making during his first offseason at the helm led to speculation that the game had passed him by, and owner Wilson as well. The hiring of coach Dick Jauron was equally uninspired and put two former Ivy Leaguers in charge in a league in which the ability to quote Winston Churchill pales in comparison to having the stamina to go all night in the film room.

A year later, even the harshest critic would have to agree that it seems as though the Ivy Leaguers might know what they're doing after all. The honest, plain-talking Jauron was a refreshing change from the guarded, grumpy regimes of Gregg Williams and Mike Mularkey (who, to our knowledge, has still not confirmed that Roscoe Parrish broke his wrist in training camp in 2005). The much maligned 2006 draft class had a significant impact in their rookie year, and the first-day picks in the 2007 draft should help fill some of the remaining holes in the starting lineup.

The Bills still aren't a playoff team, though, and some of Levy's personnel decisions continue to make observers scratch their heads. The Bills lost significant talent to free agency, exacerbated those losses by trading away their workhorse running back and a starting linebacker, and did nothing on draft day to solve a gaping hole at cornerback.

Levy likes to say that talent without character is destined to fail, but the Bills are still paying the price for their last few character-driven personnel moves. In 2005, vet-

---

BILLS PROSPECTUS

2006 Record: 7–9

DVOA Estimated Wins: 7.9 (16th)

Pythagorean Wins: 7.7 (17th)

DVOA: −2.1% total (16th), 0.9% weighted (17th)

Offense: −8.7% DVOA (24th)

Defense: −0.7% DVOA (15th)

Special Teams: 5.9% DVOA (2nd)

Variance: 15.5% (17th)

2006: Rookies on defense, young skill players on offense provide hope for end to a seven-year playoff drought.

2007: More holes to fill as last of the old guard leave.

2007 Mean Projection: 6.2 wins

The Brohm Closet (0–4): 21%

Bad Team (5–6): 36%

Mediocre (7–8): 30%

Playoff Contender (9–10): 11%

Super Bowl Contender (11+): 3%

Projected Average Opponent: 8.6% DVOA (1st in NFL)

eran wide receiver Eric Moulds led a midseason player revolt that unseated starting quarterback J. P. Losman in favor of Kelly Holcomb. When the Levy regime took over at season's end, Moulds was sent packing and Losman was reinstated as the starter.

Lee Evans was able to step into the role of lead receiver last year, but Moulds's absence was felt farther down the depth chart. The Bills threw 32.5 percent of their passes to the number-one receiver, a higher percentage than any team except for Houston.

Only four teams threw fewer balls to their second option. That's because, in his return to Buffalo, Peerless Price couldn't recapture the big-play magic that earned him a fat contract in Atlanta a few years ago. He struggled to get open and specialized in short sideline routes that ended at the point of reception. Thirty-four percent of passes to Price traveled less than six yards through the air, and he ranked 70th in yards after catch.

The Bills did not do anything to upgrade their wide receiver depth this offseason, with Marv Levy and Assistant GM Tom Modrak preaching the value of internal improvement at the skill positions. That means the Bills are counting heavily on an improved showing from Roscoe Parrish. Parrish would certainly do more to stretch opposing defenses; his average of 5.3 yards after catch was double that of Price, and 14 percent of his passes from Losman were bombs over 25 yards. Sam Aiken and Josh Reed will both be given yet another chance to show improvement as well.

Receiver depth isn't the only concern about the passing game. Losman's development in 2006 allowed him to firm up his grasp on the starting job, but his decision making in the pocket and his receiver selection still need to improve. Levy threw Kelly Holcomb in as part of the Takeo Spikes deal, so the only other veteran quarterback on the roster is longtime Brett Favre caddy Craig Nall, but despite claiming that "J. P. is still the man," the Bills spent a first-day pick on Stanford's Trent Edwards.

With their passing game having been sabotaged by a character issue in 2005, it was the running game's turn last year. Running back Willis McGahee frustrated coaches and fans all year with his blasé attitude. After getting stuffed on a key 4th-and-short early in the year, McGahee claimed he didn't know it was fourth down. He capped the year by complaining bitterly about the city of Buffalo in a series of interviews, calling the women of Buffalo ugly and suggesting that the team move to Toronto, where there was stuff to do.

Sure enough, McGahee was shipped off to enjoy the dazzling nightlife of Baltimore, where the level of female companionship might finally be up to the standards set for McGahee in college. The greater Baltimore area has produced three Miss America contestants in the past ten years, rivaling Miami's four over the same span. The city of Buf-

| \multicolumn{6}{l}{**2007 Bills Schedule**} |

Week	Opp	Week	Opp	Week	Opp
1	DEN	7	BAL	13	at WAS
2	at PIT	8	at NYJ	14	MIA
3	at NE	9	CIN	15	at CLE
4	NYJ	10	at MIA	16	NYG
5	DAL (Mon.)	11	NE	17	at PHI
6	BYE	12	at JAC		

falo has produced just one pageant contestant over the same period.

While McGahee ponders Baltimore's HBAR (Hot Babes Above Replacement), Buffalo will try to figure out how to replace him in the backfield. Anthony Thomas, who has struggled with injuries whenever he's been asked to carry the load, is the only option on the roster with significant NFL experience, so the Bills used their first-round pick on California running back Marshawn Lynch. Lynch's past involvement in a drive-by shooting and a domestic incident raises questions as to whether Levy is already rethinking his policy.

One reason for Levy's possible change in approach is the realization that the Bills are still trying to cope with the fallout from a character issue that occurred four years ago, when perennial Pro Bowl guard Ruben Brown became frustrated with the direction in which the Bills franchise was headed and ripped the team in the press. The move came at the height of former team president Tom Donahoe's reign of terror, and the Bills shipped Brown out in the offseason.

Since Brown's departure, the Bills' offensive line has been terrible. The team has seen its ranking in Adjusted Sack Rate steadily decline—from 22nd in 2004 to 27th in 2005, and 29th last season. The team's performance on runs up the middle, as judged by Adjusted Line Yards, has also slipped each year, bottoming out at 30th in 2006.

Our game charters tagged Buffalo guards Mike Gandy, Chris Villarrial, Duke Preston, Aaron Merz, and Tutan Reyes with 16 blown blocks leading directly to sacks last year. Manning the right guard position for the Bears, Brown was tagged with just two all season.

It's no surprise then that Buffalo upgraded their line via free agency this past offseason. The Bills acted early to land Washington guard Derrick Dockery, Oakland tackle Langston Walker, and journeyman tackle Jason Whittle, but while the Bills were throwing left tackle money at Dockery, other teams were snapping up Buffalo's free-agent defensive stalwarts. The longest-tenured member of the Buffalo defense, middle linebacker London Fletcher-Baker, inked a deal with Washington. Even more damaging was the defection of cornerback Nate Clements. Considered the top free-agent corner available, Clements barely lasted a few hours on the open market before San Francisco landed him with an $80 million offer.

Curiously, while the negative repercussions of the Bills' earliest character-based move appear to have rippled through to the defense, it is there that the approach seems to have produced its first positive results.

In their first draft together, Levy and Modrak used six picks on defense. It seemed as though Buffalo was once again overvaluing character and selling talent short, as they very likely could have waited to draft most of the players chosen, including first-rounders Donte Whitner and John McCargo (McCargo might have been available a round later, and the Bills could have traded down a few slots for Whitner). Yet four of those six rookies ended up starting at least half their games: Whitner, fourth-round safety Ko Simpson, fifth-round defensive tackle Kyle Williams, and sixth-round linebacker Keith Ellison (table 1). The only other team to regularly start as many as four rookies in 2006 was Green Bay, and only one of those rookies (A. J. Hawk) was on defense.

Table 1. Buffalo's Defensive Rookies in 2006

Player	Round	Games	Starts
Donte Whitner	1	15	14
John McCargo	1	5	0
Ashton Youboty	3	3	1
Ko Simpson	4	16	15
Kyle Williams	5	16	11
Keith Ellison	6	14	7
Total		**69**	**48**

Whitner played a big role in run support, amassing some gaudy tackle numbers. Williams played as well as or better than the veterans on the Bills' defensive line, which admittedly isn't saying much. Ellison also received expanded playing time when Angelo Crowell went down to injury, displaying accurate tackling and contributing an interception.

Each rookie contributor allowed Buffalo to jettison another expensive veteran brought in by the Donahoe administration. Once Whitner and Simpson were given the keys to the safety position, the Bills released Troy Vincent. Ellison's contributions allowed the team to deal Takeo Spikes to Philadelphia for defensive line help. There was no one left to cut from the middle of the defensive line, so Kyle Williams's fast development made the loss of tackles Pat Williams and Ron Edwards to free agency and Sam Adams to the salary cap, all of whom went on to start elsewhere, a little less painful. With their slimmed-down defensive pay-

roll, Buffalo had some money to invest in the offensive line this offseason.

The youth movement in the Buffalo defense will continue as the team turned to the 2007 draft to help replace Fletcher-Baker. The Bills claim that Penn State tackle machine Paul Posluszny was the second-ranked player overall on their entire draft board, and he fell to them in the second round. The versatile Posluszny can fill either Spikes's or Fletcher-Baker's position and will also give Levy an excuse to break out all of his old Shane Conlan stories.

At cornerback, however, the Bills are counting on the ever popular "internal improvement" as they fill Nate Clements's cornerback spot with some combination of Youboty and veteran Kiwaukee Thomas. The Bills didn't just pass on the draft's highest-rated corners, they passed on the chance to add cornerback depth in the sixth and seventh rounds as well. Indeed, the team's strong start in the draft seems to have been undermined by some odd priorities in the later rounds. Unless the team has one heck of a minicamp scheduled, internal improvement won't pick up the slack.

Buffalo had a strong rookie class in 2006, but it's possible that they overreacted to their drafting prowess and sacrificed too many veterans in the offseason. The young defense may take a step back without a veteran presence on the field to settle things down. The offense still has some major holes and desperately needs Lynch to be ready for the NFL from day one.

All of which makes it unlikely that the Bills' playoff drought will end anytime soon. Last year pushed the current drought past the team's 1982–87 run to tie it with the 1967–73 period for longest dry spell in team history. Of the 32 teams in the league, only Detroit and Arizona have an active streak of missing the playoffs as long as Buffalo's.

Buffalo's regular-season record compares favorably with the other teams that missed the playoffs for seven straight years (table 2), but the current Bills have seen a similar amount of turmoil at leadership positions.

For the Bills to return to the playoffs, they must prevent their defense from backsliding too far and adequately

Table 2. Playoffs? You Want to Talk to Me About Playoffs?

Team	Win Pct	# of Coaches	# of Passing Leaders	# of Rushing Leaders
2000–06 Bills	.411	4	4	3*
1967–73 Bills	.265	4	5	3
1982–87 Bills	.307	4	3	4
1999–2006 Cardinals	.320	3*	5	5
2000–06 Lions	.295	6	3	3

* Cardinals will have fourth coach and Bills fourth leading rusher during 2007 season.

replace McGahee, and their solutions to the personnel problems they created on the offensive line and at receiver must work. That's asking a lot, without considering perhaps the most important factor: Each of the previous Buffalo teams returned to the postseason only after finding a franchise quarterback. The fifth quarterback of the 1970s era Bills teams was Joe Ferguson, and the 1980s Bills returned to the playoffs after giving Jim Kelly the job. If the development of J. P. Losman continues to exceed Football Ousiders projections, he might be able to bring the Bills out of the desert. If not, this playoff drought might put the franchise record out of reach.

Shawn Krest

Missed Tackles Are Better than Nothing

Week 6 in Detroit: On the second snap of the game, the Lions' Kevin Jones gets the ball on a run to the right. He eludes Buffalo linebacker Angelo Crowell after a two-yard gain. The next defender in position to tackle Jones is Nate Clements, 46 yards downfield.

Week 13 in Buffalo: Late in the first quarter, San Diego's LaDainian Tomlinson runs left just shy of midfield. The first member of the Bills' defense to appear on-screen is Ko Simpson, who misses a tackle at the five-yard line as Tomlinson heads in for a 51-yard touchdown.

Vince Young, Samkon Gado, and Travis Henry found holes running against the Bills' defense, going untouched for 46, 35, and 45 yards respectively. All three were eventually taken down by defensive backs.

Who is missing from the picture? The Buffalo defensive linemen. While missed tackles are obviously discouraging, their absence underscores a more serious defensive shortcoming. The fact that the linemen aren't around when the ballcarrier arrives shows that the undersized Bills ends and tackles were blown off the ball by opposing lines. Put simply, even getting into position to miss a tackle is a tough job in the NFL. Too often, the Buffalo line wasn't up to the task.

As part of the Football Outsiders game charting project, I've broken down film on every Buffalo Bills game over the last two years. Very early on in the tape study, I noticed that Nate Clements misses an awful lot of tackles, and a good chunk of London Fletcher-Baker's gaudy tackle numbers seem to result from his jumping on the pile after all the work is done. I began tracking several tackling statistics for the Bills, including Misses, On-Tops (or "Fletchers"), and yards dragged by a ballcarrier after the initial hit. (Unfortunately, collecting this information takes time that isn't available to all our game charters, so we only have it for Buffalo and their opponents.)

One statistic that came out of these observations is what I call Missed Tackle Yards, which includes all yards gained by a back after first contact with a defender. Looking at run plays in Buffalo games, it is striking how few yards the Bills gave up due to missed tackles relative to their total yards allowed. At first glance, the numbers may seem to say just the opposite, as Buffalo's total Missed Tackle Yards is nearly as large as the total yardage. However, a long run often has multiple missed tackles close to the line of scrimmage. For example, if a lineman misses a running back in the backfield, and a second lineman misses him just past the line of scrimmage, a ten-yard gain could result in 20 missed-tackle yards. The Bills, for example, racked up 61 Missed Tackle Yards on the 45-yard Travis Henry run mentioned earlier. Line two of the table shows that Bills opponents have more than 250 more Missed Tackle Yards than total yards. While there is no league average, since these numbers aren't charted for every team, multiple misses on long gains and a Missed Tackle Yards total greater than a team's total yardage allowed appears to be the norm (table 3).

Table 3. Yards from Missed Tackles

	Run Plays	Yards Allowed	Missed Tackle Yards	Ratio of Missed Yards to Total
Bills defense	472	2393	2348	0.98
Bills opponents	427	1602	1857	1.16

The Bills missed-tackle yardage is artificially high due to notoriously sloppy tacklers Fletcher-Baker and Clements. Isolating the numbers to just missed-tackle yards by the defensive lines shows how badly the Bills' front four were cleared out on run plays (table 4).

Table 4. Yards from Missed Tackles by Defensive Linemen

	Yards Allowed	Missed Tackle Yards	Ratio of Miss Yds/Yds
Bills line	2393	895	37.4%
Opposing lines	1602	689	43.0%

As I said above, Missed Tackle Yards includes all yards added onto a play after first contact. Those could come after an actual missed tackle or could result from a running back moving the pile. If we just look at pure misses and throw out the dragged defender yardage, we again see that Buffalo linemen were knocked out of position more often than opposing front fours (table 5).

The comparison of the Bills' defensive line with that of the team's opponents is skewed slightly because the opponents were playing against the Bills' offensive line, which

Table 5. Missed Tackles by Defensive Line

	Missed Tackles	Yards
Bills line	67	478
Bills team	165	1254
Line's % of total	40.6%	38.1%
Opposing lines	62	363
Opposing teams	146	890
Lines' % of total	42.5%	40.8%

struggled in 2006. However, as J. P. Losman would testify, much of the Bills' offensive line problem was on pass protection. While not great on running plays, the Bills' offensive line was closer to middle of the pack than bottom of the barrel.

Buffalo coaches were forced to juggle downfield personnel to help mitigate the line's struggles. The string of injuries to the linebackers—London Fletcher-Baker and Angelo Crowell each missed time—was most likely a result of their increased workload all season long. In addition, rookie safety Donte Whitner found himself heavily involved in stopping the run. He was involved in 17.1 percent of all Buffalo run tackles, the highest percentage of any safety in the league. Part of this may have been that more running backs were making it all the way downfield to his position, but the team also put Whitner in the box frequently.

Whitner's average run tackle came 4.5 yards past the line of scrimmage, ranking him sixth among safeties with a significant number of tackles. With Whitner crowding the line, Bills coaches often shifted fellow rookie safety Ko Simpson deeper to protect against play-action. His average run tackle—11.8 yards—was third-worst among safeties.

The true indication that Buffalo defenders couldn't compete with bigger linemen was the number of long runs, on which opposing backs were untouched until deep downfield. Opposing backs had more than twice as many yards before contact as Buffalo ballcarriers, thanks to the gaping holes torn in the Bills' front (table 6).

Table 6. Yards Before Contact on Run Plays

	Yds Pre-Contact	Total Yds	Pct
Buffalo line	783	2393	32.7%
Opposing line	315	1602	19.7%

Losing the line-of-scrimmage battle leads to big plays. Comparing the ten longest run plays by the Bills and their opponents (table 7), we see that opposing backs had an average of nearly seven extra yards before first contact. While opponents gained 129 more yards on their long plays than did the Bills, Buffalo linemen only had seven more Missed Tackle Yards.

Table 7. Untouched Yards on Ten Longest Run Plays

	Yards	Untouched Yards	DL Missed Tackle Yards	Miss Tackle Yards %
Bills defense	370	167	56	15.1%
Opposing defenses	241	99	49	20.3%

Expanding the list to the 25 longest runs of the season (table 8), the Bills gave up more than 200 more yards than their opponents, but the front four had only 23 more Missed Tackle Yards.

Table 8. Untouched Yards on 25 Longest Run Plays

	Yards	Untouched Yards	DL Missed Tackle Yards	Miss Tackle Yards %
Bills defense	643	278	148	23.0%
Opposing defenses	435	162	125	28.7%

The smaller Bills front four was no match against opposing offensive lines. Even against running backs, the Bills' defensive line was often overpowered. Bills linemen had twice as many ankle tackles as their opponents, a sign that ballcarriers were breaking through the defender's initial contact.

The Bills traded linebacker Takeo Spikes for near 300-pound tackle Darwin Walker over the offseason. A natural assumption would be that Walker's size will help plug holes at the line, a departure from the team's stated strategy of having small speedy linemen chase down plays, but Walker is much more of a pass-rusher, and his 59 percent Stop Rate on runs was the lowest among NFL defensive tackles with at least 25 plays. Incumbent defensive tackles Tim Anderson and Larry Tripplett also ranked in the bottom six. All of which means that Buffalo's front four might have trouble getting into position to miss tackles again in 2007.

Shawn Krest

Bills 2006 Stats by Week

Wk	vs.	W–L	PF	PA	YDF	YDA	TO	Total	Off	Def	ST
1	@NE	L	17	19	240	319	+2	23.5%	5.4%	-14.1%	4.0%
2	@MIA	W	16	6	171	282	+1	40.0%	12.8%	-13.5%	13.7%
3	NYJ	L	20	28	475	256	-3	-25.9%	-4.3%	22.7%	1.1%
4	MIN	W	17	12	298	330	+2	10.2%	15.3%	-7.4%	-12.5%
5	@CHI	L	7	40	145	351	-4	-98.3%	-59.4%	33.2%	-5.7%
6	@DET	L	17	20	242	397	-2	-33.2%	-28.4%	24.1%	19.3%
7	NE	L	6	28	255	265	-4	-29.5%	-24.6%	0.2%	-4.7%
8	BYE										
9	GB	W	24	10	184	427	+4	36.1%	14.1%	-6.4%	15.6%
10	@IND	L	16	17	162	384	+2	-52.4%	-52.5%	11.5%	11.5%
11	@HOU	W	24	21	403	397	+1	-15.5%	-3.0%	19.0%	6.5%
12	JAC	W	27	24	241	323	0	26.3%	17.7%	8.9%	17.5%
13	SD	L	21	24	230	335	-2	7.7%	-25.2%	-25.0%	7.9%
14	@NYJ	W	31	13	318	275	+2	42.6%	7.6%	-38.4%	-3.4%
15	MIA	W	21	0	286	212	0	52.8%	-4.2%	-49.4%	7.6%
16	TEN	L	29	30	368	396	-2	-3.9%	12.8%	32.0%	15.3%
17	@BAL	L	7	19	253	327	-2	-25.0%	-26.4%	4.7%	6.1%

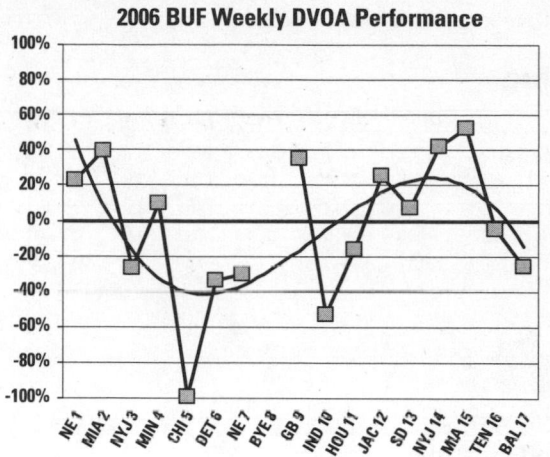

2006 BUF Weekly DVOA Performance

Trends and Splits

	Offense	Rank	Defense	Rank
Total DVOA	-8.7%	24	-0.7%	15
Unadjusted VOA	-10.5%	26	3.1%	20
Weighted Trend	-9.9%	23	-3.1%	10
Variance	5.6%	22	5.5%	21
Passing	-5.7%	21	-10.6%	6
Rushing	-11.8%	27	9.7%	29
First Down	-10.8%	21	-13.9%	6
Second Down	3.6%	12	18.2%	32
Third Down	-23.7%	29	-5.3%	10
Red Zone	-8.6%	19	3.7%	16
Late and Close	-12.8%	24	-12.3%	7

Five-Year Performance

	2006	2005	2004	2003	2002
W-L	7-9	5-11	9-7	6-10	8-8
Pythagorean Wins	7.7	5.2	11.0	6.7	7.6
Estimated Wins	7.9	5.5	11.6	6.7	6.6
Total DVOA	-2.1%	-20.4%	29.8%	-7.7%	-10.5%
Rank	16	28	4	22	25
Offense	-8.7%	-18.6%	-5.8%	-18.8%	-0.2%
Rank	24	30	22	29	20
Defense	-0.7%	8.9%	-28.1%	-12.8%	7.6%
Rank	15	26	1	7	24
Special Teams	5.9%	7.2%	7.5%	-1.7%	-2.6%
Rank	2	1	1	24	24

Strategic Tendencies

Formations		Rank	Run/Pass		Rank	Defense		Rank	Other		Rank
3+ WR	47%	15	Runs, all plays	46%	10	Sacks by LB	16%	22	Run with 2+ RB	47%	27
4+ WR	19%	3	Runs, first half	47%	7	Sacks by DB	3%	26	Run with 2+ TE	43%	7
2+ TE	29%	10	Runs, first down	55%	14	Rush 6+	2.9%	31	Play action	12%	28
Single back	63%	7	Runs, power sit.	69%	11	Rush 7+	0.5%	29	Go for it on 4th	0.69	26
Empty back	0.9%	25	Runs, behind 2H	33%	15	Rush 3	0.5%	32	Offensive Pace	31.2	20
Max protect	18%	2	Pass, ahead 2H	40%	20	CB1 on WR1	55%	5	Defensive Pace	31.3	25

The Bills were one of only four teams that we did not record using a five-wide receiver formation at any time (Chicago, Oakland, and San Francisco were the others).... Buffalo threw to the middle of the field less often than any other team.... Buffalo receivers dropped only 12 passes, the lowest total in the league. Tight end Robert Royal, who was a drop machine with Washington in 2005, led the Bills with just three drops in 2006.... Eight sacks by the Buffalo defense were marked as "QB Fault." No other defense had more than five. Buffalo was also the only defense that was never credited with a Coverage Sack.... The Bills ran just 60 play-action fakes, 30th in the NFL, and when they did run them, they weren't very good at them. They ranked 30th in DVOA (-31.2%) and 31st in net yards per play-action pass (4.2).

Passing

Player	DPAR	DVOA	Plys	NtYds	Avg	YAC	C%	TD	Int
J. P. Losman	21.3	-2.8%	427	2704	6.3	4.7	62.8%	19	13

Rushing

Player	DPAR	DVOA	Plys	Yds	Avg	TD	Fum	Suc
Willis McGahee*	13.8	-1.7%	259	996	3.8	6	4	45%
Anthony Thomas	-4.5	-24.4%	107	378	3.5	2	1	37%
J. P. Losman	-4.3	-37.3%	32	135	4.2	1	13	—
Peerless Price	-0.5	-44.3%	5	18	3.6	0	0	—
Josh Reed	0.1	-26.5%	4	13	3.3	0	0	—

Receiving

Player	DPAR	DVOA	Plys	Ctch	Yds	Y/C	YAC	TD	C%
WR									
Lee Evans	34.3	23.2%	137	82	1292	15.8	4.3	8	60%
Peerless Price	1.0	-12.4%	77	49	399	8.1	2.6	3	64%
Josh Reed	8.4	12.5%	48	34	410	12.1	4.4	2	71%
Roscoe Parrish	0.0	-14.5%	40	23	320	13.9	5.3	2	58%
Andre' Davis*	-2.7	-73.9%	7	2	13	6.5	2.5	0	29%
TE									
Robert Royal	4.2	4.7%	39	23	233	10.1	4.4	3	59%
Brad Cieslak	-0.2	-16.5%	9	6	46	7.7	7.8	0	67%
RB									
Willis McGahee*	-1.7	-21.4%	28	18	156	8.7	10.7	0	64%
Anthony Thomas	4.0	24.5%	24	22	139	6.3	6.7	0	92%
Daimon Shelton*	-2.5	-53.9%	10	7	35	5.0	3.9	0	70%

Offensive Line

Year	Yards	ALY	Rank	Power	Rank	10+ Yds	Rank	Stuff	Rank	Sack	ASR	Rank
2004	3.86	3.98	25	57%	22	17%	19	27%	25	39	7.8%	21
2005	3.80	4.09	16	63%	18	12%	25	20%	4	43	8.8%	27
2006	3.74	3.94	26	69%	11	13%	26	24%	16	47	9.4%	29

Year	LE	Rank	LT	Rank	Mid	Rank	RT	Rank	RE	Rank
2004	5.10	4	4.71	10	3.88	25	3.02	32	3.63	20
2005	3.32	26	4.07	23	4.05	18	4.34	13	4.78	6
2006	4.57	8	4.36	14	3.73	30	3.92	27	3.42	27

In past years, the Bills may have put too much trust in offensive line coach Jim McNally's reputation. While he may be a skilled teacher and motivator, he can't take five guys from a tailgate and get them to protect a young quarterback. So, after three years of replacement-level linemen such as Bennie Anderson, Mike Gandy, Greg Jerman, and Tutan Reyes, Buffalo finally decided to try surrounding McNally with talent.

Well, one talent, anyway. The Bills brought in three veteran linemen on the first day of free agency. They made guard Derrick Dockery, the best run-blocker in Washington last year, the highest-paid player in team history. They also added tackle Langston Walker from Oakland and backup tackle Jason Whittle from Minnesota, but Whittle is veteran filler, and signing linemen away from Oakland isn't exactly a recipe for success.

Jason Peters is a converted tight end playing left tackle who just might be the best athlete on the field. Before he became a starter, he was often the first player downfield on the kickoff coverage unit. Duke Preston has been too versatile for his own good. The team has shuffled him across the line to fill holes, keeping him from getting comfortable in any one spot. He'll start off at guard, unless center Melvin Fowler springs a leak. Terrance Pennington and Aaron Merz earned playing time in their rookie years and will help provide experienced depth.

Defensive Front Seven

Defensive Line	Age	Pos	Plys	TmPct	Rk	Stop	Dfts	StpRt	Rk	AvYd	Rk	Sack	Hit	Hur	Runs	RuStp	RuYd	Pass	PaStp	PaYd
Chris Kelsay	28	DE	65	7.6%	20	47	20	72%	61	2.3	64	6	8	17	47	72%	2.4	18	72%	2.1
Aaron Schobel	30	DE	58	6.8%	26	46	24	79%	31	0.1	8	13.5	10	26	33	73%	3.1	25	88%	-3.9
Ryan Denney	30	DE	57	6.6%	29	43	14	75%	52	1.5	36	6	4	7	42	69%	2.6	15	93%	-1.6
Kyle Williams	24	DT	53	6.2%	19	40	9	75%	46	2.8	61	1	3	6	47	74%	2.6	6	83%	4.2
Larry Tripplett	28	DT	37	4.3%	57	26	10	70%	59	2.1	44	2.5	8	6	28	61%	3.1	9	100%	-1.2
Tim Anderson	27	DT	33	4.1%	61	20	4	61%	69	3.1	68	0	2	3	30	63%	2.9	3	33%	4.7
Anthony Hargrove	24	DE	20	2.7%	—	10	5	50%	—	5.3	—	1.5	0	0	15	53%	5.5	5	40%	4.4
Darwin Walker	*30*	*DT*	*39*	*4.3%*	*58*	*27*	*15*	*69%*	*61*	*0.8*	*12*	*5.5*	*6*	*7*	*29*	*59%*	*2.8*	*10*	*100%*	*-4.8*

Linebackers	Age	Pos	Plys	TmPct	Rk	Stop	Dfts	StpRt	AvYd	Sack	Hit	Hur	Runs	RuStp	Rk	RuYd	Rk	Tgts	Suc%	Rk	PaYd	Rk
L. Fletcher-Baker*	32	ILB	161	18.8%	4	89	40	55%	5.1	2	2	1	81	59%	69	4.0	79	61	54%	36	6.0	38
Angelo Crowell	26	OLB	90	14.0%	30	50	16	56%	5.1	2	0	1	44	66%	42	3.5	58	40	46%	64	7.3	75
Takeo Spikes*	31	OLB	73	11.3%	59	43	5	59%	4.2	1	0	0	50	62%	58	4.3	84	19	65%	10	3.5	6
Keith Ellison	23	OLB	61	8.1%	87	35	12	57%	4.5	1	0	2	34	71%	25	3.1	30	29	81%	1	2.4	1

Year	Yards	ALY	Rank	Power	Rank	10+ Yds	Rank	Stuff	Rank	Sack	ASR	Rank
2004	3.68	3.77	3	42%	1	15%	12	29%	5	45	8.8%	4
2005	4.59	4.46	26	76%	29	19%	20	22%	25	38	7.7%	9
2006	4.83	4.76	29	69%	22	18%	24	20%	29	40	8.1%	6

Year	LE	Rank	LT	Rank	Mid	Rank	RT	Rank	RE	Rank
2004	3.30	4	4.83	27	3.58	3	4.15	13	3.55	12
2005	3.67	10	4.37	18	4.43	25	4.60	28	5.91	32
2006	5.28	30	5.11	28	4.84	30	4.15	15	4.11	17

Defensive end Aaron Schobel ranked among the league leaders with 14 sacks. However, half of them came in three games: a blowout of the Jets, a blowout loss to the Packers, and a 14-point win over Green Bay. In a four-game stretch of games decided by a total of ten points, Schobel had just one sack.

Not to pick solely on Schobel, Ryan Denney had three of his six sacks in one game against the Dolphins. While Chris Kelsay has been the starter at left end, Denney has been making the big plays. Denney's Amazonian reach allows him to bat down passes at the line, and, appropriately, his NBA height creates matchup problems for opposing linemen.

On the inside, Kyle Williams, Larry Tripplett, and Tim Anderson struggled against the run. Darwin Walker adds a big body, but he was a better pass-rusher than run stopper in Philadelphia.

At linebacker, the big names from the Tom Donahoe era have been purged. In place of London Fletcher-Baker and Takeo Spikes are Angelo Crowell, Keith Ellison, and second-rounder Paul Posluszny. Ellison didn't start for much of the year, but he was the NFL's top-rated linebacker in our pass coverage stats. Crowell and Ellison's performance helped make Fletcher-Baker and Spikes expendable. Bumped from safety, Coy Wire also saw playing time at linebacker, his college position, in late 2006.

Defensive Secondary

Secondary	Age	Pos	Plys	TmPct	Rk	Stop	Dfts	RuYd	Rk	RuStp	Rk	Tgts	Tgt%	Rk	Dist	Suc%	Rk	PaYd	Rk	PD	Int
Nate Clements*	28	CB	92	10.7%	19	42	21	10.4	69	32%	62	93	21%	18	10.7	59%	13	6.4	16	18	3
Terrence McGee	26	CB	89	11.1%	15	40	16	6.0	30	50%	25	82	20%	27	11.2	43%	73	8.2	56	11	0
Kiwaukee Thomas	30	CB	51	5.9%	—	27	14	6.3	—	50%	—	41	9%	—	7.6	51%	—	6.9	—	5	0
Donte Whitner	22	SS	111	13.8%	5	58	11	4.5	8	56%	10	35	8%	26	10.6	58%	23	5.8	11	4	1
Ko Simpson	24	FS	81	9.4%	44	10	6	11.8	78	7%	80	23	5%	71	15.8	45%	58	8.9	51	4	2
Coy Wire	29	SS	15	1.7%	—	5	1	5.0	—	50%	—	5	1%	—	1.3	33%	—	6.2	—	0	0
Jason Webster	30	CB	55	13.6%	3	19	8	8.7	41	40%	45	57	25%	6	11.0	38%	79	10.1	78	7	2

Year	Pass D Rank	DVOA vs. #1 WR	Rank	DVOA vs. #2 WR	Rank	DVOA vs. Other WR	Rank	DVOA vs. TE	Rank	DVOA vs. RB	Rank
2004	1	-10.0%	5	-2.7%	11	11.2%	28	-39.7%	2	-64.2%	1
2005	15	6.8%	16	1.2%	22	11.5%	28	-8.5%	11	4.8%	21
2006	6	-22.1%	2	18.5%	27	-2.3%	18	0.8%	20	11.4%	23

Teams often retire the jerseys of the great players from their past. The Bills are apparently taking that one step further and retiring Nate Clements's position. Clements once described his position as "big play corner," and when he left for San Francisco's $80 million contract offer, Buffalo did nothing to fill the hole he left on the roster. It seems that the Bills plan on playing without a right cornerback in 2007, big play or little.

On the other hand, they've seen more of Ashton Youboty than the rest of us. Thus far, Youboty hasn't been on the field long enough to earn the obvious nickname of "Shake" from Chris Berman. He started one game, played in another, and dressed for a third. While his rookie year was essentially a washout due to preseason injury and an illness in his family, Buffalo coaches swear that he's showing well in practice, and their lack of offseason moves seems to indicate they think he's ready to step into Clements's spot. If not, the Bills also re-signed veteran Kiwaukee "the Ming of Beers" Thomas, who filled in last year. At the other corner spot, Terrence McGee struggled defending the double move and was benched for a short stretch at midseason.

(continued next page)

Defensive Secondary (continued)

The Bills are in better shape at safety, especially considering that the two starters—Donte Whitner and Ko Simpson—are both second-years with potential for improvement. No safety in the NFL was involved in a higher percentage of his team's running plays than Whitner (17.1 percent), but with a less experienced cornerback group in front of him, Whitner may not be able to spend as much time in the box in 2007, and that will lead to some growing pains in pass coverage. Special-teamer Jim Leonhard is the only other veteran safety on the roster, and the Bills added John Wendling in the sixth round of the draft. Wendling capped a pedestrian three-year career at Wyoming with an impressive combine performance, generally not the best prescription for a solid NFL career. Note: As we went to press, the Bills signed free-agent Jason Webster, one of the worst starting cornerbacks in the league in 2006.

Special Teams

Year	DVOA	Rank	FG/XP	Rank	Net Punt	Rank	Punt Ret	Rank	Net Kick	Rank	Kick Ret	Rank	Hidden	Rank
2004	7.5%	1	-3.7	22	8.0	5	11.6	1	10.5	6	18.0	2	-1.2	15
2005	7.2%	1	3.6	11	7.5	5	0.4	12	3.8	12	27.2	1	8.9	4
2006	5.9%	2	8.5	4	16.1	1	6.6	3	-2.0	25	5.5	6	-2.2	16

Offense and defense are usually more consistent from year to year than special teams, but not in Buffalo. The Bills have ranked first or second in our special teams ratings for three straight years. No other team has even ranked in the top ten all three years.

Punter Brian Moorman is one of the best in the business. He flirted with the mythical 40-yard net-punting average in 2006, falling short by 0.8 yards—and remember, for half the year his distance is limited by the weather at his home stadium. Until the freezing temperatures come, Moorman is good for at least one 60-yarder a game, making the Bills one of the few teams in the league that can bring the crowd back into the game with a punt.

Special teams wizard Bobby April took advantage of Moorman's leg strength to build one of the league's best coverage squads. Wide receiver Sam Aiken and defensive end Anthony Hargrove led the charge down the field last year. Peters was a coverage man before he earned a starting job on the offensive line. Count on April once again to build a shut-down coverage unit from the spare parts on offense and defense. The Bills held the Colts to zero return yards in their game last season. When Pacman Jones was instilling strip-club levels of terror in the hearts of opposing special-teamers late last season, Buffalo held him to negative return yardage. Meanwhile, Terrence McGee and Roscoe Parrish flirted with team records for return yardage on kicks and punts respectively. Kicker Rian Lindell rounds out the special teams; he has the highest career field-goal percentage in Bills team history.

Coaching Staff

Head coach Dick Jauron wasn't a popular choice with the fans, but his low-key, straight-talking manner was a good fit for a team that is young at so many key positions. It's hard to imagine one of the coaches from the Tom Donahoe era saying, "It didn't work so it wasn't the right decision," or "You make the calls and live with them. Of course you second-guess yourself," when his decision making was challenged by the media in a postgame press conference. Jauron had a similar soft hand with the players, using teaching instead of punishment as his motivational technique.

Both coordinators showed an ability to make midseason adjustments to cover up personnel shortcomings. Steve Fairchild shuffled the offensive line over the bye week, switching three of the five positions and starting a rookie, Terrance Pennington, at right tackle for the rest of the season. He also found a way to get Lee Evans open consistently on the left sideline for big plays and allowed J. P. Losman's development not only to continue but to accelerate.

On defense, Perry Fewell's troops were exposed by the Bears in a 40–7 October loss. In response, Fewell was able to use his rookie safeties creatively and hide left corner Terrence McGee's coverage shortcomings. At linebacker, Takeo Spikes struggled early to regain his old form after his 2005 Achilles injury. Injuries haunted the position all season, forcing Fewell to rely on a sixth-round draft pick in Keith Ellison. Fewell's scheming worked, as the defense finished on a roll in the second half of the season, holding the potent Colts offense to 17 points and shutting out Miami.

Cincinnati Bengals

At Football Outsiders, we have a million stats to tell you how and why football teams win and lose, and to rate their level of success. Yet, none of our formulas is as simple and effective a measure of the success of the Marvin Lewis era in Cincinnati as this: In 2006, the Bengals went 8–8, and the team and its fans universally viewed the season as a failure.

The Bengals were the NFL's most beaten-up and kicked-around franchise in the 1990s. It was a mantle they inherited from the 1980s Tampa Bay Buccaneers, and one they have passed on to the Arizona Cardinals in the current decade.

When Lewis went .500 his first two seasons, he was hailed as a hero in the Queen City. When the Bengals went 11–5 in his third season, he nearly became a legend. After just four seasons, Lewis is already the third-winningest head coach in franchise history (a history that includes the legendary Paul Brown, as well as two different coaches, Forrest Gregg and Sam Wyche, who took the Bengals to the Super Bowl).

The euphoria of 2005 lasted all of two plays in the AFC Divisional game against Pittsburgh—long enough for Carson Palmer's shredded knee to hit the turf at Paul Brown Stadium. The team made few changes that offseason, placing its faith in Palmer's ability to heal. When he was the opening-day starter and led Cincinnati to a 3–0 start, all appeared well.

Unfortunately for the Bengals, the only thing about the first three weeks that would prove indicative of the rest of the season was the streak itself. Cincinnati's 3–0 start was followed by a 1–5 stretch, which was followed by a four-game winning streak, which was followed by a three-game slide. Had the Bengals won even one of those final three games, they most likely would have made the playoffs at 9–7.

The contrast between the Bengals' offense and defense mirrored their habit of blowing hot and cold

BENGALS PROSPECTUS	
2006 Record: 8–8	
DVOA Estimated Wins: 8.6 (10th)	
Pythagorean Wins: 9.1 (10th)	
DVOA: 8.8% total (11th), 7.7% weighted (11th)	
Offense: 14.6% DVOA (4th)	
Defense: 7.1% DVOA (25th)	
Special Teams: 1.3% DVOA (12th)	
Variance: 9.6% (28th)	
2006: Welcome back, Carson. Can you play D?	
2007: Indy did it, why can't we?	
2007 Mean Projection: 8.7 wins	
The Brohm Closet (0–4): 4%	
Bad Team (5–6): 12%	
Mediocre (7–8): 28%	
Playoff Contender (9–10): 34%	
Super Bowl Contender (11+): 21%	
Projected Average Opponent: 0.7% DVOA (16th in NFL)	

through the schedule. The offense was outstanding (4th in DVOA); the defense was awful (25th in DVOA). When the Bengals mine the 2006 season for positives, they will most likely all be found on the offensive side of the ball.

Palmer, whose career was thought to be in jeopardy at various points following his injury, returned strong. He started all 16 games and set a team record with 4,035 passing yards. Though his numbers weren't quite as outstanding as those in 2005, his DPAR (97.2 points above replacement level) and DVOA (27.6%, 6th in the league) still placed him among the NFL's elite throwers.

Palmer seemed to gain confidence as the season wore on and his numbers over the second half were greatly improved. The Bengals' passing game ranked 11th in DVOA over the season's first nine weeks but was second only to that of the Colts from Week 10 on. Overall, the passing game was slightly better in 2006 than it had been in 2005. The marked improvement contributes heavily to our lofty projection for Palmer in 2007.

With Palmer and the offense back in full swing, this was a team that won big—with an average margin of victory in its eight wins of nearly two touchdowns—but lost close. The average spread in the Bengals' eight losses was more than five points smaller than in their victories. Indeed, close games were their death knell, as they went 1–3 in contests decided by three points or fewer and 2–5 in those decided by seven points or fewer. While Cincinnati was 3–4 overall against playoff teams in 2006, the league's better offenses gave the Bengals' defense fits. Cincinnati played five teams that finished in the top ten in offensive DVOA: Indianapolis, San Diego, New Orleans, New England, and Kansas City. Though the Bengals went 2–3 in those contests, they surrendered an average of 29.4 points, and that includes holding the Chiefs to ten points after knocking out quarterback

2007 Bengals Schedule

Week	Opp	Week	Opp	Week	Opp
1	BAL (Mon.)	7	NYJ	13	at PIT
2	at CLE	8	at PIT	14	STL
3	at SEA	9	at BUF	15	at SF (Sat.)
4	NE (Mon.)	10	at BAL	16	CLE
5	BYE	11	ARI	17	at MIA
6	at KC	12	TEN		

Trent Green in Week 1. Clearly this was a team whose defense was pushed around by any competent offense.

Some of Cincinnati's close losses can be attributed to misfortune. The Bengals dropped one game when a phantom roughing-the-passer call kept Tampa Bay's game-winning touchdown drive alive. They fell to the Broncos when the potential game-tying extra point slipped through the holder's hands in the final minute. If either of those things doesn't happen, Cincinnati probably makes the playoffs as well.

Some of Cincinnati's other missteps were self-induced. The team's off-the-field troubles with the law—nine players arrested in a nine-month span—are well documented and don't merit retelling here, but the story certainly dogged the Bengals in 2006, especially because they weren't performing as well on the field. Some of the incidents will have a very real effect on Cincinnati in 2007. They will be without talented third receiver Chris Henry for the first eight games due to a league-imposed suspension. Middle linebacker Odell Thurman was suspended for all of last season, and his status for 2007 is very much up in the air as we go to press.

Under Lewis, the Bengals have paid precious little attention to past misdeeds when drafting players. Several of the arrests that dogged the club last season were related to incidents that occurred prior to the team signing the involved players. The collective effect put the club under a microscope entering the 2007 draft. As the league's poster children for character issues, the Bengals went out of their way to avoid drafting players with red flags in their past.

Cincinnati's first pick, cornerback Leon Hall, certainly fit the bill. Hall was a three-year starter at Michigan who has never been in trouble and who is routinely described as mature. He was also, according to many observers, the best corner in the draft, yet he fell to the Bengals with the 18th pick. He'll enter the depth chart as the nickel corner and could end up starting immediately for a secondary that struggled last season.

It should be noted that some of the gambles the Bengals have made on players with character issues show signs of working out. The team was without a third-round selection in this year's draft after using the pick in the 2006 supplementary draft on Ahmad Brooks, a linebacker with first-round talent whose off-field conduct got him bounced from the University of Virginia.

Brooks is penciled in as the starting middle linebacker heading into his second season. As a rookie last year, he started several games at midseason after Brian Simmons was injured, but inattention to detail earned him a seat on the bench for three of the final seven games. Still, there have been no off-the-field issues and linebackers coach Rickey Hunley has been impressed with Brooks's work ethic this offseason. He looks like the player who can finally stop Cincinnati's revolving door at middle linebacker—where Lewis has used seven different starters in his four seasons.

The Bengals have the makings of a decent defensive line with ends Justin Smith and Robert Geathers combining for 18 sacks—part of the team's overall improvement from 30th to 17th in Adjusted Sack Rate. Cincinnati felt strong enough about the development of second-year player Domata Peko that the team opted to release 34-year-old run-stuffing tackle Sam Adams. The signing of former Denver starter Michael Meyers as a free-agent also contributed to this decision.

Depth at linebacker—where the team might find itself in the unenviable position of relying on Thurman—and in the secondary is a concern. Promising linebacker David Pollack's career is in jeopardy following a fractured vertebra last season. Though Cincinnati did not select a single linebacker in the draft, the Bengals did sign free-agent Ed Hartwell, a dynamic player whose career has been derailed by injuries. At safety, free-agent Kevin Kaesviharn is gone to New Orleans, which leaves very little on the roster behind starters Dexter Jackson and Madieu Williams.

Hall was drafted to address a lack of depth at corner, where there was precious little play-making from the starters in 2006. The top three corners on the roster a year ago combined for just one interception. As a group, the secondary was lousy against first and third/fourth receivers but respectable against number two wideouts. Second-year corner Johnathan Joseph shows promise, and if Hall proves worthy of his pre-draft hype, the Bengals will have a pair of good young corners to go with veteran Deltha O'Neal.

The Cincinnati defense could certainly benefit from some of the continuity that has been a hallmark of the offense. When all the first-teamers were healthy, the Bengals started the same 11 players on offense for three straight seasons, a remarkable achievement in the free-agency era.

Though there will be at least two changes on the offensive line in 2007 (center Rich Braham retired and guard Eric Steinbach, one of the players who was arrested last year, was allowed to leave as a free agent), as many as nine starters could return.

The key skill players—Palmer, receivers Chad Johnson and T. J. Houshmandzadeh, and running back Rudi Johnson—will all return, but the last member of that group has to be a concern. By traditional measures, Rudi Johnson had a good year in 2006—1,309 yards and 12 touchdowns vs. 1,458 yards and 12 scores in 2005—but his rushing average dropped by half a yard per carry, and he fumbled more times (six) than he had in his entire career through 2005 (five). When your feature back drops from third to 31st in DVOA over the space of a year, alarms start going off.

Part of the drop can be attributed to the offensive line, and perhaps the changes there—Andrew Whitworth and Eric Ghiaciuc are slated to take over for Braham and Steinbach—will help. Steinbach banked a big-money deal to join division rival Cleveland, but the Bengals viewed him as expendable in part because of Whitworth's development. Cincinnati felt strongly enough about their offensive line situation that they didn't draft a lineman until guard Dan Santucci of Notre Dame in the sixth round.

Rudi Johnson is edging toward 30 and the Bengals may be ready to shift some of the load to backup Kenny Watson, a six-year veteran with all of 167 career carries who was re-signed to a multiyear deal as an unrestricted free agent this offseason. He's certainly a better bet to get a look than Chris Perry, a former first-round pick who hasn't been able to stay healthy and hasn't contributed much when he has been in the lineup. Cincinnati even tried Perry as a kick returner last season with little success. Another option is Kenny Irons, a highly productive tailback at Auburn whom the Bengals selected in the second round of the draft.

Because this is an offense driven by the passing game, the Bengals don't need a dominant running attack to win.

Palmer deftly balances the abilities of his top two receivers, something that he probably doesn't get enough credit for. Ask the Cowboys, Eagles, and 49ers how failure to manage the ego of a top wideout can torpedo an offense. Palmer also managed to get third wideout Henry 15 touchdown receptions the past two seasons, including nine on just 36 catches last year.

Palmer won't have quite the variety of weapons to throw to this season. Henry's suspension and the departure of fourth wideout Kelley Washington to New England have turned a deep position into a thin one. Reggie McNeal, a former Texas A&M quarterback and another Bengal who has had his legal issues, will be counted on to help fill the void during Henry's suspension, but an injury to either Chad Johnson or Houshmandzadeh could be devastating.

It also goes without saying that Palmer must stay healthy for Cincinnati to have any chance to contend. For the second straight year, the backup situation is bleak. At press time, the depth chart at quarterback consisted of Palmer, Doug Johnson, and fourth-round rookie Jeff Rowe, a project from Nevada.

The story of how Palmer and Chad Johnson once drove to Indianapolis to watch Peyton Manning and Marvin Harrison play on *Monday Night Football* is often told during Cincinnati broadcasts. The visit must have had some effect. The resemblance between the teams' offenses is growing. In addition to Palmer and Johnson, the Bengals have Houshmandzadeh in the role of Reggie Wayne and Rudi Johnson as Edgerrin James/Joseph Addai. Cincinnati may be trying to copy another page out of the Colts' blueprint: winning a championship with an offense-heavy team. After so many years of leading an outstanding defense on offensively challenged teams in Baltimore, Lewis finds himself in the opposite situation in Cincinnati. He can only hope this scenario works out as well for him as it did for Tony Dungy last year. Failing that, he might want to give his old boss Brian Billick a call and offer to trade teams.

Russell Levine

Bengals 2006 Stats by Week

Wk	vs.	W–L	PF	PA	YDF	YDA	TO	DVOA Total	Off	Def	ST
1	@KC	W	23	10	236	289	+2	44.6%	-3.4%	-40.9%	7.1%
2	CLE	W	34	17	481	301	+1	25.4%	22.5%	-8.3%	-5.4%
3	@PIT	W	28	20	246	365	+2	-4.8%	-27.5%	-16.8%	5.9%
4	NE	L	13	38	279	424	-1	-21.5%	4.3%	27.6%	1.8%
5	BYE										
6	@TB	L	13	14	314	310	+1	-33.8%	-16.1%	22.2%	4.6%
7	CAR	W	17	14	342	277	+1	9.4%	22.5%	8.6%	-4.4%
8	ATL	L	27	29	331	420	-1	-1.0%	27.8%	43.4%	14.6%
9	@BAL	L	20	26	275	374	-3	-9.9%	27.0%	28.6%	-8.4%
10	SD	L	41	49	545	431	-1	14.9%	63.5%	39.0%	-9.6%
11	@NO	W	31	16	385	595	+3	10.4%	11.0%	4.3%	3.7%
12	@CLE	W	30	0	388	203	+4	74.1%	31.9%	-40.7%	1.5%
13	BAL	W	13	7	294	316	+1	58.8%	51.8%	0.1%	7.1%
14	OAK	W	27	10	439	223	-2	23.2%	22.6%	-4.4%	-3.8%
15	@IND	L	16	34	278	394	0	-47.1%	-33.2%	19.2%	5.3%
16	@DEN	L	23	24	343	287	-2	15.2%	-11.3%	-22.4%	4.1%
17	PIT	L	17	23	295	482	+2	-4.2%	35.0%	37.7%	-1.5%

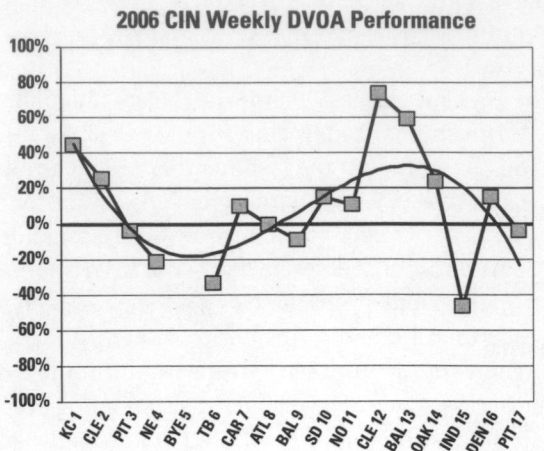

2006 CIN Weekly DVOA Performance

Trends and Splits

	Offense	Rank	Defense	Rank
Total DVOA	14.6%	4	7.1%	25
Unadjusted VOA	12.7%	7	8.0%	25
Weighted Trend	18.8%	3	12.0%	30
Variance	7.1%	12	6.9%	15
Passing	28.9%	2	17.6%	27
Rushing	-2.5%	15	-4.8%	13
First Down	20.7%	4	11.1%	27
Second Down	19.7%	3	2.0%	17
Third Down	-7.7%	23	7.3%	17
Red Zone	35.1%	3	7.6%	21
Late and Close	16.8%	6	27.1%	32

Five-Year Performance

	2006	2005	2004	2003	2002
W-L	8-8	11-5	8-8	8-8	2-14
Pythagorean Wins	9.1	9.7	8.1	7.0	3.8
Estimated Wins	8.6	10.3	9.4	7.6	3.4
Total DVOA	8.8%	18.9%	11.5%	-5.7%	-29.2%
Rank	11	9	10	21	29
Offense	14.6%	19.6%	4.7%	5.9%	-3.6%
Rank	4	5	11	10	22
Defense	7.1%	1.0%	-2.9%	12.7%	17.4%
Rank	25	20	14	31	30
Special Teams	1.3%	0.4%	3.9%	1.1%	-8.1%
Rank	12	14	7	15	32

Strategic Tendencies

Formations		Rank	Run/Pass		Rank	Defense		Rank	Other		Rank
3+ WR	56%	6	Runs, all plays	43%	21	Sacks by LB	7%	28	Run with 2+ RB	78%	1
4+ WR	8%	21	Runs, first half	41%	28	Sacks by DB	14%	4	Run with 2+ TE	13%	31
2+ TE	10%	31	Runs, first down	48%	28	Rush 6+	10.9%	9	Play action	10%	31
Single back	33%	31	Runs, power sit.	72%	5	Rush 7+	1.5%	15	Go for it on 4th	0.70	25
Empty back	1.6%	19	Runs, behind 2H	35%	12	Rush 3	5.3%	10	Offensive Pace	28.2	2
Max protect	8%	26	Pass, ahead 2H	46%	9	CB1 on WR1	33%	29	Defensive Pace	32.2	30

Cincinnati had the most net yards per pass (15.7) and highest DVOA (56.0%) on play-action passes in the NFL, yet they rarely used them. Arizona was the only team we recorded with fewer play-action fakes. . . . The Bengals ranked 30th in using two-running back/two-tight end power sets, behind only Arizona and Seattle. . . . The Bengals were the league's best passing team when only two wide receivers were on the field, surpassing even Indianapolis with a 64.5% DVOA and 10.7

net yards per pass. Cincinnati was least effective passing with four wide receivers (−22.6% DVOA, 8.9 net yards per pass).... Carson Palmer had the highest second-quarter DVOA of any NFL quarterback (59.6%).... Cincinnati had the third-highest DVOA on screen passes but ranked only 25th in how often they were used.... Although Chad Johnson was the sixth most targeted receiver in the NFL, Palmer threw to T. J. Houshmandzadeh more often than Johnson on third down, and with more success. Houshmandzadeh converted 21 of 47 opportunities, Johnson 10 of 34.... Despite their generally poor run defense up the middle, the Bengals ranked fourth in defensive DVOA on draw plays.

Passing

Player	DPAR	DVOA	Plys	NtYds	Avg	YAC	C%	TD	Int
Carson Palmer	97.3	27.6%	516	3787	7.3	4.4	62.8%	28	12

Rushing

Player	DPAR	DVOA	Plys	Yds	Avg	TD	Fum	Suc
Rudi Johnson	15.6	-2.5%	341	1309	3.8	12	6	44%
Kenny Watson	5.3	41.0%	25	138	5.5	1	0	67%
Jeremi Johnson	2.4	24.6%	15	56	3.7	1	0	50%
Carson Palmer	1.0	-8.7%	14	47	3.4	0	15	—
Chris Perry	2.6	44.3%	10	57	5.7	0	0	7%
Chad Johnson	-0.6	-40.0%	6	24	4.0	0	0	—
T. J. Houshmandzadeh	-0.9	-64.6%	3	6	2.0	0	0	—

Receiving

Player	DPAR	DVOA	Plys	Ctch	Yds	Y/C	YAC	TD	C%
WR									
Chad Johnson	31.4	15.5%	152	87	1375	15.8	3.5	7	68%
T. J. Houshmandzadeh	31.4	20.7%	132	90	1081	12.0	3.5	9	57%
Chris Henry	9.2	3.6%	75	36	605	16.8	4.6	9	48%
Kelley Washington*	4.3	36.7%	12	9	115	12.8	4.9	1	75%
Tab Perry	2.4	44.5%	6	5	81	16.2	9.4	0	83%
Antonio Chatman	-0.1	-17.7%	5	3	22	7.3	3.7	0	60%
TE									
Reggie Kelly	6.5	17.9%	33	21	254	12.1	3.9	1	64%
Tony Stewart*	3.2	17.9%	18	14	120	8.6	3.7	1	78%
RB									
Kenny Watson	7.7	43.7%	32	23	213	9.3	11.5	0	72%
Rudi Johnson	-1.5	-19.0%	31	23	124	5.4	5.0	0	74%
Chris Perry	0.6	2.4%	11	9	42	4.7	4.7	0	82%
Jeremi Johnson	-1.2	-37.4%	9	6	37	6.2	5.0	0	67%

Offensive Line

Year	Yards	ALY	Rank	Power	Rank	10+ Yds	Rank	Stuff	Rank	Sack	ASR	Rank
2004	4.15	4.20	16	58%	20	18%	13	26%	21	31	5.7%	7
2005	4.29	4.51	4	70%	8	14%	21	23%	10	22	3.7%	2
2006	3.97	4.43	10	72%	5	9%	29	25%	27	36	5.9%	12

Year	LE	Rank	LT	Rank	Mid	Rank	RT	Rank	RE	Rank
2004	4.51	11	4.47	14	4.22	19	3.96	20	3.93	15
2005	3.26	28	4.57	11	4.63	3	4.78	3	4.35	13
2006	4.19	16	4.44	13	4.34	18	5.29	1	3.89	18

The injuries that plagued Cincinnati's offensive line in 2006 may prove to be a blessing in disguise. Youngsters Eric Ghiaciuc at center and guard/tackle Andrew Whitworth got valuable playing time that will serve them well this season when they take over as starters for the departed Rich Braham and Eric Steinbach. The club felt strongly enough about Whitworth's ability to play inside that they made no effort to re-sign Steinbach, who is viewed as one of the league's better guards. Despite the injury-related lineup shuffles, the offensive line performed well as a whole, giving Carson Palmer enough protection to keep him healthy all season and opening enough holes for Rudi Johnson to plow for 1,309 yards. The biggest concern for the unit is the health of left tackle Levi Jones, who is trying to recover from a knee injury that caused him to miss ten games a season ago. When healthy, Jones and Willie Anderson form one of the league's better tackle tandems.

Defensive Front Seven

Defensive Line	Age	Pos	Plys	TmPct	Rk	Stop	Dfts	StpRt	Rk	AvYd	Rk	Sack	Hit	Hur	Runs	RuStp	RuYd	Pass	PaStp	PaYd
Justin Smith	28	DE	83	9.6%	5	63	25	76%	50	1.7	50	7.5	13	17	64	75%	2.6	19	79%	-1.3
John Thornton	31	DT	46	5.7%	28	34	9	74%	49	2.7	60	2	0	5	35	77%	2.1	11	64%	4.8
Bryan Robinson	33	DT	44	5.1%	39	31	11	70%	58	2.8	62	3	5	12	35	71%	2.6	9	67%	3.8
Domata Peko	23	DT	43	5.0%	41	32	7	74%	48	1.9	37	2.5	2	5	37	78%	2.1	6	50%	0.5
Robert Geathers	24	DE	42	4.8%	56	35	20	83%	15	0.8	18	10.5	8	7	27	78%	2.7	15	93%	-2.7
Michael Myers	*31*	*DT*	*61*	*7.3%*	*9*	*41*	*11*	*67%*	*63*	*2.4*	*54*	*2*	*2*	*3*	*52*	*67%*	*2.5*	*9*	*67%*	*1.8*

Linebackers	Age	Pos	Plys	TmPct	Rk	Stop	Dfts	StpRt	AvYd	Sack	Hit	Hur	Runs	RuStp	Rk	RuYd	Rk	Tgts	Suc%	Rk	PaYd	Rk
Landon Johnson	26	OLB	111	12.8%	45	50	13	45%	6.0	0.5	2	1	57	61%	61	3.8	63	45	28%	97	9.7	97
Caleb Miller	27	OLB	95	10.9%	63	49	12	52%	5.2	1	1	2	56	63%	56	3.6	59	30	39%	82	7.3	80
Brian Simmons*	32	ILB	65	10.9%	64	34	11	52%	5.6	0	3	3	35	66%	45	3.5	50	22	45%	69	8.4	88
Rashad Jeanty	23	OLB	57	8.8%	80	30	5	53%	4.9	0	2	1	41	61%	62	3.2	35	18	48%	54	6.7	67
Ahmad Brooks	23	OLB	31	5.2%	—	17	3	55%	5.7	1	2	1	19	58%	—	3.8	—	6	33%	—	7.3	—
Edgerton Hartwell	*29*	*ILB*	*40*	*9.9%*	*—*	*24*	*2*	*60%*	*5.2*	*0.5*	*0*	*2*	*28*	*75%*	*—*	*3.4*	*—*	*6*	*30%*	*—*	*5.3*	*—*

Year	Yards	ALY	Rank	Power	Rank	10+ Yds	Rank	Stuff	Rank	Sack	ASR	Rank
2004	4.68	4.55	29	71%	26	18%	21	23%	17	37	7.3%	13
2005	4.46	4.56	29	64%	19	16%	13	20%	28	28	4.9%	30
2006	4.03	4.24	16	56%	7	16%	18	26%	10	35	6.1%	22

Year	LE	Rank	LT	Rank	Mid	Rank	RT	Rank	RE	Rank
2004	4.39	18	5.34	31	4.70	29	3.47	2	4.50	25
2005	5.57	32	4.46	23	4.50	27	4.13	18	4.35	19
2006	3.41	8	4.55	17	4.68	27	3.57	9	3.46	9

When a team is as poor defensively as the 2006 Bengals were, one might reasonably expect them to spend a host of draft picks on that side of the ball. Yet, after adding a cornerback in the first round, the Bengals selected offensive players with two of their next three picks. Perhaps the team's brain trust just didn't feel there was defensive value at the spots at which they were drafting. Then again, maybe Marvin Lewis—who knows a thing or two about defense, after all—has reason for optimism, particularly with regard to the front seven. The Bengals staged a terrific turnaround at midseason after being unable to stop the run for the season's first half, improving from 24th over the season's first nine weeks to fifth over the course of the second half in DVOA against the run.

Of course, that improvement came as the defense was being torched by the pass. The front four generated a decent pass rush with ends Robert Geathers and Justin Smith (the latter of whom has a major incentive to come up with a big year in 2007 after being hit with the franchise tag and subsequently signing a one-year deal); it's the linebackers that need to improve. There is help on the way in the form of Ed Hartwell, who is looking to recapture the form that made him a standout when he played for Lewis in Baltimore. If Hartwell can stay healthy, he should greatly improve the ability of a unit that had trouble making plays close to the line of scrimmage and also help cover some of the mistakes that second-year player Ahmad Brooks makes in the middle, making him exactly the type of steadying presence an otherwise young group of linebackers needs. Either that or he'll just be an endless presence in the trainer's room.

Defensive Secondary

Secondary	Age	Pos	Plys	TmPct	Rk	Stop	Dfts	RuYd	Rk	RuStp	Rk	Tgts	Tgt%	Rk	Dist	Suc%	Rk	PaYd	Rk	PD	Int
Deltha O'Neal	30	CB	47	7.2%	61	21	9	7.0	47	33%	57	57	16%	56	13.0	51%	40	6.8	25	7	1
Johnathan Joseph	23	CB	78	9.0%	45	37	14	3.3	3	67%	3	83	17%	49	10.7	53%	36	7.5	41	16	0
Tory James*	34	CB	57	6.6%	70	21	13	11.3	74	29%	65	76	16%	54	12.7	44%	72	9.8	76	13	4
Madieu Williams	26	FS	95	10.9%	26	41	13	8.0	62	43%	39	42	8%	25	9.5	69%	3	4.0	1	10	3
Dexter Jackson	30	SS	59	9.1%	54	27	12	6.4	37	55%	12	37	10%	17	10.0	40%	68	10.0	63	5	1
Kevin Kaesviharn*	31	FS	69	9.1%	52	31	20	8.5	69	44%	36	35	8%	35	12.6	56%	28	6.6	25	8	6
Keiwan Ratliff	26	CB	19	2.2%	—	7	4	11.7	—	0%	—	17	3%	—	5.1	23%	—	8.2	—	1	0

Year	Pass D Rank	DVOA vs. #1 WR	Rank	DVOA vs. #2 WR	Rank	DVOA vs. Other WR	Rank	DVOA vs. TE	Rank	DVOA vs. RB	Rank
2004	10	-22.8%	4	-18.5%	2	0.7%	18	22.2%	27	16.8%	27
2005	13	-26.3%	1	2.5%	24	-15.2%	8	24.7%	27	-36.7%	1
2006	27	10.7%	26	-8.6%	9	24.6%	28	-8.4%	12	17.5%	26

Cornerbacks Deltha O'Neal and Tory James were outstanding in 2005, but they seriously declined in 2006. That created a major problem in the secondary, one the Bengals never really solved. James is gone, and it wouldn't be a surprise to see rookie Leon Hall starting opposite second-year man Johnathan Joseph by midseason. At safety, the Bengals need Dexter Jackson and Madieu Williams to stay healthy, although Keiwan Ratliff may be ready to make a greater contribution in his fourth season. Williams in particular is excellent in coverage and can help cover the deficiencies of the corners, while Jackson is a savvy veteran who is usually in excellent position. Still, even at full health, this is a secondary that needs an assist from the pass rush in order to be successful, as none of the starters is going to run with a top receiver all over the field.

Special Teams

Year	DVOA	Rank	FG/XP	Rank	Net Punt	Rank	Punt Ret	Rank	Net Kick	Rank	Kick Ret	Rank	Hidden	Rank
2004	3.9%	7	9.9	3	3.3	14	0.6	12	14.1	2	-5.0	22	-22.8	32
2005	0.4%	15	5.3	6	-4.9	24	-2.8	21	1.0	16	3.6	11	-10.6	30
2006	1.3%	12	2.2	11	9.7	5	-3.4	28	7.4	8	-8.0	28	2.4	13

Cincinnati's most notorious failure in 2006 came courtesy of the special teams: the botched extra point that cost the team a shot at overtime in a critical Week 16 loss to Denver. Nevertheless, that's a fluke play, and the Bengals had decent special teams overall, combining excellent coverage units with a season-long struggle to find a consistent return man (running back and former first-round pick Chris Perry was not the answer). Free agency has robbed the Bengals of several special-teams standouts—players such as Marcus Wilkins and Tony Stewart—so the coverage and return units could struggle early as new faces are broken in. Kicker Shayne Graham found a few extra yards on his kickoffs last year—his 63.9-yard average was his highest since 2002 and his 13 touchbacks more than doubled his career total—but he also missed five of 30 field goals and two extra points. Punter Kyle Larson bounced back with an excellent season after a poor 2005.

Coaching Staff

Given that Marvin Lewis has overseen a complete change in culture in Cincinnati, it will probably take more than one disappointing season to hurt his standing with the team's faithful. Still, Lewis is poised to become a victim of his own success. The division title in 2005 raised expectations to the point that 8-8 is no longer an acceptable result, particularly when that mediocre record is accompanied by a host of off-the-field issues. Lewis and the front office seem to have been genuinely embarrassed by the string of player arrests, and it's unlikely they will be taking a chance on too many players with character issues anytime in the near future. Lewis's entire staff returns nearly intact, with only wide receivers coach Hue Jackson moving on, to take the offensive coordinator job in Atlanta.

Much like Tony Dungy in Indianapolis, Lewis is a defensive mind who has come to terms with leading a team with an explosive offense, and he deserves credit for allowing Bob Bratkowski to run an attacking offense while he and defensive coordinator Chuck Bresnahan try to bring some stability to the defense. If Lewis is indeed modeling his team after Dungy's Colts, he needs to be careful to avoid Dungy's fate in Tampa Bay, where he oversaw the transformation of a sadsack franchise only to be fired for failing to meet rising expectations.

Cleveland Browns

April 28, 2007, might have been the best day for Browns fans since the franchise returned to Cleveland in 1999. A team that had made the playoffs just once in eight seasons (and lost a heartbreaker that time) exceeded even the most optimistic fans' expectations: Cleveland bolstered its offensive line by drafting Joe Thomas, then engineered a trade to select its quarterback of the future, Brady Quinn.

Thomas was the third overall pick and will therefore make $15 million to $20 million more on his rookie contract, but Quinn is the real key to this draft. Quinn instantly becomes the face of the franchise, its most recognizable name, and the player fans will hang their hopes on for the future.

Of course, first-round quarterbacks always make the fans of their new teams excited, and they don't always work out. Houston fans were once excited about David Carr. Detroit fans were once excited about Joey Harrington. Baltimore fans were once excited about Kyle Boller. We could go on all day. Many college football fans doubt Quinn because he had some of his worst outings in some of Notre Dame's biggest games, most notably in the final game of his college career, going 15-of-35 for 148 yards, two touchdowns, and two interceptions against LSU while JaMarcus Russell was carving up Notre Dame's vastly inferior defense.

Fortunately for Cleveland fans, there's some good evidence that Quinn won't disappoint the way Carr, Harrington, Boller, and so many other highly regarded college quarterbacks have. Last year, we introduced a system for projecting quarterbacks based on their college stats. David Lewin has an update on that system later in the book, but where the Browns are concerned, the bottom line is that Quinn started 46 games at Notre Dame and completed 58 percent of his passes. The first-round quarterbacks who were most similar to Quinn in terms of their college numbers were Carson Palmer, Donovan McNabb, and Jay Cutler, each of whom started 45 games and completed between 57 and 59 percent of their passes. It's too early to say how Cutler will turn out, but if Quinn plays like Palmer or McNabb, he will make the Dawg Pound very happy.

He won't be an instant fix, however. Quinn should be a good NFL quarterback some day, but he could spend part of 2007 holding a clipboard, especially if he holds out. If he doesn't show up to training camp on time, he probably won't be ready to start the opener. Even if Quinn is in camp on time, coach Romeo Crennel and his staff know they'll be out of a job if the Browns aren't better this season, so there's a chance they'll decide three-year veteran Charlie Frye is more ready to win right away than Quinn.

Frye hasn't shown much ability as a professional quarterback thus far in his NFL career, but the Browns think highly enough of him that he would have been the starter if Quinn hadn't slipped so far in the draft. Imagine the emotional roller coaster ride Frye went on during the draft. When Cleveland picked Thomas, he must have been ecstatic: Not only had his coaches given him a vote of confidence by passing on Quinn, but they had also added the tackle who would be protecting his blind side. Then the Browns traded back into the first round, took Quinn, and showed that they do not, in fact, see Frye as their quarterback of the future.

No matter who plays quarterback, we are still talking about a Browns' offense that was 31st in the league in offensive DVOA in 2006. Although Thomas should improve

---

BROWNS PROSPECTUS

2006 Record: 4–12

DVOA Estimated Wins: 4.8 (31st)

Pythagorean Wins: 4.4 (30th)

DVOA: −21.3% total (30th), −25.7% weighted (32nd)

Offense: −18.5% DVOA (31st)

Defense: 5.0% DVOA (21st)

Special Teams: 2.3% DVOA (10th)

Variance: 13.2% (22nd)

2006: Another lousy season has Cleveland losing patience with Romeo Crennel.

2007: With Joe Thomas and Brady Quinn in the mix, this team is heading in the right direction—but is still probably a year away.

2007 Mean Projection: 7.6 wins

The Brohm Closet (0–4): 8%

Bad Team (5–6): 22%

Mediocre (7–8): 34%

Playoff Contender (9–10): 25%

Super Bowl Contender (11+): 10%

Projected Average Opponent: 0.1% DVOA (14th in NFL)

their offensive line immediately, overall the Browns' offensive personnel isn't markedly better now than it was a year ago. The Browns' receiving corps is one of the NFL's biggest question marks. No one doubts the raw talent in Cleveland—particularly tight end Kellen Winslow, the sixth overall pick in the 2004 draft, and wide receiver Braylon Edwards, the third overall pick in the 2005 draft—but many doubt whether that raw talent will ever translate into excellence on the field.

Edwards occasionally flashed his athleticism in 2006. The 75-yard catch he had in Week 2 against the Bengals was a thing of beauty; he used his speed to break in to the clear, then used his power to bulldoze Bengals safety Kevin Kaesviharn at the end of the play. When Edwards made plays like that, Cleveland fans cheered, but they also asked why he couldn't do it more often. Edwards had trouble getting open at times, and our game charting showed that 17 percent of passes thrown to Edwards were defensed. Out of all wide receivers with at least 75 passes, only Randy Moss had a higher percentage of passes defensed, and we're not sure Moss was even trying to catch those balls.

Winslow is a more complex case than Edwards. In the spring of 2004, the NFL was ready to label Winslow its next big star. One year, two games, and two major injuries later, the pendulum had swung so far in the other direction that Winslow was about to be labeled the league's next big bust. In 2006, Winslow finally got the chance to show what kind of player he is, and he was one of the best tight ends in the NFL. He finished sixth among NFL tight ends with a 15.5 DPAR, and he had a respectable DVOA of 7.8% despite playing for the abysmal Cleveland offense and its overall passing DVOA of –18.1%.

Winslow was regarded as a freakishly strong and fast athlete at the University of Miami, but it's his superior route-running that separates him from other athletic tight ends. Many inexperienced players don't understand the nuances of how to get open or where to position themselves on the field, but when the Browns faced 3rd-and-7, Winslow could be found exactly eight yards past the line of scrimmage. Winslow has the keen understanding of the game that comes from being around it his whole life. It's way too early to say Quinn-to-Winslow could do for the Browns what Fouts-to-Winslow did for Kellen Sr.'s San Diego Chargers, but we're looking forward to their pairing.

Wide receiver Joe Jurevicius should be a good match for the inexperienced Quinn, as well. A year ago, Jurevicius took less money than he could have made elsewhere to play in Cleveland because he grew up in the area. There must have been times last season when he regretted that decision. When a veteran free agent agrees to play for less than fair market value, it's usually because he wants to earn a ring, not finish 4–12. Still, Jurevicius was Cleveland's best

2007 Browns Schedule					
Week	Opp	Week	Opp	Week	Opp
1	PIT	7	BYE	13	at ARI
2	CIN	8	at STL	14	at NYJ
3	at OAK	9	SEA	15	BUF
4	BAL	10	at PIT	16	at CIN
5	at NE	11	at BAL	17	SF
6	MIA	12	HOU		

receiver last year, and the presence of a reliable veteran of his ilk should help Edwards, Winslow, and Quinn. Unfortunately, the 32-year-old Jurevicius will be long gone before those guys are in their primes.

The Browns saved money on Jurevicius last year, but they spent a fortune upgrading their offensive line with results so disastrous that they decided the offensive line was their top priority in this year's draft. Free-agent left tackle Kevin Shaffer signed a seven-year, $36 million contract with $12 million guaranteed, but the Browns discovered that Shaffer was only effective in the zone-blocking scheme he was part of in Atlanta. Shaffer struggled in the Browns' blocking schemes, and after Cleveland drafted Thomas, he asked to be traded.

The other expensive offensive line upgrade was center LeCharles Bentley, who signed a virtually identical deal to the one Shaffer received and never played a snap. Bentley blew out his knee during the first scrimmage of training camp. That injury combined with a subsequent staph infection may have ended his career.

Cleveland has been somewhat star-crossed on defense, too. Cornerback Leigh Bodden is one of the league's best defensive backs when he's healthy, but that isn't very often. A variety of injuries has caused Bodden to miss 21 games in his four-year career, and he's been hobbled in several other games. When he's healthy, though, he's amazing. Bodden is strong enough to knock receivers off their routes as soon as they come off the line of scrimmage, and he's fast enough to stay with them on every step on deep passes. Bodden is so good that he sometimes reaches Champ Bailey territory, when the opposing quarterback simply stops looking at the receiver he's covering.

Cleveland hired Crennel because he had so much success as the coordinator of the Patriots' defense, but aside from Bodden playing the Ty Law role, these Browns don't look much like those Patriots. Ted Washington, the nose tackle who is listed at 365 pounds and probably weighs more, manned the middle of the Browns' line in 2006 the way he did in New England in 2003, but he's 39 years old now and way, way past his prime. It's extraordinary that

Washington's knees haven't broken down by this point, and he deserves respect just for that, but he's really not a good player anymore, and the Browns will improve defensively if Shaun Smith can beat him out for the starting nose tackle job.

Last year's first-round draft pick, outside linebacker Kamerion Wimbley, was a bright spot. He led the team with 11 sacks and came on very strong late in the year, recording eight sacks in the last nine games and generally looking like a terror. With Wimbley rushing opposing quarterbacks and Bodden taking away the other team's number-one receiver, Crennel has two big parts in place. Linebacker D'Qwell Jackson has also shown promise, but 14-year veteran linebacker Willie McGinest, who followed Crennel from New England to Cleveland, is pretty much done.

The young players such as Jackson, Wimbley, Thomas, and Quinn are a lot like the Browns as a whole: They have a lot of potential, but they also have a lot to prove. This year, the Browns should show signs of improvement. Next year they should finally get back to the playoffs.

Michael David Smith

How Important Is Offensive Line Continuity?

Script supervisors are in charge of continuity in a movie. They make sure that all of the details are the same in every take of a scene, even if the scene is shot over several days. Their job also entails making certain that the principle players are in their proper places during each take. The Cleveland Browns' offensive line has been in desperate need of a script supervisor since 2000. Last summer, during their "Who Wants to Be an NFL Center" phase, it looked like Ed Wood Jr. was in charge of continuity. Fortunately, *Plan 9 from Philadelphia,* aka Hank Fraley, ended up providing some stability by starting all 16 games for the Browns. They would need it. In all, Cleveland still used nine different starters on the line. The most consecutive games that any group managed to start together was six. For an assortment of reasons, the Browns broke continuity six times in the 2006 season. By their recent standards this was par for the course.

Since 2000, the Browns have used 34 different starters on the offensive line, the most in football over that period. By comparison, the Broncos, Colts, and Titans have used only 15 different starters over the same period. Since 2000, the longest continuous stretch of games in which the Browns were able to field the same five linemen was ten games during their playoff season of 2002. On average,

their longest continuity "streak" in each of the previous seven seasons is less than seven games. In all, the Browns have switched personnel on the line 42 times in the last seven years. That is the fifth-most over that span. The Jets made a league-low 18 changes over that time.

How much does continuity matter? To help answer this, we created a measure of offensive line continuity and applied it to every team in each season since 2000 and for each franchise cumulatively since 2000. The components of this continuity score were the number of unique offensive line starters in each season, the longest streak of games with the same starting line in each season, and the number of times continuity was broken by changing one of the starting linemen. In order to weigh each component equally, we subtracted the number of unique starters from 21, resulting in a maximum possible value of 16. The longest streak was left as is, again with a maximum possible of 16. We subtracted the number of breaks in continuity from 16 to, once again, give a maximum of 16. We then added the three component scores together, resulting in a maximum possible score of 48 in an individual season. We used a similar process to derive a value for the entire seven-year span for each franchise (five years for the Texans) that would give results on a similar scale.

Seventeen teams since 2000 have scored a perfect 48 in an individual season. The worst individual seasons all came from 2003 and belonged to the 49ers, Chargers, and Raiders, all of whom had a continuity score of 21. The best seven-year total is the Titans' 44, which is nearly two standard deviations better than the league average over that span. The lowest seven-year total is the Browns' 19, which is a little more than two standard deviations below the league average.

Using these continuity scores for every team in the league, we ran a number of correlations to attempt to gauge the importance of continuity. We examined seven statistics: wins, offensive DVOA, adjusted line yards, adjusted sack rate, drive success rate, points per drive, and false starts. After looking at all 222 team seasons, we found the correlations intriguing enough to pursue further; they ranged in strength from a low of 0.19 to a high of 0.38.

Just lining up all the continuity scores with the offensive statistics that continuity might logically affect and running correlations neglects an important fact of NFL life: Not every team's skill position players are created equal. Some teams have Peyton Manning throwing to Reggie Wayne or a dynamic game-changing running back such as LaDainian Tomlinson. Other teams have Charlie Frye and Reuben Droughns.

To get a sense of what was happening for each team over the seven-year period regarding their own ebbs and flows with continuity, we ran correlations on each individual franchise. This would eliminate the problem of comparing a Colts offense with a poor continuity score (still very good) to a Cardinals offense with a similarly poor continuity score (not so good). The results show many teams with some very strong correlations, including several in the 0.80 and 0.90 ranges, an indication that offensive line continuity is indeed important to a line's collective performance. Overall, no less than 80 percent of teams showed a positive correlation when correlating continuity with wins, offensive DVOA, drive success rate, and points per drive. Additionally, 22 of 32 teams saw their adjusted line yards increase and their adjusted sack rate decrease in seasons in which their continuity increased from the previous season, and 21 teams saw a general decline in false starts as continuity improved. The fact that continuity does not affect adjusted sack rate as much as the other statistics matches previous research showing that individual quarterbacks are more responsible for their own sacks than most fans realize.

A single-year continuity score of 41 or better represents a mark that is more than one standard deviation above the mean. A score of 26 or less is greater than one standard deviation below average. Forty-two seasons since 2000 have fallen into the former group (excellent), and 31 comprise the latter (poor), leaving 149 seasons in the middle (average) (table 1).

Table 1. Single-Season Stats Compared to Continuity Score

Continuity	Wins	Off. DVOA	Adj. Line Yards	Adj. Sack Rate	DSR	Pts/Drive	False Starts
Excellent	9.6	4.9%	4.23	5.9%	0.678	1.87	21
Average	8.0	-0.9%	4.12	6.7%	0.662	1.70	23
Poor	5.7	-8.5%	3.99	7.4%	0.647	1.49	26

Not shown in the table is the fact that 29 of the 42 "excellent" continuity teams made the postseason, while only five of 31 "poor" continuity teams made the postseason. This is not due to a handful of ultra-successful franchises heavily weighting the "excellent" list year after year and a few lousy teams dominating the "poor" list. Twenty-three different franchises contribute to the excellent continuity group

while 21 different franchises contribute at least one season to the poor continuity group. The Giants and Dolphins are the only teams that have been in the average range for all seven seasons.

What do these trends look like when we examine continuity over seven seasons? They are similar and a bit stronger, with correlations ranging in strength from 0.37 to 0.64. When we look at the stats by team, the importance of continuity becomes even clearer. Six franchises qualify as "excellent" (more than one standard deviation above the mean), four as "poor" (more than one standard deviation below the mean), and the other 22 as "average" (table 2).

Table 2. Seven-Year Stats Compared to Continuity Score

Continuity	Wins	Off. DVOA	Adj. Line Yards	Adj. Sack Rate	DSR	Pts/Drive	False Starts
Excellent	9.5	20.9%	4.26	5.6%	0.692	1.96	19
Average	8.0	-2.2%	4.13	6.7%	0.661	1.68	24
Poor	5.5	-20.2%	3.85	8.2%	0.627	1.39	24

The "excellent" continuity group had 25 combined postseason trips, with all six teams making it at least twice. The four franchises in the "poor" continuity group made just one postseason trip (the 2002 Browns).

So, is good line play more a function of having the best players or just having the healthiest? Of course, it must be some combination, but these continuity trends are hard to ignore. Continuity does not measure whether the new lineman is a top pick or a star free agent or some guy off the practice squad. It is only concerned with how long that player remains in the starting lineup. Given the importance of continuity, it might be better to play a consistent line game after game and year after year instead of constantly tinkering in an attempt to make small gains in talent.

Of course, trying to keep a consistent line does not mean actually being able to keep a consistent line. A team's offensive line health in one season does not predict that team's offensive line health for the next season. A team with a strong continuity score in one season, poor or excellent, usually regresses to average in the following season. Perhaps that is good news for the Browns and their fans.

Jason McKinley

Browns 2006 Stats by Week

Wk	vs.	W–L	PF	PA	YDF	YDA	TO	DVOA Total	Off	Def	ST
1	NO	L	14	19	186	326	-1	-24.7%	-45.9%	-15.9%	5.3%
2	@CIN	L	17	34	301	481	-1	-38.9%	-31.8%	11.0%	3.9%
3	BAL	L	14	15	288	340	-2	14.4%	10.3%	-2.3%	1.7%
4	@OAK	W	24	21	283	240	-2	-0.1%	7.0%	24.4%	17.3%
5	@CAR	L	12	20	248	288	-3	-27.0%	-31.9%	14.2%	19.2%
6	BYE										
7	DEN	L	7	17	165	347	-1	-23.5%	-19.3%	6.3%	2.1%
8	NYJ	W	20	13	267	193	+2	16.5%	-1.2%	-43.6%	-25.9%
9	@SD	L	25	32	293	381	-1	-24.1%	-31.6%	21.3%	28.8%
10	@ATL	W	17	13	236	343	+1	-6.9%	-25.1%	-19.2%	-1.0%
11	PIT	L	20	24	302	338	+1	28.3%	-5.7%	-26.7%	7.3%
12	CIN	L	0	30	203	388	-4	-93.3%	-67.6%	23.6%	-2.2%
13	KC	W	31	28	438	417	0	7.2%	38.4%	31.0%	-0.3%
14	@PIT	L	7	27	294	528	-1	-56.4%	-0.7%	49.8%	-5.9%
15	@BAL	L	17	27	236	373	+1	1.6%	-5.7%	-2.3%	5.0%
16	TB	L	7	22	187	355	-2	-103.3%	-72.4%	16.3%	-14.5%
17	@HOU	L	6	14	306	179	-2	-27.7%	-37.5%	-12.0%	-2.2%

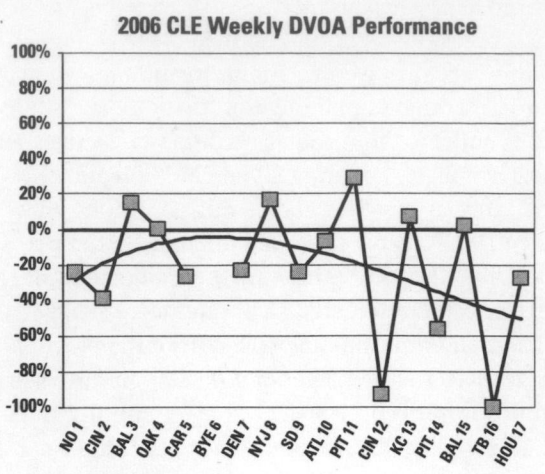

2006 CLE Weekly DVOA Performance

Trends and Splits

	Offense	Rank	Defense	Rank
Total DVOA	-18.5%	31	5.0%	21
Unadjusted VOA	-22.7%	31	5.2%	23
Weighted Trend	-18.8%	31	6.7%	20
Variance	8.1%	7	5.5%	22
Passing	-18.0%	29	3.8%	16
Rushing	-19.3%	30	6.3%	25
First Down	-9.2%	20	7.8%	25
Second Down	-30.3%	31	-7.3%	9
Third Down	-19.0%	28	18.2%	26
Red Zone	-8.9%	20	10.8%	24
Late and Close	-35.6%	31	15.4%	29

Five-Year Performance

	2006	2005	2004	2003	2002
W-L	4-12	6-10	4-12	5-11	9-7
Pythagorean Wins	4.4	5.6	4.9	5.8	8.7
Estimated Wins	4.8	6.3	5.5	6.6	8.4
Total DVOA	-21.3%	-17.1%	-19.0%	-9.8%	-0.2%
Rank	30	24	27	23	16
Offense	-18.5%	-13.5%	-12.5%	-12.6%	-6.6%
Rank	31	26	27	25	25
Defense	5.0%	5.4%	8.4%	-2.7%	-4.4%
Rank	21	24	23	14	10
Special Teams	2.3%	1.7%	1.9%	0.1%	2.1%
Rank	10	8	12	20	11

Strategic Tendencies

Formations		Rank	Run/Pass		Rank	Defense		Rank	Other		Rank
3+ WR	44%	22	Runs, all plays	39%	30	Sacks by LB	71%	1	Run with 2+ RB	62%	15
4+ WR	12%	12	Runs, first half	43%	21	Sacks by DB	5%	20	Run with 2+ TE	38%	13
2+ TE	29%	9	Runs, first down	47%	29	Rush 6+	8.6%	17	Play action	21%	11
Single back	56%	14	Runs, power sit.	74%	3	Rush 7+	1.3%	17	Go for it on 4th	0.85	17
Empty back	4.6%	7	Runs, behind 2H	28%	26	Rush 3	13.8%	2	Offensive Pace	33.5	31
Max protect	10%	20	Pass, ahead 2H	50%	4	CB1 on WR1	63%	2	Defensive Pace	29.3	4

Five percent of Cleveland's running plays were draws (14th in the NFL), but the Browns had the worst DVOA in the league on draw plays. . . . The only formation in which the Browns had a positive offensive DVOA was the goal-line set, and that was just ten short-yardage plays. Cleveland's worst formation was the four-wide receiver set, from which the Cleveland DVOA (both rushing and passing) was −75.0%. . . . The tight end was the Browns' most targeted receiver in almost all formations, a stat that is even more exaggerated in long-yardage situations. . . . Cleveland allowed nine sacks with the pass-rusher untouched, second in the league to Oakland. . . . Cleveland had only one sack by a linebacker (Andra Davis) and only 1.5 sacks by defensive backs (Brodney Pool with a full sack and Sean Jones with a half sack). . . . The Browns had the second-slowest offensive pace since 1998, the first year for which we have pace stats. The slowest offense also played last year, in Jacksonville.

Passing

Player	DPAR	DVOA	Plys	NtYds	Avg	YAC	C%	TD	Int
Charlie Frye	-17.3	-22.4%	392	2194	5.6	4.4	64.5%	10	8
Derek Anderson	-8.5	-28.5%	116	730	6.3	6.1	56.9%	5	15

Rushing

Player	DPAR	DVOA	Plys	Yds	Avg	TD	Fum	Suc
Reuben Droughns*	-6.8	-20.1%	219	761	3.5	4	5	42%
Jason Wright	-0.3	-17.0%	62	189	3.0	0	1	33%
Charlie Frye	2.8	-9.5%	40	215	5.4	3	8	—
Jerome Harrison	-3.7	-61.5%	20	60	3.0	0	1	92%
Trent Smith*	-1.4	-51.0%	8	14	1.8	0	0	76%
Lawrence Vickers	-1.8	-105.7%	3	2	0.7	0	0	48%
Braylon Edwards	-0.2	-32.9%	3	7	2.3	0	0	—
Dennis Northcutt*	-0.5	-60.6%	3	32	10.7	0	1	—
Derek Anderson	0.4	7.5%	3	48	16.0	0	2	—
Jamal Lewis	*3.7*	*-9.9%*	*314*	*1130*	*3.6*	*9*	*4*	*42%*

Receiving

Player	DPAR	DVOA	Plys	Ctch	Yds	Y/C	YAC	TD	C%
WR									
Braylon Edwards	1.4	-13.7%	125	61	884	14.5	5.2	6	62%
Joe Jurevicius	11.9	12.1%	65	40	495	12.4	3.2	3	49%
Dennis Northcutt*	-4.8	-31.4%	45	22	228	10.4	4.3	0	33%
Joshua Cribbs	-2.8	-43.7%	15	10	91	9.1	4.9	0	67%
Travis Wilson	0.1	-10.8%	6	2	32	16.0	2.5	0	49%
Tim Carter	*-5.2*	*-31.5%*	*49*	*22*	*253*	*11.5*	*1.8*	*2*	*58%*
TE									
Kellen Winslow	14.7	6.6%	120	89	875	9.8	3.7	3	74%
Steve Heiden	1.3	-8.4%	46	36	249	6.9	4.1	2	78%
RB									
Reuben Droughns*	1.4	-2.5%	34	28	168	6.0	7.6	0	82%
Jerome Harrison	-1.0	-24.1%	14	9	47	5.2	6.3	0	86%
Jason Wright	0.0	-9.9%	11	6	82	13.7	14.3	0	55%
Trent Smith*	-3.8	-73.8%	11	8	21	2.6	2.1	0	64%
Lawrence Vickers	2.6	55.3%	7	6	60	10.0	10.3	0	73%
Jamal Lewis	*-0.4*	*-13.3%*	*26*	*18*	*115*	*6.4*	*7.4*	*0*	*69%*

Offensive Line

Year	Yards	ALY	Rank	Power	Rank	10+ Yds	Rank	Stuff	Rank	Sack	ASR	Rank
2004	3.79	3.67	30	64%	14	17%	15	30%	30	42	8.9%	27
2005	3.86	3.89	21	48%	31	17%	16	19%	3	46	7.9%	24
2006	3.29	3.70	31	74%	3	7%	31	28%	31	54	9.1%	27

Year	LE	Rank	LT	Rank	Mid	Rank	RT	Rank	RE	Rank
2004	4.38	15	3.33	30	3.72	28	3.74	25	3.24	26
2005	3.05	29	4.18	18	3.84	24	4.12	16	4.14	14
2006	0.06	32	4.27	18	3.54	32	4.26	13	3.59	23

If first-round draft pick Joe Thomas does anything short of starting 16 games at left tackle as a rookie, the Browns' front office will be disappointed. Of all the prospects in this year's draft, Thomas was advertised as the most prepared to start immediately.

Playing next to Thomas will be left guard Eric Steinbach, who signed a seven-year, $49.5 million contract with the Browns that includes $17 million guaranteed. Steinbach, who started the last four years in Cincinnati, is a fierce run blocker and a versatile lineman who has also played center and tackle. Combine Steinbach's free-agent contract and the big money that Thomas will get as the third overall pick, and the left side of the line in Cleveland will be extremely expensive—but it has the potential to be worth the money.

The ridiculously low left-end number for Adjusted Line Yards is a sample size issue, not a problem with the players Thomas and Steinbach are replacing. The Browns only had a running back go around the left end eight times, 15 runs less than any other team and 40 runs less than the NFL average.

On the right side, the Browns signed guard Seth McKinney as a free agent from Miami. He's no more than an adequate player, and he missed all of 2006, but he'll probably start now that Cleveland has cut Joe Andruzzi, who started the last two years but was mostly a disappointment as a free-agent signing from New England. Tackles Ryan Tucker and Kevin Shaffer will compete for the starting job at right tackle.

As for center Hank Fraley, the offensive line stats show a strange dichotomy in runs up the middle: The Browns were excellent when they only needed a yard or two, but they were otherwise terrible. Cleveland seemingly went through a hundred centers last year during training camp before trading with Philadelphia for Fraley. He is an adequate player, but not as good as the player who was supposed to start at center: last year's big free-agent signing, LeCharles Bentley, who might never play again due to a staph infection.

Our injury expert Will Carroll says Bentley's medical difficulties are the apex of a growing problem in the NFL: Community-Acquired MRSA, or Methicillin-resistant Staphylococcus aureus. Bentley tore his patellar tendon early in training camp, which cost him the 2006 season, but his recovery was further complicated by an MRSA infection after surgery.

(continued next page)

Offensive Line *(continued)*

Reporters will use the words *staph infection,* which make this illness sound much less damaging than it truly is. MRSA is specific bacterial strain that is resistant to antibiotics, so treatment is difficult and lengthy. Bacterial infections aren't the scourge that they once were, due to the prevalence of antibiotics. A post-surgical infection that would have been lethal a century ago is now merely an annoyance, but drug-resistant strains of bacteria are threatening to undo that progress. While MRSA is seldom deadly, it can be life-threatening if not treated aggressively. If you want to know why MRSA is so problematic, consider its other common name: flesh-eating bacteria.

Both the Browns and the St. Louis Rams had internal outbreaks of MRSA last year, although the Browns' received much more attention because of the Bentley situation. The increase in MRSA infections in sports mirrors that of its spread in the general population, but certain things about the NFL and sports in general increase MRSA's ability to take hold and even thrive. First, the communal nature of facilities, especially locker rooms, showers, towels, and whirlpools, provides effective vectors for transmitting the infection. Second—let's face it, athletes aren't clean people. They throw towels down, reuse razors, share personal care products, and simply don't think about the need for disinfecting many surfaces.

The Browns acknowledged having five cases of MRSA over the last three years, but many think that the incidence rate is higher. One of those infected, tight end Kellen Winslow, may have suffered damage internally from the infection, necessitating offseason surgery. Both the Browns and Washington Redskins have gone as far as repainting, resurfacing, and instituting new locker room and training room protocols to prevent further outbreak. League-wide, this is likely to be a larger problem than will be reported, especially for teams that play on or have artificial turf practice surfaces. While cases such as Bentley's potentially career-ending infection are likely to be rare, infection is likely to be the cause of several missed games until broader infection control protocols are in place league-wide.

Defensive Front Seven

Defensive Line	Age	Pos	Plys	TmPct	Rk	Stop	Dfts	StpRt	Rk	AvYd	Rk	Sack	Hit	Hur	Runs	RuStp	RuYd	Pass	PaStp	PaYd
Ted Washington	39	DT	52	6.3%	17	42	5	81%	29	2.5	56	0	1	1	51	80%	2.5	1	100%	2.0
Alvin McKinley*	29	DT	47	6.5%	13	34	8	72%	55	2.3	49	1	6	6	46	72%	2.5	1	100%	-9.0
Simon Fraser	24	DE	40	4.9%	54	32	7	80%	26	2.2	62	4.5	1	4	27	81%	3.1	13	77%	0.5
Orpheus Roye	34	DE	33	7.1%	24	24	5	73%	58	2.5	68	1	3	6	27	70%	2.8	6	83%	1.3
Nick Eason	27	DT	25	3.7%	68	19	5	76%	44	2.9	65	0	3	6	23	78%	2.5	2	50%	7.0
Ethan Kelley	27	DT	17	3.0%	—	16	1	94%	—	2.0	—	0	1	0	17	94%	2.0	0	0%	0.0
Robaire Smith	*30*	*DT*	*46*	*5.6%*	*29*	*30*	*8*	*65%*	*66*	*3.4*	*70*	*0.5*	*0*	*1*	*36*	*75%*	*2.4*	*10*	*30%*	*6.9*

Linebackers	Age	Pos	Plys	TmPct	Rk	Stop	Dfts	StpRt	AvYd	Sack	Hit	Hur	Runs	RuStp	Rk	RuYd	Rk	Tgts	Suc%	Rk	PaYd	Rk
Andra Davis	29	ILB	98	13.6%	35	58	18	59%	4.9	1	4	2	64	73%	12	3.5	57	33	42%	76	6.0	39
D'Qwell Jackson	24	ILB	86	12.9%	44	48	9	56%	5.3	0	1	0	69	61%	63	4.0	73	19	53%	42	6.1	43
Kamerion Wimbley	24	OLB	63	7.7%	90	49	27	78%	1.9	11	16	19	37	84%	1	2.5	9	10	83%	—	2.9	—
Willie McGinest	36	OLB	48	6.7%	—	33	14	69%	3.1	4	7	5	34	71%	—	2.9	—	12	61%	—	3.0	—
Leon Williams	24	ILB	37	4.5%	—	19	8	51%	4.3	1	2	2	25	48%	—	3.6	—	7	42%	—	6.9	—
Chaun Thompson	27	OLB	26	3.2%	—	16	7	62%	3.0	2	1	1	22	59%	—	3.5	—	2	50%	—	9.0	—

Year	Yards	ALY	Rank	Power	Rank	10+ Yds	Rank	Stuff	Rank	Sack	ASR	Rank
2004	4.34	4.65	31	67%	23	12%	7	21%	27	32	6.2%	25
2005	4.40	4.49	28	70%	25	16%	15	20%	29	23	5.4%	28
2006	4.73	4.71	27	58%	9	20%	26	21%	24	28	5.1%	30

Year	LE	Rank	LT	Rank	Mid	Rank	RT	Rank	RE	Rank
2004	4.23	15	4.35	14	4.88	31	4.18	16	4.60	27
2005	3.80	13	4.93	30	4.66	31	3.53	3	4.88	27
2006	5.00	26	5.03	27	4.60	22	4.54	22	5.48	32

To build a 3-4 defensive line like the one Romeo Crennel is assembling in Cleveland, you need an enormous nose tackle who can clog the middle of the line and two big, strong ends who are stout against the run. The pass rush from the line is less important. With Ted Washington at nose tackle and Orpheus Roye and Robaire Smith at end, Cleveland has three players who look the part more than they play the part. Roye, Smith, and Washington are all big, and they're all smart, experienced players who understand their role in a 3-4 front, but they're awfully slow coming out of their stances. At 29, Smith is the baby of the group. Roye is old by defensive line standards, but he's still five years younger than Washington. When Washington retires, the NFL ought to ship his body directly to the Smithsonian.

Opinion was divided when Cleveland drafted outside linebacker Kamerion Wimbley in the first round in 2006, but he was one of the best defensive rookies in the league last year. No starting linebacker in the NFL had a better Stop Rate on running plays. Willie McGinest, the longtime Patriot, is a 14-year veteran and a fine player for Wimbley to learn from, but he doesn't have much gas left in the tank. Cleveland signed Antwan Peek as a free agent from Houston, and Crennel thinks he can make an impact where McGinest hasn't. Peek wasn't particularly productive in Houston last year, but the Browns think he struggled because Houston's switch back to a 4-3 alignment left him without a position. The starting inside linebackers, Andra Davis and D'Qwell Jackson, are both good athletes who are still getting better; Davis is better against the run; Jackson, when covering the pass. Overall, linebacker is probably the Browns' best position group.

Defensive Secondary

Secondary	Age	Pos	Plys	TmPct	Rk	Stop	Dfts	RuYd	Rk	RuStp	Rk	Tgts	Tgt%	Rk	Dist	Suc%	Rk	PaYd	Rk	PD	Int
Daven Holly	25	CB	67	9.3%	33	22	12	7.1	49	56%	16	85	22%	16	13.1	41%	76	8.9	69	8	5
Brodney Pool	23	FS	62	7.5%	60	30	17	7.6	56	48%	27	51	11%	2	9.5	42%	66	7.6	37	8	1
Ralph Brown*	29	CB	43	5.2%	80	20	12	4.6	14	56%	17	48	11%	80	9.2	48%	60	7.8	48	9	0
Leigh Bodden	26	CB	44	9.5%	31	21	8	10.4	70	45%	36	47	19%	38	13.7	60%	10	6.8	24	13	2
Sean Jones	25	SS	127	15.5%	2	61	18	5.6	23	56%	11	42	9%	20	13.4	51%	47	8.3	43	13	5
Brian Russell*	29	FS	56	9.1%	53	15	5	10.7	77	27%	68	31	8%	27	12.9	47%	55	7.2	31	4	1
Gary Baxter	29	CB	24	15.6%	—	7	2	8.1	—	14%	—	25	29%	—	15.7	47%	—	10.1	—	4	1
Jereme Perry	26	CB	18	2.9%	—	10	5	0.0	—	0%	—	21	6%	—	12.9	50%	—	8.4	—	5	0
Kenny Wright	*30*	*CB*	*51*	*6.3%*	*73*	*22*	*11*	*9.1*	*62*	*33%*	*60*	*66*	*15%*	*61*	*11.1*	*46%*	*69*	*8.3*	*58*	*13*	*1*

Year	Pass D Rank	DVOA vs. #1 WR	Rank	DVOA vs. #2 WR	Rank	DVOA vs. Other WR	Rank	DVOA vs. TE	Rank	DVOA vs. RB	Rank
2004	20	12.5%	22	7.3%	21	15.2%	30	-10.8%	11	-8.3%	11
2005	23	-1.6%	12	-27.4%	3	52.4%	32	-15.4%	6	9.2%	24
2006	16	-16.8%	5	0.0%	16	-5.1%	16	-25.6%	4	9.9%	21

At *Pro Football Prospectus*, we absolutely love Leigh Bodden. Cleveland's DVOA against number-one receivers indicates that he's great. Our game charting numbers indicate that he's great. Our own subjective viewings of the Browns indicate that he's great. Most fans have never heard of him because he plays for the Browns and gets hurt a lot, but we'd love to see him stay healthy and get the recognition he deserves. The Browns' other starting cornerback, Daven Holly, wasn't ready when he was forced into the lineup after Gary Baxter suffered serious injuries to both knees, but he improved as the 2006 season wore on. Holly will battle rookie Eric Wright for a starting job this season, and the Browns hope one of them can team with Bodden to give the team a good pair of corners.

The Browns aren't as strong at safety. Brian Russell, who started last season, signed in Seattle, and Brodney Pool, who will replace him in the starting lineup, is young and inexperienced. The other starting safety, Sean Jones, has good numbers against the run, but that's partly because safeties tend to make plays when the defense is giving up a lot of yardage.

Special Teams

Year	DVOA	Rank	FG/XP	Rank	Net Punt	Rank	Punt Ret	Rank	Net Kick	Rank	Kick Ret	Rank	Hidden	Rank
2004	1.9%	12	1.0	14	5.1	12	5.7	6	1.1	13	-1.9	16	0.2	12
2005	1.7%	8	3.7	10	-6.2	26	7.9	3	2.6	14	2.3	14	5.0	10
2006	2.3%	10	-5.2	27	6.9	8	2.2	9	-0.2	20	9.7	4	4.7	10

One of the real bright spots for Cleveland last year was the way Josh Cribbs developed into a top-flight kick returner. The former Kent State quarterback is speedy, elusive, and smart. His most complete game was probably Week 5 against Carolina, when he returned four kickoffs for a 29.8-yard average and two punts for a 21.5-yard average, and caught both passes thrown to him for 18 total yards. College quarterbacks turned NFL receivers are an increasingly common sight, and the Browns look as though they got one of the best when they signed Cribbs as an undrafted free agent in 2005. With Dennis Northcutt now in Jacksonville, Cribbs may have to add punt returns to his duties on a full-time basis.

Punter Dave Zastudil had an outstanding season and was a great free-agent signing from Baltimore. Zastudil is one of the best in the league at pinning opponents deep into their own territory; last year he landed 28 kicks inside the 20-yard line and had only seven touchbacks. Kicker Phil Dawson had a disappointing season, going just 6-of-12 from 40 to 49 yards. He'll need to beat undrafted rookie Jon Peattie from the University of Miami in a training camp battle if he wants to keep his job.

Coaching Staff

Romeo Crennel hired Rob Chudzinski as his new offensive coordinator this offseason, and the indications are that Chudzinski wants to make Kellen Winslow the focal point of the passing game. Chudzinski spent the last two years as the tight ends coach in San Diego, where tight end Antonio Gates flourished. Chudzinski was the University of Miami's offensive coordinator and tight ends coach when Winslow played there, including in 2003, when Winslow won the John Mackey Award as the best tight end in college football.

Offensive line coach John Marshall is another new addition, and he might have the most important job of any coach on the staff. He has to juggle, among other things, a rookie in Joe Thomas, a high-priced free agent in Eric Steinbach, and a high-priced free agent who's angry about being demoted in Kevin Shaffer. If Cleveland's line is in sync this season, Marshall should get a lot of credit.

Defensive coordinator Todd Grantham is a longtime defensive line coach, usually for teams that run 3-4 fronts, which means his philosophy should be similar to Romeo Crennel's. Neither he nor Crennel has been able to do much with the defense in Cleveland, though.

Denver Broncos

Who knew what to think of the 2006 Denver Broncos? Remember Week 1, when they were taking on the rebuilding Rams? Picking Denver in that game looked like the safest bet of the NFL's opening weekend—until the Broncos took an ugly 18–10 loss.

And remember how great the Denver defense looked? The Broncos won their next five games without giving up more than seven points in any of them.

And remember how Peyton Manning picked that defense apart in the seventh game? It was a 34–31 loss that exposed the Broncos' defense as a good but not great unit that could shut down bottom-of-the-barrel offenses such as the Raiders' and Browns', but not high-powered offenses such as the Colts' and Chargers'.

And remember Jake Plummer? He made so many mistakes in September that Mike Shanahan neutered him, forcing him to throw short, safe passes again and again before finally benching him in favor of Jay Cutler in December.

Ultimately, the Broncos were a mediocre team: a little above average on defense, a little below average on offense, almost exactly average on special teams. They played about as well as you would expect them to play within their own division (two wins over the Raiders, two losses to the Chargers, a split with the Chiefs). But a surprisingly weak 1–3 record against the NFC West, culminating in a Week 17 loss to the 49ers, cost them a wild-card berth.

If there's one untold story of the Broncos' 2006 season, it's that it was the year when the vaunted Denver running attack ground to a halt. We've been hearing for a decade now that the Broncos have such an incredible offensive line that they can just plug any runner in at any time, but an injury to left tackle Matt Lepsis in the sixth game of the season devastated that offensive line, and running back

Tatum Bell tried to dance around too much behind the line of scrimmage, making him a bad fit for Denver's one-cut system. Overall, the Broncos' running game was actually below average last year.

Bell is gone now, as is right tackle George Foster. The two were traded to the Detroit Lions in exchange for Dre' Bly, a move that should make the pass defense—the strength of the Broncos last year—even better. Pairing Bly with Champ Bailey gives the Broncos one of the best cornerback tandems we'll ever see, a pair that has made a combined nine Pro Bowls and is still in top form.

Bly was always given the most challenging assignment in the Lions' secondary. Until head coach Rod Marinelli and his Tampa-influenced zone coverage schemes, no cornerback in the league spent as much time covering the opposing teams' number-one receivers as Bly did in Detroit. Now that he's playing with Bailey, he'll get a reprieve from that task, while taking on the added responsibility of having opposing quarterbacks throw in his direction as they avoid Bailey. Bly is a ball hawk who occasionally takes too many chances and therefore gets beaten when he takes on elite receivers, but playing opposite Bailey, he won't take on as many elite receivers. That means Bly should be among the league leaders in interceptions this season.

Bly turned 30 during the offseason, so it's a bit surprising that the Broncos gave in to his contract demands, signing him to a five-year, $33 million deal with $16 million guaranteed. Bly and Bailey (who's 29) will be a great duo this season, but they'll be an expensive and aging pairing in the not-too-distant future.

Of course, just because the Broncos' combo of Bly and Bailey looks good on paper doesn't mean it will work out

---

BRONCOS PROSPECTUS

2006 Record: 9–7

DVOA Estimated Wins: 7.0 (22nd)

Pythagorean Wins: 8.4 (14th)

DVOA: −3.9% total (18th), −10.2% weighted (21st)

Offense: −8.3% DVOA (23rd)

Defense: −3.7% DVOA (12th)

Special Teams: 0.7% DVOA (15th)

Variance: 16.7% (14th)

2006: Broncos miss the playoffs thanks to Plummer's failures and Cutler's learning curve.

2007: They're no better this year than they were last year, but an easy schedule could lead to the postseason.

2007 Mean Projection: 8.7 wins

The Brohm Closet (0–4): 4%

Bad Team (5–6): 14%

Mediocre (7–8): 27%

Playoff Contender (9–10): 34%

Super Bowl Contender (11+): 22%

Projected Average Opponent: −3.6% DVOA (29th in NFL)

2007 Broncos Schedule

Week	Opp	Week	Opp	Week	Opp
1	at BUF	7	PIT	13	at OAK
2	OAK	8	GB (Mon.)	14	KC
3	JAC	9	at DET	15	at HOU (Thu.)
4	at IND	10	at KC	16	at SD (Mon.)
5	SD	11	TEN (Mon.)	17	MIN
6	BYE	12	at CHI		

on the field. When the Baltimore Ravens signed Samari Rolle as a free agent in 2005, they thought pairing Rolle with Chris McAllister would make it almost impossible to pass against them. As it turns out, Rolle had lost a step by the time he joined the Ravens at age 29 and has actually been the weak link in the Ravens' great defense.

The pass defense will get even better if the Broncos can put some pressure on opposing quarterbacks. Over the last two years, Denver's pass rush has been among the worst in the league (they finished 26th and 32nd in Adjusted Sack Rate), but new assistant head coach Jim Bates, who will be calling the plays on defense, plans to emphasize the need to improve that woeful pass rush. Last year, rookie Elvis Dumervil led the team with 8.5 sacks as a part-time player. This year, expect Bates to give Dumervil more playing time, and Dumervil to respond by making the Broncos' pass rush better.

More help for the pass rush came during the draft, when the Broncos had just four picks but used three of them on defensive linemen Jarvis Moss of Florida in the first round, Tim Crowder of Texas in the second round, and Marcus Thomas of Florida in the fourth round. The addition of those three makes the Denver defense younger, as does the loss of middle linebacker Al Wilson. The team's defensive captain and a five-time Pro Bowler, Wilson suffered a serious neck injury in December and was released in April. He'll be missed, but he had already lost some of the speed that once made him one of the game's elite linebackers. D. J. Williams could move from outside linebacker to the middle to take Wilson's place, although the Broncos hope middle linebacker Nate Webster will finally be healthy and ready to play. Over the past three years, two in Cincinnati and one in Denver, Webster has only been healthy enough to play in eight regular-season games.

Changes are coming on offense, too. Denver signed running back Travis Henry to a five-year deal that included $12 million in guarantees. That was a surprising signing for Denver, not only because the Broncos hadn't invested a lot of resources into running backs in the past due to the belief that any back could succeed behind their offensive line, but because Henry is far from a superstar and, just a few

seasons ago, served a four-game suspension for violating the league's substance-abuse policy.

On the other hand, when they sent Tatum Bell to Detroit in the Bly trade, we knew the Broncos would add a running back and, among the free agents available, Henry was probably the best. Better backs such as Thomas Jones and Willis McGahee were available via trade, but the Broncos didn't want to give up the necessary draft picks to acquire them. Then again, Mike Bell looked good as an undrafted rookie last year, and while Henry is expected to get the bulk of the carries, it's not at all clear that Henry is a better option than Bell.

If Bell looks better than Henry in training camp, we could see a running back controversy. And don't completely rule out the possibility of a quarterback controversy. Denver signed Patrick Ramsey to a two-year, $5 million deal to back up Jay Cutler, and Mike Shanahan's other moves this offseason (signing Henry, trading for Bly) indicate that he's looking to win now. If Cutler shows early in the year that he's not ready to win now, Shanahan won't be shy about replacing him. Just ask Plummer or Bubby Brister.

Cutler might spend a little time looking over his shoulder at Ramsey, but he has one big reason to feel good about the coming year: wide receiver Javon Walker. The best decision any team made during the 2006 NFL draft wasn't the New Orleans Saints selecting Reggie Bush or the Tennessee Titans taking Vince Young. The single best move on draft day took place when the Broncos traded a second-round pick to the Green Bay Packers for Walker.

It didn't look like a slam-dunk decision at the time. Walker was coming off a serious knee injury that ended his 2005 season after just one game, and some questioned his commitment when he threatened to sit out 2006 in a contract dispute. In Denver, Walker was healthy and committed, and he kept an otherwise sinking Bronco offense afloat. Cutler's DVOA was 36.2% on passes to Walker but −20.3% when throwing to anyone else. For Plummer, the dichotomy was even greater; his DVOA was 62.9% on passes to Walker and −36.3% otherwise.

Many wide receivers rely on their speed as young players and then become possession receivers as they get older, learning to run more precise routes when they lose a step. The 28-year-old Walker is in his prime and thus combines both abilities. He still has blazing speed (that knee injury healed just fine), but he has learned to run routes that allow the quarterback to know exactly where he'll be. When Plummer was the quarterback, Walker mostly turned short passes into long gains. When the stronger-armed Cutler went under center, Walker ran deep routes.

Shanahan traded for Walker because he knew he needed to add another wide receiver to help the team deal with the inevitable decline of Rod Smith. A three-time Pro

Bowler, Smith is one of the best players in the history of the Broncos' franchise, with 849 catches for 11,389 yards during his career, but he doesn't have much left in his 37-year-old body, as evidenced by his career-low 9.8 yards per catch last year. The collapse in Smith's performance was sudden, but it is not temporary, and at this point Smith is more of a liability than an asset. Shanahan was smart to see Smith's decline coming and make the deal for Walker when he did.

Another liability is the Broncos' return game. It's not clear who will return punts and kickoffs for Denver in 2007, an area in which they struggled in 2006. About the best thing that can be said for the Broncos' returners is that, with the Mile High elevation, there are more touchbacks in Denver than any other NFL city, thus diminishing the impact of the return game. Elsewhere on special teams, the Broncos are looking around for an upgrade over Paul Ernster, who handled kickoffs and punts, but field goal kicker Jason Elam is still going strong at age 37, providing stability at that position in Denver for the last 15 years.

Despite all their offseason changes, the Broncos aren't much better or much worse than they were a year ago. Instead, they are more likely to make the playoffs because they've stood still while the other teams in their division fell backward. San Diego handed the car keys to one of the worst head coaches in NFL history. With an overworked running back and a deteriorating line, Kansas City is primed for collapse. Oakland has a rookie quarterback, a new offensive coaching staff, and the same terrible linemen as last year. Getting to the postseason in Cutler's second year would be a big achievement, and it's within the Broncos' grasp.

Michael David Smith

ACL Recovery

There was a time, not long ago, when the football world feared an abbreviation. The NFL did not want to hear about the ACL. A player, especially a skill position player, was considered to be done if he tore or ruptured his anterior cruciate ligament. Yet in the course of just a few decades, ACL repair has gone from the brutal type of carpentry practiced on Broadway Joe Namath to the precise techniques used to repair a franchise quarterback such as Donovan McNabb or a speedy wide receiver such as Javon Walker. These improvements have changed how those both inside and outside the game view the injury.

While we covered the topic of ACL recovery in *Pro Football Prospectus 2006*, the information we learned over the course of last season makes this a worthwhile topic again. What was the difference between the injuries suf-

fered by Carson Palmer and Daunte Culpepper? Why did Javon Walker return to become the Broncos' top weapon while Mark Bradley never established himself as even the fourth option in the Bears offense? How did Deuce McAllister stay productive while showing all the signs of early-stage ACL recovery we expect to see in a running back?

There were decades of medical progress between Joe Namath and Donovan McNabb. Namath had state-of-the-art care both when he had his initial knee injury at the University of Alabama and during his pro career with the New York Jets. However, that same surgery today looks primitive. Here's the amazing thing: Though commonly thought of as an ACL repair, Namath's vaunted knee surgery was a medial mensicectomy (the removal of the meniscus); his ACL was fine. After a similar surgery, today's athlete would walk off the table and be back in the game within weeks.

The eight-inch incision Dr. James Nicholas made on Namath's leg is a relic replaced on today's athletes by much smaller scars and, in some cases, the small punctures that are used to insert an arthroscope. Surgeons are using new techniques, such as making more complete repairs with only arthroscopes and smaller "keyhole" or semi-open incisions. They are also using a newer technique that combines ACL repair with one of the more controversial surgeries: microfracture. Using a patented methodology, surgeons are reattaching the ACL into "bleeding beds" created by drilling holes into the bone at the anchor point. These microfractures allegedly allow for more rapid healing. In a study done in 2006 at the Stone Clinic in San Francisco, doctors using this procedure returned all of the 41 subjects to their previous level of activity in an average of three months. That level of activity is a far cry from a professional athlete's, and there is no evidence that this technique has been used on a professional player, but that is probably not far off.

In training camp last year, the Dolphins' Daunte Culpepper sounded as confident as his coach, Nick Saban. They expected big things, saw no problems, and experienced no setbacks, but the fact is that Culpepper never felt fully recovered from the ACL tear he suffered with the Vikings in 2005. What we didn't know at the time was that, while Carson Palmer had only minor damage aside from his ACL, Culpepper had devastation in several structures. The more structures that are damaged—ACL, posterior cruciate ligament (PCL), medial collateral ligament (MCL), meniscus, patellar tendon—the longer and more difficult the recovery is going to be. It is this designation—ACL only or ACL plus—that is notable. It's one thing to give a car an oil change, another to rebuild the entire engine. Worse, it's not enough to repair the structure; any competent surgeon can do that. It has to be functional first and then usable by the athlete, a function that goes beyond anatomy and gets to feel and even confidence. One thing to note here is that most surgeons aren't repairing the external stabilizers—the lateral collateral ligament (LCL) and MCL—since there are other structures in place that are actually the primary stabilizers. Repair of a redundant structure makes anatomical sense, but it only slows a functional recovery.

The differences between Culpepper and Palmer weren't apparent in most stories. Peter King had a now-famous conversation with Palmer during last year's training camp, after which he reported that Palmer looked nervous and admitted to not feeling ready. Palmer had to deal with standard physical concerns, as well the knowledge that the donor of the Achilles tendon used to replace his ACL was a young woman killed in a drunken driving accident.

Once the surgery is done, it's not enough simply to be repaired. The surgeon and then the team of physical therapists and athletic trainers that manage the rehabilitation and recovery of the athlete have to get that knee to *feel* right again. The medical term for the body's ability to sense and control itself within space is *proprioception*. If you stand up and close your eyes, you can sense where your arms and legs are. Assuming there's no wall close by, you can even walk around, all because of your innate proprioception.

It is this sense that comes back last in almost any significant athletic surgery. An athlete saying that his knee just doesn't "feel" right isn't being obtuse; instead, he's being very, very specific. His body is still trying to reestablish proprioception, to learn where and how the part works now. Doctors, trainers, and therapists have learned that getting the athlete to use the "new knee" as quickly as possible after surgery helps the healing process. By using things such as immediate weight bearing, closed chain therapy, and functional plyometrics in very early stages, players are seeing not only quicker healing times, but a full return of proprioception. This was the type of work that the Broncos' medical staff was doing early and often with Walker.

How do you measure proprioception? With a post-ACL NFL player, it's easier than you'd think. The first thing to return is straight-line speed. Seeing a player run is no indication, though the Dolphins showed a lot of video of Culpepper running to try to show people that he was fine. Not seeing him stop, plant, or dodge defenders during games should have been the red flag we were looking for. The next thing to return is acceleration. There was no problem in getting Deuce McAllister up to speed during training camp and the first weeks of the season, but in watching him, it was clear that he was limited. McAllister remained productive because he could stay behind his blockers and burst, but he couldn't cut or juke.

These skills are the next to return. After acceleration comes the ability to make cuts in which the player changes directions in one plane. Javon Walker showed this in the very early weeks, getting open by making a quick stop or a lateral cut to shake his defender. By the middle of the season, he'd gotten back the cuts and jukes (yes, these are the technical terms therapists are using) that allowed him to make multiple, quick moves and get more yards after the catch. On the other hand, Mark Bradley never got back to the cut stage before suffering another injury, this time a sprained right ankle. Preseason games don't tell us much, but if you can see this type of movement from your players, you'll know where they stand on the continuum of recovery.

While ACL repair has come a long way, getting better, stronger, and faster, just like the NFL players it rebuilds, tearing an ACL is still a devastating injury. As the NFL community has learned, surgery is simply not enough. The return of function rather than simply the rebuilding of anatomy is now the focus and the difference between a player coming back and a player coming back to the Pro Bowl.

Will Carroll

Broncos 2006 Stats by Week

Wk	vs.	W–L	PF	PA	YDF	YDA	TO	Total	Off	Def	ST
								DVOA			
1	@STL	L	10	18	259	320	-5	-37.4%	-53.5%	-16.5%	-0.5%
2	KC	W	9	6	318	276	+1	-18.5%	-18.1%	-19.5%	-20.0%
3	@NE	W	17	7	400	370	0	40.1%	38.2%	-6.3%	-4.4%
4	BYE										
5	BAL	W	13	3	222	257	+1	64.9%	9.0%	-47.1%	8.8%
6	OAK	W	13	3	235	244	+1	36.2%	14.6%	-10.2%	11.4%
7	@CLE	W	17	7	347	165	+1	-11.1%	-9.7%	-6.0%	-7.4%
8	IND	L	31	34	396	437	-1	3.7%	37.6%	35.6%	1.7%
9	@PIT	W	31	20	336	499	+6	80.4%	58.6%	-5.7%	16.2%
10	@OAK	W	17	13	264	244	-1	-42.3%	-29.3%	6.1%	-6.8%
11	SD	L	27	35	326	342	+1	-16.7%	-8.8%	6.5%	-1.4%
12	@KC	L	10	19	244	382	0	-46.3%	-21.5%	19.6%	-5.2%
13	SEA	L	20	23	302	370	-4	-45.4%	-51.4%	-4.6%	1.3%
14	@SD	L	20	48	328	419	0	-59.9%	-9.1%	47.8%	-3.0%
15	@ARI	W	37	20	362	295	0	32.8%	11.8%	-8.2%	12.8%
16	CIN	W	24	23	287	343	+2	-7.1%	-35.8%	-29.4%	-0.7%
17	SF	L	23	26	325	360	-2	-19.4%	-42.9%	-14.8%	8.7%

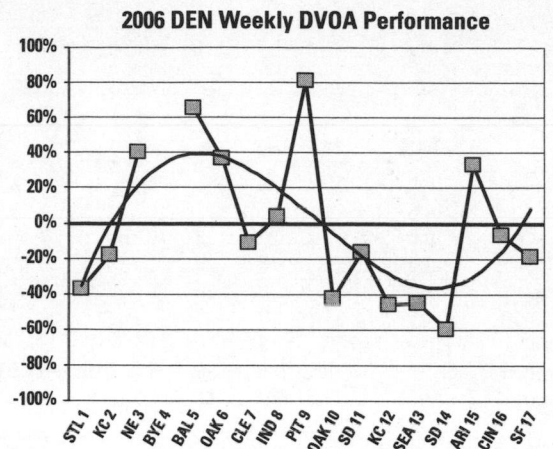

2006 DEN Weekly DVOA Performance

Trends and Splits

	Offense	Rank	Defense	Rank
Total DVOA	-8.3%	23	-3.7%	12
Unadjusted VOA	-4.5%	21	0.6%	13
Weighted Trend	-11.4%	26	0.9%	14
Variance	10.3%	3	5.1%	28
Passing	-9.4%	22	-4.6%	10
Rushing	-7.4%	21	-2.7%	15
First Down	-8.7%	19	-8.2%	10
Second Down	3.2%	13	12.8%	27
Third Down	-24.4%	30	-20.3%	5
Red Zone	-3.4%	18	-15.2%	6
Late and Close	-5.9%	21	2.2%	18

Five-Year Performance

	2006	2005	2004	2003	2002
W-L	9-7	13-3	10-6	10-6	9-7
Pythagorean Wins	8.4	11.7	10.1	10.2	9.2
Estimated Wins	7.0	11.7	10.6	9.8	9.5
Total DVOA	-3.9%	30.7%	22.6%	14.5%	16.2%
Rank	18	2	7	8	6
Offense	-8.3%	23.4%	11.3%	8.6%	17.0%
Rank	23	4	10	8	5
Defense	-3.7%	-10.5%	-13.7%	-7.1%	-1.1%
Rank	12	6	5	11	13
Special Teams	0.7%	-3.2%	-2.4%	-1.2%	-1.8%
Rank	15	28	24	22	20

Strategic Tendencies

Formations		Rank	Run/Pass		Rank	Defense		Rank	Other		Rank
3+ WR	39%	30	Runs, all plays	49%	7	Sacks by LB	19%	19	Run with 2+ RB	62%	16
4+ WR	9%	19	Runs, first half	48%	6	Sacks by DB	0%	30	Run with 2+ TE	32%	20
2+ TE	32%	6	Runs, first down	60%	6	Rush 6+	10.5%	11	Play action	20%	15
Single back	48%	22	Runs, power sit.	63%	16	Rush 7+	2.7%	7	Go for it on 4th	1.11	8
Empty back	3.7%	8	Runs, behind 2H	40%	5	Rush 3	5.0%	15	Offensive Pace	31.1	19
Max protect	16%	6	Pass, ahead 2H	42%	17	CB1 on WR1	54%	6	Defensive Pace	31.5	27

Denver was the worst offense in the league in the first quarter (−38.4% DVOA). . . . The Broncos ranked 30th in frequency of draw plays, and only Cleveland had a lower DVOA on draws. . . . Only Buffalo threw over the middle less often than Denver. . . . The Denver offense ranked fourth in screens as a percent of all passes. . . . The Broncos went four-wide twice as often with Jay Cutler compared with Jake Plummer, and for good reason: Cutler had a far better DVOA in those situations (41.7% for Cutler, −26.2% for Plummer). . . . Denver ran 38 percent of the time when they used three wide receivers, the highest percentage in the league. . . . Denver was fifth in percentage of sacks by defensive backs in 2005 but didn't have a single sack by a defensive back in 2006.

Passing

Player	DPAR	DVOA	Plys	NtYds	Avg	YAC	C%	TD	Int
Jake Plummer*	4.8	-9.8%	316	1878	5.9	5.1	55.4%	11	13
Jay Cutler	3.7	-7.2%	137	913	6.7	5.2	59.1%	9	5

Rushing

Player	DPAR	DVOA	Plys	Yds	Avg	TD	Fum	Suc
Tatum Bell*	10.9	-2.2%	233	1031	4.4	2	3	40%
Mike Bell	14.8	5.4%	157	677	4.3	8	1	51%
Jake Plummer*	0.0	-21.6%	20	123	6.2	1	7	—
Damien Nash*	-0.4	-18.8%	18	66	3.7	0	0	50%
Cecil Sapp	2.4	31.3%	10	80	8.0	0	0	14%
Javon Walker	4.5	52.6%	9	123	13.7	1	0	—
Jay Cutler	-10.9	-245.5%	9	10	1.1	0	8	—
Kyle Johnson	1.2	57.3%	5	30	6.0	0	0	53%
Travis Henry	*12.1*	*-2.8%*	*270*	*1211*	*4.5*	*7*	*3*	*43%*

Receiving

Player	DPAR	DVOA	Plys	Ctch	Yds	Y/C	YAC	TD	C%
WR									
Javon Walker	21.0	10.1%	126	69	1084	15.7	15.7	8	55%
Rod Smith	-4.1	-22.1%	94	52	512	9.8	9.8	3	55%
Brandon Marshall	2.3	-6.0%	37	20	309	15.5	15.5	2	54%
David Kircus	-0.7	-19.5%	27	9	187	20.8	20.8	0	33%
Brandon Stokley	*2.2*	*17.5%*	*11*	*8*	*85*	*10.6*	*10.6*	*1*	*50%*
TE									
Tony Scheffler	5.4	8.6%	37	18	286	15.9	15.9	4	49%
Stephen Alexander	-0.2	-12.6%	35	18	160	8.9	8.9	2	51%
Nate Jackson	0.5	0.2%	6	5	49	9.8	9.8	0	83%
Daniel Graham	*2.2*	*-3.2%*	*34*	*21*	*235*	*11.2*	*11.2*	*2*	*62%*
RB									
Tatum Bell*	-6.7	-52.0%	31	24	115	4.8	4.8	0	74%
Mike Bell	0.3	-7.6%	27	20	158	7.9	7.9	0	77%
Kyle Johnson	-0.9	-23.5%	11	7	37	5.3	5.3	1	57%
Cecil Sapp	-1.0	-27.3%	10	8	34	4	4	0	64%
Damien Nash*	1.2	32.2%	7	4	41	10	10	0	80%
Travis Henry	*-4.8*	*-51.1%*	*25*	*18*	*78*	*4*	*4*	*0*	*72%*

Offensive Line

Year	Yards	ALY	Rank	Power	Rank	10+ Yds	Rank	Stuff	Rank	Sack	ASR	Rank
2004	4.49	4.48	8	56%	27	17%	16	21%	5	17	3.8%	3
2005	4.71	4.62	2	68%	9	23%	5	21%	5	23	4.7%	4
2006	4.44	4.23	18	63%	16	21%	7	25%	19	31	5.7%	9

Year	LE	Rank	LT	Rank	Mid	Rank	RT	Rank	RE	Rank
2004	5.45	2	3.97	25	4.56	10	4.28	13	4.52	7
2005	5.28	2	4.39	15	4.85	1	4.45	11	3.27	25
2006	2.65	30	4.04	24	4.64	6	4.46	8	3.44	25

Can left tackle Matt Lepsis return to form after a torn ACL cut short his 2006 season? That's the biggest question facing the offensive line in Denver. Lepsis hadn't missed a game since 1998, and the Broncos missed him greatly after he went down for the season in the sixth game. Mike Shanahan's decision to draft Notre Dame left tackle Ryan Harris in the third round this year is an indication that he doesn't plan on having the 33-year-old Lepsis around much longer. Harris started all 45 games of his Notre Dame career and should be ready to play as a rookie, though not at the high level the Broncos have come to expect from Lepsis.

Center Tom Nalen is 36 and can't last much longer either. The departure of Nalen and Lepsis will mark the end of an era for Denver, which has had one of the league's best offensive lines for most of the last decade but is starting to decline up front. The ideal scenario for Shanahan would be to have Nalen and Lepsis continue to play at a high level for at least another year, allowing Harris to start at right tackle as a rookie before moving to left tackle when Lepsis retires. If Harris isn't ready to go right away, the Broncos will resort to starting Adam Meadows, who has played just three games in the last three years, at right tackle. That could be trouble.

Ben Hamilton has started every game at left guard the last five years and will be back again in 2007, but Cooper Carlisle, who started every game the last two years, signed with the Raiders in the offseason. Chris Kuper and Montrae Holland will compete to replace Carlisle at right guard.

Defensive Front Seven

Defensive Line	Age	Pos	Plys	TmPct	Rk	Stop	Dfts	StpRt	Rk	AvYd	Rk	Sack	Hit	Hur	Runs	RuStp	RuYd	Pass	PaStp	PaYd
Ebenezer Ekuban	31	DE	64	8.2%	14	46	20	72%	64	2.2	61	7	4	9	52	69%	3.2	12	83%	-2.4
Michael Myers*	31	DT	61	7.3%	9	41	11	67%	63	2.4	54	2	2	3	52	67%	2.5	9	67%	1.8
Kenard Lang	32	DE	37	4.4%	65	26	8	70%	67	2.1	57	6	4	4	26	65%	3.5	11	82%	-1.5
John Engelberger	32	DE	35	4.2%	70	28	6	80%	25	1.7	49	1	1	2	27	78%	2.0	8	88%	0.6
Demetrin Veal	26	DT	33	3.9%	63	25	8	76%	45	2.9	66	1.5	6	1	25	76%	3.3	8	75%	1.8
Gerard Warren	29	DT	30	3.8%	66	20	9	67%	64	1.0	17	2.5	3	3	22	59%	2.4	8	88%	-2.9
Elvis Dumervil	23	DE	19	2.8%	—	16	14	84%	—	-0.1	—	8.5	1	8	7	71%	7.9	12	92%	-4.7
Alvin McKinley	29	DT	47	6.5%	13	34	8	72%	55	2.3	49	1	6	6	46	72%	2.5	1	100%	-9.0

Linebackers	Age	Pos	Plys	TmPct	Rk	Stop	Dfts	StpRt	AvYd	Sack	Hit	Hur	Runs	RuStp	Rk	RuYd	Rk	Tgts	Suc%	Rk	PaYd	Rk
Al Wilson*	30	ILB	107	13.6%	34	61	16	57%	5.1	1	1	1	68	69%	30	3.5	54	40	50%	49	8.3	87
Ian Gold	29	OLB	95	12.1%	52	48	17	51%	4.3	0	4	3	56	61%	64	2.8	18	49	46%	65	6.0	35
D. J. Williams	25	OLB	78	9.3%	75	42	12	54%	4.0	1	4	1	48	73%	14	2.5	8	44	42%	75	5.7	26
Patrick Chukwurah*	28	OLB	17	2.3%	—	12	7	71%	2.5	4.5	2	4	8	75%	—	4.3	—	1	0%	—	8.0	—
Warrick Holdman	32	OLB	71	8.8%	79	31	5	44%	5.5	1	1	5	38	58%	75	3.1	31	33	34%	92	9.1	93

Year	Yards	ALY	Rank	Power	Rank	10+ Yds	Rank	Stuff	Rank	Sack	ASR	Rank
2004	3.83	3.94	6	68%	24	12%	8	27%	7	38	7.6%	12
2005	3.89	4.06	15	70%	24	13%	8	19%	31	28	4.9%	31
2006	4.18	4.42	22	76%	29	13%	5	22%	20	35	5.6%	27

Year	LE	Rank	LT	Rank	Mid	Rank	RT	Rank	RE	Rank
2004	3.95	10	3.95	6	4.22	16	3.73	6	2.81	5
2005	5.51	31	3.85	9	3.95	11	3.96	13	3.47	8
2006	5.06	27	4.60	19	4.38	18	4.10	13	3.75	12

The Denver defensive line will look very different in 2007. The incumbent starters at defensive end, Kenard Lang and Ebenezer Ekuban, could easily lose their jobs in training camp to the Broncos' first two draft picks, Jarvis Moss and Tim Crowder. Elvis Dumervil, who led the team in sacks as a rookie part-time defensive end last year, will also get a shot at a starting job. The 32-year-old Lang is the oldest of the group and probably in the most danger of being cut. Moss was the first-round pick Denver traded up to acquire and is the most likely to earn a starting job.

At defensive tackle, the Broncos added yet another free agent from the Browns, signing Alvin McKinley to play alongside his former Cleveland teammate Gerard Warren. Warren was a bust in Cleveland, but he's been much better in Denver, making plays and showing the natural athleticism that made scouts fall in love with him when he was in college. Rookie Marcus Thomas will round out the three-man tackle rotation.

It's still not clear how new assistant head coach for defense, Jim Bates, will shuffle the linebackers to make up for the loss of Al Wilson, the longtime starter in the middle. Denver still has two good linebackers in D. J. Williams and Ian Gold. Gold will start on the weak side. Williams could move to the middle, and Louis Green, who has spent most of his career playing special teams, could try to earn a job on the strong side, or veterans Nate Webster and Keith Burns could compete for playing time. Even though Wilson started to decline last year, missing tackles he would have made in past years, it's still a long way down from Wilson to Green, Webster, Burns, or whoever else becomes the Broncos' third starting linebacker after Williams and Gold.

Defensive Secondary

Secondary	Age	Pos	Plys	TmPct	Rk	Stop	Dfts	RuYd	Rk	RuStp	Rk	Tgts	Tgt%	Rk	Dist	Suc%	Rk	PaYd	Rk	PD	Int
Champ Bailey	29	CB	110	13.1%	5	53	29	4.7	17	55%	18	86	18%	46	13.5	62%	5	5.8	6	16	10
Darrent Williams*	25	CB	94	12.0%	10	32	15	6.7	43	39%	47	82	18%	45	11.4	48%	61	7.9	50	8	4
D. Foxworth	24	CB	61	7.3%	60	24	11	6.9	45	35%	54	59	12%	78	8.5	47%	62	8.4	60	6	1
John Lynch	36	FS	90	10.8%	29	34	12	4.6	9	50%	24	22	4%	75	12.3	58%	24	6.0	15	6	0
Nick Ferguson	33	SS	38	7.3%	63	11	4	7.4	53	21%	74	20	7%	47	12.6	55%	31	8.4	45	3	1
Karl Paymah	25	CB	16	1.9%	—	5	1	7.0	—	33%	—	20	4%	—	17.1	60%	—	5.7	—	2	0
Curome Cox	26	SS	18	2.2%	—	8	4	9.3	—	17%	—	13	3%	—	12.3	61%	—	6.4	—	5	1
Dre' Bly	30	CB	76	9.0%	43	39	15	4.7	18	70%	2	89	19%	35	12.4	50%	53	7.6	44	19	3

(continued next page)

Defensive Secondary *(continued)*

Year	Pass D Rank	DVOA vs. #1 WR	Rank	DVOA vs. #2 WR	Rank	DVOA vs. Other WR	Rank	DVOA vs. TE	Rank	DVOA vs. RB	Rank
2004	4	4.7%	17	5.9%	20	6.7%	22	-45.4%	1	-39.9%	3
2005	5	-2.5%	11	-12.1%	9	-33.3%	3	-47.4%	1	9.4%	25
2006	10	-15.8%	6	-16.7%	6	-19.2%	10	-2.2%	18	16.7%	25

With Champ Bailey and Dre' Bly starting at cornerback and John Lynch at free safety, the Broncos have a plethora of Pro Bowlers in the defensive backfield. Strong safety Nick Ferguson doesn't have the NFL résumé of his three teammates, but he played well early last year. Ferguson missed the last six games of 2006 with a knee injury, but he's expected to be back in the starting lineup in September.

The problem is that these Broncos are long in the tooth. Lynch is 35, Ferguson is 32, Bly is 30, and Bailey is 29. Domonique Foxworth, a 24-year-old who's entering his third season in the league, has shown flashes of talent, but he hasn't been consistent enough.

Note that Bly's strong numbers against the run are a product of Detroit's move toward the Tampa-2 scheme. The previous year, Bly rarely stopped a running back within ten yards of the line of scrimmage. Bailey, on the other hand, has been strong against the run for two years and rarely gets credit for being not just a shutdown corner, but a well-rounded one.

Special Teams

Year	DVOA	Rank	FG/XP	Rank	Net Punt	Rank	Punt Ret	Rank	Net Kick	Rank	Kick Ret	Rank	Hidden	Rank
2004	-2.4%	24	2.3	11	-5.9	27	-2.5	21	-4.6	23	-3.3	18	-5.5	24
2005	-3.1%	28	-6.8	26	1.0	16	-3.8	24	-4.3	23	-4.4	22	3.2	12
2006	0.7%	15	6.0	7	3.1	14	-1.7	17	-0.1	19	-3.4	20	-13.5	30

Although he has lost some leg strength and no longer kicks off, kicker Jason Elam was as accurate as ever at the age of 36, missing just two field goals on the season. Elam is one of Mike Shanahan's favorites and won't be going anywhere any time soon.

It was surprising that punter Todd Sauerbrun returned to the Broncos by signing a one-year contract in April. Reports out of Denver indicated that there was bad blood between Sauerbrun and Shanahan when Sauerbrun left the team after serving a four-game suspension for using a banned dietary supplement at the start of the 2006 season. Sauerbrun played two regular-season games and three playoff games for the Patriots last year and showed he still has a strong leg. He should be an improvement over Paul Ernster, who punted and kicked off in Denver last year. Denver was league average in net punting because of good coverage. Ernster, judged by punts alone, was worth an estimated −4.3 points of field position, 27th in the league.

The late Darrent Williams returned punts last year, and Quincy Morgan and Brian Clark shared the kickoff return responsibilities. The Broncos were mediocre in the return game last year and probably will be mediocre in 2007 as well.

Coaching Staff

Jim Bates spent 2006 out of football, frustrated that no team offered him a head coaching job after he had spent many years as one of the league's most respected assistants. Mike Shanahan lured him back to coaching by offering him complete control of the defense as the Broncos' assistant head coach, and Bates plans to reshape the defense, making it more aggressive and getting more sacks and turnovers. Bob Slowik has the title of defensive coordinator, but Bates runs the defense. It's a family reunion, because Bates's son Jeremy is in his second year coaching the Denver wide receivers and quarterbacks.

Mike Shanahan runs the show on offense, though last year he seemed to delegate more to assistant head coach Mike Heimerdinger and offensive coordinator Rick Dennison. (Yes, the Broncos have two men with the title of assistant head coach *and* two men with the title of coordinator.) New special teams coach Scott O'Brien has a wealth of experience coaching special teams in the NFL, with stints in Cleveland (1991–95), Baltimore (1996–98), and Carolina (1999–2004), and is widely considered one of the best in the business. He spent the last two years as Miami's coordinator of football operations and assistant to the head coach but decided not to follow Nick Saban to Alabama.

Houston Texans

Once upon a time, Brian Billick and Jon Gruden were known as offensive geniuses. Now they run the defense-oriented Ravens and Bucs. Tony Dungy and Marvin Lewis were once considered defensive gurus. Now they run the league's top two offenses in Indianapolis and Cincinnati.

When these four coaches were coordinators, each was known for a specific system. They all brought those systems with them to their new teams, where, assuming their systems could win with lesser talent, they concentrated on personnel acquisitions on the other side of the ball. Sometimes, as in the case of Dungy and Gruden, that personnel was already there when they arrived. Three of the four have since won the Super Bowl as a head coach.

The latest coordinator turned head coach to fall into this pattern is Gary Kubiak, who came to Houston last year after 11 seasons in charge of the Denver offense. In Kubiak's first season as the Texans' head coach, the Houston offense improved to 16th in DVOA, although the Texans would have been 21st without their two inexplicable wins over the inconsistent Jaguars—but the defense was terrible. Now, while Houston concentrates its draft resources on defensive players with superstar-level potential, the offense is spinning its wheels. Kubiak may think that his system can overcome a lack of offensive talent, but after a year and a half of backtracking and contradictory moves, it's hard to figure out what that system even is. Kubiak may not be emulating Billick and Gruden on purpose, but Houston is headed in that direction.

The organization's concentration on defense started even before Kubiak and general manager Rick Smith took over last spring. When the Texans made defensive tackle Amobi Okoye their first selection in the this year's draft, it marked the fourth straight year in which the Texans used a first-round pick on a defensive lineman. That would add up to one heck of a line if it wasn't for the fact that the first two guys flopped. They were taken with higher draft picks, but defensive end Mario Williams is essentially the replacement for Jason Babin, and Okoye is essentially the replacement for Travis Johnson.

Over the last four years, based on the standard draft value chart, the Texans have spent six times more draft value on defensive players than on offensive players (table 1). For their trouble, they've had the worst defense in the AFC for two straight seasons. Only five of the 16 defensive players taken by Houston in the last four drafts are in the Texans' projected 2007 starting lineup.

When the Texans made the controversial decision to take Williams ahead of running back Reggie Bush with last year's first overall pick, they admitted that Bush would adapt to the NFL sooner than Williams would. That's precisely what happened. Bush was all over the weekly highlights during the Saints' miracle season. Even on his own team, Williams was overshadowed by middle linebacker DeMeco Ryans, the second-round pick who won Defensive Rookie of the Year. That doesn't mean Williams was a flop or a mistake. He showed plenty of talent in his first season, and he could still develop into an All-Pro pass-rusher who is playing for years after Bush has hung up his cleats.

Cornerback Dunta Robinson took a step backward last year compared with his fine first two seasons, but he still has the talent to be one of the league's top cornerbacks. The Texans have now added Okoye, the 20-year-old wunderkind who is 6-foot-2, 300 pounds, mentally sharp, and not yet done growing. If these players develop as most scouts expect, the Houston defense of 2010 will be anchored around four Pro Bowl–level stars. The Texans

---

TEXANS PROSPECTUS

2006 Record: 6–10

DVOA Estimated Wins: 5.8 (28th)

Pythagorean Wins: 5.1 (28th)

DVOA: −20.1% total (28th), −13.5% weighted (25th)

Offense: −2.5% DVOA (17th)

Defense: 15.5% DVOA (31st)

Special Teams: −2.1% DVOA (23rd)

Variance: 14.0% (19th)

2006: Four years in, the expansion Texans return to square one.

2007: They've moved to the front edge of square one. We suppose this counts as progress.

2007 Mean Projection: 6.0 wins

The Brohm Closet (0–4): 26%

Bad Team (5–6): 34%

Mediocre (7–8): 28%

Playoff Contender (9–10): 10%

Super Bowl Contender (11+): 3%

Projected Average Opponent: 1.5% DVOA (10th in NFL)

Table 1. Houston Draft Picks, 2003–2006

Year	Picks	Value*	Current Starters
			Offense
2004	2	9	None
2005	3	322	None
2006	5	658	T Eric Winston, TE Owen Daniels
2007	3	269	WR Jacoby Jones (?)
Total	**13**	**1258**	
			Defense
2004	7	2094	CB Dunta Robinson, SS Glenn Earl
2005	3	1018	None
2006	2	3580	DE Mario Williams, LB DeMeco Ryans
2007	4	1387	DT Amobi Okoye
Total	**16**	**8079**	

* Total value based on typical "draft value" chart.

look like one of those teams that could take a huge defensive leap forward in two or three years if they make the right free-agent moves to replace their below-average supporting cast as their young talents mature.

This would be even more exciting if the 2006 season wasn't such a wasted year on offense. Nearly every decision made in the first year of the Kubiak-Smith era was negated by a decision made this past offseason. Until the Texans made a big splash by trading for young quarterback Matt Schaub in March, every move made with the offense seemed to have the goal of reaching mediocrity as quickly as possible and then staying there indefinitely.

Conventional wisdom says that Kubiak and offensive coordinator Mike Sherman needed a year to install their system and teach it to the players. If this is true, it might have been a good idea actually to keep the same players. The Texans go into 2007 with new starters at quarterback, running back, left tackle, and wide receiver.

The first decision Kubiak had to make after his arrival in Houston was what to do about David Carr. The transition to a new head coach and a new offensive scheme was the perfect time to change the starting quarterback. Kubiak decided, however, that Carr could learn his system. He gave him a vote of confidence, and owner Bob McNair gave Carr an $8 million option bonus.

Within months, it was clear that Kubiak had changed his mind. He had no confidence in Carr's ability to make decisions or avoid a pass rush. The offense was entirely built around short throws that wouldn't require multiple reads. Carr completed 68.3 percent of his passes in an offense that scared nobody. The bad Texans defense led to bad starting field position for the offense, and without any big plays, the Texans would consistently stall and punt

after two or three first downs. When the season was over, the Texans made the big trade for Schaub and waived Carr, officially acknowledging that the $8 million bonus was a total waste of money.

In Atlanta, the talented Schaub sat behind Michael Vick for three years, waiting for his chance. To obtain his services, the Texans had to switch places with the Falcons in the first round and then give up second-round picks this year and next. Is Schaub really better than the talent Houston could have taken with two second-round picks?

Atlanta used Houston's second-round pick on offensive lineman Justin Blalock. With the very next selection, Miami took BYU quarterback John Beck. Michigan State quarterback Drew Stanton was chosen three picks later. With their original selection, the Texans could have chosen Beck or Stanton and still had next year's second-round pick to build with.

Wide receivers Sidney Rice, Dwayne Jarrett, and Steve Smith were also available at that point in the draft. Trent Edwards, from Stanford, did not go until late in the third round and was still available when Houston used the 73rd pick on wide receiver Jacoby Jones, a small-school receiver who was generally perceived as a second-day talent. Are Schaub and Jones really better than Edwards, Sidney Rice, and a 2008 second-round pick? Edwards is a third-round talent, but three years ago, that's exactly what scouts thought of Schaub.

The argument in favor of Schaub is that the experience he gained on the Atlanta bench has made him far more ready for the starting lineup than any rookie quarterback. That would be a strong argument if the Texans were a team that was ready for contention but had a hole at quarterback, but that's not where this team is at all. Will players such as Williams, Okoye, and Jones really be ready for prime time that far ahead of Beck or Stanton?

At least the Schaub trade is forward-looking. Other moves made by the Texans over the last year amount to a whole lot of running in place.

Before the 2006 season, the Texans traded a fifth-round pick to Buffalo for the services of 33-year-old wide receiver Eric Moulds. They started him for a year instead of a younger receiver they could develop, and then cut him after the season. According to media reports, the Texans were disappointed in Moulds's production, but Moulds actually had his best season in years. Moulds finally accepted that he was no longer a deep threat in his old age, and the Texans threw him tons of short- and medium-length passes. He caught 74 percent of them, the highest catch rate in the league.

In effect, the Texans designed an offense that would use this veteran possession receiver strictly as a possession receiver, and then got upset when he turned out to be nothing more than a possession receiver. They traded away a fifth-round pick and got 16 games of space-holding.

Even space-holding is better than nothing, though, and that's what the Texans have now because they did nothing to replace Moulds. Top receiver Andre Johnson will now start opposite either unexceptional slot receiver Kevin Walter or third-round reach pick Jones. The scouting report on Jones says that he is fast and can run crisp routes but has trouble dealing with physical defenders and doesn't like to go over the middle. Does that sound like a player who fits the current Houston offense built around short passes and yards after the catch?

Houston fans also have to ask why a rebuilding team doesn't have room for a 34-year-old wide receiver who has lost the speed of his youth, but does have room for a 30-year-old running back who has lost the speed of his youth. Unsatisfied with last year's committee, aka "four guys who are not Reggie Bush," the Texans lured free-agent running back Ahman Green away from Green Bay with a four-year, $23 million contract that includes $8 million guaranteed in the first season.

Green was a great running back once upon a time, but that time ended two years ago. Green's DVOA was slightly above average last year, due to a difficult schedule, but he's averaged less than four yards per carry for two seasons now. The chances that Green will be worth this contract in 2007 are small. The chances that Green will be worth this contract two years from now—or will even still be playing in Houston when he's 32—are nonexistent. Once again, the Texans have added a veteran where a rebuilding team should be adding either a top draft pick or a cheap later-round pick with potential.

Wasn't Kubiak supposed to bring with him the Denver philosophy of building an offensive line and using interchangeable running backs behind it? If that's the case, there isn't a lot of building going on. Rookie right tackle Eric Win-

2007 Texans Schedule					
Week	**Opp**	**Week**	**Opp**	**Week**	**Opp**
1	KC	7	TEN	13	at TEN
2	at CAR	8	at SD	14	TB
3	IND	9	at OAK	15	DEN (Thu.)
4	at ATL	10	BYE	16	at IND
5	MIA	11	NO	17	JAC
6	at JAC	12	at CLE		

ston entered the starting lineup at midseason last year and looks promising, but the Texans' interior line remains the same as it was two years ago. With second-year tackle Charles Spencer still recovering from a broken leg, the Texans signed free-agent left tackle Jordan Black, who had replaced Willie Roaf in Kansas City last year. The Chiefs had finished in the top five in Adjusted Line Yards for five straight years. Black was one of the reasons they dropped to 17th in 2006.

A Denver-style zone-blocking scheme would require smaller, more agile linemen. When does Kubiak plan on adding some? Denver starters such as Tom Nalen, Matt Lepsis, and Ben Hamilton all weigh 290 pounds or less. Black and Winston both weigh 310 pounds. Starting guard Chester Pitts weighs 320 pounds. The only lineman under 290 pounds on the current Houston roster is practice squad center Chris White.

The Houston offense will still be better than the defense in 2007, but neither unit is going to be better than the league average. In future years, that will change. Houston fans have something to look forward to. Ask the fans in Chicago or Baltimore, and they'll tell you a team full of defensive superstars can be a lot of fun to watch. They will also remind you that promising young quarterbacks don't always turn out to be as good as advertised.

Aaron Schatz

Texans 2006 Stats by Week

Wk	vs.	W–L	PF	PA	YDF	YDA	TO	Total	Off	Def	ST
								DVOA			
1	PHI	L	10	24	241	441	+1	-26.7%	9.3%	34.9%	-1.0%
2	@IND	L	24	43	299	515	-1	-30.9%	-6.7%	29.3%	5.1%
3	WAS	L	15	31	261	495	-1	-65.2%	-10.5%	58.3%	3.5%
4	MIA	W	17	15	276	289	-2	-33.5%	-11.4%	25.7%	3.6%
5	BYE										
6	@DAL	L	6	34	234	352	-3	-53.1%	-35.0%	15.0%	-3.1%
7	JAC	W	27	7	349	220	+2	61.3%	39.3%	-21.5%	0.5%
8	@TEN	L	22	28	427	197	-5	-30.7%	4.9%	15.7%	-19.8%
9	@NYG	L	10	14	251	285	0	-21.8%	9.5%	28.4%	-2.9%
10	@JAC	W	13	10	306	322	+4	39.8%	5.3%	-43.3%	-8.8%
11	BUF	L	21	24	397	403	-1	1.4%	14.8%	17.5%	4.2%
12	@NYJ	L	11	26	334	304	-1	-11.5%	-2.5%	8.6%	-0.3%
13	@OAK	W	23	14	124	302	+3	-58.3%	-52.1%	13.0%	6.8%
14	TEN	L	20	26	240	418	+2	-14.0%	15.8%	29.6%	-0.2%
15	@NE	L	7	40	198	230	-4	-91.8%	-57.4%	6.0%	-28.4%
16	IND	W	27	24	354	319	+1	10.4%	33.3%	19.8%	-3.1%
17	CLE	W	14	6	179	376	+2	-10.5%	-22.0%	-4.0%	7.5%

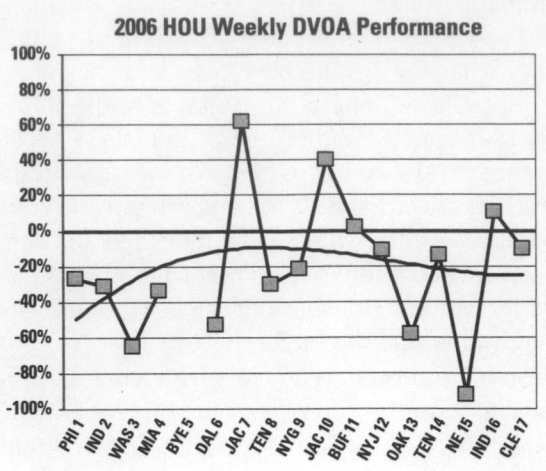

2006 HOU Weekly DVOA Performance

Trends and Splits

	Offense	Rank	Defense	Rank
Total DVOA	-2.5%	17	15.5%	31
Unadjusted VOA	-2.4%	17	15.0%	31
Weighted Trend	-2.6%	19	7.5%	23
Variance	6.9%	13	5.3%	25
Passing	-2.8%	18	23.9%	31
Rushing	-2.1%	14	6.5%	26
First Down	-14.4%	25	2.1%	18
Second Down	7.8%	9	17.7%	31
Third Down	3.9%	15	39.8%	31
Red Zone	25.0%	8	6.8%	19
Late and Close	7.2%	12	10.8%	25

Five-Year Performance

	2006	2005	2004	2003	2002
W-L	6-10	2-14	7-9	5-11	4-12
Pythagorean Wins	5.1	3.7	7:1	4.5	3.7
Estimated Wins	5.8	3.6	7.6	5.8	2.1
Total DVOA	-20.1%	-34.8%	-4.0%	-21.1%	-39.8%
Rank	28	31	18	29	31
Offense	-2.5%	-17.3%	0.4%	-12.9%	-37.8%
Rank	17	29	15	27	32
Defense	15.5%	21.2%	0.8%	10.6%	4.1%
Rank	31	32	18	28	20
Special Teams	-2.1%	3.6%	-3.7%	2.3%	2.0%
Rank	23	3	29	8	12

Strategic Tendencies

Formations		Rank	Run/Pass		Rank	Defense		Rank	Other		Rank
3+ WR	40%	27	Runs, all plays	44%	17	Sacks by LB	43%	8	Run with 2+ RB	68%	9
4+ WR	5%	28	Runs, first half	43%	19	Sacks by DB	14%	4	Run with 2+ TE	31%	25
2+ TE	30%	7	Runs, first down	51%	22	Rush 6+	11.8%	7	Play action	21%	9
Single back	44%	27	Runs, power sit.	71%	8	Rush 7+	2.6%	8	Go for it on 4th	0.75	22
Empty back	6.5%	3	Runs, behind 2H	31%	23	Rush 3	5.1%	14	Offensive Pace	32.1	27
Max protect	14%	9	Pass, ahead 2H	37%	23	CB1 on WR1	46%	13	Defensive Pace	31.3	24

Something about the AFC South makes teams avoid the four-wide receiver set. The only two offenses that went four-wide less often than Houston were Indianapolis and Jacksonville.... Houston's defense ranked third in Adjusted Sack Rate on first down but 30th in ASR on third down.... The miserable Houston defense improved to league average on play-action passes (12.4% DVOA; the NFL average was 12.7% DVOA).... Houston's defense was horrible against screen passes (56.5% DVOA), and only San Francisco and Tennessee faced more screen passes.

Passing

Player	DPAR	DVOA	Plys	NtYds	Avg	YAC	C%	TD	Int
David Carr	10.3	-8.3%	440	2516	5.7	4.8	68.6%	11	12
Sage Rosenfels	9.5	39.6%	39	268	6.9	5.3	69.2%	3	1
Matt Schaub	*5.9*	*40.7%*	*27*	*200*	*7.4*	*3.8*	*66.7%*	*1*	*1*

Rushing

Player	DPAR	DVOA	Plys	Yds	Avg	TD	Fum	Suc
Ron Dayne	12.3	4.9%	151	612	4.1	5	1	54%
Wali Lundy	1.9	-10.0%	124	476	3.8	4	1	39%
David Carr	2.7	-4.8%	40	212	5.3	2	16	—
Chris Taylor	2.2	7.6%	28	123	4.4	1	4	33%
Jameel Cook	0.9	30.6%	3	18	6.0	0	0	25%
Andre Johnson	0.2	-30.0%	3	14	4.7	0	0	—
Ahman Green	*20.6*	*4.4%*	*266*	*1063*	*4.0*	*5*	*2*	*43%*
Matt Schaub	*1.3*	*46.1%*	*3*	*24*	*8.0*	*0*	*0*	*—*

Receiving

Player	DPAR	DVOA	Plys	Ctch	Yds	Y/C	YAC	TD	C%
WR									
Andre Johnson	16.5	0.1%	164	103	1155	11.2	4.1	5	63%
Eric Moulds	10.9	6.3%	77	57	557	9.8	3.6	1	74%
Kevin Walter	2.4	2.6%	21	17	160	9.4	2.7	0	81%
Andre' Davis	*-2.7*	*-73.9%*	*7*	*2*	*13*	*6.5*	*2.5*	*0*	*29%*
TE									
Owen Daniels	11.1	20.1%	51	34	352	10.4	5.0	5	67%
Jeb Putzier	0.4	-9.6%	22	13	125	9.6	5.6	0	90%
Mark Bruener	2.9	30.2%	10	9	62	6.9	2.8	2	59%
RB									
Wali Lundy	1.3	-2.3%	39	33	204	6.2	8.1	0	85%
Jameel Cook	-5.9	-50.5%	26	18	107	5.9	5.6	0	69%
Ron Dayne	-0.9	-19.2%	18	14	77	5.5	6.1	0	100%
Vonta Leach	4.2	122.8%	6	6	61	10.2	7.3	1	78%
Ahman Green	*2.6*	*-0.8%*	*63*	*46*	*375*	*8.2*	*9.2*	*1*	*83%*

Offensive Line

Year	Yards	ALY	Rank	Power	Rank	10+ Yds	Rank	Stuff	Rank	Sack	ASR	Rank
2004	3.86	4.16	19	67%	11	13%	31	25%	20	50	10.4%	30
2005	4.06	4.43	8	50%	30	12%	27	26%	21	68	12.9%	32
2006	4.00	4.18	21	71%	8	14%	22	20%	2	43	9.3%	28

Year	LE	Rank	LT	Rank	Mid	Rank	RT	Rank	RE	Rank
2004	4.93	7	3.85	27	4.37	13	3.97	18	2.86	30
2005	4.16	17	4.14	22	4.62	4	3.75	23	4.35	12
2006	4.23	15	2.66	32	4.41	14	4.25	14	4.20	14

For four years, the offensive line was Dom Capers's white whale. The Texans brought Gary Kubiak in because he was an accomplished fisherman who could hook the big prize, but the coaching staff is still floating around in deep waters, with neither whales nor Aloha Stadium in sight.

The issue is not that the offensive line failed to improve in 2006, but that it actually declined, giving back the run-blocking improvements of the year before. As we point out in the Cleveland chapter, continuity does a lot to improve an offensive line, but if the Texans are going to devote the time to build continuity, do they really want to do it with Chester Pitts and Fred Weary? Right tackle Eric Winston is a promising prospect. So is left tackle Charles Spencer, if he can recover from last year's broken leg. Then again, calling that injury simply a "broken leg" is like saying that Houston summers are "a tad moist." It was a devastating injury, as uncommon as it was violent. Spencer is not coming back from a simple broken leg like Steve Smith did two years ago; he's coming back from an injury that resulted in the top of his tibia being held together by eight screws and two plates. The Texans needed to move forward as if Spencer's not coming back, which they did by signing Kansas City tackle Jordan Black.

What the Texans really need to do is put Winston and either Spencer or Black together with a couple of young interior linemen of mid-range talent, rather than the holdovers drafted by the last administration, and then let that group grow and develop together over several seasons. Perhaps fifth-round pick Brandon Frye will be one of those young linemen. The Virginia Tech product is mobile enough for a zone-blocking scheme, but it needs a ton of work on technique. At least having a new quarterback will give Houston fans an idea of how much they can blame David Carr for the 272 sacks he took over five seasons. We suspect it's a lot; our game charters consistently made comments about Carr holding on to the ball too long, looking to scramble when there was no opening, and even falling down while dropping back to pass.

Defensive Front Seven

Defensive Line	Age	Pos	Plys	TmPct	Rk	Stop	Dfts	StpRt	Rk	AvYd	Rk	Sack	Hit	Hur	Runs	RuStp	RuYd	Pass	PaStp	PaYd
Mario Williams	22	DE	51	6.3%	36	42	15	82%	19	1.7	46	4.5	4	14	37	86%	1.9	14	71%	1.2
Anthony Weaver	27	DE	41	5.4%	47	36	15	88%	8	1.1	28	1	3	4	32	88%	1.1	9	89%	1.1
Anthony Maddox	29	DT	37	6.1%	20	22	7	59%	70	2.9	64	2	1	3	32	59%	3.2	5	60%	0.6
N. D. Kalu	32	DE	22	2.9%	—	17	7	77%	—	1.8	—	2	6	5	17	76%	2.9	5	80%	-2.0
Thomas Johnson	26	DT	19	3.4%	—	12	2	63%	—	2.6	—	0	5	2	18	67%	2.6	1	0%	4.0
Jeff Zgonina	*37*	*DT*	*35*	*4.9%*	*45*	*25*	*6*	*71%*	*56*	*2.1*	*45*	*0*	*0*	*1*	*30*	*73%*	*2.2*	*5*	*60%*	*1.6*

Linebackers	Age	Pos	Plys	TmPct	Rk	Stop	Dfts	StpRt	AvYd	Sack	Hit	Hur	Runs	RuStp	Rk	RuYd	Rk	Tgts	Suc%	Rk	PaYd	Rk
DeMeco Ryans	23	ILB	164	20.3%	2	86	28	52%	5.1	3.5	5	7	91	63%	55	3.5	56	48	48%	56	7.4	81
Morlon Greenwood	29	ILB	117	14.5%	26	63	20	54%	4.6	1	0	3	75	59%	72	3.5	53	30	47%	63	6.2	45
Shantee Orr	26	OLB	28	3.5%	—	20	9	71%	2.5	1.5	1	2	14	79%	—	2.1	—	14	50%	—	4.8	—
Jason Babin	27	OLB	25	3.3%	—	16	8	64%	2.6	5	3	5	16	63%	—	4.9	—	0	0%	—	0.0	—
Shawn Barber	*32*	*OLB*	*53*	*7.2%*	*94*	*25*	*12*	*47%*	*5.3*	*0*	*1*	*1*	*24*	*54%*	*86*	*3.2*	*34*	*27*	*43%*	*72*	*6.3*	*51*

Year	Yards	ALY	Rank	Power	Rank	10+ Yds	Rank	Stuff	Rank	Sack	ASR	Rank
2004	4.50	4.40	24	47%	2	17%	18	22%	21	24	5.4%	31
2005	4.66	4.73	31	67%	23	16%	12	18%	32	37	8.1%	6
2006	4.32	4.36	19	77%	30	15%	13	21%	25	28	5.6%	26

Year	LE	Rank	LT	Rank	Mid	Rank	RT	Rank	RE	Rank
2004	3.78	7	5.05	28	4.45	24	4.17	14	4.70	29
2005	4.83	25	4.89	29	4.51	28	6.18	32	3.73	14
2006	5.45	32	4.12	10	4.02	8	4.75	25	4.72	25

Anyone who was expecting Mario Williams immediately to become Reggie White had to be disappointed with his mere 4.5 sacks, all of which came during a five-game stretch from Week 4 through Week 9. Don't be discouraged—every other number says Williams had an excellent rookie season. He did a lot to hurry the quarterback and was excellent against the run. The Texans improved significantly last year in stopping runs over left tackle or up the middle, which are the two directions most likely to be affected by the right defensive end, and Williams was one of the top-ten defensive ends in Stop Rate on running plays. A good example of Williams's excellent play came in the Week 6 game against Dallas. On 1st-and-10 in the second quarter, the Texans switched up their defense with Williams on the offense's right side. When the Cowboys handed the ball to Marion Barber and he went to run around the left end, Williams threw tight end Jason Witten aside like a rag doll and came all the way around the back of the offensive line to tackle Barber after a gain of just three yards. Williams's only weakness is that he does not have Julius Peppers–like versatility in pass coverage, something the Texans exacerbated by getting cute with way too many zone blitzes.

Anthony Weaver had a reasonable season at left defensive end, but Houston's defensive tackles were horrible—those excellent Adjusted Line Yards numbers up the middle are generally tackles by Williams and middle linebacker DeMeco Ryans. First-round pick Amobi Okoye will go right into the starting lineup at tackle, and ex-Miami tackle Jeff Zgonina will provide depth if his aged body can make it through training camp. Behind the defensive line, Ryans was like a piece of filet mignon sandwiched between two slices of moldy pumpernickel. Bringing free-agent veteran Shawn Barber over from Philadelphia won't really improve things. Undrafted free-agent inside linebacker Jon Abbate is a real gamer and has a great backstory, helping Wake Forest to the best season in school history, but he's slow and, even in the best-case scenario, would just be a backup to Ryans.

Defensive Secondary

Secondary	Age	Pos	Plys	TmPct	Rk	Stop	Dfts	RuYd	Rk	RuStp	Rk	Tgts	Tgt%	Rk	Dist	Suc%	Rk	PaYd	Rk	PD	Int
Dunta Robinson	25	CB	96	11.9%	11	47	19	4.6	15	46%	32	95	22%	11	11.7	55%	20	7.0	30	10	2
Demarcus Faggins	28	CB	41	7.4%	57	19	11	11.3	73	25%	71	59	21%	23	14.0	44%	71	10.1	77	11	2
Lewis Sanders*	29	CB	43	9.5%	—	14	6	7.8	—	25%	—	40	17%	—	11.9	53%	—	6.0	—	5	0
Dexter McCleon	34	CB	29	3.6%	—	8	5	5.9	—	43%	—	29	7%	—	5.4	40%	—	8.6	—	1	1
C. C. Brown	24	FS	78	10.3%	37	21	7	10.6	76	27%	67	26	6%	59	13.2	57%	25	6.1	16	3	1
Glenn Earl	26	SS	73	9.7%	41	24	9	6.1	30	38%	51	26	6%	60	12.6	39%	71	7.5	36	3	1
Jason Simmons	31	FS	39	4.8%	77	12	6	6.1	32	43%	41	23	5%	68	9.6	31%	76	9.2	56	1	1
Jamar Fletcher	*28*	*CB*	*41*	*6.0%*	*75*	*15*	*9*	*6.5*	*37*	*50%*	*26*	*48*	*13%*	*75*	*10.4*	*39%*	*77*	*10.2*	*79*	*6*	*3*

Year	Pass D Rank	DVOA vs. #1 WR	Rank	DVOA vs. #2 WR	Rank	DVOA vs. Other WR	Rank	DVOA vs. TE	Rank	DVOA vs. RB	Rank
2004	18	-9.4%	6	16.8%	28	-17.8%	8	-1.1%	15	-25.2%	4
2005	30	30.6%	31	24.8%	31	10.2%	26	28.7%	30	-1.1%	16
2006	31	10.7%	27	-5.5%	12	14.9%	24	-1.8%	19	25.2%	29

The Houston secondary is a festival of replacement-level talent with one bright exception, cornerback Dunta Robinson. Robinson was extremely streaky in 2006, playing well against teams such as the Cowboys and then struggling against the mediocre receivers of the Titans and Dolphins. When all was said and done, he ended up with better charting numbers than he had in 2005, going from 41st to 20th in Success Rate and from 52nd to 30th in average yards per pass. As for the rest of these veterans, there's no reason to waste a paragraph delineating shades of mediocrity. The Texans drafted South Carolina cornerback Fred Bennett in the fourth round, and he has extreme strengths and weaknesses. He's a tall, athletic leaper with great cover skills, but he doesn't like contact and can't tackle. Fifth-round safety Brandon Harrison, from Stanford, has excellent physical tools and underdeveloped skills.

Special Teams

Year	DVOA	Rank	FG/XP	Rank	Net Punt	Rank	Punt Ret	Rank	Net Kick	Rank	Kick Ret	Rank	Hidden	Rank
2004	-3.7%	29	-5.9	29	-5.3	26	-2.6	22	-2.7	21	-5.3	23	5.9	6
2005	3.6%	3	-8.2	28	-0.4	18	-4.8	29	11.9	2	22.9	2	8.2	6
2006	-2.1%	23	-0.8	18	-6.1	27	3.0	6	-2.6	26	-6.1	26	-7.5	25

The Texans had excellent special teams in 2005 for two reasons: strong kickoff coverage and Pro Bowl kick returner Jerome Mathis. Kicker Kris Brown was no different than he was in 2005, but the coverage team collapsed. Opposing kickoff returns went from 7.0 points worth of field position below average in 2005 to 3.8 points above average in 2006. Mathis missed almost the entire year with a stress fracture in his foot, and his replacement, reserve cornerback Dexter Wynn, was much better at returning punts than kicks. The good news is that once stress fractures heal, they have a tendency not to recur, so Mathis should be back in 2007. Punter Chad Stanley has been below average for years and needs to be replaced.

Coaching Staff

Other than head coach Gary Kubiak, there are very few well-known names on the Houston Texans coaching staff. Offensive coordinator Mike Sherman failed as the head coach and general manager in Green Bay. He was a better head coach than he gets credit for, but he really was bad with personnel decisions, and the fact that he keeps convincing Kubiak to bring in ex-Packers should be a bit disconcerting to Texans fans. Quarterbacks coach Kyle Shanahan has a well-known name, but it belongs to his dad, and defensive coordinator Richard Smith has a well-known name, but that's because half the people in America are named Smith. Smith was defensive coordinator in Miami two years ago. When the Texans fired Dom Capers and hired Kubiak, Nick Saban replaced Smith with Capers, and Smith came to Houston. Perhaps they also traded houses.

Indianapolis Colts

Conventional wisdom says that the NFL is a copycat league, but the 2006 Indianapolis Colts won the Super Bowl with an uncopyable blueprint.

Tampa Bay's Super Bowl win kick-started the spread of the ubiquitous Tampa-2 defense. When the Steelers won it all, every team went looking for a college quarterback who could convert to receiver and run gadget plays. The 2001 Patriots showed how to build a champion by smartly signing lower-cost veteran free agents, and by 2004, even the guy who cleans wastebaskets at Gillette Stadium was a head coaching candidate somewhere.

The 2006 Colts, however, are sui generis. It would be nearly impossible to build a team with a similar roster, and, even then, it would be even harder to actually win a championship with it. You can't plan on drafting one of the top quarterbacks in NFL history. It's difficult to surround that quarterback with talented offensive weapons, then keep all those players healthy every single year. You can't count on a Super Bowl opponent stuck with a gaping black hole at the most important position on the field.

And most importantly, you cannot expect that a defense as pathetic as the 2006 Indianapolis Colts' will suddenly shut down opponents when the calendar turns to January.

That shocking defensive turnaround made this championship possible, but there would be no opportunity for such a turnaround if Peyton Manning did not virtually guarantee the Colts a playoff spot every single year. The entire Colts franchise revolves around Manning, so it's hard to remember that one of the greatest quarterbacks who ever lived would be playing for another team under slightly different circumstances.

Imagine an alternate universe in which Peyton Manning decided to come out as a junior. Would we be talking about Manning and Hall of Fame–bound wideout Keyshawn Johnson, backed by a Bill Belichick–designed defense, winning multiple Super Bowls for the New York Jets and head coach Bill Parcells?

(Even stranger, since the Jets would not have traded down with St. Louis, we would also be talking about Orlando Pace as the anchor of the Oakland Raiders offensive line . . . but I digress.)

From 1998 to 2005, seven teams used the first overall draft pick on a quarterback. Unless there's a dramatic breakthrough in San Francisco this year, it is safe to say that only two of those teams actually got a top-tier, franchise quarterback out of the deal. The Bengals and Colts are contenders every season because their worst seasons happened to randomly align with the senior years of the two best quarterback prospects of the last decade.

When a team lucks into a franchise quarterback, it has the challenge of surrounding him with worthwhile talent. Through a combination of smart scouting and serendipity, the Colts ended up with Marvin Harrison instead of Alex Van Dyke, and Reggie Wayne instead of Freddie Mitchell. Of course, taking Edgerrin James over Ricky Williams was entirely smart scouting.

Year after year, the media criticized Manning for poor play in January, and year after year it was ridiculous. First of all, Manning played well in recent postseasons, with the glaring exception of the 2003 AFC Championship game. Second, without Manning, the Colts wouldn't be playing in January year after year to begin with.

No, the problem was always the defense. All of the money spent on offensive firepower didn't leave a lot left over for the defense, but Tony Dungy made do with younger, cheaper talent and his Tampa-2 defensive scheme. Strong drafting led to gradual defensive improvement, and everything came together in 2005. The Colts

---

COLTS PROSPECTUS

2006 Record: 12–4

DVOA Estimated Wins: 10.6 (6th)

Pythagorean Wins: 9.6 (9th)

DVOA: 19.5% total (7th), 21.8% weighted (4th)

Offense: 33.7% DVOA (1st)

Defense: 11.3% DVOA (27th)

Special Teams: −2.9% DVOA (25th)

Variance: 17.3% (11th)

2006: The 2005 Colts finish what they started, 12 months later than expected.

2007: There is no way to know what to expect from this defense in 2007.

2007 Mean Projection: 8.9 wins

The Brohm Closet (0–4): 2%

Bad Team (5–6): 13%

Mediocre (7–8): 27%

Playoff Contender (9–10): 34%

Super Bowl Contender (11+): 24%

Projected Average Opponent: 2.5% DVOA (6th in NFL)

finally had a top-ten defense, even stopping the run to a reasonable extent, and dominated the league all year—only to slip in the playoffs against the Steelers.

Last year, the Colts were back to their old ways. They gave up points by the bucketful. Opposing offenses played "keep away from Manning." The Colts got lucky when opposing kickers missed 11 field goals, three more than against any other team. Indianapolis started the season 9–0, but seven of those wins came by a touchdown or less. Two of them were by a single point each over the 0–4 Titans and the 3–5 Bills.

By the second half of the season, the Colts were getting trampled on a weekly basis by everyone from Maurice Jones-Drew (not a surprise) to Travis Henry (reasonable) to Ron Dayne (incomprehensible). The Colts made the play-offs, but nobody picked them to win it all. Despite the greatness of Manning, the Colts would get trampled by an opposing rushing attack, by Larry Johnson, or LaDainian Tomlinson, or the Maroney-Dillon combo.

Instead, the Colts played as if they had been keeping the 2005 defense locked in the basement for 11 months, waiting for the right time to unleash their monster upon the world. They demolished the Chiefs and baffled the Ravens. The defense wasn't quite as good in the final two games, but it was good enough for Manning to win a shootout with the rival Patriots, then pick apart an over-cautious Chicago zone in the Super Bowl.

When the defense finally came alive, the cry went out from the Colts and their fans: "Nobody believed in us!" Given the circumstances, *of course* nobody believed in them. As we point out in the second essay of this chapter, the Colts went against everything we've learned about why teams win in the playoffs. The numbers came up each time the Colts won another playoff game, but let's go through them one more time for the sake of posterity:

- The Colts had the lowest Pythagorean winning percentage of any Super Bowl champion (.600), narrowly dipping below the 1980 Raiders (.602). The 1988 49ers were the only other champion below .650.

- The Colts gave up 360 points during the regular season. No other team had ever even been to the Super Bowl after allowing more than 340 points, and the 1983 Raiders (338) were the only other Super Bowl champion ever to allow more than 310 points.

- The Colts allowed 5.33 yards per carry during the regular season. This is not only the highest rushing average ever allowed by a Super Bowl champion, it is the highest regular-season rushing average allowed by *any NFL team* since the 1961 expansion Minnesota Vikings gave up 5.41 yards per carry. No team had ever allowed five yards per carry and made it to the Super Bowl, and the 1997 Broncos (4.73) were

2007 Colts Schedule					
Week	Opp	Week	Opp	Week	Opp
1	NO (Thu.)	7	at JAC (Mon.)	13	JAC
2	at TEN	8	at CAR	14	at BAL
3	at HOU	9	NE	15	at OAK
4	DEN	10	at SD	16	HOU
5	TB	11	KC	17	TEN
6	BYE	12	at ATL (Thu.)		

the only Super Bowl champion to allow more than 4.4 yards per carry during the regular season.

- Opposing quarterbacks had a regular-season completion percentage of 64.3 percent against the Colts. Before that, the 1993 Cowboys (60.2 percent) were the only Super Bowl champion to allow a completion percentage higher than 59 percent, and the 1994 Chargers (62.9 percent) were the only conference champion to allow a completion percentage higher than 61 percent.

- The Colts did no better in our advanced stats. From 1996 to 2006, the only other team to make the Super Bowl with a positive defensive DVOA (i.e. giving up more offense than average) was the 1998 Denver Broncos at 0.4%. The Colts ranked 27th in defensive DVOA, the only conference champion ever ranked 20th or below.

- No dome-based team had ever made the Super Bowl without playing all their playoff games indoors.

What on earth happened? The postseason return of free safety Bob Sanders is certainly part of the explanation, but not all of it. Sanders is tremendously important to the Colts' run defense, largely because he has the talent to clean up the tackling mistakes of the linebackers in front of him. But if Sanders alone is the difference, why wasn't he the difference during the regular season? The Colts allowed more yards per carry in the four regular season games with Sanders (5.55) than in the 12 regular season games without him (5.27).

Whether it was the return of Sanders, increased intensity from the Colts' defenders, or just bad game plans from the Chiefs and Ravens, it all combined with a bit of luck and a dash of Rex Grossman to create an unprecedented championship run. Immediately after the Super Bowl, conventional wisdom flipped from "Peyton will never be a winner" to "Will the Colts be a dynasty?"

One championship is a tough task. Two in a row is even harder, but the Colts certainly go into the 2007 season as one of the NFL's top contenders. The Colts will go into every season as one of the NFL's top contenders as long as number 18 is still lining up under center. The Colts have put a championship-level offense on the field for four straight seasons, and they retain ten of 11 starters from 2006. The only change is at running back, where Dominic Rhodes left as a free agent and Joseph Addai has graduated to the starting position.

The only thing that could derail the Colts' offense would be injury, and last year that was very nearly the case. Ben Utecht is a useful player, but the Colts were lucky when Dallas Clark's torn ACL turned out to be a misread MRI and actually a much less significant MCL injury. It is not a coincidence that the Colts went 11–1 with Clark in the lineup and 1–3 in the four games he missed in December. If Clark's knee injury had been season-ending, as originally thought, we would be writing about the fourth New England championship in six years, and Peyton Manning would still have his unwarranted "can't win the big one" rep.

Most of the Colts' skill players have excellent injury records through a combination of great conditioning, good luck, and the more-than-occasional dip out of bounds to avoid a tackle. Peyton Manning has started every single Colts game since the moment he entered the NFL. Reggie Wayne hasn't missed a game in five years. Marvin Harrison has missed just two games in eight years, and one of those was simply to rest for the playoffs.

Nonetheless, a clean injury record in the past is no guarantee of an injury-free future. Many writers criticized the Colts for using their first-round pick on wide receiver Anthony Gonzalez rather than a defensive player, but Gonzalez doesn't just give Manning another weapon. Gonzalez provides depth in case Harrison suddenly succumbs to the effects of age, and, without him, the Colts would be one injury away from starting a scrub such as Aaron Moorehead or John Standeford.

This smart decision to address receiver depth makes the decision not to address running back depth all the more puzzling. Unless the Colts sign a veteran off the waiver wire during training camp, Addai goes into the season backed up by two undrafted youngsters: rookie Clifton Dawson from Harvard and second-year back DeDe Dorsey from that little-known NAIA football factory Lindenwood University. The Colts have done well with undrafted backs in the past, including Rhodes and James Mungro, but it's never a wise idea to depend on undrafted players before they prove something on the field. Without a committee partner, Addai will get more carries, and more carries means a greater chance of injury, and an injured Addai is a big problem because he has no committee partner.

Of course, the Colts could play a third-string tackle at running back and still have no problem scoring, but figuring out which Colts' defense will show up in 2007 is nearly impossible. Other than a small third-down rebound, there are no indicators hidden in last year's regular-season numbers that suggest defensive improvement in 2007. What impact does the postseason performance have on expectations for the Colts' defense in the upcoming season? Anybody who says they know the answer to this question is either kidding themselves or wearing a Colts uniform. You can't make a projection based on similarities to teams of the past when there are no similar teams in the past.

The Colts are not the first team with a below-average defense to play well during the postseason, but there is a difference between below average and *waaaay* below average. Nine teams since 1978 ranked in the bottom half of the league in net yards allowed per play, then cut that number by at least half a yard in multiple postseason games (table 1). For some of these teams, the improvement continued into the next season, but are these teams really similar to the 2006 Colts? The 1984 49ers were below average, sure, but that was because they ranked 15th in a 28-team league. Only the 1985 Dolphins were almost as bad as the 2006 Colts were during the regular season, and, after a slight improvement in two playoff games, their defense was actually worse the next year.

Table 1. Below-Average Defenses Improving in the Postseason, 1978–2006

		Regular Season		Postseason			Next Season	
Year	Team	NetYd/ Play	Rank	Net Yd/ Play	G	Dif	NetYd/ Play	Rank
1984	SF	5.0	15	3.2	3	−1.8	4.7	6
2000	OAK	5.2	20	3.7	2	−1.5	5.1	19
1996	NE	5.0	17	3.7	3	−1.3	4.6	5
2006	IND	5.7	28	4.7	4	−1.0	—	—
1986	CLE	5.0	19	4.0	2	−1.0	4.7	8
1986	WAS	5.1	20	4.2	3	−0.9	4.9	12
2001	NE	5.3	24	4.7	3	−0.6	5.2	19
1985	MIA	5.6	24	5.0	2	−0.6	5.7	27
1996	JAC	5.1	21	4.5	3	−0.6	5.1	21

If Sanders's return keyed the great defense in the playoffs, does a full year of Sanders mean improved defense throughout the regular season? Possibly, but what are the odds of him actually playing a full year? Sanders has missed half of the Colts' regular-season games since he was drafted. His rookie year, he missed the first month with a foot injury and the last month with a knee injury. He had knee and back issues in 2005, then the knee injury in 2006. For good measure, he missed three games of his senior year at Iowa with a knee injury and missed the Senior Bowl when he hurt his foot in practice.

Sanders is 5-foot-8, the only starting safety in the league under 5-foot-10. He hits like a truck, but unfortunately he's a small truck who is constantly hitting much bigger trucks. All that kinetic energy has to go somewhere, and when some of it inevitably goes back into Sanders's body, there's a good chance something is going to break. If you've ever seen a pickup crash into a semi, you know which truck is going to spend more time in the shop.

Figuring out this defense gets even more confusing when we consider the large amount of turnover during the past offseason. Linebacker Cato June is gone, as is safety Mike Doss and both starting cornerbacks, Jason David and Nick Harper. The loss of both cornerbacks is not the problem it might seem at first glance. The cornerbacks are less important in the Colts' Tampa-2 scheme than they might be on other teams, because they so often play zone coverage. The Colts already had two youngsters waiting in the wings, new starters Marlin Jackson and Kelvin Hayden, and a surprising number of recent teams have turned over both cornerback positions in the same offseason without any problems. The Eagles went to the Super Bowl after replacing Bobby Taylor and Troy Vincent with Sheldon Brown and Lito Sheppard in 2004.

Still, the offseason departures exacerbate this team's problem with defensive depth. Jackson and Hayden can replace David and Harper, but who replaces Jackson and Hayden? The Colts drafted three defensive backs, and one of them might be NFL-ready by midseason, but that's not something the team should count on. Jackson was the main backup for Sanders, and given Sanders's injury history, that's a bigger problem than filling Jackson's place in the nickel. Freddie Keaiho replaces June, but who replaces Keaiho if one of the linebackers goes down? Given this team's dependence on the front four to generate a pass rush, what on earth would they do if Dwight Freeney were to get injured for the first time in his NFL career?

Probability is not certainty. But that doesn't mean that a team that defies probability one year will defy probability the next year. With a mean projection of 8.9 wins, it looks like we're expecting a Colts collapse, but our system actually expects them to remain the same team as last year: great on offense, horrible on defense. The 2006 Colts are a dramatic outlier in the history of NFL champions. The odds are still strong that a team that gives up five yards per run won't win a title, that a dome team will struggle to win outside on a cold January night, and that you can't give up 22.5 points per game and expect to take home the Lombardi Trophy. If the Colts revert to last year's defensive level and sneak into the playoffs at 10–6, they are not going to overcome these obstacles a second time.

If the postseason defense is the true Colts' defense, however, this team will be in the mix until the end—and this time, we won't have to hear the endless chatter about whether Peyton Manning is clutch enough to win.

Aaron Schatz

Why Doesn't Bill Polian's Sh . . . Wait, It Does Work in the Playoffs?

In their book *Baseball Between the Numbers,* our Baseball Prospectus colleagues Nate Silver and Dayn Perry took a look at what aspects of regular season performance drive postseason success. They found that the best predictors were the performance of a team's closer, the strikeout rates of its pitchers, and the performance of the team's defense. Offensive performance showed no such significance in predicting postseason success.

With this work in mind, I decided to do similar research on predicting performance in the NFL playoffs. I could have used traditional stats and gone all the way back to the first Super Bowl, but our advanced DVOA metric does a better job of adjusting for context, and can be broken up by splits that allow us to see if teams that succeed in certain situations during the regular season are more likely to succeed in the playoffs.

The initial results of my research, which utilized data from 1997 to 2005, ran in an article on FootballOutsiders.com in January. For *Pro Football Prospectus 2007,* I've since updated the research with data from both 1996 and 2006. As you might imagine, this year's playoffs have changed things a bit.

To begin, I needed a simple metric that would measure the success of each team in the playoffs; the BP guys called theirs Playoff Score Points, and so have I. The idea is to reward teams that win the Super Bowl over all else, but also to note the performance of teams that perform well without winning it all. In that vein, each team was given:

- 2 points for winning a playoff game at home
- 3 points for winning a playoff game on the road
- 5 points for winning the Super Bowl

I recognize that this system might appear to slightly penalize teams that get a first-round bye, but I would argue that those teams simply didn't need to perform as well once they made it to the playoffs as a team attempting to go from the Wild Card to the Super Bowl did. Furthermore, a team that wins two home games and the Super Bowl would earn nine points; a team that won three road games but lost the Super Bowl would receive the same figure. It's not outlandish to suggest that both of those teams played very well. The maximum number of points a team can receive is 14, which Pittsburgh achieved in 2005; the minimum, obviously, is zero. Forty percent of the teams that have made it to the playoffs over the last nine years (44 out of 108) have not earned a single point.

After compiling the Playoff Score Points for each playoff team since 1996, I ran correlation coefficients comparing

PSP to 100 different regular season metrics. These metrics represented overall team play as well as specific splits taken from the new Football Outsiders premium stat database, which should be fully unveiled by the time you buy this book.

The original study, conducted before the 2006 playoffs, had five key findings:

- Teams with very good regular season defenses enjoyed playoff success, while an effective regular season offense had no relationship to success.

- Teams with strong run defense enjoyed the most success.

- Defensive performance on first down was key.

- Much like third down performance from season-to-season, third down performance in the regular season did not carry over into the playoffs.

- Also echoing typical season-to-season fluctuations, an accurate regular season kicker won't necessarily be an accurate postseason kicker (think Gary Anderson).

Based on these five precepts, the original article stated that "...it's hard to recommend teams like Indianapolis, New Orleans, the New York Jets, Seattle, or Dallas."

So, how big of a shock was it that the Colts won? Let's go through the team-specific tenets above.

- Of the 132 playoff teams from 1996 to 2006, the Colts defensive DVOA (+11.3%) was 126th. As mentioned in the first essay of this chapter, the 1998 Broncos were the only team to win the Super Bowl without an above-average defense. The average defensive DVOA of the nine other Super Bowl winners was −18.5%; that's an elite-level defense (the 2006 Bears were at −20.3%).

- The Colts had the third-worst rush defense DVOA of the 132 teams. Only the 2004 Vikings and 2006 Jets were worse. Keep in mind that the ten worst rush defenses in the sample won a total of six playoff games—and four of those wins belonged to last year's Colts.

- The Colts had reasonable success stopping the pass on first down (−6.8%), but their performance overall on first down defense (+6.2%) was mediocre because of their poor overall run defense

In short, the Colts didn't bend the rules. They snapped the rules over their knees and built new ones in their place. Before the 2006 playoffs, the offensive correlations ranged from +.051 to +.075, while the defensive correlations ranged from −.174 to −.242. That most extreme correlation, −.242, was run defense; in fact, if the Colts are excluded from the study, the correlation between rushing defense and playoff success bounces back up to .25. The new correlations (table 2) still see offensive performance as being less relevant to playoff success than defensive performance, but the gap has narrowed dramatically. It's impossible to overstate how unlikely the 2006 Colts' run was, considering what had been successful over the previous ten postseasons.

While these figures aren't exact correlations or even close to it, remember that the small sample size of the NFL, even across the 16-game regular season, almost always results in lower coefficients and more variability than in other sports.

Offensively, the statistic most indicative of playoff success is Third Quarter DVOA. Its correlation to Playoff Score Points is .223; the next highest correlation is .169 for Home DVOA. Why Third Quarter DVOA? One theory is that teams who do well offensively in the third quarter do an excellent job of making halftime adjustments and come out ahead of the opposition defense for the second half. Included amongst the ten best third quarter offenses are, amazingly, five Super Bowl champions: the 2004 Patriots, last year's Colts, the 1996 Packers, the 2005 Steelers, and the 1998 Broncos. The 2004 and 2005 Colts also show up in the top ten, which shows that this is a repeatable skill.

On the defensive side (table 3), first-down performance still has the best correlation with playoff success. It makes sense that the ability to stop the run inside the red zone is important—not because of idle chatter about teams inflicting their will and other media nonsense, but because field goals are worth half as much as touchdowns. Even the Colts lousy run defense was slightly above-average inside the red zone (−1.0%).

As noted earlier, kicking accuracy is too voluble for regular season success to be predictive of postseason success, no matter how much karma Adam Vinatieri brings to the locker room. There is a facet of special teams that does look very kindly upon Super Bowl dreams, though: punt returns. Regular-season performance on punt returns, measured

Table 2. Correlation to Playoff Success, Before and After 2006 Playoffs

Offensive Performance	Before 2006	After 2006	Defensive Performance	Before 2006	After 2006
Offensive DVOA	0.069	0.133	Defensive DVOA	−0.225	−0.179
Offensive Weighted DVOA	0.051	0.105	Defensive Weighted DVOA	−0.226	−0.183
Offensive Passing DVOA	0.062	0.133	Defensive Passing DVOA	−0.174	−0.152
Offensive Rushing DVOA	0.075	0.090	Defensive Rushing DVOA	−0.242	−0.174

Table 3. Defensive Split Correlations

1st Down Passing DVOA	−0.280
1st Down Total DVOA	−0.248
1st Down DVOA	−0.248
2nd Down Total DVOA	−0.222
Late and Close DVOA	−0.215
Road DVOA	−0.209
Red Zone DVOA	−0.206
Red Zone Rushing DVOA	−0.191

by the value of field position gained over an average team, had a correlation of +.248 with Playoff Score Points, higher than any offensive split. Again, five of the 11 Super Bowl winners tracked showed up in the top ten punt returning teams: the 1996 Packers, 2000 Ravens, 2005 Steelers, 2001 Patriots, and 1997 Broncos. Last year's Colts ranked in the top half, 47th out of 132.

Beyond Regular-Season Performance

A popular piece of conventional wisdom said that the Colts lacked the experience needed to win the big one; alternately, the Patriots knew "how to close out games" because they'd won in the past. A good case-in-point was the AFC Championship Game, where Troy Brown's awareness allowed Marlon McCree to intercept Tom Brady's last-gasp fourth-down pass solely so Brown could strip McCree, recover the ball, and get the Patriots a first down. He knew how to win.

The problem is, quantifying "experience" is difficult. Simply using age won't give us the whole story. The 2006 Saints were an inexperienced playoff team, but they weren't a particularly young one. On the other hand, the 2004 Patriots were a young team, but they had two Super Bowl runs in their recent history. While none of the correlations (table 4) stand out as obvious indicators, there appears to be some evidence that a veteran defense might have a little to do with winning playoff teams. Not sure if Troy Brown's crafty play would fit in there.

Table 4. Correlation of PSP and Average Age

All Offense	0.034	All Defense	0.211
Skill Position	−0.081	Secondary	0.138
Offensive Line	0.125	Front Seven	0.179

There's a quick-and-dirty method for quantifying actual playoff experience. For each playoff team, I calculated "experience" by looking at their previous five seasons, awarding one point for each playoff appearance, four for each Super Bowl appearance, and four more for each Super Bowl victory. While this doesn't account for player turnover, the most experienced playoff teams by this measure were the 1996 Cowboys, 1998 Packers, and the 2005 and 2006 Patriots.

The correlation between this playoff experience measure and Playoff Score Points? +.01; in other words, virtually nil. So, when some commentator tells you in January that the Colts are favored because they learned how to win in the 2006 playoffs, feel free to ignore him. At least until the Colts decide to break the rules. Again.

Bill Barnwell

Colts 2006 Stats by Week

Wk	vs.	W–L	PF	PA	YDF	YDA	TO	Total	Off	Def	ST
1	@NYG	W	26	21	327	433	+1	-9.5%	19.1%	42.1%	13.6%
2	HOU	W	43	24	515	299	+1	38.4%	49.1%	5.9%	-4.8%
3	JAC	W	21	14	272	297	+2	36.3%	29.7%	-2.1%	4.5%
4	@NYJ	W	31	28	352	321	+3	10.5%	31.8%	0.9%	-20.5%
5	TEN	W	14	13	320	277	-1	-30.7%	-0.9%	26.5%	-3.2%
6	BYE										
7	WAS	W	36	22	452	325	0	17.3%	44.2%	5.0%	-21.9%
8	@DEN	W	34	31	437	396	+1	28.9%	70.7%	52.3%	10.5%
9	@NE	W	27	20	354	349	+3	31.8%	19.0%	-20.1%	-7.2%
10	BUF	W	17	16	384	162	-2	61.9%	44.7%	-26.4%	-9.2%
11	@DAL	L	14	21	335	342	-2	-45.9%	-30.3%	13.7%	-1.9%
12	PHI	W	45	21	420	300	+2	104.2%	83.1%	-9.2%	11.9%
13	@TEN	L	17	20	451	382	0	10.4%	24.8%	15.9%	1.5%
14	@JAC	L	17	44	339	447	0	-55.0%	32.4%	54.9%	-32.5%
15	CIN	W	34	16	394	278	0	79.4%	38.2%	-39.9%	1.4%
16	@HOU	L	24	27	319	354	-1	0.7%	41.9%	49.2%	8.0%
17	MIA	W	27	22	354	399	0	33.7%	48.6%	15.6%	0.7%
18	KC	W	23	8	435	126	0	100.3%	17.0%	-76.2%	7.1%
19	@BAL	W	15	6	261	244	+2	67.4%	6.2%	-50.4%	10.8%
20	NE	W	38	34	455	319	0	34.1%	26.8%	-20.8%	-13.5%
21	@CHI	W	29	17	430	265	+2	38.3%	35.5%	-22.1%	-19.3%

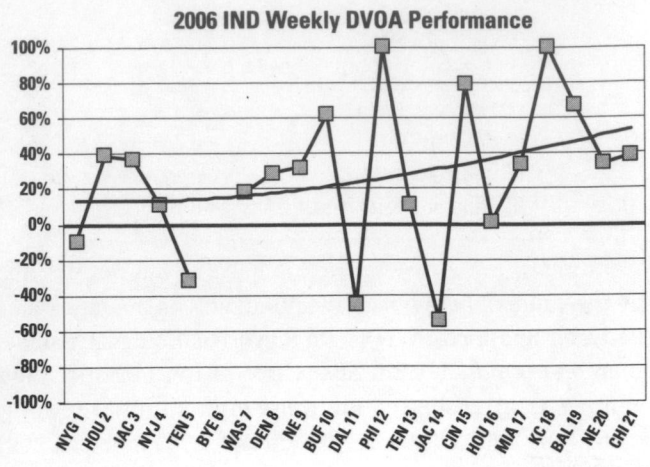

2006 IND Weekly DVOA Performance

Trends and Splits

	Offense	Rank	Defense	Rank
Total DVOA	33.7%	1	11.3%	27
Unadjusted VOA	32.2%	1	13.5%	30
Weighted Trend	35.8%	1	10.5%	28
Variance	7.2%	10	7.6%	11
Passing	56.8%	1	5.4%	19
Rushing	7.4%	6	15.7%	31
First Down	28.8%	2	6.2%	23
Second Down	20.2%	2	6.4%	22
Third Down	71.6%	1	30.1%	30
Red Zone	25.1%	7	18.6%	29
Late and Close	35.9%	3	2.1%	17

Five-Year Performance

	2006	2005	2004	2003	2002
W-L	12-4	14-2	12-4	12-4	10-6
Pythagorean Wins	9.6	12.7	11.5	10.6	9.0
Estimated Wins	10.6	12.7	12.0	10.5	8.1
Total DVOA	19.5%	33.5%	33.8%	19.8%	-2.0%
Rank	7	1	3	5	19
Offense	33.7%	26.9%	39.9%	17.3%	5.5%
Rank	1	1	1	2	15
Defense	11.3%	-8.8%	3.5%	-1.3%	5.5%
Rank	27	8	19	15	23
Special Teams	-2.9%	-2.2%	-2.5%	1.3%	-2.1%
Rank	25	25	25	14	21

Strategic Tendencies

Formations		Rank	Run/Pass		Rank	Defense		Rank	Other		Rank
3+ WR	78%	1	Runs, all plays	43%	20	Sacks by LB	4%	31	Run with 2+ RB	9%	32
4+ WR	2%	31	Runs, first half	41%	29	Sacks by DB	0%	30	Run with 2+ TE	36%	18
2+ TE	22%	24	Runs, first down	55%	13	Rush 6+	2.7%	32	Play action	26%	4
Single back	90%	1	Runs, power sit.	60%	22	Rush 7+	0.5%	32	Go for it on 4th	0.66	30
Empty back	0.4%	30	Runs, behind 2H	31%	21	Rush 3	1.1%	30	Offensive Pace	29.6	9
Max protect	13%	3	Pass, ahead 2H	48%	6	CB1 on WR1	34%	27	Defensive Pace	33.3	32

The Colts ran just 148 offensive drives in 2006, the lowest total in the nine seasons for which we have drive stats. The second-lowest total belonged to last year's Colts, 156 drives. One reason is that the Colts defense faced the fourth-slowest pace since 1998 last year. Three of the four slowest defensive paces belong to the Colts in 2003, 2005, and 2006 (the other is the

2005 Jets). Teams tried to slow things down against the Colts in the past, but last year the run defense was so bad that the slowdown occurred without teams even trying.... The Colts used three-wide-receiver sets more often than any other team. They came out in a three-wide set on 73 percent of first downs. Seattle ranked second in three-wide sets on first down with just 45 percent.... Despite all these three-wide sets, the Colts almost never used four wide receivers. When they did, they actually ran the ball 10 of 18 times.... In formations with only two wideouts, the Colts ran the ball 68 percent of the time, more often than any other team.... The Colts rarely used two running backs (including a tight end in a fullback role) and, when they did, they still threw the ball 60 percent of the time, well above the league-wide average of 41.5 percent.... The Colts gave up no Coverage Sacks and had the fewest number of passes marked Hit in Motion. The defense, on the other hand, was tied for first place in passes marked Hit in Motion.... The Colts used play-action more than any other team in the AFC, although they were behind Atlanta and Philadelphia overall. Their DVOA on play-action was 47.5%, third in the NFL, but this was actually *less* than the Colts' overall passing DVOA (56.7%).... On defense, the Colts were completely sucked in by the play-action fake. Indianapolis allowed 7.6 net yards per pass on play-action fakes (DVOA: 42.1%) but just 5.3 net yards per pass when the quarterback dropped back without a play-action fake (DVOA: –4.3%).... Fifteen percent of all runs against Indianapolis were marked as draw plays. No other defense was above ten percent.

Passing

Player	DPAR	DVOA	Plys	NtYds	Avg	YAC	C%	TD	Int
Peyton Manning	174.8	58.0%	553	4305	7.8	3.9	65.5%	31	9

Rushing

Player	DPAR	DVOA	Plys	Yds	Avg	TD	Fum	Suc
Joseph Addai	36.1	19.7%	226	1074	4.8	7	2	62%
Dominic Rhodes*	0.6	-13.1%	187	641	3.4	5	2	49%
Peyton Manning	4.5	50.5%	10	54	5.4	4	2	—
Ran Carthon	0.5	36.4%	3	4	1.3	1	0	58%

Receiving

Player	DPAR	DVOA	Plys	Ctch	Yds	Y/C	YAC	TD	C%
WR									
Marvin Harrison	44.3	28.9%	148	95	1366	14.4	2.9	12	63%
Reggie Wayne	46.1	35.0%	137	86	1314	15.3	2.3	9	64%
Aaron Moorehead	-0.2	-17.1%	16	8	82	10.3	1.1	1	73%
Brandon Stokley*	2.2	17.5%	11	8	85	10.6	3.6	1	50%
TE									
Dallas Clark	7.9	9.2%	57	30	367	12.2	4.6	4	53%
Ben Utecht	7.3	10.1%	53	37	377	10.2	4.9	0	70%
Bryan Fletcher	7.2	32.4%	25	18	202	11.2	4.1	2	72%
RB									
Joseph Addai	10.5	29.6%	50	40	325	8.1	7.6	1	80%
Dominic Rhodes*	-0.1	-10.7%	47	36	251	7.0	6.2	0	77%

Offensive Line

Year	Yards	ALY	Rank	Power	Rank	10+ Yds	Rank	Stuff	Rank	Sack	ASR	Rank
2004	4.65	4.85	1	46%	32	15%	27	19%	4	14	3.5%	2
2005	3.95	4.71	1	54%	29	9%	32	18%	1	20	3.6%	1
2006	4.13	4.56	5	60%	22	10%	28	20%	4	15	3.4%	1

Year	LE	Rank	LT	Rank	Mid	Rank	RT	Rank	RE	Rank
2004	5.42	3	5.04	4	4.92	1	4.21	15	4.39	8
2005	5.28	1	4.75	5	4.45	5	5.24	1	4.58	10
2006	4.56	9	5.45	2	4.72	5	4.56	5	3.64	21

The Colts' offensive line has long been an enigma. It would always rate highly in our offensive line stats, but had a tendency to fold in big games. It was difficult to figure out what portion of their high rating was good blocking, and how much of it was a product of Peyton Manning's excellent play-fakes and ability to get passes off before taking a sack. The Colts' line played well in last year's playoffs, but it remains an enigma. Center Jeff Saturday was rightly lauded for his great postseason, but then, Saturday was never the problem when the Indianapolis line had a bad day. Neither was left tackle Tarik Glenn. The questions revolve around the guards and right tackle. Guard Jake Scott was a strong run-blocker in the first half of the season—he flat-out embarrassed Denver lineman Mike Myers when the Colts beat the Broncos—but couldn't clear holes in the second half of the year. Scott and Ryan Lilja were the guards who self-destructed when asked to pull to block blitzing linebackers in the playoff loss to Pittsburgh two years ago, but last year our game charters felt that right tackle Ryan Diem and second tight end Ben Utecht were the weak links in Indianapolis's pass blocking.

(continued next page)

Offensive Line *(continued)*

If the Colts do need an upgrade at line, they have talent waiting in the wings. Tackle Charlie Johnson was a sixth-round steal a year ago. When an injury to Diem forced him into the lineup during the Super Bowl, nobody noticed, and that's the highest compliment a rookie lineman can get. The Colts also traded up to take tackle Tony Ugoh in the second round of this year's draft. General manager Bill Polian obviously thought it was important to find an heir apparent for the 31-year-old Glenn at the line's most important position, because Ugoh is the first offensive lineman taken by Indianapolis on the first day of the draft since the late Brandon Burlsworth eight years ago.

Defensive Front Seven

Defensive Line	Age	Pos	Plys	TmPct	Rk	Stop	Dfts	StpRt	Rk	AvYd	Rk	Sack	Hit	Hur	Runs	RuStp	RuYd	Pass	PaStp	PaYd
Robert Mathis	26	DE	69	8.4%	11	53	30	77%	46	1.6	39	10.5	8	15	46	74%	2.9	23	83%	-1.0
Raheem Brock	29	DT	52	6.3%	16	38	16	73%	51	1.9	38	3	8	1	41	71%	2.4	11	82%	0.0
Anthony McFarland	30	DT	41	5.0%	40	32	12	78%	37	1.7	32	2.5	2	0	33	79%	1.9	8	75%	0.9
Dwight Freeney	27	DE	31	3.8%	75	28	12	90%	4	-0.5	4	5.5	9	33	23	87%	1.2	8	100%	-5.4
Josh Thomas	26	DE	22	2.7%	—	15	3	68%	—	3.0	—	1	4	3	18	72%	2.9	4	50%	3.5
Darrell Reid	25	DT	15	2.0%	—	13	6	87%	—	3.3	—	0	2	0	12	83%	4.1	3	100%	0.0

Linebackers	Age	Pos	Plys	TmPct	Rk	Stop	Dfts	StpRt	AvYd	Sack	Hit	Hur	Runs	RuStp	Rk	RuYd	Rk	Tgts	Suc%	Rk	PaYd	Rk
Cato June*	28	OLB	147	17.9%	6	79	33	54%	5.2	1	2	0	92	60%	67	4.6	92	38	47%	61	7.6	85
Gary Brackett	27	ILB	125	17.4%	9	60	12	48%	4.8	0	1	0	91	56%	80	3.5	49	37	39%	83	7.3	79
Gilbert Gardner*	25	OLB	52	6.8%	97	29	8	56%	3.3	0	0	0	30	60%	65	2.9	20	12	47%	—	4.1	—
Robert Morris	32	ILB	36	4.7%	—	21	5	58%	4.0	0	1	0	28	71%	—	2.7	—	5	0%	—	9.8	—

Year	Yards	ALY	Rank	Power	Rank	10+ Yds	Rank	Stuff	Rank	Sack	ASR	Rank
2004	4.82	4.58	30	52%	6	19%	22	23%	19	45	8.1%	7
2005	4.47	4.22	20	60%	14	19%	19	26%	14	46	8.4%	2
2006	5.37	4.80	31	81%	32	23%	30	21%	21	25	6.1%	21

Year	LE	Rank	LT	Rank	Mid	Rank	RT	Rank	RE	Rank
2004	4.55	22	4.49	18	4.67	28	4.75	30	3.85	16
2005	4.96	28	4.50	25	4.07	15	4.39	23	3.91	16
2006	1.87	1	4.96	26	4.99	32	5.71	32	3.22	8

There are few surprises in the individual numbers above. The Colts' linebackers were awful against the run, and the defensive ends concentrated on rushing the passer, which is why right end Dwight Freeney makes his average play behind the line of scrimmage. As we explain later in the book in the "Beyond Sacks" essay, Freeney's high total of hits and hurries show that his lower sack total wasn't evidence of a down season.

There is a surprise here, but it comes in the total defensive front seven numbers. Ranking the Colts number one against runs around the left end is completely at odds with the conventional wisdom that Freeney can't play the run because he only cares about getting to the quarterback. This is not a case of Dwight Freeney turning into an amazing run-stopper. A run "at" Freeney would probably be listed as left tackle or left guard, while an "end" run is usually a sweep, a stretch, or a pitch. Picture Dwight Freeney doing his outside spin move around the left tackle. If the offense runs behind the guard and tackle, he's taken himself out of the play. If the offense runs around the end, it will run straight into Freeney as he's on his way towards the quarterback. That's exactly what happened with two Clinton Portis attempts in Week 7. First Portis took a pitch to the left, but Freeney was already so far upfield that Portis had to change his angle and attempt to go even wider. By the time he tried to turn the corner, linebacker Gilbert Gardner was right there for a six-yard loss. Later in the game, on a run with the right guard pulling to the left, Freeney was once again past the play, but he was able to reach back and get just enough of Portis to force him to take a wider angle, which ran smack into linebacker Cato June.

That left-end ranking is also a product of small sample size. The Colts faced only 18 left-end runs by running backs, fewer than any other team and far fewer than the NFL average of 47. The low total was not a quirk of the official scorer at the RCA Dome, because the Colts' offense was third in the league with 70 left end runs. It was a quirk of the Colts' defense: Why run around the left end when going up the middle is so darn easy? It remains to be seen if the Colts will play in September the way they did in January, with Freeney twisting inside as often as he went outside, and the whole front seven run-blitzing when the other team gave an obvious signal that it would run up the middle, such as wearing Chiefs uniforms.

Defensive Secondary

Secondary	Age	Pos	Plys	TmPct	Rk	Stop	Dfts	RuYd	Rk	RuStp	Rk	Tgts	Tgt%	Rk	Dist	Suc%	Rk	PaYd	Rk	PD	Int
Nick Harper*	33	CB	84	10.9%	16	39	18	6.9	46	50%	27	76	22%	14	10.3	55%	23	5.9	8	13	3
Jason David*	25	CB	63	7.7%	51	22	9	10.1	68	28%	66	75	21%	21	14.4	50%	55	6.4	17	11	2
Antoine Bethea	23	SS	93	13.0%	10	19	5	10.2	74	22%	73	23	6%	52	23.6	76%	1	4.2	2	3	1
Kelvin Hayden	24	CB	33	4.3%	—	13	5	5.7	—	57%	—	21	7%	—	8.9	33%	—	7.6	—	1	0
Marlin Jackson	24	FS	76	10.6%	33	25	8	8.0	61	31%	61	20	6%	63	9.6	33%	75	9.8	60	1	1
Mike Doss*	26	SS	31	10.1%	—	14	5	6.5	—	35%	—	13	8%	—	13.5	65%	—	3.4	—	3	2
Matt Giordano	25	FS	21	3.4%	—	8	1	7.7	—	40%	—	9	2%	—	15.1	64%	—	5.5	—	2	1
Bob Sanders	26	FS	30	14.7%	—	15	5	6.3	—	57%	—	8	8%	—	13.7	29%	—	14.8	—	1	1

Year	Pass D Rank	DVOA vs. #1 WR	Rank	DVOA vs. #2 WR	Rank	DVOA vs. Other WR	Rank	DVOA vs. TE	Rank	DVOA vs. RB	Rank
2004	21	1.0%	13	-1.0%	16	3.3%	20	13.4%	21	26.5%	29
2005	4	-7.3%	6	-14.7%	7	-3.7%	15	-1.1%	18	-4.2%	12
2006	19	20.0%	29	7.8%	17	-13.1%	12	1.2%	21	-3.9%	13

The two starting cornerbacks are gone and the starting free safety barely played during the regular season. Do these stats have anything to do with the Indianapolis secondary in 2007? New starting corner Marlin Jackson played safety most of last season. Kelvin Hayden's poor pass coverage numbers in limited playing time don't say much about his true ability to be a starting cornerback, but neither does his ability to catch a lame duck pass that Rex Grossman just tossed up for grabs. If Daymeion Hughes can learn the scheme quickly, it wouldn't be shocking to see him starting by midyear. Hughes is a high-floor, low-ceiling prospect who dropped into the third round because of slow workout times, which is less of an issue in zone coverage. He was excellent in run support at California.

Antoine Bethea has the highest Success Rate among all safeties, but don't get too excited. As you can tell from his run support numbers and the average distance of the passes he covered, he was playing centerfield, not trying to stay man-to-man with tight ends and slot receivers. He was involved in a high percentage of Indianapolis's defensive plays because somebody had to clean up all the non-tackles on running plays when Bob Sanders wasn't around. When adjusted for games played, Chris Hope of the Titans and Sean Jones of the Browns were the only safeties involved in a higher percentage of defensive plays than Sanders was.

One thing should remain the same in 2007: A better DVOA defending number-two receivers than number-one receivers is somewhat emblematic of the Tampa-2 defensive scheme. When the defense is playing zone coverage the majority of the time, a number-one receiver is going to find the holes and the quarterback is going to look for him first. Opposing offenses also like to switch up formations to try to exploit holes in the coverage. The Jaguars used wide receiver Matt Jones as an H-back, the Bengals put T. J. Houshmandzadeh in the slot, and nearly every opponent used lots and lots of motion.

Special Teams

Year	DVOA	Rank	FG/XP	Rank	Net Punt	Rank	Punt Ret	Rank	Net Kick	Rank	Kick Ret	Rank	Hidden	Rank
2004	-2.5%	25	-5.3	27	-1.2	18	-1.4	19	-9.9	29	3.1	11	-1.5	17
2005	-2.2%	25	5.3	7	3.8	12	-2.2	18	-9.7	29	-9.9	28	10.0	3
2006	-2.9%	25	4.8	8	-9.7	29	2.5	8	-15.2	30	0.5	14	10.0	4

When it comes to ranking in special teams, the Colts sure are consistent. They just aren't very good. The Colts signed Adam Vinatieri to the largest kicker contract in history because they wanted someone more consistent on field goals and better on kickoffs than Mike Vanderjagt. They got exactly what they wanted—Vinatieri's kickoffs were worth exactly zero points after adjusting for weather and altitude—but screwed it up with another year of horrible coverage teams. Oakland was the only team to give up more value on kickoff returns, so Devin Hester's touchdown to start the Super Bowl was no surprise. Punter Hunter Smith, like Vinatieri, is a reasonably skilled player doomed by the ten teammates who share the field with him. The bad special teams play is just one more problem that Peyton Manning and the offense have to continuously overcome. It helps that opponents have given the Colts the gift of bad kicking for two years, which is one of the reasons they've won more than their share of close games.

Coaching Staff

There are a number of head coaches and coordinators across the league who worked under Dungy in Tampa Bay. The Colts have been hugely successful ever since he came to the team in 2002. Yet for some reason, no team has put two and two together and offered a higher position to a member of the Indianapolis staff. Part of the problem is that a lot of these guys are too old for their first head coaching position. Offensive coordinator Tom Moore is 69 years old, and most people don't even think he really plans the offense. The real coordinator is that guy who hosted *Saturday Night Live.* Offensive line coach Howard Mudd has a resume featuring not just these lines but the Seattle lines that blocked for Chris Warren, but he's already 65. Defensive coordinator Ron Meeks is 53, so perhaps he still has a shot, but he doesn't come as a package deal with Bob Sanders and Dwight Freeney. One young coach worth watching might be the offensive quality control guy and assistant to Mudd, longtime NFL tight end Pete Metzelaars.

Jacksonville Jaguars

In the sports world, one of the common criticisms of statistical analysis is that it does not consider elements such as leadership and character, but just because statistical analysis doesn't consider leadership and character does not mean that statistical *analysts* don't believe that these are important elements of a successful team. The reason leadership and character are called "intangibles" is that they are intangible. They cannot be measured with numbers, and, therefore, we don't try to measure them with numbers. We have to consider these elements subjectively, separate from the numbers. The acknowledgement that statistics cannot account for intangibles is a better solution than the creation out of thin air of some ridiculous "leadership and character" rating.

Why do we mention this now? Because other than the general randomness of the universe, intangibles are the only possible explanation for why a team that played as well as the 2006 Jacksonville Jaguars would finish 8–8 and out of the playoffs.

The Jaguars went 12–4 in 2005, but they were not a great team. They were a good team with an absurdly easy schedule, and New England pummeled them in the postseason. They were almost guaranteed to decline in 2006. But while Jacksonville's record declined, their actual play on the field did not; the 8–8 Jaguars of 2006, ranked sixth in DVOA, were a better team than the 12–4 Jaguars of 2005, who ranked tenth.

Entering the 2006 season, the biggest question in Jacksonville was how the team would cope with the abrupt retirement of wide receiver Jimmy Smith. Not only was Smith the face of the franchise, he was also still the team's best offensive player, even at the age of 36. Because he waited until May to make his announcement, the team had no opportunity to replace him through the draft.

JAGUARS PROSPECTUS

2006 Record: 8–8

DVOA Estimated Wins: 9.6 (7th)

Pythagorean Wins: 10.8 (5th)

DVOA: 22.0% total (6th), 19.2% weighted (5th)

Offense: 4.3% DVOA (12th)

Defense: −17.9% DVOA (3rd)

Special Teams: −0.2% DVOA (19th)

Variance: 30.5% (1st)

2006: How does a team with this much talent lose to Houston twice?

2007: A top Super Bowl contender, if they can get their heads screwed on straight.

2007 Mean Projection: 11.8 wins

The Brohm Closet (0–4): 1%

Bad Team (5–6): 2%

Mediocre (7–8): 2%

Playoff Contender (9–10): 21%

Super Bowl Contender (11+): 74%

Projected Average Opponent: −3.1% DVOA (28th in NFL)

How could the Jaguars stay productive on offense without Smith? First, quarterback Byron Leftwich had to stay healthy, continue his development, and move on from his dependence on Smith as his go-to receiver. Second, one of Jacksonville's trio of tall young receivers—quarterback conversion experiment Matt Jones, first-round disappointment Reggie Williams, and underdog Ernest Wilford—had to step forward and take Smith's place as the team's number-one option.

Neither of these things happened in 2006. Leftwich struggled with an ankle injury and had the worst DVOA of his career. After six games, he was replaced by backup David Garrard. The Jaguars won five of their next seven games without Garrard playing any better than Leftwich had, and head coach Jack Del Rio exacerbated the quarterback controversy with noncommittal statements about whether or not Leftwich was healthy enough to play and/or would be getting his job back.

Of course, it didn't matter who was throwing the ball, because none of the Jacksonville receivers stepped up either. After some encouraging early play, Williams went back to his habits of dropping passes and disappearing in coverage. Jones was in and out of the lineup with nagging injuries. Wilford caught less than half his intended passes. Not one of the Jags three young wideouts managed to get to 650 yards receiving, let alone the 1,023 that Smith compiled in his final season.

So, the quarterback and wide receiver positions were having problems, but every other area of the team improved. Rashean Mathis blossomed into a Pro Bowl cornerback in his fourth season. His new partner, Brian Williams, was an improvement over 2005 starter Kenny Wright. Defensive end Bobby McCray emerged with a huge season after starter Reggie Hayward tore his Achilles tendon. The front seven

2007 Jaguars Schedule

Week	Opp	Week	Opp	Week	Opp
1	TEN	7	IND (Mon.)	13	at IND
2	ATL	8	at TB	14	CAR
3	at DEN	9	at NO	15	at PIT
4	BYE	10	at TEN	16	OAK
5	at KC	11	SD	17	at HOU
6	HOU	12	BUF		

stuffed the run despite midseason injuries to defensive tackle Marcus Stroud and middle linebacker Mike Peterson.

Meanwhile, the offense overcame its mediocre passing attack with a championship-quality running game. Left tackle Khalif Barnes took a step forward in his second year, while the rest of the offensive line coalesced and strengthened in its fourth year together. After years of trying to find a smaller and shiftier partner for veteran Fred Taylor, the Jaguars finally hit the jackpot with 2006 second-round pick Maurice Jones-Drew. In previous years, with an average line and an average Taylor, the Jaguars' run-first philosophy was a detriment to their success. With the explosive Jones-Drew joining a more rested Taylor behind an improved line, that philosophy became an asset.

When everything went right, the Jaguars were a juggernaut. They went 5–3 against playoff teams. They demolished the Jets 41–0. They stomped the Giants 26–10. They embarrassed the Indianapolis run defense in a 44–17 victory that had conventional wisdom writing off the Colts' chances of wining the Super Bowl. (Whoops.) Yet, somehow, this same collection of talent lost to Houston twice and choked away an 8–5 record with a three-game losing streak that ended their season without a playoff berth.

Through 13 games, Jacksonville had the highest game-to-game variance in the 11-year history of DVOA. That variance dropped a bit when the Jaguars ended the season with two close losses to above-average teams, two results that "made sense," but they still rank fourth all-time, behind the 2003 49ers, 2005 49ers, and 2003 Bills.

What was going on here? This wasn't bad luck, like when the Philadelphia Eagles lost a game on a 62-yard field goal. When the Jaguars lost, they lost because they played like garbage. Every unit on the Jaguars took its turn costing the team wins. Garrard handed games to Houston and Tennessee via interceptions. Fred Taylor and Maurice Jones-Drew somehow gained just 19 yards on ten carries in an overtime loss to Washington. Underwhelming quarterbacks such as ex-Jaguar Mark Brunell and J. P. Losman humiliated the vaunted Jacksonville secondary. The run defense, the only element of this team that had remained consistent all season, finally buckled in Jacksonville's final two losses.

Head coach Jack Del Rio blamed the inconsistency on a lack of leadership and the rash of injuries, but the Jaguars went back and forth between winning and losing no matter who was in the lineup. The Jaguars were 5–5 with Garrard starting at quarterback and 3–3 with Leftwich starting. They were 7–7 with Matt Jones and 1–1 without Matt Jones. They were 2–2 with both Marcus Stroud and Mike Peterson in the lineup, 2–2 with neither one in the lineup, and 4–4 when one was healthy and the other was not.

As for leadership, perhaps Del Rio should look in the mirror. The number-one motivational leader in an NFL locker room is the head coach. The number-two motivational leader is the starting quarterback, but he doesn't earn as much respect if the head coach is continuously jerking him around. The most important thing the Jaguars need to do in 2007 is to make Leftwich the quarterback, boost his confidence, and see if he can take that next step of improvement that he should have taken last year were it not for the injuries.

NFL fans, scouts, and analysts are split about whether Leftwich can truly be a successful NFL quarterback. Leftwich's detractors point to three issues: his elongated delivery, which gives the defense extra time to disrupt the pass; his decision-making skills; and his lack of mobility. The first two are real issues that Leftwich must face going forward, but the third problem is dramatically overexaggerated.

Because Leftwich is African-American and doesn't run around like Michael Vick, people tend to speak of him as if he were some sort of Bledsoe-esque statue. Garrard's mobility and Leftwich's purported lack thereof was a major factor in Del Rio's decision to continue to start Garrard even though Leftwich could have returned from his injury late in the season. In fact, Leftwich compares favorably to Caucasian quarterbacks such as Carson Palmer and Ben Roethlisberger, who are considered to be reasonably mobile. Here are the rushing numbers and Adjusted Sack Rates for these four quarterbacks over the past three seasons. Can you tell which one is Leftwich?

	ASR	Runs	Yds
A	4.8%	66	135
B	5.3%	111	372
C	8.4%	110	318
D	6.5%	80	508

How would you rank the mobility of these four quarterbacks? Quarterback D is clearly the most mobile. Quarterback A can avoid the rush, but doesn't scramble. Quarterback C can scramble, but can't avoid the rush. Quarterback B can do both. Quarterback D is Garrard, of course, but Quarterback B is Byron Leftwich (Palmer is A, Roethlisberger is C). David Garrard's mobility is supposed to help him avoid the pass rush, but Leftwich took fewer sacks playing behind the same offensive line. The man is not a gazelle out there, but when we look at the results, it is clear that Byron Leftwich's mobility is not a significant problem.

Garrard may have been slightly better than the hobbled Leftwich last year, and he's a nice quarterback to have on your bench as backup, but nobody really thinks that David Garrard is a starting NFL quarterback. A writer who says "David Garrard should be starting over Byron Leftwich" is really making a statement about Leftwich, not Garrard. In Leftwich, the Jaguars have a young quarterback with a reasonably high ceiling. He deserves another shot to make this team his without having to look over his shoulder.

There's not much we can learn about Jacksonville's 2007 prospects by making historical comparisons with other inconsistent teams. In the 11 years of DVOA, there was only one other team that combined a mediocre record with high DVOA and an extreme variance: the 1997 Detroit Lions, who ranked seventh in DVOA but went just 9–7. That team collapsed to 5–11 the following year, but it was a team with aging talent. The Jaguars' talent is just reaching its peak.

Another way to look at Jacksonville's season is to look at Pythagorean wins. Teams that outscore opponents 371–274 should win an average of 10.8 games. The Jaguars won only eight, which makes them one of 22 teams since 1978 to underperform the Pythagorean projection by at least 2.5 wins. These teams improved the following year by an average of more than three wins—but that's because most of them were 3–13 or 4–12 to begin with, and those teams are usually going to win more games the next year anyway. The only other team on that list that had at least eight wins was the 1989 Cincinnati Bengals, who went 9–7 the next season.

Looking for similar teams in NFL history doesn't give a strong feeling about which way the Jaguars will go, but the *PFP* win projection system sure does. Only New England has a better projection for 2007. The list of positive indicators goes on and on and on. The Jaguars' offense and defense were both worse on third down last year than they were overall, which suggests that both units will improve as their third-down performances fall back in line. The team's top skill players are in their second and third years, which

is when skill players generally mature. Slow-paced offenses tend to be better the next year than fast-paced offenses, and the Jaguars had the slowest offensive pace since 1998. Teams with wide receiver and tight end injuries tend to improve the following year. Defenses that are strong against the run overall but mediocre against the run in the red zone tend to improve. Kickoff distance is a better indicator of success than field-goal percentage.

On top of all of that, the Jaguars went into the offseason with three major holes and filled all three. They signed Baltimore right tackle Tony Pashos on the first day of free agency, solving the one weakness on the offensive line. They needed a new free safety when Deon Grant signed with Seattle, and took Florida's Reggie Harris in the first round of a safety-rich draft. They had the worst punting in the NFL last year, and while they shouldn't have blown a fourth-round pick to replace Chris Hanson with rookie punter Adam Podlesh, at least they replaced Chris Hanson.

This team has scary talent on defense, and the only starter past his prime is safety Donovin Darius. If he falters, the Jaguars already have his replacement ready in Gerald Sensabaugh. On offense, most of the pieces are there, led by a stalwart offensive line and an excellent running game. The last missing piece is a better passing game, and the Jaguars have made a move to try to jump-start their air attack by replacing conservative offensive coordinator Carl Smith with former Arizona State head coach Dirk Koetter, who is known as a passing guru.

The last thing the Jaguars have to do is figure out what intangible problems created last year's inconsistency. If they can solve their psychological dilemmas and add improvement from Leftwich, Jones, and second-year tight end Marcedes Lewis, this team will be a top-five Super Bowl contender. Even if everyone plays at the exact same level as a year ago, solving the consistency issues would virtually assure this team a wild-card playoff spot. This team just has too much talent to be losing to the Houston Texans twice a year. Statistical analysis can't tell us what works to emotionally motivate a football team, but if this talent can't win ten games in 2007, we'll know what doesn't work: whatever Jack Del Rio was doing before Jacksonville fired him.

Aaron Schatz

Jaguars 2006 Stats by Week

Wk	vs.	W–L	PF	PA	YDF	YDA	TO	DVOA Total	Off	Def	ST
1	DAL	W	24	17	307	323	+2	29.3%	9.0%	-29.0%	-8.8%
2	PIT	W	9	0	362	153	+1	87.1%	-8.1%	-87.1%	8.0%
3	@IND	L	14	21	297	272	-2	-1.1%	-10.4%	-27.0%	-17.8%
4	@WAS	L	30	36	307	481	0	-52.6%	-30.2%	23.2%	0.9%
5	NYJ	W	41	0	312	177	+4	112.9%	27.3%	-76.0%	9.6%
6	BYE										
7	@HOU	L	7	27	220	349	-2	-70.2%	-36.8%	28.2%	-5.3%
8	@PHI	W	13	6	285	227	-1	42.6%	2.6%	-34.0%	5.9%
9	TEN	W	37	7	342	262	+3	77.3%	22.0%	-46.1%	9.2%
10	HOU	L	10	13	322	306	-4	-51.6%	-57.4%	-7.6%	-1.8%
11	NYG	W	26	10	414	247	+2	69.9%	28.0%	-34.3%	7.6%
12	@BUF	L	24	27	323	241	0	-8.5%	12.1%	5.4%	-15.2%
13	@MIA	W	24	10	353	309	+1	62.7%	53.9%	-3.9%	4.8%
14	IND	W	44	17	447	339	0	102.7%	47.1%	-29.0%	26.7%
15	@TEN	L	17	24	396	98	-4	-3.9%	-31.9%	-37.2%	-9.2%
16	NE	L	21	24	339	359	-1	7.5%	36.0%	17.6%	-10.9%
17	@KC	L	30	35	397	395	+2	14.7%	24.5%	2.4%	-7.4%

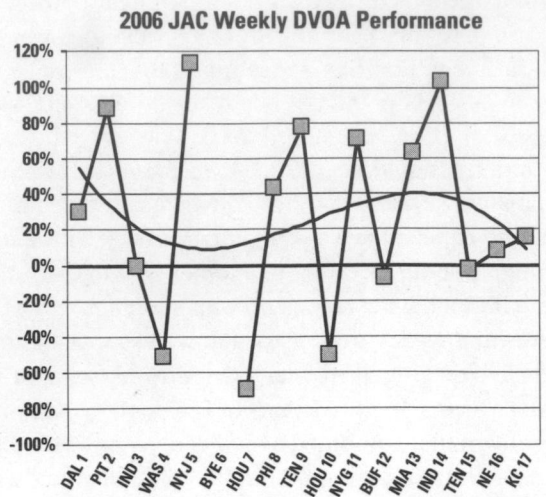

2006 JAC Weekly DVOA Performance

Trends and Splits

	Offense	Rank	Defense	Rank
Total DVOA	4.3%	12	-17.9%	3
Unadjusted VOA	8.5%	10	-10.3%	5
Weighted Trend	8.0%	12	-10.8%	8
Variance	9.7%	6	10.5%	2
Passing	-5.3%	20	-23.6%	3
Rushing	12.8%	3	-11.5%	7
First Down	22.3%	3	-16.6%	5
Second Down	-12.1%	26	-6.5%	11
Third Down	-4.5%	19	-35.9%	2
Red Zone	6.9%	13	-13.1%	9
Late and Close	-21.3%	28	-9.8%	10

Five-Year Performance

	2006	2005	2004	2003	2002
W-L	8-8	12-4	9-7	5-11	6-10
Pythagorean Wins	10.8	10.7	7.3	6.3	8.4
Estimated Wins	9.6	10.3	8.6	8.2	8.1
Total DVOA	22.0%	17.0%	0.4%	1.2%	-3.5%
Rank	6	10	14	16	20
Offense	4.3%	6.6%	-3.7%	-1.4%	7.1%
Rank	12	10	18	15	9
Defense	-17.9%	-10.2%	-4.5%	-7.6%	9.3%
Rank	3	7	9	10	25
Special Teams	-0.2%	0.3%	-0.5%	-5.0%	-1.3%
Rank	19	15	17	29	18

Strategic Tendencies

Formations		Rank	Run/Pass		Rank	Defense		Rank	Other		Rank
3+ WR	42%	24	Runs, all plays	52%	2	Sacks by LB	15%	24	Run with 2+ RB	48%	26
4+ WR	1%	32	Runs, first half	50%	5	Sacks by DB	3%	25	Run with 2+ TE	44%	5
2+ TE	34%	5	Runs, first down	61%	3	Rush 6+	8.6%	18	Play action	16%	23
Single back	63%	8	Runs, power sit.	65%	14	Rush 7+	2.3%	10	Go for it on 4th	0.85	18
Empty back	0.8%	26	Runs, behind 2H	40%	4	Rush 3	3.4%	22	Offensive Pace	34.0	32
Max protect	11%	18	Pass, ahead 2H	32%	30	CB1 on WR1	51%	7	Defensive Pace	30.5	13

Thanks to that great running game, the Jaguars ran the slowest offense in the nine years for which we have situation-neutral pace numbers. . . . In 2005, the Jaguars used four or more wide receivers 15 percent of the time. Last year, they used four or more wide receivers on only ten plays. Jacksonville ranked 24th in using three or more wide receivers, but ninth in using exactly three. . . . Jacksonville was second in percentage of run plays that were draws, behind St. Louis, and ran more draw plays in short-yardage situations than any other team. . . . Only five quarterbacks with at least 75 shotgun snaps had a higher DVOA under center than in shotgun, and two of them were Byron Leftwich and David Garrard (see Tampa Bay chapter for details). . . . Jacksonville's defense was the beneficiary of 37 drops, tied for second in the league.

Passing

Player	DPAR	DVOA	Plys	NtYds	Avg	YAC	C%	TD	Int
David Garrard	12.0	-2.5%	241	1597	6.6	5.4	60.2%	10	9
Byron Leftwich	3.6	-8.8%	183	1106	6.0	5.3	59.0%	7	5
Quinn Gray	5.5	53.6%	22	155	7.0	NA	59.1%	0	0

Rushing

Player	DPAR	DVOA	Plys	Yds	Avg	TD	Fum	Suc
Fred Taylor	23.1	12.0%	231	1146	5.0	5	2	44%
Maurice Jones-Drew	26.0	23.6%	166	941	5.7	13	1	51%
David Garrard	8.1	18.9%	37	260	7.0	0	4	—
Alvin Pearman	1.4	3.6%	19	89	4.7	1	0	67%
Byron Leftwich	-2.3	-43.5%	16	49	3.1	2	2	—
LaBrandon Toefield	-1.4	-45.1%	10	22	2.2	0	0	60%
Reggie Williams	-1.5	-60.3%	7	33	4.7	0	1	—
Rich Alexis	-0.9	-94.1%	3	5	1.7	0	0	42%
Dennis Northcutt	*-0.5*	*-60.6%*	*3*	*32*	*10.7*	*0*	*1*	—

Receiving

Player	DPAR	DVOA	Plys	Ctch	Yds	Y/C	YAC	TD	C%
WR									
Reggie Williams	3.3	-9.9%	91	52	616	11.8	4.7	4	54%
Matt Jones	7.5	-1.5%	76	41	643	15.7	4.4	4	57%
Ernest Wilford	2.3	-10.7%	74	36	524	14.6	3.4	2	49%
Cortez Hankton	-1.0	-28.9%	11	5	48	9.6	0.0	0	45%
Dennis Northcutt	*-4.8*	*-31.4%*	*45*	*22*	*228*	*10.4*	*4.3*	*0*	*33%*
TE									
George Wrighster	2.5	-6.5%	63	39	353	9.1	2.7	3	62%
Marcedes Lewis	1.4	-1.5%	21	13	126	9.7	4.4	1	62%
Kyle Brady*	-1.0	-30.0%	8	5	37	7.4	2.4	0	63%
Jermaine Wiggins	*1.8*	*-8.2%*	*67*	*46*	*390*	*8.5*	*2.6*	*1*	*69%*
RB									
Maurice Jones-Drew	8.3	17.1%	62	46	436	9.5	9.6	2	74%
Fred Taylor	5.3	25.0%	28	23	242	10.5	10.3	1	82%
Derrick Wimbush	-0.1	-12.2%	5	4	23	5.8	3.0	0	80%

Offensive Line

Year	Yards	ALY	Rank	Power	Rank	10+ Yds	Rank	Stuff	Rank	Sack	ASR	Rank
2004	4.13	4.14	20	51%	29	18%	9	27%	23	32	6.2%	10
2005	3.94	3.83	25	61%	21	19%	13	27%	24	32	5.7%	10
2006	5.13	4.66	2	65%	14	23%	5	22%	9	30	7.0%	19

Year	LE	Rank	LT	Rank	Mid	Rank	RT	Rank	RE	Rank
2004	2.81	29	4.32	20	4.29	16	3.81	23	4.53	6
2005	3.70	24	4.15	21	4.17	15	2.45	32	1.80	32
2006	4.60	7	5.22	3	4.72	4	3.92	26	4.42	11

Ingredients: Four collegiate linemen and one undrafted veteran, preferably with Hawaiian flavor. Marinate veteran in Cajun spices for five years, allowing the flavor of his talent to emerge. Add collegiate linemen to dish gradually, encouraging flavors to develop, and learn to work together as one delicious unit. Left tackle will be the strongest ingredient, so feel free to add it last. Wait 365 days and finish with a liberal dose of agile young running back. Voila! The recipe for a great offensive line. Warning: Maurice Williams may not ripen properly. Replace with either fenugreek or Baltimore Greek.

Jacksonville built an offensive line the way offensive lines should be built. The resulting group won't make headlines, and maybe not even Pro Bowls, they just do the job, and that allows guys such as Maurice Jones-Drew to shine. The only problem was Williams, who simply never developed as well as the other linemen, but the Jaguars filled that hole by signing former Baltimore right tackle Tony Pashos on the first day of free agency. When it comes to 2007's best match of free agent and team need, the Pashos signing and the Adalius Thomas signing in New England are neck and neck for the grand prize. Fifth-rounder Uche Nwaneri is a nice developmental prospect for when 33-year-old right guard Chris Naeole finally shows his age.

Defensive Front Seven

Defensive Line	Age	Pos	Plys	TmPct	Rk	Stop	Dfts	StpRt	Rk	AvYd	Rk	Sack	Hit	Hur	Runs	RuStp	RuYd	Pass	PaStp	PaYd
John Henderson	28	DT	56	7.2%	10	39	16	70%	60	1.0	18	3.5	2	2	43	65%	1.6	13	85%	-0.8
Paul Spicer	32	DE	51	6.6%	30	40	16	78%	35	1.1	27	3	7	12	41	78%	1.0	10	80%	1.4
Bobby McCray	26	DE	36	5.0%	53	30	20	83%	14	-0.1	7	10	7	13	20	85%	1.0	16	81%	-1.6
Rob Meier	33	DT	30	3.9%	65	25	13	83%	21	0.2	4	5	2	7	21	81%	1.4	9	89%	-2.7
Marcus Stroud	29	DT	22	4.1%	—	17	6	77%	—	0.0	—	2.5	2	6	15	73%	1.7	7	86%	-3.4
Tony McDaniel	22	DT	18	3.4%	—	13	4	72%	—	3.7	—	1	0	3	11	73%	2.5	7	71%	5.4
Marcellus Wiley*	33	DE	16	2.8%	—	13	6	81%	—	0.8	—	0	1	5	12	75%	0.8	4	100%	1.0

(continued next page)

Defensive Front Seven (*continued*)

Linebackers	Age	Pos	Plys	TmPct	Rk	Stop	Dfts	StpRt	AvYd	Sack	Hit	Hur	Runs	RuStp	Rk	RuYd	Rk	Tgts	Suc%	Rk	PaYd	Rk
Daryl Smith	25	ILB	96	12.4%	51	63	24	66%	4.3	3	1	4	53	66%	39	3.1	26	42	65%	11	4.7	14
Clint Ingram	22	OLB	70	10.3%	69	31	10	44%	5.1	1.5	1	2	37	54%	87	3.8	65	36	38%	87	6.6	65
Nick Greisen	28	OLB	37	4.8%	—	26	9	70%	2.5	0	1	2	23	70%	—	2.2	—	16	59%	23	4.6	12
Mike Peterson	31	ILB	33	13.7%	—	21	8	64%	3.5	0	1	3	24	63%	—	2.6	—	12	80%	—	3.7	—

Year	Yards	ALY	Rank	Power	Rank	10+ Yds	Rank	Stuff	Rank	Sack	ASR	Rank
2004	4.10	4.17	14	63%	19	15%	13	25%	12	36	8.1%	8
2005	3.96	4.09	18	59%	10	13%	7	21%	27	47	8.8%	1
2006	3.52	3.65	3	69%	25	15%	12	27%	6	35	7.2%	13

Year	LE	Rank	LT	Rank	Mid	Rank	RT	Rank	RE	Rank
2004	4.65	23	4.56	22	4.02	10	4.42	24	3.95	19
2005	3.66	8	4.28	17	4.31	22	3.78	10	3.83	15
2006	3.12	5	3.12	4	4.00	6	2.90	4	4.12	18

It seemed strange in 2005 when the Jaguars' defense built around two highly regarded tackles was below average against runs up the gut, but the Jags rebounded with a great performance against the run in 2006. It was even better during the weeks that left tackle Marcus Stroud was healthy. With Stroud in the lineup, the Jaguars stuffed 30 percent of runs, allowing 3.91 Adjusted Line Yards up the middle and 1.78 ALY on runs behind right tackle (Stroud's side). When Stroud was injured from Week 5 to Week 10, the Jaguars stuffed just 23 percent of runs, allowing 4.13 ALY both up the middle and behind right tackle. John Henderson may have played five more games, but our game charters made many more positive comments about Stroud.

Everyone knows that the Jaguars' tackles are great, but their ends do not get nearly the credit they deserve, especially Bobby McCray, who moved into the starting lineup when Reggie Hayward tore his Achilles tendon. McCray has wicked speed around the edge, but also had a good year against the run and made plays when dropped into coverage on zone blitzes. McCray is unhappy about his contract, and held out of minicamps rather than sign the $1.85-million restricted free-agent tender offered by the team. His contract situation is unlikely to affect the regular season, but, long term, McCray needs to get paid. The other starting end, Paul Spicer, is known more as a run-stopper, but did his share to harass opposing quarterbacks last year. Hayward's status is up in the air; he wasn't healthy enough to participate in minicamp, and an Achilles injury damages quickness more than any other skill, a real problem for a pass-rush specialist.

Inside linebacker Mike Peterson has the easier injury recovery after tearing his pectoral muscle against the Jets early last year. Daryl Smith did a good job replacing Peterson inside, but when rookie Clint Ingram was forced into the lineup to replace Smith on the outside, he played like a rookie forced into the lineup. Peterson will be back this year, Smith will go back outside, and Ingram will stay in the starting lineup at weak-side linebacker, hopefully having been improved by his experience last year.

The Jaguars took Hampton linebacker Justin Durant in the second round of the draft, and he is now the heir apparent to Peterson. He's athletic and quick with great awareness, although he's a bit undersized. "Great awareness but undersized" worked very well for Tedy Bruschi, Zach Thomas, and London Fletcher-Baker, so the Jaguars have a nice prospect on their hands. Fourth-round pick Brian Smith is a DE/OLB tweener who belongs in a 3-4 defense and doesn't make sense for this team.

Defensive Secondary

Secondary	Age	Pos	Plys	TmPct	Rk	Stop	Dfts	RuYd	Rk	RuStp	Rk	Tgts	Tgt%	Rk	Dist	Suc%	Rk	PaYd	Rk	PD	Int
Rashean Mathis	27	CB	82	10.6%	21	44	22	6.6	39	65%	6	94	22%	12	12.3	57%	16	6.3	13	19	8
Brian Williams	28	CB	66	9.1%	42	20	13	6.1	31	33%	56	77	19%	40	13.9	55%	26	7.4	36	10	1
Deon Grant*	28	FS	70	9.1%	55	21	11	6.3	36	29%	64	37	8%	32	15.6	53%	34	9.0	53	6	2
Terry Cousin	32	CB	39	8.1%	—	16	7	7.0	—	42%	—	32	11%	—	10.1	56%	—	7.6	—	4	1
Donovan Darius	32	SS	50	10.3%	36	19	3	7.5	55	41%	45	23	8%	36	12.6	53%	38	7.3	33	2	0
George Sensabaugh	24	SS	39	5.0%	74	16	10	4.4	6	54%	16	20	4%	77	15.6	66%	6	8.9	52	4	2
Scott Starks	24	CB	21	2.7%	—	12	5	2.8	—	67%	—	18	4%	—	7.0	59%	—	6.3	—	1	1

Year	Pass D Rank	DVOA vs. #1 WR	Rank	DVOA vs. #2 WR	Rank	DVOA vs. Other WR	Rank	DVOA vs. TE	Rank	DVOA vs. RB	Rank
2004	12	-4.2%	10	0.1%	17	-8.6%	15	-9.1%	12	5.2%	18
2005	9	-6.3%	7	-13.1%	8	3.0%	21	-18.9%	4	-0.4%	18
2006	3	-9.5%	11	-41.6%	1	-54.0%	1	2.1%	22	-22.0%	5

No team wants to enter the draft with a gaping roster hole so large that it virtually demands that a player at that position be chosen first. The Jaguars got off easy, because the position they had to fill happened to be the deepest one in the draft. The Jaguars traded down four spots and still got the player they wanted, Florida free safety Reggie Nelson. He'll go straight into the starting lineup to replace departed free-agent Deon Grant (now in Seattle). Nelson has outstanding range and the best pass coverage skills of this year's four first-round safeties. He's not the strongest tackler in the world, but he doesn't shy away from contact, another reason why he's a good fit for a Jacksonville defense that likes to blitz its safeties.

Last year, we wrote that Rashean Mathis "rarely plays up to his physical skills" but "is young and talented with room for improvement." Consider that improvement achieved, as Mathis made his first Pro Bowl in his fourth season. At the other corner, Brian Williams was not as good last year as he was in Minnesota a year earlier, but he was much better than the man he replaced in Jacksonville, Kenny Wright. Terry Cousin still does a fine job at nickelback. Donovin Darius is a locker room leader, but backup Gerald Sensabaugh was actually the better player at strong safety in 2006, and the changing of the guard could come soon. Fifth-round pick Josh Gattis, a hard-hitter from Wake Forest, provides depth at both safety positions.

Special Teams

Year	DVOA	Rank	FG/XP	Rank	Net Punt	Rank	Punt Ret	Rank	Net Kick	Rank	Kick Ret	Rank	Hidden	Rank
2004	-0.5%	17	-5.0	25	-2.0	19	-0.4	17	9.8	8	-5.4	25	11.3	3
2005	0.6%	13	-6.6	24	-3.3	23	0.2	14	6.8	6	6.2	7	8.7	5
2006	-0.2%	19	1.4	12	-21.2	32	-2.5	23	12.9	2	8.1	5	12.3	2

Josh Scobee has developed into one of the top kickoff men in the league, and the Jaguars also had strong kickoff coverage in 2006. Scobee is nothing special on field goals, but, as we explain in the Arizona chapter, kickoff distance is the much more consistent skill. The coverage teams may get even better this year with the addition of seventh-round pick Chad Nkang out of Elon College. He's a former fullback who falls halfway between linebacker and safety, and his best role might be as an all-purpose special teams tackling monster along the lines of Larry Izzo or Larry Whigham. Maurice Jones-Drew was great on kick returns in 2006, but Alvin Pearman has been mediocre on punt returns for two years now. If Jones-Drew is going to carry the ball more, the Jaguars could use somebody new to do both jobs, possibly seventh-round speed demon John Broussard from San Jose State.

You may notice a pattern here: The seventh round is where you use draft picks for special teams. The Jaguars didn't get this entirely right in the 2007 draft. Chris "Keep Choppin' Wood" Hanson was the worst punter in the league last year and had to go, but using the second pick of the fourth round on a punter is still a colossal waste of resources. Maryland punter Adam Podlesh has both distance and accuracy, and will make a fine professional, but there's no reason to believe he'll be better than Miami seventh-round pick Brandon Fields or whichever free-agent punter from NFL Europa ends up with the Patriots—especially when the punt coverage was as bad as Hanson's was. The Jaguars gave up two 82-yard punt return touchdowns last year, and, even after adjusting for Hanson's poor kicks, only Arizona gave up more value than the Jaguars did on punt returns.

Coaching Staff

Defensive coordinator Michael "not David" Smith is one of the more underrated assistant coaches in the NFL and has done a great job shaping this defense to the talent he has. The other two coordinators will be new. Offensive coordinator Dirk Koetter, the former head coach at Arizona State, is considered a passing guru, but he may not be the best man to handle the quarterback controversy between Byron Leftwich and David Garrard. With the Sun Devils last year, he so mangled the quarterback decision that it torpedoed his 2006 season and led to his dismissal. Koetter at first named Sam Keller his starter only to change his mind days before the season in favor of Rudy Carpenter. Keller immediately transferred to Nebraska, while Carpenter's uneven play was one of the reasons for Arizona State's struggles. New special teams coordinator Joe DeCamillis was in Atlanta the last three seasons. The Falcons had top-ten special teams units his first two years, but dropped to 28th last year, primarily because of the Michael Koenen kicker/punter experiment.

Kansas City Chiefs

When Trent Green was carted off the Arrowhead Stadium field with a severe concussion in Week 1, it looked as though the Chiefs' 2006 season was about to go down the tubes. Green's injury handed the starting quarterback job to Damon Huard, who had thrown exactly one pass in the previous five seasons. Kansas City lost its first two games, and the outlook was bleak.

Then, after the Chiefs' Week 3 bye, something extraordinary happened: Huard wasn't just good filling in for Green, he was great. The Chiefs won five of their next six games, and, all of a sudden, they looked like contenders.

It didn't last. When Green returned to health, head coach Herm Edwards benched Huard. That was a mistake: Huard's DVOA of 36.0% was second only to Peyton Manning's among the 45 quarterbacks who threw at least 100 passes last year. Green's DVOA of 3.4% was 21st, placing him just behind Jason Campbell and just ahead of Eli Manning. The Chiefs still managed to get into the playoffs, but they didn't just lose the Wild Card playoff game in Indianapolis, they were humiliated, running Larry Johnson into a wall of defenders again and again apparently without a Plan B prepared in case it didn't work.

That loss represented more than just the Kansas City offense collapsing and Tony Dungy out-coaching Herm Edwards. It also represented the Chiefs' last chance to win with their current nucleus of players. Huard got Kansas City into the playoffs one last time, but now the Chiefs are a rebuilding team.

Consider Tony Gonzalez. Gonzalez was outstanding yet again in 2006. He was the best tight end in the NFL, leading the league in DPAR and coming in second in DVOA, and was the favorite target of both Green and Huard, but Gonzalez is about to go from an asset to a lia-

bility. During the offseason, Gonzalez turned 31, and the Chiefs signed him to a five-year contract extension that guarantees him close to $18 million. Even though Gonzalez is a durable player who has missed just two games in his career, everything we know about the way athletes age tells us that Gonzalez is in for a steep decline just as his share of the Chiefs' salary cap expands.

Consider the offensive line, which was great a few years ago, but has since fallen apart. The line had some problems in 2005, but Larry Johnson ran so well that few noticed the cracks in the wall. Last year, left tackle Willie Roaf retired and the line was thoroughly mediocre. This offseason, guard Will Shields also retired. Roaf and Shields were two of the most talented linemen in recent NFL history. They both had that rare blend of power and quickness that allowed them to excel in short-yardage running situations, to get out ahead on sweeps, and to deal with speedy pass rushers. With both gone in 2007, the line could be atrocious. As a result, the Chiefs now project as one of the worst offenses in the league.

Even before Shields retired, our projections showed the Kansas City offense collapsing. The reason is easily summed up in one number: 416. In the past, we've written a great deal about the way running backs who carry the ball 370 or more times in a season frequently decline or get injured the following year. Johnson hit 370 with a game and a half to spare last year, then kept going, setting a new NFL record for carries with 416.

Herm Edwards loves the power running game and loves having one featured back who carries the mail in his offense. Just ask Curtis Martin, who suffered a steep decline after carrying the ball 371 times for Edwards in 2004. When Edwards arrived in Kansas City last year, he didn't object to offensive coordinator Al Saunders leaving for the Redskins because Edwards prefers a straightforward offense while Saunders likes a fancier attack. Edwards handed Johnson the ball 30 or more times in six different games, and used him the way the late Michigan coach Bo Schembechler liked to use his running backs. Even facing eight in the box, Edwards and offensive coordinator Mike Solari would pound Johnson into the line, over and over again.

If Edwards doesn't want Johnson on injured reserve halfway through the season, he needs to get Michael Bennett more involved. Bennett is a former college track star, and, in terms of straight-line speed, he is probably the fastest running back in the NFL. Teams usually played pass when Johnson left the field, giving Bennett room to run. In response, Bennett posted a 19.6% DVOA, but on only 36 carries. It's surprising that the Chiefs didn't take more advantage of that.

Even if Bennett could step in for Johnson without missing a beat, or even if Johnson could get through another 400-carry season without getting hurt, it's hard to see how the Chiefs could be nearly as good in 2007 as they were in 2006. There's still that declining offensive line. There's still the aging Tony Gonzalez. If Huard is the starter, he'll be hard-pressed to repeat last year's great performance. If Brodie Croyle is the starter, you know Edwards is already thinking about 2008.

We haven't even gotten to the defense, which declined last year after a promising 2005 and often looked like a disorganized mishmash of Edwards's philosophies and those of defensive coordinator Gunther Cunningham. Outside linebacker Kendrell Bell, in particular, never looked like a good fit in the Chiefs' defense and has been a disappointment since signing as a big-money free agent two years ago. Jared Allen was their best defensive player last season, but he is unhappy with his contract and will serve a four-game suspension to start the season following a pair of drunk driving

2007 Chiefs Schedule

Week	Opp	Week	Opp	Week	Opp
1	at HOU	7	at OAK	13	SD
2	at CHI	8	BYE	14	at DEN
3	MIN	9	GB	15	TEN
4	at SD	10	DEN	16	at DET
5	JAC	11	at IND	17	at NYJ
6	CIN	12	OAK		

convictions. Ty Law and Patrick Surtain would have been the best pair of corners in the league if they had teamed up five years ago, but both players are past their expiration date.

Middle linebacker Kawika Mitchell started every game the last two years, but he signed a free-agent deal with the Giants, and the Chiefs got themselves an upgrade. With Napoleon Harris as the starting middle linebacker, the Vikings had the best run defense in the league last year. Harris was also good against the pass, with 2.5 sacks and three interceptions. The addition of Harris as a free agent will stem the tide to a certain degree, but unless Harris turns into the unholy spawn of Bob Sanders and Brian Urlacher, Kansas City's defense won't be any better than the mediocre unit it was last season. Combine that with the almost certain decline of the offense, and the Chiefs are a team heading in the wrong direction.

The Chiefs have had bad luck in recent seasons. Last year they had a playoff game in Indianapolis just as the Colts figured out how to stop the run. In 2005, they were a very good team that missed the playoffs thanks to some bad breaks in some important games. For the three years before that, they were basically the 2006 Colts minus the defensive turnaround in the playoffs. However, all signs indicate that, in 2007, they won't just be unlucky, they'll be bad.

Michael David Smith

Chiefs 2006 Stats by Week

Wk	vs.	W–L	PF	PA	YDF	YDA	TO	DVOA Total	Off	Def	ST
1	CIN	L	10	23	289	236	-2	-39.6%	-41.4%	-10.7%	-8.9%
2	@DEN	L	6	9	276	318	-1	11.3%	-9.7%	-10.4%	10.7%
3	BYE										
4	SF	W	41	0	333	165	+4	123.2%	31.8%	-63.6%	27.8%
5	@ARI	W	23	20	301	298	-1	-31.4%	-34.3%	1.7%	4.5%
6	@PIT	L	7	45	213	457	-2	-79.1%	-36.3%	45.6%	2.8%
7	SD	W	30	27	355	349	+2	38.8%	28.4%	-29.4%	-19.0%
8	SEA	W	35	28	499	240	-1	30.5%	30.1%	-5.7%	-5.4%
9	@STL	W	31	17	317	452	+3	27.7%	23.5%	6.9%	11.0%
10	@MIA	L	10	13	265	306	+1	-13.7%	2.0%	3.2%	-12.5%
11	OAK	W	17	13	292	326	+1	-8.0%	22.5%	28.6%	-1.8%
12	DEN	W	19	10	382	244	0	48.7%	26.0%	-12.7%	10.0%
13	@CLE	L	28	31	417	438		-25.7%	31.4%	56.5%	-0.6%
14	BAL	L	10	20	276	376	-2	-20.7%	-3.0%	20.0%	2.3%
15	@SD	L	9	20	241	353	0	13.9%	-22.8%	-35.3%	1.4%
16	@OAK	W	20	9	292	307	+4	0.9%	3.6%	6.5%	3.8%
17	JAC	W	35	30	395	397	-2	-5.3%	25.9%	27.0%	-4.3%
18	@IND	L	8	23	126	435	0	-82.2%	-75.4%	-5.1%	-11.9%

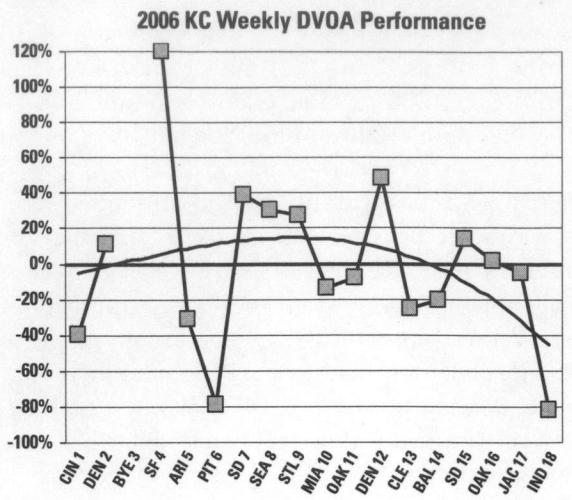

2006 KC Weekly DVOA Performance

Trends and Splits

	Offense	Rank	Defense	Rank
Total DVOA	4.8%	11	2.8%	18
Unadjusted VOA	3.8%	12	1.1%	15
Weighted Trend	10.5%	10	8.9%	26
Variance	6.6%	16	8.7%	6
Passing	14.0%	10	6.0%	22
Rushing	-3.1%	17	-0.4%	19
First Down	6.6%	10	1.6%	17
Second Down	-3.4%	21	-1.8%	14
Third Down	14.0%	10	11.9%	20
Red Zone	24.4%	9	6.3%	18
Late and Close	11.4%	8	-0.9%	16

Five-Year Performance

	2006	2005	2004	2003	2002
W-L	9-7	10-6	7-9	13-3	8-8
Pythagorean Wins	8.5	10.0	9.0	11.4	9.5
Estimated Wins	8.4	11.1	9.3	10.4	9.9
Total DVOA	3.4%	27.5%	11.4%	25.9%	19.6%
Rank	13	4	11	1	5
Offense	4.8%	23.7%	28.7%	27.0%	33.3%
Rank	11	2	2	1	1
Defense	2.8%	-5.7%	16.7%	6.7%	16.2%
Rank	18	12	30	24	29
Special Teams	1.3%	-2.0%	-0.5%	5.5%	2.5%
Rank	13	23	18	1	10

Strategic Tendencies

Formations		Rank	Run/Pass		Rank	Defense		Rank	Other		Rank
3+ WR	46%	19	Runs, all plays	49%	5	Sacks by LB	25%	15	Run with 2+ RB	46%	28
4+ WR	14%	8	Runs, first half	50%	4	Sacks by DB	16%	3	Run with 2+ TE	50%	3
2+ TE	36%	2	Runs, first down	61%	4	Rush 6+	9.3%	14	Play action	19%	18
Single back	63%	6	Runs, power sit.	74%	2	Rush 7+	3.5%	5	Go for it on 4th	0.93	15
Empty back	1.2%	24	Runs, behind 2H	36%	11	Rush 3	2.1%	26	Offensive Pace	31.8	23
Max protect	9%	25	Pass, ahead 2H	36%	25	CB1 on WR1	38%	23	Defensive Pace	30.6	15

Kansas City ranked 27th in use of two running backs, but third in use of a power set with two running backs and two tight ends. . . . Kansas City gained an average of 11 yards on screen passes, the only offense to average more than ten. . . . Larry Johnson dropped ten passes, the most among running backs. The only other running backs with more than seven were guys who were thrown almost twice as many passes, Steven Jackson and Brian Westbrook. Johnson's ten drops accounted for half of the charted incomplete passes thrown his way. . . . The Chiefs had the fewest passes defensed in the NFL, and only Indianapolis was the beneficiary of fewer dropped passes by opposing offenses. . . . Kansas City rarely rushed more than six defenders on first or second down, but rushed at least six on 17 percent of third downs, which ranked fifth in the NFL. . . . Herman Edwards has the lowest career Aggressiveness Index (.59) of any active head coach with at least two years of experience.

Passing

Player	DPAR	DVOA	Plys	NtYds	Avg	YAC	C%	TD	Int
Damon Huard	52.0	34.5%	244	1760	7.2	5.4	60.7%	11	1
Trent Green*	15.6	3.4%	198	1210	6.1	4.0	61.1%	7	9
Brodie Croyle	-3.5	-112.8%	7	13	1.9	0.0	42.9%	0	1

Rushing

Player	DPAR	DVOA	Plys	Yds	Avg	TD	Fum	Suc
Larry Johnson	42.1	9.9%	416	1789	4.3	17	2	44%
Michael Bennett	4.6	19.3%	36	200	5.6	0	1	20%
Trent Green*	-0.8	-30.5%	11	57	5.2	0	5	—
Dee Brown	-4.0	-120.8%	10	24	2.4	0	1	45%
Ronnie Cruz	0.0	-12.7%	5	19	3.8	0	0	58%
Eddie Kennison	0.3	-9.2%	4	16	4.0	0	0	—
Damon Huard	-5.4	-234.3%	4	3	0.8	0	8	—
Derrick Ross	-0.6	-48.4%	3	8	2.7	0	0	46%
Samie Parker	-0.1	-32.5%	3	7	2.3	0	0	—
Dante Hall*	-0.7	-50.5%	3	11	3.7	0	0	—

Receiving

Player	DPAR	DVOA	Plys	Ctch	Yds	Y/C	YAC	TD	C%
WR									
Eddie Kennison	18.6	13.0%	101	53	860	16.2	2.3	5	52%
Samie Parker	15.8	20.0%	68	41	561	13.7	3.0	1	60%
Dante Hall*	2.1	-6.8%	40	26	204	7.8	2.8	2	65%
Rod Gardner	-4.0	-79.5%	9	2	17	8.5	3.0	0	22%
TE									
Tony Gonzalez	30.2	35.5%	104	73	900	12.3	3.9	5	70%
Jason Dunn	-0.1	-13.4%	10	4	40	10.0	7.5	0	40%
RB									
Larry Johnson	4.1	2.0%	67	41	410	10.0	11.6	2	61%
Kris Wilson	2.3	0.9%	24	15	132	8.8	5.2	3	63%
Michael Bennett	1.1	8.2%	12	9	77	8.6	8.2	0	75%
Ronnie Cruz	0.0	-13.3%	5	2	20	10.0	12.0	0	40%

Offensive Line

Year	Yards	ALY	Rank	Power	Rank	10+ Yds	Rank	Stuff	Rank	Sack	ASR	Rank
2004	4.60	4.73	3	70%	8	16%	23	18%	2	32	6.1%	9
2005	4.79	4.62	3	68%	10	21%	7	19%	2	32	6.6%	15
2006	4.34	4.24	17	74%	2	21%	8	24%	15	41	7.5%	21

Year	LE	Rank	LT	Rank	Mid	Rank	RT	Rank	RE	Rank
2004	4.82	8	4.35	19	4.81	2	3.96	19	4.95	3
2005	5.18	3	4.59	10	4.44	7	4.26	14	4.61	9
2006	3.53	24	4.58	12	4.57	8	2.57	32	4.69	8

Right guard Will Shields has retired, and with John Welbourn slated to take his place, the Chiefs will suffer a steep drop-off. Left guard Brian Waters is still playing at a high level, but he's the only top-notch player left on what was once a great offensive line. Center Casey Wiegmann has started every game over the last five years and will be back again this year, but he's not as quick getting to the second level as he used to be, and with Shields no longer next to him, Wiegmann will be less effective this season. Free-agent acquisition Damion McIntosh, who played the last three years in Miami and four years before that in San Diego, is now the left tackle. McIntosh is a better run blocker than he is a pass blocker. Chris Terry was just a part-time backup last year, but he will likely start at right tackle this year. In general, the Chiefs' offensive line isn't as good as the stats would suggest. The great power running stat, in particular, says more about Larry Johnson than it does about the offensive line; Johnson is one of the best in the league at putting his shoulder down and barreling through the line for a yard or two.

Defensive Front Seven

Defensive Line	Age	Pos	Plys	TmPct	Rk	Stop	Dfts	StpRt	Rk	AvYd	Rk	Sack	Hit	Hur	Runs	RuStp	RuYd	Pass	PaStp	PaYd
Jared Allen	25	DE	86	10.7%	3	71	30	83%	18	1.6	40	7.5	11	13	61	82%	2.8	25	84%	-1.1
Tamba Hali	24	DE	68	8.5%	9	48	26	71%	66	1.1	29	8	1	7	46	67%	2.6	22	77%	-1.9
James Reed	30	DT	39	5.2%	35	30	7	77%	41	2.3	50	1	7	1	35	74%	2.7	4	100%	-1.5
Jimmy Wilkerson	26	DT	23	3.5%	—	18	7	78%	—	1.2	—	0	1	1	19	74%	1.4	4	100%	0.3
Ron Edwards	28	DT	21	2.6%	—	18	6	86%	—	1.0	—	2.5	2	2	16	81%	2.1	5	100%	-2.4
Alfonso Boone	*31*	*DT*	*26*	*4.3%*	*59*	*20*	*7*	*77%*	*40*	*1.6*	*30*	*2*	*1*	*1*	*24*	*75%*	*2.3*	*2*	*100%*	*-6.5*

Linebackers	Age	Pos	Plys	TmPct	Rk	Stop	Dfts	StpRt	AvYd	Sack	Hit	Hur	Runs	RuStp	Rk	RuYd	Rk	Tgts	Suc%	Rk	PaYd	Rk
Kawika Mitchell*	28	ILB	108	13.5%	38	49	15	45%	5.8	1.5	3	5	69	51%	92	4.3	86	33	35%	90	8.8	90
Derrick Johnson	25	OLB	81	12.4%	50	51	18	63%	3.9	4.5	1	2	40	73%	17	2.7	13	41	51%	45	6.5	62
Kendrell Bell	27	OLB	48	6.0%	—	29	10	60%	3.5	1	1	1	32	66%	—	2.7	—	18	62%	14	3.0	2
Keyaron Fox	25	OLB	47	5.9%	—	20	7	43%	7.2	1	1	2	22	59%	—	3.7	—	17	31%	95	6.3	55
Donnie Edwards	*34*	*ILB*	*152*	*18.9%*	*3*	*82*	*27*	*54%*	*5.5*	*2.5*	*2*	*3*	*80*	*59%*	*71*	*4.0*	*76*	*55*	*54%*	*38*	*5.9*	*30*
Napoleon Harris	*28*	*ILB*	*64*	*9.9%*	*72*	*32*	*15*	*50%*	*5.0*	*2.5*	*4*	*7*	*35*	*60%*	*66*	*3.3*	*38*	*21*	*34%*	*91*	*8.8*	*91*

Year	Yards	ALY	Rank	Power	Rank	10+ Yds	Rank	Stuff	Rank	Sack	ASR	Rank
2004	4.63	4.01	8	67%	22	25%	29	29%	4	42	8.9%	2
2005	4.10	3.87	10	65%	20	21%	27	25%	16	28	5.0%	29
2006	4.15	4.23	15	63%	13	17%	22	28%	5	32	5.6%	28

Year	LE	Rank	LT	Rank	Mid	Rank	RT	Rank	RE	Rank
2004	4.53	20	4.55	21	3.87	6	4.28	19	2.87	6
2005	3.37	7	3.86	10	3.99	14	3.84	11	4.47	21
2006	4.43	19	4.18	12	3.92	3	4.77	27	5.01	30

The key to the front seven will be how well the two free-agent linebackers, Napoleon Harris and Donnie Edwards, can be integrated into Herm Edwards's defense. Harris had a great year as the middle linebacker in Minnesota last season and should be a solid addition. There aren't many 255-pounders who can pursue opposing running backs as well as Harris can, although the Chiefs will want to limit how much they use Harris in pass coverage. Edwards is a playmaker who has been a very good linebacker for years, but at age 34 it seems inevitable that he'll slow down soon. Edwards will move from 3-4 inside linebacker in San Diego to 4-3 outside linebacker in Kansas City, but he's been so versatile in his career that he shouldn't have a problem with the position switch. Derrick Johnson, the only holdover among the three starting linebackers, is lightning fast but doesn't fly around the field the way a player with his athleticism should.

Defensive end Tamba Hali, the Chiefs' 2006 first-round draft pick, was a good-looking rookie who led the team with eight sacks. He'll need to be even better at the start of 2007, as defensive end Jared Allen will miss the first four games because of a league suspension. The Chiefs added two defensive tackles on the first day of the draft, Turk McBride of Tennessee in the second round and Tank Tyler of North Carolina State in the third. That's not much of a vote of confidence in the projected starters, James Reed and Ron Edwards, even though our stats indicate that the defensive tackle position was far from the Chiefs' biggest need. Kansas City was fifth in stuffing opposing runners and third in Adjusted Line Yards up the middle.

Defensive Secondary

Secondary	Age	Pos	Plys	TmPct	Rk	Stop	Dfts	RuYd	Rk	RuStp	Rk	Tgts	Tgt%	Rk	Dist	Suc%	Rk	PaYd	Rk	PD	Int
Patrick Surtain	31	CB	74	9.2%	36	34	14	4.6	16	50%	22	47	12%	77	10.4	51%	45	6.9	28	6	1
Ty Law	33	CB	78	9.7%	30	29	12	4.8	20	38%	50	75	20%	30	8.7	43%	74	8.6	64	10	4
Lenny Walls*	28	CB	31	3.9%	—	8	2	11.0	—	25%	—	38	10%	—	12.0	42%	—	8.9	—	4	0
Sammy Knight*	32	SS	86	10.7%	30	40	13	5.2	13	54%	15	32	8%	29	11.4	64%	9	5.5	9	5	1
Greg Wesley	29	FS	75	10.7%	31	24	12	7.7	58	32%	59	26	8%	33	18.4	53%	36	13.2	77	6	3
Jarrad Page	23	FS	39	4.9%	76	16	7	7.4	52	27%	66	23	6%	65	13.7	63%	12	5.1	3	5	3
Jon McGraw	*28*	*SS*	*35*	*4.2%*	*78*	*11*	*8*	*7.0*	*47*	*67%*	*3*	*33*	*7%*	*46*	*10.1*	*31%*	*77*	*12.5*	*75*	*2*	*0*

Year	Pass D Rank	DVOA vs. #1 WR	Rank	DVOA vs. #2 WR	Rank	DVOA vs. Other WR	Rank	DVOA vs. TE	Rank	DVOA vs. RB	Rank
2004	28	28.4%	27	-1.1%	15	4.0%	21	27.5%	29	28.2%	30
2005	16	-4.1%	10	3.2%	25	-41.5%	2	22.4%	25	11.9%	27
2006	22	-19.8%	3	9.7%	20	35.9%	31	-18.1%	9	-4.4%	12

Before the draft, the Chiefs' front office identified the secondary as an important area to upgrade given the advancing ages of starting cornerbacks Ty Law and Patrick Surtain. As the draft played out, however, the Chiefs never took a defensive back, so now they must pray that Law and Surtain can find the fountain of youth. There's plenty of evidence that Law has already lost his effectiveness. With the New York Jets in 2005, Law ranked 80th out of 83 cornerbacks in Success Rate. Last year in Kansas City, Law ranked 74th out of 81, and opponents clearly threw at Law and avoided Surtain.

There had been some talk that the Chiefs would trade eight-year veteran Greg Wesley, who has spent his entire career in Kansas City, but he appears set to start again at free safety. Sammy Knight, who started last season at strong safety, was released over the offseason, making the Chiefs' secondary a little younger. Last year's two rookie safeties, Jarrad Page and Bernard Pollard, played more on special teams than on defense, but one of them will likely start at strong safety alongside Wesley in 2007.

Special Teams

Year	DVOA	Rank	FG/XP	Rank	Net Punt	Rank	Punt Ret	Rank	Net Kick	Rank	Kick Ret	Rank	Hidden	Rank
2004	-0.5%	18	-4.9	24	-15.5	32	3.2	10	-5.1	26	19.1	1	-4.2	20
2005	-2.0%	24	-0.6	20	1.0	15	-2.9	22	-14.1	31	4.9	8	2.8	13
2006	1.3%	13	-3.6	24	14.4	2	2.2	10	-3.2	27	-2.2	16	7.9	6

Punter Dustin Colquitt is one of the best in the league; he has a strong leg and is excellent at directional punting, landing 23 punts inside the 20-yard line last year with just five touchbacks. The Chiefs used a fifth-round pick to make UCLA's Justin Medlock the first kicker taken in this year's draft, and in May they sent incumbent kicker Lawrence Tynes to the Giants for an undisclosed draft pick. Medlock should be an improvement on kickoffs, but not necessarily on field goals.

Longtime return man Dante Hall was traded to the Rams, but that's not as big a loss to the Chiefs' special teams as it was made out to be. It's been a few years since Hall played well enough to merit the media attention he gets. Wide receivers Jeff Webb and Eddie Kennison, running back Michael Bennett, and cornerback Benny Sapp will all get a chance to replace Hall on returns. Two little-noted free-agent signings could make a big difference on special teams. Long snapper J. P. Darche was signed from Seattle, and safety Jon McGraw was rescued from Detroit. The Chiefs' coaching staff has raved about Darche's abilities, while the coverage units should be aided by the addition of McGraw, who played well on the Lions' special teams last year.

Coaching Staff

Herm Edwards retained most of the assistants when he replaced Dick Vermeil last year, but just because Vermeil had a good staff in place doesn't mean that Edwards was right to keep the staff around. As a former assistant to Tony Dungy, Edwards comes from a Cover-2 defensive background, which isn't a great fit with defensive coordinator Guenther Cunningham, who likes to blitz more than Edwards does. Offensive coordinator Mike Solari doesn't seem like the right fit for Edwards, either. Solari spent seven years working under Al Saunders, who is known for his incredibly complex passing attack and detailed playbook. Edwards likes to run Larry Johnson into the line again and again, and Solari would wisely prefer to open things up. If the Chiefs don't make it back to the playoffs this year, the uneasy marriage between Edwards and his staff is likely to come to an end.

Miami Dolphins

The Nick Saban era was like a relationship anyone can fall into. You know this guy at work who's really happy because his girlfriend has really gone places—sure, she has no fashion sense and wears hoodies and these gigantic rings everywhere, but she's so well-loved that she can curse at television personalities and shove cameramen and everyone just thinks it's charming. She has a friend who she swears is *perfect* for you. You're a little skeptical because you've been set up before (the one with the mustache comes to mind), but eventually you go for it. At first, things are great—she's a little bit of a control freak, but you really like her and she seems to really like you. Then, after a couple of dates ... she gets bored.

She starts talking about her friend across town that she hasn't seen in a while and she wants to "get together with." You get suspicious and start spending a little less time together to give her "space." Those 16-hour days you used to spend together become ten-hour days, some of which actually involve Cleo Lemon. She denies her disinterest, saying she's totally committed and wants to take things to the next level, but you hesitate on having her move in, telling her, "let's not make plans for after this season, babe." The same awful cycle of denial and gossip continues and then one day, you wake up and there she is on TV, holding a press conference about how she's fallen in love with the University of Alabama and they're signing an eight-year lease together.

With that January 3 press conference, Saban became the first NFL head coach to voluntarily leave for a college job since Al Groh went from the Jets to Virginia in 2001. While the move hurt Dolphins fans, it was inevitable and for the best: Saban's skill set and motivational tactics lend themselves to college players, not professional ones. His career as an NFL head coach is over. There will be a Patriots scout stationed in Alabama for about the next eight seasons, but it's time for the Dolphins to move on.

Saban's replacement, former Chargers offensive coordinator Cam Cameron, inherits a house that even Under Armour might write off. Cameron's defensive coordinator, Dom Capers, actually makes more money than he does. His star player, 2006 Defensive Player of the Year Jason Taylor, turns 33 on September 1. Middle linebacker Zach Thomas turns 34 the same day.

Not only are Taylor and Thomas old, but the rest of the Dolphins' front seven were feeling a little creaky in 2006. From 2001 to 2006, the average age of a starter on an NFL front seven was 27.6 years old; last year's Dolphins' front seven averaged 31.3 years old (table 1), which tied Miami's own 2005 group as the oldest front seven in that six-year span.

The good thing for Cameron is that the age might not be a problem. The Miami defense has continued to play well the last couple years despite the advancement of time. The secondary is younger this year, albeit less talented, and there are younger players in the front seven who will see their roles expanded. The Dolphins will likely start 25-year-old Matt Roth at defensive end, and 24-year-old outside linebacker Channing Crowder will play more in passing situations. The team also hopes that former Texas star defensive tackle Rodrique Wright, a first-round talent who went in the seventh round of the 2006 draft after tearing his rotator cuff, will work his way into the rotation after missing all of his rookie season. However, the biggest addition to the Dolphins' defense will be another elder statesman: former All-Pro linebacker Joey Porter, who signed with Miami after Pittsburgh made him a salary cap casualty.

There was talk at the end of last season that Porter had lost a step because his sack total had gone down; if that's

---

DOLPHINS PROSPECTUS

2006 Record: 6–10

DVOA Estimated Wins: 7.2 (21st)

Pythagorean Wins: 7.2 (19th)

DVOA: −3.9% total (17th), 0.2% weighted (19th)

Offense: −12.2% DVOA (28th)

Defense: −8.9% DVOA (7th)

Special Teams: −0.7% DVOA (21st)

Variance: 13.0% (23rd)

2006: Pick your favorite spectre hanging over the season: Daunte Culpepper, Wayne Huizenga, Nick Saban, Dan Marino ...

2007: The only thing worse than one Chris Chambers is two Chris Chambers.

2007 Mean Projection: 5.6 wins

The Brohm Closet (0–4): 31%

Bad Team (5–6): 37%

Mediocre (7–8): 24%

Playoff Contender (9–10): 7%

Super Bowl Contender (11+): 1%

Projected Average Opponent: 5.4% DVOA (2nd in NFL)

Table 1. Oldest Front Sevens, 2001–2006

Year	Team	Avg Age	Wins	AdjSack %	AdjLine Yd	Power	10+ Yds	Stuff
2005	MIA	31.3	9	8.0%	3.64	54%	19%	28%
2006	MIA	31.3	6	7.9%	3.87	66%	11%	23%
2002	OAK	31.0	11	6.4%	4.11	61%	16%	24%
2006	TB	30.9	4	4.7%	4.21	74%	15%	24%
2006	CLE	30.7	4	5.0%	4.71	58%	20%	23%
2003	WAS	30.4	5	4.8%	4.50	63%	15%	20%
2004	MIA	30.3	4	7.2%	4.25	50%	20%	23%
2003	SEA	30.1	10	6.6%	4.24	65%	9%	20%
2004	DAL	30.1	6	6.0%	4.44	61%	17%	22%
2006	WAS	30.1	5	4.3%	4.77	62%	18%	21%
Oldest 10		**30.6**	**6**	**6.1%**	**4.27**	**61%**	**16%**	**23%**
All Defenses		**27.6**	**8**	**6.5%**	**4.14**	**64%**	**17%**	**25%**

NOTE: Age based on opening day starters.

the case, it wasn't borne out by his pass coverage numbers from our game charting project, which were virtually identical to 2005. The bigger concern is that Pittsburgh linebackers from the Bill Cowher regime have tended to go bust after leaving the Steel City—ask Kansas City fans about Kendrell Bell sometime. Porter is guaranteed $20 million regardless, unless the Dolphins can find a clause about beating AFC offensive tackles up inside casinos.

The other advantage of the Porter signing is that it allowed the Dolphins to use their first-round pick on the franchise quarterback they've needed since...Wait a minute...instead of drafting Brady Quinn with the ninth overall pick—to the surprise of everyone including, and most emphatically, Brady Quinn—the Dolphins chose Ohio State wideout Ted Ginn Jr. and his 4.28, 40 time, opting to grab BYU quarterback John Beck in the second round instead. While wide receiver was undoubtedly a need for the Dolphins after the loss of Wes Welker and the struggles of Chris Chambers, drafting Ginn was a shocking, bold move.

Ginn represents a scouting conflict that has come up frequently in sabermetric discussions of baseball, but has yet to be addressed in football outside of David Lewin's quarterback projection system: the difference between tools and skills. Ginn's speed and potential as a returner are unquestioned, but his aptitude as a wide receiver is another case entirely. A typical scouting report comes from Rob Rang of NFLDraftScout.com, who wrote, "I see a player who lacks size, courage over the middle, and is both a sloppy route-runner and an inconsistent pass catcher." It's one thing to be a sloppy route-runner when you primarily run three routes, as Ginn did at Ohio State; doing it in the NFL is a ticket to Canada.

Chambers is a similar player, albeit a better one. He is probably the best leaper in the NFL, has great speed, and is capable of amazing catches that show up in *SportsCenter* montages. On the other hand, *SportsCenter* doesn't show the 94 passes intended for him that went incomplete last year, most in the league. All those incomplete passes led to Chambers having the worst DVOA and DPAR of any regular wide receiver in football by a wide margin. While it's easy to chalk this up to Joey Harrington, Chambers has yet to have a year in which he catches even a league-average percentage of the passes thrown to him. Since Chambers has played with five different starting quarterbacks, Occam's Razor would suggest that this is the wide receiver's fault.

How much is raw speed an indicator that a wide receiver will blossom in the NFL? Ginn's measurables (table 2) all match up very well to those of Texans receiver Jerome Mathis, who was a Pro Bowl return man his rookie season before getting hurt in a motorcycle accident before the 2006 season. Both before and after his injury, Mathis has had no role in a Texans' passing attack that desperately needs a receiver across from Andre Johnson. The only significant difference between the two is that Mathis played for Hampton and was never on television, while Ginn played for Ohio State and has Dan Fouts's number in his cell phone.

Table 2. Fastest 40-Yard Dashes by WR at Combine, 1999–2007

Year	Name	Ht	Wt	40	Vert	Jump	School
1999	Rondel Menendez	5′ 9″	178	4.24	37.0	9′ 9″	Eastern Kentucky
2005	Jerome Mathis	5′ 11″	181	4.28	35.5	10′ 3″	Hampton
2007	Ted Ginn*	5′ 11″	178	4.28	34.5	9′ 2″	Ohio St
2002	Aaron Lockett	5′ 7″	155	4.31	35.0	9′ 11″	Kansas State
2001	Santana Moss	5′ 9″	181	4.31	42.0	n/a	Miami
2002	Tim Carter	5′ 11″	190	4.32	39.0	10′ 6″	Auburn
2005	Troy Williamson	6′ 1″	203	4.32	37.0	n/a	South Carolina
2007	Carl Berman	5′ 9″	166	4.32	38.5	10′ 9″	Indiana St
1999	Karsten Bailey	5′ 11″	205	4.33	40.0	10′ 1″	Auburn
2001	Chris Chambers	5′ 11″	210	4.33	45.0	11′ 2″	Wisconsin

* Ginn did not attend combine—numbers are those provided by NFL for a campus workout.

2007 Dolphins Schedule

Week	Opp	Week	Opp	Week	Opp
1	at WAS	7	NE	13	NYJ
2	DAL	8	NYG	14	at BUF
3	at NYJ	9	BYE	15	BAL
4	OAK	10	BUF	16	at NE
5	at HOU	11	at PHI	17	CIN
6	at CLE	12	at PIT (Mon.)		

Perhaps consequently, Ginn was a first-round pick, while Mathis was not.

Some might look at the table and see the names of Santana Moss and Chambers as proof that Ginn's skills will translate to NFL success. However, Moss was many times the route runner Ginn was, and Chambers's leaping ability far surpasses Ginn's.

In early June, Miami turned rumor into reality by finally sending a fifth-round pick to Kansas City for quarterback: Trent Green. Green struggled in 2006 after returning from the gruesome concussion he suffered in Week 1, but he represents a likely upgrade over Joey Harrington and the leftover bits and pieces of Daunte Culpepper. Still, it's not a sure bet by any stretch that Green will turn the Dolphins' offense around; he won't be operating behind the old Chiefs offensive line, nor will he have Tony Gonzalez and Eddie Kennison running patterns for him. Chambers is likely to get better with or without Green, solely because it's impossible for him to play much worse than he did last year, but putting Green under center won't suddenly turn Chambers into an elite receiver. The losses of Welker and Randy McMichael, meanwhile, mean that the Dolphins' offense is likely to attempt a vertical passing attack that only Al Davis could love.

It won't matter much if Green is only keeping the seat warm. The selection of Beck in the second round was an astute one. As a four-year starter with a completion percentage over 62 percent, Beck projects to be about as good as Quinn according to our college quarterback forecasting system. Even allowing for the fact that Beck played in a spread offense while Quinn played in more of a pro-style scheme, Beck should be at least a capable NFL starter. However, since Beck went on a Mormon mission during college, he is entering the league at the advanced age of 26. If he's going to avoid the Chris Weinke career path, he needs to get the starting job and begin impressing people as soon as possible.

It's a shame that the team has yet to put together a cohesive passing attack, because if they did, Ronnie Brown would run for 1,500 yards. While Brown has been limited to 207 and 241 carries over his first two seasons due to Ricky

Williams and a fluke hand injury, he remains an explosive runner with all the skills needed to be an elite-caliber back. Losing underrated left tackle Damion McIntosh won't help, but the reuniting of offensive line coach Hudson Houck and Cam Cameron might fit better schematically than Houck and Saban.

In the past, the Dolphins have traded draft picks to shore up their skill position personnel by adding mediocrities such as Lamar Gordon and A. J. Feeley, thus costing the team opportunities to add real playmakers. From 2002 to 2006, the Dolphins traded away five first-day draft picks, picks that could not only have netted them better players at the desired positions, but also turned into Pro Bowlers at other spots as well. The first of two first-round picks traded for Ricky Williams turned into Pro Bowl defensive end Charles Grant; the second could've been used on the top running back in that year's draft, Larry Johnson. One year of Feeley was acquired in exchange for the pick that became wide receiver Reggie Brown; holding on to the pick and taking Brown could've saved the Dolphins from reaching for Ginn.

It seems strange that a team with so many flaws could've been talked about as a Super Bowl contender before the 2006 season, but the Dolphins seemed to have a lot more of the crucial parts than they actually did. This team has much lower expectations for 2007, and they're likely to meet them. Their schedule is too tough, they have too many holes on offense, and, unless they figure out a way to put Marty Booker's brain in Ted Ginn's body, they just spent their first-round pick on a special teams guy. John Beck may throw passes as well as Brady Quinn, but how often will Ted Ginn actually be catching them?

Bill Barnwell

Will Cam Cameron Revolutionize the Miami Offense?

The Miami Dolphins have been built around defense since the end of the Dan Marino era, ranking in the top-ten in defensive DVOA every season since 1997. The Dolphins offense, meanwhile, has ranked in the bottom half of the league every year since 1999, with the exception of 2002 when it ranked 13th. DVOA goes back to 1996, and the Dolphins have never had a top-ten offense during that span.

With this in mind, the Dolphins hired Cam Cameron as their new head coach. In the five years Cameron was offensive coordinator in San Diego, the Chargers offense never had a negative DVOA. In each of the past three years, the San Diego offense ranked sixth in the league or higher.

The Dolphins clearly hope that Cameron's presence can jumpstart their long moribund offense. They aren't the only team that hired a head coach with a specific unit in mind. San Diego hired Norv Turner because they needed an offensive mind who could replace Cameron, while Dallas hired Wade Phillips with the hope that he can improve their 3-4 defense.

Does a new head coach with a reputation on one side of the ball really bring quick improvement to that specific unit? To find out, we looked at every new coach hired between 1997 and 2006, excluding midseason replacements such as Mike Tice and coordinators promoted from within, such as Mike Martz in St. Louis or Dave Campo in Dallas.

So, based on our research, can Dolphins fans expect their offense to catapult to the top of the league in Cameron's first season? The answer to that is clearly no. The average improvement on offense for teams hiring an offense-minded head coach is an insignificant 0.6% DVOA. The average improvement on defense with a defense-minded coach is only slightly better, 1.4% DVOA. Needless to say, these extremely modest improvements are not exactly what an organization is hoping for when they spend millions on a new head coach.

Although neither offenses nor defenses show much improvement when a new coach takes the reins, there is a marked difference in the average starting point between the two types. For the purposes of this study, 30 teams hired offensive-minded coaches and 31 hired defensive-minded coaches. The offensive-minded coaches took over teams with an average offensive DVOA the previous season of –9.5%, while the defensive coaches took over teams that were exactly league-average (–0.02%, to be precise). This past offseason was no different. Pittsburgh and Dallas, the two teams that hired former defensive coordinators, averaged –3.4% DVOA in 2006. (Remember, a negative DVOA favors the defense.) Even with the influence of San Diego's powerful offense, the ineptitude in Atlanta, Arizona, Miami, and Oakland gives the average team that hired an offense-minded coach a –7.7% DVOA.

San Diego is a special case, but teams generally seem to only hire offensive coaches when they have a below-average offense. Only three of the 30 offensive head coaches in the study joined teams with an above-average offense in the previous season: Dennis Erickson and Steve Mariucci in San Francisco, and Dick Vermeil in Kansas City. Fourteen out of the 31 teams who hired a defensive coach had an above-average defense the season before.

Regression to the mean is a powerful force, and this discrepancy between offensive and defensive coaches hints that defensive coaches are providing a much greater return. It is a simple law of statistics that all teams trend back towards average over time. Consider that, of the ten

defensive-minded coaches who took over teams with a defensive DVOA of 5.0% or worse, nine saw improvement in their first season. These improvements were modest for the most part—only three were greater than ten points of DVOA—but this performance is still better than the performance for similar offenses. Only six of the bottom ten teams who hired offensive-minded head coaches improved, even though those coaches were taking over comparatively worse units.

Of course, a team does not hire a head coach merely for one year. An instant improvement is nice, but how do these teams look two or three years down the line?

The sample for multiple years is a bit more limited, since we only have one year of data for last year's new coaches, and some coaches get fired after just one or two years. Still, the data appears instructive. The average defense with a new defensive head coach was better by 2.3% DVOA two years later, and better by 5.0% DVOA after three years. These averages are held down by two specific teams: the Jets under Herm Edwards, whose defense was more than 20 DVOA points worse after two years and just as bad in year three, and the Bills under Gregg Williams, 20 points worse after two years. The only other coach with a decline greater than one DVOA point in both seasons is Bill Belichick, whose 2001 and 2002 defenses were both worse than Pete Carroll's last defense in 1999.

The teams that hire offensive coordinators as coaches see units that improve more over time, but with a major caveat. The improvement after two years is 6.6% DVOA, and over three years, it averages 11% DVOA. However, one-third of offensive head coaches hired between 1997 and 2004 did not even make it to their third season and are not included in these numbers. Among those fired after two years were Chan Gailey, Norv Turner, and Steve Spurrier, all of whom had actually improved their offenses at that point. Of the coaches who made it three years, only Steve Mariucci (in San Francisco) and Dan Reeves saw substantial declines, but both had impressive seasons the year before and would have successful offensive teams in future years.

It's interesting that Gailey, Turner, and Spurrier all have reputations as poor head coaches, but the three teams that fired them all saw their offenses improve while they were head coach, then experienced significant declines in offense the year after they were fired. The Cowboys offense tanked in Troy Aikman's last season. The Redskins found no magic in the first year of Joe Gibbs's return. And Oakland just wants to ignore the second Art Shell era.

The uneven results of those three coaches highlights one problem with this method of evaluating the potential for success of an extraordinary coordinator such as Cameron. In this study, Shell is treated the same as Mike Holmgren. We have not introduced a way to separate an "offensive genius" from a pedestrian coach with an offensive background. Not enough coaches were coordinating the year before to use previous year's DVOA as a predictor. Any subjective separation of coaches based on reputation would be colored by their success or lack thereof as a head coach. Marty Mornhinweg, for example, had a sterling reputation when he was hired by Detroit, but was a national punch-line after his embarrassing tenure as head coach. Now, after a successful season coordinating in Philadelphia, he has regained his status as innovative offensive mind. Further, some of the best initial improvements came from coaches who were not highly successful in their previous stop. Scott Linehan and Dick Jauron oversaw the 21st ranked offense and defense respectively in 2005. In his first year as head coach, Linehan oversaw a nearly 16-point improvement in the DVOA of the St. Louis offense, while Jauron spearheaded a nine-point improvement in Buffalo's defense.

Still, our results indicate that a defensive-minded head coach might be able to get more immediate results. This should not be too surprising because defense varies more from year to year. Substantial jumps in offensive performance are simply rarer. Then again, the fact that defensive coaches take over better units makes their improvement relatively more impressive. Again, thanks to our friend regression to the mean, it is more difficult to improve from average to above-average than from below-average to average.

Only three of the 11 offensive coaches who took over a team within five points of the Dolphins' 2006 offensive DVOA improved the offense by more than seven points the next season (table 3). One of these teams was the 2006 Saints, but, as we learn in the New Orleans chapter, a team that lost a

Table 3. Improvement in First Year with Offense-Oriented Head Coach

Year	Team	New Coach	DVOA Y−1	DVOA
2006	GB	McCarthy	−7.0%	−6.3%
1999	SEA	Holmgren	−7.1%	−2.5%
2004	WAS	Gibbs	−7.2%	−17.0%
2004	OAK	Turner	−11.1%	0.1%
1999	BAL	Billick	−11.7%	−18.8%
2007	MIA	Cameron	−11.8%	—
2002	WAS	Spurrier	−11.9%	−7.1%
1997	SD	Gilbride	−12.7%	−29.2%
2001	DET	Mornhingweg	−12.9%	−14.0%
2006	NO	Payton	−13.4%	13.7%
2004	NYG	Coughlin	−13.8%	−6.8%

season to a hurricane should not be considered a statistical predictor for anything. Another was the 2004 Raiders, who added Randy Moss. The third example, and maybe the best hope for Miami, was the 2004 Giants. Tiki Barber reached an elite level under new coach Tom Coughlin, and the offense improved by seven DVOA points despite the growing pains of rookie quarterback Eli Manning. If Cameron can do the same for Ronnie Brown, then maybe Miami can defy the odds.

Ultimately, both offensive and defensive coaches see gains made over two and three years, so it looks as though Dolphins fans are going to get the offensive improvement they so desperately desire. They simply need to be patient about it. By the end of the decade, the Dolphins will likely have a much improved offense thanks to the hire of Cam Cameron.

Ned Macey

Dolphins 2006 Stats by Week

Wk	vs.	W–L	PF	PA	YDF	YDA	TO	Total	Off	Def	ST
1	@PIT	L	17	28	278	342	-1	-8.1%	-19.4%	1.5%	12.8%
2	BUF	L	6	16	282	171	-1	-52.1%	-20.1%	11.8%	-20.2%
3	TEN	W	13	10	289	316	+2	-8.3%	-14.7%	-12.7%	-6.3%
4	@HOU	L	15	17	289	276	+2	15.6%	-3.3%	-15.0%	3.9%
5	@NE	L	10	20	283	213	-2	-25.5%	-20.5%	-6.7%	-11.7%
6	@NYJ	L	17	20	395	272	-3	-18.3%	-15.4%	1.3%	-1.7%
7	GB	L	24	34	448	346	-2	-8.2%	-4.0%	2.6%	-1.7%
8	BYE										
9	@CHI	W	31	13	298	292	+4	41.3%	-9.9%	-49.0%	2.2%
10	KC	W	13	10	306	265	-1	-0.7%	-11.5%	-11.5%	-0.8%
11	MIN	W	24	20	261	361	+1	-26.1%	-20.1%	-3.0%	-9.0%
12	@DET	W	27	10	395	220	0	46.2%	4.6%	-35.4%	6.2%
13	JAC	L	10	24	309	353	-1	-45.2%	4.6%	42.7%	-7.1%
14	NE	W	21	0	315	189	+3	85.6%	22.3%	-57.6%	5.8%
15	@BUF	L	0	21	212	286	0	-53.5%	-57.0%	-3.7%	-0.2%
16	NYJ	L	10	13	253	324	+1	-14.6%	-25.3%	-8.1%	2.7%
17	@IND	L	22	27	399	354	0	-0.3%	-5.0%	9.2%	13.9%

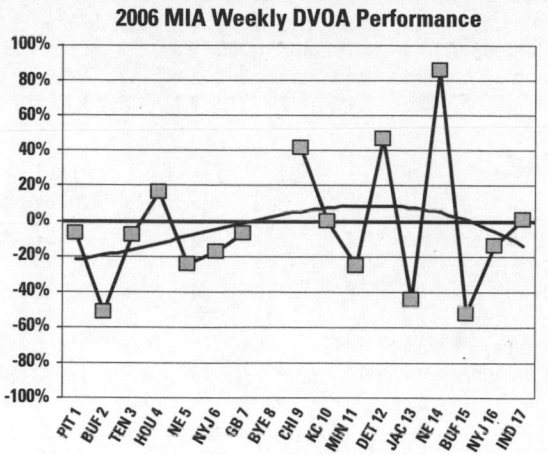

2006 MIA Weekly DVOA Performance

Trends and Splits

	Offense	Rank	Defense	Rank
Total DVOA	-12.2%	28	-8.9%	7
Unadjusted VOA	-10.7%	27	-9.9%	6
Weighted Trend	-11.0%	24	-10.2%	9
Variance	2.8%	32	5.4%	24
Passing	-11.9%	24	1.0%	12
Rushing	-12.0%	28	-19.5%	3
First Down	-11.9%	23	-24.5%	1
Second Down	-23.0%	30	-8.3%	8
Third Down	3.1%	16	17.6%	25
Red Zone	-28.6%	28	-2.9%	11
Late and Close	-13.3%	25	-1.5%	14

Five-Year Performance

	2006	2005	2004	2003	2002
W-L	6-10	9-7	4-12	10-6	9-7
Pythagorean Wins	7.2	8.0	5.7	9.6	10.1
Estimated Wins	7.2	8.8	6.6	9.6	10.4
Total DVOA	-3.9%	3.2%	-14.0%	12.5%	24.9%
Rank	17	13	23	10	4
Offense	-12.2%	-7.5%	-28.9%	-8.0%	6.2%
Rank	28	21	31	20	13
Defense	-8.9%	-7.9%	-9.8%	-18.1%	-16.1%
Rank	7	10	7	4	2
Special Teams	-0.7%	2.8%	5.0%	2.5%	2.6%
Rank	21	4	4	7	9

Strategic Tendencies

Formations		Rank	Run/Pass		Rank	Defense		Rank	Other		Rank
3+ WR	57%	5	Runs, all plays	38%	31	Sacks by LB	12%	26	Run with 2+ RB	53%	22
4+ WR	14%	11	Runs, first half	41%	27	Sacks by DB	6%	18	Run with 2+ TE	43%	8
2+ TE	25%	19	Runs, first down	49%	23	Rush 6+	10.0%	12	Play action	15%	24
Single back	64%	5	Runs, power sit.	70%	9	Rush 7+	1.6%	13	Go for it on 4th	0.68	29
Empty back	2.3%	14	Runs, behind 2H	24%	31	Rush 3	1.6%	28	Offensive Pace	30.0	12
Max protect	18%	3	Pass, ahead 2H	41%	19	CB1 on WR1	40%	21	Defensive Pace	30.1	8

More than two-thirds of all Miami passes came from a shotgun formation, the highest percentage in the league.... Miami had a 22.6% DVOA passing the ball with four wide receivers (12th in the NFL) and a negative passing DVOA in every other formation.... Miami had the league's worst DVOA on play-action passes (−54.4%) and gained just four yards per play-action pass.... Miami led the league in dropped passes with 46. Wide receiver Chris Chambers and tight end Randy McMichael were tied for fourth among individual receivers with 11 each.... Miami's defense faced the lowest number of screen passes in the NFL, and for good reason, as it posted the fifth-best DVOA against screens (−44.7%).... The Dolphins were tied for second in most sacks against a max protect blocking scheme.

Passing

Player	DPAR	DVOA	Plys	NtYds	Avg	YAC	C%	TD	Int
Joey Harrington*	5.7	-9.9%	386	2122	5.5	4.0	57.8%	12	15
Daunte Culpepper	1.4	-11.2%	133	785	5.9	6.7	60.9%	2	3
Cleo Lemon	8.4	14.9%	65	388	6.0	3.2	58.5%	2	1
Trent Green	*15.6*	*3.4%*	*198*	*1210*	*6.1*	*4.0*	*61.1%*	*7*	*9*

Rushing

Player	DPAR	DVOA	Plys	Yds	Avg	TD	Fum	Suc
Ronnie Brown	3.5	-10.3%	241	995	4.1	5	4	46%
Sammy Morris	-2.2	-19.3%	92	403	4.4	1	2	42%
Travis Minor*	1.5	7.2%	19	74	3.9	0	0	0%
Joey Harrington*	-2.2	-50.6%	12	28	2.3	0	4	—
Chris Chambers	3.4	35.6%	8	95	11.9	0	0	—
Daunte Culpepper	-0.1	-14.7%	7	23	3.3	1	3	—
Lee Suggs	0.7	9.6%	6	26	4.3	0	0	39%
Marty Booker	0.3	-10.1%	3	19	6.3	0	0	—
Trent Green	*-0.8*	*-30.5%*	*11*	*57*	*5.2*	*0*	*5*	*—*

Receiving

Player	DPAR	DVOA	Plys	Ctch	Yds	Y/C	YAC	TD	C%
WR									
Chris Chambers	-19.8	-33.6%	153	59	677	11.5	3.1	4	61%
Wes Welker*	9.6	0.1%	100	67	687	10.3	3.8	1	67%
Marty Booker	16.7	13.6%	90	55	747	13.6	4.8	6	39%
Derek Hagan	2.7	-3.1%	37	21	221	10.5	2.2	1	57%
TE									
Randy McMichael*	13.9	11.1%	96	62	640	10.3	4.9	3	65%
Justin Peelle	1.8	3.6%	18	16	116	7.3	3.9	1	89%
David Martin	*3.9*	*5.3%*	*36*	*21*	*198*	*9.4*	*3.5*	*2*	*47%*
RB									
Ronnie Brown	5.3	16.6%	38	33	276	8.4	7.7	0	87%
Sammy Morris	-4.1	-33.3%	35	21	162	7.7	7.1	0	60%
Darian Barnes*	-1.9	-63.3%	7	3	22	7.3	5.0	0	43%

Offensive Line

Year	Yards	ALY	Rank	Power	Rank	10+ Yds	Rank	Stuff	Rank	Sack	ASR	Rank
2004	3.45	3.48	32	73%	4	17%	18	30%	32	52	8.5%	25
2005	4.35	4.33	11	71%	6	19%	14	23%	8	26	4.8%	5
2006	4.18	4.22	20	70%	9	19%	10	25%	18	41	7.0%	20

Year	LE	Rank	LT	Rank	Mid	Rank	RT	Rank	RE	Rank
2004	2.53	32	3.26	31	3.52	32	3.45	30	4.10	12
2005	5.00	6	5.13	1	4.21	13	4.21	15	3.92	17
2006	3.43	25	4.66	10	4.05	24	4.76	2	4.91	6

It was a tale of two lines in Miami last season. Free-agent signing L. J. Shelton became the new starting left tackle, with incumbent Damion McIntosh moving to right guard, Rex Hadnot shifting to center, and Seth McKinney going to the bench. The result was a line that didn't do the newly immobile Daunte Culpepper any favors (21 sacks in Culpepper's four games) and struggled to open up holes for Ronnie Brown. After a Week 5 loss to New England, the Dolphins threw their hands up and changed everything. Shelton went to right guard, while McIntosh, who'd been injured the first three weeks of the season, went back to left tackle. At the time, Nick Saban said, "Damion is probably a better left tackle than he was a guard." Oops.

Miami's Adjusted Line Yards went from 3.75 before the change to a slightly-above-average 4.15 after. While McIntosh isn't regarded as an elite left tackle, he's always looked good according to our metrics, and Kansas City—a team that knows something about linemen—signed him to a six-year free-agent contract. Back in Miami, Vernon Carey will move over from the right side to man left tackle, where he struggled in a short stint as a rookie. Shelton will likely move to right tackle despite his ineptitude at pass blocking, which will be magnified on the outside.

Left guard Jeno James, who struggled through injuries before going on injured reserve, was cut in the offseason. His likely replacement is either Arizona refugee Chris Liwienski or James's 2006 replacement, utility lineman Kendyl Jacox. Former Notre Dame guard Dan Stevenson could occupy the right side. Stevenson was drafted by the Patriots in the sixth round in 2006, but ended up on the Miami practice squad at midseason. If he starts on opening day of 2007, it will be his first NFL game.

Also arriving is center Samson Satele, drafted in the second round out of Hawaii. Satele isn't the fastest offensive lineman, but he's stout at the point of attack, an excellent pass defender, and a leader on the line. If Satele wins the job at center, he'll push Hadnot to right guard. Satele didn't cut his hair once in four years at Hawaii, which shows his dedication, at the very least to his gimmick. Former Chiefs reserve center Jonathan Ingram also saw some time with the first team during minicamp.

Defensive Front Seven

Defensive Line	Age	Pos	Plys	TmPct	Rk	Stop	Dfts	StpRt	Rk	AvYd	Rk	Sack	Hit	Hur	Runs	RuStp	RuYd	Pass	PaStp	PaYd
Jason Taylor	33	DE	73	8.9%	6	53	30	73%	59	1.0	26	13.5	9	21	43	63%	2.7	30	87%	-1.4
Vonnie Holliday	32	DT	67	8.2%	5	56	19	84%	20	1.4	27	7	4	4	52	85%	2.3	15	80%	-1.9
Kevin Carter*	34	DE	47	5.8%	43	45	15	96%	1	0.6	11	5.5	4	5	37	95%	1.4	10	100%	-2.2
Keith Traylor	38	DT	39	5.5%	32	36	10	92%	3	0.5	7	4	0	3	33	91%	1.2	6	100%	-3.0
Matt Roth	25	DE	37	4.5%	63	29	9	78%	36	1.6	41	3.5	1	1	28	82%	1.9	9	67%	0.9
Jeff Zgonina*	37	DT	35	4.9%	45	25	6	71%	56	2.1	45	0	0	1	30	73%	2.2	5	60%	1.6
David Bowens*	30	DE	16	2.0%	—	16	16	100%	—	-1.1	—	5	0	1	4	100%	2.0	12	100%	-2.2
Dan Wilkinson	34	DT	16	3.1%	—	15	0	94%	—	1.8	—	0	0	1	13	92%	2.2	3	100%	0.0

Linebackers	Age	Pos	Plys	TmPct	Rk	Stop	Dfts	StpRt	AvYd	Sack	Hit	Hur	Runs	RuStp	Rk	RuYd	Rk	Tgts	Suc%	Rk	PaYd	Rk
Zach Thomas	34	ILB	173	21.2%	1	105	24	61%	4.2	3	0	5	116	66%	46	3.5	52	62	65%	8	6.5	60
Channing Crowder	24	OLB	108	13.2%	40	57	9	53%	4.2	1	4	2	82	55%	84	3.8	67	28	32%	94	6.2	48
Donnie Spragan	31	OLB	49	6.0%	—	33	5	67%	3.8	1.5	1	3	30	73%	—	3.1	—	19	59%	20	4.2	9
Joey Porter	*30*	*OLB*	*60*	*8.7%*	*81*	*43*	*18*	*72%*	*2.1*	*7*	*4*	*5*	*40*	*68%*	*35*	*2.6*	*10*	*21*	*74%*	*2*	*4.9*	*17*

Year	Yards	ALY	Rank	Power	Rank	10+ Yds	Rank	Stuff	Rank	Sack	ASR	Rank
2004	4.40	4.28	18	50%	4	20%	23	23%	20	36	8.2%	6
2005	3.70	3.64	3	54%	3	19%	21	28%	5	49	8.3%	3
2006	3.55	3.87	6	66%	16	11%	2	24%	17	47	8.4%	4

Year	LE	Rank	LT	Rank	Mid	Rank	RT	Rank	RE	Rank
2004	4.75	26	3.99	8	4.48	25	3.94	10	3.75	15
2005	2.87	4	4.03	14	3.41	1	4.40	24	4.05	17
2006	3.68	12	4.47	16	4.03	9	3.24	5	3.07	5

Undersized defensive linemen aren't supposed to age well. Despite being only 255 pounds and turning 32 as the season started, Jason Taylor had the best season of his career in 2006. Perhaps buoyed by his cameo in *Jackass 2*, Taylor was the best pass rusher in the NFL that didn't fail a steroid test during the season, something he reminded the media about before they voted him Defensive Player of the Year. While his Stop Rate is low for an end, it's because the Dolphins use him in a hybrid DE/OLB role. Taylor's success had a cascading effect on the performance of the rest of the defense, specifically Kevin Carter. While Carter's lost a step, he still has the craftiness and footwork needed to be an effective end, especially given that the protection shielded towards Taylor. Carter's move to Tampa Bay pushes Matt Roth into the lineup. If Roth's going to be a useful player, he'll have his chance to show it this year because, as he did for Carter, Taylor will leave him with single blockers.

Defensive tackles Keith Traylor and Vonnie Holliday also had excellent years clogging up the middle, but they're a combined 70 years old, and Traylor, in particular, needs to log fewer snaps. Integrating Rodrique Wright and Fred Evans into the lineup is a necessity following Jeff Zgonina's move to Houston. Paul Solail, a 334-pound fourth-rounder from Utah, is a project, but Traylor makes the perfect mentor. Cameron also called him "the skinniest 340 [pounder] I've ever seen," which begs many questions.

Talk is that the Dolphins will rest Zach Thomas on nickel and dime situations by using Channing Crowder instead, but one look at Crowder's game charting numbers tells you that such a move is ill-advised. Crowder remains more of an athlete than a football player at this point. While defensive coordinator Dom Capers is foaming at the mouth over the idea of integrating Joey Porter with Taylor on the pass rush, the only starting Steelers linebacker during the Bill Cowher Era who improved after he left the Steel City was Kevin Greene—who, perhaps not coincidentally, did so under Dom Capers.

Defensive Secondary

Secondary	Age	Pos	Plys	TmPct	Rk	Stop	Dfts	RuYd	Rk	RuStp	Rk	Tgts	Tgt%	Rk	Dist	Suc%	Rk	PaYd	Rk	PD	Int
Will Allen	29	CB	69	9.0%	44	34	16	4.1	7	63%	8	82	20%	32	11.1	51%	47	7.4	35	10	1
Andre' Goodman	29	CB	46	6.0%	76	26	9	5.0	23	57%	15	54	13%	70	14.7	58%	15	8.7	65	8	0
Renaldo Hill	29	FS	94	11.5%	22	28	11	6.7	45	33%	58	49	10%	8	14.0	59%	22	5.9	13	9	2
Travis Daniels	25	CB	39	6.4%	72	12	5	6.7	42	23%	73	48	14%	64	13.4	49%	57	8.0	55	2	1
Yeremiah Bell	25	SS	77	9.4%	45	38	21	5.3	16	54%	18	47	10%	15	11.0	62%	16	7.4	34	10	0
Travares Tillman	30	SS	46	6.4%	68	16	6	5.5	20	45%	33	19	5%	70	11.6	47%	54	7.6	38	2	0
Jason Allen	24	FS	15	1.8%	—	4	3	10.5	—	0%	—	12	2%	—	15.5	67%	—	7.6	—	2	1

(continued next page)

Defensive Secondary (*continued*)

Year	Pass D Rank	DVOA vs. #1 WR	Rank	DVOA vs. #2 WR	Rank	DVOA vs. Other WR	Rank	DVOA vs. TE	Rank	DVOA vs. RB	Rank
2004	5	-3.5%	11	38.0%	32	-27.7%	2	-12.5%	10	-5.6%	12
2005	11	17.3%	25	1.0%	20	-21.1%	6	-5.9%	14	-14.7%	7
2006	12	1.5%	18	-3.0%	15	18.8%	27	3.3%	24	-12.3%	11

The virtual swap of Will Allen for Sam Madison ended up being a good one for the Dolphins. While Allen isn't a great player, the Dolphins' pass rush masks his weaknesses in coverage and allows his excellent instincts and reads to come to the forefront. Andre' Goodman and Travis Daniels split time across from Allen, and neither one can stay healthy. Daniels joined Saban on the trek from LSU to Miami, which means he's no longer coach's favorite, but Goodman's May shoulder surgery hands him the starting job. Last year's first-round selection, Jason Allen, was drafted as a cornerback, but played as a nickel back and reserve safety. He was moved back to corner during minicamp, but, as Dolphins beat writer Alex Marvez of the *South Florida Sun-Sentinel* wrote, "Let's just say it couldn't go any worse than it [did] at safety." It might be too early to call Allen a bust, but with new management not beholden to the pick, he might be the first 2006 first-round pick to be cut. Safety Renaldo Hill's first year in teal and coral was an excellent one, as he moved over from corner and represented a serious improvement over the departed Lance Schulters. If Jackson can't stay healthy, Hill might be pushed back to corner and Travares Tillman would start at safety. Tillman might also step in if Yeremiah Bell doesn't get better at run support.

Special Teams

Year	DVOA	Rank	FG/XP	Rank	Net Punt	Rank	Punt Ret	Rank	Net Kick	Rank	Kick Ret	Rank	Hidden	Rank
2004	4.7%	4	2.2	12	6.2	9	4.5	8	8.1	9	6.6	7	4.0	9
2005	3.1%	4	0.3	16	10.1	2	-0.9	16	7.8	3	1.0	16	-10.1	29
2006	-0.7%	21	-10.6	31	2.3	15	-1.7	18	10.3	5	-4.3	23	-4.0	22

Kicker Olindo Mare had a strange year. His vaunted leg strength was still there on kickoffs, and his six touchbacks against Indianapolis in the final week moved him ahead of New England's Stephen Gostkowski for the league lead in kickoff value. On field goals, however, Mare's accuracy disappeared when he was stretched out of his comfort zone, which tops out around 42 to 44 yards. Front offices always see the field goals first, so Miami traded Mare to New Orleans, where he'll replace John Carney and see his raw numbers bounce back in a dome. His replacement, former Giants kicker Jay Feely, doesn't have nearly the leg strength Mare does. Punter Donnie Jones was snapped up by the Rams after the Dolphins offered him the lowest restricted free agency tender possible, but Dolphins fans should not be sad to see him gone. Jones had the lowest punt value in the league last year, worth -7.4 points of field position compared to an average punter. Miami was only average in net punting because the coverage unit was so strong; they did not allow a return above 28 yards and forced three fumbles. Jones will be replaced by this year's seventh-round pick, Michigan punter Brandon Fields, who led the nation in punting in 2004, but struggles for consistency and form.

While Wes Welker was a solid return man, the return units would enjoy an immediate boost from a healthy Ted Ginn. This spring he was considering immobilizing his foot to speed up the healing process, which doesn't bode well. If Ginn can't go or gets hurt again, Az-Zahir Hakim would take over.

Coaching Staff

Cam Cameron, like many other new head coaches, represents someone far different than the man he replaced. While Nick Saban was a defense-minded authoritarian who demanded as much control as possible, Cameron is an offensive coach who knows his role within the organizational hierarchy. He will be calling the plays and serving as offensive coordinator as well, with Mike Mularkey going from head coach to offensive coordinator to tight ends coach over two seasons. Cameron has been particularly hard on Ronnie Brown and Chris Chambers since his appointment. Cameron's prior experience with Dolphins offensive line coach Hudson Houck in San Diego will hopefully expedite the line's development. Defensive coordinator Dom Capers remains the football coaching equivalent of baseball's quadruple-A player—too good to be a defensive coordinator, not good enough to be a head coach. Miami will reap the benefits until someone gets the itch to not develop any offensive players for four seasons.

New England Patriots

After the Patriots' dramatic loss to the Colts in the AFC Championship game, a roundtable discussion on the popular website Boston Sports Media Watch raised a provocative question: Was 2006 a successful season for the New England Patriots?

Running down the team's list of accomplishments makes it very difficult to say no. The Patriots won 12 games en route to the AFC East crown, ranked fifth in the league in total DVOA, won two playoff games, including a victory against the Chargers in San Diego, and were a couple of key third-down conversions away from another trip to the Super Bowl. Running back Laurence Maroney, their 2006 first-rounder, enjoyed a successful rookie season until a late-season shoulder injury; 2005 first-rounder Logan Mankins earned consideration for the Pro Bowl at guard; and cornerback Asante "Get Paid" Samuel had a breakout season that saw him intercept ten passes in the regular season and three more in the post-season.

On the other hand, there are plenty of arguments that the Patriots' season was not successful. The team won those 12 games in a mediocre division, often struggling against easily-beatable teams (witness their yearly loss to Miami as well as a close win over Detroit). While they did beat San Diego in the playoffs, it took some unbelievable fumble luck for them to do so, and, although they dominated Indianapolis for two quarters, the same Patriots team that "knew how to win" in the San Diego game flat out blew their trip to the Super Bowl.

There were signs of degradation amongst the Patriots' players for the first time since the 2002 season. The linebackers struggled throughout the season, with Tedy Bruschi losing a noticeable step in pass coverage, and Mike Vrabel losing about three or four. The late signing of Junior Seau did little to mitigate these problems, and Tully Banta-Cain failed

---

PATRIOTS PROSPECTUS

2006 Record: 12–4

DVOA Estimated Wins: 11.0 (4th)

Pythagorean Wins: 12.2 (3rd)

DVOA: 23.2% total (5th), 27.4% weighted (2nd)

Offense: 12.3% DVOA (6th)

Defense: −8.4% DVOA (9th)

Special Teams: 2.5% DVOA (8th)

Variance: 18.8% (7th)

2006: One day, we'll look back at the idea of Reche Caldwell as a number-one receiver and laugh.

2007: The team with something for everyone: notably, losses.

2007 Mean Projection: 12.1 wins

The Brohm Closet (0–4): 0%

Bad Team (5–6): 1%

Mediocre (7–8): 2%

Playoff Contender (9–10): 20%

Super Bowl Contender (11+): 77%

Projected Average Opponent: 1.8% DVOA (9th in NFL)

---

to emerge as much more than a situational pass rusher. The Patriots secondary continued to remain one of the most injury-prone in football, with seemingly everyone except for Samuel missing time at one point or another. In addition, while the Patriots' first-rounders were doing well, their second-rounders struggled dramatically. Despite a wide-open competition for wide receivers, 2006 second-rounder Chad Jackson never settled into the offense, tore his ACL in the AFC Championship game, and will likely spend 2007 on injured reserve. Marquise Hill, their 2004 second-rounder, only played four games, and was unable to crack the rotation at defensive end. Wide receiver Bethel Johnson, the second-round pick from 2003, was traded to New Orleans for defensive tackle Jonathan Sullivan in a bust-for-bust challenge trade. Sullivan was summarily cut and probably drowned his disappointments in a 64 oz. Coke and a box of donuts.

These performance issues were compounded by the front office's failure to anticipate the 2006 free-agent market and its boom in spending. As a result, the Patriots missed the opportunity to lock up both Samuel and wide receiver Deion Branch at below-market rates. Branch refused to sign with the team and was dealt to Seattle for a first-round pick as the 2006 season started, while Samuel has yet to sign his franchise tender at press time and could be traded as well. The Patriots ended up giving a contract similar to Branch's demands to Wes Welker, a useful player with nowhere near Branch's ability. The front office's failure to anticipate Branch's departure and the loss in performance of the linebackers resulted in castoffs and limited players such as receiver Reche Caldwell and linebacker Eric Alexander struggling to play key roles in the playoffs.

A sign that the Patriots viewed the 2006 season as a disappointment internally is that they didn't stand pat in

2007 Patriots Schedule

Week	Opp	Week	Opp	Week	Opp
1	at NYJ	7	at MIA	13	at BAL (Mon.)
2	SD	8	WAS	14	PIT
3	BUF	9	at IND	15	NYJ
4	at CIN (Mon.)	10	BYE	16	MIA
5	CLE	11	at BUF	17	at NYG (Sat.)
6	at DAL	12	PHI		

the offseason like they did after 2005. No longer patiently waiting for their long-term plan to bear fruit, the Patriots went out and added parts for a team designed to win now.

Their first move was signing Ravens linebacker Adalius Thomas to a five-year, $35-million contract to play outside in the Pats' 3-4 alignment. Though Thomas recorded 11 sacks last season, he's likely to be employed more as a pass defender as opposed to a pass rusher in 2007; any Patriots fan who is disappointed by that should think back to Dallas Clark and the AFC Championship Game. With Thomas playing the pass, Vrabel can concentrate on using the skills he still has: rushing the passer and stopping the run.

The Patriots' next move was to raid the division rival Dolphins for the few desirable parts of their offense. Free-agent acquisition Sammy Morris will serve as an all-purpose running back, occasionally playing halfback, splitting time with Heath Evans at fullback, and contributing on special teams. Slot receiver and return man Wes Welker was acquired for a second-round pick. Welker is not a unique player, but he is a useful one, and will give the Patriots more in 2007 than a rookie wide receiver who might have been taken with that pick.

Adding Welker was just the first step in a massive reconstruction of the Patriots' wide receiver corps. The Patriots signed former Saints and Eagles receiver Donte' Stallworth to a deal valued at six years and $30.5 million, but with only $3.5 million guaranteed. The contract will likely be renegotiated after the 2007 season because of a prohibitively expensive bonus due, but bringing in such a skilled receiver while making such a small commitment is an absolute coup for the Patriots. Stallworth's speed and ability to stretch the field and Welker's ability to get open in the slot and poke holes in zones will give Tom Brady two fantastic new targets to exploit.

The Patriots liked the Stallworth move so much that they decided to do it again a month later. Rumor had linked Randy Moss to the Patriots off and on for over a year. On the second day of the draft, just 24 hours after reports said the deal was officially dead, the Patriots dealt a fourth-round pick to the Raiders for Moss. They made their final decision after Moss agreed to restructure his contract by

waiving his right to several million dollars in bonuses, allowing the Patriots to cut him if his oversized personality can't fit within the organization, without the move costing them any salary cap space. While Moss isn't the same player he was when he left Minnesota, he's still a fantastic athlete with the ability to leap over smaller defensive backs (hello, Justin Miller, Ashton Youboty, and Andre' Goodman) and be a dominant force in the red zone. The Patriots' offense was already third in the league in passing inside the red zone last year (46.2% DVOA), and the addition of Moss makes Brady downright spoiled for choice inside the 20. Moss, Stallworth, and Welker are locks to make the team, with Caldwell, Jackson, playoff hero Jabar Gaffney, and Kelley Washington (signed as a free agent from Cincinnati) all competing for the other two or three wide receiver spots available. They might want to start buttering up backup quarterback Matt Cassel now.

The reason for all these moves? The core of this Patriots team is now entering its prime (table 1). While guys such as Bruschi, Vrabel, and Rodney Harrison are aging rapidly and becoming supplementary parts, the team's star players are in the 27–30 range, where they can be expected to be at their peak. The additions the team made this offseason are mostly like-minded; guys such as Morris, Stallworth, Welker, Moss, and Thomas can be expected to offer a lot over the next two to three seasons. By 2011, Brady will be 34, Matt Light 33, Richard Seymour 31, and Samuel,

Table 1. Patriots (Mostly) at Their Peak

Pos	Name	2007 Age
	Key Holdovers	
QB	Tom Brady	30
TE	Ben Watson	27
LT	Matt Light	29
C	Dan Koppen	28
DE	Richard Seymour	28
DE	Ty Warren	26
DT	Vince Wilfork	26
CB	Asante Samuel	26
CB/S	Eugene Wilson	27
	2007 Additions	
RB	Sammy Morris	30
WR	Randy Moss	30
WR	Donte' Stallworth	27
WR	Kelley Washington	28
WR	Wes Welker	26
TE	Kyle Brady	35
LB	Adalius Thomas	30
CB	Tory James	34
S	Brandon Meriweather	23

Vince Wilfork, and Ty Warren all 30. The Patriots' window of opportunity is over these next three seasons, with a particular focus (as evidenced by Moss's and Stallworth's contracts) on 2007.

On paper, the 2007 Patriots have the strongest roster of the Belichick era. The only glaring weakness is a lack of depth at certain important positions. A serious injury to Brady or Maroney would put this team in a very sticky situation. Samuel's return is in doubt at press time, and his absence would leave the Patriots awfully thin at cornerback. The Patriots still didn't do much to solve their depth issues at linebacker, merely upgrading one starting position from Banta-Cain to Thomas. Of course, we could come up with a similar list of potential pitfalls for any team, but none of them enjoy the likelihood of success that the Patriots do. That makes New England the clear favorite to win Super Bowl XLII.

Bill Barnwell

New England's Sore Spot

If the New England defensive backs had a clubhouse, the inside would probably look like the surgical set from *M*A*S*H*. Not only have players such as Ty Law, Rodney Harrison, Eugene Wilson, and Randall Gay all gone down over the last three seasons for significant lengths of time due to injury, but the guys replacing them have gone down too. This has led to a converted linebacker playing safety, a wide receiver playing cornerback, and a football card for Earthwind Moreland.

If the Patriots had suffered a rash of injuries in a lone season, that could be chalked up to some bad luck. Even if it had been two seasons in a row, that would be within the realm of random chance. Three seasons, though, is a trend.

To gather information about injuries, we took the NFL-issued Injury Reports from 2002 to 2006 and tracked trends across teams and positions. We measured injuries with two different metrics: a **Total** metric, which is the number of times a player from a team appeared on the injury report, regardless of the severity, and a **Weighted** metric that scored a team's injury status based upon the severity of the injury. With this weighted metric, a team was given four points per game when a player was marked as out, three when a player was marked as doubtful, two for questionable, and one for probable. This matches up with the NFL's definition of the injuries, as a doubtful player is expected to miss the game 75 percent of the time, a questionable player 50 percent of the time, and a probable player 25 percent. An "out" player appearing in a game is actually a prerequisite for sainthood on behalf of the team's trainer.

Of course, the list isn't always used that way. For example, the Patriots listed Tom Brady as probable each week from 2004 to 2006, despite Brady playing in every game over that timeframe. This would raise questions about whether the Patriots defensive back injuries are being overreported. We checked for that by going through the official NFL gamebooks to see whether the injury report matched what actually happened in the game. We noted whether a player started, served as a substitute, or didn't play at all. Take Patriots' defensive backs that were listed as questionable, for example; if the Patriots were overreporting their injuries, they would be expected to participate more than 50 percent of the time. In reality, Patriots' defensive backs played *less* often than defensive backs listed as questionable by other teams (table 2).

Table 2. Gameplay of DBs Listed as Questionable, 2002–2006

	Patriots	Pct	Other	Pct
Did Not Play	54	48%	608	45%
Substituted	28	25%	324	24%
Started	30	27%	421	31%

The average NFL secondary averaged 408 weighted points on their injury reports. Per table 3, the Patriots had the most injury-plagued secondary in football over the past five seasons. The Browns were second, but we'll get to them in a moment.

Table 3. Top-Ten Teams by Weighted DB Injuries, 2002–2006

Team	Prob	Ques	Doub	Out/IR	Total	Weighted
NE	20	112	11	136	279	821
CLE	25	92	8	137	262	781
CIN	66	49	5	126	246	683
GB	58	46	5	100	209	565
IND	101	116	23	34	274	538
CHI	27	52	11	91	181	528
STL	50	43	9	82	184	491
ARI	38	24	5	95	162	481
DET	23	44	9	83	159	470
SF	34	33	17	79	163	467
Average	**40**	**46**	**9**	**62**	**158**	**408**

The 2004–2006 Patriots have three of the top-ten most defensive back injury-laden seasons of the last five years (table 4). In 2004, they were third in the league in defensive back injuries; in 2005, they were first, and in 2006, second. The only team to have a season as bad as the 2005 or 2006 Patriots was Cleveland last year, when the Browns had

Table 4. Ten Worst Injury-Hit Seasons for DBs, 2002–2006

	Year	Team	Total	Weighted
1	2006	CLE	105	331
2	2006	NE	94	283
3	2005	NE	94	280
4	2005	DEN	77	220
5	2006	CIN	64	203
6	2006	GB	63	198
7	2004	CHI	57	180
8	2004	CIN	68	172
9	2004	NE	56	171
10	2003	GB	55	170

more defensive back injuries than any other team from the last five years. In 2005, the Browns ranked third in defensive back injuries. What's different about the Cleveland Browns of the past two seasons? Their new head coach, Romeo Crennel, formerly of the New England Patriots.

There are several possible explanations for these high injury totals, but none of them hold up to close scrutiny. It's not that the secondary is getting hurt making tackles against the run. When Patriots' defensive backs make a tackle, their Average Yards per Run are generally, well, average, so they're not hitting particularly close to the line. Furthermore, there's no real pattern to the injuries that the

players were suffering—Rodney Harrison went down while running with a Colts receiver, while Eugene Wilson went down during Super Bowl XXXVIII while playing special teams. Another argument might be that the Patriots are so frequently ahead that their defensive backs are on the field more often, but other successful teams such as San Diego and Philadelphia haven't had the same problem. There is no statistical correlation between passes attempted against a defense and that defense's defensive back injury rate.

Harrison's injuries are sometimes attributed to his advancing age, but the younger players such as Gay get hurt, too. There is no correlation between injuries and a secondary's average age on the opening day of the season. There's a slight correlation (+.15) between defensive back injuries in one season and an increase in team wins the following season.

More likely, it's something not obvious from watching game film. Perhaps the Patriots under Belichick and Browns under Crennel view defensive backs as eminently replaceable and draft and acquire injury-prone ones to gain a sense of arbitrage. Maybe the defensive backs they acquire aren't training properly and are suffering nagging injuries in camp or practice that linger onto the season and begin to cascade. It's hard to say, but with these trends, don't expect the injured secondaries of New England or Cleveland to heal up anytime soon.

Bill Barnwell

Patriots 2006 Stats by Week

Wk	vs.	W–L	PF	PA	YDF	YDA	TO	DVOA Total	Off	Def	ST
1	BUF	W	19	17	319	240	-2	-12.8%	-8.3%	8.1%	3.6%
2	@NYJ	W	24	17	358	337	-1	11.6%	15.3%	3.7%	0.0%
3	DEN	L	7	17	370	400	0	-22.3%	12.3%	40.2%	5.5%
4	@CIN	W	38	13	424	279	+1	63.1%	33.4%	-26.0%	3.7%
5	MIA	W	20	10	213	283	+2	33.3%	14.4%	-16.5%	2.4%
6	BYE										
7	@BUF	W	28	6	265	255	+4	46.9%	14.2%	-25.1%	7.7%
8	@MIN	W	31	7	430	284	+2	67.6%	53.6%	-21.5%	-7.5%
9	IND	L	20	27	349	354	-3	-3.2%	-16.0%	-17.9%	-5.1%
10	NYJ	L	14	17	377	278	-1	-25.1%	-7.9%	12.6%	-4.6%
11	@GB	W	35	0	357	120	0	97.9%	27.8%	-62.7%	7.3%
12	CHI	W	17	13	352	324	-1	22.7%	6.7%	-10.2%	5.8%
13	DET	W	28	21	363	361	+2	24.7%	-0.4%	-17.7%	7.4%
14	@MIA	L	0	21	189	315	-3	-65.4%	-38.0%	30.0%	2.6%
15	HOU	W	40	7	230	198	+4	95.8%	-0.3%	-57.8%	38.3%
16	@JAC	W	24	21	359	339	+1	21.0%	45.5%	25.2%	0.7%
17	@TEN	W	40	23	414	342	+3	31.1%	47.1%	-8.8%	-24.8%
18	NYJ	W	37	16	358	347	+1	45.1%	11.9%	-16.3%	16.8%
19	@SD	W	24	21	327	352	+1	-25.3%	-44.6%	-13.3%	6.0%
20	@IND	L	34	38	319	455	0	17.9%	-13.1%	-13.4%	17.6%

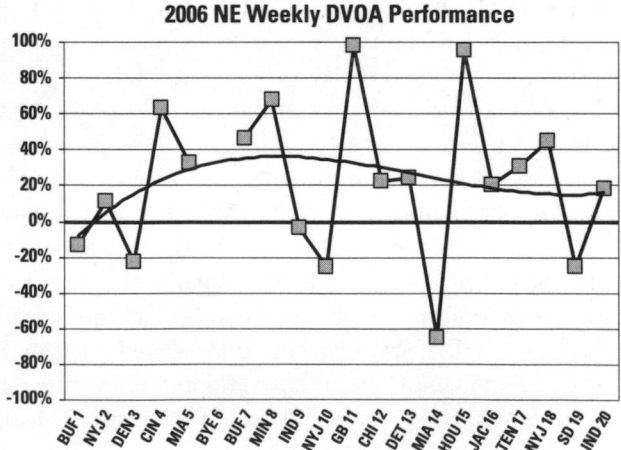

2006 NE Weekly DVOA Performance

Trends and Splits

	Offense	Rank	Defense	Rank
Total DVOA	12.3%	6	-8.4%	9
Unadjusted VOA	11.6%	8	-12.5%	3
Weighted Trend	12.2%	7	-12.5%	5
Variance	5.9%	18	7.7%	10
Passing	20.6%	6	-9.9%	7
Rushing	3.8%	8	-6.4%	10
First Down	19.6%	5	-22.7%	2
Second Down	-9.6%	25	3.2%	18
Third Down	31.7%	3	1.8%	14
Red Zone	37.3%	2	-35.2%	3
Late and Close	-3.2%	18	-18.9%	4

Five-Year Performance

	2006	2005	2004	2003	2002
W-L	12-4	10-6	14-2	14-2	9-7
Pythagorean Wins	12.2	9.1	12.4	11.4	8.9
Estimated Wins	11.0	8.9	13.1	11.6	9.3
Total DVOA	23.2%	3.4%	35.7%	22.8%	12.6%
Rank	5	12	1	3	10
Offense	12.3%	12.8%	24.2%	0.4%	7.1%
Rank	6	7	4	14	10
Defense	-8.4%	10.5%	-11.3%	-22.0%	0.3%
Rank	9	27	6	2	15
Special Teams	2.5%	1.1%	0.2%	0.4%	5.8%
Rank	8	12	16	17	3

Strategic Tendencies

Formations		Rank	Run/Pass		Rank	Defense		Rank	Other		Rank
3+ WR	50%	11	Runs, all plays	45%	13	Sacks by LB	49%	7	Run with 2+ RB	35%	30
4+ WR	10%	16	Runs, first half	45%	14	Sacks by DB	5%	24	Run with 2+ TE	64%	1
2+ TE	43%	1	Runs, first down	49%	24	Rush 6+	6.6%	22	Play action	14%	26
Single back	71%	3	Runs, power sit.	82%	1	Rush 7+	1.2%	18	Go for it on 4th	1.20	4
Empty back	7.6%	2	Runs, behind 2H	36%	8	Rush 3	9.0%	4	Offensive Pace	30.2	15
Max protect	8%	27	Pass, ahead 2H	49%	5	CB1 on WR1	37%	24	Defensive Pace	29.1	3

Since 1996, no head coach has been as aggressive on fourth down as Bill Belichick (Aggressiveness Index: 1.75). . . . New England used more than five blockers on only 42 percent of pass plays, the second lowest percentage in the NFL behind Seattle. Every other AFC team used more than five blockers on at least half of their pass plays. . . . Tom Brady faced six or more pass rushers more often than any other quarterback in the NFL and had the most incompletes classified as Hit in Motion. . . . The Patriots led the league in DVOA with four wide receivers (67.9%), but were only seventh with 6.6 yards per play from that formation. That's because they often used the four-wide set to convert third downs with only one to six yards to go. . . . The Patriots came out 28 times with two running backs and three tight ends, not counting kneeldowns. No other team used this formation more than 17 times. . . . The Patriots' defense ranked second in Adjusted Sack Rate on first down (11.9 percent), but 28th in Adjusted Sack Rate on third or fourth down (4.5 percent). The Patriots ranked second in sacks classified as Blown Blocks, behind San Diego. . . . New England blitzed far less in 2006 than in 2005, when they sent at least six pass rushers on 17 percent of pass plays, which was second in the league. . . . The Jets and Patriots were tied for the league's best DVOA against play-action passes (-35.5%), but the Patriots allowed more yards per play-action pass (5.7) than the Jets (4.5).

Passing

Player	DPAR	DVOA	Plys	NtYds	Avg	YAC	C%	TD	Int
Tom Brady	75.9	19.6%	516	3345	6.5	5.1	62.0%	24	12
Matt Cassel	-3.4	-88.4%	8	15	1.9	5.0	62.5%	0	0

Rushing

Player	DPAR	DVOA	Plys	Yds	Avg	TD	Fum	Suc
Corey Dillon*	15.6	5.2%	199	812	4.1	13	2	52%
Laurence Maroney	9.1	-1.9%	175	749	4.3	6	1	46%
Heath Evans	0.0	-13.7%	27	117	4.3	0	1	45%
Tom Brady	1.9	-6.3%	26	121	4.7	0	12	—
Kevin Faulk	3.3	22.4%	25	123	4.9	1	0	56%
Patrick Pass*	-2.7	-95.5%	6	21	3.5	0	1	73%
Chad Jackson	0.9	22.5%	4	22	5.5	0	0	—
Sammy Morris	*-2.2*	*-19.3%*	*92*	*403*	*4.4*	*1*	*2*	*42%*

Receiving

Player	DPAR	DVOA	Plys	Ctch	Yds	Y/C	YAC	TD	C%
WR									
Reche Caldwell	15.6	9.2%	102	61	767	12.6	3.5	4	60%
Troy Brown	4.2	-6.3%	76	44	386	8.8	4.3	4	56%
Doug Gabriel	8.0	8.3%	54	30	428	14.3	5.6	3	58%
Jabar Gaffney	3.1	8.5%	20	11	142	12.9	2.2	1	68%
Chad Jackson	4.9	23.5%	19	13	152	11.7	4.4	3	55%
Wes Welker	*9.6*	*0.1%*	*100*	*67*	*687*	*10.3*	*3.8*	*1*	*67%*
Randy Moss	*0.8*	*-13.7%*	*97*	*42*	*553*	*13.2*	*2.7*	*3*	*70%*
Donte' Stallworth	*12.2*	*7.3%*	*78*	*38*	*725*	*19.1*	*5.4*	*5*	*49%*
Kelley Washington	*4.3*	*36.7%*	*12*	*9*	*115*	*12.8*	*4.9*	*1*	*75%*
TE									
Benjamin Watson	5.7	-2.2%	91	49	643	13.1	4.1	3	54%
Daniel Graham*	2.2	-3.2%	34	21	235	11.2	4.5	2	62%
David Thomas	5.7	46.1%	16	11	159	14.5	8.3	1	69%
Kyle Brady	*-1.0*	*-30.0%*	*8*	*5*	*37*	*7.4*	*2.4*	*0*	*63%*
RB									
Kevin Faulk	8.3	19.5%	56	43	356	8.3	5.7	2	77%
Laurence Maroney	3.6	12.2%	30	22	194	8.8	9.3	1	73%
Corey Dillon*	3.0	24.0%	16	15	147	9.8	12.2	0	94%
Heath Evans	-0.4	-17.2%	9	7	34	4.9	3.4	1	78%
Sammy Morris	*-4.1*	*-33.3%*	*35*	*21*	*162*	*7.7*	*7.1*	*0*	*60%*

Offensive Line

Year	Yards	ALY	Rank	Power	Rank	10+ Yds	Rank	Stuff	Rank	Sack	ASR	Rank
2004	4.42	4.60	4	69%	9	16%	21	22%	11	26	4.7%	5
2005	3.53	3.79	26	77%	3	10%	31	26%	23	28	4.8%	7
2006	4.22	4.37	12	82%	1	16%	13	21%	7	29	5.6%	8

Year	LE	Rank	LT	Rank	Mid	Rank	RT	Rank	RE	Rank
2004	4.99	5	4.83	5	4.29	15	5.21	2	4.57	5
2005	4.08	18	2.40	31	3.83	25	4.53	8	3.56	22
2006	5.05	4	4.23	20	4.55	10	3.75	30	2.82	31

The Patriots' dramatic split in effectiveness running to the left side as opposed to the right has a bit to do with injuries and a bit to do with talent. Most of New England's running plays go behind left tackle Matt Light and left guard Logan Mankins, but the performance on the right side of the line has deteriorated since 2004. While Nick Kaczur is penciled in as the starting right tackle, he's been pretty average so far in his career, while injury replacement Ryan O'Callaghan is a project that wasn't ready when he entered the starting lineup last year. O'Callaghan will be pushed by former Alabama tackle Wesley Britt, who looked better than either O'Callaghan or Kaczur in his one start against the Bengals last year. Right guard Stephen Neal missed time with a shoulder injury, and took a step back from his 2005 form.

There is much better news on the rest of the line. Center Dan Koppen is one of the more underrated offensive linemen in football. A Pro Bowl appearance in 2007 is not out of the question, and he'll have a fun rivalry going against the Jets' Nick Mangold for the next five years or so. Tackle Matt Light made it to his first Pro Bowl last year as an injury replacement for Jonathan Ogden. Light struggled with speed rushers at the beginning of the season, perhaps feeling tentative on the leg he broke halfway through 2005, but he improved in the second half of the year, culminating in the lockdown Light put on Dwight Freeney in the AFC Championship Game. The most promising player on the entire line, though, is Mankins—the operative word is "mauler," and Will Shields's retirement opens up a Pro Bowl slot for Mankins starting immediately.

Defensive Front Seven

Defensive Line	Age	Pos	Plys	TmPct	Rk	Stop	Dfts	StpRt	Rk	AvYd	Rk	Sack	Hit	Hur	Runs	RuStp	RuYd	Pass	PaStp	PaYd
Ty Warren	26	DE	86	12.3%	1	71	17	83%	17	1.2	33	7	7	9	74	81%	1.9	12	92%	-3.1
Vince Wilfork	26	DT	53	8.8%	2	45	7	85%	17	2.0	41	1	3	4	48	85%	2.1	5	80%	1.0
Richard Seymour	28	DE	50	6.7%	28	41	18	82%	22	1.0	21	4	9	11	32	75%	2.3	18	94%	-1.4
Jarvis Green	28	DE	34	4.6%	62	32	15	94%	2	-0.4	5	7.5	6	6	23	96%	2.0	11	91%	-5.3
Mike Wright	25	DT	31	4.2%	60	27	5	87%	12	1.8	34	1	1	1	25	88%	1.9	6	83%	1.5

Linebackers	Age	Pos	Plys	TmPct	Rk	Stop	Dfts	StpRt	AvYd	Sack	Hit	Hur	Runs	RuStp	Rk	RuYd	Rk	Tgts	Suc%	Rk	PaYd	Rk
Tedy Bruschi	34	ILB	119	17.1%	12	71	20	60%	4.3	2	3	5	80	68%	34	3.4	47	45	55%	33	6.2	46
Mike Vrabel	32	OLB	93	12.5%	49	56	18	60%	4.0	4.5	4	9	50	76%	7	2.8	15	35	49%	52	5.8	28
Junior Seau	38	ILB	70	13.7%	33	41	10	59%	4.5	1	3	5	48	75%	10	2.8	14	18	28%	98	9.1	94
Rosevelt Colvin	30	OLB	60	8.1%	88	48	22	80%	0.8	9	19	20	33	73%	15	2.3	5	24	73%	3	3.0	4
Tully Banta-Cain*	27	OLB	33	4.4%	—	20	11	61%	4.0	5	6	9	18	61%	—	3.6	—	4	43%	—	4.6	—
Adalius Thomas	*30*	*OLB*	*91*	*12.0%*	*54*	*60*	*28*	*66%*	*3.9*	*10.5*	*10*	*13*	*36*	*72%*	*20*	*4.4*	*90*	*35*	*61%*	*16*	*4.6*	*13*

Year	Yards	ALY	Rank	Power	Rank	10+ Yds	Rank	Stuff	Rank	Sack	ASR	Rank
2004	3.80	4.39	23	57%	10	7%	1	20%	31	46	8.0%	9
2005	3.73	4.29	22	76%	28	9%	1	21%	26	33	6.0%	25
2006	3.91	3.99	8	68%	21	17%	20	24%	18	44	7.8%	10

Year	LE	Rank	LT	Rank	Mid	Rank	RT	Rank	RE	Rank
2004	5.91	31	4.15	10	4.43	23	4.06	11	2.49	2
2005	4.29	19	4.41	20	4.20	20	4.51	27	4.72	24
2006	3.30	7	4.33	15	4.15	12	2.83	2	4.05	16

Ty Warren didn't actually outplay Richard Seymour last year. Warren's game charting numbers are better, but Seymour attracts two blockers on every play, freeing Warren up. That being said, Warren's pass rushing technique improved dramatically in 2006 as his already-strong first step was supplemented by better use of his hands to gain leverage on the defensive line. Seymour continued to be Seymour—if Julius Peppers isn't the best defensive lineman in football, it's because Seymour is. While Vince Wilfork is the right nose tackle for this system, the Patriots would probably benefit from adding more depth beyond Mike Wright. The Patriots drafted Miami defensive tackle Kareem Brown in the fourth round. Brown had antagonized 2004 draftee Wilfork while they were both at the U with comments such as "you better enter the draft, because I'm going to take your job next year." Brown will probably be a little bit more reserved this year.

Adding Adalius Thomas will have a cascading effect on the responsibilities of the Patriots' linebackers. Mike Vrabel will play on the inside, hopefully allowing him to use his instincts more. His past experience playing alongside Tedy Bruschi means that they'll both know where the other is, but the Patriots already struggled against slot receivers last year, and it's hard to see Vrabel and Bruschi getting better at stopping them. Thomas, only two years younger than Vrabel, will need every ounce of foot speed he possesses to keep up with Dallas Clark come playoff time. Eric Alexander, whom the Patriots used to try to cover Clark last year, is stretched as a regular linebacker and might give way to the returning Junior Seau, who still plays the run well, but wasn't much better in coverage in 2006.

Defensive Secondary

Secondary	Age	Pos	Plys	TmPct	Rk	Stop	Dfts	RuYd	Rk	RuStp	Rk	Tgts	Tgt%	Rk	Dist	Suc%	Rk	PaYd	Rk	PD	Int
Asante Samuel	26	CB	88	12.6%	7	40	20	8.4	57	38%	51	101	23%	8	12.9	60%	11	5.9	9	26	10
Ellis Hobbs	24	CB	52	7.5%	54	17	8	14.0	80	14%	78	78	18%	48	14.6	55%	24	7.7	46	9	2
Chad Scott	33	CB	45	6.9%	66	12	5	7.1	50	20%	75	56	14%	69	13.1	51%	46	8.5	61	9	2
Artrell Hawkins	30	SS	63	9.7%	40	15	9	6.2	33	35%	56	28	6%	55	17.4	52%	43	10.0	64	2	1
Rodney Harrison	35	SS	53	11.4%	23	22	6	5.6	24	45%	34	27	9%	24	7.6	65%	8	5.3	6	2	1
James Sanders	24	FS	41	5.5%	73	18	7	6.2	34	55%	14	20	4%	76	11.8	56%	29	6.4	19	1	1
Eugene Wilson	27	FS	26	14.0%	—	6	3	9.2	—	20%	—	19	15%	—	8.1	32%	—	13.3	—	2	0
Tory James	*34*	*CB*	*57*	*6.6%*	*70*	*21*	*13*	*11.3*	*74*	*29%*	*65*	*76*	*16%*	*54*	*12.7*	*44%*	*72*	*9.8*	*76*	*13*	*4*

Year	Pass D Rank	DVOA vs. #1 WR	Rank	DVOA vs. #2 WR	Rank	DVOA vs. Other WR	Rank	DVOA vs. TE	Rank	DVOA vs. RB	Rank
2004	6	-39.6%	1	29.4%	29	7.5%	24	-23.4%	5	22.4%	28
2005	29	18.0%	26	15.2%	30	10.7%	27	8.0%	22	8.1%	22
2006	7	-13.8%	9	24.9%	29	-18.9%	11	-34.0%	3	5.9%	18

(continued next page)

Defensive Secondary (*continued*)

It was another injury-filled year in the Patriots' secondary. Starting safeties Eugene Wilson and Rodney Harrison and nickel back Randall Gay missed most of the season, while the Philip Rivers–christened "Sorriest Corner in Football," Ellis Hobbs, played a majority of the year with a broken wrist. Fill-ins such as James Sanders, Rashad Baker, Antwain Spann, and Troy Brown were unable to sufficiently replace the lost starters. The Patriots made two moves to alleviate these concerns over the offseason, signing cornerback Tory James from Cincinnati and drafting Miami safety Brandon Meriweather in the first round. The concerns over Meriweather's character are overstated, and he has the versatility and football smarts the Patriots look for in their defenders. The next time Harrison gets hurt, Meriweather is likely to take his job and keep it.

As for Samuel, his season was as good as advertised according to our game charters. He led the league with 26 passes defensed, four more than any other cornerback. The issue of re-signing him is better addressed elsewhere, but if he doesn't show up to training camp, the Patriots will probably move Wilson onto a corner and start Artrell Hawkins at safety until Harrison gets hurt. It's belaboring the point, but Harrison's yearly injury is an inevitability at this point, and the Patriots have prepared for it.

The Patriots have struggled against number-two receivers for three years now and gave up huge games to guys such as Mike Furrey, Marty Booker, and Jerricho Cotchery (twice) in 2006. This is probably schematic, not the fault of any particular defensive back.

Special Teams

DVOA	Rank	FG/XP	Rank	Net Punt	Rank	Punt Ret	Rank	Net Kick	Rank	Kick Ret	Rank	Hidden	Rank
0.2%	16	12.8	1	-4.2	25	-9.1	31	-1.5	16	3.1	10	-4.1	19
1.1%	12	0.1	17	-0.4	19	1.7	10	0.6	17	4.7	9	-6.2	23
2.5%	8	-5.5	28	-5.9	25	4.9	4	4.9	11	16.6	1	3.7	11

The Patriots have finally developed excellent return units, and that's due more to the blockers than the return men being used. The retirement of linebacker/safety Don Davis and the advancing age of theoretical linebacker Larry Izzo are reasons to think the blocking on returns will decline some in 2007, but adding Wes Welker to the lineup immediately makes him the primary return man and a likely upgrade on the combination of Troy Brown and Kevin Faulk.

While the Patriots missed Adam Vinatieri's magic playoff beans, Stephen Gostkowski proved to be a more-than-adequate replacement. Some early-season hiccups were forgotten by the time the playoffs rolled around, as Gostkowski hit all eight field goals he attempted, including a 50-yarder against the Chargers that Vinatieri simply doesn't have the leg to kick. He was also excellent on kickoffs, the aspect of the kicking game that stays steady from year-to-year (see the Arizona chapter).

Coaching Staff

The Patriots' staff remains relatively unchanged for the first time in several seasons. The only departure was wide receivers coach Brian Daboll, who joined Eric Mangini in New York and was replaced by director of pro personnel Nick Caserio. Caserio was the quarterback at John Carroll University, where one of his wide receivers was Patriots offensive coordinator and quarterbacks coach Josh McDaniels. McDaniels's offensive scheme was limited last year by the struggles of the Patriots' wide receivers. With another new group of receivers coming in, the playbook probably won't be expanded until 2008, at which point McDaniels will likely be a head coaching candidate. Dean Pees remains the defensive coordinator in name, but the defense is Bill Belichick's baby. Their task in 2007 is to limit the roles of players such as Vrabel, Bruschi, and Harrison to the things they do well while integrating the new additions into the lineup.

New York Jets

Jets fans will be the first to tell you about all the awful events that have befallen their franchise since Super Bowl III. Joe Namath's knees. Being stuck in Giants Stadium. Mark Gastineau roughing the passer. Dan Marino's fake spike. Herman Edwards. We won't even get into the draft picks, or we'll be here all day. Jets fans go beyond having a sense of humor about these things; they've come to embrace their team's poor fortune as if they've developed some sort of mutated Stockholm Syndrome. After the first 21st-century Jets team was broken up following the 2005 season, the inexperienced Eric Mangini was hired as head coach, and Curtis Martin proved unable to answer the bell, Gang Green once again had very low expectations heading into last season.

Then the magic happened. For the first time in what seemed like forever, the Jets got lucky.

Let's not chalk up all of the 2006 Jets' success to luck. DVOA's Estimated Wins peg them to have "earned" 7.7 wins, and Pythagoras bumps them up to 8.7. Maybe luck handed the Jets a couple of extra wins, but no one on the planet expected the Jets to win eight games last season, never mind ten. You know those post-season NFL Network commercials that mock fans' deluded preseason expectations? They couldn't even film a Jets version, the expectations were that low. Still, while the Jets and Eric Mangini deserve credit for doing as well as they did, ultimately some of it was indeed the simple magic of lucky bounces.

The Jets' good fortune manifested itself most obviously on defense. The Jets had the sixth-ranked defense in the NFL going by points allowed, but finished a lowly 26th in defensive DVOA. How can there be such a large disparity? Here are five reasons why: (1) **The Jets played the fifth-easiest schedule of opposing offenses in the league.** Oak-

---

JETS PROSPECTUS

2006 Record: 10–6

DVOA Estimated Wins: 7.7 (18th)

Pythagorean Wins: 8.7 (12th)

DVOA: −4.3% total (19th), 0.9% weighted (18th)

Offense: 2.8% DVOA (14th)

Defense: 10.3% DVOA (26th)

Special Teams: 3.2% DVOA (5th)

Variance: 15.2% (10th)

2006: A core of promising young talent rides to the playoffs on luck and Mangenius.

2007: A core of still-improving young talent misses the playoffs when luck snaps back to normal.

2007 Mean Projection: 8.8 wins

The Brohm Closet (0–4): 3%

Bad Team (5–6): 12%

Mediocre (7–8): 28%

Playoff Contender (9–10): 34%

Super Bowl Contender (11+): 23%

Projected Average Opponent: 2.7% DVOA (4th in NFL)

---

land (worst offense in the league), Cleveland (31st), and Minnesota (29th) were all on the Jets docket last season. Miami (28th) was on the schedule twice. Those teams averaged 12.6 points. The rest of the teams on the Jets' schedule averaged over 21 points. (2) **The Jets and their opposition both played at a slow pace.** While the Jets' offensive pacing was mostly their choice, their opposition's slow pace was a direct result of the Jets having the worst run defense in the NFL. With teams loading up on the run and taking their time, and the Jets moving at their own glacial pace, Jets' games featured only 346 drives in 2006, fewer than the total in the games of any team except Houston and Indianapolis. Fewer drives mean fewer points. As for the offense, many Jets fans blamed this frustrating strategy on former offensive coordinator Paul Hackett, but it has continued under both his successor Mike Heimerdinger and current coordinator Brian Schottenheimer. (3) **Only one defensive touchdown was scored against the Jets.** That's pretty impressive, but defensive touchdowns are given up, or in this case prevented, by the offense, not the defense. The Jets allowing only one was luck, and in no way reflected skill on the part of the defense. (4) **The Jets opponents had a poor field goal percentage and poor average kickoff distance.** The latter is more subtle; by getting better field position from the opposing kickoffs, the Jets were more likely to pin their opponents back in their end of the field on a subsequent punt, making it that much harder for the opponent to score.

Like average kickoff distance, the poor field goal percentage is also random and uncontrollable; if you want to believe that it's because Jonathan Vilma knows exactly what to say to get under a kicker's skin, and Bryan Thomas has a way of giving holders the heebie-jeebies, that's fine, but opposition field goal percentage is a number that always regresses to the mean. (5) **The Jets recovered 75**

2007 Jets Schedule

Week	Opp	Week	Opp	Week	Opp
1	NE	7	at CIN	13	at MIA
2	at BAL	8	BUF	14	CLE
3	MIA	9	WAS	15	at NE
4	at BUF	10	BYE	16	at TEN
5	at NYG	11	PIT	17	KC
6	PHI	12	at DAL (Thu.)		

Table 1. . . . And Yards for All

Featured Runner	Team	Avg vs Jets		Avg vs All Others		Game Rank
		Yds/ Game	Yds/ Carry	Yds/ Game	Yds/ Carry	
Chris Brown	TEN	64	4.0	23	3.7	1
Corey Dillon	NE	89	5.7	46	3.8	1, 2
Willis McGahee	BUF	138	6.5	72	3.3	1, 2
Joseph Addai	IND	84	4.2	66	4.8	5
Fred Taylor	JAC	111	5.3	69	4.9	2
Ronnie Brown	MIA	119	5.9	70	3.8	2, 4
Kevin Jones	DET	86	5.7	55	3.6	4
Reuben Droughns	CLE	125	3.8	49	3.4	1
Thomas Jones	CHI	121	5.3	73	4.0	1
Wali Lundy	HOU	11	1.4	36	4.0	10
Ahman Green	GB	102	7.3	74	3.8	5
Chester Taylor	MIN	38	3.5	84	4.0	12
Justin Fargas	OAK	79	4.6	39	3.6	2
Averages		**89.8**	**4.9**	**58.2**	**3.9**	

NOTE: Game Rank lists how these games compare to each back's single-game yardage totals for the season. For division rivals, averages include two games against the Jets.

percent of fumbles recovered on defense. While fumbling is not a random event, fumble recovery is. No team is consistently better than average at recovering fumbles. Flip a coin 20 times. If heads comes up 15 of those 20 times, does it mean it has a 75 percent chance of happening on the 21st flip? Of course not. Fumble recoveries are about the same.

The Jets cannot expect to enjoy any of this luck in 2007. Their rough 2007 schedule brings the NFC East and AFC North to town, replacing the patsies from 2006 with offensive powerhouses including Cincinnati, Philadelphia, and Dallas. The Jets can expect to give up more defensive touchdowns, the kickers facing them are very likely to be more effective, and it's a near-impossibility that they will recover 75 percent of the balls that hit the ground again. The Jets also were better on third down than they were overall on both offense and defense in 2006, a strong negative indicator.

The smart moves made by the front office are the best reason to believe that the Jets can limit this decline. The front office had another offseason to add personnel that fits the team's 3-4 scheme, and the incumbent personnel has another training camp to practice it. However, even if overall defense were to improve to match its strong performance on third downs, which would be contrary to what we know about the consistency of third-down performance, the results on the field would still likely be worse. In the 11 years for which we have DVOA stats, the 2006 Jets had the second-largest gap between their rank in DVOA and their rank in points allowed. Only the 2003 Jets' gap was wider, and, while they were actually even stingier in 2004, the five teams with the next largest disparities gave up far more points the following year, even if their DVOA improved.

The run defense is almost guaranteed to improve, because the 2006 Jets were dead last in defense DVOA against the run. They didn't get as much press for their struggles against the run as Indianapolis did because the Colts' raw yards per carry were higher, but, since the Jets were in closer games than the Colts, New York's inability to stop the run was more harmful.

Take a look at how each team's featured running back did against the Jets as opposed to all other opponents (table 1). Of the 13 backs, the Jets kept exactly two below their regular season average yards per game: Wali Lundy and Chester Taylor. The other 11 were all better against the Jets, and the difference was usually significant. Five runners posted their best game of the season against the Jets, while three more posted their second-best game. Reuben Droughns posted his only game over 100 yards against the Jets; Willis McGahee, his only two. All together, the backs featured in table 1 were an entire yard per carry better against the Jets than against the rest of the league.

The Jets' run defense did improve as the season went on, mainly because defensive lineman Dewayne Robertson went from abhorrent to near competency. Robertson's development will be the key for the team's front seven in 2007. Fellow lineman Kimo von Oelhoeffen struggled mightily following his acquisition via free agency, so the Jets went on a defensive lineman spree in the offseason. New to Gang Green in 2007 are defensive ends David Bowens, Michael "Badstreet" Haynes, Kenyon Coleman, Bobby Hamilton, and surprisingly enough, former Cardinals third-overall pick defensive tackle Andre Wadsworth, who hasn't appeared in an NFL game in over six years. While none will turn the tide by themselves, the group can be effective if Mangini effectively employs each in roles and situations that fit their skill sets, something at which his mentor, Bill Belichick, excels.

Another key to the run defense is the selection of Michigan middle linebacker David Harris in the second round of this year's draft. Harris is a perfect fit for the Jets' needs on defense as he's a stout defender against the run and has great instincts. The Jets' first-round pick, corner-back Darrelle Revis, should start immediately, allowing the shaky Justin Miller to move into the slot, and Hank Poteat to move into his old Foxboro apartment.

Offensively, the Jets benefited from another piece of luck. In his seventh season, quarterback Chad Pennington finally managed to play in all 16 regular season games for the first time in his pro career. After winning the job in training camp, Pennington was effective during the season, but the Jets offense was defined by his limitations, and will be for as long as he remains the starter. Pennington is the football equivalent of veteran finesse pitchers Jamie Moyer and Tom Glavine; he compensates for his utter lack of velocity by doing everything else well. The Jets' offensive scheme involves a lot of slants, screens, and play-action passes (Pennington fakes the handoff well enough to consider applying for an NEA grant). These plays keep Pennington in his comfort range. As the game wears on and safeties creep up, the Jets begin to go deep with the out and go patterns that Pennington simply cannot throw all game. While Pennington can be a championship-caliber quarterback at this level of play, counting on him to play 16 games again is simply wishcasting.

The season also saw two unheralded young players emerge at the expense of sour, ineffective veterans. At wide receiver, the disappointing Justin McCareins showed up to camp out of shape. Mangini responded by permanently assigning McCareins to his doghouse and gave his spot to former kick returner Jerricho Cotchery, who'd impressed the coaches with his offseason work ethic. Cotchery proceeded directly to his breakout season, catching 82 passes to McCareins's 23.

At tailback, Derrick Blaylock spent the season making Will Shields's and Willie Roaf's Hall of Fame cases that much stronger, while training camp acquisition Kevan Barlow averaged a woeful 2.8 yards per carry and didn't have a run longer than 12 yards all season. Instead, fourth-rounder Leon Washington saw his role expanded as the season went along and played like the poor man's Tiki Barber (or, if you prefer, the "Weekend Today" man's Tiki Barber). He was above-average in both the running and passing games, was an excellent pass blocker for a rookie, and contributed on special teams. The trade for former Bears running back Thomas Jones gives Mangini and Schottenheimer two backs with distinct skills, allowing them to utilize Jones and Washington in situations that specifically suit their respective strengths and create mismatches.

As for the Jets' outlay on offensive linemen in the first round of the 2006 draft, both D'Brickashaw Ferguson and Nick Mangold showed promise over the course of the season. In particular, Mangold's fierce play and ability to pick up the line calls peg him as a Pro Bowl–caliber center as

early as next season, while Ferguson showed signs of brilliance at left tackle, but struggled with consistency. Both look more like success stories so far than, say, Oakland left tackle Robert Gallery, and can be expected to be two of the Jets' parts that will improve this season.

Unfortunately for Jets fans, improvement does not necessarily mean a return trip to the playoffs. The Jets' schedule strength ranked 21st in 2006, but we're projecting it to rank fourth in 2007. Combine the tougher schedule with luck reverting to normal, and the Jets could improve their play on the field but actually win fewer games. This will feel awfully familiar to Mangini, because he went through the same thing as an assistant on the 2002 Patriots. A 9–7 record may seem like a step backwards, but Mangini knows the next step in the pattern. It involves the Lombardi Trophy.

Bill Barnwell

David Bowens's Perfect Season

You could get eye strain looking for David Bowens's contributions on a stat sheet. According to NFL.com, he recorded 13 tackles and seven assists last season, but those numbers are inflated by a handful of special teams tackles. On defense, he made just nine tackles and five assists. He registered five sacks, a high total for a bit player, and broke up one pass, but the rest of his statistical résumé could fit on an index card. Why would the Jets invest $6.2 million over three years in a player with so little to offer?

Bowens's season was better than his raw stats suggest. Examine each of Bowens's tackles, sacks, and passes defensed closely, and you'll discover that he had an uncanny knack for making crucial plays:

Week 2 vs. Buffalo: On 3rd-and-12 at the Dolphins 35-yard line in the third quarter, J. P. Losman threw a short pass in the right flat to Josh Reed. Bowens hustled out from his defensive end position to help Taveras Tillman stop Reed for an eight-yard gain, forcing a field goal.

Week 4 vs. Houston: Bowens stopped Ron Dayne for a one-yard gain on 3rd-and-4 just before halftime.

Week 5 vs. New England: Bowens and Matt Roth stuffed Laurence Maroney for a three-yard loss on 2nd-and-4, effectively ending a Patriots first-quarter drive. In the third quarter, Bowens dropped into zone coverage and broke up a pass intended for Kevin Faulk on 3rd-and-9. Then, in the fourth quarter, Bowens recovered a Faulk fumble on a punt return, giving the Dolphins one last shot to beat the Patriots. As a special teams play, this doesn't add to Bowens's Defeat total, but it was a crucial play nonetheless.

Week 6 vs. the Jets: On 3rd-and-9 from the Dolphins 23-yard line in the third quarter, the Jets ran Leon Washington off right end. Bowens and Tillman teamed up again, this time stopping Washington for an eight-yard gain. The Jets settled for a field goal.

Week 7 vs. Green Bay: Early in the first quarter, Jason Taylor sacked Brett Favre, forcing a fumble. Bowens recovered the loose ball, and the Dolphins scored a touchdown on the next play.

Week 9 vs. Chicago: Bowens sacked Rex Grossman for a six-yard loss on 3rd-and-8 in the third quarter of Miami's Grossman piñata party.

Week 11 vs. Minnesota: Bowens sacked Brad Johnson on 3rd-and-7 on the Vikings' first possession after halftime.

Week 12 vs. Detroit: Bowens sacked Jon Kitna for an eight-yard loss late in the fourth quarter with the Dolphins sitting on a comfortable lead.

Week 13 vs. Jacksonville: Bowens earned a half-sack as he and Kevin Carter carved up David Garrard on 3rd-and-16 in the first quarter, and another half-sack when he joined Vonnie Holliday to make a wishbone out of Garrard in the third quarter.

Week 14 vs. New England: Tom Brady tossed a wideout screen to Troy Brown in the second quarter. Bowens recognized the play immediately and tackled Brown for a loss of one.

Week 15 vs. Buffalo: Bowens sacked J. P. Losman on 3rd-and-9, a play that should have ended Buffalo's first drive—except that Zach Thomas came in after Bowens had Losman already down and drew a roughing the passer penalty. Later in the game, Bowens once again sniffed out a screen when Losman dumped the ball to Anthony Thomas on 3rd-and-18. Bowens and Zach Thomas derailed the A-Train after a six-yard gain.

Week 16 vs. Jets: The Jets surrendered on 3rd-and-14 by running a draw play to Washington. Bowens stopped him for a two-yard gain. In the fourth quarter, Chad Pennington threw an incomplete backwards pass, and when Jerricho Cotchery hopped on the fumble, Bowens hopped on him for a three-yard loss.

Individually, Bowens's appearances on the stat sheet don't stand out. Look at them together, and we see something remarkable: In our statistics, Bowens went a perfect 16-for-16 registering Defeats. That is, all of his tackles, sacks, and passes defensed resulted either in a loss of yardage, a turnover, or a stop on third down. Bowens is the only defender with over ten plays to be "perfect" since we began counting Defeats three years ago.

Not all of Bowens's tackles were game-changing plays—it doesn't take Lee Roy Selmon to stop a draw play on 3rd-and-14, and Bowens's garbage-time sack against the Lions had no impact on the final score—but every objective stat includes some borderline data. As a pass rush specialist, Bowens saw a lot of action on third downs, putting him in position to register some extra Defeats. Still, there are many pass rush specialists in the NFL, and none came close to Bowens's accomplishment. Sixteen defeats is an impressive total, no matter how you slice it. Bowens's teammate Kevin Carter had 15 Defeats, and he played many more snaps. Dwight Freeney and Mike Rucker had 12 Defeats apiece. Dozens of every-down linemen around the league finished last season with fewer defeats than Bowens.

Bowens's 2006 Defeat total is typical for him. In 2005, he recorded 23 tackles on defense and six sacks, registering 12 Defeats. In 2004, he racked up 36 tackles, six sacks, and 17 Defeats. By breaking down his Defeats, we discover that Bowens is much more than just a pass rusher and makes many meaningful stops in pass coverage. Bowens made only four Defeats in run defense in 2006, but most of them came on "surprise" runs, delays, and draws in long-yardage situations. Add the draw play Defeats to the coverage Defeats, and you get an image of Bowens as the pass rusher who isn't fooled, the defender who attacks hard but attacks smart. That image is backed up by game charting and tape study.

When it came to sacks and big plays, Bowens was the equal of many of the league's best full-time starters in 2006. But what about the small plays? The flip side of Bowens's 16-for-16 season is a dearth of routine plays. The tackles Bowens didn't make tell another story, that of a limited defender who gets blocked too easily to make an every-down contribution. One Defeat per week doesn't make a player a starter or take him to the Pro Bowl. It does make him a valuable role player. The Jets have two solid starters at defensive end in Shaun Ellis and Bryan Thomas. They needed a reliable contributor off the bench. If Bowens can provide 16 more big plays in part-time duty this year, the Jets will be satisfied.

Mike Tanier

Jets 2006 Stats by Week

Wk	vs.	W–L	PF	PA	YDF	YDA	TO	Total	Off	Def	ST
								DVOA			
1	@TEN	W	23	16	393	328	+1	18.2%	23.2%	-9.4%	-14.4%
2	NE	L	17	24	358	337	-1	-8.6%	12.5%	17.6%	-3.5%
3	@BUF	W	28	20	256	475	+3	14.6%	25.9%	15.0%	3.7%
4	IND	L	28	31	321	352	-3	-5.1%	-8.6%	15.6%	19.1%
5	@JAC	L	0	41	177	312	-4	-107.8%	-58.7%	37.2%	-11.9%
6	MIA	W	20	17	272	395	+3	6.6%	11.6%	4.2%	-0.9%
7	DET	W	31	24	398	386	+1	2.7%	27.6%	32.2%	7.3%
8	@CLE	L	13	20	193	297	-2	-51.5%	-45.4%	27.4%	21.2%
9	BYE										
10	@NE	W	17	14	278	377	+1	39.0%	19.9%	-10.4%	8.7%
11	CHI	L	0	10	264	284	-2	-20.3%	-14.4%	7.2%	1.3%
12	HOU	W	26	11	304	334	+1	-6.5%	-2.6%	13.0%	9.1%
13	@GB	W	38	10	441	351	+1	42.1%	42.5%	-0.1%	-0.4%
14	BUF	L	13	31	275	318	-2	-58.5%	-35.5%	29.7%	6.8%
15	@MIN	W	26	13	391	307	-1	20.9%	16.7%	7.6%	11.7%
16	@MIA	W	13	10	324	253	-1	-6.2%	0.9%	-1.6%	-8.7%
17	OAK	W	23	3	266	209	+3	44.9%	25.1%	-14.6%	5.2%
18	@NE	L	16	37	347	358	-1	-13.1%	-1.0%	14.1%	2.1%

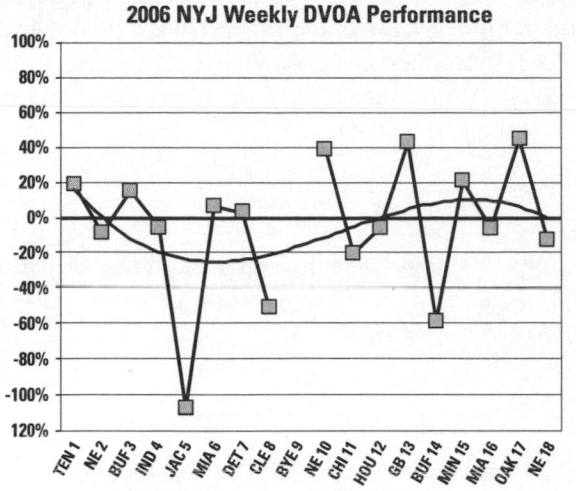

2006 NYJ Weekly DVOA Performance

Trends and Splits

	Offense	Rank	Defense	Rank
Total DVOA	2.8%	14	10.3%	26
Unadjusted VOA	0.2%	16	4.5%	22
Weighted Trend	3.8%	14	7.7%	24
Variance	7.7%	9	2.4%	32
Passing	9.5%	12	5.2%	18
Rushing	-3.9%	18	16.0%	32
First Down	0.3%	14	18.9%	32
Second Down	-2.6%	20	11.7%	28
Third Down	14.7%	9	-7.0%	8
Red Zone	-2.7%	17	11.7%	26
Late and Close	18.3%	5	14.3%	28

Five-Year Performance

	2006	2005	2004	2003	2002
W-L	10-6	4-12	10-6	6-10	9-7
Pythagorean Wins	8.7	4.5	10.2	7.5	8.6
Estimated Wins	7.7	5.2	11.3	7.6	9.5
Total DVOA	-4.3%	-20.0%	26.4%	-5.6%	12.9%
Rank	19	27	5	20	9
Offense	2.8%	-19.3%	20.0%	4.8%	18.6%
Rank	14	31	5	11	4
Defense	10.3%	0.6%	-4.1%	12.2%	11.0%
Rank	26	18	11	29	26
Special Teams	3.2%	-0.1%	2.3%	1.9%	5.4%
Rank	5	18	9	11	4

Strategic Tendencies

Formations		Rank	Run/Pass		Rank	Defense		Rank	Other		Rank
3+ WR	50%	10	Runs, all plays	48%	8	Sacks by LB	54%	6	Run with 2+ RB	63%	13
4+ WR	17%	4	Runs, first half	45%	15	Sacks by DB	19%	2	Run with 2+ TE	18%	30
2+ TE	15%	29	Runs, first down	63%	1	Rush 6+	15.5%	2	Play action	18%	19
Single back	47%	23	Runs, power sit.	56%	27	Rush 7+	4.6%	2	Go for it on 4th	0.83	19
Empty back	2.5%	12	Runs, behind 2H	42%	2	Rush 3	25.4%	1	Offensive Pace	30.2	14
Max protect	15%	8	Pass, ahead 2H	45%	13	CB1 on WR1	41%	19	Defensive Pace	30.7	17

The Jets didn't just rush three defenders more often than any other team, they were off the charts. Cleveland rushed only three men on 14 percent of its opponents' pass plays, and every other NFL team was below 10 percent. Since the Jets also blitzed more than almost any other team, they used the conventional four pass rushers on less than 60 percent of their opponents' pass plays. Every other team rushed four defenders on at least 78 percent of opposing pass plays. . . . The Jets ranked third in using draw plays, but posted a meager 4.6% DVOA on those plays, which ranked 20th. . . . The Jets spread the

(continued next page)

Strategic Tendencies (continued)

ball around on third down less than any other offense. Andre Johnson of Houston led the league as his team's most frequent third-down target, but Jerricho Cotchery was second and Laveranues Coles was eighth. . . . The Jets' defense ranked second in Coverage Sacks and second in sacks with Rusher Untouched, but was tied with Washington for the least number of sacks classified as Blown Blocks. . . . The Jets defense was ranked 28th in passes defensed. . . . The Jets and Patriots were tied for the league's best DVOA against play-action passes (−35.5%) but the Jets allowed fewer yards per play-action pass (4.5) than the Patriots (5.7).

Passing

Player	DPAR	DVOA	Plys	NtYds	Avg	YAC	C%	TD	Int
Chad Pennington	52.3	10.2%	479	3185	6.6	4.4	65.3%	17	15
M. Tuiasosopo	-6.4	-116.6%	13	68	5.2	2.7	46.2%	1	2

Rushing

Player	DPAR	DVOA	Plys	Yds	Avg	TD	Fum	Suc
Leon Washington	17.4	16.0%	151	650	4.3	4	1	49%
Kevan Barlow*	-1.7	-14.9%	131	368	2.8	6	1	42%
Cedric Houston	4.9	-4.0%	113	374	3.3	5	0	45%
Derrick Blaylock*	-5.7	-70.9%	25	44	1.8	0	0	40%
Chad Pennington	2.5	-1.4%	24	119	5.0	0	7	—
Brad Smith	4.7	11.7%	18	103	5.7	0	0	—
B. J. Askew*	-1.2	-54.7%	6	11	1.8	0	0	57%
Jerricho Cotchery	0.3	-15.2%	5	25	5.0	0	0	—
Thomas Jones	25.7	5.7%	296	1210	4.1	6	1	48%
M. Tuiasosopo	-0.2	-25.5%	4	29	7.3	0	1	—

Receiving

Player	DPAR	DVOA	Plys	Ctch	Yds	Y/C	YAC	TD	C%
WR									
Laveranues Coles	14.8	-0.2%	151	91	1080	11.9	3.0	6	66%
Jerricho Cotchery	23.5	13.0%	125	82	960	11.7	4.3	6	60%
Justin McCareins	5.0	4.0%	39	23	345	15.0	4.1	1	59%
Tim Dwight	2.2	2.6%	19	16	112	7.0	3.6	0	84%
Brad Smith	-0.8	-23.2%	14	9	64	7.1	4.1	0	64%
TE									
Chris Baker	9.7	20.7%	45	31	300	9.7	4.0	4	69%
Sean Ryan	-2.4	-57.5%	9	6	44	7.3	3.3	0	67%
RB									
Leon Washington	3.3	10.1%	31	25	265	10.6	11.0	0	81%
B. J. Askew*	-0.2	-11.4%	12	9	50	5.6	5.3	0	75%
Kevan Barlow*	-2.8	-63.1%	10	7	21	3.0	4.4	0	56%
Derrick Blaylock*	-0.2	-13.4%	9	5	29	5.8	5.2	0	88%
Cedric Houston	-0.7	-29.8%	8	7	43	6.1	8.1	0	40%
James Hodgins	-1.4	-62.6%	5	2	9	5	4.0	0	70%
Thomas Jones	-6.2	-34.0%	47	36	154	4	6.5	0	66%
Darian Barnes	-1.9	-63.3%	7	3	22	7	5.0	0	43%

Offensive Line

Year	Yards	ALY	Rank	Power	Rank	10+ Yds	Rank	Stuff	Rank	Sack	ASR	Rank
2004	4.70	4.83	2	84%	1	14%	30	18%	3	31	6.7%	15
2005	3.46	3.86	24	71%	7	11%	30	27%	26	53	10.2%	31
2006	3.40	3.96	25	56%	27	8%	30	25%	23	34	6.6%	17

Year	LE	Rank	LT	Rank	Mid	Rank	RT	Rank	RE	Rank
2004	4.93	6	4.71	11	4.63	5	5.17	3	5.33	1
2005	2.15	32	4.17	19	3.79	26	4.76	4	4.36	11
2006	2.77	29	4.65	11	3.94	27	4.72	3	3.76	20

In the 2006 draft, the Jets became only the second team (after the 1975 Rams) to take two offensive linemen in the first round. While left tackle D'Brickashaw Ferguson and center Nick Mangold didn't represent a significant performance upgrade on Jason Fabini and Kevin Mawae last year, they will be a lot better than that pair starting this year and for about the next 12. Ferguson had shaky moments in 2006, particularly as a pass blocker, but he also showed flashes of brilliance and is on the Pro Bowl track, not the Robert Gallery track. Mangold didn't get the cameras on him every time he made a mistake the way Ferguson did, but he was still the better player of the two his first season. While Pete Kendall filled in at center and guard in 2005, he remained at left guard all season in 2006 and did an excellent job pulling in the running game. Kendall was shopped around following fears that he might hold out, and, although he hadn't been traded at press time, he didn't participate in the Jets' "voluntary" offseason program. The Jets would replace him with former Dolphins washout Wade Smith or a free agent, perhaps local boy Joe Andruzzi. Right tackle Anthony Clement beat out Adrian Jones for the starting gig, but when Pennington went down, Clement was usually the one who was standing around looking confused. His starting job isn't under threat yet, but that's only because the Jets don't have a better option.

Defensive Front Seven

Defensive Line	Age	Pos	Plys	TmPct	Rk	Stop	Dfts	StpRt	Rk	AvYd	Rk	Sack	Hit	Hur	Runs	RuStp	RuYd	Pass	PaStp	PaYd
Dewayne Robertson	26	DT	63	7.8%	7	51	11	81%	28	2.0	43	2.5	3	9	57	79%	2.6	6	100%	-2.8
Shaun Ellis	30	DE	61	7.6%	21	44	13	72%	62	2.1	59	5	0	10	50	68%	3.2	11	91%	-2.7
Kimo von Oelhoffen	36	DT	29	3.6%	69	20	2	69%	62	2.0	42	1	0	2	26	65%	2.6	3	100%	-3.0
Kenyon Coleman	*28*	*DE*	*33*	*4.2%*	*69*	*24*	*7*	*73%*	*57*	*2.1*	*58*	*4*	*1*	*3*	*24*	*67%*	*3.0*	*9*	*89%*	*-0.1*
David Bowens	*30*	*DE*	*16*	*2.0%*	*—*	*16*	*16*	*100%*	*—*	*-1.1*	*—*	*5*	*0*	*1*	*4*	*100%*	*2.0*	*12*	*100%*	*-2.2*

Linebackers	Age	Pos	Plys	TmPct	Rk	Stop	Dfts	StpRt	AvYd	Sack	Hit	Hur	Runs	RuStp	Rk	RuYd	Rk	Tgts	Suc%	Rk	PaYd	Rk
Jonathan Vilma	25	ILB	121	15.0%	23	59	15	49%	5.0	0	3	3	81	56%	82	4.0	80	37	56%	30	6.1	42
Victor Hobson	27	OLB	103	12.8%	46	54	20	52%	5.0	6	7	8	58	59%	73	4.7	93	37	47%	59	7.1	73
Eric Barton	30	OLB	102	12.7%	47	56	15	55%	3.8	4.5	1	3	79	56%	81	4.0	77	22	40%	80	6.9	72
Bryan Thomas	28	OLB	78	9.7%	73	44	17	56%	3.9	8.5	4	19	44	66%	43	3.2	33	16	45%	68	7.3	78
Brad Kassell	27	ILB	20	2.5%	—	9	1	45%	5.3	0	0	1	13	46%	—	3.8	—	9	53%	—	5.7	—
Matt Chatham	30	OLB	19	2.4%	—	12	3	63%	2.7	0	0	2	14	71%	—	1.9	—	7	50%	—	5.6	—

Year	Yards	ALY	Rank	Power	Rank	10+ Yds	Rank	Stuff	Rank	Sack	ASR	Rank
2004	3.68	3.89	4	61%	15	15%	11	28%	6	36	6.6%	21
2005	4.04	4.46	27	83%	32	12%	4	20%	30	30	6.6%	20
2006	4.65	4.99	32	67%	18	14%	8	16%	32	35	6.3%	18

Year	LE	Rank	LT	Rank	Mid	Rank	RT	Rank	RE	Rank
2004	2.71	1	4.74	26	4.02	9	3.46	1	4.29	22
2005	4.81	24	4.63	27	4.35	24	5.03	29	3.54	9
2006	5.12	29	5.30	30	4.61	24	5.67	31	4.54	22

We wrote in last year's book that the Jets would struggle to fit into the 3-4 defense, and they did; Dewayne Robertson wasn't stout enough to be a 3-4 nose tackle, while former Steelers end Kimo von Oelhoffen was a disaster in his first season in New York. With a paucity of stud 3-4 linemen available both in free agency and the draft, the Jets went for quantity and hoped that spotting their linemen better would improve the team's play. The big signing was former Cowboys end Kenyon Coleman, but this team desperately needs a nose tackle.

The linebackers weren't much better. Inside linebacker Jonathan Vilma, who looked like a star in the 4-3, struggled to make plays with guards crawling all over him in the 3-4. Eventually, the Jets started pushing Vilma farther off the line of scrimmage to try to give him more space, to the point at which he was almost serving as a third safety. Fellow inside linebacker Eric Barton served as the run plugger, but that's not a role in which he's particularly effective. As a result, the Jets used a second-round pick on David Harris of Michigan, who may have been the best run-stopping linebacker in the whole draft. Harris will take Barton's job at some point this season. Outside linebacker Bryan Thomas slimmed down last year and was effective as a pass rusher and run stunter, but still gets lost in coverage. Victor Hobson remains the starter on the other side.

Defensive Secondary

Secondary	Age	Pos	Plys	TmPct	Rk	Stop	Dfts	RuYd	Rk	RuStp	Rk	Tgts	Tgt%	Rk	Dist	Suc%	Rk	PaYd	Rk	PD	Int
Andre Dyson	28	CB	70	9.3%	35	23	13	9.7	65	26%	68	71	16%	52	10.7	46%	68	6.8	26	9	4
Justin Miller	23	CB	59	7.3%	59	24	12	5.2	24	50%	24	61	13%	71	9.6	55%	27	7.5	42	5	0
Kerry Rhodes	25	FS	106	13.2%	9	40	19	5.7	25	32%	60	47	9%	18	10.9	56%	27	5.8	12	11	4
David Barrett	30	CB	42	6.4%	71	12	7	7.5	53	27%	67	46	11%	79	13.2	51%	42	7.6	45	7	3
Erik Coleman	25	SS	97	12.0%	17	23	10	8.4	68	21%	75	43	8%	34	12.3	62%	15	6.2	17	2	1
Hank Poteat	30	CB	39	6.0%	—	11	6	6.5	—	30%	—	43	8%	—	11.5	52%	—	6.1	—	4	0
Drew Coleman	25	CB	23	2.9%	—	7	4	5.0	—	0%	—	34	7%	—	8.8	48%	—	8.5	—	3	0
Eric Smith	24	SS	17	2.2%	—	9	5	3.0	—	50%	—	13	3%	—	12.0	76%	—	5.9	—	3	2

Year	Pass D Rank	DVOA vs. #1 WR	Rank	DVOA vs. #2 WR	Rank	DVOA vs. Other WR	Rank	DVOA vs. TE	Rank	DVOA vs. RB	Rank
2004	19	31.3%	31	16.7%	27	-16.1%	11	-16.2%	8	-3.9%	13
2005	8	14.7%	21	-38.1%	2	-19.1%	7	10.5%	23	-22.2%	4
2006	18	-0.4%	15	12.8%	25	3.2%	21	-20.3%	7	6.9%	20

(continued next page)

Defensive Secondary *(continued)*

Kerry Rhodes had a breakout year under Mangini, showing impeccable instincts on the blitz and a playmaker's flair with four interceptions and three forced fumbles. If he plays at that level again, he'll fit in comfortably as the backup to Ed Reed in next year's Pro Bowl. Free safety Erik Coleman has struggled to live up to his performances as a rookie, and 2007 is likely his last opportunity to return to that level before he gets tossed overboard. Rookie safety Eric Smith looked good in his limited play. If it comes down to an argument over how to spell their first name, you know who Mangini will side with.

In this year's draft, the Jets traded up to grab Pittsburgh corner Darrelle Revis, leaving the higher-ranked (by most observers) Leon Hall on the board. Revis is fast, but he plays slower than his 40 time and is unlikely to develop into an elite corner. He will, however, be a good corner as soon as he steps into the starting lineup. He has great instincts and ball skills, and, with Justin Miller moving into the slot, Revis won't need to cover Ted Ginn or Roscoe Parrish. Miller's been a project at cornerback since he entered the league and has yet to make significant strides. He will benefit from being placed in the slot. Andre Dyson will start on the other side, with Hank Poteat and David Barrett in reserve.

Special Teams

Year	DVOA	Rank	FG/XP	Rank	Net Punt	Rank	Punt Ret	Rank	Net Kick	Rank	Kick Ret	Rank	Hidden	Rank
2004	2.3%	9	0.9	15	7.5	6	-1.6	20	4.9	10	1.7	12	-5.4	23
2005	0.0%	18	-2.4	21	4.8	9	-4.5	28	-6.7	26	8.5	4	-9.0	28
2006	3.2%	5	0.4	15	7.9	7	-2.6	24	-1.1	21	14.3	2	6.7	8

The Jets' kick return unit was special in 2006. While the top-ranked Patriots consistently garnered solid returns, the Jets and Justin Miller were more spectacular. Miller's most memorable return was a 103-yarder for a touchdown with 2:20 left against the Colts in Week 4 that gave the Jets a 28–24 lead . . . that the defense relinquished anyway. Miller scored two touchdowns and had eight returns over 40 yards on the season. Revis takes over on punt returns from Leon Washington, which should be a plus as well.

Punter Ben Graham is one of the more fun players in football—the 34-year-old ex-Australian Rules footballer has a giant leg that booms punts ten yards over returners' heads, and he is one of the few punters more likely to rough than be roughed. He signed a six-year extension in the offseason. As for our favorite whipping boy, well, kicker Mike Nugent improved last year to the level that Doug Brien was at two seasons ago. He'll be competent for a number of seasons, but he's still going to be a wasted pick.

Coaching Staff

Eric Mangini's press conferences aren't as entertaining as Herman Edwards's. That is about the only way in which the Jets' coaching didn't improve in 2006. Mangini put every position up for grabs, found roles for players such as Leon Washington, Jerricho Cotchery, Bryan Thomas, and Kerry Rhodes, and the time-management issues that had plagued the Jets under Edwards mysteriously disappeared. While the 2006 team wasn't perfect, Mangini clearly was the right hire.

Offensive coordinator Brian Schottenheimer got some press with regards to the Miami opening. He's probably not ready for a head coaching gig, but you might have said that about Mangini heading into last year, too. Schottenheimer built an offense around the strengths of the personnel he had: the play-action pass and running behind Kendall. Bob Sutton returns as defensive coordinator, but, much like Belichick in New England, Mangini's the man who's actually charge of the defense. Looking for a future coordinator on the staff? Former AFC East DE/LB Bryan Cox is managing the defensive linemen, and may end up replacing Sutton in a couple years' time.

Oakland Raiders

The 2006 Oakland Raiders were a joke. That's not just our way of saying they were a bad team (although they certainly were). It's meant literally: The words "2006 Oakland Raiders" can make football fans burst into laughter. Consider just a few of the things that made last year's Raiders the butt of jokes around the league: (1) Offensive coordinator Tom Walsh had been out of coaching for more than a decade and had most recently managed a bed and breakfast. (2) Wide receiver Jerry Porter feuded with head coach Art Shell, a feud that culminated with Shell accusing Porter of cheering against the Raiders while he stood on the sideline during a game. Porter denied cheering against his own team, saying that would have been impossible because he wasn't even watching the game. (3) The Raiders had three nationally televised games and lost them by a combined score of 63-9, and the only memorable play any Raider made in any of those games came when defensive end Tyler Brayton kneed Seahawks tight end Jerramy Stevens in the groin, earning an ejection. (4) The offensive line was a sieve, ranking dead last in Adjusted Sack Rate, despite having a head coach (Shell) and an offensive line coach (Jackie Slater) who were Hall of Fame offensive linemen themselves.

We could go on, but let's go into some more detail about that offensive line. The biggest problem was at the most important position, left tackle, where Robert Gallery missed six games and was ineffective when he did play. Gallery was the most highly touted offensive line prospect in years when the Raiders drafted him out of Iowa in 2004, and his failure to develop into a solid player is a major disappointment for the Raiders. His contract is also a major strain on their salary cap.

As bad as Gallery has been, the line was even worse without him. In the six games Gallery missed, he was replaced by Chad Slaughter, a 6-foot-8, 340-pounder who looks like a prototypical NFL left tackle when he stands on the sidelines but clearly doesn't belong there when the game starts. A guy as big as Slaughter can always find a job in the NFL, but any team that starts him at left tackle is going to see their quarterback get, well, slaughtered.

The Raiders tried a few different guard combinations but never found a good one. Kevin Boothe and Paul McQuistan were both rookies who should have been learning on the bench, but the Raiders were so desperate for warm bodies on the line that Boothe started 14 games and McQuistan started six. Neither played well, nor did Barry Sims, who played part of the year at guard and part at tackle.

Center Jake Grove is a decent player who could be a good player if he had better teammates. Grove made the line calls and often appeared to have communication problems with his teammates, especially the rookie guards on either side of him. ESPN analyst Ron Jaworski cited those communication problems as the biggest reason for the offensive line's weakness last year.

The most talented member of last year's Oakland offensive line—not that being the best player on the Raiders' line is anything special—was right tackle Langston Walker, a massive player who showed surprising quickness when asked to get to the second level on running plays. Walker signed with the Buffalo Bills as a free agent in the offseason. Still, despite the loss of Walker, the line can't help but get at least a little better thanks to the addition of Cooper Carlisle, who started all 16 games at guard for the Broncos last year, and new offensive line coach Tom Cable. Cable spent last year with the Falcons and will implement a zone-blocking scheme similar to the one the Falcons ran, which seems like a better fit for the Raiders' personnel.

RAIDERS PROSPECTUS

2006 Record: 2–14

DVOA Estimated Wins: 3.9 (32nd)

Pythagorean Wins: 2.7 (32nd)

DVOA: −30.0% total (32nd), −25.4% weighted (31st)

Offense: −35.6% DVOA (32nd)

Defense: 8.6% DVOA (8th)

Special Teams: −3.0% DVOA (26th)

Variance: 10.0% (26th)

2006: Snicker, chortle, guffaw.

2007: They couldn't possibly be worse, but don't expect them to be much better.

2007 Mean Projection: 6.5 wins

The Brohm Closet (0–4): 19%

Bad Team (5–6): 32%

Mediocre (7–8): 31%

Playoff Contender (9–10): 14%

Super Bowl Contender (11+): 4%

Projected Average Opponent: −3.0% DVOA (27th in NFL)

2007 Raiders Schedule

Week	Opp	Week	Opp	Week	Opp
1	DET	7	KC	13	DEN
2	at DEN	8	at TEN	14	at GB
3	CLE	9	HOU	15	IND
4	at MIA	10	CHI	16	at JAC
5	BYE	11	at MIN	17	SD
6	at SD	12	at KC		

The development of the offensive line will dictate how soon we see rookie quarterback JaMarcus Russell, whom the Raiders selected with the first pick in the draft. If Cable can whip his troops into shape—at least enough to make them resemble a professional offensive line—new head coach Lane Kiffin can feel confident that when he puts Russell on the field, he won't be risking the quarterback's future. If the line looks as bad in 2006 as it did in 2007, Russell should warm the bench.

Although Raiders owner Al Davis has fired three head coaches in the last five years, the early indications are that he'll give Kiffin all the time he needs to develop Russell properly. When Davis hired Kiffin, then 31, off the staff of the University of Southern California, Kiffin became not just the youngest coach in the league right now, but the youngest coach in the history of the league, and Davis wants Kiffin to grow into the job.

Kiffin was a surprising choice both because of his age, and because coaches rarely go directly from college assistant to professional head coach. Davis has never hesitated to hire young coaches, though. Davis himself spent three seasons as the Raiders' head coach starting in 1963, when he was 33 years old, and Davis hired four of the 16 other men who have become NFL head coaches at age 35 or younger: Kiffin, John Madden, Mike Shanahan, and Jon Gruden. Davis clearly has an eye for young coaching talent, as Madden, Shanahan, and Gruden all coached teams to championships, although only Madden won his Super Bowl ring with the Raiders.

The list of NFL head coaches who have started before age 35 includes two who are now in the Pro Football Hall of Fame, Madden and Don Shula, but it also includes several who were in over their heads, such as Harland Svare of the Los Angeles Rams, who went 14–31–3 in the 1960s, and Shula's son, David, who went 19–52 in the 1990s with the Cincinnati Bengals. It's too soon to say where Kiffin falls, but he has a huge job ahead of him rebuilding the Raiders' offense, which wasn't just the worst in the league in 2006, it was among the worst any league observer could ever remember seeing. The Raiders' offensive DVOA of −35.5% was light years behind the Browns' 31st ranked offense, which had a DVOA of −18.2%. In the 11 years of DVOA, only three offenses were worse: the 2002 Texans, 2004 Bears, and 2005 49ers.

The best player on the Raiders' offense last year, by a wide margin, was wide receiver Ronald Curry, who ranked 20th in the league in DVOA and 25th in DPAR. Doing that in the 2006 Raiders' offense is miraculous. The rest of the receiving corps is a question mark. With Randy Moss gone, the Raiders have eliminated a big headache, but also a big talent. Kiffin should be able to develop a better rapport with Porter than Shell had, but it remains to be seen if Porter can get his head in the game after catching just one pass last year. Alvis Whitted was terrible in 2006, and new addition Mike Williams was always overweight and out of shape during two years in Detroit.

With the disarray the Raiders' offense was in last year, it would have been easy for the defense to pack it in. Instead, the defense excelled. The dichotomy between the Raiders' offense and defense was demonstrated in many games, but the best example being when the Raiders played the Houston Texans in an ugly December game. The Raiders' defense forced Texans quarterback David Carr to fumble three times and sacked him for more negative yards (37) than they allowed him to gain passing (32)—but the offense turned the ball over five times, and the Raiders still lost.

That the defense continued to play well despite the offense throwing games away is a credit, first and foremost, to defensive coordinator Rob Ryan (who might have been a better choice than Kiffin to get the head job), and it's also a credit to the talent the Raiders have assembled on defense. The most talented player may be strong safety Michael Huff, who had a great rookie year after the Raiders took him with the seventh overall pick. The Raiders were often criticized for passing on Matt Leinart to take Huff, but Huff will be an outstanding player for a long time. With Huff, free safety Stuart Schweigert, and cornerbacks Fabian Washington and Nnamdi Asomugha, the Raiders have one of the youngest secondaries in the league, and one of the best.

That secondary is aided by the pass rush of defensive end Derrick Burgess. After starting his career with four disappointing, injury-plagued years in Philadelphia, Burgess has become a pass-rushing demon in Ryan's Oakland defense, recording 27 sacks over the last two years. Rookie defensive end Quentin Moses, a third-round pick out of Georgia, has a very good chance of winning a starting job opposite Burgess. Although Moses fell in the draft after a disappointing senior season, he has the natural ability to become the same kind of edge rusher as Burgess. Defensive tackle Warren Sapp had ten sacks last year, his most since 2000, and, after losing 49 pounds over the offseason, he should continue to rush the passer well even at age 35.

The Raiders' defense isn't perfect. Much like his father, Buddy, Rob Ryan runs a defense in which the linebackers either blitz or drop into deep pass coverage. Either way, that leaves the middle of the field open. For that reason, Oakland struggles to stop passes to opposing running backs. The run defense is only average, with defensive tackle Terdell Sands getting pushed around far more than a 6-foot-7, 335-pounder should.

The problems with the defense are minor, however, and they pale in comparison to the problems on offense. Kiffin has an enormous task ahead of him in revitalizing the offensive line and developing Russell into a big-time player. He might get things turned around eventually, but not in 2007.

Michael David Smith

Raiders 2006 Stats by Week

Wk	vs.	W–L	PF	PA	YDF	YDA	TO	DVOA Total	Off	Def	ST
1	SD	L	0	27	129	302	-1	-37.0%	-53.3%	-11.9%	4.4%
2	@BAL	L	6	28	162	264	-5	-55.0%	-64.9%	-6.7%	3.3%
3	BYE										
4	CLE	L	21	24	240	283	+2	-48.9%	-15.9%	16.2%	-16.8%
5	@SF	L	20	34	370	330	-4	-58.5%	-27.8%	17.8%	-12.9%
6	@DEN	L	3	13	235	244	-1	-65.9%	-40.9%	14.2%	-10.8%
7	ARI	W	22	9	395	224	-3	34.8%	-35.3%	-60.9%	9.2%
8	PIT	W	20	13	98	360	+3	14.7%	-52.5%	-57.2%	10.0%
9	@SEA	L	0	16	185	371	0	-63.1%	-38.1%	23.5%	-1.5%
10	DEN	L	13	17	244	264	+1	7.3%	-23.5%	-30.2%	0.5%
11	@KC	L	13	17	326	292	-1	-11.6%	-2.3%	11.6%	2.3%
12	@SD	L	14	21	245	260	-1	-9.8%	-11.7%	-15.3%	-13.4%
13	HOU	L	14	23	302	124	-3	-10.4%	-37.7%	-53.3%	-26.1%
14	@CIN	L	10	27	223	439	+2	-53.2%	-49.1%	4.0%	0.0%
15	STL	L	0	20	260	251	-5	-41.5%	-47.2%	-8.8%	-3.0%
16	KC	L	9	20	307	292	-4	-12.2%	-26.3%	-9.4%	4.6%
17	@NYJ	L	3	23	209	266	-3	-66.0%	-49.8%	15.4%	-0.7%

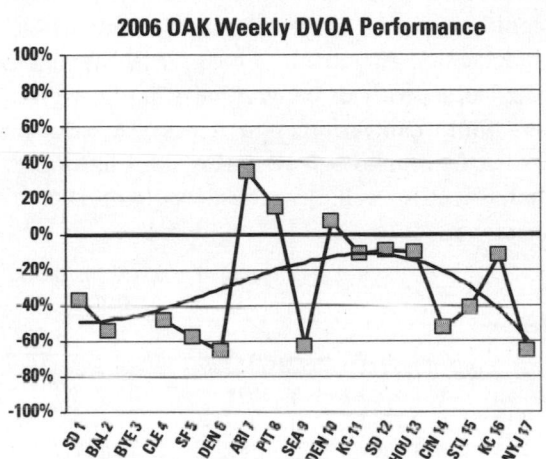

2006 OAK Weekly DVOA Performance

Trends and Splits

	Offense	Rank	Defense	Rank
Total DVOA	-35.6%	32	-8.6%	8
Unadjusted VOA	-37.1%	32	-4.2%	11
Weighted Trend	-33.3%	32	-11.0%	6
Variance	3.5%	31	7.3%	12
Passing	-47.6%	32	-16.7%	5
Rushing	-21.6%	31	-2.3%	16
First Down	-42.1%	32	-5.5%	16
Second Down	-34.3%	32	-9.8%	7
Third Down	-25.7%	31	-12.2%	6
Red Zone	-58.7%	32	-0.3%	13
Late and Close	-57.6%	32	-5.7%	12

Five-Year Performance

	2006	2005	2004	2003	2002
W-L	2-14	4-12	5-11	4-12	11-5
Pythagorean Wins	2.7	5.5	5.1	4.9	11.5
Estimated Wins	3.9	7.4	6.2	5.8	11.7
Total DVOA	-30.0%	-6.0%	-16.3%	-17.9%	30.9%
Rank	32	20	25	28	2
Offense	-35.6%	-0.1%	0.1%	-11.1%	24.4%
Rank	32	13	16	24	2
Defense	-8.6%	2.4%	14.7%	8.4%	-6.4%
Rank	8	23	26	25	7
Special Teams	-3.0%	-3.5%	-1.8%	1.7%	0.1%
Rank	26	29	22	12	15

Strategic Tendencies

Formations		Rank	Run/Pass		Rank	Defense		Rank	Other		Rank
3+ WR	40%	26	Runs, all plays	41%	26	Sacks by LB	6%	29	Run with 2+ RB	63%	14
4+ WR	4%	30	Runs, first half	46%	11	Sacks by DB	6%	19	Run with 2+ TE	37%	15
2+ TE	27%	14	Runs, first down	54%	15	Rush 6+	6.9%	21	Play action	11%	30
Single back	55%	15	Runs, power sit.	58%	25	Rush 7+	0.7%	26	Go for it on 4th	1.42	2
Empty back	0.0%	32	Runs, behind 2H	29%	25	Rush 3	6.8%	6	Offensive Pace	30.7	16
Max protect	13%	14	Pass, ahead 2H	47%	8	CB1 on WR1	37%	25	Defensive Pace	31.5	26

Oakland's offensive DVOA in the fourth quarter was −70.4%, more than twice as bad as any other team. The Raiders had 24 fourth-quarter turnovers, while no other team had more than 16.... Oakland passed the ball on 83 percent of their plays from a three-wide-receiver formation, the highest percentage in the league.... Oakland was the only team for which we did not record a single empty backfield formation. We also never recorded the Raiders in a five-wide set, because the Raiders could never find five receivers who were all out of Art Shell's doghouse at the same time.... The Raiders had at least six blockers on 78 percent of pass plays, the highest percentage in the NFL. Fat lot of good that did them: Oakland also led the league with 38 Blown Blocks leading directly to sacks.... Oakland's defense started its average drive at the opponent's 35-yard line, which was the worst starting field position for defense in the past four years. The Raider defense didn't allow many touchdowns, but also didn't force as many turnovers, punts, or three-and-outs as we might expect from a team that ranked so well in yards allowed and DVOA. They did a lot of bending without breaking, and gave up a lot of field goals as a result.

Passing

Player	DPAR	DVOA	Plys	NtYds	Avg	YAC	C%	TD	Int
Andrew Walter	-30.4	-36.9%	275	1407	5.1	3.4	53.5%	3	7
Aaron Brooks*	-15.8	-30.5%	190	926	4.9	3.9	57.9%	3	11
M. Tuiasosopo*	-6.4	-116.6%	13	68	5.2	2.7	46.2%	1	2

Rushing

Player	DPAR	DVOA	Plys	Yds	Avg	TD	Fum	Suc
Justin Fargas	1.1	-12.6%	178	652	3.7	1	1	40%
LaMont Jordan	2.8	-8.1%	114	434	3.8	2	0	34%
Zack Crockett	0.8	-11.7%	39	158	4.1	0	2	39%
ReShard Lee	-1.3	-22.0%	21	72	3.4	2	1	52%
Aaron Brooks*	0.4	-15.5%	18	125	6.9	0	5	—
Andrew Walter	-7.6	-170.7%	9	30	3.3	0	13	—
M. Tuiasosopo*	-0.2	-25.5%	4	29	7.3	0	1	—
Dominic Rhodes	0.6	-13.1%	187	641	3.4	5	2	49%
Justin Griffith	-2.3	-44.1%	19	106	5.6	1	2	52%

Receiving

Player	DPAR	DVOA	Plys	Ctch	Yds	Y/C	YAC	TD	C%
WR									
Randy Moss*	0.8	-13.7%	97	42	553	13.2	2.7	3	70%
Ronald Curry	17.2	14.4%	89	62	727	11.7	3.3	1	43%
Alvis Whitted	-8.8	-36.7%	63	27	303	11.2	1.1	0	43%
Johnnie Morant	-4.3	-68.6%	12	7	70	10.0	3.4	0	58%
Mike Williams	-0.8	-21.7%	18	8	99	12.4	2.4	1	44%
TE									
Randal Williams	-3.9	-23.4%	57	28	293	10.5	2.3	0	58%
Courtney Anderson	3.4	0.5%	43	25	285	11.4	3.3	2	49%
John Madsen	0.2	-14.0%	19	11	146	13.3	3.0	1	58%
Tony Stewart	3.2	17.9%	18	14	120	8.6	3.7	1	78%
RB									
ReShard Lee	1.3	0.2%	25	20	138	6.9	6.7	0	80%
Justin Fargas	-1.2	-21.7%	21	13	91	7.0	6.8	0	62%
Zack Crockett	-3.1	-46.6%	17	10	53	5.3	4.2	0	63%
LaMont Jordan	-1.9	-34.2%	16	10	74	7.4	9.6	0	59%
Dominic Rhodes	-0.1	-10.7%	47	36	251	7.0	6.2	0	77%
Justin Griffith	4.8	22.4%	28	23	168	7.3	6.2	3	82%

Offensive Line

Year	Yards	ALY	Rank	Power	Rank	10+ Yds	Rank	Stuff	Rank	Sack	ASR	Rank
2004	4.09	4.24	14	74%	3	18%	11	23%	13	30	5.3%	6
2005	3.75	4.06	17	64%	16	11%	28	25%	15	44	7.8%	23
2006	3.74	3.84	29	58%	25	15%	18	28%	30	72	12.4%	32

Year	LE	Rank	LT	Rank	Mid	Rank	RT	Rank	RE	Rank
2004	4.44	13	4.49	13	4.15	20	5.56	1	3.25	25
2005	4.31	13	4.41	13	4.13	16	3.74	24	3.51	24
2006	4.37	13	3.65	30	3.89	28	4.39	10	3.09	28

The departure of head coach Art Shell and co-offensive line coaches Jackie Slater and Irv Eatman will be good for the line. Last year, linemen frequently complained that they didn't know what was expected of them, which is not surprising as they were taking orders from three different coaches. New offensive line coach Tom Cable, previously with the Falcons, is installing a zone-blocking scheme. That made the Raiders a great fit for free-agent guard Cooper Carlisle, who comes from the zone-blocking Broncos and has been handed one of the starting guard positions. Paul McQuistan, who showed some promise as a rookie from Weber State last year, is expected to earn the other.

The Raiders will be in decent shape at guard. The bad news is at tackle, where Robert Gallery and Barry Sims are the likely starters. The Raiders can't feel comfortable about having that pair protecting JaMarcus Russell. Mario Henderson, a third-round tackle from Florida State, was the only offensive lineman the Raiders drafted this year. He has potential, but probably won't be ready to go as a rookie. Incumbent starter Jake Grove will battle free-agent addition Jeremy Newberry for the starting job at center. Newberry was once a good center for the 49ers, but injuries have limited him to just 11 games over the last three years, and Grove is the favorite to win the job.

Defensive Front Seven

Defensive Line	Age	Pos	Plys	TmPct	Rk	Stop	Dfts	StpRt	Rk	AvYd	Rk	Sack	Hit	Hur	Runs	RuStp	RuYd	Pass	PaStp	PaYd
Tommy Kelly	29	DE	68	8.3%	13	56	19	82%	20	1.8	53	3.5	3	4	60	80%	2.3	8	100%	-2.0
Derrick Burgess	29	DE	50	6.1%	38	41	17	82%	23	1.0	22	11	4	12	34	76%	3.2	16	94%	-3.6
Warren Sapp	35	DT	47	5.8%	26	45	19	96%	1	0.2	3	10	9	11	33	97%	2.0	14	93%	-4.1
Terdell Sands	28	DT	45	5.5%	31	39	13	87%	13	1.3	25	1	1	2	39	85%	1.5	6	100%	0.0
Tyler Brayton	28	DE	44	5.4%	48	25	6	57%		3.3	76	0	0	5	42	57%	3.2	2	50%	6.0
Bobby Hamilton	36	DE	32	3.9%	72	25	4	78%	38	2.7	71	0	0	1	29	79%	2.4	3	67%	5.3
Lance Johnstone	34	DE	16	2.9%	—	9	6	56%	—	3.2	—	2	2	2	12	50%	3.3	4	75%	2.8

Linebackers	Age	Pos	Plys	TmPct	Rk	Stop	Dfts	StpRt	AvYd	Sack	Hit	Hur	Runs	RuStp	Rk	RuYd	Rk	Tgts	Suc%	Rk	PaYd	Rk
Kirk Morrison	26	ILB	128	15.7%	19	82	33	64%	3.5	1	0	0	101	63%	53	3.1	29	29	67%	6	3.5	7
Thomas Howard	24	OLB	108	13.3%	39	56	19	52%	4.9	0	1	1	71	56%	78	4.1	81	28	59%	22	4.4	10
Sam Williams	27	OLB	38	5.0%	—	22	8	58%	3.4	1	1	2	27	63%	—	2.8	—	8	13%	—	7.3	—
Robert Thomas	27	OLB	30	3.7%	—	22	8	73%	2.4	0	0	1	24	79%	—	1.6	—	1	100%	—	0.0	—

Year	Yards	ALY	Rank	Power	Rank	10+ Yds	Rank	Stuff	Rank	Sack	ASR	Rank
2004	3.70	4.29	19	61%	14	9%	3	21%	29	26	5.9%	28
2005	4.11	4.42	25	63%	17	16%	16	24%	20	36	7.2%	15
2006	4.06	4.11	11	61%	11	16%	16	25%	13	34	7.4%	11

Year	LE	Rank	LT	Rank	Mid	Rank	RT	Rank	RE	Rank
2004	3.89	8	5.09	30	4.21	14	4.70	28	3.46	8
2005	3.67	9	4.42	21	4.53	29	4.35	21	5.09	30
2006	3.94	15	3.38	5	4.14	11	4.63	23	4.59	23

In a move that had been rumored to be in the works for ages, the Raiders fired personnel executive Michael Lombardi in May. When the team you've assembled is coming off a 2-14 season, it's hard to argue that you deserved to keep your job, but there's one thing that Lombardi was good at: drafting linebackers. Lombardi drafted all three members of the Raiders' talented starting trio: Sam Williams (2003, third round), Kirk Morrison (2005, third round), and Thomas Howard (2006, second round).

The defensive line is much better at rushing the passer than at stopping the run, and, unfortunately, so is rookie defensive end Quentin Moses. The weight starting tackle Warren Sapp has lost will only tip the balance further in that direction. Fifth-round pick Jay Richardson, a defensive end from Ohio State, is an intriguing rookie. He's a good enough athlete to play linebacker, but at 6-foot-5 and 276 pounds, he's built more like a defensive lineman. He looks like the kind of athlete who could play all over the field, the way Adalius Thomas did in Baltimore. We're confident Rob Ryan will find the right way to use him.

Defensive Secondary

Secondary	Age	Pos	Plys	TmPct	Rk	Stop	Dfts	RuYd	Rk	RuStp	Rk	Tgts	Tgt%	Rk	Dist	Suc%	Rk	PaYd	Rk	PD	Int
Fabian Washington	24	CB	55	7.7%	50	20	12	12.5	77	18%	76	77	25%	5	14.1	50%	52	7.1	33	13	4
Nnamdi Asomugha	26	CB	70	9.2%	38	29	20	11.2	72	33%	61	61	19%	41	13.5	51%	41	7.8	47	19	8
Michael Huff	24	SS	76	9.3%	47	40	14	4.0	4	60%	6	37	11%	5	8.6	53%	33	6.8	27	2	0
Stuart Schweigert	26	FS	103	12.6%	14	19	5	9.8	73	19%	76	26	7%	41	12.3	51%	46	7.1	30	4	0
Tyrone Poole*	35	CB	19	2.9%	—	10	6	5.0	—	100%	—	25	9%	—	13.5	51%	—	8.8	—	5	1
Stanford Routt	24	CB	17	2.1%	—	5	3	16.3	—	0%	—	17	5%	—	8.1	35%	—	6.8	—	1	1
Chris Carr	24	CB	16	2.0%	—	7	3	5.8	—	50%	—	16	5%	—	8.6	63%	—	3.8	—	2	1

Year	Pass D Rank	DVOA vs. #1 WR	Rank	DVOA vs. #2 WR	Rank	DVOA vs. Other WR	Rank	DVOA vs. TE	Rank	DVOA vs. RB	Rank
2004	32	19.1%	24	-1.2%	14	39.9%	32	8.2%	18	3.5%	17
2005	27	16.6%	24	4.8%	26	22.0%	31	1.3%	19	20.7%	31
2006	5	-30.5%	1	22.1%	28	-22.4%	7	-19.6%	8	12.1%	24

This is a good unit, both at cornerback (Nnamdi Asomugha and Fabian Washington are the starters) and at safety (Michael Huff at strong safety and Stuart Schweigert at free safety). The Raiders' defense often uses one of the safeties to help out against the opposition's number-one receiver, and Huff fit that part perfectly, a big reason why Oakland was the best in the league in that category. Asomugha is a 2003 first-round pick who had been something of a disappointment, but he had by far the best season of his career in 2006, intercepting eight passes after getting none in three previous seasons. The Raiders are thrilled with the starting four. The only real question is who will be the fifth defensive back on the field in the nickel package. A pair of rookies, fourth-round pick John Bowie from Cincinnati and fifth-round pick Eric Frampton from Washington State, will vie for that job.

Special Teams

Year	DVOA	Rank	FG/XP	Rank	Net Punt	Rank	Punt Ret	Rank	Net Kick	Rank	Kick Ret	Rank	Hidden	Rank
2004	-1.8%	22	6.0	6	-2.7	23	-5.0	27	-0.2	15	-8.7	30	19.9	1
2005	-3.5%	29	-8.0	27	-7.8	28	-6.1	31	-7.5	27	8.7	3	-5.4	22
2006	-3.0%	26	-0.6	17	-8.1	28	-3.0	26	-15.9	31	9.8	3	2.2	14

Both kicker Sebastian Janikowski and punter Shane Lechler suffered last season from the Raiders' terrible coverage teams. Janikowski had average kick value, but returns against the Raiders were worth 16.9 points. That was the worst kick coverage in the league by a huge margin. How huge? The Colts' kickoff coverage team was woefully bad, yet the Colts allowed just 15.4 points of returns on 82 kickoffs. The Raiders allowed 16.9 on only 48. Lechler had an off year by his standards, accomplishing the rare feat of booting the ball into the end zone for a touchback as many times (19) as he pinned the other team inside the 20-yard line, but the main reason the Raiders had a negative value on punts is that the coverage units gave up huge returns.

Chris Carr, the second-year backup defensive back from Boise State, handled all the return duties last year. Carr has speed and is very good at returning kickoffs, but doesn't have a feel for returning punts. He'll probably be replaced on punt returns by third-round pick Johnnie Lee Higgins, a wide receiver from Texas-El Paso who was one of the fastest players in this year's draft.

Coaching Staff

When Lane Kiffin became the new head coach, his approach to building the staff was simple: fire the offensive assistants and keep the defensive assistants. It was the right approach. The defensive staff, including coordinator Rob Ryan, linebackers coach Don Martindale, defensive line coach Keith Millard, and defensive backs coach Willie Brown, has done great work in Oakland. Ryan seems likely to become a head coach eventually. If he does, it will be a major loss for the Raiders. The most important offensive assistant is quarterbacks coach John DeFilippo, who will be tasked with showing JaMarcus Russell the ropes. Like Kiffin, DeFilippo is a young coach (at 29, he's three years younger than Kiffin) with a relatively light résumé. DeFilippo spent the past two seasons as an offensive quality control assistant for the Giants and the two before that as the quarterbacks coach at Columbia.

Pittsburgh Steelers

The Pittsburgh Steelers' "one for the thumb" campaign for a fifth Super Bowl title took 26 years, but it took a few months for things to begin to unravel. From the moment Ben Roethlisberger crashed his motorcycle in the middle of downtown Pittsburgh, everything went wrong for the 2006 Steelers. Pittsburgh stumbled to a 2–6 start before rallying to finish 8–8. The disappointing season became the final chapter in one era of Steelers history and ushered in a makeover for 2007 that is among the most drastic ever for a recent Super Bowl champion.

The biggest change, of course, is the retirement of 15-year head coach Bill Cowher. His replacement, rookie head man Mike Tomlin, is the fourth coaching apple to fall from the Tony Dungy tree—a crop that has already produced one Super Bowl coach (Chicago's Lovie Smith) and another that has taken two teams to the playoffs (Kansas City's Herman Edwards). Tomlin's persona, which follows the quiet approach favored by Dungy, is a 180-degree turn away from the fiery Cowher.

Tomlin has enjoyed a meteoric rise in NFL coaching circles. After playing wide receiver at William and Mary, he pursued a coaching career as a college assistant, spending six years at various schools. As the head coach in Tampa Bay, Dungy hired Tomlin to coach his defensive backs in 2001 following Edwards's departure to the New York Jets. At the time, Tomlin had been coaching defense for just three years (he spent his first three years coaching receivers). It was Tomlin's personality that won him the job in Tampa as much as his coaching acumen. Five years later, he earned the defensive coordinator job in Minnesota, and, just a year later, he finds himself one of the youngest head coaches in recent NFL history.

Nearly everyone who is asked about him says that Tomlin is incredibly bright and captivates any audience he comes in contact with. At just 35, Tomlin finds himself in charge of one of the NFL's most storied franchises, one that is just a year removed from a championship and has a fan base that is hungry for more. His leadership abilities will face an immediate test. The offensive captain, Pro Bowl guard Alan Faneca, has demanded a trade. The defensive captain, linebacker Joey Porter, was released in the offseason. Even special teams captain Sean Morey is gone, signing with Arizona to play for ex-Steelers offensive coordinator Ken Whisenhunt.

Faneca is unhappy with his contract, but he's also upset that Pittsburgh chose Tomlin over Russ Grimm, the longtime Steelers offensive line coach who was a finalist for the head-coaching job. When Faneca showed up for a mandatory minicamp, the relief was short-lived. He promptly blasted the organization for failing to offer him a fair deal, declared that 2007 would be his last year with the Steelers, then sat out a practice.

The Steelers chose to head off a similar confrontation with Porter, a volatile player who was the emotional spark plug for the Pittsburgh defense much the way Ray Lewis is for Baltimore's. Director of football operations Kevin Colbert made a straight business decision, opting to rid himself of Porter rather than face a potential season-long distraction as he headed into the final year of his contract. Porter recently turned 30 and is one of many players the Steelers were faced with having to re-sign following the 2007 season. Colbert decided Porter could more easily be replaced than, say, safety Troy Polamalu. Colbert probably didn't anticipate that Faneca could end up providing the same type of distraction as Porter, but now he must bank on the fact that Faneca will be playing for his next contract—if not from the Steelers then from some other NFL team—and hope that Faneca plays up to his usual elite standard.

Taken together, the departures and unhappiness leave Tomlin facing a potential leadership vacuum and a tense

---

STEELERS PROSPECTUS

2006 Record: 8–8

DVOA Estimated Wins: 8.5 (12th)

Pythagorean Wins: 9.1 (11th)

DVOA: 7.5% total (12th), 8.5% weighted (9th)

Offense: 5.2% DVOA (10th)

Defense: −6.5% DVOA (10th)

Special Teams: −4.2% DVOA (30th)

Variance: 17.5% (10th)

2006: Repeat dreams crash along with Big Ben.

2007: Meet the new boss, not the same as the old boss.

2007 Mean Projection: 9.1 wins

The Brohm Closet (0–4): 2%

Bad Team (5–6): 9%

Mediocre (7–8): 26%

Playoff Contender (9–10): 36%

Super Bowl Contender (11+): 26%

Projected Average Opponent: 2.1% DVOA (7th in NFL)

2007 Steelers Schedule

Week	Opp	Week	Opp	Week	Opp
1	at CLE	7	at DEN	13	CIN
2	BUF	8	at CIN	14	at NE
3	SF	9	BAL (Mon.)	15	JAC
4	at ARI	10	CLE	16	at STL (Thu.)
5	SEA	11	at NYJ	17	at BAL
6	BYE	12	MIA (Mon.)		

locker room in his first season. Fortunately, Tomlin's demeanor is perfectly suited to such a task. Much like the other head coaches who learned under Dungy, Tomlin will not try to win over the team through intimidation and is unlikely to butt heads with his new charges. Instead, he will rely on his skills as a teacher and motivator—invaluable assets for a coach who has at times worked with players who were older than him.

Tomlin is not the only member of the organization facing a challenge that is more about psychology than it is about football. There is no bigger question mark on the Steelers than quarterback Ben Roethlisberger, who has already experienced tremendous highs and lows in a three-year NFL career.

Roethlisberger's 2006 season was one he'd like to forget for many reasons, and it proved to be a microcosm of the Steelers' collective struggles. First came the motorcycle crash that nearly killed him, then the emergency appendectomy just before the start of the season, and then his wildly inconsistent on-field performance. Roethlisberger went from 8.9 yards per pass and nine interceptions in 2005 to 7.5 yards per pass and 23 interceptions in 2006, dropping from third in quarterback DVOA to 15th.

Roethlisberger's injuries from his June 12 accident sounded horrific—facial fractures, missing teeth, a severe concussion—but the public never saw the quarterback in that condition. By the time he made his first public appearances, Roethlisberger appeared healed—outwardly at least—and Steelers Nation breathed a considerable sigh of relief. The appendectomy that caused him to miss the season-opener seemed little more than a cruel twist of fate. Roethlisberger was pronounced fit to start in Week 2, but it was immediately apparent that this was not the same cocksure, unflappable player that had led the Steelers deep into the playoffs in his first two seasons. His first three starts produced three losses, zero touchdown passes, seven interceptions, and a microscopic quarterback rating.

Roethlisberger finally appeared to be "back" in a Week 5 win over Kansas City in which he went 16-of-19 with two touchdowns and zero interceptions in a 45–7 rout, but it was a mirage. Another outstanding performance was fol-

lowed by two miserable ones, including the nadir of the Steelers' season: a 20–13 loss at Oakland in which Roethlisberger threw four interceptions—two of which were returned for touchdowns—and the Steelers wasted a defensive performance in which they allowed just 98 total yards.

At times, the Good Ben/Bad Ben dichotomy was on display in the same game. The following week, at home against Denver, Roethlisberger was brilliant at times, awful at others. He kept one play alive for several seconds before finally spotting running back Willie Parker in the end zone for a touchdown. He used his feet to keep two others alive before throwing interceptions inside the Denver five-yard line, both on balls thrown into double coverage.

That loss dropped Pittsburgh to 2–6 and the Steelers seemed to be headed for one of the all-time worst performances by a defending Super Bowl champion. Cowher may have done one of the best coaching jobs of his career to coax his team to an 8–8 finish and an improbable run at a playoff spot, even as Roethlisberger continued his uneven play. The effort may have also exhausted Cowher enough to seal his decision to step down.

Thus it falls to Tomlin to heal Roethlisberger's battered psyche on a team that needs its quarterback to become the leader of the offense—a role that's usually automatic on most NFL teams. Because of Roethlisberger's early-career success on veteran-laden teams, he didn't need to assume the added burden of being the locker-room leader. Entering his fourth season, that is no longer the case. With Jerome Bettis and Cowher gone, and Faneca unhappy, the Steelers will lean on Roethlisberger in a way they didn't the last three years.

Not all the signs are encouraging. In an April interview, Roethlisberger suggested that his relationship with Cowher wasn't great and that he was looking forward to being a "rookie" along with Tomlin. It was a strange comment about the coach who stuck with Roethlisberger even when his play probably merited a seat on the bench last season.

Still, the Steelers will sink or swim with Roethlisberger in 2007. New offensive coordinator Bruce Arians is willing to give him more responsibility to call audibles and blocking adjustments at the line. The Steelers will continue to feature four-receiver sets that utilize Roethlisberger's downfield arm, as they step away from the power-run game that was the hallmark of the Cowher era, a transformation that actually began last season following the retirement of future Hall of Fame running back Jerome Bettis. Pittsburgh's play selection showed a dramatic change from 2005 to 2006 (table 1).

The signs that Cowher had lost faith in the power-run game were evident during that key Week 9 loss to Denver. In that contest, the Steelers faced a situation in which they nearly always turned to the ground game in the past. Trailing

Table 1. Pittsburgh Play Selection by Situation, 2005–2006

2005	Pct	Rk	2006	Pct	Rk
Runs, all plays	56%	1	Runs, all plays	44%	18
Runs, first half	50%	2	Runs, first half	45%	12
Runs, first down	66%	1	Runs, first down	54%	16
Runs, power sit.	74%	5	Runs, power sit.	63%	19
Runs, behind 2H	37%	2	Runs, behind 2H	26%	29
Pass, ahead 2H	17%	32	Pass, ahead 2H	27%	32

by four early in the fourth quarter, the Steelers had the ball at their own 9-yard line. Instead of trying to grind out a first down on the ground, Pittsburgh called three consecutive pass plays that resulted in a batted ball, a near-interception, and a sack. The ensuing punt set the Broncos up with the field position that led to the clinching touchdown.

The Steelers aren't going to be transformed overnight into a pass-first team, but the changes ushered in by Arians and Tomlin represent a continuation of the team's offensive transformation, a decision based more on personnel than philosophy. Cowher's offenses were built around the bruising Bettis and a powerhouse offensive line. Willie Parker is a smaller, quicker back, and the offensive line is in transition with the retirement of center Jeff Hartings and likely departure of Faneca following the 2007 season. The line dropped from 12th in 2005 to 22nd in Adjusted Line Yards last season, and the only new addition of note is guard Sean Mahan, who wasn't exactly part of a stellar unit in Tampa Bay.

While Roethlisberger was the most visible symbol of Pittsburgh's problems last year, he was hardly alone. Parker ran for 1,495 yards and 13 touchdowns, but his six fumbles tied for the league lead among running backs. Rookie receiver Santonio Holmes showed promise as an explosive playmaker and punt-returner, but his inability to hold onto the ball was also a concern. He fumbled five times in a four-game span at midseason, though he did not fumble again the rest of the way.

Arians and Tomlin may believe that this team is no longer suited to dominating opponents at the line of scrimmage and will benefit from being more aggressive—and unpredictable—on offense. Parker is a big-play back—the Steelers have gone from last in the NFL to third in runs of ten-plus yards in the space of two years, an improvement that coincides with Parker's emergence as the starter. Holmes has the speed and ability to be the Steelers' primary downfield threat, a role the team needs to fill after the departures of Antwaan Randle El and Plaxico Burress the last two years. Spreading things out could benefit both the passing game and the rushing attack, creating even more lanes for Parker to slash through for big gains.

Najeh Davenport is a nice change-of-pace back for Parker, and offseason free-agent signing Kevan Barlow will probably end up being the third-down back, but Barlow can hardly be counted upon in the wake of his performance the last two years with San Francisco and the Jets.

On defense, Tomlin was expected to effect more changes because of his 4-3, Tampa-2 pedigree, but he opted to retain defensive coordinator Dick LeBeau. That move suggests the team will retain LeBeau's preferred 3-4, zone-blitz scheme. Pittsburgh's first two choices in the April draft addressed both the loss of Porter, and the need for versatility on a defense that could ultimately utilize both formations.

Pittsburgh's first-round selection was outside linebacker Lawrence Timmons of Florida State, an undersized, speedy defender who can cover a lot of ground. Tomlin, who had Derrick Brooks in Tampa Bay for three seasons, drew an immediate comparison between Timmons and the Buccaneers' perennial Pro-Bowler (and fellow former Seminole). The Steelers can use Timmons as a speed-rusher if they stick with the 3-4 or an all-over-the-field tackler in a 4-3.

The Steelers may have found a steal with their second-round pick. Linebacker/defensive end LaMarr Woodley is another versatile defender who can excel at the speed-rush. Playing on one of the nation's best defenses at Michigan last season, Woodley terrorized quarterbacks coming off the edge and enjoyed a great night against Penn State left tackle Levi Brown, who was the fifth pick in the draft. He needs to be more consistent and disappeared in some of the Wolverines' bigger games, but he has to potential to produce double-digit sacks in the NFL.

Following those two selections, Pittsburgh looked for some help for the offense and special teams. The third-round pick, tight end Matt Spaeth from Minnesota, is a huge (6-foot-7) target with great hands, plus excellent run-blocking skills. He should earn playing time as the Steelers employ more two tight-end sets. Incumbent Heath Miller is the far more athletic tight end and will get the lion's share of the attention in the passing game, but Spaeth has enough all-around skills to contribute right away. Spaeth and the 6-foot-5 Miller are appealing targets on a team where the top four receivers are 6-foot-1 or shorter. Spaeth also makes Jerame Tuman, who never developed into anything more than a role player, expendable.

By selecting the Lombardi (Woodley), Mackey (Spaeth), and Ray Guy (punter Daniel Sepulveda, taken in the fourth round) award winners, the Steelers gave the appearance that they were selecting players out of the *Street & Smith's* guide the way teams did back in the early days of the draft, but the picks represented value and addressed needs, and the top four selections should all be valuable contributors this season.

The Steelers are a team in transition, and not just because of the change atop the coaching staff. As we have noted, this is a team that was shifting its offensive philosophy even before Cowher stepped down. Tomlin will continue to lead that evolution, using his leadership skills to win over the locker room and build on the positives that came out of the 6–2 finish to last season. If he can quell the brewing discontent from Faneca and, most importantly, coax Roethlisberger back into form, the Steelers should experience an upswing that will make 2006 look like an aberration. Pittsburgh's reign atop the NFL may have been a short one, but the quick overhaul that included the arrival of Tomlin and the departure of Porter and the drafting of his replacements could have the team right back in the playoffs in 2007 in what should be a tight AFC North race with Baltimore and Cincinnati.

Russell Levine

Steelers 2006 Stats by Week

Wk	vs.	W–L	PF	PA	YDF	YDA	TO	Total	Off	Def	ST
1	MIA	W	28	17	342	278	+1	7.3%	13.4%	-13.6%	-19.8%
2	@JAC	L	0	9	153	362	-1	-41.3%	-53.6%	-12.2%	0.1%
3	CIN	L	20	28	365	247	-2	23.5%	-18.5%	-47.0%	-5.1%
4	BYE										
5	@SD	L	13	23	288	361	-1	14.4%	-6.1%	-22.4%	-1.9%
6	KC	W	45	7	457	213	+2	85.2%	44.7%	-49.7%	-9.2%
7	@ATL	L	38	41	473	399	-1	20.1%	38.4%	8.4%	-9.8%
8	@OAK	L	13	20	360	98	-3	-9.0%	-41.9%	-34.4%	-1.6%
9	DEN	L	20	31	499	336	-6	-62.1%	5.4%	56.8%	-10.7%
10	NO	W	38	31	467	513	+3	28.4%	53.4%	13.0%	-12.0%
11	@CLE	W	24	20	338	302	-1	-41.4%	-22.3%	6.0%	-13.1%
12	@BAL	L	0	27	172	275	-3	-61.1%	-30.8%	27.1%	-3.2%
13	TB	W	20	3	267	254	+3	27.3%	-10.5%	-39.9%	-2.0%
14	CLE	W	27	7	528	294	+1	19.4%	42.8%	15.6%	-7.7%
15	@CAR	W	37	3	306	240	+2	74.4%	30.4%	-20.3%	23.7%
16	BAL	L	7	31	251	359	0	-28.6%	-14.6%	14.0%	0.0%
17	@CIN	W	23	17	482	295	-2	22.6%	34.2%	13.2%	1.6%

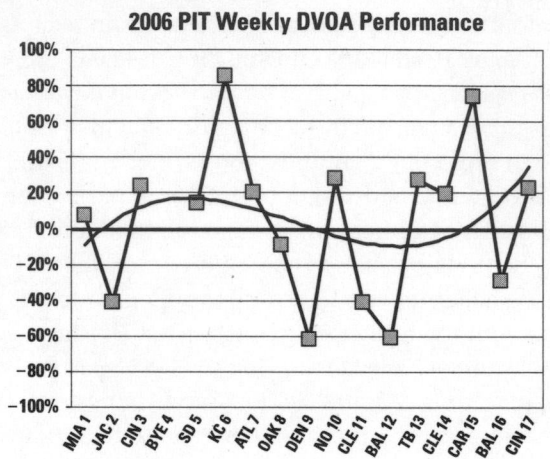

2006 PIT Weekly DVOA Performance

Trends and Splits

	Offense	Rank	Defense	Rank
Total DVOA	5.2%	10	-6.5%	10
Unadjusted VOA	0.9%	14	-7.9%	8
Weighted Trend	11.0%	9	-0.4%	12
Variance	10.6%	2	8.2%	9
Passing	16.7%	8	3.0%	14
Rushing	-7.2%	20	-18.0%	4
First Down	2.4%	12	-7.9%	11
Second Down	-0.2%	19	-19.4%	3
Third Down	18.5%	7	15.6%	23
Red Zone	-19.6%	24	-4.0%	10
Late and Close	-3.1%	17	3.6%	19

Five-Year Performance

	2006	2005	2004	2003	2002
W-L	8-8	11-5	15-1	6-10	10-5-1
Pythagorean Wins	9.1	11.6	11.5	7.2	9.2
Estimated Wins	8.5	11.6	12.1	7.6	8.7
Total DVOA	7.5%	28.1%	34.8%	-2.0%	7.3%
Rank	12	3	2	19	14
Offense	5.2%	11.5%	15.0%	-9.3%	5.8%
Rank	10	8	8	22	14
Defense	-6.5%	-15.1%	-17.6%	-3.8%	-6.0%
Rank	10	2	3	13	9
Special Teams	-4.2%	1.4%	2.3%	3.5%	-4.4%
Rank	30	9	10	3	28

Strategic Tendencies

Formations		Rank	Run/Pass		Rank	Defense		Rank	Other		Rank
3+ WR	46%	20	Runs, all plays	44%	18	Sacks by LB	56%	5	Run with 2+ RB	64%	12
4+ WR	23%	1	Runs, first half	45%	12	Sacks by DB	13%	7	Run with 2+ TE	42%	9
2+ TE	26%	18	Runs, first down	54%	16	Rush 6+	3.9%	28	Play action	14%	25
Single back	53%	17	Runs, power sit.	63%	19	Rush 7+	0.7%	24	Go for it on 4th	1.13	7
Empty back	2.0%	17	Runs, behind 2H	26%	29	Rush 3	6.9%	5	Offensive Pace	32.9	30
Max protect	7%	30	Pass, ahead 2H	27%	32	CB1 on WR1	58%	3	Defensive Pace	31.7	28

Pittsburgh threw to the middle of the field on 23 percent of its passes, second in the NFL to the Giants. . . . It was a hard year for Ben Roethlisberger, but one positive trend continued: Roethlisberger had a 39.3% DVOA in the first quarter, second in the NFL behind Peyton Manning. He was fifth in his rookie year and led the league with a first-quarter DVOA over 100% in 2005. . . . Pittsburgh threw to Hines Ward almost twice as often as anyone else on first down. . . . The Steelers ran a very low number of play-action fakes, even though they are known as a running team and ranked second in DVOA on play-action passes (54.1%). . . . Pittsburgh ran the second-highest number of two-running-back sets, and their defense saw the fourth-highest number of two-running-back sets run against it. . . . Pittsburgh's defense led the league in sacks marked Rusher Untouched and tied for the lead in incomplete passes marked Hit in Motion.

Passing

Player	DPAR	DVOA	Plys	NtYds	Avg	YAC	C%	TD	Int
Ben Roethlisberger	42.7	6.6%	465	3252	7.0	5.3	60.4%	18	21
Charlie Batch	18.0	63.0%	53	479	9.0	7.4	58.5%	5	0

Rushing

Player	DPAR	DVOA	Plys	Yds	Avg	TD	Fum	Suc
Willie Parker	21.6	1.1%	337	1495	4.4	13	6	44%
Najeh Davenport	-3.3	-32.6%	60	221	3.7	1	1	57%
Ben Roethlisberger	0.0	-17.3%	23	105	4.6	2	5	—
Verron Haynes	0.1	-12.2%	15	78	5.2	0	1	75%
Nate Washington	0.3	1.3%	3	8	2.7	0	0	—
Charlie Batch	-2.0	-175.3%	3	20	6.7	0	1	—
Kevan Barlow	*-1.7*	*-14.9%*	*131*	*368*	*2.8*	*6*	*1*	*42%*

Receiving

Player	DPAR	DVOA	Plys	Ctch	Yds	Y/C	YAC	TD	C%
WR									
Hines Ward	16.0	3.8%	127	75	996	13.3	4.8	6	57%
Santonio Holmes	19.6	18.4%	86	49	824	16.8	6.5	2	59%
Nate Washington	15.2	20.1%	69	35	624	17.8	3.4	4	51%
Cedrick Wilson	4.8	-4.3%	69	37	504	13.6	3.4	1	54%
TE									
Heath Miller	7.5	9.0%	55	34	393	11.6	5.3	5	62%
Jerame Tuman	3.6	63.4%	7	7	73	10.4	5.3	1	100%
RB									
Willie Parker	2.1	0.5%	42	31	222	7.2	7.9	3	74%
Verron Haynes	-0.2	-11.2%	22	18	95	5.3	4.2	0	71%
Najeh Davenport	7.0	61.8%	21	15	193	12.9	11.9	1	82%
Dan Kreider	-0.2	-12.9%	13	8	62	7.8	6.6	0	62%
Kevan Barlow	*-2.8*	*-63.1%*	*10*	*7*	*21*	*3.0*	*4.4*	*0*	*56%*

Offensive Line

Year	Yards	ALY	Rank	Power	Rank	10+ Yds	Rank	Stuff	Rank	Sack	ASR	Rank
2004	4.22	4.59	5	69%	10	11%	32	22%	10	36	9.5%	28
2005	4.18	4.29	12	68%	12	18%	15	23%	9	32	7.7%	22
2006	4.38	4.16	22	63%	19	24%	3	25%	22	49	7.9%	24

Year	LE	Rank	LT	Rank	Mid	Rank	RT	Rank	RE	Rank
2004	4.41	14	4.82	6	4.80	3	3.66	29	3.98	14
2005	5.01	5	2.71	30	4.41	9	4.48	10	4.96	4
2006	4.02	19	4.05	23	4.43	13	3.66	31	4.05	16

Pittsburgh fans are probably more concerned about the offensive line than any other area of the team heading into the 2007 season. Center Jeff Hartings retired, and there has been much gnashing of teeth about the three potential free agents among the remaining starters: guards Alan Faneca and Kendall Simmons, and tackle Max Starks. Faneca, the unit's best player, is all but gone following the season given his acrimonious negotiations with the team during the past offseason. Despite his stellar reputation, Faneca had an uneven 2006, which could factor into the team's decision to focus its priorities elsewhere. The Steelers would like to re-sign at least one of the other would-be departures up front, and the smart

(continued next page)

Offensive Line (continued)

money is on Simmons after Starks's struggles in 2006. Simmons could end up starting at center or guard this season as the Steelers try out all their options to replace Hartings. Chukki Okobi is probably the odds-on favorite to win the competition.

Despite the potential turnover, the Steelers opted not to address the offensive line until day two of the draft, when they selected guard Cameron Stephenson of Rutgers in the fifth round. He joins free-agent signee Sean Mahan from Tampa Bay as a new face up front. Mahan is another guard/center who could end up starting or backing up at either position. Given the recent decline in the line's performance—from 5th to 12th to 22nd in Adjusted Line Yards since 2004—and the team's move away from the power ground game in general, now could be a good time to start remaking the unit into a quicker, more athletic bunch that can better open lanes for slashing tailback Willie Parker and keep quarterback Ben Roethlisberger on his feet.

Defensive Front Seven

Defensive Line	Age	Pos	Plys	TmPct	Rk	Stop	Dfts	StpRt	Rk	AvYd	Rk	Sack	Hit	Hur	Runs	RuStp	RuYd	Pass	PaStp	PaYd
Aaron Smith	31	DE	66	8.4%	12	58	14	88%	7	1.7	51	4.5	3	5	56	89%	2.0	10	80%	0.3
Brett Keisel	29	DE	60	7.6%	18	46	11	77%	47	1.9	54	5.5	5	8	44	73%	2.6	16	88%	-0.3
Casey Hampton	30	DT	42	5.7%	27	35	7	83%	23	2.4	52	0	1	0	37	89%	1.7	5	40%	7.2

Linebackers	Age	Pos	Plys	TmPct	Rk	Stop	Dfts	StpRt	AvYd	Sack	Hit	Hur	Runs	RuStp	Rk	RuYd	Rk	Tgts	Suc%	Rk	PaYd	Rk
James Farrior	32	ILB	134	17.0%	14	79	27	59%	4.7	4	4	7	75	71%	24	3.3	40	39	38%	86	6.2	44
Larry Foote	27	ILB	93	11.8%	56	65	16	70%	3.5	4	1	7	59	75%	11	2.8	16	28	58%	26	6.6	63
Clark Haggans	30	OLB	82	11.1%	62	55	21	67%	3.2	6	3	5	54	72%	21	3.4	42	14	48%	—	6.6	—
Joey Porter*	30	OLB	60	8.7%	81	43	18	72%	2.1	7	4	5	40	68%	35	2.6	10	21	74%	2	4.9	17

Year	Yards	ALY	Rank	Power	Rank	10+ Yds	Rank	Stuff	Rank	Sack	ASR	Rank
2004	3.41	3.39	1	65%	21	16%	14	33%	1	42	8.7%	5
2005	3.41	3.66	4	56%	6	12%	5	28%	6	47	8.2%	4
2006	3.31	3.92	7	63%	14	10%	1	26%	8	39	6.9%	15

Year	LE	Rank	LT	Rank	Mid	Rank	RT	Rank	RE	Rank
2004	3.92	9	3.47	1	3.41	1	3.71	5	2.48	1
2005	4.20	18	3.47	6	3.62	3	3.66	5	3.68	13
2006	2.00	2	4.77	22	3.94	4	4.11	14	4.68	24

Will they or won't they? Whether or not the Steelers stick with the 3-4 or mix in some 4-3 and Cover-2, the team's defensive personnel seems well adapted to playing either scheme. The three incumbent linemen, ends Aaron Smith and Brett Keisel and nose tackle Casey Hampton, will again anchor the front seven. The only question is if Smith will move inside on occasion as somebody—presumably rookie end/linebacker LaMarr Woodley—puts a hand down next to him. Smith probably prefers to remain outside, but after receiving a hefty contract extension in the offseason, he'll do whatever the coaching staff asks. The other rookie linebacker, first-round pick Lawrence Timmons, may be a bit of a project due to his lack of playing time in college, but his athleticism instantly upgrades this unit, and he could become a sideline-to-sideline tackling force.

Regardless of their alignment, the Steelers will continue to generate a pass rush with their linebackers while the linemen absorb double-teams and stop the run. That has long been the formula in Pittsburgh, and it worked once again in 2006 as the Steelers ranked fourth in DVOA against the run. Secondary struggles hampered the defense last season, and, with the same secondary returning, the Steelers may look to create more pressure on the passer with the front three (or four) in order to ease the burden on their corners and safeties.

Defensive Secondary

Secondary	Age	Pos	Plys	TmPct	Rk	Stop	Dfts	RuYd	Rk	RuStp	Rk	Tgts	Tgt%	Rk	Dist	Suc%	Rk	PaYd	Rk	PD	Int
Ike Taylor	27	CB	75	9.5%	32	27	10	4.7	19	50%	23	90	20%	29	12.8	45%	70	9.2	72	14	2
Deshea Townsend	32	CB	53	6.7%	67	31	18	8.8	60	0%	81	84	19%	42	9.7	50%	51	7.4	40	9	2
Bryant McFadden	26	CB	63	8.0%	48	25	13	6.3	35	25%	69	68	15%	63	13.2	51%	44	7.9	49	9	3
Troy Polamalu	26	SS	86	13.4%	7	46	20	3.5	3	58%	8	32	8%	30	9.0	60%	19	6.5	23	6	3
Ryan Clark	27	FS	75	11.7%	21	28	13	6.6	44	44%	37	30	8%	37	12.1	60%	18	6.6	26	4	1
Tyrone Carter	31	FS	41	5.2%	—	15	8	6.5	—	36%	—	15	3%	—	8.9	54%	—	10.3	—	1	0
Anthony Smith	24	FS	18	2.3%	—	5	2	8.8	—	0%	—	15	3%	—	15.6	54%	—	11.8	—	4	2

Year	Pass D Rank	DVOA vs. #1 WR	Rank	DVOA vs. #2 WR	Rank	DVOA vs. Other WR	Rank	DVOA vs. TE	Rank	DVOA vs. RB	Rank
2004	3	-7.4%	9	-14.4%	3	-22.3%	3	-13.6%	9	6.1%	19
2005	6	-13.6%	4	-4.6%	15	-9.5%	9	-7.6%	12	20.2%	30
2006	14	23.8%	30	17.6%	26	-50.6%	2	-6.0%	14	-24.9%	2

Mike Tomlin's background as a secondary coach will be put to the test with Pittsburgh's cornerbacks. At his first minicamp, Tomlin reinstalled Ike Taylor as his number-one corner. Taylor earned a fat contract extension last year, only to land on the bench after routinely getting burned and missing tackles. Our charting stats ranked 85 corners based on yards per catch allowed; only 11 of them were worse than Taylor. Much like quarterback, cornerback is a position with a large psychological component, and some players can no longer perform after a loss of confidence. That appears to be what happened to Taylor last season. He has the physical tools to return to form and, in Tomlin, an excellent teacher and advocate (early on at least), which should help boost his confidence. Deshea Townsend and Bryant McFadden will battle for the other starting spot, with the loser becoming the nickel back. Ricardo Colclough, a second-round pick in 2004, has yet to develop into a reliable corner and missed much of last season with a neck injury. He was pronounced fit during offseason workouts, but probably doesn't fit into the team's future plans as he enters the final year of his rookie contract.

Strong safety Troy Polamalu can occasionally miss a tackle by being overaggressive at the line of scrimmage, but he has few peers, particularly in run support. He'll become a free agent after the season, and the need to re-sign him is one reason why perennial Pro Bowl guard Alan Faneca has been left wanting this offseason. Safety is fast becoming the new impact defensive position in the NFL, especially in light of the impact Bob Sanders had on the Colts' playoff run last year. Polamalu is a game-changing player at the position. Ryan Clark and second-year Anthony Clark are expected to compete for the starting spot at free safety, where either can serve in a complementary role to Polamalu.

Special Teams

Year	DVOA	Rank	FG/XP	Rank	Net Punt	Rank	Punt Ret	Rank	Net Kick	Rank	Kick Ret	Rank	Hidden	Rank
2004	2.3%	10	3.1	9	13.8	2	-1.3	18	2.4	12	-4.8	20	-7.4	26
2005	1.4%	10	0.9	14	-3.2	22	12.4	1	-1.6	20	-0.1	17	0.0	15
2006	-4.2%	30	-4.4	25	0.5	19	-5.4	30	-10.2	28	-5.0	24	-2.5	17

Many a Steelers fan cringed when Pittsburgh traded up to select punter Daniel Sepulveda in the fourth round, but, when a team feels an unshakable urge to draft a specialist, it might as well draft one who was a linebacker in high school. Sepulveda was a two-time winner of the Ray Guy award as the nation's best punter while at Baylor. His powerful left leg should provide a huge upgrade over the aged Chris Gardocki, who was the third-worst punter in the league last year if we measure only punt value and not coverage (-5.8 points). Sepulveda may not turn out to be Robo-Punter in human form, but it's doubtful those same Steelers fans will regret this pick when he's booming kicks this fall—and occasionally making an open-field tackle afterwards. Sepulveda can't help the return game, however, which was miserable last season. Santonio Holmes is the Steelers' most explosive returner and seems to have cured the fumble problems that plagued him at midseason, but can he be a full-time return man if he also becomes a starting receiver? Kicker Jeff Reed missed seven field goals, but all seven were at home, where the swirling winds and poor footing make field goals an adventure for every kicker in the league.

Coaching Staff

New Pittsburgh head coaches come along about as often as Halley's comet. Mike Tomlin has a lot to live up to after the team's previous two leaders, Chuck Noll and Bill Cowher, lasted a combined 38 years and racked up five Super Bowl titles. Tomlin is about the same age as both of those legendary figures were when they were hired by the Steelers, and no doubt hopes to lay down similar roots in the Steel City. Rather than clean house when he was hired in January, he opted to retain six of Cowher's assistants, and both of his coordinators are holdovers from Cowher's final Pittsburgh staff. Bruce Arians was promoted from wide receivers coach to offensive coordinator after Ken Whisenhunt became the new head coach in Arizona. This is Arians's second stint as an NFL offensive coordinator, so we know he favors an aggressive attack that will continue the departure from the run first, second, and third approach that marked much of Cowher's tenure. Tomlin's most interesting choice for retention was defensive coordinator Dick LeBeau, whose 3-4, zone-blitz approach is a departure from the 4-3, Cover-2 defenses that Tomlin has always been associated with. The willingness to keep LeBeau signals that Tomlin is not married to a single system, but will rather tailor his team's approach to match the skills on the roster.

San Diego Chargers

When the Chargers fired Marty Schottenheimer in February, he didn't look angry or sad or shocked. He looked relieved. A 14–2 regular season made the Chargers the favorites to win the Super Bowl, but all the breaks went against San Diego in their divisional round playoff loss to New England. Although the Chargers initially said they'd keep Schottenheimer around for the 2007 season, it quickly became apparent that his long-running feud with general manager A. J. Smith could not be resolved. Firing a coach after a 14–2 season might seem crazy, but Schottenheimer's relationship with Smith was universally described as "dysfunctional," and these two guys weren't going to be able to work together effectively for another year.

But was Norv Turner the right person to take over? That's the single biggest question facing San Diego this year, and all indications are that the answer is a resounding no.

In our first book, *Pro Football Prospectus 2005,* we featured an essay called "In Defense of Mike Martz." It used various statistical arguments to counter many of the misconceptions about the former Rams' head coach. Using the same set of data, we attempted to forge a defense of Norv Turner. It was useless. After nine seasons as coach of the Redskins and Raiders, Turner's record is defenseless.

Let's start with Pythagorean wins, the projection based solely on points scored and allowed. This number is admittedly limited in what it conveys about head coaches, but the theory is that coaches whose teams outperform their Pythagorean projections over a number of years have been particularly successful. There are inherent pitfalls with this method. For example, an extremely dominant team will have a difficult time reaching its projection, and an extremely weak team will more easily beat its projection. But

which coach did the better job? Based on performance vs. Pythagorean wins, the coach of the weak team was better.

If we want to use the Pythagorean projection to identify poor coaching, we're not looking for coaches who couldn't meet a good projection. We want to find the coaches who couldn't win enough games to match a *bad* projection.

One hundred fourteen men have coached at least 64 games since the 1950 AAFC-NFL merger. Forty-nine of these coaches have a losing career record. Out of all those coaches, only eight had a losing record and still fell short of their teams' Pythagorean projection by at least one half-win every 16 games. Norv Turner is one of those eight coaches (table 1).

Is that poor record just due to poor luck? Looking at Turner's record in close games gives an indication that it is not. Norv Turner–coached teams that have allowed their opponents to get the ball when down by a single score in the fourth-quarter have gone 37–23. The league average would point to a record no worse than 41–19. That is the *average* expectation, not good or great. Four wins may not seem like a lot, but given Turner's long career, there is less than a 10 percent chance that this poor won-loss record is due to bad luck.

Looking at blown leads places Turner in historically poor company. In NFL history, 383 coaches have held a lead at some point in the fourth quarter (believe it or not, there have been 23 who haven't). Adjusting for era, Norv Turner grades out as the ninth-worst head coach of all time at holding fourth-quarter leads of any size. (We need to adjust for era because the league average at holding leads has shifted dramatically as various rule changes and strategy changes have taken effect.) Turner is one of 11 coaches with a record of futility in holding fourth-quarter leads for whom there is less than a five percent chance that their

---

CHARGERS PROSPECTUS

2006 Record: 14–2

DVOA Estimated Wins: 12.0 (1st)

Pythagorean Wins: 12.1 (4th)

DVOA: 29.9% total (2nd), 25.7% weighted (3rd)

Offense: 24.0% DVOA (2nd)

Defense: −1.5% DVOA (14th)

Special Teams: 4.4% DVOA (3rd)

Variance: 9.2% (29th)

2006: A very good team with lousy luck in its playoff loss to New England.

2007: Uh-oh. The Chargers got Norved.

2007 Mean Projection: 8.6 wins

The Brohm Closet (0–4): 3%

Bad Team (5–6): 14%

Mediocre (7–8): 31%

Playoff Contender (9–10): 34%

Super Bowl Contender (11+): 18%

Projected Average Opponent: −1.3% DVOA (17th in NFL)

Table 1. Head Coaches with a Career Losing Record

Coach	Wins Per 16 Games	Pyth Wins per 16 Games
Neill Armstrong	7.5	8.0
Lindy Infante	6.0	6.6
Norv Turner	6.6	7.2
Dennis Erickson	6.7	7.4
Joe Bugel	4.8	5.6
Dan Henning	5.5	6.5
David Shula	4.3	5.4
Monte Clark	6.9	8.0

bad record is simply due to bad luck because of its large sample size (table 2).

Turner's teams fared better defending two-score leads, but still were slightly below average. Turner's teams have won 48 of 58 games with a two-score lead, not significantly different from the league average that suggests 49 wins in 58 games. All these records together, however, suggest that Norv Turner–coached teams tend to do well when things start well but fold in tight situations.

Turner's supporters will surely trot out the argument that his numbers are bound to look bad because he took over horrible teams. He coached the 1994 Redskins following their 4–12 season and the 2004 Raiders after their 4–12 campaign. Yet his efforts still suffer by comparison with similar teams. Thirty-seven teams went 4–12 between 1978 and 2001. Looking ahead to the next five seasons, those teams would average 7.4 wins per year with two playoff appearances, including at least one trip to the divisional round. In Turner's first five years, the Redskins averaged 6.5

Table 2. Worst Head Coaches at Holding Fourth-Quarter Leads

Coach	Record	Binomial
Monte Clark	50–20	2.7%
Joe Bugel	24–13	1.6%
Norv Turner	58–23	1.4%
June Jones	21–11	1.4%
Norm Van Brocklin	72–27	1.3%
Tommy Prothro	36–17	0.7%
Otto Graham	19–11	0.6%
Dan Henning	39–21	0.3%
Mike Riley	14–12	0.2%
Marion Campbell	34–19	0.2%
David Shula	18–13	0.1%

NOTE: Coaches are ranked by binomial distribution, which combines record with frequency to determine the likelihood that results are due to chance.

wins per year and made zero playoff appearances. Since the start of free agency in 1993, Turner's Redskins are one of only three 4–12 teams out of 17 not to make the post-season in the five subsequent years.

This time Turner is not saddled with a team coming off a poor season. The Chargers were 14–2 in 2006. They should be able to withstand any storm and be a contender for years to come, right? Thirteen teams finished with a 14–2 record between 1978 and 2001. In the next five seasons, these teams would average only 9.3 wins per year and make an average of two playoff appearances, including at least two trips to the divisional round. That is really not all that much better than the performance of the 4–12 teams in their next five years. The window of opportunity may be closing faster than the Chargers think.

Why do people keep hiring Norv Turner as a head coach if he is as bad as it appears? For starters, it helps to have a Hall of Fame quarterback telling everyone who will listen that Turner is the greatest thing that ever happened to him. Troy Aikman, who played for Turner when Turner was the Cowboys' offensive coordinator, makes it sound as though he thinks he'd be flipping burgers at McDonald's if Turner hadn't molded him. But is that realistic? Aikman played well enough at UCLA to be the first pick in the draft, and that was before he ever worked with Turner, and it's not like Aikman fell apart without Turner calling the plays; Aikman made the Pro Bowl in each of his first three seasons after Turner left for the Redskins.

While Aikman routinely pledges his allegiance to Turner, perhaps the most telling statement about Turner comes from another Hall of Fame player he coached. After the Chargers hired their new head coach, Jerry Rice, who played for Turner in Oakland, said of Turner, "He could not motivate the players. He had no control."

Is there any hope for San Diego? Of course there is: This might be the most talented team in the league. In running back LaDainian Tomlinson, San Diego has a superstar who is beloved by coaches and teammates and relishes the responsibility of carrying the team on his shoulders. In quarterback Philip Rivers, San Diego has a young player who looked very promising in his first season as a starter and is likely to get better. In tight end Antonio Gates, San Diego has a player who is already one of the best in the league at his position and, at age 27, still has a few years left in his prime. In the first round of the draft, the Chargers took receiver Craig Davis, who some scouts said had the best hands in this year's NFL draft.

While the skill position players get most of the attention, the guys blocking for them are even more important. In a league in which fullbacks are becoming an endangered species, Lorenzo Neal is still extremely effective. Neal

2007 Chargers Schedule

Week	Opp	Week	Opp	Week	Opp
1	CHI	7	BYE	13	at KC
2	at NE	8	HOU	14	at TEN
3	at GB	9	at MIN	15	DET
4	KC	10	IND	16	DEN (Mon.)
5	at DEN	11	at JAC	17	at OAK
6	OAK	12	BAL		

is 36 years old, but playing for Turner could rejuvenate him: Turner will use Neal in much the same way he used Moose Johnston with the Cowboys. Like Neal, Johnston was mostly a lead blocker, but he averaged 37 catches a year in the three years Turner was his offensive coordinator; it wouldn't be surprising to see Neal get close to that many catches this year.

In addition to having a great fullback blocking for a Hall of Fame running back, there's another respect in which Turner's San Diego offense resembles his Dallas offense: It has the best offensive line in football. The Chargers already had a good offensive line before they got one of the steals of the 2006 draft, selecting left tackle Marcus McNeill in the second round. In a year in which many of the old standbys at left tackle, such as Jonathan Ogden and Walter Jones, began to decline, McNeill established himself as the best player in the league at the most important line position. The Chargers' entire line was outstanding and ranked first in the league in adjusted line yards.

San Diego also has some good linemen on the other side of the ball. The Chargers' three starting defensive linemen do a great job of keeping blockers away from the linebackers. That's not usually the role of 3-4 linemen the way it is of 4-3 defensive tackles; then again 3-4 teams usually don't have a group of defensive linemen as overpowering as the Chargers' trio of Luis Castillo, Jamal Williams, and Igor Olshansky.

Last year, San Diego's biggest problem on defense was an inability to stop the opposing team's number-one receiver. Their DVOA of 12.7% against number-one receivers ranked 25th in the league. As the season wore on, however, rookie Antonio Cromartie looked like he might develop into the kind of player who can shut down those top receivers. Cromartie is an amazing athlete and a hard hitter and looks like yet another great draft pick for A. J. Smith. On the other hand, we don't want to get carried away: Cromartie didn't start a single game last year and started only one game in his entire college career at Florida State thanks to injuries and the Seminoles' depth at cornerback. He's still got quite a bit of work to do. The Chargers' secondary also got a little better in the 2007 draft, when they traded up in the second round to nab safety Eric Weddle of Utah.

At linebacker, the Chargers have one great player and many question marks. The great player is Shawne Merriman, who led the league in sacks despite missing four games. Merriman just turned 23 in May, and he already has 27 sacks in his 27 career games. He has the potential to be one of the game's truly elite players for several years. Merriman's four-game suspension for steroid use was one of the biggest stories of the 2006 NFL season, but it's a bigger story than we can get into here. What we can say is that Merriman is enormously important to the Chargers, and there was a huge drop-off when the Chargers had to replace Merriman with Carlos Polk at outside linebacker.

Indeed, you won't see many 3-4 teams with less depth at linebacker than these Chargers. The Chargers' second-best linebacker in 2006 was Donnie Edwards. Edwards started all 16 games last season, and, even though he's 34 years old, he's still very effective, especially against the pass. Unfortunately, Edwards signed with Kansas City as a free agent, which is a major loss for this defense. Edwards's departure makes it all the more significant that the Chargers were able to hire Ron Rivera as their linebackers coach this offseason. As the Bears' defensive coordinator the last three seasons, Rivera had a good enough reputation that he was considered for several head-coaching jobs. That the Chargers signed him as a position coach was a major coup.

Still, that coup won't be enough to compensate for the major loss at the top of the coaching staff. Although firing Schottenheimer might have been the right way to deal with the dysfunctional relationship in the Chargers' front office, hiring Turner was not the right way to replace him. Quite simply, the Chargers won't be as good in 2007 as they were in 2006.

Jason McKinley
Michael David Smith

Chargers 2006 Stats by Week

Wk	vs.	W–L	PF	PA	YDF	YDA	TO	DVOA Total	Off	Def	ST
1	@OAK	W	27	0	302	129	+1	34.8%	16.8%	-18.9%	-0.9%
2	TEN	W	40	7	476	218	+2	86.5%	38.6%	-40.2%	7.7%
3	BYE										
4	@BAL	L	13	16	284	207	+2	44.0%	8.5%	-34.5%	1.0%
5	PIT	W	23	13	361	288	+1	34.0%	12.2%	-14.5%	7.3%
6	@SF	W	48	19	421	306	+2	42.4%	43.1%	-3.6%	-4.4%
7	@KC	L	27	30	349	355	-2	-17.4%	-10.6%	20.6%	13.8%
8	STL	W	38	24	419	412	+1	43.3%	41.3%	11.8%	13.9%
9	CLE	W	32	25	381	293	+1	31.7%	37.6%	-12.6%	-18.5%
10	@CIN	W	49	41	431	545	+1	22.1%	54.7%	43.3%	10.7%
11	@DEN	W	35	27	342	326	-1	39.7%	29.8%	-0.8%	9.0%
12	OAK	W	21	14	260	245	+1	2.8%	19.9%	21.0%	3.9%
13	@BUF	W	24	21	335	230	+2	1.0%	-2.3%	-16.5%	-13.1%
14	DEN	W	48	20	419	328	0	94.7%	73.6%	-4.7%	16.5%
15	KC	W	20	9	353	241	0	28.8%	-12.3%	-31.8%	9.3%
16	@SEA	W	20	17	340	314	+2	23.8%	2.1%	-15.1%	6.6%
17	ARI	W	27	20	387	444	0	-12.5%	35.3%	59.8%	12.0%
18	BYE										
19	NE	L	21	24	352	327	-1	71.3%	14.7%	-59.0%	-2.3%

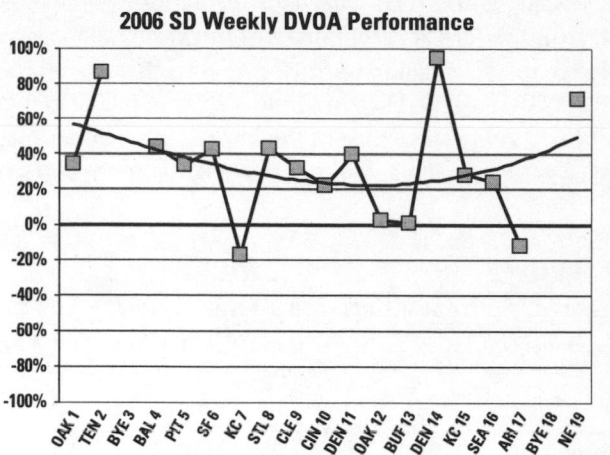

2006 SD Weekly DVOA Performance

Trends and Splits

	Offense	Rank	Defense	Rank
Total DVOA	24.0%	2	-1.5%	14
Unadjusted VOA	26.7%	2	-5.1%	10
Weighted Trend	24.9%	2	4.3%	16
Variance	5.8%	20	7.2%	13
Passing	26.3%	3	-3.0%	11
Rushing	22.0%	1	0.4%	22
First Down	15.1%	6	-10.8%	7
Second Down	39.0%	1	3.8%	19
Third Down	17.6%	8	10.0%	18
Red Zone	63.0%	1	44.1%	32
Late and Close	40.5%	2	-17.3%	5

Five-Year Performance

	2006	2005	2004	2003	2002
W-L	14-2	9-7	12-4	4-12	8-8
Pythagorean Wins	12.1	10.7	11.2	4.9	7.1
Estimated Wins	12.0	10.9	10.7	6.1	7.4
Total DVOA	29.9%	21.5%	19.9%	-14.8%	-4.4%
Rank	2	6	8	24	22
Offense	24.0%	18.1%	19.0%	0.8%	2.3%
Rank	2	6	6	13	17
Defense	-1.5%	-3.1%	-3.9%	12.2%	5.2%
Rank	14	16	12	30	22
Special Teams	4.4%	0.2%	-3.0%	-3.4%	-1.5%
Rank	3	16	26	27	19

Strategic Tendencies

Formations		Rank	Run/Pass		Rank	Defense		Rank	Other		Rank
3+ WR	36%	31	Runs, all plays	50%	4	Sacks by LB	69%	2	Run with 2+ RB	76%	3
4+ WR	9%	17	Runs, first half	46%	10	Sacks by DB	2%	29	Run with 2+ TE	31%	24
2+ TE	24%	20	Runs, first down	63%	2	Rush 6+	4.6%	27	Play action	20%	14
Single back	33%	32	Runs, power sit.	73%	4	Rush 7+	0.5%	31	Go for it on 4th	0.89	16
Empty back	3.1%	11	Runs, behind 2H	34%	14	Rush 3	0.8%	31	Offensive Pace	31.8	25
Max protect	14%	11	Pass, ahead 2H	39%	22	CB1 on WR1	44%	16	Defensive Pace	30.9	19

San Diego had the NFL's highest offensive DVOA in the fourth quarter (52.9%), committing no fumbles and just one interception. Every other team had at least five fumbles or interceptions in the fourth quarter. . . . San Diego recovered nine of 13 offensive fumbles, the highest percentage in the league. . . . In the "no duh" department, San Diego was ranked first in rushing DVOA when two running backs were in the game (24.9%). They also ranked first in passing DVOA with two running backs in the game (40.8%). Only Cincinnati used two running backs more often. . . . While still ranked an impressive eighth,

(continued next page)

Strategic Tendencies *(continued)*

San Diego's rushing DVOA was not as good with only one back on the field (11.0%), and the Chargers were actually 26th in passing DVOA from one-back formations (−8.0%).... The Chargers defense had the highest Adjusted Sack Rate in the NFL on first down (12.6 percent), but were below average on third and fourth down (6.4 percent).... San Diego led the league in sacks against a max protect scheme, and led the league in defensive sacks marked as Blown Blocks.... San Diego's defense was second in incomplete passes tipped at the line of scrimmage.... Marty Schottenheimer is one of the more aggressive coaches of the last decade (career Aggressiveness Index: 1.18), although he wasn't in 2006. Norv Turner has a career AI of .83, making him slightly more conservative than average on fourth down.

Passing

Player	DPAR	DVOA	Plys	NtYds	Avg	YAC	C%	TD	Int
Philip Rivers	85.2	28.4%	459	3228	7.0	4.8	61.9%	22	9

Rushing

Player	DPAR	DVOA	Plys	Yds	Avg	TD	Fum	Suc
LaDainian Tomlinson	52.6	24.0%	348	1815	5.2	28	2	49%
Michael Turner	20.7	46.5%	80	502	6.3	2	0	55%
Lorenzo Neal	6.1	19.3%	29	140	4.8	1	1	49%
Philip Rivers	-7.5	-59.9%	24	60	2.5	0	8	—
Andrew Pinnock	0.8	39.0%	4	25	6.3	0	0	39%
Vincent Jackson	0.7	11.7%	3	16	5.3	0	0	—

Receiving

Player	DPAR	DVOA	Plys	Ctch	Yds	Y/C	YAC	TD	C%
WR									
Eric Parker	19.2	26.6%	70	48	659	13.7	2.5	0	69%
Vincent Jackson	7.5	5.5%	56	27	453	16.8	2.7	6	71%
Keenan McCardell*	9.6	13.2%	51	36	437	12.1	2.3	0	48%
Malcom Floyd	0.2	-14.3%	32	15	210	14.0	3.1	3	47%
TE									
Antonio Gates	26.9	22.8%	120	71	924	13.0	4.3	9	59%
B. Manumaleuna	4.3	31.5%	17	14	91	6.5	4.7	3	82%
RB									
LaDainian Tomlinson	9.5	12.7%	80	56	508	9.1	9.5	3	70%
Lorenzo Neal	-5.4	-48.3%	26	17	83	4.9	6.0	0	65%

Offensive Line

Year	Yards	ALY	Rank	Power	Rank	10+ Yds	Rank	Stuff	Rank	Sack	ASR	Rank
2004	4.25	4.19	17	71%	7	20%	6	24%	16	19	4.1%	4
2005	4.49	4.39	9	78%	2	20%	11	24%	14	30	5.8%	12
2006	5.38	4.82	1	73%	4	29%	1	18%	1	28	6.3%	15

Year	LE	Rank	LT	Rank	Mid	Rank	RT	Rank	RE	Rank
2004	2.87	28	5.10	3	4.12	21	4.74	7	3.48	23
2005	4.39	12	4.86	3	4.04	19	4.52	9	5.81	1
2006	5.90	2	5.08	4	4.34	17	4.48	7	5.81	1

Already very good before the 2006 season, the Chargers' line turned into one of the truly elite units in the league with the addition of rookie left tackle Marcus McNeill. Everyone thought D'Brickashaw Ferguson, selected by the Jets with the fourth pick in 2006, was the best lineman in last year's draft, but if their rookie years were any indication, McNeill is the one who's going to have the truly great career. Right tackle Shane Olivea is a solid run blocker, though nowhere near the naturally gifted talent McNeill is. Mike Goff and Kris Dielman are a good pair of guards and help cover for center Nick Hardwick, the weak spot on the line. Hardwick sometimes struggles against bigger defensive tackles, but there's no shame in being the weak spot of the best offensive line in football. The only question about the Chargers' line is whether it has the depth to withstand an injury. Last year the five starters on the line combined to miss just one game. Cory Withrow, a one-time starter for the Minnesota Vikings, is the backup center and can play guard in a pinch. Roman Oben, the 12-year veteran best known in San Diego as the return on the last draft pick acquired in the Eli Manning-Philip Rivers trade, backs up both tackles.

Defensive Front Seven

Defensive Line	Age	Pos	Plys	TmPct	Rk	Stop	Dfts	StpRt	Rk	AvYd	Rk	Sack	Hit	Hur	Runs	RuStp	RuYd	Pass	PaStp	PaYd
Jamal Williams	31	DT	71	8.8%	1	55	6	77%	39	2.2	47	2	0	1	67	76%	2.5	4	100%	-2.8
Luis Castillo	24	DE	40	8.0%	16	31	17	78%	43	0.8	16	7.5	2	6	26	69%	2.4	14	93%	-2.4
Jacques Cesaire	27	DE	38	4.7%	61	30	10	79%	33	1.9	55	4	1	4	26	77%	3.5	12	83%	-1.6
Igor Olshansky	25	DE	35	5.4%	49	28	8	80%	27	2.3	66	1.5	6	7	30	80%	2.7	5	80%	0.4
Derreck Robinson	25	DE	17	2.1%	—	13	5	76%	—	1.2	—	1.5	0	0	10	60%	3.8	7	100%	-2.4
Ryon Bingham	26	DT	15	1.9%	—	9	3	60%	—	2.5	—	1.5	1	2	13	54%	3.3	2	100%	-3.0

Linebackers	Age	Pos	Plys	TmPct	Rk	Stop	Dfts	StpRt	AvYd	Sack	Hit	Hur	Runs	RuStp	Rk	RuYd	Rk	Tgts	Suc%	Rk	PaYd	Rk
Donnie Edwards*	34	ILB	152	18.9%	3	82	27	54%	5.5	2.5	2	3	80	59%	71	4.0	76	55	54%	38	5.9	30
Shaun Phillips	26	OLB	74	10.5%	66	54	24	73%	1.6	11.5	7	13	35	57%	77	3.2	36	10	67%	—	3.7	—
Shawne Merriman	23	OLB	72	11.9%	55	57	26	79%	1.3	17	5	12	34	71%	26	2.2	4	19	53%	40	5.3	19
Randall Godfrey	34	ILB	60	9.2%	76	44	11	73%	2.8	4	1	2	42	79%	2	2.6	12	15	78%	—	4.5	—
Stephen Cooper	28	ILB	53	6.6%	98	28	6	53%	4.1	2	1	3	37	54%	88	3.9	71	10	76%	—	11.0	—
Marques Harris	25	OLB	27	3.6%	—	20	11	74%	2.5	3	2	4	16	69%	—	4.9	—	8	57%	—	5.4	—
Carlos Polk	30	OLB	26	3.2%	—	18	4	69%	4.2	2	0	2	21	71%	—	2.7	—	4	57%	—	8.9	—
Matt Wilhelm	26	ILB	15	1.9%	—	12	6	80%	3.2	0	0	0	7	100%	—	0.3	—	6	88%	—	6.6	—

Year	Yards	ALY	Rank	Power	Rank	10+ Yds	Rank	Stuff	Rank	Sack	ASR	Rank
2004	3.74	4.24	16	62%	16	8%	2	21%	28	29	5.5%	30
2005	3.60	3.92	14	67%	21	14%	11	27%	11	46	8.0%	7
2006	4.05	4.20	13	78%	31	15%	11	23%	19	61	9.0%	3

Year	LE	Rank	LT	Rank	Mid	Rank	RT	Rank	RE	Rank
2004	4.43	19	4.27	12	4.41	22	3.86	8	3.86	17
2005	5.24	30	3.85	8	3.96	12	3.75	9	3.57	10
2006	4.52	20	4.18	13	4.30	17	4.31	18	3.06	4

When the Chargers drafted defensive end Luis Castillo in 2005, he looked more like a big guy who could help out against the run than an every-down player. He has developed into an outstanding pass rusher, recording seven sacks in 2006, a very impressive total for a 3-4 defensive lineman who played only ten games. The other end, Igor Olshansky, is more the kind of player Castillo was expected to be, a plugger against the run who doesn't generate much of a pass rush. Jamal Williams is the prototypical 3-4 nose tackle. He weighs 348 pounds and is awfully hard to budge in the middle of the line, but you usually won't notice him unless the play goes directly at him.

Outside linebacker Shawne Merriman is the Chargers' best defensive player and maybe the best defensive player in the league, although the fact that he tested positive for steroids puts an asterisk next to his league-leading 17 sacks. With Donnie Edwards gone to Kansas City as a free agent, Merriman is the only linebacker on the Chargers' roster that new coordinator Ted Cottrell can feel completely confident about, although Shaun Phillips, who starts opposite Merriman, gives the Chargers another strong speed-rusher off the edge.

Run defense was a problem last year, and that's mostly the fault of the inside linebackers, which is why the Chargers didn't make much of an effort to re-sign last year's starters, Edwards and Randall Godfrey. Matt Wilhelm and Stephen Cooper were backups at inside linebacker last year, and should be the starters in 2007. They're both good athletes, but a bit undersized. That description also applies to the two linebackers the Chargers drafted. Inside linebacker Anthony Waters, the third-round pick out of Clemson, probably won't start, but should provide good depth. Brandon Siler of Florida lasted until the seventh round, but he was a very consistent player until he suffered a knee injury in 2006, so he could be a steal if healthy.

Defensive Secondary

Secondary	Age	Pos	Plys	TmPct	Rk	Stop	Dfts	RuYd	Rk	RuStp	Rk	Tgts	Tgt%	Rk	Dist	Suc%	Rk	PaYd	Rk	PD	Int
Quentin Jammer	28	CB	98	12.2%	9	39	17	4.3	10	31%	63	111	24%	7	10.9	48%	58	6.5	18	19	4
Drayton Florence	27	CB	80	10.0%	28	40	16	6.8	44	39%	48	96	20%	24	10.8	55%	22	7.6	43	17	3
Antonio Cromartie	23	CB	19	2.4%	—	8	1	9.2	—	33%	—	40	8%	—	18.3	59%	—	8.6	—	4	0
Marlon McCree	30	FS	65	9.2%	49	24	11	8.6	70	37%	54	30	7%	50	11.3	30%	79	11.7	72	3	1
Terrence Kiel*	27	SS	55	7.3%	62	18	7	6.5	40	46%	31	23	5%	72	13.7	48%	53	11.1	69	3	0
Clinton Hart	30	SS	36	4.5%	—	18	8	6.3	—	63%	—	14	3%	—	16.1	71%	—	9.7	—	6	3
Bhawoh Jue	28	FS	16	2.7%	—	5	3	12.3	—	0%	—	13	3%	—	23.1	55%	—	6.9	—	4	0

Year	Pass D Rank	DVOA vs. #1 WR	Rank	DVOA vs. #2 WR	Rank	DVOA vs. Other WR	Rank	DVOA vs. TE	Rank	DVOA vs. RB	Rank
2004	15	-8.2%	7	-9.0%	6	-13.3%	12	-9.0%	13	-9.7%	9
2005	21	10.2%	18	-1.8%	19	9.2%	24	-8.7%	10	11.1%	26
2006	11	5.2%	23	-9.8%	8	1.1%	19	-8.4%	11	-3.2%	14

From the moment he entered the league, Quentin Jammer was supposed to develop into the next great shut-down cornerback, but he's just never going to do that. Jammer isn't a bad player—he starts every game and doesn't make too many glaring mistakes—but opposing quarterbacks aren't afraid to throw in his direction. Cornerback Antonio Cromartie showed a lot of promise as a rookie, enough that he should probably be the favorite to beat out Drayton Florence for the other starting cornerback spot. With Jammer and Cromartie starting, the Chargers might have the most athletic pair of corners in the league, but certainly not the best. Chargers General Manager A. J. Smith must really, really like strong safety Eric Weddle, the second-round pick out of Utah, considering that he traded a second-round pick, two third-round picks, and a fifth-round pick to move up in this year's draft and select him. Marlon McCree is firmly entrenched in one starting safety spot, and the Chargers certainly hope Weddle can beat out Clinton Hart as the other starter. Safety was the Chargers' biggest weakness on defense last year, and you don't make that kind of draft-day trade for a player at your weakest position if you don't think he can provide an immediate upgrade.

Special Teams

Year	DVOA	Rank	FG/XP	Rank	Net Punt	Rank	Punt Ret	Rank	Net Kick	Rank	Kick Ret	Rank	Hidden	Rank
2004	-3.0%	26	-3.7	23	1.9	16	-4.5	25	-17.2	32	5.8	8	9.9	4
2005	0.2%	16	6.0	5	4.5	10	-4.4	26	-8.7	28	4.1	10	10.8	2
2006	4.4%	3	7.8	6	10.8	4	-3.4	27	8.4	6	2.4	10	-12.4	29

The outstanding San Diego special teams were often overlooked last year, perhaps because the Chargers didn't have any kick returns for touchdowns, and that's the one aspect of great special teams that gets on *SportsCenter*. Although he didn't score any touchdowns, Michael Turner is a fairly good kickoff return man in addition to being the league's most reliable backup running back. Eric Parker broke a few long punt returns, but was nothing special overall. That's why punt returns are the one area of special teams in which the Chargers were below average.

Kicker Nate Kaeding got a long-term contract extension prior to 2006 and rewarded the Chargers with an outstanding season. Kaeding had his best year on both kickoffs and field goals, and the Chargers can feel comfortable about their kicking situation for years to come. Mike Scifres doesn't have the strongest leg in the league, but he is an absolutely amazing directional punter. He can kick the ball to the five-yard line and have it bounce back toward him time and time again. His ratio of 35 kicks inside the 20-yard line to just two touchbacks is superhuman.

Coaching Staff

From the players' standpoint, the change from Marty Schottenheimer to Norv Turner will be more about practice methods and less about game plans. Turner was the Chargers' offensive coordinator in 2001, and the offense in San Diego hasn't changed much since then, so there won't be too steep a learning curve. Cottrell says he doesn't plan to change much about the defense Wade Phillips ran in San Diego last year. Schottenheimer was at his best as a coach when managing his players, but that's where Turner has been at his worst in his past jobs. There's no way to say for sure how a very good team will adjust to a new staff, but if the Chargers don't advance further in the playoffs this season than they did last season, it will be hard not to call firing Schottenheimer a mistake.

Tennessee Titans

Born on the doomed planet Krypton, Vince Young came to Earth in a tiny spacecraft built by his loving father Jor-El. The craft landed in Houston, Texas, where the radiation from our yellow sun imbued Young with incredible powers. Off the field, he's a mild-mannered athlete with a dubious Wonderlic score, but on the gridiron, he becomes *Vince Young, Quarterback of Tomorrow.*

The NFL hype machine stopped just short of anointing Young the league's newest superhero last year. Perhaps it was because he was sharing the late-season spotlight with Tony Romo, who trumped Young by both winning games and dating half the VH-1 Top Twenty Countdown. Young didn't quite achieve Next Big Thing status, but he was showered with laurels, including a Rookie of the Year award, a trip to Honolulu, and a portrait on the box of our favorite video game. Most of the accolades were deserved—though we could argue for Joseph Addai or Marques Colston as Rookie of the Year, Young was a worthy choice—but the sudden success placed Young on a perilous perch. With great hype comes great (often unrealistic) expectations, and when Young was selected to the Pro Bowl, his development timetable suddenly accelerated. Second-year quarterbacks are expected to have growing pains, but Pro Bowl quarterbacks don't have that luxury.

What Young did off the field was invaluable to the Titans organization. In the wake of the bungled dismissals of stars Eddie George and Steve McNair, the Titans earned a national reputation as a cap-strapped outpost devoid of marquee talent. Young gave fans a reason to buy season tickets and kids a jersey worth wearing.

What Young did on the field was noteworthy, but not historic. The Titans' 8–5 record with Young at the helm is

---

TITANS PROSPECTUS

2006 Record: 8–8

DVOA Estimated Wins: 6.8 (24th)

Pythagorean Wins: 6.0 (25th)

DVOA: −13.0% total (24th), 2.4% weighted (15th)

Offense: −9.3% DVOA (26th)

Defense: 6.2% DVOA (24th)

Special Teams: 2.4% DVOA (9th)

Variance: 16.9% (13th)

2006: With an exciting base of young talent, Tennessee begins to emerge from salary cap purgatory.

2007: Pacman Jones makes it rain . . . on the parade of optimistic Titans fans.

2007 Mean Projection: 6.9 wins

The Brohm Closet (0–4): 15%

Bad Team (5–6): 29%

Mediocre (7–8): 31%

Playoff Contender (9–10): 19%

Super Bowl Contender (11+): 6%

Projected Average Opponent: 2.1% DVOA (8th in NFL)

---

impressive, but it comes with a small constellation of asterisks. The Titans beat the Redskins when both of Washington's starting defensive tackles were injured. They beat the Eagles during Philly's midseason confidence crisis, when Donovan McNabb got hurt and Jeff Garcia had not yet slathered his joints in WD-40. They erased a 21–0 deficit to defeat the Giants in the game that introduced the world to Mathias Kiwanuka's catch-and-release sack technique. The Titans' last five wins came by a total of 16 points, a sure sign that Dame Fortune was smiling on them.

Young played well during the Titans' six-game winning streak late in the season; his passing DVOA was −16.0% through Week 10, but 9.7% during the streak. He wasn't dominating, however, and neither were the Titans, as their average margin of defeat indicates. Unfortunately, fans and sportswriters love winning streaks and dramatic come-from-behind victories. Young and the Titans provided both at the end of last season. Had they caught fewer breaks, the Titans would have enjoyed a 4–2 stretch that showed they were an improving team with an exciting young passer. Instead, Young became the Leader and Winner who helped his franchise turn the corner. It's a classic case of too much success, too soon.

The late-season winning streak was great for morale and ticket sales, but the Titans are still a rebuilding team, and Young is still a work in progress. The team has some pieces in place—an improving offensive line, a quality coaching staff, some good defensive players—but they don't have the talent to compete for a division title against the Colts and Jaguars. Young's talent is undeniable, and he was a better-than-expected decision maker last season, but he still made rookie mistakes, and his strange slingshot

2007 Titans Schedule

Week	Opp	Week	Opp	Week	Opp
1	at JAC	7	at HOU	13	HOU
2	IND	8	OAK	14	SD
3	at NO	9	CAR	15	at KC
4	BYE	10	JAC	16	NYJ
5	ATL	11	at DEN (Mon.)	17	at IND
6	at TB	12	at CIN		

delivery led to some fumbles and off-target passes. The Titans are built for another .500-at-best finish, but their impatient fan base is expecting much more.

The Titans did their best to temper fan enthusiasm in March by letting several key free agents walk. Running back Travis Henry and receivers Drew Bennett and Bobby Wade accounted for 2,487 yards of total offense and 12 touchdowns last season. They weren't great players who could form the core of a championship-caliber offense, but all three were capable veterans and viable weapons for Young. The Titans will replace Henry with two young backs who didn't even play full-time in college, 2006 second-rounder LenDale White and 2007 second-rounder Chris Henry (no relation). Tennessee will likewise be hard-pressed to replace Bennett and Wade from within, as Brandon Jones, Roydell Williams, Justin Gage, and Jonathan Orr are slot receiver types; only Jones has potential as a top wideout. Rookies Paul Williams, Chris Davis, and Joel Filani are midrange prospects who will need time to develop. Even if David Givens recovers from his knee injury by midseason, the Titans still have the weakest receiving corps in the league. If his receivers aren't open, Young will be tempted to tuck and run more often, which will play to his worst instincts.

Each free-agent departure was a blow to Titans optimism, but the Pacman Jones saga was the haymaker that knocked it to the canvas. On February 19, the Titans cornerback was involved in an incident at a Vegas nightclub that included R&B singer Nelly, $81,000 in cash, several dancers, a hair stylist, a cactus, a bottle of Dom Perignon, and, sadly, a gun that may or may not have been wielded by a member of Jones's entourage. While that story was still percolating, reports surfaced that Jones was arrested twice in Georgia in 2006 for possession of marijuana and obstruction of justice. Jones never reported those arrests to the NFL, which was a direct violation of the league's code-of-conduct policy. Commissioner Roger Goodall needed a poster boy for his crackdown on bad behavior, and Jones got posterized. The league suspended Jones for the 2007 season.

Without Jones, the Titans will lose much of the ground they gained defensively last year. Before Jones stepped up, the Titans had been without a true shutdown cornerback since Samari Rolle started to slip after the 2003 season. The Titans couldn't count on their cornerbacks in man coverage, and they didn't have anyone to rush the quarterback except end Kyle Vanden Bosch. That left the defense in a double bind that forced coordinator Jim Schwarz to play lots of Cover-2 and other vanilla schemes. The philosophy wasn't bend-but-don't-break, it was break-but-don't-shatter.

Circumstances changed as Jones started to adjust to life in the NFL. He didn't develop into a technically perfect defender, but he was so gifted as a freelancer and big-play threat that opposing quarterbacks were reluctant to throw his way. Suddenly, the Titans had options. They could blitz a little more. They could put a safety in the box more often. Jones, Bullock, and Vanden Bosch gave the Titans a Pro Bowl performer at each defensive level. Like the offense, the Titans defense went from awful to acceptable in the second half of the season, and Jones was the difference maker.

Without Jones, the Titans face the same predicament that vexed them in 2004 and 2005. Defenders such as Bulluck, Vanden Bosch, safety Chris Hope, and linebacker David Thornton can keep the Titans from bottoming out, but the team is very weak at cornerback and defensive tackle, two critical positions. Rookie safety Michael Griffin will bolster the secondary, but he hardly offsets the loss of Jones. It will be another season of soft zones and conservative calls in Tennessee. Quarterbacks will find the pickings easy.

The forecast for 2007 looks grim, but it's easy to imagine the Titans leaping into contention in 2008. The most important ingredient to the team's long-term success isn't Young or Jones, but new general manager Mike Reinfeldt. Reinfeldt helped build a Super Bowl nucleus in Seattle. More impressively, he managed to keep that nucleus together despite the limitations of the salary cap. Reinfeldt's arrival signals the start of a new era of Titans football, an era that may not include head coach Jeff Fisher.

Fisher cannot be blamed for the cap purge that left the team uncompetitive in 2004 and 2005, but the coach who assured ownership that he could "handle" Jones before the 2005 draft ultimately failed to keep the team's second most important player on the straight-and-narrow. Rumors swirled last season that Fisher was squabbling with then-GM Floyd Reese, and that owner Bud Adams overruled Fisher and inserted Young into the lineup. New general manager Mike Reinfeldt wants to distance himself from the mistakes of the Reese era: the McNair lockout fiasco, the cap management nightmare, the first-round gambles on troublemakers such as Jones and defensive tackle Albert Haynesworth. If the Titans falter out of the gate, Reese's loyalty to Fisher may look like one more mistake.

If the Titans don't make the playoffs, Adams will almost certainly allow Fisher's contract to expire. Reinfeldt will then be free to pick his own coach: offensive coordinator Norm Chow (both men have a USC connection), one of the Ryan twins, maybe even Bill Cowher. Anyone but Chow will arrive with a new scheme for Young to learn. Constant change is like kryptonite for a developing passer. The Titans need Young. Young needs continuity. Five years from now, Young could be a legitimate superstar, a quarterback rather than a "playmaker." He could also be seated on a folding chair between Randall Cunningham and Kordell Stewart at a Scramble-o-holics Anonymous meeting. Everything is

riding on this season. It's a heck of a time to lose several free agents and have your best defender suspended.

The Titans will provide plenty of drama during this otherwise mediocre season. We'll watch Young struggle to come of age, Fisher fight for his job, Reinfeldt pull strings and plot behind the scenes, and Pacman wrestle his demons as he tries to stay off the police blotter. It may lack the grandeur of a Superman epic, but the story of the 2007 Titans will make an interesting episode of *Smallville*.

Mike Tanier

Titans 2006 Stats by Week

Wk	vs.	W–L	PF	PA	YDF	YDA	TO	Total	Off	Def	ST
								DVOA			
1	NYJ	L	16	23	328	393	-1	-63.0%	-32.7%	25.7%	-4.6%
2	@SD	L	7	40	218	476	-2	-74.6%	-52.9%	17.6%	-4.0%
3	@MIA	L	10	13	316	289	-2	-19.3%	-17.5%	3.0%	1.1%
4	DAL	L	14	45	229	396	-2	-103.4%	-41.4%	51.8%	-10.1%
5	@IND	L	13	14	277	320	+1	31.4%	3.8%	-21.8%	5.7%
6	@WAS	W	25	22	344	305	+2	-0.3%	-1.4%	-1.5%	-0.4%
7	BYE										
8	HOU	W	28	22	197	427	+5	-3.5%	-10.8%	14.7%	22.0%
9	@JAC	L	7	37	262	342	-3	-58.8%	-37.7%	22.9%	1.8%
10	BAL	L	26	27	367	421	+1	24.2%	30.4%	-4.3%	-10.5%
11	@PHI	W	31	13	293	390	+2	49.2%	1.7%	-32.0%	15.5%
12	NYG	W	24	21	343	287	0	29.3%	21.6%	-0.8%	6.9%
13	IND	W	20	17	302	451	0	-3.5%	-4.1%	2.2%	2.0%
14	@HOU	W	26	20	418	240	-2	-11.5%	5.8%	26.5%	9.2%
15	JAC	W	24	17	98	396	+4	6.2%	-26.5%	-27.6%	5.1%
16	@BUF	W	30	29	396	368	+2	-15.1%	20.3%	23.0%	-12.4%
17	NE	L	23	40	342	414	-3	-38.1%	-12.1%	39.4%	13.4%

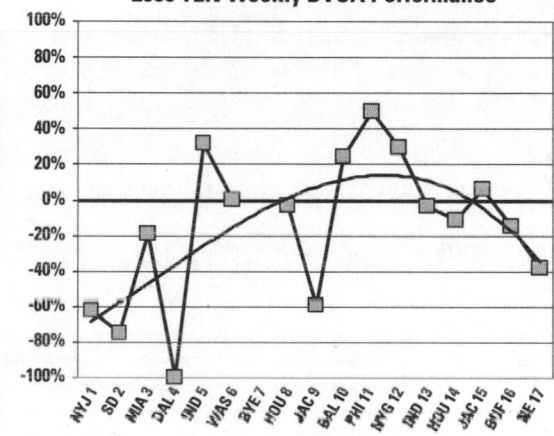

2006 TEN Weekly DVOA Performance

Trends and Splits

	Offense	Rank	Defense	Rank
Total DVOA	-9.3%	26	6.2%	24
Unadjusted VOA	-6.6%	22	12.1%	29
Weighted Trend	0.6%	17	2.3%	15
Variance	5.5%	23	5.2%	27
Passing	-16.7%	27	4.7%	17
Rushing	-2.8%	16	7.7%	28
First Down	-15.0%	26	4.9%	20
Second Down	-5.5%	23	9.4%	25
Third Down	-3.7%	18	3.2%	16
Red Zone	8.6%	11	7.1%	20
Late and Close	-5.1%	19	-7.1%	11

Five-Year Performance

	2006	2005	2004	2003	2002
W-L	8-8	4-12	5-11	12-4	11-5
Pythagorean Wins	6.0	4.9	5.8	10.7	9.2
Estimated Wins	6.8	5.3	5.4	10.6	9.0
Total DVOA	-13.0%	-18.6%	-21.1%	23.3%	8.1%
Rank	24	25	28	2	12
Offense	-9.3%	-6.2%	-6.7%	14.3%	9.5%
Rank	26	18	24	4	6
Defense	6.2%	14.3%	10.6%	-8.9%	1.7%
Rank	24	30	24	9	17
Special Teams	2.4%	1.9%	-3.9%	0.1%	0.2%
Rank	9	7	30	19	14

Strategic Tendencies

Formations		Rank	Run/Pass		Rank	Defense		Rank	Other		Rank
3+ WR	49%	12	Runs, all plays	49%	6	Sacks by LB	17%	21	Run with 2+ RB	41%	29
4+ WR	6%	25	Runs, first half	51%	3	Sacks by DB	12%	9	Run with 2+ TE	38%	14
2+ TE	28%	12	Runs, first down	56%	12	Rush 6+	6.6%	24	Play action	26%	3
Single back	65%	4	Runs, power sit.	67%	13	Rush 7+	2.0%	11	Go for it on 4th	0.97	13
Empty back	1.4%	22	Runs, behind 2H	43%	1	Rush 3	9.1%	3	Offensive Pace	29.4	8
Max protect	20%	1	Pass, ahead 2H	37%	24	CB1 on WR1	41%	17	Defensive Pace	31.0	20

Tennessee ran the ball with considerably more effectiveness in one-back sets (8.3% DVOA, ranked tenth), than two-back sets (−13.8% DVOA, ranked 26th). . . . In late and close situations, Tennessee's defense was much more effective against formations with three and four wide receivers (−56.6% and −32.2% DVOA, respectively) than against those with two receivers (50.8% DVOA). No other team had a similar split. . . . Offenses used both screen passes and draw plays against the Titans defense at more than twice the league-average rate. The Titans also faced play-action more often than any other team in the AFC, and behind only the Cowboys and Giants in the entire league. . . . Tennessee's defense had an above-average Adjusted Sack Rate of 7.3 percent on both first and second down, but had an Adjusted Sack Rate of 2.4 percent on third and fourth down, the lowest in the league except for Washington. . . . Titans' quarterbacks faced at least five pass rushers on 38 percent of passes, third behind Denver and Oakland, and faced at least six pass rushers on 12 percent of passes, second behind New England. These percentages were exactly the same for both Kerry Collins and Vince Young.

Passing

Player	DPAR	DVOA	Plys	NtYds	Avg	YAC	C%	TD	Int
Vince Young	9.6	-6.9%	353	2051	5.8	5.0	52.4%	12	12
Kerry Collins	-8.4	-34.6%	90	527	5.9	5.1	46.7%	1	6

Rushing

Player	DPAR	DVOA	Plys	Yds	Avg	TD	Fum	Suc
Travis Henry*	12.1	-2.8%	270	1211	4.5	7	3	43%
Vince Young	7.3	-0.8%	75	551	7.3	7	9	—
LenDale White	-1.2	-18.6%	62	244	3.9	0	1	40%
Chris Brown*	-1.2	-20.8%	41	156	3.8	0	1	0%
Ahmard Hall	-0.3	-19.3%	7	21	3.0	0	0	0%

Receiving

Player	DPAR	DVOA	Plys	Ctch	Yds	Y/C	YAC	TD	C%
WR									
Drew Bennett*	6.6	-4.4%	97	46	737	16.0	3.3	3	57%
Bobby Wade*	11.2	15.0%	58	33	461	14.0	4.8	2	50%
Brandon Jones	6.8	4.2%	54	27	384	14.2	2.9	4	47%
Roydell Williams	-0.5	-18.7%	21	8	121	15.1	4.8	0	38%
David Givens	-2.3	-32.4%	20	8	104	13.0	6.4	0	29%
Courtney Roby	-1.7	-51.3%	7	2	28	14.0	1.0	0	40%
Justin Gage	*-1.3*	*-38.8%*	*8*	*4*	*68*	*17.0*	*4.0*	*0*	*50%*
TE									
Bo Scaife	1.5	-8.4%	56	29	371	12.8	5.0	2	52%
Ben Troupe	-0.5	-14.8%	29	13	150	11.5	7.3	2	45%
Ben Hartsock	-1.2	-25.0%	15	6	68	11.3	8.2	0	40%
RB									
Travis Henry*	-4.8	-51.1%	25	18	78	4.3	5.9	0	72%
Ahmard Hall	-0.2	-12.4%	21	15	138	9.2	8.8	0	71%
LenDale White	-3.2	-50.6%	20	14	60	4.3	6.7	0	22%
Chris Brown*	-2.9	-93.0%	9	2	4	2.0	0.0	0	70%

Offensive Line

Year	Yards	ALY	Rank	Power	Rank	10+ Yds	Rank	Stuff	Rank	Sack	ASR	Rank
2004	4.42	4.21	15	51%	28	18%	12	25%	18	44	8.2%	23
2005	3.78	3.93	20	62%	19	13%	23	26%	18	31	4.6%	3
2006	4.29	3.93	27	67%	13	22%	6	24%	14	29	6.0%	13

Year	LE	Rank	LT	Rank	Mid	Rank	RT	Rank	RE	Rank
2004	3.19	26	4.21	21	4.36	14	4.61	10	3.66	19
2005	3.77	22	3.61	26	3.92	22	4.66	7	2.80	30
2006	3.82	20	3.37	31	4.08	23	4.24	15	3.61	22

The Titans' line coalesced when Jacob Bell moved from right tackle to left guard to replace the injured Zach Pillar, and David "Big Country" Stewart replaced Bell at tackle. Bell was overmatched by speed rushers at tackle, but he was a quick, athletic second-level blocker on the interior. Stewart, an incredibly strong mauler in the Kyle Turley mold, blossomed into a star in his second season. "It is scary how good this kid can be," offensive coordinator Norm Chow said at midseason. "We see him getting better and better."

Like Stewart, left tackle Michael "Kanga" Roos is a second-year player on the rise. Roos was flagged for nine false starts as a rookie, but he cut that total to four last year and made few mistakes in pass protection. Roos excels at engulfing his defender on the backside of runs; many of Travis Henry's biggest gains came on cutbacks after Roos completely shut down the right side of the defensive line.

Center Kevin Mawae proved that the Jets released him prematurely after the 2005 season. The six-time Pro Bowl participant stabilized the line and proved that he still has the strength and leverage to block most defensive tackles one-on-one. Mawae still has a year or two left before his odometer turns over. Rookie Leroy Harris, a four-year starter at North Carolina State, will be groomed as Mawae's replacement.

Defensive Front Seven

Defensive Line	Age	Pos	Plys	TmPct	Rk	Stop	Dfts	StpRt	Rk	AvYd	Rk	Sack	Hit	Hur	Runs	RuStp	RuYd	Pass	PaStp	PaYd
Kyle Vanden Bosch	29	DE	77	8.8%	7	53	20	69%	71	2.5	67	6.5	19	29	63	68%	3.0	14	71%	0.2
Robaire Smith*	30	DT	46	5.6%	29	30	8	65%	66	3.4	70	0.5	0	1	36	75%	2.4	10	30%	6.9
Randy Starks	24	DT	42	4.8%	47	33	15	79%	35	1.6	31	3	1	4	33	82%	2.1	9	67%	0.0
Tony Brown	27	DT	35	4.9%	42	30	10	86%	15	2.0	40	1.5	4	7	30	87%	2.2	5	80%	0.6
Travis LaBoy	26	DE	32	4.5%	64	24	11	75%	55	1.0	23	3.5	5	8	25	72%	1.8	7	86%	-2.0
Albert Haynesworth	26	DT	32	5.3%	33	28	7	88%	11	1.1	20	2	3	8	27	85%	1.9	5	100%	-2.8

Linebackers	Age	Pos	Plys	TmPct	Rk	Stop	Dfts	StpRt	AvYd	Sack	Hit	Hur	Runs	RuStp	Rk	RuYd	Rk	Tgts	Suc%	Rk	PaYd	Rk
Keith Bulluck	30	OLB	152	17.4%	10	83	22	55%	4.8	2.5	1	2	100	49%	94	4.8	95	47	64%	12	4.5	11
David Thornton	29	OLB	113	12.9%	42	59	20	52%	5.6	0	1	0	60	53%	90	5.3	97	54	55%	32	6.1	41
Peter Sirmon*	30	ILB	91	10.4%	67	41	14	45%	5.0	0.5	0	2	61	46%	97	4.4	89	37	48%	55	6.2	47
Stephen Tulloch	22	ILB	38	4.3%	—	21	5	55%	4.1	0.5	0	0	22	73%	—	2.8	—	17	28%	96	6.3	52
Gilbert Gardner	25	OLB	52	6.8%	97	29	8	56%	3.3	0	0	0	30	60%	65	2.9	20	12	47%	—	4.1	—

Year	Yards	ALY	Rank	Power	Rank	10+ Yds	Rank	Stuff	Rank	Sack	ASR	Rank
2004	4.80	4.15	12	48%	3	26%	32	26%	11	32	6.7%	19
2005	4.38	3.92	13	54%	5	24%	29	23%	24	41	7.4%	12
2006	4.47	4.57	25	69%	24	18%	25	20%	28	26	5.7%	25

Year	LE	Rank	LT	Rank	Mid	Rank	RT	Rank	RE	Rank
2004	5.39	30	3.62	3	3.77	4	4.52	26	4.62	28
2005	4.09	16	2.25	1	3.86	9	4.44	26	5.09	29
2006	4.94	24	4.00	9	4.51	20	4.16	16	5.26	31

Keith Bulluck is one of the five best linebackers in the game, a tremendous all-purpose defender with outstanding range and great ability as a pass rusher. Strong-side linebacker David Thornton is a consummate pro who shines in pass coverage and makes many tackles in pursuit. Inside linebacker Peter Sirmon was a solid two-down run defender who retired in the offseason; either Steven Tulloch or free-agent Ryan Fowler will replace him. The Titans linebackers would be better if they got more support from their defensive line. Bulluck, Thornton, and Sirmon made too many of their tackles five or more yards down the field last year because they had to work so hard to fend off offensive linemen.

The Titans invested several high draft picks in their defensive line from 2002 through 2004, but have seen few results. Tackle Albert Haynesworth, who was once billed as the next Reggie White, is best known for stomping on the helmetless head of Cowboys' lineman Andre Gurode. Haynesworth sometimes flashes elite talent, but is lazy and undisciplined. Tackle Randy Starks can be disruptive when fresh, but is often forced to play too many snaps. End Travis LaBoy is a high-motor player who is too small to hold up against the run. End Antwan Odom played well against the run in limited action, but he missed the start and end of the season with two separate injuries to his right leg. Starks, Odom, and LaBoy are entering their fourth seasons, so they are past the prospect stage and won't get significantly better.

Kyle Vanden Bosch was constantly double-teamed after registering 12.5 sacks in 2005. That dropped his sack total to 6.5, but he led the league in quarterback hits and ranked fourth in hurries, proving that opposing offenses can't stop him, they can only hope to slow him down. Vanden Bosch hasn't missed a start since the triad injury that wiped out his 2003 season. On a defense with the ability to exploit those double teams, he would consistently ring up double-digit sack totals.

Defensive Secondary

Secondary	Age	Pos	Plys	TmPct	Rk	Stop	Dfts	RuYd	Rk	RuStp	Rk	Tgts	Tgt%	Rk	Dist	Suc%	Rk	PaYd	Rk	PD	Int
Pacman Jones*	24	CB	75	9.2%	40	36	15	10.0	67	35%	55	69	16%	53	12.3	63%	2	5.4	1	14	4
Reynaldo Hill	29	CB	61	7.4%	55	24	5	9.2	63	42%	43	78	19%	44	15.3	53%	35	8.7	66	6	2
Chris Hope	27	SS	136	15.6%	1	59	21	5.2	15	51%	22	57	11%	3	12.2	47%	56	8.7	49	12	5
Cortland Finnegan	23	CB	63	7.2%	62	28	14	9.5	64	46%	33	49	10%	81	8.9	63%	3	6.3	14	6	0
Lamont Thompson	29	FS	83	9.5%	43	31	8	8.1	64	36%	55	42	9%	22	17.0	40%	70	13.2	79	6	3
Vincent Fuller	25	FS	15	1.7%	—	8	3	3.8	—	75%	—	6	1%	—	2.2	36%	—	6.5	—	0	0
Nick Harper	*33*	*CB*	*84*	*10.9%*	*16*	*39*	*18*	*6.9*	*46*	*50%*	*27*	*76*	*22%*	*14*	*10.3*	*55%*	*23*	*5.9*	*8*	*13*	*3*

Year	Pass D Rank	DVOA vs. #1 WR	Rank	DVOA vs. #2 WR	Rank	DVOA vs. Other WR	Rank	DVOA vs. TE	Rank	DVOA vs. RB	Rank
2004	23	5.2%	18	7.8%	22	-0.3%	17	22.5%	28	-1.7%	15
2005	32	27.5%	30	41.5%	32	-9.0%	11	11.4%	24	42.0%	32
2006	17	4.2%	21	-5.5%	13	3.1%	20	-20.5%	6	-2.4%	15

With Pacman Jones suspended, free-agent acquisition Nick Harper is the Titans' top cornerback. Harper played in the Colts' Cover-2 system, but he's solid in man coverage and in run support, though he struggles against bigger receivers. Reynaldo Hill found himself in the crosshairs last year when opponents started avoiding Jones. Hill didn't adjust and was headed for a role as a nickel corner before Jones's suspension. Sophomore Cortland Finnegan blitzed well as a nickel corner and kept his receivers off the scoresheet. He should push Hill.

Rookie Michael Griffin will probably supplant Finnegan as the nickel defender this season. Griffin was drafted as a safety, but he played some cornerback at Texas. He is effective when playing close to the line of scrimmage as a man defender or blitzer, but makes mistakes in zone coverage and can get caught flat-footed on deep passes, so it may take a year for Griffin to replace Lamont Thompson at free safety.

Safety Chris Hope led the Titans in interceptions and was second on the team in tackles. Hope is a field general who always seems to be around the ball, but he was forced to make too many clean-up tackles last season.

Special Teams

Year	DVOA	Rank	FG/XP	Rank	Net Punt	Rank	Punt Ret	Rank	Net Kick	Rank	Kick Ret	Rank	Hidden	Rank
2004	-3.9%	30	-5.0	26	5.1	11	-14.1	32	-1.6	17	-7.1	27	-4.3	21
2005	2.0%	7	-3.2	23	2.6	13	2.7	9	7.1	5	2.5	13	4.1	11
2006	2.4%	9	-1.4	20	4.2	12	12.4	1	-1.9	24	1.1	12	9.4	5

The Titans lost their best kickoff returner, Bobby Wade, to free agency. Their top punt returner was Pacman Jones. Rookie Chris Henry, a running back with track-star speed, will get a chance to return kicks. Fellow rookie Chris Davis will challenge Courtney Roby and Cortland Finnegan on punt returns. Kicker Rob Bironas nailed a 60-yard field goal against the Colts, but missed a 23-yard chip shot in the season finale against the Patriots and was just 5-of-10 outside 40 yards. The Titans signed rookie free-agent John Vaughn to challenge his fellow Auburn alum Bironas. Rookie Michael Griffin blocked eight kicks in college and is expected to be an immediate force on the coverage units. Colby Bockwoldt and Casey Cramer are the best players on otherwise average coverage units.

Coaching Staff

Offensive coordinator Norm Chow did an excellent job of adapting his offense to Vince Young's strengths. Chow incorporated more shotgun formations into his game plans to accommodate Young and introduced a variety of options and designed rollouts to exploit Young's running ability. Chow kept his formations and personnel groupings simple, but the Titans' offense was never predictable.

Jim Schwartz has been the Titans' defensive coordinator for six years and has been trying to make chicken soup from chicken feathers for the last three. Schwartz doesn't like to put players in untenable situations, so he has emphasized conservative schemes during the team's extended rebuilding period. Schwartz will be calling a lot of Cover-2 again this season despite being without his best cornerback.

Strength and conditioning coach Steve Watterson has been with the organization for over 20 years and is one of the most decorated conditioning coaches in the field. He was named Professional Strength and Conditioning Coach of the Year in 1992, won the President's Award from the Professional Football Strength and Coaches Society in 2002, and earned numerous other obscure accolades in the fitness and nutrition field. He has designed rehabilitation equipment for leg and shoulder injuries and training regimens for everyone from Olympians to auto racer A. J. Foyt. If running back LenDale White shows up for camp out of shape, it's not because Watterson wasn't trying.

Arizona Cardinals

The Chicago Cardinals were one of the original franchises that formed the American Professional Football Association in 1920. They played through the change from the APFA to the NFL, moving to St. Louis in 1960 and then to Arizona in 1988. Out of 1,149 regular-season games in the 87 years of Cardinals football, the most remarkable game of all—and certainly the most remarkable press conference of all—took place on Monday night, October 16, 2006.

On that night, the 1–4 Cardinals hosted the undefeated Chicago Bears in Arizona's first Monday Night appearance since 1999. The Cardinals were double-digit underdogs, but they came out white-hot against the NFL's best defense, scoring 20 points in the first half on Matt Leinart touchdown passes to Bryant Johnson and Anquan Boldin and two Neil Rackers field goals.

The Cardinals were on their way to an amazing upset, but the Bears had other ideas. Rising above a singularly awful performance by quarterback Rex Grossman—four interceptions and 10.7 quarterback rating—Chicago defenders returned fumbles by Leinart and Edgerrin James for touchdowns, Robbie Gould answered Rackers's second-half field goal, and Devin Hester returned a punt for Chicago's third non-offensive touchdown to put the Bears up, 24–23, with less than three minutes remaining.

On Arizona's final drive, Leinart moved his team 39 yards in nine plays with more poise than anyone had a right to expect from a rookie in his second NFL start, giving Rackers a chance to win the game with a 40-yard field goal . . . which Rackers missed, wide left. Grossman took a knee three times to end the game, and the Bears walked off the field still undefeated. Cardinals Head Coach Dennis

CARDINALS PROSPECTUS	
2006 Record: 5–11	
DVOA Estimated Wins: 6.2 (27th)	
Pythagorean Wins: 6.0 (26th)	
DVOA: −17.6% total (26th), −7.0% weighted (20th)	
Offense: −7.5% DVOA (21st)	
Defense: 5.4% DVOA (23rd)	
Special Teams: −4.8% DVOA (32nd)	
Variance: 19.3% (6th)	
2006: The Cardinals are who we thought we were.	
2007: They seem to be on the right track, but the numbers say to postpone the ass-crowning ceremonies.	
2007 Mean Projection: 6.0 wins	
The Brohm Closet (0–4): 25%	
Bad Team (5–6): 35%	
Mediocre (7–8): 24%	
Playoff Contender (9–10): 12%	
Super Bowl Contender (11+): 3%	
Projected Average Opponent: −2.2% DVOA (22nd in NFL)	

Green walked a few hundred steps to the post-game press room and his date with immortality.

"If you want to crown them, then crown their ass! But they are who they thought they were—and we let 'em off the hook," Green yelled after giving his podium microphone a swift bat for dramatic effect, then stormed out of the press room. Such goofy hubris endeared Green to nobody except *SportsCenter*, YouTube, and bloggers eager for material, especially after he made offensive coordinator Keith Rowen the fall guy by firing him two days later. After a 1–7 start, the Cardinals managed to post a .500 record in the second half of the season, but that came too late to help their coach.

It was Green's second straight 5–11 coaching performance, putting his Cardinals record at 16–32 overall. The front office had seen enough. Fired on New Year's Day, Green accepted his fate more willingly than one might expect. "I wasn't as disappointed as a lot of people think because we didn't play like we thought we would play," Green told ESPNews in mid-March. "We left five games on the table that we should have won in the 2006 season, [and] we did the exact same thing in 2005 and 2004. My frustration level was very high."

At a certain point, a team's escape from the cellar comes down to coaching and competitive mind-set. The Cardinals spent the Green era fumbling through supposed solutions, but could never overcome their (and their coach's) limitations. With a new stadium, a new big-money free-agent running back, and a glamorous new franchise quarterback, more was expected. The Cardinals have been everybody's preseason darlings for two years now, but few organizations in sports do a better job of showing the difference between a team on paper and a team on the field

2007 Cardinals Schedule

Week	Opp	Week	Opp	Week	Opp
1	at SF (Mon)	7	at WAS	13	CLE
2	SEA	8	BYE	14	at SEA
3	at BAL	9	at TB	15	at NO
4	PIT	10	DET	16	ATL
5	at STL	11	at CIN	17	STL
6	CAR	12	SF		

than the Arizona Cardinals. Green seemed bored—sometimes, downright antagonized—by fundamental issues such as conditioning, veteran leadership, and continuity. He burned through coaches like crazy, employing three offensive coordinators, three offensive line coaches, two special teams coaches, two receivers coaches, and two defensive line coaches in his three-year term.

On the eve of his first training camp as Arizona's head coach in 2004, Green released veteran lineman Pete Kendall, who had been the team's starting center. Kendall went to the playoffs with the Jets that year. Replacement Alex Stepanovich didn't measure up. Green juggled quarterbacks Josh McCown and Shaun King, even after the team found momentum with McCown in 2004. Free-agent acquisitions such as James and quarterback Kurt Warner did little to help, because the foundation was always off-kilter. James went from the team with the best Adjusted Line Yards ranking (Indianapolis) to the worst, and his stats told the story. Wide receivers Anquan Boldin and Larry Fitzgerald could rack up all the numbers they wanted, but the team was still treading water.

The weight of expectation now moves to Ken Whisenhunt, who was hired as the head coach two weeks after Green was axed. A former tight end with the Falcons, Redskins, and Giants, "Whizzie" became Pittsburgh's offensive coordinator in 2004 after three years as the Steelers' tight ends coach. It was Whisenhunt's goal to bring the ground game back to the Steel City. Pittsburgh ranked last in the league in rushing DVOA in 2003 and 31st in rushing yardage, the worst showing in team history, and finished the season with a 6–10 record. The 2004 Steelers, a 15–1 machine, ranked eighth in rushing DVOA and second in rushing yardage. The team's rushing attempts went up precipitously—a NFL-high 618 in 2004 after just 446 in 2003—but Jerome Bettis, the leading rusher in both seasons, carried the rock only four more times in the later campaign.

Willie Parker took over as Pittsburgh's leading rusher in 2005, but still accounted for less than half of the team's total carries. In 2006, however, Parker's 337 carries represented 72 percent of Pittsburgh's total, and Whisenhunt was unhappy with the running back's more conventional

workload and the team's pass-centric approach. Whisenhunt likes his backs to work in pairs or by committee, so when he says that he wants the Cardinals to run the ball 600 times in 2007 (and there have been words to that effect), James need not worry about having to bear a Larry Johnson–style workload.

As Whisenhunt told Ed Bouchette of the *Pittsburgh Post-Gazette* in February of 2004, there are specific ways in which he accomplishes his goals. "You want to strive for balance, but the running game especially establishes a mental toughness, a physical toughness with your team . . . I think you have to reestablish the fact that no matter what the situation is, you can run the ball and try to be successful doing that."

With the hire of assistant head coach Russ Grimm, his ex-teammate in Washington and co-staffer in Pittsburgh, Whisenhunt will also bring his philosophy of intelligent toughness to Arizona's oft-beleaguered offensive line. "It's never as simple as replacing one guy with another," he said. "It's getting the right person and getting everybody on the same page. We have enough weapons on this offense. If we can address a couple of the issues we talked about . . . it's going to make everybody better."

Ironically, the offensive line finally found continuity in Green's last few weeks as head coach. Arizona fielded five different line combinations in the opening nine games, a stretch that saw them go 1–8 and allow 26 sacks. From week 10 on, the Cardinals started the same line every game—from left to right: Leonard Davis, Milford Brown, Nick Leckey, Deuce Lutui, and Reggie Wells—went 4–3, allowed only nine sacks, and saw James post his only three 100-plus-yard games of the season. Arizona's offensive line was in last place in Adjusted Line Yards after eight games (3.42), but ranked sixth in the NFL over the final eight weeks (4.70).

This seems like it should be a positive indicator for the Arizona offense in 2007, but that turns out not to be the case. From 2000 through 2005, a dozen different offensive lines improved by 0.75 Adjusted Line Yards or more between Weeks 1–9 and Weeks 10–17. Half of these teams actually saw their offensive DVOA ratings drop by more than five percentage points the following season (table 1). Even more shocking is the identity of the team with the greatest second-half improvement in Adjusted Line Yards since 2000: The 2005 Arizona Cardinals. Arizona's offensive line improved in Adjusted Line Yards by more than *50 percent* during the second half of 2005, and barely any of that improvement carried over into 2006. The hiring of Grimm and presence of 2007 fifth-overall pick Levi Brown gives hope to this line in the long term, but last year's second half does nothing to provide hope for the short term.

On the defensive side of the ball, coordinator Clancy Pendergast and assistant defensive backs coach Rick Cour-

Table 1. Biggest Offensive Line Improvement in Weeks 10–17, 2000–2005

Team	Year	ALY Wk 1–9	ALY Wk 10–17	ALY Change	DVOA Yr1	DVOA Yr2	DVOA Change
ARI	2005	2.57	3.93	1.36	−11.3%	−8.0%	3.3%
NYJ	2002	3.39	4.65	1.27	18.6%	6.0%	−12.6%
CIN	2003	3.55	4.63	1.07	5.9%	3.0%	−2.9%
JAC	2000	3.71	4.73	1.02	6.6%	1.1%	−5.5%
NYJ	2005	3.45	4.29	0.85	−19.3%	2.3%	21.6%
DET	2004	3.61	4.46	0.85	−4.5%	−12.6%	−8.1%
OAK	2004	3.89	4.73	0.85	0.1%	0.6%	0.4%
KC	2000	3.56	4.40	0.84	10.1%	5.1%	−5.0%
PHI	2005	3.30	4.11	0.81	−9.2%	19.3%	28.5%
CIN	2000	3.26	4.07	0.81	−23.2%	−13.2%	10.0%
TB	2005	3.60	4.41	0.80	−6.9%	−18.4%	−11.6%
TEN	2003	3.27	4.04	0.78	14.3%	−8.4%	−22.7%

NOTE: Three teams had similar improvement in 2006: Arizona (+1.28 ALY), New Orleans (+1.09 ALY), and Houston (+1.02 ALY).

tright are the only two coaching survivors of the post-Green purge. Pendergast came on board with Green, and the Arizona defense rose from the worst DVOA in the league in 2003 to an above-average rating in 2004. Since then, however, the Cardinals dropped from 15th to 17th in 2005 and 23rd in 2006. Last year, the Cardinals ranked 22nd against number-one receivers, and 18th against running backs in the passing game. When your division rivals feature Steven Jackson and Frank Gore, that's a problem.

Whisenhunt is used to physical defenses, and he's going to want a front seven that finishes better than the 2006 Cardinals, who were 10th in Adjusted Line Yards, and 19th in Adjusted Sack Rate. Defensive ends Bert Berry and Chike Okeafor are effective but aging. The linebackers are still putting it together, though Karlos Dansby is a great young player. The secondary is led by a criminally under-rated *PFP* favorite strong safety Adrian Wilson, who was finally named to the Pro Bowl as a starter for the first time in 2006. Cornerback Antrel Rolle, Arizona's first-round pick in 2005, played only five games as a rookie because of a knee injury. Last year, in his first full season, he got a real education from opposing receivers. Rolle and Baltimore's Chris McAlister were tied with a league-leading seven pass interference penalties. Pass interference is often an indicator of close coverage, so those penalties show both Rolle's potential and need for more discipline. His three face mask penalties, however, only show his need for more discipline.

It's not easy to erase a culture of losing. Whisenhunt has what it takes to do the job, but what do the players think? Larry Fitzgerald, who knew Green as a Vikings ball-boy years ago, was none too happy about the switch, but fellow receiver Anquan Boldin finds intriguing possibilities in a coach who used Hines Ward in multiple roles. Whisen-hunt sees similarities between the two versatile receivers, Ward and Boldin. Boldin, a quarterback in high school, will play more from the slot under his new coach, and could be throwing passes in certain gadget plays. Matt Leinart will benefit from his new coach's experience with Ben Roethlis-berger; Whisenhunt knows how to groom a young quarterback for success.

Green never understood that successful teams are built from the lines out, and the fact that the Cardinals selected linemen in the first two rounds of this year's draft—Penn State tackle Levi Brown and Michigan defensive tackle Alan Branch—speaks to a more fundamental approach. Brown will replace Reggie Wells at right tackle, protecting the lefty Leinart's blind side. Branch will help an interior line that ranked 28th in defensive Adjusted Line Yards in the Mid-Guard area.

The front office spent a couple hundred thousand dollars on new weight room equipment and hired strength and conditioning coach John Lott (the guy who's famous for getting in the faces of bench-pressers at the Scouting Combine). Before, players would make a show of working out at the team facility, while scheduling their real work with their own personal trainers. Now, Lott will put together custom programs for maximum results.

In *Pro Football Prospectus 2006,* we described the Cardinals as having, "an average defense, a decent passing threat powered by two excellent young receivers, a solid kicking game, and one of the worst rushing attacks in NFL history." Last year, the defense regressed (despite the presence of Adrian Wilson, the secondary looks like a long-term project), and, although James and a slightly improved line took the Cardinals' running game out of the historical muck over the final seven weeks, there's no guarantee that will carry over to 2007. Not much has changed on the roster for 2007. Rather, any potential improvement must come about because of improved coaching and motivation. Ken Whisenhunt might be the right man for the job, but because his predecessor ran in place for three seasons, he will have his work cut out for him.

Doug Farrar

Is Field-Goal Percentage Useless?

Going into the 2006 season, the Arizona Cardinals fans didn't know if their team's offensive line would be able to block for their expensive new free-agent running back. They didn't know when their famous rookie quarterback would finally get into the starting lineup, and they didn't know if their defense would be any good. There was only one sure thing that Arizona fans knew about their team: The kicker was money. The year before, Neil Rackers had set a single-season NFL record with 40 field goals and led the league with a 95 percent field-goal percentage. He even hit six of seven kicks from 50 yards or more.

So it was a little surprising when Rackers missed field goals of 51 and 53 yards against Seattle in Week 2. Three weeks later, he missed a 51-yarder against Kansas City. The next week, he missed two field goals against Chicago, including a 40-yarder that would have won the game with less than a minute left. After eight games, Rackers had a field-goal percentage of 67 percent. He was better over the second half of the year, but still finished the season having converted only 76 percent of his field goal attempts. Instead of leading the league, he was 27th. There was no injury involved—Rackers finished second in the league in average kickoff distance, behind Denver's altitude-aided Paul Ernster. What happened to Rackers's accuracy?

The answer, believe it or not, is nothing. Rackers's year-to-year inconsistency is emblematic of a remarkable fact about kickers: There is virtually no correlation between a field-goal kicker's performance between one year and the next, yet average kickoff distance shows more consistency from year-to-year than almost any other individual statistic in the NFL.

The variable performance of field-goal kickers is easily apparent when looking at the league leaders in field-goal percentage. Only two players appeared in the top ten for field-goal percentage in both 2005 and 2006: San Diego's Nate Kaeding and Baltimore's Matt Stover. Cleveland's Phil Dawson, second to Rackers in 2005, saw his accuracy dive-bomb to 72 percent in 2006. Chicago's Robbie Gould was below average in 2005, then hit 24 straight field goals to start 2006.

Remember when Mike Vanderjagt was perfect for the entire 2003 season? The year before he hit just 74 percent of his field goals, and the year after he hit just 80 percent.

The numbers for kickoff distance are completely different. Rackers has finished either first or second in the NFL for three straight years. Josh Scobee of the Jaguars and Olindo Mare of the Saints (formerly of the Dolphins) have ranked in the top ten all three years. Except for his rookie year, when he played only five games, former New Orleans and Minnesota punter/kickoff specialist Mitch Berger never ranked lower than sixth in kickoff distance in his 12-year career.

The difference between field goals and kickoffs is just as apparent if we use our advanced metrics, which take into account field-goal distance, weather, and altitude. On kickoffs, there are seven kickers who have been worth at least one point more than average for three straight seasons. On field goals, there are only two, and Baltimore's Matt Stover is the only kicker who has been consistently at the top of the league. From 2005 to 2006, 16 different kick-

Table 2. Biggest Swings in Kicker Value, 2005–2006

Kicker	Change	Kicker	Change
FG/XP Value			
Neil Rackers	−21.1	Jason Hanson	+10.1
Joe Nedney	−15.3	Phil Dawson	−9.0
Jason Elam	+12.8	Josh Scobee	+8.0
Robbie Gould	+12.3	Sebastian Janikowski	+7.4
Olindo Mare	−10.9	Kris Brown	+5.9
Mike Vanderjagt	−10.9	Adam Vinatieri	+5.5
John Kasay	+10.7	Jeff Reed	−5.4
John Carney	+10.7	Matt Bryant	−5.2
Gross Kickoff Value			
Dave Rayner	+9.6	Nate Kaeding	+5.8
Jason Hanson	+6.4	Shayne Graham	+5.3
Rob Bironas	−6.1		

ers either declined or improved on field goals by five points or more, but only five had a similar swing in kickoff value (table 2).

Measuring every kicker from 1999 to 2006 who had at least ten field goal attempts in each of two consecutive years, the year-to-year correlation of field-goal percentage is an insignificant .05. Our advanced field-goal measurement isn't much better, with a year-to-year correlation of .08.

Perhaps field-goal percentage swings wildly from year to year, but if we look at a kicker's career numbers, surely we'll discover that some kickers are consistently better on field goals than others, right? Actually, no. Career numbers don't provide much better correlation. For kickers with at least three years of experience, the correlation between past career percentage and field-goal percentage the next season is .10. If we measure kickers with five or more years experience, that correlation actually drops to .06. Even for football, where stats are more erratic from year to year than in any of the other three major team sports due to the small samples resulting from the 16-game season, these correlations are meaningless.

What about the idea that certain kickers have "more leg" and can hit longer field goals more reliably than their "short-legged" brethren? Since the introduction of the special teams–only k-ball in 1999, the year-to-year correlation of field-goal percentage on kicks of 40 yards or more is −.10. In other words, a kicker who is above-average on longer field goals in one year is actually more likely to be *below*-average the following year. There isn't even a correlation from year to year in the number of attempts a kicker gets from 40 yards or more, or even from 50 yards or more. The only way to get a correlation coefficient of at least .20 (actually, exactly .20) is to compare career field-goal percentage below 40 yards to next year's field-goal percentage below 40 yards, but even that is only mildly significant.

On the other hand, the year-to-year correlation of average kickoff distance—looking at the same time period, with the same minimum of ten kickoffs per year—is .61. That makes average kickoff distance one of the most predictable individual stats in the entire NFL, at any position. The year-to-year correlation of our advanced kickoff metric—which adjusts for weather and altitude and treats touchbacks and out-of-bounds kickoffs differently than other kicks—is .50, which still ranks among the most predictable stats in football, and much higher than any correlation for field-goal percentage.

This dramatic difference in consistency between field goals and kickoffs means that NFL teams are generally signing and drafting kickers based on the wrong skill. Vanderjagt has been the worst kickoff man in the NFL over the last decade, but Dallas signed him because he could hit field goals. When he couldn't hit field goals, the Cowboys cut him halfway through the year and ate his signing bonus. The Indianapolis Colts signed Adam Vinatieri to a five-year, $12-million contract based on his history of hitting clutch field goals for the rival New England Patriots. Vinatieri, however, is no more consistent than any other kicker. He has never had two straight seasons with a field-goal percentage higher than 80 percent.

The Patriots replaced Vinatieri with rookie Stephen Gostkowski, and the New England media ripped the team after Gostkowski missed four of his first 12 professional field-goal tries. The rookie stabilized after that, going 12-for-14 the rest of the year. More importantly, he was a beast on kickoffs. Gostkowski was sixth in the league, averaging 65.5 yards per kickoff, and would have been better if not for the cold New England weather. In our numbers, adjusted for weather and altitude, Gostkowski was third behind Mare and Scobee. Gostkowski will be up and down on field goals for the rest of his career, just like Vinatieri, but he's probably going to have a high kickoff average every single year, just like Neil Rackers.

These mistaken decisions continued in the most recent offseason. Olindo Mare was awful on field goals last year, hitting just 72 percent of his attempts, so Miami dealt him to New Orleans for a sixth-round pick. Mare's booming kickoffs will give the Saints more advantage in field position than Reggie Bush's punt returns, and his field-goal accuracy will be fine, especially because the Saints play 11 games indoors.

Does this mean that there is absolutely no such skill as field-goal accuracy? Not necessarily. As the great baseball analyst Bill James pointed out in an article called "Underestimating the Fog," not proving that something exists is not the same as proving that it does not exist. James was writing about clutch hitting in baseball, but the same thing applies to field-goal accuracy. We don't know whether field-goal accuracy is a true skill. What we do know is that the statistic we currently use to measure it, field-goal percentage, is almost completely useless as a predictor of future performance on a year-to-year basis.

No kickoff is as important as a field goal to win the game in the final seconds, but it's impossible to tell which kickers will be most trustworthy in that scenario from year to year. If teams want to guarantee value from the kicker position, they should find a kicker whose kickoffs will impact field position for an entire game. We would recommend Neil Rackers, but he's already taken.

Aaron Schatz

Cardinals 2006 Stats by Week

Wk	vs.	W–L	PF	PA	YDF	YDA	TO	Total	Off	Def	ST
1	SF	W	34	27	393	367	-1	-42.2%	-0.9%	34.6%	-6.8%
2	@SEA	L	10	21	256	341	+2	-49.9%	-38.0%	6.9%	-4.9%
3	STL	L	14	16	357	372	-2	-27.0%	-33.7%	-5.2%	1.4%
4	@ATL	L	10	32	187	405	-3	-91.5%	-78.8%	-0.8%	-13.5%
5	KC	L	20	23	298	301	+1	14.8%	-7.4%	-34.2%	-12.0%
6	CHI	L	23	24	286	168	+4	48.7%	3.0%	-77.3%	-31.6%
7	@OAK	L	9	22	224	395	+3	-71.5%	-54.3%	5.4%	-11.8%
8	@GB	L	14	31	218	383	-1	-80.2%	-16.0%	63.2%	-1.0%
9	BYE										
10	DAL	L	10	27	295	434	-3	-48.7%	-20.2%	24.1%	-4.4%
11	DET	W	17	10	338	213	+1	26.1%	19.9%	-14.8%	-8.6%
12	@MIN	L	26	31	412	412	-4	-14.6%	12.1%	39.7%	13.0%
13	@STL	W	34	20	316	394	+3	40.4%	20.1%	-23.0%	-2.6%
14	SEA	W	27	21	345	348	+2	6.9%	7.1%	9.5%	9.3%
15	DEN	L	20	37	295	365	0	-35.7%	-10.8%	21.9%	-3.1%
16	@SF	W	26	20	372	223	+1	14.1%	15.5%	-0.4%	-1.8%
17	@SD	L	20	27	444	387	0	37.4%	53.7%	14.1%	-2.2%

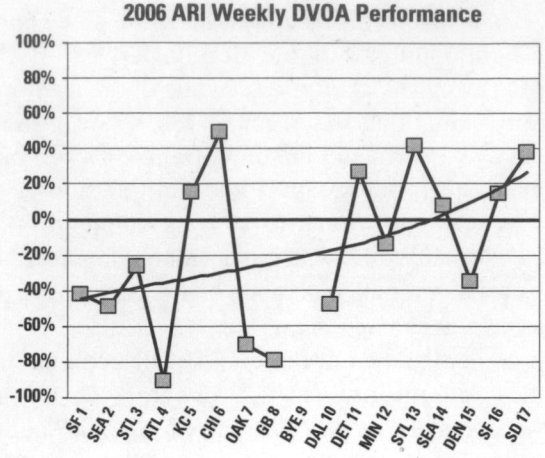

2006 ARI Weekly DVOA Performance

Trends and Splits

	Offense	Rank	Defense	Rank
Total DVOA	-7.5%	21	5.4%	23
Unadjusted VOA	-3.9%	20	2.3%	18
Weighted Trend	3.4%	15	7.1%	21
Variance	9.8%	5	9.9%	3
Passing	1.5%	15	15.7%	26
Rushing	-17.9%	29	-6.2%	12
First Down	-22.8%	30	-6.4%	13
Second Down	2.2%	16	16.8%	30
Third Down	6.6%	14	12.0%	21
Red Zone	-12.6%	21	-16.4%	5
Late and Close	8.2%	11	11.3%	26

Five-Year Performance

	2006	2005	2004	2003	2002
W-L	5-11	5-11	6-10	4-12	5-11
Pythagorean Wins	6.0	6.0	6.8	2.6	4.0
Estimated Wins	6.2	6.3	5.0	3.5	3.1
Total DVOA	-17.6%	-12.3%	-21.6%	-42.8%	-41.9%
Rank	26	22	29	32	32
Offense	-7.5%	-11.5%	-22.5%	-22.2%	-16.2%
Rank	21	23	30	32	28
Defense	5.4%	-1.5%	-2.3%	18.6%	20.6%
Rank	23	17	15	32	31
Special Teams	-4.8%	-2.3%	-1.4%	-1.9%	-5.1%
Rank	32	26	21	25	29

Strategic Tendencies

Formations		Rank	Run/Pass			Rank	Defense		Rank	Other		Rank
3+ WR	66%	2	Runs, all plays	41%		24	Sacks by LB	26%	12	Run with 2+ RB	24%	31
4+ WR	16%	6	Runs, first half	42%		26	Sacks by DB	13%	6	Run with 2+ TE	43%	6
2+ TE	26%	16	Runs, first down	53%		18	Rush 6+	3.7%	29	Play action	9%	32
Single back	83%	2	Runs, power sit.	56%		26	Rush 7+	0.5%	30	Go for it on 4th	0.59	32
Empty back	0.6%	28	Runs, behind 2H	31%		22	Rush 3	3.6%	20	Offensive Pace	30.9	17
Max protect	5%	32	Pass, ahead 2H	46%		10	CB1 on WR1	44%	15	Defensive Pace	29.4	5

Arizona set up in formations with one wide receiver only 3.3 percent of the time, and ran the ball on 91 percent of those plays. When Arizona used this formation in the second half of the Chicago game, Dennis Green also held up a large sign that said "This is a run up the middle".... In standard two-wide-receiver sets, Arizona threw only 12 percent of its passes to the running back, doing so less often than any other team. The NFL average was 23 percent, and the league leader was New Orleans at 40 percent.... With only two wide receivers on the field, Kurt Warner (68.0% DVOA) was notably better than Matt Leinart (–28.0% DVOA). Leinart was better than Warner in other sets, and the two ended up with the exact same overall passing DVOA.... Including running plays, Arizona had a below-average offensive DVOA in every formation with two wide receivers or fewer, and an above-average DVOA in every formation with three wide receivers or more. . . . Only Seattle ran fewer screens as a percentage of total passes than Arizona. The Cardinals also ran the lowest number of play-fakes in the NFL. . . . The Arizona defense ranked seventh in Adjusted Sack Rate on first down (7.6%), but last on second down (4.8%), and 24th on third and fourth down (5.1%). . . . Only the Rams had a worse defensive DVOA against screen passes than the Cardinals' 115.4%. . . . For the second straight year, Arizona ranked both 30th in rushing seven defenders and 20th in rushing three.

Passing

Player	DPAR	DVOA	Plys	NtYds	Avg	YAC	C%	TD	Int
Matt Leinart	28.4	4.0%	370	2373	6.4	4.1	57.8%	11	11
Kurt Warner	13.1	4.1%	168	1259	7.5	5.8	64.3%	6	5

Rushing

Player	DPAR	DVOA	Plys	Yds	Avg	TD	Fum	Suc
Edgerrin James	3.7	-11.5%	337	1162	3.4	6	3	45%
Marcel Shipp	2.7	12.9%	17	41	2.4	4	0	0%
J. J. Arrington	-3.4	-81.6%	14	19	1.4	0	0	55%
Matt Leinart	1.4	2.0%	14	63	4.5	2	8	—
Obafemi Ayanbadejo	1.9	21.5%	9	37	4.1	0	0	33%
Kurt Warner	-3.2	-94.8%	6	6	1.0	0	9	—
Anquan Boldin	-0.7	-56.8%	5	28	5.6	0	1	—
Terrelle Smith	*-1.4*	*-51.0%*	*8*	*14*	*1.8*	*0*	*0*	*76%*

Receiving

Player	DPAR	DVOA	Plys	Ctch	Yds	Y/C	YAC	TD	C%
WR									
Anquan Boldin	18.7	3.8%	152	83	1203	14.5	5.5	4	62%
Larry Fitzgerald	27.6	22.3%	111	69	946	13.7	2.7	6	55%
Bryant Johnson	16.9	21.3%	74	40	740	18.5	5.8	4	54%
Troy Walters	4.3	4.0%	35	23	209	9.1	3.6	2	66%
TE									
Adam Bergen	-5.9	-49.6%	24	15	111	7.4	2.6	1	70%
Leonard Pope	1.0	-6.6%	23	16	161	10.1	4.8	0	63%
RB									
Edgerrin James	-4.8	-25.6%	60	38	217	5.7	4.2	0	63%
Obafemi Ayanbadejo	0.6	-4.3%	19	17	141	8.3	7.4	0	80%
Marcel Shipp	0.5	0.1%	11	6	60	10.0	7.7	0	89%
J. J. Arrington	2.4	51.3%	10	8	58	7.3	5.4	0	55%
Terrelle Smith	*-3.8*	*-73.8%*	*11*	*8*	*21*	*2.6*	*2.1*	*0*	*64%*

Offensive Line

Year	Yards	ALY	Rank	Power	Rank	10+ Yds	Rank	Stuff	Rank	Sack	ASR	Rank
2004	3.62	3.71	29	47%	31	16%	25	29%	29	39	6.9%	18
2005	3.01	3.26	32	41%	32	11%	29	32%	32	45	6.3%	14
2006	3.34	4.05	23	56%	26	4%	32	25%	25	36	6.2%	14

Year	LE	Rank	LT	Rank	Mid	Rank	RT	Rank	RE	Rank
2004	2.95	27	4.45	17	3.67	30	3.41	31	4.07	13
2005	3.84	21	2.23	32	3.58	30	3.16	28	3.20	27
2006	4.08	17	3.96	26	4.25	21	3.77	29	3.46	24

Most teams who lose their left tackles to huge contracts in free agency are in big trouble, but the Arizona Cardinals are the exception to this rule for a number of reasons. First, that Leonard Davis, the left tackle in question, took his seven blown blocks and ten penalties to Dallas for seven years, $49.6 million, and $18.75 million guaranteed says more about the money burning a hole in Jerry Jones's pocket than it does about Davis's abilities. Second, new offensive line coach Russ Grimm, a near–Hall of Fame guard with Joe Gibbs's Redskins a generation ago, was instrumental in making Pittsburgh's line one of the most physical and effective in the league in his six years there.

Third, quarterback Matt Leinart is a lefty, which puts the responsibility for his blind side on the right tackle. Fourth, the right tackle will be former Penn State mauler Levi Brown, who was selected by the Cardinals with the fifth-overall pick in this year's draft. The Nittany Lions averaged almost two yards per carry more in 2006 when Brown was in the lineup than during the two games missed following arthroscopic surgery on his knee. This is great news for Edgerrin James. Brown will need finishing work as a pass blocker, but he's already better than any tackle the Cards have on the roster, including the man he'll replace, Reggie Wells.

Ex-Bears and Bills tackle Mike Gandy will occupy Davis's old spot at left tackle, while Wells may move to left guard. Ex-Cowboys backup center Al Johnson will give Nick Leckey a run as the main man in the middle. Guards Milford Brown and Deuce Lutui are both under contract through 2009, and both did well down the stretch last year. Lutui, a rookie in 2006, seems to have elite potential. The future looks bright for this much-maligned offensive line, but, as we showed earlier in the chapter, the Cardinals should expect one step back before the line takes three steps forward.

Defensive Front Seven

Defensive Line	Age	Pos	Plys	TmPct	Rk	Stop	Dfts	StpRt	Rk	AvYd	Rk	Sack	Hit	Hur	Runs	RuStp	RuYd	Pass	PaStp	PaYd
Chike Okeafor	31	DE	62	7.5%	22	45	24	73%	60	0.7	15	8.5	12	9	43	63%	2.4	19	95%	-3.0
Bertrand Berry	32	DE	25	4.8%	58	18	14	72%	63	-0.5	3	6	4	8	16	56%	2.4	9	100%	-5.8
Chris Cooper	30	DE	26	3.9%	73	22	6	85%	11	1.6	38	2	2	2	18	78%	2.7	8	100%	-0.9
Antonio Smith	26	DE	26	3.1%	77	20	8	77%	44	1.0	25	2.5	3	5	21	71%	2.0	5	100%	-2.8
Darnell Dockett	26	DT	55	6.6%	11	40	15	73%	53	2.7	58	2	6	4	46	72%	3.1	9	78%	0.8
Kendrick Clancy*	29	DT	29	5.1%	37	21	4	72%	54	2.2	48	1	0	2	28	71%	2.5	1	100%	-5.0
Gabe Watson	24	DT	17	2.7%	—	9	3	53%	—	2.6	—	1	0	2	13	46%	2.7	4	75%	2.3

Linebackers	Age	Pos	Plys	TmPct	Rk	Stop	Dfts	StpRt	AvYd	Sack	Hit	Hur	Runs	RuStp	Rk	RuYd	Rk	Tgts	Suc%	Rk	PaYd	Rk
Gerald Hayes	27	ILB	100	13.8%	31	53	15	53%	5.5	1	2	4	58	67%	36	3.6	60	45	45%	66	6.4	59
Karlos Dansby	26	OLB	85	11.7%	58	53	23	62%	4.5	8	1	3	40	73%	16	2.9	19	33	40%	81	10.4	98
Orlando Huff	29	OLB	74	8.9%	78	34	5	46%	5.4	0	0	1	46	52%	91	4.0	78	37	38%	88	8.9	92
Calvin Pace	27	OLB	26	3.1%	—	15	4	58%	3.5	1	0	2	16	56%	—	3.3	—	8	88%	—	5.5	—

Year	Yards	ALY	Rank	Power	Rank	10+ Yds	Rank	Stuff	Rank	Sack	ASR	Rank
2004	4.75	4.30	20	59%	12	25%	30	24%	13	37	5.9%	29
2005	4.07	3.76	8	59%	12	22%	28	30%	2	37	6.7%	19
2006	4.23	4.31	18	66%	17	17%	21	25%	14	38	5.9%	23

Year	LE	Rank	LT	Rank	Mid	Rank	RT	Rank	RE	Rank
2004	4.66	24	4.43	17	4.28	19	3.78	7	5.39	31
2005	2.51	1	4.38	19	4.44	26	3.68	6	2.34	1
2006	3.30	6	4.56	18	4.76	28	4.39	19	4.34	20

New defensive line coach Ron Aiken has an interesting mix of talent to work with. He also has injury and age concerns staring him in the face. Defensive ends Bert Berry and Chike Okeafor are the line's two best players, but Berry has missed a total of 14 games over the last two seasons. As a result, Berry has just 12 sacks in those two seasons combined after racking up 14.5 in 2004 alone. Okeafor led the team in sacks last year, and really stepped it up after Berry was lost for the season, racking up 6.5 sacks in his last five games. Okeafor, Berry, and top backup Chris Cooper are all in their thirties, so the Cardinals had better start looking for depth at the edges.

Kendrick Clancy and Darnell Dockett were Arizona's primary interior linemen last season. Clancy's job is to take double teams so that his teammates can make plays, and Dockett is an aggressive and athletic tackle. For the second straight year, the Cards drafted a Michigan defensive tackle, and both 2006 fourth-rounder Gabe Watson and 2007 second-rounder Alan Branch bring concerns to the table. Watson needs to control his weight and focus on conditioning. Branch dropped from his expected place in the top-ten overall picks due to inconsistent results and a reputation for taking plays off.

Of the linebackers, only Karlos Dansby has shown anything approaching All-Pro play. Middle linebacker Gerald Hayes displays some ability, but Arizona's rank of 28th in Adjusted Line Yards up the middle is about more than just the line. Orlando Huff's weak-side designation was entirely appropriate, and that is a position the team will look to upgrade. Whisenhunt has publicly expressed a desire to implement more 3-4 schemes with his new team. "I want us to be more flexible," he told ESPN.com's Len Pasquarelli in April. "I think it will give us a little different look, and some maneuverability, so we'll see how it works." However, Whisenhunt and defensive coordinator Clancy Pendergast, who has preferred the 4-3 in the past, might find such ingenuity a hard go with their current linebacker corps.

Defensive Secondary

Secondary	Age	Pos	Plys	TmPct	Rk	Stop	Dfts	RuYd	Rk	RuStp	Rk	Tgts	Tgt%	Rk	Dist	Suc%	Rk	PaYd	Rk	PD	Int
Antrel Rolle	25	CB	98	11.8%	12	39	10	4.9	21	52%	21	100	22%	15	12.1	54%	31	6.3	15	14	1
Eric Green	25	CB	54	6.9%	65	28	10	3.0	2	57%	14	56	13%	72	12.1	55%	25	8.0	53	8	0
David Macklin*	29	CB	38	5.2%	79	13	6	13.1	79	14%	77	50	12%	76	11.3	54%	30	8.0	54	6	1
Adrian Wilson	28	SS	92	11.1%	24	59	30	3.4	2	77%	2	44	9%	21	9.0	52%	44	7.2	32	10	4
Robert Griffith	37	FS	90	10.9%	28	20	8	10.3	75	16%	78	28	5%	67	20.0	48%	52	9.8	61	8	3
Aaron Francisco	24	FS	31	3.7%	—	10	4	7.5	—	40%	—	11	2%	—	20.2	47%	—	11.9	—	3	2
Terrence Holt	27	FS	81	9.6%	42	20	10	8.9	71	17%	77	28	5%	66	15.5	63%	11	6.3	18	4	3
Roderick Hood	26	CB	22	3.9%	—	10	5	2.7	—	67%	—	30	11%	—	11.7	59%	—	8.1	—	0	0
Ralph Brown	29	CB	43	5.2%	80	20	12	4.6	14	56%	17	48	11%	80	9.2	48%	60	7.8	48	9	0

Year	Pass D Rank	DVOA vs. #1 WR	Rank	DVOA vs. #2 WR	Rank	DVOA vs. Other WR	Rank	DVOA vs. TE	Rank	DVOA vs. RB	Rank
2004	13	-7.4%	8	-2.6%	12	-17.0%	9	11.1%	20	8.7%	21
2005	12	15.3%	22	-2.0%	18	-6.2%	14	-15.9%	5	-26.5%	3
2006	26	10.5%	25	12.0%	24	31.0%	29	-3.0%	17	2.4%	17

With the exception of strong safety Adrian Wilson, no member of Arizona's 2006 defensive backfield should feel too safe. The front office addressed a secondary that finished 26th in DVOA against the pass by signing free safety Terrence Holt and cornerback Roderick Hood to five-year, $15-million contracts. Holt was an aggressive player for the Lions and led the Detroit secondary in tackles with 76. Hood will battle it out with Eric Green and Antrel Rolle at cornerback. He was a nickel corner in Philadelphia, but will get a chance to start with the Cardinals. Green has moments of spectacular play (especially in the *Monday Night Football* loss to the Bears), but those moments have not been frequent enough. Rolle, the team's first-round draft pick in 2005, has the best chance of starting, but he needs to take a step forward this season. Though he finished 15th in yards per pass allowed, Rolle is vulnerable to the deep ball and collects far too many penalty flags.

As for longtime *PFP* favorite Wilson, last year he was the only NFL player with five sacks and four interceptions, he forced a career-high four fumbles, and he had two 99-yard touchdowns—one a fumble return, the other an interception return. If Wilson played in New York or Dallas, he'd be a perennial Pro Bowler, but he was only named to the starting roster for the first time last year. In the 1960s and early 1970s, another Cardinals safety named Wilson—Hall of Famer Larry—became the first prominent advocate of the safety blitz with the St. Louis franchise, to the point that urban legend had him inventing the maneuver. Adrian Wilson set the pace with a record eight sacks on safety blitzes in 2005, and tied Kerry Rhodes of the Jets for the league lead with five in 2006. He also led all defensive backs with nine quarterback hurries last year. Quite simply, he's as good a strong safety as there is in the NFL.

Special Teams

Year	DVOA	Rank	FG/XP	Rank	Net Punt	Rank	Punt Ret	Rank	Net Kick	Rank	Kick Ret	Rank	Hidden	Rank
2004	-1.4%	21	6.2	5	-6.1	28	-7.6	29	11.2	5	-12.3	31	-9.1	27
2005	-2.3%	26	20.0	1	-5.7	25	-2.3	20	-20.7	32	-4.7	24	-5.2	21
2006	-4.8%	32	-1.2	19	-20.0	31	-3.8	29	0.5	16	-3.5	22	-8.3	26

Neil Rackers's off-year on field goals is discussed earlier in the chapter. His kickoffs were good, but Arizona's kickoff and punt coverage teams were not. The 10.4-yard discrepancy between punter Scott Player's gross and net punting average (44.9 to 34.5) was the second-largest in the NFL behind Oakland's Shane Lechler at 11.1. Fourth receiver Troy Walters was an acceptable, if unspectacular, punt returner, and backup running back J. J. Arrington was the team's primary kick returner. Arrington broke a 99-yard return against the Vikings in November, but the Cardinals drafted Michigan receiver Steve Breaston in the fifth round in the hope that the all-purpose threat could continue the productivity that made him a scoring threat on punt and kickoff returns in each of his collegiate seasons. Special teams coach Kevin Spencer, another import from the Steelers' staff, will try to get things on track with a total unit that ranked last in special teams DVOA in 2006.

Coaching Staff

The transition from Dennis Green to Ken Whisenhunt couldn't be more drastic. Green, who could be kindly called "mercurial," blew through assistant coaches at an impressive rate and, at times, didn't seem to grasp fundamentals. Whisenhunt is a graduate of one of the most stable coaching staffs of the modern era (it just happened to split apart all at the same time). He brings an intensity and accountability learned from his Steelers days, and his staff will uphold those principles. Expect a Cardinals team that looks more like a real football squad and less like a fantasy team come to life. Green made the Cardinals a flashy, surface-level preseason pick last year, but, over time, Whisenhunt could turn this scattered, underachieving franchise into an actual winner.

Atlanta Falcons

The Falcons are a football team with basketball problems. To understand their predicament, it helps to switch sports for a few moments.

In the NBA, one-man franchises are fairly common. A down-and-out organization enters the draft lottery, selects a talented college freshman (or high school kid, or embryo), and hands him the keys to the city. Before long, the team is .500, the kid is an all-star, and he is making as much from sneaker endorsements as he is from playing the game. The kid makes money, the team makes money, the fans are exhilarated by highlight-film dunks, and everyone is happy... for a year or two.

Then the trouble starts. The young phenom suddenly stops developing. Often he reaches the limits of his athletic ability while still struggling with the fundamentals. He can dunk, hit the three-pointer, and block a shot, but his passing and team defense stink. The team can't get past the first round of the playoffs, partly because their superstar has a major hole in his game, and partly because that superstar comes equipped with a big ego and a bigger cap number. He's exciting, but he isn't a championship-caliber performer.

Unfortunately, the superstar's popularity with fans and his value as a season ticket/jersey salesman make him more important to the guys who sign the checks than any of his teammates, or even the coach. The franchise owners, afraid to trade the superstar, try to make the world revolve around him. Instead of acquiring better players, they assemble a "supporting cast" of performers whose style of play meshes with the star's. Instead of hiring the best available coaches, they hire coaches who can relate to/handle/mollycoddle the star. That just makes his ego bigger and further hinders his development. The cycle continues until the wins dry up completely.

The scenario above describes the relationship between the 76ers and Allen Iverson, the Raptors and Vince Carter, the Rockets and Steve Francis, and other NBA players and teams over the last decade. NFL teams rarely find themselves in such a parasitic relationship with a player: the rosters are too big, the salary cap too hard, and the team-oriented nature of the game too ingrained in the minds of fans, players, and execs. The Falcons, however, have become an NBA-style one-man franchise; their identity has been totally subsumed by Michael Vick.

When NBA teams are grasping for ways to improve, they often hire savior coaches from college hoops powerhouses. So it only makes sense that the Falcons hired Louisville coach Bobby Petrino to wrest them from the doldrums. Petrino arrived in Atlanta with the kind of resume and reputation to make Falcons fans quickly forget the unfulfilled expectations of the Jim Mora era. At Louisville, he earned a reputation as an offensive wunderkind. His system, which made pro prospects out of mobile passers such as Chris Redman, Stefan LeFors, and Brian Brohm, seems tailor-made for Vick. Petrino sounded energetic and charismatic in his opening press conferences. He talked about installing his complicated offense in three stages so the team could easily absorb it. He revealed that Vick would be free to audible, a right the quarterback never had when Greg Knapp coordinated the offense. It was just the fresh start that the Falcons needed after a season of rumored squabbles between Mora, his assistants, and ownership, a season that ended with Mora "joking" he would take the University of Washington job in a heartbeat while Vick hinted that he wanted the season finale to end early so he could attend a New Year's Eve bash.

The Vick-Petrino honeymoon was short-lived, however. Just days after Petrino took over, Vick tried to board an airplane carrying a water bottle with a secret compartment

---

FALCONS PROSPECTUS

2006 Record: 7–9

DVOA Estimated Wins: 7.4 (19th)

Pythagorean Wins: 6.9 (20th)

DVOA: −8.3% total (21st), −11.5% weighted (24th)

Offense: −2.1% DVOA (16th)

Defense: 2.4% DVOA (17th)

Special Teams: −3.8% DVOA (28th)

Variance: 18.5% (8th)

2006: Another year of Vick 24-7 leaves the Falcons at 7–9.

2007: Bobby Petrino won't end this cycle of frustration and mediocrity.

2007 Mean Projection: 7.6 wins

The Brohm Closet (0–4): 8%

Bad Team (5–6): 24%

Mediocre (7–8): 31%

Playoff Contender (9–10): 26%

Super Bowl Contender (11+): 11%

Projected Average Opponent: −1.9% DVOA (20th in NFL)

that smelled suspiciously like Tommy Chong's ashtray. Legally, the incident was more smoke than fire (if you will), as authorities found no illicit substances in Vick's possession, but Bottlegate fanned speculation that Petrino would give Matt Schaub a chance to compete for the starting job, speculation that didn't evaporate until Schaub was traded to the Texans.

A month after Bottlegate, defensive end Patrick Kerney voided the final two years of his contract and became a free agent. Before signing with the Seahawks, Kerney fired a thinly-veiled parting shot at Vick. "Your performance on the field on Sunday is just a byproduct of a year-round commitment. How do you treat your body? How do you handle yourself in the offseason? What's your devotion to your teammates, even away from the locker room?" While Kerney was reading the fine print in Seattle, Vick was reading wine labels: The multi-talented quarterback opened The Tasting Room, a gourmet restaurant in which he has an ownership stake. "I can't play football forever. I'm going to have to become an entrepreneur and make my money grow. This is a step in a different direction." Petrino never commented about the restaurant, but he couldn't have been thrilled that his quarterback was tending investments and chilling cabernet instead of focusing on that three-stage offensive installation program.

In late April, just when it appeared that Vick maxed out his potential for causing distractions, animal abuse investigators raided a Virginia property owned by Vick. The investigators found mistreated animals and evidence of dog fighting. Vick claimed that a cousin (no, not Aaron Brooks) was using the property and he was unaware of any suspicious activity. Vick may be exonerated, just as he was after Bottlegate, but the fact remains: this sort of thing never happens to Peyton Manning or Donovan McNabb.

As exasperating as Vick can be, Petrino has no choice but to try to corral him and finally turn him into a consistent player. The "Trade Vick, Start Schaub" talk made for interesting speculation in February, but it was unrealistic. Vick costs the Falcons roughly $10 million in cap space, making him almost impossible to trade or cut. Behind him, the Falcons lack the talent base to be competitive. The Vick-less Falcons would be a cap-strapped 5–11 team. For all his faults, Vick is an equalizer; his lightning strike scrambles and bombs allow the Falcons to beat up the league's bottom feeders while shocking the occasional contender. As mediocre as the Falcons are with him, they would be terrible without him. Half the general managers in the NBA can nod sympathetically at this predicament.

Petrino knows what every careful observer has known for years: The Falcons won't be a great team until Vick starts mixing his big plays with a greater quantity of medium and small ones. In late March, Petrino began reciting a mantra

2007 Falcons Schedule

Week	Opp	Week	Opp	Week	Opp
1	at MIN	7	at NO	13	at STL
2	at JAC	8	BYE	14	NO
3	CAR	9	SF	15	at TB
4	HOU	10	at CAR	16	at ARI
5	at TEN	11	TB	17	SEA
6	NYG (Mon.)	12	IND		

that Mora, Knapp, and Dan Reeves chanted for years: "What I would like to change about Michael is his first instinct, when he decides to take the game over and go win it by running the ball. . . . He's still going to have the ability to take off and go. We'd like that to be his third instinct instead of his first."

Petrino's task seems simple enough, but the coach is just one voice in Vick's ear. To be heard, the coach will have to shout above Vick's agent, his entourage, his business partners, his fans, and that pitchfork-waving devil that's always scrambling around his shoulders. There's also owner Arthur Blank, who invested a ton of money in Vick and is determined to keep his star happy at all costs. Blank insisted over the offseason that Vick doesn't have a personal pipeline to the owner's office, and that he never sided with his quarterback in a disagreement with his coaches. Still, Petrino won't be issuing Blank an "either he goes or I go" ultimatum without first packing a suitcase and checking airfare.

Petrino would have enough to worry about if Vick were his only problem, but the Falcons have numerous other issues. The Falcons' defense, mediocre last season, will be worse this year without Kerney. Mora's efforts to rebuild the defense in 2005 and 2006 left the team bloated with overpriced veterans such as linebackers Ed Hartwell and Ike Reese, safety Lawyer Milloy, and defensive end John Abraham. Hartwell and Reese were released in March (to be fair, we wrote approvingly about both signings at the time). Only Abraham still plays at a high level. A large amount of cap money is invested in players such as Milloy, Abraham, linebacker Keith Brooking, and cornerback DeAngelo Hall, leaving the Falcons with little wiggle room to try to make upgrades. Defensive tackle Grady Jackson, one of the best defenders on the roster, filed a lawsuit against the team in March over leaked medical information, so his future is in doubt. New defensive coordinator Mike Zimmer will build on the cheap. With rookie defensive end Jamaal Anderson replacing Kerney, and Brooking once again playing out-of-position at middle linebacker, the Falcons won't win many games by stopping opponents.

The receiving corps also needs immediate attention. Former first-round picks Michael Jenkins and Roddy White dropped numerous passes last year, and Ashley Lelie is gone after one forgettable season. The receivers became the go-to excuse for Vick apologists, who claimed that Vick would win a Super Bowl if only he had reliable targets (and a system to fit his talents, and a line to better protect him, and on and on). Vick boosters overstated the issue, but White and Lelie were pretty bad, and Jenkins is a glorified number two, not a number one. Free-agent Joe Horn and veteran Brian Finneran join Jenkins and White this year. Both players have strong track records, but are old and coming off injuries. Petrino must find a mix of receivers that works, and he must do so while fitting the players around his jigsaw puzzle quarterback; a Vick receiver must be able to block for scrambles, react to bad balls, and accept his role as a bit player in someone else's story. Joe Horn certainly wasn't satisfied with his bit role in the Miracle of New Orleans.

The list goes on—the Falcons' offensive line must adapt to a new blocking scheme. The return teams aren't very good. The Falcons' roster is filled with effective-but-fading veterans such as running back Warrick Dunn, Abraham, and Brooking, plus enigmatic perma-prospects such as Hall, Jenkins, and White. The Falcons can rebuild on the fly, but only if Petrino can turn Vick into a complete quarterback. If Vick harnesses his Steve Young-level talent, the Falcons can win with a mediocre defense, and no one will notice if a receiver drops a pass or two or the punter has to double as a kicker.

It could happen. Shaquille O'Neal became a complete player; he even improved a little as a foul shooter. Rip Hamilton stopped trying to be a one-man show and became a champion in Detroit. Still, the NBA offers a dozen Stephon Marbury failures for every Rasheed Wallace success story. Petrino will do his best, but the only person who can change Vick is Vick, the entrepreneur, bottle smuggler, and sometime quarterback. The Falcons will be a sub-.500 team until Vick finally gets the bulletin about focusing on football, playing within a system, and mastering all that boring stuff like footwork and delivery. Unfortunately for the Falcons, they could be below .500 for a long time.

Mike Tanier

The Great Koenen Experiment

KICKER WANTED: No exp. necessary. Will train! Must work cheap. Very cheap. Send (brief) resume to Rich McKay, 4400 Falcon Parkway, Flowery Branch, Ga.

The Falcons didn't run a classified like that in the *Atlanta Journal-Constitution*. They probably didn't want to pay the publication fee. If they had run some want ads, they might have started the 2006 season with a real kicker on the roster. Instead, they tried to hearken back to the days of eight-track tapes and sweater-wearing presidents by making Michael Koenen a full-time punter and kicker.

Kicking on a Budget

The Falcons faced a bit of a money crunch last year. They blew major scratch on free agents such as John Abraham, Lawyer Milloy, and Ed Hartwell in 2005 and 2006, and it takes a lot of dough to keep Michael Vick in fake water bottles. Owner Arthur Blank and GM McKay were forced to economize at some positions to pay for their binge-spending at others. You know your deadbeat cousin who bought the speedboat and plasma TV, then ate nothing but ramen noodles for eight months? He spent last year working for the Falcons as a cap consultant.

A decent kicker costs about as much as Vick spends on earrings, but that was too rich for the Falcons. Blank knows a thing or two about bargain hunting from his hardware store days, so he sent McKay on a dumpster dive for kickers. McKay emerged from the alley behind the convenience store with Tony Yelk and Zac Derr. Notice the short surnames: The Falcons wanted to cut down on jersey letter-sewing costs. Derr and Yelk couldn't kick field goals if you stood them on the crossbar, so McKay auditioned mysterious individuals such as Carlos Martinez, Seth Marler, E. J. Cochrane, and Miro Kesic. If he kicked in the World League or Arena League, spent time on a practice squad, came from a Division III program, or was willing to kick for food, he tried out for the Falcons last summer.

Eventually, McKay and coach Jim Mora stumbled on a brilliant idea: Let the punter do it. Koenen kicked a few field goals in college and nailed a 58-yarder against the Patriots in 2005. Given a chance to pull double-duty in camp, Koenen outkicked Yelk and Kesic, which is like outsmarting Spongebob and Patrick. Koenen broke camp as a double-duty kicker-punter. "Quite frankly, it saves some cap room that we can use in other spots," Jim Mora said, "but by no means do we want to sacrifice the chance to score three points for some more cap room."

After two weeks and four missed chip-shot field goals, the Koenen experiment ended. The Falcons had traded 12 points for some cap room.

A Historically Bad Idea

When teams decide to squeeze nickels, they always look to the little guys with the single-bar facemasks. Old school football men have always been suspicious of specialists earning top dollar. "They are paid anywhere from $10,000 to $20,000 for four months' work, just for their ability in putting the ball out on the opponents' two-yard line, or booting a 45-yard field goal or getting 40-for-40 extra points," *The Sporting News* lamented back in 1965.

Back then, position players usually kicked and punted, though a handful of specialists were taking the league by storm. Players such as Danny Villanueva, who later founded Telemundo, and Don Chandler, who played for the great Giants teams of the late 1950s, were clearly better kickers than the backup defensive ends they replaced, but they expected to earn a living. In 1964, Chandler asked the Giants for time off so he could concentrate on his insurance business. The Giants balked, traded him, and handed the kicking chores to rookie quarterback Bob Timberlake, who went 1-for-19 on field goals. "I put the excitement back in the extra point," Timberlake said the following year. At least Mora didn't ask D. J. Shockley to kick last year.

Coaches and GMs soon learned to love their kicking specialists, and by the mid-1970s, most teams employed both a kicker and a punter. Occasionally, a team would economize and make one player handle both chores. The Eagles started 1978 with Nick Mike-Mayer as their kicker, but when he got hurt midseason, they asked punter Mike Michel to pull double duty. The Eagles were in the playoff chase for the first time in over a decade, but free-spending owner Leonard Tose couldn't fit a real kicker into his cocktails-and-casinos budget (though he did sign an extra punter on the cheap). The Eagles went five weeks without kicking a field goal, and Michel missed 3 of the 12 extra points he attempted.

Miraculously (literally, as this was the Miracle at the Meadowlands season), the Eagles made the playoffs. On a rainy day in Atlanta, Michel missed three field goals and an extra point, allowing the Falcons to beat the Eagles 14–13. "It's something I've got to live with all year," Michel said after the game. "But I'll come back. It's just something that happens. What else can you say?" Ironically, Atlanta's kicker that day was former Philadelphia bartender Tim Mazzetti. Remember Vince Papale from *Invincible*? Half of the specialists in the NFL in the late 1970s were former Philly bartenders. Those were some tough bars. Clearly Tose had his own methods of scouting.

Michel never kicked again, and no one in Atlanta remembered what happened in 1978. If they had, they would have re-signed Todd Peterson. Or maybe Mike-Mayer.

Michel wasn't the last two-way kicker-punter. That honor goes to an interesting character named Frank Corral.

Corral was pretty good in double duty in 1980 and 1981, but his $125,000 salary was high for a kicker of that era. The Rams signed a young kicker and punter to compete with Corral in 1982, but Corral assumed his job was secure and merely went through the motions in camp. Coach Ray Malavasi cut him. Corral (who was born in Chihuahua, Mexico) was livid. "Ray can say that I'm a dumb, dirty, bean-eating Mexican," he said at the time, "but don't fool the public and tell them I can't kick anymore." John Misko, the young punter who replaced Corral, didn't need to play the race card. "Let's face it, he's not Ray Guy," Misko said.

Corral never kicked or punted in the NFL again. In the 1960s, teams and the reporters who covered them lamented that specialist kickers made too much money. By the 1980s, it was cheaper and more effective to employ two young specialists than one overpriced veteran. In 2006, one innovative organization decided to change the course of history.

Kicking It Old School

Luckily, the Koenen story had a happy ending. The Falcons won both games in which he pretended to be a kicker, so none of those missed chip shots cost the team a victory, and the Falcons realized the error of their ways and went searching for a real kicker. They didn't have to look far. The team heard rumors that a guy with strange clothes and a funny accent was practicing field goals in public parks around Atlanta. Once they realized it wasn't Borat, the Falcons rushed out and signed 46-year-old Morten Andersen, who likes to work out in a Vikings helmet, Giants pants, Saints shoulder pads, and a Pro Bowl jersey. He'll probably add a Falcons cup to his wardrobe this year.

Andersen is a real, professional kicker, not a kid with a big leg who can nail 50-yarders in August. Modern kickers train specifically for their task. As he explained to the *Journal-Constitution*, Andersen keeps a journal of every aspect of every kick he makes: "get-off time from snap to kick, sideline routine, arousal control, focus, setup, breathing, approach, steps, contact, follow-through, head and hips." For most of us, proper arousal control leads to extra-long get-off time. Apparently the opposite is true for kickers.

Andersen allowed Koenen to concentrate on his punting, but Koenen did add a coda to his kicking career when he nailed a 51-yarder against the Cardinals. Hey, maybe the kid deserves another shot. The Falcons could spend the extra cash on a linebacker, or a handler/pedicurist/sommelier for Vick.

Or they could just accept the fact that, in the 21st century, punters punt, kickers kick, and professional football teams must pay for both services.

Mike Tanier

Falcons 2006 Stats by Week

Wk	vs.	W–L	PF	PA	YDF	YDA	TO	Total	Off	Def	ST
								DVOA			
1	@CAR	W	20	6	385	215	+2	64.0%	28.3%	-38.2%	-2.5%
2	TB	W	14	3	382	351	+1	-19.9%	5.8%	-0.5%	-26.1%
3	@NO	L	3	23	112	326	0	-94.5%	-58.0%	11.0%	-25.6%
4	ARI	W	32	10	405	187	+3	86.7%	-3.7%	-71.3%	19.1%
5	BYE										
6	NYG	L	14	27	377	439	0	-48.5%	-38.4%	13.0%	2.9%
7	PIT	W	41	38	399	473	+1	-12.0%	12.9%	34.5%	9.7%
8	@CIN	W	29	27	420	331	+1	20.0%	34.9%	9.3%	-5.6%
9	@DET	L	14	30	319	435	-2	-48.5%	-11.6%	28.0%	-8.9%
10	CLE	L	13	17	343	236	-1	-29.6%	-33.8%	-0.9%	3.3%
11	@BAL	L	10	24	186	328	+1	-18.6%	12.8%	16.7%	-14.8%
12	NO	L	13	31	333	427	0	-45.0%	-24.0%	25.7%	4.7%
13	@WAS	W	24	14	369	381	+2	25.1%	21.7%	-9.4%	-5.9%
14	@TB	W	17	6	280	282	+1	-22.1%	-9.3%	-1.8%	-14.6%
15	DAL	L	28	38	376	352	-1	13.0%	16.3%	9.1%	5.8%
16	CAR	L	3	10	177	194	-2	-14.5%	-19.5%	-10.9%	-5.9%
17	@PHI	L	17	24	378	393	0	-2.6%	25.9%	28.9%	0.3%

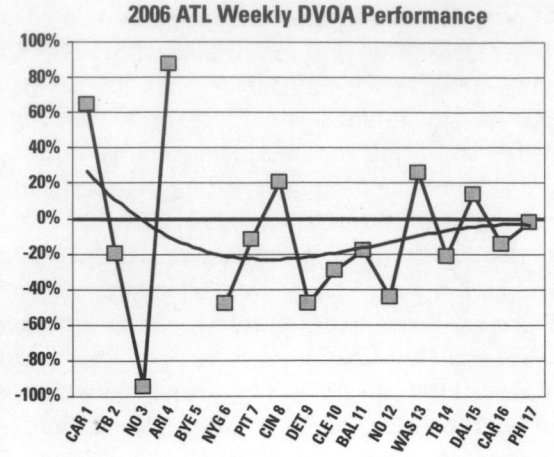

2006 ATL Weekly DVOA Performance

Trends and Splits

	Offense	Rank	Defense	Rank
Total DVOA	-2.1%	16	2.4%	17
Unadjusted VOA	0.7%	15	1.1%	14
Weighted Trend	-1.1%	18	8.2%	25
Variance	6.8%	15	6.8%	16
Passing	-17.0%	28	5.5%	20
Rushing	9.5%	5	-1.1%	17
First Down	-0.1%	16	-6.6%	12
Second Down	2.5%	15	5.4%	20
Third Down	-12.3%	24	15.7%	24
Red Zone	-25.4%	26	0.3%	14
Late and Close	19.6%	4	-1.7%	13

Five-Year Performance

	2006	2005	2004	2003	2002
W-L	7-9	8-8	11-5	5-11	9-6-1
Pythagorean Wins	6.9	8.3	8.1	4.9	10.3
Estimated Wins	7.4	7.9	8.0	5.5	9.0
Total DVOA	-8.3%	-3.5%	-2.7%	-17.4%	15.9%
Rank	21	17	17	26	7
Offense	-2.1%	5.1%	-6.2%	-9.9%	8.1%
Rank	16	11	23	23	8
Defense	2.4%	10.9%	0.5%	9.1%	-3.4%
Rank	17	28	17	26	11
Special Teams	-3.8%	2.3%	4.0%	1.5%	4.4%
Rank	28	5	6	13	6

Strategic Tendencies

Formations		Rank	Run/Pass		Rank	Defense		Rank	Other		Rank
3+ WR	43%	23	Runs, all plays	53%	1	Sacks by LB	18%	20	Run with 2+ RB	59%	17
4+ WR	6%	27	Runs, first half	53%	2	Sacks by DB	11%	11	Run with 2+ TE	31%	23
2+ TE	24%	21	Runs, first down	60%	5	Rush 6+	12.8%	5	Play action	27%	1
Single back	50%	19	Runs, power sit.	59%	23	Rush 7+	4.0%	3	Go for it on 4th	1.16	5
Empty back	0.6%	29	Runs, behind 2H	42%	3	Rush 3	3.1%	23	Offensive Pace	29.6	10
Max protect	10%	21	Pass, ahead 2H	30%	31	CB1 on WR1	57%	4	Defensive Pace	32.0	29

Atlanta's offense led the league in sacks marked as Blitz or Overall Pressure.... Even though they are a run-first offense, the Falcons inexplicably dropped from fourth in 2005 to 23rd in 2006 in frequency of runs in power situations.... On offense, only Philadelphia ran play-action fakes more often than Atlanta. One might think that it would help to see play-action so much in practice, but apparently not: On play-action, the Atlanta defense ranked 31st in DVOA (49.9%), ahead of only Tampa Bay, and 31st in yards per play-action pass attempt (8.5), ahead of only Green Bay.... Then again, perhaps the Falcons spent more time practicing screen passes. Atlanta had the second worst offensive DVOA on screen passes (–108.6%) but the best defensive DVOA on screen passes (–65.2%).... Atlanta was the NFL's worst defense in the first quarter (32.0%

DVOA).... The Atlanta defense ranked 13th in close and late situations, but the breakdown is stunning. The Falcons were above-average against the run when ahead or behind by eight or fewer points in the second half (−6.2% DVOA, ranked 12th). They were great against the pass in the third quarter of close games (−28.9% DVOA, ranked 7th) but against the pass in the fourth quarter of close games they completely imploded (59.3% DVOA, ranked 31st).... The Atlanta defense led the league in Coverage Sacks and passes tipped at the line, and was tied for the league lead on incompletes caused by hitting the quarterback while his hand was in motion.... Opposing offenses dropped fewer passes against Atlanta than against any defense except Indianapolis.

Passing

Player	DPAR	DVOA	Plys	NtYds	Avg	YAC	C%	TD	Int
Michael Vick	-6.5	-16.7%	388	2164	5.6	4.1	52.6%	20	11
Matt Schaub*	5.9	40.7%	27	200	7.4	3.8	66.7%	1	1
Joey Harrington	*5.7*	*-9.9%*	*386*	*2122*	*5.5*	*4.0*	*57.8%*	*12*	*15*

Rushing

Player	DPAR	DVOA	Plys	Yds	Avg	TD	Fum	Suc
Warrick Dunn	12.6	-3.9%	286	1140	4.0	4	1	39%
Michael Vick	32.4	27.6%	119	1038	8.7	2	9	—
Jerious Norwood	21.3	35.8%	99	633	6.4	2	0	53%
Justin Griffith*	-2.3	-44.1%	19	106	5.6	1	2	52%
Matt Schaub*	1.3	46.1%	3	24	8.0	0	0	—
Ovie Mughelli	*2.3*	*26.5%*	*12*	*50*	*4.2*	*0*	*0*	*41%*
Joey Harrington	*-2.2*	*-50.6%*	*12*	*28*	*2.3*	*0*	*4*	*—*

Receiving

Player	DPAR	DVOA	Plys	Ctch	Yds	Y/C	YAC	TD	C%
WR									
Michael Jenkins	-1.4	-17.7%	83	39	436	11.2	2.4	7	47%
Ashley Lelie*	-1.4	-18.0%	68	28	430	15.4	2.3	1	41%
Roddy White	-0.5	-16.4%	64	30	509	17.0	2.6	0	47%
Joe Horn	*19.7*	*31.7%*	*61*	*37*	*679*	*18.4*	*4.4*	*4*	*59%*
TE									
Alge Crumpler	15.3	10.0%	103	56	780	13.9	4.4	8	54%
Dwayne Blakley	-1.5	-31.6%	14	6	76	12.7	3.2	0	43%
RB									
Justin Griffith*	4.8	22.4%	28	23	168	7.3	6.2	3	82%
Warrick Dunn	4.2	20.2%	27	22	164	7.5	7.1	1	81%
Jerious Norwood	1.0	2.8%	15	12	102	8.5	7.1	0	80%

Offensive Line

Year	Yards	ALY	Rank	Power	Rank	10+ Yds	Rank	Stuff	Rank	Sack	ASR	Rank
2004	4.36	4.52	6	72%	5	16%	22	18%	1	49	11.6%	31
2005	4.49	4.46	7	65%	14	20%	12	24%	13	39	8.0%	25
2006	4.64	4.30	13	59%	23	23%	4	25%	24	47	10.4%	31

Year	LE	Rank	LT	Rank	Mid	Rank	RT	Rank	RE	Rank
2004	4.49	12	4.78	7	4.59	9	4.57	11	3.50	22
2005	5.17	4	4.75	4	3.93	21	4.74	5	5.05	2
2006	4.53	10	3.71	28	4.50	11	4.27	12	4.67	9

Former line coach Alex Gibbs, a guru of the zone blocking scheme, insisted that his lineman weigh less than 300 pounds. Gibbs conducted weekly weigh-ins to keep his linemen from growing too portly, a practice which didn't sit well with many of the players. "You had different guys starving themselves," guard Kynan Forney said in April. "That's crazy to me. We're not naturally sleek and lean."

Bobby Petrino and new line coach Mike Summers prefer bigger blockers. As if to signal the philosophical change, the team signed guard Toniu Fonoti, who would have a hard time weighing less than 300 on a kilogram scale. Fonoti couldn't overcome injuries and bad footwork in three seasons with the Chargers and one with the Vikings, but he will challenge Forney and Tyson Clabo at left guard. Second-round pick Justin Blaylock will battle journeyman Gibbs disciple P. J. Alexander at right guard.

Second-year tackle Quinn Ojinnaka took most of the snaps at right tackle during the team's April minicamp in place of Todd Weiner, who was nursing minor injuries. Ojinnaka may move to the left side to replace Wayne Gandy, a 36-year old who was flagged for holding four times last year. Ojinnaka is another Gibbs holdover: quick (he played some tight end at Syracuse), smart, but a little sleek and lean. Weiner, Vick's blindside defender, is still a capable starter.

Center Todd McClure, who hasn't missed a start since 2001, is the Falcons' unsung hero. Opponents often unveil new fronts and blitz packages when facing Vick, forcing McClure to make line calls to counter strategies he hasn't seen on tape. He's also a great shotgun snapper who executes direct snaps to Warrick Dunn and other running backs several times per season.

Defensive Front Seven

Defensive Line	Age	Pos	Plys	TmPct	Rk	Stop	Dfts	StpRt	Rk	AvYd	Rk	Sack	Hit	Hur	Runs	RuStp	RuYd	Pass	PaStp	PaYd
Chauncey Davis	24	DE	39	4.8%	57	26	9	67%	74	3.1	75	1	1	5	32	66%	3.3	7	71%	2.1
Paul Carrington	25	DE	36	4.8%	59	28	7	78%	42	2.2	60	3	1	2	29	76%	2.8	7	86%	-0.6
Rod Coleman	31	DT	36	4.8%	48	28	19	78%	38	1.7	33	6	8	6	15	60%	2.9	21	90%	0.9
Grady Jackson	34	DT	36	4.5%	53	29	16	81%	30	0.1	2	1	1	4	33	79%	0.3	3	100%	-2.0
Jon Babineaux	25	DT	32	4.0%	62	27	11	84%	19	1.8	36	1	1	6	25	88%	1.8	7	71%	2.0
John Abraham	29	DE	19	4.7%	—	14	9	74%	—	-0.1	—	4	6	9	13	62%	2.5	6	100%	-5.7
Patrick Kerney*	31	DE	18	4.0%	—	12	7	67%	—	2.8	—	5	4	12	8	63%	4.3	10	70%	1.6

Linebackers	Age	Pos	Plys	TmPct	Rk	Stop	Dfts	StpRt	AvYd	Sack	Hit	Hur	Runs	RuStp	Rk	RuYd	Rk	Tgts	Suc%	Rk	PaYd	Rk
Keith Brooking	32	ILB	138	17.1%	11	72	13	52%	5.3	2	2	5	88	66%	41	4.0	74	46	39%	84	7.3	76
Michael Boley	25	OLB	95	11.8%	57	58	23	61%	3.8	3.5	1	4	49	63%	54	2.9	22	35	44%	71	6.8	71
Demorrio Williams	27	OLB	91	11.3%	61	49	17	54%	5.5	1	3	7	52	71%	22	3.8	64	25	56%	29	6.0	36
Ed Hartwell*	29	ILB	40	9.9%	—	24	2	60%	5.2	0.5	0	2	28	75%	—	3.4	—	6	30%	—	5.3	—

Year	Yards	ALY	Rank	Power	Rank	10+ Yds	Rank	Stuff	Rank	Sack	ASR	Rank
2004	3.98	4.39	22	63%	18	14%	10	22%	23	48	8.9%	3
2005	4.88	4.76	32	67%	22	20%	23	24%	18	37	7.1%	17
2006	3.84	4.15	12	56%	6	12%	4	25%	11	38	7.8%	8

Year	LE	Rank	LT	Rank	Mid	Rank	RT	Rank	RE	Rank
2004	6.00	32	3.59	2	4.25	17	3.90	9	5.01	30
2005	4.87	26	5.03	31	4.77	32	4.41	25	4.73	25
2006	5.07	28	3.55	8	4.21	15	3.59	10	4.98	29

When it comes to stirring controversy, the Falcons defensive line can give Michael Vick a run for his money. The line even has its own alleged animal abuser in Jonathan Babineaux, the reserve tackle accused of killing his girlfriend's pitbull after a domestic squabble. Grady Jackson, the team's best lineman, is suing the Falcons. He claims that the team leaked confidential medical information about Jackson when he was a free agent, lowering his free-agent leverage and forcing him to return to Atlanta. The team needs the king-sized Jackson and may try to settle the lawsuit quietly. Babineaux, however, may be thrown to the animal rights activists as a peace offering.

End John Abraham terrorized the Panthers in the 2006 season opener (two sacks, two forced fumbles), then spent the rest of the year battling the groin injury that has plagued him since 2003. When healthy, Abraham is an exceptional pass rusher, but can get pushed around against the run. Rookie Jamaal Anderson will battle Chauncey Davis for the left end position vacated by Patrick Kerney, who is now in Seattle. Anderson, who started his college career at wide receiver, is a tremendous size-speed prospect who needs to refine his technique. Davis is a solid run defender.

Keith Brooking was a Pro Bowl–caliber outside linebacker early in his career, but he's a liability at middle linebacker. Brooking is at his best when blitzing and attacking the line of scrimmage. When forced to read, react, or defend multiple gaps, he's indecisive and tries to run around blockers. He is also a step slow in pass coverage. Outside linebackers Demorrio Williams and Michael Boley are players on the rise. Boley is the team's best coverage linebacker. Williams is a speedster who is at his best when pursuing plays from the backside. Williams tore a pectoral muscle in minicamp and may not be ready for the start of the season. Marcus Wilkins, a free agent from the Bengals who was signed as a kick gunner, could be thrust into the lineup in Williams's place.

Defensive Secondary

Secondary	Age	Pos	Plys	TmPct	Rk	Stop	Dfts	RuYd	Rk	RuStp	Rk	Tgts	Tgt%	Rk	Dist	Suc%	Rk	PaYd	Rk	PD	Int
DeAngelo Hall	24	CB	75	9.3%	34	38	17	4.5	12	45%	37	92	20%	26	13.4	54%	28	8.5	63	13	4
Chris Crocker	27	FS	57	7.1%	67	20	6	7.5	54	35%	57	51	10%	13	16.7	46%	57	13.2	78	6	1
Allen Rossum	32	CB	34	4.2%	—	11	3	7.1	—	33%	—	40	9%	—	12.2	36%	—	12.4	—	3	0
Lawyer Milloy	34	SS	102	12.7%	13	42	12	5.2	14	50%	23	32	7%	49	7.8	40%	67	9.4	59	4	0
Kevin Mathis*	33	FS	23	5.7%	72	11	6	8.2	66	40%	48	27	11%	1	8.8	55%	30	6.6	24	4	0
Jimmy Williams	23	CB	21	3.2%	—	12	4	2.7	—	67%	—	17	4%	—	10.0	55%	—	7.3	—	1	0
Lewis Sanders	*29*	*CB*	*43*	*9.5%*	*—*	*14*	*6*	*7.8*	*—*	*25%*	*—*	*40*	*17%*	*—*	*11.9*	*53%*	*—*	*6.0*	*—*	*5*	*0*

Year	Pass D Rank	DVOA vs. #1 WR	Rank	DVOA vs. #2 WR	Rank	DVOA vs. Other WR	Rank	DVOA vs. TE	Rank	DVOA vs. RB	Rank
2004	16	6.1%	19	-2.0%	13	-9.5%	14	17.3%	26	10.1%	24
2005	20	7.5%	17	-5.6%	14	0.9%	19	25.3%	28	-0.1%	19
2006	20	28.2%	31	27.8%	31	-3.9%	17	3.9%	25	-22.6%	3

Jim Mora said it best after the Falcons narrowly beat the Steelers in Week 7, "There's an area between the hashmarks called the middle of the field, and, when the safety's in the middle of the field and they throw a skinny post in there, he's supposed to make the play." Mora was moved to state the obvious after Chris Crocker decided to protect the giant Falcons logo at midfield instead of covering Hines Ward on what proved to be a 74-yard touchdown-scoring skinny post.

With Crocker and 20th century star Matlock Milloy covering as much ground as two garden slugs, it's no wonder the Falcons cornerbacks couldn't cover anyone deep. Jason Webster spent the first half of the season smothered in creamed chip beef; he was released in early May. Jimmy Williams replaced him in the Steelers game and promptly gave up a touchdown. When Williams was hurt late in the season, 5-foot-9 punt returner Allen Rossum was thrust into the lineup at cornerback. The results included a 30–14 loss to the Lions and a 31–13 loss to the Saints.

DeAngelo Hall is the Falcons' best cornerback, and he's a threat to play Pick-Six every time an opposing quarterback makes a mistake. Unfortunately, Hall is an undisciplined defender who gambles too often, gets poor position on his receivers, and misses tackles. Williams showed some promise as last season wore on and will open camp as the starter opposite Hall. Rookie Chris Houston is incredibly fast and excelled in press coverage at Arkansas, but he's short (5-foot-9), and inexperienced in zone coverage. Houston turned heads at the Combine with his 4.39 40-time and chiseled physique, but Hall has shown that it takes more than speed and athleticism to succeed as an NFL cornerback.

As for those safeties, the Falcons couldn't land LaRon Landry in the draft and may have to suffer through another season with Crocker and Milloy. If Houston develops quickly, or Sanders is better than advertised, Williams may be moved to free safety to challenge Crocker.

Special Teams

Year	DVOA	Rank	FG/XP	Rank	Net Punt	Rank	Punt Ret	Rank	Net Kick	Rank	Kick Ret	Rank	Hidden	Rank
2004	4.0%	6	-5.3	28	7.4	7	11.3	2	10.0	7	0.1	14	-6.0	25
2005	2.4%	5	4.2	9	7.6	4	-4.5	27	15.9	1	-9.2	26	-14.4	32
2006	-3.8%	28	-14.8	32	-11.1	30	-0.7	16	12.4	3	-8.0	27	-3.8	21

DeAngelo Hall is a dangerous return man with outstanding quickness and creativity in the open field. Unfortunately, the former coaching regime thought he was too important on defense to play special teams, so Allen Rossum returned kicks and punts. Rossum is a locker room leader and a high-character guy, but he will turn 33 next season and is no longer a big-play threat. Petrino will probably allow Hall to return punts. Jerious Norwood, Adam Jennings, and rookie Laurent Robinson also have return skills.

We discussed the Great Koenen Experiment earlier in the chapter, but, after that was over, Michael Koenen still had a season-long hangover. After great kickoffs and punts in 2005, he had okay kickoffs and below-average punts in 2006. He will hopefully be back on the right track this year. Morten Andersen won't return for a 743rd NFL season, so veterans Aaron Elling and Billy Cundiff will battle for the placekicker spot. Both struggled kicking field goals in the past, and their most recent teams employed them as kickoff specialists—an area Koenen already covers for Atlanta.

Coaching Staff

Petrino's offense includes a little of everything. At Louisville, he often used spread formations and executed lots of spread options and other "quarterback on the move" plays that suit Michael Vick's talents. At the same time, Petrino also likes to line up a big running back in the I-formation and let him hammer the defense. It's a complex scheme that may take a year or two to install. New defensive coordinator Mike Zimmer helmed the Cowboys defense from 2000 through 2006. Zimmer's strength is fitting his scheme to accommodate the available personnel. Zimmer ran a hybrid 3-4 scheme in Dallas over the past three seasons, but he'll use a more traditional 4-3 alignment in Atlanta. Quarterback coach Bill Musgrave survived the regime change and returns for a second season as the Sisyphus of NFL coaches. Musgrave appeared to have some influence on Michael Vick midway through last season; Vick was more settled in the pocket and made great decisions with the ball against the Steelers and Bengals. Everything came unglued at the end of the season, of course, but that probably had more to do with the three-ring circus that surrounds Vick than with Musgrave's coaching.

Carolina Panthers

It's easy to determine why the Panthers fell short of expectations last year. They had the worst third down offense in the NFL, whether measured by DVOA (−31.6%) or by conventional stats (31 percent conversion rate). It's hard to reach the playoffs if you can't convert at least one third down in three, and the Panthers can blame early-season losses to the Falcons (2-of-12 on third downs), Vikings (3-of-14), and Bengals (2-of-11) on their inability to sustain drives.

The Panthers came by their third-down futility honestly. Most bad third down offenses are also bad on first and second down; the offense digs itself lots of 3rd-and-15 holes that it isn't capable of climbing out of. The Panthers, however, were above average on first down (14th in DVOA) and second down (10th). When third down arrived, everything went kablooey, whether they were facing third-and-short (26th in DVOA), third-and-medium (29th), or third-and-long (30th).

A lot had to go wrong for the Panthers to be so bad on third down. Their woes started when center Justin Hartwig and left tackle Travelle Wharton got hurt in the season opener. Those injuries forced offensive coordinator Dan Henning to juggle linemen, leading to lots and lots of punting. Henning moved Jordan Gross from right tackle to left tackle, inserted Geoff Hantgartner at center, and pulled Jeremy Bridges off the waiver wire to fill the void at right tackle. The rebuilt line was terrible for the first half of the year. Hantgartner was slow and indecisive at the snap, leaving the Panthers vulnerable against interior blitzes. Bridges took a few weeks to round into shape. Gross, a solid right tackle, was marginal at best on the left side. Poor line play affected the entire Panthers offense, but the problems were most obvious on third down, as it soon became clear that the Panthers couldn't run or throw on third-and-short. Opposing defenders blew through the Panthers line easily, and the team lacked a push-the-pile running back who could break tackles in the backfield and convert short-yardage opportunities. As a result, the Panthers were 13-of-22 (59 percent, 29th in the NFL) when running on 3rd-and-1 or 2.

The best way to convert on third-and-short is to run the ball, but a team like the Panthers could have overcome their difficulties on the ground by throwing in short yardage situations. A few play-action bombs to Steve Smith not only would have produced big gains, but would also have loosened things up for the backs, but the Panthers couldn't throw on 3rd-and-short, converting just 4-of-12 first downs (33 percent, 30th in the NFL) and averaging a bombless 3.83 yards per pass. The offensive line was again the culprit; Henning couldn't count on Hantgartner and company to stop defenders long enough for Jake Delhomme to take a deep drop and Smith to beat a jam.

As a result, the Panthers were forced to use max protection schemes on 3rd-and-medium-to-long. Tight end Kris Mangum and fullbacks Brad Hoover or Nick Goings were often on the field on 3rd-and-10 situations. Sometimes, they were in the backfield in Henning's full house formation, an alignment teams only use on passing downs if they are afraid their quarterback will be mutilated. Sometimes, Henning deployed Mangum and the tight ends in empty backfield formations, lining them up as blockers flanking Gross or Bridges. No matter what Henning did to disguise his intentions, opponents knew that the only men they needed to worry about in long-yardage situations were Smith, Keyshawn Johnson, and DeAngelo Williams, if he was on the field.

Delhomme tried to make opponents pay if they loaded up to stop the top weapons, attempting 50 third

PANTHERS PROSPECTUS

2006 Record: 8–8

DVOA Estimated Wins: 7.9 (14th)

Pythagorean Wins: 6.9 (21st)

DVOA: 2.9% total (14th), 7.5% weighted (12th)

Offense: −4.3% DVOA (19th)

Defense: −10.0% DVOA (5th)

Special Teams: −2.8% DVOA (24th)

Variance: 13.6% (20th)

2006: Panthers implode on third downs, consider move to CFL.

2007: 20 of 22 starters return, but is that a good thing?

2007 Mean Projection: 8.9 wins

The Brohm Closet (0–4): 3%

Bad Team (5–6): 11%

Mediocre (7–8): 28%

Playoff Contender (9–10): 33%

Super Bowl Contender (11+): 25%

Projected Average Opponent: −2.8% DVOA (26th in NFL)

Table 1. Jake Delhomme Sacks and Interceptions, 2006

	Sacks per Pass Attempt		Interceptions per Pass Attempt	
	1st/2nd Down	3rd Down	1st/2nd Down	3rd Down
Delhomme	3.0%	10.3%	1.6%	5.1%
NFL Average	5.7%	8.7%	2.7%	3.5%

2007 Panthers Schedule

Week	Opp	Week	Opp	Week	Opp
1	at STL	7	BYE	13	SF
2	HOU	8	IND	14	at JAC
3	at ATL	9	at TEN	15	SEA
4	TB	10	ATL	16	DAL (Sat.)
5	at NO	11	at GB	17	at TB
6	at ARI	12	NO		

down passes to Mangum, Hoover, Goings, Michael Gaines, and other players who shouldn't have been running pass routes in long-yardage situations, such as Keary Colbert. The results were predictable: lots of four-yard passes on 3rd-and-10.

With his protection crumbling around him and only two or three reliable receivers on the field, Delhomme began to press on third down. He'd either try to force-feed passes to Smith and Keyshawn, or hold the ball too long, waiting for his top targets to break free. Delhomme suffered just 10 sacks on 311 first and second down attempts, but he was sacked 12 times on 117 third down attempts. He was picked off five times on early downs, but threw six interceptions on third down (table 1).

Considering how bad the Panthers were on third down, it's amazing that they managed to accomplish as much as they did. The Panthers were 6–4 entering Week 11, and they were about to face the Redskins, who had just given up on Mark Brunell, and the Eagles, who had just lost Donovan McNabb. The Panthers' third down foibles betrayed them in both games. They lost to the Redskins 17–13, going 6-for-16 on third down. Trailing by four with three minutes left, the Panthers actually attempted a draw to Williams on 3rd-and-10, a sure sign that they were flailing offensively. The Panthers then lost to the Eagles on Monday night, converting 4-of-13 third downs. With the score tied in the fourth quarter of that game, Delhomme tried to hit Goings on a seam route on 3rd-and-7, but he missed Goings by a mile and Brian Dawkins intercepted the pass. The play encapsulated the Panthers' third down woes nicely: Delhomme was pressured, a non-playmaker (Goings) was not only on the field but running a deep route, and Delhomme made a bad decision while trying to force a play. Delhomme hurt his wrist against the Eagles and missed three weeks. By the time he returned, the Panthers were out of the playoff picture.

There's often a silver lining to this kind of third down futility. Our research shows that teams which perform disproportionately poorly on third downs compared to early downs tend to bounce back the following year. In fact, the third down correction is a major component of our projection system, and it's our best tool for identifying surprise contenders. The Panthers certainly believe that they can

solve their problems without making a major overhaul. After all, Wharton and Hartwig will be back, Williams emerged as a major playmaker as the season progressed, and the Panthers offense only has to be above average to complement their defense and propel the team into the playoffs.

Our projections assume that the Panthers will return to relative third down competency. They also give the team a boost for facing a relatively easy schedule in 2007, but our statistical enthusiasm is tempered by several factors.

First, there's the switch from Henning to Jeff Davidson at offensive coordinator. Henning became the fall guy for the team's third down problems last season. His game plans weren't terrible—the multiple formations, reverses and screens, and innovations such as using Williams as a short-yardage quarterback kept the team from becoming too predictable—but Henning deserves some blame for not getting the backup linemen ready to play, and his loyalty to players such as Hoover, Mangum, and Chris Weinke left the Panthers with too many creaky veteran role players. All we know about Davidson is that he's a shoot from the tree of Belichick who called the plays for the Browns after Maurice Carthon resigned at midseason last year, he likes to run the ball, and he likes to use multiple formations. So the Panthers offense won't look very different on the surface. Similarities and pedigree aside, however, Davidson is a new coordinator, and teams often suffer through an adjustment period when changing systems.

Second, there are multiple cracks in the Panthers' pillar-of-strength defense. Julius Peppers is one of the best players in the league, and the Panthers front four is still a dominant unit, but the team lacks playmakers in the back seven. The team is counting on Dan Morgan to return from his umpteenth concussion to solidify their linebacker corps, and they will try to squeeze one more year from safety Mike Minter before he retires. Both players are on the downside, as is defensive end Mike Rucker. Journeymen Na'il Diggs and Shaun Williams were retained to play key roles this season because the cap-strapped Panthers didn't have the cash to pursue better players via free agency. There's some young talent around, including linebacker Thomas Davis and cornerback Richard Marshall, but there is little depth.

The plan this season is for Peppers and the front four to terrorize opponents so they cannot pick on the linebackers and safeties. It worked last year, but it will only take a few injuries or dips in performance for the Panthers to slip to the middle of the pack.

The Panthers proudly announced in early March that 21 of last season's 22 starters were returning in 2007, with retired tight end Mangum the only exception. Retaining the team's best players was something of an accomplishment for the organization. As the offseason began, the Panthers were over the salary cap, Keyshawn was threatening retirement, and it appeared that players such as Diggs and Minter could end up elsewhere. But continuity can be a mixed blessing. The Panthers announced their nearly-set lineup at a time when teams with money to spend were still acquiring starting-caliber talent. The Peppers-Smith nucleus of top talent is good enough to keep the Panthers at or around .500, but a lineup full of Hoovers and Diggses isn't built to suddenly go 13–3 and run away with the conference. When the Panthers did make a change to their starting lineup by releasing Keyshawn after the draft, it was a smart long-term move that will hurt the team in 2007: Drew Carter hasn't proven himself as a starter, and rookie Dwayne Jarrett is an enigma. An awful lot is riding on the health of the older defenders and the return of Hartwig and Wharton, two linemen who bear little resemblance to Mike Webster and Anthony Munoz.

The short-term prognosis for the Panthers may be disappointing, but the long term-forecast is worse. Rucker and Minter are as good as gone. Peppers has two years left on his contract but eats up double-digit cap space; he could be asked to restructure after the season. Delhomme may have peaked, and new backup David Carr isn't the quarterback to build a franchise around (just ask the Houston Texans). The Panthers need to win now, but they lack the talent to do it. Improving on third down isn't enough. The Panthers must get younger, faster, and better. They are none of those things in 2007.

Mike Tanier

The Long and Short of It

Steve Smith is a tremendous deep threat. You know it, we know it, and opposing cornerbacks know it, which is why they can often be seen playing 15 yards off of him.

Smith is also a great weapon on short passes. When those cornerbacks give him a huge cushion, Smith and Jake Delhomme hook up on a "smoke" pass, Smith makes a cut or two, and the Panthers pick up some substantial yardage. Smith is also effective on wide receiver screens,

Table 2. Lowest Percentage of Medium Routes, 2005–06

Player	Charted Passes	Pct Medium Routes
Kevin Curtis	124	26.7%
Steve Smith	289	28.4%
Bernard Berrian	127	29.5%
Antwaan Randle El	133	31.4%
Marcus Robinson	115	31.5%
Isaac Bruce	197	32.6%
Reche Caldwell	145	32.6%
Terrell Owens	244	32.9%
Justin McCareins	141	33.3%
Andre Johnson	278	33.9%

NOTE: Minimum 100 charted passes.

where he can set up his blockers and use his open-field creativity to produce big gains.

The Panthers love to throw deep to Smith, and they love to throw short to him. They aren't as excited about using him on medium-length routes. Over the last two seasons, only 28.4 percent of the passes thrown to Smith traveled between 6 and 15 yards in the air (table 2). That's by far the lowest percentage for any starting wide receiver, and the second-lowest percentage of any player who was thrown to 100 or more times in the last two years.

The other receivers on the list include bomb specialists (Berrian and Robinson), guys who catch lots of short passes in conservative systems (Johnson and McCareins), and players who share Smith's reputation as open field terrors (Owens and Randle El). The list is also dominated by slot receivers or one-year starters with small data samples. If we extend the list to find a few more two-year starters, we run into Chris Chambers (34.2 percent) and Santana Moss (35.0 percent) as players who share Smith's general screens-and-bombs usage pattern.

With Smith concentrating on long and short passes, you might guess that Keyshawn Johnson was among the league leaders in medium passes. He ranks 11th in table 3, but that ranking is a bit misleading, since he sits behind a number of role players and part-timers. When we only consider receivers who were full-time starters in each of the last two seasons, Keyshawn moves up to fifth behind Joe Horn, Deion Branch, Hines Ward, and Laveranues Coles. His time in Dallas doesn't affect his status—he was actually thrown a higher percentage of medium-length passes with the Cowboys than with the Panthers.

The Panthers created a simple dichotomy between their speed and possession receivers: Smith handled the short and long stuff, while Keyshawn caught everything in between. Most teams don't distribute their passes that neatly. Many teams throw a high percentage of their deep

Table 3. Highest Percentage of Medium Routes, 2005–06

Player	Charted Passes	Pct Medium Routes
Joe Jurevicius	149	55.4%
Brandon Lloyd	167	51.8%
Joe Horn	164	51.8%
Chris Henry	125	51.8%
Cedric Wilson	122	51.6%
Deion Branch	226	51.2%
Hines Ward	241	49.2%
Dez White	132	49.1%
Laveranues Coles	282	48.1%
Samie Parker	126	48.1%
Keyshawn Johnson	258	48.0%

NOTE: Minimum 100 charted passes.

passes to slot receivers and favor the tight end as a mid-range target. Other teams rarely throw short passes to wideouts. Furthermore, teams throw different percentages of short, medium, and long passes depending on their philosophies and the game situations they find themselves in. The Panthers rarely used their tight ends in the passing game, their slot receivers weren't major components in the offense, and the team threw a roughly league-average amount of each type of pass. As a result, it's easy to see a distinct split between Smith and Keyshawn.

That split may not be as pronounced this year. With Keyshawn gone, the Panthers lack a true possession receiver to catch all those medium-length passes. Rookie Dwayne Jarrett has a possession receiver's skill set—size, hands, lack of speed—but he lacks the experience needed to get open against zone coverage. Drew Carter is more of a home run threat than a mid-range target. Smith may be asked to use his speed to set up defenders on 10–15 yard hooks and crossing routes more often.

Smith should benefit from a change in roles. New offensive coordinator Jeff Davidson vows to get Smith more involved in the offense. That usually means that Smith will be targeted for more short passes; after all, you can only throw so many bombs. Such a well-defined game plan can become too predictable. Anyone who watched the Redskins last year knows that there's such a thing as too many wide receiver screens. The Panthers will miss Keyshawn, but with Smith running more medium range routes and Carter playing an increased role as a deep threat, their offense will be far more diverse. Smith will have no problem hauling in those extra throws; his percentage may have been low, but Smith was still targeted for 82 medium-length passes in the last two years, a little less than three per game for the games in which he was healthy. That's just enough action to keep him involved on 3rd-and-10, and the Panthers need their best player to be a factor if they hope to shake the third down blues in 2007.

Mike Tanier

Panthers 2006 Stats by Week

Wk	vs	W–L	PF	PA	YDF	YDA	TO	Total	Off	Def	ST
1	ATL	L	6	20	215	385	-2	-54.8%	-44.2%	14.3%	3.7%
2	@MIN	L	13	16	271	365	0	-4.7%	1.8%	1.5%	-5.0%
3	@TB	W	26	24	350	209	-1	-2.6%	-3.5%	3.5%	4.4%
4	NO	W	21	18	324	407	-1	33.9%	39.1%	5.3%	0.1%
5	CLE	W	20	12	288	248	+3	7.7%	4.5%	-23.3%	-20.1%
6	@BAL	W	23	21	414	292	0	37.9%	13.1%	-28.2%	-3.4%
7	@CIN	L	14	17	277	342	-1	-3.2%	-7.6%	-1.2%	3.2%
8	DAL	L	14	35	204	414	-2	-40.5%	0.2%	20.2%	-20.5%
9	BYE										
10	TB	W	24	10	318	212	+2	15.5%	7.2%	-11.4%	-3.0%
11	STL	W	15	0	411	111	-1	68.0%	-34.2%	-104.8%	-2.5%
12	@WAS	L	13	17	264	253	-1	-6.5%	-34.3%	-23.4%	4.4%
13	@PHI	L	24	27	377	402	-2	19.0%	16.0%	8.3%	11.3%
14	NYG	L	13	27	463	307	-3	12.3%	-8.8%	-19.4%	1.7%
15	PIT	L	3	37	240	306	-2	-70.3%	-24.9%	16.9%	-28.6%
16	@ATL	W	10	3	194	177	+2	11.8%	-20.1%	-23.3%	8.6%
17	@NO	W	31	21	313	297	+2	65.9%	28.1%	-39.8%	-2.0%

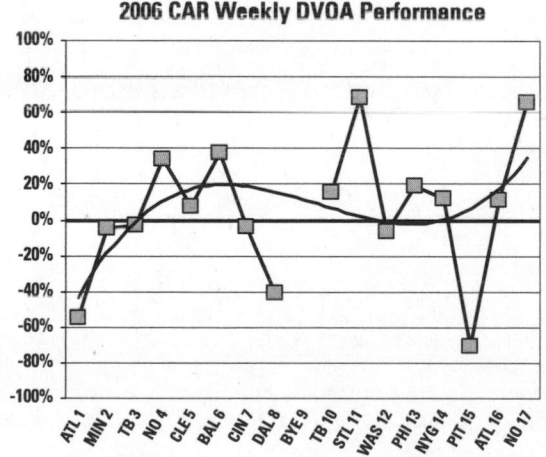

2006 CAR Weekly DVOA Performance

Trends and Splits

	Offense	Rank	Defense	Rank
Total DVOA	-4.3%	19	-10.0%	5
Unadjusted VOA	-2.7%	18	-6.1%	9
Weighted Trend	-5.8%	20	-15.9%	4
Variance	5.0%	25	8.8%	5
Passing	-2.3%	17	-5.7%	9
Rushing	-6.8%	19	-14.7%	6
First Down	0.3%	15	-10.3%	8
Second Down	7.5%	10	-12.2%	6
Third Down	-34.5%	32	-6.3%	9
Red Zone	-16.4%	23	14.6%	28
Late and Close	-7.5%	23	-1.2%	15

Five-Year Performance

	2006	2005	2004	2003	2002
W-L	8-8	11-5	7-9	11-5	7-9
Pythagorean Wins	6.9	11.6	8.4	8.6	6.5
Estimated Wins	7.9	9.9	8.6	7.9	7.0
Total DVOA	2.9%	14.0%	2.3%	0.4%	-9.2%
Rank	14	11	12	17	24
Offense	-4.3%	-3.2%	0.8%	-7.2%	-22.9%
Rank	19	15	13	.18	31
Defense	-10.0%	-14.9%	-3.8%	-7.1%	-13.8%
Rank	5	3	13	12	3
Special Teams	-2.8%	2.3%	-2.3%	0.6%	-0.2%
Rank	24	6	23	16	16

Strategic Tendencies

Formations		Rank	Run/Pass		Rank	Defense		Rank	Other		Rank
3+ WR	49%	13	Runs, all plays	41%	25	Sacks by LB	23%	16	Run with 2+ RB	76%	2
4+ WR	14%	10	Runs, first half	44%	18	Sacks by DB	5%	22	Run with 2+ TE	19%	29
2+ TE	13%	30	Runs, first down	44%	31	Rush 6+	9.2%	15	Play action	18%	20
Single back	39%	30	Runs, power sit.	50%	31	Rush 7+	1.0%	20	Go for it on 4th	0.62	31
Empty back	4.8%	6	Runs, behind 2H	19%	32	Rush 3	5.8%	8	Offensive Pace	31.8	24
Max protect	14%	10	Pass, ahead 2H	44%	14	CB1 on WR1	20%	32	Defensive Pace	30.2	11

In 2005, Carolina ranked in the top ten in all the run-frequency categories except for runs when behind in the second half. In 2006, Carolina was near the bottom of the league in all of these categories.... Carolina's passing game was great in the first two quarters (25.2% DVOA, ranked fourth), but imploded in the second half (–26.1% DVOA, ranked 30th).... Carolina ran the most three-running back sets with 36, more than twice the number of any other team. Surprisingly, they threw the ball 67 percent of the time in such formations, and, despite the full backfield, Jake Delhomme was sacked twice.... Carolina's offense ranked 31st in DVOA on play-action (–38.1%), ahead of only Miami.... Carolina's pass defense had a –58.6% DVOA in the first quarter. No other pass defense was better than –33.0%. From the second quarter on, Carolina's pass defense had a DVOA of 11.1%, 22nd in the NFL. The run defense was consistently good in all four quarters.... Carolina forced a three-and-out on 33 percent of drives, the highest figure in the league.

Passing

Player	DPAR	DVOA	Plys	NtYds	Avg	YAC	C%	TD	Int
Jake Delhomme	22.5	-1.6%	431	2632	6.1	4.7	61.0%	17	11
Chris Weinke*	-5.2	-24.5%	96	570	5.9	4.2	58.3%	2	0
Brett Basanez	1.4	14.6%	11	56	5.1	1.2	54.5%	0	4
David Carr	10.3	-8.3%	440	2516	5.7	4.8	68.6%	11	12

Rushing

Player	DPAR	DVOA	Plys	Yds	Avg	TD	Fum	Suc
DeShaun Foster	11.4	-4.0%	227	900	4.0	3	3	45%
DeAngelo Williams	6.4	-3.3%	121	501	4.1	1	1	47%
Brad Hoover	-0.5	-20.3%	22	73	3.3	1	1	30%
Nick Goings	-0.5	-25.2%	11	52	4.7	0	0	30%
Eric Shelton	-0.9	-48.3%	8	23	2.9	0	0	44%
Steve Smith	0.7	-8.4%	8	61	7.6	1	1	—
Jake Delhomme	0.4	-2.4%	4	26	6.5	0	6	—
Chris Weinke*	-1.5	-139.6%	3	15	5.0	0	2	—
David Carr	2.7	-4.8%	40	212	5.3	2	16	—

Receiving

Player	DPAR	DVOA	Plys	Ctch	Yds	Y/C	YAC	TD	C%
WR									
Steve Smith	22.5	9.0%	139	83	1166	14.0	5.2	8	60%
Keyshawn Johnson*	6.8	-7.5%	128	70	821	11.7	2.8	4	55%
Drew Carter	1.7	-10.9%	51	28	357	12.8	2.4	3	55%
Keary Colbert	-2.3	-45.9%	12	5	56	11.2	4.4	0	60%
Taye Biddle	0.4	-5.4%	5	3	37	12.3	2.0	0	42%
TE									
Kris Mangum*	-1.1	-18.2%	33	21	170	8.1	3.8	1	64%
Michael Gaines	-2.1	-24.9%	28	15	146	9.7	3.8	0	54%
RB									
DeShaun Foster	-7.1	-40.6%	46	32	159	5.0	4.9	0	92%
DeAngelo Williams	10.9	48.0%	36	33	313	9.5	10.5	1	69%
Brad Hoover	-2.1	-22.6%	29	20	122	6.1	3.5	0	70%
Nick Goings	2.8	28.7%	15	10	107	10.7	7.3	1	67%

Offensive Line

Year	Yards	ALY	Rank	Power	Rank	10+ Yds	Rank	Stuff	Rank	Sack	ASR	Rank
2004	3.80	3.94	26	61%	16	15%	26	25%	19	33	5.8%	8
2005	3.62	4.17	13	60%	22	12%	26	22%	6	27	5.6%	9
2006	3.98	4.02	24	50%	31	17%	12	25%	26	32	6.4%	16

Year	LE	Rank	LT	Rank	Mid	Rank	RT	Rank	RE	Rank
2004	4.37	16	3.91	26	3.89	24	4.72	9	3.08	27
2005	3.72	23	4.60	9	4.07	17	4.03	20	4.70	8
2006	4.64	5	4.32	16	4.12	22	4.41	9	2.43	32

Offensive line coach Dave Magazu helped develop such line prospects as Dan Koppen and Chris Snee while coaching at Boston College. Magazu prefers "B.C." style linemen: small, quick, and tenacious. Rookie center Ryan Kalil fits that description, with exceptional quickness and footwork. The second-round pick from USC should thrive in the zone-blocking scheme that Magazu and coordinator Jeff Davidson plan to emphasize. If Kalil develops quickly, Justin Hartwig will move from center to guard. Geoff Hantgartner, last year's overmatched starter at center, should stick as a super sub.

Jordan Gross, a former first-round pick, never looked comfortable at left tackle last year, jumping offsides six times and blowing several blocks. Strong pass rushers can rag doll him. He may be a lifer on the right side. Left guard Mike Wahle, the team's best lineman, had an off year in 2006, but it's hard to block effectively when the players to your left and right are getting beaten consistently. Like Kalil, Wahle is a natural zone and second-level blocker. Wahle missed the final three games of 2006 with a shoulder injury, but participated in May minicamp.

Jeremy Bridges signed with the Panthers in early September and became their starting right tackle in Week 3 after a knee injury felled left tackle Travelle Wharton and Gross had to go back to the left side. Bridges played well enough to earn a contract extension in December, and, if Wharton is able to regain his form, Bridges will provide depth at both tackle positions.

Defensive Front Seven

Defensive Line	Age	Pos	Plys	TmPct	Rk	Stop	Dfts	StpRt	Rk	AvYd	Rk	Sack	Hit	Hur	Runs	RuStp	RuYd	Pass	PaStp	PaYd
Julius Peppers	27	DE	63	7.9%	17	49	34	78%	40	0.9	19	13	8	32	35	74%	2.6	28	82%	-1.3
Kris Jenkins	28	DT	42	5.3%	34	37	10	88%	10	0.7	11	3	4	7	35	86%	1.4	7	100%	-2.9
Mike Rucker	32	DE	38	5.5%	46	31	12	82%	24	0.7	13	5.5	9	15	31	77%	2.3	7	100%	-6.7
Maake Kemoeatu	28	DT	35	4.4%	55	25	5	71%	57	2.4	55	0	0	4	31	71%	2.3	4	75%	3.5
Al Wallace*	33	DE	23	2.9%	—	15	8	65%	—	3.4	—	2.5	4	3	15	60%	3.1	8	75%	4.0
Damione Lewis	29	DT	20	2.5%	—	20	12	100%	—	-0.4	—	4.5	3	5	8	100%	2.3	12	100%	-2.2

Linebackers	Age	Pos	Plys	TmPct	Rk	Stop	Dfts	StpRt	AvYd	Saok	Hit	Hur	Runs	RuStp	Rk	RuYd	Rk	Tgts	Suc%	Rk	PaYd	Rk
Chris Draft*	31	ILB	108	13.6%	36	73	30	68%	3.1	5.5	0	0	68	75%	9	2.1	2	35	54%	35	5.4	20
Thomas Davis	24	OLB	91	13.1%	41	45	13	49%	5.5	1.5	8	8	48	46%	98	5.3	98	54	52%	43	6.3	54
Na'il Diggs	29	OLB	63	8.5%	83	41	12	65%	3.0	0	0	1	50	66%	40	2.8	17	21	68%	4	3.0	3
James Anderson	24	OLB	20	2.5%	—	11	7	55%	4.8	2	2	0	10	50%	—	3.6	—	8	40%	—	8.6	—

Year	Yards	ALY	Rank	Power	Rank	10+ Yds	Ronk	Stuff	Rank	Saok	ASR	Rank
2004	4.13	4.04	9	74%	28	21%	25	23%	18	34	6.6%	22
2005	3.52	3.68	6	46%	1	13%	6	26%	13	45	7.5%	11
2006	3.97	4.03	9	48%	2	16%	17	28%	3	41	8.0%	7

Year	LE	Rank	LT	Rank	Mid	Rank	RT	Rank	RE	Rank
2004	2.93	3	4.65	25	4.12	13	4.76	31	2.80	4
2005	3.93	14	3.42	5	3.93	10	3.40	2	3.13	7
2006	3.55	10	4.67	20	4.02	7	4.53	21	3.51	10

Julius Peppers led all defensive linemen with 34 defeats last season and is sixth in the NFL with 65 defeats over the last three seasons (the top five: Jason Taylor [85], Aaron Schobel [76], Osi Umenyiora [67], Robert Mathis [67], and Leonard Little [66]). Peppers was also second in the NFL with 32 hurries in 2006. Peppers also improved as a run defender last season and performed well when dropping into zone coverage. The Panthers can afford to use Peppers as an all-purpose threat because left end Mike Rucker and tackle Kris Jenkins also rush the passer effectively. Jenkins bounced back from two injury-ruined seasons last year to prove that he's still one of the best interior linemen in the NFL. Rucker is a tactician who beats his opponents with multiple moves and perfect hand technique.

(continued next page)

Defensive Front Seven (*continued*)

Maake Kemoeatu, signed to replace Brentson Buckner as the team's nose tackle, was an oversized bust who couldn't occupy double teams. He may play a reduced role this season. Damione Lewis was a disappointment as a first-round pick in St. Louis, but was very effective as a wave defender. Rookie end Charles Johnson will replace Al Wallace and is Rucker's heir apparent.

Because their defensive line is the best in the NFL, the Panthers can get by with some very ordinary linebackers. Na'il Diggs is adequate against the run, but leaves the field on passing downs. Chris Draft showed great range when Dan Morgan got hurt, but he missed too many tackles and didn't fill gaps well. Draft signed with the Rams as a free agent. Thomas Davis returned to his natural linebacker position last year after spending his rookie season at safety and struggled to readjust. Davis has outstanding speed and should be a natural in pass coverage, but he was often out of position. Rookie Jon Beason is a lot like Morgan: explosive, tough against the run, and frequently injured.

Morgan is the X-factor of the front seven. He signed a one-year, incentive-laden deal with the team and hopes to prove that he can bounce back from multiple concussions. If Morgan is healthy, head coach John Fox and his staff will be able to fit players such as Diggs and Davis around him to form a quality linebacker corps.

Defensive Secondary

Secondary	Age	Pos	Plys	TmPct	Rk	Stop	Dfts	RuYd	Rk	RuStp	Rk	Tgts	Tgt%	Rk	Dist	Suc%	Rk	PaYd	Rk	PD	Int
Chris Gamble	24	CB	78	10.5%	23	42	18	4.1	6	63%	7	58	16%	51	12.7	52%	37	9.2	73	11	3
Richard Marshall	23	CB	82	10.3%	26	43	20	3.8	5	62%	10	70	18%	47	13.2	59%	12	6.2	11	10	3
Ken Lucas	28	CB	55	8.5%	—	28	13	6.2	—	52%	—	42	13%	76	14.8	53%	36	6.6	—	10	3
Mike Minter	33	FS	88	11.1%	25	28	13	7.2	49	43%	38	32	7%	42	13.4	53%	37	7.8	40	4	1
Shaun Williams*	30	SS	77	12.9%	11	31	8	6.5	42	46%	30	26	8%	28	15.2	62%	14	5.4	7	6	2
Colin Branch*	27	SS	16	2.0%	—	6	4	5.7	—	50%	—	8	2%	—	16.8	50%	—	17.6	—	1	1

Year	Pass D Rank	DVOA vs. #1 WR	Rank	DVOA vs. #2 WR	Rank	DVOA vs. Other WR	Rank	DVOA vs. TE	Rank	DVOA vs. RB	Rank
2004	8	4.2%	16	0.6%	18	-18.3%	7	-31.4%	3	-9.1%	10
2005	2	-17.1%	2	-26.7%	4	3.9%	22	-1.2%	17	-3.8%	13
2006	9	-16.9%	4	11.5%	22	-20.9%	8	12.8%	28	-20.6%	7

Fourth-year veteran Chris Gamble is a size-speed specimen who regressed in 2006 after playing at a Pro Bowl level in 2005. Gamble's surname is appropriate: He makes a lot of mistakes while freelancing and trying to bait the quarterback into a bad decision. Richard Marshall, last year's second-round pick, filled in for the injured Ken Lucas midway through the season and then replaced him in the starting lineup for good. Marshall excels in press coverage and uses his long arms to break up deep passes. Now playing the nickel role, Lucas is a smart veteran with good instincts who has trouble keeping up with quicker receivers.

Free safety Mike Minter plans to retire after this season. He spent much of 2006 chasing down receivers after 20-yard gains, and the Panthers must limit his man coverage responsibilities if they hope to wring one more year out of him. The Panthers released strong safety Shaun Williams and backup Colin Branch, leaving sophomore Nate Salley as the likely starter. Salley started at Ohio State for three seasons, but wasn't a top prospect because he had slow reactions in coverage and missed too many tackles. He played sparingly last season. If Salley isn't the answer, the Panthers may re-sign Branch or promote free-agent signing Deke Cooper to the starting lineup.

Special Teams

Year	DVOA	Rank	FG/XP	Rank	Net Punt	Rank	Punt Ret	Rank	Net Kick	Rank	Kick Ret	Rank	Hidden	Rank
2004	-2.3%	23	-0.5	17	4.9	13	-5.0	26	-8.1	27	-4.9	21	4.6	7
2005	2.4%	6	0.7	15	7.3	6	6.4	6	7.5	4	-8.0	25	-4.4	20
2006	-2.8%	24	11.5	1	0.8	18	-15.3	32	-1.8	23	-11.6	30	-2.6	18

Kicker John Kasay bounced back from a miserable 2005 season to go 18-for-18 on field goal attempts under 50 yards last year. Kasay will turn 38 this season, but he still has enough leg for long attempts (he hit a 54-yarder last season) and is adequate on kickoffs.

Punter Jason Baker led the NFL with 98 attempts; that will happen when your offense cannot convert on third down. Baker finished third in the NFL with a net average of 39.0 yards per punt. He was aided by a punt coverage team that allowed just 6.4 yards per return, the fourth-lowest total in the NFL. Special teams captain Carl Hankton was a cap casualty, but the Panthers have plenty of gunners to choose from among Nick Goings, Kevin McCadam, James Anderson, and Deke Cooper.

DeAngelo Williams showed promise as a kick returner early in the season, but appeared tentative when he returned from an October ankle injury. Chris Gamble has the tools to excel as a punt returner, but wasn't productive last season, generating just one return longer than 20 yards. Wide receiver Steve Smith is one of the best return men in the NFL, of course, but the Panthers don't want to risk injuring him. Rookie Ryne Robinson holds the Mid-Atlantic Conference record with seven career punt return touchdowns, but the 5-foot-9, 180-pound Robinson must prove that he's tough enough to survive in the NFL.

Coaching Staff

Dan Henning may be gone as offensive coordinator, but John Fox retained several assistants from Henning's offensive staff, including offensive line coach Dave Magazu, who was responsible for tight ends under Henning, and assistant head coach/running backs coach Jim Skipper. The most important returning coach is Mike McCoy, who holds the title Quarterbacks Coach/Passing Game Coordinator. McCoy has been Jake Delhomme's coach since 2003, and was the person who relayed plays from Henning to Delhomme via the helmet headset. Continuity can be a mixed blessing for a new coordinator; Jeff Davidson knows his coaches have a good rapport with the players, but it may be difficult to institute changes with a staff full of Henning protégés.

It can be hard for a defensive coordinator to gain notice when working for a defensive-minded coach. In his first season at the helm of the Panthers defense, Mike Trgovac helped the team reach the Super Bowl. Trgovac is a players' favorite who has put his own stamp on John Fox's system, adding some zone blitzes and occasional three-man fronts to the defensive mix. Trgovac was lucky to get an opportunity as a coordinator. When Jack Del Rio left after the 2002 season, Fox wanted to hire Jim Mora Jr. Mora put Fox on hold to talk to the Falcons, so Trgovac (then the defensive line coach) took the initiative to assume Del Rio's responsibilities. He's been the coordinator ever since.

Chicago Bears

It was Super Bowl Sunday. The Chicago Bears had the ball at their own 38-yard line with less than 12 minutes to go. They trailed the Indianapolis Colts by five points. The Bears were one touchdown drive away from taking a fourth-quarter lead in the Super Bowl. On a first down play, Rex Grossman dropped back, looked deep, and threw a pass well over the head of Muhsin Muhammad. Indianapolis cornerback Kelvin Hayden caught the ball and tiptoed down the sideline for the game-clinching touchdown.

Grossman's truly awful play made him the convenient scapegoat for the loss, but the Super Bowl was not lost on the memorable interception by Hayden. The Bears lost the championship to the Colts when defensive tackle Tommie Harris ruptured his hamstring in Week 13 against Minnesota. Absent Harris, the dominant Bears defense ceased to exist, and the pressure to compensate was thrust on a young quarterback who was not ready to handle it.

The loss of a defensive tackle is rarely crippling, but Harris had very quietly developed into arguably the league's best player at his position. Through and including Harris's last game against Minnesota, the Bears never had a below-average defensive performance (based on single-game DVOA). The next three weeks were all below average. In the playoffs, the Bears only rated as an above-average defense in the weather-hampered NFC Championship Game against New Orleans. In the Super Bowl, they kept the score down by forcing field goals, but the Bears defense was overwhelmed. They allowed 190 yards on the ground.

> ## BEARS PROSPECTUS
>
> **2006 Record:** 13–3
>
> **DVOA Estimated Wins:** 10.8 (5th)
>
> **Pythagorean Wins:** 12.4 (2nd)
>
> **DVOA:** 24.0% total (4th), 12.2% weighted (7th)
>
> **Offense:** −4.2% DVOA (18th)
>
> **Defense:** −20.6% DVOA (2nd)
>
> **Special Teams:** 7.6% DVOA (1st)
>
> **Variance:** 28.4% (2nd)
>
> **2006:** The best team in a bad conference still gets to go to the Super Bowl.
>
> **2007:** Signs point toward a decline that Rex Grossman will only exacerbate.
>
> ---
>
> **2007 Mean Projection:** 8.3 wins
>
> **The Brohm Closet (0–4):** 4%
>
> **Bad Team (5–6):** 17%
>
> **Mediocre (7–8):** 32%
>
> **Playoff Contender (9–10):** 32%
>
> **Super Bowl Contender (11+):** 16%
>
> **Projected Average Opponent:** −3.8% DVOA (30th in NFL)

Without Harris, the Bears defense is mediocre. With him, it is dominant. Even after losing him for the last four games, the Bears finished with a DVOA of −20.3%, second in the league. The −20% threshold is crossed by only one or two teams each year, and is rarely crossed by the same team in back-to-back seasons. Only 17 teams since 1996 have had a defensive DVOA of −20% or better[1] (table 1). The Bears, who had a defensive DVOA of −21.8% in 2005, are only the third team in the last eleven seasons to reach −20% in consecutive seasons. The other teams to achieve back-to-back seasons at that level were Baltimore and Tampa Bay, each of which, unlike Chicago, won the Super Bowl in the second of those two seasons. The Bears defied the odds last season by declining only 1.7% from the year before. On average, teams with a −20% or better defensive DVOA decline by more than 11 percentage points of DVOA the next season.

The Bears will get Harris back this season, along with the rest of their preferred starting lineup from last year, but recent history suggests they are still almost certain to decline defensively. The problem is that defenses are not consistent from season to season, and teams are likely to regress toward the mean. Barring a rash of devastating injuries, the Bears will still likely be a good defense, but they are unlikely to be outstanding.

There is room for the Bears' offense to more than make up for the decline likely to be experienced by their defense, but that means that the team will need Rex Grossman to show considerable development in his second full season as the starter. The offense took great strides in 2006,

---

1. Reminder: a negative DVOA favors the defense, so defenses get "better" when they move further below zero, and "decline" when they move closer to the league average of zero.

Table 1. Dominant Defenses, One Year Later

Team	Year	DVOA	DVOA Y+1	Rk Y+1	Change
GB	1996	−24.1%	−13.1%	5	−11.0%
SF	1997	−23.5%	−3.8%	15	−19.7%
MIA	1998	−25.7%	−13.7%	9	−12.0%
TB	1999	−24.3%	−17.9%	4	−6.4%
BAL	1999	−21.5%	−30.0%	1	8.5%
TEN	2000	−28.4%	7.2%	25	−35.6%
BAL	2000	−30.0%	−17.2%	4	−12.8%
PHI	2001	−21.5%	−13.8%	4	−7.7%
TB	2001	−20.3%	−33.6%	1	13.3%
TB	2002	−33.6%	−21.3%	3	−12.3%
NE	2003	−22.0%	−11.3%	6	−10.7%
BAL	2003	−28.4%	−19.3%	2	−9.1%
TB	2003	−21.3%	−7.0%	8	−14.3%
BUF	2004	−28.1%	8.9%	26	−37.0%
CHI	2005	−21.8%	−20.2%	2	−1.6%

but they were still a below-average group, thanks in large part to Grossman's erratic quarterbacking. Grossman was healthy for 16 games last season, but his performance was uneven to say the least. In the build-up to the Super Bowl, it was often stated that Grossman had seven games with a passer rating of 100 or higher and three games with a rating of ten or lower. This fueled a sense that there was a "Good Rex/Bad Rex" dichotomy. This perception arose in large part from Grossman's ability to post strong conventional numbers against bad defenses. Grossman played seven of his 16 games against teams that ranked among the league's ten-worst pass defenses and posted five of his seven 100-plus quarterback ratings against those bottom-feeders.

DVOA adjusts for opposing defense, and a look at DVOA shows that last season was not a case of Good Rex/Bad Rex but Not-on-Tape Rex/On-Tape Rex. Once opposing defensive coordinators had enough tape to spot Grossman's tendencies, they easily schemed to confuse him, and what started as a promising season quickly turned into a disaster. Through four games, Grossman had a DVOA of 51.5%. The rest of the season, it was −32.6%. No player in the history of DVOA has ever seen a decline like that after four weeks.

Grossman's extreme splits make him a unique case, but it may still be instructive to see how other quarterbacks with severe post-Week 4 declines fared in their next season. Before last season, 18 quarterbacks had seen a post-Week 4 decline of at least 40 points of DVOA. Of those, 14 attempted at least 100 passes the next season. In the first season, these quarterbacks averaged 38.3% DVOA through four weeks, but −16.3% from Week 5 on, for a total DVOA of 1.3%. The next season, DVOA was almost unchanged from the previous year, averaging −0.6% (table 2).

The Bears could do worse than having Grossman play at the mediocre level he averaged a season ago. Unfortu-

nately, a closer look shows that Grossman could be heading for a fall. Of the seven players in table 2 who improved their overall DVOA the next season, six had started at least 35 games before the season at issue. Of the seven players who declined the next year, only two had started 35 games. The six relatively new starters declined by an average of 13.5 percentage points of DVOA the next season.

Were Grossman to fall that far, his passing DVOA would be −24.8%, which would have ranked 39th in the league last season. Only eight quarterbacks threw 100 passes in 2006 with a DVOA of −20% or worse. Six of them were the platoon quarterbacks for the offensively inept Raiders, Browns, and Buccaneers. The other two were Drew Bledsoe, who is now out of the game, and Seneca Wallace, a career backup.

The Bears' offseason has left Grossman with a similar supporting cast to the one he struggled with a season ago. Thomas Jones was shipped off to the Jets, leaving Cedric Benson as the primary running back. Jones and Benson were equally effective a season ago, and the trade will only cause a major change if Benson suffers an injury. On draft day, the Bears used their first-round pick on the best tight end from the Class of '07, Greg Olsen. The Miami product is an impressive athlete, but he will hardly revolutionize the passing game. In addition, he is a poor blocker, which means he may struggle for every-down playing time. If Olsen only plays on obvious passing downs, he will no longer create the mismatches that favor an athletic tight end.

The other reason for concern is that the Bears' exceptional special teams cannot possibly be as successful as they were last season. Devin Hester garnered most of the

Table 2. Hot QB Starts Followed by Big Fades, 1996–2006

Year	Player	Wk 1–4	Wk 5–17	Total	Fade	Y+1
2006	R. Grossman	51.5%	−32.6%	−11.3%	−84.2%	—
1999	B. Johnson	70.3%	−3.1%	13.8%	−73.4%	7.3%
2004	M. Brunell	11.1%	−57.7%	−22.8%	−68.8%	10.1%
2003	D. Bledsoe	38.4%	−27.9%	−11.9%	−66.2%	−2.0%
2001	B. Griese	39.4%	−23.4%	−7.7%	−62.8%	11.6%
1999	D. Bledsoe	39.0%	−22.2%	−5.8%	−61.2%	3.9%
1999	K. Warner	81.1%	25.4%	35.1%	−55.7%	17.2%
2000	T. Couch	8.3%	−41.0%	−13.1%	−49.3%	−27.7%
2000	T. Banks	18.4%	−30.1%	−6.2%	−48.4%	−11.6%
1997	J. George	49.1%	1.2%	13.1%	−47.9%	−17.4%
2004	K. Warner	27.8%	−20.0%	−0.5%	−47.8%	8.7%
2005	D. McNabb	28.6%	−18.7%	2.2%	−47.3%	25.7%
1997	T. Dilfer	45.6%	−0.7%	10.3%	−46.3%	−18.1%
1997	D. Bledsoe	40.1%	−6.0%	5.6%	−46.1%	9.7%
2000	R. Johnson	38.9%	−4.7%	6.7%	−43.6%	26.2%
Average		**38.3%**	**−16.3%**	**1.3%**	**−54.6%**	**−0.6%**

2007 Bears Schedule

Week	Opp	Week	Opp	Week	Opp
1	at SD	7	at PHI	13	NYG
2	KC	8	DET	14	at WAS (Thu.)
3	DAL	9	BYE	15	at MIN (Mon.)
4	at DET	10	at OAK	16	GB
5	at GB	11	at SEA	17	NO
6	MIN	12	DEN		

publicity, and he was certainly spectacular, but the Bears were above average in every facet of special teams play. Their most important player may have been Robbie Gould, who emerged as an excellent field goal kicker in his second year. Gould also increased his kickoff distance, which, along with excellent coverage spearheaded by Brendon Ayanbadejo and Adrian Peterson, gave Chicago the best net kickoffs in the league.

The 2006 Bears' 7.6% special teams DVOA was the third best rating of the last decade. The only two teams ahead of them, the 2002 Saints and 1998 Cowboys, saw their special teams ratings drop to –1.2% and 1.7%, respectively, the next season. The Bears could avoid some of this fall if Hester assumes primary kick-return duties. A season ago, Hester returned 20 kicks, while Rashied Davis returned 32. Still, even Hester's 100 Speed rating in Madden 2007 won't stop the Chicago special teams from declining somewhat in the actual 2007 season.

This gloomy tone shows just how far the franchise has come since Lovie Smith was hired three seasons ago. At that point, Bill Swerski and da Superfans would have given anything for multiple division championships and a Super Bowl appearance. The Bears had two playoff appearances in the 11 years between Ditka and Smith. Now the Bears would likely consider anything short of the Super Bowl a disappointment. A failure to make the playoffs would be a disaster.

The likely step back this season is most disheartening because the team's long-term success is far from secured. Linebacker Lance Briggs's ongoing contract dispute highlights what will be an extremely difficult task for General Manager Jerry Angelo over the next several seasons. The Bears climbed into the defensive elite in 2005 with a talent base primarily made up of young draft picks, but as those players begin to reach free agency, the Bears will have to determine who they can afford, and who can most easily be replaced. Briggs will almost certainly be gone after this season, when the Bears will also have to make decisions about both their starting cornerbacks, Nathan Vasher and Charles Tillman. Harris and fellow defensive tackle Tank Johnson's contracts expire a year later. Meanwhile, All-Pro middle linebacker Brian Urlacher turns 30 after this sea-

son, and the aging process might not be kind to a player so dependent on speed.

The need to pay these high-impact defenders will limit the Bears' ability to improve the offense. Grossman and wide receiver Bernard Berrian are both free agents after this season, while Muhsin Muhammad is comfortably into his mid-30s. Four-fifths of the offensive line will be 30 or older this year, and tackle Fred Miller and guard Ruben Brown are already past their prime.

The window for success in the NFL is exceedingly small unless you can consistently draft and develop new talent. Angelo deserves a great deal of credit for assembling this roster, but odds are against sustained excellence unless he develops an Ozzie Newsome-like ability to consistently field top level defenses despite personnel turnover. If Angelo thinks Briggs is truly expendable, he is certainly not following the model set by his old employers in Tampa Bay. That team held on to most of its high-impact players through their prime years. Presumably, Harris will be re-signed, but, after that, it is anyone's guess.

With so much potential upheaval, the pressure is on this year's team to cash in while the talent level is so high. It will be difficult to do that without improved quarterback play, and the signs indicate that Grossman will be unable to provide that. He obviously has physical talent, but successful quarterbacks also have to be able to make the right decisions under pressure, and, so far, Grossman has come up very short in that area. Smith stuck with Grossman despite his poor play a season ago, a decision that didn't cost them until the Super Bowl. If the defense and Grossman both regress this season, the losses will start to mount. At that point, this talented team may be placed in the inconsistent hands of Brian Griese, and the Bears will again be looking for their quarterback of the future.

Ned Macey

The Worst Quarterback Ever to Win a Super Bowl

Lots of people rooted for Rex Grossman in the Super Bowl. Bears fans rooted for Grossman. Gamblers who took the points rooted for Grossman. Ma and Pa Grossman, no doubt, rooted for their boy Rex.

But one man rooted harder for Grossman than anyone else. If the Bears could pull off a win, Grossman would replace Trent Dilfer as the Worst Quarterback Ever to Win a Super Bowl.

When Dilfer led the Ravens to victory in Super Bowl XXXV, he had no idea what a dubious distinction he would earn. It only took two or three years for Dilfer to become a talk-radio argument stopper. "Of course the home team can win with Tony Armless at quarterback. The Ravens won with Dilfer, didn't they?" As the Bears defense and special teams dragged Grossman into the playoffs, Dilfer became Grossman's litmus test. Every time the Bears won a game in which Grossman threw four picks or completed just six passes, Bears fans prayed a novena to Saint Trent, patron of custodial quarterbacks.

Six years of criticism have taken their toll on Dilfer's legacy and reputation. The storyline of the 2000 Ravens has been warped, the details forgotten. In our dim memories, the Ravens won every game 10–3, their lone touchdown on a Ray Lewis fumble recovery or Jermaine Lewis punt return. When not handing off to Jamal Lewis or Priest Holmes, Dilfer could be seen picking his nose, drooling down his chin, or tossing the ball into the arms of a waiting defender. Dilfer was a hopeless bumbler, a first-round bust who accomplished nothing in Tampa Bay, got lucky in Baltimore, and earned his place at the absolute bottom of the pantheon of Super Bowl champions.

But was Dilfer really that bad?

Before he arrived in Baltimore, Dilfer had established himself as a pretty good NFL quarterback. He threw for 43 touchdowns and just 26 interceptions in 1997 and 1998 combined. He made the Pro Bowl while leading the Bucs to a 10–6 record in 1997—their first winning record in 16 years. He even won a playoff game that year, throwing for 181 yards and a touchdown in a 20–10 victory over the Lions.

In 1999, Dilfer threw for 1,619 yards, 11 touchdowns, and 11 interceptions before getting hurt in Week 12 against the Seahawks. The Bucs were 6–3 under Dilfer, but his relationship with offensive coordinator Mike Shula soured after Dilfer was benched for one midseason game. When the Bucs got hot with rookie Shaun King under center, they decided not to pick up a $4.2-million option on his contract. Before he left, Dilfer called the Bucs "the most frustrating team on earth," saying that they were making him the "fall guy" for the team's shortcomings.

That offseason, Dilfer signed with the Ravens. He was expected to push Tony Banks for a starting job, but Dilfer played poorly in the preseason and started the year on the bench.

The Ravens jumped out to a 5–1 record, but by October their offense disappeared. Completely. They won two games without scoring a touchdown. They then lost two games by 10–3 and 14–6 scores, extending their streak to 16 quarters without scoring a touchdown. Exasperated, Brian Billick turned to Dilfer in the fourth quarter of the 14–6 loss to the Titans. Dilfer missed an exchange with Priest Holmes in his first series. He threw an interception in his second. He fumbled in his third. Despite the inauspicious debut, Dilfer became the Ravens' new starter.

Dilfer failed to lead the Ravens to the end zone in his first start, a 9–6 loss to the Steelers. He completed 11-of-24 passes for 151 yards and an interception. The *Baltimore Sun* described him as "merely mediocre," which was still a step up from Banks. It was Halloween and the Ravens had not scored a touchdown since September 24th. The team was falling out of the playoff race and closing in on several records for offensive futility.

Then, in Week 10 against the Bengals, Dilfer hit Brandon Stokley for a touchdown. The *Sun* described the scene: "Pandemonium ruled for a few unworldly moments. Quarterback Trent Dilfer danced in front of the Ravens' bench, index fingers shooting flares into the sky." Dilfer threw three touchdown passes in a rout that day. The next week, he threw for 281 yards and two touchdowns in a come-from-behind win over the Titans. In Week 12, he was 18-of-24 for 242 yards and two touchdowns in a win over the Cowboys. Dilfer was hot, and the Ravens were back in the playoff hunt.

Seven touchdowns and three wins can do a lot for a quarterback's reputation. "Dilfer is the man, close to being THE MAN," *Sun* writer Mike Preston wrote after the Titans game. Dilfer was praised for his leadership, his competitive fire, and all the other things he always seemed to lack in Tampa Bay. Tight end Shannon Sharpe compared his comfort zone with Dilfer to the relationship he shared with John Elway in Denver. Receiver Qadry Ismail credited Dilfer with reinvigorating the Ravens' downfield passing attack. "He reminds me of Brett Favre when it come to the deep game."

The man. Elway. Favre. Trent Dilfer.

It didn't take long for the Elway comparisons to evaporate. Dilfer began cooling just a few weeks after he got hot. He threw two touchdowns each against the Browns and Chargers, but Billick was clearly scaling down his offense, emphasizing the running game and counting on his defense to win games. Dilfer was left with very little to do. He suffered through a terrible game against the Cardinals: 12-of-22 passes, 70 yards, one interception. Critics noted that Dilfer didn't have the arm strength to connect on sideline routes and that he was starting to force passes. The Ravens were looking for other options at quarterback for the next season. A rumor circulated that the team would try to lure Brad Johnson away from the Redskins.

The Ravens faced the Broncos in the Wild Card round of the playoffs; the weather was icy, and wind gusts topped 25 miles per hour. It wasn't a day for passing, and the Ravens weren't about to try. Dilfer completed just 9 of 18 passes for 190 yards and a touchdown, and the Ravens won 21–3. Dilfer had another low-impact game in the divisional round against the Titans, completing just five passes for 117 yards in a 24–10 win. "Regardless of Dilfer's numbers, the Ravens use him successfully within a conservative structure," the *Baltimore Sun* opined.

In the AFC title game, Dilfer completed just nine passes, but one of them set a record. Facing 3rd-and-18 from the Ravens' four yard line, Dilfer read a Raiders blitz on a play called Rip Double Slant. Dilfer threw a quick slant to Sharpe, hoping to give the punter some room. Sharpe blew past his defender, picked up some blocks downfield, and raced 96 yards for the longest touchdown catch in playoff history. The Ravens were headed to the Super Bowl—in Tampa, the city that had turned its back on Dilfer. Dilfer completed 12-of-25 passes for 153 yards and a touchdown to Stokley in Super Bowl XXXV, but his performance was overshadowed by the defense as the Ravens romped over the Giants 34–7.

Dilfer's late-season swoon and handoff-jockey act in the playoffs overshadowed the midseason hot streak that kept the Ravens in the playoff hunt. "If you were to ask anybody across the league, they would probably say the Ravens won in spite of Trent," Doug Williams would later say of Dilfer. In the public's mind, Dilfer was no longer a fiery leader or a guy who could ignite the deep passing game. The Ravens realistically surmised that they didn't have an all-time great under center, so they went shopping on the free-agent market. When Elvis Grbac became available, the team offered him a five-year contract. "It ain't John Elway they're replacing," Williams noted, ironically echoing Sharpe's earlier praise. Dilfer became the only quarterback ever to be released the year after winning the Super Bowl.

Six years later, Dilfer is still active, and still something of a punchline. Had he lost Super Bowl XXXV, Dilfer would be lumped in with guys like Joe Kapp, Vince Ferragamo, and Stan Humphries, quarterbacks who had their moments but weren't qualified to win a championship. If the Ravens let him hang around for a few years and go 10–6 every year (he was, after all, better than the Grbacs and Jeff Blakes who replaced him), his resume would resemble those of Jim McMahon or Jim Plunkett, good-but-not-great passers who did what they had to do, earning high marks for competitiveness and leadership. Instead, Dilfer became a backup in Seattle. He never got another chance to prove that he was more than just a guy who stood there and cheered for men named Lewis.

Rex Grossman couldn't win the Super Bowl and erase Dilfer from our collective consciousness. That's because he wasn't as good as Dilfer, at least not from Week 6 on. Maybe he'll get another shot, but he'll have to be better than he was for most of 2006. To be the Worst Quarterback Ever to Win the Super Bowl, you have to be a pretty darn good quarterback.

Mike Tanier

Bears 2006 Stats by Week

Wk	vs.	W–L	PF	PA	YDF	YDA	TO	Total	Off	Def	ST
								DVOA			
1	@GB	W	26	0	361	267	+2	66.9%	16.0%	-22.3%	28.5%
2	DET	W	34	7	383	245	+2	35.3%	21.7%	-8.5%	5.2%
3	@MIN	W	19	16	325	286	0	20.3%	4.9%	-9.2%	6.2%
4	SEA	W	37	6	362	230	+2	56.3%	15.9%	-40.9%	-0.5%
5	BUF	W	40	7	351	145	+4	109.6%	30.1%	-68.9%	10.7%
6	@ARI	W	24	23	168	286	-4	-58.7%	-93.2%	-13.3%	21.2%
7	BYE										
8	SF	W	41	10	402	248	+5	111.2%	29.9%	-61.6%	19.7%
9	MIA	L	13	31	292	298	-4	-33.6%	-47.4%	-17.4%	-3.6%
10	@NYG	W	38	20	352	249	0	38.4%	1.6%	-39.1%	-2.4%
11	@NYJ	W	10	0	284	264	+2	29.4%	-5.9%	-37.9%	-2.6%
12	@NE	L	13	17	324	352	+1	11.0%	-6.1%	-21.7%	-4.6%
13	MIN	W	23	13	107	346	0	0.6%	-58.8%	-38.5%	20.9%
14	@STL	W	42	27	372	433	+1	79.6%	46.4%	2.9%	36.1%
15	TB	W	34	31	446	357	-1	2.9%	22.4%	6.3%	-13.2%
16	@DET	W	26	21	354	327	0	-10.5%	-5.0%	16.2%	10.7%
17	GB	L	7	26	316	377	-5	-81.3%	-84.2%	-6.2%	-3.3%
18	BYE										
19	SEA	W	27	24	371	306	-1	-29.6%	-18.6%	8.8%	-2.2%
20	NO	W	39	14	340	375	+4	53.7%	9.4%	-26.5%	17.7%
21	IND	L	17	29	265	430	-2	-7.1%	-33.0%	-16.5%	9.3%

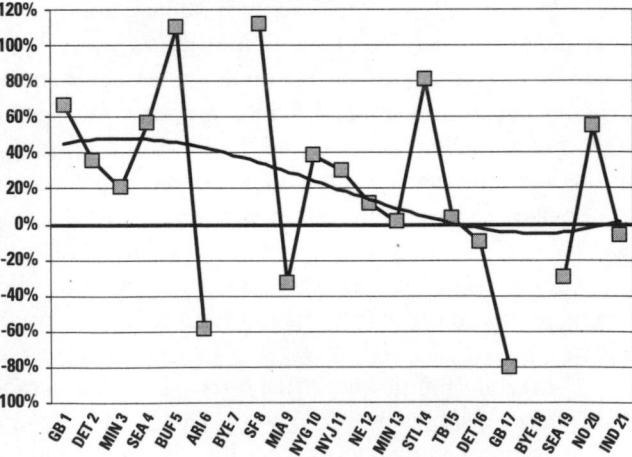

2006 CHI Weekly DVOA Performance

Trends and Splits

	Offense	Rank	Defense	Rank
Total DVOA	-4.2%	18	-20.6%	2
Unadjusted VOA	-3.5%	19	-26.5%	2
Weighted Trend	-11.3%	25	-17.1%	2
Variance	16.4%	1	5.6%	19
Passing	-10.6%	23	-24.6%	2
Rushing	2.4%	9	-15.2%	5
First Down	-11.4%	22	-6.3%	14
Second Down	11.1%	6	-29.6%	1
Third Down	-13.8%	25	-32.8%	4
Red Zone	1.2%	16	-1.2%	12
Late and Close	6.4%	13	-26.0%	3

Five-Year Performance

	2006	2005	2004	2003	2002
W-L	13-3	11-5	5-11	7-9	4-12
Pythagorean Wins	12.4	10.3	4.8	6.1	5.3
Estimated Wins	10.8	8.5	4.4	6.2	6.3
Total DVOA	24.0%	2.3%	-30.2%	-17.8%	-16.3%
Rank	4	14	31	27	27
Offense	-4.2%	-16.8%	-36.5%	-20.3%	-15.1%
Rank	18	28	32	30	27
Defense	-20.6%	-21.8%	-4.5%	0.4%	4.5%
Rank	2	1	10	18	21
Special Teams	7.6%	-2.7%	1.9%	2.9%	3.3%
Rank	1	27	11	5	7

Strategic Tendencies

Formations		Rank	Run/Pass		Rank	Defense		Rank	Other		Rank
3+ WR	40%	28	Runs, all plays	46%	11	Sacks by LB	3%	32	Run with 2+ RB	71%	7
4+ WR	5%	29	Runs, first half	42%	24	Sacks by DB	8%	16	Run with 2+ TE	36%	16
2+ TE	26%	17	Runs, first down	58%	10	Rush 6+	8.9%	16	Play action	21%	12
Single back	49%	20	Runs, power sit.	71%	7	Rush 7+	1.0%	21	Go for it on 4th	0.77	20
Empty back	0.2%	31	Runs, behind 2H	36%	9	Rush 3	1.3%	29	Offensive Pace	28.0	1
Max protect	12%	16	Pass, ahead 2H	42%	18	CB1 on WR1	47%	11	Defensive Pace	31.3	23

The Chicago offense had the fastest pace in the league, possibly because they couldn't wait to get their defense back onto the field. . . . We never recorded Chicago using a five-wide set. . . . Rex Grossman had the worst fourth quarter DVOA (–54.5%) of any starting quarterback not wearing a Raiders uniform. . . . Chicago was much more effective running from one-back formations (19.9%, ranked second), than with two backs on the field (–5.2%, ranked 13th). . . . Chicago was one of three offenses for whom no sack was marked as a Coverage Sack (the others were Indianapolis and Miami). . . . Chicago executed the fewest draw plays as a percentage of all running plays (less than one percent). However, on the rare occasions they used a draw, they had a league-best DVOA of 69.8%. Chicago also had the best defensive DVOA against draws (–62.1%). . . . Chicago's defense ranked fifth in Adjusted Sack Rate on first down (7.8%), 13th on second down (6.9%), and 27th on third or fourth down (4.7%). . . . The Bears faced the most passes marked as Overthrown and the most passes marked as Thrown Behind. . . . Chicago grabbed a league-high 11 interceptions on passes on which the quarterback was hurried.

Passing

Player	DPAR	DVOA	Plys	NtYds	Avg	YAC	C%	TD	Int
Rex Grossman	4.0	-11.3%	479	3052	6.4	4.8	54.7%	23	20
Brian Griese	-4.3	-45.7%	32	198	6.2	5.7	56.3%	1	2

Rushing

Player	DPAR	DVOA	Plys	Yds	Avg	TD	Fum	Suc
Thomas Jones*	25.7	5.7%	296	1210	4.1	6	1	48%
Cedric Benson	17.9	15.1%	157	647	4.1	6	0	47%
Adrian Peterson	3.2	60.4%	10	41	4.1	2	0	43%
Jason McKie	-0.5	-32.8%	8	18	2.3	0	0	67%
Rex Grossman	1.2	15.8%	5	24	4.8	0	7	—

Receiving

Player	DPAR	DVOA	Plys	Ctch	Yds	Y/C	YAC	TD	C%
WR									
Muhsin Muhammad	12.9	1.5%	117	60	863	14.4	3.1	5	51%
Bernard Berrian	0.8	-13.9%	102	51	775	15.2	4.0	6	50%
Rashied Davis	-1.9	-20.1%	56	22	303	13.8	2.7	2	39%
Mark Bradley	7.7	37.4%	23	14	282	20.1	8.1	3	61%
Justin Gage*	-1.3	-38.8%	8	4	68	17.0	4.0	0	50%
TE									
Desmond Clark	15.5	16.5%	80	45	626	13.9	4.6	6	56%
John Gilmore	0.0	-12.6%	12	6	38	6.3	3.7	2	50%
Gabe Reid	-2.7	-58.6%	10	4	37	9.3	4.3	0	40%
RB									
Thomas Jones*	-6.2	-34.0%	47	36	154	4.3	6.5	0	66%
Jason McKie	-3.4	-25.2%	38	25	162	6.5	6.3	0	77%
Cedric Benson	1.0	8.2%	10	8	54	6.8	9.5	0	80%
Adrian Peterson	-0.7	-38.9%	6	6	85	14.2	12.2	0	100%

Offensive Line

Year	Yards	ALY	Rank	Power	Rank	10+ Yds	Rank	Stuff	Rank	Sack	ASR	Rank
2004	3.72	3.79	28	64%	15	14%	29	27%	24	66	11.9%	32
2005	4.41	4.12	15	55%	28	23%	4	26%	22	31	7.5%	21
2006	4.07	4.46	9	71%	7	12%	27	21%	6	25	4.6%	6

Year	LE	Rank	LT	Rank	Mid	Rank	RT	Rank	RE	Rank
2004	4.23	18	4.43	18	3.86	27	4.25	14	1.80	32
2005	4.00	19	4.33	16	4.28	12	4.06	19	3.21	26
2006	3.65	22	4.71	8	4.80	1	4.11	21	4.28	13

The most underappreciated factor in the Bears' Super Bowl run was a proficient offensive line that opened holes against eight-man fronts and kept a barrage of blitzers off of Rex Grossman. The Bears like to pound the ball up the middle, and that is where they run most effectively. Center Olin Kreutz is a physical player in the middle of the line who deserved Pro Bowl selection. Roberto Garza took over full-time at guard last year, pushing Terrence Metcalf to the bench in a move that made the line more athletic. The Bears looked for a replacement for guard Ruben Brown this past offseason, but decided to re-sign the 35-year-old to a one-year deal. Josh Beekman, a fourth-round pick out of Boston College, could push Brown for playing time this year and is expected to replace him in 2008. Tackle John Tait holds his own against speed rushers and excels in run blocking. Tait used to play on the right in Kansas City, but he has completely adjusted to the left tackle position in Chicago. The weak link is Fred Miller at right tackle. The aging veteran has never been particularly quick and, at this point in his career, is merely competent. This group remained healthy nearly all season; only Tait missed any starts. Depth is questionable behind the starters with Beekman and Metcalf solid inside options, but revolving door tackle John St. Clair as the top reserve on the outside.

Defensive Front Seven

Defensive Line	Age	Pos	Plys	TmPct	Rk	Stop	Dfts	StpRt	Rk	AvYd	Rk	Sack	Hit	Hur	Runs	RuStp	RuYd	Pass	PaStp	PaYd
Alex Brown	28	DE	52	6.4%	34	39	18	75%	53	0.7	14	7	8	10	40	68%	2.8	12	100%	-6.2
Adewale Ogunleye	30	DE	48	6.7%	27	40	18	83%	16	1.3	34	6.5	8	14	33	82%	2.4	15	87%	-1.1
Mark Anderson	24	DE	31	3.8%	74	28	19	90%	3	-2.6	1	12	1	4	13	92%	0.5	18	89%	-4.9
Ian Scott*	26	DT	30	3.9%	64	24	5	80%	31	1.8	35	0	1	2	19	74%	2.1	11	91%	1.5
Tommie Harris	24	DT	28	4.6%	52	24	12	86%	14	0.9	14	5	9	9	21	81%	2.0	7	100%	-2.6
Tank Johnson	26	DT	27	3.8%	67	23	9	85%	16	0.5	8	3.5	8	7	22	82%	1.3	5	100%	-2.8
Alfonso Boone*	31	DT	26	4.3%	59	20	7	77%	40	1.6	30	2	1	1	24	75%	2.3	2	100%	-6.5
Israel Idonije	27	DE	15	2.3%	—	11	4	73%	—	2.3	—	0	0	2	10	70%	2.4	5	80%	2.0
Anthony Adams	*27*	*DT*	*23*	*3.2%*	*—*	*16*	*7*	*70%*	*—*	*0.6*	*—*	*2*	*3*	*4*	*18*	*67%*	*2*	*5*	*80%*	*-4.4*

Linebackers	Age	Pos	Plys	TmPct	Rk	Stop	Dfts	StpRt	AvYd	Sack	Hit	Hur	Runs	RuStp	Rk	RuYd	Rk	Tgts	Suc%	Rk	PaYd	Rk
Brian Urlacher	29	ILB	152	18.7%	5	93	33	61%	4.5	0	10	6	87	72%	18	3.1	28	38	59%	24	5.9	29
Lance Briggs	27	OLB	143	17.6%	8	94	37	66%	5.4	1	1	10	74	77%	5	3.4	45	65	54%	37	5.5	23
Hunter Hillenmeyer	27	OLB	49	6.4%	—	30	9	61%	4.8	0	1	3	22	86%	—	1.4	—	18	60%	18	6.5	61

Year	Yards	ALY	Rank	Power	Rank	10+ Yds	Rank	Stuff	Rank	Sack	ASR	Rank
2004	4.40	3.90	5	63%	17	22%	28	32%	3	34	6.8%	18
2005	3.97	3.72	7	59%	11	20%	25	29%	4	40	7.3%	13
2006	4.21	3.85	4	63%	15	22%	28	29%	2	40	6.5%	16

Year	LE	Rank	LT	Rank	Mid	Rank	RT	Rank	RE	Rank
2004	4.03	12	4.28	13	3.84	5	3.67	4	3.63	14
2005	3.07	5	3.30	4	4.09	16	3.71	7	2.93	3
2006	4.09	16	3.52	7	3.99	5	4.18	17	3.09	6

The defense's decline after the injury to defensive tackle Tommie Harris makes what was widely considered one of the best front sevens in football look a little shakier. Rather than a group of very good players, the Bears have a few outstanding players and a number of others who are merely dependable. Harris and middle linebacker Brian Urlacher are indisputably outstanding football players. The Bears appear to think that Lance Briggs may benefit from playing next to Urlacher and are willing to let him leave after this season. Briggs certainly looks outstanding when the tape rolls. Against the run, he has the highest Stop Rate of any linebacker with at least 50 plays. Against the pass, Briggs is arguably the best coverage line-backer in football. To replace him, the Bears drafted Michael Okwo, a speedy linebacker out of Stanford. On the defensive line, Harris's backups Alfonso Boone and Ian Scott were allowed to leave. In their place, the Bears signed undersized tackle Anthony Adams from San Francisco, who should be a good addition in a one-gap system such as the Tampa-2. Second-year tackle Dusty Dvoraceck missed his rookie season with a foot injury, but is expected to contribute in 2007. Defensive tackle Tank Johnson and defensive ends Alex Brown and Adewale Ogunleye are the players who appeared to be merely dependable once the double-teams Harris demanded were no longer necessary. Brown, in particular, makes fewer plays than someone with his athleticism should make, although he remains a solid run defender. The Bears were helped immensely by defensive end Mark Anderson's unexpected emergence as a dominant pass rusher, and he should share time equally with Ogunleye and Brown this year. Second-round defensive end Dan Bazuin, like Anderson, is an under-sized pass rusher. Israel Idonije provides depth at both end and tackle.

Defensive Secondary

Secondary	Age	Pos	Plys	TmPct	Rk	Stop	Dfts	RuYd	Rk	RuStp	Rk	Tgts	Tgt%	Rk	Dist	Suc%	Rk	PaYd	Rk	PD	Int
Nathan Vasher	26	CB	56	7.9%	49	23	12	7.9	54	9%	79	88	20%	25	9.4	56%	18	5.7	4	5	3
Charles Tillman	26	CB	95	13.4%	4	42	19	4.5	13	52%	20	108	26%	2	12.5	61%	7	6.2	12	14	5
Ricky Manning	26	CB	56	7.3%	58	27	17	5.0	22	45%	35	63	14%	66	8.2	47%	63	9.1	70	11	5
Danieal Manning	25	FS	71	8.7%	57	16	10	16.3	80	10%	79	26	5%	73	18.4	68%	5	6.5	20	9	2
Chris Harris	25	FS	56	10.0%	39	25	7	5.3	17	57%	9	21	6%	57	17.8	50%	48	6.8	28	5	2
Devin Hester	25	CB	8	1.0%	—	1	1	9.0	—	0%	—	15	3%	—	11.3	46%	—	5.4	—	0	0
Todd Johnson*	29	SS	25	4.1%	—	10	4	5.2	—	36%	—	10	3%	—	14.9	67%	—	3.0	—	3	0
Mike Brown	29	SS	26	8.5%	—	13	4	4.8	—	64%	—	9	5%	—	8.2	53%	—	6.7	—	1	0

Year	Pass D Rank	DVOA vs. #1 WR	Rank	DVOA vs. #2 WR	Rank	DVOA vs. Other WR	Rank	DVOA vs. TE	Rank	DVOA vs. RB	Rank
2004	11	17.1%	23	-29.6%	1	-16.4%	10	-26.0%	4	-14.2%	7
2005	1	-6.3%	8	-8.4%	13	-51.7%	1	-35.6%	2	-17.9%	5
2006	2	-3.7%	14	-30.1%	3	-24.8%	5	-48.5%	1	-21.3%	6

Cornerbacks Nathan Vasher and Charles Tillman have very similar statistical profiles from our game-charting stats, but opposing teams clearly think Tillman is the weaker link. Tillman is the more physical corner, but he struggles at times against quicker receivers and will get beat deep. Vasher is more technically sound and more likely to keep the play in front of him. Nickel back Ricky Manning Jr. gets plenty of interceptions thanks to his gambling style, but he's really not very good. Fifth-round pick Corey Graham is an intriguing talent out of New Hampshire who could be the replacement for Vasher or Tillman down the line. The corners may be set, but safety is a different proposition. Mike Brown is excellent when on the field, but he has missed 28 games over the past three seasons and cannot be counted on to stay healthy. Danieal Manning, the second-round pick a year ago, played well, but, when he made a mistake, it went for big yardage—most notably when Reggie Wayne caught a 51-yard touchdown during the Super Bowl. Chris Harris, who showed such promise as a rookie, regressed badly last season and will struggle for playing time this year. The Bears traded a sixth-round pick for Adam Archuleta, who was terrible in Washington, but excelled for Lovie Smith when he coached him in St. Louis. Archuleta provides good insurance for Brown if he goes down again this year. Rookie Kevin Payne, a fifth-round pick from Louisiana-Monroe, is a big-hitter who provides depth.

Special Teams

Year	DVOA	Rank	FG/XP	Rank	Net Punt	Rank	Punt Ret	Rank	Net Kick	Rank	Kick Ret	Rank	Hidden	Rank
2004	1.9%	11	-7.6	30	14.1	1	9.5	4	-2.2	19	-2.7	17	12.6	2
2005	-2.6%	27	-12.0	32	-2.5	20	-2.3	19	5.2	10	-3.9	21	14.9	1
2006	7.6%	1	8.8	3	2.0	16	11.7	2	18.9	1	3.4	9	11.0	3

The Devin Hester hype-meter may get out of control this season. No recent kick returner has been able to consistently score touchdowns every single year, and Hester's six touchdown returns last season are already a record. Still, Hester is a spectacle to behold in the open field. Even if he is contained more often this season, his impact will be felt, as it was in the Super Bowl when the Colts squib-kicked for most of the game after Hester's opening return touchdown. The Bears also

(continued next page)

Special Teams (*continued*)

have exceptional coverage teams, a solid punter in Brad Maynard, and a good kicker in Robbie Gould. The special teams were historically good a season ago and should remain an asset this season as well. That said, Bears fans who expect Gould's massive improvement as a placekicker to hold in 2007 need to look at Neil Rackers's numbers for 2005 and 2006 (or the placekicking essay in the Arizona chapter).

Coaching Staff

Lovie Smith is an outstanding football coach. The linebackers he coached in Tampa Bay were excellent. The defenses he coached in St. Louis were very good. The team he now runs as a head coach made it to the Super Bowl. In the wake of that success, Smith let defensive coordinator Ron Rivera leave in a sign of philosophical differences between the head coach and defensive coordinator. Smith is more of a true believer in the Cover-2 scheme, while Rivera wanted to blitz more often. The Bears were forced out of their Cover-2 last season, particularly after the Harris injury limited the run defense. To replace Rivera, Smith promoted Bob Babich, a longtime college coach who moved to the NFL to work for Smith in St. Louis. The move signals Smith's complete control over the defense. Offensively, Ron Turner returns as the coordinator despite struggling last year to find the right balance between protecting Grossman and letting him play. The Bears were not afraid to let Grossman throw the ball in 2006, but were too concerned with running or throwing short passes on first down in order to keep Grossman out of second-and-long situations. If the offense sputters again this year, Chicago's failures may be blamed on Turner.

Dallas Cowboys

Let's just say not everybody was sad to see Bill Parcells retire. During a television interview, running back Julius Jones said the former Cowboys head coach had him "running like a robot" last season. Defensive end Marcus Spears, fearful of being labeled a bust after a so-so start to his career, accused the Tuna of misusing him in Dallas's version of the 3-4 defense.

Wade Phillips is now The Guy in Dallas, and in addition to implementing his version of the 3-4, he will also face potentially serious challenges on the other side of the ball. Specifically, a suspect offensive line and a quarterback who may or may not be over the team's wild-card round loss, one in which he played an instrumental role. There are also questions about Phillips, who is making his third run at being an NFL head coach, and whether he will be anything more than a "yes man" for owner Jerry Jones.

Wade Phillips started his NFL coaching career in 1976 with the Houston Oilers, working with the defensive line under his father, legendary head coach Bum Phillips. Since then, he has been a defensive coordinator six times, and twice a head coach before coming to Dallas. His most successful season came in 1999, when he led the Buffalo Bills to an 11–5 record. That accomplishment was overshadowed by an unpopular late-season change at quarterback. Phillips got the bright idea to bench Doug Flutie, who had started 15 games (and won ten of them), for Rob Johnson. The Bills promptly lost in the first round of the playoffs. Phillips would lose his job following the 2000 season, but, in retrospect, it's a miracle he wasn't fired the minute he thought Johnson could quarterback an NFL team.

Phillips has had much more success as a defensive coordinator. In his most recent gig, as coordinator in San Diego, Phillips took a unit that was 30th in defensive DVOA the season before he arrived and, within three years, molded it into one of the league's most feared defenses during last year's 14-2 run.

The Cowboys have featured the 3-4 defense since 2003, but a Wade Phillips 3-4 is different from a Bill Parcells 3-4. Under the Tuna, the Cowboys defensive ends were run stoppers first. In fact, the Cowboys ranked eighth against the run last year, but the pass defense struggled. That's where Phillips's version of the 3-4 comes in. Phillips will expect the defensive ends to focus on pressuring the quarterback and will create schemes to put them in position to do just that. Luis Castillo's success under Phillips in San Diego—he had seven sacks in 2006—has to be good news for Spears, who has been desperate to become more involved in the pass rush. Last season, the Chargers finished in the top third of the league against the pass, and much of that was a function of the front seven's ability to get to the quarterback (the linebackers accounted for 42 of the team's 61 sacks).

While struggling in 2006, the Dallas pass defense is poised for a turnaround this season. One reason is that Dallas's personnel are comparable to San Diego's. The Chargers have Shaun Phillips and Shawne Merriman at outside linebacker; the Cowboys have DeMarcus Ware and Greg Ellis (and first-round pick, Anthony Spencer, who is already drawing parallels to Merriman). At inside linebacker, Dallas's Bradie James and Akin Ayodele are upgrades over San Diego's Randall Godfrey and Stephen Cooper. The defensive line is what differentiates the two teams: The Chargers have arguably the best nose tackle in football in Jamal Williams, and he's flanked by Castillo and Igor Olshansky. The Cowboys' nose tackle, Jason Ferguson, is serviceable, but he doesn't control the line of scrimmage like Williams. Ends

---

COWBOYS PROSPECTUS

2006 Record: 9–7

DVOA Estimated Wins: 8.6 (11th)

Pythagorean Wins: 9.8 (7th)

DVOA: 9.7% total (10th), 7.8% weighted (10th)

Offense: 9.9% DVOA (8th)

Defense: −0.1% DVOA (16th)

Special Teams: −0.2% DVOA (20th)

Variance: 17.5% (9th)

2006: Tony Romo is the greatest thing since sliced bread.

2007: What if Tony Romo turns out to be the unwanted end-pieces of the sliced bread?

2007 Mean Projection: 6.4 wins

The Brohm Closet (0–4): 20%

Bad Team (5–6): 33%

Mediocre (7–8): 30%

Playoff Contender (9–10): 13%

Super Bowl Contender (11+): 4%

Projected Average Opponent: 2.7% DVOA (5th in NFL)

2007 Cowboys Schedule

Week	Opp	Week	Opp	Week	Opp
1	NYG	7	MIN	13	GB (Thu.)
2	at MIA	8	BYE	14	at DET
3	at CHI	9	at PHI	15	PHI
4	STL	10	at NYG	16	at CAR (Sat.)
5	at BUF (Mon.)	11	WAS	17	at WAS
6	NE	12	NYJ (Thu.)		

Spears and Chris Canty, meanwhile, came into the league with high expectations two years ago, but have yet to live up to them.

If San Diego's front seven gets a slight edge, Dallas makes up the difference in the secondary, which is the Chargers' biggest weakness. In Dallas, cornerback Terence Newman quietly had another productive season, and number-two cornerback Anthony Henry was functional. The Cowboys safeties are far superior in pass coverage compared to their counterparts in San Diego—as long as you are talking about the Cowboys safeties in 2007, not 2006. Roy Williams, often criticized as a liability in the passing game, ranked 21st in Success Rate out of 80 ranked safeties in 2006. Dallas has since added free-agent safety Ken Hamlin from Seattle, who ranked 17th. Hamlin should allow Williams to make more plays near the line of scrimmage and avoid the mistakes that plagued Keith Davis (12.2 yards per pass) and Pat Watkins (16.0 yards per pass) a year ago.

The Dallas defense will have to show improvement under Phillips to compensate for the potential problems facing the offense. Tony Romo may have caused a sensation in the metro area when he was handed the quarterback job midway through the season, but he remains a largely unknown quantity and will be playing behind an offensive line that raises concerns of its own. Then again, one of those concerns was quelled, at least in part, when Romo became the starter.

In 2005, the Cowboys offense ranked 28th in Adjusted Sack Rate. That offseason, the Cowboys jettisoned offensive tackles Torrin Tucker and Rob Pettiti—who combined for 16 blown blocks leading to sacks—and signed guard Kyle Kosier. That led to mild improvement, up to 23rd in Adjusted Sack Rate, but some of the blame for these poor blocking statistics should fall on the quarterback. No, not the guy who ended Dallas's season on a botched hold of a game-winning field-goal attempt, the guy who lost his job to that guy—that's right, the now-retired Drew Bledsoe.

As pointed out in the "Pregame Show" essay earlier in the book, Bledsoe was sacked once every 11.6 dropbacks, while the more mobile Romo was sacked once every 17.0

dropbacks, even though the Cowboys started the same five offensive linemen in all 16 games. Sack numbers, and even Adjusted Sack Rate, mask the fact that pass protection is heavily dependent on the passer who is being protected. Bledsoe's immobility exacerbated Dallas's leaky front five; Romo's elusiveness—at least compared to Bledsoe—masked some of its shortcomings. Nonetheless, 18 of the sacks the Cowboys' quarterbacks absorbed were directly attributable to blown blocks, so the offensive line isn't completely absolved of negligence.

Romo got a vote of confidence when Dallas owner Jerry Jones passed on Brady Quinn in the draft, though Jones admitted afterwards that the team did consider drafting Quinn. Interestingly, Cowboys fans were split on the idea of taking the former Notre Dame star, even though Romo is coming off a Pro Bowl season and is only 27 years old. Quinn is now in Cleveland and Romo, who is in the last year of his contract, will almost certainly get a raise. If Quinn emerges as a star in a few years, there is sure to be criticism. Not because Quinn is guaranteed to be a franchise quarterback, but because Romo may never be more than an adequate NFL starter.

Last season, Romo was a victim of his early success; he was picking up bad habits because *everything* he did worked. ESPN NFL analyst Ron Jaworski pointed out that, during the Cowboys' Week 13 victory over the Giants, Romo was missing open targets, forcing throws into tight coverage, and completing passes that had no business being completed. The Cowboys won anyway. Jaworski predicted that Romo had a bad game in his near future; the only question was if he would learn from it. A week later against the Saints, Romo finished 16-for-33 for 249 yards, with a touchdown and two interceptions. Based on how he played for the remainder of the season, he didn't seem to have learned from it.

There was so much attention paid to the way Chicago's Rex Grossman fell apart in the second half of last year that nobody noticed Tony Romo starting to fall apart as well. In his first six games, through the Thanksgiving blowout of Tampa Bay, Romo averaged 8.5 net yards per pass with a DVOA of 46.0%, totaling 12 touchdowns, and five interceptions. Beginning with that game against the Giants and through the rest of the regular season, Romo averaged 6.7 net yards per pass with a DVOA of –11.5%, while totaling six touchdowns, and eight interceptions. Romo also couldn't hold onto the ball; he fumbled six times over the last three weeks of the regular season. That presaged the great Romo blunder, the fumbled extra-point snap that cost Dallas its season in the Wild Card Game against Seattle.

Based on our similarity scores, the most similar quarterbacks to Romo at this stage in his career are Jim Kelly,

Scott Mitchell, Trent Green, Erik Kramer, and Shane Matthews. Certainly, it is encouraging when your starting quarterback is compared to Kelly, a Hall of Famer, and Green, who made multiple Pro Bowls—but it's important to note that Kelly and Romo are similar primarily because neither one took an NFL snap until the age of 26. Unlike Romo, however, Kelly wasn't carrying a clipboard; he was competing in the USFL. The remaining names on the list are certain to give nightmares to Jerry Jones, and those nightmares will feature Brady Quinn hoisting the Lombardi Trophy in front of Cleveland City Hall.

There are other reasons to expect a step backwards from the Dallas offense. Despite Sean Payton's success in New Orleans last season, offenses often start out slow when a new coordinator is installing a new system. The Cowboys' new offensive coordinator, Jason Garrett, is considered a rising star in the coaching ranks, but he's in his first year on the job in Dallas, which means an adjustment period for both players and coach. (On the upside, the Cowboys won't have to memorize a 700-page playbook like the rival Redskins did last year.) Dallas also has to deal with the law of third-down rebounds: Last year they ranked 13th in DVOA on first down, 11th on second down, but were second only to Indianapolis on third down. There's also the question of injuries, as in the total absence of them in 2006. Dallas started the same five offensive linemen for 16 straight games. The chances of that happening again are miniscule. Remember that it was an offensive line injury, to left tackle Flozell Adams, that started the downward slide of the 2005 Cowboys. Finally, there's the risk involved in starting two wide receivers over the age of 33; the fact that one of them is a crazy person multiplies that risk by some unimaginable exponent.

All of this put together tells us that, barring 17 weeks of near perfect, injury-free football, the Cowboys might take a few steps back in 2007. On the upside, Dallas could be in position to take the next quarterback who is cursed to fall down the draft board because we named our 0–4 win category after him. Brian Brohm, anyone? Anyone?

Ryan Wilson

Adding an Offensive Lineman

Last year saw the free-agent market for offensive linemen explode. What seemed like silly money for Steve Hutchinson in 2005 was given out to inconsistent guards such as Derrick Dockery in 2006. One explanation is that the struggles of Oakland tackle Robert Gallery and former Buffalo tackle Mike Williams have helped to invalidate the long-held belief that highly-drafted linemen were sure things. The Dallas Cowboys were one team that perceived free agency as the safer bet, handing a $49.6-million deal with over $18 million guaranteed to former Arizona first-round pick Leonard Davis this offseason, even though they may switch him from tackle to guard. While we won't be able to judge Davis's impact on the Dallas offensive line until he lines up, what we can do is look at the past and determine whether it's more effective to draft an offensive lineman in the first round or acquire a veteran instead.

From 1997 through 2005, 34 offensive linemen were chosen in the first round of the draft, and 82 starting offensive linemen changed teams in the offseason via a trade or through free agency. For each transaction, we compared the acquiring team's rushing DVOA, Adjusted Line Yards, and Adjusted Sack Rate for the year before the transaction to its average performance in the two years afterwards. To attempt to isolate the value of adding a player, we also tracked a control team for each statistic for each of the 116 transactions. The control team was the team with the most similar rushing DVOA, Adjusted Line Yards, or Adjusted Sack Rate to the acquiring team in the season before the acquisition that did not add a new offensive lineman in either of the two following years.

Drafting a Offensive Lineman

Those 34 teams did not benefit, at least in the short term, from drafting a first-rounder (table 1). On average, the teams saw their rushing DVOA and Adjusted Line Yards decline very slightly, while their buddies who didn't add an offensive lineman had even more slightly improved ground games. The trend was reversed in pass protection with Adjusted Sack Rate, but it's clear that these teams are not improving their offensive line play within two years of their selection.

The two most extreme cases are worth noting. The biggest drop in rushing DVOA came after the 49ers drafted tackle Kwame Harris, while the most successful pick was Raiders tackle/guard Matt Stinchcomb. While Harris has no doubt struggled over the course of his NFL career to date, most of the drop in San Francisco's rushing attack

Table 1. Effects of Drafting an Offensive Lineman

Type	Year 0	Year 1	Year 2	Avg	Diff	Match %
Rushing DVOA	−4.2%	−5.9%	−6.2%	−6.1%	−1.9%	
Control	−4.4%	−5.6%	−2.4%	−4.0%	+0.4%	79%
Adjusted Line Yards	4.04	3.98	4.03	4.01	−.03	
Control	4.06	4.03	4.15	4.09	+.03	68%
Adjusted Sack Rate	7.13%	7.27%	6.84%	7.06%	−.08%	
Control	7.32%	7.45%	7.53%	7.49%	+.17%	58%

NOTE: **Avg** is the average of Years 1 and 2, the two seasons after adding the new lineman; **Diff** is the difference between Year 0, the year before adding the new lineman, and **Avg**; **Match%** notes the percentage of control teams that saw their performance head in the same direction as the variable team, regardless of whether it was an improvement or a decline.

Table 2. Effects of Adding a Veteran Offensive Lineman

Type	Year 0	Year 1	Year 2	Avg	Diff	Match %
Rushing DVOA	−7.9%	−6.2%	−4.2%	−5.2%	+2.7%	
Control	−7.8%	−3.4%	−4.4%	−3.9%	+3.9%	56%
Adjusted Line Yards	3.93	4.01	4.10	4.05	+.12	
Control	3.93	4.10	4.08	4.09	+.16	70%
Adjusted Sack Rate	7.30%	6.95%	6.73%	6.84%	−.46%	
Control	7.31%	6.82%	6.74%	6.78%	−.53%	64%

was due to the salary cap constraints that cost the 49ers most of their team and, eventually, led to the hiring of Mike Nolan. Meanwhile, Stinchcomb arrived shortly after Jon Gruden and Rich Gannon. The resulting schematic change had much more to do with the Raiders' success than adding an effective but injury-prone first-round lineman.

Acquiring a Veteran Starting Offensive Lineman

Signing a free agent or trading for a older offensive lineman (table 2) proved to be a much more fruitful expenditure. Across the board, adding a veteran led to a better rushing attack and fewer sacks, in each of the two years following the signing.

What's also interesting, though, is that the control group in all sets almost always outperforms the group of teams actively trying to improve by acquiring an offensive lineman. This matches our research on offensive line continuity in the Cleveland Browns chapter, which says that teams that keep their lines together outperform those who shuffle things around.

The tackle/guard split in rushing DVOA shows that adding a tackle isn't always an effective move. Of the 47 centers and guards who changed hands, 27 saw their new teams' rushing DVOA improve. Thirty six teams added new tackles, but only 16 teams saw improvement. This could be because elite tackles such as Orlando Pace and Walter Jones

rarely hit the market, and teams are left filling gaps with tackles who don't really represent a significant upgrade on what they already have. The only truly elite tackle who changed hands in this timeframe was Willie Roaf, who left New Orleans for a third-round pick after disagreements with management and proceeded to help Kansas City's rushing DVOA rise by 12.4%.

As with the biggest gain among teams drafting linemen, the biggest gain among teams adding a veteran had little to do with the lineman himself. Adam Timmerman, a very solid offensive lineman by all regards, left Green Bay after 1998 to join the Rams. His arrival in St. Louis in 1999 coincided with the rise of the Greatest Show on Turf, as Marshall Faulk and Kurt Warner dominated defenses across the league. Did Timmerman help? Surely. Warner needed time to throw, and Timmerman was the best interior lineman the Rams had that season. Was he even one of the biggest reasons why the Rams offense improved dramatically in 1999? Surely not.

Adding an offensive lineman, whether through the draft, via free agency, or a trade, is by no means a sure bet to immediately improving a rushing attack. Instead, the solution appears to be schematic and/or coaching-related. In fact, of the top-ten single-season improvements in rushing DVOA from 1997 to 2005, six of them involved a new offensive coordinator in his first season with the team, and two others involved an offensive coordinator in his second season. For a team that needs to improve its rushing attack, the solution might not be to draft an offensive lineman, but rather to sack an offensive coordinator.

Bill Barnwell

Cowboys 2006 Stats by Week

Wk	vs.	W–L	PF	PA	YDF	YDA	TO	DVOA Total	Off	Def	ST
1	JAC	L	17	24	323	307	-2	-9.5%	2.6%	4.3%	-7.8%
2	WAS	W	27	10	367	245	0	30.4%	3.6%	-39.1%	-12.3%
3	BYE										
4	@TEN	W	45	14	396	229	+2	87.3%	53.8%	-31.2%	2.4%
5	@PHI	L	24	38	369	406	-3	-31.5%	-29.6%	-5.2%	-7.1%
6	HOU	W	34	6	354	232	+3	46.9%	12.6%	-28.7%	5.6%
7	NYG	L	22	36	379	328	-2	-32.7%	-28.3%	5.1%	0.8%
8	@CAR	W	35	14	414	204	+2	46.8%	35.2%	3.6%	15.2%
9	@WAS	L	19	22	378	300	+1	-11.9%	16.6%	11.8%	-16.6%
10	@ARI	W	27	10	434	295	+3	50.0%	27.5%	-16.8%	5.8%
11	IND	W	21	14	342	335	+2	65.1%	11.5%	-64.1%	-10.5%
12	TB	W	38	10	435	211	+2	56.8%	58.1%	5.3%	3.9%
13	@NYG	W	23	20	365	396	-1	-5.2%	17.7%	26.1%	3.2%
14	NO	L	17	42	347	536	-2	-56.2%	1.4%	59.7%	2.1%
15	@ATL	W	38	28	352	376	+1	1.2%	13.9%	16.3%	3.5%
16	PHI	L	7	23	201	426	-2	-33.0%	-20.5%	10.5%	-1.9%
17	DET	L	31	39	365	362	-3	-23.2%	-8.6%	24.7%	10.0%
18	@SEA	L	20	21	284	332	+1	2.5%	-16.6%	0.0%	19.1%

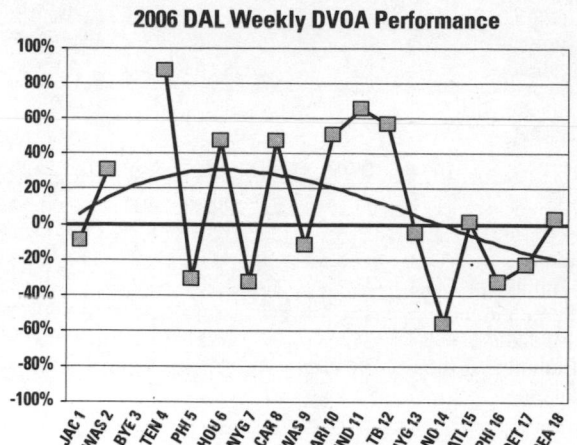

2006 DAL Weekly DVOA Performance

Trends and Splits

	Offense	Rank	Defense	Rank
Total DVOA	9.9%	8	-0.1%	16
Unadjusted VOA	13.9%	4	3.6%	21
Weighted Trend	11.8%	8	5.5%	18
Variance	6.2%	17	8.2%	7
Passing	14.0%	9	8.3%	24
Rushing	5.7%	7	-9.3%	8
First Down	1.9%	13	12.8%	30
Second Down	5.0%	11	-17.3%	4
Third Down	33.6%	2	2.6%	15
Red Zone	7.5%	12	10.8%	23
Late and Close	12.1%	7	9.9%	24

Five-Year Performance

	2006	2005	2004	2003	2002
W-L	9-7	9-7	6-10	10-6	5-11
Pythagorean Wins	9.8	8.5	5.1	9.0	4.3
Estimated Wins	8.6	8.2	6.6	8.2	5.2
Total DVOA	9.7%	1.7%	-14.3%	4.2%	-25.6%
Rank	10	15	24	14	28
Offense	9.9%	-3.0%	-2.8%	-8.6%	-22.6%
Rank	8	14	17	21	30
Defense	-0.1%	-5.4%	12.8%	-13.7%	0.6%
Rank	16	13	25	6	16
Special Teams	-0.2%	-0.7%	1.3%	-0.8%	-2.4%
Rank	20	22	13	21	22

Strategic Tendencies

Formations		Rank	Run/Pass		Rank	Defense		Rank	Other		Rank
3+ WR	41%	25	Runs, all plays	45%	14	Sacks by LB	61%	3	Run with 2+ RB	67%	10
4+ WR	11%	15	Runs, first half	42%	22	Sacks by DB	0%	30	Run with 2+ TE	22%	27
2+ TE	21%	26	Runs, first down	58%	8	Rush 6+	12.0%	6	Play action	21%	10
Single back	48%	21	Runs, power sit.	63%	17	Rush 7+	3.8%	4	Go for it on 4th	1.51	1
Empty back	4.8%	4	Runs, behind 2H	33%	16	Rush 3	2.6%	25	Offensive Pace	30.0	11
Max protect	12%	17	Pass, ahead 2H	35%	26	CB1 on WR1	41%	18	Defensive Pace	30.6	14

Since 1996, the only head coach more aggressive on fourth down than Bill Parcells was Bill Belichick. During his three years in Buffalo, incoming head coach Wade Phillips was league-average in taking risks on fourth down.... On first down, Dallas lined up with the standard two wide receivers more often than any other team, and the Dallas defense faced the standard two wide receivers more often than any other team.... Including both running and passing, Dallas posted a positive DVOA in all formations except for four-wide sets.... Has T.O. stopped complaining about getting the ball yet? Only four wide receivers were thrown a higher percentage of their team's passes in 2006 than Owens's 27 percent. Owens also led the league in dropped passes.... The Dallas defense saw the second most play-action fakes in the NFL, tied with Tennessee and trailing only the Giants.

Passing

Player	DPAR	DVOA	Plys	NtYds	Avg	YAC	C%	TD	Int
Tony Romo	50.9	19.8%	337	2761	8.2	4.5	65.3%	19	13
Drew Bledsoe*	-7.5	-23.1%	169	1066	6.3	5.4	53.3%	7	8
Brad Johnson	*1.7*	*-12.3%*	*436*	*2559*	*5.9*	*4.9*	*61.9%*	*9*	*15*

Rushing

Player	DPAR	DVOA	Plys	Yds	Avg	TD	Fum	Suc
Julius Jones	14.0	-1.6%	267	1084	4.1	4	1	45%
Marion Barber	30.9	35.9%	135	654	4.8	14	0	56%
Tony Romo	0.1	-17.8%	21	109	5.2	0	8	—
Tyson Thompson	-1.8	-46.1%	13	30	2.3	1	0	13%
Lousaka Polite	-0.6	-41.0%	7	18	2.6	0	0	38%
Drew Bledsoe*	0.4	-4.5%	7	29	4.1	2	3	—
Terry Glenn	-0.5	-56.9%	3	11	3.7	0	0	—
Brad Johnson	*-0.3*	*-18.9%*	*21*	*83*	*4.0*	*1*	*9*	*—*

Receiving

Player	DPAR	DVOA	Plys	Ctch	Yds	Y/C	YAC	TD	C%
WR									
Terrell Owens	27.3	12.1%	152	85	1180	13.9	4.3	13	56%
Terry Glenn	25.9	19.1%	111	70	1047	15.0	3.7	6	63%
Patrick Crayton	16.5	37.3%	48	36	519	14.4	5.2	4	75%
Sam Hurd	0.2	-12.7%	11	5	75	15.0	2.6	0	45%
TE									
Jason Witten	18.2	20.1%	91	64	754	11.8	4.0	1	70%
Anthony Fasano	-1.2	-21.6%	24	14	126	9.0	4.1	0	58%
RB									
Marion Barber	5.2	27.4%	32	23	196	8.5	6.8	2	72%
Julius Jones	5.7	63.6%	15	9	142	15.8	16.3	0	60%
Lousaka Polite	-1.7	-43.9%	8	2	21	10.5	6.0	0	25%

Offensive Line

Year	Yards	ALY	Rank	Power	Rank	10+ Yds	Rank	Stuff	Rank	Sack	ASR	Rank
2004	3.99	3.99	24	56%	25	16%	20	29%	28	37	6.8%	16
2005	3.76	3.87	23	60%	23	14%	19	25%	17	52	9.5%	28
2006	4.21	4.47	8	63%	17	15%	20	23%	11	37	7.9%	25

Year	LE	Rank	LT	Rank	Mid	Rank	RT	Rank	RE	Rank
2004	5.47	1	4.75	9	3.62	31	3.72	27	2.93	29
2005	3.32	27	3.61	27	4.34	11	4.08	17	3.13	29
2006	3.66	21	5.57	1	4.37	16	4.12	20	4.78	7

In 2006, the Cowboys were a much-improved run-blocking team, but their pass blocking remained suspect. With that in mind, the club signed free-agent Leonard Davis in March. We're not so sure that will help. With Arizona last year, Davis was responsible for eight Blown Blocks that led to sacks—tied for third most in the league. In 2005, Davis led the NFL with 12 false start flags and was second behind Rams tackle Alex Barron with eight in 2006. Dallas will move Davis from left tackle to right guard, which should mitigate some of the concerns about his inability to operate in space, but it won't make him any less fidgety.

Davis will replace Marco Rivera, who played the last two seasons with a balky back, but the Cowboys' other four starting offensive linemen will return. Andre Gurode turned in a Pro Bowl effort after the club made him strictly a center last year (he played both center and guard in previous seasons). Guard Kyle Kosier replaced Larry Allen last year, and their styles couldn't be more different. Allen was known for mauling defenders; Kosier relies on athleticism and excels in the run game in which he can use his quickness to get to the second-level defenders. Against the pass, Kosier and left tackle Flozell Adams struggled to protect the quarterback's blind side at times and were inconsistent against elite pass rushers, even when double-teaming them.

Defensive Front Seven

Defensive Line	Age	Pos	Plys	TmPct	Rk	Stop	Dfts	StpRt	Rk	AvYd	Rk	Sack	Hit	Hur	Runs	RuStp	RuYd	Pass	PaStp	PaYd
Marcus Spears	24	DE	48	6.1%	39	32	3	67%	73	2.7	70	1	2	6	43	65%	2.9	5	80%	0.8
Jason Ferguson	33	DT	47	6.0%	21	35	5	74%	47	2.4	53	0	1	3	46	74%	2.5	1	100%	0.0
Chris Canty	25	DE	34	4.3%	66	27	7	79%	30	1.7	45	1	3	4	30	80%	2.0	4	75%	-0.8
Kenyon Coleman*	28	DE	33	4.2%	69	24	7	73%	57	2.1	58	4	1	3	24	67%	3.0	9	89%	-0.1
Jay Ratliff	26	DE	21	2.8%	—	17	10	81%	—	0.4	—	4	3	5	14	71%	2.9	7	100%	-4.6
Jason Hatcher	25	DE	15	2.2%	—	13	5	87%	—	0.4	—	2.5	0	4	12	83%	2.8	3	100%	-9.3

Linebackers	Age	Pos	Plys	TmPct	Rk	Stop	Dfts	StpRt	AvYd	Sack	Hit	Hur	Runs	RuStp	Rk	RuYd	Rk	Tgts	Suc%	Rk	PaYd	Rk
Bradie James	26	ILB	112	14.2%	28	53	17	47%	5.3	0	0	4	57	56%	79	3.5	55	47	59%	25	6.4	57
Akin Ayodele	28	ILB	85	10.8%	65	53	14	62%	4.9	1	2	2	53	75%	8	3.3	41	23	60%	19	6.3	53
DeMarcus Ware	25	OLB	80	10.2%	70	59	27	74%	2.0	11.5	11	25	47	72%	19	2.9	21	13	74%	—	3.6	—
Greg Ellis	32	OLB	34	7.7%	—	28	10	82%	1.0	4.5	4	17	22	82%	—	2.4	—	8	38%	—	5.1	—
Kevin Burnett	25	OLB	26	3.3%	—	10	7	38%	6.6	1	0	1	7	71%	—	4.6	—	21	43%	74	9.4	96
Al Singleton	32	OLB	22	2.8%	—	13	2	59%	2.8	1	0	1	18	61%	—	2.7	—	5	60%	—	3.6	—

Year	Yards	ALY	Rank	Power	Rank	10+ Yds	Rank	Stuff	Rank	Sack	ASR	Rank
2004	4.16	4.46	26	61%	13	17%	17	22%	25	33	6.3%	24
2005	4.16	4.63	30	74%	27	12%	3	24%	22	39	8.1%	5
2006	3.81	4.37	20	60%	10	11%	3	21%	22	34	7.2%	12

Year	LE	Rank	LT	Rank	Mid	Rank	RT	Rank	RE	Rank
2004	4.90	28	4.60	24	4.33	21	4.28	20	4.51	26
2005	4.49	23	4.21	16	4.58	30	5.47	31	4.72	23
2006	5.42	31	4.22	14	4.11	10	4.87	29	3.98	14

Last year, Greg Ellis moved from defensive end to linebacker. The transition wasn't easy for the ten-year veteran, and tearing his Achilles in Week 10 didn't help. It's unclear if Ellis will ever make his way back into the starting lineup. For the second year in a row, the Cowboys used a first-round pick on an outside linebacker, taking Purdue's Anthony Spencer. Spencer is an exciting player and a natural pass rusher, but he will need to improve his coverage skills. That Dallas drafted him raises questions about the team's 2005 first-round pick, outside linebacker Bobby Carpenter. Last year, Carpenter was a man without a position—the club moved him to inside linebacker in training camp, he barely played at the start of the season, and he eventually saw time at every linebacker position. After Ellis's injury, Carpenter showed flashes of potential, but since he is not a true pass rusher, he might be better suited to playing inside in Wade Phillips's 3-4 defense.

Outside linebacker DeMarcus Ware is an amazing talent still learning the nuances of the position after coming to the Cowboys as an undersized and unbelievably quick defensive end. He registered 11.5 sacks last season and proved that he can run with tight ends in passing situations. Safety Roy Williams gets most of the recognition, but Ware is the heart of this defense. Big things were expected of inside linebacker Bradie James after he signed a long-term deal prior to last season, but 2006 was a disappointment. He often looked lost in pass coverage and could eventually be replaced by Carpenter. The other inside linebacker, Akin Ayodele, was a free-agent signing who moved from an outside position in Jacksonville's 4-3 scheme. He had a very underrated season in his first year in Dallas and should improve further in new defensive coordinator Brian Stewart's system. The defensive line's success will depend largely on nose tackle Jason Ferguson. If he can draw double teams, defensive ends Marcus Spears and Chris Canty, as well as the outside linebackers, will have an easier time getting to the quarterback.

Defensive Secondary

Secondary	Age	Pos	Plys	TmPct	Rk	Stop	Dfts	RuYd	Rk	RuStp	Rk	Tgts	Tgt%	Rk	Dist	Suc%	Rk	PaYd	Rk	PD	Int
Terence Newman	29	CB	72	9.1%	41	23	8	6.0	29	38%	49	68	16%	50	13.4	55%	21	8.3	59	10	1
Anthony Henry	31	CB	102	12.9%	6	37	14	8.4	56	24%	72	110	26%	3	11.6	51%	43	6.5	19	22	2
Roy Williams	27	SS	72	9.1%	50	30	13	5.4	18	47%	29	52	11%	4	15.8	59%	21	8.8	50	9	5
Aaron Glenn	35	CB	29	3.7%	—	11	8	0.0	—	0%	—	35	8%	—	10.4	52%	—	6.9	—	6	1
Pat Watkins	25	FS	43	6.2%	69	15	6	7.9	60	26%	69	19	4%	74	20.8	52%	45	16.0	80	6	3
Tony Parrish	32	SS	18	3.7%	—	5	2	10.0	—	18%	—	9	3%	—	6.6	24%	—	8.6	—	0	0
Keith Davis	29	FS	18	2.4%	—	0	0	6.7	—	0%	—	8	2%	—	14.2	31%	—	12.2	—	0	0
Ken Hamlin	26	FS	107	13.3%	8	44	14	8.1	63	45%	35	48	9%	19	13.7	62%	17	6.5	22	9	3

Year	Pass D Rank	DVOA vs. #1 WR	Rank	DVOA vs. #2 WR	Rank	DVOA vs. Other WR	Rank	DVOA vs. TE	Rank	DVOA vs. RB	Rank
2004	26	20.4%	25	33.1%	30	-20.9%	5	10.5%	19	0.8%	16
2005	7	11.9%	19	-59.8%	1	-23.5%	4	37.5%	31	-7.1%	11
2006	24	1.5%	17	9.0%	19	37.2%	32	-5.4%	15	6.2%	19

Cornerback Terence Newman enters the last year of his rookie contract. He would leave a gaping hole in the secondary if he didn't return in 2008. Newman only had one interception in 2006, but that's not an indictment on his ball skills; teams threw away from him, preferring to target the other cornerback, Anthony Henry. Throwing at Henry isn't picking on a

(continued next page)

Defensive Secondary (continued)

weakling, however; Henry had good charting numbers and ranked second behind New England's Asante Samuel in passes defensed.

Strong safety Roy Williams's pass-coverage deficiencies have been somewhat exaggerated, and he continues to be excellent against the run. During offseason minicamp, the Cowboys even experimented with using him as a linebacker in a nickel package. The problem in Dallas was not Williams, but that the Cowboys teamed Williams with two players who duplicate his skill set, veteran Keith Davis and rookie Pat Watkins. Watkins's failures were very noticeable in Week 5, as he gave up two touchdowns when left in one-on-one coverage with Philadelphia receivers. Given that pre-draft scouting reports had Watkins as a "safety/linebacker tweener," he never should have been in that position in the first place. free-agent signing Ken Hamlin has a skill set much more suited for pass coverage, although the front office is clearly not sold on him, having offered the former Seattle starter a mere one-year contract. If the team lets Hamlin walk after the season, critics will wonder why the Cowboys didn't address this need during the 2007 draft, when quality safeties littered the draft board.

Special Teams

Year	DVOA	Rank	FG/XP	Rank	Net Punt	Rank	Punt Ret	Rank	Net Kick	Rank	Kick Ret	Rank	Hidden	Rank
2004	1.3%	13	-1.8	20	-2.7	24	0.4	15	17.3	1	-5.3	24	-12.1	30
2005	-0.7%	22	-9.4	31	5.7	7	-7.3	32	4.8	11	1.8	15	-6.6	24
2006	-0.2%	20	-7.3	30	-2.8	22	1.8	11	6.5	9	0.5	13	-3.3	19

Mike Vanderjagt didn't even make it out of November. After signing a three-year deal, the most accurate kicker in NFL history was jettisoned in favor of Martin Gramatica (ouch). Gramatica proved to be an upgrade, but the season wasn't decided by a missed field goal; instead, it was a botched hold. Go figure. Gramatica will be challenged in camp by sixth-round pick Nicholas Folk from Arizona. Punter Mat McBriar had his best season as a professional, averaging 48 yards per punt, but he is sometimes too good, out-kicking his coverage. Both return teams were adequate, but nothing spectacular, with a mix of players taking turns: Terence Newman and Patrick Crayton on punts, Miles Austin and Tyson Thompson on kickoffs. Second-year reserve defensive back Abram Elam may also see some time returning kicks and punts in 2007.

Coaching Staff

Last year we wrote that 2006 might be Bill Parcells's last season, as he had lost his two most trusted assistants to other gigs, and it was. As Jerry Jones conducted the job search, an odd thing happened: He named Jason Garrett the offensive coordinator before naming Wade Phillips the head coach days later. Usually, one of the perks of being a head coach is that you get to put together your staff. Not in Dallas, apparently. Joining Garrett is defensive coordinator Brian Stewart. Stewart, who originally got into coaching through the NFL's Minority Coaching Fellowship Program, was the Chargers' secondary coach under Phillips, and is familiar with the 3-4 scheme. Other than Phillips, assistant head coach Tony Sparano might have the most important job. Sparano, who has been with the team for five seasons, handles the offensive line, a unit that will play a large part in Dallas's success or failure in 2007.

Detroit Lions

Matt Millen the executive will be remembered for two things: his complete ineptitude and his fetish for first-round wide receivers. The easy punch lines surrounding the latter sometimes obscure the magnitude of the former. Millen has overseen one of the worst teams in modern NFL history and somehow remains employed. The development of a powerful passing attack dominates his thinking to the point of obsession. He may finally have the quality passing attack he has always wanted, but years of poor personnel decisions have created a team so devoid of talent elsewhere that it would take a miracle worker to turn it around. Second-overall pick Calvin Johnson may be a great player, but he won't be working any miracles with the 2007 Lions.

In most situations, the best early-round draft strategy is to take the best player available. Injuries are too common and NFL careers too short to go after needs at the top of the draft. In that sense, each of Millen's four top-ten picks spent on wide receivers is justifiable. Hindsight is 20/20, but the Lions took each player in a draft position that matched conventional wisdom at the time. Not a single pick was a "reach" in that each was considered a top prospect. Still, the top-ten is a dangerous place to pick, as it is rife with draft busts that all the draftniks in the world were convinced would succeed. Quite simply, a quality GM is able to differentiate between Peyton Manning and Ryan Leaf, and Millen all too often finds the Leafs. Charles Rogers and Mike Williams, the Lions' top picks in the 2003 and 2005 drafts, both had red flags out of college, but Millen was wowed by their upside. Rogers had a positive drug test at the combine, while Williams had slow timed speed and had sat out a year before the draft. The problem was not the choice to draft wide receivers; the Lions never

had an overabundance of those. The problem was that Millen twice chose receivers who were colossal busts.

Millen's draft decisions were further hampered by a clear fixation on the receiver position. The Lions have drafted in the top ten for each of the past six drafts, and they have taken four wide receivers, one quarterback, and one linebacker. A total of ten receivers have been drafted in the first ten picks during this time. So, while Millen has used four out of six picks on receivers, the other teams in the top ten have used only six out of 54 picks on receivers. Among those other 54 picks have been nine quarterbacks, eight offensive tackles, seven cornerbacks and six defensive tackles.

Maybe it is an amazing coincidence that Millen was drafting the best player available, and four times it happened to be a wide receiver. More likely, Millen has chased these explosive "playmakers" at the top of the draft and overvalued their ability.

This explanation is buttressed by the amount of time and expense Millen has put into the offensive passing attack. His coaching hires have all hinted at his desire for explosive offense. First came Marty Mornhinweg, a disciple of the West Coast offense and supposed passing game guru. After Marty appeared to be overwhelmed by his head coaching role, he was tossed aside for his mentor Steve Mariucci. Three lackluster offensive years later, Millen finally hired a "defensive" coach in Rod Marinelli. That hire was more about attitude and leadership than defensive scheming, and Millen quickly threw out big money to lure in Mike Martz as the offensive coordinator. Nobody signifies explosive passing attacks like Martz.

To help these coaches out, Millen has consistently sought out what he considers to be explosive wide

---

LIONS PROSPECTUS

2006 Record: 3–13

DVOA Estimated Wins: 5.6 (29th)

Pythagorean Wins: 5.6 (27th)

DVOA: −20.6% total (29th), −17.6% weighted (29th)

Offense: −9.2% DVOA (25th)

Defense: 14.2% DVOA (30th)

Special Teams: 2.8% DVOA (6th)

Variance: 8.1% (31st)

2006: New coaching staff, same Matt Millen.

2007: Holes on the offensive and defensive lines will not be filled by wide receiver Calvin Johnson.

2007 Mean Projection: 7.1 wins

The Brohm Closet (0–4): 13%

Bad Team (5–6): 27%

Mediocre (7–8): 32%

Playoff Contender (9–10): 22%

Super Bowl Contender (11+): 6%

Projected Average Opponent: −2.3% DVOA (24th in NFL)

2007 Lions Schedule

Week	Opp	Week	Opp	Week	Opp
1	at OAK	7	TB	13	at MIN
2	MIN	8	at CHI	14	DAL
3	at PHI	9	DEN	15	at SD
4	CHI	10	at ARI	16	KC
5	at WAS	11	NYG	17	at GB
6	BYE	12	GB (Thu.)		

receivers. Millen acquired a team in transition in 2001. Two years before he was hired, the Lions featured twin 1,000-yard receivers in Germane Crowell and Johnnie Morton, as well as an aging Herman Moore. Moore and Crowell suffered major injuries in Millen's first season, and the Lions finished 2–14 despite 1,154 yards from Morton.

Millen responded by cutting Morton for salary cap space, drafting Charles Rogers, and signing Bill Schroeder and Az Hakim to big-money free-agent contracts. Rogers is arguably the biggest draft bust in NFL history, as he never showed an ability to separate from NFL-caliber cornerbacks, had constant injury problems, and eventually was suspended for repeated positive drug tests. The injuries were bad luck beyond Millen's control, but the very next selection in that year's draft was Andre Johnson, who went on to become a Pro Bowl receiver for Houston. Millen and his staff failed to notice that Rogers lacked precise route-running skills and willfully ignored the drug problems. Schroeder and Hakim were both bitter disappointments. The three combined for just 225 catches in a total of eight seasons on the Lions roster. The next two years saw the selection of the two Williamses, Roy and Mike. Roy has emerged as a star player, but Mike was shipped out after two years in a draft-day trade with the Raiders. Despite the two big free-agent contracts and the three top-ten picks, Roy Williams ended the 2005 season starting across from the eminently forgettable Scottie Vines.

The 2006 season saw the first glimpse of a dynamic passing game. Roy Williams took the proverbial next step, and one-time Rams safety Mike Furrey turned out to be a hidden gem once he switched back to offense. The result may have been promising, but the various roster machinations that it took to get there highlight Millen's incompetence.

The Lions broke camp with the two Williamses, Furrey, Corey Bradford, Shaun Bodiford, Devale Ellis, and Eddie Drummond active. Bradford, signed away from Houston as a free agent, was the opening-day starter opposite Roy Williams. After Week 1, the Lions once again signed the available Hakim and shipped Ellis back to the practice squad. Bradford struggled early, dropping a few passes, and was released after Week 3. On October 18, the Lions tried to slip Bodiford through waivers to the practice squad, but he was scooped up by Green Bay. Nine days later, they released Hakim and gave Kevin Kasper a chance. A few weeks later, Kasper was released, and the Lions re-signed Bradford. During all this roster movement, Martz was goofing around with backup quarterback Josh McCown as a slot receiver. McCown had more receptions than Mike Williams until Week 15.

The selection of a team's sixth receiver is not exactly a general manager's most important task, but this complete chaos is telling. Millen seemed more intent on appeasing Martz's fancy than looking out for the long-term interests of the team. If your team is floundering, why are you letting an unproven but intriguing talent such as Bodiford go to acquire has-beens and never-weres such as Hakim and Kasper? If Bradford is not good enough to be on the team after Week 3, why bother re-signing him before Week 10 to take playing time away from Mike Williams or rookie Devale Ellis?

Despite these troubles, Roy Williams and Furrey proved to be two of the rare productive players the Lions have had under Millen. The two combined for the third highest DPAR among receiver tandems in 2006. Millen deserves full credit for Williams, but Furrey was a complete accident. The Lions had stockpiled a gaggle of players who once played for Mike Martz. Nobody expected this sort of output from Furrey. Martz himself never had Furrey above sixth on the depth chart in St. Louis until he switched him from wide receiver to safety and made him a starter on defense. The acquisitions of Hakim, Arlen Harris, and Lamar Gordon, all former Rams, did not pay equal dividends.

Despite this impressive output by his receivers, Millen's team still stumbled to a 3–13 record thanks to the league's worst rushing attack and third worst defense. Such pitiful results can hardly be a surprise when so little is invested in areas outside the passing game, a lesson Millen should have finally learned in 2006, but likely didn't.

The running game struggled due to what is perhaps the league's most incompetent offensive line. Left tackle Jeff Backus and center Dominic Raiola were Millen's first two draft picks in 2000 and 2001 and have been fixtures of mediocrity ever since—which actually makes them the bright spots on this line. The Lions have not taken an offensive lineman on the first day of the draft since taking Raiola in the second round. This strategy has left them desperate to fill holes.

Free agents Damien Woody and Rick DeMulling never even came close to living up to their big-money contracts. Before last season, the Lions played "sign an injured lineman," inking free agents Barry Stokes, Rex Tucker, and Ross Verba. The Lions have continued this depressing trend in 2007, signing former Ravens guard Edwin Mulitalo, who turns 33 in September and missed most of last season with a torn triceps. Mulitalo's best days appear to be behind him. Last year, the Lions stuffed the numerous gaps created by injury with roster filler such as Jonathan Scott and Frank Davis. The result was the worst run-blocking line in the league and the second most sacks allowed.

The offensive line situation became so desperate that the Lions felt obligated to take the bold move of shipping their top asset, cornerback Dre' Bly, to Denver for offensive tackle George Foster. The oversized Foster was not sufficiently athletic for Denver's blocking scheme, but he is a decent lineman if he plays in a limited space. Foster is unlikely to make a Pro Bowl, but he is an upgrade for the offensive line.

The offensive line woes are largely attributable to a lack of investment on draft day, but at least the Lions have used some first-day picks on the defense. Second-year weakside linebacker Ernie Sims is Millen's only first-round defensive pick, but the Lions have filled the defense with second and third-round selections. Defensive tackle Shaun Rogers is the only premium player, but under Millen the Lions have also drafted probable starters Cory Redding, Kalimba Edwards, Stanley Wilson, and Daniel Bullocks. If linebackers Teddy Lehman or Boss Bailey could ever stay healthy, they might find spots over hard-working but limited talents Paris Lenon and Alex Lewis.

Of course, most of these players were around this past season when the defense was abysmal, proving that, even when the Lions spend their valuable draft picks on positions of need, their poor talent evaluation brings in only mediocre players. The easy excuse for last season's struggles is that Rogers was suspended four games after testing positive for a banned substance and then lost for the year following knee surgery, but there was no significant difference between Detroit's defense before and after Rogers left the lineup; Detroit's defensive DVOA was 15.7% before Rogers's suspension, and 13.3% afterwards. The defense has since lost Bly, arguably their best individual defender. Bly was not made for the Cover-2 defense employed by the Lions last year and was well off his performance from the year before. Still, he was a better solution than the oft-injured Fernando Bryant or the recently signed Travis Fisher, who finished last among all 81 ranked cornerbacks in Success Rate as judged by our game charters.

The Lions remain a terrible football team, but the franchise's decision-makers proceed as if they are not to blame. Last year's failures are blamed on poor character and poor coaching. The Lions appear to truly believe that once Mari-

nelli gets rid of enough "bad apples," heart and hard work will magically make this team a winner. Listen to a Marinelli press conference, and it becomes clear he has watched *Hoosiers* one time too many. In pursuit of this vision, the Lions cast off Bly, Mike Williams, and defensive linemen James Hall and Marcus Bell. The failure of the offensive line was blamed in part on line coach Larry Beightol, and the defensive struggles were put on coordinator Donnie Henderson. These moves cement the power of Martz and Marinelli. Beightol was widely respected but clashed with Martz. Marinelli was allowed to hire his son-in-law Joe Barry, a fellow former Tampa Bay coach, as defensive coordinator.

Millen has effectively hitched his reputation to these two coaches. Marinelli recommends former Tampa Bay defensive end Dwayne White; Millen gives him a huge contract. Martz wants former Rams receiver Shaun McDonald; Millen signs him. The embattled GM basically has no choice. He is on his third coaching regime and sports a career record of 24–72. The last team this bad over a six-year span was the 1983–1988 Buccaneers, who went 21–74. The only other teams to fail to win 30 games in six years during the free-agent era were the 1997–2002 and 1998–2003 Bengals. Of course, the Bengals provide some hope to Lions fans who fear that Millen will never leave. After the 2003 season, Cincinnati hired Marvin Lewis as head coach, and they have not been below .500 since despite Mike Brown's continued presence as final decision-maker in the front office. Of course, it didn't hurt that they had a number-one pick in a year when a franchise quarterback was entering the draft, though it's to their credit that they had the simple sense to draft him.

For six years, Matt Millen has proven to have no eye for talent and no ability to successfully make major or minor decisions with regard to roster construction. He has consistently chased after a high-powered passing attack and now has seemingly abdicated his role to the whims of the notoriously fickle Martz. If Calvin Johnson is as good as advertised—and he does appear to be freakishly good—Millen may finally have a top-ten passing offense. A team built around a high-powered passing attack just won the Super Bowl, but nobody is going to mistake Jon Kitna for Peyton Manning. The rest of the team is low on talent, with a poor offensive line and weak defense. Lions games may be more fun to watch this year, but the season is likely to end with another high draft pick. Lions fans can only hope that this pick will be used by a brand new general manager—on something other than a wide receiver.

Ned Macey

Lions 2006 Stats by Week

Wk	vs.	W–L	PF	PA	YDF	YDA	TO	Total	Off	Def	ST
									DVOA		
1	SEA	L	6	9	251	264	0	-40.9%	-27.9%	-3.4%	-16.4%
2	@CHI	L	7	34	245	383	-2	-42.7%	1.1%	36.1%	-7.6%
3	GB	L	24	31	424	400	+1	6.6%	30.9%	17.2%	-7.1%
4	@STL	L	34	41	370	427	+1	-30.6%	-17.5%	28.2%	15.1%
5	@MIN	L	17	26	217	336	-1	-51.2%	-40.5%	21.1%	10.4%
6	BUF	W	20	17	397	242	+2	9.2%	16.2%	-7.9%	-14.9%
7	@NYJ	L	24	31	386	398	-1	-30.8%	11.0%	38.6%	-3.2%
8	BYE										
9	ATL	W	30	14	435	319	+2	9.2%	13.7%	12.3%	7.8%
10	SF	L	13	19	251	315	-3	-32.0%	-31.2%	7.6%	6.8%
11	@ARI	L	10	17	281	338	-1	-62.4%	-30.7%	39.8%	8.1%
12	MIA	L	10	27	220	395	0	-65.9%	-32.7%	33.2%	0.0%
13	@NE	L	21	28	361	363	-2	-12.4%	-16.6%	0.9%	5.0%
14	MIN	L	20	30	280	328	-4	-38.8%	-31.9%	25.5%	18.6%
15	@GB	L	9	17	142	303	+1	-17.5%	-69.2%	-37.3%	14.5%
16	CHI	L	21	26	327	354	0	23.5%	29.3%	16.3%	10.5%
17	DAL	W	39	31	362	365	+2	21.3%	19.5%	-2.6%	-0.9%

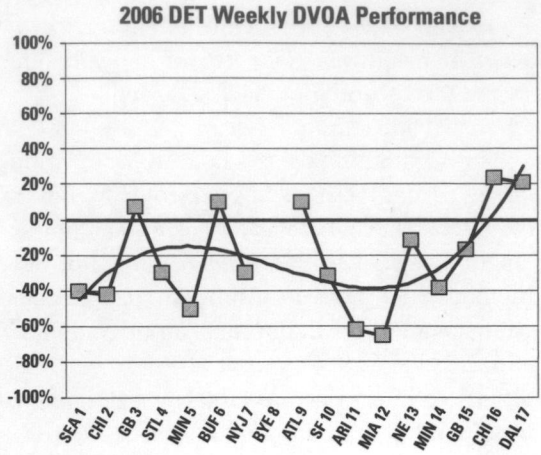

2006 DET Weekly DVOA Performance

Trends and Splits

	Offense	Rank	Defense	Rank
Total DVOA	-9.2%	25	14.2%	30
Unadjusted VOA	-14.3%	29	9.5%	27
Weighted Trend	-11.6%	27	11.5%	29
Variance	8.0%	8	4.1%	30
Passing	0.7%	16	20.6%	30
Rushing	-27.0%	32	7.6%	27
First Down	-19.7%	28	6.3%	24
Second Down	2.0%	17	16.3%	29
Third Down	-5.6%	21	26.7%	29
Red Zone	-24.5%	25	10.5%	22
Late and Close	-13.6%	26	6.7%	21

Five-Year Performance

	2006	2005	2004	2003	2002
W-L	3-13	5-11	6-10	5-11	3-13
Pythagorean Wins	5.6	5.2	6.4	4.9	4.6
Estimated Wins	5.6	5.8	7.7	5.6	3.6
Total DVOA	-20.6%	-19.3%	-5.0%	-24.6%	-35.4%
Rank	29	26	19	31	30
Offense	-9.2%	-13.1%	-4.5%	-22.1%	-20.3%
Rank	25	24	19	31	29
Defense	14.2%	1.8%	4.9%	5.8%	21.6%
Rank	30	21	20	23	32
Special Teams	2.8%	-4.3%	4.4%	3.3%	6.6%
Rank	6	32	5	4	2

Strategic Tendencies

Formations		Rank	Run/Pass		Rank	Defense		Rank	Other		Rank
3+ WR	61%	4	Runs, all plays	31%	32	Sacks by LB	5%	30	Run with 2+ RB	53%	21
4+ WR	22%	2	Runs, first half	34%	32	Sacks by DB	9%	13	Run with 2+ TE	31%	22
2+ TE	21%	25	Runs, first down	36%	32	Rush 6+	6.2%	25	Play action	11%	29
Single back	61%	9	Runs, power sit.	37%	32	Rush 7+	0.6%	27	Go for it on 4th	0.74	24
Empty back	3.2%	10	Runs, behind 2H	27%	27	Rush 3	3.5%	21	Offensive Pace	28.9	6
Max protect	9%	24	Pass, ahead 2H	63%	1	CB1 on WR1	50%	8	Defensive Pace	30.7	16

With Mike Martz as coordinator, the Lions rankings changed dramatically in many of the stats listed above. Compared to 2005, they ran far more three-wide and four-wide sets, ran the offense at a much faster pace, and were more conservative on fourth downs. They dropped from eighth to 27th in runs when behind in the second half, and rose from 18th to first in passes when ahead in the second half. They passed in the latter situation 25 percent more often than any other offense in 2006. . . . The Lions were the only team to run in less than half of all power situations and the only team to run on less than 44 percent of first downs. . . . Detroit's offense ranked 27th in frequency of play-action fakes, but they were much more successful on play-action passes (28.1% DVOA) than non-play-action passes (–3.6% DVOA). Philadelphia and Cincinnati were the only other teams to average more than nine yards per pass attempt when using play-action. . . . Detroit's offense led the league in Coverage Sacks. . . . On first down, the Lions threw to Roy Williams 50 percent more often than Mike Furrey. On second and third down, they threw to Furrey 30 percent more often than Williams. . . . Detroit's secondary had the highest number of passes defensed when the target was the opposing team's number-one wide receiver, at a rate almost 60 percent better than league average. . . . Detroit's defense was last in the league in tipped passes. . . . On offense, the Lions recovered only four of 21 fumbles, the worst percentage in the league. On defense, the Lions recovered 16 of 23 fumbles, the second-highest percentage in the league (behind Houston).

Passing

Player	DPAR	DVOA	Plys	NtYds	Avg	YAC	C%	TD	Int
Jon Kitna	49.8	4.6%	594	3825	6.4	4.7	62.6%	21	21

Rushing

Player	DPAR	DVOA	Plys	Yds	Avg	TD	Fum	Suc
Kevin Jones	-5.6	-22.3%	181	688	3.8	6	4	40%
Arlen Harris	0.3	-17.9%	49	158	3.2	1	0	0%
Jon Kitna	-1.9	-29.3%	28	153	5.5	2	11	—
Aveion Cason	1.1	-4.1%	24	94	3.9	0	0	80%
Brian Calhoun	-3.9	-179.9%	7	13	1.9	0	1	0%
Tatum Bell	*10.9*	*-2.2%*	*233*	*1031*	*4.4*	*2*	*3*	*40%*
T. J. Duckett	*-0.6*	*-20.8%*	*38*	*133*	*3.5*	*2*	*1*	*39%*

Receiving

Player	DPAR	DVOA	Plys	Ctch	Yds	Y/C	YAC	TD	C%
WR									
Roy Williams	29.1	14.2%	151	82	1310	16.0	16.0	7	54%
Mike Furrey	25.8	12.5%	146	98	1086	11.1	11.1	6	67%
Az-Zahir Hakim*	-0.6	-18.2%	27	17	147	8.6	8.6	0	56%
Corey Bradford	0.2	-13.7%	25	14	166	11.9	11.9	0	63%
Mike Williams*	-0.8	-21.7%	18	8	99	12.4	12.4	1	44%
Eddie Drummond	-3.2	-64.8%	10	2	10	5.0	5.0	0	44%
Devale Ellis	-1.8	-47.7%	9	4	41	10.3	10.3	0	20%
Shaun McDonald	*0.1*	*-14.1%*	*19*	*13*	*136*	*10.5*	*10.5*	*1*	*68%*
TE									
Dan Campbell	11.7	44.1%	32	21	308	14.7	14.7	4	66%
Marcus Pollard*	-0.6	-17.3%	17	12	100	8.3	8.3	0	70%
Casey FitzSimmons	1.3	9.3%	10	7	71	10.1	10.1	0	71%
Sean McHugh	0.7	16.0%	5	3	25	8.3	8.3	0	50%
RB									
Kevin Jones	13.2	22.1%	78	61	520	8.5	8.5	2	78%
Arlen Harris	0.6	-5.1%	25	18	132	7.3	7.3	0	72%
Cory Schlesinger*	-1.7	-41.0%	11	8	36	4.5	4.5	0	89%
Aveion Cason	-2.9	-66.7%	10	5	26	5.2	5.2	0	60%
Shawn Bryson	5.4	116.3%	9	8	98	12.3	12.3	1	73%
Tatum Bell	*-6.7*	*-52.0%*	*31*	*24*	*115*	*4.8*	*4.8*	*0*	*74%*

Offensive Line

Year	Yards	ALY	Rank	Power	Rank	10+ Yds	Rank	Stuff	Rank	Sack	ASR	Rank
2004	4.50	4.08	21	60%	18	23%	1	30%	31	37	6.8%	17
2005	3.71	4.15	14	61%	20	14%	22	28%	28	30	5.7%	11
2006	3.62	3.66	32	37%	32	18%	11	29%	32	63	9.8%	30

Year	LE	Rank	LT	Rank	Mid	Rank	RT	Rank	RE	Rank
2004	2.67	31	4.60	12	4.42	11	3.92	22	3.92	16
2005	4.24	15	4.39	14	3.86	23	4.69	6	3.93	16
2006	3.57	23	3.90	27	3.83	29	4.18	17	2.91	30

What a disaster this is. Dominic Raiola and Jeff Backus both started every game at center and left tackle respectively. The other 48 starts were spread between nine different players at the three positions. The Lions were last in the league in Adjusted Line Yards, but were saved the indignity of also ranking last in Adjusted Sack Rate thanks to Jon Kitna. Kitna had never been sacked more than 37 times in a single season before going down 63 times last year. Had David Carr been back there, the Lions could have easily topped 70 sacks allowed. Backus is a mediocre left tackle who got a huge contract probably because of how he compares to the rest of his teammates on film. Raiola struggles to get a push up the middle. Guard Damien Woody was fat and out of shape before going on injured reserve. Rex Tucker did not have the agility to play right tackle. Sadly, these are the more talented players. The Dre' Bly trade brought in George Foster, who is the sort of enormous right tackle Mike Martz prefers, but Foster never lived up to his first-round status in Denver. Edwin Mulitalo was signed from Baltimore and is an upgrade at guard if he is healthy, but his age makes that an unlikely proposition. Woody has reportedly already lost a great deal of weight. Tackle Jonathan Scott struggled as a rookie, but he has physical tools. The Lions' biggest offensive challenge will be getting adequate play out of some combination of these players. The importation of Foster and Mulitalo and a recommitted Woody certainly increases the talent.

Defensive Front Seven

Defensive Line	Age	Pos	Plys	TmPct	Rk	Stop	Dfts	StpRt	Rk	AvYd	Rk	Sack	Hit	Hur	Runs	RuStp	RuYd	Pass	PaStp	PaYd
Cory Redding	27	DE	49	5.8%	42	41	21	84%	12	0.3	9	8	2	5	35	89%	1.5	14	71%	-2.7
Kalimba Edwards	28	DE	40	4.8%	60	27	15	68%	72	2.8	72	3	5	10	31	61%	3.5	9	89%	0.2
Marcus Bell*	28	DT	40	5.9%	24	25	6	63%	68	2.8	63	1	3	1	34	65%	3.0	6	50%	1.8
James Hall*	30	DE	24	6.5%	—	21	8	88%	—	-0.3	—	5	4	5	18	83%	2.3	6	100%	-8.2
Jared DeVries	30	DE	24	3.3%	—	19	7	79%	—	1.1	—	0	3	6	17	82%	2.0	7	71%	-1.1
Shaun Rogers	28	DT	21	6.7%	—	20	8	95%	—	-0.9	—	3	3	9	15	100%	0.2	6	83%	-3.5
Dewayne White	*28*	*DE*	*50*	*6.0%*	*40*	*43*	*22*	*86%*	*9*	*1.0*	*24*	*5*	*12*	*14*	*34*	*82%*	*2.2*	*16*	*94%*	*-1.4*

Linebackers	Age	Pos	Plys	TmPct	Rk	Stop	Dfts	StpRt	AvYd	Sack	Hit	Hur	Runs	RuStp	Rk	RuYd	Rk	Tgts	Suc%	Rk	PaYd	Rk
Ernie Sims	23	OLB	126	15.0%	24	59	14	47%	5.3	0.5	0	2	78	59%	70	3.4	46	42	40%	79	6.6	66
Paris Lenon	30	ILB	76	9.0%	77	46	15	61%	3.9	0	3	2	45	73%	13	2.4	6	35	51%	48	6.0	40
Boss Bailey	28	OLB	69	8.2%	86	30	7	43%	5.4	1	1	1	47	49%	95	4.0	75	15	37%	—	9.4	—
Alex Lewis	26	OLB	41	7.1%	—	28	6	68%	4.0	0	2	1	25	76%	—	3.2	—	16	44%	70	5.8	27

Year	Yards	ALY	Rank	Power	Rank	10+ Yds	Rank	Stuff	Rank	Sack	ASR	Rank
2004	3.78	4.06	10	79%	31	12%	5	26%	10	38	6.1%	27
2005	4.23	4.07	16	63%	16	18%	18	28%	7	31	6.0%	24
2006	4.23	4.50	24	71%	27	16%	15	20%	30	30	5.8%	24

Year	LE	Rank	LT	Rank	Mid	Rank	RT	Rank	RE	Rank
2004	4.24	16	4.10	9	3.98	8	4.28	18	3.87	18
2005	3.68	11	4.83	28	3.65	5	4.07	16	4.64	22
2006	3.88	14	5.59	32	4.60	23	4.05	12	4.48	21

The pleasant surprise of the season was Cory Redding's development at defensive tackle after All-Pro Shaun Rogers was lost for the season after knee surgery. Redding provided the only pass rush on the team and held his own despite being undersized. If Rogers is healthy, he joins with Redding and Shaun Cody to give Detroit an above-average tackle rotation. Defensive end Kalimba Edwards struggled after signing a big contract. He totaled only three sacks and was a downright liability against the run. Ex-Tampa free agent Dewayne White should take over one defensive end position, offering a more balanced set of skills and a more consistent pass rush. The other side will be manned by Edwards or Jared DeVries, the latter of whom has limited skills but hangs in there against the run. Second-round pick Ikaika Alama-Francis out of Hawaii has more potential than either, but he's a project who never played football until 2003. He has size, speed, and a nonstop motor, so the sooner he develops, the better. Rookie linebacker Ernie Sims made a lot of plays last year, but most of them were well downfield, as he would get lost in traffic and struggled to disengage from blockers. He is fast and has upside, but his collegiate history of concussions is still a concern. Some combination of Paris Lenon, Teddy Lehman, Boss Bailey, and Alex Lewis will start at the other two linebacker positions. Lehman and Bailey have the most talent, but both are constantly injured. The middle is most problematic, as Bailey has proven inept there. Lenon may hold onto the job. He had a strong year against the run in 2006, and his solid pass coverage ability makes him a respectable option in the Cover-2.

Defensive Secondary

Secondary	Age	Pos	Plys	TmPct	Rk	Stop	Dfts	RuYd	Rk	RuStp	Rk	Tgts	Tgt%	Rk	Dist	Suc%	Rk	PaYd	Rk	PD	Int
Dre' Bly*	30	CB	76	9.0%	43	39	15	4.7	18	70%	2	89	19%	35	12.4	50%	53	7.6	44	19	3
Jamar Fletcher*	28	CB	41	6.0%	75	15	9	6.5	37	50%	26	48	13%	75	10.4	39%	77	10.2	79	6	3
Fernando Bryant	29	CB	52	9.9%	29	21	7	7.1	51	50%	28	45	16%	55	9.9	47%	64	6.7	22	5	0
Stanley Wilson	25	CB	40	5.9%	—	19	6	5.2	—	58%	—	44	12%	—	8.8	55%	—	4.8	—	4	0
Jon McGraw*	28	SS	35	4.2%	78	11	8	7.0	47	67%	3	33	7%	46	10.1	31%	77	12.5	75	2	0
Terrence Holt*	27	FS	81	9.6%	42	20	10	8.9	71	17%	77	28	5%	66	15.5	63%	11	6.3	18	4	3
Daniel Bullocks	24	FS	73	9.3%	48	30	8	6.5	41	49%	26	26	6%	64	11.8	52%	42	8.2	42	3	0
Kenoy Kennedy	30	SS	62	11.8%	19	21	8	6.4	38	45%	32	18	6%	51	15.3	40%	69	12.3	73	3	2
Travis Fisher	*29*	*CB*	*31*	*7.1%*	*63*	*8*	*2*	*10.4*	*71*	*60%*	*11*	*45*	*20%*	*34*	*10.6*	*33%*	*81*	*10.9*	*80*	*1*	*0*

Year	Pass D Rank	DVOA vs. #1 WR	Rank	DVOA vs. #2 WR	Rank	DVOA vs. Other WR	Rank	DVOA vs. TE	Rank	DVOA vs. RB	Rank
2004	24	1.6%	14	13.4%	26	-3.1%	16	14.9%	24	-2.3%	14
2005	17	20.0%	27	-8.5%	12	-21.5%	5	-4.6%	15	-1.1%	17
2006	30	-15.0%	8	32.4%	32	34.8%	30	20.3%	31	11.0%	22

The departure of Dre' Bly leaves an enormous hole in the secondary. Bly was a poor fit for the Cover-2, but he was still the most talented cornerback on the team. Most Cover-2 teams are weak against number-one receivers, but that was the one place where the Detroit secondary was strong, and a lot of that was Bly. Stanley Wilson, a 2005 third-rounder, impressed in his time on the field last year and should earn one starting position. Fernando Bryant has battled injuries and ineffectiveness since he arrived in Detroit in 2004, but he likely remains the second best option. When Bryant's inevitable injury comes, the Lions will struggle. Travis Fisher, a free agent addition from the Rams, had the worst numbers of any cornerback in the league in multiple game-charting metrics last year. At safety, Kenoy Kennedy is generally solid in coverage but is starting to lose a step. Terrence Holt was allowed to leave as a free agent, an under-the-radar move that could hurt because of Holt's very solid coverage skills and Kennedy's advancing age. Fortunately, Holt's replacement, Daniel Bullocks, last year's second-round pick out of Nebraska, may already be a more complete safety and will certainly be much stronger against the run. The Lions also used this year's second-round pick on a defensive back, safety Gerald Alexander from Boise State, who was considered a reach by draft analysts, but has exceptional physical skills.

Special Teams

Year	DVOA	Rank	FG/XP	Rank	Net Punt	Rank	Punt Ret	Rank	Net Kick	Rank	Kick Ret	Rank	Hidden	Rank
2004	4.4%	5	-0.8	18	-9.2	30	10.5	3	11.8	4	13.6	3	-3.4	18
2005	-4.3%	32	-2.7	22	-8.6	30	0.3	13	-11.2	30	-3.2	19	6.6	9
2006	2.8%	6	8.3	5	4.0	13	1.5	12	5.9	10	-3.5	21	-7.0	24

The retirement of special teams coach Chuck Priefer could hurt one of this team's few consistent strengths. Detroit's special teams suffered through a terrible 2005 season because of injuries to kicker Jason Hanson and return man Eddie Drummond, but the Lions have otherwise had a top-ten special teams unit every year since 1998. Healthy again in 2006, the 36-year-old Hanson hit three field goals of 50 or more yards and had one of his best seasons ever in terms of kickoffs. Hanson has now played for seven different head coaches without ever leaving Detroit. Punter Nick Harris is coming off his best year with the Lions, putting both kicking positions in sure feet. Drummond has shown flashes of game-breaking potential, but that potential has not borne consistent results, partly because of those nagging injuries. After five years with the Lions, Drummond has yet to play a full season. New free agent receiver Shaun McDonald may take over on punt returns, but he was mediocre in St. Louis.

Coaching Staff

The first year of the Rod Marinelli era has to be considered a disappointment. Marinelli's lack of head-coaching experience was apparent, as he showed little imagination with game or clock management in 2006 and pretty much played by the book. Then again, the Lions' best quarter on offense and defense was the third, so maybe Marinelli excels at halftime adjustments. The defense's failings were particularly troubling due to Marinelli's background as a defensive-line coach. Marinelli fired defensive coordinator Donnie Henderson after the season and brought in Jon Barry—Marinelli's son-in-law, but more importantly, a fellow Tampa-2 adherent. Offensive coordinator Mike Martz continued to soil his once-pristine reputation as offensive genius. Martz last oversaw a top-ten offense in 2001, and he has not had an above-average running game since then. Meanwhile, the Rams had both this year, the first after Martz's departure from St. Louis, despite very little personnel turnover. Martz is still good for making big plays in the passing game, but his running offense is too creative for its own good, and the offense as a whole takes too many negative plays. The Lions allowed 63 sacks, threw 22 interceptions, and lost 17 fumbles in their first year under Martz. That accounts for over ten percent of Detroit's offensive plays. At this point, a Martz-coached offense should be viewed with the same skepticism as one coached by Mike Mularkey.

Green Bay Packers

T he low point of 2006 in Green Bay, Wisconsin, came on December 3rd. That day, the Packers fell behind the New York Jets 31–0 in the first half on their way to a 38–10 loss that dropped them to 4–8 overall, and 1–5 at Lambeau Field. Brett Favre was out there throughout the meaningless fourth quarter, presumably wondering why he had come back for such a pathetic season.

Over the next four weeks, the Packers rebounded and brought substantial hope for the franchise in 2007. After the season Favre decided, again, to postpone retirement. His return puts him in position to take all the major career passing records from Dan Marino. Favre has already passed Marino to set the all-time record for completions. He needs just six passing touchdowns to catch Marino in that category, and should do that by midseason. By the end of the year, Favre will be marching towards the all-time passing yardage record, for which he is currently 3,861 yards behind Marino. Much media attention will be focused on those impressive feats, but the more interesting story is that Favre may be marching back into the playoffs at the same time.

A skeptic would immediately point out that Green Bay's feel-good finish deserves an asterisk. The four-game run started with wins over San Francisco and Detroit, ranked 29th and 27th respectively in DVOA. The Packers then toppled a Minnesota team in Green Bay that was giving rookie quarterback Tarvaris Jackson his first professional start in a driving rainstorm, and ended the run with a win over a Bears team that had already clinched home field advantage in the playoffs. For a franchise with only one sub-.500 record since 1992, this is hardly the stuff of legends.

Still, the 2006 season was a massive improvement over an embarrassing 2005 campaign in which the Packers limped home with a 4–12 record. That season cost head

coach Mike Sherman his job, as GM Ted Thompson brought a new Mike into town, Mike McCarthy. The crucial change, however, took place the year before, when Sherman was stripped of his GM duties, and Thompson was hired to run the team.

According to many accounts, Thompson and McCarthy were ready to unload their veterans and rebuild the team that offseason and there was much speculation that the front office secretly hoped Favre would opt for retirement. Of course, Thompson and McCarthy could not show their long-time quarterback the door and guarantee their own physical safety in Favreville. So when Favre decided to return for 2006, Thompson made a slight deviation from his previous move of importing younger free agents. Before Favre's decision to return, Thompson had signed defensive tackle Ryan Pickett from St. Louis and safety Marquand Manuel from Seattle, both of whom were 26 years old when they signed. After Favre's announcement, Thompson made a bold move by acquiring talented but often-injured cornerback Charles Woodson who was almost 30 and had missed 13 games the previous two seasons. The net result of these moves was a rebuilt defense that had enormous potential. This rebuilt defense, combined with what have now been three solid drafts, and the remaining holdovers from the strong Green Bay teams of the early part of the decade, has the Packers in position to make a run at the playoffs.

The draft record of the Packers during the Mike Sherman era is embarrassing. Sherman assumed the general manager duties in 2001 after Ron Wolfe's departure, and he oversaw the Packers' drafts from that year through 2004. Those drafts should have formed the core of this year's Packers team. Instead, they produced only two projected starters: defensive end Aaron Kampman and linebacker

PACKERS PROSPECTUS

2006 Record: 8–8

DVOA Estimated Wins: 7.7 (17th)

Pythagorean Wins: 6.2 (23rd)

DVOA: −0.6% total (15th), 6.5% weighted (13th)

Offense: −5.9% DVOA (20th)

Defense: −9.3% DVOA (6th)

Special Teams: −3.9% DVOA (29th)

Variance: 22.9% (3rd)

2006: Late-season run brings Favre back for one more go.

2007: There should be more to watch than just Favre's record-setting.

2007 Mean Projection: 9.5 wins

The Brohm Closet (0–4): 2%

Bad Team (5–6): 8%

Mediocre (7–8): 20%

Playoff Contender (9–10): 36%

Super Bowl Contender (11+): 34%

Projected Average Opponent: −4.7% DVOA (31st in NFL)

Nick Barnett. To be generous, Sherman did also draft wide receiver Javon Walker, whose trade to Denver netted the draft pick used on starting guard Daryn Colledge, but it was Sherman's failure to sign Walker to a long-term contract that forced the trade which brought in a lesser talent.

This lack of team-drafted talent in its prime has forced the Packers to explore all possible options to field frontline starters. First, they continue to ride with some of their veteran stalwarts on offense. The middle of their offensive line left as free agents after the 2004 and 2005 seasons, but other key contributors remain. Favre is the obvious one, but he still has the same two tackles who have protected him for years, as well as his top receiver since 2002, Donald Driver. Tight end Bubba Franks has been starting since 2000, though his performance began to slip last year.

As a second step, Thompson did an admirable job acquiring veteran free agents before the 2006 season. Pickett fortified the middle of the defensive line with good if unspectacular play. Manuel arrived from Seattle as another experienced player, who, while disappointing on some levels, was a significant upgrade over the other available choices. The big impact move, however, was the Woodson signing. Woodson may no longer be among the game's best cornerbacks, if he ever was, but the high-risk gamble ended up working out. He teamed with Al Harris to form one of the best starting cornerback tandems in football in 2006. Woodson may have been more good than great, but in 2005 the other starting cornerback was Ahmed Carroll, who was repeatedly toasted at nickelback last year and released midseason. Signing Manuel and Woodson meant that of the *nine* defensive backs the Packers drafted between 1999 and 2004, not one was a starter in 2006. Harris came in a trade from Philadelphia in 2002, and safety Nick Collins was chosen in 2005, the first Thompson draft.

The Packers have also supplemented their roster by grabbing freely available talent. In Sherman's defense, many of these finds date from his tenure. Cullen Jenkins was undrafted out of Central Michigan, out of football for a season, and eventually allocated to NFL Europe before finally sticking with the Packers as a free agent in 2004. Late last season, Jenkins switched from defensive tackle to defensive end and did wonders for the run defense. He is now the proud owner of a $16-million extension. The Packers also received important contributions last year from defensive tackle Colin Cole, cornerback Patrick Dendy, running back Noah Herron, and fullback Brandon Miree, all of whom were either undrafted or released by other teams. Intriguing wideouts Carlyle Holiday and Ruvell Martin—two undrafted free agents who saw their first playing time last season—hope to continue this trend of young, freely available talent developing into important contributors.

2007 Packers Schedule

Week	Opp	Week	Opp	Week	Opp
1	PHI	7	BYE	13	at DAL (Thu.)
2	at NYG	8	at DEN (Mon.)	14	OAK
3	SD	9	at KC	15	at STL
4	at MIN	10	MIN	16	at CHI
5	CHI	11	CAR	17	DET
6	WAS	12	at DET (Thu.)		

Finally, the Packers have been forced to push the fruit of their recent drafts directly into the fire. Nowhere was this more obvious than on last year's offensive line. The Packers struggled mightily after guards Mike Wahle and Marco Rivera left as free agents before the 2005 season. Thompson addressed this enormous need in the following year's draft, taking Daryn Colledge and Jason Spitz in the second and third round respectively. The two were both starting by Week 3, and were often joined by guard Tony Moll, who filled in when minor injuries struck various linemen. Even though the Packers let center Mike Flanagan walk before the season, the line improved substantially with the two rookies in the lineup, moving back into the top half of the league in Adjusted Line Yards after falling to 30th in 2005.

The offensive line was not the only place where unproven players were pushed into the lineup in 2006. Second-year player Brady Poppinga took over at one outside linebacker position while top draft choice A. J. Hawk manned the other. Corey Williams, a two year backup, took over a starting defensive tackle position in October. On the offensive side of the ball, second-round rookie wide receiver Greg Jennings became a starter in Week 2.

The vast majority of the Packers' 2006 contributors return for 2007, the notable exception being running back Ahman Green, who signed with Houston as a free agent. This patchwork assembly necessitated by the barren drafts has created an odd mix of young and old, particularly on offense. The Packers only have a handful of players who are under 30 and have more than one year experience starting in the league. The only offensive players that fit that description are Bubba Franks and center Scott Wells. The rest of the offense is either aging or unproven.

The oldest player is Favre, who looked revitalized last year after throwing 29 interceptions in 2005. In his first year as head coach, Mike McCarthy did a great deal to make Favre more comfortable. A zone-blocking scheme and healthy Green improved the running game. Additionally, the Packers often played out of a tight formation, giving more players responsibility for blitz pickup and giving Favre more confidence to stay in the pocket. Favre would still be jittery at times, but the wholesale collapses in pass protection that marked 2005 were noticeably absent in 2006. The resulting output was a pretty mediocre offense, but considering three of the top six linemen and the second and third most productive wide receivers were rookies, mediocre was somewhat commendable.

It's here on offense that this team has the most room for improvement. It is easy to construct a scenario in which this unit coalesces into the sort of solid offense the Packers have enjoyed throughout most of the Favre era. That scenario would see Colledge and Spitz improve in their second season as the starting interior linemen, Jennings and Martin turn into reliable receivers that provide big play potential opposite Donald Driver, and rookie running back Brandon Jackson, a second-round pick out of Nebraska, step in and contribute immediately like numerous rookie runners have done before.

None of these propositions is unreasonable, but the likelihood of all of them happening at once is low. Last year's offense was severely hampered by the lack of a reliable second option behind Driver. As a result, Favre threw passes to Driver whether he was open or not. Only Rams receiver Torry Holt was thrown more passes in 2006 than Driver's 173. No other receiver was within 20 of those two. Driver had never been targeted more than 146 times before. His previous career-low Catch Rate was 59 percent. This past season it was 53 percent. Driver had only six more catches last year than 2005 despite having an additional 27 passes thrown his way.

The tight formations that helped protect Favre also allowed defenses to key two men on Driver when he was split wide. Without more people putting pressure on the defense all across the field, Driver will likely be overwhelmed again, and, at age 32, he is in danger of losing a step. Further compounding Driver's troubles, Green was the third most frequent target for Favre. It is doubtful that Jackson will be as adept in the passing game, which could lead to more passes to a double-covered Driver. In order to keep opposing defenses honest, Favre will have to place more faith in Jennings and Martin in the hope that at least one of them can play well consistently.

These weaknesses in the offense were exacerbated in the red zone, where the Packers' offense suddenly became the second-worst in all of football. Almost all of the problems were in the passing game. Green Bay's 19th ranking in red zone rushing was actually higher than its overall rank, but Favre completed fewer than 40 percent of his passes inside his opponent's 20. Nearly one-third of those attempts went to Driver, only 37 percent of which were completed. If Favre had just been replacement level in the red zone (with a red zone DPAR of 0), he would have ranked seventh in the league in overall DPAR, right behind Tom Brady. Historically, Favre has had no problems in the red zone, per his

reputation, but the underlying causes of last year's struggles—no reliable second receiver, the decline of Franks, a continued lack of confidence in his pass protection—have not changed during this offseason.

Favre apparently wanted more aggressive steps taken this past offseason to provide him with offensive weapons, but the sort of aggressive moves Thompson made for the defense before the 2006 season were nowhere to be found in 2007. The "major" free-agent acquisition was Frank Walker, a fringe cornerback who may or may not play regularly. The first-round draft pick was once again spent on a defensive player. The offense saw nothing but the departure of Green and drafting of Jackson. Favre wanted to add Randy Moss, but Moss went to New England for a mere fourth-round pick and a limited salary.

Favre is correct that the offense will show only modest gains, but that does not mean Favre will not go out a winner. Offense is not even half the game, and the Green Bay defense is developing into a very good unit. That defense ranked an impressive eighth in overall DVOA last year, and third in weighted DVOA. As noted above, these numbers are probably a bit misleading due to some fortunate scheduling quirks, but the Packers have a number of reasons to believe the defense will be that good this season. First, their impressive late-season run also coincided with the entrance of Jenkins into the starting line-up over Kabeer Gbaja-Biamila, who is no longer a dynamic pass rusher and had become an outright liability against the run. Second, the Packers were breaking in a number of new players who understandably played better as the season went along. Only Harris, Collins, Kampman, and Barnett were regular starters throughout both 2005 and 2006. Third, Bob Sanders was also in his first season as defensive coordinator, and he grew as a play-caller throughout the season. Finally, this year's first-round pick, defensive tackle Justin Harrell, will boost a potentially formidable defensive line if he stays healthy.

The Packers defense still has one major problem for next season: it is too reliant on aging cornerbacks. Harris is 33, and Woodson is a 30-year-old with a history of injuries. Behind them is Dendy, who is merely adequate as a nickelback and would be picked on repeatedly if forced to start regularly. The safeties struggle in coverage, particularly Manuel, which puts additional pressure on the corners. After an injury to Favre, the worst-case scenario for the Packers would be a major injury to Harris or Woodson.

Still, a defense with Harris, Kampman, Hawk, and an emerging playmaker like Jenkins has a great deal to recommend it. The Packers have to deal with the third-down regression effect, as they were the best defense in the NFL on third down, but 10th on second down and 22nd on first down. However, depth built through the draft with selections such as Harrell could easily keep the Packers defense in the top-ten. Even a small decline would actually look like surprising improvement to the majority of fans who don't realize how well the Green Bay defense was playing by the end of last season.

Thompson has put in place a number of quality players that could push the Packers into the playoffs. Two final holes may have been filled by the controversial 2007 draft in which both Harrell and Jackson were selected well before expected. If Thompson is right about both players, then the Packers become a complete team with a potentially excellent defense. If Thompson is wrong, then the defense will regress, and Favre will spend his final season handing off to Vernand Morency in losing efforts.

The Packers appear to have a wide range of possible outcomes this season, but one thing in their favor is a very favorable schedule. Minnesota and Detroit are awful, while Chicago is almost sure to regress. Their interdivisional games come against the AFC West and NFC East, two divisions that our projections say will be less daunting than in years past. A league-average team could easily win nine or ten games against this schedule, and the Packers are certainly that good.

The season-long celebration of Favre will be a proper tribute to one of the game's great quarterbacks. Ironically, his team's success will largely be determined by whether or not his defense reaches an elite level. He may be upset that his potential final season will not likely feature great personal statistics. A quarterback and team leader, however, should care most about the team's record, and it appears that Favre can end his career with a playoff berth if he merely oversees a league-average offense. After two disappointing seasons, Favre should be happy to get another shot in January no matter how he gets there.

Ned Macey

Packers 2006 Stats by Week

Wk	vs.	W–L	PF	PA	YDF	YDA	TO	DVOA Total	Off	Def	ST
1	CHI	L	0	26	267	361	-2	-51.6%	-13.7%	6.9%	-31.0%
2	NO	L	27	34	285	380	+1	16.6%	-6.9%	-24.7%	-1.2%
3	@DET	W	31	24	400	424	-1	-18.1%	4.7%	30.6%	7.8%
4	@PHI	L	9	31	318	398	-1	-25.1%	-22.3%	-3.4%	-6.2%
5	STL	L	20	23	336	327	-2	-27.9%	-1.2%	23.5%	-3.1%
6	BYE										
7	@MIA	W	34	24	346	448	+2	17.6%	8.5%	-3.9%	5.2%
8	ARI	W	31	14	383	218	+1	80.7%	52.1%	-18.8%	9.8%
9	@BUF	L	10	24	427	184	-4	-27.8%	-7.0%	14.0%	6.7%
10	@MIN	W	23	17	394	312	+2	25.5%	18.3%	-2.6%	4.5%
11	NE	L	0	35	120	357	0	-74.6%	-54.7%	8.5%	-11.4%
12	@SEA	L	24	34	316	382	0	-31.6%	-28.6%	-13.7%	-16.6%
13	NYJ	L	10	38	351	441	-1	-58.3%	-15.7%	34.3%	-8.3%
14	@SF	W	30	19	420	340	+3	36.5%	16.2%	-14.1%	6.2%
15	DET	W	17	9	303	142	-1	9.7%	-55.6%	-71.4%	-6.0%
16	MIN	W	9	7	319	104	-2	24.9%	-24.6%	-61.6%	-12.0%
17	@CHI	W	26	7	373	316	+5	108.3%	14.8%	-91.2%	2.3%

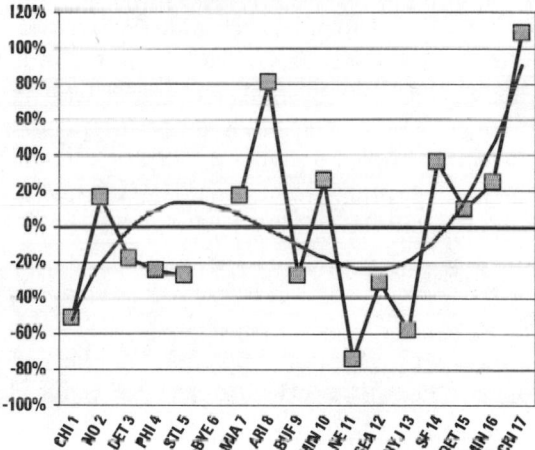

2006 GB Weekly DVOA Performance

Trends and Splits

	Offense	Rank	Defense	Rank
Total DVOA	-5.9%	20	-9.3%	6
Unadjusted VOA	-7.5%	23	-9.4%	7
Weighted Trend	-7.1%	21	-17.0%	3
Variance	7.1%	11	12.2%	1
Passing	-4.3%	19	-17.0%	4
Rushing	-8.1%	23	-0.5%	18
First Down	-29.2%	31	5.8%	22
Second Down	9.5%	8	-7.0%	10
Third Down	13.2%	11	-39.9%	1
Red Zone	-47.4%	31	-13.9%	7
Late and Close	-18.4%	27	-10.9%	8

Five-Year Performance

	2006	2005	2004	2003	2002
W-L	8-8	4-12	10-6	10-6	12-4
Pythagorean Wins	6.2	6.7	9.0	11.3	9.8
Estimated Wins	7.7	6.0	8.4	10.2	9.2
Total DVOA	-0.6%	-12.9%	1.6%	21.8%	7.9%
Rank	15	23	13	4	13
Offense	-5.9%	-7.0%	17.1%	10.5%	2.1%
Rank	20	20	7	7	18
Defense	-9.3%	2.1%	16.4%	-9.5%	-9.3%
Rank	6	22	29	8	5
Special Teams	-3.9%	-3.8%	0.9%	1.9%	-3.4%
Rank	29	30	14	10	25

Strategic Tendencies

Formations		Rank	Run/Pass		Rank	Defense		Rank	Other		Rank
3+ WR	47%	16	Runs, all plays	39%	28	Sacks by LB	14%	25	Run with 2+ RB	75%	4
4+ WR	6%	26	Runs, first half	39%	30	Sacks by DB	2%	28	Run with 2+ TE	36%	17
2+ TE	22%	23	Runs, first down	47%	30	Rush 6+	7.9%	19	Play action	18%	21
Single back	45%	25	Runs, power sit.	63%	18	Rush 7+	0.7%	22	Go for it on 4th	1.08	10
Empty back	3.3%	9	Runs, behind 2H	32%	18	Rush 3	5.2%	13	Offensive Pace	28.4	3
Max protect	17%	4	Pass, ahead 2H	50%	3	CB1 on WR1	69%	1	Defensive Pace	29.7	6

Compared to 2005, the Packers dropped significantly in using four-wide sets (from 5th to 18th) and two-tight end sets (from 4th to 23rd).... Green Bay set up in 55 four-wide sets but only ran from the formation once.... Green Bay ranked second in three-running back sets, although the third running back was most often tight end Bubba Franks motioning into the backfield. Unlike top-ranked Carolina, which threw the ball 67 percent of the time from these formations, Green Bay ran the ball on every play but one.... The Green Bay offense had the most Overthrown passes in the league, 22 percent more than second place Miami.... On third down, Green Bay used a standard formation with two wide receivers more often than any other offense.... Green Bay's defense was one of three that faced only five pass rushers on more than half of all pass plays.

Passing

Player	DPAR	DVOA	Plys	NtYds	Avg	YAC	C%	TD	Int
Brett Favre	46.7	4.3%	611	3748	6.1	5.9	56.1%	18	18
Aaron Rodgers	-4.0	-67.5%	15	28	1.9	4.2	40.0%	0	0

Rushing

Player	DPAR	DVOA	Plys	Yds	Avg	TD	Fum	Suc
Ahman Green*	20.6	4.4%	266	1063	4.0	5	2	43%
Vernand Morency	5.6	-1.2%	96	434	4.5	2	2	40%
Samkon Gado	-1.9	-22.6%	56	210	3.8	1	1	67%
Noah Herron	3.2	6.5%	37	150	4.1	1	0	25%
Brett Favre	-4.4	-79.1%	10	30	3.0	1	7	—
Donald Driver	-1.8	-57.1%	7	16	2.3	0	0	—

Receiving

Player	DPAR	DVOA	Plys	Ctch	Yds	Y/C	YAC	TD	C%
WR									
Donald Driver	16.9	0.1%	172	92	1270	13.8	5.3	8	53%
Greg Jennings	-6.5	-24.1%	105	45	632	14.0	6.9	3	43%
Ruvell Martin	7.3	11.8%	43	21	358	17.0	4.2	1	49%
Koren Robinson	0.6	-9.6%	16	7	89	12.7	2.7	0	60%
Carlyle Holiday	2.3	9.9%	15	9	126	14.0	4.1	0	44%
Robert Ferguson	-3.0	-50.1%	13	5	31	6.2	-0.2	1	40%
Chris Francies	-0.9	-40.7%	5	2	16	8.0	4.0	0	38%
TE									
Bubba Franks	-6.5	-30.4%	53	25	234	9.4	4.4	0	58%
David Martin*	3.9	5.3%	36	21	198	9.4	3.5	2	47%
Donald Lee	0.1	-11.8%	21	10	150	15.0	9.6	0	48%
RB									
Ahman Green*	2.6	-0.8%	63	46	375	8.2	9.2	1	83%
Noah Herron	5.3	20.1%	35	29	211	7.3	6.9	2	73%
Samkon Gado	-3.0	-37.0%	23	17	85	5.0	4.7	0	94%
Vernand Morency	1.8	9.0%	18	17	114	6.7	7.5	0	69%
William Henderson*	-1.5	-25.0%	18	12	62	5.2	4.9	0	67%
Brandon Miree	-0.2	-11.7%	13	9	57	6.3	3.2	0	74%

Offensive Line

Year	Yards	ALY	Rank	Power	Rank	10+ Yds	Rank	Stuff	Rank	Sack	ASR	Rank
2004	4.41	4.32	12	74%	2	20%	5	22%	9	14	2.8%	1
2005	3.41	3.59	30	67%	13	14%	18	25%	16	27	4.8%	6
2006	4.11	4.27	16	63%	18	15%	19	24%	17	24	3.7%	3

Year	LE	Rank	LT	Rank	Mid	Rank	RT	Rank	RE	Rank
2004	3.54	25	4.47	15	4.38	12	5.08	4	4.19	11
2005	2.88	30	4.41	12	3.34	31	4.06	18	3.80	19
2006	4.63	6	4.84	7	4.02	26	4.28	11	3.43	26

Zone blocking, that latest NFL fad, was installed in Green Bay in 2006 with some positive results. Rookie guards Jason Spitz and Daryn Colledge both played well after being thrown into the fire. Colledge is probably the slightly better player because he's quicker, but both were excellent finds for the Packers. Center Scott Wells showed flashes of potential in his first year as full-time center and should grow with the young guards. Tackles Chad Clifton and Mark Tauscher continue their run as solid, workmanlike bookends, but Clifton is starting to get beat more often in pass protection. The best surprise was rookie Tony Moll, who filled in across the line and proved invaluable for his versatility. Rookie Allen Barbre, a fourth-round pick from Missouri Southern State, could step in at tackle if one of the veterans is injured. Predictably for a line with so many young players, it got better as the season progressed. Game charters listed the Packers as having blown 14 blocks, but only six were by the starting offensive linemen. That was a big improvement over 2005, but the line will have to take another step forward this season if the Packers hope to make the playoffs.

Defensive Front Seven

Defensive Line	Age	Pos	Plys	TmPct	Rk	Stop	Dfts	StpRt	Rk	AvYd	Rk	Sack	Hit	Hur	Runs	RuStp	RuYd	Pass	PaStp	PaYd
Aaron Kampman	28	DE	89	11.1%	2	62	28	70%	69	1.7	44	15.5	18	24	68	63%	3.6	21	90%	-4.4
Ryan Pickett	28	DT	70	8.8%	3	51	8	73%	52	3.2	69	0	2	3	59	73%	3.1	11	73%	3.6
Kabeer Gbaja-Biamila	30	DE	41	5.1%	51	31	14	76%	51	1.2	30	6.5	13	16	32	69%	3.4	9	100%	-6.7
Colin Cole	27	DT	38	5.1%	38	24	4	63%	67	2.7	57	1	1	1	36	64%	2.6	2	50%	3.5
Corey Williams	27	DT	38	4.8%	49	28	13	74%	50	1.3	26	7	4	4	21	67%	2.7	17	82%	-0.3
Cullen Jenkins	26	DT	34	4.9%	46	27	17	79%	33	0.3	6	6	7	10	20	75%	2.4	14	86%	-2.6
Mike Montgomery	24	DE	16	2.9%	—	12	2	75%	—	2.9	—	1.5	4	4	12	75%	3.5	4	75%	1.3

Linebackers	Age	Pos	Plys	TmPct	Rk	Stop	Dfts	StpRt	AvYd	Sack	Hit	Hur	Runs	RuStp	Rk	RuYd	Rk	Tgts	Suc%	Rk	PaYd	Rk
A. J. Hawk	23	OLB	126	15.8%	18	77	26	61%	4.1	3.5	2	5	74	66%	38	3.8	68	46	52%	44	5.6	25
Nick Barnett	26	ILB	113	15.1%	21	62	22	55%	4.5	2	3	13	68	62%	59	3.8	66	53	47%	60	6.7	68
Brady Poppinga	28	OLB	63	7.9%	89	40	10	63%	4.5	1	2	5	41	71%	23	3.0	23	32	53%	39	8.6	89

Year	Yards	ALY	Rank	Power	Rank	10+ Yds	Rank	Stuff	Rank	Sack	ASR	Rank
2004	4.60	4.10	11	56%	9	26%	31	26%	8	40	6.9%	16
2005	3.95	4.35	24	64%	18	13%	9	24%	17	35	7.3%	14
2006	4.17	4.50	23	53%	4	14%	7	21%	26	46	8.1%	5

Year	LE	Rank	LT	Rank	Mid	Rank	RT	Rank	RE	Rank
2004	4.17	13	3.63	4	4.50	26	3.63	3	3.60	13
2005	4.14	17	5.10	32	4.27	21	4.01	14	4.45	20
2006	4.60	23	4.82	24	4.68	26	3.66	11	4.28	19

At Football Outsiders, we prefer defensive ends that play both the run and the pass, which is one reason why we love Aaron Kampman. He made more plays in the running game than any other 4-3 end and still finished second in the NFL in sacks, second in quarterback hits, and sixth in hurries. Kabeer Gbaja-Biamila used to be a pass-rush specialist who made up for his poor run play by terrorizing quarterbacks. His quick first step has slowed just a touch, and his complete ineffectiveness against the run eventually cost him his job. Cullen Jenkins replaced him late in the year and is much more of a two-way player and a potential emerging star. Inside, tackle Ryan Pickett struggles to get penetration, but rarely is taken out of plays. First-round pick Justin Harrell from Tennessee is an amazing physical specimen whose only flaw is a history of injuries. Corey Williams and Colin Cole have been stretched as starters, but are valuable members of the tackle rotation. If healthy, the Packers will have one of the top defensive lines in the league.

(continued next page)

Defensive Front Seven *(continued)*

At linebacker, A. J. Hawk was the can't-miss prospect everyone expected. The only question now is whether he will emerge as a consistent Pro Bowl-caliber player, or just a very good long-term starter. He can run. He can hit. He can cover. For now, he can also be blocked, but it was still an impressive rookie season. Middle linebacker Nick Barnett never lived up to the hype of his rookie year, but the Packers finally realized he was a good if not great player and signed him to an extension. Strongside linebacker Brady Poppinga fills holes well, but does nothing outstanding. He may be challenged by Abdul Hodge, last year's third-round pick who fought injuries throughout his rookie season.

Defensive Secondary

Secondary	Age	Pos	Plys	TmPct	Rk	Stop	Dfts	RuYd	Rk	RuStp	Rk	Tgts	Tgt%	Rk	Dist	Suc%	Rk	PaYd	Rk	PD	Int
Al Harris	33	CB	57	7.1%	64	22	8	16.6	81	9%	80	67	16%	58	13.9	63%	4	6.1	10	15	3
Charles Woodson	31	CB	80	10.0%	27	46	24	4.3	9	65%	5	87	20%	31	10.0	54%	34	5.9	7	18	8
Nick Collins	24	FS	94	11.8%	20	36	19	7.3	50	43%	40	47	10%	9	13.7	45%	59	9.4	58	13	3
Patrick Dendy	25	CB	34	5.7%	—	9	4	6.3	—	0%	—	44	14%	—	14.0	50%	—	9.6	—	7	3
Marquand Manuel	28	SS	83	10.4%	35	29	11	4.8	11	53%	19	28	6%	54	14.2	43%	63	11.5	70	3	1
Ahmad Carroll*	24	CB	8	3.3%	—	3	1	6.0	—	0%	—	15	11%	—	16.0	50%	—	9.9	—	0	1

Year	Pass D Rank	DVOA vs. #1 WR	Rank	DVOA vs. #2 WR	Rank	DVOA vs. Other WR	Rank	DVOA vs. TE	Rank	DVOA vs. RB	Rank
2004	29	12.4%	21	-10.6%	5	9.0%	27	45.2%	32	40.1%	32
2005	22	-4.9%	9	7.5%	28	9.5%	25	25.8%	29	8.3%	23
2006	4	-15.2%	7	-37.5%	2	-11.4%	13	-35.3%	2	23.9%	28

Al Harris has been one of the five best cornerbacks in the league for the past several seasons. It is a great injustice that he has never made a Pro Bowl while DeAngelo Hall has made two. Unfortunately, Harris is already 32 years old. He has amazing technique and physicality, but, at some point, his lack of speed will start to cause problems. On the other side, a healthy Charles Woodson was a pleasant surprise in 2006. Woodson is extremely inconsistent, ranging from frequently beaten gambler to dominating presence on a week-to-week basis, but the net result was an above-average number-two cornerback. Ahmad Carroll's remains were peeled off the turf in Philadelphia, and he was released the next week. Patrick Dendy stepped in at nickel back, but he is merely serviceable. Frank Walker, signed from the Giants, doesn't promise to offer much more.

Safety was a bigger problem, where free-agent acquisition Marquand Manuel struggled in coverage and run defense. Nick Collins looked good by comparison, but his coverage skills in particular leave something to be desired. The Packers grabbed Aaron Rouse in the third round of this year's draft to help in run defense. The Virginia Tech product plays well close to the line of scrimmage, but he won't change the fact that the Packers' safeties are a liability in pass coverage.

Special Teams

Year	DVOA	Rank	FG/XP	Rank	Net Punt	Rank	Punt Ret	Rank	Net Kick	Rank	Kick Ret	Rank	Hidden	Rank
2004	0.9%	14	5.0	7	-1.2	17	0.4	14	0.0	14	1.2	13	7.6	5
2005	-3.8%	30	-8.7	29	-6.2	27	7.9	4	-3.1	21	-12.1	30	-8.6	27
2006	-3.9%	29	-5.9	29	-4.9	23	-2.3	22	3.4	14	-13.5	31	-14.4	31

The Packers special teams were bad enough on their own, and they received no help from Lady Luck. Opponents were an amazing 26-of-27 on field goals, with the only miss a 52-yard attempt by Miami's Olindo Mare. The Packers broke in Dave Rayner's big leg as place kicker, which paid off on kickoffs but cost them on field goals. Rayner will have a camp battle with sixth-round pick Mason Crosby out of Colorado. Scouts say Crosby's long-range field goals and booming kickoffs are not a product of altitude, but we'll believe it when we see it at sea level. Nine years after a memorable punt return touchdown against Ohio State helped him win the Heisman Trophy, Charles Woodson finally got a chance to be a regular punt returner in the NFL and was merely average. The bigger problem was on kickoff returns, where the Packers were the worst in the league. Vernand Morency and Koren Robinson were equally bad, meaning much of the problem was the blocking. Punter Jon Ryan has a big enough leg, but he put too many punts into the end zone in his first season. He did, however, complete a 16-yard pass on a fake punt in his first career NFL game.

Coaching Staff

Mike McCarthy had a rather undistinguished résumé before coming to Green Bay for his first head-coaching job. The offense he guided in San Francisco was hardly a juggernaut. Nonetheless, he and offensive coordinator Joe Philbin did a great job developing the Packers' young offensive talent, particularly on the offensive line. One critique is their pass-happy ways. The Packers threw more in the first two quarters than all but two teams. They also struggled mightily in the red zone and will need to develop more creative ways to get the ball into the end zone. Defensive coordinator Bob Sanders may only be the second most important person with that name in the NFL, but the coaching lifer did a good job in his first year as an NFL coordinator. Sanders rarely blitzed out of fear of putting his safeties in man coverage, but it did not affect the team's ability to generate a pass rush. At times, however, his coverage schemes would become predictable. The whole staff deserves some blame for the inconsistent play of the team overall.

Minnesota Vikings

Great football teams run the ball and stop the run. Talking heads shout this refrain at us every season. All the pretty passing in the world is rendered meaningless if a team cannot control the line of scrimmage. At Football Outsiders, we pride ourselves on our unconventional wisdom, but even we argue that line play is often underrated.

All that is well and good, but without a competent passing game, even the best running team in the league is going to get stuffed by a front-loaded defense. We are not living in 1975. The modern NFL is a passing league. Sadly, the Vikings have not gotten the message.

The Vikings have made major investments in their offensive and defensive lines in recent years, but they still posted a mediocre 6–10 record in 2006. The Vikings drafted four linemen in the first round between 2002 and 2005. They signed free-agent defensive tackle Pat Williams to a sizable contract two years ago, and broke the bank for offensive guard Steve Hutchinson before last season. Long-time center Matt Birk remains highly compensated. The net result of this amazing investment was an incomparable run defense, but not much else.

The Vikings' rush defense DVOA of −33.6% in 2006 was the best in the NFL since the incredible 2000 Baltimore Ravens. Minnesota's defensive tackle tandem of Kevin and Pat Williams was simply impossible to contain. Both players require a constant double team, and obviously a team cannot have four players assigned to block two. Kevin is the more complete player, and a fine run defender in his own right, but Pat Williams is a sight to behold defending the run. Somehow this man weighing a good 30 pounds more than his listed 317 is able to slice through seams and constantly break through to his opponent's backfield. Pat Williams is not just a player that occupies blockers; he blows up the offensive line.

The impact of the two Williams can hardly be overstated. Last year, the Ravens were proud owners of the NFL's second best Adjusted Line Yards average on runs up the middle at 3.78. The Vikings allowed just 2.95. The difference between those two teams was equal to the difference between Baltimore and 24th ranked Washington.

Of course, the run defense was not solely about the two Williamses. Both were on the team a season ago when the team's run defense was roughly league average. Kenechi Udeze somehow recorded no sacks despite starting 16 games at defensive end last year, but he is a sound run defender who had missed most of the 2005 season with an injury. Even more importantly, defensive coordinator Mike Tomlin let E. J. Henderson loose at weakside linebacker, the Derrick Brooks position in the Tampa-2. Henderson, a disappointment early in his career, emerged as a run-stopping force in a system that allowed him to attack the line of scrimmage. The new system also emphasized run support by its cornerbacks, allowing Antonio Winfield to arguably supplant Ronde Barber as the best run defense corner in football.

The 2000 Ravens are one of the three teams in the last 11 years to have a better run defense DVOA than the 2006 Vikings, but the Vikings had a lot more in common with the other two: the 1998 and 1999 San Diego Chargers, who wasted their amazing defensive play on some of the worst quarterbacks in NFL history. Like those Chargers teams, the rest of the Vikings' units ranged from mediocre to downright horrendous. While the defensive line excelled against the run, they put no pressure on opposing quarterbacks.

Teams quickly learned that running against the Vikings was a futile endeavor and turned to the air. The turning point came on *Monday Night Football* against the Patriots in Week 7. The Patriots called passing plays on 28

VIKINGS PROSPECTUS

2006 Record: 6–10

DVOA Estimated Wins: 7.9 (15th)

Pythagorean Wins: 6.6 (22nd)

DVOA: −9.0% total (22nd), −11.1% weighted (22nd)

Offense: −15.9% DVOA (29th)

Defense: −10.6% DVOA (4th)

Special Teams: −3.6% DVOA (27th)

Variance: 7.7% (32nd)

2006: Vikings spend the season showing how difficult it is to win without a passing game.

2007: Gluttons for punishment, the Vikings try to beat the odds again.

2007 Mean Projection: 7.5 wins

The Brohm Closet (0–4): 10%

Bad Team (5–6): 25%

Mediocre (7–8): 33%

Playoff Contender (9–10): 24%

Super Bowl Contender (11+): 9%

Projected Average Opponent: −2.1% DVOA (21st in NFL)

of their 34 first half plays and built a 17–0 lead. By the end of the season, the Vikings had faced 348 rushes and a staggering 628 pass attempts. Since the liberalization of passing rules in 1978, 86 different teams with losing records still faced at least 55 percent passes, but no losing team had ever faced 60 percent passes. Last year, Vikings opponents passed 64 percent of the time.

Despite all those pass attempts, the Vikings totaled only 30 sacks. After adjusting for opponent quality and opportunity with Adjusted Sack Rate, the Vikings had the second worst pass rush in all of football last year. Clearly, the loss of defensive end Erasmus James to a torn ACL was a problem, but James is not exactly Reggie White. The Vikings, despite Tomlin's Tampa-2 pedigree, were also not afraid to blitz. They brought at least six rushers more often than all but two other teams according to our game-charting stats. Tomlin brought linebackers for the most part, but to little effect.

Tomlin's blitz-happy ways often left his cornerbacks in single coverage, but Winfield and rookie Cedric Griffin held up remarkably well. Stalwart safety Darren Sharper saw a major decrease in interceptions but remained effective controlling the middle of the field. The rest of the pass defense was extremely problematic. Cornerback Fred Smoot again proved incapable of stopping anyone and quickly lost his job to Griffin. Between two poor years on the field and the "Love Boat" incident, Smoot has been among the worst free-agent signings of recent years.

A more consistent problem was with the linebackers. Henderson, so dominant against the run, struggled in coverage. He was targeted early and often, more than any linebacker besides Antonio Pierce and Lance Briggs (the latter of whom actually excels in coverage). Equally bad were middle linebacker Napoleon Harris and safety Dwight Smith.

The good news is that the Vikings seem to understand why they struggled. Smoot was released, the most predictable divorce since Britney and K-Fed. Harris was allowed to walk as well, opening up the door for second-year linebacker Chad Greenway who tore his ACL before the 2006 season. Greenway has good speed and should be an upgrade in pass defense at middle linebacker.

Also, the Vikings have a bevy of safety prospects to compete with Smith. They imported Mike Doss from Indianapolis and re-signed Tank Williams, who missed last season with a fractured knee. They also hope for continued development from 2006 draftee Greg Blue.

All the defense in the world will not help if the Vikings passing offense remains so inept. Head coach Brad Childress is best known for the years he served under the pass-happy Andy Reid in Philadelphia. Before that, however, he was offensive coordinator in Wisconsin during the Ron Dayne era. He clearly likes to pound the football. To help,

2007 Vikings Schedule					
Week	**Opp**	**Week**	**Opp**	**Week**	**Opp**
1	ATL	7	at DAL	13	DET
2	at DET	8	PHI	14	at SF
3	at KC	9	SD	15	CHI (Mon.)
4	GB	10	at GB	16	WAS
5	BYE	11	OAK	17	at DEN
6	at CHI	12	at NYG		

the Vikings imported Hutchinson, welcomed back Birk from injury and acquired free agent Chester Taylor from the Ravens. Pound the football the Vikings did. Taylor had at least 24 carries seven times in the first 11 games.

The problem for the Vikings was that quarterback Brad Johnson and a pedestrian group of receivers posed no threat to opposing defenses. So, as the Vikings made it clear they were going to run the ball, more and more teams stacked the box. The Vikings were consistently running the ball into eight-man fronts, and the results were as expected. Despite their major investment in the running game, the Vikings' rushing attack ranked 23rd in the league according to DVOA. That high-priced offensive line will never get a chance to show its worth unless there's an increase in talent in the passing game.

Unfortunately, this offensive dysfunction was not remedied in the offseason. The Vikings passed on Brady Quinn in the draft and did not make a run at David Carr, Trent Green, or any of the other experienced free-agent passers. Rather, the Vikings have decided that Tarvaris Jackson is their quarterback. The Vikings moved up in the 2006 draft to acquire the Alabama State product and now place the future of the team on his very unproven shoulders.

Competent play from Jackson is extremely unlikely. In limited playing time as a rookie, Jackson was terrible. He has adequate NFL skills, but he is not some übertalent that can be expected to break out once he gains some experience. He has a strong arm and solid mobility, but neither skill is overwhelming. Meanwhile, he has major accuracy problems, and, last season, he immediately fled the pocket when his first read was covered. Perhaps Childress sees Donovan McNabb when he looks at Jackson. The perennial Pro Bowler was equally terrible his first season before busting out in his second year. McNabb, however, is one of the game's top physical talents and was a big-time performer at a top major college. Jackson is, at best, a decent talent who played at an I-AA school.

Despite placing so much faith in Jackson, the Vikings failed to surround him with any game-changing receivers. The team's best receiver a season ago, Travis Taylor, was not re-signed. The Minnesota receiver with the most touchdowns, Marcus Robinson, was released before last season ended. Neither is a great player, but both are better than what the Vikings have left. The current depth is topped by frustrating drop machine Troy Williamson. The rest of the corps will be filled out by the winners of "Replacement-Level Death Match 2007," starring Billy McMullen, Cortez Hankton, Bobby Wade, and Randy Hymes. The Vikings drafted Sidney Rice, a player with great physical talent but unrefined technique, despite the disappointment of Williamson, a player who came out of college with great physical talent but unrefined technique. Rice may develop into a great receiver, but it will certainly not be this season.

Instead, the Vikings' major offensive upgrade was the drafting of running back Adrian Peterson. Peterson was the proverbial "best player available," and some scouts compare him to the great Eric Dickerson. If Peterson can remain healthy, he certainly has the potential to be the rare game-changing running back. No running back, however, is likely to be successful running into eight-man fronts all the time. Ronnie Brown's lack of success in Miami should hint at the problems Peterson may face. Peterson is probably more talented, but Brown's two seasons with −9.5% DVOA or worse should scare Vikings fans everywhere.

Peterson will join the Williamses, Winfield, Hutchinson, and a handful of other extremely talented players whose great play will be undermined by a bumbling passing game. Maybe Childress is right about Jackson. Maybe he is the next Donovan McNabb, but the evidence indicates he is the next Charlie Frye. The defense already played at a high level last season, and the running game already had quality names on paper, but the lack of a passing game held the Vikings to a 6–10 finish. With Jackson under center, this show is going to be a rerun nobody wants to watch.

Ned Macey

Vikings 2006 Stats by Week

Wk	vs.	W–L	PF	PA	YDF	YDA	TO	DVOA			
								Total	Off	Def	ST
1	@WAS	W	19	16	309	266	0	-14.3%	-24.6%	-17.3%	-7.0%
2	CAR	W	16	13	365	271	0	-0.2%	-0.7%	-4.3%	-3.9%
3	CHI	L	16	19	286	325	0	-7.5%	-2.8%	3.1%	-1.6%
4	@BUF	L	12	17	330	298	-2	-26.9%	-19.7%	10.2%	3.0%
5	DET	W	26	17	336	217	+1	22.8%	-5.5%	-39.3%	-11.1%
6	BYE										
7	@SEA	W	31	13	332	290	+3	44.4%	-14.4%	-44.7%	14.1%
8	NE	L	7	31	284	430	-2	-53.1%	-25.5%	28.4%	0.8%
9	@SF	L	3	9	238	133	-2	12.4%	-32.6%	-44.2%	0.8%
10	GB	L	17	23	312	394	-2	-14.8%	-5.5%	8.4%	-1.0%
11	@MIA	L	20	24	361	261	-1	5.0%	-8.4%	-13.6%	-0.1%
12	ARI	W	31	26	412	412	+4	-7.6%	22.2%	14.8%	-15.0%
13	@CHI	L	13	23	346	107	0	11.4%	-36.4%	-72.1%	-24.3%
14	@DET	W	30	20	328	280	+4	16.8%	2.8%	-30.3%	-16.2%
15	NYJ	L	13	26	307	391	+1	-35.9%	-17.7%	0.4%	-17.8%
16	@GB	L	7	9	104	319	+2	-25.6%	-60.8%	-30.5%	4.7%
17	STL	L	21	41	293	416	-2	-66.3%	-45.0%	34.3%	13.0%

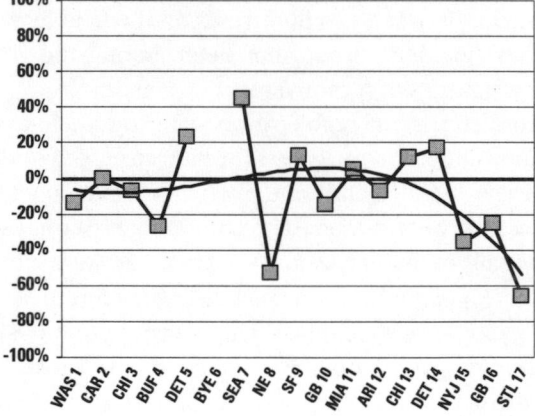

2006 MIN Weekly DVOA Performance

Trends and Splits

	Offense	Rank	Defense	Rank
Total DVOA	-15.9%	29	-10.6%	4
Unadjusted VOA	-14.2%	28	-12.1%	4
Weighted Trend	-17.8%	30	-11.0%	7
Variance	4.0%	27	8.2%	8
Passing	-23.2%	30	3.5%	15
Rushing	-7.7%	22	-33.6%	1
First Down	-13.1%	24	-20.0%	4
Second Down	-19.8%	29	-6.0%	12
Third Down	-15.2%	26	0.9%	13
Red Zone	-29.6%	29	-39.7%	2
Late and Close	-25.3%	29	-38.4%	1

Five-Year Performance

	2006	2005	2004	2003	2002
W-L	6-10	9-7	8-8	9-7	6-10
Pythagorean Wins	6.6	6.9	8.2	9.5	6.8
Estimated Wins	7.9	7.8	8.6	8.9	6.2
Total DVOA	-9.0%	-7.2%	-0.5%	7.7%	-12.4%
Rank	22	21	15	13	26
Offense	-15.9%	-5.9%	26.3%	15.9%	8.5%
Rank	29	17	3	3	7
Defense	-10.6%	0.6%	23.8%	3.0%	15.4%
Rank	4	19	32	21	28
Special Teams	-3.6%	-0.6%	-3.1%	-5.2%	-5.4%
Rank	27	20	27	31	30

Strategic Tendencies

Formations		Rank	Run/Pass		Rank	Defense		Rank	Other		Rank
3+ WR	47%	17	Runs, all plays	43%	22	Sacks by LB	33%	11	Run with 2+ RB	54%	20
4+ WR	9%	18	Runs, first half	47%	9	Sacks by DB	7%	17	Run with 2+ TE	40%	11
2+ TE	28%	13	Runs, first down	52%	20	Rush 6+	13.8%	3	Play action	19%	16
Single back	58%	11	Runs, power sit.	68%	12	Rush 7+	1.2%	19	Go for it on 4th	1.01	12
Empty back	1.3%	23	Runs, behind 2H	31%	20	Rush 3	4.8%	17	Offensive Pace	32.9	29
Max protect	10%	22	Pass, ahead 2H	45%	11	CB1 on WR1	36%	26	Defensive Pace	28.5	1

Minnesota threw to the right side of the field more often than any offense except for San Francisco and Seattle.... The Vikings only ran draws on three percent of their running plays (ranked 28th) and posted DVOA of -17.9% (ranked 26th) on those draws.... Minnesota quarterbacks led the league in interceptions when hurried.... Minnesota's defense had the lowest percentage of passes defensed compared to total passes. However, they also tied with Philadelphia as the defense which forced the most throwaways.... The Minnesota pass rush was average with 1 to 6 yards to go (7.2% ASR), but the worst in the league with 7-plus yards to go (4.2% ASR).

Passing

Player	DPAR	DVOA	Plys	NtYds	Avg	YAC	C%	TD	Int
Brad Johnson*	1.7	-12.3%	436	2559	5.9	4.9	61.9%	9	15
Tarvaris Jackson	-11.9	-44.6%	80	437	5.5	6.5	58.8%	2	0
Brooks Bollinger	5.1	36.7%	18	104	5.8	8.0	72.2%	0	4

Rushing

Player	DPAR	DVOA	Plys	Yds	Avg	TD	Fum	Suc
Chester Taylor	7.4	-9.4%	303	1219	4.0	6	4	46%
Artose Pinner	3.9	8.0%	43	190	4.4	3	1	34%
Mewelde Moore	3.8	33.7%	24	131	5.5	0	0	35%
Brad Johnson*	-0.3	-18.9%	21	83	4.0	1	9	—
Ciatrick Fason	5.1	55.2%	18	99	5.5	1	0	40%
Tarvaris Jackson	0.6	-9.5%	15	77	5.1	1	3	—
Tony Richardson	0.2	-11.5%	5	12	2.4	0	0	52%
Bethel Johnson*	-0.6	-62.2%	4	8	2.0	0	0	—

Receiving

Player	DPAR	DVOA	Plys	Ctch	Yds	Y/C	YAC	TD	C%
WR									
Travis Taylor	8.4	0.3%	86	56	647	11.6	3.2	3	65%
Troy Williamson	-1.0	-16.3%	76	37	455	12.3	5.3	0	50%
Marcus Robinson	-0.3	-15.9%	58	29	384	13.2	4.1	4	49%
Billy McMullen	5.1	4.5%	42	24	306	12.8	4.2	2	57%
Bethel Johnson*	1.4	-3.6%	19	9	156	17.3	8.1	0	47%
Martin Nance	-2.9	-75.3%	7	4	33	8.3	3.5	0	57%
Bobby Wade	*11.2*	*15.0%*	*58*	*33*	*461*	*14.0*	*4.8*	*2*	*50%*
TE									
Jermaine Wiggins*	1.8	-8.2%	67	46	390	8.5	2.6	1	69%
Jim Kleinsasser	-3.0	-40.2%	16	7	47	6.7	2.3	0	67%
Jeff Dugan	-1.2	-26.5%	13	8	40	5.0	3.9	1	62%
Richard Owens	-0.7	-24.3%	9	6	45	7.5	3.2	1	44%
Visanthe Shiancoe	*-0.2*	*-13.9%*	*14*	*12*	*81*	*6.8*	*3.3*	*0*	*86%*
RB									
Mewelde Moore	5.3	9.4%	62	46	468	10.0	10.0	1	74%
Chester Taylor	2.1	-2.2%	51	42	288	7.0	7.3	0	82%
Tony Richardson	3.4	34.6%	14	13	111	9.0	6.6	0	93%
Ciatrick Fason	-0.3	-20.5%	5	3	19	6.0	7.0	0	60%

Offensive Line

Year	Yards	ALY	Rank	Power	Rank	10+ Yds	Rank	Stuff	Rank	Sack	ASR	Rank
2004	4.70	4.50	7	71%	6	18%	10	23%	12	45	7.9%	22
2005	3.75	3.55	31	63%	17	21%	9	28%	27	55	10.2%	30
2006	4.20	4.30	14	68%	12	16%	14	24%	13	43	7.6%	22

Year	LE	Rank	LT	Rank	Mid	Rank	RT	Rank	RE	Rank
2004	3.79	22	5.28	2	4.59	8	4.78	6	3.80	17
2005	4.84	7	5.09	2	3.11	32	2.72	30	3.75	20
2006	3.00	27	4.85	6	4.33	19	4.54	6	5.15	5

The Vikings offensive line was not a bad unit in 2006, but this supposed strength of the offense was still disappointing. The most troubling aspect of the line was its failure in pass protection. Playing in front of jittery quarterback Brad Johnson, they rarely held firm. As a result, Johnson sensed pressure even if the danger was not imminent, throwing the ball away at every opportunity. Left guard Steve Hutchinson got an enormous contract, and, while he played well at times, he was far from dominating. The Vikings keep pretending that Bryant McKinnie is a dominant left tackle, but he is simply a solid player who can get beat on the outside rush. Center Matt Birk was not nearly as proficient as he used to be after missing the 2005 season due to injury. Those three, however, still provide a solid core. The right side was more troubling. Artis Hicks, brought from Philadelphia by Brad Childress, appeared to be merely a stopgap solution at right guard. The right tackle position, where Marcus Johnson struggled all season, was even more of a problem. Ryan Cook took over late in the year, but he may have trouble against quicker defensive ends.

Defensive Front Seven

Defensive Line	Age	Pos	Plys	TmPct	Rk	Stop	Dfts	StpRt	Rk	AvYd	Rk	Sack	Hit	Hur	Runs	RuStp	RuYd	Pass	PaStp	PaYd
Darrion Scott	26	DE	48	6.5%	33	34	15	71%	65	1.2	31	5.5	2	3	35	74%	1.4	13	62%	0.7
Pat Williams	35	DT	47	6.4%	15	43	16	91%	6	0.6	10	1	2	5	43	91%	0.9	4	100%	-2.3
Kevin Williams	27	DT	44	5.9%	23	40	19	91%	7	1.0	19	5	8	11	26	92%	1.2	18	89%	0.8
Kenechi Udeze	24	DE	30	4.1%	71	27	16	90%	6	1.7	48	0	5	13	25	100%	0.9	5	40%	5.8
Spencer Johnson	26	DT	15	2.3%	—	14	3	93%	—	1.7	—	0	2	3	13	100%	1.5	2	50%	3.0

Linebackers	Age	Pos	Plys	TmPct	Rk	Stop	Dfts	StpRt	AvYd	Sack	Hit	Hur	Runs	RuStp	Rk	RuYd	Rk	Tgts	Suc%	Rk	PaYd	Rk
E. J. Henderson	27	OLB	115	15.5%	20	61	27	53%	4.9	3	4	13	49	78%	3	2.0	1	63	41%	77	6.8	70
Napoleon Harris*	28	ILB	64	9.9%	72	32	15	50%	5.0	2.5	4	7	35	60%	66	3.3	38	21	34%	91	8.8	91
Ben Leber	29	OLB	53	7.6%	91	42	14	79%	3.0	3	0	3	31	77%	4	3.4	48	22	51%	46	5.9	31
Dontarrious Thomas	27	ILB	22	3.0%	—	13	3	59%	4.0	1	0	2	13	62%	—	2.8	—	6	36%	—	9.9	—

Year	Yards	ALY	Rank	Power	Rank	10+ Yds	Rank	Stuff	Rank	Sack	ASR	Rank
2004	4.54	4.71	32	74%	29	16%	16	19%	32	39	6.7%	20
2005	3.93	4.07	17	72%	26	17%	17	23%	23	33	6.4%	22
2006	2.97	2.78	1	47%	1	23%	29	40%	1	30	4.8%	31

Year	LE	Rank	LT	Rank	Mid	Rank	RT	Rank	RE	Rank
2004	4.68	25	5.35	32	4.89	32	4.53	27	3.51	10
2005	4.44	22	4.00	13	4.15	17	4.18	20	3.07	5
2006	2.08	3	2.56	1	2.95	1	2.84	3	3.10	7

As the main article shows, the Vikings were amazing against the run but suspect against the pass. The Vikings struggled mightily getting to the quarterback on defense. They blitzed linebackers constantly, had a dominant inside pass rusher in Kevin Williams, and were still one of the worst pass rushes in football. Kenechi Udeze was a major culprit, with no sacks despite being a starting defensive end. The struggles got to Udeze, who became trigger happy with constant offsides penalties. The Vikings even resorted to lining up linebacker Ben Leber at defensive end on obvious passing downs, but he also had limited success. The pass rush problems have not been solved this offseason, unless defensive end Erasmus James returns from injury to become a dominant pass rusher. Fourth-round pick Brian Robison is quick with a non-stop motor, but expecting the next Mark Anderson is overly optimistic, and the flexibility he showed moving between linebacker and defensive end at Texas won't be utilized by this defensive scheme. The lack of a pass rush from the line combined with new defensive coordinator Leslie Frazier's studies under Philadelphia coordinator Jim Johnson likely means an even heavier dose of blitzes in 2007.

One of Frazier's biggest tasks will to keep E. J. Henderson productive. The fifth-year linebacker struggled early in his career before finding his footing on the weak side last season. He should be an excellent blitzing weapon for Frazier. Chad Greenway was supposed to start at middle linebacker a year ago but missed the season with a torn ACL. He's more versatile than Napoleon Harris, who left for Kansas City in free agency, but, even if he is technically no longer a rookie, he is still inexperienced. The Vikings are likely trading run defense for pass defense, but that is a trade they can afford to make. One other positive about this unit is its impressive depth. With James's return, Darrion Scott will mix in the rotation at both defensive end positions, and Dontarrious Thomas is a quality fourth linebacker.

Defensive Secondary

Secondary	Age	Pos	Plys	TmPct	Rk	Stop	Dfts	RuYd	Rk	RuStp	Rk	Tgts	Tgt%	Rk	Dist	Suc%	Rk	PaYd	Rk	PD	Int
Antoine Winfield	30	CB	103	13.9%	1	51	22	2.6	1	73%	1	95	20%	33	10.5	56%	17	7.1	32	15	4
Fred Smoot*	28	CB	69	10.7%	20	24	13	6.1	33	63%	9	98	23%	10	8.1	42%	75	6.7	21	7	1
Cedric Griffin	25	CB	49	7.6%	52	24	11	8.6	59	40%	46	61	14%	65	11.7	58%	14	7.1	31	9	2
Dwight Smith	29	FS	87	12.5%	15	33	16	4.6	10	55%	13	39	8%	31	9.3	43%	64	8.5	47	7	4
Darren Sharper	32	SS	77	10.4%	34	28	10	5.9	28	39%	50	39	7%	43	12.8	69%	4	5.3	4	10	4
Ronyell Whitaker	28	CB	10	1.4%	—	5	3	0.0	—	100%	—	21	4%	—	9.7	38%	—	16.2	—	0	0
Mike Doss	26	SS	31	10.1%	—	14	5	6.5	—	35%	—	13	8%	—	13.5	65%	—	3.4	—	3	2

Year	Pass D Rank	DVOA vs. #1 WR	Rank	DVOA vs. #2 WR	Rank	DVOA vs. Other WR	Rank	DVOA vs. TE	Rank	DVOA vs. RB	Rank
2004	30	30.5%	30	8.9%	24	8.8%	26	34.5%	30	9.9%	23
2005	19	4.0%	14	-24.8%	5	-2.8%	16	24.6%	26	20.1%	29
2006	15	3.2%	19	-18.9%	5	18.7%	26	-7.9%	13	-13.8%	10

In 2005, Brian Williams stepped in for an ineffective Fred Smoot at cornerback to save the defense. Prior to last season, Williams left in free agency, and Smoot got another opportunity with a new coaching staff. Once again, Smoot was replaced, this time by rookie Cedric Griffin. Like Williams before him, Griffin answered the call and played extremely well. The other starting corner, Antoine Winfield, remains a solid cover man and great run defender, but in trying to avoid giving up the big play, he too often allows the underneath throw. Third-round pick cornerback Marcus McCauley was a potential draft steal. The Fresno State product has very good physical skills and many draft guides projected him as a second-rounder. He will be a natural fit if the Vikings retain a base Cover-2 scheme and should beat out Ronyell Whitaker, who struggled in limited action a season ago, for the nickel back position. Safety Darren Sharper's interceptions were down last year, so he did not get his Pro Bowl berth, but the veteran was still extremely effective in coverage. Training camp should feature a fierce battle between Dwight Smith, Mike Doss, Tank Williams, and Greg Blue for the other starting safety position. All are incomplete players, and the Vikings could consider playing the intriguing Blue in the base defense but using Doss or Williams as a nickel safety on passing downs.

Special Teams

Year	DVOA	Rank	FG/XP	Rank	Net Punt	Rank	Punt Ret	Rank	Net Kick	Rank	Kick Ret	Rank	Hidden	Rank
2004	-3.1%	27	-2.7	21	2.5	15	3.9	9	-13.8	30	-8.3	29	-5.4	22
2005	-0.6%	21	-8.8	30	-9.4	31	4.4	8	6.7	7	3.4	12	-1.2	17
2006	-3.6%	27	-3.4	23	-5.3	24	2.7	7	-12.8	29	-2.6	17	-3.8	20

For a team that wanted to play low-scoring, field position games, the Vikings were severely hampered by poor special teams play in 2006. They were only above average on punt returns, where do everything running back Mewelde Moore excelled. Bethel Johnson got the kick return job halfway through the season, but has since signed with Philadelphia as a free agent. The Vikings drafted fifth-round receiver Aundrae Allison, who has good kick returning skills, from East Carolina in this year's draft. If he is not up to the challenge, the Vikings will likely be left using whatever mediocre talent ends up as the fifth-string wide receiver. The free-agent signing of place kicker Ryan Longwell prior to last season was supposed to strengthen the Vikings while weakening their division rivals in Green Bay. Instead, the Vikings got a player on the downside of his career who struggled on kickoffs and field goals and has clearly lost leg strength. The punting game was little better with Chris Kluwe, who traded a little distance for more hang time, but remained mediocre.

Coaching Staff

Brad Childress waited a long time for a head coaching job, but he apparently failed to spend that time preparing for the opportunity. The play-calling in his first season was unimaginative, and both offensive and defensive players were questioning it by midseason. He was also extremely conservative on fourth downs. Defensive coordinator Mike Tomlin became an immediate star with his imaginative schemes, and he parlayed his success into the Steelers' head coaching position. To replace Tomlin, the Vikings hired Leslie Frazier, who worked with Childress in Philadelphia. Frazier loves to blitz, which created tension with Marvin Lewis when Frazier was defensive coordinator in Cincinnati. After two years working for the league's most infrequent blitzer, Tony Dungy, Frazier might be able to remain aggressive without taking unnecessary risks. The assistant coach with the most pressure on him may be quarterbacks coach Kevin Rogers, who has been given the responsibility of developing Tarvaris Jackson.

New Orleans Saints

The 2006 New Orleans Saints engineered the greatest franchise reversal in NFL history. It doesn't qualify as the greatest improvement by simply counting regular season wins. That honor belongs to the 1999 Indianapolis Colts, who went from 3–13 to 13–3 in Peyton Manning's second season. However, the Saints were the first 3–13 team to go to a conference championship the following season, and the spiritual reversal of the franchise far surpassed any numerical turnaround.

The Miracle of New Orleans goes past the emotional lift that the Saints gave their battered city. Remember, the Saints were in trouble before Hurricane Katrina ever hit. Their fan base was dwindling, and the team was considering a move to San Antonio or Los Angeles. To keep the team, the state of Louisiana was forced to make a deal that would pay owner Tom Benson if the Saints failed to sell enough tickets. On the field, the Saints were mired in mediocrity, their roster consisting of Joe Horn and a bunch of would-be fantasy football superstars who couldn't take their games to the next level.

Now, following their miracle 2006 season, the Saints are one of the most popular teams in the NFL, and feature two of the league's marquee players. Drew Brees is the very model of the All-American quarterback. Reggie Bush might be one of the ten best athletes who ever played the game and has charisma to spare. For the 2007 season, the Saints have sold out their luxury suites for the first time in history and suddenly have a waiting list for season tickets.

Nobody knows what will happen to the city of New Orleans in the future (actually, nobody knows what is happening to the city *now*; when is the last time you saw something about Katrina reconstruction on the news?), but the Saints are committed to staying in the city through at least 2010 and now have the largest, most fervent fan base in franchise history.

Nobody expected this, least of all us. In *Pro Football Prospectus 2006*, the Saints had the worst projection out of all 32 teams. We gave them a 59 percent chance of winning less than five games and a four percent chance of winning more than eight. So how did this turnaround happen? How did general manager Mickey Loomis and head coach Sean Payton completely rebuild both the roster and the psyche of this team in a single offseason? Along with good fortune and a few propitious bounces, these are the principal factors that brought about the Miracle of New Orleans:

The hurricane was a colossal variable that nobody could account for. Obviously, Hurricane Katrina played a part in the Saints' collapse to 3–13 in 2005, but there was no way to tell how large of a part. There was plenty of evidence that they would be bad in 2005 even before the hurricane hit. The Saints had a bunch of mediocre veterans mixed in with second-level offensive stars and an army of completely failed defensive tackle prospects. Still, if the 3–13 Saints of 2005 were really more of a 7–9 team, a division title in 2006 isn't really all that surprising. There's really no way to know how much of last season's improvement was simply the Saints reverting to how they would have played in 2005 if Hurricane Katrina had never happened.

Drew Brees's shoulder was fine. We knew that Drew Brees was a top-ten quarterback when healthy, so that wasn't the surprise. The surprise was that he saw no ill effects from injuring his shoulder in the final game of 2005. Chad Pennington was screwed up for a couple of seasons with the same injury, so we assumed that Brees would have similar

SAINTS PROSPECTUS

2006 Record: 10–6

DVOA Estimated Wins: 9.1 (8th)

Pythagorean Wins: 10.3 (6th)

DVOA: 11.0% total (9th), 11.4% weighted (8th)

Offense: 13.4% DVOA (5th)

Defense: 3.2% DVOA (19th)

Special Teams: 0.7% DVOA (14th)

Variance: 16.6% (15th)

2006: They didn't make the Super Bowl, but that doesn't make the Miracle of New Orleans any less impressive.

2007: The offense will score, the defense will regress.

2007 Mean Projection: 7.4 wins

The Brohm Closet (0–4): 9%

Bad Team (5–6): 27%

Mediocre (7–8): 33%

Playoff Contender (9–10): 23%

Super Bowl Contender (11+): 9%

Projected Average Opponent: 1.1% DVOA (11th in NFL)

2007 Saints Schedule

Week	Opp	Week	Opp	Week	Opp
1	at IND (Thu.)	7	ATL	13	TB
2	at TB	8	at SF	14	at ATL (Mon.)
3	TEN (Mon.)	9	JAC	15	ARI
4	BYE	10	STL	16	PHI
5	CAR	11	at HOU	17	at CHI
6	at SEA	12	at CAR		

problems. The Miami Dolphins assumed the same thing, which is why they chose trading for Daunte Culpepper over signing Brees as a free agent. Whoops.

The 2006 draft may be the best in Saints history. We knew that the Saints got lucky when Reggie Bush dropped into their laps, but we had no idea that an obscure seventh-rounder from Hofstra named Marques Colston would instantly become one of the four or five best possession receivers in the game. We didn't know that fourth-round guard Jahri Evans from the even more obscure Division II Bloomsburg University of Pennsylvania could go right into the starting lineup. And we didn't know that rookie safety Roman Harper would be a big part of the team's 4–1 start (although he went down for the year with a torn ACL in Week 5).

Along with the great rookies of 2006 came the maturation of other recent Saints draft picks. "2005 first-rounder Jammal Brown has the makings of an excellent tackle," we wrote last year, and by 2006 that excellent tackle was officially made. When veteran wide receiver Horn went down with injuries, 2004 second-rounder Devery Henderson moved into the starting lineup and finally fulfilled his potential as a deep threat, averaging 23 yards per reception and leading the league in DVOA for receivers with at least 50 passes.

Deuce McAllister is better now. The fact is that the pre-ACL injury McAllister was an overrated football player, a boom-and-bust runner who had a few too many stuffs at the line. The only season in which he had enough big plays to offset the negative value of all those zero- and one-yard gains was 2003. Sure, he's looked impressive since then, but people tend to mistake great athletes for effective football players. They are two different things, otherwise Carl Lewis would have played in three Super Bowls.

When the ACL injury in 2005 robbed him of some of his lateral movement, McAllister had to change his style. From the very start of last season, he charged ahead instead of shaking and baking in search of the big hole that never appeared. Suddenly, all that power people talked about emerged because he was running downhill instead of sideways, and he was getting his team to second-and-short instead of second-and-long. By the last few weeks, McAllister's lateral movement had returned, but the more effective style never changed.

The Saints rebuilt the linebacking corps. Dallas had a lot of linebackers, and neither Scott Fujita nor Scott Shanle fit into their 3-4 scheme. Payton grabbed Fujita in free agency, then dealt a meaningless seventh-round pick to his old team for Shanle, instantly upgrading the Saints' weakest unit. The third part of the upgrade came with the trade of wide receiver Donte' Stallworth for Mark Simoneau. Simoneau was nowhere near as good as Jeremiah Trotter in Philadelphia, but he was a much better option than guys such as Jay Foreman and Alfred Fincher.

The Saints had young talent at defensive end. We knew that Will Smith was a good player, while veteran Charles Grant still had unrealized potential. The bigger surprise was that the Saints didn't miss Darren Howard as much as we expected.

Sean Payton was an excellent head coach. We're writers, not therapists, and we're not fond of dipping our toes in the tides of psychoanalysis. Nonetheless, it seems pretty clear that Payton is an outstanding motivator who did an excellent job of changing this franchise's overall mood and getting the players to believe in themselves. It didn't hurt that his offensive game plans clearly had opponents guessing, especially when those opponents were the Dallas Cowboys.

Payton is not the first head coach to look like a genius in his first year, of course. Jim Haslett looked like a genius too. So did Jim Mora, Nick Saban, and many other head coaches who flamed out within a few years. No matter how interesting we find the story of the 2006 New Orleans Saints, there is a reason this book is called *Pro Football Prospectus 2007*. Are the Saints a magical one-year fluke, or is this team set to contend for the next few seasons?

Since 1972, 12 different teams have won four or fewer games in one year and ten or more the next. Two of those teams played last year, the Saints and Jets. Of the other ten, only the 1974–76 Baltimore Colts won more games in the third year, going from 10–4 to 11–3. Excluding the strike-year 1982 Jets, these ten teams declined by an average of 2.7 wins the year after their miracle turnarounds (table 1).

So history says that the Saints will probably go 7–9, and so does our win projection system. In this case, history doesn't mean much, and the win projection system probably has a Mardi Gras hangover. If we learned anything in 2006, we learned that you shouldn't use a team that lost a season to a hurricane to judge the results of statistical analysis—and vice versa.

The Saints offense should be as spectacular in 2007 as it was in 2006. In fact, considering that Reggie Bush didn't really get the hang of playing in the NFL until midseason, this year's offense might even be more spectacular. The only serious concern is the third-down rebound effect. The Saints' DVOA was 13.4% overall, but 30.1% on third down, a combination that usually presages decline.

On the other hand, consistency breeds success, especially on the offensive line. Ten of 11 offensive starters from the second half of the season return, 11 of 12 if we include Bush in the mix. The one new starter for 2007, free agent Eric Johnson, should be a major upgrade over last year's tight ends until he inevitably breaks himself.

Every single member of the Saints offense is either playing at his peak right now or not even there yet. Thirty-year-old guard Jamar Nesbit is the only starter older than 28. Joe Horn is gone, but after two injury-plagued years, he's not the same Joe Horn that put up 1,200-yard seasons for Saints teams of the past.

The outlook is not so rosy on defense. Last year's offense was all young talent on the way up, led by one ticked-off Drew Brees with something to prove. The defense, on the other hand, was made up of cornerback Mike McKenzie, two nice ends, and a bunch of guys playing over their heads. Fujita is a good linebacker, but not the Pro Bowl–level monster he was in the first half of 2006. Simoneau looked good last year at times, but at times he looked like the same replacement-level player that Philadelphia gave up on. Defensive tackle Hollis Thomas has health issues. Tackle Brian Young and outside linebacker Shanle are workman-like players, but nothing special. There's very little depth behind defensive ends Grant and Smith.

Table 1. From Losers to Winners . . . to Mediocrity?

Team	Year 1	Year 2	Year 3
1998–2000 Indianapolis Colts	3–13	13–3	10–6
1998–2000 St. Louis Rams	4–12	13–3	10–6
2003–2005 San Diego Chargers	4–12	12–4	9–7
1987–1989 Cincinnati Bengals	4–11	12–4	8–8
1975–1977 New England Patriots	3–11	11–3	9–5
1991–1993 San Diego Chargers	4–12	11–5	8–8
1974–1976 Baltimore Colts	2–12	10–4	11–3
1980–1982 New York Jets	4–12	10–5–1	6–3
2005–2007 New Orleans Saints	3–13	10–6	—
1999–2001 New Orleans Saints	3–13	10–6	7–9
2005–2007 New York Jets	4–12	10–6	—
1988–1990 Green Bay Packers	4–12	10–6	6–10

The Saints did address their biggest issue on defense, the raging inferno created by opposing receivers burning cornerback Fred Thomas. When Indianapolis low-balled restricted free agent Jason David, the Saints swept in and took him away with a new four-year contract. The Colts had given David the lowest-level tender, so the Saints only had to give up a fourth-round pick. The 25-year-old David is just entering his prime, and he's certainly faster than Thomas. On the other hand, like fellow Indianapolis refugee Nick Harper (who signed with Tennessee), David is going from the Colts' Tampa-2 zone coverage to a defense that primarily plays man-to-man, and there's no guarantee that he'll play as well in one scheme as he did in the other.

As for the rest of the cornerbacks, Jason Craft had a spectacular year as the nickel corner, but that year doesn't fit in with the rest of his career at all and is thus unlikely to be repeated. It was great to see Mike McKenzie return to the high level of play he established back in Green Bay, but he had not played that well in three years, so his performance may not be sustainable either. With a healthy Harper alongside Josh Bullocks, the Saints will at least have a nice young pair of safeties.

Oddly enough, the one reason for optimism on defense is the same reason for pessimism on offense: third downs. The Saints' defense was 3.2% DVOA overall, 25.6% on third downs. Poor third-down teams tend to rebound because problems on third down are usually obvious, and the front office will make these holes the highest offseason priority. The replacement of Thomas with David is a prime example of why the third-down rebound trend exists.

The 2007 prognosis for the Saints looks very similar to another recent year-after-miracle team, the 2000 Rams. The 2000 Rams had the fourth-highest offensive DVOA ever, a better offense than the two St. Louis teams that made it to the Super Bowl, but went 10–6 because their defense disintegrated, falling from 3rd to 26th. They lost the division to another team making a dramatic turnaround. Saints fans know all about this, because it was their team that beat out the Rams for the 2000 NFC West title.

So if the 2007 Saints are the 2000 Rams, who gets to be the 2000 Saints: the Bucs, the Panthers, or the Falcons? "None of the above," say the optimistic Saints fans—and after last year, why should there be any other kind?

Aaron Schatz

Onside Kickin' It

The Cowboys had just given up another touchdown to the Saints to fall behind by 18 points late in the third quarter. Time was running out; a three-score deficit made every possession from that point on critical. The Cowboys set up for the return, hoping to at least get good field position to start their comeback, then watched in disbelief as Billy Cundiff's surprise onside kick was recovered by the Saints. Four plays later, it was a 25-point game and essentially over.

There are two kinds of onside kicks: the kind you expect and the kind you don't. Both should be in every team's arsenal, but some teams have never even attempted the latter except on the practice field.

Seventy-eight "surprise" onside kicks have been attempted in the NFL since 1996. Fifty-five of them were recovered by the kicking team, a 71 percent success rate. Jimmy Johnson was among the first to embrace this play. In his four seasons with the Dolphins, his team utilized it six times. That still stands as the most attempts authorized by any head coach over the last 11 years. During Johnson's four years with the Dolphins, the rest of the league combined to use it just 13 times. Since Johnson retired from coaching, use of the play has increased to more than eight times per season on average, perhaps because of the success Johnson had with it.

Before the play became en vogue, Jeff Fisher's Titans had surprise onside kicks attempted against them in three consecutive seasons from 1998 to 2000 without attempting any themselves. Since then, Fisher has stopped worrying and come to love the surprise onside kick, calling for five of them. The play has been successful every time.

Most teams have put this play on at least once in the last 11 seasons, but not even the Titans run it as gleefully as the Atlanta Falcons. Mostly under the guidance of special teams' coordinator Joe DeCamillis, the Falcons have attempted 11 surprise onside kicks in the last 11 years, recovering ten of them. Joe DeCamillis is coaching Jacksonville's special teams in 2007, which means the Jaguars may try a surprise onside kick this year for the first time since their inaugural season in 1995.

In order to have a high rate of success, surprise onside kicks must actually be a surprise to the receiving team. That element of surprise is supplied by the state of the game when the play is run. The median situation in which a surprise onside kick is ordered up is late in the second quarter of a tie game. The first half of a deadlocked game would seem to be no time to be risking field position, but consider the relative risks involved.

The 71 percent recovery rate for surprise onside kicks is higher than the league average conversion rate for a 3rd- or 4th-and-1 play. A coach needs to reframe the issue and ask which risk is greater: The 29 percent chance that the opposition will recover a surprise onside kick in his team's territory, or the near certainty that the opposition will gain possession of a standard kickoff, likely downing the ball somewhere around their own 30 yard line.

In the "Statistical Toolbox" at the front of the book, there is a graph that shows the average value of field position over the last five seasons, based on the likelihood that the offense or defense will have the next score. We can use those numbers to perform a cost-benefit analysis on the standard kickoff vs. the surprise onside kick.

Having the ball at your own 40-yard line, which is generally where a surprise onside kick would be recovered, is worth roughly .94 points. If the other team has the ball at your 40-yard line, that's worth roughly –2.13 points. Combining those numbers with the 71 percent recovery rate indicates that a surprise onside kick will put the kicking team in a position from which the next score averages 0.05 points in their favor, and that doesn't even take into account the added bonus of removing a possession from the opposition.

In 2006, the average standard kickoff from the 30-yard line ended at the return team's 27.4-yard line. (We've removed both onside kicks and end-of-half squibs in this measurement.) Based on the numbers from the past five years, the average next score from this position is .24 points for the return team. So a surprise onside kick, on average, puts the kicking team in position to score .31 points more than a standard kickoff.

That's not a high number, but it is a positive one, and it indicates that the surprise onside kick is a good strategy. Most NFL coaches are risk-averse, but it must be very tempting to occasionally try to maintain possession at the risk of losing field position.

Curiously, the winning percentage of teams in games in which they employ this play is only .408. Knowing how successful the play is, that may seem surprisingly low. However, from 1996 through 2006, 51 of the 76 teams that have used the surprise onside kick, more than two-thirds, have had a lower DVOA than their opponents. In addition, 57 percent of these attempts have come on the road. Trying to beat a better team in their building can necessitate a risk of this nature, but it can only help so much. The play was successful for the team with the lower DVOA on the road 20 times, but that team only won six of those games. One good play for an overmatched team does not equal victory.

It is interesting to note that the two teams that have faced the highest number of surprise onside kicks since 1996 are Indianapolis and St. Louis. Both teams have been known for much of that time for their fast-break, high-scoring offenses, and both have had poor special teams during those years as measured by DVOA. This must play into the thought process of opposing teams. Taking away a possession from an offense gives them one less opportunity to score. Combined, the Colts and Rams have faced 19 surprise onside kicks and been burned 14 times (74 percent success for the kicking team). In their case, facing this play more often did not lead to stopping it more often. On the other hand, as discussed, in most cases Indianapolis and St. Louis were still the better team and were usually playing at home when this tactic was employed against them. So, they still combine for an 11–6 record in games in which teams attempted surprise onside kicks against them, despite their inability to stop it successfully.

The surprise onside kick gives the kicking team another possession, takes one away from the opposition, and forces other teams to wonder if the team might try a surprise onside kick again in the future. When facing a team that is known to have employed the surprise onside kick, front line blockers have to watch the ball all the way off the kicker's foot, rather than turning back early to get a head start on positioning within their blocking assignments. It's easy to believe that the split second lost can have a negative effect on the eventual return. Unfortunately, that is difficult to quantify.

The expected onside kick is a whole different story. The decision process regarding when to use it is much simpler, but the execution is much harder. In this case, everyone knows that the kicking team must maintain possession or the game will almost certainly end in their defeat. Both teams act accordingly, thus the rate of success is much lower for expected onside kicks than for surprise onside kicks. How much lower? Of 516 attempts since 1996, only 85 have been successful. That 16.5 percent success rate is almost literally a roll of the dice (there is a 16.7 percent chance that a given number will turn up on a single roll of a six-sided die). That is not much to pin a team's hopes on, but the play becomes necessary approximately every six games in the NFL.

A rule change from 2002 actually makes it even more difficult for a kicking team to recover an onside kick. Prior to that season, certain onside attempts that went out of bounds could actually be re-kicked. The original rule made no sense (why reward a team with another shot after they screwed up the first one) and the rule change makes for a small split in the data. From 1996–2001 the rate of recovery of expected onside kicks was 18.5 percent; since then, it is 13.7 percent. A more recent rule change may make it even more difficult to recover expected onside kicks. Now, teams must always line up with at least four players on each side of the ball. No longer can a team line up eight players on one side and have them sprint into the scrum. This rule change has not been around long enough to produce meaningful data, but it is probably reasonable to assume that the success rate will be driven further down because of it.

Do any splits exist that temper this low success rate and help the kicking team increase their rate of recovery? To dispel one common misperception, there really is not a strong advantage for recovery of expected onside kicks on artificial turf versus grass. The rate of recovery on artificial surfaces is 18 percent in 215 attempts compared to 16 percent in 301 attempts on grass. Nor is there any real difference between kicking at home (16.4 percent) versus on the road (16.6 percent). However, there actually is one split that noticeably increases the odds in favor of the kicking team. If the game is within reason at the moment of the kick, the kicking team's chances increase quite a bit.

Most expected onside kick attempts have zero chance of actually helping the kicking team win (Philadelphia, for example, tried an onside kick when down by 27 points with five seconds to play against the Colts in 1996). Conversely, onside kicks in one-score games have helped teams win even when they were attempted with as little as 26 seconds remaining. Separating kicks that happen during one-score deficits with a minimum of 26 seconds left from those that happen with the outcome already decided gives a much bigger spread than expected. The 194 "meaningful" onside kicks were recovered 42 times, or 22 percent. The 322 "meaningless" onside kicks have been recovered by the kicking team just 43 times, or 13 percent. Apparently, desperation is a powerful motivator.

No matter how the expected onside kick success rate is split, it is still awfully low, but one kicker has consistently beaten the odds: Jeff Wilkins of the Rams. Since 1996, Wilkins has attempted 17 expected onside kicks. The Rams have recovered eight of those (including two of three in the postseason). Statistically, the chance that this is just dumb luck is about 300 to one. For comparison, the next best kicker at expected onside kicks has been Neil Rackers, with five out of 12. That is quite good, but he would still need to hit three of his next five to match Wilkins.

No individual kicker or franchise has been especially cursed at recovering their own expected onside kicks. This is mostly because the odds of recovery are so low to begin with that it would take incredibly bad luck over a great deal of attempts to stand out as particularly awful. For example, the worst franchise at recovering their own expected onside kicks has been the Carolina Panthers at one recovery in 20 attempts. That sounds bad, but when the odds are only 16 percent to begin with a team that recovers only one out of 20 attempts is well within reason. The worst kicker has been Todd Sauerbrun, but his zero for 14 run is not particularly dire either.

The Chargers are the one team with a particularly poor record of recovering their opponent's expected onside kicks. They have allowed seven out of 21 attempts to be recovered by the kicking team, including two out of six attempts in meaningful situations as described above. As difficult as recovery is, of course, teams do not get points simply for recovering an onside kick. To that end, even though the Chargers have been poor at preventing opponents' expected onside kicks, they have actually gone on to lose only one game after allowing a successful one.

In reality, if a team is lining up for an expected onside kick the game is pretty much over. Of the more than 500 expected onside kicks attempted in the last 11 seasons, only ten recoveries actually contributed to a come-from-behind win. The Rams and Cowboys are the only teams to win more than one such game (each with two), and only the Steelers have lost two games in which their failure to capture an opponent's expected onside kick contributed to the loss.

Based on the information above, surprise onside kicks are much more important than expected onside kicks from a strategic standpoint. Given its 71 percent success rate, it is surprising that the play is not used more often. Of course, if it were used more, the success rate would logically decrease as it would be less surprising. Based on the cost/benefit analysis above, the surprise onside kick would no longer be advantageous at a success rate of 62 percent or lower. Field position is critical, but possessions are more so. A surprise onside kick that works is essentially a turnover. How many coaches have a play drawn up for their defense that results in a turnover 71 percent of the time?

Jason McKinley

Saints 2006 Stats by Week

Wk	vs.	W–L	PF	PA	YDF	YDA	TO	Total	Off	Def	ST
								DVOA			
1	@CLE	W	19	14	326	186	+1	11.4%	-12.2%	-25.1%	-1.5%
2	@GB	W	34	27	380	285	-1	10.6%	-1.7%	-0.9%	11.4%
3	ATL	W	23	3	326	229	0	61.1%	19.0%	-44.0%	-2.0%
4	@CAR	L	18	21	407	324	-1	-27.0%	26.4%	45.2%	-8.2%
5	TB	W	24	21	314	406	+1	-15.7%	1.9%	32.5%	14.9%
6	PHI	W	27	24	373	325	0	19.8%	25.3%	17.7%	12.3%
7	BYE										
8	BAL	L	22	35	403	293	-4	-34.8%	-10.6%	22.7%	-1.5%
9	@TB	W	31	14	363	226	+1	43.6%	30.8%	-11.5%	1.3%
10	@PIT	L	31	38	513	467	-3	-27.7%	30.3%	51.7%	-6.3%
11	CIN	L	16	31	595	385	-3	-12.5%	6.4%	4.5%	-14.4%
12	@ATL	W	31	13	427	333	0	53.7%	34.3%	-19.9%	-0.5%
13	SF	W	34	10	375	202	+3	45.3%	15.9%	-19.5%	9.9%
14	@DAL	W	42	17	536	347	+2	67.7%	69.4%	-5.4%	-7.1%
15	WAS	L	10	16	270	354	-1	-42.1%	-30.5%	11.6%	0.0%
16	@NYG	W	30	7	359	142	+3	73.5%	11.8%	-63.2%	-1.5%
17	CAR	L	21	31	297	313	-2	-48.9%	-17.7%	36.5%	5.2%
18	BYE										
19	PHI	W	27	24	435	355	-1	33.3%	34.7%	5.4%	4.0%
20	@CHI	L	14	39	375	340	-4	-24.6%	7.2%	15.0%	-16.8%

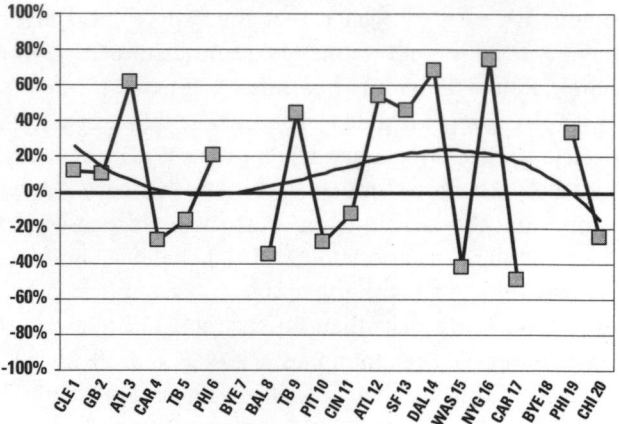

2006 NO Weekly DVOA Performance

Trends and Splits

	Offense	Rank	Defense	Rank
Total DVOA	13.4%	5	3.2%	19
Unadjusted VOA	13.8%	5	3.1%	19
Weighted Trend	16.4%	5	4.6%	17
Variance	5.7%	21	9.7%	4
Passing	22.8%	4	5.8%	21
Rushing	2.3%	10	0.2%	21
First Down	13.3%	7	-5.8%	15
Second Down	2.5%	14	0.9%	15
Third Down	30.1%	4	25.6%	28
Red Zone	4.3%	14	-17.2%	4
Late and Close	1.9%	14	5.6%	20

Five-Year Performance

	2006	2005	2004	2003	2002
W-L	10-6	3-13	8-8	8-8	9-7
Pythagorean Wins	10.3	3.6	6.6	8.4	9.0
Estimated Wins	9.1	5.4	6.1	8.1	9.1
Total DVOA	11.0%	-23.0%	-17.3%	-1.2%	8.3%
Rank	9	30	26	18	11
Offense	13.4%	-13.4%	-7.8%	4.2%	1.4%
Rank	5	25	26	12	19
Defense	3.2%	7.6%	15.2%	4.1%	3.1%
Rank	19	25	27	22	19
Special Teams	0.7%	-2.0%	5.7%	-1.2%	10.0%
Rank	14	24	3	23	1

Strategic Tendencies

Formations		Rank	Run/Pass		Rank	Defense		Rank	Other		Rank
3+ WR	48%	14	Runs, all plays	43%	19	Sacks by LB	22%	17	Run with 2+ RB	57%	19
4+ WR	14%	9	Runs, first half	42%	23	Sacks by DB	3%	27	Run with 2+ TE	32%	21
2+ TE	22%	22	Runs, first down	48%	26	Rush 6+	7.4%	20	Play action	23%	7
Single back	45%	26	Runs, power sit.	54%	30	Rush 7+	1.4%	16	Go for it on 4th	1.40	3
Empty back	7.7%	1	Runs, behind 2H	27%	28	Rush 3	1.9%	27	Offensive Pace	28.5	4
Max protect	11%	19	Pass, ahead 2H	43%	15	CB1 on WR1	39%	22	Defensive Pace	32.3	31

New Orleans ran the most five-wide sets in the NFL, although these sets often had one or two running backs as wide receivers. . . . Only Indianapolis and San Diego had more plays with non-wide receivers lined up as wide receivers. Not a surprise: Reggie Bush was lined up as a wide receiver more than twice as often as any other running back in the NFL. Definitely a surprise: Aaron Stecker was lined up as a wide receiver more often than any running back except for Bush, LaDainian Tomlinson, and Brian Westbrook. . . . When only two players lined up as wide receivers, New Orleans threw to a running back 40 percent of the time, compared to a league average of 23 percent. . . . With two running backs in the backfield, New Orleans ran the ball only 29 percent of the time, the lowest percentage in the NFL. League average was 41 percent. . . . Marques Colston ranked fourth in the NFL in the percentage of his team's passes thrown his way on third down. . . . New Orleans' defense had the third highest number of coverage sacks behind Atlanta and the New York Jets. . . . The Saints defense was the beneficiary of 37 drops, tied for second in the league.

Passing

Player	DPAR	DVOA	Plys	NtYds	Avg	YAC	C%	TD	Int
Drew Brees	105.7	28.3%	553	4322	7.8	5.5	64.6%	26	11
Jamie Martin	-4.5	-51.9%	24	185	7.7	NA	66.7%	1	1

Rushing

Player	DPAR	DVOA	Plys	Yds	Avg	TD	Fum	Suc
Deuce McAllister	26.5	9.9%	245	1061	4.3	11	2	53%
Reggie Bush	5.8	-3.4%	154	559	3.6	6	2	43%
Drew Brees	-7.7	-105.5%	16	57	3.6	0	7	—
Mike Karney	2.5	25.3%	11	33	3.0	1	0	38%
Jamaal Branch	0.4	-1.1%	10	29	2.9	0	0	44%
Aaron Stecker	0.7	49.9%	4	11	2.8	0	0	62%
Fred McAfee	1.4	116.7%	3	12	4.0	1	0	17%

Receiving

Player	DPAR	DVOA	Plys	Ctch	Yds	Y/C	YAC	TD	C%
WR									
Marques Colston	25.5	17.4%	115	70	1038	14.8	5.2	8	61%
Joe Horn*	19.7	31.7%	61	37	679	18.4	4.4	4	59%
Devery Henderson	20.2	39.9%	54	32	745	23.3	4.9	5	61%
Terrance Copper	5.3	2.9%	42	23	388	16.9	4.3	3	55%
Jamal Jones	3.6	42.5%	10	6	108	18.0	2.3	1	60%
John Owens	0.7	1.1%	5	4	44	11.0	1.0	0	80%
TE									
Mark Campbell	-1.1	-20.0%	29	18	164	9.1	4.3	0	62%
Billy Miller	-2.4	-31.2%	22	14	129	9.2	2.5	0	62%
Ernie Conwell*	-0.3	-19.2%	13	8	57	7.1	2.4	1	64%
Eric Johnson	*3.6*	*-0.1%*	*49*	*34*	*292*	*8.6*	*4.1*	*2*	*69%*
RB									
Reggie Bush	5.7	-1.2%	122	89	748	8.4	7.9	2	73%
Deuce McAllister	0.8	-5.6%	36	30	198	6.6	6.5	0	68%
Aaron Stecker	2.9	8.8%	28	19	190	10.0	3.6	0	83%
Mike Karney	3.2	18.0%	20	15	96	6.4	5.4	2	75%
Jamaal Branch	-0.3	-20.7%	6	5	14	2.8	NA	1	83%

Offensive Line

Year	Yards	ALY	Rank	Power	Rank	10+ Yds	Rank	Stuff	Rank	Sack	ASR	Rank
2004	4.04	3.88	27	58%	21	21%	3	26%	22	42	7.6%	19
2005	3.78	4.01	18	57%	25	14%	20	23%	7	41	7.3%	18
2006	3.99	4.37	11	54%	30	13%	25	22%	8	23	4.1%	4

Year	LE	Rank	LT	Rank	Mid	Rank	RT	Rank	RE	Rank
2004	3.61	24	3.53	29	3.87	26	5.01	5	2.99	28
2005	2.17	31	3.20	28	4.44	8	3.71	25	3.82	18
2006	4.38	12	4.12	21	4.55	9	3.91	28	4.43	10

The shocking truth is that the New Orleans offensive line did not improve dramatically between 2005 and 2006. The run blocking was a bit better, but that's been a gradual process over the last couple of seasons, not a sudden change. The gigantic improvement in Adjusted Sack Rate is primarily the result of blocking for Drew Brees, a quarterback who knows how to throw the ball away, rather than Aaron "Hey, Let's Run Backwards Ten Yards" Brooks. Tackles Jamaal Brown and Jon Stinchcomb are definitely better blocking for the run than they are protecting quarterbacks from pass rushers. Right guard Jahri Evans went from Division II to the NFL without a hiccup, and the Browns would like to revoke the trade that sent Jeff Faine to the Saints when ex-New Orleans center LeCharles Bentley signed with Cleveland. Left guard Jamar Nesbit is the oldest member of the line (he's 31, the others are 28 or younger), so the Saints addressed interior line depth in the draft. Both Andy Alleman (third-round, Akron) and Jermond Bushrod (fifth-round, Towson, great all-time name) are college tackles who project as guards in the NFL. The backups at tackle are Zach Strief, a colossal, somewhat promising project in his second year, and Rob Petitti, who was awful as a starter for the 2005 Cowboys. One number is sure to change in 2007: Now that Deuce McAllister has his lateral movement back and Reggie Bush has gotten used to the NFL, it is a safe bet that the Saints will have more double-digit runs this year.

Defensive Front Seven

Defensive Line	Age	Pos	Plys	TmPct	Rk	Stop	Dfts	StpRt	Rk	AvYd	Rk	Sack	Hit	Hur		Runs	RuStp	RuYd		Pass	PaStp	PaYd
Charles Grant	29	DE	71	9.7%	4	54	17	76%	49	1.7	47	5.5	14	21		47	70%	2.9		24	88%	-0.7
Will Smith	26	DE	54	8.4%	10	45	23	83%	13	-0.1	6	11	8	6		38	76%	1.8		16	100%	-4.9
Brian Young	30	DT	48	6.6%	12	40	12	83%	22	0.6	9	5.5	10	17		39	79%	2.2		9	100%	-6.3
Hollis Thomas	33	DT	45	8.2%	6	36	10	80%	32	2.2	46	3.5	2	3		37	81%	2.4		8	75%	0.9
Rondey Leisle	26	DT	17	2.7%	—	13	3	76%	—	3.3	—	0	1	0		13	85%	2.6		4	50%	5.5

Linebackers	Age	Pos	Plys	TmPct	Rk	Stop	Dfts	StpRt	AvYd	Sack	Hit	Hur		Runs	RuStp	Rk	RuYd	Rk		Tgts	Suc%	Rk	PaYd	Rk
Scott Fujita	28	OLB	103	14.1%	29	62	22	60%	5.2	3.5	5	4		54	65%	50	4.4	88		36	61%	15	4.8	16
Scott Shanle	28	OLB	99	13.5%	37	51	13	52%	5.4	4	1	0		58	53%	89	4.3	85		40	59%	21	5.1	18
Mark Simoneau	30	ILB	63	8.6%	82	38	7	60%	4.6	1	3	5		45	69%	31	3.0	25		14	56%	—	5.6	—
Brian Simmons	*32*	*ILB*	*65*	*10.9%*	*64*	*34*	*11*	*52%*	*5.6*	*0*	*3*	*3*		*35*	*66%*	*45*	*3.5*	*50*		*22*	*45%*	*69*	*8.4*	*88*

Year	Yards	ALY	Rank	Power	Rank	10+ Yds	Rank	Stuff	Rank	Sack	ASR	Rank
2004	4.64	4.51	27	81%	32	21%	24	20%	30	37	6.3%	23
2005	4.34	4.10	19	78%	31	24%	30	26%	12	26	6.0%	26
2006	4.59	4.25	17	48%	3	23%	31	28%	4	38	7.8%	9

Year	LE	Rank	LT	Rank	Mid	Rank	RT	Rank	RE	Rank
2004	3.96	11	4.54	19	4.88	30	4.20	17	3.51	9
2005	3.18	6	4.51	26	4.31	23	4.03	15	3.59	11
2006	4.59	22	4.89	25	4.20	14	3.51	8	4.03	15

Like everything else in New Orleans, stats for the front seven improved across the board in 2006, but this is the unit that is most likely to regress in 2007. It is possible that defensive tackle Hollis Thomas is so good at stuffing the run that he is personally responsible for the Saints' dramatic improvement in power situations, but since the rest of the line was the same, that improvement is more likely to have been a bit of a fluke. The pass rush numbers, however, are not, because defensive ends Charles Grant and Will Smith are right in their primes. After Cincinnati made middle linebacker Brian Simmons a salary cap casualty, the Saints signed the nine-year veteran to compete with Mark Simoneau in the middle. Simmons is probably better than Simoneau, but his stats suggest that neither is going anywhere near the Pro Bowl. Outside linebackers Scott Fujita and Scott Shanle did a good job in pass coverage, but Shanle in particular could be pushed around on running plays. The easiest way for the front seven to torpedo a Saints repeat is not on the field, but off the field: with the exception of Simmons and Simoneau at middle linebacker, the depth for the Saints front seven is terrible.

Defensive Secondary

Secondary	Age	Pos	Plys	TmPct	Rk	Stop	Dfts	RuYd	Rk	RuStp	Rk	Tgts	Tgt%	Rk	Dist	Suc%	Rk	PaYd	Rk	PD	Int
Mike McKenzie	31	CB	43	5.9%	78	25	13	13.1	78	60%	12	60	15%	59	15.6	61%	6	6.9	27	9	2
Fred Thomas	34	CB	67	11.3%	14	29	14	6.6	40	43%	42	99	30%	1	16.6	51%	48	9.3	74	12	1
Jason Craft	31	CB	49	6.7%	68	21	8	12.3	76	42%	44	52	14%	68	13.9	64%	1	5.5	2	6	1
Josh Bullocks	24	FS	78	10.7%	32	24	6	7.3	51	30%	62	36	7%	40	18.1	44%	62	13.0	76	6	2
Omar Stoutmire*	33	SS	56	9.4%	46	27	7	5.4	19	52%	21	24	7%	48	12.5	53%	39	8.2	41	6	2
Roman Harper	25	SS	31	13.6%	—	15	5	8.1	—	33%	—	21	16%	—	7.8	62%	—	5.2	—	3	0
Jason David	*25*	*CB*	*63*	*7.7%*	*51*	*22*	*9*	*10.1*	*68*	*28%*	*66*	*75*	*21%*	*21*	*14.4*	*50%*	*55*	*6.4*	*17*	*11*	*2*
Kevin Kaesviharn	*31*	*FS*	*69*	*9.1%*	*52*	*31*	*20*	*8.5*	*69*	*44%*	*36*	*35*	*8%*	*35*	*12.6*	*56%*	*28*	*6.6*	*25*	*8*	*6*

Year	Pass D Rank	DVOA vs. #1 WR	Rank	DVOA vs. #2 WR	Rank	DVOA vs. Other WR	Rank	DVOA vs. TE	Rank	DVOA vs. RB	Rank
2004	25	29.5%	29	-5.5%	7	-9.8%	13	17.0%	25	8.8%	22
2005	26	24.7%	29	12.3%	29	-7.0%	12	7.7%	21	4.4%	20
2006	21	40.6%	32	-4.7%	14	-33.7%	4	-4.4%	16	-14.8%	9

The best news for the secondary is the replacement of starting cornerback Fred Thomas with ex-Colts free agent Jason David. Although Thomas performed reasonably well during 2005 and the first few weeks of 2006, he was horrible over the second half of last year. From Week 8 on, Thomas had a success rate of 42 percent and allowed 14.7 yards per pass. He gave up eight completions over 25 yards, including four to Chad Johnson in Week 11. For both Philadelphia and Chicago, the first item on the postseason game plan was "throw long wherever you see Fred Thomas," directly resulting in a 75-yard touchdown pass to Donte' Stallworth and a 33-yard touchdown pass to Bernard Berrian. As for the other cornerbacks, Mike McKenzie returned to the high level of play from his days in Green Bay, but Jason Craft's league-leading Success Rate screams "fluke," since his Success Rate in 2005 was just 45 percent. Craft also allowed 11.3 yards per pass in 2005, far more than he allowed in 2006.

Strong safety Roman Harper was excellent over the first few weeks of his rookie year, before he was felled by a torn ACL. His recovery is proceeding on schedule, and he should be back to team with free safety Josh Bullocks this year. The secondary is the opposite of the front seven, with tons of depth. Besides Thomas and Craft, backup cornerbacks include ex-Rams starter DeJuan Groce, third-round pick Usama Young, who was a four-year starter at Kent State, and fifth-rounder David Jones, a speedy long-term project from Division II Wingate. The safeties will be backed up by former starter Jay Bellamy as well as Kevin Kaesviharn, a free agent whose departure will not be missed by the copy editors of Ohio's great newspapers.

Special Teams

Year	DVOA	Rank	FG/XP	Rank	Net Punt	Rank	Punt Ret	Rank	Net Kick	Rank	Kick Ret	Rank	Hidden	Rank
2004	5.7%	3	1.9	13	11.7	3	4.8	7	4.2	11	10.9	5	2.7	10
2005	-2.0%	23	-6.7	25	10.0	3	-0.6	15	0.1	18	-14.5	32	-7.0	25
2006	0.7%	14	2.7	10	6.3	9	-1.9	19	0.4	17	-3.3	19	12.8	1

This unit has gone through many changes over the last two years. Veteran punter and kickoff specialist Mitch Berger suffered a groin injury last year in training camp, and the Saints replaced him with Billy Cundiff on kickoffs and rookie Steve Weatherford on punts. Forty-two-year-old John Carney remained for field goals and had an excellent year, nailing 25 of 27 attempts. All three may be gone for 2007. The Saints dealt a sixth-round pick to Miami for Olindo Mare, who had a bad year on field goals, but has been one of the NFL's best kickoff artists for years. Given the erratic nature of field-goal percentage (see Arizona chapter) and the fact that New Orleans plays 11 games indoors, Mare is unlikely to have a poor year on field goals again. Weatherford will compete in camp with ex-Jacksonville punter Chris Hanson. According to our numbers, Hanson was the second-worst punter in the league while Weatherford was above average, so the Saints will either waste their time with a camp battle, or make a big mistake by declaring Hanson the winner. Longtime Saints veteran and New Orleans native Michael Lewis still handles most kickoff and punt returns, with Reggie Bush always available as a special secret weapon when a big return is necessary enough to risk an injury. If the Saints want to replace Lewis, other candidates for returns include wideout Terrance Copper and rookie running back Antonio Pittman.

Coaching Staff

It's hard to go overboard in praising the performance of Sean Payton and the new Saints coaching staff in 2006. On top of their roster construction and motivational skills, Payton deserves lots of credit for how well he used Reggie Bush as a decoy. Bush may not have had great numbers for most of the season, but he was an incredible asset for the New Orleans offense. Defensive coordinator Gary Gibbs, the former linebackers coach in Dallas, did a good job with limited talent. Payton is really the offensive mind on this staff, but this offseason the Saints hired Doug Marrone as nominal offensive coordinator. Marrone did an excellent job with the Jets offensive line in recent years and will also supervise that unit in New Orleans.

New York Giants

Tom Coughlin enters his fourth year as head coach of the New York Giants in 2007. When he was hired, the team was four years removed from a Super Bowl appearance, and Jim Fassel had just put the finishing touches on a 4–12 season. The Giants had stopped responding to Fassel's laid-back, player-friendly style, and Coughlin's no-nonsense attitude was expected to bring much-needed discipline to New York. After all, this was the guy known for fining players for not showing up *early enough* to team meetings. That discipline would form a more cohesive team and naturally lead to more wins . . . or so the thinking went.

It didn't work. Under Coughlin, the Giants have made two playoff appearances in three years, but only managed one winning season. Following an 8–8 record and a wild-card playoff loss to the Eagles last year, speculation had Coughlin on the way out of New York. Instead, the Giants gave him a one-year deal, which is an indication of the team's lack of long-term confidence in their head coach. In the wake of Coughlin's return, there were rumors that the short-term contract is just a stop-gap. A number of big-name head coaches may be available a year from now, including Bill Cowher and Marty Schottenheimer. Many people believe that the Giants intend to hire Bill Belichick as their head coach for 2008, based on the extremely popular but totally unfounded rumors that Belichick can get out of his contract after 2007. Of course, any of these men would want total control of the organization, and one has to wonder what the league office would say if the Giants were to hand Jerry Reese his pink slip after just one year as the third African-American general manager in NFL history. Whatever happens next season, Coughlin enters 2007 as a lame duck, and, if the organization has no confidence in its coach, why should the players?

A head coach on a one-year contract creates obvious continuity issues, but continuity is just one of many issues facing the Giants in 2007. While the media and fan focus never strays far from quarterback Eli Manning, much of New York's success in 2007 will depend on two units that struggled through injuries and inconsistent play last year: the offensive line and the secondary. The Giants started the 2006 season 6–2, then proceeded to lose six of seven games before beating the Redskins in Week 17 to sneak into the playoffs. Part of that early-season success can be attributed to favorable matchups, but the midseason implosion had more to do with bad luck and poor execution than with strength of schedule.

Then again, that 6–2 run masked an ominous start. The Giants were 1–2 entering their Week 4 bye. They had held Peyton Manning to 276 yards (25-of-41), one touchdown, and an interception in the Week 1 Manning Bowl, but they still came up short against the Colts, and the defense was thoroughly exploited by Donovan McNabb and Matt Hasselbeck in the subsequent two weeks. Defensive coordinator Tim Lewis admitted that during the team's embarrassing 42–30 Week 3 loss to the Seahawks, the Giants secondary blew coverages on four out of the five touchdown passes. If not for a remarkable fourth-quarter comeback against the Eagles, the Giants would have been 0–3.

To Lewis's credit, the Giants played their best defense of the year coming out of that bye week, as the team reeled off four straight victories, but, while the coordinator's scheme is certainly a critical component to a defense's success, the players executing that scheme are even more important. Last year, the four starters in the Giants' secondary—cornerbacks Sam Madison and Corey Webster and safeties Will Demps and Gibril Wilson—each ranked in the bottom half of the league in Success Rate.

GIANTS PROSPECTUS

2006 Record: 8–8

DVOA Estimated Wins: 9.0 (9th)

Pythagorean Wins: 7.8 (16th)

DVOA: 11.1% total (8th), 5.9% weighted (14th)

Offense: 8.6% DVOA (9th)

Defense: −2.1% DVOA (13th)

Special Teams: 0.4% DVOA (16th)

Variance: 12.2% (24th)

2006: Tiki's final year goes to waste thanks to injuries and a defensive meltdown.

2007: Last player to lose respect for Tom Coughlin, please turn off the lights.

2007 Mean Projection: 7.0 wins

The Brohm Closet (0–4): 14%

Bad Team (5–6): 29%

Mediocre (7–8): 31%

Playoff Contender (9–10): 19%

Super Bowl Contender (11+): 6%

Projected Average Opponent: 3.0% DVOA (3rd in NFL)

2007 Giants Schedule

Week	Opp	Week	Opp	Week	Opp
1	at DAL	7	SF	13	at CHI
2	GB	8	at MIA	14	at PHI
3	at WAS	9	BYE	15	WAS
4	PHI	10	DAL	16	at BUF
5	NYJ	11	at DET	17	NE (Sat.)
6	at ATL (Mon.)	12	MIN		

To be fair, some of the secondary's struggles last year were related to the front seven's inability to rush the passer. Much as a quarterback relies on his offensive line to protect him, a secondary relies on its defensive line to pressure the quarterback. Under Lewis, New York has relied primarily on its defensive ends for that purpose, which makes sense when you consider the team has two of the league's best pass rushers at the position in Michael Strahan and Osi Umenyiora. In 2006, however, the Giants suffered through a series of injuries that decimated the pass rush, which, in turn, undermined the pass coverage. Strahan was put on injured reserve in December after trying to return from an early-season foot injury because promising backup Justin Tuck had landed on the IR a month earlier with a Lis Franc foot sprain of his own. Umenyiora missed five weeks with a torn hip flexor. Linebacker LaVar Arrington ruptured his Achilles during Week 7, in what would prove to be his last game with the Giants. Even Madison and Webster each missed four games due to injury. Consequently, the Giants defense ranked 25th in sacks and rushed six or more defenders only three percent of the time—fewer than every team except the Bills and Colts.

The good news for 2007 is that everybody should be healthy heading into training camp, and the emergence of rookie Mathias Kiwanuka in the wake of last year's injuries has allowed New York to restructure its defense for the better with minimal outside help. Kiwanuka, the team's first-round pick in 2006, filled in admirably at defensive end while Strahan and Umenyiora were on the shelf (save for his embarrassing, game-changing aborted sack against Tennessee in Week 12). Given his athleticism, he'll move to strongside linebacker this year. There he'll team up with lone free agent signee Kawika Mitchell, who comes over from Kansas City, to surround middle man Antonio Pierce, the unit's most consistent player. Strahan and Umenyiora will then reclaim their end positions and resume their roles terrorizing opposing quarterbacks. The question is if that improved pass rush will mask a still-mediocre secondary. First-round pick cornerback Aaron Ross will help, and Webster is entering just his third season, which means he hasn't reached his potential, but, at 33, Sam Madison is on the downside of his career, and Demps's limited physical skills will always be an issue in pass coverage.

On the other side of the ball, the offensive line is undergoing a similar overhaul. Left tackle Luke Petitgout, perhaps best known for his predilection for false starts, was a salary cap casualty and is now in Tampa Bay. Gone as well is Petitgout's backup Bob Whitfield, who was thrust into action when Petitgout broke a leg at midseason, did not play well, and has since retired. In Petitgout's place is David Diehl, who was a left guard until Coughlin benched Whitfield before the final regular-season game against Washington. In the NFL, guards are guards for a reason: They are often to short, too slow, or both, to play tackle. Offensive line coach Pat Flaherty told *USA Today* he wasn't one of those coaches who believes that a guard can play tackle in the NFL, but offered this lukewarm qualification: "I am not going to say I don't think [Diehl] can make the move.... but I don't think that's the only choice."

Flaherty was referring to Guy Whimper, the team's 2006 fourth-round pick, but Whimper was a project pick who is still extremely raw. He's faster than Diehl, and has longer arms, but his footwork is extremely poor; as Russ Lande of *GM Jr.* put it a year ago, Whimper "usually stops his feet as soon as he makes contact on blocks and it leads to him losing that block." That does not sound like the player you want protecting the franchise quarterback. Giants fans were left scratching their heads during the draft when the team didn't address the position until it selected Adam Koets in the sixth round. While the Oregon State product is known as a good pass-protector, he gets pushed around on running plays way too often. The Giants might also try to acquire a veteran tackle during training camp, but then, how many teams are dealing from a surplus of left tackles? The only obvious trade candidate is Cleveland's Kevin Shaffer, and he won't be on the market if the Browns can convince him to move to the other side of the line.

Despite the injury to Petitgout, Manning was sacked only 25 times in 2006 (sixth best in the NFL), but he forced a lot of throws based on the *perception* of pressure, whether it actually existed or not. One knock on the fourth-year quarterback is that he struggles with his accuracy. Some of that is due to poor footwork, which can be the result of not feeling comfortable enough in the pocket to set his feet before throwing. In addition to the shakeup on the line, the Giants could provide Manning with better protection through a change in blocking schemes. Last season, only Arizona used max-protect blocking less often than the Giants. New offensive coordinator Kevin Gilbride could leave more players in to block, but that would also mean fewer pass-catching options downfield.

Losing the NFL's third-best running back according to DPAR certainly exacerbates the passing-game issues. Tiki

Barber decided to retire at 31, in part because of Coughlin's overbearing demeanor. Replacing Barber won't be easy. Since 2004, Barber finished no lower than seventh in rushing DPAR.

New York showed interest in free-agent running backs Tatum Bell and Travis Henry this offseason, but opted instead to promote third-year back Brandon Jacobs from his role as a short-yardage specialist. They also traded wideout Tim Carter to Cleveland for Reuben Droughns, a somewhat similar, but older back who will back up Jacobs.

On the surface, this leaves the Giants to replace a Hall of Famer with an unproven backup and a veteran on the downside of his career. Economically, however, this was the right move; in part-time duty, Jacobs ranked ahead of Bell and Henry in rushing DPAR and DVOA. Droughns is a different story, however. After back-to-back 1,200-yard rushing seasons in 2004 (with the Broncos) and 2005 (with the Browns), Droughns managed only 758 yards on 3.4 yards per carry last season, lost his job to Jason Wright, and ended the year on the Browns' special teams unit while finishing last in the league in rushing DPAR. Much of Droughns's success in Denver and struggles in Cleveland can be attributed to his offensive lines. In 2004, the Broncos finished eighth in Adjusted Line Yards; last season, the Browns finished 31st. The good news is that the Giants offensive line ranked fourth last season, so Droughns is a cheap alternative who could succeed in a limited role. The bad news is that there is a good chance the offensive line will regress in 2007, so it could be Cleveland all over again for Droughns. Maybe Barber got out at the right time.

The stories coming out of Giants training camp will say that success in 2007 hinges on Eli Manning's development, but Eli Manning is not the problem and Eli Manning is not the solution. All the improvement in the world won't allow him to block for himself. Manning won't be playing in the secondary, he won't be motivating the team in Tom Coughlin's place, and he won't be in the trainer's room keeping this team healthier than it was in 2006. Those are the issues that will decide if the Giants are competitive in 2007.

Ryan Wilson

Giants 2006 Stats by Week

Wk	vs.	W–L	PF	PA	YDF	YDA	TO	DVOA Total	Off	Def	ST
1	IND	L	21	26	433	327	-1	50.2%	40.0%	-26.2%	-16.1%
2	@PHI	W	30	24	404	451	0	-4.5%	2.4%	8.3%	1.5%
3	@SEA	L	30	42	348	333	-1	-7.8%	1.8%	19.7%	10.1%
4	BYE										
5	WAS	W	19	3	411	164	0	45.7%	17.9%	-27.4%	0.4%
6	@ATL	W	27	14	424	329	0	59.3%	18.6%	-36.6%	4.0%
7	@DAL	W	36	22	328	379	+2	64.7%	23.5%	-38.7%	2.6%
8	TB	W	17	3	251	174	+1	40.4%	-7.4%	-41.4%	6.3%
9	HOU	W	14	10	285	251	0	1.6%	21.5%	10.3%	-9.5%
10	CHI	L	20	38	249	352	0	-13.6%	-13.9%	-1.9%	-1.0%
11	@JAC	L	10	26	247	414	-2	-29.5%	-8.3%	20.0%	-1.1%
12	@TEN	L	21	24	287	343	0	-31.4%	1.4%	28.3%	-4.5%
13	DAL	L	20	23	396	365	+1	26.1%	35.2%	4.6%	-4.6%
14	@CAR	W	27	13	463	307	+3	18.2%	-4.1%	-9.1%	13.1%
15	PHI	L	22	36	358	382	-2	-11.2%	0.8%	20.3%	8.2%
16	NO	L	7	30	142	359	-3	-60.0%	-59.0%	-3.5%	-4.5%
17	@WAS	W	34	28	355	393	+2	21.1%	41.7%	23.5%	2.9%
18	@PHI	L	20	23	305	323	-1	10.9%	18.3%	-5.9%	-13.3%

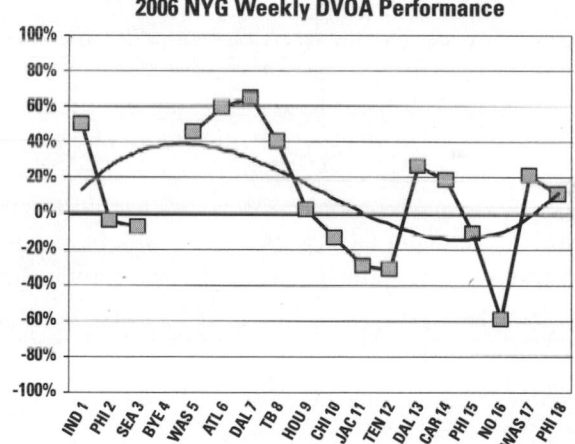

2006 NYG Weekly DVOA Performance

Trends and Splits

	Offense	Rank	Defense	Rank
Total DVOA	8.6%	9	-2.1%	13
Unadjusted VOA	9.5%	9	2.1%	16
Weighted Trend	5.4%	13	0.5%	13
Variance	5.8%	19	5.4%	23
Passing	6.0%	14	1.7%	13
Rushing	11.3%	4	-6.4%	11
First Down	5.1%	11	-10.1%	9
Second Down	11.2%	5	-2.3%	13
Third Down	11.4%	12	13.2%	22
Red Zone	29.7%	4	11.5%	25
Late and Close	11.2%	9	8.4%	22

Five-Year Performance

	2006	2005	2004	2003	2002
W-L	8-8	11-5	6-10	4-12	10-6
Pythagorean Wins	7.8	10.7	6.7	4.0	9.3
Estimated Wins	9.0	10.4	6.4	5.6	8.1
Total DVOA	11.1%	20.3%	-12.1%	-21.1%	0.8%
Rank	8	8	22	30	15
Offense	8.6%	9.0%	-6.8%	-13.8%	5.4%
Rank	9	9	25	28	16
Defense	-2.1%	-6.9%	5.9%	2.3%	0.3%
Rank	13	11	21	20	14
Special Teams	0.4%	4.4%	0.7%	-5.1%	-4.3%
Rank	16	2	15	30	27

Strategic Tendencies

Formations		Rank	Run/Pass		Rank	Defense		Rank	Other		Rank
3+ WR	51%	7	Runs, all plays	44%	16	Sacks by LB	19%	18	Run with 2+ RB	58%	18
4+ WR	6%	24	Runs, first half	45%	13	Sacks by DB	9%	12	Run with 2+ TE	29%	26
2+ TE	20%	27	Runs, first down	53%	19	Rush 6+	3.1%	30	Play action	17%	22
Single back	60%	10	Runs, power sit.	71%	6	Rush 7+	0.7%	25	Go for it on 4th	1.07	11
Empty back	2.0%	16	Runs, behind 2H	33%	17	Rush 3	4.9%	16	Offensive Pace	31.0	18
Max protect	6%	31	Pass, ahead 2H	42%	16	CB1 on WR1	45%	14	Defensive Pace	29.1	2

The Giants' defense was the beneficiary of the most dropped passes in the league by an absurd margin. We recorded 57 dropped passes against the Giants; the next highest total against a single team was 37. Numerous charters worked on Giants games, and the Giants' offense had a perfectly average number of dropped passes, so this doesn't seem to be a result of charter bias. It's just very, very strange. . . . The Giants forced opposing quarterbacks to throw the ball away less often than any other defense. . . . The Giants faced more play-action passes than any defense. . . . The Giants ran the ball 94 percent of the time when only one wide receiver was on the field, the highest percentage in the NFL. . . . The Giants threw to the middle of the field more than any other team, and to the left less than any other team. . . . The Giants used the screen pass more than any other offense and were very successful, with a 51.5% DVOA. . . . Eli Manning faced six or more pass rushers more often than any quarterback in the NFL other than Tom Brady. . . . Given Manning's propensity to throw a "jump ball" to Plaxico Burress, it is no shock to learn Burress was fourth among receivers in passes overthrown. . . . As a team, the Giants ranked third in passes overthrown, tied for second in passes underthrown, and first in passes thrown behind the receiver as he was running his pattern. Think Eli Manning has accuracy issues?

Passing

Player	DPAR	DVOA	Plys	NtYds	Avg	YAC	C%	TD	Int
Eli Manning	27.9	-1.1%	519	3057	5.9	4.5	58.0%	24	17

Rushing

Player	DPAR	DVOA	Plys	Yds	Avg	TD	Fum	Suc
Tiki Barber	39.9	14.9%	327	1665	5.1	5	3	50%
Brandon Jacobs	15.0	17.7%	96	424	4.4	9	2	57%
Eli Manning	-3.9	-71.2%	11	33	3.0	0	9	—
Reuben Droughns	*-6.8*	*-20.1%*	*219*	*761*	*3.5*	*4*	*5*	*42%*

Receiving

Player	DPAR	DVOA	Plys	Ctch	Yds	Y/C	YAC	TD	C%
WR									
Plaxico Burress	13.0	1.4%	121	63	988	15.7	3.6	10	52%
Amani Toomer	8.6	9.6%	50	32	360	11.3	1.4	3	64%
Tim Carter*	-5.2	-31.5%	49	22	253	11.5	1.8	2	58%
David Tyree	1.4	-7.6%	33	19	197	10.4	2.3	2	63%
Sinorice Moss	-3.5	-59.4%	11	5	25	5.0	4.3	0	45%
Michael Jennings	-0.5	-25.9%	8	5	49	9.8	7.6	0	45%
TE									
Jeremy Shockey	7.9	-2.1%	115	66	623	9.4	2.9	7	57%
Visanthe Shiancoe*	-0.2	-13.9%	14	12	81	6.8	3.3	0	86%
RB									
Tiki Barber	7.2	7.6%	81	58	465	8.0	8.4	0	72%
Brandon Jacobs	5.8	87.1%	14	11	149	13.5	16.0	0	79%
Jim Finn	-0.6	-17.6%	14	8	54	6.8	5.4	0	57%
Reuben Droughns	*1.4*	*-2.5%*	*34*	*28*	*168*	*6.0*	*7.6*	*0*	*82%*

Offensive Line

Year	Yards	ALY	Rank	Power	Rank	10+ Yds	Rank	Stuff	Rank	Sack	ASR	Rank
2004	4.51	4.39	9	57%	23	22%	2	24%	15	52	9.9%	29
2005	4.84	4.36	10	56%	27	27%	1	26%	19	28	5.2%	8
2006	4.99	4.61	4	71%	6	19%	9	25%	20	25	5.4%	7

Year	LE	Rank	LT	Rank	Mid	Rank	RT	Rank	RE	Rank
2004	4.59	9	3.23	32	4.62	6	3.93	21	5.09	2
2005	4.45	11	4.62	7	4.45	6	4.41	12	4.00	15
2006	5.27	3	3.69	29	4.45	12	4.65	4	5.46	3

In 2006, the Giants returned all five offensive linemen from the year before, and that consistency helped them finish in the top ten in Adjusted Line Yards and Adjusted Sack Rate. Now left tackle Luke Petitgout is in Tampa Bay via free agency, and his backup, Bob Whitfield, has retired. Barring a late-summer trade for a veteran, David Diehl will be tasked with protecting Eli Manning's blind side. Diehl does have experience at tackle—in addition to a couple of starts last season, he played right tackle earlier in his career—but like most tackles-turned-guard, Diehl struggled with one-on-one matchups, sometimes requiring the tight end to stay in and block. Second-year left tackle Guy Whimper will also be in the mix. Facing Osi Umenyiora every day in practice last season had to be great training, but Whimper is still raw…and his name is Whimper. When the book closes on the 2007 season, we will probably be asking why the Giants chose not to use the draft to address their gaping void at left tackle. Shaun O'Hara, who signed a five-year, $19-million deal in March, is serviceable at center, and right guard Chris Snee quietly turned in another productive season last year. Right tackle Kareem McKenzie excels against the run, but he led the Giants in Blown Blocks in 2006 for the second straight year. Grey Ruegamer provides depth at the interior line positions and could challenge Rich Seubert, who's currently penciled in as the starter at left guard.

Defensive Front Seven

Defensive Line	Age	Pos	Plys	TmPct	Rk	Stop	Dfts	StpRt	Rk	AvYd	Rk	Sack	Hit	Hur	Runs	RuStp	RuYd	Pass	PaStp	PaYd
Mathias Kiwanuka	24	DE	50	5.9%	41	35	14	70%	60	3.0	74	4	8	8	36	69%	2.8	14	71%	3.6
Fred Robbins	30	DT	49	5.8%	25	45	26	92%	5	-0.2	1	6	8	5	36	89%	0.9	13	100%	-3.4
Barry Cofield	23	DT	47	5.5%	30	36	8	77%	42	1.1	21	1.5	2	2	38	76%	1.4	9	78%	-0.1
Michael Strahan	36	DE	41	8.6%	8	37	15	90%	5	0.8	17	3	5	7	33	91%	1.2	8	88%	-0.9
Osi Umenyiora	26	DE	33	5.7%	45	26	12	79%	34	0.5	10	6	4	11	24	75%	2.3	9	89%	-4.3
William Joseph	28	DT	22	2.6%	—	20	10	91%	—	0.6	—	2	6	2	16	94%	1.0	6	83%	-0.3
Marcus Bell	*28*	*DT*	*40*	*5.9%*	*24*	*25*	*6*	*63%*	*68*	*2.8*	*63*	*1*	*3*	*1*	*34*	*65%*	*3.0*	*6*	*50%*	*1.8*

Linebackers	Age	Pos	Plys	TmPct	Rk	Stop	Dfts	StpRt	AvYd	Sack	Hit	Hur	Runs	RuStp	Rk	RuYd	Rk	Tgts	Suc%	Rk	PaYd	Rk
Antonio Pierce	29	ILB	150	17.7%	7	81	32	54%	5.7	1	2	3	77	70%	27	3.6	61	69	47%	62	7.3	77
Carlos Emmons*	34	OLB	63	9.9%	71	27	4	43%	5.0	1	0	0	42	50%	93	4.3	87	21	62%	13	3.4	5
Brandon Short	30	OLB	46	9.7%	—	26	7	57%	4.1	2	1	0	36	58%	—	4.1	—	7	38%	—	6.8	—
Gerris Wilkinson	24	OLB	24	2.8%	—	13	5	54%	3.3	0	0	0	18	56%	—	2.7	—	10	61%	—	2.7	—
LaVar Arrington*	29	OLB	19	6.0%	—	13	4	68%	2.8	1	0	1	9	78%	—	1.4	—	12	55%	—	4.7	—
Reggie Torbor	26	OLB	16	1.9%	—	13	6	81%	0.9	1	2	3	10	90%	—	1.7	—	5	40%	—	7.8	—
Kawika Mitchell	*28*	*ILB*	*108*	*13.5%*	*38*	*49*	*15*	*45%*	*5.8*	*1.5*	*3*	*5*	*69*	*51%*	*92*	*4.3*	*86*	*33*	*35%*	*90*	*8.8*	*90*

Year	Yards	ALY	Rank	Power	Rank	10+ Yds	Rank	Stuff	Rank	Sack	ASR	Rank
2004	4.38	4.52	28	54%	7	16%	15	23%	16	41	7.8%	10
2005	3.88	3.76	9	59%	13	20%	24	25%	15	41	6.5%	21
2006	3.74	3.85	5	70%	26	17%	19	26%	9	32	6.2%	19

Year	LE	Rank	LT	Rank	Mid	Rank	RT	Rank	RE	Rank
2004	4.85	27	4.38	15	4.27	18	4.18	15	5.73	32
2005	5.19	29	3.29	3	3.76	8	2.92	1	3.67	12
2006	3.55	9	3.00	2	4.25	16	2.82	1	4.84	27

As has been the case throughout the Tim Lewis era, the Giants relied primarily on the defensive line to generate a pass rush last year. Seventy-two percent of their sacks came from the front four, a full ten percentage points above the league average. Fourth-round rookie defensive tackle Barry Cofield came out of nowhere to help solidify the middle, but it was

(continued next page)

Defensive Front Seven (continued)

Fred Robbins who anchored the unit. Robbins was the only defensive tackle in the NFL who made his average tackle behind the line of scrimmage in 2006. Michael Strahan enters his 15th season, but he still is one of the league's best defensive ends according to our numbers. Osi Umenyiora—whom the Chargers tried to acquire as part of the Eli Manning-Philip Rivers draft-day trade—is coming back from injury, but this could be the year he finally eclipses Strahan as the Giants' next great sack machine.

The linebacker corps has been completely overhauled from a season ago. LaVar Arrington, who missed most of last season with an Achilles tear anyway, and Carlos Emmons have been released. Kansas City's Kawika Mitchell was signed as a free agent to replace Arrington, and Mathias Kiwanuka will move to outside linebacker. Even filling in as a defensive end for the injured Strahan and Umenyiora during his rookie season, Kiwanuka dropped into coverage enough to tally two interceptions, but dropping into a zone and covering a tight end or running back are two different things. Kiwanuka's challenge will be to improve his pass-coverage skills. Pierce, a former undrafted free agent, has made himself into one of the league's best middle linebackers through exhaustive film study, telling NFL.com's Pat Kirwan that he struggles with teammates who don't want to be around the team facility all the time in preparation for the 2007 season. Pierce is the glue to this unit; he's one of the most intelligent players in the league, and he is responsible for setting the defense. Last year's second-round pick, Gerris Wilkinson, has a lot of potential, and could challenge Mitchell with a solid training camp or replace Kiwanuka if the DE-to-LB transformation does not work.

Defensive Secondary

Secondary	Age	Pos	Plys	TmPct	Rk	Stop	Dfts	RuYd	Rk	RuStp	Rk	Tgts	Tgt%	Rk	Dist	Suc%	Rk	PaYd	Rk	PD	Int
Corey Webster	25	CB	56	8.8%	46	24	11	3.7	4	55%	19	74	19%	36	12.5	46%	66	7.9	51	8	1
R. W. McQuarters	31	CB	63	7.4%	56	24	10	7.4	52	44%	39	65	13%	73	10.3	54%	29	5.6	3	7	2
Sam Madison	33	CB	48	7.6%	53	19	9	6.1	32	30%	64	58	16%	57	14.7	50%	49	8.5	62	8	2
Will Demps	28	SS	108	12.8%	12	38	16	6.6	43	41%	46	53	10%	10	10.7	45%	60	8.7	48	7	2
Gibril Wilson	26	SS	112	14.1%	4	50	16	5.1	12	48%	28	52	11%	7	9.8	52%	41	6.0	14	11	2
Kevin Dockery	23	CB	39	5.3%	—	12	8	0.0	—	0%	—	44	10%	—	12.1	40%	—	10.7	—	5	2
James Butler	29	FS	19	2.6%	—	7	4	18.3	—	33%	—	12	2%	—	17.7	74%	—	4.9	—	4	0
Jason Bell	29	CB	18	2.3%	—	7	6	3.0	—	67%	—	8	2%	—	16.3	40%	—	9.4	—	3	1

Year	Pass D Rank	DVOA vs. #1 WR	Rank	DVOA vs. #2 WR	Rank	DVOA vs. Other WR	Rank	DVOA vs. TE	Rank	DVOA vs. RB	Rank
2004	22	-1.7%	12	33.6%	31	8.3%	25	3.0%	17	13.7%	26
2005	18	4.8%	15	-8.8%	10	-2.2%	17	-32.6%	3	-3.1%	14
2006	13	-10.6%	10	-10.9%	7	3.4%	22	18.8%	30	-18.0%	8

Aaron Ross from the University of Texas was the Giants' first-round pick this year, and he will be given every opportunity to earn a starting job at cornerback. That's what watching film of Sam Madison will do to a general manager. Corey Webster wasn't much better last year, and the Giants have to hope he takes a big leap forward in his third season. Nickel back R. W. McQuarters had far better numbers than either starter, one of the more surprising results from last year's game charting. Dime back Kevin Dockery had abhorrent numbers, one of the least surprising results from the game charting.

New York re-signed strong safety Gibril Wilson to a one-year deal in May, but both he and free safety Will Demps had similar struggles in the passing game, ranking in the bottom half of the league in our Success Rate statistic. Wilson is best against the run or when the Giants send him after the quarterback; Arizona's Adrian Wilson (no relation) was the only defensive back with more hurries or hits. Nonetheless, depending on how well the new linebackers pick up the scheme, Wilson could have additional pass-coverage responsibilities in 2007.

Special Teams

Year	DVOA	Rank	FG/XP	Rank	Net Punt	Rank	Punt Ret	Rank	Net Kick	Rank	Kick Ret	Rank	Hidden	Rank
2004	0.7%	15	-1.0	19	-2.0	21	-3.7	24	-2.0	18	12.7	4	-1.2	16
2005	4.4%	2	7.0	4	0.5	17	6.2	7	3.8	13	8.5	5	2.5	14
2006	0.4%	16	0.8	13	11.3	3	-2.3	21	3.1	15	-10.5	29	-1.3	15

The Giants thought so much of kicker Jay Feely last year that they released him without a replacement in mind. In late May, Kansas City traded Lawrence Tynes to the Giants in exchange for an undisclosed draft pick. Tynes isn't particularly good at either kickoffs or field goals and he'll have a training camp battle with former Ohio State star Josh Huston for the job. Punter Jeff Feagles enters his 20th season, but he might be best known as the guy who sold his number-10 jersey to Eli Manning for a Florida vacation. A year later, he sold his number-17 to Plaxico Burress for a new outdoor kitchen. Feagles is still a respectable punter, but New York's high value on net punting is primarily the result of excellent coverage, led as always by gunner David Tyree. New York ranked near the bottom of the league in both kick and punt returns. In addition to shoring up the secondary, Aaron Ross is also a dangerous return man. He will team with second-year wide receiver Sinorice Moss, who missed most of training camp and ten regular season games last year recovering from a quadriceps injury.

Coaching Staff

The odds that Tom Coughlin will be out of a job by the end of the year range between "definite" and "you're kidding, right?" The question is what becomes of first-year coordinators Kevin Gilbride and Steve Spagnuolo. Will they stay, or will the front office clean house and start over? If the Giants decide to wipe the slate clean, it means the players will have to learn a completely new system in 2008. Meanwhile, Gilbride isn't new to the team, just new to the offensive coordinator's job. The previous three years he served as quarterbacks coach, and he worked with Coughlin in Jacksonville. (And yes, Gilbride is the guy Buddy Ryan slugged during a 1994 game when both were coaches in Houston. Good times.) Spagnuolo joins the Giants from division rival Philadelphia, where he coached the linebackers. Perhaps it's just coincidence, but the Eagles' linebackers were the weakest part of their defense last year. Hopefully Spagnuolo has a little more luck in New York. Pat Flaherty has 25 years of NFL experience, and he'll need every bit of it to mold the offensive line into a decent pass-blocking unit. Anything less would be disastrous for Eli Manning and the team's already miniscule playoff chances.

Philadelphia Eagles

For a team that goes out of its way to avoid controversy, the Eagles sure spend a lot of time in the middle of it. Owner Jeffrey Lurie and team president Joe Banner aren't spotlight seekers like Jerry Jones of the Cowboys or Dan Snyder of the Redskins. They rarely spend top dollar on flashy free agents or meddle in on-field affairs. They adhere carefully to a fiscally responsible plan of cap management that keeps the team in contention and out of financial trouble year after year. For their efforts, they are portrayed as bean counters, too obsessed with the bottom line to worry about a championship.

Coach Andy Reid cultivates a public image as a taciturn, unflappable executive. He grunts his way through boilerplate press conferences, refuses to blame his players or assistants for his team's failings, and keeps his own confidence on most football matters. For his troubles, he's often portrayed as arrogant and aloof. When Reid's adult sons got into trouble with guns and drugs in February, observers were quick to label the saturnine coach as too out-of-touch to manage his family, much less his team.

Quarterback Donovan McNabb, taking a cue from Reid, works hard to keep a lid on whatever controversial pot is simmering in the Eagles locker room or the local media. He's gracious, upbeat, and usually boring when interviewed, giving carefully measured responses to sometimes loaded questions. He isn't the type of guy who rides his motorcycle without a helmet or dabbles in dog fighting. McNabb's career-long effort to take the high road has made him a favorite target for media axe-grinders from Rush Limbaugh to Terrell Owens. When McNabb refuses to speak, his critics speak for him, or they comb his mother's blog in search of smear material.

Ironically, the Lurie-Reid-McNabb Eagles take such a corporate approach to the sport of football that they make themselves perfect lightning rods for controversy. Reid and McNabb's frequent silence creates a void on the talk-radio airwaves and the sports blogosphere, a void often filled by the most creative columnist or conspiracy theorist. In seven years together, Reid, McNabb, and the front office have experienced enough success to keep them in the media forefront, but they haven't earned the benefit of the doubt that comes with a Super Bowl ring. The Eagles are in an unenviable place where every win is taken for granted, but every loss is further evidence that the coach/quarterback/franchise is fatally flawed and unwilling to make the necessary improvements.

The 2006 season proved to be a fertile spawning ground for crackpot theories. The Eagles jumped out to a 4–1 start, then suffered through a run of tough opponents and bad luck that led to three straight losses. The Eagles were 5–4 when McNabb tore his ACL in a Week 10 loss to the Titans. Jeff Garcia, after taking two games to shake off some rust, turned the season around with a second-half comeback against the Panthers on Monday night. The win touched off a five-game winning streak that vaulted the Eagles into the playoffs. Garcia played well throughout the hot streak, aided by the game plans of offensive coordinator Marty Mornhinweg, who took over the play calling from Reid in Week 10.

Garcia and Mornhinweg were an unlikely pair of heroes, castoffs who didn't set the world ablaze during stops in Cleveland and Detroit. For fans who only saw the worst in McNabb and Reid, though, the new quarterback and play caller were hailed as saviors. Finally, a quarterback who throws accurate short passes! Finally, a coordinator who calls running plays! Finally, real leadership! To read the Philly papers or listen to the bar room rhetoric, you wouldn't have thought that Reid and McNabb had led the Eagles to within a field goal of a championship two years ago.

EAGLES PROSPECTUS

2006 Record: 10–6

DVOA Estimated Wins: 11.6 (3rd)

Pythagorean Wins: 9.8 (8th)

DVOA: 24.3% total (3rd), 17.4% weighted (6th)

Offense: 19.8% DVOA (3rd)

Defense: −6.4% DVOA (11th)

Special Teams: −1.9% DVOA (22nd)

Variance: 13.4% (21st)

2006: The best NFC franchise of the 21st century returns to the postseason.

2007: The Eagles cannot allow a chemistry issue to derail the team like it did two years ago.

2007 Mean Projection: 11.0 wins

The Brohm Closet (0–4): 1%

Bad Team (5–6): 3%

Mediocre (7–8): 9%

Playoff Contender (9–10): 25%

Super Bowl Contender (11+): 63%

Projected Average Opponent: −1.3% DVOA (18th in NFL)

Closer inspection reveals that Garcia and Mornhinweg did not, in fact, rescue a mediocre team from their stubborn head coach and bumbling quarterback. The Eagles may have been .500 when Garcia started his first game, but they were far better than their record showed. The Eagles surrendered a 24–7 fourth quarter lead to the Giants in Week 2 thanks to an improbable series of events. The Eagles dominated the game, earning a DVOA of 41.7% to the Giants' –4.5%, but they lost their only fumble while the Giants recovered three of their own (including one in the end zone). Factor in a few ill-timed penalties and one badly-timed blitz, and the Eagles lost 30–24 in overtime. In Week 7, the Buccaneers beat the Eagles on a 62-yard field goal by Matt Bryant, the first successful field goal over 58 yards since the introduction of the special-teams-only k-ball in 1999. The Eagles didn't dominate that game (though they still led in DVOA 11.1% to 0.9%), but it was another fluky loss.

Fans and mainstream analysts rarely attribute wins and losses to luck, so, for many, these losses proved that the Eagles lacked character, swagger, or some other intangible. In fact, the Eagles were just unlucky, and they could have had seven wins by the time Garcia took the reins. Under Garcia, the Eagles' luck changed. Passes from McNabb that the receivers dropped became highlight-film completions. Interceptions that McNabb threw became Garcia passes that bounced off defenders' chests. Suddenly, the team started winning the close games that they lost early in the year. Garcia played well and Mornhinweg adjusted well to his new quarterback's strengths, but the Eagles didn't get better late in the year. Their fortunes just evened out.

Garcia cooled off by the time the Eagles made the playoffs, yet the team still beat the Giants and came within one drive of defeating the Saints to reach the NFC title game. In the minds of many fans, Garcia's December efforts ignited a quarterback controversy. Cooler heads recognized that McNabb was the superior player but valued Garcia as an insurance policy. The talk-radio wonks clucked their tongues and waited: If Reid released Garcia, it would be "proof" that he was more concerned with McNabb's fragile psyche than with winning football games.

Just before the start of the free agency period, the Eagles informed Garcia that his services were no longer required. To hammer home the point, the team signed third-string quarterback A. J. Feeley for second-string money. The tealeaf readers howled: Reid and McNabb were closing ranks and excising a threat to McNabb's status. Then Reid's sons got into legal trouble, and experts speculated that the head coach might resign. Some even suggested that a change might do the team some good. When Reid announced he would take a month off to attend to family matters, fans fretted that the team would sit on its hands through free agency and arrive unprepared for the draft.

2007 Eagles Schedule

Week	Opp	Week	Opp	Week	Opp
1	at GB	7	CHI	13	SEA
2	WAS (Mon.)	8	at MIN	14	NYG
3	DET	9	DAL	15	at DAL
4	at NYG	10	at WAS	16	at NO
5	BYE	11	MIA	17	BUF
6	at NYJ	12	at NE		

General Manager Tom Heckert, the team's groundhog (he's only heard from once a year, usually in February) reassured fans that he could mind the shop until Reid returned.

While McNabb silently rehabbed his knee and Reid worked from home, the Eagles launched into a surprisingly active offseason. Their free-agent losses were significant: Cornerback Rod Hood was the best nickel defender in the NFL, safety Michael Lewis had a miserable 2006 season, but had been a Pro Bowl–caliber performer in seasons past, and receiver Donte' Stallworth was the team's best deep threat. In years past, the Eagles would absorb those defections, shrug their shoulders, and look to their bench for reinforcements. Reid (running the team by telephone) and the front office moved with more urgency this year. They added free-agent defensive tackles Montae Reagor and Ian Scott to bolster a run defense that collapsed during the team's midseason swoon. They signed receiver Kevin Curtis to replace Stallworth. They even executed a major trade, sending tackle Darwin Walker to the Bills for Takeo Spikes, a major upgrade to their linebacker corps.

As the draft approached, the team had one major need, a safety to replace Lewis and apprentice under 33-year-old Brian Dawkins. It seemed to be an easy need to fill in a safety-rich draft. Reid was back at work. McNabb was jogging in a pool somewhere. All was quiet in South Philly.

The peace wouldn't last. On draft day, the Eagles traded their first-round pick to the hated Cowboys. Then they traded up in the second round. Analysts expected them to take a safety. Fans hoped for a receiver such as Dwayne Jarrett. Reid didn't throw a curveball, he threw a boomerang. The Eagles selected Kevin Kolb, a quarterback of the future. An unforeseeable future.

Fans booed. Jaws dropped. Reid claimed that he was unable to contact McNabb before making the selection. McNabb didn't return phone calls from the press. Suddenly, there was real silence from McNabb, not the "no comment" comments he usually used to soft-peddle controversies. The corporate, business-as-usual Eagles tried to explain that they just took the best player on their board. They claimed that their needs at safety and elsewhere weren't that severe. No one bought it.

In early May, McNabb broke his silence. He admitted he was shocked by the Kolb selection, then assumed his usual "company man" demeanor, saying all the right things. Observers noted that McNabb called his own press conference, independent of the team, and that he used his own press agent, a former Eagles employee who was terminated at the end of last season. The Eagles were a teapot, and there appeared to be a Category Five tempest roiling inside: Lurie and Banner mad at McNabb for hiring a dismissed (some believe disgraced) ex-Eagles publicist, McNabb mad at Reid for drafting Kolb, Reid disappointed that McNabb couldn't deliver a championship. McNabb and the team were also involved in behind-the-scenes negotiations for a contract extension, and talks were in limbo in the weeks leading up to the draft. The contract angle, and McNabb's implied anger that the team leaked news of the stalled talks, added yet another layer to the innuendo-laden drama.

The Eagles enter the 2007 season with questions swirling about McNabb's future and Reid's ability to juggle work and family responsibilities. They also enter the season as the best team in their division and perhaps the best team in the NFC. Their fans may have entered the offseason with a long wish list, but the Eagles didn't need to make a major overhaul. They only needed minor improvements to stay in the Super Bowl picture. They didn't make all the right moves, but, with the additions of Spikes and the defensive tackles, they are better than they were last year, and last year's team was far better than its 10–6 record indicated.

Our mean projection for the Eagles is 11 wins, and they will have no trouble meeting that expectation. They possess one of the best offensive lines in football, a deep defensive front seven, a secondary good enough to survive another year without rookie reinforcements, great special teams, and, yes, one of the five best quarterbacks in the NFL in McNabb. Even in the unlikely event that McNabb's knee isn't ready for the season opener, the Eagles have proven that they can win a game or two with Feeley (or any other quality backup) in the lineup. After earning a playoff berth, the Eagles will once again find themselves in a post-season sweepstakes that hasn't been kind to them. Lurie, Banner, and Reid are often criticized for building 11–5 caliber teams year after year instead of reaching for the brass ring with a free-agent splurge. The Eagles learned from the Terrell Owens fiasco that such risks can lead to heavy losses, and the Colts and Steelers proved over the last two seasons that playoff persistence can eventually pay off.

The Eagles outlook would be even rosier if not for all of the distractions. If there really is a rift between McNabb and Reid, it could easily divide the team. The Eagles collapsed under the weight of the Owens fiasco in 2005; if players start choosing camps in the locker room, then 2007 will be a very long season, one that could end with McNabb (who is due $9 million in 2008) or Reid leaving Philadelphia.

It's very likely, though, that the latest Lurie-Reid-McNabb controversy is composed of ten percent miscommunication and ruffled feathers and 90 percent media-generated hot air. For Reid and McNabb, professionalism isn't an act. It's what makes them who they are. When the hitting starts, the quarterback and the coach will be on the same page, and the Eagles will be poised for another winning season, another division crown, and another crack at a championship.

Mike Tanier

Do Trap Games Exist?

Last year Andy Reid was spared the indignity of facing the Minnesota Vikings in Brad Childress's debut season as Vikings coach, but he'll go head-to-head with his former offensive coordinator in 2007 when the Eagles travel to Minnesota in Week 8. Making this visit to the Minneapolis Metrodome to face a team that may be worse than its 6–10 record of last year is hardly the equal of playing the Patriots in a freezing Foxboro Stadium, which the Eagles will do a month later. Still, it comes between two tougher home games: A matchup with the defending NFC champion Chicago Bears, and a divisional game against the Dallas Cowboys.

When Week 8 comes around, talking heads and odds-makers alike will identify this as a "trap game." The theory behind the trap game is that it's hard to stay on an emotional high game after game, so teams are prone to let up against lesser opponents when they're facing them between games against higher quality opponents. The trap game concept is not unique to the NFL—in fact, the idea makes even more sense in basketball, where there isn't a week of preparation between each game—and it makes a certain amount of sense. But does the trap game phenomenon really exist?

A quick statistical reality check should show us if NFL teams should really be worried about trap games. Giving this supposition as wide a berth as possible, we'll define a trap game as any game against a sub-.500 opponent slotted between two games against opponents who, on the season, posted records above .500. Going by these criteria, there have been 474 trap games since 1983. Since we're only interested in how good teams deal with this problem, we'll focus on how teams that finished the season over .500 performed in these games.

It turns out that good teams win trap games just as often as they win other games. Contending teams went

389–85 overall in trap games, good for a .820 winning percentage (table 1). In all other games against sub-.500 teams, the same contenders posted a .815 winning percentage (table 2), meaning they were actually more likely to win trap games than other games.

Table 1. Winning Teams in Trap Games, 1983–2006

	All Traps	Home Traps	Road Traps
Win Pct	.820	.889	.747
W–L	389–85	217–27	172–58

Table 2. Winning Teams in Non-Trap Games Against Sub-.500 Teams, 1983–2006

	All Games	Home Games	Road Games
Win Pct	.815	.880	.751
W–L	1601–359–3	861–115–2	740–244–1

While these contenders were far more likely to win a supposed trap game at home than on the road, their home-road splits again largely mirrored their performance in non-trap games against sub-.500 teams. As you can see from tables 1 and 2, the additional pressure (or lack thereof) of the trap didn't mean much. Despite the hype, the overall effect is nil. It's possible that the existence of the myth itself has lessened the impact of a trap game.

Besides the game against the Vikings, the Eagles have a textbook trap game earlier in the season, hosting the Lions on September 23. That game falls in between two nationally televised games against division opponents; the Eagles host the Redskins on *Monday Night Football* in Week 2 and play the Giants at the Meadowlands on *Sunday Night Football* two weeks later. Conventional wisdom suggests this is a trap game of tremendous proportions. Not only are the games that surround it crucial intra-division contests, both of which will be broadcast on national television, but Philly will have a shortened week heading into the game against the Lions.

Are divisional trap games different from trap games in general? Since 1983, winning teams are 53–13 in trap games sandwiched between two divisional opponents. That's a slightly lower percentage (.803) than their record in trap games overall, but good teams are still winning 80 percent of these games.

While we found that success in trap games hasn't been more difficult to come by overall, for some coaches it has. One big name in particular hasn't been particularly sharp in these situations, including a trap game loss to the Lions late last year.

- Bill Parcells: 20–6 (.769)
- Herman Edwards: 5–2 (.714)
- Mike Tice: 2–3 (.400)

Others have performed better in trap games:

- Bill Belichick: 17–0 (1.000)
- Bill Cowher: 12–1 (.932)
- Marty Schottenheimer: 18–2 (.900)
- Andy Reid: 4–0 (1.000)

Andy Reid's 4–0 record in trap games is actually part of a larger streak. The Eagles have won 20 straight trap games since 1991.

The Eagles play four prime-time games in 2007: Three against division rivals, plus a trip to New England. Their games against cupcakes such as Minnesota and Detroit won't be any harder just because they come in between.

Alex Carnevale

Eagles 2006 Stats by Week

Wk	vs.	W–L	PF	PA	YDF	YDA	TO	Total	Off	Def	ST
1	@HOU	W	24	10	441	241	-1	26.7%	37.0%	11.9%	1.5%
2	NYG	L	24	30	451	404	0	41.7%	29.3%	-12.6%	-0.2%
3	@SF	W	38	24	416	392	+1	31.9%	33.9%	-0.4%	-2.3%
4	GB	W	31	9	398	318	+1	51.3%	20.9%	-23.0%	7.4%
5	DAL	W	38	24	406	369	+3	50.6%	11.1%	-44.7%	-5.1%
6	@NO	L	24	27	325	373	0	16.2%	33.0%	4.3%	-12.5%
7	@TB	L	21	23	506	196	-4	11.1%	8.0%	-4.6%	-1.6%
8	JAC	L	6	13	227	285	+1	14.2%	4.5%	-10.7%	-1.0%
9	BYE										
10	WAS	W	27	3	400	278	+1	54.6%	14.3%	-35.0%	5.3%
11	TEN	L	13	31	390	293	-2	-41.3%	-21.5%	2.5%	-17.3%
12	@IND	L	21	45	300	420	-2	-76.6%	-3.5%	56.2%	-16.9%
13	CAR	W	27	24	402	377	+2	26.7%	37.5%	12.2%	1.3%
14	@WAS	W	21	19	263	415	+1	36.4%	25.4%	-11.4%	-0.4%
15	@NYG	W	36	22	382	358	+2	51.6%	40.4%	-11.1%	0.2%
16	@DAL	W	23	7	406	221	+2	73.0%	30.8%	-31.5%	10.6%
17	ATL	W	24	17	393	378	0	28.1%	50.3%	20.8%	-1.4%
18	NYG	W	23	20	323	305	+1	10.7%	14.5%	7.2%	3.4%
19	@NO	L	24	27	355	435	+1	-2.2%	16.3%	16.2%	-2.3%

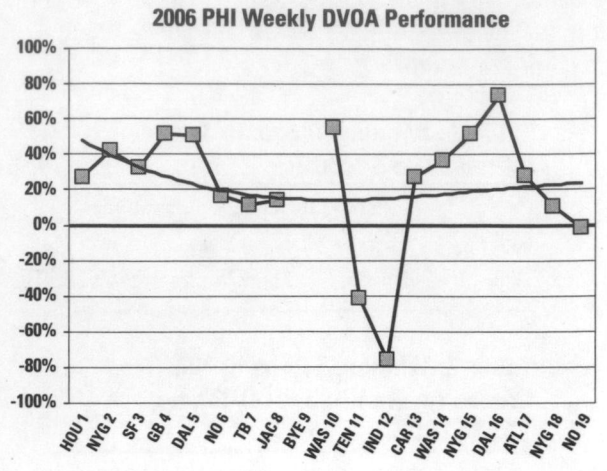

2006 PHI Weekly DVOA Performance

Trends and Splits

	Offense	Rank	Defense	Rank
Total DVOA	19.8%	3	-6.4%	11
Unadjusted VOA	19.2%	3	-3.5%	12
Weighted Trend	17.1%	4	-2.7%	11
Variance	3.6%	30	5.5%	20
Passing	22.1%	5	-8.3%	8
Rushing	16.8%	2	-4.6%	14
First Down	32.8%	1	2.4%	19
Second Down	10.7%	7	-15.4%	5
Third Down	8.5%	13	-8.6%	7
Red Zone	27.6%	5	-13.4%	8
Late and Close	55.9%	1	-12.3%	6

Five-Year Performance

	2006	2005	2004	2003	2002
W-L	10-6	6-10	13-3	12-4	12-4
Pythagorean Wins	9.8	5.9	11.5	10.4	12.5
Estimated Wins	11.6	7.4	11.4	10.3	10.7
Total DVOA	24.3%	-4.7%	22.9%	15.6%	24.9%
Rank	3	18	6	7	3
Offense	19.8%	-9.2%	14.8%	11.1%	6.7%
Rank	3	22	9	6	12
Defense	-6.4%	-4.6%	-2.2%	0.1%	-13.8%
Rank	11	14	16	17	4
Special Teams	-1.9%	0.0%	5.9%	4.7%	4.4%
Rank	22	17	2	2	5

Strategic Tendencies

Formations		Rank	Run/Pass		Rank	Defense		Rank	Other		Rank
3+ WR	51%	8	Runs, all plays	41%	23	Sacks by LB	10%	27	Run with 2+ RB	51%	23
4+ WR	11%	14	Runs, first half	38%	31	Sacks by DB	13%	8	Run with 2+ TE	21%	28
2+ TE	19%	28	Runs, first down	48%	27	Rush 6+	10.9%	8	Play action	27%	2
Single back	54%	16	Runs, power sit.	62%	21	Rush 7+	2.3%	9	Go for it on 4th	1.15	6
Empty back	2.1%	15	Runs, behind 2H	36%	10	Rush 3	3.7%	19	Offensive Pace	28.9	5
Max protect	8%	29	Pass, ahead 2H	48%	7	CB1 on WR1	40%	20	Defensive Pace	31.1	21

Philadelphia led the league in play-action passes and gained a league-best 9.6 yards per play-action pass. However, the Eagles were just ninth in DVOA on play-action (31.4%) because they converted only 4 of 13 play-action passes on third down, with five sacks and an interception.... In formations with only one wide receiver, Philadelphia threw the ball 48 percent of the time, the most of any team. . . . Philadelphia had the highest DVOA in the league on running plays with only one running back in the game (25.9%). . . . The NFC East loves the screen pass. The Eagles were tied with the Redskins for the second-highest number of screen passes in the NFL, with the Giants in first place. . . . The Eagles defense forced seven intentional grounding passes, or one-quarter of all intentional grounding passes in the entire NFL. No other defense forced more than two. . . . The Eagles' defense ranked third in sacks listed as Rusher Untouched, behind the Steelers and Jets. . . . The Eagles were tied with the Vikings as the defense which forced the most throwaways.

Passing

Player	DPAR	DVOA	Plys	NtYds	Avg	YAC	C%	TD	Int
Donovan McNabb	56.7	25.5%	314	2508	8.0	7.4	57.3%	18	5
Jeff Garcia*	27.3	19.4%	188	1273	6.8	4.1	61.7%	10	2
A. J. Feeley	11.8	60.0%	38	334	8.8	7.3	68.4%	3	0

Rushing

Player	DPAR	DVOA	Plys	Yds	Avg	TD	Fum	Suc
Brian Westbrook	34.3	19.4%	240	1217	5.1	7	1	48%
Correll Buckhalter	5.7	0.9%	83	345	4.2	2	1	58%
Donovan McNabb	11.1	57.9%	24	217	9.0	3	3	—
Ryan Moats	1.2	-3.4%	22	69	3.1	0	0	47%
Jeff Garcia*	0.8	-8.8%	15	87	5.8	0	6	—
Thomas Tapeh	-0.6	-35.1%	5	9	1.8	0	0	37%
Reno Mahe*	-0.3	-43.1%	4	18	4.5	0	0	53%
Reggie Brown	2.0	92.2%	3	24	8.0	1	4	—
Bethel Johnson	-0.6	-62.2%	4	8	2.0	0	0	—

Receiving

Player	DPAR	DVOA	Plys	Ctch	Yds	Y/C	YAC	TD	C%
WR									
Reggie Brown	18.2	14.4%	92	46	816	17.7	4.0	8	50%
Donte' Stallworth*	12.2	7.3%	78	38	725	19.1	5.4	5	49%
Hank Baskett	7.3	10.2%	43	22	464	21.1	7.6	2	65%
Greg Lewis	8.4	20.0%	37	24	348	14.5	3.4	2	51%
Jason Avant	-2.8	-45.6%	15	7	68	9.7	5.0	1	47%
Kevin Curtis	16.1	27.4%	57	40	479	12.0	3.0	4	52%
Bethel Johnson	1.4	-3.6%	19	9	156	17.3	8.1	0	47%
TE									
L. J. Smith	8.6	3.3%	80	50	611	12.2	5.2	5	63%
Matt Schobel	3.3	9.3%	22	14	214	15.3	8.4	2	64%
RB									
Brian Westbrook	12.5	11.9%	109	77	700	9.1	8.0	4	71%
Correll Buckhalter	7.3	44.7%	28	24	260	10.8	10.3	1	86%
Thomas Tapeh	-3.2	-33.3%	25	16	85	5.3	4.4	1	64%
Reno Mahe*	-2.3	-89.6%	6	5	23	5.0	3.4	0	83%

Offensive Line

Year	Yards	ALY	Rank	Power	Rank	10+ Yds	Rank	Stuff	Rank	Sack	ASR	Rank
2004	4.47	4.17	10	65%	13	19%	7	28%	27	36	6.6%	13
2005	4.12	3.79	27	60%	11	20%	10	26%	20	44	6.6%	16
2006	4.68	4.62	3	62%	21	16%	17	20%	3	28	5.9%	11

Year	LE	Rank	LT	Rank	Mid	Rank	RT	Rank	RE	Rank
2004	4.29	17	4.46	16	4.60	7	3.73	26	3.50	21
2005	4.27	14	4.69	6	3.74	28	3.67	26	3.53	23
2006	4.49	11	4.25	19	4.72	3	4.21	16	5.48	2

Right guard Shawn Andrews earned the first of what could be many Pro Bowl appearances last season. Andrews is a devastating run blocker who got to show off his talents in the second half of the season when the Eagles offense became more conservative. Andrews's season ended at the worst possible time: He injured his neck in the second quarter of the playoff game against the Saints. Backup Scott Young couldn't clear any room for Brian Westbrook at the goal line in the fourth quarter of that game, forcing the Eagles to settle for a 24-yard field goal instead of a touchdown that would have given them the lead. Young then jumped offsides to negate a 4th-and-10 completion in the final two minutes of the game. Andrews is expected back for the start of camp. Young's future is less certain.

Tackles William (formerly Tra) Thomas and Jon Runyan have been the team's starters since 2000. Thomas is starting to slip athletically, and he was never a technically perfect lineman, but he can still neutralize most of the league's pass rushers. Runyan still plows opponents in the running game and gets the job done in pass protection. Winston Justice, last year's second-round pick, is waiting in the wings to replace Thomas. Andy Reid is almost fetishistic about offensive line depth; the team kept ten linemen on the active roster for much of the season. Youngsters such as guard Max Jean-Giles and center Nick Cole will be battle-ready if the Eagles suffer a spate of line injuries.

Defensive Front Seven

Defensive Line	Age	Pos	Plys	TmPct	Rk	Stop	Dfts	StpRt	Rk	AvYd	Rk	Sack	Hit	Hur	Runs	RuStp	RuYd	Pass	PaStp	PaYd
Trent Cole	25	DE	64	7.1%	25	48	25	75%	54	0.9	20	8	9	20	43	79%	1.7	21	67%	-0.6
Mike Patterson	24	DT	58	6.4%	14	47	15	81%	27	1.3	24	1.5	3	2	47	79%	1.7	11	91%	-0.7
Darren Howard	31	DE	39	4.3%	67	31	15	79%	29	1.7	52	5	3	15	23	83%	2.2	16	75%	1.1
Darwin Walker*	30	DT	39	4.3%	58	27	15	69%	61	0.8	12	5.5	6	7	29	59%	2.8	10	100%	-4.8
Juqua Thomas	29	DE	29	3.2%	76	18	14	62%	76	2.3	63	6.5	5	11	13	31%	5.2	16	88%	-0.1
Ian Scott	*26*	*DT*	*30*	*3.9%*	*64*	*24*	*5*	*80%*	*31*	*1.8*	*35*	*0*	*1*	*2*	*19*	*74%*	*2.1*	*11*	*91%*	*1.5*

Linebackers	Age	Pos	Plys	TmPct	Rk	Stop	Dfts	StpRt	AvYd	Sack	Hit	Hur	Runs	RuStp	Rk	RuYd	Rk	Tgts	Suc%	Rk	PaYd	Rk
Jeremiah Trotter	30	ILB	117	12.9%	43	66	12	56%	4.7	0	0	4	78	65%	47	3.5	51	38	33%	93	7.9	86
Dhani Jones	29	OLB	76	8.4%	84	36	7	47%	4.5	0.5	2	3	42	48%	96	4.7	94	29	67%	5	4.2	8
Matt McCoy	25	OLB	60	7.1%	96	30	10	50%	4.8	2	0	0	36	56%	83	4.1	83	18	50%	50	6.6	64
Shawn Barber*	32	OLB	53	7.2%	94	25	12	47%	5.3	0	1	1	24	54%	86	3.2	34	27	43%	72	6.3	51
Omar Gaither	23	ILB	52	5.7%	99	27	10	52%	4.1	1.5	1	1	28	57%	76	3.1	27	25	45%	67	6.0	34
Takeo Spikes	*31*	*OLB*	*73*	*11.3%*	*59*	*43*	*5*	*59%*	*4.2*	*1*	*0*	*0*	*50*	*62%*	*58*	*4.3*	*84*	*19*	*65%*	*10*	*3.5*	*6*

Year	Yards	ALY	Rank	Power	Rank	10+ Yds	Rank	Stuff	Rank	Sack	ASR	Rank
2004	4.31	4.17	13	51%	5	17%	19	24%	15	47	7.2%	14
2005	3.77	3.66	5	56%	7	20%	26	30%	1	31	5.8%	27
2006	4.28	4.41	21	53%	5	13%	6	24%	16	40	9.3%	1

Year	LE	Rank	LT	Rank	Mid	Rank	RT	Rank	RE	Rank
2004	3.32	5	4.54	20	4.29	20	4.41	23	4.20	21
2005	2.79	3	4.11	15	3.68	6	3.92	12	4.24	18
2006	4.19	17	5.27	29	4.57	21	4.81	28	3.03	3

Defensive coordinator Jimmy Johnson used a two-platoon approach on the defensive line in the opening weeks of last season, with his backups playing almost as many snaps as his starting four. This year, Johnson has so much depth that he may shift lines like a hockey coach.

Defensive end Jevon Kearse is now 30 and coming off a fractured tibia. He lost considerable weight rehabbing his injury, but he's expected to be at full strength—and full bulk—for the start of camp. Kearse is most effective when limited to about 25 snaps per game. The Eagles should be able to accommodate him; their defensive end depth chart includes Trent Cole (converted linebacker and disruptive edge rusher), Darren Howard (solid run defender when fresh), Juqua Thomas (steady all-purpose role player), rookie Victor Abiamiri (hard-working weight room specimen), and Jerome McDougle (star-crossed former first-round pick who will probably be released).

Johnson has even more options at tackle. Free agent Ian Scott, formerly of Chicago, is a stout run defender. Ex-Colts free agent Montae Reagor is a penetrator who can play end in the unlikely event that the Eagles need a body there. Mike Patterson is undersized and wears down late in games, but he's technically sound and makes plays in pursuit. The 2006 first-round pick, Broderick Bunkley, held out for the first 13 days of camp last season and slipped out of the defensive line rotation early in the year when it was clear that he was unprepared for the NFL. He has since lost 25 pounds in the off-season and appears to have regained Johnson's trust. Third-stringer LaJuan Ramsey can contribute as a wave defender.

While the Eagles like to stockpile linemen, they often think of linebackers as replaceable parts. Takeo Spikes is the first high-profile linebacker the team has acquired in seven years under Andy Reid. Spikes, who came over from Buffalo in exchange for defensive tackle Darwin Walker, has been slowed by injuries over the past two seasons, but he was healthy and playing at a Pro Bowl level by the end of last year. Spikes is the only guaranteed starter among the linebacker corps. Jeremiah Trotter has become a liability in pass coverage, so Johnson wants second-year defender Omar Gaither to challenge him in the middle. Chris Gocong, a converted end who spent last season on the injured reserve with a neck injury, will battle rookie Stewart Bradley on the strong side. Spikes's arrival ended the Eagles career of Dhancin' Dhani Jones. Jones was a true Renaissance man. Unfortunately, they didn't play football during the Renaissance. Jones now works as an advance man for Al Gore. If he does for the environment what he did for the Eagles defense, we'll all be underwater in ten years.

Defensive Secondary

Secondary	Age	Pos	Plys	TmPct	Rk	Stop	Dfts	RuYd	Rk	RuStp	Rk	Tgts	Tgt%	Rk	Dist	Suc%	Rk	PaYd	Rk	PD	Int
Lito Sheppard	26	CB	44	6.0%	77	25	13	5.6	27	43%	41	54	15%	62	12.3	60%	9	6.6	20	13	6
Sheldon Brown	28	CB	60	6.6%	69	25	12	8.1	55	33%	59	66	14%	67	13.6	54%	33	8.9	68	8	1
Brian Dawkins	34	FS	109	12.0%	18	39	24	7.8	59	30%	63	50	11%	6	10.2	55%	32	5.4	8	7	4
Joselio Hanson	26	CB	38	4.2%	—	11	6	7.6	—	27%	—	43	9%	—	11.9	52%	—	7.3	—	10	0
Roderick Hood*	26	CB	22	3.9%	—	10	5	2.7	—	67%	—	30	11%	—	11.7	59%	—	8.1	—	0	0
Michael Lewis*	27	SS	57	7.2%	65	31	12	4.0	5	59%	7	27	10%	16	10.1	22%	80	9.0	54	7	2
Sean Considine	26	SS	73	8.0%	59	29	11	8.3	67	38%	52	17	4%	78	13.7	63%	13	6.5	21	2	1
Quintin Mikell	27	FS	18	2.0%	—	6	2	6.4	—	36%	—	7	1%	—	10.5	18%	—	10.5	—	1	0

Year	Pass D Rank	DVOA vs. #1 WR	Rank	DVOA vs. #2 WR	Rank	DVOA vs. Other WR	Rank	DVOA vs. TE	Rank	DVOA vs. RB	Rank
2004	14	21.7%	26	-3.1%	9	-18.3%	6	-22.9%	6	-20.2%	5
2005	24	16.2%	23	-4.4%	17	15.3%	29	-12.2%	8	-16.0%	6
2006	8	-4.2%	13	11.9%	23	-19.9%	9	-8.8%	10	-22.2%	4

Cornerback Lito Sheppard missed three of the first four games of last season with an ankle injury and missed the Saints playoff game with a dislocated elbow. In between, he may have been the Eagles' best defender. Sheppard registered last-second, game-saving interceptions against the Cowboys and Panthers last year while generally shutting down his side of the field. His terrible charting numbers in 2005 (79th in Success Rate, 81st in average yards per pass) were clearly the product of playing with nagging injuries. Fellow cornerback Sheldon Brown took a step back from his excellent 2005 season and will be pushed in camp by former Giants starter William James. The Eagles will miss nickel back Roderick Hood, who led NFL cornerbacks in average yards per pass in 2005, was hampered by a heel injury in 2006, then signed with Arizona this offseason. Diminutive Joselio Hanson was abused when forced into duty as a nickel defender last season.

Free safety Brian Dawkins has one foot on the field and the other in the Hall of Fame. He still hits hard and has tremendous instincts in coverage, but coordinator Jimmy Johnson wants to use him more as an in-the-box safety to compensate for his diminishing speed. Strong safety Sean Considine replaced the ineffective Michael Lewis last season, but didn't impress. Rookie fifth round pick C. J. Gaddis, a Clemson alum like Dawkins, will push Considine. Lewis signed with San Francisco as a free agent.

Special Teams

Year	DVOA	Rank	FG/XP	Rank	Net Punt	Rank	Punt Ret	Rank	Net Kick	Rank	Kick Ret	Rank	Hidden	Rank
2004	5.9%	2	10.1	2	11.1	4	1.9	11	12.1	3	-0.4	15	4.1	8
2005	0.0%	17	-0.2	19	5.5	8	-0.9	17	-1.4	19	-3.1	18	-1.4	18
2006	-1.9%	22	-5.1	26	-6.0	26	-2.7	25	7.9	7	5.4	25	-15.2	32

Just before the start of last year's playoffs, the Eagles re-signed Koy Detmer, the backup quarterback the team released at the end of training camp. Detmer was signed exclusively to hold for field goal attempts. What seemed at first like an act of roster micro-management by Andy Reid and special teams coach John Harbaugh became a stroke of genius after Tony Romo played hot potato with a potential game-winning field goal for the Cowboys in the playoffs. Less than 24 hours after Romo's blunder, the Eagles needed a 38-yard field goal on a drizzly January day to beat the Giants. Detmer's hold was perfect, as was David Akers's kick. A less experienced holder might also have executed a clean hold, but the detail-oriented Eagles weren't about to leave it up to chance.

Akers set a career high in kickoff average last season (65.5 yards per kick), but missed a sub-30 yard field goal attempt for the first time in his career. Overall, he's still one of the best at his position, and worried Eagles fans will gain solace from our essay on placekickers in the Arizona chapter. Incumbent punter Dirk Johnson may be pushed by Saverio Rocca, a 6-foot-5, 265-pound, 34-year-old Australian footie star who allegedly can hang punts in the air for 5.4 seconds or more. Long-time return man Reno Mahe was not re-signed in the offseason. Former University of Colorado star and Olympic skier Jeremy Bloom spent last season on the injured reserve and will get a chance to demonstrate his punt return skills this year. Free agent Bethel Johnson, a speedster who never caught on as a receiver in New England, was the favorite to return kicks before fracturing his tibia in a May minicamp.

(continued next page)

Special Teams (*continued*)

Mike Bartrum, the Eagles' long snapper since 2000, suffered a severe neck injury in the Colts game and may retire. He was replaced by John Dorenbos, who snapped for the Bills and Titans before arriving in Philly. Dorenbos, a part-time magician, will also replace Dhani Jones as the Eagles' resident eccentric.

The Eagles' biggest special teams problem was entirely out of their hands: Opposing kickers hit 10-of-12 field goals from 44 yards or beyond and were perfect from 40 yards in.

Coaching Staff

Offensive coordinator Marty Mornhinweg took over the play calling from Andy Reid in two stages last year. First, he assumed command of the two-minute offense. Then, after the Eagles' bye week, he took over the rest. Mornhinweg is slower to abandon the run than Reid was and is more likely to play for a field goal late in a half. Reid still plays a major role in game-planning, but he seemed to relish the opportunity to take the headset off and do more hands-on coaching on the sidelines. Reid may have a reputation as an emotionless mumbler, but he showed the world his animated, passionate side at times last year.

Former special teams coordinator John Harbaugh was transferred to secondary coach, a better career track position (special teams coordinators rarely advance to head coach). Rory Segrest, Harbaugh's assistant last year, will now handle the kicking units. Segrest has a short résumé: A year under Harbaugh, four years at Samford University, and three at Southeast Missouri State as a position coach. The Eagles special teams were among the league's best for five seasons under Harbaugh, but they slipped in the last two seasons because of injuries and the team's inability to find a true return specialist. Segrest must get the kicking and return units playing the way they did from 2000 through 2004.

St. Louis Rams

When Scott Linehan became the head coach of the St. Louis Rams in January of 2006, the hope was that he would bring some consistency to the Gateway City after six years of Mike Martz's mercurial personality and boom-or-bust schemes. When Jim Haslett replaced Larry Marmie as the Rams' defensive coordinator a week later, fans anticipated that Haslett could rebound from a six-year stint as the Saints' head coach, which started with a Coach of the Year award after the 2000 season and ended with the aftermath of Hurricane Katrina in 2005, to set the Rams' defense right. Marmie, last seen as the assistant coach turning Seattle's secondary into a nice, gooey creamsicle, led the Rams to 28th- and 29th-place finishes in defensive DVOA in his two years as defensive coordinator in St. Louis. Given his long defensive coaching history with the Raiders, Saints, and Stealers, Haslett had the pedigree to turn that around.

By the end of the 2005 season, the St. Louis offense barely resembled that of the "Greatest Show on Turf" era. Linehan's challenge was to reform the ramblin', gamblin' Rams into something more reliable. Martz had a predilection for the kind of play-calling hubris that a coach can only afford to exhibit when he has a wealth of Hall of Fame personnel at his disposal, which hadn't been the case with the Rams since their last Super Bowl appearance at the end of the 2001 season.

The Rams led the league in Offensive DVOA three straight years from 1999 to 2001, then finished no higher than 14th from 2002 to 2005. As Marshall Faulk got hurt and started to slow down, the running game became an afterthought. During that four-year period, no St. Louis back gained more than 1,000 rushing yards in a season. The resulting disproportionate emphasis on the passing attack put far too much pressure on quarterback Marc Bul-

ger. As a result, the Rams descended into a flashy sort of softness and got their collective teeth kicked in on a regular basis.

Linehan's mostly successful history as an offensive coordinator with the Vikings and Dolphins convinced ownership that he was their man. High-percentage passes would replace the seven-step-drop-and-bomb idea, running between the tackles would no longer be a sin, and Faulk replacement Steven Jackson would be given the opportunity to match his predecessor's unrivaled rushing/receiving artistry. The playbook would be reduced drastically in size, but far more of it would be used.

Bulger noticed the difference right away. "Last year we'd run about 10 percent of the plays in the playbook," he told *USA Today* in November. "Now, we probably run 90 percent of it."

It worked in many ways. A depleted offensive line finished sixth in Adjusted Line Yards after ranking 22nd in 2005. Bulger played in all 16 games for the first time in his career and finished second in the league in DPAR behind Peyton Manning. Jackson had 90 receptions, breaking Faulk's team record for running backs, and gained the fifth-most total yards in NFL history with 2,334. The Rams finished sixth in Offensive DVOA, up from 16th the year before.

And yet, there was the one bugaboo that had followed Linehan through his career as an offensive "mastermind": His schemes assure multiple trips to the red zone, but result in a mysterious inability to do much once there. In 2004, his last of three seasons as Minnesota's offensive coordinator, the Vikings offense ranked third in the NFL with a DVOA of 28.0%, but in the red zone, that DVOA sank to −7.9%, which was 20th in the league.

As we pointed out in *Pro Football Prospectus 2005*, this discrepancy had a lot to do with a desire to get cute as the

RAMS PROSPECTUS

2006 Record: 8–8

DVOA Estimated Wins: 7.4 (20th)

Pythagorean Wins: 7.6 (18th)

DVOA: −5.0% total (20th), −11.4% weighted (23rd)

Offense: 12.3% DVOA (7th)

Defense: 12.9% DVOA (29th)

Special Teams: −4.4% DVOA (31st)

Variance: 16.6% (16th)

2006: Scott Linehan fixes the offense, but the defense and special teams are still lousy.

2007: Steven Jackson won't decline, and the defense won't improve.

2007 Mean Projection: 5.8 wins

The Brohm Closet (0–4): 29%

Bad Team (5–6): 34%

Mediocre (7–8): 24%

Playoff Contender (9–10): 10%

Super Bowl Contender (11+): 2%

Projected Average Opponent: −1.6% DVOA (19th in NFL)

2007 Rams Schedule

Week	Opp	Week	Opp	Week	Opp
1	CAR	7	at SEA	13	ATL
2	SF	8	CLE	14	at CIN
3	at TB	9	BYE	15	GB
4	at DAL	10	at NO	16	PIT (Thu.)
5	ARI	11	at SF	17	at ARI
6	at BAL	12	SEA		

end zone got close. Gadget plays, ignoring reliable red zone targets, and a resistance to run when needed sank the Vikings inside of the 20. When Linehan moved to Miami in 2005, the problem went with him. The Dolphins ranked 21st overall with an offensive DVOA of –7.5% under Linehan, but their red zone performance was an even worse –27.9%, which ranked 26th. Linehan finally solved the problem in St. Louis with a sixth-ranked red zone DVOA of 26.2%, but it took several games of the 2006 season for him to get there.

Haslett's defense, on the other hand, was a disaster. Despite the coaching change, the Rams finished 29th in defensive DVOA for the second straight season in 2006. The run defense was especially worrisome—only the regular-season, non–Bob Sanders version of the Indianapolis Colts was more porous on runs up the middle. The pass defense was almost as bad, and it was bad consistently, finishing 26th in defensive DVOA over the first nine weeks of the season, and 26th in defensive DVOA over the final eight. Split that DVOA by any down, yardage, or scoreboard scenario, and the Rams were one of the worst defenses in the league.

The first game of the Linehan/Haslett era seemed to play to past trends. After watching their first-string offense fail to score a touchdown in any of its 11 preseason possessions, the Rams beat the Broncos, 18–10, as a result of six Jeff Wilkins field goals and five turnovers caused by the defense. Linehan opined that style points didn't matter in winning, but going 0 for 5 inside the 20 wasn't a good sign. It was the first time the Rams won without scoring a touchdown since moving to St. Louis in 1995.

The Rams' first touchdown of 2006 came in the second quarter of the second game, but a defensive implosion wasted the score in what turned out to be a 20–13 loss to San Francisco. St. Louis had the ball almost ten minutes more than the 49ers, but gave up 95 more yards than they gained. The offense finally hit its stride in a Week 4 game against the Lions. Linehan modified his conservative approach when forced into a shootout with Martz, now Detroit's offensive coordinator. The 41–34 St. Louis win proved that the new Rams could still score, and that their coach could effectively mix his approach with the talent on his team. Over a five-game stretch that began with that

Detroit game, the St. Louis offense averaged a DVOA of 22.3%, but again the defense sabotaged those efforts, averaging a DVOA of 17.1% over the same span (remember, positive DVOA numbers favor offense). The Rams went 2–3 over that stretch, and the three losses were the first of five straight that effectively ended their season.

And so it went. Each time the offense got on track, the defense would come crashing in like Bluto, Flounder, and the Delta gang, erasing any chance of success. When the Rams went on a three-game winning streak at the end of the season, it seemed more like a consolation prize than a barometer of future success. In beating the Raiders, Redskins, and Vikings, St. Louis "overwhelmed" teams with a combined record of 13–35.

Given how much the Rams have to fix on defense, it's easy to forget about the renewed effectiveness of the offense. As the season progressed, Linehan brought his thought process around to the idea that the team he inherited had enough talent to trust with more than just picking away at the end zone, and Bulger enjoyed his best season as a result. Meanwhile, Jackson's productivity and the diversity of his workload points to a very bright future. You can ride a horse of a running back year after year if you consistently send him out of the backfield on screens instead of slamming him into a wall of defensive linemen 400 times. With Bulger and Jackson, the Rams offense is once again built on the foundation of a strong running game and a passing attack that utilizes the backfield, which was one of the primary characteristics of the attack once led by Warner and Faulk.

The Rams have a pair of tight ends who could be very productive: Joe Klopfenstein showed potential as a rookie last year and is now teamed with free agent Randy McMichael, who played for Linehan in Miami. At the age of 34, Isaac Bruce finished 12th in DPAR among receivers with over 50 passes thrown to his area—an impressive rebound from his rank of 70th in 2005. Despite that down year in 2005, Bruce's trends indicate that he could be productive into his late thirties, much like Jerry Rice and Tim Brown. Number-one wideout Torry Holt matched Bruce's 1,000-yard season, though his DPAR dropped from 18th to 42nd, in large part because his catch rate dropped from 63 percent to 52 percent. The offensive line improved in run support, despite the fact that right tackle Alex Barron was the only lineman that started all 16 games. On defense, former Panthers linebacker Will Witherspoon manned the middle admirably, and defensive end Leonard Little amassed 13 sacks, the second-highest total in his nine-year career.

Where the cracks start to show is in the great void of talent around Witherspoon and Little. Signing former Panthers linebacker Chris Draft was a good call, as was drafting Adam Carriker in the first round of this year's draft. The Nebraska defensive lineman comes to the NFL with

Richard Seymour comparisons—as such, he'll move inside from end to tackle and man the 3-technique, crashing through lines and making plays as opposed to soaking up offensive linemen so that others get the stats. St. Louis also picked Michigan State nose tackle Cliff Ryan in the fifth round on the recommendation of defensive assistant Mike Cox. If Ryan can complement Carriker, the Rams will finally have the great interior line they've been lacking for years.

So, things do appear to be moving in the right direction. Why, then, do our projections forecast the Rams to once again be one of the worst teams in the league in 2007? First, Linehan turned the Rams' offense around with good fortune in the injury category. Everyone from the opening-day starting lineup played in all 16 games except for left tackle Orlando Pace, who missed eight games, and guard Adam Timmerman, who missed three. The Rams also got 16 games from their two slot receivers and their backup tight end. Even Drew Bennett and Randy McMichael, the new bodies in the lineup, went injury-free in 2006 for their previous teams. The chances of any team repeating a virtually injury-free season are somewhere between infinitesimal and nonexistent.

Expecting carbon copies of Bulger's career year and Jackson's total yardage season for the ages is reasonable, but risky. Regression to the mean works both ways. The offensive line was effective with seven different starting lineups—three different left tackles, four left guards, three centers and two right guards, as the Rams shuffled constantly to find the best options—but history tells us that positional consistency is the key to long-term line success. Band-Aids only work for so long.

Speaking of regression to the mean, the Rams' 23.0% DVOA on third down was fifth-best in the league. Third down performance is notoriously volatile and highly prone to revert to average, which means that not only is there very little room for improvement there, but there's a very good chance of a decline. Similarly, the potential for improvement in the red zone is minimal, because it already happened last season.

A league-average defense would make St. Louis a winning team, but the new acquisitions come with no guarantees. Meanwhile, the defensive backfield will almost certainly counteract any improvement managed by the front seven. Last year's St. Louis secondary finished 25th in overall pass defense DVOA, and 28th against number-one receivers, and that was before the Rams acquired historically atrocious cornerback Mike Rumph this past offseason. Trading with Kansas City to get return man Dante Hall is supposed to improve the Rams' special teams, which have been near the bottom of the league for years, but Hall's formerly stellar numbers have declined fairly significantly in each of the last three seasons. Combine all of these factors

and that forecast begins to look a lot less pessimistic and a lot more realistic.

The 2007 St. Louis Rams appear to be a team very much in transition, doing the best it can with what it has, and looking to build toward the future. There's no shame in that—all teams go through these down times—but any hope the organization and its fans has for 2007 had best be tempered by the reality of incremental progress.

Doug Farrar

False Starts: Separating Fact from Fiction

Since 2002, no team has been flagged for more false starts than the St. Louis Rams. In those five seasons, the Rams have drawn 188 false start penalties in 96 games. Rams right tackle Alex Barron led the league in false start penalties last year, but the Rams offensive line was home to the league leaders long before Barron came to St. Louis. As the Rams know all too well, in the hidden, fluid game of field position, false starts can be an absolute killer. They turn good situations—2nd-and-3, 3rd-and-1—into bad ones. Reasonable third downs become 3rd-and-long. If the situation's already difficult, well, you might as well warm up the punter.

When watching a game on television, one will invariably hear the announcers say that the worst thing about false starts is that they are mental mistakes. If your left tackle can't block Jevon Kearse, well, that's understandable. If he can't sit still on the line of scrimmage, that's not. These explanations are dependent upon the player, and sound a lot like the justifications for turning down the people who wanted to join Project Mayhem in *Fight Club*: If the player is young, he's too young; if he's new, he's too new; old, too old, and fat, well, they say the line hasn't gelled yet. If the violation occurs near an end zone, the opposing team's fans are given credit for disabling the line's abilities to hear the snap count and signals. It's a very paint-by-numbers analysis.

Being paint-by-numbers is fine if the theories espoused are correct. That's where we come in. From 2002 through 2006, 3,891 false start penalties were committed by offenses around the NFL. That's over three per game. Breaking down those 3,891 penalties allows us to see whether the tenets of false starts listed above are actually true.

1. Teams on the road commit more false start penalties than those at home because of the noise of the crowd.

You can imagine that it's pretty easy to check for this; sure enough, 55 percent of all false start penalties are committed by the road team. That's not a staggering difference, but it's enough to lend some credence to the idea.

The other half of the theory's a little more difficult. It's hard to quantify crowd noise, but we can try by testing a number of different theories:

2. Indoor stadiums, because they're louder, are the home of more false start penalties than outdoor stadiums.

This is almost definitely true. Of those 3,891 false start penalties, 32 percent of them occurred in domes. (It should also be noted that while Dallas doesn't play in a true dome, the acoustics of the Texas Stadium have much more in common with a dome than an outdoor stadium, so they're being included as a "dome" team for the purposes of the study.) Counting Dallas, eight teams in the NFL play in domed stadiums, and one of them, New Orleans, only played half its home schedule in a dome in 2005. That means that less than 25 percent of NFL games occurred in a dome over our five-year sample, yet 32 percent of the false start penalties occurred in those games.

Curiously, only 55 of the false starts committed in domes were committed by the road team—exactly the same percentage that were committed by road teams in open-air stadiums. Thus, while domes do increase the incidence of false start penalties, they do so across the board instead of just hurting the visitors.

3. Teams suffer more false start penalties when they're deep in their own territory.

Let's first break the field into five sections, and consider the absolute distance of a team from scoring a touchdown: 0–20 yards, 21–40 yards, 41–60 yards, 61–80 yards, and 81–100 yards. The last group would be inside a team's own 20.

Comparing the percentage of plays that are flagged for false starts within a given zone to the percentage of all plays that are flagged for false starts, we see that there's not a significant difference between the two. False starts occur on 2.62 percent of plays when a team has the ball inside their own 20, compared to on 2.39 percent of all plays regardless of field position. That is a slight increase, but not a meaningful one. In fact, false start penalties occur on a relatively consistent basis no matter where the ball is on the field.

4. No, you misunderstood me. I meant *deep* in their own territory.

Okay, let's break it down even further. Take that 81–100 group and break it down into 81–90 yards away from the end zone, and 91–100 yards away. Is there a disproportionate amount of false starts happening in that latter ten-yard range?

Not really. False starts occur on 2.9 percent of plays within the ten; while that's above the average of 2.39 percent, it's again not a significant enough difference to make a serious dent.

Does the increased crowd noise, compressed area in which to work, and general game-situation pressure related to being inside the ten make it harder to get off a play inside the ten and cause more false starts? Most likely. Why aren't the results showing up here? Probably because teams are very conservative inside their own ten. Most plays are runs, the protection schemes are simpler, and the snap counts are quicker. If teams operated the same way within their own ten as they did on the opponent's ten, chances are that the crowd noise would play a bigger factor.

5. There are more false starts in the fourth quarter because of the pressure.

No. Twenty-seven percent of all plays occur in the fourth quarter, but only 24 percent of false starts do.

6. Younger offensive linemen commit more false starts because of their inexperience.

The correlation between the average age of the five starters on an offensive line and that team's false starts varies; they were strongly correlated in 2006 and 2003, but barely at all in 2002, 2004 and 2005. Age has not shown itself over the course of the 159 teams studied to be an effective indicator of the propensity to commit false starts.

7. Offensive lines that stay together commit fewer false starts together.

Looking at the upheaval on an offensive line brought out very little as well. In 2002 and 2003, changes among the offensive line were a relatively strong (–.24) indicator of false starts; in 2004 and 2005, it showed no correlation; 2006 saw its return to being a strong indicator (–.39), as offensive lines in flux like Seattle and St. Louis committed plenty.

Some of the conventional wisdom about false starts is true. Being on the road hurts, and being in a loud dome hurts, too. They just don't hurt more when you mix them together. Everything else appears to be incorrect: Field position has little to do with false starts, younger offensive lines don't jump more, and eating at a steakhouse together for three years doesn't help, either.

What about what we said in the introduction to this essay, though—are false starts *really* an absolute killer? Do teams who commit more false starts lose more often?

8. False starts are a stronger indicator of a losing team than any other penalty.

In their 1998 book *The Hidden Game of Football: The Next Edition*, analysts Bob Carroll, Pete Palmer, and John Thorn made a remarkable discovery: There is no clear connection between avoiding penalties and winning games. The idea that there's nothing wrong with penalties is completely counterintuitive. It can't possibly be true, can it?

No, actually, it can't possibly be true. At least, it isn't true in today's NFL. Perhaps *Hidden Game* was wrong because it was only looking at the 1997 season, or perhaps the NFL has changed over the past decade, but teams with fewer penalties do in fact win more games. Over the past five seasons, the 25 single-season teams with the fewest penalties have averaged 1.5 wins more than the 25 with the most penalties. During that period, the overall correlation between losses and penalties was .21.

Not all penalties are created equal, however. Penalties on defense or special teams have a negligible effect on wins and losses. Over the past five seasons, the correlation between defensive penalties and losses is almost zero, while the correlation between offensive penalties and losses is .31. The 25 teams with the most offensive penalties averaged 6.2 wins, while the 25 teams with the most defensive penalties averaged 7.9 wins.

Defensive penalties are often a byproduct of good defensive play. Defensive linemen trying to anticipate the snap count will get a head start on the pass rush more often than they will pick up encroachment penalties. A cornerback who does a good job blanketing his receiver is bound to draw the occasional flag, especially because every official in the league seems to have a completely different interpretation of the pass interference guidelines.

The definition for offensive holding is certainly nebulous, but other offensive penalties are just outright mistakes. The rulebook is clear that seven men must be on the line of scrimmage. Receivers have to follow specific guidelines when they go in motion. There's no judgment call when the offense can't get a play off before the play clock hits zero. When an offensive lineman jumps early, that's his own fault. False starts and delay of game have a higher correlation with losing than any other penalties, and false starts are a much larger problem because they are far more common (table 1). Since 2002, 29 teams were called for a false start an average of once per game or less. Those teams averaged 8.7 wins. Eighteen teams were called for a false start twice a game or more. Those teams averaged 7.3 wins.

Over the past five seasons, the teams with the most false starts have one thing in common: horns on their helmets. The 2005 Rams had 46 false starts, the highest total of the

Table 1. Penalties vs. Losses, 2002–2006

Penalty	Annual Total for Avg Team	Correl to Losses	Correl Year-to-Year
False Starts	22.9	0.23	0.35
Delay of Game	2.8	0.23	0.35
Offensive Holding	12.7	0.17	−0.08
Illegal Form./Shift/Motion	2.3	0.06	0.01
Off. Pass Interference	1.9	−0.01	0.07
All Offensive Penalties	**58.1**	**0.31**	**0.30**
Def. Pass Interference	6.2	0.08	0.18
Roughing Passer	3.4	0.06	−0.04
Defensive Holding	4.3	0.05	0.12
Offside/Encroach/N. Zone	11.2	−0.06	0.31
Illegal Contact	2.7	−0.07	0.04
All Defensive Penalties	**43.1**	**0.03**	**0.15**
Kickoff/Punt Penalties	**18.2**	**0.06**	**0.20**

last five years. Last year's Rams had 40 false starts, and the 2004 Rams had 36. Those are three of the top five totals in recent years. (That other team with the horns, the Vikings, has seasons ranked 4th, 9th, and 12th.) The Rams are the only offense called for 30 false starts or more every year since 2002. That problem is likely to continue.

9. False starts are more consistent from season to season than any other penalty.

Offensive lines that stay together may commit fewer false starts together, but players who commit false starts tend to keep committing false starts: Oakland's Robert Gallery, Tampa Bay's Luke Petitgout, and, above all, the Cowboys' new big-money free agent Leonard Davis, who has 26 false starts over the last three seasons. False starts and delay of game are not just the penalties that correlate best with losing. They are also the penalties that correlate best from year to year. For five years, the Rams have ranked in the top six for false starts. It's a hard pattern to escape, and there's no reason to believe that this is the year they will do it.

Bill Barnwell
Aaron Schatz

Rams 2006 Stats by Week

Wk	vs.	W–L	PF	PA	YDF	YDA	TO	Total	Off	Def	ST
1	DEN	W	18	10	320	259	+5	41.5%	-0.9%	-35.0%	7.5%
2	@SF	L	13	20	265	360	0	-44.4%	-26.5%	14.9%	-3.1%
3	@ARI	W	16	14	372	357	+2	19.9%	3.5%	-14.8%	1.6%
4	DET	W	41	34	427	370	-1	14.2%	25.8%	3.0%	-8.6%
5	@GB	W	23	20	327	336	+2	29.3%	44.7%	14.1%	-1.2%
6	SEA	L	28	30	419	393	-1	-23.5%	14.0%	35.7%	-1.8%
7	BYE										
8	@SD	L	24	38	412	419	-1	-7.8%	27.1%	32.5%	-2.5%
9	KC	L	17	31	452	317	-3	-14.7%	16.8%	29.8%	-1.6%
10	@SEA	L	22	24	299	283	+1	-33.8%	-4.3%	18.6%	-11.0%
11	@CAR	L	0	15	411	111	-1	-55.9%	-74.4%	-15.1%	3.4%
12	SF	W	20	17	349	319	+2	-22.5%	2.3%	29.6%	4.7%
13	ARI	L	20	34	394	316	-3	-52.0%	-16.4%	42.0%	6.4%
14	CHI	L	27	42	433	372	-1	-82.2%	36.5%	63.0%	-55.7%
15	@OAK	W	20	0	251	260	+5	20.0%	12.2%	1.3%	9.2%
16	WAS	W	37	31	579	336	0	-7.1%	38.5%	23.5%	-22.2%
17	@MIN	W	41	21	416	293	+2	83.2%	62.3%	-19.8%	1.1%

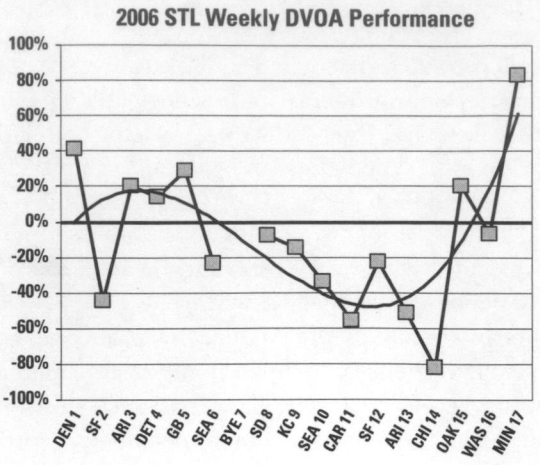

2006 STL Weekly DVOA Performance

Trends and Splits

	Offense	Rank	Defense	Rank
Total DVOA	12.3%	7	12.9%	29
Unadjusted VOA	13.4%	6	6.4%	24
Weighted Trend	14.1%	6	19.0%	31
Variance	9.8%	4	6.4%	17
Passing	19.9%	7	14.1%	25
Rushing	2.1%	11	11.7%	30
First Down	7.4%	9	12.6%	29
Second Down	11.5%	4	14.9%	28
Third Down	23.0%	5	10.2%	19
Red Zone	26.2%	6	3.8%	17
Late and Close	11.0%	10	11.6%	27

Five-Year Performance

	2006	2005	2004	2003	2002
W-L	8-8	6-10	8-8	12-4	7-9
Pythagorean Wins	7.6	6.4	6.1	10.8	6.5
Estimated Wins	7.4	5.1	5.6	9.2	8.2
Total DVOA	-5.0%	-21.8%	-23.0%	9.0%	-1.6%
Rank	20	29	30	12	18
Offense	12.3%	-3.6%	0.7%	-3.2%	-3.7%
Rank	7	16	14	16	23
Defense	12.9%	14.0%	16.1%	-14.4%	-2.7%
Rank	29	29	28	5	12
Special Teams	-4.4%	-4.1%	-7.5%	-2.2%	-0.6%
Rank	31	31	32	26	17

Strategic Tendencies

Formations		Rank	Run/Pass		Rank	Defense		Rank	Other		Rank
3+ WR	50%	9	Runs, all plays	39%	29	Sacks by LB	25%	14	Run with 2+ RB	50%	24
4+ WR	17%	5	Runs, first half	43%	20	Sacks by DB	9%	14	Run with 2+ TE	40%	10
2+ TE	27%	15	Runs, first down	49%	25	Rush 6+	15.8%	1	Play action	20%	13
Single back	58%	12	Runs, power sit.	63%	20	Rush 7+	5.5%	1	Go for it on 4th	0.69	26
Empty back	0.8%	27	Runs, behind 2H	25%	30	Rush 3	5.3%	11	Offensive Pace	30.1	13
Max protect	13%	15	Pass, ahead 2H	51%	2	CB1 on WR1	34%	28	Defensive Pace	31.2	22

Torry Holt was overthrown on more incompletes than any receiver in the league. . . . The Rams led the league in incomplete passes thrown ahead of the receiver as he was running his pattern, with Isaac Bruce being the most common intended receiver on such incompletes. . . . Torry Holt (10) and Steven Jackson (9) were both among the NFL's top dozen players in dropped passes, but the Rams as a team were league-average because everyone else combined to drop only ten passes. . . . Fourteen percent of St. Louis runs were draw plays, which led the league. The NFL average was 5 percent. The Rams had a 41.2% DVOA on draw plays. . . . Marc Bulger tied Peyton Manning for the fewest passes tipped at the line. . . . The Rams had the worst defense in the NFL against screen passes (126.7% DVOA). . . . Defensive coordinator Jim

Haslett blitzed more than he did in his previous job as New Orleans head coach, and far more than his St. Louis predecessor Larry Marmie. The Rams led the league in blitzing six or more defenders last year. They were 21st in that category in 2005, and the Saints were 11th. St. Louis was the only NFL team to blitz at least six on more than 10 percent of first downs.

Passing

Player	DPAR	DVOA	Plys	NtYds	Avg	YAC	C%	TD	Int
Marc Bulger	108.8	27.4%	580	3935	6.8	4.9	63.8%	24	7

Rushing

Player	DPAR	DVOA	Plys	Yds	Avg	TD	Fum	Suc
Steven Jackson	36.2	10.2%	346	1528	4.4	13	2	48%
Stephen Davis	2.5	1.9%	40	177	4.4	0	1	47%
Marc Bulger	1.7	11.7%	7	53	7.6	0	5	—
Tony Fisher*	-1.3	-79.5%	6	9	1.5	0	0	33%
Kevin Curtis*	-0.9	-55.1%	4	4	1.0	0	0	—
Kay-Jay Harris	-0.5	-91.6%	3	9	3.0	0	0	67%
Travis Minor	*1.5*	*7.2%*	*19*	*74*	*3.9*	*0*	*0*	*0%*

Receiving

Player	DPAR	DVOA	Plys	Ctch	Yds	Y/C	YAC	TD	C%
WR									
Torry Holt	11.5	-5.7%	179	93	1192	12.8	2.9	10	59%
Isaac Bruce	24.9	13.9%	126	74	1098	14.8	3.7	3	70%
Kevin Curtis*	16.1	27.4%	57	40	479	12.0	3.0	4	52%
Shaun McDonald*	0.1	-14.1%	19	13	136	10.5	1.2	1	68%
Drew Bennett	*6.6*	*-4.4%*	*97*	*46*	*737*	*16.0*	*3.3*	*3*	*57%*
TE									
Joe Klopfenstein	2.5	-2.0%	34	20	226	11.3	4.8	1	59%
Aaron Walker	3.4	89.3%	6	5	68	13.6	6.2	0	83%
Randy McMichael	*13.9*	*11.1%*	*96*	*62*	*640*	*10.3*	*4.9*	*3*	*65%*
RB									
Steven Jackson	14.6	15.9%	110	90	806	9.0	8.6	3	82%
Tony Fisher*	3.0	31.4%	18	14	159	11.4	10.8	0	78%
Stephen Davis	1.1	2.5%	17	12	90	7.5	5.1	1	71%
Madison Hedgecock	-1.0	-27.3%	10	7	29	4.1	2.3	0	70%

Offensive Line

Year	Yards	ALY	Rank	Power	Rank	10+ Yds	Rank	Stuff	Rank	Sack	ASR	Rank
2004	4.31	4.31	13	66%	12	17%	17	21%	6	50	7.8%	20
2005	4.13	3.87	22	57%	26	21%	8	30%	31	46	7.4%	19
2006	4.36	4.50	6	63%	20	16%	15	25%	21	49	7.9%	23

Year	LE	Rank	LT	Rank	Mid	Rank	RT	Rank	RE	Rank
2004	4.14	19	4.02	23	4.23	18	4.73	8	4.59	4
2005	3.52	25	4.16	20	4.18	14	3.08	29	3.67	21
2006	2.44	31	4.34	15	4.76	2	4.11	22	5.35	4

The St. Louis line had a major problem with continuity last year, using seven different starting combinations. Original starting center Andy McCollum suffered a season-ending knee injury in the first game, a torn triceps put left tackle Orlando Pace on injured reserve in November, and guard Adam Timmerman's rib injury led to his eventual release. Sophomore right tackle Alex Barron was the only Rams lineman to start all 16 games at the same position, and he's still raw, as evidenced by his 8 blown blocks and 13 false starts.

How then to explain St. Louis' ranking of 6th in Adjusted Line Yards, after the Rams were below average for four straight seasons? Line coach Paul Boudreau, a 20-year NFL veteran, did a fine job in his first season with the Rams. Mark Setterstrom and Richie Incognito surprised with powerful run blocking inside. Adam Goldberg did a decent job of replacing Pace, and the Rams often left extra blockers in the backfield to help on pass protection. In addition, Marc Bulger's ability to dump passes off to running back Steven Jackson kept opposing front sevens honest. Second-year fullback Madison Hedgecock helped with solid blocking in the backfield.

Defensive Front Seven

Defensive Line	Age	Pos	Plys	TmPct	Rk	Stop	Dfts	StpRt	Rk	AvYd	Rk	Sack	Hit	Hur	Runs	RuStp	RuYd	Pass	PaStp	PaYd
Leonard Little	33	DE	62	8.0%	15	53	26	85%	10	0.6	12	13	17	26	41	83%	2.2	21	90%	-2.4
Jimmy Kennedy	28	DT	40	5.2%	36	33	13	83%	24	1.5	28	1	1	0	36	81%	1.9	4	100%	-2.0
La'Roi Glover	33	DT	38	4.9%	43	29	10	76%	43	0.8	13	5.5	1	7	32	72%	2.7	6	100%	-8.8
Victor Adeyanju	24	DE	36	6.2%	37	25	6	69%	70	3.6	77	1	1	1	31	71%	3.2	5	60%	6.4
Jason Fisk*	35	DT	21	2.7%	—	10	2	48%	—	3.4	—	0	1	0	19	53%	2.2	2	0%	14.5
Brandon Green	27	DE	18	2.9%	—	13	5	72%	—	2.1	—	0.5	1	5	16	69%	2.9	2	100%	-5.0
James Hall	*30*	*DE*	*24*	*6.5%*	*—*	*21*	*8*	*88%*	*—*	*-0.3*	*—*	*5*	*4*	*5*	*18*	*83%*	*2.3*	*6*	*100%*	*-8.2*

(continued next page)

Defensive Front Seven (continued)

Linebackers	Age	Pos	Plys	TmPct	Rk	Stop	Dfts	StpRt	AvYd	Sack	Hit	Hur	Runs	RuStp	Rk	RuYd	Rk	Tgts	Suc%	Rk	PaYd	Rk
Will Witherspoon	27	ILB	122	15.8%	17	75	19	61%	3.9	3	3	5	77	65%	49	3.0	24	54	49%	53	7.6	83
Brandon Chillar	25	OLB	56	7.3%	92	31	8	55%	4.6	2	2	0	42	64%	52	3.4	43	18	39%	85	5.9	33
Pisa Tinoisamoa	26	OLB	37	7.0%	—	23	10	62%	3.5	2	2	2	19	63%	—	4.5	—	18	54%	34	5.4	22
Dexter Coakley*	35	OLB	33	4.3%	—	15	5	45%	4.5	0	1	0	19	53%	—	3.8	—	13	40%	—	8.4	—
Chris Draft	31	ILB	108	13.6%	36	73	30	68%	3.1	5.5	0	0	68	75%	9	2.1	2	35	54%	35	5.4	20

Year	Yards	ALY	Rank	Power	Rank	10+ Yds	Rank	Stuff	Rank	Sack	ASR	Rank
2004	4.59	4.27	17	76%	30	22%	27	24%	14	36	7.0%	15
2005	4.90	4.28	21	77%	30	27%	31	29%	3	41	7.6%	10
2006	4.94	4.73	28	67%	20	21%	27	19%	31	34	6.5%	17

Year	LE	Rank	LT	Rank	Mid	Rank	RT	Rank	RE	Rank
2004	4.35	17	5.07	29	3.97	7	4.38	21	4.48	24
2005	3.70	12	4.43	22	4.15	18	4.38	22	5.49	31
2006	4.97	25	4.79	23	4.89	31	4.48	20	3.61	11

The myth of the Super Bowl–era Rams is that those teams hit the gravy train with a flashy aerial offense that hid other flaws. In truth, St. Louis made the big games at the end of the 1999 and 2001 seasons the same way just about everyone else does—with both quality offense *and* quality defense. Unfortunately, the defense hasn't been anywhere near postseason caliber since 2003, and the front four has been the main culprit. Defensive end Leonard Little was once again a cut above—actually, five or six cuts above—the rest of the front four. He was tied for fifth in the NFL with 13 sacks, the second-highest total of his career. He also was third in quarterback hits and tied for fourth in hurries. Defensive tackle La'Roi Glover still has the ability to rush the passer, but was on the field too much for a man who will be 33 this season. Nobody else on the defense had more than three sacks, and the rest of the line was a nonfactor in quarterback pressure.

Drafting defensive tackle Adam Carriker with the 13th overall pick should go a long way toward solving St. Louis's woes against the run. Carriker will pay immediate dividends as a 3-technique tackle. Though he primarily played defensive end at Nebraska, he's got the size, athleticism, and toughness to succeed. Watch out for Michigan State tackle Cliff Ryan as well; the fifth-round pick is a favorite of new defensive assistant Mike Cox, who coached Ryan in college. The Rams signed ex-Lions end James Hall to provide some pass rush and run support from the right side.

Middle linebacker Will Witherspoon was one of 2006's notable defenders, in that he came to a new team, moved inside after four years spent primarily as a weak side linebacker in Carolina, and performed well with little help in front of him and question marks on either side. Pisa Tinoisamoa and Dexter Coakley split time on the weak side last year due to Tinoisamoa's injuries, and Brandon Chillar was decent on the strong side, but the Rams recognized a need for more. To that end, they went back to the Carolina well and signed veteran free agent Chris Draft, who was one of the best run-stopping linebackers in the league last year as Dan Morgan's replacement in the middle. Draft would be a great strong-side option.

Defensive Secondary

Secondary	Age	Pos	Plys	TmPct	Rk	Stop	Dfts	RuYd	Rk	RuStp	Rk	Tgts	Tgt%	Rk	Dist	Suc%	Rk	PaYd	Rk	PD	Int
Fakhir Brown	30	CB	77	11.4%	13	21	8	6.5	36	25%	70	82	23%	9	11.2	49%	56	7.4	37	12	3
Tye Hill	25	CB	48	6.2%	74	17	12	12.2	75	36%	52	62	15%	60	13.6	48%	59	9.5	75	6	3
Travis Fisher*	29	CB	31	7.1%	63	8	2	10.4	71	60%	11	45	20%	34	10.6	33%	81	10.9	80	1	0
Corey Chavous	31	SS	95	12.3%	16	42	11	7.1	48	54%	17	43	10%	14	9.6	50%	49	7.1	29	6	1
Oshiomogho Atogwe	26	FS	84	10.9%	27	23	10	12.2	79	24%	72	31	7%	45	17.7	56%	26	10.1	65	6	3
Ron Bartell	25	FS	23	3.0%	80	11	8	5.8	26	50%	25	24	6%	62	10.8	60%	20	5.6	10	7	3
Jerome Carter	25	SS	17	2.5%	—	6	3	6.8	—	25%	—	12	2%	—	12.4	59%	—	6.5	—	2	2
Todd Johnson	29	SS	25	4.1%	—	10	4	5.2	—	36%	—	10	3%	—	14.9	67%	—	3.0	—	3	0
Mike Rumph	28	CB	13	3.7%	—	7	5	16.5	—	50%	—	18	9%	—	15.1	50%	—	10.0	—	0	4
Lenny Walls	28	CB	31	3.9%	—	8	2	11.0	—	25%	—	38	10%	—	12.0	42%	—	8.9	—	4	0

Year	Pass D Rank	DVOA vs. #1 WR	Rank	DVOA vs. #2 WR	Rank	DVOA vs. Other WR	Rank	DVOA vs. TE	Rank	DVOA vs. RB	Rank
2004	27	8.4%	20	7.9%	23	19.3%	31	14.8%	23	31.0%	31
2005	28	37.8%	32	1.6%	23	5.8%	23	-9.1%	9	-13.5%	8
2006	25	10.8%	28	10.1%	21	-24.0%	6	3.1%	23	25.4%	30

St. Louis's inability to stop the run defined the defense, but the secondary wasn't much better. A sluggish pass rush was only part of the problem. Cornerback Tye Hill, the team's 2006 first-round pick, started ten games and showed some improvement on the left side as the season went on. Veteran Fakhir Brown was the team's best cornerback last season. Strong safety Corey Chavous finished second on the team in tackles, which tells you a little about his talent and a lot about the inefficiency of the front seven. In fact, the three leading tacklers behind Will Witherspoon were all defensive backs: Chavous, free safety Oshiomogho Atogwe, and Brown. Chavous is also credited with the further development of second-year man Atogwe, whose three picks, five forced fumbles, and seven passes defensed indicated significant improvement from his rookie campaign. Atogwe was also the only Rams starter with an above-average Success Rate.

The Rams didn't bother re-signing free-agent nickel back Travis Fisher, who had the worst Success Rate in the NFL last year, but apparently they have some sort of quota requirement for horrible nickel backs. That's the only possible explanation for their signing Mike Rumph. Over his five seasons with the 49ers and Redskins, Rumph has proven to be quite possibly the worst cover corner of his era. His only serious competition was Ahmad Carroll, who was waived by Jacksonville after an arrest in early May. Rumph has no such extracurricular concerns, but the Football Outsiders staff is seriously considering the introduction of a "Mike Rumph Variable" to our team projection system, a statistic that would pinpoint those players whose defensive "contributions" prove to have the most negative effect on their teams.

Special Teams

Year	DVOA	Rank	FG/XP	Rank	Net Punt	Rank	Punt Ret	Rank	Net Kick	Rank	Kick Ret	Rank	Hidden	Rank
2004	-7.5%	32	0.4	16	-8.4	29	-8.1	30	-14.4	31	-13.7	32	-10.6	29
2005	-4.1%	31	8.9	3	-13.4	32	-3.5	23	-6.1	25	-10.2	29	7.9	7
2006	-4.4%	31	4.1	9	0.0	20	-0.1	14	-16.0	32	-13.7	32	-11.5	28

The Rams were among the league's worst in yards per return last year, finishing 27th in the NFL on punts, and 26th on kickoffs. In our stats, which take into account the specific circumstances of each kick, they were actually average on punt returns, but dead last in the league on kickoff returns. Enter Dante Hall, the former Chiefs return specialist who electrified the league from 2002 to 2004. The Rams picked up Hall for a 2007 fifth-round draft pick, and Scott Linehan does not seem concerned that Hall's production has declined. He should be. From 2002 to 2004, Hall averaged 13.5 yards per punt return, 25 yards per kick return, and scored nine return touchdowns. Over the last two seasons, his punt-return average has dropped to 7.5, his kickoffs to 23.4, and he's scored only twice on returns.

Because of their return issues, St. Louis finished 31st in special teams DVOA, but, when the offense had trouble scoring, kicker Jeff Wilkins was the team's saving grace. The Rams began the season 2–1 despite scoring two touchdowns in their first three games. Wilkins scored all 18 points in the season-opening win over Denver and proceeded to outscore the offense 15–14 over the next two weeks. Wilkins made 32-of-37 field goals overall, including 3-of-3 from 50 or more yards, and his 131 points were the second-highest total of his 13-year career.

Veteran punter Matt Turk had a net average of 38.3, seventh-highest in the NFL, and he dropped 26 punts inside the 20-yard line with only five touchbacks. Unfortunately, talks were stalling with the free-agent Turk and the Rams went out and signed former Dolphins punter Donnie Jones. Why they chose Jones is a mystery. Our numbers rate him as the NFL's worst punter in 2006, with –7.4 points on punts alone. It could be that Scott Linehan will keep the Mike Martz tradition of undervaluing special teams alive and well.

Coaching Staff

Defensive coordinator Jim Haslett will have several more quality players this season. That's the good news for Haslett. The bad news is that Rams Nation is very impatient for improvement on a defense that has finished 28th, 29th, and 29th again in defensive DVOA over the last three seasons. Haslett must motivate a defense that hasn't recovered from a series of subpar drafts and the departure of ex-coordinator Lovie Smith.

The most prominent off-field change for St. Louis is not on the coaching staff but in the front office, as former Panthers executive Tony Softli takes the role of vice president of player personnel from Charley Armey. Armey came to St. Louis with Dick Vermeil in 1997 and was a key part of the brain trust that put the Rams' Super Bowl teams together. If Softli can live up to Armey's five best decisions with the Rams, he'll have done very well for himself. Armey signed an Arena League quarterback named Kurt Warner in December 1997, spotted smallish linebacker London Fletcher from John Carroll University and signed him as an undrafted free agent in 1998, pulled the trigger on the trade that brought Marshall Faulk from Indianapolis to St. Louis, got starting defensive ends Grant Wistrom and Leonard Little in the first and third rounds of the 1998 draft, and signed former Packers guard Adam Timmerman in 1999. Softli, who worked briefly with Linehan on the University of Washington coaching staff in the early 1990s, has a tough act to follow.

San Francisco 49ers

It's not often that rampant optimism surrounds a team that went 7–9 in the NFL's worst division, and rose from 32nd to 29th in team DVOA, but the 2007 San Francisco 49ers have received as many warm fuzzies from preseason pundits as any team in the NFL. There are several reasons for this: What the 49ers did in free agency, what the 49ers did in the draft, and what the 49ers have been doing in the front office over the last couple of seasons.

There's also the matter of the disaster inherited by head coach Mike Nolan and vice president of player personnel Scot McCloughan when they came on board before the 2005 season. The formerly elite franchise had been run into the ground by the questionable decision-making and petty infighting of the Terry Donahue/Dennis Erickson era. Nolan and McCloughan were charged with the rebirth of a 2–14 team that finished 2004 with a total DVOA of −46.1%, the worst to that point in the history of the statistic. No San Francisco team had lost 14 games since 1979, the first year of Bill Walsh's tenure.

The new administration had a plan, but things would get worse before they got better. The 49ers selected quarterback Alex Smith with the first overall pick in the 2005 draft, then watched as he went without a touchdown pass in his first eight professional games. That year, four 49ers quarterbacks combined to accomplish . . . well, nothing. The team doubled its win total with a couple of tight victories, but its overall DVOA slipped even further to −56.6%, the only DVOA under −50% ever recorded, a near-untouchable mark of futility. Smith's rookie performance produced the single worst quarterback rating in the history of our data: −66.5 DPAR.

To be fair, it wasn't all Smith's fault. His most prolific receiver, Brandon Lloyd, had a "career year" with 48 catches for 733 yards. Lloyd's catch rate of 44 percent was well behind the curve of San Francisco's receiver corps even given the Terrible Offense Factor and Rookie Quarterback Excuse. Among running backs, only rookie Frank Gore and erstwhile backup Maurice Hicks posted positive DPAR numbers, though Kevan Barlow led the team in carries.

The offensive line ranked 29th in Adjusted Line Yards and 31st in Adjusted Sack Rate. Smith was sacked 29 times in seven starts. The defense was little better, ranking 31st in DVOA.

However, the first draft presided over by Nolan and McCloughan would come up trumps in time. In addition to Smith and Gore, the 49ers also selected offensive linemen Adam Snyder and David Baas, who started 13 games combined in their rookie season. Their 2006 draft take is also brimming with potential, as tight end Vernon Davis and outside linebacker Manny Lawson have the capacity for All-Pro play.

For Smith, several moves made a world of difference before the 2006 season. The most obvious were the hire of offensive coordinator Norv Turner and the arrival of backup quarterback Trent Dilfer (who was acquired from Cleveland for fellow quarterback Ken Dorsey). Turner has been a menace as a head coach (as explored in the San Diego chapter), but he does exhibit an ability to develop quarterbacks and make offenses go, if that's all he's doing. Dilfer unselfishly helped Matt Hasselbeck become an elite quarterback in Seattle when it was determined that Hasselbeck was Mike Holmgren's long-term solution. After his unsuccessful attempt to revive his career as a starter in Cleveland in 2005, Dilfer came to San Francisco to mentor Smith as he had Hasselbeck. Turner and Dilfer pulled Smith out of the bottomless pit he dug in his rookie season. Turner, San Francisco's fourth offensive coordinator in four years, followed the undistinguished

---

49ERS PROSPECTUS

2006 Record: 7–9

DVOA Estimated Wins: 6.2 (26th)

Pythagorean Wins: 5.1 (29th)

DVOA: −19.8% total (27th), −17.3% weighted (28th)

Offense: −7.8% DVOA (22nd)

Defense: 12.1% DVOA (28th)

Special Teams: 0.1% DVOA (18th)

Variance: 20.2% (4th)

2006: Frank Gore is the first of the 49ers' new guard to blossom.

2007: They won't improve by three wins again, but one or two more wins might take this division.

2007 Mean Projection: 8.1 wins

The Brohm Closet (0–4): 5%

Bad Team (5–6): 19%

Mediocre (7–8): 31%

Playoff Contender (9–10): 30%

Super Bowl Contender (11+): 14%

Projected Average Opponent: −5.2% DVOA (32nd in NFL)

tenures of Greg Knapp, Ted Tollner, and Mike McCarthy by shelving the West Coast Offense and going with the deep ball, which got Smith out of shellshock and comfortable in his own skin. Dilfer helped with the on-field maturation process and gave Smith a sounding board.

The results weren't world-beating per se, but Smith's DPAR did make a huge climb from −66.5 to 1.5 in his second season. Smith accomplished this despite the fact that he had no receivers who finished in the top 35 in DPAR. His favorite wideout (Antonio Bryant, who had replaced Lloyd after he was traded to Washington) missed the season's last two games as part of a four-game substance abuse suspension. The man who picked up the slack as a receiver, running back, and franchise keystone was Frank Gore.

In his second season, Gore was an absolute revelation. With Barlow traded to the Jets, Gore set the all-time franchise record with 1,695 rushing yards and led the team in receptions. He made the acquisition of veteran guard Larry Allen look like a stroke of genius, and stabilized the offense with the further help of fullback Moran Norris. Norris had been waived by the Saints and Texans and, after five years in the league, had developed a reputation as little more than a second-string blocker and special teams spare part. In 2006, he found out that his true home was between Gore and a drastically improved offensive line. The team agreed when it signed Norris to a three-year extension in the offseason.

The primary problem with the offensive line in 2005 was injuries. With so many players shuffling in and out, there was never a hope for continuity. In 2006, the line of (from left to right) Jonas Jennings, Allen, Eric Heitmann, Justin Smiley, and Kwame Harris started 11 of 16 games. Partly as a result, San Francisco ranked seventh in Adjusted Line Yards, and the Adjusted Sack Rate rose just enough (24th in 2006) to give Smith a chance. San Francisco ranked second in the NFL in 10+ Yards, a statistic that recognizes rushing yardage beyond the offensive line. Twenty-six percent of the team's rushing yards came after the running back was more than 10 yards from the line of scrimmage; only the Chargers, with 29 percent, were better in 2006.

The unit holding San Francisco back last year was the defense, which finished 29th in DVOA against the pass and 24th against the run, but two players rose above the malaise. Free-agent cornerback Walt Harris had an all-time out-of-nowhere season with eight interceptions after *totaling* eight picks from 2000 to 2005 with the Bears, Colts, and Redskins. Strong side linebacker Brandon Moore surprised with a career-high 92 tackles and a Stop Rate of 68 percent, the best of the team's linebackers. Moore and Harris tied for the team lead with 19 Defeats (plays that result in a turnover, a loss of yardage, or a failed third-down conversion). Everywhere else, the San Francisco defense was in

2007 49ers Schedule

Week	Opp	Week	Opp	Week	Opp
1	ARI (Mon.)	7	at NYG	13	at CAR
2	at STL	8	NO	14	MIN
3	at PIT	9	at ATL	15	at CIN (Sat.)
4	SEA	10	at SEA (Mon.)	16	TB
5	BAL	11	STL	17	at CLE
6	BYE	12	at ARI		

transition. There was neither the quantity of starting-caliber linebackers nor the quality of interior linemen that would allow Nolan to run the full-time 3-4 defense he prefers.

These individual sets of improvements, which led to the team's rise to near-prominence, meshed with the harmonious environment now present in the front office after the bitter years that preceded Nolan's and McCloughan's tenures. Over the previous decade, two salary cap purges reflected a desperate need to replace aging personnel, and an obvious inability to do it wisely. The franchise is now in the hands of able executives with a mission: Build the team's nucleus through the draft and strike at the free-agent market when appropriate complementary players become available.

With the NFL's salary cap ramped up to $109 million in 2007, the 49ers launched into their plan. Phase One: Find up to seven new starters on defense, beginning with former Buffalo cornerback Nate Clements, who signed the richest contract of any defensive player in NFL history: eight years and $80 million overall, with $22 million in guarantees. San Francisco then signed former Eagles strong safety Michael Lewis before the rest of the NFL could take a breath. With the secondary filled in, the front office turned its attention towards the front seven. Former Ravens nose tackle Aubrayo Franklin, who Nolan knows from his days as the Ravens' defensive coordinator, will man the point in the full-time 3-4. Free-agent linebacker Tully Banta-Cain brings his experience playing for the Patriots, one of the elite defenses in the history of the 3-4.

These moves could bring a toughness and efficiency to San Francisco's defense not seen in years. The 28-year-old Clements is an elite player and hasn't missed a game in his six-year NFL career, though he's far better against the pass than the run. If Harris can come close to his 2006 performance, the 49ers will have a pass coverage unit that ranks among the league's best. Lewis was one of the best safeties against the run in 2006, ranking fifth in rushing yards allowed per play and seventh in Stop Rate.

Phase Two: Impress once again on Draft Weekend. For the third straight year, Nolan and McCloughan put together a draft strategy that drew raves. Nolan and his staff coached the South team in the 2007 Senior Bowl, and it was there that Ole Miss linebacker Patrick Willis really caught his eye. Nolan compared Willis favorably to 2006 Defensive Rookie of the Year DeMeco Ryans of the Texans after he saw the linebacker calling the signals for his team and being taught by assistant head coach Mike Singletary. It was no surprise, then, when Willis was selected by the 49ers with the 11th overall pick. Two players with enormous raw potential were next off the board: offensive tackle Joe Staley from Central Michigan, and Washington State speedburner receiver Jason Hill.

On the second day of the draft, the 49ers augmented their passing game and made a distinct divisional statement by trading one of their three fourth-round picks to Seattle for Matt Hasselbeck's favorite target, receiver Darrell Jackson. For the first time in his young NFL career, Alex Smith will have real weapons at his disposal in Jackson and free-agent deep threat Ashley Lelie. If Jackson can stay healthy, Lelie can overcome a disappointing past with the Broncos and Falcons, and Hill can find a way to match his physical gifts with an understanding of the pro game, there just might be evidence of a passing attack in the Bay Area once again. Add a healthy Vernon Davis to the mix, and that passing attack could be downright dangerous—especially in a division in which the only potentially dominant secondary is the one Smith will face in practice.

For Smith, the challenge will be to continue his growth despite Turner's departure for San Diego. There's no doubt that Smith has Turner to thank for his development. Turner worked with him on everything from his mental approach to simple mechanical things such as the height of his non-throwing arm and his timing under center as a player who was used to taking the ball from the shotgun. However, Smith will be surrounded by more talent than ever. He'll also have Jim Hostler, his former quarterbacks coach, as his new offensive coordinator. Hostler will run an offense very similar to Turner's, so Smith won't have to learn a new system.

Things look very encouraging in San Francisco, but all of this nebulous improvement still has to translate on the field. While anyone who has followed the progress of the new 49ers' administration cannot help but be impressed, it is generally easier for teams to rise from the depths of the NFL to mediocrity than it is for the middle class to find the NFL's top level. For the first time, the team that Nolan and his crew assembled will face expectations of real success. The NFC West is ripe for the picking, and our projections give San Francisco the best chance to win the division, by a fraction over Seattle. In 2008, that gap will be more than just a fraction. The franchise that was in complete chaos a couple of years ago could soon be the NFC West's dominant force.

Doug Farrar

How the Bears Earned Nate Clements $80 Million

Through the first quarter of the 2006 season, Nate Clements was on pace for perhaps the worst contract year in NFL history. By year's end, he was the top free-agent corner and landed an $80-million payday from San Francisco after just a dozen hours on the market.

The reason for the remarkable turnaround? The Chicago Bears.

To explain Clements's season, I'm going to use some unique statistics. As noted in the Buffalo chapter, I charted every Bills game for the Football Outsiders game charting project and kept additional stats that were not part of the standard charting. Those numbers included:

- **Missed Tackles:** An unblocked defender makes an attempt at tackling a ballcarrier but does not get credited with the tackle. It could be a running back bouncing off of a defensive lineman and changing directions, it could be a stiff-arm, or it could be a complete whiff in the open field.

- **Tackle Accuracy:** This is tackles made (as credited by the NFL statisticians) as a percentage of all tackle attempts (tackles plus Missed Tackles).

- **Missed Tackle Yards:** This is a count of any yards that came after a Missed Tackle, including yards that a tackler was dragged by a ballcarrier.

- **Whiffed Tackle Yards:** A subset of Missed Tackle Yards, this is a count of yards added solely by whiffs on tackle attempts (essentially Missed Tackle Yards minus yards dragged by ballcarrier). These are all of the yards gained by ballcarriers between a missed tackle and an eventual successful tackle, out of bounds, or touchdown.

- **Double Coverage:** Two defenders in tackling position when the ball arrives. This does not include a safety who just happens to be in the area, but rather a defender actually trying to cover the intended receiver. Of course, that distinction is a judgment call for the charter.

- **Draped Coverage:** Coverage in which the defender is making contact with the receiver as the ball arrives, but avoids an interference flag.

These stats exist only for the Bills and their opponents, but they can give us extra insight into San Francisco's new big-money corner.

Through the first four weeks of the season, Clements had missed more than half his attempted tackles (12 of 23). Another miss during the 40–6 Week 5 beatdown by the Bears gave Clements 13 missed tackles, after which offenses

Table 1. Nate Clements Charting Stats, 2006

	Weeks 1–4	Weeks 5–17
Missed Tackles	12	9
Wiffed Tackle Yards	94	62
Tackle Accuracy	53.6%	83.9%
Average Missed Tackle Yards	4.4	3.1
Completion Percentage	69%	53%

Table 2. Buffalo Double Coverage Schemes

Gave extra help to...	Weeks 1–4	Weeks 5–17
Nate Clements	9	16
Terrence McGee	2	14
Kiwaukee Thomas	1	9

gained a total of 104 additional yards. Both numbers led the Buffalo defense at the time. Clements also ranked 13th on the Bills (out of 15 eligible tacklers) in Missed Tackle Yards. In addition, the completion percentage against Clements's pass coverage was slightly better than the completion percentage for screen passes thrown to uncovered receivers.

The Nate Clements reclamation project began the following week (table 1). Clements missed fewer tackles in the final eleven games combined than he did in the first five, and allowed only half as many Missed Tackle Yards. He tightened up his coverage as well.

Clements also regained the big-play ability that had eluded him in the season's first five weeks. Up to the Bears game, he had just six tackles on which he stopped the ball-carrier in his tracks, doing so on 21 percent of tackle attempts. From the Bears game on, Clements earned stopped ballcarriers in their tracks 15 times, a frequency rate of 27 percent. All three of his interceptions and both of his fumble recoveries came in the latter part of the season. In addition, after getting burned by receivers three times in the first four weeks, Clements was beaten deep just twice in the final 12 games.

What did the Bears do to wake up Nate Clements? They realized that Terrence McGee, the Bills corner on the other side, struggles against double moves. Throughout the game, receivers juked their way past McGee for long gains, making Chicago quarterback Rex Grossman look like a future candidate for Super Bowl MVP.

Throughout his career, Clements has been the anti-Deion. Instead of shutting down one side of the field as elite corners are often credited with doing, Clements has tried to bait opposing quarterbacks into throwing his way by leaving a wide cushion and crashing the play as the ball arrives. Clements has intercepted 23 passes over his six-year career using that technique, returning five for scores, but it has also resulted in some spectacular misses and big plays in the other direction.

Of course, quarterbacks were more willing to gamble in Clements's direction when tidy tackler Antoine Winfield was covering the other side of the field. Twelve of Clements's

picks came when he shared the backfield with Winfield. In recent years, Clements has had lesser talent manning the other corner position, making him work harder to lure passers into throwing his way.

Paired with McGee, and with rookie safeties behind him, Clements left even bigger cushions and broke later, but, as we've seen, proved unable to effectively close that distance. Once McGee's double-move secret was out, however, Clements saw less action. Opponents threw at Clements 22 percent of the time in the first five weeks, but that fell to 17.7 percent over the rest of the season. McGee struggled with injuries as the year went on and saw his playing time dip, so the decrease in Clements's work rate wasn't perfectly balanced by an increase in McGee's, but the numbers of both McGee and his replacements on a game-by-game basis support the fact that quarterbacks were looking away from Clements.

McGee's struggles also impacted the Bills' defensive strategy. Instead of using safeties and linebackers to help fill the space Clements left between himself and his receiver, the Bills rotated the help to the lesser corners on the opposite side (table 2).

Since opponents weren't gambling his way anyway, Clements shrunk his cushion. He had nearly three times as many Draped Coverages in the final 12 games as he had in the first 4.

You can see the impact of the Bears strategy on Bills opponents by looking at the way teams used their receivers when playing against Buffalo. In 2005, when Clements was baiting quarterbacks away from McGee, Bills opponents threw 29.8 percent of passes to their number-one receivers, who were typically covered by Clements; that was the highest percentage in the AFC and ranked third in the league. In 2006, this number fell to 25.5 percent, which ranked 21st in the NFL.

Following the Bears' lead, Bills opponents picked on Nate Clements's teammates in the defensive backfield. No longer tasked with hiding their shortcomings, Clements was able to play it safe and clean up his tackling statistics. By allowing opposing quarterbacks to share the wealth, Nate Clements was able to accumulate quite a large share of it for himself.

Nate Clements has always been a gambler. His willingness to risk big plays in the other direction in search of an interception earned him a me-first label in Buffalo. However, in his contract year, a time when just about everyone becomes a me-first player, Clements was willing to not just sacrifice his personal numbers to help the team but devastate them for the first quarter of the season. That he actually wound up hurting the team in the process was of no matters. The 49ers wisely ignored that portion of the season altogether in preparing their contract offer. With Pro Bowler Walt Harris across from Clements and ample cornerback

depth behind them, there shouldn't be a talent mismatch in the 49ers' secondary that needs hiding. San Francisco also has experienced safeties playing behind Clements and Harris. The perfect storm that plagued Clements in early 2006—a pair of rookie safeties, an overmatched cornerback sharing the backfield, and a new coordinator still tinkering with personnel and schemes—isn't likely to strike in San Francisco.

Shawn Krest

49ers 2006 Stats by Week

Wk	vs.	W–L	PF	PA	YDF	YDA	TO	DVOA Total	Off	Def	ST
1	@ARI	L	27	34	393	367	-1	0.3%	16.9%	18.8%	2.2%
2	STL	W	20	13	360	265	0	30.6%	-1.1%	-27.2%	4.5%
3	PHI	L	24	38	392	416	-1	-33.2%	-2.1%	32.1%	1.0%
4	@KC	L	0	41	165	333	-4	-133.2%	-72.6%	39.6%	-21.0%
5	OAK	W	34	20	330	370	+4	4.6%	17.9%	14.6%	1.3%
6	SD	L	19	48	306	421	-2	-35.0%	-10.0%	32.3%	7.3%
7	BYE										
8	@CHI	L	10	41	248	402	-5	-101.8%	-48.9%	42.7%	-10.1%
9	MIN	W	9	3	133	238	+2	-17.1%	-34.5%	-6.7%	10.6%
10	@DET	W	19	13	315	251	+3	-9.6%	-11.7%	-8.7%	-6.6%
11	SEA	W	20	14	416	303	+4	30.0%	25.2%	-14.6%	-9.8%
12	@STL	L	17	20	319	349	-2	12.4%	14.7%	1.3%	-1.0%
13	@NO	L	10	34	202	375	-3	-50.1%	-31.4%	17.1%	-1.6%
14	GB	L	19	30	340	420	-3	-43.2%	-10.3%	32.1%	-0.8%
15	@SEA	W	24	14	390	300	+2	25.8%	20.8%	-3.7%	1.3%
16	ARI	L	20	26	223	372	-1	-31.1%	-16.7%	34.4%	20.0%
17	@DEN	W	26	23	360	325	+2	14.1%	-14.8%	-25.2%	3.7%

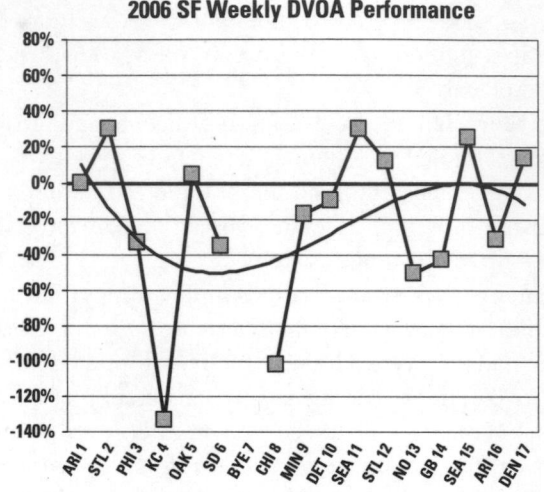

2006 SF Weekly DVOA Performance

Trends and Splits

	Offense	Rank	Defense	Rank
Total DVOA	-7.8%	22	12.1%	28
Unadjusted VOA	-8.8%	24	10.9%	28
Weighted Trend	-7.5%	22	10.5%	27
Variance	6.9%	14	5.2%	26
Passing	-13.9%	26	18.1%	29
Rushing	-2.1%	13	5.8%	24
First Down	-4.2%	18	11.1%	28
Second Down	-14.3%	27	7.0%	23
Third Down	-4.5%	20	22.1%	27
Red Zone	-15.0%	22	12.0%	27
Late and Close	-5.2%	20	-10.4%	9

Five-Year Performance

	2006	2005	2004	2003	2002
W-L	7-9	4-12	2-14	7-9	10-6
Pythagorean Wins	5.1	3.2	3.4	9.2	8.4
Estimated Wins	6.2	1.6	2.3	7.5	9.2
Total DVOA	-19.8%	-56.6%	-46.1%	2.0%	13.1%
Rank	27	32	32	15	8
Offense	-7.8%	-39.8%	-22.3%	8.3%	19.3%
Rank	22	32	29	9	3
Defense	12.1%	18.0%	22.9%	1.4%	2.5%
Rank	28	31	31	19	18
Special Teams	0.1%	1.3%	-0.9%	-5.0%	-3.7%
Rank	18	11	19	28	26

Strategic Tendencies

Formations		Rank	Run/Pass		Rank	Defense		Rank	Other		Rank
3+ WR	39%	29	Runs, all plays	47%	9	Sacks by LB	40%	9	Run with 2+ RB	69%	8
4+ WR	7%	23	Runs, first half	47%	8	Sacks by DB	22%	1	Run with 2+ TE	39%	12
2+ TE	29%	11	Runs, first down	58%	9	Rush 6+	6.6%	23	Play action	22%	8
Single back	47%	24	Runs, power sit.	55%	28	Rush 7+	0.7%	23	Go for it on 4th	0.75	21
Empty back	2.3%	13	Runs, behind 2H	35%	13	Rush 3	5.2%	12	Offensive Pace	32.0	26
Max protect	15%	7	Pass, ahead 2H	34%	28	CB1 on WR1	46%	12	Defensive Pace	30.3	12

San Francisco threw the ball to the right side of the field 53 percent of the time, second only to Seattle. . . . San Francisco, Buffalo, Chicago, and Oakland are the only teams for whom we did not record a single five-wide receiver set. . . . Alex Smith had the worst DVOA of any starting quarterback in the second quarter last year. . . . Smith led the league in passes thrown away due to pressure. . . . The 49ers had an 11.0% DVOA on play-action passes and a –22.1% DVOA on other passes. . . . San Francisco's defense had the fewest incompletes caused by hitting the quarterback while his hand was in motion.

Passing

Player	DPAR	DVOA	Plys	NtYds	Avg	YAC	C%	TD	Int
Alex Smith	2.5	-11.9%	439	2696	6.1	5.4	58.8%	16	16

Rushing

Player	DPAR	DVOA	Plys	Yds	Avg	TD	Fum	Suc
Frank Gore	34.2	9.8%	312	1696	5.4	8	5	47%
Michael Robinson	-1.9	-23.5%	38	116	3.1	2	0	52%
Alex Smith	-2.9	-30.5%	32	161	5.0	2	10	—
Maurice Hicks	-1.0	-23.0%	29	82	2.8	0	0	60%
Bryan Gilmore	2.2	19.0%	7	94	13.4	0	1	—
Arnaz Battle	0.9	12.1%	4	28	7.0	0	0	—

Receiving

Player	DPAR	DVOA	Plys	Ctch	Yds	Y/C	YAC	TD	C%
WR									
Antonio Bryant*	6.2	-4.6%	91	40	733	18.3	4.1	3	70%
Arnaz Battle	12.3	6.6%	86	60	692	11.5	4.2	3	44%
Bryan Gilmore	-7.2	-49.3%	31	8	150	18.8	4.3	1	33%
Taylor Jacobs	-2.5	-44.3%	12	4	29	7.3	0.3	0	26%
Darrell Jackson	17.6	9.1%	112	63	968	15.4	4.0	10	68%
Ashley Lelie	-1.4	-18.0%	68	28	430	15.4	2.3	1	41%
TE									
Eric Johnson*	3.6	-0.1%	49	34	292	8.6	4.1	2	69%
Vernon Davis	-3.0	-25.4%	42	20	265	13.3	5.8	3	48%
RB									
Frank Gore	4.1	-0.7%	86	61	405	8.0	7.3	1	71%
Maurice Hicks	5.6	66.3%	15	13	137	10.5	10.8	1	87%
Michael Robinson	-1.7	-34.5%	12	9	47	5.2	4.8	0	71%
Moran Norris	0.3	-4.1%	7	5	36	7.2	7.6	2	75%

Offensive Line

Year	Yards	ALY	Rank	Power	Rank	10+ Yds	Rank	Stuff	Rank	Sack	ASR	Rank
2004	3.50	3.62	31	56%	26	16%	24	28%	26	52	8.4%	24
2005	4.14	3.66	29	58%	24	24%	3	28%	29	48	10.1%	29
2006	4.99	4.48	7	55%	28	26%	2	21%	5	35	6.8%	18

Year	LE	Rank	LT	Rank	Mid	Rank	RT	Rank	RE	Rank
2004	2.78	30	4.07	22	3.72	29	3.66	28	2.60	31
2005	3.94	20	3.17	29	3.69	29	3.95	22	3.19	28
2006	6.01	1	4.30	17	4.40	15	4.04	23	4.34	12

The offensive line was the biggest improvement for the 49ers in 2006, as they moved up from 29th to 7th in Adjusted Line Yards. Frank Gore's ascent to the big time had a lot to do with that, but the Niners ranked 3rd in 10+ Yards in 2005 and second in 2006. In other words, Gore's productivity in the open field was fairly consistent over his first two seasons, it was the play in the trenches that changed. Most people thought that the signing of future Hall of Fame guard Larry Allen prior to last season was a stopgap at best. Allen went back and forth with Dallas head coach Bill Parcells over conditioning and other issues and refused a pay cut before his release in March of 2006. After signing a two-year contract with San Francisco a few days later, the man who may go down as the greatest lineman of his generation got to work on his professional rebirth. Allen helped the left side of the line take enormous strides forward. Right guard Justin Smiley had a great year as

(continued next page)

Offensive Line (continued)

well, playing most of the season through a torn labrum he suffered in the second game. There's a shakeup coming, however. The 49ers underestimated Smiley's value in initial negotiations on a contract extension, and other teams have already expressed interest in a trade. Reports indicate that a trade for a 2008 second-round draft pick could mean Smiley's departure, and both Allen and Smiley are in the last years of their current contracts.

Left tackle Jonas Jennings and right tackle Kwame Harris have struggled with different issues. For Jennings, it's been injuries, which have caused him to miss 16 games in his two seasons with the 49ers. For Harris it's been a simple lack of consistency. It's well known that the team isn't averse to a trade, and San Francisco's move to acquire a second first-round pick and take Central Michigan tackle Joe Staley in this year's draft speaks to the need for improvement at the position. Should Harris be moved, Staley would most likely start on the right side. If he lives up to his potential, Staley could make multiple Pro Bowls. Center Eric Heitmann broke his right leg in the mid-December win over the Seahawks, and missed the final two games of the season. He's expected to be ready for training camp. If not, Tony Wragge is a good backup.

Defensive Front Seven

Defensive Line	Age	Pos	Plys	TmPct	Rk	Stop	Dfts	StpRt	Rk	AvYd	Rk	Sack	Hit	Hur	Runs	RuStp	RuYd	Pass	PaStp	PaYd
Marques Douglas	30	DE	63	7.6%	19	48	15	76%	48	2.0	56	3	2	5	55	73%	2.6	8	100%	-2.3
Bryant Young	35	DE	53	6.4%	35	42	13	79%	32	1.7	43	5.5	6	13	43	77%	2.2	10	90%	-0.8
Melvin Oliver	24	DE	43	5.2%	50	32	6	74%	56	2.9	73	1	2	2	40	78%	2.9	3	33%	3.3
Ronald Fields	26	DE	29	4.3%	68	19	4	66%	75	2.6	69	0	1	2	27	67%	2.5	2	50%	3.0
Isaac Sopoaga	26	DT	26	3.3%	70	24	6	92%	4	0.9	15	1.5	1	2	19	89%	1.7	7	100%	-1.3
Anthony Adams*	27	DT	23	3.2%	—	16	7	70%	—	0.6	—	2	3	4	18	67%	2.0	5	80%	-4.4
Aubrayo Franklin	27	DT	18	2.7%	—	13	2	72%	—	2.9	—	0	1	1	14	79%	2.6	4	50%	4.3

Linebackers	Age	Pos	Plys	TmPct	Rk	Stop	Dfts	StpRt	AvYd	Sack	Hit	Hur	Runs	RuStp	Rk	RuYd	Rk	Tgts	Suc%	Rk	PaYd	Rk
Brandon Moore	28	ILB	94	11.3%	60	64	19	68%	3.0	6.5	7	13	61	69%	32	3.3	39	27	57%	28	5.9	32
Derek Smith	32	ILB	70	10.4%	68	28	4	40%	6.1	0	0	2	56	45%	99	5.0	96	21	43%	73	6.0	37
Manny Lawson	23	OLB	60	7.2%	93	33	10	55%	5.8	2.5	1	2	29	62%	57	5.3	99	20	58%	27	5.6	24
Jeff Ulbrich	30	ILB	59	7.1%	95	27	7	46%	6.4	0	0	0	38	58%	74	3.8	69	18	47%	58	6.4	56
Hannibal Navies	30	OLB	18	5.8%	—	4	2	22%	10.6	0	0	0	7	29%	—	5.0	—	6	45%	—	4.4	—
Tully Banta-Cain	27	OLB	33	4.4%	—	20	11	61%	4.0	5	6	9	18	61%	—	3.6	—	4	43%	—	4.6	—

Year	Yards	ALY	Rank	Power	Rank	10+ Yds	Rank	Stuff	Rank	Sack	ASR	Rank
2004	4.17	4.45	25	72%	27	13%	9	22%	22	29	5.2%	32
2005	4.04	4.31	23	60%	15	16%	14	27%	10	28	4.9%	32
2006	4.33	4.64	26	67%	19	15%	10	21%	27	34	6.2%	20

Year	LE	Rank	LT	Rank	Mid	Rank	RT	Rank	RE	Rank
2004	5.16	29	4.38	16	4.21	15	5.04	32	4.19	20
2005	4.89	27	3.61	7	3.99	13	5.11	30	5.05	28
2006	4.23	18	4.13	11	4.80	29	4.73	24	4.93	28

It's been Mike Nolan's desire to switch to a full-time 3-4 defense in San Francisco, and, after two years of tinkering, he might finally have the horses to do it. First-round draft pick Patrick Willis of Ole Miss has never played in a 3-4, so he'll get a crash course. Nolan isn't worried about the young man who so impressed him at the Senior Bowl. Willis will compete with Derek Smith to start at weakside inside linebacker. Smith, a productive veteran, was bothered by a muscle strain that affected his eyesight last season.

There are no such positional battles on the strong side, where Brandon Moore had a superlative season in 2006. Manny Lawson, a rookie last year, was a pass-rushing specialist on North Carolina State's dominant 2005 defensive line. He's still learning the fine points of the linebacker position, but he has the raw talent and pure athleticism to excel outside in a 3-4. Opposite Lawson is free-agent signing Tully Banta-Cain, who had a productive season for New England last year in his first year as a regular starter after three years playing primarily on special teams. He's best when rushing the passer, and the 49ers should avoid dropping him into coverage too often.

Nolan needed a prototype nose tackle for his optimal scheme, so he reached back to his past as Baltimore's defensive coordinator and signed Aubrayo Franklin. Like Banta-Cain, Franklin is used to playing in an elite 3-4. He's a strong tackle with some playmaking ability. Backup Isaac Sopoaga is a raw bulldozer with limited mobility but some potential. Bryant Young and Marques Douglas are productive veterans at the ends. The 49ers wanted to use more of second-year end Melvin Oliver, but he tore his ACL at minicamp and is out for the year.

Defensive Secondary

Secondary	Age	Pos	Plys	TmPct	Rk	Stop	Dfts	RuYd	Rk	RuStp	Rk	Tgts	Tgt%	Rk	Dist	Suc%	Rk	PaYd	Rk	PD	Int
Walt Harris	33	CB	84	10.8%	18	38	19	4.3	11	44%	40	81	19%	37	10.8	52%	38	5.8	5	21	8
Shawntae Spencer	25	CB	73	10.8%	17	30	14	6.2	34	47%	31	81	22%	13	13.0	50%	50	8.8	67	9	1
Keith Lewis	26	SS	70	8.4%	58	24	15	7.6	57	25%	70	36	7%	38	10.5	52%	40	9.1	55	4	2
Mark Roman	30	FS	60	7.2%	64	30	18	6.4	39	42%	42	29	6%	56	14.5	65%	7	7.6	39	7	1
Sammy Davis	27	CB	37	5.5%	—	12	2	7.2	—	50%	—	29	8%	—	14.5	39%	—	10.5	—	6	0
Chad Williams	28	SS	25	3.2%	79	12	10	0.1	1	86%	1	28	6%	53	9.4	36%	74	8.3	44	2	1
Mike Adams*	26	FS	59	7.1%	66	15	4	6.3	35	28%	65	27	6%	61	12.1	37%	73	9.9	62	2	0
Nate Clements	28	CB	92	10.7%	19	42	21	10.4	69	32%	62	93	21%	18	10.7	59%	13	6.4	16	18	3
Michael Lewis	27	SS	57	7.2%	65	31	12	4.0	5	59%	7	27	10%	16	10.1	22%	80	9.0	54	7	2

Year	Pass D Rank	DVOA vs. #1 WR	Rank	DVOA vs. #2 WR	Rank	DVOA vs. Other WR	Rank	DVOA vs. TE	Rank	DVOA vs. RB	Rank
2004	31	48.0%	32	-2.9%	10	13.5%	29	37.6%	31	-10.9%	8
2005	31	23.2%	28	-18.7%	6	-6.6%	13	45.9%	32	12.7%	28
2006	29	1.0%	16	-5.8%	11	-7.5%	14	34.4%	32	26.6%	31

If everything breaks right, the 49ers will have one of the most formidable cornerback duos in the NFL. The questions surrounding Walt Harris and Nate Clements are whether Harris's eight-interception season was a fluke or a harbinger, and how long it takes Clements to become the kind of player who can justify the richest defensive contract in NFL history. For Harris, who totaled eight interceptions from 2000 through 2005, the concern is that he was the beneficiary of mistakes by less-than-stellar opposing signal callers. Harris had two picks each from backups Marques Tuiasosopo of Oakland and Seneca Wallace of Seattle, one from Denver's Jake Plummer, who was backing up Jay Cutler in the season finale, one from a rookie (Cutler himself), and one from the fossilized version of Brad Johnson. That's the template for a one-off career year, which is compounded by the fact that Harris turned 33 in August—cornerbacks his age generally have more of a past than a future. Clements, on the other hand, should thrive in San Francisco. There's an improving defense in front of him, and the threat of Harris makes it more likely that quarterbacks will look his way. However, as detailed in the accompanying essay by Shawn Krest, Clements is a player who likes to bait quarterbacks, leave open pockets, and crash plays, which can lead to big plays when he misses.

The 49ers also signed former Eagles safety Michael Lewis to a six-year contract despite pass coverage problems that caused Lewis to lose his starting job to Sean Considine in mid-October. New San Francisco defensive coordinator Greg Manusky sees Lewis as more of a blitzing safety, which makes sense based on the Eagles' preference to use Lewis on rushing downs. Mark Roman, who signed a three-year extension to stay in San Francisco, played well on the strong side last year and will move to free safety.

Special Teams

Year	DVOA	Rank	FG/XP	Rank	Net Punt	Rank	Punt Ret	Rank	Net Kick	Rank	Kick Ret	Rank	Hidden	Rank
2004	-0.9%	19	2.4	10	6.7	8	0.4	16	-8.6	28	-6.0	26	-10.5	28
2005	1.3%	11	12.8	2	2.0	14	0.8	11	5.9	9	-13.9	31	7.7	8
2006	0.1%	18	-0.1	16	1.8	17	-0.3	15	-1.4	22	0.2	15	-11.3	27

San Francisco's special teams were better than average in 2005 and possibly the only thing that kept the team from a winless season that year. Last year, as everything else improved, special teams actually struggled a bit. Kicker Joe Nedney's field goal percentage dropped to 82 percent from 92, though he overcame a slow start, especially in kickoff distance, made ten-of-ten field goals in December, and was generally consistent. Punter Andy Lee finished seventh in the NFL with a 44.8 yards-per-punt gross average and 17th in net average with 36.8 yards per punt. Lee was the highest-rated punter in our numbers for pure punt value, but only Arizona and Jacksonville gave up more value than San Francisco on punt returns. As for the 49ers' own returns, they were very average, with backup running back Maurice Hicks on kickoffs and rookie receiver Brandon Williams on punts. Given all the new receivers on the depth chart, perhaps the 49ers will be more open to trying Arnaz Battle as the regular punt-return man. Battle returned seven punts last season, one for 60 yards.

Coaching Staff

The culture established by Mike Nolan was best expressed by defensive end Bryant Young, who decided to stay in San Francisco for a 14th season. As the last link to San Francisco's Super Bowl years, Young has seen it all. "We're on the verge, the cusp of just being right there," he said after signing a one-year extension on March 1. "I thought we left something on the table last year, and, with the addition of a few more pieces, we're going to be right in the mix. Part of [his decision to return] is wanting to be part of finishing [the] work and leaving the 49ers organization like I found it." When Nolan came on board in 2005, the notion of a new 49ers dynasty was utterly ridiculous. Now, there's an amazing amount of optimism surrounding this 7–9 team. What makes Nolan's squad different than the usual worst-to-first entrants is the fact that both attention and money has been paid to unglamorous positions such as defensive tackle and offensive guard. No mention of Nolan's ability to turn things around is complete without mentioning the front office, especially personnel chief Scot McCloughan. The coaching staff is important, but Vince Lombardi in his prime would have had difficulty succeeding with what Nolan inherited. This is now a team built aggressively, but also for the long haul.

Seattle Seahawks

On the surface, the 2006 Seattle Seahawks look like a team that followed the first Super Bowl appearance in franchise history with a third consecutive NFC West title and a near-return to the NFC Championship game. In the Divisional round, they battled the Chicago Bears, the NFC's best team, at Soldier Field, only to lose in overtime. They broke the Super Bowl Loser's Curse in half, and you could be forgiven for thinking that the drop-off from 2005 wasn't so severe. After all, with a few more lucky breaks, the Seahawks could have been in their second straight Super Bowl.

That, in a nutshell, is why advanced statistical analysis matters. The 2005 and 2006 Seahawks teams were about as different as two teams could be while still making the playoffs in both seasons with most of the same players. All you had to do was to look under the hood. The Seahawks finished 25th in overall DVOA in 2006, after placing fifth in 2005. The offense, third in DVOA during the team's Super Bowl season, fell to 27th.

Seattle began 2006 3–0, but those wins introduced the problems that would plague the team all season. The offensive line looked terrible, both in a 9–6 squeaker over the dismal Lions and a 21–10 win over the hapless Cardinals. The third win was a 42–30 shootout over the Giants, a game Seattle led 42–3 in the fourth quarter before a total defensive collapse. Combine that impotent offensive line and defensive collapse, and you get Seattle's fourth game, a 37–6 pasting at the hands of the Bears. The Seahawks couldn't handle Chicago on either side of the ball. The offensive line was bullied by the Bears' front seven—especially defensive tackle Tommie Harris—and the defensive line was pushed around by running backs Thomas Jones and Cedric Benson.

Injuries and inconsistency added to the overall malaise (running back and 2005 MVP Shaun Alexander broke a

bone in his left foot in the Giants game and missed the next six weeks), but the bottom line was clear. In 2005, the Seahawks controlled the game up front with aggression and purpose; in 2006, the team was reactive, tentative, and often a step slow. In the NFL, success starts in the trenches, and that was where the 2006 Seattle Seahawks didn't measure up. Seattle had no answer for the loss of left guard Steve Hutchinson to the Vikings, and their mostly undersized defensive tackle rotation, so effective in 2005, struggled mightily when Marcus Tubbs missed 11 games and was placed on injured reserve in early November.

The most humiliating and debilitating loss of the season came in Week 7, when Minnesota stomped the Seahawks 31–13 at Qwest Field. Not only did Minnesota running back Chester Taylor set a franchise record with a 95-yard touchdown run—as Hutchinson practically walled off half the Seattle defense by himself—but Vikings linebacker E. J. Henderson rolled into Matt Hasselbeck's right leg early in the second half, spraining the quarterback's medial collateral ligament. Hasselbeck missed a month, and the Seahawks went 2–2 under backup Seneca Wallace. The loss to Minnesota ended a 12-game home winning streak for the Seahawks. By the time both Hasselbeck and Alexander had returned to the backfield, it was late November.

Still, Seattle managed an 8–4 record by the three-quarter mark of the season. Remaining talent was a factor, but this was not an 8–4 team. An amazing four wins came on late Josh Brown field goals, and the Broncos were the only team Seattle beat that finished the season with a winning record. Most of all, Seattle benefited from its residence in the NFL's worst division. Add the ratings for all four teams, and three divisions had a negative DVOA last year: the NFC North, NFC South, and NFC West. The NFC West's combined

2007 Seahawks Schedule

Week	Opp	Week	Opp	Week	Opp
1	TB	7	STL	13	at PHI
2	at ARI	8	BYE	14	ARI
3	CIN	9	at CLE	15	at CAR
4	at SF	10	SF (Mon.)	16	BAL
5	at PIT	11	CHI	17	at ATL
6	NO	12	at STL		

-57.1% DVOA was more than three times worse than the South, and more then ten times worse than the North. That being said, the Seahawks could only muster a 3–3 record in their division. The 49ers, the one team in the NFC West unquestionably on the rise last season, swept the Seahawks decisively. Seattle had to play most of their starters in the season finale against a moribund Tampa Bay squad just to avoid a .500 record, and their 1–3 end to the season eclipsed any overt joy about a return to the playoffs. The Seahawks were lucky to be there, and they knew it.

Of course, they needed even more luck to get past the Cowboys in the Wild Card round. Up 21–20 with less than two minutes left, the Seahawks watched Tony Romo botch the hold on what would have been a gimme 19-yard game-winning field goal by Martin Gramatica. Defensive back Jordan Babineaux's clutch stop of Romo before he could score with the ball sent the Seahawks to Chicago, their eventual season's end, and an uncertain future.

Questions about this team's direction have only been magnified by its offseason moves. Seattle's free-agent shopping spree was almost more notable for the players they let go and didn't get than for their acquisitions. Desperate to shore up an offensive line that finished 30th in Adjusted Line Yards in 2006, Seattle set its sights on Chargers free-agent guard Kris Dielman. The Seahawks flew Dielman up to Seattle in owner Paul Allen's private plane and gave him the full dog-and-pony show, but Dielman flew coach back to San Diego and re-signed with the team that had the NFL's best offensive line in 2006. In their effort to replace tight end Jerramy Stevens, released after one too many scrapes with the law, the Seahawks were outbid by Denver for the services of former New England standout Daniel Graham. Patchwork solutions at both guard positions don't inspire confidence, even in the short term, and the idea that 35-year-old tight end Marcus Pollard can replace Stevens is downright laughable.

Just as laughable was the notion of trading Darrell Jackson—Seattle's most productive receiver this decade—to division rival San Francisco for a paltry mid-fourth round pick. Seattle fortified the 49ers' biggest need, and took away

Matt Hasselbeck's primary target, because team president Tim Ruskell didn't think Jackson was a "character fit."

There have also been extensive changes on the defensive side of the ball. Ruskell signed defensive end Patrick Kerney, a favorite from his days as Atlanta's assistant GM, to a six-year, $39.5-million contract. Kerney's signing paved the way for Grant Wistrom's release. Wistrom had signed a six-year, $30-plus-million deal of his own back in 2004, but never lived up to it. The 30-year-old Kerney missed the final seven games of the 2006 season with a torn pectoral muscle, but he racked up 4.5 sacks in that abbreviated season, while Wistrom had only four in 16 games.

In, the secondary, Seattle made no attempt to re-sign free agent Ken Hamlin, allowing the 2003 second-round draft pick to join the Dallas Cowboys. In his stead, former Jacksonville free safety Deon Grant received a great deal of money—a $30-million, six-year contract, with an $11.1 million signing bonus, the latter believed to be the largest ever given to any player at his position. The Seahawks then signed former Vikings and Browns safety Brian Russell. Russell, who is known for his versatility and heady play, may replace strong safety Michael Boulware, who was benched for several games last year due to blown coverages. Hamlin and Boulware have more pure physical talent than their successors, but the Seahawks hope that the veteran savvy of Grant and Russell will more than make up for any athletic discrepancies, as the Seahawks missed Marquand Manuel's ability to read plays and get everyone in the right spots after Manuel signed with the Packers before the 2006 season.

The defensive line will go the way of Marcus Tubbs, or Cal defensive tackle Brandon Mebane, whom the Seahawks selected in the third round of this year's draft. Tubbs had microfracture surgery on his left knee in the offseason. Head coach Mike Holmgren has expressed optimism about Tubbs's recovery, but the microfracture procedure (in which knee cartilage is restored by creating small fractures in the adjoining areas) has ended more than one NFL career. Seattle's run defense fell apart without Tubbs's ability to take on multiple blockers, as did its capacity to have other defenders flow through holes and harass opposing quarterbacks. The Seahawks ranked sixth in the NFL with 41 sacks last year after leading the league with 50 in 2005, but nine of those 41 came against the Raiders in a single game. Tubbs wasn't playing against the Raiders, which says more about that Oakland offensive line than anything else. Mebane provides more run support in rotation, and a marginal insurance policy, should Tubbs be unable to recover.

Seattle's front office appears to have a surprising level of confidence in an offense that imploded in 2006. Last year was the first season since 2001 that the offense was below league average, but the team blames much of that on injuries. Hasselbeck and Alexander missed significant time, tackles Walter Jones and Sean Locklear were nicked up, with Locklear missing five games, veteran center Robbie Tobeck was lost for the season after eight games, alleged Hutchinson replacement Floyd Womack went down with his usual litany of boo-boos, and receivers Darrell Jackson and D. J. Hackett were out for weeks at a time, as well. Continuity was impossible, and productivity was a catch-as-catch-can prospect.

On defense, it was the same story. By the time the Seahawks started their playoff run, the secondary was so banged up that Ruskell was signing street free agents to cover Terry Glenn and Bernard Berrian. Seattle lost 59 starter-games to injury, the most of any playoff team. This year, the thought seems to be that, with a fairly healthy team in a weak division, the Seahawks can make up the ground they lost last year.

There's some validity to that concept, but there are signs that suggest their window is closing quickly. The offensive line features two outstanding tackles in Jones and Locklear, but the players inside are probably either too old (right guard Chris Gray) or too young (guard Rob Sims and center Chris Spencer) to return to 2005's level of dominance. Matt

Hasselbeck will be 32 in September, and he's not the sort of quarterback who can function at an All-Pro level without a great line (not that many can). Shaun Alexander will be a very old 30 in August. His catches have decreased every season since 2002, and mixing catches and carries is the surest way to extend the life of any back. The wide receiver situation is still unresolved after the Jackson trade, and last September's trade for Deion Branch meant that the Seahawks had no first-round pick in this year's draft with which to address any of their numerous issues. Maryland cornerback Josh Wilson, taken in the second round with the 55th overall pick, is a fast, undersized player (Ruskell likes small cornerbacks) with surprising pop behind his tackles. He'll be on the return teams right away, and in nickel coverages soon after.

For all the concerns, it could still work out for the 2007 Seahawks. The Rams, Cardinals, and 49ers each have reason to be optimistic, but our projections show that only San Francisco is ready to challenge Seattle for the division title. A 9–7 record may be enough for the Seahawks to rule the ghetto of the NFL for one more season. Nevertheless, the ground beneath their feet is shifting. The Seahawks can no longer plan solely for the here and now.

Doug Farrar

Seahawks 2006 Stats by Week

Wk	vs.	W–L	PF	PA	YDF	YDA	TO	DVOA Total	Off	Def	ST
1	DET	W	9	6	264	251	0	-10.0%	-26.7%	-14.7%	2.0%
2	@ARI	W	21	10	341	256	+2	6.5%	-8.4%	-27.5%	-12.7%
3	NYG	W	42	30	333	348	+1	9.5%	13.4%	3.7%	-0.1%
4	@CHI	L	6	37	230	362	+2	-50.8%	-30.7%	21.7%	1.6%
5	BYE										
6	@STL	W	30	28	393	419	+1	13.2%	9.5%	4.8%	8.5%
7	MIN	L	13	31	290	332	-3	-54.7%	-45.2%	3.4%	-6.1%
8	KC	L	28	35	240	499	+1	-52.1%	-21.0%	31.0%	0.0%
9	@OAK	W	16	0	371	185	0	14.7%	22.4%	8.5%	0.8%
10	STL	W	24	22	283	299	-1	29.9%	-4.3%	-14.3%	19.8%
11	@SF	L	14	20	303	416	-4	-67.3%	-36.8%	30.7%	0.2%
12	GB	W	34	24	382	316	0	16.3%	-18.1%	-19.2%	15.3%
13	@DEN	W	23	20	302	270	+4	27.6%	-10.8%	-38.7%	-0.3%
14	@ARI	L	21	27	348	345	-2	-28.9%	-4.7%	21.0%	-3.2%
15	SF	L	14	24	300	390	-2	-57.6%	-28.7%	28.5%	-0.4%
16	SD	L	17	20	314	340	-2	-0.4%	-27.2%	-18.6%	8.2%
17	@TB	W	23	7	344	287	+1	1.8%	15.5%	24.5%	10.8%
18	DAL	W	21	20	332	284	-1	5.1%	-7.3%	-24.1%	-11.7%
19	@CHI	L	24	27	306	371	+1	36.7%	16.9%	-10.7%	9.2%

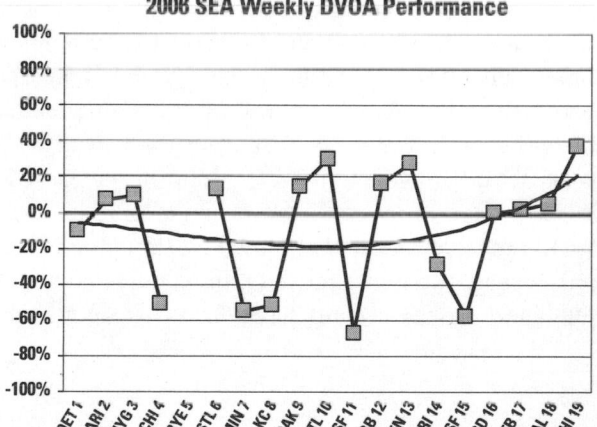

2006 SEA Weekly DVOA Performance

Trends and Splits

	Offense	Rank	Defense	Rank
Total DVOA	-11.7%	27	4.1%	20
Unadjusted VOA	-9.4%	25	2.2%	17
Weighted Trend	-12.5%	28	5.9%	19
Variance	3.9%	28	4.8%	29
Passing	-11.9%	25	6.8%	23
Rushing	-11.5%	26	1.1%	23
First Down	-17.3%	27	5.5%	21
Second Down	-7.0%	24	5.4%	21
Third Down	-7.1%	22	-0.9%	12
Red Zone	3.0%	15	23.3%	31
Late and Close	-29.7%	30	9.2%	23

Five-Year Performance

	2006	2005	2004	2003	2002
W-L	9-7	13-3	9-7	10-6	7-9
Pythagorean Wins	7.8	12.3	7.9	10.0	7.6
Estimated Wins	6.3	11.7	7.6	10.0	6.8
Total DVOA	-13.1%	26.2%	-5.0%	14.4%	-3.9%
Rank	25	5	20	9	21
Offense	-11.7%	23.4%	2.6%	13.3%	6.9%
Rank	27	3	12	5	11
Defense	4.1%	-3.5%	6.3%	-0.9%	11.4%
Rank	20	15	22	16	27
Special Teams	2.6%	-0.6%	-1.3%	0.2%	0.5%
Rank	7	21	20	18	13

Strategic Tendencies

Formations		Rank	Run/Pass		Rank	Defense		Rank	Other		Rank
3+ WR	61%	3	Runs, all plays	46%	12	Sacks by LB	35%	10	Run with 2+ RB	66%	11
4+ WR	16%	7	Runs, first half	42%	25	Sacks by DB	5%	23	Run with 2+ TE	10%	32
2+ TE	8%	32	Runs, first down	54%	17	Rush 6+	6.0%	26	Play action	19%	17
Single back	41%	28	Runs, power sit.	70%	10	Rush 7+	0.6%	28	Go for it on 4th	0.68	28
Empty back	1.6%	18	Runs, behind 2H	38%	7	Rush 3	5.7%	9	Offensive Pace	29.0	7
Max protect	8%	28	Pass, ahead 2H	34%	27	CB1 on WR1	48%	9	Defensive Pace	30.1	9

In the "Everything Old Is New Again" department, Seattle led the NFC with 43 dropped passes. Darrell Jackson and Denver's Javon Walker tied for second in drops by an individual receiver, behind Terrell Owens. . . . Seattle left behind only five blockers more often than any other offense (62 percent of pass plays). The Seahawks also faced 6-plus pass rushers on only 4.5 percent of pass plays, the lowest percentage in the league, so leaving behind only five blockers makes some sense. . . . Seattle lined up without a tight end more often than any other team. . . . Seattle ran the ball out of a four-wide receiver set more often than any other team, doing so on 33 percent of all plays in this formation. (Indianapolis actually had a higher percentage of runs from that formation, but Seattle lined up four-wide nearly ten times as often as the Colts.) . . . Seattle threw to the right side more often than any other team. . . . The Seahawks ran the fewest screen passes in the league and were horrible on the few they tried (–136.4% DVOA). . . . Mack Strong Gets Old, Exhibit A: Seattle had an 8.7% rushing DVOA with one running back on the field, but a –22.2% DVOA with two running backs on the field. Shaun Alexander and Maurice Morris were used in these formations with similar frequency, so the halfbacks are not the issue. . . . Mack Strong Gets Old, Exhibit B: Seattle's offense ranked second behind Oakland in Blown Blocks. Strong had six, the highest of any nonlineman in the NFL last year. Even more shocking is the fact that the great Walter Jones was second in the league with nine Blown Blocks, which is evidence of how much his ankle was bothering him during the season. . . . Seattle's defense ranked third in Adjusted Sack Rate on third or fourth down (10.0%), but ranked 25th on first down (5.8%) and 27th on second down (5.3%). . . . Seattle's defense led the NFL in sacks when rushing only three defenders.

Passing

Player	DPAR	DVOA	Plys	NtYds	Avg	YAC	C%	TD	Int
Matt Hasselbeck	7.3	-8.8%	368	2220	6.0	3.5	57.1%	18	15
Seneca Wallace	-7.6	-25.1%	141	851	6.0	3.5	58.2%	8	7

Rushing

Player	DPAR	DVOA	Plys	Yds	Avg	TD	Fum	Suc
Shaun Alexander	-0.5	-13.3%	252	901	3.6	7	5	43%
Maurice Morris	2.4	-11.5%	161	604	3.8	0	1	40%
Mack Strong	4.8	21.7%	33	149	4.5	1	0	60%
Matt Hasselbeck	4.2	41.8%	14	112	8.0	0	3	—
Seneca Wallace	3.4	44.1%	10	123	12.3	0	5	—
Deion Branch	1.2	20.2%	4	30	7.5	0	0	—
Marquis Weeks	-0.6	-55.4%	3	8	2.7	0	0	60%

Receiving

Player	DPAR	DVOA	Plys	Ctch	Yds	Y/C	YAC	TD	C%
WR									
Darrell Jackson*	17.6	9.1%	112	63	968	15.4	4.0	10	68%
Deion Branch	8.2	-3.0%	101	53	725	13.7	3.4	4	56%
D. J. Hackett	22.7	38.1%	66	45	610	13.6	4.3	4	52%
Nate Burleson	0.2	-14.2%	37	18	192	10.7	1.9	2	67%
Bobby Engram	7.3	15.8%	36	24	290	12.1	2.7	1	49%
TE									
Jerramy Stevens*	-2.1	-20.9%	48	22	231	10.5	2.7	4	46%
Itula Mili*	-3.1	-38.5%	18	10	69	6.9	3.2	0	80%
Will Heller	1.3	32.3%	5	4	32	8.0	2.0	1	56%
Marcus Pollard	*-0.6*	*-17.3%*	*17*	*12*	*100*	*8.3*	*4.7*	*0*	*70%*
RB									
Mack Strong	-9.7	-52.4%	44	29	159	5.5	4.1	0	66%
Maurice Morris	-4.3	-53.0%	20	11	46	4.2	3.9	0	55%
Shaun Alexander	-6.2	-81.8%	16	12	46	3.8	3.7	0	75%

Offensive Line

Year	Yards	ALY	Rank	Power	Rank	10+ Yds	Rank	Stuff	Rank	Sack	ASR	Rank
2004	4.62	4.37	10	61%	17	20%	4	21%	7	34	6.3%	11
2005	4.92	4.49	6	81%	1	25%	2	27%	25	27	5.9%	13
2006	3.70	3.81	30	70%	10	14%	23	26%	28	49	8.7%	26

Year	LE	Rank	LT	Rank	Mid	Rank	RT	Rank	RE	Rank
2004	4.55	10	5.31	1	4.26	17	3.97	16	3.76	18
2005	4.21	16	3.76	24	4.72	2	5.22	2	4.71	7
2006	4.29	14	4.00	25	3.66	31	3.93	25	2.97	29

In 2005, the same five linemen started every important regular season and postseason game for the Seahawks team that went to Super Bowl XL. Eight different line combinations took the field for the Seahawks in their follow-up year, with dismal results. Losing left guard Steve Hutchinson, who poison-pilled his way to Minnesota, was a big blow, but it's hard to know the real effect of his departure given all the injuries suffered by his former teammates. All-World left tackle Walter Jones suffered a sprained ankle in the season opener against Detroit, and it bothered him all season. Floyd Womack, who replaced Hutchinson at left guard, never displayed a fraction of his predecessor's effectiveness and missed several games with various injuries starting in the season's second week. Chris Spencer, the team's first-round draft pick in 2005, played left guard before moving to center because of Robbie Tobeck's hip injury, starting there for the rest of the season. Tom Ashworth was a decent replacement at right tackle when Locklear missed five games with a high ankle sprain. Rob Sims flashed potential in the preseason and started the last three games of the regular season at left guard.

This offseason, the Seahawks tried to offer Chargers guard Kris Dielman the money they didn't want to give Hutchinson the year before, but Dielman returned to San Diego. Tobeck retired, leaving Spencer and little else at center. Jones and Sims will endeavor to reestablish the dominant left side of 2005. Thirty-seven-year-old Chris Gray will try to hold up for one more year at right guard unless he has to replace Spencer. Spencer does not need additional surgery on his troublesome shoulder, but it's not known know how he'll respond to the rigors of a full season. Locklear signed a first-round tender as a restricted free agent and is effective when healthy. Womack is back in a utility role, and third-year tackle Ray Willis might finally factor into the team's plans somewhere on the right side, but the fact that the Seahawks could not restock talent on the line has to be a huge concern.

Defensive Front Seven

Defensive Line	Age	Pos	Plys	TmPct	Rk	Stop	Dfts	StpRt	Rk	AvYd	Rk	Sack	Hit	Hur	Runs	RuStp	RuYd	Pass	PaStp	PaYd
Bryce Fisher	30	DE	46	5.7%	44	36	13	78%	37	1.7	42	4	5	11	35	80%	1.9	11	73%	0.9
Grant Wistrom*	31	DE	39	4.9%	55	30	10	77%	45	1.6	37	4	1	3	30	73%	2.2	9	89%	-0.6
Rocky Bernard	28	DT	37	4.6%	50	35	17	95%	2	0.3	5	3.5	4	8	30	97%	1.3	7	86%	-4.0
Chartric Darby	32	DT	37	4.6%	51	29	16	78%	36	1.1	22	3.5	4	4	31	77%	2.1	6	83%	-4.0
Russell Davis	32	DT	32	4.9%	44	29	4	91%	8	1.0	16	3	0	3	26	92%	2.0	6	83%	-3.5
Darryl Tapp	23	DE	24	3.0%	—	20	8	83%	—	0.6	—	3	7	6	19	79%	2.1	5	100%	-5.2
Craig Terrill	27	DT	15	2.7%	—	12	4	80%	—	2.0	—	3	0	3	9	78%	2.6	6	83%	1.2
Patrick Kerney	*31*	*DE*	*18*	*4.0%*	*—*	*12*	*7*	*67%*	*—*	*2.8*	*—*	*5*	*4*	*12*	*8*	*63%*	*4.3*	*10*	*70%*	*1.6*
Brandon Green	*27*	*DE*	*18*	*2.9%*	*—*	*13*	*5*	*72%*	*—*	*2.1*	*—*	*0.5*	*1*	*5*	*16*	*69%*	*2.9*	*2*	*100%*	*-5.0*

Linebackers	Age	Pos	Plys	TmPct	Rk	Stop	Dfts	StpRt	AvYd	Sack	Hit	Hur	Runs	RuStp	Rk	RuYd	Rk	Tgts	Suc%	Rk	PaYd	Rk
Lofa Tatupu	25	ILB	132	16.4%	16	81	22	61%	4.2	1.5	2	7	84	68%	33	3.2	32	34	65%	9	6.3	49
Julian Peterson	29	OLB	97	12.1%	53	60	27	62%	3.5	10	5	11	52	60%	68	3.8	62	26	60%	17	6.7	69
Leroy Hill	25	OLB	95	12.6%	48	49	10	52%	5.4	2	1	3	62	55%	85	4.5	91	27	51%	47	7.5	82

Year	Yards	ALY	Rank	Power	Rank	10+ Yds	Rank	Stuff	Rank	Sack	ASR	Rank
2004	4.50	4.30	21	69%	25	22%	26	22%	24	36	6.1%	26
2005	3.47	3.55	1	54%	4	14%	10	27%	8	50	7.8%	8
2006	4.73	4.03	10	69%	23	29%	32	27%	7	41	7.1%	14

Year	LE	Rank	LT	Rank	Mid	Rank	RT	Rank	RE	Rank
2004	4.54	21	3.85	5	4.51	27	4.47	25	3.41	7
2005	3.94	15	3.93	11	3.64	4	3.53	4	2.40	2
2006	3.81	13	4.77	21	4.17	13	3.38	6	2.92	2

It is sometimes hard to quantify the value of the individual in a team sport, but there are times when disparity in numbers points out such value in graphic terms. In the 11 regular season games defensive tackle Marcus Tubbs missed in 2006, the Seahawks defense averaged 147 rushing yards allowed and 4.8 yards per carry. In the five games Tubbs played, that average dropped to 82 yards per game and 3.9 yards per carry. Seattle's fast, undersized front seven revolves around a space-eater such as Tubbs who can soak up double teams and allow his teammates to fly through lanes and make plays. Tubbs himself doesn't make the tackles—you'll notice he didn't even make the 15-play minimum that would put his name in the table above—but, without Tubbs in the lineup, there wasn't enough strength to power that speed. Tubbs underwent microfracture surgery on his left knee in the offseason. The Seahawks are optimistic about Tubbs's recovery, but it's usually basketball players, not 320-pound linemen, who return to action after this procedure. The pursuit ability of Rocky Bernard and the toughness of Chuck Darby personify the rest of Seattle's interior rotation. They'll need Tubbs or third-round draft pick Brandon Mebane to solidly man the inside for optimal results. Seattle doesn't blitz a lot, but the defense consistently puts up high sack numbers. Replacing defensive end Grant Wistrom with former Falcons pass-rush specialist Patrick Kerney, and the further development of second-year end Darryl Tapp, should ensure continued success.

Seattle's linebacker corps, the team's most glaring weakness before the 2005 season, is now among the best in the league, though the Seahawks' inability to cover elite tight ends remained unsolved last season. Former 49ers' All-Pro Julian Peterson flourished in his first season with the Seahawks, leading the team in sacks and proving to be reasonably adept in pass coverage. Peterson took over the role that Leroy Hill played in his 2005 rookie season, and Hill struggled more than anyone among the front seven last year as a result. In 2005, Hill was a forward-moving pass-rushing force, picking up 7.5 sacks, but he wasn't built to backpedal and cover, which is what Seattle asked him to do last year. Lofa Tatupu roams the middle of Seattle's defense, and he's its unquestioned leader. An amazingly intuitive player who impressed from his first NFL minicamp, Tatupu has great tackling ability and can cover as well as any middle linebacker—he's especially impressive in deep coverage. However, he's slightly undersized for his position, and Tubbs's injury affected him the most. He's the one who needs those open lanes to do his job.

Defensive Secondary

Secondary	Age	Pos	Plys	TmPct	Rk	Stop	Dfts	RuYd	Rk	RuStp	Rk	Tgts	Tgt%	Rk	Dist	Suc%	Rk	PaYd	Rk	PD	Int
Marcus Trufant	27	CB	79	10.5%	22	29	7	9.8	66	46%	34	78	19%	39	16.3	37%	80	9.2	71	10	1
Kelly Herndon*	31	CB	84	10.5%	24	50	23	4.3	8	59%	13	83	19%	43	11.6	55%	19	8.2	57	12	1
Kelly Jennings	25	CB	42	5.2%	81	12	5	7.0	48	33%	58	57	13%	74	14.3	46%	67	6.7	23	7	1
Ken Hamlin*	26	FS	107	13.3%	8	44	14	8.1	63	45%	35	48	9%	19	13.7	62%	17	6.5	22	9	3
Michael Boulware	26	SS	46	5.7%	71	20	6	5.5	22	41%	43	33	7%	44	16.2	74%	2	10.8	67	5	2
Jordan Babineaux	25	SS	55	7.3%	61	18	6	9.0	72	24%	71	27	6%	58	8.4	53%	35	7.5	35	4	1
Deon Grant	28	FS	70	9.1%	55	21	11	6.3	36	29%	64	37	8%	32	15.6	53%	34	9.0	53	6	2
Brian Russell	29	FS	56	9.1%	53	15	5	10.7	77	27%	68	31	8%	27	12.9	47%	55	7.2	31	4	1

Year	Pass D Rank	DVOA vs. #1 WR	Rank	DVOA vs. #2 WR	Rank	DVOA vs. Other WR	Rank	DVOA vs. TE	Rank	DVOA vs. RB	Rank
2004	17	28.8%	28	5.2%	19	-31.6%	1	-17.8%	7	10.8%	25
2005	25	12.9%	20	6.1%	27	1.7%	20	4.9%	20	-8.5%	10
2006	23	8.8%	24	-7.2%	10	15.5%	25	17.8%	29	-1.4%	16

Seattle's 2007 pass coverage unit will hardly resemble the 2006 version—at least, that's the idea—and it will start with the coaching staff. Former Falcons head coach and 49ers defensive coordinator Jim Mora Jr. has replaced defensive assistant Larry Marmie as the man in charge of the secondary. Mora will return to the city in which he grew up, make the squad assignment-correct, and deflect all the "Will He Replace Holmgren?" questions that will be thrown at him. Mora's new-look secondary will not include Ken Hamlin, the free safety who recovered from serious head injuries in 2005 to post a quality season in his contract year. The Seahawks were looking for more consistency from the position and allowed Hamlin, who is known as a risk-taker, to sign with the Cowboys. The Seahawks benched safety Michael Boulware for several games in the middle of the year after consistent coverage lapses—he proved especially prone to bite on play-fakes—and his job is not at all secure. To bolster the safety ranks, Seattle signed Deon Grant and Brian Russell from the Jaguars and Browns, respectively. Minicamp reports indicate that Mora's acumen and Grant's ability to help put his battery-mates in the right place have made a difference already.

Marcus Trufant and Kelly Jennings are the projected starters at left and right cornerback. Trufant is moving back to the left side, where he's more comfortable, after two seasons on the right designed to protect his right shoulder. Whatever it takes, Trufant needs to rebound from an abysmal season in which his Success Rate dropped from 26th to 80th among cornerbacks. He also has to figure out how to stop Torry Holt, who completely owns Trufant and shows up on the schedule twice a year. Jennings, Seattle's first-round pick in 2006, got burned a bit early on, but proved his talent as the season progressed. Much will be expected from him, and better safety help will mean a lot to Trufant and Jennings. Jordan Babineaux and Kelly Herndon filled different roles last year. Babineaux has been the team's ultimate utility man, filling in at corner and safety when needed. He replaced Boulware during his benching. Herndon was a nickel corner miscast as a sometime starter, and the Seahawks waived him for cap purposes on June 1. Maryland cornerback Josh Wilson, Seattle's top pick in 2007, will make an impact on special teams and could be an early fit in nickel packages.

Special Teams

Year	DVOA	Rank	FG/XP	Rank	Net Punt	Rank	Punt Ret	Rank	Net Kick	Rank	Kick Ret	Rank	Hidden	Rank
2004	5.9%	2	10.1	2	11.1	4	1.9	11	12.1	3	-0.4	15	4.1	8
2005	0.0%	17	-0.2	19	5.5	8	-0.9	17	-1.4	19	-3.1	18	-1.4	18
2006	-1.9%	22	-5.1	26	-6.0	26	-2.7	25	7.9	7	-5.4	25	-15.2	32

All hail Josh Brown, the Vinatieri of the Left Coast. The Seahawks put the franchise tag on their kicker after he won four games in 2006 with last-second field goals. It wasn't just the game-winners that made this season Brown's best. His 64.9 yards-per-kickoff average and 12 touchbacks were career highs. The Seahawks' punting was dramatically improved last year thanks to rookie punter Ryan Plackemeier, the 2005 Ray Guy Award winner from Wake Forest. Nate Burleson, signed as a wide receiver, was relegated to special teams after a series of early dropped passes, and he excelled in his new role. Between Brown's field goals and Burleson's 90-yard game-saving punt return touchdown in the second game against the Rams, it's safe to say that special teams saved Seattle's season. Rookie cornerback Josh Wilson is a highly regarded returner who set his school's record for kick return average. Wilson could take over the return duties if Burleson returns to a full-time receiver role.

Coaching Staff

A year after taking his second NFL team to a Super Bowl, Mike Holmgren turned in what may have been the best coaching performance of his career. He endured enormous personnel churn due to injury and free agency loss and still had his Seahawks within an overtime field goal of their second straight NFC Championship game. Yes, this was accomplished in an abysmal division, but when you lose 59 starter-games to injury, you get a pass in that department. Holmgren will face further challenges in 2007, and a few rumors have him bailing after this season, but the extension he signed in 2006 has him under contract through 2008. Those rumors stem from the decision to lowball Hutchinson and the Darrell Jackson trade, neither of which met with Holmgren's approval. Gil Haskell is the team's offensive coordinator, but it's very obviously Holmgren's show from a play-calling perspective. Quarterbacks coach Jim Zorn, Seattle's first franchise signal-caller from 1976 through 1984, is a highly regarded advisor with a bright coaching future.

In 1997, defensive coordinator John Marshall led the 49ers to the NFL's best defensive DVOA ranking by a wide margin. He was assisted by secondary coach Jim Mora Jr. Marshall and Mora will reprise their roles a decade later for the Seahawks and hope for similar results. The Seahawks run a basic Cover-2/Tampa-2 defense with few obvious wrinkles. It's not schematically dominant like the defenses of Dick LeBeau and Bill Belichick, but it allows for new players to pick up the system quickly. Bruce DeHaven, a 20-year veteran who has served with the Bills, 49ers, and Cowboys, will run special teams. He replaces Bob Casullo, who signed on with the Buccaneers.

Tampa Bay Buccaneers

The most successful era in Tampa Bay Buccaneers history ended unceremoniously last season. From 1996 through 2005, the Bucs were among top-ten defenses in the league in points allowed every year and missed the top ten in yards allowed just once in that span. They were also among the top ten in the NFL in defensive DVOA every year, topping the league twice and finishing second and third in two other seasons. The Bucs as a team had their ups and downs over the last decade, particularly during the last four seasons, but their defense was rock steady. It was an era of defensive dominance so long and thorough that the Bucs' scheme became a brand name, and "Tampa-2" copycats proliferated around the league.

Last season, the Bucs defense finished 22nd in the league in DVOA, 21st in points allowed, and 17th in yards allowed. Call it what you want—the Dungy-Gruden era, the Monte Kiffin era, the Derrick Brooks era—but it's over. Brooks and defensive coordinator Kiffin might still be around, but the magic is gone.

Tampa Bay's 2006 defensive collapse can't be written off as a one-year aberration. A glance at the depth chart shows that many of the team's defensive stars are either gone or nearing the end of their warranties. Brooks made the Pro Bowl as a gold watch alternate at linebacker, but at times last year he flipped from the weak to the strong side of the defensive formation to compensate for his declining speed. Defensive end Simeon Rice, now 33 years old, played in just eight games and recorded two sacks before getting shelved with a shoulder injury. Middle linebacker Shelton Quarles, 36, missed time with numerous injuries last year and suffers from a hip condition that will soon end his career. Big names such as Warren Sapp, John Lynch, Dexter Jackson, and Donnie Abraham moved on

years ago. Cornerback Ronde Barber is still playing at a high level, but he will be 32 when the season starts, and his twin brother is now a TV news correspondent. When last season ended, these graybeards were surrounded by an unexciting collection of homegrown commodities (safety Jermaine Philips, linebacker Ryan Nece) and humdrum journeymen from the Buy Three Get One Free aisle of the free-agent market (cornerbacks Juran Bolden and Will Allen, tackle Chris Hovan). There will be no return to glory for the Tampa defense in 2007.

The funny thing about the Bucs defensive collapse last year was that no one noticed it. Most observers were too busy examining the sinkhole created by the Bucs offense to realize that there was trouble on the other side of the ball. It's true that the Bucs offense was far worse than the defense, but that's not new. The Bucs defense spent the last decade picking up the slack and pulling the team over .500. Gruden's offense provided plenty of slack this season, but the aging defense threw its back out while bending to pick it up.

Entering the season, the Bucs were optimistic about their offense. The unit had finished a subpar 19th in the NFL in DVOA in 2005, but featured promising youngsters such as running back Cadillac Williams and a relatively capable young quarterback in Chris Simms. The offensive line was in its usual state of flux, but Jon Gruden had a mix of veterans and high draft choices to choose from as he performed his annual patch job. The Bucs appeared to have a middle-of-the-pack offense, enough to compete in the NFC South when paired with their typical top-ten defense.

The season started inauspiciously for Simms and the offense, as they managed just 142 yards in a shutout loss to the Ravens. After three interceptions, Gruden benched

---

BUCCANEERS PROSPECTUS

2006 Record: 4–12

DVOA Estimated Wins: 5.1 (30th)

Pythagorean Wins: 3.6 (31st)

DVOA: −23.0% total (31st), −23.0% weighted (30th)

Offense: −18.0% DVOA (30th)

Defense: 5.1% DVOA (22nd)

Special Teams: 0.1% DVOA (17th)

Variance: 8.2% (30th)

2006: Fans weren't chanting "Bruuuce." They were booing.

2007: Derrick Brooks, Ronde Barber, and Shelton Quarles await a visit from the *Cocoon* aliens.

2007 Mean Projection: 9.0 wins

The Brohm Closet (0–4): 4%

Bad Team (5–6): 10%

Mediocre (7–8): 26%

Playoff Contender (9–10): 33%

Super Bowl Contender (11+): 26%

Projected Average Opponent: −2.7% DVOA (25th in NFL)

2007 Buccaneers Schedule

Week	Opp	Week	Opp	Week	Opp
1	at SEA	7	at DET	13	at NO
2	NO	8	JAC	14	at HOU
3	STL	9	ARI	15	ATL
4	at CAR	10	BYE	16	at SF
5	at IND	11	at ATL	17	CAR
6	TEN	12	WAS		

Simms in favor of rookie Bruce Gradkowski. Simms was back in Week 2, but he surrendered three more interceptions in a 14–3 loss to Atlanta. Simms drew the bulk of the criticism, but he was just part of an overall offensive collapse: Williams gained just 59 yards and averaged 2.6 yards per rush in the first two games, and the offensive line was so bad that Gruden was already dipping into the bench after the Ravens loss.

The offense showed some signs of life in Week 3, but just as Simms started to find his rhythm against a good Panthers defense, he suffered a vicious hit that led to an emergency splenectomy. Gradkowski, a fleet-footed sixth-round pick who leapfrogged Tim Rattay on the depth chart during training camp, took over the reins of the offense, and fooled opponents for a few weeks, but soon exhausted the portion of the playbook that he could execute. The offense bumbled through Weeks 8 to 14, scoring more than 14 points only once, never netting more than 200 passing yards, and turning the ball over 16 times. When Rattay replaced Gradkowski at the end of the year, the offense bounced back a bit, but by that time the team was jockeying for draft position.

Given these circumstances, it was easy to overlook the Bucs' problems on defense. After all, the defense played well in a 14–13 win over the Bengals in Week 6 and a 17–3 loss to the Giants in Week 8. Against the Eagles in Week 7, the defense provided its own offense, with Barber scoring two touchdowns on returns to help the team to a 23–21 win. Unfortunately, the Bucs defense couldn't sustain that level of performance. In Week 9 against the Saints, they allowed 314 passing yards and forced no sacks or turnovers. In Week 12 against the Cowboys, they allowed 435 total yards and five passing touchdowns. Other subpar outings included Week 10 against the Panthers (16.7% DVOA for the game) and Week 15 against the Bears (34.6%). Those DVOAs show that the Bucs defense wasn't allowing points and yardage because it was always on the field and battling poor field position because of the failures of the offense. They were giving up those points and yards because they weren't very good, and, befitting an older unit, lost steam as the year went on.

The clearest signal that the Bucs defense was ready for the bulldozer came in October, when the Bucs raised a white flag and traded defensive tackle Anthony "Booger" McFarland to the Colts for a second-round draft pick. McFarland, the Bucs first-round pick in 1999, was one of the team's few youngish stars, a sub–Pro Bowl performer who was the closest thing the team had to an heir apparent to Brooks and company on defense. When McFarland left, the Bucs faced a depressing *Children of Men* scenario on defense: Brooks and his peers played out the string not knowing if another generation would arrive to carry their mantle.

To their credit, Jon Gruden and general manager Bruce Allen recognized that their team's greatest needs this offseason were on defense and made major additions through the draft and free agency in an effort to overhaul the unit. The moves weren't enough to rebuild the elite Bucs defense of 1996 to 2005, but they will keep the Bucs near the middle of the pack. With a soft schedule and more competent quarterbacking in 2007, the Bucs may be surprise contenders for the NFC South crown.

Linebacker Cato June was the first big-name defensive reinforcement to arrive in Tampa when he was signed away from the Colts to facilitate Brooks's full-time move to the strong side. June finished sixth in the NFL with 141 total tackles, but tackle totals are a poor statistic to use when evaluating defenders. Indeed, many of June's tackles were made downfield while playing for a terrible run defense. Despite that statistical inflation, June is an excellent pass defender who played in a nearly identical system in Indy, and by allowing Brooks to move to a position where speed is less essential, his arrival upgrades two positions.

Gruden and Allen added more new faces on the defensive line. End Gaines Adams, the best defender in the draft, fell into the team's lap with the fourth overall pick. Adams, a natural pass rusher on the right side of the line, will be a situational player this year, then replace Rice in 2008. Free agent Kevin Carter, who will turn 34 at the start of the season, can still be productive as a wave defender and may play tackle on passing downs. Tackle Ryan Sims, a former first-round bust acquired in a trade with the Chiefs, and free-agent defensive end/linebacker Patrick Chukwarah, a favorite of new line coach Larry Coyer during their days together in Denver, give Kiffin plenty of warm bodies to build around on the front four.

On offense, the Bucs made two major moves, signing Jeff Garcia to compete with Chris Simms at quarterback and Luke Petitgout to provide experience at left tackle. Gruden's rebuilding project on offense was a study in hedged bets. His efforts to land Garcia and Jake Plummer (who retired instead of reporting to the Bucs, thus voiding their trade with Denver) sent a clear no-guarantees message to Simms, clouding the team's quarterback situation.

If Garcia wins the starting job (a distinct possibility) and Simms languishes on the bench for a year, the Bucs will be at a quarterback crossroads in 2008. Garcia will be 38. Simms will probably be out of the picture. Where does Gradkowski fit in? As for Petitgout, he will fill the left tackle slot and prevent a meltdown on the line, but he's just one placeholder on an offense loaded with veteran placeholders including fullback Mike Alstott, wide receiver Ike Hilliard, tight end Anthony Becht, center John Wade, running back Michael Pittman, and Garcia.

By the time the dust settled on their offseason, the Bucs had spent a lot of money and effort to climb out of their 4–12 hole, but they only managed to climb to the .500 level. They may win nine or ten games because the youngsters of the NFC West still can't tie their shoes correctly, but that's a gift from the NFL schedule-makers, not a sign that the Bucs have turned the corner.

Rather, Tampa Bay will face yet another daunting rebuilding project next offseason, a Sisyphean pattern that can ultimately be traced back to the head coach. Gruden lacks the patience to rebuild. He's always looking for the next Brad Johnson–Rich Gannon shortcut at quarterback (hence Garcia), and his rosters are glutted with Hilliard-types because young receivers usually struggle to master his complex strain of the West Coast Offense. In the years since the Bucs won the Super Bowl, Kiffin has kept the team competitive by wringing everything he could out of his cadre of defensive superstars, but, despite the additions of Adams and June, Kiffin is running low on elite players. The Bucs need a change of philosophy to become perennial contenders again. That may mean that the next rebuilding project will have to include a change of head coaches.

Mike Tanier

Gunner Gruden

Tampa Bay head coach Jon Gruden announced in March that he was adding shotgun formations to his offensive playbook. Gruden, a West Coast Offense hardliner, resisted using the shotgun for years because it didn't fit the quick-drop, quick-release principles carried down from Mount Sinai by Bill Walsh in the early 1980s. Fellow West Coast acolytes such as Mike Shanahan and Andy Reid lapsed into heresy long ago, but Gruden held firm. After witnessing last season's offensive collapse, however, Gruden decided it was time to make some changes. It's about time.

The Buccaneers are the only team that didn't throw a single pass from the shotgun last year (table 1). The Texans, coached by Gary Kubiak (another old-school West Coast disciple), used the formation for just one Hail Mary play. The Bears, like the Bucs, are adding more shotgun forma-

tions to their scheme this season. The Seahawks, coached by West Coast stalwart Mike Holmgren, only used the formation regularly when freewheeling backup quarterback Seneca Wallace was playing. The Raiders, of course, didn't actually have an offense last year. Most other teams lined up in the shotgun in long-yardage or two-minute situations. The most prolific shotgun teams, such as the Patriots, Dolphins, and Colts, deployed the formation on 2nd-and-5, 3rd-and-short, or even as a wrinkle on 1st-and-10.

A look at shotgun data from 2006 reveals a remarkable trend: Of the 27 teams that threw more than 10 percent of their passes from the shotgun, 22 had a higher DVOA on passes from the shotgun than on passes from under center (table 1). Factor in running plays from both formations, and the league DVOA on shotgun plays was 15.2% in 2006. The DVOA on under-center plays was −3.1%. Shotgun plays gained an average of 6.4 yards, while under-center plays gained an average of just 5.0 yards.

This wide split between the two formations made us skeptical; we worried that DVOA might be measuring some component of offense inaccurately. Perhaps, because shotgun formations are most common on 3rd-and-long, DVOA was granting teams too much credit for succeeding in long-yardage situations. Perhaps the system was being too generous on passes thrown against prevent defenses in the fourth quarter, passes which are often thrown from the shotgun. Peyton Manning and Michael Vick were among the most prolific shotgun quarterbacks in the league; perhaps Manning's passing and Vick's running were warping the data.

Table 1. Use of Shotgun, 2006

Team	Pct of Passes from Shotgun	Pass DVOA		Team	Pct of Passes from Shotgun	Pass DVOA	
		Shotgun	Under Center			Shotgun	Under Center
TB	0.0%	0.0%	−22.7%	WAS	30.2%	25.1%	5.7%
HOU	0.2%	−137.2%	−4.8%	NYJ	32.0%	34.9%	−4.9%
CHI	1.1%	−141.5%	−12.2%	SD	33.1%	32.0%	26.8%
SEA	4.8%	−146.1%	−8.6%	BUF	33.4%	−9.2%	−0.4%
OAK	8.1%	−32.6%	−38.8%	BAL	34.0%	34.9%	2.2%
KC	12.6%	−4.2%	20.5%	TEN	39.7%	11.7%	−28.0%
SF	13.2%	−9.9%	−12.7%	ARI	41.1%	19.8%	−5.4%
CIN	14.5%	11.4%	30.3%	STL	42.5%	38.6%	19.4%
CAR	18.0%	14.3%	−11.9%	JAC	44.6%	−10.7%	2.0%
DET	20.1%	14.1%	2.3%	ATL	49.9%	−1.7%	−23.7%
DEN	22.4%	−34.9%	17.0%	NYG	50.5%	5.1%	−7.5%
DAL	24.6%	16.7%	2.4%	GB	51.5%	12.2%	−6.6%
NO	26.9%	64.9%	10.3%	PIT	53.6%	15.8%	9.7%
PHI	28.3%	17.0%	26.0%	NE	55.8%	26.3%	9.6%
MIN	28.6%	6.1%	−20.3%	IND	56.0%	73.4%	41.2%
CLE	28.9%	−10.4%	−29.0%	MIA	64.7%	7.3%	−30.4%

Table 2. Shotgun DVOA Splits, 2006

Down	Overall		First Half Only		Passing Only		RB Runs Only	
	Shotgun	Under Center	Shotgun	Under Center	Shotgun	Under Center	Shotgun	Under Center
1st Down	8.4%	−3.1%	12.9%	−9.0%	7.7%	3.2%	14.7%	2.1%
2nd Down	11.0%	−1.7%	23.9%	−4.2%	10.1%	1.2%	25.3%	−3.2%
3rd Down	21.6%	−6.2%	14.5%	−2.7%	17.4%	−16.9%	−9.6%	1.4%

In an effort to isolate any biases in the system, we ran the shotgun and under-center data by down, then checked the first-half data (to eliminate garbage-time production). We then analyzed rushing and passing plays separately, eliminating scrambles from the rushing data to remove any Vick effect. The results (table 2) are hard to argue with: any way you slice it, the shotgun emerges as the better formation.

The further we dug into the data, the more shocking the disparity became between the two formations. On 3rd-and-long (7 yards or more), the DVOA for all shotgun plays was 34.4%; on plays under center, it was −21.5%. Remember that DVOA is situation dependent, so a six-yard gain on 3rd-and-7 isn't a positive play. The only way to earn a high DVOA on 3rd-and-long is to generate a lot of first downs. In these long-yardage situations, the difference between shotgun and traditional formations is the difference between success and failure. The shotgun only proved ineffective on third-down running plays, excluding scrambles. On third-down runs, however, selection bias skews the data in favor of under-center formations: Most third-down runs from the shotgun are draw plays in long-yardage situations, safe plays that have a low likelihood of converting for a new set of downs.

The disparity between the two formations isn't driven by Manning, or any other individual quarterback. Most quarterbacks who attempt a high number of passes from both formations are far more effective from the shotgun (table 3). We expect players such as Manning and Vince Young (who played in a shotgun offense in college) to have wide splits, but Brad Johnson and Chad Pennington? The

shotgun seems to favor everyone: hard-throwing youngsters, savvy field generals, scramblers, pocket passers, and creaky old veterans alike. The only two players in 2006 who were significantly better under center rather than in shotgun were Byron Leftwich and Carson Palmer, and Leftwich was far better in shotgun than under center in both 2004 and 2005. Palmer and David Garrard are the only two quarterbacks who were better under center in each of the past two seasons.

So why are shotgun plays so much more effective? The shotgun is designed to protect the quarterback, an effect which is most noticeable on third down, when defenses sack the quarterback on 10 percent of plays when the quarterback is under center, but just 7.8 percent of plays from the shotgun. Still, those lower sack totals only account for a small part of the disparity between the formations. There are many other possible factors at work: Hurry-up offensive schemes (usually executed from the shotgun), easier pre-snap reads for the quarterback from his backfield position, and the element of surprise when the quarterback lines up deep on 2nd-and-4. Whatever the causes, the formation disparity isn't a one-year phenomenon. The splits between shotgun and under-center formations were present, though not as pronounced, in 2005, and roughly similar to last year's splits in 2004.

Are we suggesting that under-center formations should be scrapped? Should NFL teams hire Urban Meyer clones as offensive coordinators? That may be taking things too far. If teams started executing 75 percent of their

Table 3. Shotgun DVOA by Quarterback, 2006

Player	Shotgun	Under Center	Diff	Player	Shotgun	Under Center	Diff	Player	Shotgun	Under Center	Diff
Byron Leftwich	−23.3%	1.2%	−24.5%	Jon Kitna	14.1%	2.3%	11.8%	Peyton Manning	73.3%	42.3%	31.0%
Carson Palmer	7.0%	30.5%	−23.5%	Tom Brady	26.0%	12.4%	13.6%	Matt Leinart	22.1%	−12.0%	34.1%
J. P. Losman	−9.2%	0.0%	−9.2%	Eli Manning	6.6%	−7.5%	14.1%	Brad Johnson	20.0%	−20.6%	40.6%
David Garrard	−7.0%	0.2%	−7.2%	Marc Bulger	40.6%	19.7%	20.9%	Joey Harrington	7.1%	−35.2%	42.3%
Donovan McNabb	19.8%	26.8%	−7.0%	Brett Favre	16.0%	−6.6%	22.6%	Drew Brees	65.9%	16.2%	49.7%
Philip Rivers	33.9%	26.2%	7.7%	Tony Romo	39.5%	15.1%	24.4%	Chad Pennington	46.0%	−4.2%	50.2%
Charlie Frye	−15.5%	−25.1%	9.6%	Mark Brunell	31.8%	6.4%	25.4%	Vince Young	21.9%	−30.5%	52.4%
Jeff Garcia	28.5%	18.1%	10.4%	Steve McNair	29.7%	3.3%	26.4%	Daunte Culpepper	11.7%	−54.8%	66.5%
Ben Roethlisberger	12.2%	0.9%	11.3%	Michael Vick	3.0%	−27.1%	30.1%				

NOTE: Minimum 75 pass attempts in shotgun formation.

plays from the shotgun, defenses would find a way to adapt. Still, the data indicates that Gruden is taking a step in the right direction, a step that many of his peers took a few seasons ago when they became more daring in their deployment of shotgun formations. As per table 3, Jeff Garcia, who may be the Bucs' starting quarterback this season, was more effective from the shotgun than from under center last year. If your quarterback likes the shotgun, and final-four teams such as the Colts and Saints are thriving thanks in part to the shotgun, then it's time to add the shotgun to the playbook. Jon Gruden may be a hardliner, but he's no fool.

Mike Tanier

Buccaneers 2006 Stats by Week

Wk	vs.	W–L	PF	PA	YDF	YDA	TO	Total	Off	Def	ST
								DVOA			
1	BAL	L	0	27	142	271	-3	-34.9%	-48.4%	-12.8%	0.7%
2	@ATL	L	3	14	351	382	-1	-42.2%	-24.1%	5.4%	-12.7%
3	CAR	L	24	26	209	350	+1	-5.7%	-5.0%	8.7%	7.9%
4	BYE										
5	@NO	L	21	24	406	314	-1	2.4%	11.7%	-2.3%	-11.5%
6	CIN	W	14	13	310	314	-1	4.0%	-8.5%	-24.7%	-12.2%
7	PHI	W	23	21	196	506	+4	0.9%	-12.6%	-0.4%	13.0%
8	@NYG	L	3	17	174	251	-1	-51.8%	-60.0%	-14.7%	-6.6%
9	NO	L	14	31	226	363	-1	-62.9%	-35.6%	24.2%	-3.1%
10	@CAR	L	10	24	222	318	2	36.0%	20.2%	16.7%	1.0%
11	WAS	W	20	17	359	252	-1	1.7%	-8.8%	-5.8%	4.6%
12	@DAL	L	10	38	211	435	-2	-58.5%	-4.8%	56.3%	2.6%
13	@PIT	L	3	20	254	267	-3	-37.9%	-49.3%	-13.5%	-2.1%
14	ATL	L	6	17	272	280	-1	-10.1%	-22.9%	-6.2%	6.6%
15	@CHI	L	31	34	357	446	-1	-8.8%	6.3%	34.6%	19.5%
16	@CLE	W	22	7	355	187	+2	46.8%	-4.8%	-50.2%	1.3%
17	SEA	W	22	7	287	344	-1	-35.9%	-0.2%	28.3%	-7.4%

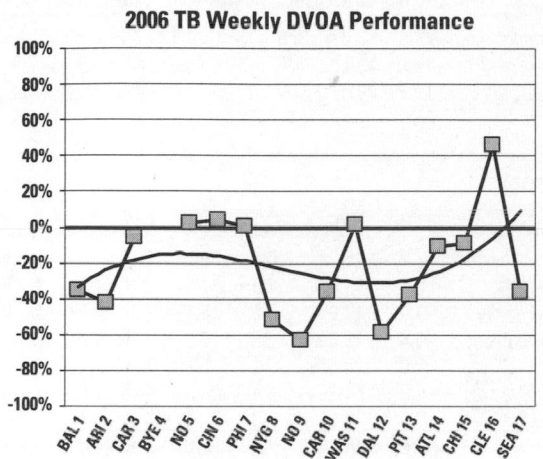

2006 TB Weekly DVOA Performance

Trends and Splits

	Offense	Rank	Defense	Rank
Total DVOA	-18.0%	30	5.1%	22
Unadjusted VOA	-21.0%	30	8.8%	26
Weighted Trend	-17.0%	29	7.5%	22
Variance	4.3%	26	6.1%	18
Passing	-23.9%	31	17.8%	28
Rushing	-10.8%	25	-7.3%	9
First Down	-22.3%	29	13.0%	31
Second Down	-14.6%	28	1.3%	16
Third Down	-15.7%	27	-3.8%	11
Red Zone	-30.2%	30	20.1%	30
Late and Close	-1.6%	16	16.7%	30

Five-Year Performance

	2006	2005	2004	2003	2002
W-L	4-12	11-5	5-11	7-9	12-4
Pythagorean Wins	3.6	8.9	7.9	9.2	12.7
Estimated Wins	5.1	8.1	7.9	9.4	12.0
Total DVOA	-23.0%	1.3%	-2.3%	11.2%	34.0%
Rank	31	16	16	11	1
Offense	-18.0%	-6.9%	-5.6%	-4.6%	-2.5%
Rank	30	19	21	17	21
Defense	5.1%	-8.7%	-7.0%	-21.3%	-33.6%
Rank	22	9	8	3	1
Special Teams	0.1%	-0.6%	-3.6%	-5.4%	2.9%
Rank	17	19	28	32	8

Strategic Tendencies

Formations		Rank	Run/Pass		Rank	Defense		Rank	Other		Rank
3+ WR	45%	21	Runs, all plays	41%	27	Sacks by LB	16%	23	Run with 2+ RB	71%	6
4+ WR	7%	22	Runs, first half	45%	16	Sacks by DB	8%	15	Run with 2+ TE	50%	2
2+ TE	35%	4	Runs, first down	52%	21	Rush 6+	10.6%	10	Play action	12%	27
Single back	52%	18	Runs, power sit.	64%	15	Rush 7+	1.9%	12	Go for it on 4th	1.10	9
Empty back	1.6%	21	Runs, behind 2H	29%	24	Rush 3	2.7%	24	Offensive Pace	31.3	21
Max protect	13%	12	Pass, ahead 2H	33%	29	CB1 on WR1	3%	30	Defensive Pace	30.0	7

(continued next page)

Strategic Tendencies *(continued)*

Tampa Bay ran the most power sets featuring two running backs and two tight ends.... Only 55 percent of Gradkowski's third- and fourth-down completions converted for a new set of downs, the lowest percentage in the league.... Tampa Bay's offense led the league in passes tipped at the line.... Joey Galloway was underthrown 13 times, second in the NFL behind Miami's Chris Chambers. No other receiver was underthrown more than eight times.... Tampa Bay's defense ranked second against screen passes (−53.2% DVOA) and sixth against draw plays (−26.6% DVOA), but it was the league's worst defense against the play-action fake (52.0% DVOA).... Jon Gruden was one of the league's most aggressive coaches on fourth down after being one of the most conservative (.59 AI) in 2005.

Passing

Player	DPAR	DVOA	Plys	NtYds	Avg	YAC	C%	TD	Int
Bruce Gradkowski	-29.0	-32.9%	326	1518	4.7	4.6	54.3%	9	2
Chris Simms	-13.0	-40.1%	105	553	5.3	4.2	55.2%	1	7
Tim Rattay*	19.3	29.0%	102	728	7.1	4.5	60.8%	4	9
Jeff Garcia	*27.3*	*19.4%*	*188*	*1273*	*6.8*	*4.1*	*61.7%*	*10*	*2*

Rushing

Player	DPAR	DVOA	Plys	Yds	Avg	TD	Fum	Suc
Cadillac Williams	-2.4	-16.2%	225	799	3.6	1	2	40%
Mike Alstott	0.1	-14.8%	60	171	2.9	3	1	68%
Michael Pittman	4.2	7.0%	49	242	4.9	1	1	49%
Bruce Gradkowski	-0.4	-18.8%	35	167	4.8	0	9	—
Earnest Graham	2.0	28.8%	11	59	5.4	0	0	39%
Michael Clayton	-0.9	-51.1%	5	41	8.2	0	1	—
Chris Simms	0.4	0.9%	3	8	2.7	1	0	—
Jeff Garcia	*0.8*	*-8.8%*	*15*	*87*	*5.8*	*0*	*6*	*—*
B. J. Askew	-1.2	-54.7%	6	11	1.8	0	0	57%

Receiving

Player	DPAR	DVOA	Plys	Ctch	Yds	Y/C	YAC	TD	C%
WR									
Joey Galloway	5.8	-9.3%	141	62	1057	17.0	4.3	7	44%
Michael Clayton	-3.8	-23.9%	65	33	360	10.9	5.4	1	62%
Ike Hilliard	-0.4	-16.9%	55	34	339	10.0	4.1	2	51%
Maurice Stovall	1.7	5.7%	13	7	102	14.6	4.0	0	71%
Paris Warren	1.8	25.8%	7	5	63	12.6	3.0	0	54%
TE									
Alex Smith	-3.6	-22.7%	53	35	250	7.1	3.4	3	69%
Anthony Becht	-3.2	-31.2%	26	18	115	6.4	2.8	1	66%
Jerramy Stevens	*-2.1*	*-20.9%*	*48*	*22*	*231*	*10.5*	*2.7*	*4*	*46%*
RB									
Michael Pittman	5.8	6.8%	77	48	408	8.5	6.3	0	62%
Cadillac Williams	-1.0	-12.8%	44	30	196	6.5	6.9	0	68%
Mike Alstott	-7.4	-46.6%	38	21	85	4.0	5.0	0	55%
B. J. Askew	*-0.2*	*-11.4%*	*12*	*9*	*50*	*5.6*	*5.3*	*0*	*75%*

Offensive Line

Year	Yards	ALY	Rank	Power	Rank	10+ Yds	Rank	Stuff	Rank	Sack	ASR	Rank
2004	4.03	4.04	23	56%	24	18%	14	24%	14	44	8.6%	26
2005	4.21	4.00	19	75%	5	22%	6	29%	30	41	8.2%	26
2006	3.68	3.88	28	64%	15	14%	21	26%	29	33	5.8%	10

Year	LE	Rank	LT	Rank	Mid	Rank	RT	Rank	RE	Rank
2004	3.79	23	3.78	28	4.04	22	3.97	17	4.38	9
2005	4.46	9	4.61	8	3.97	20	3.48	27	2.73	31
2006	2.97	28	4.06	22	4.02	25	4.14	18	4.11	15

The Bucs haven't fielded a quality offensive line since they lost left tackle Roman Oben after the 2003 season, but this year's line is brimming with young talent. The team spent their top two draft picks on linemen in 2006. Second-round pick Jeremy Trueblood became the starting right tackle in Week 4, and first-rounder Davin Joseph (who originally won a starting job before getting hurt in camp) took over at right guard a week later. Both players took their lumps, particularly Trueblood, who allowed five sacks and committed six false starts, but by season's end, both were showing progress. Joseph, who played left tackle at Oklahoma, has Pro Bowl potential.

Left tackle Luke Petitgout is best known as the Giants lineman who was flagged for five false starts against the Seahawks in 2005. Petitgout had a total of ten false starts that season, but jumped only three times in 2006. He's not an elite left tackle, but he's steady. He'll replace Anthony Davis, who was named Best Supporting Actor for his role as a minor obstacle in Julius Peppers's highlight video.

Rookie Arron Sears played every offensive line position but center at Tennessee. He projects as the Bucs' starter at left guard. Dan Buenning will move from guard to center to compete with John Wade, a starter since 2003 who has never been more than adequate.

Defensive Front Seven

Defensive Line	Age	Pos	Plys	TmPct	Rk	Stop	Dfts	StpRt	Rk	AvYd	Rk	Sack	Hit	Hur	Runs	RuStp	RuYd	Pass	PaStp	PaYd
Greg Spires	33	DE	54	6.5%	32	42	11	78%	41	1.4	35	5	5	9	45	73%	2.4	9	100%	-3.9
Chris Hovan	29	DT	52	6.3%	18	46	14	88%	9	1.2	23	2	6	7	50	88%	1.6	2	100%	-10.0
Dewayne White*	28	DE	50	6.0%	40	43	22	86%	9	1.0	24	5	12	14	34	82%	2.2	16	94%	-1.4
Ellis Wyms	28	DT	30	4.4%	54	20	9	67%	65	2.7	59	5	2	1	20	60%	4.1	10	80%	-0.1
Simeon Rice	33	DE	20	4.8%	—	14	8	70%	—	2.0	—	2	5	13	14	79%	1.3	6	50%	3.5
Jovan Haye	25	DT	17	3.6%	—	11	1	65%	—	2.9	—	0	2	2	16	63%	2.9	1	100%	2.0
Kevin Carter	*34*	*DE*	*47*	*5.8%*	*43*	*45*	*15*	*96%*	*1*	*0.6*	*11*	*5.5*	*4*	*5*	*37*	*95%*	*1.4*	*10*	*100%*	*-2.2*

Linebackers	Age	Pos	Plys	TmPct	Rk	Stop	Dfts	StpRt	AvYd	Sack	Hit	Hur	Runs	RuStp	Rk	RuYd	Rk	Tgts	Suc%	Rk	PaYd	Rk
Derrick Brooks	34	OLB	125	15.1%	22	79	19	63%	5.0	0	0	1	87	70%	28	3.9	70	47	49%	51	6.4	58
Shelton Quarles*	36	ILB	106	17.0%	13	63	21	59%	3.8	2.5	3	2	80	65%	48	3.2	37	22	35%	89	7.6	84
Ryan Nece	28	OLB	65	8.4%	85	38	8	58%	3.4	1.5	3	5	44	66%	44	2.4	7	16	56%	31	6.3	50
Barrett Ruud	24	ILB	47	5.7%	—	24	2	51%	6.4	0	0	0	35	63%	—	3.5	—	8	38%	—	6.8	—
Cato June	*28*	*OLB*	*147*	*17.9%*	*6*	*79*	*33*	*54%*	*5.2*	*1*	*2*	*0*	*92*	*60%*	*67*	*4.6*	*92*	*38*	*47%*	*61*	*7.6*	*85*
Patrick Chukwurah	*28*	*OLB*	*17*	*2.3%*	*—*	*12*	*7*	*71%*	*2.5*	*4.5*	*2*	*4*	*8*	*75%*	*—*	*4.3*	*—*	*1*	*0%*	*—*	*8.0*	*—*

Year	Yards	ALY	Rank	Power	Rank	10+ Yds	Rank	Stuff	Rank	Sack	ASR	Rank
2004	4.02	4.19	15	59%	11	17%	20	21%	26	45	9.2%	1
2005	3.29	3.62	2	59%	9	10%	2	27%	9	36	7.0%	18
2006	3.92	4.21	14	74%	28	15%	14	24%	15	25	5.4%	29

Year	LE	Rank	LT	Rank	Mid	Rank	RT	Rank	RE	Rank
2004	4.22	14	3.99	7	4.09	11	4.72	29	4.35	23
2005	2.70	2	4.47	24	3.46	2	3.73	8	4.77	26
2006	3.63	11	3.44	6	4.47	19	5.02	30	3.87	13

Rookie defensive end Gaines Adams grew up a Buccaneers fan and idolized Simeon Rice. Now he will battle his former hero for the starting job on the right side of the line. Rice missed the second half of last season with a shoulder injury and is in the last year of his contract. Whoever loses the starting job will still get ample playing time as a designated pass rusher. Adams is eager to challenge the two-time Pro Bowl defender. "May the best man play," he said at a post-draft press conference. Greg Spires will platoon with Kevin Carter at left end. Spires is an effective run defender who doesn't rush the passer well. Carter, who turns 34 in September, must be kept fresh but can still get to the quarterback. Chris Hovan and Ellis Wyms are quick penetrators in the middle of the defensive line, but neither player is a standout pass rusher. Coordinator Monte Kiffin may move Carter inside on passing downs and use ex-Broncos free agent Patrick Chukwurah as a pass-rushing end.

Ryan Sims, the sixth overall pick in the 2002 draft, was a major disappointment in Kansas City. He battled ankle, foot, and other injuries and often appeared out of shape. The Bucs hope he can compete for a role as a run-plugging nose tackle. Kiffin has had success with reclamation projects in the past: Hovan appeared to be a lost cause in Minnesota two seasons ago, but was rejuvenated in Tampa.

Shelton Quarles started at middle linebacker for eight years in one of the best defenses in the NFL, but was always overshadowed by brighter stars such Rice and Derrick Brooks. In late April, the Bucs released Quarles, who reportedly suffered several concussions in 2005 and missed four games last season with a knee injury. "He personified the Tampa-2," Ronde Barber said after the release. "When teams were studying our defense, what they were doing was studying Shelton Quarles." Barrett Ruud, Nebraska's all-time leading tackler, played well in relief of Quarles last season and is the favorite to start in the middle.

Defensive Secondary

Secondary	Age	Pos	Plys	TmPct	Rk	Stop	Dfts	RuYd	Rk	RuStp	Rk	Tgts	Tgt%	Rk	Dist	Suc%	Rk	PaYd	Rk	PD	Int
Ronde Barber	32	CB	115	13.9%	2	49	22	5.3	26	49%	30	95	21%	19	11.3	46%	65	7.9	52	16	3
Juran Bolden*	33	CB	76	9.2%	39	37	14	5.3	25	44%	38	93	21%	20	11.9	54%	32	7.4	38	10	1
Jermaine Phillips	28	SS	112	13.5%	6	55	15	4.5	7	61%	4	48	10%	11	13.3	44%	61	9.2	57	8	2
Phillip Buchanon	27	CB	33	4.5%	—	11	4	9.0	—	29%	—	38	8%	—	12.2	47%	—	8.2	—	6	2
Will Allen	29	FS	75	9.0%	56	20	7	8.2	65	41%	44	27	5%	69	14.5	30%	72	12.4	74	3	0
Torrie Cox	27	CB	24	2.9%	—	13	4	4.1	—	71%	—	26	6%	—	16.2	45%	—	9.0	—	2	0
Kalvin Pearson	27	FS	28	3.4%	—	14	4	2.9	—	67%	—	4	1%	—	-0.3	25%	—	6.0	—	0	0

(continued next page)

Defensive Secondary *(continued)*

Year	Pass D Rank	DVOA vs. #1 WR	Rank	DVOA vs. #2 WR	Rank	DVOA vs. Other WR	Rank	DVOA vs. TE	Rank	DVOA vs. RB	Rank
2004	7	-25.7%	3	9.8%	25	3.0%	19	13.6%	22	-18.3%	6
2005	14	-9.3%	5	-4.6%	16	19.2%	30	-6.1%	13	-1.4%	15
2006	28	3.7%	20	7.9%	18	-37.4%	3	9.4%	26	21.5%	27

Cornerback Ronde Barber and safety Jermaine Phillips are the sure things in the secondary. Barber still plays the run extremely well and excels at breaking up short passes. Phillips is similar to former Bucs All-Pro John Lynch. He is a big-hitting run defender who can make receivers hear footsteps, though Phillips lacks Lynch's instincts in deep zone coverage.

Juran Bolden, last year's starter opposite Barber, was released after the draft. Former starting cornerback Brian Kelly missed all but two games last season with turf toe, then held out of offseason workouts in search of a contract extension. If he returns, he's a lock to regain his starting job. Philip Buchanon, who played surprisingly well in nickel duties last season, signed a one-year contract in March. Buchanon, an exceptional athlete, washed out of Oakland and Houston because he made too many mental mistakes and freelanced too often. He's a poor man's Terrell Buckley, who was a poor man's Deion Sanders.

Free safety Will Allen had an awful season in 2006, but rookie Sabby Piscitelli is more of a strong safety or nickel line-backer than the kind of deep defender the Bucs need in the Tampa-2 system. Instead, Allen will be pushed by Kalvin Pearson, a journeyman who spent three seasons on the Browns practice squad, and Alan Zemaitis, a big cornerback from Penn State who spent last season on the inactive list.

Special Teams

Year	DVOA	Rank	FG/XP	Rank	Net Punt	Rank	Punt Ret	Rank	Net Kick	Rank	Kick Ret	Rank	Hidden	Rank
2004	-3.9%	30	-5.0	26	5.1	11	-14.1	32	-1.6	17	-7.1	27	-4.3	21
2005	2.0%	7	-3.2	23	2.6	13	2.7	9	7.1	5	2.5	13	4.1	11
2006	2.4%	9	-1.4	20	4.2	12	12.4	1	-1.9	24	1.1	12	9.4	5

Entering Week 7 against the Eagles, Matt Bryant had never kicked a field goal longer than 50 yards in his five-year career. In the first six weeks of the season, he missed two 43-yard attempts and a 45-yarder, and his longest successful kick traveled just 28 yards. Needless to say, his 62-yard game-winning field goal against the Eagles came as a bit of a surprise. The shocking kick saved Bryant's job for a season, but the Buccaneers signed rookie free agent Garrett Rivas to challenge Bryant in camp. Rivas, a four-year starter at Michigan, is a marksman who lacks ideal leg strength.

The Buccaneers haven't gotten much from their return game in the last 31 years; they are still waiting for the first kick-off return touchdown in franchise history. Michael Pittman will handle kicks for another season; ball security is his specialty. Buchanon was once one of the most dangerous punt returners in the NFL, but he did little with 18 attempts in relief of Ike Hilliard last season. Justin Gatlin, an Olympic sprinter who last played football as a Tennessee freshman in 2003, earned a post-draft tryout with the team. If he sticks, it will be as a return man.

Coaching Staff

Jon Gruden's version of the West Coast Offense evolved over the past two seasons to meet the needs of his personnel. Gruden uses more two-tight end sets than most traditionalists, and the Bucs use a lot of max protect schemes to compensate for the poor quality of their offensive line. Gruden has always been more run-oriented than West Coast adherents such as Andy Reid, but, when his offense is firing on all cylinders, the running game is balanced with a short passing game that uses multiple formations to flood zones and get the ball to receivers in space. If the offensive line jells this season, Gruden will be able to use more three- and four-receiver spreads, allowing him to open up the offense.

Defensive coordinator Monte Kiffin is now 67 years old and the father of an NFL head coach. Despite his age and the proliferation of Tampa-2 copycats throughout the league, Kiffin still has some tricks up his sleeve. The Bucs started blitzing and using more man coverage last year to compensate for their personnel shortcomings. New defensive line coach/assistant head coach Larry Coyer was the Broncos defensive coordinator for four years, knows Kiffin's system, and also isn't afraid to add some blitzes to the mix. Coyer's defense in Denver finished fifth in DVOA in 2004 and sixth in 2005 before dropping to 12th last season.

Washington Redskins

How much distance separated the Washington Redskins from the Indianapolis Colts in 2006?

The question seems ridiculous, doesn't it? The Redskins went 5–11 and were effectively out of the playoff race before late October. After the season ended, a three-part series in *The Washington Post* detailed a season of infighting in the front office and on the field from a franchise that clearly had too many cooks stirring the pot. The Colts, on the other hand, won the Super Bowl.

The gap between these teams seems like a chasm, but look closer at the two rosters as they stood at the beginning of the 2006 season. The difference between the 2006 Redskins and the 2006 Colts came down to Peyton Manning, Marvin Harrison, and luck.

In last year's book, we called Washington "a Super Bowl contender, as long as they can keep their starters on the field," and noted that it would only take a few injuries to turn this team into a loser. That's exactly what happened—not a few injuries, but an astonishing cascade of injuries, affecting nearly every unit on the field. The Redskins aren't the only NFL team with depth problems. As detailed in the Indianapolis chapter, the Colts don't have much depth either, but they certainly have more than the Redskins and, for the most part, their stars have never been hurt. The ones that were hurt in 2006 got healthy in time for the playoffs. The rest is history.

Allow us for a moment to use that classic analytical staple, the position-by-position comparison. Manning and Harrison would destroy their Washington counterparts, but let's set them aside for the moment and analyze the rest of the original projected 2006 lineups for each team.

When Santana Moss and Reggie Wayne were teammates at Miami, scouts generally thought Moss was the better player, and they've both been spectacular professionals.

Dallas Clark and Chris Cooley are both excellent receiving tight ends. Ben Utecht and Mike Sellers are a wash, as are a healthy Brandon Stokley and Antwaan Randle El.

There's no reason to believe that Joseph Addai and Dominic Rhodes provide a better running game than a healthy Clinton Portis and Ladell Betts. In fact, even with Portis fighting injuries, the two Washington backs earned 35.7 DPAR rushing last year; Addai and Rhodes combined for 36.7 DPAR. On the offensive line, the Colts were better at center (Jeff Saturday) and right guard (Jake Scott), the Redskins were better at left guard (Derrick Dockery) and right tackle (Jon Jansen), and it's reasonable to consider left tackles Tarik Glenn and Chris Samuels equal.

The Colts had better defensive ends, the Redskins better defensive tackles—remember, we're talking here about a *healthy* Cornelius Griffin and Joe Salave'a. Middle linebacker Lemar Marshall is better than, or at least equal to, Gary Brackett. Most scouts would take Cato June over Warrick Holdman, but Marcus Washington is easily better than Rob Morris or Gilbert Gardner.

Shawn Springs had the best numbers of any NFL cornerback in the first year of the Football Outsiders game charting project; although Carlos Rogers was inexperienced, a healthy Springs and Rogers are a better duo than Nick Harper and Jason David. At the start of the year, you would have taken Adam Archuleta over Antoine Bethea, although it certainly didn't turn out that way. Bob Sanders is amazing, but Sean Taylor isn't exactly chopped liver. And while the Colts have a better kicker and punter, the Redskins have far superior return teams.

Unfortunately, that Washington starting lineup never saw the field. The injuries started in the preseason and never ended. Combine that with bickering between coaches and

---

REDSKINS PROSPECTUS

2006 Record: 5–11

DVOA Estimated Wins: 6.8 (23rd)

Pythagorean Wins: 6.1 (24th)

DVOA: −11.6% total (23rd), −16.5% weighted (27th)

Offense: 4.2% DVOA (13th)

Defense: 17.6% DVOA (32nd)

Special Teams: 1.7% DVOA (11th)

Variance: 9.6% (27th)

2006: This is what happens when a team with no depth gets hit by a rash of injuries.

2007: Here comes the rebound . . . as long as they can keep their starters on the field.

2007 Mean Projection: 8.2 wins

The Brohm Closet (0–4): 5%

Bad Team (5–6): 16%

Mediocre (7–8): 32%

Playoff Contender (9–10): 32%

Super Bowl Contender (11+): 15%

Projected Average Opponent: 0.9% DVOA (13th in NFL)

2007 Redskins Schedule

Week	Opp	Week	Opp	Week	Opp
1	MIA	7	ARI	13	BUF
2	at PHI (Mon.)	8	at NE	14	CHI (Thu.)
3	NYG	9	at NYJ	15	at NYG
4	BYE	10	PHI	16	at MIN
5	DET	11	at DAL	17	DAL
6	at GB	12	at TB		

players, coaches and coaches, and between the team and the media, and the Redskins crumbled.

Despite the attention paid to Clinton Portis's various injuries, the offense actually escaped relatively unscathed, and played much better than it seems at first glance. Washington's offense ranked 13th in DVOA, but only 20th in points scored for reasons out of their control. Since the defense couldn't get turnovers, the offense ranked 24th in average starting field position. Many drives that should have scored three points instead scored zero thanks to Nick Novak's prolonged midseason slump.

The really big injuries came on defense, and many of them were suffered by a single player, Shawn Springs. Springs missed the first five games recovering from abdominal surgery, struggled all year with hamstring problems, then broke his scapula in Week 16. Even when he wasn't 100 percent, the defense was better with him (13.0% DVOA) than without him (22.1% DVOA).

Springs's absence shifted every one else into a role they didn't fit. Carlos Rogers wasn't ready to be the number-one cornerback. Kenny Wright went from a below-average nickel back to a horrible starter. Mike Rumph went from not playing to playing, always a bad move. Adam Archuleta, whose strength is stopping the run, spent most of his time providing deep pass coverage. Soon he was benched for Vernon Fox, a special teams lifer with only five career starts and none since 2003.

When Griffin and Salave'a fought nagging injuries and Andre Carter didn't live up to his contract, the pass rush suffered as well, finishing last in Adjusted Sack Rate. Put it all together, and you have a pass defense that was not just bad, but monumentally, historically bad.

In 11 years of DVOA stats, going back to 1996, no defense ever was worse than 60% DVOA against third-down passes. Washington was over 70% (table 1). Washington wasn't the worst third-down defense overall, since they were reasonable against the run, but "second-worst third-down defense of the decade" is not something Gregg Williams wants to put on his business cards.

This is where the silver lining comes in. Extreme third-down performance is a very strong indicator for a rebound

the following season, and it doesn't get much more extreme than the 2006 Washington third-down pass defense.

The other nine teams in table 1 improved their overall defensive DVOA by an average of –8.8% the following season. If we expand the list to look at the 25 worst third-down pass defenses from 1996 to 2005, the average improvement is –9.3% DVOA. Every single one of those 25 teams improved in overall defense the following season, except for the 1997–98 Bengals.

The Redskins have three powerful trends working in their favor. First, there is natural regression towards the mean. Any team this bad at one particular skill will probably move closer to league average the following year. Second, there is what Bill James dubbed the "Plexiglas Principle": Teams that significantly improve or decline in one season have a tendency to relapse or bounce back in the next. The Redskins didn't go from average to awful; they went from great to awful. The 2005 Redskins ranked third in the league in defensive DVOA on third down. The year before, the Redskins were number one in the NFL.

The third-down principle is less about third-down defense on its own, however, and more about third downs compared to overall defense. This is the third trend that points towards improvement. The Redskins still had a below-average defense on first and second down, but it was far better than their third-down defense. That puts Washington on another list, the teams with the largest gap between third-down and overall defensive DVOA (table 2). You may recognize this table from the 2005 San Diego chapter; with a couple of exceptions—primarily from 1997, when this trend inexplicably disappeared for one season—it's a who's who of turnaround defenses. (The 2003 Chargers would be 14th.)

Before we have Washington fans calling for playoff tickets, we should point out that the Redskins have the worst overall defense on that list. They may not be bouncing back to the same place they were two years ago, especially if their offseason free-agent moves backfire once again.

Table 1. Worst Defensive DVOA on Third Down, 1996–2006

Year	Team	vs Pass	All Plays
2006	WAS	72.0%	48.8%
2002	DET	59.2%	45.2%
2000	MIN	56.0%	49.0%
1996	BAL	55.6%	32.7%
2001	ATL	50.9%	43.3%
2003	DET	49.3%	31.3%
2002	SF	48.0%	41.8%
1996	JAC	47.8%	27.6%
2001	MIN	46.3%	31.8%
2000	CIN	44.1%	35.2%

Table 2. Top 10 Defenses Worse on Third Down, 1996–2006

Year	Team	Def All	Def 3rd	Dif	PA	PA Y + 1	Dif
1996	KC	−4.6%	38.2%	42.8%	300	232	−68
2002	SF	2.5%	41.8%	39.3%	351	337	−14
2001	ATL	7.6%	43.3%	35.7%	377	314	−63
2002	PIT	−6.0%	28.3%	34.3%	345	327	−18
2004	CAR	−3.8%	30.0%	33.9%	339	259	−80
1997	JAC	1.7%	35.4%	33.7%	318	338	20
2006	WAS	17.6%	48.8%	31.3%	376	—	—
2000	CLE	11.0%	42.0%	31.0%	419	319	−100
1996	STL	−4.6%	26.4%	31.0%	409	359	−50
2002	NE	0.3%	30.1%	29.8%	346	238	−108

This year's big catch was former Buffalo middle linebacker London Fletcher-Baker. Fletcher-Baker had a great year with the Bills, leading the league with 40 Defeats (our stat combining turnovers, plays that lose yardage, and third-down stops). But Fletcher-Baker is a slightly undersized, read-and-react player, and Williams generally looks for linebackers who attack more. There's always the chance that Williams will adjust his scheme to fit Fletcher-Baker, but he certainly hasn't adjusted his schemes to fit any of Washington's big-name free agents in the past. Just ask Adam Archuleta.

Except for linebacker Lemar Marshall going to the bench to make room for Fletcher-Baker, the defense is no better prepared for injuries than it was a year ago, and many of the injuries from 2006 give players an increased chance of getting hurt in 2007. Broken shoulder bones heal easily, but Springs has now been dealing with groin and hamstring problems for two years. The Redskins simply can't afford to lose him for large stretches of time. Behind Springs and Rogers are two free-agent signings, Cardinals refugee David Macklin and prodigal son/yachtsman Fred Smoot. It is unlikely that a return to Washington will help Smoot recapture past glories after two bad years in Minnesota, and Macklin was target number one for Arizona opponents. First-round pick LaRon Landry should be an improvement on Archuleta and Fox, but unless the Redskins are planning to play a predominantly Cover-2 scheme, the cornerbacks are still going to play a more important role than the safeties.

On offense, there are both good and bad indicators. Dockery was the best player on the offensive line last year, and a significant loss to free agency. The Redskins didn't draft a single offensive lineman, and, as we go to press, Dockery's prospective replacement is five-year veteran Mike Pucillo, who played for three teams in the last three years. At receiver, Antwaan Randle El is still better suited for the slot, Brandon Lloyd is still despised by his coaches and teammates, and there's little depth behind Randle El, Lloyd, and Santana Moss.

On the other hand, Clinton Portis's broken hand will be fully healed, and quarterback Jason Campbell can only get better. "Matt Leinart will be much better with a year of experience" is going to be a common statement by people who pick the Arizona Cardinals to surprise, and there's no reason why that same logic can't apply to Jason Campbell—especially given the complexity of the Al Saunders playbook.

There's a good chance that Washington bounces back to 8–8 or even better. That doesn't look like "a Super Bowl contender if they avoid injuries." Then again, the bar is set a little lower in the NFC. If everything goes right, this team has the talent to play deep into January. Even if they run into a couple of problems, the third-down rebound effect alone puts them in competition for a wild card. If the injuries start piling up, however, it's 2006 all over again.

Aaron Schatz

What Makes a Hall of Fame Wide Receiver?

The record book for NFL wide receivers has undergone a radical transformation in recent years. Before 1990, there was only one 100-reception season in NFL history and two more in the short existence of the AFL. Since 1990, the 100-reception mark has been reached 47 times. These changes have created a seemingly impossible task for Hall of Fame selectors.

Consider the case of Fred Biletnikoff. The Oakland great retired from football in 1978. At that time, he ranked sixth in all-time receiving yards. When he was elected to the Hall of Fame in 1988, he had fallen to 12th. Today, he ranks 39th, behind Andre Rison, Muhsin Muhammad, and Tony Martin, among others.

The case of Art Monk receives even more press intention because Monk retired with the most catches in NFL history. He has already fallen to sixth and is in danger of getting passed by Isaac Bruce, Terrell Owens, and Torry Holt over the next several seasons. Monk has already fallen out of the top ten in all-time receiving yards despite retiring in third place.

The selectors can no longer simply compare a candidate's career stats to those of the current Hall of Famers because of how radically the context for those statistics has changed. They did not respond immediately to the new reality, inducting Steve Largent and Charlie Joiner in 1995 and 1996, respectively, based on their career numbers. When they retired, Largent and Joiner ranked first and second in career receiving yards. Today, they rank 8th and 13th respectively. After Largent and Joiner's election, the rules of the game changed. No longer were great all-time numbers enough; wide receiver candidates had to have something special.

Since Joiner's enshrinement, four wide receivers have entered the Hall of Fame off the regular ballot: Lynn Swann, Jon Stallworth, James Lofton, and Michael Irvin. (A fifth receiver, Tommy McDonald, was elected as a senior candidate.) Swann, Stallworth, and Irvin all won at least three Super Bowls, and the selectors tend to become mesmerized by those shiny Super Bowl rings. Lofton's career statistics were so outstanding—he currently ranks third in receiving yards—that he somehow avoided the fate of many of his peers (and even he had to wait ten years for enshrinement).

Those peers have formed a web of confusion that the selectors seem unable to untangle. Between 1983 and 2000, Andre Reed, Irvin Fryar, Art Monk, Gary Clark, Stanley Morgan, Harold Jackson, Andre Rison, Drew Hill, Anthony Miller, and Harold Carmichael all retired with more receiving yards than Biletnikoff. All but Hill played in at least three Pro Bowls, the same number as Joiner, Stallworth, and Swann.

This group of receivers is running short on time for enshrinement because their incredible achievements will soon be overshadowed by even more dominant numbers. Cris Carter is eligible for the Hall of Fame this year, Jerry Rice and Tim Brown in 2010. Active players such as Marvin Harrison, Isaac Bruce, Terrell Owens, Randy Moss, and Torry Holt will all retire with better numbers than Monk and his contemporaries, while Rod Smith, Keenan McCardell, Keyshawn Johnson, Eric Moulds, Joey Galloway, and Muhsin Muhammad will retire with numbers similar to Monk's.

Clearly, traditional numbers are insufficient to determine who belongs in the Hall of Fame. The selectors' recent strategy of looking only at intangibles, namely Super Bowls, is equally flawed. We would love to have DPAR numbers dating back to the NFL's inception to shed light on this issue, but we only have 1996 to 2006, which is of little value for the players already eligible. Instead, we are mostly limited to the same information that the selectors have: catches, yards, and touchdowns. The selection process should not merely be about numbers, but developing a better system to deal with seemingly equivalent numbers will help towards ending this logjam. Here are five suggestions to the selectors as they consider wide receivers going forward.

All Numbers Are Not Created Equal

The selectors intuitively understand that the NFL was a different game in the 1970s than it is today, but they seem unable to quantify the size of the difference. For perspective, in 1972, the average team completed 5.3 passes per game to all of its wide receivers for a total of 86 yards per game.

Today, Marvin Harrison averages 6.0 catches and 79.7 yards per game all by himself. Such an enormous discrepancy makes it hard to compare Harold Carmichael to Harrison, and it should be no surprise that Harrison's career stats far outstrip Carmichael's.

To solve this problem, we have simply adjusted each player's career stats to the offensive environment of 2006. The research originally began with the AFL-NFL merger in 1970, but we extended the study back to 1968 in order to include the full careers of two stars from the seventies (Harold Jackson and Charlie Joiner). Each season was adjusted individually. When we add them together, we get an all-time leaderboard that takes into account the offensive environment each player played in (table 3).

It is a credit to the Hall of Fame selectors that the top three eligible players in adjusted yards have all been enshrined. Art Monk's career statistics appear to regain their luster. Marvin Harrison is still outstanding, but the favorable wide receiver environment of today has clearly inflated his regular stats. The biggest beneficiaries are players from the early part of the 1970s. Jackson and Carmichael, who are nowhere near the top 20 in actual catches and yards, are now fighting to make the top ten.

Separate Players with High Peaks

One of the big knocks on Art Monk's candidacy is that he caught 60 12-yard hitches a year for over a decade but never dominated the game. To sort out receivers with particularly low peak value, we have put together a list of players based on their totals in their best six seasons. Yes, six is somewhat arbitrary, but wide receivers do not have the attrition issues of running backs, and most great receivers have at least six great years. Since we have no one measurement for receiver value, we'll use adjusted yards as the measure of a receiver's "best" seasons (table 4). This adjustment seems to confirm the traditional assessment of Monk. He ranks fifth in receptions, but is 23rd in peak-season yards.

Owens, Moss, and Harrison have put up amazing raw touchdown numbers, so amazing that these numbers survive the translation to rank just below Jerry Rice. Touchdowns are very important, but the presence of Carl Pickens and Joey Galloway should give some pause about just *how* important. That peak-season touchdown list is the only one of the six in either table 3 or table 4 on which Lynn Swann makes an appearance.

These peak score translations boost the candidacies of Sterling Sharpe, Lynn Swann, and Michael Irvin, but they help Cliff Branch the most. His career total of 501 catches is somewhat pedestrian, but he was outstanding between 1974 and 1980, with six of those seven seasons represented in this study.

Table 3. Adjusted All-Time WR Leaders

Player	Rec	Player	Yds	Player	TD
Jerry Rice	1,633	Jerry Rice	22,978	Jerry Rice	195
Steve Largent	1,182	Charlie Joiner	15,984	Cris Carter	126
Charlie Joiner	1,156	James Lofton	15,972	Marvin Harrison	119
Art Monk	1,145	Steve Largent	15,952	Steve Largent	115
Cris Carter	1,107	Harold Jackson	14,936	Terrell Owens	111
Tim Brown	1,091	Tim Brown	14,538	Harold Carmichael	100
Andre Reed	1,037	Henry Ellard	14,056	Tim Brown	98
James Lofton	1,011	Art Monk	13,669	Randy Moss	98
Harold Jackson	1,007	Cris Carter	13,544	Harold Jackson	95
Harold Carmichael	1,000	Andre Reed	13,344	Nat Moore	89
Marvin Harrison	999	Marvin Harrison	13,255	Andre Reed	87
Henry Ellard	908	Irvin Fryar	12,868	Mark Clayton	87
Irvin Fryar	907	Isaac Bruce	12,857	Cliff Branch	86
Isaac Bruce	864	Stanley Morgan	12,691	Andre Rison	85
Keenan McCardell	844	Harold Carmichael	12,679	Irvin Fryar	83
Jimmy Smith	841	Cliff Branch	11,928	James Lofton	82
Rod Smith	833	Jimmy Smith	11,812	Stanley Morgan	80
Cliff Branch	820	Michael Irvin	11,696	Wes Walker	80
Drew Pearson	816	Terrell Owens	11,371	Charlie Joiner	78
John Stallworth	800	Gary Clark	11,285	Isaac Bruce	76

Table 4. Peak-Adjusted WR Performance

Player	Rec	Player	Yds	Player	TD
Marvin Harrison	638	Jerry Rice	9,365	Jerry Rice	86
Jerry Rice	635	Cliff Branch	8,751	Terrell Owens	77
Steve Largent	630	Steve Largent	8,737	Randy Moss	75
Cris Carter	596	Marvin Harrison	8,678	Marvin Harrison	73
Art Monk	594	Torry Holt	8,500	Cliff Branch	70
Cliff Branch	592	James Lofton	8,492	Mark Clayton	70
Harold Carmichael	592	Harold Jackson	8,223	Harold Carmichael	65
Charlie Joiner	574	Michael Irvin	8,138	Andre Rison	65
Sterling Sharpe	566	Randy Moss	8,083	Sterling Sharpe	65
Drew Pearson	559	Harold Carmichael	7,898	Cris Carter	61
John Stallworth	557	Drew Pearson	7,894	Steve Largent	57
Torry Holt	555	Charlie Joiner	7,826	Isaac Curtis	57
Jimmy Smith	551	John Stallworth	7,794	Lynn Swann	55
James Lofton	535	Isaac Bruce	7,755	Harold Jackson	55
Tim Brown	532	Jimmy Smith	7,634	John Stallworth	54
Rod Smith	528	Stanley Morgan	7,511	Nat Moore	51
Michael Irvin	527	Henry Ellard	7,494	Carl Pickens	51
Harold Jackson	522	Terrell Owens	7,472	Joey Galloway	50
Terrell Owens	522	Tim Brown	7,437	Wes Walker	50
Andre Rison	515	Rod Smith	7,360	Rod Smith	50

Great Receivers Do Not Have to Play with Great Quarterbacks

Even after calculating these translated stats, the decision about who to let in and who to exclude is difficult. Irvin Fryar and Henry Ellard have the same number of adjusted catches. Fryar has more touchdowns, but Ellard has more yards. Deciding which of the two is better is a normative judgment that has to be made by the selectors. One thing they should consider is the relative quality of each receiver's quarterbacks.

The Hall of Fame has welcomed in 18 modern wide receivers to date. Of those 18, fully 12 have spent some substantial part of their career with a Hall of Fame quarterback. The only two certain inductees not currently enshrined are Jerry Rice and Marvin Harrison. Rice played with two Hall of Fame quarterbacks, and Harrison's quarterback has a pretty good chance of being enshrined someday himself.

This consistent selection of receivers who teamed with Hall of Fame quarterbacks is absurd. Intuitively, among two players who have amassed similar statistics, the one who played without the benefit of a Hall of Fame quarterback was probably the more impressive player. Harold Jackson, for instance, had his only brush with a Hall of Fame quarterback when he caught some passes from Joe Namath on the Rams. The quarterbacks in his best seasons were Norm Snead, John Reaves, and Steve Grogan.

Tim Brown is an equally good example. Brown's raw career numbers certainly merit enshrinement, but these adjustments move him from sure thing to solid contender. Still, his peak score is pretty mediocre, hinting at a long career of continued excellence but little dominance. In Brown's 16 years on the Raiders, however, six different quarterbacks led the team in passing. Brown led his team in receiving yards every year between 1992 and 1999 despite receiving passes from Jay Schroeder, Jeff Hostetler, Jeff George, Donald Hollas, and Rich Gannon. Meanwhile, Jerry Rice was catching passes from Joe Montana, Steve Young, and Jeff Garcia.

More Wide Receivers Is Not a Bad Thing

It is sometimes written that the explosion of wide receiver numbers makes receivers interchangeable, and, therefore, fewer receivers from recent years should be enshrined. In fact, the opposite is true. The increase in wide receiver numbers means that they have a larger impact on games. The Hall of Fame consistently recognizes quarterbacks and running backs in high quantities in part because of the amount of times they touch the ball. The modern NFL is a passing league, so more receivers should be recognized, not fewer.

The amazing transformation of the wide receiver position was hinted at above, but it warrants a bit of elabora-tion. Before the liberalization of the passing rules in 1978, the average team completed fewer than six passes per game to its wide receivers. The rule change made life easier for wide receivers, but that also meant that wide receivers played a more important role in deciding who won or lost. The total passes to receivers increased to over nine catches per game through the late 1980s and early 1990s and has been above ten every year since 1993 (table 5).

Table 5. Average Receptions by Wide Receivers, per Game per Team

Years	Rec/Game
1970–1977	5.61
1978–1987	7.47
1988–1993	9.67
1994–2006	10.69

The NFL has currently inducted 25 halfbacks and 23 quarterbacks from the modern era into the Hall of Fame, but only 18 wide receivers. Only two Hall of Fame receivers started their careers after the liberalization of passing rules, just as wide receivers were becoming so important. Nobody is suggesting a massive increase in wide receivers—we'll happily vote for the massive increase in offensive linemen to come first—but we should not be too concerned about a modest increase that reflects the larger role of wide receivers over the past 30 years.

Super Bowls Should Be a Tie-Breaker, Not a Basis for Candidacy Itself

The recent inductions of Stallworth, Swann, and Irvin reconfirm the selectors' long-held belief that Super Bowl rings somehow make the player. Sadly, this is a trend that has accelerated in recent years as selectors have become unable to distinguish between receivers with such similar statistics. Wide receivers are growing more and more important to team success, but a wide receiver will never win a Super Bowl by himself. For all of Jerry Rice's greatness, his teams won only one Super Bowl over his last 15 seasons.

The selection of Lynn Swann is hopefully the low point in Hall of Fame election history. Nobody wants to say intangibles do not count, but it is probably a good idea to count tangibles along with them. When it comes to quantifiable performance on the field, Swann belongs nowhere near Canton. Swann scores poorly in adjusted career totals and adjusted peak. He played with a Hall of Fame quarterback and across from another Hall of Fame receiver. His election was based on a couple of highlight reel catches, amazing Super Bowl performances, and a heaping dose of sentimentality. Deion Branch cannot supply the highlight reel catches, but he matches Swann's production in the Super Bowl and his production in the regular season. Nobody would argue that Branch, if he retired today, would belong anywhere near Canton.

Conclusion: Art Monk, Re-re-re-revisited

After all these fancy numbers and shots taken at the excellent Hall of Fame selectors, you're probably hoping for a surefire list of who deserves to be enshrined. Sorry to disappoint. The NFL selection process is about more than just numbers, and the process is generally effective. Intangible attributes such as impact on opposing coaches' schemes, blocking ability, and team leadership are important parts of the evaluation of Hall of Fame candidates. Still, while we will not give a straight in or out list, we will leave you with general thoughts on the possibilities.

Last year, the preliminary list of candidates included ten players who still remain unelected: Cliff Branch, Harold Carmichael, Gary Clark, Mark Clayton, Isaac Curtis, Mark Duper, Henry Ellard, Art Monk, Drew Pearson, and Andre Reed. The most notable absentee is Harold Jackson, who actually becomes eligible for the senior list next year and would be a worthy candidate no matter how he is enshrined. Of the players who played the majority of their career in the 1970s, Jackson, Carmichael, and Branch would all be solid selections.

The 1900s present the Art Monk problem. He has developed into a lightning rod for Hall of Fame discussion. No shame would fall upon Canton if Monk were selected, but he is impossible to distinguish from Ellard. Surprisingly, Andre Reed does not come out too well in our rankings and is far from a certain selection. Irving Fryar seems to be just below these three. Of the three, Ellard may be the most impressive because of both his consistent status as the best player on his offense and his big play ability. Still, these three are hard to separate, and no ranking is right or wrong.

Obviously Rice will be enshrined, and Cris Carter and Tim Brown should join him as well. As for active and recently retired players, Harrison will be enshrined, but the jury is likely out on touchdown machines Owens and Moss. (Certainly, consideration of intangibles has to include consideration of a player's attitude and effect on teammates *off* the field.) Isaac Bruce, Jimmy Smith, and Rod Smith should have inner-circle memberships to the Hall of Very Good, with Bruce (along with his younger teammate, Torry Holt) as the best candidate to make the actual Hall.

The Hall of Fame selectors need not follow all our advice, but it would be nice if they started considering some of these elements as soon as this year's election. Cris Carter's presence on the ballot may force Monk, Ellard, and Reed further into the background, and it would be highly unusual for the selectors to enshrine two wide receivers in one year. Tim Brown and Jerry Rice come two years later, pushing Monk et al further down (and conceivably off) the list of finalists.

That fate is not just for some of these players, and we can only hope that selectors develop an understanding of great performance within the context of a given era, or qualified individuals will have to come through the back door as senior selections like the eminently worthy Harold Jackson.

Ned Macey

Redskins 2006 Stats by Week

Wk	vs.	W–L	PF	PA	YDF	YDA	TO	DVOA Total	Off	Def	ST
1	MIN	L	16	19	266	309	0	-12.8%	4.3%	9.0%	-8.1%
2	@DAL	L	10	27	245	367	0	-36.9%	-36.6%	13.1%	12.8%
3	@HOU	W	31	15	495	261	+1	35.3%	46.3%	11.2%	0.2%
4	JAC	W	36	30	481	307	0	57.1%	43.3%	-4.0%	9.8%
5	@NYG	L	3	19	164	411	0	-47.5%	-16.1%	24.0%	-7.4%
6	TEN	L	22	25	305	344	-2	-30.6%	-3.6%	22.8%	-4.3%
7	@IND	L	22	36	325	452	0	-27.0%	-3.9%	31.6%	8.5%
8	BYE										
9	DAL	W	22	19	300	378	-1	-7.2%	15.9%	25.8%	2.7%
10	@PHI	L	3	27	278	400	-1	-49.5%	-25.9%	15.8%	-7.9%
11	@TB	L	17	20	252	359	+1	-26.4%	-11.7%	16.3%	1.6%
12	CAR	W	17	13	253	264	+1	-15.8%	-15.3%	-10.9%	-11.4%
13	ATL	L	14	24	381	369	-2	-39.1%	-8.5%	29.0%	-1.6%
14	PHI	L	19	21	415	263	-1	-18.5%	-0.8%	31.5%	13.8%
15	@NO	W	16	10	354	270	+1	45.0%	14.7%	-24.6%	5.7%
16	@STL	L	31	37	336	579	0	-23.1%	9.1%	39.7%	7.5%
17	NYG	L	28	34	393	355	-2	-11.1%	31.6%	50.2%	7.5%

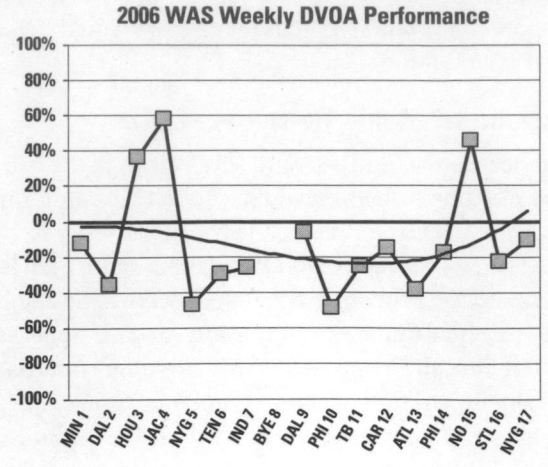

2006 WAS Weekly DVOA Performance

Trends and Splits

	Offense	Rank	Defense	Rank
Total DVOA	4.2%	13	17.6%	32
Unadjusted VOA	5.7%	11	22.2%	32
Weighted Trend	0.9%	16	19.4%	32
Variance	5.1%	24	3.6%	31
Passing	8.9%	13	36.2%	32
Rushing	0.1%	12	-0.1%	20
First Down	9.6%	8	9.4%	26
Second Down	1.4%	18	7.0%	24
Third Down	-2.0%	17	48.8%	32
Red Zone	-25.8%	27	2.8%	15
Late and Close	-6.7%	22	19.2%	31

Five-Year Performance

	2006	2005	2004	2003	2002
W-L	5-11	10-6	6-10	5-11	7-9
Pythagorean Wins	6.1	9.9	7.1	5.6	6.4
Estimated Wins	6.8	10.4	6.8	5.6	7.7
Total DVOA	-11.6%	20.9%	-5.8%	-15.6%	-7.7%
Rank	23	7	21	25	23
Offense	4.2%	5.1%	-17.0%	-7.2%	-7.1%
Rank	13	12	28	19	26
Defense	17.6%	-14.4%	-15.0%	10.3%	-6.1%
Rank	32	4	4	27	8
Special Teams	1.7%	1.4%	-3.9%	1.9%	-6.7%
Rank	11	10	31	9	31

Strategic Tendencies

Formations		Rank	Run/Pass		Rank	Defense		Rank	Other		Rank
3+ WR	47%	18	Runs, all plays	50%	3	Sacks by LB	26%	12	Run with 2+ RB	50%	24
4+ WR	12%	13	Runs, first half	53%	1	Sacks by DB	5%	21	Run with 2+ TE	34%	19
2+ TE	30%	8	Runs, first down	59%	7	Rush 6+	12.9%	4	Play action	24%	5
Single back	56%	13	Runs, power sit.	55%	29	Rush 7+	3.0%	6	Go for it on 4th	0.75	23
Empty back	1.6%	20	Runs, behind 2H	40%	6	Rush 3	3.8%	18	Offensive Pace	31.7	22
Max protect	9%	23	Pass, ahead 2H	39%	21	CB1 on WR1	48%	10	Defensive Pace	30.2	10

Washington was the most unpredictable team in 2006 when it came to the run vs. the pass. In each formation, Washington had a more even split between runs and passes than any other offense.... Washington ran the most screen plays as a percent of total passes, with an above-average 22.7% DVOA.... The 2006 Redskins ran when behind in the second half more than twice as often as they did in 2005, when they were ranked 31st at 18 percent.... Washington's defense was tied for the fewest sacks categorized as Blown Blocks last year.... The Redskins forced a turnover once every 17.2 drives, which was the first time in our seven years of drive stats that a defense had ever forced a turnover less often than once every 13 drives. . . . Although the Redskins were last in defensive DVOA last year, they still managed to force a three-and-out punt on 26 percent of drives, which ranked 11th in the NFL. Apparently, that first series was their only shot at stopping anybody.

Passing

Player	DPAR	DVOA	Plys	NtYds	Avg	YAC	C%	TD	Int
Mark Brunell	29.6	13.0%	259	1691	6.5	6.1	62.5%	8	4
Jason Campbell	14.8	3.6%	206	1242	6.0	5.0	53.4%	10	6

Rushing

Player	DPAR	DVOA	Plys	Yds	Avg	TD	Fum	Suc
Ladell Betts	22.7	7.1%	245	1157	4.7	4	4	46%
Clinton Portis	13.0	7.8%	127	523	4.1	7	0	44%
T. J. Duckett*	-0.6	-20.8%	38	133	3.5	2	1	39%
Antwaan Randle El	1.7	-12.1%	19	118	6.2	0	0	—
Jason Campbell	3.6	20.5%	17	114	6.7	0	1	—
Mike Sellers	4.1	38.9%	12	51	4.3	0	0	45%
Mark Brunell	-4.6	-104.6%	9	31	3.4	0	5	—
Santana Moss	0.7	-13.2%	7	82	11.7	0	1	—
Rock Cartwright	-3.2	-217.1%	5	20	4.0	0	1	38%
Derrick Blaylock	*-5.7*	*-70.9%*	*25*	*44*	*1.8*	*0*	*0*	*40%*

Receiving

Player	DPAR	DVOA	Plys	Ctch	Yds	Y/C	YAC	TD	C%
WR									
Santana Moss	8.9	-2.0%	100	54	767	14.2	4.3	6	54%
Antwaan Randle El	-2.5	-21.0%	63	32	351	11.0	2.3	3	51%
Brandon Lloyd	-4.1	-25.9%	58	24	388	16.2	2.5	0	41%
James Thrash	3.1	6.5%	20	12	151	12.6	1.7	1	60%
TE									
Chris Cooley	12.5	8.0%	95	57	734	12.9	7.4	6	60%
RB									
Ladell Betts	5.6	9.7%	64	53	445	8.4	8.5	1	83%
Clinton Portis	-0.8	-16.0%	26	17	170	10.0	10.9	0	65%
Mike Sellers	-2.2	-28.2%	22	18	105	5.8	5.0	1	82%
Derrick Blaylock	*-0.2*	*-13.4%*	*9*	*5*	*29*	*5.8*	*5.2*	*0*	*88%*

Offensive Line

Year	Yards	ALY	Rank	Power	Rank	10+ Yds	Rank	Stuff	Rank	Sack	ASR	Rank
2004	3.89	4.06	22	47%	30	14%	28	25%	17	38	6.6%	14
2005	4.39	4.50	5	65%	15	16%	17	24%	11	31	6.9%	17
2006	4.41	4.28	15	55%	29	16%	16	24%	12	19	4.4%	5

Year	LE	Rank	LT	Rank	Mid	Rank	RT	Rank	RE	Rank
2004	3.87	21	4.02	24	3.95	23	4.39	12	4.36	10
2005	4.45	10	4.27	17	4.38	10	4.00	21	5.02	3
2006	4.05	18	4.95	5	4.58	7	3.94	24	3.86	19

A lot of silly money was thrown at free-agent offensive linemen this past offseason, but there's no doubt that Washington is going to miss left guard Derrick Dockery, who signed with Buffalo. Offensive line positions do not correlate perfectly to the specific directions in our Adjusted Line Yards numbers, but the two directions in which the left guard will have the most influence are behind left tackle and up the middle. Those happened to be the two directions in which Washington was in the league's top-ten last year. The two possible candidates to replace Dockery are journeymen Todd Wade and Mike Pucillo. Wade tore knee ligaments while playing for the Houston Texans in 2005, then signed with the Redskins, but barely saw the field last year. In 2005, Wade led Houston in Blown Blocks, which made him the worst pass-blocker on the league's worst pass-blocking team. He was a tackle then, so perhaps he'll do better at guard. Pucillo has bounced from Buffalo to Cleveland to Washington with just 18 career starts in five seasons.

On a team full of high-priced contracts, tackles Jon Jansen and Chris Samuels are two players who have earned their salaries. Unfortunately, both are in their early 30s, as are center Casey Rabach, right guard Randy Thomas, and Wade. The team chose not to add depth in the draft, although it is hard to add depth with only four picks. Washington's depth chart reads like the transactions section of the newspaper following cut-down day at the end of training camp, and if any of the starters get injured, Jason Campbell might want to request a bigger flak jacket.

Defensive Front Seven

Defensive Line	Age	Pos	Plys	TmPct	Rk	Stop	Dfts	StpRt	Rk	AvYd	Rk	Sack	Hit	Hur	Runs	RuStp	RuYd	Pass	PaStp	PaYd
Andre Carter	28	DE	59	7.3%	23	47	16	80%	28	1.2	32	6	8	9	46	78%	2.2	13	85%	-2.0
Cornelius Griffin	31	DT	53	7.5%	8	43	6	81%	26	2.3	51	1	2	2	46	80%	2.5	7	86%	1.3
Kedric Golston	24	DT	48	6.0%	22	38	9	79%	34	2.9	67	0.5	1	2	41	80%	3.4	7	71%	0.3
Phillip Daniels	34	DE	41	5.1%	52	32	9	78%	39	2.3	65	3	1	13	32	78%	2.7	9	78%	1.1
Joe Salave'a	32	DT	18	2.8%	—	12	3	67%	—	2.1	—	0	1	3	17	71%	1.8	1	0%	7.0
Demetric Evans	28	DE	17	2.1%	—	10	6	59%	—	2.7	—	2	0	3	13	54%	2.8	4	75%	2.3
Renaldo Wynn	33	DE	15	2.0%	—	12	5	80%	—	3.4	—	0	1	3	14	86%	2.1	1	0%	21.0

Linebackers	Age	Pos	Plys	TmPct	Rk	Stop	Dfts	StpRt	AvYd	Sack	Hit	Hur	Runs	RuStp	Rk	RuYd	Rk	Tgts	Suc%	Rk	PaYd	Rk
Lemar Marshall	31	ILB	108	14.3%	27	63	15	58%	5.4	1.5	4	6	73	64%	51	4.1	82	40	47%	57	9.2	95
Marcus Washington	30	OLB	97	13.8%	32	59	19	61%	4.1	2.5	9	8	65	62%	60	3.9	72	33	66%	7	4.7	15
Warrick Holdman*	32	OLB	71	8.8%	79	31	5	44%	5.5	1	1	5	38	58%	75	3.1	31	33	34%	92	9.1	93
Rocky McIntosh	25	OLB	15	1.9%	—	10	2	67%	3.4	0	0	0	12	75%	—	2.9	—	3	100%	—	1.3	—
L. Fletcher-Baker	*32*	*ILB*	*161*	*18.8%*	*4*	*89*	*40*	*55%*	*5.1*	*2*	*2*	*1*	*81*	*59%*	*69*	*4.0*	*79*	*61*	*54%*	*36*	*6.0*	*38*

Year	Yards	ALY	Rank	Power	Rank	10+ Yds	Rank	Stuff	Rank	Sack	ASR	Rank
2004	3.18	3.47	2	56%	8	12%	6	32%	2	39	6.9%	17
2005	4.23	3.87	11	57%	8	27%	32	24%	19	35	6.3%	23
2006	4.71	4.78	30	62%	12	18%	23	21%	23	19	4.6%	32

Year	LE	Rank	LT	Rank	Mid	Rank	RT	Rank	RE	Rank
2004	2.86	2	4.58	23	3.45	2	4.39	22	2.61	3
2005	4.39	21	3.94	12	3.72	7	4.10	17	3.12	6
2006	4.52	21	5.42	31	4.62	25	4.76	26	4.75	26

Last offseason, just like those that preceded it, the Redskins went on a free-agent spending spree to shore up identified areas of need. Hoping to resuscitate a moribund pass rush, the team signed defensive end Andre Carter to a six-year, $30-million contract. Instead, the pass rush became even more moribund, finishing last in Adjusted Sack Rate with 11 fewer sacks than the next-to-last place Vikings. Obviously, Carter isn't completely responsible—his six sacks led the team—but his big contract is emblematic of a larger problem: The club's habit of letting their players walk then forking over humongous paydays for other teams' free agents.

That's what happened two years ago with linebacker Antonio Pierce, who had been the team's defensive leader and on-field coach. According to an in-depth *Washington Post* series, assistant head coach-defense Gregg Williams attributed the defenses' success more to his system than to the players. Pierce, who blossomed under Williams, was considered expendable and was allowed to sign with the rival Giants. Without Pierce, the front seven's stats have dropped each of the past two seasons. The club hopes it has found Pierce's replacement in their most recent free-agent acquisition, London Fletcher-Baker. Fletcher-Baker was the linebacker equivalent of a boom-and-bust running back in Buffalo last year: He led the NFL in Defeats, but also had a lot of plays on which he tackled running backs after significant gains. He won't have to take on quite so many runners in Washington if the tackles in front of him, Cornelius Griffin and Joe Salave'a, can stay healthy. Despite his flaws against the run, Fletcher-Baker is much better than Pierce in pass coverage, and he looks like Deion Sanders compared to Lemar Marshall, the 'Skins 2006 starter.

Washington traded up in the 2006 draft to take outside linebacker Rocky McIntosh. He saw very little playing time last season because he was slow to pick up Williams's defense. The Redskins were uncertain enough about McIntosh's progress to try to trade for Lance Briggs this offseason. Having failed to land Briggs, Washington will give McIntosh every opportunity to start this year.

Defensive Secondary

Secondary	Age	Pos	Plys	TmPct	Rk	Stop	Dfts	RuYd	Rk	RuStp	Rk	Tgts	Tgt%	Rk	Dist	Suc%	Rk	PaYd	Rk	PD	Int
Carlos Rogers	26	CB	93	12.3%	8	36	12	6.5	38	36%	53	103	25%	4	12.4	50%	54	6.9	29	9	1
Kenny Wright*	30	CB	51	6.3%	73	22	11	9.1	62	33%	60	66	15%	61	11.1	46%	69	8.3	58	13	1
Shawn Springs	32	CB	47	10.4%	25	20	12	8.6	58	22%	74	48	20%	28	11.0	52%	39	7.4	39	8	1
Sean Taylor	24	FS	116	14.4%	3	43	12	6.0	29	40%	47	46	10%	12	14.3	49%	51	10.8	68	6	1
Mike Rumph*	28	CB	13	3.7%	—	7	5	16.5	—	50%	—	18	9%	—	15.1	50%	—	10.0	—	0	4
Adam Archuleta*	30	SS	49	6.1%	70	16	5	5.5	21	40%	49	14	3%	79	12.2	30%	78	10.5	66	0	0
Vernon Fox	27	SS	40	5.0%	75	15	6	5.9	27	38%	53	10	2%	80	17.2	64%	10	5.3	5	3	1
Troy Vincent*	36	FS	23	5.1%	—	5	0	7.2	—	28%	—	0	0%	—	0.0	0%	—	0.0	—	0	0
Fred Smoot	28	CB	69	10.7%	20	24	13	6.1	33	63%	9	98	23%	10	8.1	42%	75	6.7	21	7	1
Omar Stoutmire	33	SS	56	9.4%	46	27	7	5.4	19	52%	21	24	7%	48	12.5	53%	39	8.2	41	6	2
David Macklin	29	CB	38	5.2%	79	13	6	13.1	79	14%	77	50	12%	76	11.3	54%	30	8.0	54	6	1

Year	Pass D Rank	DVOA vs. #1 WR	Rank	DVOA vs. #2 WR	Rank	DVOA vs. Other WR	Rank	DVOA vs. TE	Rank	DVOA vs. RB	Rank
2004	9	-33.3%	2	-14.0%	4	7.0%	23	-5.7%	14	8.5%	20
2005	3	-13.6%	3	1.0%	21	-9.4%	10	-14.4%	7	-29.7%	2
2006	32	4.8%	22	25.6%	30	13.2%	23	9.4%	27	30.3%	32

After the Redskins failed to take a much-needed pass rusher in this year's draft, head coach Joe Gibbs proclaimed the front seven in fine shape. The issue, he said, was the secondary: Improving the pass coverage would require quarterbacks to hold the ball longer, and sacks would naturally follow. Or so the thinking goes. To that end, Washington selected LSU's LaRon Landry with the sixth-overall pick in this year's draft. Landry will pair with 2004 fifth-overall pick, veteran Sean Taylor, to form what is possibly the greatest safety tandem ever assembled. The problem is that we were having this exact same conversation a year ago following the Redskins signing of safety Adam Archuleta to a long-term deal that included $10 million in guarantees. Archuleta proved to be the exact wrong player for Williams's scheme.

By all accounts, Landry will be a very good player, but Taylor has expressed dissatisfaction with his current contract and was a no-show for Organized Team Activities in May, as was cornerback Shawn Springs, who refused to take a pay cut and was the topic of trade talks during the early days of free agency. Springs was our top-rated cornerback in 2005, and the Redskins desperately need to keep him happy and healthy. Third-year cornerback Carlos Rogers was regularly skewered for routinely giving up big plays, but the real problem was whoever had to line up on the other side or at nickel while Springs was hurt. Washington hopes the returning Fred Smoot can help solve that problem, but Arizona free agent David Macklin definitely will not.

Special Teams

Year	DVOA	Rank	FG/XP	Rank	Net Punt	Rank	Punt Ret	Rank	Net Kick	Rank	Kick Ret	Rank	Hidden	Rank
2004	-3.9%	31	-7.8	31	-10.5	31	-3.0	23	-4.9	25	3.5	9	0.6	11
2005	1.4%	9	-0.1	18	10.1	1	-4.3	25	-3.5	22	6.2	6	-1.8	19
2006	1.7%	11	-2.9	22	4.4	11	3.7	5	0.0	18	5.1	7	3.0	12

The Redskins have had fine special teams the last two seasons, except they can't find a quality kicker and keep him healthy. Head coach Joe Gibbs loved John Hall's toughness, but his perpetually iffy hamstring kept him on the shelf for most of his four-year stint in Washington. Nick Novak couldn't hit the broad side of a barn with his field goal attempts, and his kickoffs barely averaged 60 yards. The team has finally settled on Shaun Suisham, the 16th kicker the team has used since 1995, but if he starts the season poorly, the Redskins will be looking for kicker number 17 before October.

The team signed Antwaan Randle El prior to last season as much for his ability to return punts as for his offensive versatility. His 87-yard touchdown during the Week 7 Colts game is probably what most fans remember, but he gained four more yards per punt return than Antonio Brown, Washington's primary return man in 2005. Rock Cartwright inherited the kickoff-return duties from Ladell Betts and ranked seventh in the NFC with a 24.1-yard average. Punter Derrick Frost was average but the Redskins had good punt coverage.

Coaching Staff

Joe Gibbs signed a five-year contract when he unretired in 2004, and, though rumors circulate every year that he will re-retire, every year he comes back. A year ago, the longtime offensive guru shocked the football world by turning control of his offense over to another offensive guru, new offensive coordinator Al Saunders. Saunders introduced the Redskins to his 700-page playbook with predictable results. Saunders's greatest strength is his ability to adapt his game plans to fit his personnel. The problem, however, is that the Redskins aren't familiar enough with the Saunders playbook to take full advantage. Saunders is a big proponent of using pre-snap motion to confuse the defense. He was extremely successful in Kansas City and St. Louis using that scheme, but modern defenses are often complex enough to adapt, and sometimes it looked as though the Redskins were more confused than their opponents were. Having had last year to adapt to Saunders's system, and with a quarterback capable of making all the necessary throws, the Washington offense should improve in 2007. Assistant head coach-defense Gregg Williams is on the proverbial hot seat after his unit collapse a year ago. Once thought to be a rising head-coaching candidate (again), he'll be looking for a new assistant coaching job next spring unless the third-down rebound comes to his rescue.

Quarterbacks

The most surprising thing about quarterback performance during the 2006 season may have been the lack of surprise. A shorter season naturally means that NFL stats fluctuate more than those of other American team sports, but four quarterbacks finished in the top seven for DPAR (Defense-Adjusted Points Above Replacement) in both 2005 and 2006: Peyton Manning, Carson Palmer, Tom Brady, and Drew Brees.

Strong performances are nothing new to these four quarterbacks. Palmer finished 15th in DPAR as a rookie in 2004, then second and fourth over the past two seasons. Last year was the third-straight top-ten season for Brees and the fourth-straight top-ten season for Brady. The most remarkable numbers, of course, belong to the leader of last year's Super Bowl champions. Peyton Manning has now led the league in DPAR for four straight years. He ranked 18th in his rookie year of 1998, but has ranked 6th or higher in every season since.

In this section of the book, we give the last three years' worth of numbers for the top two quarterbacks on each team's depth chart, as well as a few other quarterbacks who may prove to be important in 2007. Each quarterback also gets a projection from our KUBIAK fantasy football projection system, based on a complicated regression analysis that takes into account numerous variables including projected role, performance over the past two years, performance on third down vs. all downs, experience of the projected offensive line, historical comparables, collegiate stats, height, age, and strength of schedule.

It is difficult to accurately project statistics for a 162-game baseball season, but it is exponentially more difficult to accurately project statistics for a 16-game football season because of the small size of the data samples involved. With that in mind, we ask that you consider the listed projections not as a prediction of exact numbers, but the mean of a range of possible performances. What's important is not so much the exact number of yards and touchdowns we project, but whether or not we're projecting a given player to improve or decline. Along those same lines, rookie projections will not be as accurate as veteran projections due to lack of data.

Our quarterback projections look a bit different than our projections for the other skill positions. At running back and wide receiver, second-stringers see plenty of action, but, at quarterback, either a player starts or he does not start. We recognize that, when a starting quarterback gets injured in Week 8, you don't want to grab your *Pro Football Prospectus* to find out if his backup is any good only to find that we've projected that the guy will throw 12 passes this year. Therefore, like we did last year, we have projected all quarterbacks to start all 16 games. If Steve McNair goes down in November, you can look up Kyle Boller or Troy Smith, divide the stats by 16, and get an idea of what we think each player will do in an average week.

Last year, our quarterback projections also included an attempt to estimate each player's chances of suffering a major or minor injury. In retrospect, this was a good example of biting off more than we could chew. Trying to pin down the chance for injury to a specific percentage was a bit silly. At the same time, many readers asked us to make similar forecasts for the other positions, and there is no doubt that two players with a similar fantasy football projection won't go at the same point in the draft if one has an injury history and the other one does not.

Therefore, this year's KUBIAK projections include a new category: **Risk.** A player's Risk level indicates the likelihood that he will fall short of his listed KUBIAK projection no matter what the reason—injury, a change in playing time, decline of skills, etc. Instead of giving you some sort of "estimated risk percentage" statistic, which would be implausibly precise, we have borrowed an idea from our colleague Will Carroll and his preseason "Team Health Reports" on BaseballProspectus.com by listing each player's Risk as Green, Yellow, or Red.

The players most likely to hit their projections are marked Green, the players who are riskier, but still somewhat dependable are marked Yellow, and everyone else is marked Red. Given the amount of variability inherent in projecting a 16-game NFL season, the Red category includes about half the players starting for NFL teams as well as nearly all the second-string players (since their playing time is most likely to decrease due to coaching decisions). Roughly one-quarter of the projected starters at each position are listed as Green, and roughly one-quarter of the projected starters and a handful of second-string players are listed as Yellow, although these distributions are by no means exact.

To determine Risk, we used the current version of KUBIAK to create projections for all players for the 2001 through 2006 seasons, then compared those projections to the players' actual performances in those seasons. As our goal was to determine Risk, not general variability, we threw out all players who exceeded their projections. For the remaining underperforming players, we used a statistical regression to determine which factors correlated best with ensuing underperformance (for example, for quarterbacks these factors included past playing time, projected interceptions, and runs per pass attempt).

We should add that there are two extra colors of Risk for quarterbacks only. The five projected backup quarterbacks who are most likely to meet their KUBIAK projections if they become starters are listed as Orange. Thanks to his otherworldly consistency, Peyton Manning is marked Blue. We're not actually projecting Manning to have the most fantasy points in 2007, but unless you crash test roller coasters for a living, we would still recommend drafting Manning before any other quarterback.

How to Read the Quarterback Statistics Table

The first line (table 1) contains biographical data—each player's name, height, weight, college, draft position, birth date, and age. Height and weight are the best data we could find; weight, of course, can fluctuate during the offseason. **Age** is very simple, the number of years between the player's birth year and 2007, but birth date is provided if you want to figure out exact age.

Draft position gives draft year and round, with the overall pick number with which the player was taken in parentheses. In the sample table, it says that Steve McNair was chosen in the 1995 draft in the first round with the third-overall pick. Undrafted free agents are listed as "FA" with the year they came into the league, even if they were only in training camp or on a practice squad.

To the far right of the first line is the player's **Risk** for fantasy football in 2007.

Next we give the last three years of player stats. The majority of these statistics are passing numbers, though the final five columns on the right are the quarterback's rushing statistics.

The first few columns after the year and team the player played for are standard numbers: games (**G**), pass attempts

(**Att**), pass completions (**Cmp**), completion percentage (**C%**), passing yards (**Yds**), passing touchdowns (**TD**), and interceptions (**INT**). These numbers are official NFL totals and therefore include plays we leave out of our own metrics, such as clock-stopping spikes, and omit plays we include in our metrics, such as sacks and aborted snaps. Note that the games total includes all games the player appeared in, not just games started, which is why a backup quarterback who holds on field goals will often be listed with 16 games played.

The next column is fumbles (**FUM**), which adds together all fumbles by this player, whether turned over to the defense or recovered by the offense (explained in the essay "Pregame Show"). Even though this fumble total is listed among the passing numbers, it includes all fumbles, including those on sacks, aborted snaps, and rushing attempts. By listing fumbles and interceptions next to one another we hope to give a general idea of how many total turnovers the player was responsible for.

Next comes Adjusted Sack Rate (**ASR**). This is the same statistic you'll find in the team chapters, only here it is specific to the individual quarterback. It represents sacks per pass play (total pass plays = pass attempts + sacks) adjusted based on down, distance, and strength of schedule. For reference, the NFL average over the past three seasons is 6.8 percent.

The next two columns are Net Yards per Pass (**NY/P**), a standard stat but a particularly good one, and the player's rank (**Rk**) in Net Yards per Pass for that season. Consider the inclusion of this number our tribute to the godfather of football stats, Bud Goode. It consists of passing yards minus yards lost on sacks, divided by total pass plays.

The five columns remaining in passing stats give our advanced metrics: **DVOA** (Defense-Adjusted Value Over Average), **DPAR** (Defense-Adjusted Points Above Replacement), and **PAR** (Points Above Replacement), along with the player's rank in both DVOA and DPAR. These metrics compare each quarterback's passing performance to league-average or replacement-level baselines based on the game situations that quarterback faced. DVOA and DPAR are also adjusted based on the opposing defense. The methods used to compute these numbers are described in detail in the "Statistical Toolbox" introduction in the

Table 1. Quarterback Statistics Sample

Steve McNair Height: 6-2 Weight: 235 College: Alcorn State Draft: 1995/1 (3) Born: 14-Feb-1973 Age: 34 Risk: Yellow

Year	Team	G	Att	Cmp	C%	Yds	TD	INT	FUM	ASR	NY/P	Rk	DVOA	Rk	DPAR	Rk	PAR	Runs	Yds	TD	DPAR	DVOA
2004	TEN	8	215	129	60.0%	1343	8	9	5	6.3%	5.5	27	-18.9%	32	-6.0	32	1.9	23	128	1	3.9	18.6%
2005	TEN	14	476	292	61.3%	3161	16	11	6	3.7%	6.2	14	11.2%	13	51.3	9	60.6	32	139	1	4.5	10.6%
2006	BAL	16	468	295	63.0%	3050	16	12	7	3.0%	6.2	15	10.9%	13	47.9	12	54.5	45	119	1	6.7	34.5%
2007	BAL		494	301	61.1%	3444	21	16			6.5								39	124	1		

2005: 49% Short 35% Mid 9% Deep 7% Bomb YAC: 5.0 (14)   2006: 49% Short 38% Mid 8% Deep 5% Bomb YAC: 4.3 (34)

front of the book. The important distinctions between them are:

- DVOA is a rate statistic, while DPAR is a cumulative statistic. Thus, a higher DVOA means more value per pass play, while a higher DPAR means more aggregate value over the entire season.

- Because DPAR is defense-adjusted and PAR is not, a player whose DPAR is higher than his PAR faced a harder-than-average schedule. A player whose DPAR is lower than his PAR faced an easier-than-average schedule.

To qualify for a ranking in Net Yards per Pass, passing DVOA, and passing DPAR in a given season, a quarterback must have had 100 pass plays in that season. There are 45 quarterbacks ranked for 2006, 46 quarterbacks for 2005, and 42 quarterbacks for 2004.

The final five columns contain rushing statistics, starting with **Runs**, rushing yards (**Yds**), and rushing touchdowns (**TD**). Once again, these are official NFL totals and include kneeldowns, which means you get to enjoy statistics such as Brett Favre running 23 times for 29 yards. The final two columns give **DPAR** and **DVOA** for quarterback rushing, which are calculated separately from passing. Rankings for these statistics, as well as numbers that are not adjusted for defense (PAR and VOA) can be found on our website, FootballOutsiders.com.

The italicized row of statistics for the 2007 season is our 2007 KUBIAK projection, as detailed above. Note that KUBIAK only projects the official NFL statistics, not our advanced metrics. Again, in the interest of producing meaningful statistics, all quarterbacks are projected to start a full 16-game season, regardless of the likelihood of them actually doing so.

The final line represents data from the Football Outsiders game charting project. First, we break down charted passes based on distance: **Short** (5 yards or less), **Mid** (6–15 yards), **Deep** (16–25 yards), and **Bomb** (26 or more yards). These numbers are based on distance in the air only and include both complete and incomplete passes. Passes thrown away or tipped at the line are not included, nor are passes on which the quarterback's arm was hit by a defender while in motion. We also give Yards after Catch (**YAC**) and with the Rank in parentheses for the 45 quarterbacks who qualify. Charting data is listed for both 2005 and 2006 (there was no charting project in 2004).

A number of third- and fourth-string quarterbacks are briefly discussed at the end of the chapter in a section we call "Going Deep."

Table 2. Top 20 QB by Passing DPAR (Total Value), 2006

Rank	Player	Team	DPAR	Rank	Player	Team	DPAR
1	Peyton Manning	IND	175.0	11	Jon Kitna	DET	48.1
2	Marc Bulger	STL	108.8	12	Steve McNair	BAL	47.9
3	Drew Brees	NO	106.0	13	Brett Favre	GB	46.0
4	Carson Palmer	CIN	97.2	14	Ben Roethlisberger	PIT	42.6
5	Philip Rivers	SD	85.1	15	Mark Brunell	WAS	29.7
6	Tom Brady	NE	75.9	16	Matt Leinart	ARI	28.3
7	Donovan McNabb	PHI	57.0	17	Eli Manning	NYG	28.0
8	Damon Huard	KC	53.4	18	Jeff Garcia	PHI	27.6
9	Chad Pennington	NYJ	52.2	19	Jake Delhomme	CAR	22.5
10	Tony Romo	DAL	51.3	20	J. P. Losman	BUF	21.2

Table 3. Top 20 QB by Passing DVOA (Value per Pass), 2006

Rank	Player	Team	DVOA	Rank	Player	Team	DVOA
1	Peyton Manning	IND	58.0%	11	Tom Brady	NE	19.6%
2	Damon Huard	KC	36.0%	12	Mark Brunell	WAS	13.1%
3	Tim Rattay	TB	29.0%	13	Steve McNair	BAL	10.9%
4	Drew Brees	NO	28.4%	14	Chad Pennington	NYJ	10.2%
5	Philip Rivers	SD	28.3%	15	Ben Roethlisberger	PIT	6.6%
6	Carson Palmer	CIN	27.6%	16	Brett Favre	GB	4.0%
7	Marc Bulger	STL	27.4%	17	Matt Leinart	ARI	3.9%
8	Donovan McNabb	PHI	25.7%	18	Kurt Warner	ARI	3.9%
9	Tony Romo	DAL	20.1%	19	Jon Kitna	DET	3.9%
10	Jeff Garcia	PHI	19.7%	20	Jason Campbell	WAS	3.5%

Derek Anderson   Height: 6-6   Weight: 239 College: Oregon State   Draft: 2005/6 (213) Born: 15-Jun-1983   Age: 24   Risk: Red

Year	Team	G	Att	Cmp	C%	Yds	TD	INT	FUM	ASR	NY/P	Rk	DVOA	Rk	DPAR	Rk	PAR	Runs	Yds	TD	DPAR	DVOA
2006	CLE	5	117	66	56.4%	793	5	8	2	5.9%	5.9	22	-28.5%	41	-8.5	40	-10.7	4	47	0	0.4	7.5%
2007	CLE		424	252	59.4%	2734	19	13			5.6							40	126	1		

2006:   36% Short   43% Mid   18% Deep   3% Bomb   YAC: 6.1 (3)

Anderson is a one-half wonder. He replaced Charlie Frye in the third quarter against the Chiefs in Week 13, threw a few nice passes, ran well, benefited from some typically awful tackling by the Chiefs defense, and engineered an overtime win. That earned Anderson the starting job for the remainder of the season, but the more he played, the worse he looked. By the season finale, he was serving up four interceptions to the Bucs. Anderson can do some things Frye couldn't, like throw a ball more than 20 yards without giving it the trajectory of a weather balloon, but he's a C-minus prospect whose best attribute is his 6-foot-6 frame.

Charlie Batch   Height: 6-2   Weight: 220 College: Eastern Michigan   Draft: 1998/2 (60) Born: 5-Dec-1974   Age: 33   Risk: Red

Year	Team	G	Att	Cmp	C%	Yds	TD	INT	FUM	ASR	NY/P	Rk	DVOA	Rk	DPAR	Rk	PAR	Runs	Yds	TD	DPAR	DVOA
2005	PIT	4	36	23	63.9%	246	1	1	—	3.7%	6.7	—	27.9%	—	6.5	—	6.6	11	30	1	1.1	5.1
2006	PIT	8	53	31	58.5%	492	5	0	1	3.5%	8.6	—	63.0%	—	18.0	—	17.7	13	15	0	-2.0	-99.9%
2007	PIT		415	251	60.5%	2811	13	23			5.9							30	75	1		

2005:   55% Short   23% Mid   13% Deep   10% Bomb   YAC: 4.1 (—)   2006:   35% Short   35% Mid   18% Deep   12% Bomb   YAC: 7.4 (—)

Batch's strong effort when Ben Roethlisberger was out earned him another season as the primary backup in Pittsburgh. Though Big Ben is clearly the starter, a new coach in Pittsburgh means that Batch may get a look sooner if Roethlisberger struggles the way he did last season.

John Beck   Height: 6-2   Weight: 215 College: BYU   Draft: 2007/2 (40) Born: 21-Aug-1981 Age: 26   Risk: Red

Year	Team	G	Att	Cmp	C%	Yds	TD	INT	FUM	ASR	NY/P	Rk	DVOA	Rk	DPAR	Rk	PAR	Runs	Yds	TD	DPAR	DVOA
2007	MIA		480	297	61.7%	3090	16	12			5.6							19	15	1		

Think of Beck as "the man who must be Brady Quinn." Beck enters the league at the age of 26 following a two-year Mormon mission, making him the oldest rookie quarterback since erstwhile minor league third baseman Chris Weinke debuted at the age of 29 in 2001. Weinke was a Heisman Trophy winner who was pushed into the starting lineup for an awful Carolina team before he was ready, failed, then spent the rest of his career on the bench. Beck has three more years to work with, but a less impressive pedigree. His selling points are a quick-trigger release and excellent accuracy on short and medium distances. On the downside, Beck struggles with distance and accuracy on his deep ball. While that might not be exposed in some schemes, the Dolphins like to go deep to burners Chris Chambers and Ted Ginn. Unless Beck goes on the Tom Brady post-collegiate weightlifting program, he's not a good fit for the Dolphins offense as currently constructed.

Drew Bledsoe   Height: 6-5   Weight: 238 College: Washington State   Draft: 1993/1 (1)   Born: 14-Feb-1972   Age: 35   Risk: NA

Year	Team	G	Att	Cmp	C%	Yds	TD	INT	FUM	ASR	NY/P	Rk	DVOA	Rk	DPAR	Rk	PAR	Runs	Yds	TD	DPAR	DVOA
2004	BUF	16	450	256	56.9%	2932	20	16	9	7.8%	5.5	26	-2.0%	22	22.5	21	13.7	22	37	0	-1.4	-41.5%
2005	DAL	16	499	300	60.1%	3639	23	17	16	9.2%	6.1	15	5.3%	19	43.2	14	46.7	34	50	2	-3.2	-42.9%
2006	DAL	6	169	90	53.3%	1164	7	8	3	9.6%	5.6	30	-23.1%	39	-7.5	38	-4.0	8	28	2	0.4	-4.5%

2005:   41% Short   38% Mid   13% Deep   8% Bomb   YAC: 4.5 (29)   2006:   38% Short   44% Mid   10% Deep   8% Bomb   YAC: 5.4 (11)

The Cowboys were wise to pull Bledsoe from the starting lineup at midseason. In the Chicago chapter, there's a table listing the quarterbacks who declined the most after a strong four-week start to a season. Bledsoe appears on that list three times, which only hints at the problem. Year after year, for virtually his entire career, Bledsoe started out strong and then collapsed down the stretch. These numbers represent every year in Bledsoe's career since 1996, except for 2001 and 2006 when he did not play the entire year:

Weeks 1–9:   34.5 DPAR per season,   13.8% DVOA,   6.2 net yards per pass

Weeks 10–17:   1.9 DPAR per season,   −11.3% DVOA,   5.4 net yards per pass

Only once since 1996 did Bledsoe maintain the starting job all year without a drop in DVOA after week 9. That was in 2004, when Bledsoe had a DVOA of −3.0% in the first half of the year, −1.3% in the second half. The most egregious of Bledsoe's late-season collapses was 1999. Bledsoe had a DVOA of 32.4% over the first eight games as the Patriots got off to a 6–2 start. After Week 9, Bledsoe had a DVOA of −44.0%, the Patriots went 2–6, and head coach Pete Carroll lost his job.

If Bledsoe was that bad in the first half of the 2006 season, what on earth would he have been like if he had started for the rest of the year? By all accounts, Bledsoe is a nice guy who does a lot for charity, so let's look on the bright side: Now that he's retired, we don't have to say bad things about him anymore.

Kyle Boller

Height: 6-3 Weight: 220 College: California **Draft: 2003/1 (19) Born: 17-Jun-1981 Age: 26 Risk: Red**

Year	Team	G	Att	Cmp	C%	Yds	TD	INT	FUM	ASR	NY/P	Rk	DVOA	Rk	DPAR	Rk	PAR	Runs	Yds	TD	DPAR	DVOA
2004	BAL	16	464	258	55.6%	2559	13	11	11	6.9%	4.7	34	-2.0%	21	23.1	20	3.1	53	189	1	1.5	-12.0%
2005	BAL	9	293	171	58.4%	1799	11	12	3	10.5%	4.6	42	-25.0%	39	-15.4	40	-7.3	23	66	1	-0.6	-21.2%
2006	BAL	5	55	33	60.0%	485	5	2	3	5.0%	8.1	—	17.6%	—	7.7	—	6.3	22	34	0	-2.2	-53.5%
2007	BAL		437	280	64.1%	2836	20	20			6.1							43	134	1		
2005:	51% Short	24% Mid	17% Deep	8% Bomb		YAC: 4.5 (27)						2006:	37% Short	41% Mid	12% Deep	10% Bomb			YAC: 6.2 (—)			

Boller posted a pair of huge games at the tail end of 2005 to cap the best year of his three-season career. As a result, KUBIAK had him poised for a breakout year in 2006. His reward? A clipboard and a front-row view of Steve McNair. The Ravens went 13-3, so it's hard to argue with the decision, but we can't help wondering if Baltimore might have had similar success with Boller, who was impressive in limited action as McNair's backup. It looks like Boller's now on the backup quarterback track for good, but a team could do worse than to have a player of Boller's experience as the backup to a brittle, 34-year-old starter. Oh, and if you need someone to chuck it through the goalposts from a kneeling position on the 50-yard line, Kyle's your man.

Brooks Bollinger

Height: 6-0 Weight: 205 College: Wisconsin **Draft: 2003/6 (200) Born: 15-Nov-1979 Age: 28 Risk: Red**

Year	Team	G	Att	Cmp	C%	Yds	TD	INT	FUM	ASR	NY/P	Rk	DVOA	Rk	DPAR	Rk	PAR	Runs	Yds	TD	DPAR	DVOA
2004	NYJ	1	9	5	55.6%	60	0	0	0	9.2%	5.2	—	4.2%	—	0.7	—	0.3	1	2	0	-0.6	-117.9%
2005	NYJ	11	266	150	56.4%	1558	7	6	7	7.4%	5.3	35	-6.1%	27	9.0	27	4.8	35	135	0	-6.1	-60.6%
2006	MIN	2	18	13	72.2%	146	0	1	0	24.3%	4.3	—	36.7%	—	5.1	—	1.7	0	0	0	0.0	0.0%
2007	MIN		478	303	63.4%	3036	14	17			5.5							26	52	0		
2005:	50% Short	33% Mid	9% Deep	9% Bomb		YAC: 4.0 (39)						2006:	59% Short	29% Mid	6% Deep	6% Bomb			YAC: 8.0 (—)			

One year after he struggled mightily as the Jets starter, Bollinger finds himself with another chance to start in the NFL. He probably wasn't as bad as he looked with the Jets, but he has a hard time staying upright, as he's been sacked on nearly 11 percent of his drop-backs; that's higher than David Carr, and approaching the rarefied air of Rob Johnson. Tarvaris Jackson remains this staff's pet project, so Bollinger will have to really impress to win the job.

Tom Brady

Height: 6-4 Weight: 220 College: Michigan **Draft: 2000/6 (199) Born: 3-Aug-1977 Age: 30 Risk: Green**

Year	Team	G	Att	Cmp	C%	Yds	TD	INT	FUM	ASR	NY/P	Rk	DVOA	Rk	DPAR	Rk	PAR	Runs	Yds	TD	DPAR	DVOA
2004	NE	16	474	288	60.8%	3692	28	14	7	5.0%	7.1	9	41.6%	2	113.4	3	95.6	43	28	0	1.1	-8.1%
2005	NE	16	530	334	63.0%	4110	26	14	4	4.7%	7.1	4	30.9%	4	104.0	3	100.9	27	89	1	5.0	15.4%
2006	NE	16	516	319	61.8%	3529	24	12	12	5.1%	6.2	17	19.6%	10	75.9	6	71.1	49	102	0	1.9	-6.3%
2007	NE		517	332	64.2%	3994	30	10			7.0							37	94	1		
2005:	48% Short	32% Mid	12% Deep	8% Bomb		YAC: 5.6 (4)						2006:	52% Short	27% Mid	14% Deep	7% Bomb			YAC: 5.1 (16)			

A Week 3 loss to Denver led to ridiculous attempts on the part of the Boston media to parse the meaning of Brady's "body language." It was an awful example of journalists projecting their story onto a player, which is a Boston media specialty. Back in the real world, Tom Brady played about as well as a quarterback who lost his top receiver could be expected to play. Donte' Stallworth and Randy Moss are upgrades on Reche Caldwell and Troy Brown, but losing Corey Dillon deprives Brady of his best pass blocker in the backfield—Laurence Maroney and Sammy Morris simply don't compare.

Drew Brees

Height: 6-0 Weight: 221 College: Purdue **Draft: 2001/2 (32) Born: 15-Jan-1979 Age: 28 Risk: Green**

Year	Team	G	Att	Cmp	C%	Yds	TD	INT	FUM	ASR	NY/P	Rk	DVOA	Rk	DPAR	Rk	PAR	Runs	Yds	TD	DPAR	DVOA
2004	SD	15	400	262	65.5%	3159	27	7	7	5.0%	7.2	8	29.5%	7	75.6	9	90.7	53	85	2	4.6	4.0%
2005	SD	16	500	323	64.6%	3576	24	15	8	5.5%	6.4	10	19.8%	8	73.3	7	71.2	21	49	1	1.6	-5.3%
2006	NO	16	554	356	64.3%	4418	26	11	7	3.3%	7.6	3	28.3%	5	105.7	3	117.0	42	32	0	-7.7	-99.9%
2007	NO		558	345	61.9%	4091	26	16			6.7							25	51	0		
2005:	47% Short	34% Mid	13% Deep	6% Bomb		YAC: 4.6 (24)						2006:	55% Short	27% Mid	12% Deep	6% Bomb			YAC: 5.5 (7)			

(continued next page)

Drew Brees (*continued*)

Once upon a time, there were two quarterbacks available in the NFL draft. One quarterback was coming out of school early after an impressive bowl victory. He was mobile with a rocket arm, a gifted athlete who could revolutionize the quarterback position. The other quarterback was a three-year starter who saw his draft stock fall after he stayed in school for his senior year. He had excellent technique and leadership skills, but he was too slow to avoid the pass rush, and scouts did not know if he had the arm to make all the throws that an NFL quarterback has to make.

Wait . . . did we say "once upon a time"? Sorry, we meant *thrice* upon a time. Everything that has been said about Matt Leinart and Brady Quinn over the past two years was said about Drew Brees back in 2001. Last year, Brees completed 58 percent of all Deep or Bomb passes, meaning that the guy who scouts said couldn't make the deep throw was the most accurate quarterback in the league on the deep throw. If this is the upside for Leinart and Quinn, the Cardinals and Browns will happily take it.

Saints fans may be wondering why Brees finished so far behind Peyton Manning in both DVOA and DPAR, when their conventional stats are virtually identical. The biggest reason is that Manning was far better at moving the chains. Forty-three percent of Manning's pass attempts resulted in a first down or touchdown, compared to just 36 percent for Brees, even though Manning's average pass came with a half-yard more to go for the first down. The difference was even bigger at the goal line, the one place where Brees was terrible last year. Brees threw a touchdown pass on only 6 of 31 goal-to-go pass attempts, with two interceptions. Manning threw a touchdown pass on 15 of 30 goal-to-go pass attempts, with just one interception.

Aaron Brooks													Height: 6-4		Weight: 220	College: Virginia			Draft: 1999/4 (131)		Born: 24-Mar-1974		Age: 33		Risk: Red
Year	Team	G	Att	Cmp	C%	Yds	TD	INT	FUM	ASR	NY/P	Rk	DVOA	Rk	DPAR	Rk	PAR	Runs	Yds	TD	DPAR	DVOA
2004	NO	16	542	309	57.0%	3810	21	16	13	7.1%	6.0	19	-3.9%	24	23.2	19	33.1	58	173	4	6.9	9.1%
2005	NO	13	431	240	55.7%	2882	13	17	4	7.0%	5.8	23	-1.2%	23	23.2	22	21.0	45	281	2	13.0	41.2%
2006	OAK	8	192	110	57.3%	1105	3	8	5	11.3%	4.3	44	-30.5%	42	-15.8	42	-13.6	22	124	0	0.4	-15.5%
2007	FA		463	295	63.8%	2957	15	13			5.2							51	208	1		
2005:	35% Short		42% Mid		18% Deep		5% Bomb			YAC: 4.4 (31)				2006:		42% Short		39% Mid	9% Deep		10% Bomb	YAC: 3.9 (41)

Brooks's patented "run backwards" method of dealing with the pass rush was especially ineffective behind the Raiders' terrible offensive line. The one thing Brooks used to do well is run, and he looks as though he's lost a step. If Brooks were ever going to become an effective NFL quarterback, he would have done it by now. Still a free agent at press time, and he may be done.

Mark Brunell													Height: 6-1		Weight: 217	College: Washington			Draft: 1993/5 (118)		Born: 17-Sep-1970		Age: 37		Risk: Red
Year	Team	G	Att	Cmp	C%	Yds	TD	INT	FUM	ASR	NY/P	Rk	DVOA	Rk	DPAR	Rk	PAR	Runs	Yds	TD	DPAR	DVOA
2004	WAS	9	237	118	49.8%	1194	7	6	6	5.7%	4.3	38	-22.8%	34	-10.2	33	-8.1	19	62	0	-1.6	-39.1%
2005	WAS	16	454	262	57.7%	3050	23	10	10	5.9%	5.9	22	10.1%	15	47.0	12	48.5	42	111	0	0.3	-14.7%
2006	WAS	10	260	162	62.3%	1789	8	4	5	5.0%	6.2	14	13.0%	12	29.6	15	32.4	13	34	0	-4.6	-99.9%
2007	WAS		372	207	55.6%	2191	11	15			5.4							22	53	0		
2005:	54% Short		30% Mid		8% Deep		8% Bomb			YAC: 5.8 (3)				2006:		54% Short		26% Mid	13% Deep		7% Bomb	YAC: 6.1 (4)

It took nine weeks, but Father Time finally caught up to Brunell last season. Head coach Joe Gibbs—who has seemingly always preferred veteran quarterbacks—finally benched Brunell in favor of second-year player and former first-round pick Jason Campbell. Only a year removed from a well-deserved Pro Bowl appearance, Brunell took an offseason pay cut to stay in Washington and back up Campbell. Oddly, despite playing in only nine games in 2006, Brunell ranked 15th in DPAR, just three spots below his 2005 finish. The explanation—which should be named the Brunell Rule—is that the quarterback was relatively accurate on short routes that were turned into long gains, thanks, in part, to Santana Moss and Chris Cooley. In fact, Brunell ranked fourth in the league in yards after catch, just behind such luminaries as Daunte Culpepper and Derek Anderson. Benching Brunell was the right move, but he is still an experienced backup who, like Jon Kitna in Cincinnati in 2004, could help Campbell ease into the starting job.

Marc Bulger Height: 6-3 Weight: 215 College: West Virginia   Draft: 2000/6 (168) Born: 5-Apr-1977 Age: 30 Risk: Yellow

Year	Team	G	Att	Cmp	C%	Yds	TD	INT	FUM	ASR	NY/P	Rk	DVOA	Rk	DPAR	Rk	PAR	Runs	Yds	TD	DPAR	DVOA
2004	STL	14	485	321	66.2%	3964	21	14	5	8.0%	7.0	10	29.3%	8	92.6	6	85.8	19	89	3	2.7	7.7%
2005	STL	8	287	192	66.9%	2297	14	9	5	8.2%	6.7	9	15.0%	11	37.5	17	46.6	9	29	0	-0.5	-32.4%
2006	STL	16	588	370	62.9%	4301	24	8	5	7.7%	6.2	13	27.4%	7	108.8	2	113.6	18	44	0	1.7	11.7%
2007	*STL*		*565*	*346*	*61.2%*	*3980*	*20*	*14*			*6.1*								*21*	*53*	*0*		
2005:	*42% Short*		*31% Mid*		*19% Deep*		*8% Bomb*			*YAC: 4.3 (34)*				*2006:*		*50% Short*		*26% Mid*		*16% Deep*	*8% Bomb*	*YAC: 4.9 (20)*

According to DPAR, Bulger was the NFL's top mortal division quarterback in 2006, "mortal division" being defined as all quarterbacks not named Peyton Manning. Bulger played in all 16 games for the first time in his career in 2006 and threw fewer interceptions than he did in just 8 games the year before. His great season was assisted by several external factors. All four secondaries in the NFC West were awful. St. Louis rediscovered the running back as a receiving option, forcing opposing defenses to contend with Steven Jackson on both running and passing plays. The offensive line improved tremendously over the 2005 season and the mess that was 2004 . . . well, for half the year, at least. Bulger's numbers took a big downturn when left tackle Orlando Pace tore his triceps in Week 10. If Pace has trouble again this year, so will Bulger. In the first eight games of the 2006, Bulger had 6.8 net yards per pass, a 41.8% DVOA, and only one interception. In the final eight games, Bulger had 5.6 net yards per pass, a 13.7% DVOA, and seven interceptions.

Jason Campbell Height: 6-4 Weight: 223 College: Auburn   Draft: 2005/1 (25) Born: 31-Dec-1981 Age: 25 Risk: Green

Year	Team	G	Att	Cmp	C%	Yds	TD	INT	FUM	ASR	NY/P	Rk	DVOA	Rk	DPAR	Rk	PAR	Runs	Yds	TD	DPAR	DVOA
2006	WAS	7	207	110	53.1%	1297	10	6	1	3.2%	5.8	23	3.6%	20	14.8	23	18.4	24	107	0	3.6	20.5%
2007	*WAS*		*472*	*281*	*59.4%*	*3204*	*18*	*18*			*6.2*							*51*	*185*	*1*		
															2006:	*42% Short*	*32% Mid*	*14% Deep*	*12% Bomb*			*YAC: 5 (17)*

Campbell started the final 7 games of 2006 after not playing a down in 2005. Unsurprisingly, he was inconsistent, but most of that can be attributed to inexperience and unfamiliarity with new offensive coordinator Al Saunders's well-publicized 700-page playbook. For the first time in his pro career, Campbell will head into training camp as the unquestioned starter, which means he will take all the first-team snaps and have a chance to develop a rapport with his receivers. Additionally, the club will work with Campbell to improve his footwork, which—along with the first-team workouts—should improve his accuracy. Our college projection system likes Campbell because of his high completion rate at Auburn, and there is no reason to think he can't duplicate that in the NFL.

David Carr Height: 6-3 Weight: 223 College: Fresno State   Draft: 2002/1 (1) Born: 21-Jul-1979 Age: 28 Risk: Red

Year	Team	G	Att	Cmp	C%	Yds	TD	INT	FUM	ASR	NY/P	Rk	DVOA	Rk	DPAR	Rk	PAR	Runs	Yds	TD	DPAR	DVOA
2004	HOU	16	466	285	61.2%	3531	16	14	10	10.6%	6.3	16	-0.6%	20	27.5	18	46.3	73	299	0	5.9	-0.4%
2005	HOU	16	423	256	60.5%	2488	14	11	17	13.3%	4.2	44	-21.3%	36	-17.0	41	-18.6	56	308	1	6.0	1.2%
2006	HOU	16	442	302	68.3%	2767	11	12	16	9.1%	5.2	38	-8.3%	28	10.3	26	3.4	54	193	2	2.7	-4.8%
2007	*CAR*		*436*	*266*	*60.9%*	*2644*	*17*	*19*			*5.3*							*42*	*185*	*2*		
2005:	*49% Short*		*34% Mid*		*12% Deep*		*5% Bomb*			*YAC: 4.0 (38)*				*2006:*		*62% Short*		*26% Mid*		*7% Deep*	*5% Bomb*	*YAC: 4.8 (22)*

In 2006, the Texans treated Carr like the girlfriend they wanted to dump but couldn't, alternating between praising him and then degrading him. His Week 8 benching against the Titans for fumbling twice just made the decision to pass on Vince Young look even worse. While Gary Kubiak built an offense entirely out of dinks and dunks for Carr in 2006, the quarterback still went down once every 11.8 dropbacks, while the system held back Houston's real offensive star, wide receiver Andre Johnson. Houston finally cut bait on Carr after the season once they found a prettier quarterback in Matt Schaub. Carr went to Carolina, where he'll back up Jake Delhomme, but don't be surprised to see Carr starting again if Delhomme gets off to a slow start.

Matt Cassel
Height: 6-4   Weight: 232   College: USC   Draft: 2005/7 (230)   Born: 17-May-1982   Age: 25   Risk: Red

Year	Team	G	Att	Cmp	C%	Yds	TD	INT	FUM	ASR	NY/P	Rk	DVOA	Rk	DPAR	Rk	PAR	Runs	Yds	TD	DPAR	DVOA
2005	NE	3	24	13	54.2%	183	2	1	2	2.4%	7.2	—	-7.9%	—	0.5	—	0.7	6	12	0	0.5	0.0%
2006	NE	6	8	5	62.5%	32	0	0	0	27.2%	1.4	—	-88.4%	—	-3.4	—	-2.9	2	4	0	0.4	31.9%
2007	NE		459	278	60.7%	3234	25	11			6.3							70	315	0		

2005: 67% Short   33% Mid   0% Deep   0% Bomb   YAC: 5.5 (—)   2006: 83% Short   17% Mid   0% Deep   0% Bomb   YAC: 5.0 (—)

Six games, eight pass attempts; at this point, we need to develop an acronym to mirror baseball's LOOGY for Cassel. KAGEY (Kneeldown At Game's End guY) should do nicely. The next meaningful situation Cassel enters will be his first since high school, something the Patriots should make sure never occurs. Cassel put up a 93.5 passer rating in the preseason while leading the AFC in passing yards, but damned if we know what that means. Even if the Patriots are committed to using Cassel as their backup, they should bring in a third-string veteran with some reasonable skills in case Cassel totally bombs. And, no, Vinny Testaverde does not count.

Kellen Clemens
Height: 6-2   Weight: 215   College: Oregon   Draft: 2006/2 (49)   Born: 6-Jun-1983   Age: 24   Risk: Red

Year	Team	G	Att	Cmp	C%	Yds	TD	INT	FUM	ASR	NY/P	Rk	DVOA	Rk	DPAR	Rk	PAR	Runs	Yds	TD	DPAR	DVOA
2006	NYJ	2	1	0	0.0%	0	0	0	0	79.2%	-5.4	—	-241.3%	—	-5.1	—	-5.3	2	10	0	-0.2	-44.7%
2007	NYJ		412	243	58.8%	2934	19	16			6.3							77	349	0		

Last year's *PFP* cover boy made it into two games in garbage time as a rookie. He was sacked four times and made only one actual pass attempt. That means nothing for his long-term future, of course, and all reports out of New York say that he still looks every bit like the prospect David Lewin's system and Ron Jaworski's eyes said he was. He should easily push Marques Tuiasosopo aside to claim the primary backup role in 2007, so when Chad Pennington suffers his inevitable season-ending injury, Clemens can claim the starting job for good.

Kerry Collins
Height: 6-5   Weight: 240   College: Penn State   Draft: 1995/1 (5)   Born: 30-Dec-1972   Age: 34   Risk: Orange

Year	Team	G	Att	Cmp	C%	Yds	TD	INT	FUM	ASR	NY/P	Rk	DVOA	Rk	DPAR	Rk	PAR	Runs	Yds	TD	DPAR	DVOA
2004	OAK	14	513	289	56.3%	3495	21	20	7	5.8%	6.2	17	-11.1%	29	4.8	29	19.4	16	36	0	1.1	11.8%
2005	OAK	15	565	302	53.5%	3759	20	12	—	6.9%	5.7	24	5.8%	18	47.5	11	54.2	18	38	1	1.8	15.1%
2006	TEN	4	90	42	46.7%	549	1	6	—	2.8%	5.5	—	-34.6%	—	-8.4	—	-10.6	0	0	0	0.0	0.0%
2007	TEN		431	247	57.4%	2752	11	14			5.7							13	26	0		

2005: 41% Short   32% Mid   18% Deep   8% Bomb   YAC: 4.4 (30)   2006: 44% Short   31% Mid   17% Deep   9% Bomb   YAC: 5.1 (—)

The Titans signed Collins on August 29 of last year. Thirteen days later, just 90 minutes before kickoff against the Jets, he was announced as the team's opening-day starter. Collins was understandably out of sync against the Jets, awful against the Chargers (6-of-19, 57 yards, two picks, with Vince Young mopping up), and mediocre against the Dolphins before the curtain rose on the Vince Young era. Titans management either liked Collins's clipboard form or hated what they saw on the free-agent market, so they re-signed Collins to be Young's caddie for 2007. Collins still has the arm to be useful off the bench and should be a better player now that he has had time to break the binding on his Titans playbook.

Brodie Croyle
Height: 6-3   Weight: 205   College: Alabama   Draft: 2006/3 (85)   Born: 6-Feb-1983   Age: 24   Risk: Red

Year	Team	G	Att	Cmp	C%	Yds	TD	INT	FUM	ASR	NY/P	Rk	DVOA	Rk	DPAR	Rk	PAR	Runs	Yds	TD	DPAR	DVOA
2006	KC	2	7	3	42.9%	23	0	2	0	12.6%	1.6	—	-112.8%	—	-3.5	—	-3.6	3	-3	0	0.0	0.0%
2007	KC		452	239	52.8%	2374	15	15			4.7							23	26	0		

2006: 14% Short   71% Mid   0% Deep   14% Bomb   YAC: 0 (—)

The Chiefs' third-round pick in 2006, Croyle moves from third to second on the quarterback depth chart with the departure of Trent Green. At Alabama, Croyle was a good passer known for having a keen understanding of the offense, but the Chiefs would prefer to have him hold the clipboard for at least another year.

Daunte Culpepper
Height: 6-4   Weight: 264   College: UCF   Draft: 1999/1 (11)   Born: 28-Jan-1977   Age: 30   Risk: Red

Year	Team	G	Att	Cmp	C%	Yds	TD	INT	FUM	ASR	NY/P	Rk	DVOA	Rk	DPAR	Rk	PAR	Runs	Yds	TD	DPAR	DVOA
2004	MIN	16	548	379	69.2%	4717	39	11	9	7.5%	7.5	2	38.9%	4	136.4	2	144.4	89	406	2	11.7	7.3%
2005	MIN	7	216	139	64.4%	1564	6	12	5	13.1%	5.6	29	-19.8%	35	-6.9	36	-18.0	23	148	1	5.5	24.5%
2006	MIA	4	134	81	60.4%	929	2	3	3	14.1%	5.1	39	-11.2%	33	1.4	36	4.8	10	20	1	-0.1	-14.7%
2007	MIA		532	332	62.4%	3533	12	20			5.8							29	81	1		

2005: 47% Short   35% Mid   11% Deep   7% Bomb   YAC: 4.8 (16)   2006: 53% Short   29% Mid   11% Deep   7% Bomb   YAC: 6.7 (2)

Culpepper's health was repeatedly questioned throughout the 2006 preseason, but when the season started, he was under center. After four mediocre games, a cascade caused his shoulder to start stiffening up in practice. He never saw the field again, undergoing arthroscopic surgery on his knee in November and going on injured reserve shortly thereafter. No one's really sure whether he's actually made a throw since 2005 that didn't cause him pain. Three years removed from his brilliant 2004, and in the middle of a Trent Green/John Beck squeeze, Culpepper may never get a chance to show that he's not the same quarterback he once was.

Jay Cutler

Height: 6-4 Weight: 225 College: Vanderbilt Draft: 2006/1 (11) Born: 29-Apr-1983 Age: 24 Risk: Green

Year	Team	G	Att	Cmp	C%	Yds	TD	INT	FUM	ASR	NY/P	Rk	DVOA	Rk	DPAR	Rk	PAR	Runs	Yds	TD	DPAR	DVOA
2006	DEN	5	137	81	59.1%	1001	9	5	8	7.7%	6.1	19	-7.2%	27	3.7	32	7.1	12	18	0	-10.9	-99.9%
2007	DEN		464	283	61.1%	3174	25	17			6.1							30	66	1		
												2006:	34% Short		40% Mid		11% Deep		15% Bomb		YAC: 5.2 (14)	

Mike Shanahan traded up in the draft to select Cutler, then created a controversy by benching Jake Plummer in favor of Cutler with just five games left in the season and the Broncos still in the playoff hunt. In the end, Cutler was approximately as good as Plummer in 2006, which is to say, not very good. Still, he was just a rookie, and he seems to have developed a good rapport with Javon Walker. He should continue to improve, but Patrick Ramsey is an insurance policy if he doesn't.

Jake Delhomme

Height: 6-2 Weight: 205 College: LA-Lafayette Draft: 1998/FA Born: 10-Jan-1975 Age: 32 Risk: Yellow

Year	Team	G	Att	Cmp	C%	Yds	TD	INT	FUM	ASR	NY/P	Rk	DVOA	Rk	DPAR	Rk	PAR	Runs	Yds	TD	DPAR	DVOA
2004	CAR	16	533	310	58.2%	3886	29	15	12	5.9%	6.4	14	7.5%	14	49.4	14	71.1	25	71	1	2.4	6.6%
2005	CAR	16	435	262	60.2%	3421	24	16	12	5.8%	6.9	7	11.2%	14	47.8	10	40.3	24	31	1	-2.2	-50.2%
2006	CAR	13	431	263	61.0%	2805	17	11	6	5.2%	5.8	26	-1.6%	23	22.5	19	30.9	18	12	0	0.4	-2.4%
2007	CAR		504	305	60.5%	3286	21	16			5.8							22	39	0		
2005:	42% Short		33% Mid		15% Deep		10% Bomb		YAC: 6.1 (1)				2006:		46% Short		32% Mid		14% Deep		8% Bomb	YAC: 4.7 (25)

Joe Buck reported on a FOX pregame show in late December that Delhomme's Panthers career was over, citing Terry Bradshaw as the source of the story. Delhomme was injured at the time, and the idea that John Fox had soured on the veteran after the team's losses to the Redskins and Eagles seemed plausible enough, but the report was erroneous. An overzealous scriptwriter blew the story out of proportion, then passed it along to Buck and the crew. Delhomme is 32 and has started to acquire a Drew Bledsoe–like reputation as a gunslinger who racks up a lot of yards, but makes too many game-ruining mistakes. David Carr is waiting in the wings if Delhomme starts slow in 2007.

Trent Dilfer

Height: 6-4 Weight: 225 College: Fresno State Draft: 1994/1 (6) Born: 13-Mar-1972 Age: 35 Risk: Red

Year	Team	G	Att	Cmp	C%	Yds	TD	INT	FUM	ASR	NY/P	Rk	DVOA	Rk	DPAR	Rk	PAR	Runs	Yds	TD	DPAR	DVOA
2004	SEA	5	58	25	43.1%	333	1	3	1	5.6%	5.0	—	-36.3%	—	-6.0	—	-9.5	10	14	0	-1.2	-141.9%
2005	CLE	11	333	199	59.8%	2321	11	12	9	6.2%	6.0	20	-3.8%	25	14.9	24	7.9	20	46	0	-3.6	-72.9%
2007	SF		393	235	59.8%	2515	14	14			5.7							20	50	0		
2005:	43% Short		39% Mid		11% Deep		7% Bomb		YAC: 5.3 (10)													

Dilfer's career has three distinct chapters. He was a complete and total bust in Tampa Bay—a label he shares with Steve Young, so maybe it was more about Tampa Bay than Dilfer himself. In Baltimore, he became the patron saint of game managers and helped the Ravens win Super Bowl XXXV (discussed in detail in the Chicago chapter). For the last few years, he's been a Steve DeBerg–esque adviser of young quarterbacks in Seattle, Cleveland, and now San Francisco. He didn't take a snap in 2006, and he won't take too many in 2007, but he'll be worth a roster spot as long as Alex Smith needs his help. Dilfer might have another Matt Hasselbeck on his hands—or another Drew Brees, according to our college quarterback projection system. We can only hope that after he's done with this last phase of his NFL career, Dilfer steps into a broadcast booth somewhere. His ability to speak about the game with knowledge and humor is a skill sorely lacking on most Sunday telecasts.

Trent Edwards Height: 6-3 Weight: 223 College: Stanford   Draft: 2007/3 (92) Born: 30-Oct-1983 Age: 24   Risk: Red

Year	Team	G	Att	Cmp	C%	Yds	TD	INT	FUM	ASR	NY/P	Rk	DVOA	Rk	DPAR	Rk	PAR	Runs	Yds	TD	DPAR	DVOA
2007	BUF		436	234	55.7%	2679	17	13			5.1								34	123	1		

Edwards has a strong arm when he needs to fire passes to the sidelines, although his deep ball tends to flutter. The Stanford offensive linemen are partly to blame; they were so bad that Edwards rarely had time to set his feet on deep passes. The Bills drafted him as Plan B in case of J. P. Losman failure, and he'll likely spend the 2007 season on the bench.

Brett Favre Height: 6-2 Weight: 225 College: Southern Miss.   Draft: 1991/2 (33) Born: 10-Oct-1969 Age: 38   Risk: Green

Year	Team	G	Att	Cmp	C%	Yds	TD	INT	FUM	ASR	NY/P	Rk	DVOA	Rk	DPAR	Rk	PAR	Runs	Yds	TD	DPAR	DVOA
2004	GB	16	540	346	64.1%	4088	30	17	4	1.8%	7.3	7	22.0%	10	83.5	7	96.4	16	36	0	1.3	22.1%
2005	GB	16	607	372	61.3%	3881	20	29	10	4.1%	5.9	21	1.8%	20	40.5	15	19.6	18	62	0	-0.2	-22.2%
2006	GB	16	613	343	56.0%	3885	18	18	7	3.4%	5.9	21	4.3%	17	46.7	13	42.0	23	29	1	-4.4	-79.1%
2007	GB		577	342	59.2%	4031	23	21			6.4							19	35	1		

2005: 49% Short 30% Mid 14% Deep 7% Bomb YAC: 4.5 (25)   2006: 50% Short 30% Mid 11% Deep 9% Bomb YAC: 5.9 (5)

Conventional statistics to the contrary, Favre was not any better last year than he was during his supposedly disastrous 2005 campaign, he just did not face the same murderer's row of pass defenses. In fact, despite the constant talk about Favre's demise, this has been his level of play since 1998. Favre's passing DVOA has been between 1.0% and 7.0% seven times in the last nine years. The recent decline of the Packers has very little to do with a supposed drop-off in Favre's ability. Many fans believe Favre is no longer an above-average quarterback, but those fans have an inflated opinion of what "average" is. If you needed a quarterback for 2007 only, meaning potential would play no part in your decision, who would you rather have from the NFC? Donovan McNabb, Drew Brees, and Marc Bulger, but that's it. A repeat of last season will make him the career leader in every major quarterback counting stat, and consistent play from his defense will give him one more shot at the postseason, even without that Randy Moss trade he so desperately wanted.

A. J. Feeley Height: 6-3 Weight: 225 College: Oregon   Draft: 2001/5 (155) Born: 16-May-1977 Age: 30   Risk: Red

Year	Team	G	Att	Cmp	C%	Yds	TD	INT	FUM	ASR	NY/P	Rk	DVOA	Rk	DPAR	Rk	PAR	Runs	Yds	TD	DPAR	DVOA
2004	MIA	11	356	191	53.7%	1893	11	15	10	6.1%	4.6	36	-20.5%	33	-11.6	35	-33.0	14	13	1	-0.6	-33.3%
2006	PHI	2	38	26	68.4%	342	3	0	1	2.6%	8.2	—	60.0%	—	11.8	—	12.2	1	3	0	-0.5	-99.9%
2007	PHI		433	272	63.0%	3245	25	20			6.7							22	34	0		

2006: 80% Short 20% Mid 0% Deep 0% Bomb YAC: 7.3 (—)

Normally, Donovan McNabb's backup is the Most Popular Man in Philadelphia (MPMP). This year, Feeley will have to battle for that title with Kevin Kolb, who has youth, novelty, and the college quarterback projection system on his side. Feeley knows what Philadelphia fan adulation is like: He led the Eagles to a 4–1 record as a starter in 2002 when McNabb was injured. He then played below replacement level during his sojourn with the Dolphins, and last year's Week 17 victory against the disinterested Falcons didn't fool anyone into thinking he was anything more than a custodial backup. Chants of "Put Feeley in" will turn to chants of "Put Kolb in" by Columbus Day, assuming that McNabb isn't already hurt by then. Should McNabb stay healthy and play well all year, Feeley and Kolb will lose their MPMP status to either Phillies second baseman Chase Utley, mayor-to-be Michael Nutter, or the dude who works the midnight shift at Pat's Steaks.

Ryan Fitzpatrick Height: 6-2 Weight: 221 College: Harvard   Draft: 2005/7 (250) Born: 24-Nov-1982 Age: 25   Risk: Red

Year	Team	G	Att	Cmp	C%	Yds	TD	INT	FUM	ASR	NY/P	Rk	DVOA	Rk	DPAR	Rk	PAR	Runs	Yds	TD	DPAR	DVOA
2005	STL	4	135	76	56.3%	777	4	8	3	6.7%	5.0	39	-42.0%	44	-18.0	42	-15.7	14	64	2	1.1	-2.0%
2007	STL		459	272	59.2%	2845	18	14			5.4							48	186	2		

2005: 38% Short 33% Mid 17% Deep 12% Bomb YAC: 4.1 (36)

After a rookie year in 2005 that saw him struggle behind a patchwork offensive line and under two different coaches, Fitzpatrick was relegated to a distant third option behind Marc Bulger's durability and Gus Frerotte's experience with Scott Linehan's system. This career path normally leads to "insurance salesman," but Fitzpatrick's Harvard degree puts him instead on a route to "think tank."

Gus Frerotte

Height: 6-3　Weight: 225　College: Tulsa　　　　Draft: 1994/7 (197)　Born: 3-Jul-1971　　Age: 36　　Risk: Red

Year	Team	G	Att	Cmp	C%	Yds	TD	INT	FUM	ASR	NY/P	Rk	DVOA	Rk	DPAR	Rk	PAR	Runs	Yds	TD	DPAR	DVOA
2005	MIA	16	494	257	52.0%	2996	18	13	10	5.2%	5.4	30	-11.0%	31	4.8	29	15.1	27	61	0	0.8	-7.9%
2006	STL	1	3	1	33.3%	27	0	0	0	0.7%	9.0	—	19.3%	—	0.5	—	0.7	0	0	0	0.0	0.0%
2007	STL		461	259	56.2%	2928	14	17			5.5							21	64	0		
2005:	47% Short	30% Mid	13% Deep	10% Bomb	YAC: 5.3 (9)							2006:	0% Short	0% Mid	50% Deep	50% Bomb		YAC: 9.0 (—)				

Well, some guys are just *Football Follies* stars in the end. After 13 years in the league, Frerotte is still best-known for concussing himself by celebrating a touchdown by head-butting a concrete stadium wall in 1997. Still, he helped the Rams in 2006 by getting Marc Bulger up to speed in Scott Linehan's offense. That made him worth a roster spot. Now that Bulger has the playbook memorized, it's anyone's guess what will happen to Frerotte.

Charlie Frye

Height: 6-4　Weight: 217　College: Akron　　　　Draft: 2005/3 (67)　Born: 28-Aug-1981　Age: 26　　Risk: Red

Year	Team	G	Att	Cmp	C%	Yds	TD	INT	FUM	ASR	NY/P	Rk	DVOA	Rk	DPAR	Rk	PAR	Runs	Yds	TD	DPAR	DVOA
2005	CLE	7	164	98	59.8%	1002	4	6	6	10.9%	4.6	40	-25.0%	38	-9.3	38	-11.3	18	60	1	2.4	10.6%
2006	CLE	14	392	252	64.3%	2454	10	17	8	9.4%	5.0	41	-22.4%	38	-17.3	43	-16.9	47	215	3	2.8	-9.5%
2007	CLE		439	283	64.4%	2781	17	20			5.3							51	213	3		
2005:	40% Short	39% Mid	9% Deep	12% Bomb	YAC: 3.5 (46)							2006:	50% Short	34% Mid	8% Deep	8% Bomb		YAC: 4.4 (33)				

When Cleveland drafted Frye, it was trendy to say he was the draft's top sleeper. After all, he was a 6-foot-4 pocket passer who just looked the part of an NFL quarterback. After two professional seasons, however, it's hard to see any reason to remain optimistic about Frye. He's far too careless with the ball, both with interceptions and fumbles, and his arm has the power of a cap gun. Although 18 starts might seem too few to write him off, it seems reasonable to think that, if he had what it takes to become a solid starter, he would have shown it by now.

Jeff Garcia

Height: 6-1　Weight: 195　College: San Jose State　　　　Draft: 1999/FA　　Born: 24-Feb-1970　Age: 37　　Risk: Red

Year	Team	G	Att	Cmp	C%	Yds	TD	INT	FUM	ASR	NY/P	Rk	DVOA	Rk	DPAR	Rk	PAR	Runs	Yds	TD	DPAR	DVOA
2004	CLE	11	252	144	57.1%	1731	10	9	8	8.1%	5.9	22	-2.8%	23	11.2	24	-4.3	35	169	2	7.5	22.1%
2005	DET	6	173	102	59.0%	937	3	6	1	4.1%	5.0	38	-13.7%	34	-0.4	34	-6.1	17	51	1	-1.2	-28.6%
2006	PHI	8	188	116	61.7%	1309	10	2	6	4.1%	6.6	10	19.4%	11	27.3	18	32.1	25	87	0	0.8	-8.8%
2007	TB		429	243	56.7%	2640	18	21			5.5							43	133	1		
2005:	56% Short	26% Mid	14% Deep	4% Bomb	YAC: 4.7 (21)							2006:	50% Short	28% Mid	12% Deep	10% Bomb		YAC: 4.1 (36)				

The shooting star that was Jeff Garcia in Philadelphia is emblematic of how the Eagles operate these days. When called upon, Garcia exceeded expectations because the team adjusted its tactics better to suit him (Brian Westbrook averaged four more carries per game in Garcia's starts than in Donovan McNabb's), but when he became a free agent, the team didn't show him as much love as the fans did. Some people expect Garcia to succeed in Tampa Bay because he has what Jon Gruden's offense requires: more savvy than arm strength. Then again, these same Bucs let Brad Johnson go after the 2004 season, and he fits that description even better. Garcia should be a good backup in Tampa if he's content there, but he shouldn't threaten a healthy Chris Simms for the starting job.

David Garrard

Height: 6-1　Weight: 238　College: East Carolina　　　　Draft: 2002/4 (108)　Born: 14-Feb-1978　Age: 29　Risk: Orange

Year	Team	G	Att	Cmp	C%	Yds	TD	INT	FUM	ASR	NY/P	Rk	DVOA	Rk	DPAR	Rk	PAR	Runs	Yds	TD	DPAR	DVOA
2004	JAC	4	72	38	52.8%	374	2	1	0	7.0%	4.3	—	-9.5%	—	1.2	—	1.0	12	76	1	2.8	20.1%
2005	JAC	8	168	98	58.3%	1117	4	1	4	4.5%	6.1	17	13.2%	12	19.9	23	30.1	31	172	3	5.0	16.1%
2006	JAC	11	241	145	60.2%	1735	10	9	4	8.2%	6.2	16	-2.5%	24	12.0	25	15.9	47	250	0	8.1	18.9%
2007	JAC		443	274	61.8%	3479	21	15			6.8							64	277	2		
2005:	35% Short	40% Mid	15% Deep	10% Bomb	YAC: 3.6 (43)							2006:	45% Short	32% Mid	13% Deep	10% Bomb		YAC: 5.4 (9)				

For all the hype over Garrard as the best backup quarterback in football, he proved to be pretty average once the word "backup" was dropped from his title. Garrard is more mobile than Byron Leftwich and ranked fourth among quarterbacks in rushing DPAR last year, but his Adjusted Sack Rate was much higher than Leftwich's (5.5%). Jack Del Rio appears to have settled on Leftwich as his starter for the upcoming season, with Garrard waiting in the wings if Leftwich leaves following the 2007 campaign. Flip-flopping back and forth would almost certainly be a worse move than just picking one and sticking with him all season long. Quirky stat about quarterback-receiver partnerships: Every Jacksonville receiver with a higher DVOA on passes from Garrard in 2006 had a higher DVOA on passes from Leftwich in 2005, and vice versa.

Bruce Gradkowski

Height: 6-2 Weight: 222 College: Toledo   Draft: 2006/6 (194) Born: 27-Jan-1983 Age: 24   Risk: Red

Year	Team	G	Att	Cmp	C%	Yds	TD	INT	FUM	ASR	NY/P	Rk	DVOA	Rk	DPAR	Rk	PAR	Runs	Yds	TD	DPAR	DVOA
2006	TB	14	328	177	54.0%	1661	9	9	9	7.1%	4.3	45	-32.9%	43	-29.0	44	-26.8	41	161	0	-0.4	-18.8%
2007	TB		389	213	54.7%	2362	18	15			5.4							48	186	1		

2006: 55% Short 27% Mid 11% Deep 6% Bomb YAC: 4.6 (27)

Gradkowski seemed to do okay when he first entered the lineup. In his first three starts, he threw only one pick, and his DVOA was −8.2%. In his final eight starts, however, he threw eight picks, and his DVOA was −43.7%. In short, the league figured out what he could do and didn't have much trouble stopping it. Gradkowski has the arm and mobility to succeed, but wasn't ready to helm a complex offense with a balsa wood offensive line. He's now buried behind Chris Simms and Jeff Garcia on the depth chart, though neither one is signed past 2008. If Gradowski plays his cards right, studies hard, and shines in camp, he can stay in the Bucs plans and become a candidate to start in 2009. Still, it seems more likely that he'll become the next Shaun King, get lost in the shuffle, and spend half a decade knocking around the league.

Quinn Gray

Height: 6-3 Weight: 246 College: Florida A&M   Draft: 2002/FA   Born: 21-May-1979 Age: 28   Risk: Red

Year	Team	G	Att	Cmp	C%	Yds	TD	INT	FUM	ASR	NY/P	Rk	DVOA	Rk	DPAR	Rk	PAR	Runs	Yds	TD	DPAR	DVOA
2005	JAC	1	14	8	57.1%	100	2	0	1	4.9%	6.1	—	44.9%	—	3.0	—	4.1	3	1	0	0.4	0.0%
2006	JAC	2	22	13	59.1%	166	0	0	0	5.0%	6.7	—	53.6%	—	5.5	—	5.9	2	26	2	2.7	99.9%
2007	JAC		404	254	62.9%	3031	18	14			6.6							23	36	1		

The Jaguars signed Gray to a $1.35-million offer sheet in the offseason, scaring away potential suitors searching for a good, but affordable backup. Gray wants an opportunity to start and could be trade bait if another team's starter gets injured in camp. He's a prospect with a good arm, good size, and some mobility. He has played well in brief appearances over the past two years, but stats can be deceiving: Chiefs defenders dropped two easy interceptions in Gray's Week 17 relief stint last year. That Week 17 game is one of the few missing from game charting, which is why Gray has no stats for pass distance.

Trent Green

Height: 6-3 Weight: 217 College: Indiana   Draft: 1993/8 (222) Born: 9-Jul-1970   Age: 37   Risk: Red

Year	Team	G	Att	Cmp	C%	Yds	TD	INT	FUM	ASR	NY/P	Rk	DVOA	Rk	DPAR	Rk	PAR	Runs	Yds	TD	DPAR	DVOA
2004	KC	16	556	369	66.4%	4591	27	17	10	6.7%	7.4	3	27.7%	9	102.9	5	114.3	25	85	0	4.4	37.3%
2005	KC	16	507	317	62.5%	4014	17	10	8	6.2%	7.1	3	27.3%	7	91.1	4	102.6	35	82	0	0.4	-15.1%
2006	KC	8	198	121	61.1%	1342	7	9	5	9.5%	5.5	34	3.4%	21	15.6	22	4.9	19	59	0	-0.8	-30.5%
2007	MIA		509	304	59.8%	3038	13	16			5.2							32	110	1		

2005: 45% Short 34% Mid 15% Deep 6% Bomb YAC: 5.2 (12)   2006: 42% Short 38% Mid 15% Deep 5% Bomb YAC: 4.0 (40)

That nasty concussion Green suffered in the season opener cost him most of the season, and, although he's still got a little gas left in the tank, you have to figure 2006 was the beginning of the end. He's had a good career, but it's sad to think that "good" might have been "great" if he hadn't had to wait until his late 20s to get on the field, and if he hadn't suffered a torn ACL in the 1999 preseason. As we go to press, he still hasn't been traded to Miami, but everyone is still expecting that deal, and the projection above is based on the assumption that Green will be the starter for the Dolphins in 2007. Statistical quirk alert from the essay on fantasy football matchups later in the book: Green is the only significant quarterback of the past decade who actually has a better QB rating against the best pass defenses in football (−13.3% DVOA or lower) than he does against the worst, below-replacement-level defenses (+13.3% DVOA or higher).

Brian Griese

Height: 6-3 Weight: 215 College: Michigan   Draft: 1998/3 (91) Born: 18-Mar-1975 Age: 32 Risk: Orange

Year	Team	G	Att	Cmp	C%	Yds	TD	INT	FUM	ASR	NY/P	Rk	DVOA	Rk	DPAR	Rk	PAR	Runs	Yds	TD	DPAR	DVOA
2004	TB	11	336	233	69.3%	2632	20	12	5	6.9%	6.8	11	19.3%	11	50.4	13	60.6	30	17	0	-6.5	-93.8%
2005	TB	6	174	112	64.4%	1136	7	7	2	6.4%	5.7	25	-9.5%	30	2.8	31	1.7	13	12	0	-2.0	-70.6%
2006	CHI	6	32	18	56.3%	220	1	2	0	7.4%	5.7	—	-45.7%	—	-4.3	—	-3.9	6	-5	0	-2.4	-99.9%
2007	CHI		502	292	58.2%	3261	11	14			6.0							31	71	1		

2005: 56% Short 28% Mid 13% Deep 3% Bomb YAC: 5.1 (13)   2006: 50% Short 38% Mid 13% Deep 0% Bomb YAC: 5.7 (—)

Lovie Smith refused to turn to Griese when Rex Grossman struggled last year. The Bears made it to the Super Bowl, so it is hard to question the decision, but it would be interesting to see what might happen in 2007 if Griese were to get a fair shot at the job in training camp. (Ignore the bad stats from the final game of 2006; the Bears tossed him in during the second half when everybody else was just anxious to get to a New Year's party.) There's general agreement that Grossman has the higher upside because of his youth and superior physical tools, but Griese has had some big years. He ranked 2nd in DVOA in 2000 and 11th in 2004. His problem is consistency: He's the reverse-Saberhagen, with below-average DVOA ratings in 1999, 2001, 2003, and 2005. The Bears might have missed their chance by staying away from him in an even-numbered year.

Rex Grossman   Height: 6-1   Weight: 222   College: Florida   Draft: 2003/1 (22)   Born: 23-Aug-1980   Age: 27   Risk: Yellow

Year	Team	G	Att	Cmp	C%	Yds	TD	INT	FUM	ASR	NY/P	Rk	DVOA	Rk	DPAR	Rk	PAR	Runs	Yds	TD	DPAR	DVOA
2004	CHI	3	84	47	56.0%	607	1	3	3	6.3%	6.6	—	-18.8%	—	-2.2	—	4.2	11	48	1	-1.5	-39.9%
2005	CHI	2	39	20	51.3%	259	1	2	0	1.7%	6.3	—	-4.5%	—	1.4	—	0.1	0	0	0	0.0	0.0%
2006	CHI	16	480	262	54.6%	3193	23	20	7	4.3%	6.1	18	-11.3%	34	4.0	31	14.6	24	2	0	1.2	15.8%
2007	CHI		525	312	59.4%	3598	23	16			6.2							25	45	0		

2005: 27% Short   32% Mid   24% Deep   16% Bomb   YAC: 2.8 (—)   2006: 42% Short   32% Mid   14% Deep   12% Bomb   YAC: 4.8 (23)

We tied ourselves in knots trying to figure out a projection for Rex Grossman in 2007. KUBIAK thinks he's going to improve with experience, but it has no idea how to handle his colossal second-half implosion because, as we point out in the Chicago chapter, there isn't another quarterback in our stats whose midseason decline was as catastrophic. We tried using Grossman's 2006 stats as if the first four weeks didn't exist and ended up with the same mildly optimistic projection whether we counted September or not. Similarity scores don't help much, since very few players miss large parts of their first three years, but there are two somewhat similar quarterbacks who didn't become every-week starting quarterbacks until their third seasons. One of them was Randy Wright of the 1986 Packers (6.6 yards per pass, 53.5 completion percentage, 17 TD, 23 INT). Wright lost his job to Dan Majkowski in 1987 and was out of the league by 1989. The other similar quarterback is Jon Kitna of the 1999 Seahawks (6.8 yards per pass, 54.5 completion percentage, 23 TD, 16 INT), who has spent the last decade bouncing around the NFL as either an average starter or a very good backup. Kitna was undrafted, while Grossman still has that first-round potential, but it's not absurd to think that Grossman's career will end up looking similar.

Joey Harrington   Height: 6-4   Weight: 220   College: Oregon   Draft: 2002/1 (3)   Born: 21-Oct-1978   Age: 29   Risk: Red

Year	Team	G	Att	Cmp	C%	Yds	TD	INT	FUM	ASR	NY/P	Rk	DVOA	Rk	DPAR	Rk	PAR	Runs	Yds	TD	DPAR	DVOA
2004	DET	16	489	274	56.0%	3047	19	12	6	6.3%	5.5	28	-10.2%	28	6.5	27	17.2	48	175	0	0.3	-16.8%
2005	DET	13	330	188	57.0%	2021	12	12	7	6.3%	5.3	33	-8.3%	28	7.2	28	-4.1	24	80	0	-0.9	-26.4%
2006	MIA	11	388	223	57.5%	2236	12	15	4	3.8%	5.2	37	-9.9%	32	5.7	29	-7.3	19	24	0	-2.2	-50.6%
2007	ATL		373	213	57.1%	2205	13	15			4.8							13	31	0		

2005: 48% Short   37% Mid   10% Deep   5% Bomb   YAC: 4.8 (18)   2006: 46% Short   35% Mid   13% Deep   6% Bomb   YAC: 4.0 (39)

Thrust into the starting job four weeks into the season, Harrington played a pretty mediocre quarterback on a pretty mediocre team. There's some value to that in the same sense that an innings-eater is something you need in your pitching rotation, but Harrington wasn't exactly pushing the Dolphins towards the playoffs. Prediction: The Falcons media guide will mention that he threw for a personal-best 414 yards in Week 7 of 2006, but will not mention that it took him 62 attempts to do so.

Matt Hasselbeck   Height: 6-4   Weight: 233   College: Boston College   Draft: 1998/6 (187)   Born: 25-Sep-1975   Age: 32   Risk: Green

Year	Team	G	Att	Cmp	C%	Yds	TD	INT	FUM	ASR	NY/P	Rk	DVOA	Rk	DPAR	Rk	PAR	Runs	Yds	TD	DPAR	DVOA
2004	SEA	14	474	279	58.9%	3382	22	15	4	5.6%	6.4	13	10.3%	13	52.5	12	57.7	27	90	1	0.8	-7.6%
2005	SEA	16	449	294	65.5%	3455	24	9	4	5.1%	7.0	6	28.4%	6	88.4	5	100.1	36	124	1	4.2	14.4%
2006	SEA	12	371	210	56.6%	2442	18	15	3	8.3%	5.5	32	-8.8%	30	7.3	28	12.4	18	110	0	4.2	41.8%
2007	SEA		540	337	62.3%	3822	21	16			6.1							47	156	1		

2005: 41% Short   39% Mid   13% Deep   7% Bomb   YAC: 3.9 (42)   2006: 36% Short   41% Mid   15% Deep   8% Bomb   YAC: 3.5 (43)

Shaun Alexander wasn't the only one affected by the decline of the Seattle offensive line in 2006. Hasselbeck was the NFC's best quarterback in 2005, but last year he spent a lot of plays running for his life instead of going through his reads. He threw six fewer touchdowns and six more interceptions than he did in 2005 and took ten more sacks, despite playing four fewer games because of a midseason knee injury. (The line and his knee also made him KUBIAK's biggest miss in 2006; sorry about that, folks.) As Alexander did, Hasselbeck rebounded toward the end of the season and in the playoffs as the offense started to come together. He's got a better chance of returning to form in 2007 than most, if his health is not an issue, but he did have offseason surgery to repair a torn labrum in his nonthrowing shoulder.

Kelly Holcomb Height: 6-2 Weight: 212 College: Mid. Tenn. State Draft: 1996/FA Born: 9-Jul-1973 Age: 34 Risk: Red

Year	Team	G	Att	Cmp	C%	Yds	TD	INT	FUM	ASR	NY/P	Rk	DVOA	Rk	DPAR	Rk	PAR	Runs	Yds	TD	DPAR	DVOA
2004	CLE	4	87	59	67.8%	737	7	5	0	5.1%	7.7	—	21.4%	—	13.7	—	11.4	3	-2	0	-2.7	-48.8%
2005	BUF	10	230	155	67.4%	1509	10	8	11	7.6%	5.4	31	-11.5%	32	1.8	32	1.7	18	11	1	-2.7	-53.8%
2007	PHI		434	253	58.2%	2684	17	21			5.6							13	28	0		

2005: 64% Short 24% Mid 9% Deep 3% Bomb YAC: 5.5 (7)

That projection says Philadelphia, but there's a very good chance that Holcomb will be elsewhere in 2007. Buffalo sent him to Philadelphia in the Takeo Spikes–Darwin Walker deal, but Kevin Kolb makes him superfluous. He'll end up on a team that needs a veteran with enough experience that he could fall out of bed and be ready to run an offense within five minutes. As a starter in 2005, two-thirds of Holcomb's passes traveled five yards or less through the air, the highest percentage of short tosses in the league.

Damon Huard Height: 6-3 Weight: 215 College: Washington Draft: 1997/FA Born: 9-Jul-1973 Age: 34 Risk: Red

Year	Team	G	Att	Cmp	C%	Yds	TD	INT	FUM	ASR	NY/P	Rk	DVOA	Rk	DPAR	Rk	PAR	Runs	Yds	TD	DPAR	DVOA
2006	KC	10	244	148	60.7%	1878	11	1	8	5.3%	6.8	8	34.5%	2	52.0	9	56.4	9	9	0	-5.4	-99.9%
2007	KC		465	268	57.6%	2984	16	18			5.6							14	32	0		

2006: 47% Short 29% Mid 21% Deep 3% Bomb YAC: 5.4 (10)

Is this finally the year, after 11 seasons in the league, that Huard is going to be his team's opening-day starter? It should be. Huard's DVOA was better than Trent Green's by a huge margin last season, and Brodie Croyle sure isn't ready. Unfortunately for Huard, this long-awaited starting job comes with a front-row seat at the three-ring circus of offensive struggle: Tony Gonzalez and Eddie Kennison aging, Larry Johnson breaking down due to overuse, and the offensive line collapsing without its veteran framework.

Tarvaris Jackson Height: 6-2 Weight: 225 College: Alabama State Draft: 2006/2 (64) Born: 21-Apr-1983 Age: 24 Risk: Red

Year	Team	G	Att	Cmp	C%	Yds	TD	INT	FUM	ASR	NY/P	Rk	DVOA	Rk	DPAR	Rk	PAR	Runs	Yds	TD	DPAR	DVOA
2006	MIN	4	81	47	58.0%	475	2	4	3	8.7%	5.0	—	-44.6%	—	-11.9	—	-14.7	15	77	1	0.6	-9.5%
2007	MIN		489	286	58.5%	3363	16	16			6.0							101	607	0		

2006: 52% Short 17% Mid 22% Deep 9% Bomb YAC: 6.5 (—)

The only thing we know right now is that Jackson was not ready to contribute last season. He was unsure when to pass and when to scramble when his first option was not open, a sadly common experience for Vikings quarterbacks. Despite his lack of track record, he may be handed the reins to a team with a playoff-caliber defense. The scariest part of his performance projection is his very low college completion percentage. The windows are a lot smaller in the NFL than they were at Alabama State, and, sadly, his receivers may not be a whole lot better. Jackson is a solid athlete, but he won't be able to survive on his dynamic rushing skills alone.

Brad Johnson Height: 6-5 Weight: 226 College: Florida State Draft: 1992/9 (227) Born: 13-Sep-1968 Age: 39 Risk: Red

Year	Team	G	Att	Cmp	C%	Yds	TD	INT	FUM	ASR	NY/P	Rk	DVOA	Rk	DPAR	Rk	PAR	Runs	Yds	TD	DPAR	DVOA
2004	TB	4	103	65	63.1%	674	3	3	2	8.6%	5.6	25	-18.2%	31	-2.4	31	-1.6	5	23	0	1.1	26.4%
2005	MIN	15	294	184	62.6%	1885	12	4	5	7.2%	5.6	27	18.1%	10	39.2	16	31.4	18	53	0	1.5	11.8%
2006	MIN	15	439	270	61.5%	2750	9	15	9	5.9%	5.4	35	-12.3%	36	1.7	35	1.0	29	82	1	-0.3	-18.9%
2007	DAL		419	252	60.1%	2411	11	17			5.0							23	69	1		

2005: 54% Short 26% Mid 10% Deep 10% Bomb YAC: 4.9 (15)   2006: 36% Short 48% Mid 11% Deep 5% Bomb YAC: 4.9 (19)

The veteran quarterback helped salvage the Vikings season in 2005 and was supposed to provide stability for a new coaching staff in 2006. Instead, he seemed to hit a wall. What was most troubling was that, despite his experience and veteran leadership, he made inexcusable mistakes. A potent pass rush seemed to genuinely scare him. He is now 39 and has moved to Dallas where he will hold a clipboard behind Tony Romo. It is very impressive that a player with his limited physical skills will be on an NFL roster for a 16th season, but the Cowboys don't want him actually playing in games.

Doug Johnson Height: 6-2 Weight: 225 College: Florida Draft: 2000/FA Born: 27-Oct-1977 Age: 30 Risk: Red

Year	Team	G	Att	Cmp	C%	Yds	TD	INT	FUM	ASR	NY/P	Rk	DVOA	Rk	DPAR	Rk	PAR	Runs	Yds	TD	DPAR	DVOA
2004	TEN	3	12	6	50.0%	68	0	0	0	9.7%	4.8	—	6.9%	—	1.1	—	0.6	2	-2	0	0.0	0.0%
2007	CIN		421	257	61.1%	3037	19	16			6.3							22	44	1		

Johnson couldn't beat out Anthony Wright for the job as Carson Palmer's backup in 2006, but with Wright gone to New York, Johnson will be the primary backup in 2007; he's no great shakes, but a rusty JUGS machine would be a fantasy sleeper in this offense.

Jon Kitna Height: 6-2 Weight: 220 College: Central Washington Draft: 1997/FA Born: 21-Sep-1972 Age: 35 Risk: Green

Year	Team	G	Att	Cmp	C%	Yds	TD	INT	FUM	ASR	NY/P	Rk	DVOA	Rk	DPAR	Rk	PAR	Runs	Yds	TD	DPAR	DVOA
2004	CIN	4	104	61	58.7%	623	5	4	2	4.3%	5.2	30	5.9%	16	8.7	26	0.8	10	42	0	1.1	10.0%
2005	CIN	3	29	17	58.6%	99	0	2	0	7.4%	2.9	—	-88.4%	—	-10.6	—	-10.5	2	14	0	1.2	0.0%
2006	DET	16	596	372	62.4%	4208	21	22	11	9.6%	5.8	24	4.6%	16	49.8	11	38.4	34	156	2	-1.9	-29.3%
2007	DET		567	341	60.1%	3743	18	20			5.5							47	165	2		
2005:	100% Short	0% Mid	0% Deep	0% Bomb		YAC: 3.0 (—)						2006:	46% Short	31% Mid	17% Deep	6% Bomb			YAC: 4.7 (26)			

When you start every game at quarterback for a team that goes 3–13, you are bound to receive criticism. When you throw 22 interceptions and lose 9 fumbles, that criticism sharpens. A closer look, however, reveals that Kitna had an admirable season. He played with the league's worst running attack, a sieve for an offensive line, and a defense that always made the offense play catch-up. Kitna also had only one receiver any other team in the league wanted before the season. Despite these obstacles, Kitna ranked a solid 11th in DPAR. The sacks are a problem, but, in this case, they really are a function of the offensive line and offensive system. Kitna never took sacks at anything close to his 2006 rate before.

The Detroit media criticized Kitna for poor play in the fourth quarter, but Kitna's fourth-quarter performance was in line with his performance overall. The problem was that Kitna dominated the third quarter (35.6% DVOA), so when he returned to earth in the fourth quarter (−5.6% DVOA) it looked like a collapse. Kitna is not the problem in Detroit, but he does turn 35 this season, and it is doubtful that he will be part of the solution when the Lions are ready to compete. On the other hand, it's doubtful the Lions will ever be ready to compete.

Kevin Kolb Height: 6-3 Weight: 218 College: Houston Draft: 2007/2 (36) Born: 24-Aug-1984 Age: 23 Risk: Orange

Year	Team	G	Att	Cmp	C%	Yds	TD	INT	FUM	ASR	NY/P	Rk	DVOA	Rk	DPAR	Rk	PAR	Runs	Yds	TD	DPAR	DVOA
2007	PHI		476	274	57.5%	3593	29	15			6.7							37	76	2		

He was a surprise pick, but a surprise is not a mistake. Our projection system loves Kolb: He's a four-year starter from a Division I program with an excellent collegiate completion percentage (61.6 percent) who scouted well enough to warrant a high draft pick—according to reports on draft day, multiple teams were considering him in the second round. Our projection system doesn't know he's backing up Donovan McNabb. It doesn't know he played in shotgun offenses in high school and college. It doesn't know anything about David Klingler or Andre Ware. That's both the advantage and disadvantage of an empirical system: It's incapable of considering outside factors, but it's also unfettered by meaningless baggage and won't penalize a prospect for what another guy from the same college did 20 years ago.

Kolb's hobbies include wild hog hunting. Kolb and two dogs (Black Mouth Curs) pursue the 150-pound animals. After the dogs corner a hog, Kolb moves in with a 12-inch Bowie knife. "It's a little bit dangerous, but as long as you know what you're doing, you'll be all right," Kolb told the *Philadelphia Daily News* after the draft. In Philly, such formative experiences are considered excellent practice for dealing with talk radio host Howard Eskin, though the Eagles will probably make Kolb sign a "no hunting wild animals with a Bowie knife" clause.

It will be about five years before anyone will know how good Kolb really is, but mark it down now: he's going to be good.

Byron Leftwich Height: 6-5 Weight: 245 College: Marshall Draft: 2003/1 (7) Born: 14-Jan-1980 Age: 27 Risk: Red

Year	Team	G	Att	Cmp	C%	Yds	TD	INT	FUM	ASR	NY/P	Rk	DVOA	Rk	DPAR	Rk	PAR	Runs	Yds	TD	DPAR	DVOA
2004	JAC	14	441	267	60.5%	2941	15	10	2	5.7%	6.1	18	2.3%	18	30.2	17	43.6	39	148	2	0.1	-17.6%
2005	JAC	11	302	175	57.9%	2123	15	5	7	6.4%	6.3	13	19.3%	9	43.5	13	43.9	31	67	2	3.0	6.2%
2006	JAC	6	183	108	59.0%	1159	7	5	2	5.5%	5.8	25	-8.8%	29	3.6	33	13.5	25	41	2	-2.3	-43.5%
2007	JAC		497	315	63.3%	3780	23	10			6.8							39	94	1		
2005:	42% Short	29% Mid	19% Deep	11% Bomb		YAC: 4.3 (33)						2006:	50% Short	31% Mid	15% Deep	4% Bomb			YAC: 5.3 (13)			

Jack Del Rio's tune this offseason was somewhere between the Temptations's "Ain't Too Proud to Beg" and Otis Redding's "Security." After making a debacle of the Jaguars' quarterback situation in 2006, Del Rio was left with the proverbial egg on his face when a slimmed down Leftwich (it always happens after you dump them, right?) reemerged as the best choice for the starting job after recovering from an ankle injury. There's a ton to like here: Leftwich has lost 25 pounds, his

(continued next page)

Byron Leftwich (*continued*)

receivers (particularly Marcedes Lewis and Matt Jones) should improve in 2007, opposing defenses will have to bring safeties up to take on Maurice Jones-Drew, and the average Pro Bowl quarterback makes it to Hawaii for the first time at the age of 27. Our team projection system absolutely loves the Jaguars, and, by extension, Leftwich. Worried about his injury history, the Jaguars decided not to sign him to an extension on his original five-year rookie contract. It's very conceivable that Leftwich could enter the 2008 offseason in the same bargaining position as Drew Brees in 2006—only without a torn labrum.

Matt Leinart Height: 6-5 Weight: 225 College: USC Draft: 2006/1 (10) Born: 11-May-1983 Age: 24 Risk: Yellow

Year	Team	G	Att	Cmp	C%	Yds	TD	INT	FUM	ASR	NY/P	Rk	DVOA	Rk	DPAR	Rk	PAR	Runs	Yds	TD	DPAR	DVOA
2006	ARI	12	377	214	56.8%	2547	11	12	8	5.7%	6.1	20	4.0%	19	28.4	16	24.9	22	49	2	1.4	2.0%
2007	ARI		542	317	58.5%	3626	18	18			5.9							31	85	1		

2006:   44% Short   34% Mid   13% Deep   9% Bomb   YAC: 4.1 (38)

After watching the Cardinals in the preseason, one had to wonder if Leinart would lead the Cardinals in rushing yards, so beset was he by defenders who found no challenge in Arizona's offensive line. The third game in which he saw regular season NFL action was Arizona's incredible *Monday Night Football* loss to the Bears. Leinart's performance against a Chicago defense that still had Tommie Harris and Mike Brown was a revelation. Content to slice and dice Ron and Lovie's Cover-2 until the Arizona coaches made him stop, he showed maturity far beyond his years. Leinart had his ups and downs after that, and he'll have his ups and downs this year as Ken Whisenhunt and Russ Grimm reconstitute the Arizona offense. By the turn of the decade, however, he'll be one of the top five quarterbacks in the game.

Cleo Lemon Height: 6-2 Weight: 215 College: Arkansas State Draft: 2001/FA Born: 16-Aug-1979 Age: 28 Risk: Red

Year	Team	G	Att	Cmp	C%	Yds	TD	INT	FUM	ASR	NY/P	Rk	DVOA	Rk	DPAR	Rk	PAR	Runs	Yds	TD	DPAR	DVOA
2006	MIA	4	68	38	55.9%	412	2	1	0	7.6%	5.5	—	14.9%	—	8.4	—	7.5	3	7	0	-0.7	-67.7%
2007	MIA		428	239	55.9%	2477	14	15			5.0							19	43	0		

2006:   54% Short   29% Mid   14% Deep   4% Bomb   YAC: 3.2 (—)

Lemon got to play the better part of two full games at the end of the season, but struggled to make reads, and threw mostly checkdowns. Joe Theismann insinuated that he was a "playmaker" for obvious reasons. Cam Cameron worked with Lemon in San Diego and wasn't upset when Lemon was traded away. Cameron gave Lemon suggestions on improving his mechanics before April minicamp, but Lemon showed up without having implemented any of Cameron's suggestions. That about covers Lemon's future.

J. P. Losman Height: 6-2 Weight: 217 College: Tulane Draft: 2004/1 (22) Born: 12-Mar-1981 Age: 26 Risk: Green

Year	Team	G	Att	Cmp	C%	Yds	TD	INT	FUM	ASR	NY/P	Rk	DVOA	Rk	DPAR	Rk	PAR	Runs	Yds	TD	DPAR	DVOA
2004	BUF	4	5	3	60.0%	32	0	1	1	17.7%	5.0	—	-167.4%	—	-4.9	—	-5.2	2	15	0	0.7	36.9%
2005	BUF	9	228	113	49.6%	1340	8	8	7	9.7%	4.5	43	-44.4%	45	-31.3	44	-24.9	31	154	0	4.8	17.3%
2006	BUF	16	429	268	62.5%	3051	19	14	13	9.4%	5.7	27	-2.8%	25	21.3	20	13.3	38	140	1	-4.3	-37.3%
2007	BUF		461	269	58.3%	2992	19	14			5.4							43	159	1		

2005:   41% Short   40% Mid   8% Deep   11% Bomb   YAC: 5.4 (8)   2006:   44% Short   34% Mid   12% Deep   9% Bomb   YAC: 4.7 (24)

Losman's resurgence in 2006 mirrored the breakout campaign of wide receiver Lee Evans. It's hard to pinpoint who was the chicken and who was the egg, but the Bills won't lose any sleep over the quandary. The slightly goofy Losman can be tough to rattle: Nine of his 19 touchdown passes came against the blitz, and his yards per attempt went from 6.7 against four or fewer rushers, to 7.9 against five rushers, to 8.8 against six or more. His touchdown percentage similarly increased against an increasing rush—from 3.4 percent to 6.6 percent to 10 percent—and he got first downs on one-third of his passes against six or more rushers. That lack of fear also leads Losman to throw into double coverage more often than most other quarterbacks, which is good when the intended receiver is Evans and bad when the intended receiver is anyone else.

Eli Manning Height: 6-4 Weight: 218 College: Mississippi Draft: 2004/1 (1) Born: 3-Jan-1981 Age: 26 Risk: Green

Year	Team	G	Att	Cmp	C%	Yds	TD	INT	FUM	ASR	NY/P	Rk	DVOA	Rk	DPAR	Rk	PAR	Runs	Yds	TD	DPAR	DVOA
2004	NYG	9	197	95	48.2%	1043	6	9	3	5.5%	4.6	37	-28.4%	37	-13.3	36	-22.1	6	35	0	1.9	70.2%
2005	NYG	16	557	294	52.8%	3762	24	17	9	5.2%	6.1	19	1.8%	21	36.9	18	41.2	29	80	1	2.7	8.3%
2006	NYG	16	522	301	57.7%	3244	24	18	9	5.1%	5.6	31	-1.1%	22	27.9	17	29.9	25	21	0	-3.9	-71.2%
2007	NYG		505	300	59.4%	3219	21	14			5.8							18	39	0		

2005:   39% Short   38% Mid   15% Deep   8% Bomb   YAC: 4.7 (19)   2006:   47% Short   33% Mid   13% Deep   7% Bomb   YAC: 4.5 (28)

Last year we projected Eli Manning to complete 300 passes in 540 attempts (55.6 completion percentage) for 3,640 yards, with 22 touchdowns and 17 interceptions. We weren't far off. The good news is that Manning's completion percentage has increased in each of his first three seasons. The bad news is that the former first-overall pick has fallen behind the rest of the 2004 first-round draft class. Last season, Philip Rivers ranked 5th in DPAR and 4th in DVOA. Ben Roethlisberger, who already has one Super Bowl ring, finished 14th in DPAR and 15th in DVOA, easily his worst season as a professional. A common explanation for the early successes of Rivers and Roethlisberger is that their teams have strong running games and solid pass protection. According to our Adjusted Line Yards measure, the Giants were the 4th-best run-blocking unit in the league. In terms of Adjusted Sack Rate, New York's offensive line ranked 7th, allowing only 25 sacks on the year. Granted, the Giants need more consistency from their pass catchers, but it's not as though the Chargers and the Steelers boast a stable of big-play wideouts. Manning is a capable NFL quarterback, but he will never be his older brother, and he will never be worth the bounty that the Giants paid the Chargers for his services.

Peyton Manning   Height: 6-5   Weight: 230   College: Tennessee   Draft: 1998/1 (1)   Born: 24-Mar-1976   Age: 31   Risk: Blue

Year	Team	G	Att	Cmp	C%	Yds	TD	INT	FUM	ASR	NY/P	Rk	DVOA	Rk	DPAR	Rk	PAR	Runs	Yds	TD	DPAR	DVOA
2004	IND	16	497	336	67.6%	4557	49	10	5	3.2%	8.7	1	62.8%	1	170.1	1	189.2	25	38	0	0.8	-3.1%
2005	IND	16	453	305	67.3%	3747	28	10	5	3.4%	7.8	1	41.7%	1	112.5	1	130.0	33	45	0	-5.9	-74.8%
2006	IND	16	557	362	65.0%	4397	31	9	2	3.2%	7.6	2	58.0%	1	174.8	1	179.8	23	36	4	4.5	50.5%
2007	IND		531	344	64.9%	4263	31	13			7.4							18	35	1		
2005:	41% Short		38% Mid		13% Deep		7% Bomb			YAC: 4.6 (22)				2006:	43% Short		35% Mid		13% Deep		9% Bomb		YAC: 3.9 (42)

"Choke" is a four-letter word, an angry little expletive thrown around by individuals who need to make themselves feel superior to professional athletes. When a columnist, blogger, or talk-radio caller calls a player such as Peyton Manning a "choker," he's betraying his ignorance of the sport and insulting not just Manning, but the opponents who ostensibly stood around and waited for him to panic instead of beating him in a toe-to-toe battle. If professional athletes ever choke, it's a rare phenomenon, because few athletes who get the yips in pressure situations would ever survive the high school state finals, college bowl games, and training camp battles that define a player's early career. It was immature and petty for anyone to suggest that Manning, one of the most gifted and dedicated athletes of our generation, suddenly lost his marbles when he reached the playoffs, or the Championship Game, or when he saw Bill Belichick or Bill Cowher scowling at him from the opposite sideline. Yet Manning endured this sort of brain-dead criticism through halftime of Super Bowl XLI.

Now that Manning has his ring, the same geniuses who labeled him a choker will turn their attention to Donovan McNabb, Matt Hasselbeck, or some other star who hasn't hoisted the Lombardi Trophy yet. They'll trot out the same tired arguments and lazy insults. In doing so, they'll slowly erode the joy that should be at the core of sports fandom. Fans should celebrate victors for their accomplishments, not deride losers for their perceived shortcomings. Reaching a championship game should be perceived as an accomplishment, not a mere prelude to national-scale failure. Great players such as Manning, who spend years mastering their craft in pursuit of a title, should be held up as role models, not ridiculed. A player should not be ashamed of falling one step short of a championship, but those who earn money writing or talking about sports should be ashamed whenever they take the lazy way out by appealing to their lowest-denominator readers and listeners.

Jamie Martin   Height: 6-2   Weight: 205   College: Weber State   Draft: 1994/FA   Born: 8-Feb-1970   Age: 37   Risk: Red

Year	Team	G	Att	Cmp	C%	Yds	TD	INT	FUM	ASR	NY/P	Rk	DVOA	Rk	DPAR	Rk	PAR	Runs	Yds	TD	DPAR	DVOA
2004	STL	1	30	16	53.3%	188	0	0	0	6.3%	5.4	—	31.4%	—	5.8	—	3.6	0	0	0	0.0	0.0%
2005	STL	8	177	124	70.1%	1277	5	7	2	5.9%	6.4	11	-9.1%	29	3.2	30	7.0	9	6	0	-0.1	0.0%
2006	NO	16	24	16	66.7%	208	1	1	3	16.4%	6.4	—	-51.9%	—	-4.5	—	-5.0	0	0	0	0.0	0.0%
2007	NO		448	271	60.5%	3179	18	18			6.5							17	33	0		
2005:	56% Short		25% Mid		13% Deep		6% Bomb			YAC: 4.8 (17)												

Drew Brees hasn't exactly avoided injury over the course of his career; if he goes down, Martin gets the keys to New Orleans's high-powered attack. If this strikes you as a particularly good idea, we might ask you how Thanksgiving with Mr. Martin was last year.

Josh McCown Height: 6-4 Weight: 212 College: Sam Houston St. Draft: 2002/3 (81) Born: 4-Jul-1979 Age: 28 Risk: Red

Year	Team	G	Att	Cmp	C%	Yds	TD	INT	FUM	ASR	NY/P	Rk	DVOA	Rk	DPAR	Rk	PAR	Runs	Yds	TD	DPAR	DVOA
2004	ARI	14	408	233	57.1%	2511	11	10	12	5.9%	5.1	32	-7.6%	26	10.5	25	9.1	36	112	2	0.3	-15.6%
2005	ARI	9	270	163	60.4%	1836	9	11	5	6.0%	6.1	16	-2.5%	24	13.1	25	13.5	29	139	0	-3.6	-36.8%
2007	OAK		440	256	58.1%	2507	14	18			4.4							45	174	1		
2005:	45% Short		31% Mid		14% Deep		10% Bomb		YAC: 4.6 (23)													

McCown thought he was signing with Detroit for a chance to compete for the starting job and possibly put up big numbers in a Mike Martz offense. The competition was short-lived, with Jon Kitna almost immediately being named the starter. Instead, McCown only got on the field as a slot receiver, with two catches for 18 yards, then was dealt to Oakland with Mike Williams for a fourth-round pick. JaMarcus Russell will be much better off in the long run if he can sit on the sidelines and learn the offense while the Raiders' offensive line gets McCown killed instead.

Donovan McNabb Height: 6-2 Weight: 226 College: Syracuse Draft: 1999/1 (2) Born: 25-Jan-1976 Age: 31 Risk: Yellow

Year	Team	G	Att	Cmp	C%	Yds	TD	INT	FUM	ASR	NY/P	Rk	DVOA	Rk	DPAR	Rk	PAR	Runs	Yds	TD	DPAR	DVOA
2004	PHI	15	469	300	64.0%	3875	31	8	8	5.7%	7.3	6	35.8%	5	107.1	4	102.9	41	220	3	8.7	40.2%
2005	PHI	9	357	211	59.1%	2507	16	9	10	5.8%	6.1	18	-0.4%	22	23.2	21	30.6	25	55	1	-0.6	-26.0%
2006	PHI	10	316	180	57.0%	2647	18	6	3	7.1%	7.5	4	25.5%	8	56.7	7	68.4	32	212	3	11.1	57.9%
2007	PHI		511	315	61.8%	4221	28	14			7.4							64	242	3		
2005:	53% Short		30% Mid		10% Deep		8% Bomb		YAC: 5.9 (2)			2006:	48% Short		29% Mid		13% Deep		11% Bomb		YAC: 7.4 (1)	

McNabb has been a good quarterback for most of his career, but in the last few years he has blossomed into one of the league's best. Alas, in his eight NFL seasons he has played all 16 games only three times, most recently in 2003. He runs less than he did early in his career, but his offensive line is still only average in pass protection. Given the pass-wackiness of Andy Reid's offense, that means he takes an above-average number of sacks. McNabb's two best seasons, 2004 and 2006, coincided with the acquisitions of number-one receivers Terrell Owens (before he went all T.O. in 2005) and Donte' Stallworth, respectively. The former was the only season in which he completed more than 60 percent of his passes (64 percent, to be exact), and the latter saw him throw for a career-high 8.38 yards per attempt despite completing just 57 percent of his passes. According to our charting stats, that high yards-per-attempt figure was in part the result of McNabb's throwing an increased number of deep balls and leading the league in yards after the catch. If Kevin Curtis can be the recipient of those passes in place of Stallworth, and Reggie Brown develops into a very good possession-plus receiver, McNabb could combine 2004's efficiency with 2006's explosiveness to turn in an MVP-type season in 2007. If he stays healthy. If.

Steve McNair Height: 6-2 Weight: 235 College: Alcorn State Draft: 1995/1 (3) Born: 14-Feb-1973 Age: 34 Risk: Yellow

Year	Team	G	Att	Cmp	C%	Yds	TD	INT	FUM	ASR	NY/P	Rk	DVOA	Rk	DPAR	Rk	PAR	Runs	Yds	TD	DPAR	DVOA
2004	TEN	8	215	129	60.0%	1343	8	9	5	6.3%	5.5	27	-18.9%	32	-6.0	32	1.9	23	128	1	3.9	18.6%
2005	TEN	14	476	292	61.3%	3161	16	11	6	3.7%	6.2	14	11.2%	13	51.3	9	60.6	32	139	1	4.5	10.6%
2006	BAL	16	468	295	63.0%	3050	16	12	7	3.0%	6.2	15	10.9%	13	47.9	12	54.5	45	119	1	6.7	34.5%
2007	BAL		494	301	61.1%	3444	21	16			6.5							39	124	1		
2005:	49% Short		35% Mid		9% Deep		7% Bomb		YAC: 5.0 (14)			2006:	49% Short		38% Mid		8% Deep		5% Bomb		YAC: 4.3 (34)	

While his overall performance in 2006 painted McNair as a middle-of-the-pack player, there is little doubt that he injected the Baltimore offense with the confidence it has lacked since, well, forever. McNair surprised everyone by staying healthy enough to start all 16 games for the first time in four seasons. He also adapted himself well to Baltimore's talent, showering tight end Todd Heap with a team leading 145 passes, while resisting the urge to overuse comfort blanket Derrick Mason at the expense of 1-A receiver Mark Clayton (each saw exactly 112 balls). McNair got better as the year went along, with at least 3.7 DPAR in all but two games after the bye week. One was the Week 15 game in which he cut his hand and had to leave the game after just four passes. The other, unfortunately, was the playoff game against the Colts, in which McNair turned the ball over three times and everything good about the Ravens offense went out the window.

Kyle Orton Height: 6-4 Weight: 226 College: Purdue Draft: 2005/4 (106) Born: 14-Nov-1982 Age: 25 Risk: Red

Year	Team	G	Att	Cmp	C%	Yds	TD	INT	FUM	ASR	NY/P	Rk	DVOA	Rk	DPAR	Rk	PAR	Runs	Yds	TD	DPAR	DVOA
2005	CHI	15	368	190	51.6%	1869	9	13	—	7.7%	4.2	45	-36.0%	41	-38.9	45	-45.0	24	44	0	-4.3	-99.9%
2007	CHI		455	257	56.5%	2771	17	18			5.6							31	79	1		
2005:	52% Short		28% Mid		12% Deep		9% Bomb		YAC: 3.6 (44)														

The bearded one returned to his rightful place on the bench following some disastrous numbers as a rookie in 2005. In a league that has found a long-term place for Jamie Martin, Chris Weinke, and Doug Johnson, Orton should be able to hold onto his roster spot. If *Deadspin* ever forms a team that plays colleges in the preseason, à la basketball's Upper Deck or Athletes in Action teams, Orton will be their quarterback. Their drunk, sloppy quarterback.

Carson Palmer Height: 6-5 Weight: 230 College: USC   Draft: 2003/1 (1) Born: 27-Dec-1979 Age: 27 Risk: Green

Year	Team	G	Att	Cmp	C%	Yds	TD	INT	FUM	ASR	NY/P	Rk	DVOA	Rk	DPAR	Rk	PAR	Runs	Yds	TD	DPAR	DVOA
2004	CIN	14	432	263	60.9%	2897	18	18	2	5.0%	6.0	20	7.2%	15	39.0	15	15.7	18	47	1	3.5	51.2%
2005	CIN	16	509	345	67.8%	3836	32	12	5	3.5%	7.0	5	34.5%	2	108.3	2	108.1	34	41	1	1.6	-2.6%
2006	CIN	16	520	324	62.3%	4035	28	13	15	6.0%	6.9	7	27.6%	6	97.3	4	83.4	26	37	0	1.0	-8.7%
2007	CIN		526	337	64.0%	4146	29	14			7.0							20	39	0		

2005: 43% Short 38% Mid 12% Deep 7% Bomb   YAC: 3.9 (41)   2006: 39% Short 37% Mid 14% Deep 10% Bomb   YAC: 4.4 (31)

That Palmer was able to line up under center in Week 1 had to be a pleasant surprise for the Bengals. That he was able to remain healthy for 16 starts despite a slew of offensive line injuries had to be a major relief. Palmer led the league with 56 recorded quarterback hits—nobody else was above 50—and also had a career-high 32 sacks. Perhaps that pounding was the reason why Palmer seemed to fade in December (six touchdowns, five interceptions, only 56 percent completions). His overall performance was enough to reclaim his place among the league's elite QBs. In other words, it wasn't Carson's fault that the Bengals missed the playoffs. If KUBIAK is correct, he won't be to blame if the team falters again this year.

Chad Pennington Height: 6-3 Weight: 225 College: Marshall   Draft: 2000/1 (18) Born: 26-Jun-1976 Age: 31 Risk: Yellow

Year	Team	G	Att	Cmp	C%	Yds	TD	INT	FUM	ASR	NY/P	Rk	DVOA	Rk	DPAR	Rk	PAR	Runs	Yds	TD	DPAR	DVOA
2004	NYJ	13	370	242	65.4%	2673	16	9	5	4.4%	6.6	12	31.6%	6	77.2	8	60.5	34	126	1	5.3	15.5%
2005	NYJ	3	83	49	59.0%	530	2	3	7	9.0%	4.8	—	-26.8%	—	-5.1	—	-7.0	6	27	0	1.7	0.0%
2006	NYJ	16	485	313	64.5%	3352	17	16	7	5.8%	6.3	12	10.2%	14	52.3	8	43.8	35	109	0	2.5	-1.4%
2007	NYJ		453	292	64.5%	3192	20	14			6.2							36	106	1		

2005: 39% Short 42% Mid 12% Deep 7% Bomb   YAC: 4.5 (—)   2006: 48% Short 35% Mid 12% Deep 5% Bomb   YAC: 4.4 (32)

Pennington hushed any talk of a quarterback competition early in camp and put up statistics similar to those from earlier in his career, but his formerly average arm is now even weaker. He threw fewer deep balls than anyone except David Carr in 2006, and that was only because a brain implant shocked Carr whenever he dropped back more than two steps. It was fascinating to watch how Jets offensive coordinator Brian Schottenheimer would spend an entire game setting up opposing defenses for the one deep out Pennington had in him, much as other teams do for the play-action pass. Late in the third quarter or early in the fourth quarter of each game, Pennington would suddenly launch the ball 30 yards after 40 minutes worth of slants, screens, and curls. Pennington can be a productive quarterback at this level, but not if his arm strength drops any further (and it will, inevitably, if only because of age). The Kellen Clemens era may come sooner than anyone expects.

Jake Plummer Height: 6-2 Weight: 197 College: Arizona State   Draft: 1997/2 (42) Born: 19-Dec-1974 Age: 32 Risk: Red

Year	Team	G	Att	Cmp	C%	Yds	TD	INT	FUM	ASR	NY/P	Rk	DVOA	Rk	DPAR	Rk	PAR	Runs	Yds	TD	DPAR	DVOA
2004	DEN	16	521	303	58.2%	4089	27	20	4	3.8%	7.4	4	11.5%	12	50.4	11	72.5	62	202	1	-2.6	-27.4%
2005	DEN	16	456	277	60.7%	3366	18	7	4	4.6%	6.8	8	30.2%	5	88.0	6	93.1	46	151	2	3.1	0.0%
2006	DEN	16	317	175	55.2%	1994	11	13	7	4.8%	5.6	29	-9.8%	31	4.8	30	-5.6	36	112	1	0.0	-21.6%
2007	TB		438	255	58.3%	2831	18	16			5.8							40	137	1		

2005: 46% Short 35% Mid 10% Deep 9% Bomb   YAC: 5.5 (6)   2006: 46% Short 33% Mid 12% Deep 9% Bomb   YAC: 5.1 (15)

After Denver traded him to Tampa Bay, Plummer said he was retiring. He could change his mind if he's forced to pay back a prorated portion of his signing bonus, but we've probably seen the last of him, unless handball suddenly becomes a televised sport.

Brady Quinn Height: 6-4 Weight: 232 College: Notre Dame   Draft: 2007/1 (22) Born: 27-Oct-1984 Age: 23 Risk: Red

Year	Team	G	Att	Cmp	C%	Yds	TD	INT	FUM	ASR	NY/P	Rk	DVOA	Rk	DPAR	Rk	PAR	Runs	Yds	TD	DPAR	DVOA
2007	CLE		465	290	62.3%	3230	14	19			5.9							52	147	1		

To compare Quinn to Peyton Manning is to doom the poor kid before he even takes an NFL snap. Quinn simply isn't in the same class as Manning was as a prospect. Still, there are many similarities. Both had superlative junior seasons, fell off slightly as seniors, and became the subjects of the sort of pre-draft micromanagement that the John Becks of the world are

(continued next page)

Brady Quinn *(continued)*

never troubled with. Both were criticized for poor play in "the big game," criticism it took Manning nine years to shake. Both suddenly faced questions about their arm strength in their senior seasons, in part because both faced competition from a cannon-armed late arrival to the prospect scene. Both came to the NFL with poise, maturity, intelligence, and confidence as their calling cards; in other words, they were guys with "intangibles." Intangibles will kill you most of the time, but, in Manning's case, work habits and maturity made the difference between a good quarterback and an all-time great. In Quinn's case, they will eventually make the difference between an average quarterback and a guy who goes to multiple Pro Bowls.

Patrick Ramsey Height: 6-2 Weight: 218 College: Tulane Draft: 2002/1 (32) Born: 14-Feb-1979 Age: 28 Risk: Red

Year	Team	G	Att	Cmp	C%	Yds	TD	INT	FUM	ASR	NY/P	Rk	DVOA	Rk	DPAR	Rk	PAR	Runs	Yds	TD	DPAR	DVOA
2004	WAS	9	272	169	62.1%	1665	10	11	6	7.1%	5.2	31	-12.4%	30	1.0	30	-2.1	10	19	0	-0.1	-25.2%
2005	WAS	4	25	15	60.0%	279	1	1	2	13.5%	8.9	—	20.3%	—	3.7	—	1.7	7	3	0	-0.9	0.0%
2007	DEN		470	275	58.4%	3177	17	22			6.1							36	102	1		

2005: 50% Short 23% Mid 23% Deep 5% Bomb YAC: 9.1 (—)

In Week 12, Chad Pennington went down clutching his wrist after a hit by Mario Williams and didn't get up. He was helped off the field as the crowd held their breath. Ramsey came on the field, threw a single incomplete pass, and Pennington came back in as soon as he'd gotten some wind back into him. For this incomplete pass, Ramsey earned $1,688,000. The next time someone tells you that Patrick Ramsey hasn't gotten a fair shake, remind them that he's at least well compensated for his stillness. Ramsey's signed with the Broncos, where he'll back up Jay Cutler and probably put up numbers similar to Cutler's if called into action by an injury to the starter.

Tim Rattay Height: 6-0 Weight: 215 College: Louisiana Tech Draft: 2000/7 (212) Born: 15-Feb-1977 Age: 30 Risk: Red

Year	Team	G	Att	Cmp	C%	Yds	TD	INT	FUM	ASR	NY/P	Rk	DVOA	Rk	DPAR	Rk	PAR	Runs	Yds	TD	DPAR	DVOA
2004	SF	9	325	198	60.9%	2169	10	10	11	9.6%	5.4	29	-4.6%	25	13.1	23	5.2	12	55	0	1.9	22.8%
2005	SF	4	97	56	57.7%	667	5	6	3	9.6%	5.6	26	-30.0%	40	-7.6	37	-8.3	7	18	0	1.4	0.0%
2006	TB	4	101	61	60.4%	748	4	2	2	4.1%	6.9	6	29.0%	3	19.3	21	15.9	4	3	0	-0.9	-68.6%
2007	TEN		423	227	53.7%	2583	17	18			5.5							24	41	0		

2005: 52% Short 31% Mid 12% Deep 6% Bomb YAC: 5.3 (11)   2006: 55% Short 27% Mid 11% Deep 8% Bomb YAC: 4.5 (29)

Rattay had a poor training camp and preseason in 2006, lost the Bucs backup job to rookie hotshot Bruce Gradkowski, then sat on the bench for three months until the Gradkwoski bandwagon crashed with a resounding thud. Given a chance to play in December, Rattay was pretty good. Unfortunately, he made a smooth transition from middle-tier prospect to career backup without landing on any of the spaces in between, and no one came clamoring for his services in the offseason. Now in Tennessee, the only job he's threatening belongs to Kerry Collins.

Philip Rivers Height: 6-4 Weight: 226 College: North Carolina St. Draft: 2004/1 (4) Born: 8-Dec-1981 Age: 25 Risk: Green

Year	Team	G	Att	Cmp	C%	Yds	TD	INT	FUM	ASR	NY/P	Rk	DVOA	Rk	DPAR	Rk	PAR	Runs	Yds	TD	DPAR	DVOA
2004	SD	2	8	5	62.5%	33	1	0	0	0.0%	2.6	—	-36.8%	—	-0.7	—	0.5	5	-5	0	0.0	0.0%
2005	SD	3	22	12	54.5%	115	0	1	2	14.5%	4.0	—	-60.1%	—	-5.2	—	-6.0	1	-1	0	0.0	0.0%
2006	SD	16	460	284	61.7%	3388	22	9	8	5.5%	6.6	9	28.4%	4	85.2	5	86.6	48	49	0	-7.5	-59.9%
2007	SD		508	327	64.3%	3748	27	16			6.6							24	55	1		

2006: 45% Short 33% Mid 13% Deep 9% Bomb YAC: 4.8 (21)

Norv Turner isn't much of a tactician. Or motivator. Or talent evaluator. Or... well, anyway, one thing he's good at is finetuning a quarterback's mechanics. Rivers left college as a polished leader and reader of defenses who had an ugly delivery and a weird, wounded-ostrich motion to his backpedal. A few years later, his mechanics are better, but not flawless, and his timing and delivery on three-step drops leave something to be desired. Overall, his rookie year was a great advertisement for David Lewin's quarterback projection system, but Rivers's awkward mechanics (particularly his footwork) resulted in an almost Grossman-like inconsistency. He was exceptional against the Bengals and Broncos, horrible against the Raiders and in his second game against the Chiefs, and heavily propped up by the running game at times. Turner plans to perform a tweak here and an adjustment there on Rivers's delivery. Troy Aikman says Turner's approach works wonders. If it does, the Chargers' coach will have a Pro Bowl–caliber quarterback to pair with his superstar running back. Even Norv Turner can't mess up that combination. Right?

Aaron Rodgers   Height: 6-2   Weight: 223   College: California   Draft: 2005/1 (24)   Born: 2-Dec-1983   Age: 24   Risk: Red

Year	Team	G	Att	Cmp	C%	Yds	TD	INT	FUM	ASR	NY/P	Rk	DVOA	Rk	DPAR	Rk	PAR	Runs	Yds	TD	DPAR	DVOA
2005	GB	3	16	9	56.3%	65	0	1	2	14.6%	2.1	—	-117.7%	—	-8.3	—	-8.5	2	7	0	0.5	0.0%
2006	GB	2	15	6	40.0%	46	0	0	1	15.4%	1.6	—	-67.5%	—	-4.0	—	-5.3	2	11	0	0.6	67.4%
2007	GB		471	276	58.6%	3232	17	13			6.3							68	201	0		

2005:   55% Short   27% Mid   18% Deep   0% Bomb   YAC: 1.6 (—)   2006:   40% Short   27% Mid   27% Deep   7% Bomb   YAC: 4.2 (—)

Rodgers provides a reminder about how long we've been inundated with discussion about Brett Favre's retirement. The first-round pick in 2005, Rodgers finally got some extended playing time last year in a blowout loss to New England, only to break his foot. He looked erratic and generally overwhelmed before the injury, but 15 passes are hardly sufficient for evaluation purposes. Still, Rodgers's name popped up in trade talks over the offseason, suggesting that the current coaching staff may not be too impressed. Rodgers is less than a year older than Brady Quinn, so his future is still in front of him, but as long as Favre stays healthy, his immediate future is likely on the bench.

Ben Roethlisberger   Height: 6-4   Weight: 242   College: Miami (Ohio)   Draft: 2004/1 (11)   Born: 2-Mar-1981   Age: 26   Risk: Green

Year	Team	G	Att	Cmp	C%	Yds	TD	INT	FUM	ASR	NY/P	Rk	DVOA	Rk	DPAR	Rk	PAR	Runs	Yds	TD	DPAR	DVOA
2004	PIT	14	295	196	66.4%	2621	17	11	2	9.0%	7.4	5	40.3%	3	75.3	10	62.8	56	144	1	3.5	1.8%
2005	PIT	13	268	168	62.7%	2385	17	9	2	8.0%	7.7	2	33.5%	3	57.4	8	57.8	31	69	3	3.5	13.4%
2006	PIT	15	469	280	59.7%	3513	18	23	5	8.3%	6.4	11	6.6%	15	42.7	14	31.2	32	98	2	0.0	-17.3%
2007	PIT		515	322	62.5%	3768	19	15			6.3							40	114	2		

2005:   31% Short   47% Mid   15% Deep   7% Bomb   YAC: 5.5 (5)   2006:   36% Short   42% Mid   14% Deep   7% Bomb   YAC: 5.3 (12)

Most analysts will point to Big Ben's offseason motorcycle accident as the genesis of his difficult 2006 season, but it was his lousy performance in Super Bowl XL that started his calendar year off on the wrong foot. Roethlisberger's summer of misfortune (which also included an emergency appendectomy) appeared to merely compound the blow to his confidence suffered when he turned in the worst-ever performance by a winning Super Bowl quarterback. Roethelisberger was hardly the only problem with the 2006 Steelers, and, by some measures, he didn't even have that bad a season. DVOA and DPAR both pegged him as middle-of-the-pack. A drop-off in the team's rushing offense from 10th in 2005 to 21st certainly didn't help, as perhaps no QB in the league benefited more from his ground game in 2005 than the rookie Roethlisberger. There are enough whispers about Big Ben's work ethic to make it a concern, but the Steelers have to hope he was humbled enough by his "year from hell" to make amends in 2007. The new coaching staff's approach seems to be to put more responsibility on Roethlisberger's shoulders in the hope that he'll rise to the challenge; new offensive coordinator Bruce Arians is promising to give his QB the discretion to audible as well as have input in the offensive game plan.

Tony Romo   Height: 6-2   Weight: 227   College: Eastern Illinois   Draft: 2003/FA   Born: 21-Apr-1980   Age: 27   Risk: Red

Year	Team	G	Att	Cmp	C%	Yds	TD	INT	FUM	ASR	NY/P	Rk	DVOA	Rk	DPAR	Rk	PAR	Runs	Yds	TD	DPAR	DVOA
2006	DAL	16	337	220	65.3%	2903	19	13	8	6.5%	7.7	1	19.8%	9	50.9	10	63.8	34	102	0	0.1	-17.8%
2007	DAL		518	317	61.3%	3567	21	19			6.4							41	139	1		

2006:   37% Short   31% Mid   21% Deep   12% Bomb   YAC: 4.5 (30)

While Romo was responsible for one of the most disastrous ends to a playoff game in recent memory, the Cowboys simply would not have made it to the playoffs without him behind center. Dallas fans seem to have forgiven him, but what will they think a year from now? Every team has enjoyed an offseason to study Romo on film, so now the growing pains will come. Romo is also likely to give back some of his performance this year because his 2006 DVOA on third down (55.4%) far surpassed his DVOA on first down (1.2%) and second down (18.4%), which is one reason why KUBIAK is pretty down on him for 2007.

Sage Rosenfels   Height: 6-4   Weight: 218   College: Iowa State   Draft: 2001/4 (109)   Born: 6-Mar-1978   Age: 29   Risk: Red

Year	Team	G	Att	Cmp	C%	Yds	TD	INT	FUM	ASR	NY/P	Rk	DVOA	Rk	DPAR	Rk	PAR	Runs	Yds	TD	DPAR	DVOA
2004	MIA	3	39	16	41.0%	264	1	3	0	7.1%	5.7	—	-67.8%	—	-9.8	—	-13.3	0	0	0	0.0	0.0%
2005	MIA	4	61	34	55.7%	462	4	3	1	0.2%	7.5	—	-13.5%	—	-0.1	—	1.2	6	15	0	0.4	0.0%
2006	HOU	4	39	27	69.2%	265	3	1	0	4.3%	6.7	—	39.6%	—	9.5	—	10.5	4	5	0	-0.4	-44.9%
2007	HOU		397	250	63.0%	2279	15	15			4.8							21	55	0		

2005:   40% Short   42% Mid   11% Deep   7% Bomb   YAC: 6.1 (—)   2006:   53% Short   24% Mid   18% Deep   5% Bomb   YAC: 5.3 (—)

(continued next page)

Sage Rosenfels (*continued*)

Nobody ever expected to hear the words "Sage Rosenfels" and "quarterback controversy" in the same sentence, but that was the situation in Houston after Gary Kubiak benched David Carr for turning the ball over three times against the Titans in Week 8. Rosenfels came in for the second half and threw three touchdown passes, nearly bringing the Texans back from a 21–3 deficit. Kubiak stuck with Carr, however, and the quarterback controversy ended under bizarre circumstances a month later. Because punter Chad Stanley had a cut on his hand, Rosenfels served as Kris Brown's holder against the Jets in Week 12. Brown was short on a 59-yard field goal, and Rosenfels broke his thumb making the tackle on an attempted return by Justin Miller. One year later, Carr is gone, but Matt Schaub has arrived, which leaves us writing the same thing about Rosenfels for the third straight year: He's not starting material, but he is a better second-string option than most people give him credit for.

JaMarcus Russell Height: 6-6 Weight: 265 College: LSU Draft: 2007/1 (1) Born: 9-Aug-1985 Age: 22 Risk: Red

Year	Team	G	Att	Cmp	C%	Yds	TD	INT	FUM	ASR	NY/P	Rk	DVOA	Rk	DPAR	Rk	PAR	Runs	Yds	TD	DPAR	DVOA
2007	OAK		482	248	51.4%	3336	11	26			5.4							68	493	2		

Nobody who watches college football could have imagined a year ago that JaMarcus Russell would become the first overall selection in the 2007 NFL draft. When talking about Russell, scouts, coaches, and fans all rave about one skill in particular: arm strength. The man is gifted with an incredible arm, which can throw great distances with good accuracy. He also does a good job of avoiding the pass rush, and most reports suggest that he spends a lot more time in the film room than the other recent top picks to whom he has been compared, such as Michael Vick and Vince Young.

That being said, there is a colossal setup for failure here. Russell is going to the worst team in the NFL, where he'll play behind a tissue-paper offensive line and throw to a never-ending parade of mediocre wide receivers. Lane Kiffin, the Raiders' 31-year-old rookie head coach, has never been a head coach at any level of football. Nobody doubts that Kiffin has a great offensive mind, but there are questions as to whether he can handle the locker-room management aspect of the job. Russell has weight issues and needs to learn to handle the instant fame that comes with being the number-one overall pick, and the last thing the Raiders want is for Russell to fall into any bad habits from being around a bunch of unhappy veterans.

Most importantly, Russell made some terrible decisions with the football in his junior season at LSU and desperately needed another year of experience. Forget the specifics of the college quarterback projection system for now and just ask yourself this: How many of today's top quarterbacks came out early? Nineteen of the top 20 quarterbacks in DPAR last year stayed in college through their senior seasons. The only exception is Ben Roethlisberger. Yes, other early-entry quarterbacks such as Vince Young and Alex Smith could develop into superstars, but that has to be a pretty discouraging statistic for any Raiders fan waiting for JaMarcus Russell to save the franchise.

Matt Schaub Height: 6-5 Weight: 237 College: Virginia Draft: 2004/3 (90) Born: 25-Jun-1981 Age: 26 Risk: Red

Year	Team	G	Att	Cmp	C%	Yds	TD	INT	FUM	ASR	NY/P	Rk	DVOA	Rk	DPAR	Rk	PAR	Runs	Yds	TD	DPAR	DVOA
2004	ATL	6	70	33	47.1%	330	1	4	1	5.6%	4.3	—	-70.7%	—	-18.0	—	-14.4	8	26	0	-0.5	-32.9%
2005	ATL	16	64	33	51.6%	495	4	0	1	8.9%	6.8	—	28.9%	—	12.2	—	14.8	9	76	0	3.7	70.8%
2006	ATL	16	27	18	66.7%	208	1	2	0	6.4%	6.9	—	40.7%	—	5.9	—	4.2	7	21	0	1.3	46.1%
2007	HOU		474	296	62.4%	3175	15	14			5.8							49	167	1		

2005:	26% Short	28% Mid	28% Deep	17% Bomb	YAC: 5.9 (—)		2006:	17% Short	50% Mid	17% Deep	17% Bomb	YAC: 3.8 (—)

So who is this Schaub character? His career résumé—a poor game against the Saints in 2004, a great one against a banged-up Patriots defense in 2005, some indifferent mop-up duty in 2006, a few other cameo appearances—is good enough to generate some buzz, but not substantial enough to provide a real scouting dossier. That makes him a great dumping ground for empty rhetoric: Scribes and sports-talk yakkers can talk about his leadership/intangibles/potential all they want, but 161 regular-season attempts just aren't much of a data sample. The Texans no doubt fine-tooth-combed those 161 attempts, 193 preseason attempts, and every other scrap of info they could find before trading for Schaub and jettisoning David Carr. Schaub has the size-arm-mobility package to be a successful quarterback, but so did Carr, and so did Rob Johnson, last decade's one-game wonder turned would-be savior. We like what we've seen, and both Kubiak and KUBIAK are optimistic, but don't break ground for any Schaub statues in downtown Houston just yet.

Chris Simms Height: 6-4 Weight: 220 College: Texas Draft: 2003/3 (97) Born: 29-Aug-1980 Age: 27 Risk: Red

Year	Team	G	Att	Cmp	C%	Yds	TD	INT	FUM	ASR	NY/P	Rk	DVOA	Rk	DPAR	Rk	PAR	Runs	Yds	TD	DPAR	DVOA
2004	TB	5	73	42	57.5%	467	1	3	.2	12.5%	4.7	—	-33.1%	—	-7.6	—	-10.3	7	14	0	-0.5	-39.1%
2005	TB	11	313	191	61.0%	2035	10	7	6	8.7%	5.4	32	6.2%	17	27.5	20	27.0	19	31	0	-0.2	-20.8%
2006	TB	3	106	58	54.7%	585	1	7	0	2.5%	5.1	40	-40.1%	45	-13.0	41	-16.4	4	7	1	0.4	0.9%
2007	TB		517	321	62.2%	3414	18	12			5.9							27	50	1		

2005: 54% Short 33% Mid 8% Deep 5% Bomb YAC: 4.1 (35) 2006: 56% Short 27% Mid 12% Deep 6% Bomb YAC: 4.2 (35)

Midway through the third quarter in Week 3 against the Panthers, Simms bootlegged left on 4th-and-1 from the 2-yard line, absorbed a big hit from linebacker Adam Seward, and flipped into the end zone for a touchdown. Simms sprung up and celebrated with his teammates, suffering no apparent ill effects from the collision with Seward or the ground. Two plays into the next possession, Simms took a knee during a stoppage in play and motioned for help from the sidelines. Bruce Gradkowski finished the series. Simms entered the tunnel with trainers. The official diagnosis was cramping, not an unusual ailment on a 90-degree day.

Simms was back on the field for the next series, a bandage covering the spot on his right arm where an IV was inserted. He completed three passes for 50 yards, but looked wobbly at times. When he handed off, Simms would stagger as far away from the action as possible. Late in the fourth quarter, he was hit again, this time by Al Wallace, and he looked even woozier. Trainers iced his neck on the sidelines. Simms finished the game, but that evening he was rushed to the hospital and his spleen was removed. It wasn't clear whether the spleen ruptured on the touchdown, the Wallace hit, or on a shot he took from Kris Jenkins early in the game. What is certain is that Simms played football on a sweltering day while bleeding internally, that the situation was potentially life-threatening, and that the Buccaneers treated this serious medical condition with an IV, some ice, and a pat on the butt.

Simms was rewarded for his grit with a two-year, $7-million contract and a chance to battle Jeff Garcia for a starting job. That's the thanks you get for nearly giving your life to your employer. The Bucs owe Simms a fair chance to win the job from Garcia. Simms doesn't owe the Bucs a damn thing.

Alex Smith Height: 6-4 Weight: 212 College: Utah Draft: 2005/1 (1) Born: 7-May-1984 Age: 23 Risk: Yellow

Year	Team	G	Att	Cmp	C%	Yds	TD	INT	FUM	ASR	NY/P	Rk	DVOA	Rk	DPAR	Rk	PAR	Runs	Yds	TD	DPAR	DVOA
2005	SF	9	165	84	50.9%	875	1	11	11	13.6%	3.6	46	-97.8%	46	-66.5	46	-66.3	30	103	0	-5.8	-59.7%
2006	SF	16	442	257	58.1%	2890	16	16	10	6.9%	5.7	28	-11.9%	35	2.5	34	-3.1	44	147	2	-2.9	-30.5%
2007	SF		466	283	60.7%	3105	18	19			5.9							45	160	2		

2005: 43% Short 35% Mid 9% Deep 13% Bomb YAC: 4.7 (20) 2006: 53% Short 25% Mid 14% Deep 7% Bomb YAC: 5.4 (8)

Y. A. Tittle never did it. Neither did John Brodie. It wasn't something that Joe Montana, or Steve Young, or Jeff Garcia ever accomplished during their distinguished Bay Area careers. In 2006, Alex Smith was the first quarterback in the history of the 49ers franchise to take every regular-season snap from center.

Smith was supported in his second season by two new influences—offensive coordinator Norv Turner and backup quarterback Trent Dilfer. In his one year in San Francisco, Turner brought the "Good Norv" to the table—the coordinator that helped turn Troy Aikman into a Hall of Famer, not the coach who sank the Redskins, killed the Raiders, and may be about to do something similar to the Chargers. Dilfer, who assisted greatly in Matt Hasselbeck's development when he was a backup in Seattle, continued his gift for mentorship with Smith. Together, they helped Smith recover from the disastrous rookie campaign that came out as the least valuable season by any quarterback in the 11-year history of our advanced stats. His improvement should continue in 2007, with one of the top-three running backs in the game behind him and a new number-one receiver in Darrell Jackson.

Troy Smith Height: 6-0 Weight: 225 College: Ohio State Draft: 2007/5 (174) Born: 20-Jul-1984 Age: 23 Risk: Red

Year	Team	G	Att	Cmp	C%	Yds	TD	INT	FUM	ASR	NY/P	Rk	DVOA	Rk	DPAR	Rk	PAR	Runs	Yds	TD	DPAR	DVOA
2007	BAL		460	266	57.8%	2862	13	20			5.8							98	645	3		

The Heisman Trophy–winning quarterback from Ohio State fell to Baltimore in the fifth round because of his height, yet he's just a whisker shorter than Drew Brees. Smith is an excellent decision-maker with ample arm strength and good elusiveness. He has a chance to supplant Kyle Boller as the Ravens backup in 2008, and, even if he can't overcome his physical deficiencies, the Ravens will have risked very little.

Jim Sorgi   Height: 6-3   Weight: 194   College: Wisconsin   Draft: 2004/6 (193) Born: 3-Dec-1980   Age: 27   Risk: Red

Year	Team	G	Att	Cmp	C%	Yds	TD	INT	FUM	ASR	NY/P	Rk	DVOA	Rk	DPAR	Rk	PAR	Runs	Yds	TD	DPAR	DVOA
2004	IND	4	29	17	58.6%	175	2	0	1	6.5%	5.2	—	4.8%	—	2.6	—	1.3	8	-5	0	-0.3	-73.6%
2005	IND	5	62	43	69.4%	444	3	1	1	3.9%	6.6	—	25.8%	—	11.1	—	10.9	12	1	0	0.1	0.0%
2007	IND		414	258	62.3%	2841	26	15			6.3							19	34	0		
2005:	42% Short		48% Mid		6% Deep		3% Bomb			YAC: 4.0 (—)												

Sorgi has become a bit of a joke around the league, and he certainly doesn't mind. He famously showed up at a casting call for the new Maytag repairman, announcing that he had the perfect (in)experience for the part. He also received the lowest performance-based bonus check in the league: $189, thanks to a single snap on which he served as holder on an extra point. What isn't a joke is Sorgi's actual play on the field. The Colts didn't sit their starters at the end of the 2006 season, but when Sorgi played at the end of 2004 and 2005, he put up better numbers than most of the other men who back up the league's best quarterbacks. Colts fans don't want to see Manning ever miss a snap, but Sorgi is a better option than Matt Cassel, Doug Johnson, or Jamie Martin.

Drew Stanton   Height: 6-3   Weight: 226   College: Michigan State   Draft: 2007/2 (43) Born: 7-May-1984   Age: 23   Risk: Red

Year	Team	G	Att	Cmp	C%	Yds	TD	INT	FUM	ASR	NY/P	Rk	DVOA	Rk	DPAR	Rk	PAR	Runs	Yds	TD	DPAR	DVOA
2007	DET		525	291	55.4%	2922	9	19			4.6							62	296	0		

Whenever Michigan sports fans needed a break from complaining about Matt Millen, they complained about John L. Smith and the Michigan State football team. Stanton was standing on the fault line when Smith's earthquake of incompetence swallowed the Spartans program whole, and Stanton himself nearly ended up in the Land of the Lost. Stanton appeared to be a top prospect two years ago, but last season his game started to fall apart as the team around him packed it in for the year. He picked up some bad habits at Michigan State as a result, but he could be a very good player if he gets an opportunity to master the fundamentals in an environment conducive to learning and growth. Does that sound like Detroit to you?

Vinny Testaverde   Height: 6-5   Weight: 235   College: Miami   Draft: 1987/1 (1) Born: 13-Nov-1963   Age: 44   Risk: Red

Year	Team	G	Att	Cmp	C%	Yds	TD	INT	FUM	ASR	NY/P	Rk	DVOA	Rk	DPAR	Rk	PAR	Runs	Yds	TD	DPAR	DVOA
2004	DAL	16	495	297	60.0%	3532	17	20	7	6.2%	6.3	15	3.2%	17	36.5	16	28.7	21	38	1	0.5	-12.9%
2005	NYJ	6	106	60	56.6%	777	1	6	6	10.3%	5.6	28	-39.9%	43	-13.2	39	-12.3	7	4	2	1.4	0.0%
2006	NE	3	3	2	66.7%	29	1	0	0	0.3%	9.7	—	199.6%	—	2.5	—	2.6	8	-8	0	0.0	0.0%
2007	NE		447	268	59.9%	2969	17	14			5.9							29	35	0		
2005:	33% Short		34% Mid		23% Deep		10% Bomb			YAC: 3.6 (45)												

Vinny signed with the Patriots in midseason, but the only part of the playbook the Patriots showed him when he got to Foxboro was the section on kneeldown plays. If you happen to be in a keeper fantasy league that rewards kneeldowns, he's probably underrated, but you're a masochist.

Marques Tuiasosopo   Height: 6-1   Weight: 220   College: Washington   Draft: 2001/2 (59) Born: 22-Mar-1979   Age: 28   Risk: Red

Year	Team	G	Att	Cmp	C%	Yds	TD	INT	FUM	ASR	NY/P	Rk	DVOA	Rk	DPAR	Rk	PAR	Runs	Yds	TD	DPAR	DVOA
2005	OAK	2	26	14	53.8%	124	1	2	2	19.0%	2.6	—	-54.0%	—	-5.2	—	-6.7	2	19	0	0.9	0.0%
2006	OAK	2	13	6	46.2%	68	1	2	1	0.7%	5.2	—	-116.6%	—	-6.4	—	-5.6	4	29	0	-0.2	-25.5%
2007	NYJ		372	213	57.2%	2456	19	13			5.8							56	249	1		
2005:	39% Short		43% Mid		9% Deep		9% Bomb			YAC: 2.7 (—)			2006:	25% Short	58% Mid		17% Deep	0% Bomb		YAC: 2.7 (—)	

He hasn't played enough to allow us to form a strong opinion, but when he has played, he hasn't played well. He'll try to earn the third-string job behind Chad Pennington and Kellen Clemens.

Michael Vick   Height: 6-0   Weight: 215   College: Virginia Tech   Draft: 2001/1 (1) Born: 28-Jun-1980   Age: 27   Risk: Green

Year	Team	G	Att	Cmp	C%	Yds	TD	INT	FUM	ASR	NY/P	Rk	DVOA	Rk	DPAR	Rk	PAR	Runs	Yds	TD	DPAR	DVOA
2004	ATL	15	321	181	56.4%	2313	14	12	15	12.6%	5.6	24	-24.9%	36	-18.5	37	-14.3	120	902	3	29.2	25.9%
2005	ATL	15	387	214	55.3%	2412	15	13	11	7.6%	5.3	34	-5.9%	26	12.9	26	-0.2	102	597	6	21.7	22.4%
2006	ATL	16	388	204	52.6%	2474	20	13	9	10.5%	5.0	42	-16.7%	37	-6.5	37	3.7	123	1039	2	32.4	27.6%
2007	ATL		387	218	56.1%	2550	16	10			5.4							141	892	7		
2005:	37% Short		38% Mid		16% Deep		9% Bomb			YAC: 4.1 (37)			2006:	32% Short	39% Mid		15% Deep	14% Bomb		YAC: 4.1 (37)	

Vick is the main subject of the Atlanta chapter in this year's book, and he was the main subject of the Atlanta chapter in last year's book. There is nothing left to say about the man's on-field performance or potential. The story about Vick's involvement with dog fighting in Virginia will have a dozen twists and turns between the time we go to press and the time you read this, so there's no sense in trying to address that either. Instead, we'll take this opportunity to point out that running quarterbacks such as Vick and Vince Young come out with a fantasy Risk of Green because their rushing stats are more consistent from year to year than passing stats usually are, and, since most fantasy leagues give more points for rushing yards than passing yards, that added consistency outweighs the larger injury risk that comes with so much scrambling. If Vick has been suspended for any part of the season by the time you read this, or if he's close to a suspension, his Risk is obviously not Green.

Billy Volek Height: 6-2 Weight: 214 College: Fresno State   Draft: 2000/FA   Born: 28-Apr-1976 Age: 31   Risk: Red

Year	Team	G	Att	Cmp	C%	Yds	TD	INT	FUM	ASR	NY/P	Rk	DVOA	Rk	DPAR	Rk	PAR	Runs	Yds	TD	DPAR	DVOA
2004	TEN	10	357	218	61.1%	2486	18	10	6	9.0%	5.9	21	-10.2%	27	5.0	28	24.8	11	50	1	1.9	11.1%
2005	TEN	6	88	50	56.8%	474	4	2	3	7.9%	4.4	—	-25.5%	—	-5.1	—	-8.5	1	3	0	-0.2	0.0%
2006	SD	1	2	1	50.0%	4	0	0	0	33.1%	-0.7	—	-140.5%	—	-1.5	—	-1.3	3	-3	0	0.0	0.0%
2007	SD		442	264	59.8%	3002	23	15			6.0							21	38	0		

2005: 58% Short 25% Mid 2% Deep 15% Bomb YAC: 3.6 (—)

Within a couple of weeks last summer, Volek went from holding the first spot on the Tennessee depth chart to holding a ticket out of town, with coach Jeff Fisher calling him a liar on his way out the door. Volek actually looked pretty good in 2004, the only season he ever got extended playing time, so it is disappointing that he will probably never have a chance to be an NFL starter. If reports out of Tennessee are to be believed, he was never particularly committed to becoming a starter anyway.

Seneca Wallace Height: 5-11 Weight: 196 College: Iowa State   Draft: 2003/4 (110) Born: 6-Aug-1980   Age: 27   Risk: Red

Year	Team	G	Att	Cmp	C%	Yds	TD	INT	FUM	ASR	NY/P	Rk	DVOA	Rk	DPAR	Rk	PAR	Runs	Yds	TD	DPAR	DVOA
2005	SEA	7	25	13	52.0%	173	1	1	2	9.4%	5.0	—	-29.2%	—	-1.9	—	-1.8	6	-5	0	0.0	0.0%
2006	SEA	9	141	82	58.2%	927	8	7	5	9.2%	5.5	33	-25.1%	40	-7.6	39	-7.0	12	122	0	3.4	44.1%
2007	SEA		456	272	59.6%	2829	23	17			5.3							64	259	1		

2005: 0% Short 57% Mid 29% Deep 14% Bomb YAC: 2.8 (—)   2006: 35% Short 41% Mid 15% Deep 9% Bomb YAC: 3.5 (44)

The astute AFL historians among you will remember the name Marlin Briscoe. The first black quarterback of the modern era was short for his position (around 5-foot-9), had a rocket arm, set a Denver Broncos rookie record for touchdown passes with 14 in only 11 games in 1968, and later won two Super Bowl rings as a wide receiver with the Dolphins. He had a slightly bowlegged, scattershot running style, wore the number 15 as a quarterback, and was denied the chance to play his preferred position after one season.

A generation later, Briscoe has his near-double in Wallace. Short for his position—he's listed at 5-foot-11, which is most likely generous—and wearing the number 15, Wallace made his first four professional starts in 2006, leading the team after Matt Hasselbeck's knee injury. He went 2-2 as a starter in that span did exactly what is asked of your average backup quarterback: Don't Stink Up the Joint. However, the Seahawks have been trying to switch him to receiver ever since he came into the league. The wisdom of such a move was first displayed when he torched Ken Lucas in the 2005 NFC Championship Game. Wallace has played several different positions in practice and is probably the best athlete on the team, so the exact trajectory of his NFL career is anyone's guess. Wallace is great with the deep ball, less so with the midrange touch required in Seattle's offense. His amazing mobility is the X-Factor.

Andrew Walter Height: 6-5 Weight: 234 College: Arizona State   Draft: 2005/3 (69) Born: 11-May-1982 Age: 25 Risk: Orange

Year	Team	G	Att	Cmp	C%	Yds	TD	INT	FUM	ASR	NY/P	Rk	DVOA	Rk	DPAR	Rk	PAR	Runs	Yds	TD	DPAR	DVOA
2006	OAK	12	276	147	53.3%	1677	3	13	13	13.7%	4.4	43	-36.9%	44	-30.4	45	-32.6	14	30	0	-7.6	-99.9%
2007	OAK		451	257	56.9%	2547	14	16			4.4							25	64	1		

2006: 46% Short 32% Mid 15% Deep 7% Bomb YAC: 3.4 (45)

It's impossible to honestly evaluate Walter's 2006 performance. Most quarterbacks don't have to work with an offensive coordinator who spent a decade out of football fly-fishing and running a bed and breakfast. Most quarterbacks don't get sacked 24 times in four games, as Walter was from Weeks 6 through 9. Most don't have to throw to a wide receiver who has openly

(continued next page)

Andrew Walter *(continued)*

stated that he is going through the motions. The only way a quarterback can stand out under those circumstances is to take his Randall Cunningham pills and scramble his way onto the highlight shows. Walter isn't a scrambler. Granted, he could have shown something—he could have fumbled less, made fewer mistakes, maybe rallied the team once or twice—but Dan Marino would have struggled to put points on the board for last year's Raiders. Walter's best bet now is to work hard in camp, say all the right things, and hope he gets released in time to latch on with a real organization.

Kurt Warner				Height: 6-2		Weight: 220		College: Northern Iowa				Draft: 1998/FA			Born: 22-Jun-1971		Age: 36		Risk: Red
Year	Team	G	Att	Cmp	C%	Yds	TD	INT	FUM	ASR	NY/P	Rk	DVOA	Rk	DPAR	Rk	PAR	Runs	Yds	TD	DPAR	DVOA
2004	NYG	10	277	174	62.8%	2054	6	4	12	12.0%	5.9	23	-0.5%	19	16.9	22	20.1	13	30	1	2.6	36.8%
2005	ARI	10	375	242	64.5%	2713	11	9	9	5.5%	6.4	12	8.7%	16	36.4	19	43.4	13	28	0	-1.0	-41.5%
2006	ARI	7	168	108	64.3%	1377	6	5	9	6.8%	6.9	5	4.1%	18	13.1	24	17.5	13	3	0	-3.2	-94.8%
2007	ARI		431	245	56.8%	2828	13	18			5.8							14	29	0		
2005:	50% Short		30% Mid		16% Deep		4% Bomb			YAC: 4.5 (26)			2006:	50% Short		29% Mid		17% Deep		4% Bomb		YAC: 5.8 (6)

Warner started last season well, but was booed off the field in Week 3 after throwing three picks and fumbling a snap against the Rams. Two weeks later, Matt Leinart started, and the writing was once again on the wall for the man who lost starting jobs in St. Louis (to Marc Bulger) and New York (to Eli Manning). Warner considered retirement during the season, but decided in late December that one more year was the way to go. He's a good backup option for an Arizona team that is looking to climb the ladder, though his increasing inability to handle any manner of pressure has to be a concern.

Chris Weinke				Height: 6-4		Weight: 232		College: Florida State				Draft: 2001/4 (106)			Born: 31-Jul-1972		Age: 35		Risk: Red
Year	Team	G	Att	Cmp	C%	Yds	TD	INT	FUM	ASR	NY/P	Rk	DVOA	Rk	DPAR	Rk	PAR	Runs	Yds	TD	DPAR	DVOA
2005	CAR	3	13	7	53.8%	64	1	0	0	0.3%	4.9	—	50.4%	—	3.3	—	3.0	8	-5	0	-1.4	0.0%
2006	CAR	3	96	56	58.3%	625	2	4	2	10.2%	5.4	—	-24.5%	—	-5.2	—	-3.3	4	16	0	-1.5	-99.9%
2007	FA		413	255	61.8%	2599	14	15			5.6							26	62	1		
2005:	38% Short		38% Mid		25% Deep		0% Bomb			YAC: 1.0 (—)			2006:	46% Short		32% Mid		15% Deep		7% Bomb		YAC: 4.2 (—)

As a 28-year-old senior at Florida State in 2000, Weinke was like one of those veteran minor league outfielders who hits 35 home runs in a double-A bandbox and suddenly becomes a prospect. In reality, he was a grown man playing in a league of relative boys. In 2001, he proved that the difference between a 29-year-old rookie and a 22-year-old is that, while neither player is ready, the younger guy has a chance to get better. Weinke clung to the Panthers bench for dear life for six years, but it was clear that John Fox and Dan Henning had given up hope when Weinke threw just seven passes and split time under center with running back DeAngelo Williams on Christmas Eve in Atlanta. Released in March, he should have a fine career as a college coach.

Charlie Whitehurst				Height: 6-4		Weight: 225		College: Clemson				Draft: 2006/3 (81)			Born: 6-Aug-1982		Age: 25		Risk: Red
Year	Team	G	Att	Cmp	C%	Yds	TD	INT	FUM	ASR	NY/P	Rk	DVOA	Rk	DPAR	Rk	PAR	Runs	Yds	TD	DPAR	DVOA
2007	SD		472	273	57.9%	3287	25	15			6.2							22	33	0		

The 6-foot-4, 225-pound Whitehurst always appealed more to draft analysts who watched him in shorts and a T-shirt than the ones who watched him in a helmet and shoulder pads. With Philip Rivers emerging as a top-notch quarterback, it's safe to say Whitehurst will never become the man in San Diego.

Anthony Wright				Height: 6-1		Weight: 211		College: South Carolina				Draft: 1999/FA			Born: 14-Feb-1976		Age: 31		Risk: Red
Year	Team	G	Att	Cmp	C%	Yds	TD	INT	FUM	ASR	NY/P	Rk	DVOA	Rk	DPAR	Rk	PAR	Runs	Yds	TD	DPAR	DVOA
2005	BAL	9	266	164	61.7%	1582	6	9	5	6.5%	5.1	37	-13.2%	33	0.0	33	-5.3	18	68	0	3.9	28.7%
2006	CIN	5	3	3	100.0%	31	0	0	0	-0.9%	10.3	—	93.9%	—	1.1	—	1.1	4	-12	0	-0.7	-99.9%
2007	NYG		425	248	58.4%	2535	15	18			5.4							35	105	1		
2005:	53% Short		30% Mid		12% Deep		4% Bomb			YAC: 3.9 (40)			2006:	100% Short		0% Mid		0% Deep		0% Bomb		YAC: 10.7 (—)

Wright is one of those backup quarterbacks whose value only goes up when he doesn't play. He has been kicking around the league long enough to have been with four teams in eight seasons, amassing 19 starts along the way. His best performance by far came in a seven-start stint for the Ravens in 2005. We'll pause while you look at the numbers. The inescapable conclusion: The Giants really need Eli Manning to stay healthy.

Vince Young Height: 6-5 Weight: 233 College: Texas Draft: 2006/1 (3) Born: 18-May-1983 Age: 24 Risk: Green

Year	Team	G	Att	Cmp	C%	Yds	TD	INT	FUM	ASR	NY/P	Rk	DVOA	Rk	DPAR	Rk	PAR	Runs	Yds	TD	DPAR	DVOA
2006	TEN	15	357	184	51.5%	2199	12	13	9	6.5%	5.4	36	-6.9%	26	9.6	27	4.9	83	552	7	7.3	-0.8%
2007	TEN		497	286	57.4%	3336	20	16			6.0							96	634	5		

2006: 42% Short 29% Mid 18% Deep 10% Bomb YAC: 5.0 (18)

Last year, Young's DVOA was 21.9% on 181 attempts from the shotgun, but −30.5% on 197 attempts from under center. He threw for 1,103 yards from the shotgun, but just 948 yards from under center. Young played in a shotgun offense at Texas, of course, so it makes sense that he was more comfortable in that formation. As the numbers show, offensive coordinator Norm Chow gave Young plenty of opportunities to throw from the gun, but he didn't make a fetish of it: Young's 181 attempts came mostly in long-yardage or two-minute situations, with a handful of 1st-and-10 surprises sprinkled in. Those figures do not include Young's rushing performance, but Young was pretty dangerous when he tucked and ran regardless of formation. If Young can combine those rushing numbers with the typical passing improvement of a second-year quarterback, he could prove to be a fantasy monster of Manning/Palmer proportions.

Going Deep

Brett Basanez, CAR: Basanez was an undersized overachiever who earned Big-10 Player of the Year honors at Northwestern in 2005. He narrowly beat out Stefan LeFors for the clipboard job in Carolina, and came in for mop-up duty against the Steelers in Week 15, going 6-for-11 with 56 yards and an interception (14.6% DVOA, 1.4 DPAR). Basanez gets high marks for his football intelligence and pocket presence, but low marks for his size, arm, and spotty accuracy. The signing of David Carr bumps him down to the number-three slot.

Shane Boyd, ARI: Boyd is NFL Europe's all-time leading rusher at quarterback. If Kurt Warner and Matt Leinart both retire to become cohosts of *The New Supermarket Sweep*, Boyd would have some fantasy value.

Ken Dorsey, CLE: Dorsey won a lot of college games while surrounded by talent at Miami. Dorsey's pro career, however, has been a lesson on judging quarterbacks by how many games they won in college. Dorsey had a −23.4% DVOA in 2004, a −33.1% DVOA in 2005, and one pass attempt in 2006. In Cleveland, he is now the fourth-string at a position that does not have a fourth string.

Luke Getsy, SF: Getsy transferred to Akron from Pittsburgh after the 2003 season, sat out 2004, then went on to accumulate 6,117 passing yards over his final two collegiate seasons. He's a better fit in a West Coast–style attack than in San Francisco's vertical game, but he has potential to succeed in the right system. Said 49ers coach Mike Nolan during the team's May minicamp, "The quarterback, Getsy, or whatever his name is, got my attention." Ah, the life of the undrafted . . .

David Greene, SEA: The former Georgia Bulldog, who broke Peyton Manning's record for games won by an NCAA Division I-A quarterback with 42, has discovered the NFL ceiling. While he waits for a chance, he has developed an ability to keep sideline benches from floating into the air like few others. He's also great at clipboard-holding, keeping the hot drinks hot and the cool drinks cool, being a Gatorade taster, and making sure that Matt's and Seneca's sandwich orders don't get confused. You'll see him in preseason again, and that's about it.

Matt Gutierrez, NE: What if Tom Brady, frustrated by the Drew Henson situation, transferred to a Division I-AA school? That's the upside for Matt Gutierrez, who went to Idaho State when he couldn't beat out Chad Henne at Michigan. He has good fundamentals and leadership skills, but if you make poor decisions under pressure in Division I-AA, you are a long way off from playing in the National Football League. The Patriots actually gave Gutierrez a $10,000 signing bonus as an undrafted free agent, which is a good sign that they are taking him seriously as a long-term project.

Tim Hasselbeck, NYG: Hasselbeck hasn't thrown a pass since 2003, and he's behind both Anthony Wright and Jared Lorenzen on the Giants depth chart. If your team has more faith in Jared Lorenzen than you, it's probably time to go.

Drew Henson, MIN: Henson, like Maurice Clarett and Mike Williams before him, has learned that it is difficult to have a successful NFL career if you take a year or more off between college and the pros. It doesn't matter if you spend that time the way Henson did, playing third base in the Yankees organization, or the way Clarett did, driving around Ohio with a bottle of Grey Goose, a hatchet, and the Israeli mob on speed-dial. Henson spent the 2006 season on the Vikings practice squad, firmly behind such luminaries as Tarvaris Jackson and Brooks Bollinger, and he will never reach the first-round potential that he had in his Michigan days. One wonders if he has nightmares about the $12 million in guaranteed Yankees money that he gave up to return to the gridiron.

Chris Leak, CHI: Leak led Florida to a National Championship and holds every Gators passing record worth mentioning. He wasn't drafted because he's under six feet tall and doesn't have a great arm. He looks like a CFL prospect, but the Bears will keep him around for a year or two while they make up their mind about their other Florida alum quarterback.

Stefan LeFors, Canada: LeFors was supposed to challenge Chris Weinke for the Panthers backup job last year. Instead, he lost the clipboard derby to rookie Brett Basanez and was released in the final round of camp cuts. The Broncos and Vikings kicked his tires in mid-September, but weren't impressed. LeFors is now an Edmonton Eskimo. He has the name for it.

Jared Lorenzen, NYG: The Giants began to use Lorenzen creatively towards the end of the season as a short-yardage quarterback, as his massive frame served well on the draw play. He was the nominal number-two quarterback last season, but, with Anthony Wright in camp, he'll likely be the emergency guy in 2007. We've said it before and we'll say it again—more so than any other player, when you see Jared Lorenzen on the sideline, he looks like a fan who won a contest.

Ingle Martin, GB: With Brett Favre bitter and Aaron Rogers hurt, Ingle Martin was the Packers number-one quarterback for a short period of time during their April minicamp. It's likely the last time in his career the words "number-one quarterback" will be used to describe him without the name of a province attached to them.

Craig Nall, BUF: Nall was signed from Green Bay to compete with J. P. Losman and Kelly Holcomb, but hurt a hamstring in training camp and didn't take a snap in 2006. Now, Losman's solidified as the starter, and Nall will need to catch a break to get a look. There's a reason guys pretend they're not hurt, and it's not simply machismo.

John Navarre, IND: Between Matt Leinart and Kurt Warner, there wasn't any room for Navarre in Arizona, and he didn't see any snaps in 2006. His penchant for benchwarming evidently appealed to the Colts, who signed Navarre to not play behind Peyton Manning.

Dan Orlovsky, DET: Until Mike Martz leaves or Orlovsky gets cut, the UConn grad will always be intriguing. While Martz reportedly "totally had a crush on Orlovsky" in 2006, second-round pick Drew Stanton is "totally dreamy" and rumor has it that Martz spent an offensive meeting in April crossing out each of the 928 times he'd written "Dan" in his playbook and replacing them with "Drew." If Martz takes Orlovsky out of his Top 8, we'll know it's trouble.

J. T. O'Sullivan, CHI: O'Sullivan was talked about as a future starter in the Jake Delhomme mold back when he was in New Orleans, but he'll be playing for his sixth team in seven years and would need everything to go right (or wrong) to see playing time this season.

Jordan Palmer, WAS: Carson's kid brother is a third-tier prospect with a decent arm, but a spotty record at the mid-major level. NFC East teams must stop drafting the less-talented siblings of Pro Bowl quarterbacks; otherwise, we'll soon see Butler Cutler under center for the Eagles and Skippy Roethlisberger helming the Cowboys.

Preston Parsons, DEN: Parsons is a practice-squad regular who will be the third quarterback if Denver carries more than two. He's the best golfer on the Broncos team, so if a tie in the standings became so convoluted that the NFL decides to settle it with a one-off golf match, Parsons would probably represent the Broncos. That's the only reason you will need to know his name in 2007.

Chris Redman, ATL: Redman played for Bobby Petrino in Louisville, flunked his Quarterback of the Future tryout in Baltimore, and spent last season out of football. Petrino will give his former prize pupil one last NFL shot this season; if he's wise, Redman will parlay the exposure into a coaching gig. Redman probably still plays *Madden 2002* because it's the last version of the game in which he develops into a stud quarterback in franchise mode.

Jeff Rowe, CIN: Rowe is a unique prospect who spent much of his college career operating out of an offensive set called the "pistol," in which the quarterback lines up in a short shotgun formation with the running backs lined up behind him. He has good size and arm strength, but is still an NFL project. He should stick as the Bengals' third-stringer behind Carson Palmer and Doug Johnson.

D. J. Shockley, ATL: Like Michael Vick, Shockley is a hard-throwing scrambler who can run for big gains, but sometimes misses receivers by a mile. Unlike Vick, he's a level-headed student of the game who is too busy in the film room to dabble in dark particulates or upscale restaurants. Quarterbacks coach Bill Musgrave is quite high on Shockley, but with Joey Harrington now in town, he's still going to be number three.

Tyler Thigpen, MIN: Thigpen holds nearly every passing record for the Coastal Carolina Chanticleers. He's an undersized scrambler with bad mechanics. The Vikings are trying to collect the entire set.

Bradlee Van Pelt, HOU: There are 1,524 miles between Houston and Regina, but there's just a thumbnail's distance between holding a clipboard for the Texans and starting for the Saskatchewan Roughriders.

Jared Zabransky, HOU: The hero of Boise State's mesmerizing 2007 Fiesta Bowl victory offers an intriguing blend of great story and pure athleticism. His consistency issues as a passer led to his undrafted status, and NFL teams don't seem to know what to make of him. Is he an embryonic Jeff Garcia, or another square-peg story like Eric Crouch? Houston will be the first team to try to answer that question.

Running Backs

Conventional wisdom says that the running back committee is coming back into style in the NFL, with teams once again depending on two or three running backs rather than one featured back who carries the ball 20 times per game.

It turns out not to be true. Seventeen running backs carried the ball at least 250 times in 2006. That's the exact same number of running backs who carried the ball at least 250 times in 2005, and the exact same number of running backs who carried the ball at least 250 times in 2004. The number of running backs with at least 250 carries has bounced between 15 and 19 for the last decade, and the number of running backs with at least 100 carries has bounced between 43 and 47 over the same span. The only real difference between 2006 and previous years is that only one running back went over 350 carries in 2006... very, very, very far over.

In the following section we give the last three years' statistics as well as a 2007 KUBIAK projection for every running back who played a significant role in 2006, or is expected to play a significant role in 2007.

How to Read the Running Back Statistics Table

The first line (table 1) contains biographical data—each player's name, height, weight, college, draft position, birth date, and age. Height and weight are the best data we could find; weight, of course, can fluctuate during the offseason. **Age** is very simple, the number of years between the player's birth year and 2007, but birthdate is provided if you want to figure out exact age.

Draft position gives draft year and round, with the overall pick number with which the player was taken in parentheses. In the sample table, it says that Ahman Green was chosen in the 1998 draft in the third round with the 76th-overall pick. Undrafted free agents are listed as "FA" with the year they came into the league, even if they were only in training camp or on a practice squad.

To the far right of the first line is the player's **Risk** for fantasy football in 2007. The players most likely to match their projected stats in 2007 are marked Green, the players who are riskier, but still somewhat dependable are marked Yellow, and everyone else is marked Red. The Risk variable is explained further in the introduction to the Quarterbacks section.

Next we give the last three years of player stats. The first number is games played (**G**). This is the official NFL total and may include games in which a player appeared on special teams, but did not carry the ball or catch a pass. The next four columns are familiar: **Runs**, rushing yards (**Yds**), yards per rush (**Yd/R**) and rushing touchdowns (**TD**).

The entry for fumbles (**FUM**) includes all fumbles by this running back, no matter whether they were recovered by the offense or defense. Holding onto the ball is an identifiable skill; fumbling it so that your own offense can recover it is not. (For more on this issue, see the essay "Pregame Show" in the front of the book.) This entry combines fumbles on both carries and receptions.

The next five columns give our advanced metrics for rushing: **DVOA** (Defense-Adjusted Value Over Average), **DPAR** (Defense-Adjusted Points Above Replacement), and **PAR** (Points Above Replacement), along with the player's rank (**Rk**) in both **DVOA** and **DPAR**. These metrics compare every carry by the running back to a league-average baseline based on the game situations in which that running back carried the ball. DVOA and DPAR are also adjusted based on the opposing defense. The methods used to compute these numbers are described in detail in the "Statistical

Table 1. Running Back Statistics Sample

Ahman Green					Height: 6-0		Weight: 218	College: Nebraska				Draft: 1998/3 (76)		Born: 16-Feb-1977		Age: 30		Risk: Green	
Year	Team	G	Runs	Yds	Yd/R	TD	FUM	DVOA	Rk	DPAR	Rk	PAR	Suc%	Rec	Pass	Yds	C%	Yd/C	TD	DVOA	Rk	DPAR	Rk
2004	GB	15	259	1163	4.5	7	7	-2.8%	31	12.3	27	14.2	50%	40	51	275	78%	6.9	1	-19.6%	47	-2.5	48
2005	GB	5	77	255	3.3	0	1	-19.8%	47	-1.6	46	-3.2	39%	19	27	147	70%	7.7	0	-6.9%	30	0.3	31
2006	GB	14	266	1059	4.0	5	2	4.4%	23	20.6	17	14.1	43%	46	63	373	73%	8.1	1	-0.8%	28	2.6	27
2007	HOU		250	971	3.9	6								35	287			8.3	0				

Toolbox" introduction in the front of the book. The important distinctions between them are:

- DVOA is a rate statistic, while DPAR is a cumulative statistic. Thus, a higher DVOA means more value per play, while a higher DPAR means more aggregate value over the entire season.

- Because DPAR is defense-adjusted and PAR is not, a player whose DPAR is higher than his PAR faced a harder-than-average schedule. A player whose DPAR is lower than his PAR faced an easier-than-average schedule.

To qualify for ranking in rushing DVOA and DPAR, a running back must have had 75 carries in that season. There are 53 running backs ranked for both 2005 and 2006, and 52 for 2004.

The final rushing statistic is Success Rate (**Suc%**). This number represents running back consistency, measured by successful running plays divided by total running plays. (The definition for success is explained in the "Statistical Toolbox" introduction in the front of the book.) A player with high DVOA and a low Success Rate mixes long runs with plays on which he was stuffed at or behind the line of scrimmage. A player with low DVOA and a high success rate generally gets the yards needed, but rarely gets more. The league-average Success Rate in 2006 was 45.6 percent. Success Rate is not adjusted for the defenses a player faced.

The ten columns to the right of Success Rate give data for each running back as a pass receiver. Receptions (**Rec**) counts passes caught, while Passes (**Pass**) counts total passes thrown to this player, complete or incomplete. The next four columns list receiving yards (**Yds**), Catch Rate (**C%**), yards per catch (**Yd/C**), and receiving touchdowns (**TD**).

Our research has shown that receivers bear some responsibility for incomplete passes, even though only their catches are tracked in official statistics. Catch Rate represents receptions divided by all intended passes for this running back. The average NFL running back caught 73 percent of passes in 2006.

Finally we have receiving DVOA and DPAR, which are entirely separate from rushing DVOA and DPAR. To qualify for ranking in receiving DVOA and DPAR, a running back must have 25 passes thrown to him in that season. There are 54 running backs ranked for 2006, 53 for 2005, and 59 for 2004. Numbers without opponent adjustment (PAR and VOA) can be found on our website, FootballOutsiders.com.

The italicized row of statistics for the 2007 season is our 2007 KUBIAK projection based on a complicated regression analysis that takes into account numerous variables including projected role, performance over the past two years, projected team offense and defense, historical comparables, height, age, experience of the offensive line, and strength of schedule. Note that KUBIAK only projects the official NFL statistics, not our advanced metrics. It is difficult to accurately project statistics for a 162-game baseball season, but it is exponentially more difficult to accurately project statistics for a 16-game football season. Consider the listed projections not as a prediction of exact numbers, but the mean of a range of possible performances. What's important is less the exact number of yards we project, and more which players are projected to improve or decline. Actual performance will vary from our projection less for veteran starters and more for rookies and third-stringers, for whom we must base our projections on much smaller career statistical samples. Touchdown numbers will vary more than yardage numbers.

The main section for running backs is followed by a table with statistics for fullbacks, along with comments. Finally, in a section we call "Going Deep," we briefly discuss lower-round rookies, free-agent veterans, and practice-squad players who may play a role during the 2007 season or beyond.

Table 2. Top 20 RB by Rushing DPAR (Total Value), 2006

Rank	Player	Team	DPAR	Rank	Player	Team	DPAR
1	LaDainian Tomlinson	SD	52.9	11	Thomas Jones	CHI	25.5
2	Larry Johnson	KC	42.3	12	Fred Taylor	JAC	22.9
3	Tiki Barber	NYG	39.9	13	Ladell Betts	WAS	22.8
4	Steven Jackson	STL	36.3	14	Willie Parker	PIT	21.6
5	Joseph Addai	IND	36.1	15	Jerious Norwood	ATL	21.3
6	Frank Gore	SF	34.6	16	Ahman Green	GB	20.8
7	Brian Westbrook	PHI	34.1	17	Michael Turner	SD	20.8
8	Marion Barber III	DAL	30.8	18	Cedric Benson	CHI	17.9
9	Deuce McAllister	NO	26.4	19	Leon Washington	NYJ	17.5
10	Maurice Jones-Drew	JAC	26.0	20	Corey Dillon	NE	15.5

Table 3. Top 20 RB by Rushing DVOA (Value per Rush), 2006

Rank	Player	Team	DVOA	Rank	Player	Team	DVOA
1	Michael Turner	SD	46.7%	11	Tiki Barber	NYG	14.9%
2	Marion Barber III	DAL	35.7%	12	Fred Taylor	JAC	11.8%
3	Jerious Norwood	ATL	35.7%	13	Steven Jackson	STL	10.2%
4	LaDainian Tomlinson	SD	24.1%	14	Frank Gore	SF	10.0%
5	Maurice Jones-Drew	JAC	23.6%	15	Larry Johnson	KC	10.0%
6	Joseph Addai	IND	19.7%	16	Deuce McAllister	NO	9.8%
7	Brian Westbrook	PHI	19.1%	17	Clinton Portis	WAS	7.6%
8	Brandon Jacobs	NYG	17.7%	18	Ladell Betts	WAS	7.2%
9	Leon Washington	NYJ	16.1%	19	Thomas Jones	CHI	5.6%
10	Cedric Benson	CHI	15.1%	20	Mike Bell	DEN	5.5%

Table 4. Top 10 RB by Receiving DPAR (Total Value), 2006

Rank	Player	Team	DPAR
1	Steven Jackson	STL	14.9
2	Kevin Jones	DET	13.2
3	Brian Westbrook	PHI	12.7
4	DeAngelo Williams	CAR	10.9
5	Joseph Addai	IND	10.4
6	LaDainian Tomlinson	SD	9.4
7	Maurice Jones-Drew	JAC	8.8
8	Kevin Faulk	NE	8.2
9	Kenny Watson	CIN	7.7
10	Correll Buckhalter	PHI	7.4

Table 5. Top 10 RB by Receiving DVOA (Value per Pass), 2006

Rank	Player	Team	DVOA
1	DeAngelo Williams	CAR	48.1%
2	Correll Buckhalter	PHI	45.1%
3	Kenny Watson	CIN	43.7%
4	Joseph Addai	IND	28.9%
5	Marion Barber III	DAL	28.6%
6	Fred Taylor	JAC	24.4%
7	Justin Griffith	ATL	22.4%
8	Kevin Jones	DET	22.2%
9	Warrick Dunn	ATL	20.2%
10	Maurice Jones-Drew	JAC	19.1%

Joseph Addai   Height: 6-0   Weight: 205   College: LSU   Draft: 2006/1 (30)   Born: 3-May-1983   Age: 24   Risk: Green

Year	Team	G	Runs	Yds	Yd/R	TD	FUM	DVOA	Rk	DPAR	Rk	PAR	Suc%	Rec	Pass	Yds	C%	Yd/C	TD	DVOA	Rk	DPAR	Rk
2006	IND	16	226	1081	4.8	7	2	19.7%	6	36.1	5	39.3	62%	40	50	325	80%	8.1	1	29.6%	4	10.5	5
2007	IND		330	1430	4.3	11								57		453		7.9	1				

Addai's league-leading Success Rate was the highest posted by a rookie with over 100 carries in the last decade. Edgerrin James led the NFL with a 62 percent Success Rate in 2005 and was usually among the top five in the NFL before dropping to 26th (45 percent) last year. We're still a long way from determining where the offensive line's, quarterback's, and coach's contributions to the running game end and where the back's contribution begins, but it is fairly clear that Addai and Edge's Success Rates have had an awful lot to do with Peyton Manning and the Colts offense. That may mean that Addai is as overrated as Edge was before crashing in Arizona. Still, as long as he's a productive cog in a very successful machine, it doesn't matter that the wheel is turning him more than he is turning the wheel. Addai fits the system, and his stats will take on Edge-like proportions now that he doesn't have to share the load with Dominic Rhodes.

Shaun Alexander   Height: 5-11   Weight: 225   College: Alabama   Draft: 2000/1 (19)   Born: 30-Aug-1977   Age: 30   Risk: Red

Year	Team	G	Runs	Yds	Yd/R	TD	FUM	DVOA	Rk	DPAR	Rk	PAR	Suc%	Rec	Pass	Yds	C%	Yd/C	TD	DVOA	Rk	DPAR	Rk
2004	SEA	16	353	1696	4.8	16	5	10.6%	13	36.7	3	37.9	46%	23	38	170	61%	7.4	4	-3.2%	31	1.4	32
2005	SEA	16	370	1880	5.1	27	5	20.7%	4	57.8	2	64.7	54%	15	28	78	54%	5.2	1	-20.5%	39	-1.5	36
2006	SEA	10	252	896	3.6	7	5	-13.3%	47	-0.5	47	-0.5	43%	12	16	48	75%	4.0	0	-81.8%	—	-6.2	—
2007	SEA		250	945	3.8	6								14		56		4.0	1				

At least three factors conspired to scuttle the follow-up to Alexander's 2005 MVP season: Seattle's offensive line entering the Witness Protection Program, Mack Strong's decline as a blocking fullback, and the broken bone in Alexander's left foot that was at the very least exacerbated by an uncalled horse-collar tackle by Arizona's Antrel Rolle in Week 2. Alexander missed

(continued next page)

Shaun Alexander *(continued)*

six games due to the injury and rushed for more than 100 yards and 4 yards per carry only twice all season, which is why he ended 2006 with a lower DPAR than Justin "Son of Huggy Bear" Fargas. Alexander turns 30 in August, so Mike Holmgren had better not hold him anywhere near that 370-carry flame again, but Alexander can still be a useful player. Fantasy football players should note that, according to KUBIAK, he's not going anywhere near double-digit touchdowns again.

Mike Alstott

Height: 6-1   Weight: 248 College: Purdue   Draft: 1996/2 (35) Born: 21-Dec-1973 Age: 33   Risk: Yellow

Year	Team	G	Runs	Yds	Yd/R	TD	FUM	DVOA	Rk	DPAR	Rk	PAR	Suc%	Rec	Pass	Yds	C%	Yd/C	TD	DVOA	Rk	DPAR	Rk
2004	TB	14	67	230	3.4	2	2	-9.5%	—	1.7	—	2.1	55%	29	41	202	71%	7.0	0	-27.3%	54	-3.6	53
2005	TB	16	34	80	2.4	6	0	10.3%	—	4.8	—	5.0	56%	25	38	222	66%	8.9	1	7.3%	19	3.4	20
2006	TB	16	60	171	2.9	3	1	-14.8%	—	0.1	—	-1.9	68%	21	38	85	55%	4.0	0	-46.6%	49	-7.4	53
2007	TB		42	115	2.7	3								14		88		6.4	0				

Fan favorite, on-field liability. Alstott averaged 2.24 yards per attempt on the 38 passes thrown his way last year, meaning that the Bucs basically wasted two throws per game waiting for one of Alstott's classic "boom boom" highlights. One-third of his receptions didn't even gain positive yardage. Alstott earned 20 red zone carries and responded with a 35 percent Success Rate, far lower than Cadillac Williams's 50 percent rate on 27 carries. The one thing he did well was convert 3rd-and-1 (12 of 15 opportunities), but how special is that when the average running back converts this situation 70 percent of the time? Re-signed in March, Alstott will sell jerseys for one more year.

Mike Anderson

Height: 6-0   Weight: 230 College: Utah   Draft: 2000/6 (189) Born: 21-Sep-1973 Age: 34   Risk: Red

Year	Team	G	Runs	Yds	Yd/R	TD	FUM	DVOA	Rk	DPAR	Rk	PAR	Suc%	Rec	Pass	Yds	C%	Yd/C	TD	DVOA	Rk	DPAR	Rk
2005	DEN	15	239	1014	4.2	12	1	19.6%	5	37.0	8	36.0	55%	18	21	212	86%	11.8	1	22.4%	—	3.8	—
2006	BAL	15	39	183	4.7	1	0	18.0%	—	5.9	—	5.0	30%	9	14	54	64%	6.0	0	-35.6%	—	-1.6	—
2007	BAL		29	98	3.4	1								7		44		6.2	0				

Anderson looked like Baltimore's best option at running back entering 2006, but he barely saw the ball backing up Jamal Lewis. At 34, with Willis McGahee now in Baltimore as the new workhorse and Musa Smith still around as well, it looks like Anderson is at the end of the line.

J. J. Arrington

Height: 5-9   Weight: 214 College: California   Draft: 2005/2 (44) Born: 23-Jan-1983 Age: 24   Risk: Red

Year	Team	G	Runs	Yds	Yd/R	TD	FUM	DVOA	Rk	DPAR	Rk	PAR	Suc%	Rec	Pass	Yds	C%	Yd/C	TD	DVOA	Rk	DPAR	Rk
2005	ARI	15	112	370	3.3	2	1	-23.3%	48	-4.2	48	-3.2	38%	25	33	139	76%	5.6	0	-22.6%	43	-2.0	38
2006	ARI	16	14	19	1.4	0	0	-81.6%	—	-3.4	—	-3.8	55%	8	10	58	80%	7.3	0	51.3%	—	2.4	—
2007	ARI		63	188	3.0	1								17		115		6.7	0				

In only two years at Cal after a JuCo transfer, Arrington put up numbers that had pro scouts drooling. In his senior season, he led the nation in rushing yards and yards per carry as the only Division I-A back to run for over 100 yards in every game. Unfortunately, Arizona took him early in the second round of the 2005 draft and he fell victim to Running Behind the Arizona Line Disease as rookie. Shut out as he was in the 2006 season by the addition of Edgerrin James, Arrington can only wait and wonder what might have happened under different circumstances. A cautionary tale for Bills fans: Arrington's measurables and college statistics are remarkably similar to those of fellow Cal grad Marshawn Lynch.

Marion Barber

Height: 5-11 Weight: 218 College: Minnesota   Draft: 2005/4 (109) Born: 10-Jun-1983 Age: 24   Risk: Yellow

Year	Team	G	Runs	Yds	Yd/R	TD	FUM	DVOA	Rk	DPAR	Rk	PAR	Suc%	Rec	Pass	Yds	C%	Yd/C	TD	DVOA	Rk	DPAR	Rk
2005	DAL	13	138	538	3.9	5	3	-8.8%	34	3.5	36	0.3	41%	18	25	115	72%	6.4	0	3.1%	23	1.5	28
2006	DAL	16	135	654	4.8	14	0	35.9%	2	30.9	8	31.7	56%	23	32	196	72%	8.5	2	27.4%	5	5.2	19
2007	DAL		172	756	4.4	9								34		274		8.1	1				

Barber had a better DVOA on first down (51.5%) than Julius Jones (–1.4%). Barber was also better on second down (38.3%) than Jones (–5.2%). Jones had a higher DVOA on third downs, but he only carried the ball three times, a sample so small it's practically meaningless. Barber was effective (14.5%) on 38 third-down carries. Barber and Jones each carried the ball 52 times in the red zone, but Barber gained more yards (179 to 153) and had a higher Success Rate (64 percent to 40 percent) and DVOA (44.6% to –6.3%). Jones has a higher DVOA than Barber as a receiver, but again Jones's sample is small (15 passes). Reliable observers agree that Barber is a better pass blocker than Jones.

Despite the fact that Barber was clearly better than Jones in every facet of the game, Jones started all 16 games, with Barber contributing off the bench. There's probably some logic at work here, but we can't find it. The Cowboys tried to shop Jones in the offseason; it appears that coordinator Jason Garrett has reached the conclusion that his best running back should also be his starting running back.

Tiki Barber

Height: 5-10　Weight: 200　College: Virginia　Draft: 1997/2 (36)　Born: 7-Apr-1975　Age: 32　Risk: NA

Year	Team	G	Runs	Yds	Yd/R	TD	FUM	DVOA	Rk	DPAR	Rk	PAR	Suc%	Rec	Pass	Yds	C%	Yd/C	TD	DVOA	Rk	DPAR	Rk
2004	NYG	16	322	1518	4.7	13	5	7.0%	17	29.9	6	28.4	48%	52	79	578	66%	11.1	2	21.1%	9	11.8	6
2005	NYG	16	357	1860	5.2	9	1	17.4%	7	47.4	5	44.4	49%	54	70	530	77%	9.8	2	42.7%	1	17.8	1
2006	NYG	16	327	1662	5.1	5	3	14.9%	11	39.9	3	42.9	50%	58	81	465	72%	8.0	0	7.6%	22	7.2	11

Barber cited Tom Coughlin's gruff coaching style as one of the reasons he left the game for the NBC Television Studios. Ironically, it was Coughlin who helped Barber solve his fumbling problems and made him a perennial All-Pro late in his ten-year career. Conventional wisdom suggests the Giants rushing game will suffer following Barber's departure, but Brandon Jacobs, Barber's replacement, performed well in a limited role last season. Yes, Barber ranked 3rd in rushing DPAR and 11th in rushing DVOA, but Jacobs ranked 8th in DVOA with a higher Success Rate. Barber will be missed in 2007, but the Giants' real concern isn't who will be running the ball, it's who will be blocking for him.

Kevan Barlow

Height: 6-1　Weight: 238　College: Pittsburgh　Draft: 2001/3 (80)　Born: 7-Jan-1979　Age: 28　Risk: Red

Year	Team	G	Runs	Yds	Yd/R	TD	FUM	DVOA	Rk	DPAR	Rk	PAR	Suc%	Rec	Pass	Yds	C%	Yd/C	TD	DVOA	Rk	DPAR	Rk
2004	SF	15	244	822	3.4	7	2	-16.4%	47	-2.5	49	-7.0	37%	35	45	212	78%	6.1	0	5.9%	25	3.7	22
2005	SF	12	176	581	3.3	3	1	-26.0%	50	-7.6	50	-12.5	27%	31	42	241	74%	7.8	0	-22.1%	42	-2.5	42
2006	NYJ	12	131	370	2.8	6	1	-14.9%	48	-1.7	48	-2.4	42%	7	10	21	70%	3.0	0	-63.1%	—	-2.8	—
2007	PIT		37	135	3.7	2								7	59			7.9	0				

We're now more than three years removed from Barlow's promising early years with the 49ers. Looking at the numbers above, you would never know that Barlow averaged 4.7 yards per carry in 2002 and 5.1 yards per carry in 2003. San Francisco signed him to a contract extension before the 2004 season, and, just like that, he became slow and plodding. Rumors last August that the Jets would give up a first-rounder for Barlow were laughable; they ended up trading a fourth-round pick and even that was too much. Only one player came within a half-yard of Barlow's league-low 2.8 yards per carry last year, and that was teammate Cedric Houston. Although Barlow will go to training camp with Pittsburgh, the next time we see him will probably be on the NFL Network special "Top Ten Players Who Completely Imploded after Promising Starts."

Mike Bell

Height: 6-1　Weight: 218　College: Arizona　Draft: 2006/FA　Born: 23-Apr-1983　Age: 24　Risk: Yellow

Year	Team	G	Runs	Yds	Yd/R	TD	FUM	DVOA	Rk	DPAR	Rk	PAR	Suc%	Rec	Pass	Yds	C%	Yd/C	TD	DVOA	Rk	DPAR	Rk
2006	DEN	15	157	677	4.3	8	1	5.4%	20	14.8	23	15.1	51%	20	27	158	74%	7.9	0	-7.6%	35	0.3	35
2007	DEN		143	648	4.5	5								25	214			8.7	0				

Where did Mike Shanahan find this guy? Bell went from a player even hard-core fans had never heard of to a much-discussed part of every fantasy draft when Shanahan announced during training camp that he expected Bell to play a substantial role in the running game. The acquisition of Travis Henry means Bell probably won't get more than ten carries a game in 2007, but he's a talented player and a good fit in the Broncos' running scheme.

Tatum Bell

Height: 5-11　Weight: 213　College: Oklahoma State　Draft: 2004/2 (41)　Born: 2-Mar-1981　Age: 26　Risk: Red

Year	Team	G	Runs	Yds	Yd/R	TD	FUM	DVOA	Rk	DPAR	Rk	PAR	Suc%	Rec	Pass	Yds	C%	Yd/C	TD	DVOA	Rk	DPAR	Rk
2004	DEN	14	75	396	5.3	3	1	33.9%	2	15.5	19	17.5	57%	5	7	80	71%	16.0	0	-82.7%	—	-2.5	—
2005	DEN	15	173	921	5.3	8	3	6.7%	13	15.5	14	14.4	43%	18	28	104	64%	5.8	0	-41.8%	52	-4.7	50
2006	DEN	13	233	1025	4.4	2	3	-2.2%	30	10.9	31	10.3	40%	24	31	115	77%	4.8	0	-52.0%	53	-6.7	51
2007	DET		180	684	3.8	5								44	255			5.7	1				

Bell faded badly in the final three games of last season, rushing 42 times for a total of 127 yards and losing three fumbles. His game is built around his ability to break off 20-yard runs, and he can disappear for long stretches, so he's more effective as a committee back than as a featured performer. He's almost useless in the passing game—he's a poor blocker and his receiving numbers are awful—which makes him a very strange fit in the Mike Martz offense that emphasizes passes to running backs. Bell may emerge as Detroit's nominal starter, but Mike Martz will be able to play mix-and-match with T. J. Duckett, Brian Calhoun, and Kevin Jones (when Jones gets healthy).

Michael Bennett Height: 5-9 Weight: 209 College: Wisconsin   Draft: 2001/1 (27) Born: 13-Aug-1978 Age: 29 Risk: Red

Year	Team	G	Runs	Yds	Yd/R	TD	FUM	DVOA	Rk	DPAR	Rk	PAR	Suc%	Rec	Pass	Yds	C%	Yd/C	TD	DVOA	Rk	DPAR	Rk
2004	MIN	11	70	276	3.9	1	1	-10.5%	—	0.7	—	0.0	41%	21	23	207	91%	9.9	1	54.3%	—	7.3	
2005	MIN	16	126	473	3.8	3	4	-28.8%	52	-7.7	51	-9.1	38%	27	30	124	90%	4.6	2	-26.4%	45	-2.3	39
2006	KC	11	36	200	5.6	0	1	19.3%	—	4.6	—	4.4	20%	9	12	77	75%	8.6	0	8.2%	—	1.1	—
2007	KC		53	226	4.2	1								23		217		9.4	1				

In terms of straight-line speed, this former Wisconsin track star might be the fastest running back in the league. He was quite effective in limited action last year, and it's surprising that Herm Edwards didn't give him more opportunities to run the ball and spell Larry Johnson. Having pushed Johnson past 370 carries last year, Herm isn't going to have a choice this year.

Cedric Benson Height: 5-10 Weight: 215 College: Texas   Draft: 2005/1 (4) Born: 28-Dec-1982 Age: 24 Risk: Green

Year	Team	G	Runs	Yds	Yd/R	TD	FUM	DVOA	Rk	DPAR	Rk	PAR	Suc%	Rec	Pass	Yds	C%	Yd/C	TD	DVOA	Rk	DPAR	Rk
2005	CHI	9	67	272	4.1	0	1	-22.7%	—	-2.6	—	-1.0	28%	1	1	3	100%	3.0	0	-58.0%	—	-0.3	—
2006	CHI	15	157	647	4.1	6	0	15.1%	10	17.9	18	19.7	47%	8	10	54	80%	6.8	0	8.2%	—	1.0	—
2007	CHI		287	1164	4.1	7								43		368		8.5	1				

Only a year and a half into his career, conventional wisdom said that Benson was a bust. After a meager seven yards on six carries in Week 9, he had amassed just 215 yards on 69 carries for the season (1.7% DVOA). From that point forward, he totaled 432 yards on 88 carries (24.1% DVOA). That strong late-season run gave the Bears the confidence to trade Thomas Jones, and Benson could have a big year as Chicago's new workhorse back. Benson will play more on passing downs and needs to get more comfortable as a blocker and receiver, or Adrian Peterson will get more time on the field and start cutting into his carries. Benson's injury early in the Super Bowl was an underappreciated element of Chicago's offensive struggles in that game.

Ladell Betts Height: 5-11 Weight: 223 College: Iowa   Draft: 2002/2 (56) Born: 27-Aug-1979 Age: 28 Risk: Yellow

Year	Team	G	Runs	Yds	Yd/R	TD	FUM	DVOA	Rk	DPAR	Rk	PAR	Suc%	Rec	Pass	Yds	C%	Yd/C	TD	DVOA	Rk	DPAR	Rk
2004	WAS	16	90	371	4.1	1	0	4.6%	20	7.2	35	8.4	51%	15	25	108	60%	7.2	0	-12.5%	40	-0.5	39
2005	WAS	12	89	338	3.8	1	2	-11.2%	39	1.2	41	-1.1	39%	10	17	78	59%	7.8	1	-14.8%	—	-0.4	—
2006	WAS	16	245	1154	4.7	4	4	7.1%	18	22.7	13	23.3	46%	53	64	445	83%	8.4	1	9.7%	19	5.6	14
2007	WAS		239	1065	4.5	6								45		428		9.5	1				

With Clinton Portis suffering through an injury-plagued 2006 season, Betts started nine games and ended the season with more than 1,100 yards. He performed so well that the Redskins signed him to a long-term deal, and, with most teams going to the running-back-by-committee approach, Betts might be the team's most important signing. His ability to run the ball between the tackles helped alleviate some of the pressure on first-year starting quarterback Jason Campbell last season. Betts and Portis are very similar in stature and stats; the primary differences are Betts's occasional struggles to hold onto the ball and his wig-free wardrobe.

Derrick Blaylock Height: 5-9 Weight: 205 College: Stephen F. Austin   Draft: 2001/5 (150) Born: 23-Aug-1979 Age: 28 Risk: Red

Year	Team	G	Runs	Yds	Yd/R	TD	FUM	DVOA	Rk	DPAR	Rk	PAR	Suc%	Rec	Pass	Yds	C%	Yd/C	TD	DVOA	Rk	DPAR	Rk
2004	KC	12	118	539	4.6	8	0	25.9%	5	22.1	10	22.0	57%	25	36	244	69%	9.8	1	17.6%	15	4.6	17
2005	NYJ	7	17	53	3.1	0	0	0.0%	—	-0.4	—	-0.4	41%	3	4	17	75%	5.7	0	-89.0%	—	-1.1	—
2006	NYJ	4	25	44	1.8	0	0	-70.9%	—	-5.7	—	-4.5	40%	5	9	29	56%	5.8	0	-13.4%	—	-0.2	—
2007	WAS		19	81	4.2	2								11		62		5.7	0				

You read that right—a drop of nearly 100 percentage points of DVOA from 2004 to 2006. When he was in Kansas City, Blaylock put up DVOA numbers comparable to Larry Johnson and Priest Holmes, which shows you how great the Chiefs offensive line is. After coming to New York to replace LaMont Jordan, Blaylock didn't show any of that form.

Lorenzo Booker Height: 5-10 Weight: 191 College: Florida State   Draft: 2007/3 (71) Born: 14-Jun-1984 Age: 23 Risk: Red

Year	Team	G	Runs	Yds	Yd/R	TD	FUM	DVOA	Rk	DPAR	Rk	PAR	Suc%	Rec	Pass	Yds	C%	Yd/C	TD	DVOA	Rk	DPAR	Rk
2007	MIA		82	394	4.8	3								26		221		8.5	0				

Booker's ability to catch the ball out of the backfield, 4.42 40-time, and ACC background might have hopeful Fins fans thinking he's a poor man's Tiki Barber, but Booker's role at Florida State diminished every season, making him a prospect headed in reverse. A better comp for Booker is the player he shared a backfield with in 2005, Jets running back Leon Washington.

Chris Brown

Height: 6-3 Weight: 219 College: Colorado   **Draft: 2003/3 (93) Born: 17-Apr-1981 Age: 26 Risk: Red**

Year	Team	G	Runs	Yds	Yd/R	TD	FUM	DVOA	Rk	DPAR	Rk	PAR	Suc%	Rec	Pass	Yds	C%	Yd/C	TD	DVOA	Rk	DPAR	Rk
2004	TEN	11	220	1067	4.9	6	6	-8.0%	38	5.4	37	10.6	43%	20	33	147	61%	7.4	0	-26.1%	52	-2.5	50
2005	TEN	15	224	851	3.8	5	3	-8.7%	33	5.0	30	7.8	46%	25	47	327	68%	13.1	2	-8.5%	32	0.3	32
2006	TEN	5	41	156	3.8	0	1	-20.8%	—	-1.2	—	-0.4	0%	2	9	4	22%	2.0	0	-93.0%	—	-2.9	—
2007	*FA*		*59*	*156*	*2.6*	*0*								*12*		*97*		*8.2*	*0*				

Brown became chopped liver last season when Travis Henry started playing well and LenDale White proved capable as a change-up back. The Titans let Brown walk in March, and, as of press time, he was unsigned. He'll show up somewhere, but he won't repeat the success of 2004, when he bowled over opponents for the first five games of the year only to spend the second half of the season battling injuries.

Ronnie Brown

Height: 6-0 Weight: 232 College: Auburn   **Draft: 2005/1 (2) Born: 12-Dec-1981 Age: 25 Risk: Yellow**

Year	Team	G	Runs	Yds	Yd/R	TD	FUM	DVOA	Rk	DPAR	Rk	PAR	Suc%	Rec	Pass	Yds	C%	Yd/C	TD	DVOA	Rk	DPAR	Rk
2005	MIA	15	207	907	4.4	4	3	-15.4%	45	-1.4	45	2.5	41%	32	36	232	69%	7.3	1	25.8%	6	6.5	9
2006	MIA	13	241	1008	4.2	5	4	-10.3%	42	3.5	41	6.7	46%	33	38	276	87%	8.4	0	16.6%	13	5.3	17
2007	*MIA*		*310*	*1187*	*3.8*	*7*								*46*		*332*		*7.2*	*0*				

Like Kevin Jones in 2005, Ronnie Brown was struck down by the *PFP* Second-Year Running Back Cover Curse. The Miami offensive line gave him no holes to run through and he missed three games with a broken hand. Brown's proven to be a very inconsistent performer so far. He puts up awful performances against great defenses (11 carries for just 5 yards against Minnesota) as well as bad defenses (12 carries for 49 yards against Houston). He puts up big days against great defenses (29 carries for 157 yards against Chicago) as well as bad defenses (237 yards on 40 carries in two games against the Jets). Brown would undoubtedly benefit from a cohesive passing attack that can keep opposing safeties out of the box, but that appears to be a pipe dream at this point. Everything we said last year is still true; if Brown can avoid freak injuries and Miami can improve the offensive line, he's going to get to 1,300 yards.

Correll Buckhalter

Height: 6-0 Weight: 222 College: Nebraska   **Draft: 2001/4 (121) Born: 6-Oct-1978 Age: 29 Risk: Red**

Year	Team	G	Runs	Yds	Yd/R	TD	FUM	DVOA	Rk	DPAR	Rk	PAR	Suc%	Rec	Pass	Yds	C%	Yd/C	TD	DVOA	Rk	DPAR	Rk
2006	PHI	16	83	345	4.2	2	1	0.9%	25	5.7	36	6.7	58%	24	28	256	86%	10.7	1	44.7%	2	7.3	10
2007	*PHI*		*40*	*162*	*4.1*	*2*								*19*		*125*		*6.7*	*0*				

At one point, we thought Correll Buckhalter was a mythological character, as fictional as fairies, minotaurs, and people who actually enjoyed *Studio 60 on the Sunset Strip*. Playing a full season after missing three of the previous four with a torn ACL in one knee and a torn patellar tendon in the other knee is a real achievement. A healthy Buckhalter has never shown the ability to be a superstar, but with a DVOA that's never ranked below 25th, he makes an excellent backup—until he suffers his next horrible injury.

Michael Bush

Height: 6-2 Weight: 242 College: Louisville   **Draft: 2007/4 (100) Born: 16-Jun-1984 Age: 23 Risk: Red**

Year	Team	G	Runs	Yds	Yd/R	TD	FUM	DVOA	Rk	DPAR	Rk	PAR	Suc%	Rec	Pass	Yds	C%	Yd/C	TD	DVOA	Rk	DPAR	Rk
2007	*OAK*		*48*	*219*	*4.6*	*2*								*7*		*52*		*7.3*	*0*				

Bush earned the Darren Sproles Memorial "Everyone Loves My Selection" award for this year's draft. As a former top-ten talent who broke his leg in his first game as a senior and missed the rest of the season, he sat at the top of many draftniks' sleeper boards. Bush had foot issues before his senior year, and there have been some complications in the healing process for his leg. Furthermore, Bush reportedly hates lifting weights and struggles with his diet, which is fine if you're a talk show host, but not if you want to rehab from your broken leg and be a NFL running back. Bush has the talent, but he needs to be in the right environment to be a successful pro, and Oakland is not that environment. Recommendation to avoid.

Reggie Bush

Height: 6-0 Weight: 200 College: USC   **Draft: 2006/1 (2) Born: 2-Mar-1985 Age: 22 Risk: Yellow**

Year	Team	G	Runs	Yds	Yd/R	TD	FUM	DVOA	Rk	DPAR	Rk	PAR	Suc%	Rec	Pass	Yds	C%	Yd/C	TD	DVOA	Rk	DPAR	Rk
2006	NO	16	155	565	3.6	6	2	-3.4%	34	5.8	35	3.6	43%	88	122	742	73%	8.4	2	-1.2%	29	5.7	13
2007	*NO*		*148*	*698*	*4.7*	*5*								*93*		*859*		*9.2*	*5*				

It took Bush a while to learn how to run behind the New Orleans line, whose blocking was much better suited to the new straight-ahead style of the post-ACL injury Deuce McAllister. Bush was last in the league with –10.5 rushing DPAR after the first eight games, averaging a pathetic 2.5 yards per carry, and we were starting to wonder whether it made sense to just

(continued next page)

Reggie Bush (*continued*)

switch him to wide receiver permanently. Whether it was Bush learning to follow his blocks, or the Saints learning what running plays best suited his skills, the light switched on midseason and Bush averaged 4.8 yards per carry and earned 16.3 DPAR over the final eight games. His Success Rate was 33 percent through Week 9, 54 percent afterwards. There's no reason to believe that won't carry over into 2007. Last year's experimental projection proved to be fairly accurate, so, once again, we're projecting Bush as both a committee back and a number-three receiver and then combining the numbers.

Brian Calhoun				Height: 5-10		Weight: 203	College: Wisconsin				Draft: 2006/3 (74)		Born: 8-May-1984			Age: 23		Risk: Red	
Year	Team	G	Runs	Yds	Yd/R	TD	FUM	DVOA	Rk	DPAR	Rk	PAR	Suc%	Rec	Pass	Yds	C%	Yd/C	TD	DVOA	Rk	DPAR	Rk
2006	DET	7	7	19	2.7	0	1	-179.9%	—	-3.9	—	-3.5	0%	2	2	20	100%	10.0	0	52.3%	—	0.7	—
2007	DET		29	126	4.3	0								15		92		6.3	1				

Shawn Bryson's injury opened the door for Calhoun to get carries, but the diminutive rookie went down the next week with a torn ACL. Calhoun never seemed to endear himself to Mike Martz, and the arrival of Tatum Bell makes his role for 2007 uncertain.

Aveion Cason				Height: 5-10		Weight: 204	College: Illinois State				Draft: 2001/FA		Born: 12-Jul-1979			Age: 28		Risk: Red	
Year	Team	G	Runs	Yds	Yd/R	TD	FUM	DVOA	Rk	DPAR	Rk	PAR	Suc%	Rec	Pass	Yds	C%	Yd/C	TD	DVOA	Rk	DPAR	Rk
2005	STL	2	10	65	6.5	1	0	62.6%	—	2.8	—	3.1	60%	1	1	11	100%	11.0	0	99.9%	—	0.7	—
2006	DET	6	24	94	3.9	0	0	-4.1%	—	1.1	—	0.1	80%	5	10	26	50%	5.2	0	-66.7%	—	-2.9	—
2007	DET		20	62	3.1	1								8		79		10.1	0				

Cason rejoined the Lions last year after a couple of years in St. Louis and managed to avoid embarrassing himself when he got the chance to start the final two games of the season. He will fight to make the roster, but he has been doing that since he broke into the league in 2001. The Lions have a lot of running backs floating around whose status for 2007 depends on the whims of Mike Martz and the foot of Kevin Jones.

Zack Crockett				Height: 6-2		Weight: 240	College: Florida State				Draft: 1995/3 (79)		Born: 2-Dec-1972			Age: 35		Risk: Yellow	
Year	Team	G	Runs	Yds	Yd/R	TD	FUM	DVOA	Rk	DPAR	Rk	PAR	Suc%	Rec	Pass	Yds	C%	Yd/C	TD	DVOA	Rk	DPAR	Rk
2004	OAK	16	48	232	4.8	2	0	17.6%	—	7.4	—	8.7	61%	16	20	87	80%	5.4	0	-0.6%	—	1.0	—
2005	OAK	16	60	208	3.5	1	0	-7.7%	—	1.6	—	1.1	43%	13	18	111	72%	8.5	0	-23.5%	—	-1.3	—
2006	OAK	16	39	163	4.2	0	2	-11.7%	—	0.8	—	0.2	39%	10	17	53	59%	5.3	0	-46.6%	—	-3.1	—
2007	OAK		20	79	3.9	3								11		51		4.6	0				

The Raiders have ended the last few seasons by giving Crockett an opportunity to play Featured Back for a Day. In 2003, he got ten carries in the season finale. In 2004, he wrapped up the season with a 21-carry, 134-yard effort. In 2005, he carried 30 times in the final two games. Last year, the Zack Crockett Appreciation Day tradition ended, in part because Crockett had turned 34 and no one could pretend that he deserved ten carries in any game, even if most of his teammates had quit long before December arrived. Newcomer Justin Griffith has Crockett's skill set, and, unlike Crockett, he isn't three years older than the head coach. If Crockett sticks for one last season as Griffith's backup, we want to see him to carry the ball 40 times in his final game.

Najeh Davenport				Height: 6-1		Weight: 245	College: Miami				Draft: 2002/4 (135)		Born: 8-Feb-1979			Age: 28		Risk: Red	
Year	Team	G	Runs	Yds	Yd/R	TD	FUM	DVOA	Rk	DPAR	Rk	PAR	Suc%	Rec	Pass	Yds	C%	Yd/C	TD	DVOA	Rk	DPAR	Rk
2004	GB	11	71	359	5.1	2	0	23.3%	—	10.8	—	11.4	51%	4	4	33	100%	8.3	0	76.7%	—	1.6	—
2005	GB	5	30	105	3.5	2	1	-18.5%	—	-0.4	—	-0.1	43%	2	2	3	100%	1.5	0	-84.1%	—	-0.8	—
2006	PIT	13	60	221	3.7	1	1	-32.6%	—	-3.3	—	-4.3	57%	15	21	193	71%	12.9	1	61.8%	—	7.0	—
2007	PIT		53	251	4.7	2								12		106		8.5	0				

Despite spending more time protecting Ben Roethlisberger than actually carrying the ball, Davenport surpassed Verron Hayes on the depth chart last year and has signed on for two more years as Willie Parker's backup in Pittsburgh. If he ever turns his physical gifts into a solid DVOA, we will declare a moratorium on closet jokes, but he's got to take a step forward first.

Stephen Davis Height: 6-0 Weight: 230 College: Auburn Draft: 1996/4 (102) Born: 1-Mar-1974 Age: 33 Risk: Red

Year	Team	G	Runs	Yds	Yd/R	TD	FUM	DVOA	Rk	DPAR	Rk	PAR	Suc%	Rec	Pass	Yds	C%	Yd/C	TD	DVOA	Rk	DPAR	Rk
2004	CAR	2	24	92	3.8	0	0	10.4%	—	2.3	—	2.5	46%	2	2	32	100%	16.0	0	156.3%	—	1.9	—
2005	CAR	13	180	549	3.1	12	2	-15.2%	44	-0.7	44	0.6	39%	5	12	45	42%	9.0	0	-25.7%	—	-1.0	—
2006	STL	15	40	177	4.4	0	1	1.9%	—	2.5	—	2.3	47%	12	17	90	71%	7.5	1	2.5%	—	1.1	—
2007	STL		39	94	2.4	1								6		39		6.3	0				

Davis provided real value to the Rams in 2006 by taking Steven Jackson under his wing and advising him to lower his pads more when anticipating contact with defenders. That small piece of advice helped counteract Jackson's penchant for negative plays, and Davis proceeded to watch Jackson put up the numbers Davis himself had with the Panthers and Redskins. Bad knees make Davis's retirement a possibility, but, hey, that's what we thought last year too.

Ron Dayne Height: 5-10 Weight: 245 College: Wisconsin Draft: 2000/1 (11) Born: 14-Mar-1978 Age: 29 Risk: Red

Year	Team	G	Runs	Yds	Yd/R	TD	FUM	DVOA	Rk	DPAR	Rk	PAR	Suc%	Rec	Pass	Yds	C%	Yd/C	TD	DVOA	Rk	DPAR	Rk
2004	NYG	14	52	179	3.4	1	0	-3.7%	—	2.6	—	2.4	46%	1	4	7	25%	7.0	0	-97.1%	—	-1.6	—
2005	DEN	10	53	270	5.1	1	0	25.3%	—	8.9	—	8.0	53%	3	3	17	100%	5.7	0	-99.9%	—	-2.0	—
2006	HOU	11	151	612	4.1	5	1	4.9%	22	12.3	28	17.3	54%	14	18	77	78%	5.5	0	-19.2%	—	-0.9	—
2007	HOU		82	306	3.7	3								12		110		8.9	0				

Dayne was effective on first down (14.4% DVOA) and in the red zone (46.6% DVOA) last season. He's still a bit of a battering ram with no receiving skills, but he does have some cutback ability, and he doesn't just run up his linemen's legs like he did with the Giants. He's no feature back, but he can absorb ten carries per game, particularly inside the 20-yard line, to keep Ahman Green fresh.

Corey Dillon Height: 5-11 Weight: 225 College: Washington Draft: 1997/2 (43) Born: 24-Oct-1974 Age: 33 Risk: Red

Year	Team	G	Runs	Yds	Yd/R	TD	FUM	DVOA	Rk	DPAR	Rk	PAR	Suc%	Rec	Pass	Yds	C%	Yd/C	TD	DVOA	Rk	DPAR	Rk
2004	NE	15	345	1635	4.7	12	5	19.7%	7	50.3	2	49.5	54%	15	21	103	71%	6.9	1	0.8%	—	1.0	—
2005	NE	12	209	733	3.5	12	1	2.7%	15	16.0	13	17.8	49%	22	26	181	85%	8.2	1	18.6%	11	4.2	17
2006	NE	16	199	812	4.1	13	2	5.2%	21	15.6	21	20.8	52%	15	16	147	94%	9.8	0	24.0%	—	3.0	—
2007	FA		56	221	4.0	3								2		8		4.7	0				

Dillon's final year with the Patriots was more valuable in fantasy than reality; his three-touchdown game against Detroit in Week 13 may have pushed some fantasy teams into the playoffs, but getting 25 yards on 9 carries against a poor rush defense is no great shakes. While he was altogether serviceable, Dillon's going to be 33 and is approaching 2,500 carries. The Patriots were wise to acquiesce to his request to be cut for both performance and chemistry reasons. Dillon gets a generic projection because his public statements seem to vacillate between retirement and return, and nobody has signed him yet.

DeDe Dorsey Height: 5-10 Weight: 194 College: Lindenwood Draft: 2006/FA Born: 1-Aug-1984 Age: 23 Risk: Red

Year	Team	G	Runs	Yds	Yd/R	TD	FUM	DVOA	Rk	DPAR	Rk	PAR	Suc%	Rec	Pass	Yds	C%	Yd/C	TD	DVOA	Rk	DPAR	Rk
2007	IND		87	424	4.9	3								22		209		9.7	1				

A favorite of Bill Polian, Dorsey is an undrafted free agent out of tiny Lindenwood University, near St. Louis. He played sparingly on special teams in his first NFL season, but collected a ring after taking the field for a few snaps in the Super Bowl. With the departure of Dominic Rhodes, Dorsey becomes the primary backup to Joseph Addai, and, while Addai will assume the bulk of the carries, that means he's likely to get 50 to 80 carries in one of the most successful rushing attacks in football. Dorsey already knows the system, so he has a step up on his competitors, and, if Addai gets hurt, Dorsey's going to rush for 1,000 yards by default. He's a stash-on-the-bench fantasy sleeper.

Reuben Droughns Height: 5-11 Weight: 215 College: Oregon Draft: 2000/3 (81) Born: 21-Aug-1978 Age: 29 Risk: Red

Year	Team	G	Runs	Yds	Yd/R	TD	FUM	DVOA	Rk	DPAR	Rk	PAR	Suc%	Rec	Pass	Yds	C%	Yd/C	TD	DVOA	Rk	DPAR	Rk
2004	DEN	16	275	1240	4.5	6	5	-0.3%	26	17.0	16	21.2	51%	32	44	241	73%	7.5	2	10.6%	20	4.9	14
2005	CLE	16	309	1232	4.0	2	6	-13.2%	41	2.1	39	-0.1	44%	39	56	369	70%	9.5	0	1.6%	23	3.4	19
2006	CLE	14	220	758	3.4	4	5	-20.1%	51	-6.8	53	-4.8	42%	27	34	169	82%	6.3	0	-2.5%	32	1.4	30
2007	NYG		161	662	4.1	3								26		186		7.0	0				

(continued next page)

Reuben Droughns (continued)

Droughns gave new meaning to the term "plodder" last season. His longest play from scrimmage covered just 24 yards. He averaged 2.4 yards per carry in September and 2.2 yards per carry in November. Jamal Lewis looks like Barry Sanders when compared to Droughns. Browns coaches weren't really fooled by Droughns last season; they just didn't have anyone else. The Giants seem to think that they signed a change-up back to complement Brandon Jacobs. What they got was a replacement-level back who ran out of gas halfway through the 2005 season.

T. J. Duckett

Height: 6-0 Weight: 254 College: Michigan State   Draft: 2002/1 (18) Born: 17-Feb-1981 Age: 26   Risk: Red

Year	Team	G	Runs	Yds	Yd/R	TD	FUM	DVOA	Rk	DPAR	Rk	PAR	Suc%	Rec	Pass	Yds	C%	Yd/C	TD	DVOA	Rk	DPAR	Rk
2004	ATL	13	104	509	4.9	8	2	22.9%	6	17.5	15	17.4	61%	3	3	15	100%	5.0	0	24.4%	—	0.4	—
2005	ATL	14	121	380	3.1	8	2	-14.7%	43	-0.4	43	-3.0	39%	6	7	63	86%	10.5	0	60.5%	—	2.7	—
2006	WAS	11	38	132	3.5	2	1	-20.8%	—	-0.6	—	-1.2	39%	2	2	16	100%	8.0	0	-9.8%	—	0.0	—
2007	DET		51	160	3.1	2								6		49		8.3	0				

Washington traded for Duckett during the preseason after Clinton Portis went down with a shoulder injury. Inexplicably, the Skins gave up a conditional third-round draft pick and then parked Duckett on the bench behind Ladell Betts. The pick wasn't high enough to make this one of the worst trades of all time, just one of the most stupid. Duckett ended the year with 38 carries—just 14 more than quarterback Jason Campbell—and wisely signed with the Lions this offseason.

Warrick Dunn

Height: 5-9 Weight: 180 College: Florida State   Draft: 1997/1 (12) Born: 5-Jan-1975 Age: 32   Risk: Green

Year	Team	G	Runs	Yds	Yd/R	TD	FUM	DVOA	Rk	DPAR	Rk	PAR	Suc%	Rec	Pass	Yds	C%	Yd/C	TD	DVOA	Rk	DPAR	Rk
2004	ATL	16	265	1106	4.2	9	3	-2.6%	29	11.9	29	12.6	42%	29	39	294	74%	10.1	0	7.6%	23	3.3	24
2005	ATL	16	280	1416	5.1	3	1	22.1%	3	41.0	6	37.8	46%	29	37	220	78%	7.6	1	0.3%	26	1.8	26
2006	ATL	16	286	1140	4.0	4	1	-3.9%	35	12.6	27	5.0	39%	22	27	170	81%	7.7	1	20.2%	9	4.2	21
2007	ATL		201	823	4.1	6								19		152		8.2	1				

Dunn carried 96 times for 511 yards (5.3 yards per carry) in his first five games but 190 times for just 777 yards over the rest of the year (3.3 yards per carry). He had runs of 90 and 35 yards early in the season, but didn't break one for more than 14 yards after Week 10. Nagging second-half injuries were part of the problem, but at 32 years old, those aches and pains aren't going away. If Jerious Norwood and Dunn have not switched roles by the beginning of the season, they will have switched roles by the end.

Heath Evans

Height: 6-0 Weight: 245 College: Auburn   Draft: 2001/3 (82) Born: 30-Dec-1978 Age: 28   Risk: Red

Year	Team	G	Runs	Yds	Yd/R	TD	FUM	DVOA	Rk	DPAR	Rk	PAR	Suc%	Rec	Pass	Yds	C%	Yd/C	TD	DVOA	Rk	DPAR	Rk
2004	SEA	15	7	20	2.9	0	1	-76.5%	—	-2.5	—	-2.4	57%	2	4	12	50%	6.0	0	-88.1%	—	-2.1	—
2005	NE	6	51	192	3.8	0	0	-1.7%	—	2.7	—	2.3	38%	10	17	88	82%	8.8	0	17.6%	—	2.3	—
2006	NE	16	27	117	4.3	0	1	-13.7%	—	0.0	—	0.1	45%	7	9	34	78%	4.9	1	-17.2%	—	-0.4	—
2007	NE		20	89	4.5	0								5		31		5.9	1				

Evans serves as a hybrid halfback/fullback for the Patriots, with most of his value coming as a blocking back and on special teams. He can do this for another few years—the Patriots say two, for now.

Justin Fargas

Height: 6-1 Weight: 220 College: USC   Draft: 2003/3 (96) Born: 25-Jan-1980 Age: 27   Risk: Red

Year	Team	G	Runs	Yds	Yd/R	TD	FUM	DVOA	Rk	DPAR	Rk	PAR	Suc%	Rec	Pass	Yds	C%	Yd/C	TD	DVOA	Rk	DPAR	Rk
2004	OAK	12	35	126	3.6	1	1	6.0%	—	3.1	—	3.7	54%	11	14	68	79%	6.2	0	-26.2%	—	-1.2	—
2005	OAK	14	5	28	5.6	0	0	0.0%	—	0.7	—	0.2	40%	1	5	9	20%	9.0	0	-49.5%	—	-1.2	—
2006	OAK	16	178	659	3.7	1	1	-12.6%	45	1.1	45	0.6	40%	13	21	91	62%	7.0	0	-21.7%	—	-1.2	—
2007	OAK		58	166	2.9	0								15		117		7.6	0				

Fargas has good speed but rarely breaks into the open field to show it off. He got his first chance as a starter when LaMont Jordan went down in Week 12, but he didn't capitalize on that opportunity. Don't expect him to do much this year, either.

Ciatrick Fason

Height: 6-0 Weight: 207 College: Florida Draft: 2005/4 (112) Born: 29-Oct-1982 Age: 25 Risk: Red

Year	Team	G	Runs	Yds	Yd/R	TD	FUM	DVOA	Rk	DPAR	Rk	PAR	Suc%	Rec	Pass	Yds	C%	Yd/C	TD	DVOA	Rk	DPAR	Rk
2005	MIN	13	32	62	1.9	4	0	-16.2%	—	-0.1	—	0.3	41%	0	0	0	0%	0.0	0	0.0%	—	0.0	—
2006	MIN	5	18	99	5.5	1	0	55.2%	—	5.1	—	4.8	40%	3	5	19	60%	6.3	0	-20.5%	—	-0.3	—
2007	*MIN*		*21*	*86*	*4.2*	*1*								*4*		*54*		*12.4*	*0*				

Although it would be a boon to the proofreading industry, a backfield with Ciatrick lining up behind Tarvaris seems unlikely. The third-year back out of Florida fell behind Artose Pinner on the depth chart and is fighting to stay in the league at this point. Then again, Artose could do just as much to keep those red-inkers in the black as Ciatrick.

Kevin Faulk

Height: 5-8 Weight: 202 College: LSU Draft: 1999/2 (46) Born: 5-Jun-1976 Age: 31 Risk: Red

Year	Team	G	Runs	Yds	Yd/R	TD	FUM	DVOA	Rk	DPAR	Rk	PAR	Suc%	Rec	Pass	Yds	C%	Yd/C	TD	DVOA	Rk	DPAR	Rk
2004	NE	11	54	255	4.7	2	1	39.8%	—	11.4	—	11.2	50%	26	30	248	87%	9.5	1	46.8%	2	8.2	8
2005	NE	8	51	145	2.8	0	1	-43.8%	—	-5.6	—	-6.1	33%	29	37	260	78%	9.0	0	-7.8%	31	0.4	30
2006	NE	15	25	123	4.9	1	0	22.4%	—	3.3	—	3.4	56%	43	56	356	77%	8.3	2	19.5%	11	8.3	8
2007	*NE*		*50*	*220*	*4.4*	*2*								*27*		*262*		*9.6*	*1*				

Sometime after Week 13, Bill Belichick was digging in his office sofa for enough change to hit the vending machine when he found a piece of mangled paper stuffed under a cushion. "What's this?" the hoodied man wondered. Suddenly he realized that it was the page from the playbook containing every play the Patriots had that involved handing the ball off to Kevin Faulk. "No wonder he's only carried the ball 14 times this season!" Faulk got 27 carries over the next seven games, and there were two quarters in the Chargers playoff game in which it seemed Faulk kept Corey Dillon, Laurence Maroney, and Heath Evans off the field almost entirely. Faulk has slipped as a pass blocker, though, getting embarrassingly reverse-pancaked on more than one occasion during the playoffs. Reprising that form will bring about the end of his Patriots career right quick.

Tony Fisher

Height: 6-1 Weight: 222 College: Notre Dame Draft: 2002/FA Born: 12-Oct-1979 Age: 28 Risk: #N/A

Year	Team	G	Runs	Yds	Yd/R	TD	FUM	DVOA	Rk	DPAR	Rk	PAR	Suc%	Rec	Pass	Yds	C%	Yd/C	TD	DVOA	Rk	DPAR	Rk
2004	GB	16	65	224	3.4	0	1	-3.5%	—	2.9	—	3.8	49%	38	44	277	86%	7.3	2	15.8%	16	5.3	12
2005	GB	14	60	173	2.9	1	0	-11.8%	—	0.3	—	0.4	40%	48	64	347	75%	7.2	1	-16.3%	36	-2.0	37
2006	STL	8	6	9	1.5	0	0	-79.5%	—	-1.3	—	-1.5	33%	14	18	159	78%	11.4	0	31.4%	—	3.0	—
2007	*FA*		*20*	*60*	*3.0*	*0*								*13*		*122*		*9.4*	*1*				

Fisher didn't see the field much in the first half of the year, then hurt his knee in Week 9 and missed the remainder of the season. He's a versatile back who's useful on special teams, but remained unsigned as of press time.

DeShaun Foster

Height: 6-0 Weight: 222 College: UCLA Draft: 2002/2 (34) Born: 10-Jan-1980 Age: 27 Risk: Red

Year	Team	G	Runs	Yds	Yd/R	TD	FUM	DVOA	Rk	DPAR	Rk	PAR	Suc%	Rec	Pass	Yds	C%	Yd/C	TD	DVOA	Rk	DPAR	Rk
2004	CAR	4	59	255	4.3	2	0	-2.3%	—	3.1	—	4.6	42%	9	9	76	100%	8.4	0	-36.0%	—	0.3	—
2005	CAR	15	205	879	4.3	2	1	-8.4%	32	4.8	31	7.8	43%	34	48	372	71%	10.9	1	12.1%	16	5.1	12
2006	CAR	14	227	897	4.0	3	3	-4.0%	36	11.4	30	4.9	45%	32	46	159	70%	5.0	0	-40.6%	48	-7.1	52
2007	*CAR*		*173*	*698*	*4.0*	*3*								*32*		*217*		*6.7*	*0*				

Foster is awful in the red zone, posting DVOA ratings inside the 20-yard line of −80.5% in 2005 and −59.8% in 2006, with Success Rates of 29 and 35 percent, respectively. The Panthers were the worst goal-to-go team in the NFL last season (DVOA −73.3%) thanks in large part to their inability to cultivate a short-yardage back. A team can only throw so many fades to Keyshawn Johnson and Steve Smith; if opponents know they can stuff your running back at the goal line, they'll find a way to cover your receivers. Foster is one of several Carolina starters lined up at the excuse buffet and filling his tray with "The Line Stunk" and "Dan Henning Was Predictable" casseroles. Excuses aside, he is what he is: a big-play cutback runner who needs to provide many more big plays to keep his featured status.

Samkon Gado

Height: 5-11 Weight: 210 College: Liberty Draft: 2005/FA Born: 13-Nov-1982 Age: 25 Risk: Red

Year	Team	G	Runs	Yds	Yd/R	TD	FUM	DVOA	Rk	DPAR	Rk	PAR	Suc%	Rec	Pass	Yds	C%	Yd/C	TD	DVOA	Rk	DPAR	Rk
2005	GB	8	143	582	4.1	6	3	-10.3%	38	3.1	38	1.0	43%	10	12	77	83%	7.7	1	-14.9%	—	-0.3	—
2006	HOU	10	56	210	3.8	1	1	-22.6%	—	-1.9	—	-2.3	67%	17	23	85	74%	5.0	0	-37.0%	—	-3.0	—
2007	*HOU*		*11*	*31*	*3.0*	*1*								*5*		*61*		*11.4*	*0*				

(continued next page)

Samkon Gado *(continued)*

Liberty's favorite son is now part of a crowd in Houston that includes Ahman Green, Wali Lundy, and Ron Dayne. He's a long shot to make the roster, but it sure was a fun story while it lasted. Now he can go to medical school like he planned, and, in the end, everyone will be the better for his career change.

Nick Goings   Height: 6-0   Weight: 225   College: Pittsburgh   Draft: 2001/FA   Born: 26-Jan-1978   Age: 29   Risk: #N/A

Year	Team	G	Runs	Yds	Yd/R	TD	FUM	DVOA	Rk	DPAR	Rk	PAR	Suc%	Rec	Pass	Yds	C%	Yd/C	TD	DVOA	Rk	DPAR	Rk
2004	CAR	16	217	821	3.8	6	1	-6.8%	37	6.9	36	7.4	44%	45	60	394	75%	8.8	1	19.4%	11	8.8	7
2005	CAR	16	37	133	3.6	0	0	-20.9%	—	-0.8	—	-0.4	41%	14	20	151	70%	10.8	0	24.9%	—	3.4	—
2006	CAR	11	11	52	4.7	0	0	-25.2%	—	-0.5	—	-0.4	30%	10	15	107	67%	10.7	1	28.7%	—	2.8	—
2007	*CAR*		*20*	*74*	*3.7*	*1*								*7*	*44*			*6.4*	*0*				

Goings missed two games at the start of last season and three more at the end with thigh and shoulder injuries. When healthy, he was an invisible man on the Panthers offense, even though the team needed a power back and he filled the role adequately in 2004 and the 2005 playoffs. Heading into 2007, Goings is trapped behind DeAngelo Williams and DeShaun Foster, but can fill roles as a short-yardage runner and third-down blocker/receiver if the new offensive brain-trust gives him a chance. He may have to change his name to DeNick to get noticed.

Frank Gore   Height: 5-9   Weight: 217   College: Miami   Draft: 2005/3 (65)   Born: 14-May-1983   Age: 24   Risk: Green

Year	Team	G	Runs	Yds	Yd/R	TD	FUM	DVOA	Rk	DPAR	Rk	PAR	Suc%	Rec	Pass	Yds	C%	Yd/C	TD	DVOA	Rk	DPAR	Rk
2005	SF	14	127	608	4.8	3	1	7.8%	12	12.0	19	12.1	46%	15	22	131	68%	8.7	0	-29.8%	—	-2.3	—
2006	SF	16	312	1695	5.4	8	5	9.8%	16	34.2	7	33.8	47%	61	86	485	71%	8.0	1	-0.7%	27	4.1	23
2007	*SF*		*347*	*1627*	*4.7*	*16*								*47*	*355*			*7.6*	*1*				

A 5-foot-9, 215-pound back that shreds between the tackles, rides on Larry Allen's hip, and bounces out of trash like a cartoon character? If Emmitt Smith's ears are burning, it's because we're talking about Frank Gore. The 49ers' best player showed brief flashes of greatness in his rookie year, but his 2006 took most everyone by surprise. In the second half of the year, he was as valuable and productive a player as any in the league, gaining 1,023 yards on the ground in his last eight games. In three November games against Detroit, Seattle, and St. Louis, he rushed for a total of 505 yards on only 67 carries for 7.5 yards per carry. Stellar blocking fullback Moran Norris signed up for three more years this offseason, and we're projecting San Francisco to compete for the division title, so everything points to another great season for Gore. He set the all-time 49ers single-season rushing record last year, and this year he very well may set it again, and could even replace LaDainian Tomlinson as the most valuable commodity in fantasy football.

Earnest Graham   Height: 5-9   Weight: 225   College: Florida   Draft: 2004/FA   Born: 15-Jan-1980   Age: 27   Risk: Red

Year	Team	G	Runs	Yds	Yd/R	TD	FUM	DVOA	Rk	DPAR	Rk	PAR	Suc%	Rec	Pass	Yds	C%	Yd/C	TD	DVOA	Rk	DPAR	Rk
2004	TB	9	13	73	5.6	0	0	45.4%	—	3.1	—	3.3	77%	0	1	0	0%	0.0	0	-77.4%	—	-0.4	—
2005	TB	16	28	83	3.0	0	1	-49.9%	—	-4.1	—	-4.3	36%	0	0	0	0%	0.0	0	0.0%	—	0.0	—
2006	TB	16	11	59	5.4	0	0	28.8%	—	2.0	—	2.0	39%	1	4	4	25%	4.0	0	-89.7%	—	-1.7	—
2007	*TB*		*27*	*113*	*4.2*	*0*								*4*	*42*			*11.8*	*0*				

A short bowling ball of a runner, Graham scored two touchdowns in the 2002 Orange Bowl and led the Gators in rushing that season. He spent the last three years on the Buccaneers special teams, recording 17 tackles in 2006, and always looks good in garbage-time offensive action (he carried four times for 38 yards in the loss to the Steelers last year). He could fill a role in the backfield this year, but there are only so many opportunities to go around in Tampa, what with Mike Alstott getting a state-mandated six touches per game and all.

Ahman Green   Height: 6-0   Weight: 218   College: Nebraska   Draft: 1998/3 (76)   Born: 16-Feb-1977   Age: 30   Risk: Yellow

Year	Team	G	Runs	Yds	Yd/R	TD	FUM	DVOA	Rk	DPAR	Rk	PAR	Suc%	Rec	Pass	Yds	C%	Yd/C	TD	DVOA	Rk	DPAR	Rk
2004	GB	15	259	1163	4.5	7	7	-2.8%	31	12.3	27	14.2	50%	40	51	275	78%	6.9	1	-19.6%	47	-2.5	48
2005	GB	5	77	255	3.3	0	1	-19.8%	47	-1.6	46	-3.2	39%	19	27	147	70%	7.7	0	-6.9%	30	0.3	31
2006	GB	14	266	1059	4.0	5	2	4.4%	23	20.6	17	14.1	43%	46	63	373	73%	8.1	1	-0.8%	28	2.6	27
2007	*HOU*		*250*	*971*	*3.9*	*6*								*35*	*287*			*8.3*	*0*				

Green broke down after an exceptional 2003 campaign that saw him take 403 carries between the regular season and post-season. Predictably, two down years followed, but he rebounded to have a solid 2006 season behind a young offensive line. Green's comeback came on a one-year make-good contract that paid off when he signed a sizable deal with Houston. That may pay off as well, at least in fantasy terms, as Houston had a solid ground attack with lesser running backs last year, and the switch to the AFC South from the NFC North adds two extra games against bad run defenses to his schedule. When it comes to actual football, however, a 30-year-old running back makes absolutely no sense for a rebuilding team.

Arlen Harris

Height: 5-10 Weight: 212 College: Hofstra   Draft: 2003/FA   Born: 22-Apr-1980 Age: 27   Risk: Red

Year	Team	G	Runs	Yds	Yd/R	TD	FUM	DVOA	Rk	DPAR	Rk	PAR	Suc%	Rec	Pass	Yds	C%	Yd/C	TD	DVOA	Rk	DPAR	Rk
2004	STL	14	20	63	3.2	0	1	-20.3%	—	-0.5	—	-0.7	40%	4	4	44	100%	11.0	0	-43.4%	—	-0.7	—
2005	STL	16	13	21	1.6	1	0	-33.6%	—	-1.2	—	-1.1	0%	4	5	34	80%	8.5	0	50.9%	—	1.2	—
2006	DET	10	49	158	3.2	1	0	-17.9%	—	0.3	—	-2.2	0%	18	25	132	72%	7.3	0	-5.1%	33	0.6	34
2007	FA		24	71	2.9	1								13		93		7.3	0				

Harris has a career yards-per-carry average of 3.0 and mediocre receiving skills. Unless Mike Martz brings him back, his NFL career is likely over.

Jerome Harrison

Height: 5-10 Weight: 200 College: Washington State   Draft: 2006/5 (145) Born: 26-Feb-1983 Age: 24   Risk: Red

Year	Team	G	Runs	Yds	Yd/R	TD	FUM	DVOA	Rk	DPAR	Rk	PAR	Suc%	Rec	Pass	Yds	C%	Yd/C	TD	DVOA	Rk	DPAR	Rk
2006	CLE	10	20	60	3.0	0	1	-61.5%	—	-3.7	—	-4.2	92%	9	14	47	64%	5.2	0	-24.1%	—	-1.0	—
2007	CLE		9	42	4.5	0								8		60		7.2	0				

It was Harrison—not Reggie Bush—who led the Pac-10 in rushing in 2005, and, as a rookie last year, he gave Cleveland fans hope with a solid preseason. Once the regular season rolled around, with poor blocking in front of him, he never showed off the pure speed that made him a good college player.

Verron Haynes

Height: 5-10 Weight: 223 College: Georgia   Draft: 2002/5 (166) Born: 17-Feb-1979 Age: 28   Risk: Red

Year	Team	G	Runs	Yds	Yd/R	TD	FUM	DVOA	Rk	DPAR	Rk	PAR	Suc%	Rec	Pass	Yds	C%	Yd/C	TD	DVOA	Rk	DPAR	Rk
2004	PIT	13	55	272	4.9	0	0	29.2%	—	9.3	—	8.4	47%	18	23	142	78%	7.9	2	41.8%	—	5.1	—
2005	PIT	14	74	274	3.7	3	2	-27.7%	—	-4.0	—	-2.2	39%	11	17	113	65%	10.3	0	24.9%	—	2.5	—
2006	PIT	7	15	78	5.2	0	1	-12.2%	—	0.1	—	-0.3	75%	18	22	95	82%	5.3	0	-11.2%	—	-0.2	—
2007	PIT		52	202	3.9	1								13		118		9.4	0				

Haynes was released by the Steelers prior to the start of free agency after injuring his knee midway through the 2006 season. Najeh Davenport replaced him as the primary backup to Willie Parker, and was unspectacular, and free-agent signing Kevan Barlow is awful, so the door may be open for Haynes to return.

Chris Henry

Height: 5-11 Weight: 230 College: Arizona   Draft: 2007/2 (50) Born: 6-Jun-1985 Age: 22   Risk: Red

Year	Team	G	Runs	Yds	Yd/R	TD	FUM	DVOA	Rk	DPAR	Rk	PAR	Suc%	Rec	Pass	Yds	C%	Yd/C	TD	DVOA	Rk	DPAR	Rk
2007	TEN		140	562	4.0	4								17		127		7.4	1				

Henry was a Combine superstar who didn't get many carries in college. He backed up Mike Bell at Arizona in 2004 and 2005, then lost his starting job in 2006 because he didn't meet minimum academic requirements. Henry projects as a speedy complement to LenDale White, but he is not ready to be the starter. Still, he could open the season in that role, because White battled weight issues in the offseason and tweaked his hamstring in camp.

Travis Henry

Height: 5-9 Weight: 215 College: Tennessee   Draft: 2001/2 (58) Born: 29-Oct-1978 Age: 29   Risk: Yellow

Year	Team	G	Runs	Yds	Yd/R	TD	FUM	DVOA	Rk	DPAR	Rk	PAR	Suc%	Rec	Pass	Yds	C%	Yd/C	TD	DVOA	Rk	DPAR	Rk
2004	BUF	10	94	326	3.5	0	0	-10.6%	39	1.4	41	0.2	43%	10	14	45	71%	4.5	0	-13.8%	—	-0.2	—
2005	TEN	9	88	335	3.8	0	2	-26.7%	51	-4.3	49	-5.2	35%	13	20	117	65%	9.0	0	8.7%		0.1	—
2006	TEN	14	270	1211	4.5	7	3	-2.8%	32	12.1	29	14.4	43%	18	25	78	72%	4.3	0	-51.1%	52	-4.8	47
2007	DEN		283	1254	4.4	8								21		144		6.8	0				

In 2006, for the third time in his career, Henry rushed for over 1,000 yards but posted a negative DVOA. In 2002 and 2003, fumbles were the problem, with Henry coughing it up 18 times between the two seasons. Last year, he put just three footballs on the ground, but DVOA still wasn't crazy about him for three reasons: (1) He gets stuffed a lot, losing yardage on 10.3 percent of his carries last year. Among running backs with more than 1,000 yards, only Shaun Alexander had a higher percentage of losses. (2) He wasn't very good on third down, with a dirt-poor −53.2% DVOA and a 15 percent Success Rate on 13 carries. (3) He had some high-calorie games against sweet-tooth defenses such as the Colts (216 yards in two games), Redskins

(continued next page)

Travis Henry *(continued)*

(178 yards) and Eagles (143 yards during their midseason swoon). Now in Denver, Henry will split time with Mike Bell and whoever else Mike Shanahan takes a liking to, but could keep Bell on the bench as his tackle-breaking ability is a perfect match for the Broncos' offensive line, which will often deliver him to the second level. As long as he doesn't violate the league's substance abuse policy again, he should break 1,000 yards for the fourth time, but this time with a positive DVOA to go with that hearty helping of fantasy football value.

Noah Herron   Height: 5-11 Weight: 224 College: Northwestern   Draft: 2005/7 (244) Born: 3-Apr-1982   Age: 25   Risk: Red

Year	Team	G	Runs	Yds	Yd/R	TD	FUM	DVOA	Rk	DPAR	Rk	PAR	Suc%	Rec	Pass	Yds	C%	Yd/C	TD	DVOA	Rk	DPAR	Rk
2005	GB	5	45	121	2.7	2	0	-5.6%	—	1.8	—	-0.1	42%	0	0	0	0%	0.0	0	0.0%	—	0.0	
2006	GB	16	37	150	4.1	1	0	6.5%	—	3.2	—	3.8	25%	29	35	211	83%	7.3	2	20.1%	10	5.3	18
2007	*GB*		*43*	*169*	*3.9*	*1*								*17*		*191*		*11.3*	*1*				

This shifty back was happily living the third-down back existence when the Packers went out and added Vernand Morency. Herron ran for 106 yards against St. Louis early in the season, but, as you can see, got few opportunities besides that. Stuck behind Morency on the depth chart, he will fight rookie Brandon Jackson for playing time.

Maurice Hicks   Height: 5-10 Weight: 200 College: North Carolina A&T   Draft: 2003/FA   Born: 22-Jul-1978   Age: 29   Risk: Yellow

Year	Team	G	Runs	Yds	Yd/R	TD	FUM	DVOA	Rk	DPAR	Rk	PAR	Suc%	Rec	Pass	Yds	C%	Yd/C	TD	DVOA	Rk	DPAR	Rk
2004	SF	9	96	362	3.8	2	3	-21.9%	50	-3.5	50	-6.4	35%	16	25	154	64%	9.6	0	20.6%	10	4.0	20
2005	SF	14	59	308	5.2	3	0	12.9%	—	6.7	—	8.1	41%	12	16	47	75%	3.9	0	-53.1%	—	-3.6	—
2006	SF	16	29	82	2.8	0	0	-23.0%	—	-1.0	—	-0.6	60%	13	15	137	87%	10.5	1	66.3%	—	5.6	—
2007	*SF*		*25*	*107*	*4.2*	*1*								*11*		*76*		*6.6*	*0*				

At 5-foot-11 and 196 pounds, Hicks isn't the sort of back to take a full season of pounding in a feature role, but he's been a decent change of pace for the 49ers. We'll see how that holds up if Michael Robinson gets more touches in his second season, because the 49ers don't really need a change of pace from Frank Gore often enough for both backs to get a lot of carries.

Cedric Houston   Height: 5-11 Weight: 220 College: Tennessee   Draft: 2005/6 (182) Born: 28-Jun-1982   Age: 25   Risk: Red

Year	Team	G	Runs	Yds	Yd/R	TD	FUM	DVOA	Rk	DPAR	Rk	PAR	Suc%	Rec	Pass	Yds	C%	Yd/C	TD	DVOA	Rk	DPAR	Rk
2005	NYJ	12	81	302	3.7	2	0	1.4%	20	5.3	29	5.5	42%	8	10	66	80%	8.3	0	14.9%	—	1.0	—
2006	NYJ	8	113	374	3.3	5	0	-4.0%	37	4.9	38	4.6	45%	7	8	43	88%	6.1	0	-29.8%	—	-0.7	—
2007	*NYJ*		*41*	*153*	*3.7*	*2*								*9*		*88*		*9.8*	*0*				

This 2005 sixth-rounder was surrounded in the DVOA rankings by much more expensive brethren: The 34th-ranked back in the league was Reggie Bush, while the 37th was Warrick Dunn and the 38th was Lamont Jordan. Houston usurped most of Kevan Barlow's playing time as the season went along, but the FOX Stretching Robot, a Robosapien, or the guy in the Pinaud-Clubman logo would've done the same thing. The emergence of Leon Washington as a complementary back and the acquisition of Thomas Jones mean that Houston's not likely to see 113 carries again.

Tony Hunt   Height: 6-2 Weight: 233 College: Penn State   Draft: 2007/3 (90)   Born: 24-Nov-1985 Age: 22   Risk: Red

Year	Team	G	Runs	Yds	Yd/R	TD	FUM	DVOA	Rk	DPAR	Rk	PAR	Suc%	Rec	Pass	Yds	C%	Yd/C	TD	DVOA	Rk	DPAR	Rk
2007	*PHI*		*41*	*180*	*4.4*	*1*								*9*		*66*		*7.7*	*1*				

Hunt is the prototypical Penn State running back. He's a step slow and lacks open field moves, but he's durable, patient, and capable of pounding out yards between the tackles. Hunt lies somewhere between Curtis Enis and Leroy Thompson on the list of Nittany Lions rushing prospects. He's good enough for his projected role as a power back off the bench, and he should easily take a roster spot away from Ryan Moats while challenging Correll Buckhalter for a role in the offense.

Kenny Irons   Height: 5-11 Weight: 203 College: Auburn   Draft: 2007/2 (49) Born: 15-Sep-1983 Age: 24   Risk: Red

Year	Team	G	Runs	Yds	Yd/R	TD	FUM	DVOA	Rk	DPAR	Rk	PAR	Suc%	Rec	Pass	Yds	C%	Yd/C	TD	DVOA	Rk	DPAR	Rk
2007	*CIN*		*77*	*346*	*4.5*	*3*								*9*		*87*		*9.2*	*0*				

Durability questions kept Irons from going higher in the draft. Cincinnati took him in the second round, and he figures to get a few carries as the Bengals try to keep Rudi Johnson fresh. Auburn has a long tradition of producing NFL-caliber running backs (Bo Jackson, Johnson, Cadillac Williams, Ronnie Brown), and Irons certainly has the talent to perform at the NFL level.

Brandon Jackson Height: 5-10 Weight: 210 College: Nebraska Draft: 2007/2 (63) Born: 2-Oct-1985 Age: 22 Risk: Red

Year	Team	G	Runs	Yds	Yd/R	TD	FUM	DVOA	Rk	DPAR	Rk	PAR	Suc%	Rec	Pass	Yds	C%	Yd/C	TD	DVOA	Rk	DPAR	Rk
2007	GB		146	563	3.8	3								23		158		6.9	1				

Jackson is a complementary-back type. He's small in stature, runs better outside than inside, and was a productive receiver at Nebraska. The Huskers used him in a committee system, so he never had to take a pounding as a full-time back, and he doesn't have the downhill power of a traditional feature back. The Packers drafted him in the second round, so they expect him to play a major role. He might not be ready.

Steven Jackson Height: 6-2 Weight: 231 College: Oregon State Draft: 2004/1 (24) Born: 22-Jul-1983 Age: 24 Risk: Yellow

Year	Team	G	Runs	Yds	Yd/R	TD	FUM	DVOA	Rk	DPAR	Rk	PAR	Suc%	Rec	Pass	Yds	C%	Yd/C	TD	DVOA	Rk	DPAR	Rk
2004	STL	14	134	673	5.0	4	1	17.9%	9	19.9	11	19.1	57%	19	24	189	79%	9.9	0	41.9%	—	5.4	—
2005	STL	15	254	1046	4.1	8	3	-9.1%	35	5.4	28	7.5	42%	43	55	320	78%	7.4	2	18.7%	9	8.2	7
2006	STL	16	346	1528	4.4	13	2	10.2%	13	36.2	4	36.0	48%	90	110	806	82%	9.0	3	15.9%	14	14.6	1
2007	STL		312	1372	4.4	7								78		719		9.2	2				

Jackson's combined rushing-receiving total of 2,334 yards edged out LaDainian Tomlinson's 2,323 for tops in the NFL last year. Jackson's versatility, not to mention his new consistency, has him positioned to be the lynchpin in Scott Linehan's offense in the same way that Marshall Faulk drove Dick Vermeil's and Mike Martz's Greatest Show on Turf. Like Faulk, Jackson will last longer than most running backs because his workload is more evenly split between carries and catches. The most similar running backs in their first three seasons: Thurman Thomas, Gerald Riggs, William Andrews, and Deuce McAllister.

Brandon Jacobs Height: 6-4 Weight: 256 College: Southern Illinois Draft: 2005/4 (110) Born: 6-Jul-1982 Age: 25 Risk: Yellow

Year	Team	G	Runs	Yds	Yd/R	TD	FUM	DVOA	Rk	DPAR	Rk	PAR	Suc%	Rec	Pass	Yds	C%	Yd/C	TD	DVOA	Rk	DPAR	Rk
2005	NYG	16	38	99	2.6	7	1	-3.6%	—	2.6	—	2.2	58%	0	0	0	0%	0.0	0	0.0%	—	0.0	—
2006	NYG	15	96	423	4.4	9	2	17.7%	8	15.0	22	15.8	57%	11	14	149	79%	13.5	0	87.1%	—	5.8	—
2007	NYG		236	973	4.1	9								10		158		15.8	1				

Last season, Jacobs performed well in a specialized role behind the now-retired Tiki Barber. In 2007, he will assume the starting job, although the Giants traded for Reuben Droughns to provide support. Despite limited action, Jacobs ranked eighth in rushing DVOA, which was three spots better than Barber, while his 57 percent success rate was third best in the league, seven percentage points ahead of Barber. While there are some concerns that Jacobs might not be as effective as a full-time back, if the Giants use him properly—and can figure out the left side of their offensive line—Big Blue should continue to have one of the top running games in the NFC.

Edgerrin James Height: 6-0 Weight: 214 College: Miami Draft: 1999/1 (4) Born: 1-Aug-1978 Age: 29 Risk: Red

Year	Team	G	Runs	Yds	Yd/R	TD	FUM	DVOA	Rk	DPAR	Rk	PAR	Suc%	Rec	Pass	Yds	C%	Yd/C	TD	DVOA	Rk	DPAR	Rk
2004	IND	16	334	1548	4.6	9	5	9.9%	14	34.8	4	41.0	57%	51	60	483	85%	9.5	0	40.2%	5	14.7	1
2005	IND	15	360	1506	4.2	13	2	10.6%	0	50.0	3	51.4	62%	44	50	337	88%	7.7	1	27.3%	5	10.0	3
2006	ARI	16	337	1159	3.4	6	3	-11.5%	44	3.7	39	6.0	45%	38	60	217	63%	5.7	0	-25.6%	44	-4.8	46
2007	ARI		269	1054	3.9	6								37		260		7.0	0				

Okay, hands up...who thought this would work? When James moved from Indianapolis, the team with the NFL's top offensive line in Adjusted Line Yards in 2005, to Arizona, home of the league's worst, most prognosticators still saw a bright future for the Cardinals' running game. As we wrote in *Pro Football Prospectus 2006*, "James's play this season is going to be a fascinating test case in the debate about how important a running back is to a team." In truth, James's acquisition was an even more fascinating test case in the debate about how important an offensive line is to a running back. After rushing for 100 or more yards a total of 17 times over the 2004 and 2005 seasons, he did so just three times in 2006, and all in December, when Arizona's line started to show some signs of life.

Though the Cardinals rose from 32nd to 23rd in ALY last year, James and his compatriots bottomed out in 10+ Yard percentage, as they were the NFL's worst in breaking long runs. That wasn't the Arizona line's fault, though—the Colts finished last in 10+ Yard percentage in 2005 when James was their main man. Though in 2006 he reversed a previous tendency to wear down as the season wears on, James will be 29 when the 2007 season starts, and is wasting what little time he has left plying his trade behind an embarrassingly ineffective front five. According to new coach Ken Whisenhunt, the team will counter this by integrating another running back more often, and you have to figure that the blocking will be a little better with tackle Levi Brown and new line coach Russ Grimm around.

Larry Johnson

Height: 6-1 **Weight:** 230 **College:** Penn State   **Draft:** 2003/1 (27) **Born:** 19-Nov-1979 **Age:** 28   **Risk:** Red

Year	Team	G	Runs	Yds	Yd/R	TD	FUM	DVOA	Rk	DPAR	Rk	PAR	Suc%	Rec	Pass	Yds	C%	Yd/C	TD	DVOA	Rk	DPAR	Rk
2004	KC	10	120	581	4.8	9	0	28.0%	4	24.0	9	21.8	53%	22	28	278	79%	12.6	2	76.9%	1	13.0	4
2005	KC	16	336	1750	5.2	20	5	26.0%	2	59.8	1	61.5	55%	33	49	343	67%	10.4	1	23.8%	7	8.5	6
2006	KC	16	416	1789	4.3	17	6	-2.5%	31	15.6	20	10.6	44%	41	31	410	74%	10.0	2	-19.0%	40	-1.5	40
2007	KC		342	1200	3.5	13								33		257		7.8	1				

Only one running back regularly hit 370 carries, year after year, without breaking down: Eric Dickerson. Can Johnson possibily follow in his footsteps? He didn't take many hits in college, although the Chiefs are making up for that now. He's still young, and he has tremendous talent. Then again, the 25-year-old Edgerrin James was a tremendous young talent, and so was the 25-year-old Barry Foster, and the 27-year-old Terrell Davis, and the 27-year-old Jamal Anderson, and the 26-year-old Ricky Williams, and . . .

Funny thing is, LJ is still a late-first-round fantasy back, despite the increased risk of injury. Even if the Curse of 370 destroys his speed, you know he's still getting the rock at the goal line.

Rudi Johnson

Height: 5-10 **Weight:** 225 **College:** Auburn   **Draft:** 2001/4 (100) **Born:** 1-Oct-1979   **Age:** 28 **Risk:** Yellow

Year	Team	G	Runs	Yds	Yd/R	TD	FUM	DVOA	Rk	DPAR	Rk	PAR	Suc%	Rec	Pass	Yds	C%	Yd/C	TD	DVOA	Rk	DPAR	Rk
2004	CIN	16	361	1454	4.0	12	4	5.1%	19	30.6	5	21.8	46%	15	28	84	54%	5.6	0	-48.6%	—	-5.3	—
2005	CIN	16	337	1458	4.3	12	1	19.6%	6	48.0	4	48.8	52%	23	30	90	77%	3.9	0	-59.0%	53	-7.5	53
2006	CIN	16	341	1309	3.8	12	0	24.6%	—	2.4	—	2.0	50%	23	9	124	67%	5.4	0	-37.4%	—	-1.2	—
2007	CIN		314	1281	4.1	12								21		104		5.0	0				

Fantasy owners probably didn't think Rudi Johnson had a down year in 2006, as his yards and touchdowns stacked up well with the previous two seasons, but our stats show a sharp drop-off in DVOA and Success Rate. The Bengals' offensive line also slipped to 10th in Adjusted Line Yards from fourth in 2005. The problems came on first and second down, on which Johnson had negative DVOA figures, and not on third and fourth, as he remained proficient at converting short-yardage situations. But where was his explosiveness? Johnson had five runs of 20-plus yards, same as 2005, but incredibly not one of those went for more than 22 yards. That lack of burst could indicate that Johnson is slowing down after three straight seasons of 337 or more carries.

Greg Jones

Height: 6-1 **Weight:** 250 **College:** Florida State   **Draft:** 2004/2 (55) **Born:** 4-Apr-1981   **Age:** 26 **Risk:** Red

Year	Team	G	Runs	Yds	Yd/R	TD	FUM	DVOA	Rk	DPAR	Rk	PAR	Suc%	Rec	Pass	Yds	C%	Yd/C	TD	DVOA	Rk	DPAR	Rk
2004	JAC	16	62	162	2.6	3	1	-24.2%	—	-3.2	—	-2.2	48%	3	10	13	30%	4.3	0	-72.1%	—	-3.4	—
2005	JAC	14	151	575	3.8	4	0	0.3%	22	9.2	21	10.5	45%	10	15	65	67%	6.5	0	-11.0%	—	-0.1	—
2007	JAC		46	164	3.6	2								12		73		6.3	0				

Before he tore his left ACL during the 2006 preseason, the Jaguars were developing Jones as a halfback/fullback tweener, basically Mike Alstott without the high sales figures for licensed apparel. The injury was actually Jones's second ACL tear, as he tore his right one as a junior at Florida State in 2002. The fact that players returning from ACL injuries gain straight-line speed before shiftiness doesn't matter much for a player who never counted shiftiness as one of his biggest assets. The Jaguars have a lot of running backs floating around and fighting for spots behind Fred Taylor and Maurice Jones-Drew, but Jones has the most talent and the skill set that complements the starters best. He should make the roster if healthy.

Julius Jones

Height: 5-10 **Weight:** 211 **College:** Notre Dame   **Draft:** 2004/2 (43) **Born:** 14-Aug-1981 **Age:** 26   **Risk:** Red

Year	Team	G	Runs	Yds	Yd/R	TD	FUM	DVOA	Rk	DPAR	Rk	PAR	Suc%	Rec	Pass	Yds	C%	Yd/C	TD	DVOA	Rk	DPAR	Rk
2004	DAL	8	197	819	4.2	7	3	-0.8%	27	11.4	30	9.0	43%	17	26	109	65%	6.4	0	-17.3%	43	-1.0	42
2005	DAL	13	257	993	3.9	5	3	-7.4%	30	7.3	24	2.4	39%	35	46	218	78%	6.2	0	-19.7%	37	-2.3	40
2006	DAL	16	267	1084	4.1	4	1	-1.6%	27	14.0	24	17.7	45%	9	15	142	60%	15.8	0	63.6%	—	5.7	—
2007	DAL		227	975	4.3	6								14		172		12.5	0				

Jones started all 16 games and the Cowboys' playoff game last season, but as the season progressed, he lost carries to Marion Barber, and by Week 12 he was a starter only by dint of the fact that he was on the field for the first play of every game. He never carried the ball more than 13 times in any of Dallas's final six games (though he did get 22 carries in the Wild Card game). The Cowboys shopped Jones before the draft but couldn't find any takers in a market glutted with veteran featured backs. He could still be traded during camp to a running-back-poor team such as the Packers. Despite his impressive yardage totals, he's a pretty ordinary runner who doesn't offer much as a receiver.

Kevin Jones   Height: 5-11   Weight: 221   College: Virginia Tech   Draft: 2004/1 (30)   Born: 21-Aug-1982   Age: 25   Risk: Red

Year	Team	G	Runs	Yds	Yd/R	TD	FUM	DVOA	Rk	DPAR	Rk	PAR	Suc%	Rec	Pass	Yds	C%	Yd/C	TD	DVOA	Rk	DPAR	Rk
2004	DET	15	241	1133	4.7	5	2	1.5%	24	15.4	20	21.4	46%	28	41	180	68%	6.4	1	-19.4%	46	-2.0	45
2005	DET	13	186	664	3.6	5	2	-9.5%	36	4.2	33	0.8	43%	20	28	109	71%	5.5	0	-30.8%	48	-3.3	47
2006	DET	12	181	689	3.8	6	4	-22.3%	52	-5.6	52	-4.8	40%	61	78	520	78%	8.5	2	22.1%	8	13.2	2
2007	DET		83	345	4.2	3								31		271		8.7	0				

Among players with 75 carries, the only player with a lower rushing DVOA than Kevin Jones was Anthony Thomas. Like Jones, Thomas had by far his best season as a rookie. Needless to say, this is not a comparison Jones wants to encourage. Jones has battled nagging injuries for two seasons and lost the end of last season to a major Lisfranc injury. His status for the beginning of the season is uncertain, and the arrival of Tatum Bell should decrease his carries. One thing the Lions do have to look forward to is Jones's presence in the passing game, as he showed a good understanding of how to follow blockers on screen passes. He remains an asset, but hopes of stardom seem to have vanished.

Thomas Jones   Height: 5-10   Weight: 220   College: Virginia   Draft: 2000/1 (7)   Born: 19-Aug-1978   Age: 29   Risk: Green

Year	Team	G	Runs	Yds	Yd/R	TD	FUM	DVOA	Rk	DPAR	Rk	PAR	Suc%	Rec	Pass	Yds	C%	Yd/C	TD	DVOA	Rk	DPAR	Rk
2004	CHI	14	240	948	4.0	7	2	-2.6%	28	12.4	26	14.0	47%	56	72	427	78%	7.6	0	-3.9%	32	2.3	29
2005	CHI	15	314	1335	4.3	9	2	1.8%	19	20.3	11	19.4	41%	26	39	143	67%	5.5	0	-32.3%	50	-4.5	49
2006	CHI	16	296	1210	4.1	6	1	5.7%	19	25.7	11	26.1	48%	36	47	154	77%	4.3	0	-34.0%	47	-6.2	50
2007	NYJ		299	1130	3.8	9								27		109		4.0	0				

Jones's career has been a little strange. He has gone from first-round bust to dependable starter for a conference champion over seven professional seasons. The Jets will be his fourth team in the last six years, but his stays in both Tampa Bay and Chicago have to be considered successes. Jones ran harder and with less hesitation last season. His big runs dropped off, but he was considerably more consistent. In New York, the presence of Leon Washington could keep Jones's carries where they were last season, which would prevent an increase in his overall fantasy value. Washington is also better in the red zone, though Jones's more prototypical size may get him the red zone carries anyway.

The biggest concern surrounding the Jets' acquisition of Jones is not what he'll do in 2007, but what he'll do beyond that. The list of running backs with three-year spans in their careers that most resemble Jones's last three seasons is pretty impressive, until you look at what these guys did after those three seasons. Mike Pruitt (1900–1902) and Ricky Watters (1997–1999) each had only one more big year, and Roger Craig (1987–1989) had none. Ottis Anderson (1982–1984) spent the next four years as a part-timer before his big comeback season with the 1989 Giants. It isn't all pessimistic, however: The fifth and sixth guys on the list are Corey Dillon and Curtis Martin, each from 2000–2002.

Maurice Jones-Drew   Height: 5-8   Weight: 205   College: UCLA   Draft: 2006/2 (60)   Born: 23-Mar-1985   Age: 22   Risk: Yellow

Year	Team	G	Runs	Yds	Yd/R	TD	FUM	DVOA	Rk	DPAR	Rk	PAR	Suc%	Rec	Pass	Yds	C%	Yd/C	TD	DVOA	Rk	DPAR	Rk
2006	JAC	16	166	941	5.7	13	1	23.6%	5	26.0	10	33.4	51%	46	62	436	74%	9.5	2	17.1%	12	8.3	7
2007	JAC		239	1161	4.9	11								44		347		7.9	2				

Jones-Drew had a monster rookie season and showed far more talent than anyone expected. In *Pro Football Prospectus 2006*, we called him a "slightly better version of Alvin Pearson," which may have been the understatement of the year. Actually, he's a remarkably better version of Alvin Pearson. The most surprising of Jones-Drew's many skills is not his shiftiness or his speed; it's his ability to push piles despite his small size. Warrick Dunn is the only similar back who compares.

Since 1978, 11 running backs have scored a dozen or more touchdowns with fewer than 200 carries, and three of those players did it last year (table 6).

Maurice Jones-Drew stands out on that list as a very different type of player compared to other running backs who achieved this mark. Most of those guys were either bowling-ball fullbacks or, like Marion Barber and Corey Dillon, the member of a two-running-back committee that got the goal-line carries. The only similar back in size is Priest Holmes, and MJD gained almost a yard per carry more than everyone else on the list. Last year, Dillon had six touchdowns of just one yard, and only two on carries over ten yards. Barber had six touchdowns of just one yard, and only one on a carry over ten yards. MJD had only two touchdowns of one yard and six touchdowns on carries over ten yards, including a 32-yard touchdown run against Miami, a 48-yard touchdown run against Indianapolis, and the infamous, 74-yard, "his knee never actually hit the ground" touchdown run against New England.

(continued next page)

Maurice Jones-Drew *(continued)*

Table 6. Running Backs with Fewer Than 200 Carries and 12 or More Touchdowns, 1978–2006

Player	Year	Team	G	Runs	Yds	Yd/R	TD	Height	Weight
Pete Johnson	1984	MIA/SD	16	87	205	2.4	12	6′ 0″	252
Robb Riddick	1988	BUF	15	111	438	3.9	12	6′ 0″	195
Marion Barber	2006	DAL	16	135	654	4.8	14	5′ 11″	218
Herschel Walker	1986	DAL	16	151	737	4.9	12	6′ 1″	225
Maurice Jones-Drew	2006	JAC	16	166	941	5.7	13	5′ 8″	205
David Sims	1978	SEA	12	174	752	4.3	14	6′ 3″	216
Marcus Allen	1990	RAI	16	179	682	3.8	12	6′ 2″	210
Stephen Davis	2005	CAR	13	180	549	3.1	12	6′ 0″	230
John Riggins	1981	WAS	15	195	714	3.7	13	6′ 2″	230
Priest Holmes	2004	KC	8	196	892	4.6	14	5′ 9″	213
Corey Dillon	2006	NE	16	199	812	4.1	13	5′ 11″	225

LaMont Jordan Height: 5-10 Weight: 230 College: Maryland Draft: 2001/2 (49) Born: 11-Nov-1978 Age: 29 Risk: Red

Year	Team	G	Runs	Yds	Yd/R	TD	FUM	DVOA	Rk	DPAR	Rk	PAR	Suc%	Rec	Pass	Yds	C%	Yd/C	TD	DVOA	Rk	DPAR	Rk
2004	NYJ	16	93	479	5.2	2	0	36.0%	1	19.2	13	20.6	55%	15	16	112	94%	7.5	0	42.7%	—	4.4	—
2005	OAK	14	272	1025	3.8	9	2	2.1%	17	19.5	12	19.6	47%	70	103	563	68%	8.0	2	-0.7%	27	5.0	14
2006	OAK	10	114	434	3.8	2	0	-8.1%	38	2.8	42	0.5	34%	10	16	74	63%	7.4	0	-34.2%	—	-1.9	—
2007	OAK		189	843	4.5	4								25		178		7.0	0				

Although his numbers haven't looked good since he went from backup in New York to starter in Oakland, Jordan really hasn't been that bad when you consider the line he's running behind. He's still young enough that he could become a solid contributor if he ever plays in a halfway decent offense. This 2007 projection is fairly tentative, since we don't know how Lane Kiffin will split carries between Jordan and Dominic Rhodes.

ReShard Lee Height: 5-10 Weight: 220 College: Middle Tennessee State Draft: 2004/FA Born: 12-Oct-1980 Age: 27 Risk: Red

Year	Team	G	Runs	Yds	Yd/R	TD	FUM	DVOA	Rk	DPAR	Rk	PAR	Suc%	Rec	Pass	Yds	C%	Yd/C	TD	DVOA	Rk	DPAR	Rk
2004	DAL	14	27	128	4.7	1	0	23.4%	—	4.4	—	4.7	44%	1	3	4	33%	4.0	0	-113.3%	—	-1.5	—
2005	GB	7	11	16	1.5	0	1	0.0%	0	-4.4	-1.2	-1.2	0%	1	1	5	100%	5.0	0	13.1%	—	0.0	—
2006	OAK	16	21	72	3.4	2	1	-22.0%	—	-1.3	—	-1.0	52%	20	25	138	80%	6.9	0	0.2%	26	1.3	31
2007	OAK		9	42	4.6	1								10		52		5.3	0				

Lee is a good athlete and a versatile player who can contribute on special teams as well as line up at fullback and halfback. He's bounced around the league for years and hasn't gotten much attention, but if he ever finds the right offense, he could be a solid contributor.

Brian Leonard Height: 6-2 Weight: 226 College: Rutgers Draft: 2007/2 (52) Born: 3-Feb-1984 Age: 23 Risk: Red

Year	Team	G	Runs	Yds	Yd/R	TD	FUM	DVOA	Rk	DPAR	Rk	PAR	Suc%	Rec	Pass	Yds	C%	Yd/C	TD	DVOA	Rk	DPAR	Rk
2007	STL		61	247	4.1	4								25		219		8.7	1				

Alstott, Shmalstott. Draftniks seemed incapable of mentioning Leonard without comparing him to Mike Alstott this off-season. Some mock drafters speculated that the Buccaneers would select Leonard to serve as Alstott's protégé. Since when do fullbacks need mentors? Alstott and Leonard share some surface similarities, but Leonard is smaller, quicker, has better hands, and is less of a tackle-breaker. He can play a variety of roles: third-down back, ace-formation running back, West Coast–style fullback. The Rams plan to use him as a "move" fullback, but they gave him plenty of reps at halfback in May minicamp. Look for Leonard to get 10 to 12 touches per game. If the Rams use him as their third-down back, he is capable of Larry Centers–type numbers.

Jamal Lewis   Height: 5-11 Weight: 245 College: Tennessee   Draft: 2000/1 (5)   Born: 29-Aug-1979 Age: 28   Risk: Yellow

Year	Team	G	Runs	Yds	Yd/R	TD	FUM	DVOA	Rk	DPAR	Rk	PAR	Suc%	Rec	Pass	Yds	C%	Yd/C	TD	DVOA	Rk	DPAR	Rk
2004	BAL	12	235	1006	4.3	7	2	2.4%	21	16.2	17	14.5	46%	10	12	116	83%	11.6	0	47.1%	—	3.5	—
2005	BAL	15	269	906	3.4	3	5	-24.1%	49	-10.7	52	-9.0	41%	32	44	191	73%	6.0	1	-21.0%	41	-2.4	41
2006	BAL	16	314	1132	3.6	9	4	-9.9%	40	3.7	40	2.6	42%	18	26	115	69%	6.4	0	-13.3%	38	-0.4	37
2007	CLE		315	1219	3.9	10								20	80			4.0	0				

It's hard to believe Lewis will be just 28 when the 2007 NFL season commences, seeing as he's generally considered over-the-hill. It's hard to envision a big year from a battered power back whose cutting ability is almost nonexistent at this point, but at least Cleveland won't have to face the player that has tormented them for years. Lewis still has a nose for the goal line: His red zone Success Rate of 60 percent was well above the league average (47 percent) last year. Lewis received a one-year, $3.5-million "prove it" contract from the Browns, and could put up better raw numbers than he did in his final year in Baltimore, depending upon how the Browns line situation shakes out.

Wali Lundy   Height: 5-10 Weight: 214 College: Virginia   Draft: 2006/6 (170) Born: 8-Sep-1983 Age: 24   Risk: Red

Year	Team	G	Runs	Yds	Yd/R	TD	FUM	DVOA	Rk	DPAR	Rk	PAR	Suc%	Rec	Pass	Yds	C%	Yd/C	TD	DVOA	Rk	DPAR	Rk
2006	HOU	14	124	476	3.8	4	1	-10.0%	41	1.9	44	3.9	39%	33	39	204	85%	6.2	0	-2.3%	31	1.3	32
2007	HOU		52	195	3.7	2								21	171			8.1	1				

When you think of running back hotbeds, you probably think of South Florida, San Diego County... and South Jersey? For much of last season, the Texans featured an all-Jersey backfield of Ron Dayne and Wali Lundy, a rookie who had a shocking two-week run against the Jaguars and Titans (37 carries, 209 yards) before crashing back to earth. Lundy, the all-time touchdown leader for the Virginia Cavaliers, has a future as a third-down and change-up back. Lundy and Dayne will back up Ahman Green this year. With all due respect to the gang on the Wildwood boardwalk, Nebraska's fertile soil breeds a better brand of back.

Marshawn Lynch   Height: 5-11 Weight: 215 College: California   Draft: 2007/1 (12)   Born: 22-Apr-1986 Age: 21   Risk: Yellow

Year	Team	G	Runs	Yds	Yd/R	TD	FUM	DVOA	Rk	DPAR	Rk	PAR	Suc%	Rec	Pass	Yds	C%	Yd/C	TD	DVOA	Rk	DPAR	Rk
2007	BUF		245	1040	4.2	6								28	209			7.5	1				

Lynch has his strengths: He stays low to the ground and is difficult to tackle, has good vision and waits for blocks to develop, and is a good receiver and blocker. Unlike his predecessor Willis McGahee, Lynch doesn't hate the city of Buffalo yet, which is also a plus. Unfortunately, his 4.46 40-time is faster than he actually plays. He's a smart runner, and is likely to be a competent running back on the NFL level, but he has very little potential to break out and be a star, and that's what first-round picks are for.

Laurence Maroney   Height: 5-11 Weight: 205 College: Minnesota   Draft: 2006/1 (21)   Born: 5-Feb-1985 Age: 22   Risk: Green

Year	Team	G	Runs	Yds	Yd/R	TD	FUM	DVOA	Rk	DPAR	Rk	PAR	Suc%	Rec	Pass	Yds	C%	Yd/C	TD	DVOA	Rk	DPAR	Rk
2006	NE	14	175	745	4.3	6	1	-1.9%	29	9.1	32	11.6	46%	22	30	194	73%	8.8	1	12.2%	16	3.6	24
2007	NE		304	1411	4.6	12								43	351			8.1	1				

Maroney showed flashes of brilliance in his rookie season—it's hard to think of a running back Maroney's size that seemed as agile and smooth in his cuts around the line of scrimmage—but, like most rookie backs, Maroney learned that holes that were open in college close much faster on Sundays. He slowed down as the season went on, often going missing for long stretches during games without any reason given. It wasn't until March that the Patriots announced that Maroney had undergone surgery that revealed "fairly significant damage" to his shoulder. If Maroney's healthy, he'll enter 2007 as the starting running back, but he'll need to become a better pass blocker and more efficient runner between the tackles to become a championship-caliber halfback.

Deuce McAllister

Height: 6-1 **Weight: 232** **College: Mississippi** **Draft: 2001/1 (23)** **Born: 27-Dec-1978** **Age: 28** **Risk: Red**

Year	Team	G	Runs	Yds	Yd/R	TD	FUM	DVOA	Rk	DPAR	Rk	PAR	Suc%	Rec	Pass	Yds	C%	Yd/C	TD	DVOA	Rk	DPAR	Rk
2004	NO	14	269	1074	4.0	9	5	-6.1%	36	9.0	33	5.0	43%	34	48	228	71%	6.7	0	-24.1%	50	-3.3	51
2005	NO	5	93	335	3.6	3	0	-2.9%	25	4.5	32	4.4	44%	17	18	117	94%	6.9	0	0.2%	—	0.9	—
2006	NO	15	244	1057	4.3	10	2	9.9%	15	26.5	9	25.9	53%	30	36	198	83%	6.6	0	-5.6%	34	0.8	33
2007	NO		225	936	4.2	6								35		227		6.5	1				

As we noted in the New Orleans chapter, McAllister came back from his 2005 ACL injury as a better running back than he was before the injury. With his shake-and-bake moves slow to come back, McAllister had to charge ahead behind his blockers and ended up gaining yards on a much more consistent basis. That huge jump in Success Rate is good evidence of the change. The most similar running backs to Deuce McAllister over a three-year span: James Stewart (1997–1999), Antowain Smith (1999–2001), Tyrone Wheatley (1997–1999), Cleveland Gary (1990–1992), and Ahman Green (2004–2006).

Willis McGahee

Height: 6-0 **Weight: 228** **College: Miami** **Draft: 2003/1 (23)** **Born: 20-Oct-1981** **Age: 26** **Risk: Yellow**

Year	Team	G	Runs	Yds	Yd/R	TD	FUM	DVOA	Rk	DPAR	Rk	PAR	Suc%	Rec	Pass	Yds	C%	Yd/C	TD	DVOA	Rk	DPAR	Rk
2004	BUF	16	284	1128	4.0	13	4	1.2%	25	19.6	12	18.3	46%	22	36	169	61%	7.7	0	-12.2%	39	-0.5	40
2005	BUF	16	325	1247	3.8	5	1	-0.2%	23	20.4	10	21.7	47%	28	37	178	76%	6.4	0	-1.5%	28	1.5	28
2006	BUF	14	259	990	3.8	6	4	-1.7%	28	13.8	25	7.6	45%	18	28	156	64%	8.7	0	-21.4%	41	-1.7	41
2007	BAL		311	1290	4.2	10								31		257		8.3	0				

McGahee was the league's rushing leader after four weeks, but very few people noticed that he was also leading the NFL with 99 carries. It took him till the end of Week 14 to get his next 99. McGahee has yet to make it through a full season, and, when he is in the lineup, he's not the star-caliber back the Ravens seem to think they're getting. Almost every one of our metrics grades McGahee as a middle-of-the-pack starter. Losing Priest Holmes and Chester Taylor didn't convince the Ravens that pretty good running backs are eminently replaceable, so the Ravens gave McGahee $40 million for seven years, including a $7.5-million signing bonus. If McGahee makes it halfway through that deal without serious injury it would be victory enough; there's a distinct possibility he won't even see his $6-million option bonus in 2008. It will be interesting to see what the change in offensive lines does for his boom-and-bust tendencies; 13 percent of his carries went for negative yardage last year, and 34 percent went for five or more yards, compared to 8 percent and 26 percent for Jamal Lewis.

Travis Minor

Height: 5-10 **Weight: 203** **College: Florida State** **Draft: 2001/3 (85)** **Born: 30-Jun-1979** **Age: 28** **Risk: Red**

Year	Team	G	Runs	Yds	Yd/R	TD	FUM	DVOA	Rk	DPAR	Rk	PAR	Suc%	Rec	Pass	Yds	C%	Yd/C	TD	DVOA	Rk	DPAR	Rk
2004	MIA	11	109	388	3.6	3	0	-5.1%	35	4.2	38	3.3	37%	13	27	75	48%	5.8	0	-26.5%	53	-2.5	49
2005	MIA	16	5	17	3.4	0	0	0.0%	0	-0.2	-0.3	-0.2	0%	1	1	0	100%	0.0	0	-99.9%	—	-0.7	—
2006	MIA	16	19	74	3.9	0	0	7.2%	—	1.5	—	1.3	0%	3	3	2	100%	0.7	0	-91.2%	—	-1.1	—
2007	STL		45	143	3.2	2								12		99		8.3	0				

One of the most aptly-named football players in NFL history. The injury to Ronnie Brown got Minor onto the field, but he didn't do anything while he was there to earn more playing time or a new contract. He's moved on to St. Louis, where he's not a lock to make it through camp.

Ryan Moats

Height: 5-8 **Weight: 210** **College: Louisiana Tech** **Draft: 2005/3 (77)** **Born: 17-Dec-1982** **Age: 24** **Risk: Red**

Year	Team	G	Runs	Yds	Yd/R	TD	FUM	DVOA	Rk	DPAR	Rk	PAR	Suc%	Rec	Pass	Yds	C%	Yd/C	TD	DVOA	Rk	DPAR	Rk
2005	PHI	7	55	278	5.1	3	2	-12.1%	—	1.0	—	0.3	38%	4	6	7	67%	1.8	0	-60.9%	—	-1.7	—
2006	PHI	8	22	69	3.1	0	0	-3.4%	—	1.2	—	1.3	47%	0	1	0	0%	0.0	0	-82.5%	—	-0.3	—
2007	PHI		13	51	4.0	1								4		38		8.9	0				

Moats was taken in the third round of the 2005 draft, one round ahead of Marion Barber and Brandon Jacobs, but has scarcely done anything to justify that draft position in his two professional seasons. Ostensibly an understudy for Brian Westbrook, with the same build and water-bug style, Moats wasn't on the 45-man active roster for much of the 2006 season, while Westbrook had the best season of his career. The Eagles selected running back Tony Hunt in this year's draft, and he might ultimately push Moats out of Philadelphia.

Mewelde Moore

Height: 5-11   Weight: 209   College: Tulane   Draft: 2004/4 (119)   Born: 24-Jul-1982   Age: 25   Risk: Red

Year	Team	G	Runs	Yds	Yd/R	TD	FUM	DVOA	Rk	DPAR	Rk	PAR	Suc%	Rec	Pass	Yds	C%	Yd/C	TD	DVOA	Rk	DPAR	Rk
2004	MIN	10	65	379	5.8	0	1	33.3%	—	12.3	—	15.0	57%	27	33	238	82%	8.8	0	6.2%	24	2.8	26
2005	MIN	16	155	662	4.3	1	1	0.3%	21	9.2	20	11.8	43%	37	49	339	76%	9.2	2	28.5%	4	9.5	4
2006	MIN	16	24	131	5.5	0	0	33.7%	—	3.8	—	3.2	35%	46	62	468	74%	10.2	1	9.4%	20	5.3	16
2007	MIN		36	133	3.7	0								27		259		9.6	1				

A third-down back can have a long and successful career in the NFL, but it still seems like a curse when a player gets that label early in his career. Moore should not be so limited, but Brad Childress did not see things that way. Moore did his best Kevin Faulk impression in 2006, catching 46 passes and returning punts effectively, but he has the potential to do much more. Apparently, if Childress called the plays in Philadelphia, Correll Buckhalter would average 25 carries a game.

Vernand Morency

Height: 5-9   Weight: 212   College: Oklahoma State   Draft: 2005/3 (73)   Born: 4-Feb-1980   Age: 27   Risk: Red

Year	Team	G	Runs	Yds	Yd/R	TD	FUM	DVOA	Rk	DPAR	Rk	PAR	Suc%	Rec	Pass	Yds	C%	Yd/C	TD	DVOA	Rk	DPAR	Rk
2005	HOU	13	46	184	4.0	2	0	-8.8%	—	1.1	—	2.4	35%	10	15	87	67%	8.7	0	8.3%	—	1.3	—
2006	GB	14	96	434	4.5	2	2	-1.2%	26	5.6	37	5.3	40%	17	18	118	94%	6.9	0	9.0%	—	1.8	—
2007	GB		185	818	4.4	6								28		219		7.7	1				

The rare NFL challenge trade brought Morency to the Packers straight-up for fellow running back Samkon Gado. Everyone was waiting for Green Bay to sign a starting running back this offseason, but it slipped the collective Packers' mind, which makes Morency the starter by default. Hopefully Morency sent a thank-you card to Maurice Jones-Drew for proving that little backs can do big things. Morency is a fine receiver out of the backfield and a competent third-down back, but probably isn't suited for full-time duty. We'll sure find out.

Maurice Morris

Height: 5-11   Weight: 202   College: Oregon   Draft: 2002/2 (54)   Born: 1-Dec-1979   Age: 28   Risk: Yellow

Year	Team	G	Runs	Yds	Yd/R	TD	FUM	DVOA	Rk	DPAR	Rk	PAR	Suc%	Rec	Pass	Yds	C%	Yd/C	TD	DVOA	Rk	DPAR	Rk
2004	SEA	15	30	126	4.2	0	0	15.4%	—	3.7	—	3.9	60%	9	20	53	45%	5.9	0	-27.4%	—	-1.9	—
2005	SEA	16	71	288	4.1	1	0	10.2%	—	6.7	—	8.4	45%	5	6	48	83%	8.6	0	66.2%		2.0	
2006	SEA	16	161	604	3.8	0	2	-19.3%	50	-2.2	49	-0.2	42%	11	35	46	60%	4.2	0	-33.3%	45	-4.1	45
2007	SEA		126	509	4.1	2								24		95		4.0	1				

Morris is a versatile scatback who actually put up Seattle's first 100-yard games of 2006 while subbing for the injured Shaun Alexander. Like Alexander's, Morris's DVOA took a huge hit as the Seattle offensive line folded and, while he's a better option than Alexander as a receiver, it isn't by much. The Seahawks would be wise to feature Morris a bit more in his change-of-pace role, but, by now, Morris has shown that he's never going to be the primary back for an entire season.

Sammy Morris

Height: 6-0   Weight: 218   College: Texas Tech   Draft: 2000/5 (156)   Born: 23-Mar-1977   Age: 30   Risk: Red

Year	Team	G	Runs	Yds	Yd/R	TD	FUM	DVOA	Rk	DPAR	Rk	PAR	Suc%	Rec	Pass	Yds	C%	Yd/C	TD	DVOA	Rk	DPAR	Rk
2004	MIA	13	132	523	4.0	6	1	6.2%	18	12.4	25	11.3	45%	22	28	124	79%	5.6	0	-11.0%	37	-0.3	38
2005	MIA	16	16	58	3.6	1	0	0.0%	0	1.4	0.1	0.0	0%	8	12	54	67%	6.8	0	-22.6%	—	-0.7	—
2006	MIA	12	92	400	4.3	1	1	-11.5%	43	2.4	43	1.5	40%	21	20	162	55%	7.7	0	-53.0%	—	-4.3	—
2007	NE		41	206	5.0	2								15		121		8.0	1				

The Patriots signed him to a four-year deal because he contributes as a pass blocker, lead blocker, receiver, rusher, and on special teams. He's a useful player in small doses, but the Patriots will be in trouble if an injury to Laurence Maroney makes him the lead running back.

Jerious Norwood

Height: 6-0   Weight: 204   College: Mississippi State   Draft: 2006/3 (79)   Born: 23-Jul-1983   Age: 24   Risk: Yellow

Year	Team	G	Runs	Yds	Yd/R	TD	FUM	DVOA	Rk	DPAR	Rk	PAR	Suc%	Rec	Pass	Yds	C%	Yd/C	TD	DVOA	Rk	DPAR	Rk
2006	ATL	14	99	633	6.4	2	0	35.8%	3	21.3	15	19.0	53%	12	15	102	80%	8.5	0	2.8%	—	1.0	—
2007	ATL		205	922	4.5	6								25		232		9.4	1				

Runs of 78 and 69 yards added some fluff to Norwood's 6.4-yards-per-carry average, but his high DVOA and Success Rate prove that he was also productive on a play-for-play basis. Norwood is a quick one-cut runner who showed good vision and decisiveness after earning a rep as a backfield dancer at Mississippi State. He's not built to be an every-down back, but Norwood has the tools to be the chairman of a backfield committee.

Willie Parker   Height: 5-10   Weight: 209   College: North Carolina   Draft: 2004/FA   Born: 11-Nov-1980   Age: 27   Risk: Green

Year	Team	G	Runs	Yds	Yd/R	TD	FUM	DVOA	Rk	DPAR	Rk	PAR	Suc%	Rec	Pass	Yds	C%	Yd/C	TD	DVOA	Rk	DPAR	Rk
2004	PIT	8	32	186	5.8	0	0	36.1%	—	6.1	—	5.3	47%	3	7	16	43%	5.3	0	-70.0%	—	-1.4	—
2005	PIT	15	255	1202	4.7	4	4	-1.1%	24	14.0	16	16.7	48%	18	24	218	75%	12.1	1	47.7%	—	7.2	—
2006	PIT	16	337	1494	4.4	13	6	1.1%	24	21.6	14	15.5	44%	31	42	222	74%	7.2	3	0.5%	25	2.1	28
2007	PIT		316	1298	4.1	9								37		212		5.7	1				

On the surface, it all looks good: nearly 1,500 yards, 4.4 yards per carry, and 13 TDs. However, Parker is a boom-and-bust runner whose numbers were boosted by 12 carries of 20-plus yards (tied for second-most in the league). In a Pittsburgh offense dedicated to staying out of third-and-long, "Fast Willie's" slow starts didn't help matters. Parker posted a negative DVOA on both first and second down, and usually headed to the bench on third because Najeh Davenport is a much better blocker (just 14 of Parker's 337 carries came on third or fourth down). Perhaps Cris Collinsworth put it best during an NFL Network game against Cleveland: Parker explodes through the hole, but if there isn't a clear hole, he tends to tippy-toe around instead of just charging forward to get what he can get. His ten fumbles over the last two seasons is also a distressing trend.

Alvin Pearman   Height: 5-9   Weight: 206   College: Virginia   Draft: 2005/4 (127)   Born: 10-Aug-1982   Age: 25   Risk: Red

Year	Team	G	Runs	Yds	Yd/R	TD	FUM	DVOA	Rk	DPAR	Rk	PAR	Suc%	Rec	Pass	Yds	C%	Yd/C	TD	DVOA	Rk	DPAR	Rk
2005	JAC	16	39	149	3.8	1	0	-4.8%	—	1.5	—	0.2	36%	32	36	240	89%	7.5	0	1.2%	25	1.7	27
2006	JAC	13	19	89	4.7	1	0	3.6%	—	1.4	—	2.9	67%	2	3	12	67%	6.0	0	26.2%	—	0.6	—
2007	JAC		22	98	4.4	1								8		73		9.6	0				

Maurice Jones-Drew probably hums "Anything you can do, I can do better" whenever he walks past Pearman's locker. Pearman was limited to punt-return duties last year after Jones-Drew usurped his role in the offense. Pearson is a useful player, but he's in a duplication-of-services situation in Jacksonville and may be released in camp.

Chris Perry   Height: 6-0   Weight: 224   College: Michigan   Draft: 2004/1 (26)   Born: 27-Dec-1981   Age: 25   Risk: Red

Year	Team	G	Runs	Yds	Yd/R	TD	FUM	DVOA	Rk	DPAR	Rk	PAR	Suc%	Rec	Pass	Yds	C%	Yd/C	TD	DVOA	Rk	DPAR	Rk
2004	CIN	2	2	1	0.5	0	0	-99.9%	—	-0.6	—	-0.5	0%	3	3	33	100%	11.0	0	159.7%	—	2.4	—
2005	CIN	14	61	279	4.6	0	0	5.7%	—	5.2	—	5.2	49%	51	62	328	82%	6.4	2	-26.4%	46	-5.4	52
2006	CIN	6	10	57	5.7	0	0	44.3%	—	2.6	—	2.1	7%	9	11	42	82%	4.7	0	2.4%	—	0.6	—
2007	CIN		16	65	4.0	0								18		205		11.6	1				

Perry hasn't done much to dispel the myth that receivers and running backs from Michigan don't do well in the NFL. He was supposed to be the Bengals' third-down back after Rudi Johnson emerged as the starting tailback, but he hasn't been able to stay on the field and hasn't been very effective on third down (or any other down, for that matter) when he is able to play. Coming off ankle surgery, he faces an uncertain future in Cincinnati.

Adrian L. Peterson   Height: 6-2   Weight: 217   College: Oklahoma   Draft: 2007/1 (7)   Born: 21-Mar-1985   Age: 22   Risk: Red

Year	Team	G	Runs	Yds	Yd/R	TD	FUM	DVOA	Rk	DPAR	Rk	PAR	Suc%	Rec	Pass	Yds	C%	Yd/C	TD	DVOA	Rk	DPAR	Rk
2007	MIN		192	783	4.1	4								20		142		7.0	1				

Everyone knows that Peterson is an amazing pure runner when healthy. What we will learn over the next few months is (a) how often can he be healthy, and (b) how well he can catch the ball. The Vikings got some encouraging preliminary answers at May minicamp. Peterson participated at full-speed and said that his collarbone (which he injured during the 2006 season and re-injured in the Fiesta Bowl) felt fine. In passing drills, he ran routes and caught the ball well. If Peterson can handle a 25-carry pounding and contribute as a receiver, he'll emerge as a perennial Pro Bowler, but the Vikings must limit his role until he masters the system and proves that he can take care of his body. He should be the first overall pick in any dynasty fantasy league draft this fall.

Adrian Peterson   Height: 5-10   Weight: 210   College: Georgia Southern   Draft: 2002/6 (199)   Born: 1-Jul-1979   Age: 28   Risk: Red

Year	Team	G	Runs	Yds	Yd/R	TD	FUM	DVOA	Rk	DPAR	Rk	PAR	Suc%	Rec	Pass	Yds	C%	Yd/C	TD	DVOA	Rk	DPAR	Rk
2004	CHI	14	6	19	3.2	0	0	-52.5%	—	-1.1	—	-0.8	17%	2	2	30	100%	15.0	0	119.8%	—	1.3	—
2005	CHI	16	76	391	5.1	2	0	26.6%	1	12.9	18	14.0	53%	7	12	48	58%	6.9	0	-86.1%	—	-4.6	—
2006	CHI	16	10	41	4.1	2	0	60.4%	—	3.2	—	3.2	43%	6	6	88	100%	14.7	0	-38.9%	—	-0.7	—
2007	CHI		73	313	4.3	2								17		155		9.0	0				

This Adrian Peterson is a Football Outsiders favorite. He is a player who is extraordinary at what he is asked to do and should easily handle a bigger role this year. He was an explosive runner when called upon in 2005, and, after the emergence of Cedric Benson relegated him to third string last year, Peterson went back to being a major contributor on the Bears' league-best special teams. The Bears have had him for five years through two coaching staffs, so he might have limitations holding him back from more playing time that we've been unable to detect. Still, he has done everything asked of him to date, and it would be interesting to see what he could do with 125 carries. Here's hoping this organizational soldier gets those carries this season (unless you have Benson on your fantasy team, that is).

Artose Pinner Height: 5-10 Weight: 235 College: Kentucky   Draft: 2003/4 (99) Born: 5-Jan-1978   Age: 29   Risk: Red

Year	Team	G	Runs	Yds	Yd/R	TD	FUM	DVOA	Rk	DPAR	Rk	PAR	Suc%	Rec	Pass	Yds	C%	Yd/C	TD	DVOA	Rk	DPAR	Rk
2004	DET	9	57	174	3.1	2	0	-9.8%	—	1.1	—	1.2	58%	11	11	72	100%	6.5	0	2.5%	—	0.7	—
2005	DET	16	106	349	3.3	3	0	-5.6%	27	3.9	34	5.1	48%	21	26	181	85%	8.6	0	23.5%	8	4.4	16
2006	MIN	12	43	190	4.4	3	1	8.0%	—	3.9	—	4.7	34%	2	3	15	67%	7.5	0	-19.5%	—	-0.1	—
2007	MIN		27	99	3.7	1								7		73		10.2	0				

Of Pinner's 190 yards, 125 of them came in Week 14 against the Lions, the team that cut him before the season. He got 14 carries over the remainder of the season and finds himself in a very crowded backfield. He's a poor man's Reuben Droughns, which means he may have a very short career.

Antonio Pittman Height: 5-11 Weight: 207 College: Ohio State   Draft: 2007/4 (107) Born: 9-Dec-1985   Age: 21   Risk: Red

Year	Team	G	Runs	Yds	Yd/R	TD	FUM	DVOA	Rk	DPAR	Rk	PAR	Suc%	Rec	Pass	Yds	C%	Yd/C	TD	DVOA	Rk	DPAR	Rk
2007	NO		16	94	5.7	1								11		89		8.1	0				

Reggie Bush was "shocked" when the Saints drafted Pittman in the fourth round. Donovan McNabb was also shocked when the Eagles selected Kevin Kolb: You get the impression that NFL stars watch the draft wearing monocles that pop out of their eyes when their teams draft guys at their position. Pittman is similar to Bush: a picker and darter who is at his best once he gets out to the second level. Of course, Pittman isn't in Bush's class as an athlete. There are only so many touches to go around in New Orleans, so Pittman will pull splinter duty until someone gets hurt or Deuce McAllister moves on.

Michael Pittman Height: 6-0 Weight: 228 College: Fresno State   Draft: 1998/4 (95) Born: 14-Aug-1975 Age: 32   Risk: Yellow

Year	Team	G	Runs	Yds	Yd/R	TD	FUM	DVOA	Rk	DPAR	Rk	PAR	Suc%	Rec	Pass	Yds	C%	Yd/C	TD	DVOA	Rk	DPAR	Rk
2004	TB	13	219	926	4.2	7	6	-12.5%	42	1.9	40	2.2	42%	41	64	391	64%	9.5	3	-7.0%	33	1.0	33
2005	TB	16	70	436	6.2	1	0	7.2%	—	5.7	—	6.6	36%	36	46	300	78%	8.3	1	18.7%	10	6.3	10
2006	TB	16	50	245	4.9	1	1	7.0%	—	4.2	—	4.2	49%	47	77	405	62%	8.6	0	6.8%	23	5.8	12
2007	TB		52	226	4.3	2								29		248		8.6	1				

Pittman rushed for 159 yards on 28 carries in the Bucs' final two games, a sign that not all of Cadillac Williams's problems were caused by the offensive line. Pittman has put together a fine career as an all-purpose committee back and remains a plus as a receiver, runner, and return man.

Clinton Portis Height: 5-11 Weight: 212 College: Miami   Draft: 2002/2 (51) Born: 1-Sep-1981   Age: 26   Risk: Red

Year	Team	G	Runs	Yds	Yd/R	TD	FUM	DVOA	Rk	DPAR	Rk	PAR	Suc%	Rec	Pass	Yds	C%	Yd/C	TD	DVOA	Rk	DPAR	Rk
2004	WAS	15	343	1315	3.8	5	5	-11.3%	40	4.0	39	3.6	45%	40	57	235	70%	5.9	2	-16.0%	42	-1.6	43
2005	WAS	16	352	1516	4.3	11	3	9.8%	11	36.4	9	31.3	50%	30	41	216	73%	7.2	0	13.6%	13	5.0	13
2006	WAS	8	127	523	4.1	7	0	7.8%	17	13.0	26	12.7	44%	17	26	170	65%	10.0	0	-16.0%	39	-0.8	38
2007	WAS		234	980	4.2	4								27		277		10.1	0				

Portis is a versatile and selfless player, dangerous as a receiver and underrated as a pass-blocker. He injured his shoulder during the preseason, and, although he returned in time for Week 1, he was never quite 100 percent. Then a broken hand against the Eagles in Week 9 cost him the second half of the season. Neither injury should still be an issue in 2007, but that doesn't mean Portis will be injury-free, as he missed minicamp with knee tendinitis. Washington could have the NFC's best rushing attack in 2007, with Portis and Ladell Betts sharing carries, but given all of his recent health issues, there's no guarantee that Portis will get the greater share of those carries.

Dominic Rhodes Height: 5-9 Weight: 203 College: Midwestern State Draft: 2001/FA Born: 17-Jan-1979 Age: 28 Risk: Red

Year	Team	G	Runs	Yds	Yd/R	TD	FUM	DVOA	Rk	DPAR	Rk	PAR	Suc%	Rec	Pass	Yds	C%	Yd/C	TD	DVOA	Rk	DPAR	Rk
2004	IND	16	53	254	4.8	1	1	8.1%	—	4.6	—	4.3	45%	2	4	24	50%	12.0	0	41.4%	—	0.8	—
2005	IND	13	40	118	3.0	4	0	-10.3%	—	0.8	—	1.6	50%	13	16	88	81%	6.8	0	-0.8%	—	0.7	—
2006	IND	16	187	641	3.4	5	2	-13.1%	46	0.6	46	4.6	49%	36	47	251	77%	7.0	0	-10.7%	36	-0.1	36
2007	OAK		113	446	4.0	3								24		189		7.9	0				

When he signed with Oakland this offseason, Rhodes told reporters: "It's an honor to be here and an awesome experience to play for the Raiders." Allow us to translate from Rhodes to reality: "It's all about the Benjamins, baby." Does anyone really think Rhodes went to Oakland because he wanted to play for a winner? This is a guy who couldn't even average four yards per carry in Indianapolis. He's going to get killed behind that offensive line, and he's not even guaranteed a starting job; he'll share time with LaMont Jordan, probably as the junior partner. Honestly, we don't begrudge Rhodes his big payday. He's got his ring, and it's time to make sure he's financially set for life. We just want him to hand over his car keys before celebrating his new contract.

Michael Robinson Height: 6-2 Weight: 217 College: Penn State Draft: 2006/4 (100) Born: 6-Feb-1983 Age: 24 Risk: Red

Year	Team	G	Runs	Yds	Yd/R	TD	FUM	DVOA	Rk	DPAR	Rk	PAR	Suc%	Rec	Pass	Yds	C%	Yd/C	TD	DVOA	Rk	DPAR	Rk
2006	SF	16	38	116	3.1	2	0	-23.5%	—	-1.9	—	-1.6	52%	9	12	47	75%	5.2	0	-34.5%	—	-1.7	—
2007	SF		40	184	4.6	2								12		67		5.7	0				

Robinson played quarterback in his senior season at Penn State and showed potential as a running back in his rookie season with the Niners. He's still learning his new position and won't exactly steal carries from Frank Gore. Catch him next year at a blowout or fake punt near you.

Eric Shelton Height: 6-3 Weight: 248 College: Louisville Draft: 2005/2 (54) Born: 23-Jun-1983 Age: 24 Risk: Red

Year	Team	G	Runs	Yds	Yd/R	TD	FUM	DVOA	Rk	DPAR	Rk	PAR	Suc%	Rec	Pass	Yds	C%	Yd/C	TD	DVOA	Rk	DPAR	Rk
2006	CAR	7	8	23	2.9	0	0	-48.3%	—	-0.9	—	-1.0	44%	1	1	6	100%	6.0	0	85.2%	—	0.7	—
2007	CAR		30	99	3.3	1								0		0		0.0	0				

The Panthers were desperate for a short-yardage back last year, but they had so little faith in the 245-pound Shelton that he earned just one third-down carry, and that came late in a 37–3 loss to the Steelers. He lost three yards. Shelton doesn't offer much as a blocker or receiver, and the last coaching staff wasn't crazy about his conditioning habits. He either blows away Jeff Davidson in camp or hits the unemployment line in late August.

Marcel Shipp Height: 5-11 Weight: 228 College: Massachusetts Draft: 2001/FA Born: 8-Aug-1978 Age: 29 Risk: Red

Year	Team	G	Runs	Yds	Yd/R	TD	FUM	DVOA	Rk	DPAR	Rk	PAR	Suc%	Rec	Pass	Yds	C%	Yd/C	TD	DVOA	Rk	DPAR	Rk
2005	ARI	15	157	451	2.9	0	4	-38.0%	53	-17.2	53	-17.6	41%	35	44	255	80%	7.3	0	6.2%	21	3.4	22
2006	ARI	15	17	41	2.4	4	0	12.9%	—	2.7	—	2.5	0%	6	11	60	55%	10.0	0	0.1%	—	0.5	—
2007	ARI		72	227	3.1	1								16		95		6.0	0				

Shipp missed the entire 2004 season with a broken leg, then led the Cards in rushing in 2005 with a mere 451 yards. Now he's a decent and somewhat versatile backup who signed a three-year, $5.75-million contract to stay in the Valley of the Sun. He scored three rushing touchdowns against the Rams in December and may see more carries in 2007 as Ken Whisenhunt looks to build a two-back system like the one he had in Pittsburgh.

Kolby Smith Height: 5-11 Weight: 220 College: Louisville Draft: 2007/5 (148) Born: 15-Dec-1984 Age: 22 Risk: Red

Year	Team	G	Runs	Yds	Yd/R	TD	FUM	DVOA	Rk	DPAR	Rk	PAR	Suc%	Rec	Pass	Yds	C%	Yd/C	TD	DVOA	Rk	DPAR	Rk
2007	KC		53	181	3.4	1								10		85		8.6	0				

Michael Bush's replacement at Louisville put up the same 5.6 yards per carry Bush did in his junior season, but Smith struggled with injuries throughout his college career even though he wasn't a starter. The Chiefs' plan is to move him to fullback. Smith has the blocking ability, versatility, and body type to be successful on the NFL level, but he'll need to put on about 15 more pounds of muscle and stay healthy. He would be in the "Going Deep" section except for this little thing called "The Curse of 370"; if Larry Johnson goes down with an injury, Smith becomes the big-back committee partner for Michael Bennett.

Musa Smith

Height: 6-0 **Weight:** 232 **College:** Georgia **Draft:** 2003/3 (77) **Born:** 31-May-1982 **Age:** 25 **Risk:** Red

Year	Team	G	Runs	Yds	Yd/R	TD	FUM	DVOA	Rk	DPAR	Rk	PAR	Suc%	Rec	Pass	Yds	C%	Yd/C	TD	DVOA	Rk	DPAR	Rk
2004	BAL	9	12	48	4.0	0	0	0.6%	—	0.9	—	0.5	33%	2	4	31	50%	15.5	0	74.7%	—	1.3	—
2005	BAL	1	0	0	0.0	0	0	0.0%	—	0.0	—	0.0	0%	3	3	5	100%	1.7	0	-79.5%	—	-1.0	—
2006	BAL	12	36	153	4.3	0	1	-6.0%	—	1.7	—	0.9	33%	22	25	135	88%	6.1	0	-11.7%	—	-0.1	—
2007	BAL		60	243	4.1	3								18		133		7.6	0				

Smith has shown flashes of explosiveness in his three-year career, but hasn't been able to stay healthy. Neck surgery prematurely ended his 2006 season, but the Ravens thought enough of his recovery and potential to re-sign him to a one-year deal, presumably to serve as the primary backup to Willis McGahee.

Aaron Stecker

Height: 5-10 **Weight:** 213 **College:** Western Illinois **Draft:** 2000/FA **Born:** 13-Nov-1975 **Age:** 32 **Risk:** Red

Year	Team	G	Runs	Yds	Yd/R	TD	FUM	DVOA	Rk	DPAR	Rk	PAR	Suc%	Rec	Pass	Yds	C%	Yd/C	TD	DVOA	Rk	DPAR	Rk
2004	NO	16	58	244	4.2	2	1	-19.7%	—	-1.2	—	-0.3	36%	29	38	174	76%	6.0	0	-17.8%	44	-1.6	44
2005	NO	15	95	363	3.8	0	1	-13.8%	42	0.3	42	1.1	42%	35	48	281	73%	8.0	0	12.3%	15	4.7	15
2006	NO	12	4	11	2.8	0	0	49.9%	—	0.7	—	0.5	62%	19	28	190	68%	10.0	0	8.8%	21	2.9	26
2007	NO		16	66	4.2	0								17		128		7.4	0				

The more comfortable Reggie Bush became with the Saints' offense last season, the less we saw of Stecker in the backfield. Instead, the Saints used him in the passing game. As noted in the New Orleans chapter, Aaron Stecker was lined up as a wide receiver more often than any running back last year except for Bush, LaDainian Tomlinson, and Brian Westbrook. Look for Stecker to snag another dozen receptions this year and otherwise take over Fred McAfee's role as the Saints' running back who hangs around for a decade as a special teamer.

Chester Taylor

Height: 5-11 **Weight:** 213 **College:** Toledo **Draft:** 2002/6 (207) **Born:** 22-Sep-1979 **Age:** 28 **Risk:** Red

Year	Team	G	Runs	Yds	Yd/R	TD	FUM	DVOA	Rk	DPAR	Rk	PAR	Suc%	Rec	Pass	Yds	C%	Yd/C	TD	DVOA	Rk	DPAR	Rk
2004	BAL	16	160	714	4.5	2	1	7.8%	16	14.0	22	12.5	41%	30	36	184	78%	6.1	0	-9.6%	—	0.2	—
2005	BAL	15	117	487	4.2	0	1	-5.7%	28	3.6	35	2.7	42%	41	52	292	79%	7.1	1	-15.9%	35	-1.2	35
2006	MIN	15	303	1216	4.0	6	4	-9.4%	39	7.4	33	5.3	46%	42	51	288	82%	6.9	0	-2.2%	30	2.1	29
2007	MIN		173	718	4.1	3								35		292		8.2	1				

This former Jamal Lewis backup enjoyed a respectable first season as a feature back in Minnesota. He is a bruiser who doesn't break too many long runs, only six over 20 yards, which makes it ironic that he set the franchise record with a 95-yarder against Seattle. A rib injury slowed him down in the season's final month, but with the addition of Adrian Peterson, Taylor's durability concerns aren't an issue for the Vikings. Expect Peterson and Taylor to receive about an equal amount of carries, at least for this year.

Chris Taylor

Height: 5-11 **Weight:** 220 **College:** Indiana **Draft:** 2006/FA **Born:** 7-Nov-1983 **Age:** 24 **Risk:** Red

Year	Team	G	Runs	Yds	Yd/R	TD	FUM	DVOA	Rk	DPAR	Rk	PAR	Suc%	Rec	Pass	Yds	C%	Yd/C	TD	DVOA	Rk	DPAR	Rk
2006	HOU	4	28	123	4.4	1	2	12.0%	12	23.1	12	28.0	44%	3	28	40	82%	13.3	0	25.0%	6	5.3	15
2007	HOU		40	140	3.5	1								6		49		8.6	0				

Are you ready to play *The $25,000 Pyramid*? Here are your clues: Chris Taylor, Willie Parker, Bruce Perry, Jamaal Branch, and Eric McCoo. Do you know the category? It's "Undrafted Free-Agent Running Backs Plucked Off the Practice Squad to Play in Week 17." Parker's rapid ascencion to a starting role gives hope to players such as Taylor, but there's no room for him on a team that employs Ahman Green, Ron Dayne, and Wali Lundy.

Fred Taylor

Height: 6-1 **Weight:** 234 **College:** Florida **Draft:** 1998/1 (9) **Born:** 27-Jan-1976 **Age:** 31 **Risk:** Yellow

Year	Team	G	Runs	Yds	Yd/R	TD	FUM	DVOA	Rk	DPAR	Rk	PAR	Suc%	Rec	Pass	Yds	C%	Yd/C	TD	DVOA	Rk	DPAR	Rk
2004	JAC	14	260	1224	4.7	2	3	-3.5%	33	10.1	31	13.7	45%	36	58	345	62%	9.6	1	3.2%	28	3.8	21
2005	JAC	11	194	787	4.1	3	0	-10.1%	37	3.2	37	9.2	39%	13	18	83	72%	6.4	0	-21.5%	—	-1.1	—
2006	JAC	15	231	1146	5.0	5	0	7.6%	—	2.2	—	3.6	33%	23	3	242	100%	10.5	1	81.5%	—	1.2	—
2007	JAC		190	784	4.1	8								17		124		7.4	0				

Taylor will eclipse 10,000 rushing yards this season, an amazing accomplishment for a player who was as fragile as a Christmas ornament during his first few seasons in the league. Taylor has learned to play through nagging ailments, and the Jaguars limited his workload to a sane and reasonable 20 touches per game last year, keeping him fresh and relatively healthy

(continued next page)

Fred Taylor *(continued)*

until late in the year. Taylor had a resurgence as a receiver after dropping off badly in 2005. With Maurice Jones-Drew likely taking over the lead role in 2007, Taylor can survive for a few more years and be very effective as a committee back.

Anthony Thomas   Height: 6-2   Weight: 225   College: Michigan   Draft: 2001/2 (38)   Born: 7-Nov-1977   Age: 30   Risk: Red

Year	Team	G	Runs	Yds	Yd/R	TD	FUM	DVOA	Rk	DPAR	Rk	PAR	Suc%	Rec	Pass	Yds	C%	Yd/C	TD	DVOA	Rk	DPAR	Rk
2004	CHI	12	122	404	3.3	2	1	-31.5%	51	-9.0	52	-3.9	40%	17	23	132	74%	7.8	0	10.0%	—	2.0	—
2005	DAL	6	36	80	2.2	0	0	-28.5%	—	-2.2	—	-3.7	36%	2	4	5	50%	2.5	0	-62.6%	—	-1.2	—
2006	BUF	16	107	378	3.5	2	1	-24.4%	53	-4.5	51	-0.5	37%	22	24	139	92%	6.3	0	24.5%	—	4.0	—
2007	*BUF*		*100*	*403*	*4.0*	*3*								*23*	*177*			*7.8*	*0*				

The A-Train stayed on the tracks for all 16 games last year, a career first. His 67 carries for 260 yards were respectable raw stats, which is one reason the Bills felt comfortable dealing Willis McGahee and promising Thomas more carries. The problem is that Thomas's starts came against Green Bay (21st-ranked rush defense by DVOA), Indianapolis (32nd), and Houston (26th). History also says that Thomas can't hold up to a starter's workload. When he sprained his ankle the week McGahee came back, it was the fourth straight time Thomas had an injury interrupt a stretch of 20-carry games. Over his career, Thomas has gotten 20 carries in back-to-back games 14 times. On average, his carry total falls to 18.9 in the third week following those back-to-back games and 11.3 the week after that. There's no guarantee that Marshawn Lynch will live up to his first-round-draft status, but the Bills certainly could not go into 2007 with Anthony Thomas as their projected starter.

Tyson Thompson   Height: 6-1   Weight: 220   College: San Jose State   Draft: 2005/FA   Born: 21-May-1981   Age: 26   Risk: Red

Year	Team	G	Runs	Yds	Yd/R	TD	FUM	DVOA	Rk	DPAR	Rk	PAR	Suc%	Rec	Pass	Yds	C%	Yd/C	TD	DVOA	Rk	DPAR	Rk
2005	DAL	15	46	182	4.0	0	0	6.3%	—	3.5	—	2.8	41%	3	4	16	75%	5.3	0	-34.0%	—	-0.5	—
2006	DAL	7	13	30	2.3	1	0	-46.1%	—	-1.8	—	-1.0	13%	0	0	0	0%	0.0	0	0.0%	—	0.0	—
2007	*DAL*		*52*	*196*	*3.7*	*1*								*7*	*40*			*5.6*	*0*				

Thompson is a 220-pound speedster who showed some promise as a kick returner before fracturing his fibula against the Eagles in Week 6. He could see an expanded role in the offense if the Cowboys deal Julius Jones.

LaBrandon Toefield   Height: 5-11   Weight: 232   College: LSU   Draft: 2003/4 (132)   Born: 24-Sep-1980   Age: 27   Risk: Red

Year	Team	G	Runs	Yds	Yd/R	TD	FUM	DVOA	Rk	DPAR	Rk	PAR	Suc%	Rec	Pass	Yds	C%	Yd/C	TD	DVOA	Rk	DPAR	Rk
2004	JAC	14	51	169	3.3	0	1	-11.5%	—	0.4	—	1.6	49%	28	34	151	82%	5.4	1	1.3%	30	2.0	30
2005	JAC	9	36	142	3.9	4	0	19.6%	—	5.1	—	5.5	36%	3	7	17	43%	5.7	0	-58.6%	—	-2.1	—
2006	JAC	4	10	22	2.2	0	0	-45.1%	—	-1.4	—	-0.9	60%	0	0	0	0%	0.0	0	0.0%	—	0.0	—
2007	*JAC*		*15*	*57*	*3.8*	*2*								*5*	*29*			*6.3*	*0*				

Toefield spent most of last year on the inactive list, but the Jaguars offered him a one-year contract in the offseason to return and compete for the third running back spot. He'll fight Greg Jones for the chance to stick as a big-back alternative to Fred Taylor and Maurice Jones-Drew.

LaDainian Tomlinson   Height: 5-10   Weight: 221   College: TCU   Draft: 2001/1 (5)   Born: 23-Jun-1979   Age: 28   Risk: Yellow

Year	Team	G	Runs	Yds	Yd/R	TD	FUM	DVOA	Rk	DPAR	Rk	PAR	Suc%	Rec	Pass	Yds	C%	Yd/C	TD	DVOA	Rk	DPAR	Rk
2004	SD	15	339	1335	3.9	17	6	-4.9%	34	14.0	23	16.3	45%	53	66	441	80%	8.3	1	3.4%	27	4.1	19
2005	SD	16	339	1462	4.3	18	2	14.0%	9	40.5	7	37.5	47%	51	77	370	66%	7.3	2	-20.2%	38	-4.2	48
2006	SD	16	348	1815	5.2	28	2	24.0%	4	52.6	1	58.5	49%	56	80	508	70%	9.1	3	12.7%	15	9.5	6
2007	*SD*		*327*	*1443*	*4.4*	*17*								*44*	*305*			*7.0*	*3*				

A league MVP must make difficult decisions. When the folks from EA Sports asked Tomlinson to be the cover boy for the latest version of *Madden,* Tomlinson demurred. His reason had nothing to do with a "curse"; the video game cover model must make numerous promotional appearances, and Tomlinson understandably wanted top dollar if he was going to be forced to hang around with hardcore gamers in his free time. ("Watch, n00bzore, as I enter this cheat code and pummel you with my Amsterdam Admirals money plays.") While Tomlinson hedged over the decision, Chargers fans started an on-line petition to keep his face off the shelves at your local Best Buy. In all, over 1,600 concerned citizens signed the petition by April, many of them days after Vince Young became the face that launched a thousand consoles. Tomlinson may not have to worry about a *Madden* curse, but he did decide to become a Campbell's Soup "Mama's Boy." That soup has claimed almost as many careers as the video game. Larry Johnson is one of the other players who will hoist spoon and slurp broth in the name of commerce. We have a feeling that Al Davis was in charge of casting.

Michael Turner

Height: 5-10 **Weight:** 237 **College:** Northern Illinois   **Draft:** 2004/5 (154) **Born:** 13-Feb-1982 **Age:** 25 **Risk:** Yellow

Year	Team	G	Runs	Yds	Yd/R	TD	FUM	DVOA	Rk	DPAR	Rk	PAR	Suc%	Rec	Pass	Yds	C%	Yd/C	TD	DVOA	Rk	DPAR	Rk
2004	SD	13	20	104	5.2	0	1	10.4%	—	1.8	—	3.0	40%	4	5	8	80%	2.0	0	-195.2%	—	-4.5	—
2005	SD	16	57	335	5.9	3	0	28.2%	—	9.8	—	10.6	51%	0	1	0	0%	0.0	0	-99.9%	—	-0.1	—
2006	SD	13	80	502	6.3	2	0	46.5%	1	20.7	16	19.8	55%	3	3	47	100%	15.7	0	189.1%	—	2.3	—
2007	*SD*		*109*	*514*	*4.7*	*4*								*7*		*70*		*9.3*	*0*				

On a per-play basis, Turner has been more effective than LaDainian Tomlinson, which may say more about the Chargers' offensive line than it does about either Turner or Tomlinson. That doesn't mean that Turner is a product of the system; he has great straight-line speed, he's excellent on third downs, and he's good on special teams. Because of Turner and that great line, the Chargers are the only Super Bowl contender that could withstand a significant injury to their greatest superstar. The Chargers thought about trading Turner to a team in need of a running back (primarily Tennessee), but decided to hold on to him for one more year. He's going to be a big prize as an unrestricted free agent in 2008. It is hard to imagine the Chargers finding the money to keep him from a starting job with another team.

Leon Washington

Height: 5-9 **Weight:** 199 **College:** Florida State   **Draft:** 2006/4 (117) **Born:** 29-Aug-1982 **Age:** 25 **Risk:** Red

Year	Team	G	Runs	Yds	Yd/R	TD	FUM	DVOA	Rk	DPAR	Rk	PAR	Suc%	Rec	Pass	Yds	C%	Yd/C	TD	DVOA	Rk	DPAR	Rk
2006	NYJ	16	151	650	4.3	4	1	16.0%	9	17.4	19	16.8	49%	25	31	270	81%	10.8	0	10.1%	18	3.3	25
2007	*NYJ*		*102*	*404*	*4.0*	*3*								*24*		*189*		*8.0*	*1*				

The Jets took Washington with the pick they acquired for the rights to Herman Edwards. Jets fans felt their team would come out ahead as long as Washington could successfully transform oxygen into carbon dioxide. As a bonus, Washington served as the lone exciting thing coming out of the Jets backfield in 2006, making big plays while Kevan Barlow ran for two yards per carry and told people what a proven veteran starter he was. Washington's 64-yard scamper on a screen against the Dolphins in the mud on Christmas night pretty much pushed the Jets into the playoffs. He also contributed on special teams as a secondary returner and blocker for Justin Miller. The trade for Thomas Jones puts a legitimately valuable running back in front of him, but Washington contributes in enough ways that he'll still be valuable to the Jets in 2007.

Kenny Watson

Height: 5-11 **Weight:** 220 **College:** Penn State   **Draft:** 2001/FA **Born:** 13-Mar-1978 **Age:** 29 **Risk:** Red

Year	Team	G	Runs	Yds	Yd/R	TD	FUM	DVOA	Rk	DPAR	Rk	PAR	Suc%	Rec	Pass	Yds	C%	Yd/C	TD	DVOA	Rk	DPAR	Rk
2004	CIN	16	26	161	6.2	0	2	-2.0%	—	1.2	—	0.3	48%	25	35	171	71%	6.8	1	9.1%	22	2.7	27
2006	CIN	16	25	138	5.5	1	0	41.0%	—	5.3	—	5.3	67%	23	32	213	72%	9.3	0	43.7%	3	7.7	9
2007	*CIN*		*20*	*86*	*4.3*	*1*								*23*		*202*		*8.7*	*1*				

Watson was an unrestricted free agent this offseason, but the Bengals re-signed him to a three-year deal, presumably to ease some of the workload on Rudi Johnson. Giving Watson six to eight carries a game might restore Johnson's missing burst, and Watson has been productive in limited action throughout his career. Since the Bengals drafted Kenny Irons, Watson probably won't be the primary backup, but he's still a better third-down back than Chris Perry and a valuable special-teams contributor.

Brian Westbrook

Height: 5-8 **Weight:** 203 **College:** Villanova   **Draft:** 2002/3 (91) **Born:** 2-Sep-1979 **Age:** 28 **Risk:** Yellow

Year	Team	G	Runs	Yds	Yd/R	TD	FUM	DVOA	Rk	DPAR	Rk	PAR	Suc%	Rec	Pass	Yds	C%	Yd/C	TD	DVOA	Rk	DPAR	Rk
2004	PHI	13	177	812	4.6	3	1	8.1%	15	15.7	18	15.0	43%	73	87	703	84%	9.6	6	21.6%	8	14.4	2
2005	PHI	12	156	617	4.0	3	0	-4.5%	26	6.4	27	5.5	40%	61	103	616	64%	10.1	4	11.7%	17	10.9	2
2006	PHI	15	240	1217	5.1	7	1	19.4%	7	34.3	6	37.9	48%	77	109	699	71%	9.1	4	11.9%	17	12.5	3
2007	*PHI*		*266*	*1329*	*5.0*	*10*								*73*		*620*		*8.6*	*4*				

Brian Westbrook is the engine that makes the Eagles offense go. He and the Eagles proved that last year when they only needed one week of transition time to shift to a more run-heavy offense after Donovan McNabb's knee injury. Buoyed by a four-carry-per-game increase in his workload after McNabb's injury, Westbrook shattered his career highs in carries (240 vs. 177) and yards (1,217 vs. 812). For the last three years, Philadelphia has ranked in the top ten in pass attempts and the bottom six in rush attempts, and head coach Andy Reid has acknowledged that the team had been leaning too heavily on McNabb. "I think during those first few games there, everybody just said, 'Hey, Donovan's going to show up and win the game for us,'" said Reid, "and I think everybody pulled off just a bit." Reid and playcaller Marty Mornhinweg might stick to their run-more plan this year, particularly if questions about McNabb's knee linger into camp and preseason. Westbrook is

(continued next page)

Brian Westbrook (*continued*)

built roughly like Tiki Barber—Westbrook is a couple of inches shorter and only a couple of pounds lighter—and Barber handled over 300 carries in five of his last (and best) six seasons. Still, the Eagles don't want to take any unnecessary chances with their versatile offensive centerpiece, so they will mix in plenty of Correll Buckhalter (if he stays healthy) and third-rounder Tony Hunt to correct their offensive balance without pulling a Larry Johnson on Westbrook.

LenDale White   Height: 6-2   Weight: 235   College: USC   Draft: 2006/2 (45)   Born: 20-Dec-1984   Age: 22   Risk: Red

Year	Team	G	Runs	Yds	Yd/R	TD	FUM	DVOA	Rk	DPAR	Rk	PAR	Suc%	Rec	Pass	Yds	C%	Yd/C	TD	DVOA	Rk	DPAR	Rk
2006	TEN	13	61	244	4.0	0	1	-18.6%	—	-1.2	—	-0.3	40%	14	20	60	70%	4.3	0	-50.6%	—	-3.2	—
2007	*TEN*		*214*	*903*	*4.2*	*3*								*33*		*254*		*7.8*	*1*				

The Titans gave White five toseven carries per game for most of his rookie season to get his feet wet. He didn't do anything spectacular with them, but he held on to the ball, showed some power and a little quickness, and ripped off some fine runs against the Colts and Texans, appearing ready for a smooth transition into the starting lineup this season in place of departing free agent Travis Henry. White showed up for offseason workouts at a rotund 260 pounds, however, and the Titans drafted Chris Henry to compete/split time with him. A hamstring injury kept White out of most workouts in the Titans' May minicamp, so Henry saw significant action with the first team. White was down to 245 pounds by late May and understood the significance of Henry's presence. "I don't assume anything. Ain't nothing guaranteed to nobody. I put all the pressure on me that I'm going to be the guy, and I'm going to do everything in my power to be the guy," he told the *Nashville City Paper*. White is a minus as a receiver, but he's quick enough to be an every-down back, and his willingness to pitch in on special teams will keep him out of the doghouse, even if he doesn't shed every ounce of excess flab. White, Vince Young, and Henry could grow into the most exciting backfield in the NFL in the next few years. Or, White could just grow.

Cadillac Williams   Height: 5-11   Weight: 217   College: Auburn   Draft: 2005/1 (5)   Born: 21-Apr-1982   Age: 25   Risk: Yellow

Year	Team	G	Runs	Yds	Yd/R	TD	FUM	DVOA	Rk	DPAR	Rk	PAR	Suc%	Rec	Pass	Yds	C%	Yd/C	TD	DVOA	Rk	DPAR	Rk
2005	TB	14	290	1178	4.1	6	3	-8.4%	31	6.6	26	11.4	43%	20	25	81	80%	4.1	0	-31.6%	49	-2.9	45
2006	TB	14	225	798	3.5	1	2	-16.2%	49	-2.4	50	-5.7	40%	30	44	196	68%	6.5	0	-12.8%	37	-1.0	39
2007	*TB*		*284*	*1207*	*4.2*	*6*								*25*		*99*		*4.0*	*0*				

The swiss cheese line was part of the problem. Minor back and foot injuries were part of the problem. The non-threatening novice quarterback was part of the problem. There's plenty of blame to go around for Williams's miserable sophomore campaign, a seemingly endless string of 19-carry, 48-yard and 11-carry, 27-yard stat lines. Williams made some of his best moves just to get back to the line of scrimmage last year, and, by December, he was banged up, overworked, and lapsing into bad habits, such as not protecting the ball and tiptoeing to the line of scrimmage. Cadillac has never been a good first-down runner: His first-down DVOA was –23.5 percent in 2005 and –25.7 percent last year, meaning that he put the Bucs in too many 2nd-and-9 situations. If he can find a way to be more productive on first down, he'll make life easier on the line and the quarterback, who in turn will make life easier on him. Williams still has 1,500-yard potential if he plays as he did in 2005 and a few things go his way.

DeAngelo Williams   Height: 5-10   Weight: 217   College: Memphis   Draft: 2006/1 (27)   Born: 25-Apr-1983   Age: 24   Risk: Yellow

Year	Team	G	Runs	Yds	Yd/R	TD	FUM	DVOA	Rk	DPAR	Rk	PAR	Suc%	Rec	Pass	Yds	C%	Yd/C	TD	DVOA	Rk	DPAR	Rk
2006	CAR	13	121	501	4.1	1	1	-3.3%	33	6.4	34	6.1	47%	33	36	313	92%	9.5	1	48.0%	1	10.9	4
2007	*CAR*		*165*	*714*	*4.3*	*5*								*37*		*312*		*8.5*	*1*				

Early in 2006, the Panthers split Williams out as a wide receiver to offset the loss of Steve Smith. Late in the year, they used him as a short-yardage quarterback to improve their third-down performance. Throughout the year, they used him as a kickoff returner, although only Denver's Brian Clark and Atlanta's Allen Rossum had less value in the role. In short, the Panthers want to get Williams the ball, but they don't want to run him into the meat grinder 25 times per game. Williams is an ideal complementary back, but he also happens to be the best runner on the team, and he should relegate DeShaun Foster to the bench this season.

Garrett Wolfe Height: 5-8 Weight: 186 College: Northern Illinois Draft: 2007/3 (93) Born: 17-Aug-1984 Age: 23 Risk: Red

Year	Team	G	Runs	Yds	Yd/R	TD	FUM	DVOA	Rk	DPAR	Rk	PAR	Suc%	Rec	Pass	Yds	C%	Yd/C	TD	DVOA	Rk	DPAR	Rk
2007	CHI		47	226	4.8	1								9	66			7.0	0				

Wolfe led the nation in rushing with 1,928 yards last season at Northern Illinois. He's productive but downright tiny at 5-foot-7, 177 pounds. The Bears are talking about choosing Wolfe over Adrian Peterson as the primary backup to Cedric Benson, but linebackers are bigger in the pros than in the MAC. Wolfe also has potential as a return man, but the Bears have a guy named Hester for that job.

Dwayne Wright Height: 6-0 Weight: 228 College: Fresno State Draft: 2007/4 (111) Born: 2-Jun-1983 Age: 24 Risk: Red

Year	Team	G	Runs	Yds	Yd/R	TD	FUM	DVOA	Rk	DPAR	Rk	PAR	Suc%	Rec	Pass	Yds	C%	Yd/C	TD	DVOA	Rk	DPAR	Rk
2007	BUF		60	258	4.3	2								9	51			6.0	0				

Wright looked like a top prospect in 2003, then missed two years with a torn patella tendon. He returned to rush for 1,462 yards at Fresno State last season. He's a powerful halfback/fullback tweener in the Nick Goings mold, but he's also a 24-year-old rookie with a long injury history.

Jason Wright Height: 5-10 Weight: 210 College: Northwestern Draft: 2004/FA Born: 12-Jul-1982 Age: 25 Risk: Red

Year	Team	G	Runs	Yds	Yd/R	TD	FUM	DVOA	Rk	DPAR	Rk	PAR	Suc%	Rec	Pass	Yds	C%	Yd/C	TD	DVOA	Rk	DPAR	Rk
2004	ATL	2	3	10	3.3	0	0	46.6%	—	0.5	—	0.3	33%	0	1	0	0%	0.0	0	-126.6%	—	-0.7	—
2005	CLE	3	11	27	2.5	1	—	0.0%	0	0.2	-0.1	-0.1	0%	3	3	15	100%	5.0	0	-14.5%	—	0.0	—
2006	CLE	13	62	189	3.0	0	1	-17.0%	—	-0.3	—	-4.8	33%	6	11	82	55%	13.7	0	-9.9%	—	0.0	—
2007	CLE		44	187	4.3	1								11	91			8.4	0				

Wright is mostly a special-teams player, but he started three games at running back when Reuben Droughns was hurt. In those three games he showed why he's mostly a special-teams player.

Fullbacks

Fullbacks with at least ten carries or passes are listed below with 2006 statistics in rushing and receiving as well as 2007 projection, if applicable, and age during the 2007 season.

Name	2006	G	Runs	Yds	TD	Rec	Pass	Yds	CPct	Yd/C	TD	DVOA	Rk	DPAR	Rk	2007	RuYd	Rec	RcYd	TD	Age
B. J. Askew	NYJ	13	6	11	0	9	12	50	75%	5.6	0	-11.6%	—	-0.2	—	TB	27	16	98	1	27
Obafemi Ayanbadejo	ARI	15	9	37	0	17	19	141	89%	8.3	0	-4.4%	—	0.6	—	ARI	23	13	87	0	32
Jameel Cook	HOU	12	3	18	0	18	26	107	69%	5.9	0	-50.4%	51	-5.8	49	HOU	12	15	92	1	28
Jim Finn	NYG	16	2	14	0	8	14	54	57%	3.9	0	-17.6%	—	-0.6	—	NYG	9	6	74	1	31
Justin Griffith	ATL	16	19	106	1	23	28	168	82%	7.3	3	22.4%	7	4.8	19	OAK	92	29	186	2	26
Ahmard Hall	TEN	14	7	21	0	15	21	138	71%	6.6	0	-12.4%	—	-0.2	—	TEN	14	12	77	1	28
Madison Hedgecock	STL	16	1	2	0	7	10	29	70%	2.9	0	-27.3%	—	-1.0	—	STL	1	14	89	1	26
William Henderson	GB	14	0	0	0	12	18	62	67%	3.4	0	-25.0%	—	-1.5	—	FA	0	0	0	0	36
Brad Hoover	CAR	16	22	73	1	20	29	122	69%	6.1	0	-22.0%	42	2.0	42	CAR	56	20	121	1	31
Jeremi Johnson	CIN	16	15	56	1	6	9	37	67%	6.2	0	-37.4%	—	-1.2	—	CIN	42	5	30	3	27
Kyle Johnson	DEN	14	5	30	0	7	11	37	64%	5.3	1	-23.4%	—	-0.9	—	DEN	23	15	111	2	29
Mike Karney	NO	15	11	33	1	15	20	96	75%	4.8	2	18.0%	—	3.2	—	NO	26	15	99	2	26
Dan Kreider	PIT	15	1	5	0	8	13	62	62%	4.8	0	-12.9%	—	-0.2	—	PIT	10	11	100	1	28
Le'Ron McClain	—	0	0	0	0	0	0	0	0%	0.0	0	0.0%	—	0.0	—	BAL	64	17	135	1	23
Jason McKie	CHI	15	8	18	0	25	38	162	66%	6.5	0	-25.1%	44	-3.4	45	CHI	19	26	163	1	27
Brandon Miree	GB	10	0	0	0	9	13	57	69%	4.4	0	-11.7%	—	-0.2	—	GB	1	13	89	1	26
Ovie Mughelli	BAL	16	12	50	0	21	24	182	88%	7.6	2	21.5%	—	4.0	—	ATL	33	7	72	1	27
Lorenzo Neal	SD	16	29	140	1	17	26	83	65%	4.9	0	-48.4%	50	-5.4	48	SD	126	16	90	1	37
Tony Richardson	MIN	9	5	12	0	13	14	111	93%	7.9	0	34.6%	—	3.4	—	MIN	15	18	125	1	36
Cecil Sapp	DEN	11	10	80	0	8	10	34	80%	3.4	0	-27.3%	—	-1.0	—	DEN	106	9	92	1	29
Cory Schlesinger	DET	14	0	0	0	8	11	36	73%	3.3	0	-41.0%	—	-1.7	—	MIA	1	20	149	1	35
Daimon Shelton	BUF	14	0	0	0	7	10	35	70%	3.5	0	-53.9%	—	-2.5	—	FA	0	0	0	0	35
Mack Strong	SEA	16	33	149	1	29	43	159	67%	5.5	0	-51.2%	53	-9.2	54	SEA	125	27	176	1	36
Thomas Tapeh	PHI	16	5	9	0	16	25	85	64%	5.3	1	-32.9%	46	-3.1	44	PHI	6	16	91	0	27

Cory Anderson, HOU: This ex-Tennessee fullback and middle linebacker is strictly an interior blocker, which would make him a good guard, but he'd have to put on about 60 pounds to avoid getting pushed around. He's in camp with Houston, a team that, coincidentally, needs a guard much more than a fullback.

Deon Anderson, DAL: Anderson left Connecticut in 2005 following several off-the-field incidents, but he returned in 2006 on his own dime. We're not sure whether that's a good thing or a bad thing. Either way, Dallas is loaded at fullback, which means Anderson will need to stick as a gunner to earn a roster spot. Maybe Dallas is hoping he'll try to pay his own way again.

B. J. Askew, TB: Will somebody please explain why Tampa Bay wants all of the Jets' old tight ends and fullbacks? Anthony Becht, Doug Jolley, Jerald Sowell, and now Askew, who made noise in March about how he was going to slim down and become a halfback until he realized no one was actually going to pay him to be a halfback. With those dreams dashed, he'll continue to be a decent fullback and special-teams guy in Tampa.

Obafemi Ayanbadejo, ARI: Ken Whisenhunt's repeated assertions that his Cardinals will have a fullback who focuses on blocking make a great deal of sense, but they might spell the end for Ayanbadejo, a fair blocker who is most conversant with catching the ball out of the backfield.

Darian Barnes, NYJ: It was a bit of a surprise when Barnes beat out free-agent-signing Fred Beasley for the Miami fullback job, but it wasn't really Barnes's job either. Sammy Morris was the Miami fullback. We'd love to say that Barnes is a great player who goes unnoticed, but he's really just a nondescript player who goes unnoticed for a reason. The Jets are his fourth team in five years.

Nehemiah Broughton, WAS: Broughton tore his ACL in the spring and will miss all of the 2007 season. Well, he'll miss *participating* in the 2007 NFL season. We don't think he's going to go hibernate.

Shawn Bryson, DET: A favorite of the previous regime, Bryson did not appear to fit into Mike Martz's plans, then suffered a severe knee injury in Week 6 and was placed on injured reserve. The release of Cory Schlesinger, however, has Bryson in line to take over as the full-time fullback in 2007. There aren't a lot of snaps when you're playing fullback for Martz, but, when he is on the field, Bryson should be a factor in the passing game.

Jameel Cook, HOU: Cook's two fumbles in three weeks earned him the enmity of Texans fans. While we'd like to think his IR trip shortly thereafter wasn't related, Houston fans sure do love their football. Cook was replaced by Vonta Leach, who the Texans signed to a four-year contract in the offseason. Cook's window as an offensive starter has come and gone, but he'll stay on the roster as a special-teams guy.

Ronnie Cruz, KC: Once upon a time, Cruz was the fullback and Kris Wilson was the H-back, depending on the formation. Then Cruz blew out his knee in Week 5, and, for the rest of the year, Wilson filled both slots. That leaves Cruz fighting for playing time and maybe a spot on special teams.

Jeff Dugan, MIN: Listed under tight ends.

Heath Evans, NE: Evans serves as a hybrid halfback/fullback for the Patriots, with most of his value coming as a blocking back and on special teams. He can do this for another few years—the Patriots say two, for now.

Jim Finn, NYG: Game charters recorded 11 plays on which the Giants inexplicably motioned Finn out to a wide receiver spot. Finn was never the intended receiver on any of those plays. Meanwhile, Tiki Barber got stuffed up the middle twice while Finn was running routes, and Eli Manning took two sacks and threw an interception on the nine pass plays from that formation. Jim Finn as decoy does not work. What does work is Jim Finn as lead blocker, and he was a big part of Tiki Barber's success over the last few years. The Giants signed Houston's Vonta Leach to an offer sheet that the Texans matched, so they don't share our sentiments. Finn now gets to block for Brandon Jacobs, who outweighs Finn by roughly 20 pounds. Neither one should motion out to wide receiver. Ever.

Justin Green, BAL: With Ovie Mughelli off to Atlanta, Green will need to be fully healed from last season's knee injury to fend off Le'Ron McClain. Or, alternately, he could take out McClain's knee, Tonya Harding–style. You get the feeling Ray Lewis might know someone who could help with that.

Justin Griffith, OAK: For his career, Griffith has averaged 4.7 yards per rush on 81 rushes. The high average suggests that Griffith deserves more than one carry per game. In a parallel universe, he's having a Mike Alstott career, complete with cable television commentators who provide corny sound effects for all his highlights. Griffith will quietly assume his jack-of-all-trades role in Oakland: catching passes, blocking, and relishing the rare inside give. He deserves a bigger role, but the Raiders have lots of guys who demand the ball, whether they deserve it or not.

Ahmard Hall, TEN: Hall's high school grades weren't good enough to get him into a major college, so he joined the Marines and saw action in Kosovo and Afghanistan. After four years of active duty (and a marriage to a fellow Marine—betcha the house is always spotless), he enrolled at the University of Texas and made the football team. He was co–Big XII Sportsperson of the Year in 2005, came to the Titans in the 2006 supplemental draft, and started seven games as a 27-year-old rookie. He has the typical fullback skill set—good run blocking, adequate hands, some rushing skills, special-teams value—and life lessons that are priceless. If he's not one of your favorite players by now, then reread this paragraph.

Madison Hedgecock, STL: The rookie from North Carolina earned "Super Ram" status in the Tar Heels' weight room two years in a row, then earned a starting fullback job with the real Rams in 2006 after injuries felled Paul Smith. He's more of a pure blocking back than a real production option, but the Rams have enough weapons, and his skill set matches his team's new offense.

William Henderson, FA: The venerable Henderson was sent packing after a season that saw him lose playing time to Brandon Miree. Mark Tauscher even took his spot on local TV. (A tackle, for crying out loud!) He is expected to retire, leaving Brett Favre as the last man on the roster from Green Bay's 1996 championship season.

Brad Hoover, CAR: Hoover earned –2.4 DPAR on third downs. Most fullbacks have third-down DPAR around zero because teams rarely throw to the fullback on third down; the big guy usually catches two or three checkdown passes per year on 3rd-and-18, and those plays don't ring the DPAR bell very loudly. The Panthers threw nine passes to Hoover on third down last year (third among fullbacks), and he caught seven of them, but he only had one first down. The average yards-to-go on these plays was just 5.6, and not one 3rd-and-10 or more, making the failure to convert more costly to Hoover's DPAR because of the increased expectation of a first down in those short-yardage situations. It wasn't Hoover's fault that Jake Delhomme kept looking to him in key situations last year, but when third down comes along this year, the new Panthers offensive coaching staff may want to put someone with more playmaking ability on the field.

Oliver Hoyte, DAL: Hoyte recorded 91 tackles as a linebacker at North Carolina State in 2005, earning a reputation as a big hitter with no coverage skills. The Cowboys liked the "hitter" part and moved him to fullback, where he started five games last year. Lousaka Polite was re-signed, so maybe Wade Phillips will move Hoyte back to linebacker. Or he could play both ways. With Troy Brown probably done, we in the media definitely need a new two-way player to cover with endlessly fawning feature stories.

Nate Ilaoa, PHI: Some quick facts: (1) Ilaoa stands 5-foot-9 and weighs about 250 pounds. (2) He started his career as a wide receiver. A *really* wide receiver. (3) Actually, Ilaoa only packed on the pounds after moving to running back in Hawaii's run-'n'-shoot offense. (4) He averaged 7.6 yards per carry and caught 67 passes as a senior. Ilaoa is the roundest square peg you'll ever see. He may have to go to Canada or the Arena league to find a system that suits his skills and measurables, but we're really rooting for this guy, because unique players make the NFL fun.

Jeremi Johnson, CIN: Johnson is a decent-enough lead blocker for Rudi Johnson, but on a team loaded with receiving options, he's not likely to see the ball much. He was used more as a short-yardage runner than a receiver last year, and he's relatively fast for a man his size.

Kyle Johnson, DEN: Johnson can play fullback and tight end and is a good blocker, but he's not much of a runner or receiver and is mostly a bit player in the Broncos' offense.

Mike Karney, NO: Karney's three touchdown game in Week 14 had to win a playoff game for someone in at least one frighteningly deep fantasy league last year. That also means that there's a person out there who lost their playoff game in fantasy football because of Mike Karney; that person deserves our collective sympathy and support in their new life without fantasy football.

David Kirtman, SEA: Kirtman's one claim to NFL fame so far is that his parents live next door to Mike Holmgren in Mercer Island, Washington. That's as close as the rookie got to the big time in 2006, though he didn't have to mow Coach's lawn. Presumably.

Dan Kreider, PIT: Kreider is an old-school fullback, counted on to serve as a third guard in the Steelers' run-oriented offense. If new offensive coordinator Bruce Arians deploys his preferred four-receiver sets, Kreider's role in the Pittsburgh offense could be more limited in 2007.

John Kuhn, PIT: Kuhn spent the second half of the season on the active roster after being signed off the practice squad. He will compete in camp for a spot backing up Dan Kreider, but if Kevan Barlow makes the team, he'll probably take Kuhn's roster spot.

Vonta Leach, HOU: Leach took over for Jameel Cook last year after the latter's trip to the IR. While Leach saw only a few games worth of action, the Giants thought enough of his performance to offer a four-year, $8-million contract to the restricted free agent, and the Texans thought enough of him to match it. If bad NFL teams are consistent about anything, it's justifying the money they've spent, so Leach enters 2007 as the starter.

Reagan Mauia, MIA: Okay, remember what we said above about Eagles seventh-round pick Nate Ilaoa? In the sixth round, the Dolphins took his even larger teammate Reagan Mauia, who stands 5-foot-11 and weighs 272 pounds. Mauia has lost 20 pounds since last season, but the story gets even better: Hawaii switched him from defensive tackle to offense two years ago, making Mauia a 351-pound fullback as a junior.

Le'Ron McClain, BAL: This Alabama graduate was the first real fullback taken in this year's draft, going with the last pick of the fourth round. He has the skill set—and probably the starting job—of former Ravens fullback Ovie Mughelli.

Fred McCrary, FA: A pure lead blocker and special teamer, McCrary became expendable when the Falcons signed Ovie Mughelli. McCrary's now 33, brings very little to the table, and remained unsigned at press time.

Sean McHugh, DET: McHugh is being moved from tight end to fullback to emphasize his strengths (blocking) and bury his weaknesses (route-running and agility). Shawn Bryson gets hurt enough that McHugh is likely to become the Detroit starter at some point.

Corey McIntyre, ATL: McIntyre was a defensive end and linebacker at West Virginia, switched to fullback in the pros, and spent most of the last four years bouncing between the World League and various practice squads. He played four games as part of the Falcons' "Anyone with a Pulse" roster initiative last year.

Jason McKie, CHI: Fullbacks tend not to get their proper due until they hit the downsides of their careers. McKie emerged as a full-time starter last year and did a good job clearing lanes for the Bears' solid ground attack. A few more seasons like that, and McKie will start making the Pro Bowl in 2011, when he is not nearly as good.

Garrett Mills, NE: This fourth-round pick out of Tulsa never saw the field during his rookie year, ending up on injured reserve halfway through the 2006 season. While he can play at either fullback or tight end, the Patriots are pretty deep in both spots, which means Mills will struggle to earn a roster spot.

Brandon Miree, GB: Miree was signed away from Denver after a year on their practice squad and some time in NFL Europe. Younger and more athletic than William Henderson, Miree will be the primary fullback. The Packers increasingly went to multiple tight ends last year, a trend that will keep Miree off the field.

Ovie Mughelli, ATL: This offseason, Mughelli turned 12 career carries and one season as a full-time starter into a six-year, $18-million free-agent deal with the Falcons that made him the highest-paid fullback in NFL history. What might make Mughelli worth the money is not his blocking (though he's good—think Lorenzo Neal), but his pass-catching ability, which is among the best for NFL fullbacks.

James Mungro, FA: Mungro tore his ACL in the preseason and missed the entire 2006 campaign. He was a free agent as of presstime, although the Colts have all but said they'll re-sign him once he's fully recovered. His 114-yard performance against the Eagles in 2002 is another sign that you too could run for 100 yards behind the Colts offensive line.

Lorenzo Neal, SD: The Chargers split Neal out wide even more than the Giants did Finn, a whopping 21 times. They even threw to him twice as a wideout, though both were incomplete. Now 37 years old, Neal is still one of the best lead blockers in the game, and last year he had 6.1 DPAR, the most of any running back below 75 carries. Norv Turner will use him the same way he used Daryl Johnston in Dallas.

Moran Norris, SF: Two fullbacks have recently established themselves as great blockers to the extent that people are actually talking about them: Ovie Mughelli and Moran Norris. After being released by the Texans following the 2005 season, Norris became arguably the best blocking fullback in the league with San Francisco last year. At the 2007 Scouting Combine, Mike Nolan spoke specifically of Norris's importance to the San Francisco offense, after which the 49ers gave Norris a new three-year contract. Prior to that, Frank Gore paid for Norris's trip to Hawaii when Gore went to the Pro Bowl. When the 2008 Pro Bowl comes around, Gore probably won't have to pay Norris's way.

Josh Parry, SEA: Traded to Seattle by the Eagles before the 2006 season, Parry was supposed to provide backup for Mack Strong and serve dutifully on special teams, but he was placed on injured reserve in late November with a foot injury. He was re-signed by the team in March. At a time when fullbacks are disappearing off NFL rosters, the Seahawks have four of them.

Patrick Pass, FA: The Patriots' on-again, off-again feelings for Pass appear to be off at the moment, and he's a free agent as we go to press. He spent 11 weeks on the Physically Unable to Play list last year, came back, and disappeared again after Week 14. He's a much better receiver than blocker, but this skill set is available in a million other running backs without rings.

Andrew Pinnock, SD: Like LaDainian Tomlinson, Lorenzo Neal has his very own backup. When you see Pinnock actually carrying the ball, it's time to get in the car and go home.

Lousaka Polite, DAL: Polite lost his starting job to Oliver Hoyte in training camp and played sparingly last season. All seven of his carries came in garbage time against the Buccaneers. He's an adequate blocker with no skills as a runner or receiver.

Alan Ricard, CLE: It's a slippery slope for fullbacks: Ricard went from being a Pro Bowl alternate blocking for Jamal Lewis in 2003 to being one of the last cuts in Buffalo's camp last year. The problem is that he doesn't contribute on special teams, which makes him a poor choice as a backup fullback. It's the same reason Freddie Mitchell is a substitute teacher rather than some team's fifth wideout. Ricard caught on with Cleveland, where he'll have an opportunity to win the starting job and block for Lewis again.

Tony Richardson, MIN: Richardson's 2006 season came to an end with a broken forearm in November. The longtime lead blocker in Kansas City is starting to slip as a player. He's in the last year of his deal with Minnesota, and this might be the last year we'll see Richardson as a starting fullback.

Cecil Sapp, DEN: A featured back at Colorado State, Sapp has transitioned nicely into the role of backup fullback and special-teams player for the Broncos. His recovery from a broken leg, which ended his 2006 season, has gone well, and there was discussion in minicamp about using Sapp in a hybrid role that would see him carry the ball more often. He probably won't average eight yards per carry again, but, in Denver, magic things happen.

Cory Schlesinger, MIA: Schlesinger joined the Lions in 1995, and in his 12 years with the team, under seven different head coaches, only once did Detroit win as many as ten games. Fittingly, he joined the team when they predominately ran a one-back set, and now he leaves the team when they again run the single back. He is going to Miami, where they'll actually use a fullback. Finally necessary to the offense, it is unclear he has anything valuable left to give.

Mike Sellers, WAS: Listed under tight ends.

Daimon Shelton, FA: A good example of replacement-level talent, Shelton was not retained by the Bills in the offseason and is probably done.

Paul Smith, DEN: It was thought that Smith would be St. Louis's starting fullback in 2006, but he missed six games with various injuries and lost that role to rookie Madison Hedgecock. Smith signed with the Broncos in March.

Terrelle Smith, ARI: Smith comes over from Cleveland to fill the Dan Kreider role in Ken Whisenhunt's scheme. Going from Cleveland's rushing "attack" to Arizona's exemplifies Smith's masochistic streak. He's likely to start at fullback, but he's not going to get the ball.

Jerald Sowell, FA: The longtime Jets fullback touched the ball just once in 11 games for the Bucs last season. Once a gunner extraordinaire, Sowell didn't record a single special-teams tackle in 2006. He's done.

Mack Strong, SEA: It's never good when your longtime blocking fullback morphs from stop sign to traffic cone, but Strong's effectiveness as a blocker fell off precipitously after his first Pro Bowl season in 2005. He had six Blown Blocks in 2006, the most of any non-lineman. While that may have been symptomatic of Seattle's overall line problems—it's harder to block when you first have to choose which oncoming defender to deal with—don't be surprised if the Seahawks start rotating in other options.

Thomas Tapeh, PHI: Tapeh took over the starting fullback job last season, and, while he's not the massive lead blocker that most teams look for in a fullback, the Eagles like his hands and chipping ability. His desktop wallpaper, available on the Eagles website, isn't an action shot of him plowing over a blocker or running in the flat, but instead shows him nonchalantly holding the ball before a game. In other words, look elsewhere for a background for your computer.

Lawrence Vickers, CLE: Vickers was one of ten Browns draft picks from 2006 that made the team. He's probably not going to beat out Alan Ricard for the newly available starting fullback job, but he'll contribute on special teams.

Leonard Weaver, SEA: A fan favorite for his surprisingly elusive running style and killer stiff-arm (as displayed in the last two preseasons), Weaver saw mostly special-teams time in 2005 and missed the 2006 season with a high ankle sprain. Don't be surprised to see him in the starting eleven from time to time this year—the coaches like what he can do.

Kris Wilson, KC: Listed under tight ends.

Derrick Wimbush, JAC: Wimbush is one of the better special-teams players in the league, although he wasn't as good last year as he was in 2005. He's behind LaBrandon Toefield and Greg Jones on the fullback depth chart, but he'll have a job even if he doesn't see an offensive snap in 2007.

Going Deep

Ahmed Bradshaw, NYG: Bradshaw was the nation's sixth-leading rusher at Marshall in 2006. He's a patient runner who reads blocks well, but he's a bit undersized at 5-foot-11. The Giants took him in the seventh round and are hoping to develop him into a lesser version of Tiki Barber.

Dee Brown, FA: One of the 18 Dee Browns in professional sports, this one spent last year with the Chiefs and has yet to make plans for 2007. He carried the ball ten times for 24 yards in 2006 (−120.8 percent DVOA, −4.0 DPAR).

Rock Cartwright, WAS: Cartwright only carried the ball five times for 15 yards in 2006, and has only managed 34 touches in the last three seasons, but he has plenty of value on kick returns, on which he was worth five points of field position last year, 11th in the NFL. During the Daniel Snyder era, the Redskins have proven quite proficient at signing big-name free agents to lucrative contracts, but often struggle to fill out their roster with quality depth. Cartwright is an exception, and his special-teams contributions more than make up for his paltry rushing numbers.

Kory Chapman, IND: Chapman, formerly of Minnesota and New England, spent last year on the Colts' practice squad. The departure of Dominic Rhodes opens up a possible roster slot from which he would primarily be used as a receiver out of the backfield. If he were a better pass-blocker, he'd have a shot at real playing time.

Thomas Clayton, SF: While at Kansas State, Clayton was benched for fumbling and arguing with his coach, suspended for several rules violations, and convicted of hitting a university parking officer who was trying to put a boot on Clayton's car, which was missing a VIN number and license plates. In his spare time, he played football, but he was an undersized power back with no hands and a fumbling problem. Basically, he's Travis Henry wearing the black Spider-Man costume.

Patrick Cobbs, MIA: Cobbs led the New England Patriots in rushing last preseason. This entitled him to spend the season bouncing around NFL practice squads, which should tell you something about what it means to lead a team in rushing during the preseason. He may get a shot at the Miami backup job behind Ronnie Brown if Lorenzo Booker struggles or gets hurt.

P. J. Daniels, BAL: This 2006 fourth-round pick does all his work between the tackles. He also has good hands and blocks well, but doesn't have the speed to be a featured back. Daniels is a favorite of the Ravens' coaching staff; if Mike Anderson is let go, Daniels is probably a good chunk of the reason why.

Kenneth Darby, TB: The University of Alabama's all-time leading rushers: Shaun Alexander (3,565 yards), Bobby Humphrey (3,420 yards), and Kenneth Darby (3,139 yards). Darby looked like a first-round pick after the 2005 season, but suffered through nagging injuries and a family health crisis in 2006. He could stick as an all-purpose back and could be a training camp surprise.

Clifton Dawson, IND: Dawson, the Ivy League's all-time leading rusher, was signed by the Colts as an undrafted free agent. He'll likely spend the year on the practice squad or playing special teams while he learns the complex Colts offense, which is a tough assignment—Harvard degree or no Harvard degree.

Quinton Ganther, TEN: A second-year player from Utah, Ganther is Travis Henry–light: He's built like a Kia but tries to run like a Hummer, can break some tackles, but fumbles a lot, can catch, but isn't very crafty in the open field. He could stick with the Titans if he reinvents himself as a third-down back.

Justise Hairston, NE: Hairston made his way to Central Connecticut State by way of Rutgers. He could be useful as a short-yardage back, but he's up against a crowded backfield and is more likely to star in the future TSN reality show "You'd Prefer an Argonaut."

Andre Hall, DEN: The pride of the USF Bulls is now a third-string running back for the Broncos, which makes him about as valuable in fantasy football as, oh, half the starting running backs in the NFL. Hall spent 2006 on the practice squad, and, while he's probably too small to be an every-down back, he's the prototypical Broncos running back in that he identifies the hole, goes through it, and lets nothing get in between those two tasks. He's basically 90 percent of Tatum Bell, which is the role he could assume in 2007.

Kay Jay Harris, STL: Harris spent two years in the Texas Rangers organization, where he posted OPSs of .448 and .444. He's slightly better at football, but, at 28, he's already bouncing around the league and doesn't have much time left to make a career. Harris, Chris Weinke, Drew Henson, Josh Booty—nearly all the guys who couldn't choose between baseball and football ended up falling short of their NFL potential. Remember this when Jeff Samardzija signs with the Raiders in 2009.

Priest Holmes, KC: Despite the spinal injury that ended his 2005 season and kept him out for 2006, Holmes still talks about coming back to the Chiefs in 2007. Technically, he's under contract through 2009, and there's every chance Larry Johnson will be getting the ouchies very soon following his Curse-baiting workload in 2006, but why on earth does Holmes want to risk further injury? Doesn't he want to be somewhat pain-free when he's playing with his grandkids in 15 years?

Marlion Jackson, FA: A 240-pounder currently playing for the Las Vegas Gladiators of the Arena League, Jackson earned a spot on Atlanta's practice squad last year with a 19-carry, 95-yard exhibition performance against the Titans. He made the active roster when Jerious Norwood got hurt, carried once for two yards against the Browns, tore a pectoral muscle, and was lost for the season. With his size and special-teams value, Jackson should earn a job somewhere this season.

Kenton Keith, IND: Ahman Green's cousin went to New Mexico State, then played the last four seasons in Saskatchewan. He's yet another one of the replacement-level talents in Colts camp who may get to be one Joseph Addai injury away from football glory.

Reno Mahe, PHI: Mahe carried the ball only four times in 2006 for 18 yards (–43.1 percent DVOA, –0.3 DPAR) and caught five passes for 23 yards (–89.6% DVOA, –2.3 DPAR). Mahe was Philadelphia's return specialist, but the Eagles signed Bethel Johnson to return kicks and never see the field otherwise in his place. The Eagles ranked 24th in both punt and kick return value in 2006; that level of production can be had from a rookie for half the price of either Mahe or Johnson.

Chris Morgan, IND: See Kenton Keith. Replace first sentence with "Morgan just graduated from Indiana University of Pennsylvania."

Jamal Robertson, ATL: A mediocre kick returner and failed change-up back in San Francisco and Carolina, Robertson played one game for the Falcons as part of Atlanta's "Anyone with a Pulse" roster initiative last year.

Cory Ross, BAL: As a rookie last year, Ross saw duty as both a kick and punt returner; he'll have to compete with the Ravens' returning Sams and rookie Yamon Figurs for that role in 2007.

Derrick Ross, KC: It's nice to put up a lot of yards in NFL Europa, but when those yards come at less than four yards per carry, you probably don't have a place back home in the big leagues.

Josh Scobey, BUF: During two seasons in Seattle, Scobey was a special-teams option only and did fairly well in that role, but his return duties were taken by Nate Burleson last year. He signed with Buffalo in early May.

Jason Snelling, ATL: This Virginia product was drafted by the Falcons in the seventh round of this year's draft. Fullback is pretty set in Atlanta, and, while Snelling can play special teams, he has struggled with injuries, is epileptic, and is likely too small to make it at the NFL level. Atlanta will try him out as a power back.

Darren Sproles, SD: Sproles might be the shortest player in the league: He's listed at 5-foot-6 and looks a little smaller than that. He missed all of the 2006 season with a fractured fibula, but he should be back in 2007 and will likely take on the kickoff return duties until he gets hurt again.

Lee Suggs, FA: Suggs was nearly dealt to the Jets in the preseason, but fortuitously failed his physical so the Jets could trade for Kevan Barlow instead. Suggs went to Miami, but lasted just 36 days before being cut. His Dolphins totals: six carries for 26 yards (9.6 percent DVOA, 0.7 DPAR). Suggs didn't catch on anywhere over the off-season, but was cited for owning dangerous dogs; at least the cops know that they don't have to worry about Suggs leaving them alone.

Butchie Wallace, FA: A change-up back, Wallace spent the 2004 and 2005 seasons on the Vikings' practice squad, then played well enough for the Frankfurt Galaxy to earn a World Bowl MVP award and a shot with the Falcons for 2006, then got hurt in camp and spent last season on injured reserve. Wallace has potential as a special teamer and spot performer, but he was released in April and hasn't caught on anywhere as of press time.

Derrick Ward, NYG: In 2005 Ward had 35 carries and gained 123 yards (4.2 percent DVOA, 2.4 DPAR). Last year, thanks to a debilitating foot injury and the emergence of Brandon Jacobs, he didn't carry the ball once. He's the third-string running back and will get a few carries if Droughns gets hurt or remains crummy.

Danny Ware, TEN: Ware started as a freshman at Georgia in 2004, but he fumbled his way out of the lineup and spent his last three collegiate seasons as a committee back. The Titans signed him as a priority free agent and liked what they saw in May minicamp. He could stick on a roster with few options at running back.

Marquis Weeks, SEA: A safety at Virginia, the undrafted Weeks was signed by Seattle in 2005 and bounced back and forth from preseason standout to practice-squadder before inking a small, two-year contract before the 2006 season.

Domanick Williams, FA: This is the player who used to be known as Domanick Davis; he changed his name right before Houston released him in March. The knee injury Williams suffered in 2005 cost him all of 2006 and probably ended his career. He wouldn't have made such a big deal about the name change if he didn't want to come back to the NFL, but who is going to sign a running back with no cartilage in his knee?

Shaud Williams, BUF: Williams served primarily on special teams last year, getting only two carries. Only 18 of his 89 career carries and eight of his 20 career receptions have come on third down, which is kind of odd for a third-down back. Either he blocks well for a man of his size, or he just likes standing next to the quarterback in the shotgun. The Bills drafting Dwayne Wright likely ended his time in Buffalo.

Quincy Wilson, CIN: Wilson is a former practice-squad player who led the NFL in rushing during the 2006 preseason. Chris Perry's injury history could open the door for Wilson to make the active roster.

DeShawn Wynn, GB: Green Bay's seventh-round pick out of the University of Florida, Wynn is a 230-pound power back who prefers to run to the outside. In other words, he's a misfit. The Packers need a power back, and Wynn will find a role if he can convert his size and strength into production.

Wide Receivers

Speed, acceleration, a knowledge of defensive coverage, and good hands: These are some of the skills that an NFL wide receiver must have. Fans are forgiven if they think the list also includes "a gigantic ego."

Never in NFL history have more wide receivers made more news. Yet, for all the egotistical tendencies of most of today's top wideouts, 2006 stands out as the year of the teammates. Only a few teams had a gigantic separation between the performance of their number-one wide receiver and the performance of the rest of their wideouts: primarily, Buffalo (Lee Evans), Carolina (Steve Smith), and Denver (Javon Walker). Meanwhile, four pairs of teammates ranked among the top ten receivers in DPAR: Reggie Wayne and Marvin Harrison of the Colts, Chad Johnson and T. J. Houshmandzadeh of the Bengals, Roy Williams and Mike Furrey of the Lions, and Terrell Owens and Terry Glenn of the Cowboys. By comparison, there was only one such pair in 2005 (Johnson and Houshmandzadeh), only one in 2004 (Wayne and Brandon Stokley of the Colts, with Harrison right behind at number 12), and only two in 2003 (Wayne and Harrison, and Tennessee's Derrick Mason and Justin McCareins).

In the following section we give the last three years worth of statistics as well as a 2007 projection for every wide receiver who played a significant role in 2006, or is expected to play a significant role in 2007.

How to Read the Wide Receiver Statistics Table

The first line (table 1) contains biographical data—each player's name, height, weight, college, draft position, birth date, and age. Height and weight are the best data we could find; weight, of course, can fluctuate during the offseason. Age is very simple, the number of years between the player's birth year and 2007, but birth date is provided if you want to figure out exact age.

Draft position gives draft year and round, with the overall pick number with which the player was taken in parentheses. In the sample table, it says that Terry Glenn was chosen in the 1996 draft in the first round with the seventh-overall pick. Undrafted free agents are listed as "FA" with the year they came into the league, even if they were only in training camp or on a practice squad.

To the far right of the first line is the player's **Risk** for fantasy football in 2007. The players most likely to match their projected stats in 2007 are marked Green, the players who are riskier but still somewhat dependable are marked Yellow, and everyone else is marked Red. The Risk variable is explained further in the introduction to the Quarterbacks section.

Next we give the last three years of player stats. Note that rushing stats are not included for wide receivers, but that any receiver with at least three carries last year will have his 2006 rushing stats appear in his team's chapter.

Within the wide receiver table, the first column after the year and team for which that receiver played that year is games played (**G**). This is the official NFL total and may include games in which a player appeared on special teams but did not play wide receiver. Receptions (**Rec**) counts passes caught, while Passes (**Pass**) counts passes thrown to this player, complete or incomplete. The next four columns list receiving yards (**Yds**), Catch Rate (**C%**), yards per catch (**Yd/C**), and receiving touchdowns (**TD**).

Catch Rate, or receptions divided by total passes, is an attempt to rectify a major problem in conventional statistics, which lay the blame for incomplete passes entirely on quarterbacks. Historical study shows that receivers definitely have an impact on whether a ball is complete or incomplete. We're still working to break down the degree to which the

Table 1. Wide Receiver Statistics Sample

Terry Glenn   Height: 5-11   Weight: 195   College: Ohio State   Draft: 1996/1 (7)   Born: 23-Jul-1974   Age: 33   Risk: Yellow

Year	Team	G	Rec	Pass	Yds	C%	Yd/C	TD	YAC	Rk	DVOA	Rk	DPAR	Rk	PAR	Short	Mid	Deep	Bomb
2004	DAL	6	24	37	400	65%	16.7	2	—	—	32.6%	—	11.6	—	11.3	—	—	—	—
2005	DAL	16	62	122	1136	52%	18.3	7	3.0	62	16.9%	17	25.8	14	26.1	17%	38%	17%	28%
2006	DAL	16	70	111	1047	63%	15.0	6	3.7	38	19.1%	14	25.9	9	27.7	25%	39%	21%	16%
2007	DAL		59		834		14.1	5											

responsibility for an incomplete is shared by the quarterback and receiver, but it is clearly closer to 50-50 than it is to the 100-0 currently reflected in NFL stats. Wide receivers who are used in longer pass patterns will generally catch a lower percentage of passes. The average NFL wide receiver has caught 56 percent of passes in each of the last three seasons.

(Note: Incomplete pass does not mean dropped pass; dropped passes are not specified in publicly available play-by-play, and, while we have the data from game charting, it is not yet merged into our other statistics.)

Next comes Yards After Catch (**YAC**), based on information from the game charting project, and rank (**Rk**) in Yards After Catch. That is followed by five columns with our advanced metrics for receiving: **DVOA** (Defense-Adjusted Value Over Average), **DPAR** (Defense-Adjusted Points Above Replacement), and **PAR** (Points Above Replacement), along with the player's rank in both DVOA and DPAR. These metrics compare every pass intended for a receiver and the results of that pass to a league-average baseline based on the game situations in which passes were thrown to that receiver. DVOA and DPAR are also adjusted based on the opposing defense. The methods used to compute these numbers are described in detail in the "Statistical Toolbox" introduction in the front of the book. The important distinctions between them are:

- DVOA is a rate statistic, while DPAR is a cumulative statistic. Thus, a higher DVOA means more value per pass play, while a higher DPAR means more aggregate value over the entire season.

- Because DPAR is defense-adjusted and PAR is not, a player whose DPAR is higher than his PAR faced a harder-than-average schedule. A player whose DPAR is lower than his PAR faced an easier-than-average schedule.

To qualify for ranking in YAC, receiving DVOA, or receiving DPAR, a wide receiver must have had 50 passes thrown to him in that season. We ranked 83 receivers in 2006, 89 in 2005, and 84 in 2004.

The final four columns break down pass length based on the Football Outsiders charting project. The categories are **Short** (5 yards or less), **Mid** (6–15 yards), **Deep** (16–25 yards), and **Bomb** (26 or more yards). These numbers are based on distance in the air only and include both complete and incomplete passes. Because the charting project began in 2005, these numbers (as well as YAC) are not available for 2004.

The italicized row of statistics for the 2007 season is our 2007 KUBIAK projection based on a complicated regression analysis that takes into account numerous variables, including projected role, performance over the past two years, projected team offense and defense, projected quarterback statistics, historical comparables, height, age, and strength of schedule. Note that KUBIAK projects only the official NFL statistics, not our advanced metrics.

It is difficult to accurately project statistics for a 162-game baseball season, but it is exponentially more difficult to accurately project statistics for a 16-game football season. Consider the listed projections not as a prediction of exact numbers, but as the mean of a range of possible performances. What's important is less the exact number of yards we project, and more which players are projected to improve or decline. Actual performance will vary from our projection less for veteran starters and more for rookies and third-stringers, for whom we must base our projections on much smaller career statistical samples. Touchdown numbers will vary more than yardage numbers.

A few low-round rookies, guys listed at seventh on the depth chart, and players who are listed as wide receivers but really only play special teams are briefly discussed at the end of the chapter in a section we call "Going Deep."

Two notes regarding our advanced metrics: We cannot yet fully separate the performance of a receiver from the performance of his quarterback. Be aware that one will affect the other. In addition, these statistics measure only passes thrown to a receiver, not performance on plays when he is not thrown the ball, such as blocking and drawing double teams.

Table 2. Top 20 WR by DPAR (Total Value), 2006

Rank	Player	Team	DPAR	Rank	Player	Team	DPAR
1	Reggie Wayne	IND	46.0	11	Marques Colston	NO	25.4
2	Marvin Harrison	IND	44.3	12	Isaac Bruce	STL	24.9
3	Lee Evans	BUF	34.4	13	Jerricho Cotchery	NYJ	23.5
4	T. J. Houshmandzadeh	CIN	31.4	14	Steve Smith	CAR	22.4
5	Chad Johnson	CIN	31.4	15	D. J. Hackett	SEA	22.0
6	Roy Williams	DET	29.0	16	Jevon Walker	DEN	21.0
7	Larry Fitzgerald	ARI	27.6	17	Devery Henderson	NO	20.2
8	Terrell Owens	DAL	27.4	18	Joe Horn	NO	19.7
9	Terry Glenn	DAL	26.6	19	Santonio Holmes	PIT	19.6
10	Mike Furrey	DET	25.8	20	Eric Parker	SD	19.2

Table 3. Top 20 WR by DVOA (Value per Pass), 2006

Rank	Player	Team	DVOA	Rank	Player	Team	DVOA
1	Devery Henderson	NO	39.7%	11	Terry Glenn	DAL	20.4%
2	D. J. Hackett	SEA	35.7%	12	Samie Parker	KC	19.9%
3	Reggie Wayne	IND	35.0%	13	Bryant Johnson	ARI	19.9%
4	Joe Horn	NO	31.7%	14	Nate Washington	PIT	19.9%
5	Marvin Harrison	IND	28.9%	15	Santonio Holmes	PIT	18.3%
6	Kevin Curtis	STL	27.4%	16	Marques Colston	NO	17.3%
7	Eric Parker	SD	26.5%	17	Chad Johnson	CIN	15.5%
8	Lee Evans	BUF	23.3%	18	Reggie Brown	PHI	15.4%
9	Larry Fitzgerald	ARI	22.3%	19	Bobby Wade	TEN	14.9%
10	T. J. Houshmandzadeh	CIN	20.7%	20	Ronald Curry	OAK	14.2%

David Anderson   Height: 5-11   Weight: 195   College: Colorado State   Draft: 2006/7 (251)   Born: 28-Jul-1983   Age: 24   Risk: Red

Year	Team	G	Rec	Pass	Yds	C%	Yd/C	TD	YAC	Rk	DVOA	Rk	DPAR	Rk	PAR	Short	Mid	Deep	Bomb
2006	HOU	9	1	1	27	100%	27.0	0	22.0	—	221.9%	—	1.5	—	1.5	100%	0%	0%	0%
2007	HOU		30		327		11.0	1											

Anderson has good speed and good hands, and is a good blocker. At Colorado State, he was known for his willingness to catch the ball in traffic. He fell to the seventh round because he's short and he lacks the explosiveness to burn man coverage, but how much explosiveness do you need in the Texans' "three yards and a cloud of wide receiver screens" offense? Ignore the fact that he had just one catch as a rookie; right now, the only thing standing between him and a starting role is Kevin Walter. If he gets playing time, he's a fantasy sleeper.

Jason Avant   Height: 6-1   Weight: 210   College: Michigan   Draft: 2006/4 (109)   Born: 20-Apr-1983   Age: 24   Risk: Red

Year	Team	G	Rec	Pass	Yds	C%	Yd/C	TD	YAC	Rk	DVOA	Rk	DPAR	Rk	PAR	Short	Mid	Deep	Bomb
2006	PHI	8	7	15	68	47%	9.7	1	5.0	—	-45.6%	—	-2.8	—	-2.4	58%	17%	8%	17%
2007	PHI		15		212		14.1	1											

Avant is expected to compete with Hank Baskett for the number-three receiver position in 2007. That has been an important position in the Eagles' offense, since they have been in the bottom string of teams in usage of starting receivers over the past two years. Avant plays big and strong, which could make him an effective contributor in the slot. His strengths are blocking and going over the middle. The Eagles get fairly average production from the tight end position, and Avant could line up as a sort of mini–tight end. The Eagles gave him T.O.'s old number, which must have been some kind of rookie hazing.

Hank Baskett   Height: 6-4   Weight: 215   College: New Mexico   Draft: 2006/FA   Born: 4-Sep-1982   Age: 25   Risk: Red

Year	Team	G	Rec	Pass	Yds	C%	Yd/C	TD	YAC	Rk	DVOA	Rk	DPAR	Rk	PAR	Short	Mid	Deep	Bomb
2006	PHI	16	22	43	464	51%	21.1	2	7.6	—	10.2%	—	7.3	—	7.9	19%	38%	24%	19%
2007	PHI		34		555		16.5	4											

Take away Baskett's seven catches and 177 yards against Atlanta's atrocious secondary in a meaningless Week 17 game, and his rookie totals don't look as impressive. He'll be competing with fellow sophomore Jason Avant for playing time behind Reggie Brown and Kevin Curtis. The primary difference between the two is that Baskett is taller and faster, while Avant is the stronger possession receiver.

Arnaz Battle   Height: 6-1   Weight: 217   College: Notre Dame   Draft: 2003/6 (197)   Born: 22-Feb-1980   Age: 27   Risk: Red

Year	Team	G	Rec	Pass	Yds	C%	Yd/C	TD	YAC	Rk	DVOA	Rk	DPAR	Rk	PAR	Short	Mid	Deep	Bomb
2004	SF	14	8	15	143	53%	17.9	0	—	—	5.4%	—	1.8	—	1.1	—	—	—	—
2005	SF	10	32	54	363	59%	11.3	3	3.7	38	-11.5%	71	1.5	72	3.2	39%	52%	7%	2%
2006	SF	16	59	86	686	70%	11.6	3	4.2	28	6.6%	37	12.3	39	12.5	45%	39%	10%	6%
2007	SF		44		554		12.6	2											

Battle is a fine blocker, and his Catch Rate is great, but he's not really going to become a standout number-one receiver. Now, thanks to the Darrell Jackson trade, the 49ers don't need him to become one. If you are your quarterback's leading target in the red zone and are on third down, you just might be a possession receiver.

Drew Bennett Height: 6-5 Weight: 206 College: UCLA Draft: 2000/FA Born: 26-Aug-1978 Age: 29 Risk: Yellow

Year	Team	G	Rec	Pass	Yds	C%	Yd/C	TD	YAC	Rk	DVOA	Rk	DPAR	Rk	PAR	Short	Mid	Deep	Bomb
2004	TEN	16	80	143	1247	56%	15.6	11	—	—	8.4%	38	23.6	21	26.9	—	—	—	—
2005	TEN	13	58	109	738	53%	12.7	4	3.1	56	-10.3%	67	3.7	66	5.8	32%	46%	9%	12%
2006	TEN	16	46	97	737	47%	16.0	3	3.3	49	-4.4%	57	6.6	58	5.6	13%	45%	26%	16%
2007	STL		39		505		13.1	3											

Bennett and Vince Young never clicked. Bennett caught 16 passes for 235 yards in the three games Kerry Collins started, then caught just 30 passes for 502 yards over the last 13 games. Bennett's longest reception in 2006 covered just 39 yards after he caught a total of nine 40-plus-yard passes in 2004 and 2005. He was miscast as a number-one receiver in Tennessee when Derrick Mason left as a free agent. In St. Louis, he'll terrorize nickel corners from the slot for now and replace Isaac Bruce later.

Bernard Berrian Height: 6-1 Weight: 183 College: Fresno State Draft: 2004/3 (78) Born: 27-Dec-1980 Age: 26 Risk: Red

Year	Team	G	Rec	Pass	Yds	C%	Yd/C	TD	YAC	Rk	DVOA	Rk	DPAR	Rk	PAR	Short	Mid	Deep	Bomb
2004	CHI	16	15	44	225	34%	15.0	2	—	—	-43.5%	—	-8.1	—	-7.6	—	—	—	—
2005	CHI	11	13	25	246	52%	18.9	0	3.7	—	14.8%	—	4.7	—	3.6	30%	15%	20%	35%
2006	CHI	15	51	102	775	50%	15.2	6	4.0	35	-13.9%	69	0.8	69	1.4	25%	31%	15%	28%
2007	CHI		51		820		16.0	5											

Last year Berrian did not just develop into an extraordinary deep threat; he also became a more polished receiver in general. His abuse of poor Fred Thomas in the NFC Championship game helped punch Chicago's ticket to the Super Bowl; his headfake on Thomas while a Rex Grossman dying swan was still in the air is one of the greatest moves you will ever see. Berrian slowed down late in the season, as safeties increasingly rolled toward him. He had only one catch longer than 20 yards in his last five games. His overall totals were also held down by a rib injury that cost him one game and limited him to a single catch in two others. He needs to continue to improve his ability to make plays underneath in order to open up the deep routes on which he thrives; otherwise, he risks turning into another Ashley Lelie.

Anquan Boldin Height: 6-1 Weight: 218 College: Florida State Draft: 2003/2 (54) Born: 3-Oct-1980 Age: 27 Risk: Yellow

Year	Team	G	Rec	Pass	Yds	C%	Yd/C	TD	YAC	Rk	DVOA	Rk	DPAR	Rk	PAR	Short	Mid	Deep	Bomb
2004	ARI	10	56	104	623	54%	11.1	1	—	—	-17.3%	72	-1.3	72	0.1	—	—	—	—
2005	ARI	14	102	171	1402	60%	13.7	7	5.2	13	4.5%	40	23.0	16	27.7	37%	35%	20%	7%
2006	ARI	16	83	152	1203	55%	14.5	4	5.5	4	3.8%	42	18.7	21	18.5	28%	45%	15%	11%
2007	ARI		79		1073		13.6	6											

In the introduction to this chapter, we mention four different pairs of teammates who finished in the top ten for DPAR in 2006. Those who know about Arizona's dynamic duo of Boldin and Larry Fitzgerald might be surprised to see their names missing from that list. While Fitzgerald finished seventh in DPAR, Boldin dipped below the top ten due to a drop in Catch Rate. Boldin has the edge in two areas: He's targeted more often (he led the league in passes in 2005 and tied for fifth in 2006), and gets more yards after the catch, with only Donald Driver having more total YAC in 2006. Overall, however, Fitzgerald is the more productive receiver.

Marty Booker Height: 6-0 Weight: 212 College: LA-Monroe Draft: 1999/3 (78) Born: 31-Jul-1976 Age: 31 Risk: Yellow

Year	Team	G	Rec	Pass	Yds	C%	Yd/C	TD	YAC	Rk	DVOA	Rk	DPAR	Rk	PAR	Short	Mid	Deep	Bomb
2004	MIA	15	50	105	638	48%	12.8	1	—	—	-19.6%	74	-3.2	76	-3.9	—	—	—	—
2005	MIA	15	39	86	686	45%	17.6	3	7.1	5	0.4%	49	8.5	49	8.4	24%	38%	29%	10%
2006	MIA	14	55	90	747	61%	13.6	6	4.8	15	13.6%	23	16.7	28	16.5	30%	43%	18%	8%
2007	MIA		53		563		10.6	3											

In an ideal world, the 2006 Miami offense would have had Booker operating underneath as a possession receiver, Wes Welker being a nuisance going over the middle, Randy McMichael using his speed and athletic ability to occupy safeties and outrun linebackers, and Chris Chambers emerging as a poor man's Randy Moss in Daunte Culpepper's Comeback Player of the Year

(continued next page)

Marty Booker *(continued)*

season. Instead, Booker was the Dolphins' best receiver, and the rest of the offense imploded. When a 30-year-old receiver puts up his best numbers in five years, you shouldn't expect a repeat performance. On the other hand, a list of receivers with a similar three-year span in their careers to Booker's last three seasons is surprisingly positive: Ricky Sanders, Pat Tilley, Muhsin Muhammad, and a name that will warm the hearts of all Miami fans—Mark Duper.

Dwayne Bowe   Height: 6-3   Weight: 212   College: LSU   Draft: 2007/1 (23)   Born: 21-Sep-1984   Age: 23   Risk: Red

Year	Team	G	Rec	Pass	Yds	C%	Yd/C	TD	YAC	Rk	DVOA	Rk	DPAR	Rk	PAR	Short	Mid	Deep	Bomb
2007	KC		35		508		14.5	3											

Unlike fellow LSU receiver and first-round selection Craig Davis, Bowe is an intense player who gives his all on every play. With his size (6-foot-3, 212 pounds) and blocking skill, he gives Kansas City an excellent point man on the sweep. Bowe's biggest problem is his inability to accelerate into deeper patterns, which will limit him to a possession role, much as it does many other large receivers. He can still be effective in that role, but he'll need to improve his hands and his route running before he becomes a worthwhile starting receiver on the pro level.

Corey Bradford   Height: 6-1   Weight: 197   College: Jackson State   Draft: 1998/5 (150)   Born: 8-Dec-1975   Age: 32   Risk: Red

Year	Team	G	Rec	Pass	Yds	C%	Yd/C	TD	YAC	Rk	DVOA	Rk	DPAR	Rk	PAR	Short	Mid	Deep	Bomb
2004	HOU	15	27	54	399	50%	14.8	3	—	—	-7.4%	60	3.1	64	4.3	—	—	—	—
2005	HOU	16	34	66	436	52%	12.8	5	2.8	67	-4.9%	61	4.5	61	5.8	18%	54%	16%	12%
2006	DET	9	14	25	164	56%	11.7	0	1.4	—	-13.7%	—	0.2	—	0.3	33%	33%	25%	8%
2007	FA		11		140		12.9	1											

Bradford started in Week 1, dropped some balls over the next several weeks, and found himself released after Week 3. The Lions signed Az Hakim, decided he had nothing left, screwed around with quarterback Josh McCown as a receiver, re-signed Bradford in November, and then let him become an unrestricted free agent again in February. Bradford's best attribute was always his speed, but that is starting to disappear, which means Bradford will have trouble landing a job. Unless the Lions feel like signing him and releasing him a few more times, that is.

Mark Bradley   Height: 6-1   Weight: 201   College: Oklahoma   Draft: 2005/2 (39)   Born: 29-Jan-1982   Age: 25   Risk: Yellow

Year	Team	G	Rec	Pass	Yds	C%	Yd/C	TD	YAC	Rk	DVOA	Rk	DPAR	Rk	PAR	Short	Mid	Deep	Bomb
2005	CHI	7	18	36	230	50%	12.8	0	4.5	—	-27.7%	—	-2.8	—	-3.2	34%	38%	21%	7%
2006	CHI	10	14	23	282	61%	20.1	3	8.1	—	37.4%	—	7.7	—	8.0	32%	32%	9%	27%
2007	CHI		43		579		13.4	3											

It's a good thing Rex Grossman can throw the deep ball, because Bernard Berrian and a healthy Bradley combine to give the Bears multiple receivers who can stretch the field. While Berrian was injured for two games in November, Bradley racked up 159 yards on eight catches, proving he was fully recovered from the ACL injury that ended his 2005 season. Then a severely sprained ankle—unrelated to the ACL problem—limited him down the stretch. Bradley's emergence as a quality third receiver could do wonders for the Bears' passing game, but, as our man Will Carroll always says, "health is a skill."

Deion Branch   Height: 5-9   Weight: 193   College: Louisville   Draft: 2002/2 (65)   Born: 18-Jul-1979   Age: 28   Risk: Green

Year	Team	G	Rec	Pass	Yds	C%	Yd/C	TD	YAC	Rk	DVOA	Rk	DPAR	Rk	PAR	Short	Mid	Deep	Bomb
2004	NE	9	35	51	454	69%	13.0	4	—	—	36.2%	5	16.7	35	17.2	—	—	—	—
2005	NE	16	78	125	998	62%	12.8	5	3.2	54	19.5%	13	27.9	12	25.1	30%	44%	17%	8%
2006	SEA	14	53	101	725	52%	13.7	4	3.4	47	-3.0%	55	8.2	52	8.7	11%	62%	20%	7%
2007	SEA		59		877		14.9	6											

For $39 million over six years, with $13 million guaranteed, $23 million over the first three seasons, and their first-round draft pick in this year's draft, Branch was acquired by the Seahawks, though he was entangled in a contract dispute with New England last offseason. One season later, it's hard to know who the trade benefited. Branch struggled as he adjusted to a new offense in Seattle, and, without a first-round selection, the Seahawks had a tougher time reloading for 2007. In New England, Reche Caldwell's bug-eyed stare at the end of the Pats' playoff loss to the Colts had everyone wondering, "What if?" In the end, New England signed Donte' Stallworth for almost as much as Branch wanted—on Branch's recommendation, ironically—and the Seahawks dealt Darrell Jackson to San Francisco, hoping (and praying) that Branch will return to his Super Bowl MVP-level of productivity in 2007. Essentially, Branch is now a first-round, huge-contract draft pick, saddled with high expectations but without the "I'm just a rookie" excuse. Sound like fun?

Reggie Brown Height: 6-1 Weight: 197 College: Georgia Draft: 2005/2 (35) Born: 13-Jan-1981 Age: 26 Risk: Yellow

Year	Team	G	Rec	Pass	Yds	C%	Yd/C	TD	YAC	Rk	DVOA	Rk	DPAR	Rk	PAR	Short	Mid	Deep	Bomb
2005	PHI	16	43	90	571	51%	13.3	4	4.8	18	-14.5%	75	-0.1	78	-2.8	33%	34%	19%	13%
2006	PHI	16	46	92	816	50%	17.7	8	4.0	34	14.4%	20	18.2	23	18.2	24%	38%	19%	19%
2007	PHI		52		926		17.6	6											

Brown is entering the fabled third year, when receivers often take momentous steps forward. He took a big one last year, along with the rest of the Eagles' offense, averaging more than 17 yards per reception. While impressive, that figure also suggests that Brown was used more as a deep threat than as a complete, mature receiver last year, proving he still has room to grow. Many of the league's best receivers spend about half their time moving the chains on receptions between 6 and 15 yards. Brown's lack of development in this role is the one thing that keeps him from being a true number one. The receivers most similar to Brown in their first two professional seasons are a mildly obscure bunch: Ray Butler, Floyd Dixon, Eric Martin, Ernie Jones, and . . . wait, who is this "Terrell Owens" gentleman?

Troy Brown Height: 5-10 Weight: 196 College: Marshall Draft: 1993/8 (198) Born: 2-Jul-1971 Age: 36 Risk: Red

Year	Team	G	Rec	Pass	Yds	C%	Yd/C	TD	YAC	Rk	DVOA	Rk	DPAR	Rk	PAR	Short	Mid	Deep	Bomb
2004	NE	12	17	29	184	59%	10.8	1	—	—	5.2%	—	3.6	—	3.0	—	—	—	—
2005	NE	13	39	59	466	66%	11.9	2	5.1	16	16.1%	19	12.0	34	11.6	41%	43%	12%	3%
2006	NE	16	43	76	384	58%	8.9	4	4.3	27	-6.3%	60	4.2	62	3.1	49%	38%	7%	5%
2007	NE		9		127		13.6	1											

Brown's versatility is well known at this point, but the problem is that he's not someone you actually want playing on either side of the ball. He's never been anything but a stopgap slot corner, but last year he had no business being on defense at all, showing all the skill of the kid who shows up to intramural sports in jean shorts and a cut-off T-shirt because his parents made him play a sport. Of course, Marlon McCree might beg to differ with us. Offensively, Brown's skill set is down to running short crossing patterns. He wasn't even an asset on third down last year (–15.8% DVOA). Replaced in the offense by a similar but better player in Wes Welker, Brown can probably find a job if he wants one, or retire having played his whole career in New England; if Chevy brings back their "Our Country" campaign in 2019, expect them to use Troy Brown footage in the commercial.

Isaac Bruce Height: 6-0 Weight: 188 College: Memphis Draft: 1994/2 (33) Born: 10-Nov-1972 Age: 35 Risk: Yellow

Year	Team	G	Rec	Pass	Yds	C%	Yd/C	TD	YAC	Rk	DVOA	Rk	DPAR	Rk	PAR	Short	Mid	Deep	Bomb
2004	STL	16	89	148	1292	60%	14.5	6	—	—	11.8%	37	26.0	15	25.4	—	—	—	—
2005	STL	11	36	71	525	51%	14.6	3	3.7	36	-10.7%	69	2.3	69	3.6	27%	30%	27%	17%
2006	STL	16	74	126	1098	59%	14.8	3	3.7	39	13.9%	22	24.9	12	24.4	28%	34%	27%	11%
2007	STL		66		813		12.3	4											

After missing five games with a foot injury in 2005, Bruce experienced a great rebound last year. Of course, a large part of that rebound was created by opposing defenses that now concentrate on stopping Torry Holt before Bruce. Bruce will be 35 in November and doesn't have top-end speed anymore. Nonetheless, his craftiness with routes and angles, and his mastery of every little thing in the receiving game, make him a valuable part of the Rams' offense. His nine-catch, 148-yard performance against the Redskins in Week 16 told two tales: First, that Bruce still has it, and second, that Washington's pass defense was just as bad as the numbers said.

Antonio Bryant Height: 6-1 Weight: 192 College: Pittsburgh Draft: 2002/2 (63) Born: 9-Mar-1981 Age: 26 Risk: Red

Year	Team	G	Rec	Pass	Yds	C%	Yd/C	TD	YAC	Rk	DVOA	Rk	DPAR	Rk	PAR	Short	Mid	Deep	Bomb
2004	CLE	10	42	99	546	59%	13.0	4	—	—	5.3%	42	12.8	41	12.2	—	—	—	—
2005	CLE	16	69	123	1009	56%	14.6	4	3.3	45	8.9%	29	18.9	21	18.3	20%	46%	21%	13%
2006	SF	14	40	91	733	44%	18.3	3	4.1	33	-4.6%	58	6.2	59	5.6	15%	33%	33%	20%
2007	FA		34		548		16.0	4											

Starting with the jersey-throwing flare-up with Bill Parcells during his rookie season with Dallas, Bryant's penchant for trouble both large and small has far outweighed his production. If you're a total jerk, a Catch Rate of 38 percent on third down isn't going to cut it. The 49ers' front office agrees, and they cut Bryant on March 1, just one season after signing him to a four-year, $15-million contract. If a team wants to sign him for the 2007 season, they'll have to wait until Week 3 before benefiting from his services, because Bryant served only two games of a four-game suspension handed down by the NFL for his November arrest for drunken driving, reckless driving, and resisting arrest. San Francisco will take a reported $2.3-million-salary-cap hit and just move on.

Nate Burleson Height: 6-0 Weight: 192 College: Nevada Draft: 2003/3 (71) Born: 19-Aug-1981 Age: 26 Risk: Red

Year	Team	G	Rec	Pass	Yds	C%	Yd/C	TD	YAC	Rk	DVOA	Rk	DPAR	Rk	PAR	Short	Mid	Deep	Bomb
2004	MIN	16	68	102	1006	67%	14.8	9	—	—	35.3%	6	35.0	6	34.7	—	—	—	—
2005	MIN	12	30	52	328	58%	10.9	1	2.6	72	-0.2%	53	4.8	59	3.1	29%	46%	15%	10%
2006	SEA	16	18	37	192	49%	10.7	2	1.9	—	-14.2%	—	0.2	—	-0.1	34%	37%	20%	9%
2007	SEA		32		438		13.6	3											

Seattle's "retribution" against the Vikings in the Steve Hutchinson poison-pill derby, Burleson struggled early last season with dropped passes. However, he became a real plus in the return game and one of the primary reasons that Seattle's special-teams DVOA jumped from 21st to seventh. He may get bumped up to the slot if Bobby Engram has further issues with Graves' disease, but is probably most valuable as a return man and deep threat.

Plaxico Burress Height: 6-5 Weight: 226 College: Michigan State Draft: 2000/1 (8) Born: 12-Aug-1977 Age: 30 Risk: Green

Year	Team	G	Rec	Pass	Yds	C%	Yd/C	TD	YAC	Rk	DVOA	Rk	DPAR	Rk	PAR	Short	Mid	Deep	Bomb
2004	PIT	11	35	60	698	58%	19.9	5	—	—	36.8%	4	20.5	28	20.0	—	—	—	—
2005	NYG	16	76	166	1214	46%	16.0	7	3.3	46	-8.1%	65	7.4	52	7.0	24%	41%	25%	10%
2006	NYG	15	63	121	988	52%	15.7	10	3.6	41	1.4%	46	13.0	36	11.8	24%	37%	22%	17%
2007	NYG		52		754		14.4	6											

Sometimes it seems as though Eli Manning sees a box a foot over Plaxico Burress's head that no one else can see and thinks that, if he hits it, a mushroom will fall onto Burress and the receiver will grow to twice his normal height or spit fireballs. Of course, Manning's inaccuracy is not the only reason why Burress has a low Catch Rate. He managed to catch only 58 percent of the passes Ben Rothlisberger threw him in 2004, when Roethlisberger completed 66 percent of his passes overall. When Tommy Maddox was throwing him the ball in 2003 and 2002, Burress again caught just 48 and 54 percent of his passes even though Maddox completed 57 percent and 62 percent overall. The point: Manning's not the entire problem here.

Reche Caldwell Height: 5-11 Weight: 194 College: Florida Draft: 2002/2 (48) Born: 28-Mar-1979 Age: 28 Risk: Red

Year	Team	G	Rec	Pass	Yds	C%	Yd/C	TD	YAC	Rk	DVOA	Rk	DPAR	Rk	PAR	Short	Mid	Deep	Bomb
2004	SD	6	18	29	310	62%	17.2	3	—	—	7.3%	—	4.4	—	5.8	—	—	—	—
2005	SD	16	28	43	352	65%	12.6	1	2.6	—	0.8%	—	4.5	—	3.9	24%	41%	14%	22%
2006	NE	16	61	102	760	60%	12.5	4	3.5	44	9.2%	32	15.6	33	12.7	38%	31%	20%	11%
2007	NE		14		188		13.3	1											

Ol' Bug Eyes is a reasonably talented receiver who can move the chains. Over the last two seasons, his DVOA is 1.3 percent on first and second down, but 20.0 percent on third down. Nevertheless, Patriots fans miscast Caldwell as Deion Branch's replacement last year. Caldwell was never meant to be Mr. Right, just Mr. Right Now. With the Patriots' offseason haul and Caldwell's growing reputation as a player who hears footsteps, Caldwell might soon become Mr. Have I Introduced You to My Less Attractive Canadian Friend?

Drew Carter Height: 6-3 Weight: 200 College: Ohio State Draft: 2004/5 (163) Born: 5-Sep-1981 Age: 26 Risk: Red

Year	Team	G	Rec	Pass	Yds	C%	Yd/C	TD	YAC	Rk	DVOA	Rk	DPAR	Rk	PAR	Short	Mid	Deep	Bomb
2005	CAR	3	5	15	103	33%	20.6	1	1.6	—	-2.6%	—	1.1	—	0.3	7%	14%	21%	57%
2006	CAR	14	28	51	357	55%	12.8	3	2.4	74	-10.9%	65	1.7	65	3.7	31%	39%	12%	18%
2007	CAR		36		575		16.0	3											

Carter started in place of injured Steve Smith in September and tried to assume Smith's role in the offense catching deep bombs and quick catch-and-go smoke routes. Carter displayed the wheels and moves that served him well in the final games of the 2005 season, but also demonstrated a frustrating habit of battling the ball instead of catching it. He's a certified deep threat who can help a team as a slot receiver, but Carter will drive the Panthers to distraction if he can't hold on to the football.

Tim Carter Height: 6-0 Weight: 200 College: Auburn Draft: 2002/2 (46) Born: 21-Sep-1979 Age: 28 Risk: Red

Year	Team	G	Rec	Pass	Yds	C%	Yd/C	TD	YAC	Rk	DVOA	Rk	DPAR	Rk	PAR	Short	Mid	Deep	Bomb
2004	NYG	5	12	18	182	67%	15.2	1	—	—	43.9%	—	7.2	—	6.4	—	—	—	—
2005	NYG	15	10	24	186	42%	18.6	0	2.2	—	-9.9%	—	0.7	—	0.3	14%	36%	23%	27%
2006	NYG	16	22	49	253	45%	11.5	2	1.8	—	-31.5%	—	-5.2	—	-4.4	16%	50%	20%	14%
2007	CLE		18		218		12.3	1											

At this point, it's safe to label the former second-round pick a bust. Carter was perpetually waiting to be given a bigger role in the offense, only to get hurt as soon as he entered that role. The Giants dumped Carter off on Cleveland for running back Reuben Droughns. Plaxico Burress might miss Carter the most, since Carter was the only wideout on the team with a worse Catch Rate.

Chris Chambers   Height: 5-11   Weight: 210   College: Wisconsin   Draft: 2001/2 (52)   Born: 12-Aug-1978   Age: 29   Risk: Yellow

Year	Team	G	Rec	Pass	Yds	C%	Yd/C	TD	YAC	Rk	DVOA	Rk	DPAR	Rk	PAR	Short	Mid	Deep	Bomb
2004	MIA	15	69	138	898	50%	13.0	7	—	—	-9.2%	63	5.0	57	2.8	—	—	—	—
2005	MIA	16	82	166	1118	49%	13.6	11	4.2	29	-11.6%	72	3.9	65	4.6	28%	37%	17%	18%
2006	MIA	16	59	153	677	39%	11.5	4	3.1	54	-33.6%	82	-19.8	83	-21.9	31%	34%	24%	11%
2007	MIA		64		847		13.3	5											

Table 4. Lowest DPAR by Wide Receivers, 1996–2006

Year	Player	Team	DPAR	DVOA	Rec	Pass	Yds	TD	C%	Yd/C
2003	Az-Zahir Hakim	DET	−30.2	−70.1%	49	108	449	4	45%	9.2
2006	Chris Chambers	MIA	−19.8	−33.6%	59	153	677	4	39%	11.5
2003	Reche Caldwell	SD	−18.9	−138.2%	8	34	80	0	24%	10.0
2004	Bobby Wade	CHI	−14.4	−40.6%	42	89	481	0	47%	11.5
2003	Dez White	CHI	−14.2	−43.4%	49	107	583	3	46%	11.9
2003	Cortez Hankton	JAC	−12.1	−88.8%	17	40	166	0	43%	9.8
2003	Tim Carter	NYG	−12.0	−72.1%	26	52	309	0	50%	11.9
2003	Bill Schroeder	DET	−11.9	−52.2%	36	80	397	2	45%	11.0
2003	Marty Booker	CHI	−11.7	−39.1%	52	105	715	4	50%	13.8
1997	Charlie Jones	SD	−11.7	−38.6%	32	80	423	1	40%	13.2

Chris Chambers is the NFL player with the largest gap between his perceived and actual value. No player in the NFL has had a Catch Rate as consistently low as Chambers. That gets blamed on his quarterbacks, but, at some point, 30 Helens can't be wrong. His defenders point out his Pro Bowl selection in 2005, but that was the result of two fortuitously timed big games and the nature of Chambers's skill set, which is better for making highlight reels than winning football games. For every incredible leaping Chambers grab you see on *SportsCenter,* he lets one pass hit him in the hands, cuts his route off too short on another, and can't get past the jam on a third. He'll bounce back in 2007 because it's almost impossible for him to be this bad again, but he's simply not an elite wide receiver and has shown nary a sign he's going to become one.

(Also, to answer the question many readers may be asking: No, we're not sure why so many wide receivers had terrible years in 2003.)

Antonio Chatman   Height: 5-9   Weight: 177   College: Cincinnati   Draft: 2003/FA   Born: 12-Feb-1979   Age: 28   Risk: Red

Year	Team	G	Rec	Pass	Yds	C%	Yd/C	TD	YAC	Rk	DVOA	Rk	DPAR	Rk	PAR	Short	Mid	Deep	Bomb
2004	GB	16	22	45	246	49%	11.2	1	—	—	-18.9%	—	-0.9	—	0.3	—	—	—	—
2005	GB	16	49	86	549	57%	11.2	4	3.1	57	3.4%	45	10.1	41	7.9	35%	38%	24%	3%
2006	CIN	3	3	5	22	60%	7.3	0	3.7	—	-17.7%	—	-0.1	—	-0.4	40%	20%	20%	20%
2007	CIN		35		571		16.4	3											

Like teammate Tab Perry, Chatman was limited to just a few games in 2006 before a hamstring injury ended his season. Cleared to participate in time for the offseason program, he will compete with Perry and Skyler Green for Chris Henry's slot receiver job. It's an important camp competition to watch if you're in a fantasy league that starts three wide receivers.

Mark Clayton   Height: 5-10   Weight: 193   College: Oklahoma   Draft: 2005/1 (22)   Born: 2-Jul-1982   Age: 25   Risk: Red

Year	Team	G	Rec	Pass	Yds	C%	Yd/C	TD	YAC	Rk	DVOA	Rk	DPAR	Rk	PAR	Short	Mid	Deep	Bomb
2005	BAL	14	44	86	471	51%	10.7	2	4.5	25	-24.5%	88	-5.3	88	-5.1	42%	31%	11%	17%
2006	BAL	16	67	112	939	60%	14.0	5	5.4	5	1.9%	44	12.7	38	13.7	37%	43%	9%	10%
2007	BAL		64		976		15.4	5											

(continued next page)

Mark Clayton (*continued*)

Clayton was supposed to be the Ravens' number-two receiver after Baltimore signed Steve McNair favorite Derrick Mason last offseason. In reality, Mason and Clayton were 1 and 1A, as each saw exactly 112 balls. Clayton ranked slightly higher in DVOA, possibly because it was Mason who generally saw the tougher defensive coverage. Clayton is probably too small to be an elite receiver, but he shows the football smarts and overall skill to eventually be a consistent number one, and he'll benefit from another year of sharing the load with Mason.

Michael Clayton   Height: 6-3   Weight: 197   College: LSU   Draft: 2004/1 (15)   Born: 13-Oct-1982   Age: 25   Risk: Yellow

Year	Team	G	Rec	Pass	Yds	C%	Yd/C	TD	YAC	Rk	DVOA	Rk	DPAR	Rk	PAR	Short	Mid	Deep	Bomb
2004	TB	16	80	122	1193	66%	14.9	7	—	—	33.9%	7	39.8	4	38.6	—	—	—	—
2005	TB	14	32	55	372	58%	11.6	0	5.2	14	-20.0%	86	-1.7	84	-1.7	45%	43%	11%	0%
2006	TB	12	33	65	356	51%	10.8	1	3.2	52	-23.9%	79	-3.8	78	-3.3	33%	48%	14%	5%
2007	*TB*		*34*		*511*		*15.2*	*3*											

We saw brief glimpses of the 2004 Clayton last season, like when he caught six passes for 55 yards and a game-winning touchdown against the Bengals in Week 6. Unfortunately, we didn't see very much of that Clayton, or any Clayton, as he spent much of last year duplicating his disappearing act of 2005 before missing the end of the year with a knee injury. The Bucs tried to use Clayton to move the chains, but the results were disastrous. He was targeted 26 times on third or fourth down last year, the second highest total on the team, but converted just seven first downs for a DVOA of –39.8 percent. Clayton began pursuing various off-field business opportunities after his monstrous rookie season, and those distractions appear to have stunted his development. Maurice Stovall is breathing down Clayton's neck for playing time; if Clayton doesn't bounce back, he'll be a trivia question in ten years.

Keary Colbert   Height: 5-10   Weight: 193   College: USC   Draft: 2004/2 (62)   Born: 21-May-1982   Age: 25   Risk: Red

Year	Team	G	Rec	Pass	Yds	C%	Yd/C	TD	YAC	Rk	DVOA	Rk	DPAR	Rk	PAR	Short	Mid	Deep	Bomb
2004	CAR	15	47	92	754	51%	16.0	5	—	—	-3.4%	52	7.2	48	8.3	—	—	—	—
2005	CAR	16	25	55	282	45%	11.3	2	3.5	39	-23.3%	87	-3.1	87	-3.8	29%	37%	27%	8%
2006	CAR	12	5	12	56	42%	11.2	0	4.4	—	-45.9%	—	-2.3	—	-1.7	25%	42%	25%	8%
2007	*CAR*		*13*		*174*		*13.8*	*1*											

Colbert never stepped up to the challenge when Keyshawn Johnson was signed and Drew Carter became a challenger for the number-three receiver gig. Carter passed Colbert on the depth chart, and, by November, Colbert was on the inactive list. Motivation is an issue for Colbert, who is about to go on the David Boston tour as teams try to rekindle the fire that burned under his butt in 2004.

Laveranues Coles   Height: 5-11   Weight: 193   College: Florida State   Draft: 2000/3 (78)   Born: 29-Dec-1977   Age: 29   Risk: Yellow

Year	Team	G	Rec	Pass	Yds	C%	Yd/C	TD	YAC	Rk	DVOA	Rk	DPAR	Rk	PAR	Short	Mid	Deep	Bomb
2004	WAS	16	90	168	950	54%	10.6	1	—	—	-16.2%	71	-1.7	73	-4.2	—	—	—	—
2005	NYJ	16	73	131	845	56%	11.6	5	2.5	79	-3.4%	57	9.9	43	9.1	22%	54%	14%	10%
2006	NYJ	16	91	151	1098	60%	12.1	6	3.0	57	-0.2%	51	14.8	35	12.4	34%	43%	14%	9%
2007	*NYJ*		*78*		*1020*		*13.0*	*6*											

Coles has hitched his extrasensory wagon to Chad Pennington, which means he gets to pretend that Pennington intuitively knows that Coles is almost always going to run a slant or an in. Coles would have better numbers playing with a quarterback who was less limited, but Pennington really does go out of his way to look for him, so it evens out. Jerricho Cotchery's emergence will create more space for Coles and keep his numbers around this range as he enters his decline phase.

Marques Colston   Height: 6-5   Weight: 212   College: Hofstra   Draft: 2006/7 (252)   Born: 5-Jun-1983   Age: 24   Risk: Yellow

Year	Team	G	Rec	Pass	Yds	C%	Yd/C	TD	YAC	Rk	DVOA	Rk	DPAR	Rk	PAR	Short	Mid	Deep	Bomb
2006	NO	14	70	115	1038	61%	14.8	8	5.2	10	17.4%	16	25.5	11	27.2	33%	44%	18%	5%
2007	*NO*		*82*		*1172*		*14.2*	*7*											

To get an idea of how good Colston was as a rookie, let's look at a list of the most similar wide receiver seasons since 1978 without considering age and experience the way our similarity scores normally do. The top five seasons are Anthony Carter in 1990, Ed McCaffrey in 1999, Art Monk in 1991, Rocket Ismail in 1998, and Terance Mathis in 1995. All five of those players were at least 28 years old. A little further down the similarity list are two seasons by Hall of Famer Steve Largent from the prime of his career. The most similar rookies were Joey Galloway and Cris Collinsworth, each of whom had four more 1,000-yard seasons and a fifth season that was close. Colston is going to be one of the top receivers in the league for the next few years. Not bad for a seventh-round tweener written off in last year's "Going Deep" section as "another Marc Boerigter/Teyo Johnson type who doesn't have a role in the NFL."

Terrance Copper
Height: 5-10 Weight: 204 College: East Carolina   Draft: 2004/FA   Born: 12-Mar-1982 Age: 25   Risk: Red

Year	Team	G	Rec	Pass	Yds	C%	Yd/C	TD	YAC	Rk	DVOA	Rk	DPAR	Rk	PAR	Short	Mid	Deep	Bomb
2004	DAL	10	7	20	84	35%	12.0	1	—	—	-16.2%	—	-0.3	—	-1.2	—	—	—	—
2005	DAL	16	1	4	5	25%	5.0	0	5.0	—	-66.9%	—	-1.4	—	-1.3	75%	0%	25%	00%
2006	NO	15	23	42	385	55%	16.7	3	4.3	—	2.9%	—	5.3	—	6.3	21%	47%	21%	11%
2007	NO		22		307		14.0	1											

Half of Copper's output came in Weeks 10 and 11, when Drew Brees threw 99 passes for over 900 yards. He's your generic third or fourth receiver who does a little bit of everything but isn't refined enough to be an obvious comer. Guys like Copper have careers that depend upon having the right game at the right place at the right time. If he impresses while Robert Meachem gets in shape, he'll be the regular slot receiver, but the eventual goal in New Orleans is to have Meachem starting and Devery Henderson in the slot.

Jerricho Cotchery
Height: 6-0 Weight: 199 College: North Carolina State   Draft: 2004/4 (108) Born: 16-Jun-1982 Age: 25   Risk: Red

Year	Team	G	Rec	Pass	Yds	C%	Yd/C	TD	YAC	Rk	DVOA	Rk	DPAR	Rk	PAR	Short	Mid	Deep	Bomb
2004	NYJ	12	6	11	60	55%	10.0	0	—	—	-16.1%	—	-0.1	—	-0.3	—	—	—	—
2005	NYJ	16	19	31	251	61%	13.2	0	3.2	—	7.1%	—	4.5	—	4.6	34%	45%	10%	10%
2006	NYJ	16	82	125	961	66%	11.7	6	4.3	24	13.0%	26	23.5	13	22.1	40%	41%	18%	1%
2007	NYJ		63		820		13.1	5											

When Eric Mangini gave Cotchery a chance to win a starting spot in training camp last year, he could not possibly have fathomed that Cotchery would get close to 1,000 yards. Cotchery absolutely bedeviled the Patriots, putting up 16 catches for 291 yards and three touchdowns in his three games against them; you get the sense that goes a little bit further with Mangini than it might with other coaches. While common belief has it that Pennington turns to Coles when he's in a tight spot, Cotchery actually saw 51 passes on third down, while Coles saw only 46.

Patrick Crayton
Height: 6-1 Weight: 205 College: NW Oklahoma State   Draft: 2004/7 (216) Born: 7-Apr-1979 Age: 28   Risk: Red

Year	Team	G	Rec	Pass	Yds	C%	Yd/C	TD	YAC	Rk	DVOA	Rk	DPAR	Rk	PAR	Short	Mid	Deep	Bomb
2004	DAL	7	12	14	162	79%	13.5	1	—	—	30.2%	—	4.2	—	3.9	—	—	—	—
2005	DAL	11	22	35	341	63%	15.5	2	7.6	—	14.0%	—	6.4	—	7.0	29%	57%	11%	4%
2006	DAL	16	36	48	516	75%	14.3	4	5.2	—	37.3%	—	16.5	—	17.3	30%	51%	15%	4%
2007	DAL		36		502		14.0	3											

Crayton signed a one-year tender offer with the Cowboys in April. Last year, he caught five passes for 104 yards and a touchdown against the Cardinals when Terry Glenn was injured and earned some late-season starts when the Cowboys began using more three-receiver sets. Crayton's 77 percent Catch Rate on third down was the highest on the team, better than Glenn, Terrell Owens, Jason Witten, or any of the running backs. As the primary backup to two 30-something veterans, Crayton is a valuable commodity who may only have to bide his time on the bench for one more season.

Josh Cribbs
Height: 6-1 Weight: 192 College: Kent State   Draft: 2005/0 (0)   Born: 9-Jun-1983 Age: 24   Risk: Red

Year	Team	G	Rec	Pass	Yds	C%	Yd/C	TD	YAC	Rk	DVOA	Rk	DPAR	Rk	PAR	Short	Mid	Deep	Bomb
2005	CLE	14	1	1	7	100%	7.0	0	5.0	—	44.7%	—	0.4	—	0.2	100%	0%	0%	0%
2006	CLE	16	10	15	91	67%	9.1	0	4.9	—	-43.7%	—	-2.8	—	-2.8	36%	57%	7%	0%
2007	CLE		16		212		13.5	1											

Cribbs is a college quarterback turned receiver, and with the way Charlie Frye and Derek Anderson played in 2006, Romeo Crennel might have been tempted to put him under center. Cribbs is a solid special-teams player and will likely get more passes thrown his way in Cleveland this year.

Ronald Curry   Height: 6-2   Weight: 220 College: North Carolina   Draft: 2002/FA   Born: 28-May-1979 Age: 28   Risk: Yellow

Year	Team	G	Rec	Pass	Yds	C%	Yd/C	TD	YAC	Rk	DVOA	Rk	DPAR	Rk	PAR	Short	Mid	Deep	Bomb
2004	OAK	12	50	70	679	71%	13.6	6	—	—	29.7%	10	20.8	26	22.6	—	—	—	—
2005	OAK	2	2	2	12	100%	6.0	0	0.0	—	26.2%	—	0.5	—	-0.4	50%	50%	0%	0%
2006	OAK	16	62	89	727	70%	11.7	1	3.3	50	14.4%	19	17.2	25	18.3	33%	54%	10%	4%
2007	OAK		67		844		12.6	3											

By far the Raiders' best receiver, Curry was the only guy in Oakland who always looked like he was trying. Curry became Andrew Walter's second-most-trusted receiver over the course of the second half of the season, falling just short of any-one not wearing a Raiders jersey (there were some line judges and guys in orange pennies holding down-markers who would have put up solid reception numbers for the Raiders last year). Curry's huge split—he had 16 catches in the first half of the season and 46 in the second half, the biggest difference of any wide receiver—isn't a sign that he's a second-half player. There were 18 uninjured players from 1996 to 2005 who caught 20 more balls in the second half of a season than they had in the first half; the year after, those 18 players' splits rebounded to the NFL average. A former college quar-terback, Curry has a tremendous understanding of the game and could have a breakout season if the Raiders get some decent teammates around him. He is penciled in to start unless he gets beaten out by Mike Willi . . . oh, forget it.

Kevin Curtis   Height: 5-11 Weight: 186 College: Utah State   Draft: 2003/3 (74)   Born: 17-Jul-1978   Age: 29   Risk: Yellow

Year	Team	G	Rec	Pass	Yds	C%	Yd/C	TD	YAC	Rk	DVOA	Rk	DPAR	Rk	PAR	Short	Mid	Deep	Bomb
2004	STL	14	32	50	421	64%	13.2	2	—	—	2.0%	47	5.6	54	5.9	—	—	—	—
2005	STL	16	60	97	801	62%	13.4	6	4.6	22	-3.7%	58	7.5	51	9.3	33%	30%	21%	16%
2006	STL	16	40	57	479	70%	12.0	4	3.0	56	27.4%	6	16.1	30	15.5	51%	19%	21%	9%
2007	PHI		47		761		16.2	5											

Before signing a six-year, $32-million contract with the Eagles in mid-March, Curtis was firmly entrenched as a third-receiver option in St. Louis. In past years, that contract would have said "number-one starter for sure," but the market explosion this offseason changed all that. Still, Curtis will be featured far more in Philly than he would have been in St. Louis with the Rams de-emphasizing three-receiver sets. Curtis is a small receiver who has great straight-line speed. He's good with his routes and should fit the Eagles' offense very well.

Andre' Davis   Height: 6-1   Weight: 195 College: Virginia Tech   Draft: 2002/2 (47)   Born: 12-Jun-1979   Age: 28   Risk: Red

Year	Team	G	Rec	Pass	Yds	C%	Yd/C	TD	YAC	Rk	DVOA	Rk	DPAR	Rk	PAR	Short	Mid	Deep	Bomb
2005	NE	9	9	24	190	38%	21.1	1	6.6	—	-11.5%	—	0.6	—	0.9	12%	24%	6%	59%
2006	BUF	16	2	7	13	29%	6.5	0	2.5	—	-73.9%	—	-2.7	—	-3.0	29%	29%	29%	14%
2007	HOU		13		177		13.7	1											

It seems like just yesterday that we were talking about Davis's nice numbers in Cleveland and fantasy sleeper status with the Patriots. Last year, his primary impact was on Buffalo's special teams, where he either stopped returners dead in their tracks or completely whiffed on tackles. He's since signed with Houston, where he's a candidate to start opposite Andre Johnson just like everyone else in a Texans uniform except for Matt Schaub, Mario Williams, and Andre Johnson himself.

Craig Davis   Height: 6-1   Weight: 203 College: LSU   Draft: 2007/1 (30)   Born: 5-Oct-1985   Age: 22   Risk: Red

Year	Team	G	Rec	Pass	Yds	C%	Yd/C	TD	YAC	Rk	DVOA	Rk	DPAR	Rk	PAR	Short	Mid	Deep	Bomb
2007	SD		25		407		16.1	2											

The SEC doesn't produce particularly good receivers. The best wideouts to leave the conference since 2000 are Donte' Stallworth, Peerless Price, and Reggie Brown. The bust list is much longer: Travis Taylor, Jabar Gaffney, Josh Reed, Troy Williamson (pending), Michael Clayton (on current form), and Taylor Jacobs, among others. Scouts are split on Davis; some think he's an excellent route-runner with manufactured "Combine" speed (as opposed to football speed), while others think he needs to work on his routes but can fall back on his excellent straightaway speed. Everyone agrees that Davis is hesitant and doesn't work particularly hard, particularly when he's not seeing the ball very often. In the San Diego offense, he will be the fourth option at best on most downs, which means both San Diego fans and fantasy hawks should temper their expectations for 2007.

Rashied Davis

Height: 5-9 **Weight:** 180 **College:** San Jose State **Draft:** 2005/0 (0) **Born:** 24-Jul-1979 **Age:** 28 **Risk:** Red

Year	Team	G	Rec	Pass	Yds	C%	Yd/C	TD	YAC	Rk	DVOA	Rk	DPAR	Rk	PAR	Short	Mid	Deep	Bomb
2006	CHI	16	22	56	303	39%	13.8	2	2.7	65	-20.1%	76	-1.9	76	-2.4	30%	41%	19%	11%
2007	CHI		16		221		13.5	1											

Proof that football isn't exclusively a big-man's game, Davis is a quick player who was solid on kickoff returns and emerged as a competent slot receiver. The emergence of Devin Hester gradually pushed Davis out of kick-return duty as the 2006 season progressed. Without that special-teams contribution, he will have to improve as a receiver to remain an asset to the team.

Donald Driver

Height: 6-0 **Weight:** 188 **College:** Alcorn State **Draft:** 1999/7 (213) **Born:** 2-Feb-1975 **Age:** 32 **Risk:** Yellow

Year	Team	G	Rec	Pass	Yds	C%	Yd/C	TD	YAC	Rk	DVOA	Rk	DPAR	Rk	PAR	Short	Mid	Deep	Bomb
2004	GB	16	84	138	1208	61%	14.4	9	—	—	15.6%	29	28.2	13	30.1	—	—	—	—
2005	GB	16	86	146	1221	59%	14.2	5	4.0	33	17.5%	15	31.2	5	27.0	27%	41%	23%	10%
2006	GB	16	92	172	1295	53%	14.1	8	5.3	7	0.1%	48	16.9	26	14.3	32%	38%	19%	11%
2007	GB		81		1195		14.7	7											

Is Donald Driver the least appreciated top-flight receiver in football? He certainly is the most consistent based on his last three seasons, and none of those figures includes the defensive pass interference penalties he's drawn, which led the league from 2002 to 2006. The drop in his Catch Rate is troubling because of Driver's advancing age, but the Packers' lack of a consistent second receiver is the more likely cause. Still, he is nearing that dangerous age when wide receivers start to decline. The above projection acknowledges that risk, but Driver is in impeccable shape and has missed only one game in the past five seasons. He will not fight off aging forever, but he is a reasonable bet for at least one more productive season.

Tim Dwight

Height: 5-9 **Weight:** 180 **College:** Iowa State **Draft:** 1998/4 (114) **Born:** 13-Jul-1975 **Age:** 32 **Risk:** Red

Year	Team	G	Rec	Pass	Yds	C%	Yd/C	TD	YAC	Rk	DVOA	Rk	DPAR	Rk	PAR	Short	Mid	Deep	Bomb
2004	SD	12	2	5	31	40%	15.5	1	—	—	0.2%	—	0.6	—	0.7	—	—	—	—
2005	NE	16	19	34	332	56%	17.5	3	6.6	—	21.4%	—	8.2	—	8.1	31%	31%	14%	24%
2006	NYJ	9	16	19	112	84%	7.0	0	3.6	—	2.6%	—	2.2	—	1.8	61%	39%	0%	0%
2007	NYJ		10		118		12.0	1											

Dwight's always been a very breakable receiver, so it's no surprise that he spent all of 2006 nursing thigh injuries, playing in just nine games and returning only 14 punts. It's a catch-22: As a receiver, Dwight could provide the Jets with enough value over a full season to be worth his roster spot, but if the Jets use him as a receiver, he's going to get hurt and won't last the full season. He will have to joust with Leon Washington during camp to determine who on the team gets official use of the adjective "explosive" in 2007.

Braylon Edwards

Height: 6-3 **Weight:** 211 **College:** Michigan **Draft:** 2005/1 (3) **Born:** 21-Feb-1983 **Age:** 24 **Risk:** Red

Year	Team	G	Rec	Pass	Yds	C%	Yd/C	TD	YAC	Rk	DVOA	Rk	DPAR	Rk	PAR	Short	Mid	Deep	Bomb
2006	CLE	10	32	59	512	54%	16.0	3	5.0	10	11.3%	25	10.0	42	10.5	18%	53%	15%	18%
2006	CLE	16	61	125	884	49%	14.5	6	5.2	11	-13.7%	68	1.4	66	3.0	25%	46%	17%	13%
2007	CLE		52		951		18.1	4											

We still haven't seen the talent that made many scouts consider Edwards the best player at any position in the 2005 draft. That says a little bit about Edwards, but it probably says more about the Cleveland passing game. Edwards can become a solid NFL receiver if he ever has the right quarterback throwing to him. The player with the most similar numbers over his first two seasons is Laveranues Coles, followed by Mark Carrier, Terrell Owens, Randal Hill, and fellow 2005 draftee Mark Clayton. Hill, the 23rd pick in the 1991 draft, never had another year as good as his second one, but the first three players on the list each had a 1,000-yard season in year three.

Bobby Engram

Height: 5-10 **Weight:** 188 **College:** Penn State **Draft:** 1996/2 (52) **Born:** 7-Jan-1973 **Age:** 34 **Risk:** Yellow

Year	Team	G	Rec	Pass	Yds	C%	Yd/C	TD	YAC	Rk	DVOA	Rk	DPAR	Rk	PAR	Short	Mid	Deep	Bomb
2004	SEA	13	36	53	499	68%	13.9	2	—	—	18.9%	25	12.0	44	11.2	—	—	—	—
2005	SEA	13	67	97	778	69%	11.6	3	4.0	31	4.4%	41	13.2	29	16.2	36%	44%	13%	7%
2006	SEA	7	24	36	290	67%	12.1	1	2.7	—	15.8%	—	7.3	—	7.6	22%	53%	22%	3%
2007	SEA		48		705		14.6	4											

(continued next page)

Bobby Engram (*continued*)

Has Bobby Engram lost the qualities that have made him such an effective receiver? The Seahawks don't think so. The longtime Football Outsiders favorite (we call him "The First Down Machine," and for good reason) missed nine games in 2006 due to Graves' disease (an autoimmune disorder that causes overactivity of the thyroid gland) and posted his worst numbers last year since joining the Seahawks in 2001. When Engram was healthy and back on the field, however, he was an asset—15 first downs in seven games was evidence of that—and the team thought his continuity with Matt Hasselbeck justified a new two-year contract.

Lee Evans Height: 5-10 Weight: 197 College: Wisconsin Draft: 2004/1 (13) Born: 11-Mar-1981 Age: 26 Risk: Yellow

Year	Team	G	Rec	Pass	Yds	C%	Yd/C	TD	YAC	Rk	DVOA	Rk	DPAR	Rk	PAR	Short	Mid	Deep	Bomb
2004	BUF	16	48	75	843	64%	17.6	9	—	—	39.4%	3	26.7	14	26.9	—	—	—	—
2005	BUF	16	48	92	743	53%	15.5	7	5.8	9	-3.0%	56	7.6	50	9.7	30%	41%	8%	20%
2006	BUF	16	82	137	1292	60%	15.8	8	4.3	21	23.2%	8	34.3	3	31.8	22%	45%	16%	18%
2007	*BUF*		*77*		*1089*		*14.2*	*7*											

Every year, journalists write preseason articles about how teams will miss their departed veteran players, but when the season is over, no one ever mentions that those players were not actually missed. The Bills did just fine without Eric Moulds last year, replacing him with a true number-one receiver in Evans as opposed to the number-one reputation Moulds's career was resting upon. Evans is a stud, even if you ignore the 205-yard quarter he put up against Demarcus Faggins in Week 11. He matured into Buffalo's ace in his third pro season, putting up big games against defenses that otherwise did a good job of stopping number-one receivers (Chicago, Detroit, Baltimore, and Minnesota). While J. P. Losman would benefit from having a real option across the field from Evans, Evans himself might actually benefit more.

Robert Ferguson Height: 6-1 Weight: 209 College: Texas A&M Draft: 2001/2 (41) Born: 17-Dec-1979 Age: 27 Risk: Red

Year	Team	G	Rec	Pass	Yds	C%	Yd/C	TD	YAC	Rk	DVOA	Rk	DPAR	Rk	PAR	Short	Mid	Deep	Bomb
2004	GB	13	24	49	367	49%	15.3	1	—	—	-0.5%	—	4.6	—	4.2	—	—	—	—
2005	GB	11	27	57	366	47%	13.6	3	2.0	86	-4.7%	60	3.7	67	2.8	20%	41%	19%	20%
2006	GB	4	5	13	31	38%	6.2	1	-0.2	—	-50.1%	—	-3.0	—	-3.3	15%	54%	8%	23%
2007	*GB*		*13*		*191*		*14.3*	*1*											

NFL teams often treat their players like commodities, so it is nice to see a player such as Ferguson keep his contract despite a Lisfranc injury that cost him most of 2006. Injuries are always a concern with Ferguson, who is running out of time to prove he can be a consistent contributor. A healthy Ferguson as a third receiver could make the Packers' offense much more explosive.

Larry Fitzgerald Height: 6-2 Weight: 223 College: Pittsburgh Draft: 2004/1 (3) Born: 31-Aug-1983 Age: 24 Risk: Green

Year	Team	G	Rec	Pass	Yds	C%	Yd/C	TD	YAC	Rk	DVOA	Rk	DPAR	Rk	PAR	Short	Mid	Deep	Bomb
2004	ARI	16	58	116	780	51%	13.4	8	—	—	-13.7%	68	1.3	66	2.4	—	—	—	—
2005	ARI	16	103	165	1409	62%	13.7	10	3.4	43	13.2%	23	31.5	4	34.5	32%	31%	24%	13%
2006	ARI	13	69	111	946	62%	13.7	6	2.7	66	22.3%	9	27.6	7	28.9	28%	43%	23%	6%
2007	*ARI*		*79*		*1066*		*13.5*	*7*											

Only three receivers ranked in the top ten in DPAR in both 2005 and 2006: Bengals' wonder twins Chad Johnson and T. J. Houshmandzadeh, and Fitzgerald. This despite the fact that Fitzgerald missed three games with a hamstring injury last year. While battery mate Anquan Boldin is the yards-after-catch threat, Fitzgerald is the one who's tougher to jam at the line, who runs the more precise routes, who thrives in traffic and in the red zone—he's the prototype. Under contract with the Cardinals through the 2009 season, he could be their elite receiver for many years to come, especially as Matt Leinart matures.

Malcom Floyd Height: 6-5 Weight: 225 College: Wyoming Draft: 2004/0 (0) Born: 8-Sep-1981 Age: 26 Risk: Red

Year	Team	G	Rec	Pass	Yds	C%	Yd/C	TD	YAC	Rk	DVOA	Rk	DPAR	Rk	PAR	Short	Mid	Deep	Bomb
2004	SD	4	3	9	49	33%	16.3	1	—	—	-18.7%	—	-0.1	—	0.4	—	—	—	—
2006	SD	12	15	32	210	47%	14.0	3	3.1	—	-14.3%	—	0.2	—	0.8	26%	42%	10%	23%
2007	*SD*		*16*		*219*		*13.3*	*1*											

A big, physical receiver, Floyd didn't get much attention in college at Wyoming, but when he finally got some opportunities to play last year, he showed that he's a solid player. Floyd had ankle surgery in the offseason, but will be ready for training camp. Floyd's bigger concern might be first-round pick Craig Davis, who could take his roster spot. Floyd's put on 15 pounds of muscle to try and prevent that.

Mike Furrey   Height: 6-0   Weight: 185   College: Northern Iowa   Draft: 2003/FA   Born: 12-May-1977   Age: 30   Risk: Red

Year	Team	G	Rec	Pass	Yds	C%	Yd/C	TD	YAC	Rk	DVOA	Rk	DPAR	Rk	PAR	Short	Mid	Deep	Bomb
2004	STL	8	1	3	8	33%	8.0	0	—	—	-51.0%	—	-0.6	—	-0.5	—	—	—	—
2006	DET	16	98	146	1086	67%	11.1	6	2.9	59	12.5%	27	25.8	10	24.3	35%	44%	18%	3%
2007	DET		62		761		12.3	3											

Last year's player comment on Mike Furrey said . . . wait a minute, there wasn't one because he was a safety. In fact, he led St. Louis in interceptions in 2005. Last year he led the NFC in receptions. Furrey's emergence was so unique, it makes him difficult to project going forward. He had 21 career receptions before this season in three years in the league. If you run a similarity score for Furrey and remove his season as a safety, the numbers are encouraging. The top ten includes Donald Driver, T. J. Houshmandzadeh, and Derrick Mason. The other players on his list may not have matched the consistent performance of those three, but almost all had at least another season or two of productivity. The truth is that even in the most receiver-friendly system, 1,000-yard seasons do not grow on trees, especially when the best rookie wideout in years bumps you a slot down the depth chart. Furrey is undersized and lacks great straight-ahead speed, but he's quick and has a knack for finding holes in zone coverage. He'll give the Lions plenty of value from the slot during the next few years.

Doug Gabriel   Height: 6-2   Weight: 215   College: UCF   Draft: 2003/5 (167)   Born: 27-Aug-1980   Age: 27   Risk: Red

Year	Team	G	Rec	Pass	Yds	C%	Yd/C	TD	YAC	Rk	DVOA	Rk	DPAR	Rk	PAR	Short	Mid	Deep	Bomb
2004	OAK	16	33	79	551	42%	16.7	2	—	—	-12.6%	65	1.5	65	2.8	—			
2005	OAK	14	37	72	554	51%	15.0	3	2.7	70	8.7%	31	11.0	37	10.7	15%	51%	22%	13%
2006	NE	9	25	47	344	53%	13.8	3	5.6	—	-1.2%	35	4.1	53	2.9	32%	32%	23%	14%
2006	OAK	3	5	7	344	71%	16.8	0	5.6	—	73.0%	—	4.0	—	3.7	40%	60%	0%	0%
2007	OAK		25		306		12.3	1											

Gabriel has good speed and runs good routes. When you watch him, you think he should be a better player than he is. That's certainly what the New England Patriots thought when they traded a fifth-round pick for Gabriel right before the 2006 season began. Early on, Gabriel seemed to be emerging as Tom Brady's top target, but when his fumble turned out to be the turning point in the Patriots' Week 10 upset loss to the Jets, Gabriel disappeared into Bill Belichick's doghouse. He had one catch in the next four games, got released, and came full circle by re-signing in Oakland. According to the Boston media, Gabriel just didn't buy into the "Patriots Way," but he still has potential if the Raiders can get him to buy into the Lane Kiffin Way. Note: Gabriel's listed rankings for 2006 include his time with both New England and Oakland.

Jabar Gaffney   Height: 6-1   Weight: 193   College: Florida   Draft: 2002/2 (33)   Born: 1-Dec-1980   Age: 27   Risk: Red

Year	Team	G	Rec	Pass	Yds	C%	Yd/C	TD	YAC	Rk	DVOA	Rk	DPAR	Rk	PAR	Short	Mid	Deep	Bomb
2004	HOU	16	41	68	632	60%	15.4	2	—	—	20.9%	21	16.7	34	18.7	—	—	—	—
2005	HOU	16	55	90	492	61%	8.9	2	2.1	85	-13.4%	73	1.1	74	2.0	50%	37%	9%	4%
2006	NE	10	11	20	142	55%	12.9	1	2.2	—	8.5%	—	3.1	—	2.6	37%	26%	16%	21%
2007	NE		15		208		14.0	1											

Gaffney signed with the Eagles as a free agent, but was cut during the 2006 preseason. He quietly signed with the Patriots shortly thereafter, laid low for the regular season, then broke out during the playoffs, putting up back-to-back 100-yard performances against the Jets and Chargers that rivaled his totals for the entire regular season. With the Patriots collecting wideouts in the offseason, and Gaffney being a nonfactor on special teams, his hold on a roster spot is tenuous at best.

Justin Gage   Height: 6-4   Weight: 208   College: Missouri   Draft: 2003/5 (143)   Born: 25-Jan-1981   Age: 26   Risk: Red

Year	Team	G	Rec	Pass	Yds	C%	Yd/C	TD	YAC	Rk	DVOA	Rk	DPAR	Rk	PAR	Short	Mid	Deep	Bomb
2004	CHI	16	12	28	156	43%	13.0	0	—	—	-30.9%	—	-2.8	—	-2.3	—	—	—	—
2005	CHI	15	31	55	346	56%	11.2	2	2.5	82	0.5%	48	5.8	58	5.7	30%	41%	23%	7%
2006	CHI	8	4	8	68	50%	17.0	0	4.0	—	-38.8%	—	-1.3	—	-1.6	25%	38%	13%	25%
2007	TEN		32		359		11.1	2											

(continued next page)

Justin Gage (*continued*)

After the 2005 season, Gage was arguably ahead of Bernard Berrian on the depth chart. Unfortunately, he got hurt and then struggled in training camp. A rib injury cost him the first couple games, and Berrian took advantage of the opportunity to put a stranglehold on the number-two receiver spot. Eventually, Mark Bradley and Rashied Davis passed Gage as well. Gage has since signed with Tennessee and should compete for playing time in 2007.

Joey Galloway Height: 5-11 Weight: 197 College: Ohio State Draft: 1995/1 (8) Born: 20-Nov-1971 Age: 36 Risk: Yellow

Year	Team	G	Rec	Pass	Yds	C%	Yd/C	TD	YAC	Rk	DVOA	Rk	DPAR	Rk	PAR	Short	Mid	Deep	Bomb
2004	TB	10	33	53	416	62%	12.6	5	—	—	21.7%	20	13.0	40	12.5	—	—	—	—
2005	TB	16	83	152	1287	55%	15.5	10	4.7	19	14.0%	21	28.4	11	26.9	28%	39%	20%	13%
2006	TB	16	62	141	1057	44%	17.0	7	4.3	22	-9.3%	62	5.8	60	8.0	23%	35%	26%	16%
2007	TB		53		823		15.5	6											

Year Two of Galloway's Renaissance may well be the last; by age 35, guys such as Irving Fryar were on the downside of their late-career comebacks and had reached the 40-catch nether region between the slot and the retirement home. The most similar three-year career span to Galloway's last three seasons actually belongs to Jimmy Smith right before he retired; aging greats such as Andre Reed, John Stallworth, and Roy Green are on the list too.

Galloway would be a Hall of Famer if he could replace 1999 to 2004 with seasons that truly reflected his ability. He lost most of 1999 to a contract squabble, tore his ACL in the 2000 season opener, wasn't truly back from his injury in 2001, then fell into the Cowboys' pre-Parcells malaise for the next two seasons. He'll crack 10,000 yards this year, but he could easily be closer to 12,000 yards and 100 touchdowns if he had a typical career path.

Bryan Gilmore Height: 6-0 Weight: 200 College: Midwestern State Draft: 2000/FA Born: 21-Jul-1978 Age: 29 Risk: Red

Year	Team	G	Rec	Pass	Yds	C%	Yd/C	TD	YAC	Rk	DVOA	Rk	DPAR	Rk	PAR	Short	Mid	Deep	Bomb
2004	MIA	16	15	34	206	44%	13.7	1	—	—	-13.6%	—	0.2	—	-0.3	—	—	—	—
2005	MIA	15	5	20	105	25%	21.0	1	5.0	—	-41.3%	—	-3.4	—	-2.8	18%	59%	6%	18%
2006	SF	16	8	31	150	26%	18.8	1	4.3	—	-49.3%	—	-7.2	—	-8.0	19%	58%	15%	8%
2007	SF		13		185		14.1	1											

When you are part of a group of receivers who practically defines the word "underwhelming," you play in every game as the team's number-three receiver, and you have only one more catch (eight) than you do carries (seven), well, that's not good. Still, San Francisco saw enough in Gilmore as a special teamer to re-sign him for the new season.

Ted Ginn Height: 5-11 Weight: 178 College: Ohio State Draft: 2007/1 (9) Born: 12-Apr-1985 Age: 22 Risk: Red

Year	Team	G	Rec	Pass	Yds	C%	Yd/C	TD	YAC	Rk	DVOA	Rk	DPAR	Rk	PAR	Short	Mid	Deep	Bomb
2007	MIA		22		364		16.5	2											

Yes, the Dolphins reached for Ginn. Yes, he will need time to develop. No, he will never be a great middle-of-the-field receiver. Let's focus on what he *can* do for a moment: He can score from anywhere on the field. He can separate from all but the best cornerbacks on fly routes. He can change the game as a return man. If he learns to use his speed to set up defenders and work underneath, he can be as good as Santana Moss. That's pretty good. The Dolphins paid too much for him, but just because you pay too much for a plasma television doesn't mean that you can't enjoy the show.

David Givens Height: 6-0 Weight: 212 College: Notre Dame Draft: 2002/7 (253) Born: 16-Aug-1980 Age: 27 Risk: Red

Year	Team	G	Rec	Pass	Yds	C%	Yd/C	TD	YAC	Rk	DVOA	Rk	DPAR	Rk	PAR	Short	Mid	Deep	Bomb
2004	NE	15	56	106	874	53%	15.6	3	—	—	16.6%	27	21.4	24	19.8	—	—	—	—
2005	NE	13	59	95	738	62%	12.5	2	3.9	34	6.8%	34	13.5	28	12.3	36%	44%	11%	9%
2006	TEN	5	8	20	104	40%	13.0	0	6.4	—	-32.4%	—	-2.3	—	-2.3	47%	16%	32%	5%
2007	TEN		19		219		11.3	1											

Givens is rehabbing a serious knee injury and probably won't be at full speed by Opening Day. The Titans will never see a full return on their investment in Givens; they overpaid for him, and there's little chance that he'll become a viable number-one receiver in 2007. With Drew Bennett and Bobby Wade gone, the Titans need warm bodies with experience at wide receiver, so Givens will play a role in the offense, even if he's limping.

Terry Glenn Height: 5-11 Weight: 195 College: Ohio State   Draft: 1996/1 (7)   Born: 23-Jul-1974   Age: 33   Risk: Yellow

Year	Team	G	Rec	Pass	Yds	C%	Yd/C	TD	YAC	Rk	DVOA	Rk	DPAR	Rk	PAR	Short	Mid	Deep	Bomb
2004	DAL	6	24	37	400	65%	16.7	2	—	—	32.6%	—	11.6	—	11.3	—	—	—	—
2005	DAL	16	62	122	1136	52%	18.3	7	3.0	62	16.9%	17	25.8	14	26.1	17%	38%	17%	28%
2006	DAL	16	70	111	1047	63%	15.0	6	3.7	38	19.1%	14	25.9	9	27.7	25%	39%	21%	16%
2007	DAL		59		834		14.1	5											

There are only so many balls to go around in an offense, and a team that has two outstanding receivers, a great pass-catching tight end, a quality slot receiver, and two starting-caliber backs will find it difficult to efficiently utilize all its resources. The Cowboys may have been better served by giving Glenn a few of Terrell Owens's 152 passes, and they may have scored more points if they threw to Glenn instead of handing off to Julius Jones a few more times over the course of the season. The Cowboys face a similar bind this season: There's a fine line between an embarrassment of riches and a case of diminishing returns. The new coaching staff should emphasize getting the ball to Glenn, even if they risk detonating the neutron bomb on the other side of the field.

Anthony Gonzalez Height: 6-0 Weight: 193 College: Ohio State   Draft: 2007/1 (32)   Born: 18-Sep-1984   Age: 23   Risk: Red

Year	Team	G	Rec	Pass	Yds	C%	Yd/C	TD	YAC	Rk	DVOA	Rk	DPAR	Rk	PAR	Short	Mid	Deep	Bomb
2007	IND		29		489		17.0	3											

Don't call him "Tony" Gonzalez. The Ohio State sports information department made that mistake after a spring game when Gonzalez was a freshman. His grandmother, Lourdes Gonzalez, told the information director that she didn't want her grandson confused with the Chiefs tight end. Lourdes, no doubt, watches a lot of football. Maybe she should have called Steve Smith's grandmother and given her some pointers.

According to an article in the *Indianapolis Star* in May, Gonzalez's other grandmother was a sprinter nicknamed "Rabbit." Gonzalez is plenty fast himself, though not quite as fast as Ohio State teammate Ted Ginn Jr. Gonzalez brings the full package to Indy: speed, hands, great route-running, solid character. He just needs to bulk up and improve his blocking. Until Marvin Harrison is ready to hang up his cleats, Gonzalez will be a very dangerous third receiver.

D. J. Hackett Height: 6-2 Weight: 199 College: Colorado   Draft: 2004/5 (157) Born: 31-Jul-1981   Age: 26   Risk: Yellow

Year	Team	G	Rec	Pass	Yds	C%	Yd/C	TD	YAC	Rk	DVOA	Rk	DPAR	Rk	PAR	Short	Mid	Deep	Bomb
2005	SEA	13	28	43	400	65%	14.3	2	2.6	—	16.3%	—	9.1	—	10.2	43%	26%	11%	20%
2006	SEA	14	45	66	610	68%	13.6	4	4.3	25	38.1%	2	22.7	14	23.7	27%	52%	14%	6%
2007	SEA		59		852		14.5	6											

Perhaps you bought stock in D. J. Hackett, Inc. after he led the NFL in DPAR for receivers with fewer than 50 passes thrown to them in 2005. If so, Hackett's 2006 should have been a pleasure. If not, belly up right now (and save some pennies for Patrick Crayton, LLC, since the Cowboys' slot receiver led the NFL in that same category in 2006). One of the few beacons of consistency in an offense that seemed to be coming apart at the seams, Hackett led all Seattle receivers in DPAR in 2006 and finished second to New Orleans's Devery Henderson in DVOA. Hackett has the potential to be a lethal combination of deep threat and sure-handed possession receiver (his 67 percent Catch Rate tied for sixth-best in the league). The Seahawks placed a second-round tender on him as a restricted free agent, and the Darrell Jackson deal moves him into the starting lineup. The breakout season comes this year, followed by a nice, big, well-deserved new contract.

Derek Hagan Height: 6-2 Weight: 202 College: Arizona State   Draft: 2006/3 (82) Born: 21-Sep-1984 Age: 23   Risk: Red

Year	Team	G	Rec	Pass	Yds	C%	Yd/C	TD	YAC	Rk	DVOA	Rk	DPAR	Rk	PAR	Short	Mid	Deep	Bomb
2006	MIA	16	21	37	221	57%	10.5	1	2.2	—	-3.1%	—	2.7	—	1.6	11%	70%	11%	8%
2007	MIA		21		192		9.1	1											

Miami fans don't seem to like him very much, but Hagan showed signs of life in his rookie campaign. He will drop the occasional pass, and his routes are still a little shaky, but he has the right body type, and was pretty fearless over the middle. He's not a guaranteed star or anything, and being a draftee of the old regime doesn't do him any favors, but there's no reason to rule him out yet. Check back next year.

Az-Zahir Hakim   Height: 5-10   Weight: 189   College: San Diego State   Draft: 1998/4 (96)   Born: 3-Jun-1977   Age: 29   Risk: Red

Year	Team	G	Rec	Pass	Yds	C%	Yd/C	TD	YAC	Rk	DVOA	Rk	DPAR	Rk	PAR	Short	Mid	Deep	Bomb
2004	DET	12	31	57	533	54%	17.2	3	—	—	22.6%	19	14.1	39	13.1	—	—	—	—
2005	NO	12	34	58	489	59%	14.4	2	4.7	20	16.4%	18	12.0	33	12.0	15%	59%	26%	0%
2006	DET	6	17	27	147	63%	8.6	0	3.6	—	-18.2%	—	-0.6	—	-0.6	58%	31%	8%	4%
2007	MIA		12		158		12.8	1											

When in doubt, Mike Martz brought in an old Ram to fill a hole. Mike Furrey paid off in spades, but the rest of them were less impressive. Hakim didn't get playing time until Week 3, peaked with 92 yards against Minnesota in Week 5, and was cut three weeks after that. He later signed with San Diego, but never played. This offseason, he signed with Miami, where he hopes to extend a career that is sadly nearing an end.

Dante Hall   Height: 5-8   Weight: 187   College: Texas A&M   Draft: 2000/5 (153)   Born: 1-Sep-1978   Age: 29   Risk: Red

Year	Team	G	Rec	Pass	Yds	C%	Yd/C	TD	YAC	Rk	DVOA	Rk	DPAR	Rk	PAR	Short	Mid	Deep	Bomb
2004	KC	16	25	36	230	64%	9.2	0	—	—	-11.2%	—	1.1	—	2.1	—	—	—	—
2005	KC	16	34	51	436	67%	12.8	3	3.7	37	17.2%	16	10.8	38	10.6	45%	27%	11%	16%
2006	KC	15	26	40	204	65%	7.8	2	2.8	—	-6.8%	—	2.1	—	1.9	46%	31%	23%	0%
2007	STL		15		188		12.3	1											

Not much of a receiver, and nowhere near the return threat he once was, Hall isn't a bad player, but he's a far cry from being one of the most exciting players in the league, which he was a few years ago. Had he been traded to St. Louis in 2001, the move would have been exciting and relevant. That it happened this offseason was too little, too late. There's no role for him in the Rams' offense.

Cortez Hankton   Height: 6-0   Weight: 200   College: Texas Southern   Draft: 2003/FA   Born: 20-Jan-1981   Age: 26   Risk: Red

Year	Team	G	Rec	Pass	Yds	C%	Yd/C	TD	YAC	Rk	DVOA	Rk	DPAR	Rk	PAR	Short	Mid	Deep	Bomb
2004	JAC	12	9	9	81	100%	9.0	2	—	—	42.0%	—	3.3	—	3.7	—	—	—	—
2005	JAC	5	3	6	15	50%	5.0	0	—	—	-74.3%	—	-2.2	—	-1.9	—	—	—	—
2006	JAC	12	5	11	48	45%	9.6	0	0.0	—	-28.9%	—	-1.0	—	-0.7	20%	50%	20%	10%
2007	MIN		13		182		13.7	1											

Hankton got caught in the Vikings' wide receiver dragnet this offseason. A bit performer in Jacksonville, he'll stick in Minnesota as the fourth wideout who gets on the field in special teams.

Chris Hannon   Height: 6-4   Weight: 195   College: Tennessee   Draft: 2006/FA   Born: 18-Feb-1984   Age: 23   Risk: Red

Year	Team	G	Rec	Pass	Yds	C%	Yd/C	TD	YAC	Rk	DVOA	Rk	DPAR	Rk	PAR	Short	Mid	Deep	Bomb
2007	KC		19		190		10.0	1											

Hannon signed with the Chiefs as an undrafted free agent out of Tennessee last year; he's 6-foot-3, 210 pounds, and runs a 4.37 40, so you can understand why. He didn't play last year, but he'll see increased playing time from the beginning of the season this year, and could even start if Samie Parker's stock continues to slip. Herman Edwards has said that he's going to rotate Dwayne Bowe in, and that he's going to give Hannon and Jeff Webb playing time because, "We don't cover them in practice very well." We picture a Herman Edwards practice as resembling a kindergarten recess, but whatever works. Both Hannon and Webb spent most of last season working with quarterback Brodie Croyle, so if Croyle wins the starting job, he may find his old familiar friends a little more often than Damon Huard would.

Marvin Harrison   Height: 6-0   Weight: 175   College: Syracuse   Draft: 1996/1 (19)   Born: 25-Aug-1972   Age: 35   Risk: Green

Year	Team	G	Rec	Pass	Yds	C%	Yd/C	TD	YAC	Rk	DVOA	Rk	DPAR	Rk	PAR	Short	Mid	Deep	Bomb
2004	IND	16	86	139	1113	62%	12.9	15	—	—	14.6%	32	28.6	12	31.4	—	—	—	—
2005	IND	15	82	132	1146	62%	14.0	12	3.0	61	13.8%	22	26.6	13	31.4	28%	40%	15%	17%
2006	IND	16	95	148	1366	64%	14.4	12	2.9	62	28.9%	5	44.3	2	43.3	25%	41%	19%	15%
2007	IND		90		1272		14.2	10											

There isn't much left to say about the greatness of Marvin Harrison. Eventually, age will get him. It may be sudden, like it was for Rod Smith, or it may be gradual, like it was for Steve Largent. Until then, he'll just keep pumping out 1,200-yard seasons with double-digit touchdowns. Harrison's weakness has always been that he seems to shy away from contact, and that seems to have gotten worse over the last couple years, but perhaps that weakness and Harrison's immunity to aging are connected.

Devery Henderson Height: 5-11 Weight: 191 College: LSU Draft: 2004/2 (50) Born: 26-Mar-1982 Age: 25 Risk: Yellow

Year	Team	G	Rec	Pass	Yds	C%	Yd/C	TD	YAC	Rk	DVOA	Rk	DPAR	Rk	PAR	Short	Mid	Deep	Bomb
2005	NO	14	22	50	343	44%	15.6	3	4.6	24	-10.6%	68	1.6	70	2.0	22%	41%	20%	17%
2006	NO	13	32	54	745	59%	23.3	5	4.9	13	39.9%	1	20.2	17	22.2	19%	36%	17%	28%
2007	NO		47		749		16.1	4											

You've got your track stars, and you've got your professional wide receivers, and last year Henderson crossed the line from one to the other. Everybody knew he was fast, but the important change for Henderson came in raising his Catch Rate from 44 percent to 59 percent. There's no way he averages 23 yards per reception again, but he's going to be an important part of the New Orleans's offense and—assuming he continues to start opposite Marques Colston—a useful piece for your fantasy football team. Patriots and Giants fans disappointed in Chad Jackson and Sinorice Moss, take heart: Henderson didn't even catch a pass as a second-round rookie. Two years later, he turned into this.

Chris Henry Height: 6-4 Weight: 197 College: West Virginia Draft: 2005/3 (83) Born: 17-May-1983 Age: 24 Risk: Red

Year	Team	G	Rec	Pass	Yds	C%	Yd/C	TD	YAC	Rk	DVOA	Rk	DPAR	Rk	PAR	Short	Mid	Deep	Bomb
2005	CIN	14	31	50	422	62%	13.6	6	1.8	89	4.1%	43	6.2	57	5.1	28%	47%	9%	16%
2006	CIN	13	36	75	605	48%	16.8	9	4.6	18	3.6%	43	9.2	48	10.1	13%	49%	17%	20%
2007	CIN		25		428		16.9	3											

Even on a team of guys often on the wrong side of the law, Chris Henry stands out. So why do the Bengals continue to put up with their leading social misfit? The answer is as obvious as Henry's talent. The past two seasons he has produced 15 touchdowns on just 67 receptions, a simply ridiculous touchdown rate. Not only is Henry the only number-three receiver to appear anywhere near the touchdown reception leaders list, every other receiver with 15 or more touchdowns last year needed at least 60 more receptions to get them. Henry has been suspended for the first eight games of the 2007 season and has been threatened with banishment for the whole year, so expect 2007 to be a wasted season (figuratively, not literally).

Devin Hester Height: 5-11 Weight: 185 College: Miami Draft: 2006/2 (57) Born: 4-Nov-1982 Age: 25 Risk: Red

Year	Team	G	Rec	Pass	Yds	C%	Yd/C	TD	YAC	Rk	DVOA	Rk	DPAR	Rk	PAR	Short	Mid	Deep	Bomb
2007	CHI		12		213		17.7	2											

Hester was moved to the offensive side of the ball in April after his stunning rookie season on special teams. When the Hurricanes tried to integrate him into their offense a couple years ago, Hester wasn't able to carve out a steady role for himself, and it's not any easier to do in the NFL. He'll get a couple touchdowns because the Bears will put him in situations specifically designed to get him touchdowns, but Chicago's offense isn't really based on clearing the open spaces Hester would need to do his magic.

Johnnie Lee Higgins Height: 5-11 Weight: 186 College: UTEP Draft: 2007/3 (99) Born: 8-Sep-1983 Age: 24 Risk: Red

Year	Team	G	Rec	Pass	Yds	C%	Yd/C	TD	YAC	Rk	DVOA	Rk	DPAR	Rk	PAR	Short	Mid	Deep	Bomb
2007	OAK		18		257		14.5	1											

You're not gonna believe this: The Raiders drafted someone who's really, really fast, but not much of a football player. Though, unlike the Dolphins, Al Davis at least waited until the third round to do it. Higgins, a UTEP product, ran a wind-aided 4.29 40-yard dash on campus, which is in the Ted Ginn range, but only a 4.53 40 at the Combine. He's a speed merchant and actually has pretty good hands, but he has to work on his routes and his upper-body strength before he'll be an effective NFL receiver.

Jason Hill Height: 6-1 Weight: 204 College: Washington State Draft: 2007/3 (76) Born: 20-Feb-1985 Age: 22 Risk: Red

Year	Team	G	Rec	Pass	Yds	C%	Yd/C	TD	YAC	Rk	DVOA	Rk	DPAR	Rk	PAR	Short	Mid	Deep	Bomb
2007	SF		15		225		14.8	1											

Though offensive coordinator Norv Turner has moved on to San Diego, the 49ers will keep Turner's vertical offense, and Hill's just the kind of player who could benefit. Best known for the 4.32 40-yard dash he ran at the Combine, Hill posted solid numbers for the Cougars, with 1,000-plus yardage seasons in 2004 and 2005. He missed the final two games of his college career with a left high ankle sprain, but that didn't stop draft mavens from regarding him as perhaps the most underrated receiver in the Pac-10.

Ike Hilliard   Height: 5-11   Weight: 210   College: Florida   Draft: 1997/1 (7)   Born: 5-Apr-1976   Age: 31   Risk: Red

Year	Team	G	Rec	Pass	Yds	C%	Yd/C	TD	YAC	Rk	DVOA	Rk	DPAR	Rk	PAR	Short	Mid	Deep	Bomb
2004	NYG	16	49	81	437	60%	8.9	0	—	—	-29.6%	81	-8.3	82	-11.1	—	—	—	—
2005	TB	16	35	53	282	66%	8.1	1	2.8	68	-2.4%	55	4.4	62	4.5	63%	33%	5%	0%
2006	TB	16	34	55	339	62%	10.0	2	4.1	31	-16.9%	73	-0.4	71	1.1	51%	41%	8%	0%
2007	TB		32		328		10.3	2											

Hilliard has made a strange second career out of being Jon Gruden's hitches-and-flats guy. Hilliard regularly rings up four-catch, 34-yard stat lines, the kind we might associate with a third-down back. He ran the highest percentage of short routes of any wide receiver in 2005 and was second to Eric Moulds in 2006. His yards per catch are very low, but his Catch Rates are high, and he produces enough eight-yard gains on 2nd-and-10 to register as a near-average receiver according to our metrics. It's a nice little retirement job, but those eight-yard gains will become four-yard gains as soon as Hilliard loses another step, and that's going to happen very soon.

Carlyle Holiday   Height: 6-2   Weight: 220   College: Notre Dame   Draft: 2005/0 (0)   Born: 4-Oct-1981   Age: 26   Risk: Red

Year	Team	G	Rec	Pass	Yds	C%	Yd/C	TD	YAC	Rk	DVOA	Rk	DPAR	Rk	PAR	Short	Mid	Deep	Bomb
2006	GB	4	9	15	126	60%	14.0	0	4.1	—	9.9%	—	2.3	—	2.1	24%	59%	6%	12%
2007	GB		14		182		13.5	1											

The former Notre Dame quarterback at least brings the wide receiver pass option to the Packers' playbook. Holiday has some physical skills, but is unrefined and not a dominant athlete. He ended the season on a high note with 87 yards against the Bears' B-squad in the season finale.

Santonio Holmes   Height: 5-11   Weight: 190   College: Ohio State   Draft: 2006/1 (25)   Born: 3-Mar-1984   Age: 23   Risk: Red

Year	Team	G	Rec	Pass	Yds	C%	Yd/C	TD	YAC	Rk	DVOA	Rk	DPAR	Rk	PAR	Short	Mid	Deep	Bomb
2006	PIT	16	49	86	824	57%	16.8	2	6.5	2	18.4%	15	19.6	19	20.6	19%	61%	12%	8%
2007	PIT		59		925		15.7	4											

He may have started only four games as the Steelers' number-two receiver last year, but the monthly breakdown shows that Holmes was beginning to figure things out by the end of the season. He enjoyed his strongest month in December, when he hauled in 17 passes and averaged nearly 20 yards per reception. That kind of progression suggests a player that could someday soon push Hines Ward as the Steelers' number one.

Torry Holt   Height: 6-0   Weight: 190   College: North Carolina St.   Draft: 1999/1 (6)   Born: 5-Jun-1976   Age: 31   Risk: Yellow

Year	Team	G	Rec	Pass	Yds	C%	Yd/C	TD	YAC	Rk	DVOA	Rk	DPAR	Rk	PAR	Short	Mid	Deep	Bomb
2004	STL	16	94	137	1372	69%	14.6	10	—	—	24.8%	13	34.9	7	35.2	—	—	—	—
2005	STL	14	102	163	1331	63%	13.0	9	2.6	73	5.0%	39	22.0	18	25.3	32%	32%	26%	11%
2006	STL	16	93	179	1188	52%	12.8	10	2.9	61	-5.7%	59	11.5	42	12.9	25%	39%	22%	13%
2007	STL		89		1114		12.6	7											

From 1999 to 2005, Torry Holt had more combined DPAR than any other wide receiver in the NFL, and he led the league in DPAR as recently as 2003, but his numbers have slipped in the last two years. Before 2005 Holt had never averaged less than 14 yards per reception, and before 2006 he had never put up a Catch Rate below 60 percent. There's a reasonable argument to be made that Holt is not actually playing any worse, but that opposing defenses are no longer treating Holt and Isaac Bruce as equals, instead acknowledging that Holt is now the superior player. Certainly the Rams' offense works that way now, because no NFL receiver was thrown more passes last year than Holt's 179. On the other hand, Holt is no longer a spring chicken himself, and the nagging injuries that come with age are starting to hit. Holt had problems with loose cartilage in his knee in December, which required offseason surgery.

Perhaps the strangest part of Holt's 2006 season was how often Marc Bulger simply overthrew him. According to our game charters, Holt led the league with 26 overthrown incompletes. One-third of the incomplete passes to Holt were over-thrown, compared to just 14 percent of the incomplete passes to the other Rams wide receivers. Holt also had nine dropped passes. Put it all together, and Holt's decline looks like a combination of tighter coverage, age, and a somewhat fluky case of the dropsies. That last issue may go away this year, but the other two will not.

Joe Horn   Height: 6-1 Weight: 206 College: Itawamba J.C.   Draft: 1996/5 (135) Born: 16-Jan-1972 Age: 35 Risk: Yellow

Year	Team	G	Rec	Pass	Yds	C%	Yd/C	TD	YAC	Rk	DVOA	Rk	DPAR	Rk	PAR	Short	Mid	Deep	Bomb
2004	NO	16	94	153	1399	61%	14.9	11	—	—	25.8%	12	41.6	2	44.0	—	—	—	—
2005	NO	13	49	103	654	48%	13.3	1	2.0	87	-16.0%	81	-0.6	80	-0.4	13%	54%	25%	9%
2006	NO	10	37	61	679	61%	18.4	4	4.4	20	31.7%	4	19.7	18	20.7	17%	48%	24%	10%
2007	ATL		52		687		13.1	4											

In February, Horn insisted that he wouldn't take a pay cut to stay in New Orleans. When the Saints told him he was free to test the market, he quickly changed his tune, saying that he would be happy to take a pay cut, but that Sean Payton didn't want him back. When New Orleans radio host Bobby Hebert accused Horn of being a money-first player, Horn took shots at Hebert. For most of us, this would be odd behavior. For a Class of 1996 receiver, it's just a typical winter. The Falcons equipment staff spent most of the offseason trying to get the Price-Lelie odor off of Horn's new jersey. Even if they succeeded, Horn is 35 and coming off a lingering injury. This is the coda of his career, not the next chapter.

T. J. Houshmandzadeh   Height: 6-1 Weight: 197 College: Oregon State   Draft: 2001/7 (204) Born: 26-Sep-1977 Age: 30 Risk: Green

Year	Team	G	Rec	Pass	Yds	C%	Yd/C	TD	YAC	Rk	DVOA	Rk	DPAR	Rk	PAR	Short	Mid	Deep	Bomb
2004	CIN	16	73	109	978	67%	13.4	4	—	—	28.8%	11	31.0	11	27.5	—	—	—	—
2005	CIN	14	78	115	956	68%	12.3	7	4.2	30	24.9%	7	29.8	9	28.3	34%	49%	13%	4%
2006	CIN	14	90	132	1081	68%	12.0	9	3.5	42	20.7%	11	31.4	4	31.2	41%	38%	16%	5%
2007	CIN		77		1082		14.0	7											

Houshmandzadeh probably has the skills to be a number-one receiver for a good portion of the teams in the NFL, but he's better off remaining a number-two in Cincinnati's offense. Why? Both in number (145) and percentage (28.2) of passes, no team in the NFL throws to its second receiver more than the Bengals. What's more, Houshmandzadeh saw 22 balls in the red zone, tied for fourth-most in the league and double the number thrown to his more-celebrated teammate Chad Johnson.

Sam Hurd   Height: 6-2 Weight: 187 College: Northern Illinois   Draft: 2006/FA Born: 24-Apr-1985 Age: 22 Risk: Red

Year	Team	G	Rec	Pass	Yds	C%	Yd/C	TD	YAC	Rk	DVOA	Rk	DPAR	Rk	PAR	Short	Mid	Deep	Bomb
2006	DAL	15	5	11	75	45%	15.0	0	2.6	—	-12.7%	—	0.2	—	0.5	36%	36%	18%	9%
2007	DAL		15		213		13.7	1											

Hurd impressed Cowboys coaches with his effort on special teams as a rookie, recording 13 tackles and forcing two fumbles. As a senior at Northern Illinois, he caught 65 passes for 1,074 yards and 13 touchdowns, but he isn't a burner and doesn't have the thick frame of a traditional possession receiver. His toughness on special teams will keep him on the roster until the Cowboys decide if he's the heir apparent to Terrell Owens or just a useful spare part.

Chad Jackson   Height: 6-1 Weight: 206 College: Florida   Draft: 2006/2 (36) Born: 6-Mar-1985 Age: 22 Risk: Red

Year	Team	G	Rec	Pass	Yds	C%	Yd/C	TD	YAC	Rk	DVOA	Rk	DPAR	Rk	PAR	Short	Mid	Deep	Bomb
2006	NE	12	13	19	152	68%	11.7	3	4.4	—	23.5%	—	4.9	—	4.2	63%	5%	11%	21%
2007	NE		11		160		14.6	1											

The Patriots' second-round picks under Bill Belichick have been very big hits (Matt Light, Deion Branch, Eugene Wilson) or very big misses (Bethel Johnson, Adrian Klemm, the late Marquise Hill). Based on Jackson's talent alone, it's unclear which group he will fit into, but his health might make the decision for him. He spent all of 2006 dealing with a hamstring injury that kept him out of the preseason, and then tore his ACL in the AFC Championship Game. He could make it back in time for the regular season, but the Patriots might choose to put him on the PUP list in order to carry Jabar Gaffney. If Jackson doesn't make it back, he'll be entering his third season in 2008 with 12 career catches.

Darrell Jackson   Height: 6-0 Weight: 201 College: Florida   Draft: 2000/3 (80) Born: 6-Dec-1978 Age: 29 Risk: Green

Year	Team	G	Rec	Pass	Yds	C%	Yd/C	TD	YAC	Rk	DVOA	Rk	DPAR	Rk	PAR	Short	Mid	Deep	Bomb
2004	SEA	16	87	155	1199	56%	13.8	7	—	—	4.2%	45	20.0	29	18.7	—	—	—	—
2005	SEA	6	38	55	482	69%	12.7	3	3.3	47	23.1%	8	14.3	26	15.5	30%	35%	17%	19%
2006	SEA	13	63	112	956	56%	15.2	10	4.0	36	9.1%	33	17.6	24	18.0	24%	45%	18%	13%
2007	SF		56		791		14.1	5											

(continued next page)

Darrell Jackson (*continued*)

If Jackson's career in Seattle was a Prince song, "Tick, Tick, Bang" might have been the most appropriate title, with "Strange Relationship" a close second. Matt Hasselbeck's favorite receiver since 2003, Jackson had been at odds with the front office over alleged verbal contractual promises made to him by former team president Bob Whitsitt. The drama didn't affect his on-field production, but his health certainly did: Jackson missed nine games in 2005 and three in 2006. As a result, he hasn't broken 1,000 yards since 2004, and has been stuck in the mid-to-low 20s in DPAR since 2003. After two years of minicamp holdouts and subelite production on Jackson's part, the Seahawks decided that enough was enough and shipped him to San Francisco on draft weekend for a 2007 fourth-round pick. If he can stay healthy, he'll be Alex Smith's newest, bestest buddy.

Vincent Jackson Height: 6-5 Weight: 241 College: Northern Colorado Draft: 2005/2 (61) Born: 14-Jan-1983 Age: 24 Risk: Yellow

Year	Team	G	Rec	Pass	Yds	C%	Yd/C	TD	YAC	Rk	DVOA	Rk	DPAR	Rk	PAR	Short	Mid	Deep	Bomb
2005	SD	7	3	8	59	38%	19.7	0	1.7	—	-2.9%	—	0.6	—	0.5	29%	0%	43%	29%
2006	SD	16	27	56	453	48%	16.8	6	2.7	68	5.5%	39	7.5	55	7.8	24%	35%	13%	29%
2007	SD		48		758		15.8	5											

In the 2005 NFL draft, there were two 6-foot-5, 240-pound wide receivers. One came from USC and looked like a can't-miss prospect. The other came from Northern Colorado and looked like a long-term project. The Lions took the first one, Mike Williams, tenth overall. The Chargers took the second one, Vincent Jackson, 61st overall. Two years later, there's no comparison: Jackson is a much better receiver than Williams. This year, he's supposed to take over the number-one spot in San Diego. Another solid draft decision by A. J. Smith.

Taylor Jacobs Height: 6-0 Weight: 198 College: Florida Draft: 2003/2 (44) Born: 30-May-1981 Age: 26 Risk: Red

Year	Team	G	Rec	Pass	Yds	C%	Yd/C	TD	YAC	Rk	DVOA	Rk	DPAR	Rk	PAR	Short	Mid	Deep	Bomb
2004	WAS	15	16	27	178	59%	11.1	0	—	—	-15.2%	—	0.0	—	-0.1	—	—	—	—
2005	WAS	15	11	25	100	44%	9.1	0	1.0	—	-47.6%	—	-5.3	—	-4.9	26%	26%	13%	35%
2006	SF	8	4	12	29	33%	7.3	0	0.3	—	-44.3%	—	-2.5	—	-3.3	18%	55%	9%	18%
2007	SF		13		178		13.8	1											

This five-year veteran's greatest contribution to the 49ers may have been that the trade that brought him to San Francisco allowed the Niners to dump perennial doormat cornerback Mike Rumph off on Washington. Jacobs's value as a receiver and special teamer for the 49ers in 2006 was limited by a hamstring injury that cost him eight games. With so many new receivers on board for 2007, Jacobs will be a fifth option and special-teams contributor at best.

Dwayne Jarrett Height: 6-4 Weight: 219 College: USC Draft: 2007/2 (45) Born: 11-Sep-1986 Age: 21 Risk: Red

Year	Team	G	Rec	Pass	Yds	C%	Yd/C	TD	YAC	Rk	DVOA	Rk	DPAR	Rk	PAR	Short	Mid	Deep	Bomb
2007	CAR		41		614	·	14.9	5											

If you want to tick off Jarrett, compare him to Mike Williams. Jarrett spent the weeks leading up to the draft trying to distance himself from Williams, the former first-round bust who shares Jarrett's college (USC), measurables (6-foot-4 or so, 215 pounds, a 40-time in the 4.6 range), and reputation (great production, suspect speed and work habits). In Carolina, Jarrett must distinguish himself from Keary Colbert, another big, cocky ex-Trojan whose questionable attitude and work habits marred his career while attempting to replace Keyshawn Johnson, yet another big, cocky ex-Trojan who overcame a questionable attitude and work habits to become a star. Jarrett will get plenty of opportunities with the Panthers, and early minicamp results were encouraging. If you see a 6-foot-4 USC receiver strutting around the end zone after a touchdown on some fall Saturday, don't wonder about his future, just pencil him in as a future Carolina Panther.

Michael Jenkins Height: 6-4 Weight: 217 College: Ohio State Draft: 2004/1 (29) Born: 18-Jun-1982 Age: 25 Risk: Yellow

Year	Team	G	Rec	Pass	Yds	C%	Yd/C	TD	YAC	Rk	DVOA	Rk	DPAR	Rk	PAR	Short	Mid	Deep	Bomb
2004	ATL	16	7	20	119	35%	17.0	0	—	—	-39.5%	—	-3.0	—	-2.8	—	—	—	—
2005	ATL	14	36	71	508	51%	14.1	3	2.7	71	0.7%	46	7.4	53	7.6	18%	37%	24%	21%
2006	ATL	16	39	83	436	47%	11.2	7	2.4	73	-17.7%	74	-1.4	75	-1.1	28%	41%	20%	11%
2007	ATL		30		389		12.8	2											

Jenkins only surpassed 50 receiving yards in two games last season and has caught only five passes in a game twice in his three-year career. He's the Falcons' de facto number-one receiver, but his stats look more like those of a good slot receiver or above-average tight end. Jenkins blocks well and is a big target in the red zone, but he drops passes, doesn't react to bad throws, and has a tendency to disappear for a quarter at a time. After two years, a player like this still offers the promise of a breakout, but after three years, you pretty much know what you have. The Lions aren't the only team that whiffed multiple times when drafting wideouts in the first round.

Greg Jennings   Height: 5-11   Weight: 192   College: Western Michigan   Draft: 2006/2 (52)   Born: 21-Sep-1983   Age: 24   Risk: Red

Year	Team	G	Rec	Pass	Yds	C%	Yd/C	TD	YAC	Rk	DVOA	Rk	DPAR	Rk	PAR	Short	Mid	Deep	Bomb
2006	GB	14	45	105	632	43%	14.0	3	6.9	1	-24.1%	80	-6.5	81	-7.0	32%	36%	15%	17%
2007	GB		55		831		15.2	5											

Jennings got lost in an extraordinary rookie class, but the MAC product had an active rookie season. Through five games, he had 20 catches for 364 yards and three touchdowns (0.3 DPAR). In the sixth game of the year, he hurt his ankle, and it never fully healed. The rest of the season, Jennings totaled 25 catches for 268 yards and no touchdowns (–6.8 DPAR). He does not have great straight-ahead speed, but was still able to make plays down the field before the injury. Whether the injury or opposing defenses were the cause of his slowdown will make the difference between his being an intriguing fantasy sleeper and waiver wire fodder.

Andre Johnson   Height: 6-2   Weight: 221   College: Miami   Draft: 2003/1 (3)   Born: 11-Jul-1981   Age: 26   Risk: Yellow

Year	Team	G	Rec	Pass	Yds	C%	Yd/C	TD	YAC	Rk	DVOA	Rk	DPAR	Rk	PAR	Short	Mid	Deep	Bomb
2004	HOU	16	79	137	1142	58%	14.5	6	—	—	4.5%	44	18.4	33	22.8	—	—	—	—
2005	HOU	13	63	114	688	55%	10.9	2	3.5	40	-13.6%	74	1.6	71	4.2	31%	38%	22%	10%
2006	HOU	16	103	164	1147	63%	11.1	5	4.1	32	0.1%	50	16.5	29	14.5	42%	33%	13%	11%
2007	HOU		82		842		10.3	5											

Watching Andre Johnson play in Houston's conservative offense last year was like watching Jeff Gordon take a drive out to the local Kwik-E-Mart. No team threw a higher percentage of passes to their number-one receiver, and seemingly every one of those passes traveled about three yards through the air. With Matt Schaub behind center, Gary Kubiak is expected to open up the offense a little bit more, which will benefit both the Texans and Johnson's fantasy numbers.

Bethel Johnson   Height: 5-11   Weight: 200   College: Texas A&M   Draft: 2003/2 (45)   Born: 11-Feb-1979   Age: 28   Risk: Red

Year	Team	G	Rec	Pass	Yds	C%	Yd/C	TD	YAC	Rk	DVOA	Rk	DPAR	Rk	PAR	Short	Mid	Deep	Bomb
2004	NE	13	10	21	174	48%	17.4	1	—	—	-6.5%	—	1.3	—	2.3	—	—	—	—
2005	NE	11	4	6	67	67%	16.7	1	3.0	—	2.9%	—	0.8	—	0.6	33%	17%	0%	50%
2006	MIN	11	9	19	156	47%	17.3	0	8.1	—	-3.6%	—	1.4	—	0.9	12%	29%	18%	41%
2007	PHI		11		147		13.4	1											

Johnson is very fast, but has never developed as a receiver. He is basically a kick returner these days and will try and stick with the Eagles in that role, but a stress fracture in his foot suffered during the offseason will make that a bit more difficult.

Bryant Johnson   Height: 6-2   Weight: 214   College: Penn State   Draft: 2003/1 (17)   Born: 7-Mar-1981   Age: 26   Risk: Red

Year	Team	G	Rec	Pass	Yds	C%	Yd/C	TD	YAC	Rk	DVOA	Rk	DPAR	Rk	PAR	Short	Mid	Deep	Bomb
2004	ARI	16	49	101	537	49%	11.0	1	—	—	-27.1%	79	-7.9	81	-7.4	—	—	—	—
2005	ARI	14	40	72	432	56%	10.8	1	3.3	48	-18.7%	85	-1.5	82	0.0	25%	46%	21%	9%
2006	ARI	16	40	74	740	54%	18.5	4	5.8	3	21.3%	10	16.9	27	16.3	31%	36%	19%	13%
2007	ARI		37		590		15.9	3											

Johnson's 18.5-yards-per-catch average was third-best in the NFL last year among receivers with at least 30 catches, behind only Devery Henderson and Donte' Stallworth. Johnson looked good when filling in for an injured Larry Fitzgerald for three games, and he caught as many touchdown passes on the season as Anquan Boldin did. Johnson has never lived up to his first-round status from 2003, and he won't do so with Boldin and Fitzgerald above him, but he could be a good walk-year soldier and smart fantasy pickup in a league that goes deep at wide receiver.

Calvin Johnson   Height: 6-5   Weight: 239 College: Georgia Tech   Draft: 2007/1 (2)   Born: 25-Sep-1985   Age: 22   Risk: Red

Year	Team	G	Rec	Pass	Yds	C%	Yd/C	TD	YAC	Rk	DVOA	Rk	DPAR	Rk	PAR	Short	Mid	Deep	Bomb
2007	DET		40		641		16.0	4											

Johnson's size, speed, and physical ability made him a great prospect, but his intelligence and work habits made him a once-a-decade prospect. He's Terrell Owens after receiving a brain transplant from Marvin Harrison. Quarterback Jon Kitna was impressed with Johnson's brains and NFL-readiness after the Lions' first minicamp. "He didn't break the huddle with the baffled look that most first-year guys have," Kitna said. "Heck, there are guys who have been working on [Mike Martz's offense] for a year that still don't always know what to do, but Calvin knew where he was supposed to be. He's obviously been doing his homework."

With Johnson and Roy Williams, the Lions now have an exceptional wide receiver duo, and Mike Furrey gives them a great option as a third wideout. Before you take Johnson's arrival as a sign that the Lions are about to turn the corner, remember the Cardinals. Two great young receivers and an offensive guru do not a quality NFL team make.

Chad Johnson   Height: 6-1   Weight: 192 College: Oregon State   Draft: 2001/2 (36)   Born: 9-Jan-1978   Age: 29   Risk: Green

Year	Team	G	Rec	Pass	Yds	C%	Yd/C	TD	YAC	Rk	DVOA	Rk	DPAR	Rk	PAR	Short	Mid	Deep	Bomb
2004	CIN	16	95	169	1274	56%	13.4	9	—	—	6.7%	40	24.0	19	20.8	—	—	—	—
2005	CIN	16	97	155	1432	63%	14.8	9	3.3	51	20.6%	11	38.0	2	37.8	21%	49%	17%	12%
2006	CIN	16	87	152	1369	57%	15.7	7	3.5	43	15.5%	17	31.4	5	31.1	17%	47%	19%	17%
2007	CIN		82		1258		15.3	8											

Johnson and Carson Palmer needed some time to get back in sync at the start of the 2006 season, or perhaps Johnson was just depressed about the new rules on end-zone celebrations. He exploded in November, gaining nearly 600 yards in one of the best three-game stretches a receiver has ever produced. Predictably, he wasn't able to sustain that pace, fading at the end of the season along with Palmer. Johnson might be a better teammate than he's given credit for. Sure, he complains about wanting the ball, but is there another number-one receiver in the NFL whose partner (Houshmandzadeh) sees twice as many passes in the red zone as he does?

Keyshawn Johnson   Height: 6-4   Weight: 212 College: USC   Draft: 1996/1 (1)   Born: 22-Jul-1972   Age: 35   Risk: NA

Year	Team	G	Rec	Pass	Yds	C%	Yd/C	TD	YAC	Rk	DVOA	Rk	DPAR	Rk	PAR	Short	Mid	Deep	Bomb
2004	DAL	16	70	125	981	56%	14.0	6	—	—	13.5%	35	23.6	20	20.1	—	—	—	—
2005	DAL	16	71	130	839	58%	11.8	6	2.5	78	-0.1%	51	12.2	32	12.0	26%	51%	21%	2%
2006	CAR	16	70	128	815	55%	11.6	4	2.8	64	-7.5%	61	6.8	56	9.1	27%	44%	24%	4%

Johnson worked as an analyst for ESPN during the draft, and was very excited about the prospect of mentoring new Panthers receiver (and fellow USC alum) Dwayne Jarrett. A few days later, Carolina released Johnson and gave his starting spot to Jarrett. Johnson is now 35, an age at which many good receivers fall off the cliff and second-tier ones have been selling real estate for four years. He's been fading incrementally over the last three years, losing a few points of DVOA and tenths of a yard per catch every season. It's reasonable to assume that he still has a couple of useful 700-yard seasons in him, and he would make a great addition if a contender needed a possession receiver. Unfortunately, none did, so Johnson retired in May. While we're still working out the kinks in our pundit projection system, the operative word for him in 2007 is "bombast."

Brandon Jones   Height: 6-1   Weight: 208 College: Oklahoma   Draft: 2005/3 (96)   Born: 6-Oct-1982   Age: 25   Risk: Red

Year	Team	G	Rec	Pass	Yds	C%	Yd/C	TD	YAC	Rk	DVOA	Rk	DPAR	Rk	PAR	Short	Mid	Deep	Bomb
2005	TEN	10	23	47	299	49%	13.0	2	3.4	—	-15.8%	—	0.1	—	1.6	28%	43%	20%	9%
2006	TEN	16	27	54	384	50%	14.2	4	2.9	60	4.2%	40	6.8	57	6.8	18%	39%	21%	23%
2007	TEN		50		569		11.3	4											

Jones had a coming-out party against the Bills in Week 16, catching five passes for 101 yards, including a 29-yard catch-and-run that ignited a Titans rally. He followed that performance by catching a 53-yard pass against the Patriots in the final game of the season. Jones has all the skills you want in a number-two receiver: He's a possession type who is good on third downs (29.9 percent DVOA in 23 attempts) and has a little big-play ability. The Titans should be happy with Jones as long as they don't expect him to grow into a number-one wideout, although that's where they have him penciled in on the 2007 depth chart.

Jacoby Jones Height: 6-3 Weight: 210 College: Lane Draft: 2007/3 (73) Born: 26-Dec-1985 Age: 21 Risk: Red

Year	Team	G	Rec	Pass	Yds	C%	Yd/C	TD	YAC	Rk	DVOA	Rk	DPAR	Rk	PAR	Short	Mid	Deep	Bomb
2007	HOU		32		478		15.0	2											

Jones had an outstanding career at Lane College, then proved he could play with the big boys at the Hula Bowl. He's a great size/speed prospect, but scouts worry that his hands may be too small. He may want to spend his offseasons playing catch with Alex Smith.

Jamal Jones Height: 5-11 Weight: 212 College: North Carolina A&T Draft: 2004/FA Born: 24-Apr-1981 Age: 26 Risk: Red

Year	Team	G	Rec	Pass	Yds	C%	Yd/C	TD	YAC	Rk	DVOA	Rk	DPAR	Rk	PAR	Short	Mid	Deep	Bomb
2006	NO	12	6	10	108	60%	18.0	1	2.3	—	42.5%	—	3.6	—	3.6	33%	0%	50%	17%
2007	NO		16		219		14.0	1											

Jones didn't stand out at North Carolina A&T, where his career high in passes was 41 and he was suspended for a year for disciplinary reasons, but after two seasons on the Packers' practice squad and one on the Saints' bench, Jones is much more NFL-ready. He proved that by catching passes of 27, 23, and 41 yards in December. Jones is built more like a running back than a receiver, and he gets high grades for blocking and beating jams at the line. With the Saints' wide receivers all in a logjam, and Robert Meachem already in the doghouse, Jones has his chance.

James Jones Height: 6-1 Weight: 207 College: San Jose State Draft: 2007/3 (78) Born: 31-Mar-1984 Age: 23 Risk: Red

Year	Team	G	Rec	Pass	Yds	C%	Yd/C	TD	YAC	Rk	DVOA	Rk	DPAR	Rk	PAR	Short	Mid	Deep	Bomb
2007	GB		17		203		11.7	1											

In his career at San Jose State, Jones caught 126 passes, gained 126 yards on 24 reverses, and was 2-of-7 passing on wideout option plays. He's so versatile that he can even long snap in a pinch. For all of his talents, Jones is slow for a wide receiver and will have trouble gaining separation in the pros. He should make an exceptional special teamer, but the Packers want more from their third-round pick.

Matt Jones Height: 6-6 Weight: 242 College: Arkansas Draft: 2005/1 (21) Born: 22-Apr-1983 Age: 24 Risk: Green

Year	Team	G	Rec	Pass	Yds	C%	Yd/C	TD	YAC	Rk	DVOA	Rk	DPAR	Rk	PAR	Short	Mid	Deep	Bomb
2005	JAC	16	36	69	432	52%	12.0	5	2.8	69	-6.1%	63	4.1	64	5.0	36%	39%	10%	15%
2006	JAC	14	41	76	643	54%	15.7	4	4.4	19	-1.5%	52	7.5	54	10.1	23%	42%	23%	13%
2007	JAC		46		765		16.7	5											

Jones battled through injuries early in the season, but came on strong in December. That month, he caught six passes for 128 yards and a touchdown against the Dolphins, four passes for 69 yards and a touchdown against the Patriots, and five passes for 104 yards against the Chiefs. The former option quarterback was useless as a gadget player—0-for-4 passing, –15 yards rushing—but he emerged as a serious deep threat in the second half of the year. Jones will win a starting job this season if his hamstrings stay unstrained; even if he doesn't, he'll get plenty of playing time on a team that used the three-receiver set as its base formation last year.

Joe Jurevicius Height: 6-5 Weight: 230 College: Penn State Draft: 1998/2 (55) Born: 23-Dec-1974 Age: 32 Risk: Green

Year	Team	G	Rec	Pass	Yds	C%	Yd/C	TD	YAC	Rk	DVOA	Rk	DPAR	Rk	PAR	Short	Mid	Deep	Bomb
2004	TB	10	27	37	333	73%	12.3	2	—	—	27.6%	—	10.6	—	11.5	—	—	—	—
2005	SEA	16	55	84	694	65%	12.6	10	4.3	27	20.9%	10	20.7	20	23.5	32%	51%	13%	4%
2006	CLE	13	40	65	495	62%	12.4	3	3.2	53	12.1%	28	11.9	41	12.7	21%	65%	11%	3%
2007	CLE		43		600		13.8	4											

Jurevicius took less money than he could have gotten elsewhere to sign as a free agent in his native Cleveland, and it would be hard to blame him if he regretted that decision. Seattle's offense seemed like the perfect fit for Jurevicius, and, if he had stayed there, he would have played a bigger role on a better team. Jurevicius turns 33 this season and won't be around long enough to win much with Cleveland.

Eddie Kennison

Height: 6-1 Weight: 201 College: LSU Draft: 1996/1 (18) Born: 20-Jan-1973 Age: 34 Risk: Yellow

Year	Team	G	Rec	Pass	Yds	C%	Yd/C	TD	YAC	Rk	DVOA	Rk	DPAR	Rk	PAR	Short	Mid	Deep	Bomb
2004	KC	14	62	106	1086	58%	17.5	8	—	—	19.2%	24	24.7	17	27.1	—	—	—	—
2005	KC	16	68	108	1102	63%	16.2	5	5.2	12	27.9%	4	31.0	6	31.5	28%	41%	21%	10%
2006	KC	16	53	101	860	52%	16.2	5	2.3	77	13.0%	25	18.6	22	18.0	21%	33%	32%	14%
2007	KC		52		595		11.5	3											

Still going strong at an advanced age, Kennison might be a step slower than he was as a youngster, but he's a better route runner and has better hands. If he plays a couple more years, he could go over 10,000 career receiving yards.

Ashley Lelie

Height: 6-3 Weight: 200 College: Hawaii Draft: 2002/1 (19) Born: 16-Feb-1980 Age: 27 Risk: Red

Year	Team	G	Rec	Pass	Yds	C%	Yd/C	TD	YAC	Rk	DVOA	Rk	DPAR	Rk	PAR	Short	Mid	Deep	Bomb
2004	DEN	16	54	101	1084	53%	20.1	7	—	—	22.7%	18	25.4	16	26.5	—	—	—	—
2005	DEN	16	42	88	770	48%	18.3	1	5.1	15	0.2%	50	9.0	47	9.3	18%	35%	16%	31%
2006	ATL	15	28	68	430	41%	15.4	1	2.3	78	-18.0%	75	-1.4	74	-1.5	12%	42%	20%	26%
2007	SF		41		582		14.3	2											

Lelie didn't seem to be having a completely bust-o-licious season in the first half of 2006. In September and October, he caught 15 passes for 263 yards—not great numbers, but a promising start for a guy on a run-oriented team who was still learning the system. When he caught just three passes in four November starts, however, it became clear that his one-trick route-running style wasn't what the Falcons needed. In San Francisco, Lelie's role and expectations will be reduced, and he won't be distracted by the trade demands and salary grievances that demanded his attention last season. He should be able to get back to doing what he does best: going deep a few times per game and providing the occasional 50-yard highlight.

Greg Lewis

Height: 6-0 Weight: 180 College: Illinois Draft: 2003/FA Born: 12-Feb-1980 Age: 27 Risk: Red

Year	Team	G	Rec	Pass	Yds	C%	Yd/C	TD	YAC	Rk	DVOA	Rk	DPAR	Rk	PAR	Short	Mid	Deep	Bomb
2004	PHI	16	17	46	183	63%	10.8	0	—	—	-1.3%	25	3.6	25	3.1	—	—	—	—
2005	PHI	16	48	110	561	46%	11.7	1	2.5	76	-18.5%	84	-2.6	86	-3.7	26%	42%	16%	17%
2006	PHI	16	24	37	348	65%	14.5	2	3.4	—	20.0%	—	8.4	—	9.8	17%	56%	11%	17%
2007	PHI		17		238		13.7	1											

50. 49. 51. 47. Those are the 2006 Catch Rates of the Eagles' other four wide receivers, each among the worst in the league. Lewis's 65 percent ranks well within the league's upper third, and that's thanks to his being the only Eagles receiver primarily used as a short target. Seventy-four percent of the passes thrown to Lewis traveled 15 yards or less in the air, compared with just 61 percent, 56 percent, and 50 percent, respectively, for Reggie Brown, Donte' Stallworth, and Hank Baskett. As the Eagles' other receivers develop, their short-yardage opportunities and Catch Rates will increase, and Lewis's relevance to the offense will decline.

Brandon Lloyd

Height: 6-0 Weight: 184 College: Illinois Draft: 2003/4 (124) Born: 5-Jul-1981 Age: 26 Risk: Red

Year	Team	G	Rec	Pass	Yds	C%	Yd/C	TD	YAC	Rk	DVOA	Rk	DPAR	Rk	PAR	Short	Mid	Deep	Bomb
2004	SF	13	43	89	565	48%	13.1	6	—	—	-5.6%	57	5.4	55	4.1	—	—	—	—
2005	SF	16	48	109	733	44%	15.3	5	3.0	60	-17.7%	82	-1.7	83	-0.8	13%	55%	15%	18%
2006	WAS	15	23	58	365	41%	15.9	0	2.5	72	-25.9%	81	-4.1	80	-3.8	17%	47%	11%	25%
2007	WAS		24		355		14.8	1											

The 49ers were more than happy to unload the temperamental Lloyd last offseason. In Washington, he was expected to be the number-two receiver, but continued to suffer from mental lapses, untimely drops, and a bad attitude. It took several midseason closed-door meetings with head coach Joe Gibbs for Lloyd's on-field behavior to improve, but his production never did. After starting the first 12 games of the year, Lloyd came off the bench the following three weeks (he did not play in Week 17) and managed only five catches. For the season, he finished fifth on the team in receptions after Santana Moss, Chris Cooley, Ladell Betts, and Antwaan Randle El. If not for Adam Archuleta, Lloyd would have been the biggest bust of Washington's 2006 free-agent class.

Brandon Marshall Height: 6-4 Weight: 230 College: UCF Draft: 2006/4 (119) Born: 23-Mar-1984 Age: 23 Risk: Green

Year	Team	G	Rec	Pass	Yds	C%	Yd/C	TD	YAC	Rk	DVOA	Rk	DPAR	Rk	PAR	Short	Mid	Deep	Bomb
2006	DEN	15	20	37	309	54%	15.5	2	5.2	—	-6.0%	—	2.3	—	2.8	22%	44%	25%	8%
2007	DEN		41		559		13.6	4											

Jake Plummer might find this hard to believe, but Mike Shanahan feels loyalty to his veterans. How can we be sure of that? Because Shanahan kept Rod Smith in the starting lineup last season long after it became clear that Marshall was younger, faster, and better. The only thing stopping Marshall and Jay Cutler from becoming the next great Broncos passing combination is Marshall's behavior off the field: He was arrested on suspicion of false imprisonment and domestic violence during the offseason, and, although the charges were dropped, he had to attend anger-management classes. Let's hope Marshall can get his act together, for his sake, for the Broncos' sake, and, most important, for his girlfriend's sake.

Ruvell Martin Height: 6-5 Weight: 215 College: Saginaw Valley State Draft: 2004/FA Born: 12-Mar-1981 Age: 26 Risk: Yellow

Year	Team	G	Rec	Pass	Yds	C%	Yd/C	TD	YAC	Rk	DVOA	Rk	DPAR	Rk	PAR	Short	Mid	Deep	Bomb
2006	GB	13	21	43	358	49%	17.0	1	4.2	—	11.8%	—	7.3	—	6.0	24%	49%	17%	10%
2007	GB		41		647		15.6	3											

The transition from Saginaw Valley State to the NFL is a big one, and Martin needed time on the practice squad and in NFL Europe to make it, but three years after leaving school, and two years after catching on as an undrafted free agent, Martin filled in admirably following injuries to Robert Ferguson and Greg Jennings. Martin's built like a prototypical wide receiver, but his route running is still inconsistent. Ferguson's return may knock him down a slot on the depth chart.

Derrick Mason Height: 5-10 Weight: 190 College: Michigan State Draft: 1997/4 (98) Born: 17-Jan-1974 Age: 33 Risk: Red

Year	Team	G	Rec	Pass	Yds	C%	Yd/C	TD	YAC	Rk	DVOA	Rk	DPAR	Rk	PAR	Short	Mid	Deep	Bomb
2004	TEN	16	96	158	1168	61%	12.2	7	—	—	5.0%	43	22.1	23	25.5	—	—	—	—
2005	BAL	16	86	135	1073	64%	12.5	3	2.5	83	10.4%	26	21.6	19	20.4	35%	36%	23%	7%
2006	BAL	16	68	112	750	61%	11.0	2	2.0	80	-1.8%	53	9.9	45	11.1	31%	52%	10%	7%
2007	BAL		56		719		12.9	3											

In many ways, Mason was a perfect signing for the Ravens. Not a flashy receiver, he fits into their blue-collar offense and knows his role in a tight end–dominated passing game. He's also a good mentor for Mark Clayton, who is a similar type of receiver. Plus, Mason's history with Steve McNair provided a natural fit. The results were about what you'd expect—decent production and a willingness to cede the ball to Todd Heap and others in the red zone. Never a receiver who relies solely on speed, Mason looks to have a few good years left at age 33.

Jerome Mathis Height: 5-11 Weight: 181 College: Hampton Draft: 2005/4 (114) Born: 26-Jun-1983 Age: 24 Risk: Red

Year	Team	G	Rec	Pass	Yds	C%	Yd/C	TD	YAC	Rk	DVOA	Rk	DPAR	Rk	PAR	Short	Mid	Deep	Bomb
2005	HOU	12	5	13	65	38%	13.0	1	1.7	—	-37.0%	—	-1.8	—	-1.2	33%	33%	22%	11%
2007	HOU		16		210		13.9	1											

Mathis followed up his rookie performance as a Pro Bowl kick returner by participating in the second-most-important motorcycle accident of the 2006 offseason. In June he had surgery for a stress fracture in his left foot, although team doctors insist the injury took place during the Pro Bowl and not in the accident. Either way, surgery that was supposed to cost him the first month of the season ended up costing him the first three. So much for that idea that the Texans didn't need Reggie Bush because they already had a Pro Bowl–caliber return man. Mathis will return to the offense in 2007, and stress fractures don't have a high rate of recurrence, but don't expect anything more than a few deep routes out of him.

Keenan McCardell Height: 6-1 Weight: 191 College: UNLV Draft: 1991/12 (326) Born: 6-Jan-1970 Age: 37 Risk: Red

Year	Team	G	Rec	Pass	Yds	C%	Yd/C	TD	YAC	Rk	DVOA	Rk	DPAR	Rk	PAR	Short	Mid	Deep	Bomb
2004	SD	7	31	58	393	53%	12.7	1	—	—	-12.8%	67	1.2	68	3.4	—	—	—	—
2005	SD	16	70	108	917	65%	13.1	9	2.5	80	28.1%	3	30.8	7	28.3	28%	45%	19%	9%
2006	SD	14	36	51	437	71%	12.1	0	2.3	79	13.2%	24	9.6	47	9.5	26%	52%	16%	6%
2007	FA		11		120		11.1	1											

(continued next page)

Keenan McCardell *(continued)*

McCardell struggled with injuries throughout the 2006 season, which is what happens when you get old: You get hurt more, you take longer to recover, and you don't always make it all the way back. The Chargers phased him out of the offense as the season went along and had handed his role to Vincent Jackson by the time the playoffs rolled around. McCardell's career path has been so strange up to this point that it's hard to ever fully write him off. He might still be useful as a possession receiver, but no team should be depending upon him for production.

Justin McCareins Height: 6-2 Weight: 215 College: Northern Illinois   Draft: 2001/4 (124) Born: 11-Dec-1978 Age: 28   Risk: Red

Year	Team	G	Rec	Pass	Yds	C%	Yd/C	TD	YAC	Rk	DVOA	Rk	DPAR	Rk	PAR	Short	Mid	Deep	Bomb
2004	NYJ	16	56	90	770	62%	13.8	4	—	—	19.8%	23	20.8	27	20.0	—	—	—	—
2005	NYJ	16	43	102	713	42%	16.6	2	3.1	58	-8.6%	66	4.2	63	2.8	22%	35%	23%	20%
2006	NYJ	16	23	39	347	59%	15.1	1	4.1	—	4.0%	—	5.0	—	4.5	28%	31%	15%	26%
2007	*NYJ*		*29*		*344*		*11.9*	*2*											

Justin McCareins showed up to Eric Mangini's first training camp trying to hide his gut like he was a pregnant meerkat. While Mangini probably didn't need to sniff him to figure out what was up, he did open up a nice spot for McCareins in his doghouse. Lesson: First impressions are important. While the old regime thought McCareins was worth a second-round pick, the new doesn't thinks he's worth much at all. He avoided being a cap casualty, but will struggle to get a significant number of looks with Leon Washington, Tim Dwight, and Brad Smith all wanting the ball. Still, he's put up nice numbers in the past, and could be useful once again.

Shaun McDonald Height: 5-10 Weight: 183 College: Arizona State   Draft: 2003/4 (106) Born: 13-Jun-1981 Age: 26   Risk: Red

Year	Team	G	Rec	Pass	Yds	C%	Yd/C	TD	YAC	Rk	DVOA	Rk	DPAR	Rk	PAR	Short	Mid	Deep	Bomb
2004	STL	16	37	68	494	54%	13.4	3	—	—	-0.6%	49	6.3	50	5.5	—	—	—	—
2005	STL	16	46	74	523	62%	11.4	0	3.0	63	-0.6%	54	7.1	55	8.0	26%	53%	18%	3%
2006	STL	16	13	19	136	68%	10.5	1	1.2	—	-14.1%	—	0.1	—	0.3	42%	37%	11%	11%
2007	*DET*		*16*		*223*		*13.8*	*1*											

McDonald bolted for the Lions and a reunion with Mike Martz after seeing his catch totals plummet in 2006. He was a decent option in Martz's St. Louis offenses, but changes in the coaching staff and thus the scheme turned him into a mediocrity.

Billy McMullen Height: 6-4 Weight: 210 College: Virginia   Draft: 2003/3 (95) Born: 8-Mar-1980 Age: 27   Risk: Red

Year	Team	G	Rec	Pass	Yds	C%	Yd/C	TD	YAC	Rk	DVOA	Rk	DPAR	Rk	PAR	Short	Mid	Deep	Bomb
2004	PHI	9	3	17	24	18%	8.0	0	—	—	-79.5%	—	-7.8	—	-8.5	—	—	—	—
2005	PHI	16	18	40	268	48%	14.9	1	2.0	—	-15.5%	—	-0.1	—	0.1	42%	23%	16%	19%
2006	MIN	16	23	42	307	57%	13.3	2	4.2	—	4.5%	—	5.1	—	4.6	39%	39%	11%	11%
2007	*MIN*		*32*		*349*		*10.9*	*2*											

The Vikings traded talented rookie and undrafted free agent Hank Bassett for McMullen, a much ridiculed move that seemingly spoke to Brad Childress's prioritization of system over talent. The trade was a mistake, but McMullen ran the right routes, caught the balls thrown to him, and generally acquitted himself well. The exodus of other receivers this off-season means McMullen will get more consistent playing time in 2007. The more the Vikings ask of him, the more his limitations—namely a lack of speed—will become obvious.

Robert Meachem Height: 6-2 Weight: 214 College: Tennessee   Draft: 2007/1 (27) Born: 28-Sep-1984 Age: 23   Risk: Red

Year	Team	G	Rec	Pass	Yds	C%	Yd/C	TD	YAC	Rk	DVOA	Rk	DPAR	Rk	PAR	Short	Mid	Deep	Bomb
2007	*NO*		*28*		*448*		*15.8*	*3*											

The Saints were thrilled when Meacham was still on the board at the end of the first round of this year's draft. "He was our highest-rated player on the board when we picked—significantly," General Manager Mickey Loomis said. "To be honest, we were surprised when he was available to us at 27." Meacham is big, has good hands, and is a precise route runner. He doesn't have an exceptional burst, but he projects as a possession target who can catch 70 passes per year and be a quarterback's best friend. Unfortunately, his NFL career got off to a bad start when he came to minicamp overweight, then had arthroscopic surgery to clean out loose cartilage in his knee and to repair his medical meniscus. He should return for training camp, barring complications.

Clarence Moore   Height: 6-5   Weight: 211   College: Northern Arizona   Draft: 2004/6 (199)   Born: 24-Sep-1982   Age: 25   Risk: Red

Year	Team	G	Rec	Pass	Yds	C%	Yd/C	TD	YAC	Rk	DVOA	Rk	DPAR	Rk	PAR	Short	Mid	Deep	Bomb
2004	BAL	15	24	56	293	41%	12.2	4	—	—	-20.0%	75	-2.2	74	-4.1	—	—	—	—
2005	BAL	4	3	19	59	16%	19.7	0	1.3	—	-64.4%	—	-6.2	—	-6.1	0%	39%	39%	22%
2006	BAL	10	2	6	1	33%	0.5	1	0.0	—	-63.0%	—	-1.8	—	-1.9	50%	17%	17%	17%
2007	*BAL*		*8*		*107*		*12.6*	*0*											

Moore remains a 6-foot-5 project after three years in the league. Miami showed some interest in signing him as a restricted free agent, but he went back to the Ravens. Moore, Devard Darling, Ron Johnson, LaMont Brightful—the Ravens have a terrible record of developing young wide receivers.

Aaron Moorehead   Height: 6-3   Weight: 200   College: Illinois   Draft: 2003/FA   Born: 5-Nov-1980   Age: 27   Risk: Red

Year	Team	G	Rec	Pass	Yds	C%	Yd/C	TD	YAC	Rk	DVOA	Rk	DPAR	Rk	PAR	Short	Mid	Deep	Bomb
2004	IND	7	1	3	7	33%	7.0	0	—	—	-49.2%	—	-0.8	—	-0.8	—	—	—	—
2005	IND	2	7	11	75	64%	10.7	0	-0.5	—	-4.5%	—	0.8	—	0.9	0%	100%	0%	0%
2006	IND	12	8	16	82	50%	10.3	1	1.1	—	-17.1%	—	-0.2	—	-0.3	43%	36%	7%	14%
2007	*IND*		*16*		*216*		*13.5*	*1*											

Moorehead plays the role of "white guy who isn't anywhere near as good as Brandon Stokley, but catches ten passes because Peyton Manning is a demigod." In the event that Moorehead is not able to fulfill his duties as Mr. No Depth Indianapolis, the crown shall fall to the first runner-up, John Standeford.

Johnnie Morant   Height: 6-4   Weight: 229   College: Syracuse   Draft: 2004/5 (134)   Born: 7-Dec-1981   Age: 26   Risk: Red

Year	Team	G	Rec	Pass	Yds	C%	Yd/C	TD	YAC	Rk	DVOA	Rk	DPAR	Rk	PAR	Short	Mid	Deep	Bomb
2004	OAK	4	1	2	20	50%	20.0	0	—	—	21.1%	—	0.5	—	0.6	—	—	—	—
2006	OAK	11	7	12	70	58%	10.0	0	3.4	—	-68.6%	—	-4.3	—	-4.2	42%	50%	8%	0%
2007	*OAK*		*9*		*102*		*11.5*	*0*											

It doesn't get much worse than catching seven passes and losing fumbles on two of them. Morant had multiple "incidents" in college and has struggled to learn the Raiders' playbook, but he's a big guy who's fast, so he's gotten two years of chances. He's probably not going to make it to three.

Randy Moss   Height: 6-4   Weight: 200   College: Marshall   Draft: 1998/1 (21)   Born: 13-Feb-1977   Age: 30   Risk: Yellow

Year	Team	G	Rec	Pass	Yds	C%	Yd/C	TD	YAC	Rk	DVOA	Rk	DPAR	Rk	PAR	Short	Mid	Deep	Bomb
2004	MIN	13	49	86	767	57%	15.7	13	—	—	24.1%	15	23.1	22	21.5	—	—	—	—
2005	OAK	16	60	124	1005	48%	16.8	8	2.6	74	6.0%	36	16.9	24	16.4	13%	38%	28%	22%
2006	OAK	13	42	97	553	43%	13.2	3	2.7	67	-13.7%	67	0.8	68	0.8	12%	49%	20%	19%
2007	*NE*		*61*		*911*		*15.0*	*7*											

Even if he could be motivated to play hard, does Moss still have it? He's not the dominating physical presence he once was, as both his vertical leap and his straight-line speed seem to have lost something. Three things favor a rebound in New England: a better quarterback, a better locker room environment, and a better playing surface. Moss was always better on artificial turf than grass, and the Patriots switched to Field Turf after their midseason Mud Bowl against the Jets last year. A better Moss still won't be the Moss of olden days, however, and there's a good chance that Donte' Stallworth, not Moss, will be the best of New England's new receiver acquisitions.

Santana Moss   Height: 5-10   Weight: 185   College: Miami   Draft: 2001/1 (16)   Born: 1-Jun-1979   Age: 28   Risk: Green

Year	Team	G	Rec	Pass	Yds	C%	Yd/C	TD	YAC	Rk	DVOA	Rk	DPAR	Rk	PAR	Short	Mid	Deep	Bomb
2004	NYJ	15	45	78	838	58%	18.6	5	—	—	32.6%	8	24.6	18	22.9	—	—	—	—
2005	WAS	16	84	134	1483	63%	17.7	9	7.4	4	27.5%	5	37.2	3	36.2	41%	35%	11%	13%
2006	WAS	14	55	100	790	54%	14.4	6	4.3	26	-2.0%	54	8.9	49	10.3	31%	38%	17%	14%
2007	*WAS*		*60*		*864*		*14.4*	*6*											

The Redskins are often lambasted for their personnel philosophy, which generally eschews the draft for high-priced free agents and cap-busting trades. At first, the Moss-for-Laveranues Coles deal seemed like a one-sided trade favoring the Jets, but Moss finished 2005 ranked third in DPAR among receivers and was the primary reason the Redskins offense didn't

(continued next page)

Santana Moss *(continued)*

implode on an improbable run to the NFC Divisional Playoffs. Moss struggled last season, but that was due to constant double teams and a new 700-page offensive playbook courtesy of Al Saunders. With a year in the system and an entire off-season of working with starting quarterback Jason Campbell, Moss should return to the form that made him one of the league's best wide receivers two years ago.

Sinorice Moss
Height: 5-8 Weight: 185 College: Miami   **Draft: 2006/2 (44)   Born: 28-Dec-1983   Age: 23   Risk: Red**

Year	Team	G	Rec	Pass	Yds	C%	Yd/C	TD	YAC	Rk	DVOA	Rk	DPAR	Rk	PAR	Short	Mid	Deep	Bomb
2006	NYG	6	5	11	25	45%	5.0	0	4.6	—	-59.4%	—	-3.5	—	-3.7	70%	0%	0%	30%
2007	NYG		27		375		13.9	2											

Moss had a disappointing rookie season, missing ten games with a quadriceps injury. He was expected to see time as the number-three receiver and maybe on the return teams. Instead, the Giants were forced to rely more on Tim Carter and David Tyree (especially after losing Amani Toomer for the season on November 5), and the passing game sputtered at times. With Chad Morton no longer with the team, Moss will return kicks and punts, and, depending on Toomer's health, could move all the way up to number two on the depth chart. If Toomer is fully recovered from his ACL injury, Moss should start the season in the slot.

Eric Moulds
Height: 6-2 Weight: 210 College: Mississippi State   **Draft: 1996/1 (24)   Born: 17-Jul-1973   Age: 34   Risk: Red**

Year	Team	G	Rec	Pass	Yds	C%	Yd/C	TD	YAC	Rk	DVOA	Rk	DPAR	Rk	PAR	Short	Mid	Deep	Bomb
2004	BUF	16	88	152	1043	58%	11.9	5	—	—	-4.0%	54	11.1	45	10.5	—	—	—	—
2005	BUF	15	81	129	816	63%	10.1	4	3.2	52	-7.4%	64	6.5	56	6.8	40%	43%	10%	8%
2006	HOU	16	57	77	557	74%	9.8	1	3.6	40	6.3%	38	10.9	44	9.5	54%	36%	7%	3%
2007	FA		19		224		11.8	1											

Moulds's speed and ability to get open deep have been declining for years, leaving the Bills with a veteran possession receiver who still thought of himself as a superstar. When the Texans picked Moulds up as a salary-cap casualty, they somehow managed to convince him that he actually was a veteran possession receiver. As a result, Moulds had his best season in years, and his first positive DVOA since 2000. The fact that the Texans released him after the season only emphasizes that, despite the good year, a rebuilding team never really had anything to gain by bringing in a 33-year-old wide receiver in the first place. Moulds will end up somewhere in August, possibly Tennessee.

Muhsin Muhammad
Height: 6-2 Weight: 217 College: Michigan State   **Draft: 1996/2 (43)   Born: 5-May-1973   Age: 34   Risk: Yellow**

Year	Team	G	Rec	Pass	Yds	C%	Yd/C	TD	YAC	Rk	DVOA	Rk	DPAR	Rk	PAR	Short	Mid	Deep	Bomb
2004	CAR	16	93	160	1405	58%	15.1	16	—	—	23.8%	16	41.5	3	43.2	—	—	—	—
2005	CHI	15	64	136	750	47%	11.7	4	2.5	81	-15.8%	80	-1.0	81	-2.7	31%	35%	18%	15%
2006	CHI	16	60	117	863	51%	14.4	5	3.1	55	1.5%	45	12.9	37	12.9	21%	42%	28%	9%
2007	CHI		69		985		14.2	6											

The enormous contract Muhammad received before 2005 remains a mistake given his advanced age, but his 2006 season was at least more like what the Bears had in mind. The drops that plagued Muhammad in 2005 almost disappeared, and he provided a consistent midrange threat. As Rod Smith proved last year, when it goes for a wide receiver, it can go in a hurry. The projection appears to think Muhammad will continue to be productive for at least another season, but proceed with caution.

Martin Nance
Height: 6-5 Weight: 215 College: Miami (Ohio)   **Draft: 2006/FA   Born: 26-May-1983 Age: 24   Risk: Red**

Year	Team	G	Rec	Pass	Yds	C%	Yd/C	TD	YAC	Rk	DVOA	Rk	DPAR	Rk	PAR	Short	Mid	Deep	Bomb
2006	MIN	1	4	7	33	57%	8.3	0	3.5	—	-75.3%	—	-2.9	—	-3.0	14%	71%	0%	14%
2007	MIN		28		278		10.0	2											

Nance looked like a comer after his 2003 season at Miami of Ohio (where he played with Ben Roethlisberger), but he tore his ACL in 2004 and wasn't fully back as a senior in 2005, so he went undrafted. Buffalo picked him up, waived him, and his agent smartly directed him to Minnesota, land of no wideouts. Standing 6-foot-4 and with excellent hands, Nance is the possession receiver the Vikings lack. He got on the field in Week 17, and don't be surprised if he ends up seeing significant playing time for the Vikings this year. Worth a late-round flyer in deep fantasy leagues.

Dennis Northcutt

Height: 5-11 Weight: 175 College: Arizona **Draft: 2000/2 (32) Born: 22-Dec-1977 Age: 29 Risk: Red**

Year	Team	G	Rec	Pass	Yds	C%	Yd/C	TD	YAC	Rk	DVOA	Rk	DPAR	Rk	PAR	Short	Mid	Deep	Bomb
2004	CLE	16	55	94	806	59%	14.7	2	—	—	-5.4%	56	5.7	53	4.6	—	—	—	—
2005	CLE	16	42	77	441	55%	10.5	2	3.1	55	-18.5%	83	-1.9	85	-2.8	32%	46%	7%	16%
2006	CLE	13	22	45	228	49%	10.4	0	4.3	—	-31.4%	—	-4.8	—	-4.3	44%	37%	5%	14%
2007	JAC		12		157		12.7	1											

After seven seasons in Cleveland, Northcutt has moved on to Jacksonville, where he'll be a decent slot receiver and, if needed, a punt returner. He'll also be by far the shortest receiver in a corps of giants.

Terrell Owens

Height: 6-3 Weight: 226 College: Ten-Chattanooga **Draft: 1996/3 (89) Born: 7-Dec-1973 Age: 34 Risk: Green**

Year	Team	G	Rec	Pass	Yds	C%	Yd/C	TD	YAC	Rk	DVOA	Rk	DPAR	Rk	PAR	Short	Mid	Deep	Bomb
2004	PHI	14	77	127	1200	61%	15.6	14	—	—	23.2%	17	31.9	10	28.7	—	—	—	—
2005	PHI	7	47	92	763	51%	16.2	6	7.7	2	8.0%	32	13.6	27	11.5	32%	41%	14%	13%
2006	DAL	16	85	152	1180	56%	13.9	13	4.3	23	12.1%	29	27.3	8	28.6	36%	27%	23%	14%
2007	DAL		71		938		13.2	8											

Owens's DVOA on third and fourth downs was 43.0 percent. The raw numbers are exceptional: 43 passes, 25 catches, 409 yards, 24 first downs, four of them touchdowns. Owens was also excellent in the red zone (30.1 percent DVOA). On first and second downs, however, he was just league average. The Cowboys sometimes threw him short passes on early downs just to "get him involved," and, too frequently, he dropped them because of a hand injury that bothered him all season.

Weirder than T.O.'s case of the dropsies was his complete absence during an offseason of endless news stories involving NFL players with character problems. Owens emerged from his silence only to issue a meager vote of confidence to the new Cowboys coaching staff. There are competing theories about what was really going on. Theory 1: The NFL's most over-exposed stars play Distraction Tag, and Michael Vick is now "It." Theory 2: After running Bill Parcells out of town, Owens views Wade Philips as small game unworthy of his unique franchise-killing skills. Theory 3: Former "publicist" Kim Etheridge has him tied to a bed somewhere, a la Kathy Bates in *Misery*. From a just-desserts standpoint, we prefer Theory 3, but the truth is probably far simpler. Sometimes, even T.O. needs a T.O. from T.O.

Eric Parker

Height: 6-0 Weight: 180 College: Tennessee **Draft: 2002/FA Born: 14-Apr-1979 Age: 28 Risk: Red**

Year	Team	G	Rec	Pass	Yds	C%	Yd/C	TD	YAC	Rk	DVOA	Rk	DPAR	Rk	PAR	Short	Mid	Deep	Bomb
2004	SD	15	47	71	690	66%	14.7	4	—	—	18.8%	26	16.2	36	18.6	—	—	—	—
2005	SD	16	57	80	725	71%	12.7	3	2.9	65	28.8%	2	23.4	15	22.5	25%	49%	17%	9%
2006	SD	15	48	70	659	69%	13.7	0	2.5	71	26.6%	7	19.2	20	20.8	23%	43%	21%	13%
2007	SD		50		767		15.3	3											

Is Parker the league's most underrated receiver? You hardly ever hear him mentioned as one of the NFL's elite, but his stats say that if he got enough passes thrown his way, he'd belong in that category. Parker knows how to move the chains: Of his 48 catches last year, 35 went for first downs. Vincent Jackson will pass him on the depth chart to become San Diego's number-one receiver, but Parker will stay in the starting lineup and continue to quietly help the Chargers win games.

Samie Parker

Height: 5-10 Weight: 178 College: Oregon **Draft: 2004/4 (105) Born: 25-Mar-1981 Age: 26 Risk: Red**

Year	Team	G	Rec	Pass	Yds	C%	Yd/C	TD	YAC	Rk	DVOA	Rk	DPAR	Rk	PAR	Short	Mid	Deep	Bomb
2004	KC	4	9	13	137	69%	15.2	1	—	—	36.8%	—	4.5	—	5.0	—	—	—	—
2005	KC	12	36	58	533	62%	14.8	3	1.9	88	9.2%	28	9.5	45	9.3	13%	54%	28%	6%
2006	KC	16	41	68	561	60%	13.7	1	3.0	58	20.0%	13	15.8	32	15.0	27%	42%	22%	10%
2007	KC		35		399		11.4	2											

The Chiefs threw 20 passes to Parker on first downs last season. He caught 17 of them for 205 yards, earning a DVOA of 34.0 percent. First downs aside, Parker had a remarkably quiet year for a receiver who started 16 games. He scored just one touchdown, caught just two passes of more than 30 yards, and endured a four-game stretch in which he caught only one pass per week. The Chiefs' cloud-of-dust offense is partially to blame for Parker's low totals, but the bloom has faded from Parker's prospect rose, and he hasn't developed into the big-play receiver the Chiefs were expecting. He's a third-wideout type who will lose his job as soon as the Chiefs realize that there are better ways to move the ball than to give it to the same guy 40 times per game. Indeed, April minicamp saw Parker on the outs.

Roscoe Parrish Height: 5-9 Weight: 168 College: Miami Draft: 2005/2 (55) Born: 16-Jul-1982 Age: 25 Risk: Red

Year	Team	G	Rec	Pass	Yds	C%	Yd/C	TD	YAC	Rk	DVOA	Rk	DPAR	Rk	PAR	Short	Mid	Deep	Bomb
2005	BUF	10	15	25	148	60%	9.9	1	3.8	—	-12.6%	—	0.4	—	0.3	58%	21%	16%	5%
2006	BUF	16	23	40	320	58%	13.9	2	5.3	—	-14.5%	—	0.0	—	-0.8	37%	43%	6%	14%
2007	BUF		38		453		11.9	2											

Parrish's yards per catch on turf are double what they are on grass. He would be more productive if he could use his speed to get deep while defenses are concentrating on Lee Evans. The flip side of being fast, however, is being small. J. P. Losman threw only nine percent of his passes the 5-foot-9, 168-pounder's way, but passes to Parrish were responsible for 25 percent of the passes tipped at the line of scrimmage, perhaps because of Losman's attempt to avoid overthrowing the little guy.

David Patten Height: 5-10 Weight: 190 College: Western Carolina Draft: 1997/FA Born: 19-Aug-1974 Age: 33 Risk: Red

Year	Team	G	Rec	Pass	Yds	C%	Yd/C	TD	YAC	Rk	DVOA	Rk	DPAR	Rk	PAR	Short	Mid	Deep	Bomb
2004	NE	16	44	95	800	46%	18.2	7	—	—	15.5%	30	18.6	32	17.2	—	—	—	—
2005	WAS	9	22	53	217	42%	9.9	0	4.6	21	-40.2%	89	-8.9	89	-10.9	35%	47%	12%	7%
2006	WAS	5	1	4	25	25%	25.0	0	0.0	—	-21.7%	—	-0.2	—	-0.2	50%	0%	50%	0%
2007	NO		9		125		13.4	0											

The Redskins signed Patten in 2005 with the hope that he would be just as dangerous in Washington as he was in New England the previous four seasons. Injuries torpedoed his chances of seeing the field—last season he caught only one pass—and the club released him this March. Patten caught on with New Orleans, but a younger version of him already exists there in Terrence Copper.

Tab Perry Height: 6-2 Weight: 229 College: UCLA Draft: 2005/6 (190) Born: 20-Jan-1982 Age: 25 Risk: Red

Year	Team	G	Rec	Pass	Yds	C%	Yd/C	TD	YAC	Rk	DVOA	Rk	DPAR	Rk	PAR	Short	Mid	Deep	Bomb
2005	CIN	16	4	5	21	80%	5.2	1	10.0	—	-15.0%	—	0.0	—	0.1	100%	0%	0%	0%
2006	CIN	2	5	6	81	83%	16.2	0	9.4	—	44.5%	—	2.4	—	2.4	50%	33%	0%	17%
2007	CIN		15		205		13.6	1											

If Perry is fully recovered from the hip injury that landed him on injured reserve just two games into the 2006 season, he should resume his duties as the team's top kick-returner. With Kelley Washington gone and Chris Henry suspended through Week 9, he also gets to battle Antonio Chatman for the Bengals' slot receiver job. Right now, we're projecting Chatman in that role, but whoever gets it is a fantasy sleeper.

Jerry Porter Height: 6-2 Weight: 220 College: West Virginia Draft: 2000/2 (47) Born: 14-Jul-1978 Age: 29 Risk: Yellow

Year	Team	G	Rec	Pass	Yds	C%	Yd/C	TD	YAC	Rk	DVOA	Rk	DPAR	Rk	PAR	Short	Mid	Deep	Bomb
2004	OAK	16	64	136	998	47%	15.6	9	—	—	-9.5%	64	5.3	56	6.9	—	—	—	—
2005	OAK	16	76	142	942	54%	12.4	5	2.9	64	-4.6%	59	9.4	46	8.5	28%	43%	23%	6%
2006	OAK	4	1	4	19	25%	19.0	0	0.0	—	-33.7%	—	-0.4	—	-0.4	0%	50%	25%	25%
2007	OAK		49		671		13.7	4											

A brief recap: Last season Porter publicly lobbied for a trade, criticized the coaching staff to anyone who would listen, parked in Al Davis's spot, wore a middle-finger T-shirt to practice, got benched for the season opener, cheered for the Chargers as they blew out the Raiders, earned a four-game suspension from Davis, was sent to play on the scout team, and, unsurprisingly, spent the whole season in the doghouse. Some of his bad behavior can be explained by the circus atmosphere that Davis almost encourages, but Porter was going out of his way to be a nitwit, and 31 potential employers took note. Porter still has the talent to be a top wideout, but not even US Airways can overlook this much baggage.

Peerless Price Height: 5-11 Weight: 190 College: Tennessee Draft: 1999/2 (53) Born: 27-Oct-1976 Age: 31 Risk: Yellow

Year	Team	G	Rec	Pass	Yds	C%	Yd/C	TD	YAC	Rk	DVOA	Rk	DPAR	Rk	PAR	Short	Mid	Deep	Bomb
2004	ATL	16	45	106	575	42%	12.8	3	—	—	-26.9%	78	-8.3	83	-7.8	—	—	—	—
2005	DAL	7	6	10	96	70%	16.0	0	4.2	—	48.3%	—	4.1	—	4.1	33%	33%	11%	22%
2006	BUF	16	49	77	402	64%	8.2	3	2.6	70	-12.4%	66	1.0	67	-1.0	34%	45%	16%	4%
2007	BUF		35		295		8.3	2											

The grumpy wideout better known as "Cheerless" didn't show much hunger for contact in his return to Buffalo. Price was employed primarily on screens and swing passes, throws he would summarily run with for two yards before being taken down. He immediately stepped out of bounds after making a catch seven different times—matching the combined total for Lee Evans, Josh Reed, and Roscoe Parrish. This led to Loser League specials such as Week 10 (three catches for 13 yards) and Week 12 (three catches for ten yards), plus a ridiculous record on third down: ten passes, 32 yards, only one first down. Price's average of 8.2 yards per catch was the lowest figure for a receiver in the NFL last year; the only other qualifying receivers who averaged less than ten yards per catch were Eric Moulds and Troy Brown, both of whom are looking for work as we go to press. Bills fans should hope that Price is doing the same come September.

Antwaan Randle El   Height: 5-10 Weight: 186 College: Indiana   Draft: 2002/2 (62) Born: 17-Aug-1979 Age: 28 Risk: Yellow

Year	Team	G	Rec	Pass	Yds	C%	Yd/C	TD	YAC	Rk	DVOA	Rk	DPAR	Rk	PAR	Short	Mid	Deep	Bomb
2004	PIT	16	43	62	601	68%	14.0	3	—	—	16.1%	28	12.5	42	12.3	—	—	—	—
2005	PIT	16	35	70	558	50%	15.9	1	6.0	8	-14.8%	77	0.2	75	1.2	25%	39%	23%	13%
2006	WAS	16	32	63	351	51%	11.0	3	2.3	75	-21.0%	77	-2.5	77	-2.4	42%	23%	21%	14%
2007	WAS		42		638		15.3	3											

Randle El has proven that he is a capable number-three NFL wide receiver, and his first season in Washington did nothing to change that perception. His 2006 numbers are eerily similar to his 2005 production with the Steelers: Among the league's worst in terms of DPAR, and a 50 percent Catch Rate. Such output usually doesn't garner $10 million in guarantees on a new deal, but Randle El excels as a punt returner. He has five career punt-return touchdowns in as many seasons, including an 87-yarder against the Colts last year. Randle El is nothing more than an adequate slot receiver, but his versatility—he was a college quarterback—and his big-play return abilities make him an asset.

Josh Reed   Height: 5-10 Weight: 208 College: LSU   Draft: 2002/2 (36) Born: 1-May-1980 Age: 27 Risk: Yellow

Year	Team	G	Rec	Pass	Yds	C%	Yd/C	TD	YAC	Rk	DVOA	Rk	DPAR	Rk	PAR	Short	Mid	Deep	Bomb
2004	BUF	12	16	36	153	44%	9.6	0	—	—	-36.8%	—	-5.1	—	-5.7	—	—	—	—
2005	BUF	16	32	53	449	60%	14.0	2	6.5	6	9.9%	27	8.9	48	9.6	40%	43%	15%	2%
2006	BUF	13	34	48	410	71%	12.1	2	4.4	—	12.5%	—	8.4	—	8.2	51%	33%	11%	4%
2007	BUF		37		319		8.5	2											

Reed struggled with injuries in 2006, including a bruised kidney, but was effective when he was actually on the field. He's a little too small to get a reliable jump off the line, which means that he's unlikely to develop into anything more than a slot receiver, and could get pushed by Roscoe Parrish based upon Parrish's theoretical big-play potential.

Sidney Rice   Height: 6-4 Weight: 200 College: South Carolina   Draft: 2007/2 (44) Born: 1-Sep-1986 Age: 21 Risk: Red

Year	Team	G	Rec	Pass	Yds	C%	Yd/C	TD	YAC	Rk	DVOA	Rk	DPAR	Rk	PAR	Short	Mid	Deep	Bomb
2007	MIN		39		548		13.9	4											

Back when Steve Spurrier coached at Florida, the Gators churned out wide receiver prospects by the hectare. Many of these receivers never panned out in the NFL because they were products of the fun-'n'-gun system who didn't have the toughness or route discipline to succeed in an NFL offense. Spurrier is now at South Carolina, where he coached Rice, a big, fast, productive receiver who doesn't block well, can't take a hit, and isn't very precise as a route runner. In other words, he's Travis Taylor Junior, and he must change his stripes to succeed in a tightly controlled, short-passing offense such as the one run by Brad Childress.

Koren Robinson   Height: 6-1 Weight: 205 College: North Carolina State   Draft: 2001/1 (9) Born: 19-Mar-1980 Age: 27 Risk: Red

Year	Team	G	Rec	Pass	Yds	C%	Yd/C	TD	YAC	Rk	DVOA	Rk	DPAR	Rk	PAR	Short	Mid	Deep	Bomb
2004	SEA	10	31	67	495	46%	16.0	2	—	—	-0.3%	48	6.3	51	4.9	—	—	—	—
2005	MIN	14	22	37	347	59%	15.8	1	5.1	—	5.9%	—	4.9	—	3.6	41%	25%	13%	22%
2006	GB	4	7	16	89	44%	12.7	0	2.7	—	-9.6%	—	0.6	—	0.7	19%	38%	31%	13%
2007	GB		12		167		13.6	1											

Robinson appeared to turn his life around following various substance-abuse problems and even made the Pro Bowl as a kick-return man in 2005. Sadly, alcoholism can be a tougher opponent than anyone in the NFL, and Robinson was picked up for drunk driving during the Vikings' training camp last year. Still in the shadow of the "Love Boat" and "whizzinator" incidents, the Vikings let him go. In a lesson the Titans may want to ponder in deciding the future of Pac-Man Jones, Robinson was promptly signed by division rival Green Bay. Robinson played sparingly last year before getting hit with a one-year suspension. He will become eligible to play in late September and wants to remain with Green Bay. Hopefully he can conquer his personal demons and return as an effective role player. Still only 27, he may still have a future in the NFL.

Laurent Robinson   Height: 6-2   Weight: 199 College: Illinois State   Draft: 2007/3 (75)   Born: 20-May-1985 Age: 22   Risk: Red

Year	Team	G	Rec	Pass	Yds	C%	Yd/C	TD	YAC	Rk	DVOA	Rk	DPAR	Rk	PAR	Short	Mid	Deep	Bomb
2007	ATL		14		206		15.0	0											

Robinson caught 192 passes for 3,007 yards and 29 touchdowns in 43 games at Division I-AA Illinois State and holds a variety of school and Gateway Conference records. He's long and lean and has a reputation as a hard worker in the weight room and film rooms, but doesn't block or beat the jam well. In other words, he's a project who will probably stick as Bobby Petrino puts his stamp on the offensive personnel.

Marcus Robinson   Height: 6-3   Weight: 215 College: South Carolina   Draft: 1997/4 (108) Born: 27-Feb-1975 Age: 32   Risk: Red

Year	Team	G	Rec	Pass	Yds	C%	Yd/C	TD	YAC	Rk	DVOA	Rk	DPAR	Rk	PAR	Short	Mid	Deep	Bomb
2004	MIN	16	47	79	657	59%	14.0	8	—	—	11.9%	36	14.6	38	15.1	—	—	—	—
2005	MIN	15	31	57	515	54%	16.6	5	3.4	44	18.8%	14	12.5	31	11.8	30%	31%	24%	15%
2006	MIN	10	29	58	381	50%	13.1	4	4.1	30	-15.9%	70	-0.3	70	-0.3	33%	31%	19%	17%
2007	DET		18		254		14.0	1											

Robinson led the Vikings last year with a measly four touchdown catches, but was released on Christmas Eve, which may have been a blessing since he was spared the team's 41–21 loss in its season finale. The move came the day after Robinson had criticized Brad Childress, and, while no causal connection has been proved, it was highly suspicious. Robinson is best working down the field, but is now on the wrong side of 30. He caught on with the Lions, but was crowded out by Calvin Johnson's selection and will be their fourth receiver at best.

Ryne Robinson   Height: 5-9   Weight: 179 College: Miami (OH)   Draft: 2007/4 (118) Born: 4-Nov-1984   Age: 23   Risk: Red

Year	Team	G	Rec	Pass	Yds	C%	Yd/C	TD	YAC	Rk	DVOA	Rk	DPAR	Rk	PAR	Short	Mid	Deep	Bomb
2007	CAR		17		235		14.0	2											

Robinson holds the MAC record for punt-return touchdowns, and will start his career on special teams. The former two-sport star (he was a second-team all-MAC outfielder) was productive as a college receiver and may get some opportunities in four-wideout sets.

Courtney Roby   Height: 6-0   Weight: 189 College: Indiana   Draft: 2005/3 (68)   Born: 10-Jan-1983 Age: 24   Risk: Red

Year	Team	G	Rec	Pass	Yds	C%	Yd/C	TD	YAC	Rk	DVOA	Rk	DPAR	Rk	PAR	Short	Mid	Deep	Bomb
2005	TEN	13	21	43	289	49%	13.8	1	1.9	—	-15.7%	—	-0.1	—	0.2	11%	50%	19%	19%
2006	TEN	12	2	7	28	29%	14.0	0	1.0	—	-51.3%	—	-1.7	—	-1.9	17%	33%	17%	33%
2007	TEN		14		188		13.9	1											

One minute you're a rookie wide receiver with dreams of starting. The next minute, you are a special-teams gunner, surpassed by fellow rookies such as Brandon Jones and Roydell Williams, and forgotten by the offensive coordinator. Roby had just two catches in 12 games last year. It's okay, buddy, Karl Hankton hosts a support group on Wednesday nights.

Brad Smith   Height: 6-2   Weight: 210 College: Missouri   Draft: 2006/4 (103) Born: 12-Dec-1983 Age: 23   Risk: Red

Year	Team	G	Rec	Pass	Yds	C%	Yd/C	TD	YAC	Rk	DVOA	Rk	DPAR	Rk	PAR	Short	Mid	Deep	Bomb
2006	NYJ	16	9	14	61	64%	6.8	0	4.1	—	-23.2%	—	-0.8	—	-1.1	58%	42%	0%	0%
2007	NYJ		16		220		13.5	1											

"Slash" players are difficult to evaluate early in their careers because they are used in so many different ways. The Jets listed Smith as a wide receiver, but used all sorts of gadgetry to get him the ball on handoffs. They never threw to him deep, and he saw little action as a return man, but he was effective as a kick gunner, netting 11 special-teams tackles. Another team might have used him as a return man and deep threat, or as a trick-play quarterback, but Eric Mangini liked Smith the Decoy as much or better than he liked Smith the Ball Handler. Smith is quick, creative, and tough, but we don't know much about his hands or route skills based on last season. Still, we liked what little we saw.

Rod Smith   Height: 6-0   Weight: 200 College: Missouri Southern   Draft: 1995/FA   Born: 15-May-1970 Age: 37   Risk: Yellow

Year	Team	G	Rec	Pass	Yds	C%	Yd/C	TD	YAC	Rk	DVOA	Rk	DPAR	Rk	PAR	Short	Mid	Deep	Bomb
2004	DEN	16	79	136	1144	58%	14.5	7	—	—	7.5%	39	20.9	25	23.8	—	—	—	—
2005	DEN	16	85	126	1105	67%	13.0	6	4.9	17	19.6%	12	28.9	10	28.2	37%	50%	8%	5%
2006	DEN	16	52	94	512	55%	9.8	3	2.8	63	-22.1%	78	-4.1	79	-2.1	32%	47%	13%	8%
2007	DEN		28		374		13.4	3											

It's been a great career, but it's time for Mike Shanahan to acknowledge that Smith just doesn't belong on the field anymore. A couple years ago, Shanahan leveled with Jerry Rice and told him he couldn't guarantee him any playing time. He ought to have the same conversation with Smith.

Steve Smith   Height: 5-9   Weight: 179   College: Utah   Draft: 2001/3 (74)   Born: 12-May-1979   Age: 28   Risk: Yellow

Year	Team	G	Rec	Pass	Yds	C%	Yd/C	TD	YAC	Rk	DVOA	Rk	DPAR	Rk	PAR	Short	Mid	Deep	Bomb
2004	CAR	1	6	9	60	67%	10.0	0	—	—	6.4%	—	1.3	—	1.3	—	—	—	—
2005	CAR	16	103	150	1563	69%	15.2	12	7.5	3	32.0%	1	47.8	1	45.6	44%	27%	16%	13%
2006	CAR	14	83	139	1166	60%	14.0	8	5.2	9	9.0%	34	22.5	15	23.2	34%	30%	21%	15%
2007	CAR		88		1241		14.2	7											

What do Smith, John Huston, Teddy Roosevelt, and Ernest Hemingway have in common? A passion for shooting dangerous and nearly extinct animals, of course. In February, while new offensive coordinator Jeff Davidson was telling reporters that Smith would have an even larger role in this year's offense, Smith was polishing his pith helmet for an African safari, a trip he conveniently scheduled to align with the Panthers' conditioning program. Hey, Huston nearly blew off a Humphrey Bogart movie to blast elephants, so who cares if Smith skips a few pushups? Smith can get away with this sort of thing because he's the team's biggest star, and they know he'll be in top condition come training camp. In an unrelated note, as we went to press the Panthers cut undrafted free agent Francis Macomber.

Steven Smith   Height: 6-0   Weight: 197   College: USC   Draft: 2007/2 (51)   Born: 6-May-1985   Age: 22   Risk: Red

Year	Team	G	Rec	Pass	Yds	C%	Yd/C	TD	YAC	Rk	DVOA	Rk	DPAR	Rk	PAR	Short	Mid	Deep	Bomb
2007	NYG		24		309		13.0	1											

Remember the "other" James Stewart—not the one who played for the Jaguars and Lions, or the guy from all those Hitchcock movies, but the University of Miami product who played one year in Minnesota? What about the "other" Ricky Williams: the no-dreadlock, no-yoga, no-ganja running back who spent a year or two in Indy? This "other" Steve Smith is a precise route runner with good straight-line speed, but he's small, lacks lateral quickness, and is a product of the USC system. He's a third-receiver type at best. The Giants may be expecting something more.

Donte' Stallworth   Height: 6-0   Weight: 197   College: Tennessee   Draft: 2002/1 (13)   Born: 10-Nov-1980   Age: 27   Risk: Yellow

Year	Team	G	Rec	Pass	Yds	C%	Yd/C	TD	YAC	Rk	DVOA	Rk	DPAR	Rk	PAR	Short	Mid	Deep	Bomb
2004	NO	16	58	106	767	55%	13.2	5	—	—	-1.0%	50	10.1	46	11.4	—	—	—	—
2005	NO	16	70	129	945	54%	13.5	7	3.3	49	3.7%	44	16.1	25	15.3	21%	48%	23%	8%
2006	PHI	12	38	78	725	49%	19.1	5	5.4	6	7.3%	36	12.2	40	13.6	21%	37%	27%	15%
2007	NE		63		975		15.5	7											

It's unclear whether Stallworth's explosive season—posting a career high in DVOA and averaging nearly 20 yards per reception—was a cause or an effect of the Eagles' big-play offense in 2006. Stallworth actually had a better season in 2005, when he played in every game, than he did last year. In particular, his DPAR and Catch Rate were lower last year, and that kind of feast-or-famine inconsistency may have led the Eagles to let him leave via free agency. By the way, when Donte' Stallworth plays NFL Scrabble with Dre' Bly and Andre' Goodman, the apostrophe tile is worth five points.

Brandon Stokley   Height: 5-11   Weight: 197   College: LA-Lafayette   Draft: 1999/4 (105)   Born: 23-Jun-1976   Age: 31   Risk: Red

Year	Team	G	Rec	Pass	Yds	C%	Yd/C	TD	YAC	Rk	DVOA	Rk	DPAR	Rk	PAR	Short	Mid	Deep	Bomb
2004	IND	16	68	102	1077	67%	15.8	10	—	—	41.7%	1	38.4	5	40.8	—	—	—	—
2005	IND	15	41	67	543	61%	13.2	1	5.4	11	8.8%	30	10.7	39	12.9	42%	34%	22%	3%
2006	IND	4	8	11	85	73%	10.6	1	3.6	—	17.5%	—	2.2	—	2.5	25%	42%	17%	17%
2007	DEN		12		174		14.0	1											

While he did manage to play in four games, Stokley was on the Colts' injured list for every single week of the 2006 season with three different injuries: ankle problems in Weeks 1–5, a sprained knee in Weeks 6–14, and a torn Achilles starting in Week 15. The Colts cut him after the Super Bowl, so, in just three years, Stokley has gone from the greatest season by a third receiver in NFL history to a one-year make-good contract in Denver, the city where third receivers go to die. Since Mike Shanahan became head coach, the third receiver in Denver has averaged just 249 yards per season. Between Stokley and Rod Smith, someone is about to disappear completely; only once in the last ten seasons have four different Broncos wideouts gained at least 100 yards.

Maurice Stovall Height: 6-5 Weight: 222 College: Notre Dame Draft: 2006/3 (90) Born: 21-Feb-1985 Age: 22 Risk: Yellow

Year	Team	G	Rec	Pass	Yds	C%	Yd/C	TD	YAC	Rk	DVOA	Rk	DPAR	Rk	PAR	Short	Mid	Deep	Bomb
2006	TB	9	7	13	102	54%	14.6	0	4.0	—	5.7%	—	1.7	—	1.7	42%	42%	17%	0%
2007	TB		40		527		13.0	4											

All seven of Stovall's catches came in December, six of them after Michael Clayton got hurt against the Bears. Stovall is the perfect Jon Gruden receiver: a big target for hitches and smash routes who can also work the middle of the field and block a little. It supposedly takes three years to master Gruden's offense (or, in Clayton's case, one year to master it and two to forget it). Stovall may be ahead of schedule, and he could easily supplant Clayton as the designated possession receiver this season.

Travis Taylor Height: 6-1 Weight: 200 College: Florida Draft: 2000/1 (10) Born: 30-Mar-1978 Age: 29 Risk: Red

Year	Team	G	Rec	Pass	Yds	C%	Yd/C	TD	YAC	Rk	DVOA	Rk	DPAR	Rk	PAR	Short	Mid	Deep	Bomb
2004	BAL	10	34	80	421	43%	12.4	0	←	—	-29.1%	80	-7.8	80	-9.2	—	—	—	—
2005	MIN	16	50	90	604	56%	12.1	4	3.8	35	4.3%	42	11.1	36	9.1	32%	42%	19%	7%
2006	MIN	16	57	86	651	65%	11.4	3	3.2	51	0.3%	47	8.4	51	5.9	35%	38%	23%	5%
2007	OAK		29		351		12.3	1											

If Taylor had not been the tenth-overall selection in the 2000 draft, we might all look at his career a little differently. What we see is a touted prospect who has never had a 1,000-yard season. What we miss is a consistent receiver who was far and away the best receiver on the Vikings last year. He was one of the countless NFL players to have legal trouble in the off-season, but the Raiders brought him in to compete with a million other wide receivers and tight ends for the right to catch passes from JaMarcus Russell.

James Thrash Height: 6-0 Weight: 200 College: Missouri Southern Draft: 1997/FA Born: 28-Apr-1975 Age: 32 Risk: Red

Year	Team	G	Rec	Pass	Yds	C%	Yd/C	TD	YAC	Rk	DVOA	Rk	DPAR	Rk	PAR	Short	Mid	Deep	Bomb
2004	WAS	16	17	21	203	81%	11.9	0	—	—	32.7%	—	6.5	—	6.2	—	—	—	—
2005	WAS	12	14	30	194	47%	13.9	0	3.5	—	-12.1%	—	0.5	—	-0.1	43%	39%	9%	9%
2006	WAS	16	12	20	151	60%	12.6	1	1.7	—	6.5%	—	3.1	—	3.6	21%	47%	21%	11%
2007	WAS		11		146		13.8	1											

As far as under-the-radar, fourth-wideouts go, Thrash has been pretty reliable. He enters his 11th year in the league not because of his pass-catching prowess, but because of his special-teams abilities. When you are this far down the depth chart, being a jack of all trades only helps your chances of making the club, and Thrash has excelled on coverage teams. As a wide receiver, Thrash sported better numbers than Brandon Lloyd and Antwaan Randle El—numbers two and three on the depth chart—but some of that can be attributed to facing dime backs, safeties, and sometimes linebackers in coverage.

Amani Toomer Height: 6-3 Weight: 208 College: Michigan Draft: 1996/2 (34) Born: 8-Sep-1974 Age: 33 Risk: Red

Year	Team	G	Rec	Pass	Yds	C%	Yd/C	TD	YAC	Rk	DVOA	Rk	DPAR	Rk	PAR	Short	Mid	Deep	Bomb
2004	NYG	15	51	107	747	48%	14.6	0	—	—	-7.1%	59	4.9	59	0.6	—	—	—	—
2005	NYG	16	60	109	684	55%	11.4	7	2.6	75	0.6%	47	11.2	35	8.9	28%	48%	14%	11%
2006	NYG	8	32	50	360	64%	11.3	3	1.4	81	9.6%	31	8.6	50	9.0	26%	46%	17%	11%
2007	NYG		28		333		12.0	2											

Before tearing his ACL on November 5, Toomer was having a productive season. After he went down for the year, the Giants struggled to find a reliable number-two option after Plaxico Burress. The good news is that Toomer started working out in March and should be reading for training camp. The bad news is that he will be 33 on September 8 and is on the downside of his career. Toomer could become a reliable possession receiver if he can replicate his 64 percent Catch Rate from a season ago.

David Tyree Height: 6-0 Weight: 205 College: Syracuse Draft: 2003/6 (211) Born: 3-Jan-1980 Age: 27 Risk: Red

Year	Team	G	Rec	Pass	Yds	C%	Yd/C	TD	YAC	Rk	DVOA	Rk	DPAR	Rk	PAR	Short	Mid	Deep	Bomb
2004	NYG	16	10	17	155	59%	15.5	1	—	—	23.6%	—	4.5	—	4.1	—	—	—	—
2005	NYG	13	5	9	52	56%	10.4	1	4.4	—	-32.5%	—	-1.0	—	-1.0	44%	33%	22%	0%
2006	NYG	16	19	33	197	58%	10.4	2	2.3	—	-7.6%	—	1.4	—	0.3	45%	41%	14%	0%
2007	NYG		20		273		13.9	1											

Known mostly as a special-teams player, Tyree will head into training camp as the team's fourth or fifth wide receiver. The book on Tyree is that he is a smooth route runner who creates separation, but he just hasn't been that good when he does get open. So, instead, he's a smooth kickoff gunner who creates separation—between a returner's feet and the ground.

Bobby Wade   Height: 5-10   Weight: 193   College: Arizona   Draft: 2003/5 (139)   Born: 25-Feb-1981   Age: 26   Risk: Red

Year	Team	G	Rec	Pass	Yds	C%	Yd/C	TD	YAC	Rk	DVOA	Rk	DPAR	Rk	PAR	Short	Mid	Deep	Bomb
2004	CHI	16	42	89	481	47%	11.5	0	—	—	-40.6%	84	-14.4	84	-13.6	—	—	—	—
2005	CHI	12	10	29	80	48%	8.0	0	2.7	—	-66.0%	—	-9.4	—	-9.3	57%	38%	5%	0%
2006	TEN	16	33	58	461	57%	14.0	2	4.8	16	15.0%	18	11.2	43	10.7	41%	20%	32%	7%
2007	MIN		42		528		12.7	2											

The Vikings gave Wade a five-year, $15-million contract in March, knowing full well that they were getting a slot receiver/kick returner with a history of inconsistency. In essence, he was their Kevin Curtis consolation prize, and his salary tells us a little about the current free-agent market and a lot about the Vikings' desperation at wide receiver. It's nice that he was good in 2006, but we're still talking about the guy who was last in the league in DPAR for both 2004 and 2005. Wade's quickness in the open field is an asset, but he gets jammed easily and isn't a playbook scholar, two flaws that will really hurt his production in Brad Childress's system.

Javon Walker   Height: 6-3   Weight: 220   College: Florida State   Draft: 2002/1 (20)   Born: 14-Oct-1978   Age: 29   Risk: Yellow

Year	Team	G	Rec	Pass	Yds	C%	Yd/C	TD	YAC	Rk	DVOA	Rk	DPAR	Rk	PAR	Short	Mid	Deep	Bomb
2004	GB	16	89	144	1382	62%	15.5	12	—	—	19.9%	22	33.7	8	34.5	—	—	—	—
2005	GB	1	4	5	27	80%	6.7	0	0.5	—	0.5%	—	0.5	—	0.4	25%	75%	0%	0%
2006	DEN	16	69	126	1084	55%	15.7	8	5.0	12	10.1%	30	21.0	16	21.8	30%	38%	14%	18%
2007	DEN		69		964		13.9	6											

What a great trade that turned out to be for Denver. Walker was nothing short of spectacular last season, single-handedly keeping the Broncos' passing game afloat while both Jake Plummer and Jay Cutler struggled. Walker's recovery from a 2005 ACL tear gives hope to players such as Patriots receiver Chad Jackson, who tore his ACL in the AFC Championship game and, like Walker, relies heavily on his straight-line speed.

Mike Walker   Height: 6-2   Weight: 209   College: Central Florida   Draft: 2007/3 (79)   Born: 11-Nov-1984   Age: 23   Risk: Red

Year	Team	G	Rec	Pass	Yds	C%	Yd/C	TD	YAC	Rk	DVOA	Rk	DPAR	Rk	PAR	Short	Mid	Deep	Bomb
2007	JAC		17		261		15.0	1											

Walker played wide receiver and cornerback for Central Florida in 2004. In 2005 he became a full-time offensive player, but tore his ACL at the end of the season. Last year he came back to catch 90 passes. Walker is unpolished, but he has the speed and toughness to make it in the NFL.

Kevin Walter   Height: 6-3   Weight: 221   College: Eastern Michigan   Draft: 2003/7 (255)   Born: 4-Aug-1981   Age: 26   Risk: Green

Year	Team	G	Rec	Pass	Yds	C%	Yd/C	TD	YAC	Rk	DVOA	Rk	DPAR	Rk	PAR	Short	Mid	Deep	Bomb
2004	CIN	16	8	9	67	89%	8.4	0	—	—	4.6%	—	1.1	—	0.7	—	—	—	—
2005	CIN	16	19	29	211	66%	11.1	1	3.7	—	13.4%	—	5.6	—	5.8	38%	42%	15%	4%
2006	HOU	16	17	21	160	81%	9.4	0	2.7	—	2.6%	—	2.4	—	2.4	38%	52%	0%	10%
2007	HOU		41		357		8.7	2											

Walter is just a run-of-the-mill slot receiver, but his decision to sign with Houston a year ago sure looks like a good career move. Walter has never caught more than four passes in one game, and he didn't have a single game last year with more than 30 yards, but, as of right now, he is a starting wide receiver in the National Football League. To keep that role, he'll need to fight off David Anderson—a younger but shorter version of himself—and hope that the Texans don't find a free agent out there in July.

Troy Walters   Height: 5-7   Weight: 172   College: Stanford   Draft: 2000/5 (165)   Born: 15-Dec-1976   Age: 30   Risk: Red

Year	Team	G	Rec	Pass	Yds	C%	Yd/C	TD	YAC	Rk	DVOA	Rk	DPAR	Rk	PAR	Short	Mid	Deep	Bomb
2004	IND	5	1	1	5	100%	5.0	0	—	—	-22.6%	—	0.0	—	0.0	—	—	—	—
2005	IND	16	14	19	152	74%	10.9	3	3.4	—	27.3%	—	5.3	—	5.5	42%	50%	8%	0%
2006	ARI	15	23	35	209	66%	9.1	2	3.6	—	4.0%	—	4.3	—	3.6	60%	26%	9%	6%
2007	FA		11		129		11.8	0											

Walters is an unrestricted free agent who could benefit most teams as a fourth receiver and occasional return man. Last year in Arizona, he had his most productive season since 2003.

Hines Ward

Height: 6-0 **Weight: 205** **College: Georgia** **Draft: 1998/3 (92)** **Born: 8-Mar-1976** **Age: 31** **Risk: Yellow**

Year	Team	G	Rec	Pass	Yds	C%	Yd/C	TD	YAC	Rk	DVOA	Rk	DPAR	Rk	PAR	Short	Mid	Deep	Bomb
2004	PIT	16	80	109	1004	75%	12.6	4	—	—	30.4%	9	32.9	9	31.3	—	—	—	—
2005	PIT	15	69	114	975	61%	14.1	11	4.5	26	25.4%	6	30.4	8	30.4	24%	55%	17%	4%
2006	PIT	14	74	127	975	59%	13.2	6	4.8	14	3.8%	41	16.0	31	15.5	29%	45%	19%	7%
2007	PIT		76		1029		13.5	6											

Ward, whose downfield blocking remains without peer among receivers, was slowed by hamstring and knee injuries in 2006. He hasn't been helped by Pittsburgh's revolving door at number-two wideout, either, since his strongest skill is getting open underneath when a teammate creates space with a deeper route. With all four of the team's top receivers back this year, Ward should be freed from some of his on-field coaching duties. The list of most similar receivers to Ward over a three-year span features a couple of guys who put up over 1,200 yards the next season (Isaac Bruce, 2001–2003; Keenan McCardell, 1997–1999) but also a couple of veterans who were nearing the end of the line (Brian Blades, 1993–1995; Anthony Carter, 1988–1990; and Ernest Givins, 1991–1993).

Paris Warren

Height: 6-0 **Weight: 213** **College: Utah** **Draft: 2005/7 (225)** **Born: 6-Sep-1982** **Age: 25** **Risk: Red**

Year	Team	G	Rec	Pass	Yds	C%	Yd/C	TD	YAC	Rk	DVOA	Rk	DPAR	Rk	PAR	Short	Mid	Deep	Bomb
2006	TB	8	5	7	63	71%	12.6	0	3.0	—	25.8%	—	1.8	—	1.7	43%	43%	14%	0%
2007	TB		14		189		13.8	1											

Warren caught 156 passes for Urban Meyer's Utah team in 2003 and 2004. He climbed off the Buccaneers practice squad for a handful of games last season, catching five passes. He's a crafty possession receiver with some after-the-catch niftiness, but he isn't very big or fast.

Kelley Washington

Height: 6-3 **Weight: 218** **College: Tennessee** **Draft: 2003/3 (65)** **Born: 21-Aug-1979** **Age: 28** **Risk: Red**

Year	Team	G	Rec	Pass	Yds	C%	Yd/C	TD	YAC	Rk	DVOA	Rk	DPAR	Rk	PAR	Short	Mid	Deep	Bomb
2004	CIN	16	31	50	378	64%	12.2	3	—	—	14.8%	31	9.5	47	9.5	—	—	—	—
2005	CIN	8	10	19	101	53%	10.1	1	2.3	—	-7.2%	—	1.0	—	0.9	18%	47%	24%	12%
2006	CIN	5	9	12	115	75%	12.8	1	4.9	—	36.7%	—	4.3	—	4.6	33%	67%	0%	0%
2007	NE		12		161		13.7	1											

Lost among the wealth of receiving talent in Cincinnati, Washington will now be lost among a wealth of receiving talent in New England. Over the last two seasons, he was limited to just 19 catches by injuries and a crowded depth chart, but he was a dominant player in his only full season in college. Sure, that was in 2001, but if any team can unearth those skills at the pro level, it's the Patriots, who managed to turn Reche Caldwell and Jabar Gaffney into useful pass-catchers. Washington's newfound willingness to play special teams may come in handy in his pursuit of a roster spot.

Nate Washington

Height: 6-1 **Weight: 185** **College: Tiffin** **Draft: 2005/FA** **Born: 28-Aug-1983** **Age: 24** **Risk: Red**

Year	Team	G	Rec	Pass	Yds	C%	Yd/C	TD	YAC	Rk	DVOA	Rk	DPAR	Rk	PAR	Short	Mid	Deep	Bomb
2006	PIT	16	35	69	624	51%	17.8	4	3.4	46	20.1%	12	15.2	34	15.2	21%	38%	23%	18%
2007	PIT		26		366		14.1	2											

Last year Washington emerged from nowhere, which in this case means Tiffin University, to become Pittsburgh's third wideout in his second NFL season. Unlike first-round pick Santonio Holmes, who is clearly being groomed to be the eventual focus of the passing game, Washington is likely to always be a third or fourth receiver, but, in new coordinator Bruce Arians's offense, that could mean more playing time.

Reggie Wayne

Height: 6-0 **Weight: 203** **College: Miami** **Draft: 2001/1 (30)** **Born: 17-Nov-1978** **Age: 29** **Risk: Green**

Year	Team	G	Rec	Pass	Yds	C%	Yd/C	TD	YAC	Rk	DVOA	Rk	DPAR	Rk	PAR	Short	Mid	Deep	Bomb
2004	IND	16	77	115	1210	67%	15.7	12	—	—	40.8%	2	44.0	1	46.5	—	—	—	—
2005	IND	16	83	122	1055	68%	12.7	5	4.0	32	11.4%	24	22.6	17	28.0	32%	50%	12%	6%
2006	IND	16	86	137	1310	63%	15.2	9	2.3	76	35.0%	3	46.1	1	44.2	23%	47%	18%	13%
2007	IND		79		1082		13.8	8											

A key to annual Super Bowl contention is smart drafting at the end of each round, and there's no better example of that than Reggie Wayne. The Colts took him with the 30th pick in the 2003 draft; he was the sixth wide receiver off the board. Of the five receivers taken before Wayne, the only one who has been anywhere near as valuable is his old Miami teammate Santana

Moss. Wayne was passed over for David Terrell, Koren Robinson, Rod Gardner, and Freddie Mitchell. The only thing stranger than the idea that anyone would think Freddie Mitchell was better than Reggie Wayne is the fact that the Colts may not have chosen the best receiver available—Chad Johnson went six picks later, and Steve Smith went in the third round.

Jeff Webb

Height: 6-2 Weight: 200 College: San Diego State Draft: 2006/6 (190) Born: 31-Jan-1982 Age: 25 Risk: Red

Year	Team	G	Rec	Pass	Yds	C%	Yd/C	TD	YAC	Rk	DVOA	Rk	DPAR	Rk	PAR	Short	Mid	Deep	Bomb
2006	KC	10	3	4	23	75%	7.7	0	0.0	—	4.7%	—	0.6	—	0.7	0%	100%	0%	0%
2007	KC		20		245		12.0	1											

With Samie Parker in the process of losing his job, a spot opens up for either Webb or Chris Hannon. Herm Edwards has a reputation for favoring established veterans over younger players—for example, talking about his time coaching the Jets, Edwards stated, "The worst thing I did when I was in New York was draft Jerricho Cotchery and . . . he never got on the field." Hopefully, he's learned and will trust Webb, Hannon, and Dwayne Bowe with playing time once they're ready for it.

Wes Welker

Height: 5-9 Weight: 190 College: Texas Tech Draft: 2004/FA Born: 1-May-1981 Age: 26 Risk: Yellow

Year	Team	G	Rec	Pass	Yds	C%	Yd/C	TD	YAC	Rk	DVOA	Rk	DPAR	Rk	PAR	Short	Mid	Deep	Bomb
2005	MIA	16	29	52	434	56%	15.0	0	6.2	7	14.1%	20	9.7	44	9.2	26%	52%	15%	7%
2006	MIA	16	67	100	687	67%	10.3	1	3.8	37	0.1%	49	9.6	46	8.9	51%	36%	8%	5%
2007	NE		51		684		13.3	5											

Here's an important lesson to learn: Sometimes, players can be useful, but not worth devoting real resources to. Welker's a helpful player; he's a good underneath receiver, a solid special-teams gunner, and a decent return guy. Who does that remind you of? Right, Troy Brown, the player he's replacing on the Patriots. Brown and Welker have something else in common: The former was an eighth-round pick, the latter undrafted. That's because their skill set isn't a difficult one to find. Once one of these players wants a real contract or loses a step, you get rid of him and replace him with the next guy off the heap. Giving up a second-rounder for Welker is paying way too much; giving him a $36-million contract—as the Patriots nearly did before the Dolphins decided to simply trade him when the Pats threw in an extra seventh-round pick—would have been an astonishingly bad move from a team known for making prudent decisions on player fungibility. Remember too that the Patriots wouldn't give Deion Branch $39 million the offseason before. One day, we'll be writing essays about the Class of 2007 and the contract fairy who blessed it.

Roddy White

Height: 6-1 Weight: 201 College: UAB Draft: 2005/1 (27) Born: 2-Nov-1981 Age: 26 Risk: Red

Year	Team	G	Rec	Pass	Yds	C%	Yd/C	TD	YAC	Rk	DVOA	Rk	DPAR	Rk	PAR	Short	Mid	Deep	Bomb
2005	ATL	16	29	68	446	43%	15.4	3	2.5	77	-14.5%	76	0.2	77	-0.3	11%	53%	11%	25%
2006	ATL	16	30	64	506	47%	16.9	0	2.6	69	-16.4%	72	-0.5	72	-0.3	15%	44%	13%	28%
2007	ATL		18		314		17.2	1											

White was the honorary president of the Atlanta chapter of the Bobbles Association, and he appears to be on the express train to Bustville, but don't write him off just yet. White was seen working out just days after the Super Bowl, catching passes and running routes at the practice facility for Arena football's Georgia Force. He was one of the Falcons' best third-down receivers last year (0.5 percent DVOA on 35 passes, not bad on a team with a negative third-down DVOA), and he's the best deep threat on the roster now that Ashley Lelie is gone. On the other hand, that trip to the Arena football facility may be a sign of things to come.

Alvis Whitted

Height: 6-0 Weight: 185 College: North Carolina State Draft: 1998/7 (192) Born: 4-Sep-1974 Age: 33 Risk: Yellow

Year	Team	G	Rec	Pass	Yds	C%	Yd/C	TD	YAC	Rk	DVOA	Rk	DPAR	Rk	PAR	Short	Mid	Deep	Bomb
2004	OAK	12	9	25	227	36%	25.2	2	—	—	-0.7%	—	2.4	—	2.6	—	—	—	—
2005	OAK	15	14	26	183	54%	13.1	0	3.0	—	0.0%	—	2.5	—	2.7	17%	48%	17%	17%
2006	OAK	14	27	63	299	43%	11.1	0	1.1	82	-36.7%	83	-8.8	82	-8.3	28%	37%	24%	11%
2007	OAK		28		393		14.3	1											

The Raiders front office seems to like Whitted (they re-signed him this offseason after his contract expired), but it's hard to understand why. He's going into his tenth season in the league and has never even come close to being a productive NFL receiver. Maybe he looks good in practice or something, but it's hard to imagine how this guy has stayed gainfully employed for so long. Last year he was dead last in the league in DVOA among the 83 receivers who had enough passes thrown their way to qualify.

Ernest Wilford   Height: 6-3   Weight: 220   College: Virginia Tech   Draft: 2004/4 (120)   Born: 14-Jan-1979   Age: 28   Risk: Green

Year	Team	G	Rec	Pass	Yds	C%	Yd/C	TD	YAC	Rk	DVOA	Rk	DPAR	Rk	PAR	Short	Mid	Deep	Bomb
2004	JAC	15	19	35	271	54%	14.3	2	—	—	-5.4%	—	2.5	—	4.1	—	—	—	—
2005	JAC	16	41	74	681	55%	16.6	7	3.3	50	22.9%	9	18.9	22	21.9	21%	40%	22%	18%
2006	JAC	16	36	74	524	49%	14.6	2	3.4	45	-10.7%	64	2.3	64	3.1	19%	39%	25%	16%
2007	*JAC*		*41*		*588*		*14.2*	*5*											

When we look at the standard numbers, Wilford's 2006 doesn't seem that much worse than his 2005. Our advanced numbers tell a different story. The biggest problem was a massive drop in his Catch Rate on first down, from 67 percent to 53 percent. Was life just harder for the Jacksonville receivers without Jimmy Smith around to draw coverage? Actually, no; Matt Jones and Reggie Williams both had a slight improvement in Catch Rate in 2006. Wilford had a higher DVOA on passes from David Garrard than on passes from Byron Leftwich, but in 2005 he had a higher DVOA on passes from Leftwich, so the drop probably doesn't have anything to do with the quarterback situation either. Wilford simply had a harder time getting open last year. If he could fix that, it would be a nice step toward a Jacksonville playoff appearance.

Demetrius Williams   Height: 6-2   Weight: 191   College: Oregon   Draft: 2006/4 (111)   Born: 28-Mar-1983   Age: 24   Risk: Red

Year	Team	G	Rec	Pass	Yds	C%	Yd/C	TD	YAC	Rk	DVOA	Rk	DPAR	Rk	PAR	Short	Mid	Deep	Bomb
2006	BAL	16	22	45	396	49%	18.0	2	5.4	—	3.3%	—	5.4	—	6.0	15%	51%	22%	12%
2007	*BAL*		*22*		*304*		*13.5*	*1*											

Williams's Catch Rate indicates he hasn't conquered his difficulties fighting for the ball in traffic. Still, he'll be the third receiver and the designated deep threat in 2007 provided the Ravens don't find somebody better late in free agency.

Mike Williams   Height: 6-5   Weight: 229   College: USC   Draft: 2005/1 (10)   Born: 4-Jan-1984   Age: 23   Risk: Red

Year	Team	G	Rec	Pass	Yds	C%	Yd/C	TD	YAC	Rk	DVOA	Rk	DPAR	Rk	PAR	Short	Mid	Deep	Bomb
2005	DET	14	29	57	350	51%	12.1	1	4.6	23	-15.7%	79	-0.4	79	-1.3	27%	52%	14%	7%
2006	DET	8	8	18	99	44%	12.4	1	2.4	—	-21.7%	—	-0.8	—	-1.3	28%	33%	33%	6%
2007	*OAK*		*11*		*141*		*12.5*	*0*											

Is it over for Mike Williams after just two years? He is not a small or particularly fast man, and if you aren't fast, you can't play for Mike Martz. Williams got on the field so rarely last year that it is hard to see if he has skills that would translate into another system. Odds are against it, as slow receivers who cannot get separation are not assets in any system. The year he sat out after a judge's decision allowing Maurice Clarett to declare for the draft early was overturned may have permanently stunted his development. The trade to Oakland gives him a fresh start, but Oakland might be the least likely place for Williams to find the disciplined setup he needs. Don't bet against him showing up in Tennessee by the end of the year.

Paul Williams   Height: 6-1   Weight: 205   College: Fresno State   Draft: 2007/3 (80)   Born: 2-Dec-1983   Age: 24   Risk: Red

Year	Team	G	Rec	Pass	Yds	C%	Yd/C	TD	YAC	Rk	DVOA	Rk	DPAR	Rk	PAR	Short	Mid	Deep	Bomb
2007	*TEN*		*15*		*205*		*14.0*	*1*											

This Fresno State wideout was the Titans' third-round pick. He's a great athlete, but not a great football player at this point. The Titans' coaches were reportedly very impressed by his performance at minicamp, but he still may end up switching to defensive back, a process known as "un-Hestering."

Reggie Williams   Height: 6-3   Weight: 223   College: Washington   Draft: 2004/1 (9)   Born: 17-May-1983   Age: 24   Risk: Green

Year	Team	G	Rec	Pass	Yds	C%	Yd/C	TD	YAC	Rk	DVOA	Rk	DPAR	Rk	PAR	Short	Mid	Deep	Bomb
2004	JAC	16	27	54	268	50%	9.9	1	—	—	-36.3%	83	-7.7	79	-7.0	—	—	—	—
2005	JAC	16	35	63	445	56%	12.7	0	3.4	41	-15.2%	78	0.2	76	1.6	31%	33%	25%	11%
2006	JAC	16	52	91	616	57%	11.8	4	4.7	17	-9.9%	63	3.3	63	4.6	47%	36%	11%	5%
2007	*JAC*		*46*		*632*		*13.8*	*4*											

Williams started and finished strong last year, but, from Week 6 to Week 10, he caught just four passes for 43 yards. He still drops passes and disappears for long stretches, but he pulled himself off the Epic Bust garbage pile by becoming a decent short-range target. He's now a viable, though limited, second receiver.

Roy Williams Height: 6-2 Weight: 212 College: Texas   Draft: 2004/1 (7) Born: 20-Dec-1981 Age: 25 Risk: Yellow

Year	Team	G	Rec	Pass	Yds	C%	Yd/C	TD	YAC	Rk	DVOA	Rk	DPAR	Rk	PAR	Short	Mid	Deep	Bomb
2004	DET	14	54	118	817	46%	15.1	8	—	—	-9.0%	62	4.5	60	2.5	—	—	—	—
2005	DET	13	45	94	687	48%	15.3	8	3.4	42	5.4%	38	12.6	30	9.8	25%	46%	15%	14%
2006	DET	16	82	151	1310	54%	16.0	7	4.1	29	14.2%	21	29.1	6	27.8	17%	40%	30%	14%
2007	DET		80		1069		13.4	6											

Williams had his breakout season last year and appears headed for stardom. With only Mike Furrey on the other side, he still exploded for his first Pro Bowl season. Does that season portend a great career? The line between greatness and something less exciting is exceedingly thin. Williams's most similar player based on his first three seasons of work is Lee Evans. The next two are Peerless Price and Plaxico Burress. The rest of the top ten is an extremely impressive list featuring Reggie Wayne, Art Monk, James Lofton, Andre Reed, Tim Brown, and Anthony Miller. Just to keep Williams honest, next on the list is Kevin Johnson, late of the Browns. Williams certainly seems likely to stay successful, and, as that list indicates, the sky is the limit.

Roydell Williams Height: 6-0 Weight: 192 College: Tulane   Draft: 2005/4 (136) Born: 14-Mar-1981 Age: 26 Risk: Red

Year	Team	G	Rec	Pass	Yds	C%	Yd/C	TD	YAC	Rk	DVOA	Rk	DPAR	Rk	PAR	Short	Mid	Deep	Bomb
2005	TEN	11	21	39	299	54%	14.2	2	3.8	—	-8.9%	—	1.6	—	1.5	18%	50%	8%	24%
2006	TEN	14	8	21	121	38%	15.1	0	4.8	—	-18.7%	—	-0.5	—	-0.6	25%	35%	15%	25%
2007	TEN		37		388		10.6	2											

Williams is a star on the track and in the weight room, and he looked like a top prospect before breaking his wrist in 2005. He stayed healthy last year, but regressed as the Titans offense became more run-and-dunk oriented. Nothing is guaranteed on the Titans' receiving corps, and Williams could break camp as a starter if he proves that his route running and instincts have caught up to his raw talent. More likely, he'll settle into a role as the third or fourth wideout.

Troy Williamson Height: 6-1 Weight: 203 College: South Carolina   Draft: 2005/1 (7) Born: 30-Apr-1983 Age: 24 Risk: Yellow

Year	Team	G	Rec	Pass	Yds	C%	Yd/C	TD	YAC	Rk	DVOA	Rk	DPAR	Rk	PAR	Short	Mid	Deep	Bomb
2005	MIN	14	24	52	372	46%	15.5	2	8.8	1	-0.2%	52	4.7	60	2.3	32%	29%	10%	29%
2006	MIN	14	37	76	455	49%	12.3	0	5.3	8	-16.3%	71	-1.0	73	-2.6	28%	39%	8%	24%
2007	MIN		43		680		15.7	4											

No player could have replaced Randy Moss, but, at this point, there are questions about whether Williamson can replace Travis Taylor. Williamson has speed, but he's caught less than 50 percent of the passes thrown his way in both of his first two seasons. The new theory on his propensity for drops is that he has an eye problem. He's done analysis and exercises to improve his vision and hand-eye coordination. If Williamson can track the deep ball better, then he is an interesting sleeper as an unchallenged starter. Still, his mediocre performance over his first two seasons presents a strong case for skepticism.

Cedrick Wilson Height: 5-10 Weight: 183 College: Tennessee   Draft: 2001/6 (169) Born: 17-Dec-1978 Age: 28 Risk: Red

Year	Team	G	Rec	Pass	Yds	C%	Yd/C	TD	YAC	Rk	DVOA	Rk	DPAR	Rk	PAR	Short	Mid	Deep	Bomb
2004	SF	15	47	85	641	55%	13.6	3	—	—	14.3%	33	15.8	37	13.8	—	—	—	—
2005	PIT	16	26	53	451	49%	17.3	0	2.3	84	-5.2%	62	3.3	68	3.4	20%	41%	20%	20%
2006	PIT	15	37	69	504	54%	13.6	1	3.4	48	-4.3%	56	4.8	61	3.8	8%	59%	18%	15%
2007	PIT		39		545		14.0	3											

The development of Nate Washington, who is a younger, taller version of Wilson, probably means diminished playing time for Wilson this season. Even in four-receiver sets, the pecking order is likely to be Hines Ward, Santonio Holmes, Washington, and then Wilson.

Travis Wilson Height: 6-3 Weight: 213 College: Oklahoma   Draft: 2006/3 (78) Born: 11-Feb-1984 Age: 23 Risk: Red

Year	Team	G	Rec	Pass	Yds	C%	Yd/C	TD	YAC	Rk	DVOA	Rk	DPAR	Rk	PAR	Short	Mid	Deep	Bomb
2006	CLE	4	2	6	32	33%	16.0	0	2.5	—	-10.8%	—	0.1	—	-0.1	0%	50%	50%	0%
2007			17		252		15.0	1											

Wilson was something of a surprise as a third-round pick by the Browns in 2006, as most projections had him going late on the second day. He didn't do much as a rookie, but he'll compete with Tim Carter for the third slot on Cleveland's wide receiver depth chart.

Going Deep

Charlie Adams, HOU: Denver tried to deal Adams to Dallas last year for a fourth-round pick, but he failed his physical. The Broncos cut him and he was picked up by Houston, but spent the whole year on the practice squad. Not every receiver from Hofstra turns into Marques Colston.

Sam Aiken, BUF: Aiken was the tallest wide receiver on the Buffalo roster last year, but several drops in preseason ended his role in the offense. He primarily plays on special teams, but his tackling skills last year left something be desired.

Aundre Allison, MIN: Allison made a name for himself with some outstanding Senior Bowl practices, and Minnesota grabbed the East Carolina prospect in the fifth round of this year's draft. Like Sidney Rice, the Vikings' second-round pick, he's a natural athlete with great speed who is as raw as steak tartare. He'll need a year on the practice squad to get a grip on Brad Childress's offense.

Miles Austin, DAL: Austin was productive at Division I-AA Monmouth and earned a long look from the Cowboys as a kick gunner last season. He has good hands and might get a shot as a possession receiver if/when one of the Cowboys' starters flakes. He also may return kicks or punts.

Dallas Baker, PIT: A seventh-round pick by the Steelers, Baker was a highly productive receiver on some very good Florida teams, including last year's national champions. His size could help him stick in Pittsburgh, where the roster is full of short receivers.

Alex Bannister, FA: Bannister made the Pro Bowl in 2003 as a Seattle special-teamer, but hasn't caught a pass since 2004. After the Seahawks drafted him in 2001, he told reporters, "Randy Moss is good, but I'm trying to re-innovate the receiver position. . . . I'm trying to be great. I'm trying to be a legend." So much for that idea. He's a free agent.

Taye Biddle, CAR: A swift, skinny 175-pounder from Ole Miss, Biddle made the Panthers as an undrafted rookie and saw some late-season action as a receiver, punt returner, and gunner. He caught three of five passes for 37 yards in limited action (–5.4 percent DVOA, 0.4 DPAR). Biddle has potential as a special-teamer, but the thing the Panthers like best about him is that he's not Keary Colbert.

Jeremy Bloom, PHI: This one-time championship skier is still really fast and really raw. He spent last season on injured reserve after straining a hamstring in camp; in essence, the Eagles used IR to stash him away for a year without having to use a roster spot. Bethel Johnson's offseason injury makes it more likely Bloom will make the team.

Shaun Bodiford, GB: The Packers apparently love to scout within their own division, picking up both Koren Robinson from Minnesota and Bodiford from Detroit. This undrafted free agent was the hit of training camp with the Lions before suddenly losing favor and being released. After arriving in Green Bay, he broke his leg. He will be ready for the start of the season and is an intriguing talent stuck in a difficult fight for a position on the roster.

David Boston, TB: It feels like the former Cardinals star has been flailing forever, but he's only 28; on the other hand, he's had four catches in four seasons. Stranger things have happened, but Boston looks to be done.

Bennie Brazell, CIN: The former LSU speed merchant was Cincinnati's seventh-round pick in 2006, then spent his rookie year on injured reserve with a knee injury. He may have been the school's best performer ever in track and field, but when your college media guide describes your senior year as a breakout season and you had only 12 catches, chances are you're not going to be much of an NFL receiver.

Steve Breaston, ARI: The Cardinals aren't exactly hurting at receiver, but they did finish dead last in special-teams DVOA in 2006. That explains why they took Breaston in the fifth round of this year's draft. He's an all-purpose player who never stood out as a wideout at the college level, but his return numbers were always impressive. Breaston took four punts back for touchdowns at Michigan, including two in his freshman year.

John Broussard, JAC: Broussard is a rail-thin kick-return prospect who was productive as a receiver in his final season at San Jose State. He has pure speed, but lacks size, strength, and ball skills.

William Buchanon, OAK: A good athlete who played both receiver and cornerback at USC, Buchanon is the son of Green Bay Packers great Willie Buchanon. Oakland signed him as an undrafted free agent last year, and he made it onto the active roster toward the end of the season, but Buchanon looks to be a nonentity this year.

Greg Camarillo, SD: A little-known walk-on at Stanford, Camarillo got a chance with the Chargers because he was friends with the son of Chargers receivers coach James Lofton. He saw a little bit of action on special teams in 2006.

Jason Carter, MIN: This Texas A&M product had an impressive preseason in 2006, but didn't get any playing time in the regular season, and is likely to lose his roster spot to coach's favorite Martin Nance. If he goes elsewhere, he could hang on as a fourth receiver.

Brandon Childress, NE: "Bam" didn't see much playing time last season. This offseason the Patriots signed four million new receivers. We're guessing that didn't help his chances much. If he sticks, it will be solely as a special-teamer.

Brian Clark, DEN: An undrafted free agent out of North Carolina State, Clark became the Broncos' kickoff returner midway through 2006. The addition of Quincy Morgan gives him competition for that job.

David Clowney, GB: Green Bay's fifth-round pick is a thinly built deep threat with some return ability. He projects as a third or fourth wideout and fly-pattern specialist. You can expect to see a feature story from Packers camp about Clowney and third-round safety Aaron Rouse, as they are two of the three Virginia Tech players chosen in this year's draft.

Airese Currie, FA: A cross between Devin Hester and Samuel L. Jackson's "Mr. Glass" from *Unbreakable,* Currie was waived when Hester was switched to offense and hasn't caught on with a new team as of press time.

Devard Darling, BAL: Darling looked to have potential after finishing a solid college career at Washington State, but he was inactive for the final 15 games of 2006 and will have to compete for a roster spot in training camp.

Chris Davis, TEN: Davis didn't put up great numbers at Florida State, and he injured his groin at the Combine, limiting his participation. Tennessee took him in the fourth round anyway. He's fast and has kick-return skills, but he's small and unpolished as a receiver.

Todd Devoe, DEN: Showed promise catching nine passes and playing special teams as a rookie in 2005, but got on the field for just one game in 2006.

Eddie Drummond, DET: Drummond is a return specialist, but he actually saw some time at wide receiver in 2006. He caught two of ten passes thrown his way and gained just ten yards for a –64.8 percent DVOA and –3.2 DPAR. This demonstrates why he is a return specialist.

Devale Ellis, DET: Ellis lined up across from Marques Colston at Hofstra, and went from being an undrafted free agent to "starting" at "tight end" (Ellis weighs 170 pounds) against the Bills in Week 6. Over the entire season, he caught four of nine passes for 41 yards (–47.7 percent DVOA, –1.8 DPAR). If the Lions keep six receivers on the roster, Ellis is number six.

Mike Espy, WAS: Son of the former Secretary of Agriculture, Espy is the Redskins' fifth wideout and a case in point when talking about how bad the Redskins' depth is. If the Redskins ever try to sell cookies to raise funds, though, Espy gives them a way into the lucrative government sector. How do you think they can afford all those free-agent signings?

Yamon Figurs, BAL: Figurs is tiny, but he registered the fastest 40-yard-dash time at the NFL Combine and figures to make an immediate impact as a punt- and kick-returner for the Ravens, particularly given the tenuous legal status of incumbent B. J. Sams. Given the Ravens' horrible history of developing receivers, he's unlikely to do anything on offense.

Joel Filani, TEN: Filani caught 156 passes for 2,348 yards and 21 touchdowns in two seasons as a starter in Texas Tech's spread offense. He's a product of the system, but he has NFL size and speed. The Titans took him in the sixth round and need receivers, so he'll get a long look.

Brian Finneran, ATL: Finneran tore ligaments in his left knee for the second year in a row, this time while doing some light running as part of his rehab. Players who tear ACLs in consecutive seasons generally don't make it back, which could spell the end for this longtime Football Outsiders favorite. It really hurts to have to cancel Finneran's projection and move him into the "Going Deep" section, but it hurts Michael Vick even more. While Finneran was typecast as a slow possession receiver because of his race, he was actually a speedy receiver and deep threat, and Vick's only dependable target besides Alge Crumpler.

Chris Francies, GB: Every time Brett Favre barks at the moon about how his team needed a lazy, over-the-hill receiver to make them Super Bowl champions, he's probably thinking about playing with guys like Francies, who had two catches for 16 yards in 2006 (–47.7 percent DVOA, –1.8 DPAR).

Rod Gardner, KC: Gardner may be the only person on earth who wishes Steve Spurrier were still in the NFL. Spurrier's offense was perfect for Gardner, who went for 1,006 yards in 2002. More recently he's bounced around the league, with 13 receptions for Green Bay in 2005 and two receptions—on nine passes—for Kansas City in 2006 (–79.5 percent DVOA, –4.0 DPAR).

Skyler Green, CIN: Chris Henry's suspension leaves the slot-receiver job in Cincinnati open. Whoever gets it will have 25 catches and five touchdowns in the first half of the season, which is useful if you want to get yourself a pension. Green is behind Tab Perry and Antonio Chatman as the camp battle begins, but he'll probably stick around as a punt returner and deep threat.

Marquis Hagans, STL: The former Virginia quarterback is being converted to wideout because of his speed and small (5-foot-10) stature. He didn't make an impact on the Rams as a fifth-round rookie in 2006.

Karl Hankton, FA: Hankton, the Panthers' special-teams captain, was released in March to clear cap room and is a free agent at press time. He made 73 special-teams tackles and blocked one punt in his ten-year career, and caught three passes for 31 yards in 2006 (27.3 percent DVOA, 0.9 DPAR).

Johnathan Holland, OAK: Mr. Almost Irrelevant (the second-to-last pick in this year's draft) won several WAC sprinting championships at Louisiana Tech. He can fly, and he's tough enough to earn a job as a kick gunner.

Glenn Holt, CIN: Holt is a practice-squad guy who got a chance to play after injuries felled both Tab Perry and Antonio Chatman in 2006. He has a very, very slim chance of winning the battle to replace Chris Henry as Cincinnati's slot receiver for the first half of the season.

Randy Hymes, MIN: Hymes was not thrown a single pass in Jacksonville last year, but his agent put him in the right place for 2007: Minnesota, where there are starting wide receiver jobs to go around. Unfortunately, Hymes's agent can't make Hymes run better routes, nor did he sell the Vikings on a new quarterback. Well, maybe he did—Hymes played quarterback at Grambling, and he might be the best quarterback on the Vikings roster come training camp.

Frisman Jackson, NYJ: The Fris spent 2006 out of football, but the ex-Browns receiver is still tall and could stick if the Jets decide to let Tim Dwight go.

Adam Jennings, ATL: A tiny tough guy with track speed and a knack for wedge-busting, Jennings will probably stick with the Falcons as a special-teamer. He has potential as a receiver, but will have a hard time getting noticed on a depth chart crowded with veteran free agents and former first-round picks.

Michael Jennings, NYG: Jennings didn't actually play football at Florida State, but he has been in (and out) of the league since the 49ers signed the track star as an undrafted free agent in 2002. In addition to being released by NFL teams, Jennings also has the dubious honor of not making several NFL Europa clubs. Nevertheless, he had a big NFLE season in 2005 with 33 catches for 546 yards for the Berlin Thunder, then parlayed that and a strong 2006 training camp into a small role with the Giants. Jennings had five catches for 49 yards in 2006 (–25.9 percent DVOA, –0.5 DPAR) along with two carries for 12 yards.

Mark Jones, TB: Jones is a replacement-level punt returner who doesn't really contribute anywhere else. Tampa Bay signed Chad Owens to compete with Jones for the returning gigs.

Kevin Kasper, DET: A part of the wide receiver merry-go-round in Detroit, Kasper has been on a roster at some point in each of the past four seasons and has a total of one catch.

Jordan Kent, SEA: It's hard to know what to make of Kent from a football perspective; he focused on basketball and track in high school and only played football in his junior and senior seasons. The Seahawks deemed him worthy of a sixth-round pick due to his ridiculous athleticism—he's posted sub-4.4 40-yard times despite being 6-foot-4 and 220 pounds. He's the third collegian to letter in three sports at the same time in the last 20 years, joining Adrian Awasom of North Texas and some guy named Deion Sanders from Florida State. All in all, an interesting developmental player.

Kelvin Kight, NE: Kight is undrafted practice-squad fodder with some size and speed, but raw technique and mediocre hands. There are 100 guys like this in the league, and it seems like half of them played for the Patriots at some point last year.

David Kircus, DEN: Kircus has good speed, but is inconsistent, with a penchant for dropping easy passes. After three disappointing seasons in Detroit—is there any other kind of season in Detroit?—Kircus moved on to Denver and became a solid special-teams contributor, but managed to catch only nine of the 27 passes thrown his way (187 yards, –19.5 percent DVOA, –0.7 DPAR). More important, he was arrested for second-degree assault in May after beating someone up at a party, causing Mike Shanahan to say, "Obviously, if he didn't handle himself the right way, he won't be with us [in 2007]."

Derrick Lewis, HOU: Lewis has bounced around practice squads for a couple of years, but in between he set the Arena rookie record with 1,411 receiving yards for the Austin Wranglers in 2006. He then caught one pass for the Texans last year.

Michael Lewis, NO: The local boy got to see the rebirth of his team in 2006, and continued in his usual role as return specialist. He will probably give more of those duties to Reggie Bush and Antonio Pittman as his career winds down.

Dane Looker, STL: Looker's primary role in 2006 for the Rams was as the holder for kicker Jeff Wilkins. He didn't catch a single pass in St. Louis's new, more conservative offense, but Wilkins connected on 32 of 37 field goals and made all his extra points. If you're a reserve receiver in Scott Linehan's system, that's about as close as you're going to get to scoring any points.

Maurice Mann, MIN: Mann spent the whole year on the practice squad. The Vikings don't have much on their roster at wideout, but Mann might be even less than that.

LeRon McCoy, ARI: This 2005 seventh-round pick showed potential in his rookie season, catching 18 of 30 passes for 191 yards with a –5.3 percent DVOA and 1.9 DPAR. He then missed 2006 due to a thumb injury, and the year off compounds his weaknesses: inexperience and poor route-running.

Reggie McNeal, CIN: Cincinnati took this former Texas A&M quarterback in the sixth round of the 2006 draft and tried to convert him to receiver, but his only yardage last season came on *Monday Night Football* in Week 15, as he came in for a trick play and rushed for a first down against Indianapolis. By that point, he had already joined the Bengals' perp walk conga line, as he was charged with resisting arrest and drug possession after a skirmish outside a Houston nightclub in early December.

Lance Moore, NO: Buried deep on the Saints' depth chart, Moore was on and off the team a couple of times in 2006 and caught one pass for ten yards. He's back on the roster for now, but the selection of Robert Meachem probably killed his chance at a roster spot.

Sean Morey, ARI: The receiver-rich Cardinals certainly didn't sign Morey to take playing time away from Anquan Boldin or Larry Fitzgerald, as he caught just two passes for 29 yards last year (17.3 percent DVOA, 0.8 DPAR). Morey excels on kick coverage (31 special-teams tackles the past two seasons) and even did the job when pressed into duty as a kick returner for the Steelers in 2006. With Zak DeOssie around, Morey is no longer the only Brown alum in the NFL, but we'll still give him extra space in the book. Now, will someone please tell Bryant Gumbel that Morey isn't French-Canadian?

Quincy Morgan, DEN: A solid receiver early in his career with the Browns, Morgan has played for four teams in the last four years and didn't catch a single pass last season. He'll be on special teams.

Ben Obomanu, SEA: The Seahawks are intrigued by Obomanu's potential, and he could end up on the active roster after spending his rookie season on the practice squad. At Auburn, Obomanu and fellow receiver Devin Aromashodu tied play-by-play guys into knots.

Jonathan Orr, TEN: Orr has exceptional speed, and he played well enough in training camp last year to make Tyron Calico expendable. As it turns out, Calico was expendable to begin with; the Titans relegated Orr to the practice squad for most of the season, and he was never activated for a game. Orr will get a long look this year, but he was an enigma at Wisconsin, where he caught 47 passes as a redshirt freshman in 2002 but was never able to match those numbers. He's really a track sprinter with a helmet, but the Titans are beggars, not choosers, at wide receiver.

Kassim Osgood, SD: In his first two seasons, Osgood looked like he was going to develop into a big-play threat. Between 2003 and 2004, he totaled 28 catches for 586 yards, an average of 20.9 yards a catch. Over the last two seasons, however, the Chargers have made him a bit player. Last year, he played in all 16 games, but didn't catch a pass. He made the Pro Bowl for his special-teams work last year, and that's his ticket to a roster spot for the next couple of seasons.

Chad Owens, TB: Timmy Chang's former number-one receiver at Hawaii, Owens has made his way to Tampa Bay to return kicks and/or punts.

Willie Ponder, STL: The former Giants special team ace is doing the yeoman's work of turning the awful Rams coverage and return units around. After the trade for Dante Hall, Ponder will go from being a returner to a gunner.

Ricky Proehl, Retired: Blink, and you missed Proehl's extremely abbreviated final season. The Colts signed him late in the year so they would have someone more experienced than Aaron Moorehead come playoff time. Proehl played two games, caught three passes for 30 yards (27.8 percent DVOA), and then screwed up his hamstring so he wasn't available for the postseason anyway. You may be shocked to learn that Proehl will retire ranked 31st on the NFL's all-time list for receptions. Thanks to those three catches in 2006, he also owns two Super Bowl rings. Not a bad career.

Jamaica Rector, DAL: Rector's a tweener—he's too small to break against press coverage, but he's not explosive enough to play in the slot or stick as a returner. His best bet to keep his roster spot might be to hold T.O.'s microphone for him and hope that Owens takes him wherever he goes next.

Willie Reid, PIT: Reid was an all-purpose threat at Florida State and played in one game with the Steelers after they chose him in the seventh round of the 2006 draft. On a team with four returning contributors at receiver, he'll struggle to find playing time.

Jamel Richardson, DAL: Richardson is a 25-year-old possession receiver signed by Dallas off the roster of the Saskatchewan Roughriders.

Cliff Russell, MIA: Perhaps most famous for being German suplexed by Brian Dawkins, Russell's the Dolphins' sixth wideout and will compete with Az Hakim for a roster spot. Russell caught two passes for 14 yards in 2006 (0.5 percent DVOA, 0.2 DPAR).

Edell Shepherd, DET: Last year, Houston threw to nonstarting wide receivers 60 percent less often than the average offense, only 27 passes in total. The result: Shepherd had only three receptions and 22 yards (4.4 percent DVOA, 0.5 DPAR). He signed as a free agent with Detroit, but there isn't really room for him there.

Bobby Sippio, FA: This star of the Arena Football League's Chicago Rush has one of the greatest websites you will ever see (www.sippio.com). Among the six links at the top of the page is one entitled simply "BIRTHDAY," which links to a home video of his son's birthday party at Chuck E. Cheese set to obscure hip-hop. The former Western Kentucky star had NFL corner skills when he came out as a junior, but he went undrafted and eventually ended up in Arena as an offensive specialist. If he signs somewhere and keeps his head on straight, he's a good enough athlete to stick.

Shaine Smith, STL: Smith had 60 receptions for 951 yards and nine touchdowns as a Hofstra senior, then signed as an undrafted free agent with the Rams. Some people are talking about him as the next Marques Colston, but several teams have spent the last few months specifically looking for the next Marques Colston. If Smith was it, wouldn't some team have drafted him in the sixth or seventh round?

Michael Spurlock, ARI: Spurlock, a quarterback and occasional running back at Mississippi, made the move to receiver in the NFL. He was promoted from the practice squad in late December and caught four passes for 31 yards in Arizona's season finale against the Chargers (39.7 percent DVOA, 1.4 DPAR).

Isaiah Stanback, DAL: Some quick facts: (1) Stanback was the starting quarterback at University of Washington before suffering a Lisfranc injury in 2006. (2) He was also a track star who reached the Pac-10 championships in the 100 meters. (3) Assuming he returns from the injury, Stanback will play wide receiver for the Cowboys. (4) At minicamp, many observers thought he was the most chiseled athlete on the team, which is saying something for a team that includes Terrell Owens. Stanback is a bright, hard-working prospect with rare speed. He'll work his way onto the field as soon as his foot heals.

John Standeford, IND: John Standeford is an undrafted free agent out of Purdue who has been sitting on the Colts' practice squad for three years. As noted in the main section, he is Aaron Moorehead in training.

Derek Stanley, STL: It's a shame that the Rams and punter Matt Turk have had ongoing contract squabbles this offseason. With Stanley on board, Turk's return would ensure the Rams' status as the only NFL team in history with two Wisconsin-Whitewater grads on the same squad. If the Rams' seventh-round pick can play past his small frame (5-foot-10, 175 pounds) and somewhat raw athleticism, he could leapfrog Turk and Atlanta Braves closer Bob Wickman to become the Warhawks' most distinguished attendee since John Belushi. The practice squad seems a more likely short-term outcome.

Syndric Steptoe, CLE: Cleveland took Steptoe in the seventh round of this year's draft and will pass him off as a return specialist. He hopes to replace Dennis Northcutt, a fellow University of Arizona alum who is now in Jacksonville. "I've studied Northcutt, being from the same school," Steptoe said. Let's hope it wasn't a three-credit course.

Chansi Stuckey, NYJ: This seventh-round pick from Clemson is an odd prospect; he's small, his 40-times aren't great, and he suffered several foot injuries in college. He's tough and has great lateral quickness, but he enters the NFL with two-and-a-half strikes against him.

Courtney Taylor, SEA: Taylor was an astute sixth-round pick for a team that traded Darrell Jackson and will lose Bobby Engram to age sooner than later. Taylor is quicker than he is fast, doesn't fear traffic, and is a good option on underneath routes. That makes this Auburn product a great fit for Mike Holmgren's offense. Of his 54 catches in his senior season, 33 were for first downs, and 14 of those converted third downs. Plus, he was totally awesome in the Dandy Warhols.

David Terrell, DEN: This former Bears bust has replaced Yale legend Brian Dowling as the true B.D. The Broncos keep goofing around with him in training camp every year, but he's not coming back.

Jerheme Urban, DAL: This former Seahawks wideout spent last year on the Cowboys' practice squad. This season, he could figure as a special-teams player, perhaps even as a holder.

Todd Watkins, ARI: This former BYU wideout is a stunning physical specimen; he's 6-foot-3 and runs a 4.28 40. He spent all last year on the Cardinals' practice squad, and his role in the 2007 offense, if he makes the team, is to run in a straight line for 50 yards and then jump. Basically, he's David Lee Roth on the 1984 tour.

Darius Watts, NYG: This ex-Broncos washout caught on with the Giants in 2006, but didn't make it to the active roster until the end of the season and never caught a pass. The trade of Tim Carter might have opened up a window for Watts, but the Steve Smith selection closed it. Now Watts is dangling half out a window looking all funny.

Terrence Wilkins, FA: After a long exile in St. Louis, Wilkins returned to the Colts in 2006 and picked up a ring by playing only on special teams. He's yet to resign with the team, and he might be done.

Brandon Williams, SF: The 49ers' third-round pick in the 2006 draft, this former Wisconsin star didn't catch a single pass last season. The problem isn't his skills, but his size—if Williams was 6-foot-4 instead of 5-foot-9, he would be Calvin Johnson. If he spent the offseason working on his upper-body strength and routes, he'll be a nifty receiver out of the slot and good return man. If he hasn't, he'll still be a competent return man.

Chandler Williams, MIN: Williams is best known as the Florida International receiver who dove helmet-first into Miami safety Kenny Philips after an interception, setting the stage for one of the most disturbing brawls in college football history. Williams is a compact, quick receiver with some punt-return ability. The Vikings have about 20 guys just like him on their roster, so Williams will have to stand out early in camp.

Wallace Wright, NYJ: This undrafted North Carolina wideout played on special teams after Tim Dwight went down last year. Dwight is back, which probably means that Wright will go back to the practice squad until Dwight gets hurt again.

Walter Young, PIT: Probably the only professional football player who's outweighed by his professional baseball namesake, this Walter Young is buried way down on the depth chart and isn't likely to see much, if any, playing time in 2007, much like his professional baseball namesake.

Kevin Youngblood, CAR: A lanky possession receiver who was very productive at Clemson, Youngblood has spent three seasons kicking around NFL practice squads. He's vying for the fourth or fifth wideout spot in Carolina.

Two chapters ago, we introduced our comments on running backs by noting that, despite the conventional wisdom, NFL teams don't seem to be sharing carries among multiple running backs any more than they were a few years ago.

A similar piece of conventional wisdom says that more teams in the NFL are using the two-tight-end set, which means more catches for tight ends. This piece of conventional wisdom is accurate. In 2006, 55 different tight ends had at least a dozen receptions, the highest total in NFL history. In 2005 the total was 53 tight ends, 49 in 2004, and 50 in both 2002 and 2003.

Prior to 2002, there had never been a year in which at least 50 tight ends had a dozen receptions. This is partly due to expansion, of course, but between 1988 and 1994 there wasn't even a season in which 40 tight ends had at least a dozen catches. The two-tight-end set reached its peak popularity in the early 1980s. In 1983, 48 tight ends had a dozen or more receptions, which was the record prior to 2002 and is roughly equivalent to last year's total given the addition of four teams in the intervening 23 years.

However, last year's total of 55 tight ends with at least a dozen receptions doesn't even include Mike Sellers of Washington and Kris Wilson of Kansas City, two fullbacks who were listed as tight ends until 2006 and combined for 33 receptions last year.

In the following section we give the last three years worth of numbers as well as a 2007 projection for every tight end who played a significant role in 2006, or is expected to play a significant role in 2007. Sellers and Wilson are also listed because they qualify as tight ends in most fantasy football leagues.

As there are no numbers yet to measure tight-end blocking, our statistical tables for tight ends are identical to those for wide receivers, an explanation for which can be found in the introduction to the "Wide Receivers" section. Tight ends caught 62 percent of all passes in 2006, so the average tight end will have a higher Catch Rate than the average wide receiver. To qualify for ranking in YAC, receiving DVOA, or receiving DPAR, a tight end must have 50 passes thrown to him in a given season. We ranked 43 tight ends in 2006, 45 in 2005, and 37 in 2004. If a tight end is a particularly strong or weak blocker, his accompanying player comment will contain a mention of his abilities in that area.

A few low-round rookies, third-stringers, and players who are listed as tight ends but really only play special teams are briefly discussed at the end of the chapter in a section we call "Going Deep." Two notes regarding our advanced metrics: We cannot yet fully separate the performance of a receiver from the performance of his quarterback. Be aware that one will affect the other. In addition, these statistics measure only passes thrown to a receiver, not performance on plays when he is not thrown the ball, such as blocking and drawing double teams.

Table 1. Top 10 TE by DPAR (Total Value), 2006

Rank	Player	Team	DPAR
1	Tony Gonzalez	KC	30.8
2	Antonio Gates	SD	26.7
3	Jason Witten	DAL	17.9
4	Dallas Clark	CHI	15.6
5	Alge Crumpler	ATL	15.5
6	Kellen Winslow	CLE	15.5
7	Todd Heap	BAL	14.4
8	Randy McMichael	MIA	14.0
9	Chris Cooley	WAS	12.6
10	Dan Campbell	DET	11.7

Table 2. Top 10 TE by DVOA (Value per Play), 2006

Rank	Player	Team	DVOA
1	Dan Campbell	DET	44.2%
2	Tony Gonzalez	KC	36.9%
3	Bryan Fletcher	IND	32.8%
4	Antonio Gates	SD	22.5%
5	Chris Baker	NYJ	20.6%
6	Owen Daniels	HOU	20.2%
7	Jason Witten	DAL	19.1%
8	Reggie Kelly	CIN	17.8%
9	Dallas Clark	CHI	16.6%
10	Randy McMichael	MIA	11.2%

Stephen Alexander   Height: 6-4   Weight: 250   College: Oklahoma   Draft: 1998/2 (48)   Born: 7-Nov-1975   Age: 32   Risk: Red

Year	Team	G	Rec	Pass	Yds	C%	Yd/C	TD	YAC	Rk	DVOA	Rk	DPAR	Rk	PAR	Short	Mid	Deep	Bomb
2004	DET	16	41	76	377	54%	9.2	1	—	—	-25.8%	34	-6.0	36	-4.4	—	—	—	—
2005	DEN	16	21	36	170	58%	8.1	1	2.0	45	-26.2%	40	-3.3	41	-3.6	55%	38%	7%	0%
2006	DEN	16	18	35	160	51%	8.9	2	5.1	7	-12.6%	32	-0.2	32	-1.6	58%	33%	6%	3%
2007	DEN		21		200		9.4	2											

There is a point at which a guy simply doesn't run fast enough to be a professional football player anymore, and, for Alexander, that point came a few years ago.

Courtney Anderson   Height: 6-6   Weight: 269   College: San Jose State   Draft: 2004/7 (245)   Born: 19-Nov-1980   Age: 27   Risk: Red

Year	Team	G	Rec	Pass	Yds	C%	Yd/C	TD	YAC	Rk	DVOA	Rk	DPAR	Rk	PAR	Short	Mid	Deep	Bomb
2004	OAK	9	13	21	175	62%	13.5	1	—	—	11.6%	—	3.5	—	3.1	—	—	—	—
2005	OAK	14	24	50	303	48%	12.6	3	4.6	23	-5.6%	28	2.2	27	2.4	50%	34%	16%	0%
2006	OAK	16	25	43	285	58%	11.4	2	3.3	37	0.5%	22	3.4	25	3.4	29%	51%	13%	7%
2007	OAK		26		245		9.3	2											

It takes a pretty good player to post a positive DVOA in an offense this bad. Anderson is a huge target in the middle of the field who can get open on ten-yard crossing patterns and gain a few yards after the catch. He's a competent player on a team that has forgotten what competence looks like. With so many wide receivers and tight ends in Raiders camp this year, Anderson may not even make the team, but that loss will just be some other team's gain.

Chris Baker   Height: 6-3   Weight: 258   College: Michigan State   Draft: 2002/3 (88)   Born: 18-Nov-1979   Age: 28   Risk: Red

Year	Team	G	Rec	Pass	Yds	C%	Yd/C	TD	YAC	Rk	DVOA	Rk	DPAR	Rk	PAR	Short	Mid	Deep	Bomb
2004	NYJ	15	18	29	182	62%	10.1	4	—	—	14.1%	14	5.3	20	3.5	—	—	—	—
2005	NYJ	8	18	25	269	72%	14.9	1	7.2	2	47.5%	1	9.3	13	8.9	50%	29%	21%	0%
2006	NYJ	16	31	45	300	69%	9.7	4	4.0	25	20.7%	5	9.7	12	7.8	53%	36%	11%	0%
2007	NYJ		23		301		13.3	2											

A fine all-purpose tight end, Baker bounced back from a 2005 broken ankle with a career year. He came alive late in the season, with 13 catches for 130 yards, ten first downs, and two touchdowns in his last five games. Baker wasn't used as a seam-splitter very often in 2006, but he has the speed to surprise a safety deep if given the chance.

Anthony Becht   Height: 6-5   Weight: 272   College: West Virginia   Draft: 2000/1 (27)   Born: 8-Aug-1977   Age: 30   Risk: Red

Year	Team	G	Rec	Pass	Yds	C%	Yd/C	TD	YAC	Rk	DVOA	Rk	DPAR	Rk	PAR	Short	Mid	Deep	Bomb
2004	NYJ	16	13	28	100	46%	7.7	1	—	—	-25.4%	33	-2.4	32	-3.7	—	—	—	—
2005	TB	16	16	25	112	64%	7.0	0	3.1	38	-27.0%	41	-2.3	39	-3.5	57%	43%	0%	0%
2006	TB	16	18	26	115	69%	6.4	1	2.8	39	-31.2%	43	-3.2	40	-3.8	76%	20%	4%	0%
2007	TB		12		47		4.0	0											

Buccaneers tight ends caught 55 passes last year for 6.9 yards per reception, the lowest average in the NFL. They were targeted 83 times, so the average pass attempt to a Tampa tight end netted just 4.6 yards. It's a sign of systemic offensive collapse when more than five passes per game are dumped to players in no position to do anything with the football. Becht is a fair blocker, but an inadequate receiver who should be relegated to the bench once Jon Gruden finally sorts out his offensive line.

Adam Bergen   Height: 6-4   Weight: 263   College: Lehigh   Draft: 2005/FA   Born: 3-Sep-1983   Age: 24   Risk: Red

Year	Team	G	Rec	Pass	Yds	C%	Yd/C	TD	YAC	Rk	DVOA	Rk	DPAR	Rk	PAR	Short	Mid	Deep	Bomb
2005	ARI	16	28	43	270	65%	9.6	1	4.2	27	-8.5%	31	1.2	31	1.2	71%	24%	3%	3%
2006	ARI	14	15	24	111	63%	7.4	1	2.6	—	-49.6%	—	-5.9	—	-6.7	67%	21%	8%	4%
2007	FA		17		195		11.4	2											

Bergen went undrafted in 2005, but was wise enough to sign with a team that had a completely empty depth chart at his position, making him the Arizona starter as a rookie. The Cardinals drafted a tight end the next year, Leonard Pope, ending Bergen's time as a starter, and a very poor season that ended with a sprained MCL ended Bergen's time as a Cardinal. He's a free agent at press time.

Dwayne Blakley   Height: 6-4   Weight: 257   College: Missouri   Draft: 2003/FA   Born: 10-Aug-1979   Age: 28   Risk: Red

Year	Team	G	Rec	Pass	Yds	C%	Yd/C	TD	YAC	Rk	DVOA	Rk	DPAR	Rk	PAR	Short	Mid	Deep	Bomb
2005	ATL	15	4	7	30	57%	7.5	1	2.8	—	-20.2%	—	-0.3	—	0.1	29%	57%	14%	0%
2006	ATL	16	6	14	76	43%	12.7	0	3.2	—	-31.6%	—	-1.5	—	-0.7	27%	40%	33%	0%
2007	*ATL*		*9*		*79*		*8.8*	*1*											

Blakley, a solid H-back type, has a little speed and can catch, but probably lacks a role in Bobby Petrino's offense. Blakley has said that he doesn't play as himself or the Falcons in *Madden* because he likes to build a franchise up from the depths of mediocrity. This year, he can play as himself.

Kyle Brady   Height: 6-6   Weight: 278   College: Penn State   Draft: 1995/1 (9)   Born: 14-Jan-1972   Age: 35   Risk: Red

Year	Team	G	Rec	Pass	Yds	C%	Yd/C	TD	YAC	Rk	DVOA	Rk	DPAR	Rk	PAR	Short	Mid	Deep	Bomb
2004	JAC	11	14	23	103	61%	7.4	1	—	—	-36.9%	—	-3.4	—	-2.1	—	—	—	—
2005	JAC	16	18	26	157	69%	8.7	1	3.4	35	-46.4%	44	-5.3	44	-5.0	60%	24%	16%	0%
2006	JAC	15	5	8	37	63%	7.4	0	2.4	—	-30.0%	—	-1.0	—	-1.1	57%	43%	0%	0%
2007	*NE*		*4*		*17*		*4.3*	*1*											

Back in 1995, Brady was the player Bill Belichick coveted above all others. Everyone knew, including the New York Jets, who didn't say a word to Brady before drafting him with the ninth-overall pick, one before Belichick's Browns. A shattered Belichick traded down for the 30th pick, drafted Ohio State LB Craig Powell, and was fired after the season. Now Belichick has his man and, while his expectations are slightly lower, Brady slots in well as a wham-blocking replacement for Daniel Graham.

Mark Bruener   Height: 6-4   Weight: 260   College: Washington   Draft: 1995/1 (27)   Born: 16-Sep-1972   Age: 35   Risk: Red

Year	Team	G	Rec	Pass	Yds	C%	Yd/C	TD	YAC	Rk	DVOA	Rk	DPAR	Rk	PAR	Short	Mid	Deep	Bomb
2004	HOU	16	4	10	52	40%	13.0	0	—	—	-38.2%	—	-1.8	—	-1.5	—	—	—	—
2005	HOU	16	2	4	22	50%	11.0	0	1.0	—	-39.8%	—	-0.6	—	-0.3	75%	0%	25%	0%
2006	HOU	15	9	10	62	90%	6.9	2	2.8	—	30.2%	—	2.9	—	2.8	78%	11%	11%	0%
2007	*HOU*		*6*		*24*		*4.0*	*0*											

Let's hear it for Gary Kubiak's tight end–friendly offense; Bruener had more receptions and touchdowns in 2006 than in the previous three years put together. Of course, that's still only nine catches and two TDs. Unlike most first-round tight ends, this 12-year veteran has always been known as a blocker first. That works for the Texans, because Owen Daniels and Jeb Putzier are terrible blockers.

Dan Campbell   Height: 6-5   Weight: 263   College: Texas A&M   Draft: 1999/3 (79)   Born: 13-Apr-1976   Age: 31   Risk: Yellow

Year	Team	G	Rec	Pass	Yds	C%	Yd/C	TD	YAC	Rk	DVOA	Rk	DPAR	Rk	PAR	Short	Mid	Deep	Bomb
2004	DAL	3	2	2	16	100%	8.0	0	—	—	94.1%	—	0.9	—	0.7	—	—	—	—
2005	DAL	16	3	8	24	38%	8.0	1	6.3	—	0.5%	—	0.8	—	0.7	88%	12%	0%	0%
2006	DET	16	21	32	308	66%	14.7	4	5.2	5	44.1%	1	11.7	10	11.1	43%	32%	21%	4%
2007	*DET*		*17*		*126*		*7.6*	*2*											

In past years, Campbell was a blocker first and occasionally used as a goal-line decoy or dump-off outlet. In 2006 he randomly emerged as a downfield threat with 14.7 yards per reception, though that seems to have been more the result of good play-calling than Campbell's sudden transformation into a dynamic receiver. Still, he was a good signing by Matt Millen. Blind squirrels, nuts, and so forth.

Mark Campbell   Height: 6-6   Weight: 255   College: Michigan   Draft: 1999/FA   Born: 6-Dec-1975   Age: 32   Risk: Yellow

Year	Team	G	Rec	Pass	Yds	C%	Yd/C	TD	YAC	Rk	DVOA	Rk	DPAR	Rk	PAR	Short	Mid	Deep	Bomb
2004	BUF	12	17	30	203	57%	11.9	5	—	—	9.3%	—	4.1	—	3.0	—	—	—	—
2005	BUF	14	19	29	139	66%	7.3	0	5.1	11	-46.9%	45	-5.8	45	-3.9	78%	9%	13%	0%
2006	NO	14	18	29	164	62%	9.1	0	4.3	18	-20.0%	36	-1.1	36	0.7	71%	21%	7%	0%
2007	*NO*		*12*		*80*		*6.7*	*1*											

With Billy Miller and Eric Johnson on the roster, Campbell will be squeezed for playing time, but his blocking skills should keep him on the field in short-yardage situations and on special teams.

Dallas Clark | Height: 6-3 | Weight: 257 | College: Iowa | Draft: 2003/1 (24) | Born: 12-Jun-1979 | Age: 28 | Risk: Green

Year	Team	G	Rec	Pass	Yds	C%	Yd/C	TD	YAC	Rk	DVOA	Rk	DPAR	Rk	PAR	Short	Mid	Deep	Bomb
2004	IND	15	25	39	423	64%	16.9	5	—	—	17.2%	11	7.6	16	7.4	—	—	—	—
2005	IND	15	37	51	488	73%	13.2	4	4.9	16	32.6%	2	15.3	7	17.5	39%	35%	22%	4%
2006	IND	12	30	57	367	53%	12.2	4	4.2	20	9.2%	13	7.9	15	6.9	42%	33%	16%	9%
2007	IND		38		434		11.3	5											

We have to admit, listing Dallas Clark as a tight end for 2006 is a bit silly. Clark was always more of a receiver than a blocker, but with Brandon Stokley injured, he pretty much changed his position for the season. Game charters listed Clark working out of the slot on 414 plays last year. That was more than three times as many plays as any other tight end except for Antonio Gates, who had 185 (Alge Crumpler, Tony Gonzalez, and Chris Cooley round out the top five). Still, Clark's numbers for 2006 certainly don't look out of line with his career and won't blow anybody away. If you use the wide-receiver baseline instead of the tight-end baseline, his DVOA drops a bit to 2.9 percent, but that's fine; Clark was there to help free up Marvin Harrison and Reggie Wayne, and to take advantage of defenses whose linebackers were poor in coverage such as, say, the New England Patriots. The arrival of Anthony Gonzalez means that Clark will probably be more of a true tight end this year. Nonetheless, for Dallas Clark, being more of a tight end still means being less of a tight end than any other tight end.

Desmond Clark | Height: 6-3 | Weight: 255 | College: Wake Forest | Draft: 1999/6 (179) | Born: 20-Apr-1977 | Age: 30 | Risk: Red

Year	Team	G	Rec	Pass	Yds	C%	Yd/C	TD	YAC	Rk	DVOA	Rk	DPAR	Rk	PAR	Short	Mid	Deep	Bomb
2004	CHI	15	24	49	282	49%	11.8	1	—	—	-29.4%	35	-4.3	34	-1.6	—	—	—	—
2005	CHI	16	24	49	229	49%	9.5	2	3.0	40	-7.2%	29	1.3	30	-0.8	62%	29%	5%	5%
2006	CHI	16	45	80	626	56%	13.9	6	4.6	13	16.5%	9	15.5	4	17.4	39%	48%	9%	4%
2007	CHI		33		399		12.1	3											

The Bears finally featured Clark in the offense last year, and he responded with one of the most underappreciated performances of the NFL season. He was also Rex Grossman's best red zone target, catching six touchdowns. KUBIAK's projection splits the difference between his past two seasons, which may be correct because Clark slowed noticeably as 2006 progressed; he topped 50 receiving yards in four of the first seven games, but only once in the final nine. That decreased effectiveness was partly due to the fact that Clark was kept in for pass protection after the Bears' embarrassing loss to Miami. The addition of Greg Olsen means Clark's role in the offense shifts to primarily blocking, or, alternately, being the new house producer for the 7th Floor Crew.

Ernie Conwell | Height: 6-2 | Weight: 265 | College: Washington | Draft: 1996/2 (59) | Born: 17-Aug-1972 | Age: 35 | Risk: Red

Year	Team	G	Rec	Pass	Yds	C%	Yd/C	TD	YAC	Rk	DVOA	Rk	DPAR	Rk	PAR	Short	Mid	Deep	Bomb
2004	NO	16	10	19	102	53%	10.2	1	—	—	-23.6%	—	-1.3	—	-0.9	—	—	—	—
2005	NO	9	13	29	165	45%	12.7	1	4.7	21	-25.1%	39	-2.2	38	-1.8	27%	58%	12%	4%
2006	NO	7	8	13	57	62%	7.1	1	2.4	—	-19.2%	—	-0.3	—	0.8	77%	23%	0%	0%
2007	FA		15		157		10.2	1											

Conwell started just five games for the Saints last season and missed the second half of the season with a knee injury. Waived by the Saints in February, he's probably through.

Chris Cooley | Height: 6-3 | Weight: 265 | College: Utah State | Draft: 2004/3 (81) | Born: 11-Jul-1982 | Age: 25 | Risk: Green

Year	Team	G	Rec	Pass	Yds	C%	Yd/C	TD	YAC	Rk	DVOA	Rk	DPAR	Rk	PAR	Short	Mid	Deep	Bomb
2004	WAS	16	37	63	314	59%	8.5	6	—	—	2.1%	24	5.8	18	4.7	—	—	—	—
2005	WAS	16	71	103	774	69%	10.9	7	7.0	3	12.5%	12	16.9	4	16.4	64%	23%	10%	2%
2006	WAS	16	57	95	734	60%	12.9	6	7.4	1	8.0%	16	12.5	9	15.3	46%	33%	18%	2%
2007	WAS		62		745		12.0	6											

Easily one of the best draft picks of the second Joe Gibbs era, Cooley is one of the league's best tight ends. He led the team in receiving last season primarily because opposing defenses were double-teaming Santana Moss and quarterback Mark Brunell didn't have the arm strength to consistently get the ball down the field. Cooley has always been a reliable pass catcher (his 71 catches in 2005 were second on the team), but his blocking was much improved in 2006.

Alge Crumpler

Height: 6-2 **Weight:** 262 **College:** North Carolina **Draft:** 2000/2 (35) **Born:** 23-Dec-1977 **Age:** 29 **Risk:** Green

Year	Team	G	Rec	Pass	Yds	C%	Yd/C	TD	YAC	Rk	DVOA	Rk	DPAR	Rk	PAR	Short	Mid	Deep	Bomb
2004	ATL	14	48	74	774	65%	16.1	6	—	—	37.8%	1	23.6	4	24.6	—	—	—	—
2005	ATL	16	65	118	877	55%	13.5	5	4.3	25	2.0%	21	10.8	11	10.9	30%	45%	22%	3%
2006	ATL	16	56	103	780	54%	13.9	8	4.4	15	10.0%	12	15.3	5	17.1	24%	53%	17%	6%
2007	ATL		64		811		12.6	6											

Thirty-eight percent of the Falcons' red zone passes were directed at Crumpler. Among tight ends, only Antonio Gates was the target on a higher percentage of his team's red zone passes, and only Gates and Jeremy Shockey bested Crumpler's total of 19 red zone targets. Crumpler will remain a focal point of the Falcons' offense under Bobby Petrino, and the new coach plans to split Crumpler out as a wide receiver on occasion to create mismatches. As good as Crumpler is, the Falcons would be better off if he wasn't their top target. The team realizes this, which is why they have spent so much on Peerless Price, Ashley Lelie, Joe Horn, Michael Jenkins, and Roddy White in recent years, but Crumpler remains the top option in the passing game, in part because he's so big that the quarterback has a hard time missing him.

Owen Daniels

Height: 6-3 **Weight:** 250 **College:** Wisconsin **Draft:** 2006/4 (98) **Born:** 9-Nov-1982 **Age:** 25 **Risk:** Red

Year	Team	G	Rec	Pass	Yds	C%	Yd/C	TD	YAC	Rk	DVOA	Rk	DPAR	Rk	PAR	Short	Mid	Deep	Bomb
2006	HOU	14	34	51	352	67%	10.4	5	5.0	8	20.1%	6	11.1	11	11.7	60%	29%	9%	2%
2007	HOU		33		388		11.9	3											

Daniels started his college career at Wisconsin as a quarterback, blew out his left ACL in 2002, switched to tight end, and never caught more than 25 passes in a season with the Badgers. He was probably as surprised as the rest of us when the Texans threw to him 51 times last year. Daniels is an H-back type who fits Gary Kubiak's system well; he knows how to work underneath on rollouts and play-action passes, and is athletic enough to gain a yard or two after the catch. He's not that fast, and linebackers trampled him in the running game, but he can move the chains.

Vernon Davis

Height: 6-3 **Weight:** 253 **College:** Maryland **Draft:** 2006/1 (6) **Born:** 31-Jan-1984 **Age:** 23 **Risk:** Yellow

Year	Team	G	Rec	Pass	Yds	C%	Yd/C	TD	YAC	Rk	DVOA	Rk	DPAR	Rk	PAR	Short	Mid	Deep	Bomb
2006	SF	10	20	42	265	48%	13.3	3	5.8	3	-25.4%	41	-3.0	39	-1.0	50%	25%	10%	0%
2007	SF		49		604		12.3	5											

Calling Davis athletic is like calling Wile E. Coyote injury-prone—the statement doesn't do justice to the facts. The Maryland tight end was the star of the 2006 Scouting Combine after running a 4.38 40 and putting up more bench-press reps than D'Brickashaw Ferguson, and San Francisco happily selected him with the sixth overall pick. As a rookie, Davis missed six games with a hairline fracture of his left fibula, but showed glimpses of an extremely productive future—especially late in the season against Green Bay and Arizona, when he averaged over 20 yards per catch. With Eric Johnson gone to New Orleans, Davis could be a huge fantasy pickup, especially given the fact that the potential production of San Francisco's corps of receivers remains a mystery. Improving his 29 percent Catch Rate on third down will help.

Jeff Dugan

Height: 6-3 **Weight:** 258 **College:** Maryland **Draft:** 2004/7 (220) **Born:** 8-Apr-1981 **Age:** 26 **Risk:** Red

Year	Team	G	Rec	Pass	Yds	C%	Yd/C	TD	YAC	Rk	DVOA	Rk	DPAR	Rk	PAR	Short	Mid	Deep	Bomb
2006	MIN	7	8	13	40	62%	5.0	1	3.9	—	-26.5%	—	-1.2	—	-1.1	92%	8%	0%	0%
2007	MIN		11		104		9.8	1											

This Jeff Dugan is not the proprietor and protagonist of jeffdugan.com, whose star worked as a producer at the Discovery Channel and documented his trips chasing the ghost of Nick Drake around England and riding through Paris on a Segway. Instead, he's a replacement-level tight end who will battle Richard Owens and Visanthe Shiancoe to be the backup to Jim Kleinsasser, which sounds almost as exotic as what the other Jeff Dugan's been up to.

Anthony Fasano

Height: 6-5 **Weight:** 255 **College:** Notre Dame **Draft:** 2006/2 (53) **Born:** 20-Apr-1984 **Age:** 23 **Risk:** Red

Year	Team	G	Rec	Pass	Yds	C%	Yd/C	TD	YAC	Rk	DVOA	Rk	DPAR	Rk	PAR	Short	Mid	Deep	Bomb
2006	DAL	16	14	24	126	58%	9.0	0	4.1	—	-21.6%	—	-1.2	—	-0.6	45%	45%	5%	5%
2007	DAL		25		251		10.3	1											

Fasano's contribution to the Cowboys was far greater than his stats indicate. He played tight end, H-back, and fullback, motioning all over the formation before the snap. He was even the lead blocker in a "Dotted-I" formation that Bill Parcells pulled out of an old Hank Stram playbook (the formation had Fasano, a fullback, and Julius Jones line up perpendicular to

(continued next page)

Anthony Fasano *(continued)*

the line of scrimmage; in the video games they call it "Maryland-I"). Fasano blocked very well, ran lots of mesh routes crossing the middle of the field and tangling up the defenders covering Jason Witten or Terrell Owens, and never demanded the ball, which was good, because he wasn't going to get it very often. Fasano has the receiving skills to catch 40 passes in a different system, but he doesn't need gaudy stats to help a team.

Casey FitzSimmons   Height: 6-3   Weight: 250   College: Carrol   Draft: 2003/FA   Born: 10-Oct-1980   Age: 27   Risk: Red

Year	Team	G	Rec	Pass	Yds	C%	Yd/C	TD	YAC	Rk	DVOA	Rk	DPAR	Rk	PAR	Short	Mid	Deep	Bomb
2004	DET	16	10	14	103	71%	10.3	0	—	—	3.4%	—	1.6	—	2.1	—	—	—	—
2005	DET	14	10	17	45	59%	4.5	1	1.1	—	-28.0%	—	-1.7	—	-2.9	67%	33%	0%	0%
2006	DET	11	7	10	71	70%	10.1	0	7.3	—	9.3%	—	1.3	—	0.9	64%	18%	9%	9%
2007	*DET*		*14*		*129*		*9.5*	*0*											

FitzSimmons began last season on the inactive list but started two games late in the year after the Lions gave up on Marcus Pollard. He even caught four passes against the Falcons. He's a third tight end and special teamer.

Bryan Fletcher   Height: 6-5   Weight: 235   College: UCLA   Draft: 2002/6 (210)   Born: 23-Mar-1979   Age: 28   Risk: Green

Year	Team	G	Rec	Pass	Yds	C%	Yd/C	TD	YAC	Rk	DVOA	Rk	DPAR	Rk	PAR	Short	Mid	Deep	Bomb
2005	IND	16	18	27	202	67%	11.2	3	5.5	7	31.6%	4	7.3	16	7.9	50%	46%	4%	0%
2006	IND	14	18	25	202	72%	11.2	2	4.1	24	32.4%	3	7.2	18	7.1	52%	28%	12%	8%
2007	*IND*		*18*		*202*		*11.2*	*2*											

Occupation: Colts second tight end. Job Description: (1) Line up as the actual tight end when Dallas Clark is in the slot. (2) Block on cutback runs and in max-protect schemes. (3) Get open when everyone else is covered and be ready for that checkdown pass. Both Fletcher and Ben Utecht are effective in this role. Utecht is the better blocker, but Fletcher is much faster and more dangerous as a receiver. They'll share the role again this season, but Fletcher is the better prospect if Clark ever leaves the Colts. Someday, Fletcher might even have a season with more than 18 catches for 202 yards.

Bubba Franks   Height: 6-6   Weight: 263   College: Miami   Draft: 2000/1 (14)   Born: 6-Jan-1978   Age: 29   Risk: Red

Year	Team	G	Rec	Pass	Yds	C%	Yd/C	TD	YAC	Rk	DVOA	Rk	DPAR	Rk	PAR	Short	Mid	Deep	Bomb
2004	GB	16	34	50	361	68%	10.6	7	—	—	20.1%	8	11.4	10	12.3	—	—	—	—
2005	GB	10	25	39	207	67%	8.3	1	2.6	44	-17.8%	37	-1.2	36	-0.1	36%	42%	12%	9%
2006	GB	16	25	53	232	47%	9.3	0	4.4	17	-30.4%	42	-6.5	43	-10.1	55%	39%	2%	5%
2007	*GB*		*18*		*139*		*7.5*	*1*											

Franks has always been a little overrated because he used to catch a lot of touchdowns in goal-line situations. Now he is really offering nothing to the team. He is still under 30, but seems a step slow when blocking and struggles to get any kind of separation in the open field. He also appeared unmotivated and uninterested the last couple of seasons. If he's not out of Green Bay before the season starts—the Packers were using Donald Lee as the first-team tight end during minicamp—he's out after it's over.

Michael Gaines   Height: 6-2   Weight: 275   College: UCF   Draft: 2004/7 (232)   Born: 30-Mar-1980   Age: 27   Risk: Red

Year	Team	G	Rec	Pass	Yds	C%	Yd/C	TD	YAC	Rk	DVOA	Rk	DPAR	Rk	PAR	Short	Mid	Deep	Bomb
2004	CAR	14	4	14	34	29%	8.5	0	—	—	-74.0%	—	-6.2	—	-6.2	—	—	—	—
2005	CAR	11	12	16	155	75%	12.9	2	4.6	—	49.4%	—	6.2	—	5.9	50%	17%	25%	8%
2006	CAR	16	15	28	146	54%	9.7	0	3.8	30	-24.9%	40	-2.1	38	-1.4	45%	45%	5%	5%
2007	*CAR*		*20*		*193*		*9.7*	*2*											

Gaines, a lumbering right tackle who was accidentally issued a uniform number in the 80s, caught four passes for 54 yards in the Panthers' 37–3 loss to the Steelers. There's probably a direct correlation between the number of times a team throws to a 280-pound tight end in a game and the likelihood that they will lose by five touchdowns. Gaines was tendered as a restricted free agent because of his blocking skills; hopefully, we'll have no more of this "four catch" nonsense.

Antonio Gates

Height: 6-4 Weight: 260 College: Kent State Draft: 2003/FA Born: 18-Jun-1980 Age: 27 Risk: Green

Year	Team	G	Rec	Pass	Yds	C%	Yd/C	TD	YAC	Rk	DVOA	Rk	DPAR	Rk	PAR	Short	Mid	Deep	Bomb
2004	SD	15	81	114	964	71%	11.9	13	—	—	36.1%	2	35.3	2	39.5	—	—	—	—
2005	SD	15	89	140	1101	64%	12.4	10	4.7	18	26.7%	6	34.4	1	32.9	43%	39%	16%	2%
2006	SD	16	71	120	924	59%	13.0	9	4.3	19	22.8%	4	26.9	2	24.0	35%	41%	21%	3%
2007	SD		79		970		12.3	9											

Gates remains at the top of his game, whether he's using his speed as a deep threat, catching short passes over the middle on 3rd-and-5, or running corner routes in the end zone. He's not a great blocker, which is why he sometimes comes off the field on obvious running plays, but he's the best tight end in the league right now. We were asked on a radio show before the draft whether teams were actively scouting players such as Gates. It's unlikely that any team devotes the resources to sending a scout to watch 20 to 25 college basketball games when they could be watching football, and, for every Gates, there are a few Jai Lewises who can't stand training camp and end up playing basketball in Israel.

Tony Gonzalez

Height: 6-4 Weight: 248 College: California Draft: 1997/1 (13) Born: 27-Feb-1976 Age: 31 Risk: Yellow

Year	Team	G	Rec	Pass	Yds	C%	Yd/C	TD	YAC	Rk	DVOA	Rk	DPAR	Rk	PAR	Short	Mid	Deep	Bomb
2004	KC	16	102	141	1258	70%	12.3	7	—	—	35.9%	3	43.1	1	43.6	—	—	—	—
2005	KC	16	78	116	905	67%	11.6	2	3.5	34	19.3%	8	22.6	3	21.7	38%	43%	16%	3%
2006	KC	15	73	104	900	70%	12.3	5	3.9	28	35.5%	2	30.2	1	31.0	31%	54%	15%	0%
2007	KC		61		705		11.6	5											

Gonzalez continued to play at a high level in 2006, but it can't last forever. He's getting old and is ripe for a drop-off in 2007. Then again, that's what we said last year. It's not surprising that the Chiefs signed him to a long-term contract as a show of loyalty to a player who's had an honorable career, but showing loyalty to aging veterans isn't the way to build for the future. If the Chiefs' offense suffers dramatically from the loss of Will Shields and Trent Green, Gonzalez will likely be blamed for that which isn't his fault.

Daniel Graham

Height: 6-3 Weight: 257 College: Colorado Draft: 2002/1 (21) Born: 16-Nov-1978 Age: 29 Risk: Red

Year	Team	G	Rec	Pass	Yds	C%	Yd/C	TD	YAC	Rk	DVOA	Rk	DPAR	Rk	PAR	Short	Mid	Deep	Bomb
2004	NE	14	30	48	364	63%	12.1	7	—	—	32.5%	5	13.6	9	12.2	—	—	—	—
2005	NE	11	16	26	236	64%	14.7	3	11.9	1	16.7%	9	4.3	22	3.6	52%	32%	16%	0%
2006	NE	12	21	34	235	62%	11.2	2	4.5	14	-3.2%	27	2.2	28	3.5	53%	29%	18%	0%
2007	DEN		29		307		10.6	4											

The Broncos and Seahawks got into bidding wars for the services of Graham and defensive end Patrick Kerney. When the smoke cleared, the Seahawks had Kerney, the Broncos had Graham, and both players had a few million extra dollars in the bank. Graham's five-year, $25-million contract is a little rich, but he's one of the two or three best blocking tight ends in the league. The University of Colorado alum and son of a Broncos linebacker should be a hit with the fans.

Ben Hartsock

Height: 6-3 Weight: 264 College: Ohio State Draft: 2004/3 (68) Born: 5-Jul-1980 Age: 27 Risk: N/A

Year	Team	G	Rec	Pass	Yds	C%	Yd/C	TD	YAC	Rk	DVOA	Rk	DPAR	Rk	PAR	Short	Mid	Deep	Bomb
2004	IND	16	4	8	33	50%	8.3	0	—	—	-33.4%	—	-1.3	—	-2.4	—	—	—	—
2005	IND	6	2	2	8	100%	4.0	0	—	—	-41.8%	—	-0.5	—	-0.3	—	—	—	—
2006	TEN	6	6	15	68	40%	11.3	0	8.2	—	-25.0%	—	-1.2	—	-1.6	43%	50%	7%	0%
2007	TEN		12		121		9.8	1											

The Titans claimed Hartsock off waivers from the Colts in October. Pressed into service when Ben Troupe was hurt in November, Hartsock earned substantial playing time as a second tight end and H-back. He's an effective in-line blocker with acceptable hands and special-teams value, so he'll stick on a Titans team that frequently uses two-tight-end sets.

Todd Heap

Height: 6-5 Weight: 252 College: Arizona State Draft: 2001/1 (31) Born: 16-Mar-1980 Age: 27 Risk: Green

Year	Team	G	Rec	Pass	Yds	C%	Yd/C	TD	YAC	Rk	DVOA	Rk	DPAR	Rk	PAR	Short	Mid	Deep	Bomb
2004	BAL	6	27	44	303	61%	11.2	3	—	—	19.9%	9	8.6	13	7.5	—	—	—	—
2005	BAL	16	75	114	855	66%	11.4	7	3.4	36	10.9%	15	16.3	6	15.2	44%	36%	19%	1%
2006	BAL	16	73	116	765	63%	10.5	6	3.5	35	6.9%	17	14.4	7	14.3	43%	45%	11%	2%
2007	BAL		60		645		10.8	5											

(continued next page)

Todd Heap *(continued)*

Steve McNair learned quickly where the bread is buttered in the Baltimore passing game. Only two tight ends (Antonio Gates and Kellen Winslow) saw more than the 115 balls fired Heap's way. His Catch Rate (63 percent) indicates above-average hands, and he knows how to get open when the field gets short—his DVOA skyrocketed to 41.2 percent in the red zone.

Steve Heiden   Height: 6-5   Weight: 265   College: South Dakota State   Draft: 1999/3 (69)   Born: 21-Sep-1976   Age: 31   Risk: Yellow

Year	Team	G	Rec	Pass	Yds	C%	Yd/C	TD	YAC	Rk	DVOA	Rk	DPAR	Rk	PAR	Short	Mid	Deep	Bomb
2004	CLE	13	28	42	287	67%	10.3	5	—	—	12.6%	16	6.7	17	5.5	—	—	—	—
2005	CLE	15	43	60	401	72%	9.3	3	4.2	28	-0.2%	23	5.2	19	6.6	54%	41%	2%	4%
2006	CLE	16	36	46	249	78%	6.9	2	4.1	22	-8.4%	31	1.3	31	1.8	70%	23%	7%	0%
2007	*CLE*		*12*		*119*		*9.7*	*0*											

Heiden is painfully slow and has always been a blocker first and a receiver second, but the Browns' passing game struggled so much to get anything going downfield last year that Heiden ended up being the target of quite a few passes when no one else was open.

Will Heller   Height: 6-6   Weight: 250   College: Georgia Tech   Draft: 2003/FA   Born: 28-Feb-1981   Age: 26   Risk: Red

Year	Team	G	Rec	Pass	Yds	C%	Yd/C	TD	YAC	Rk	DVOA	Rk	DPAR	Rk	PAR	Short	Mid	Deep	Bomb
2004	TB	10	12	16	98	75%	8.2	1	—	—	-29.0%	—	-1.7	—	-1.4	—	—	—	—
2005	MIA	7	1	2	1	50%	2.0	1	0.0	—	5.9%	—	0.3	—	0.2	50%	50%	100%	100%
2006	SEA	16	4	5	32	80%	8.0	1	2.0	—	32.3%	—	1.3	—	1.5	40%	60%	0%	0%
2007	*SEA*		*13*		*87*		*6.6*	*1*											

Acquired by the Seahawks before the 2006 season, Heller had been on Tim Ruskell's radar since they both resided in Tampa Bay—Ruskell as director of player personnel and Heller as an undrafted free agent who bounced on and off the Bucs' roster. Heller's more a blocking tight end than anything else, but he will see a career-high in passes this year because the only tight end ahead of him on the depth chart is 35-year-old Marcus Pollard.

Eric Johnson   Height: 6-3   Weight: 256   College: Yale   Draft: 2001/7 (224)   Born: 15-Sep-1979   Age: 28   Risk: Red

Year	Team	G	Rec	Pass	Yds	C%	Yd/C	TD	YAC	Rk	DVOA	Rk	DPAR	Rk	PAR	Short	Mid	Deep	Bomb
2004	SF	16	82	117	825	70%	10.1	2	—	—	17.9%	10	21.9	5	20.3	—	—	—	—
2006	SF	13	34	49	292	69%	8.6	2	4.1	23	-0.1%	23	3.6	24	1.6	73%	14%	11%	2%
2007	*NO*		*22*		*223*		*10.0*	*2*											

Johnson's 82 receptions in 2004 set a franchise record for tight ends. The 49ers wanted to retain the veteran free agent this offseason, but Johnson saw the writing on the wall after San Francisco picked Vernon Davis in the 2006 draft, and, though he still led the team in DPAR and receptions by a tight end in 2006, he accepted a one-year, $2-million offer from the Saints to be their primary option at the position. Like his long-lost baseball-playing cousin Nick, he'll put up big numbers—if he can stay healthy.

Doug Jolley   Height: 6-4   Weight: 250   College: BYU   Draft: 2002/2 (55)   Born: 2-Jan-1979   Age: 28   Risk: Red

Year	Team	G	Rec	Pass	Yds	C%	Yd/C	TD	YAC	Rk	DVOA	Rk	DPAR	Rk	PAR	Short	Mid	Deep	Bomb
2004	OAK	16	27	48	313	56%	11.6	2	—	—	-4.8%	28	2.4	27	2.7	—	—	—	—
2005	NYJ	16	29	50	324	58%	11.2	1	5.5	6	-16.5%	35	-1.3	37	-2.2	60%	24%	13%	2%
2006	TB	11	1	2	7	50%	7.0	0	0.0	—	-21.4%	—	-0.1	—	0.0	0%	50%	50%	0%
2007	*FA*		*5*		*37*		*7.4*	*0*											

Remember when the Jets traded a first-round pick for Jolley and a second-round pick way back in 2005? Good times. Jolley is now a receiving tight end for hire. He saw limited action for the Bucs last season, sometimes lining up as a wide receiver. A former college quarterback, Jolley is versatile enough to play poorly at several positions. He might actually have been a worse move than the guy the Jets chose with their second-round pick that year, "the Nuge," Mike Nugent.

Reggie Kelly Height: 6-4 Weight: 255 College: Mississippi State . Draft: 1999/2 (42) Born: 22-Feb-1977 Age: 30 Risk: Red

Year	Team	G	Rec	Pass	Yds	C%	Yd/C	TD	YAC	Rk	DVOA	Rk	DPAR	Rk	PAR	Short	Mid	Deep	Bomb
2004	CIN	16	15	21	85	71%	5.7	0	—	—	-34.1%	—	-3.1	—	-3.6	—	—	—	—
2005	CIN	15	15	18	90	83%	6.0	1	2.3	—	-23.6%	—	-1.4	—	-1.9	78%	17%	6%	0%
2006	CIN	16	21	33	254	64%	12.1	1	3.9	27	17.9%	8	6.5	19	5.6	55%	21%	24%	0%
2007	CIN		15		221		14.4	2											

When the top three receivers on a team all see the ball at an above-league-average rate, chances are the tight end isn't much of a factor. Meet Reggie Kelly, a serviceable player for what the Bengals need him to do: block in the running game and not demand the ball in the huddle. All the other tight ends keep moving out to the slot, but Kelly is going the other way, lining up at fullback on at least a third of his snaps last year.

Jim Kleinsasser Height: 6-3 Weight: 272 College: North Dakota Draft: 1999/2 (44) Born: 31-Jan-1977 Age: 30 Risk: Yellow

Year	Team	G	Rec	Pass	Yds	C%	Yd/C	TD	YAC	Rk	DVOA	Rk	DPAR	Rk	PAR	Short	Mid	Deep	Bomb
2004	MIN	1	2	3	24	67%	12.0	0	—	—	28.4%	—	0.8	—	1.0	—	—	—	—
2005	MIN	16	22	28	171	79%	7.8	0	4.1	29	-16.8%	36	-0.8	35	-1.8	77%	23%	0%	0%
2006	MIN	16	7	16	47	44%	6.7	0	2.3	—	-40.2%	—	-3.0	—	-4.1	57%	29%	7%	7%
2007	MIN		19		152		7.8	1											

Kleinsasser's transition from fullback to H-back to tight end is complete despite the fact that he's still wearing number 40. As a tight end, he is exclusively a blocker. His 46 receptions in 2003 seem a long time ago and are likely more than he'll haul in over the rest of his career. The Vikings surprisingly kept him instead of Wiggins, but Kleinsasser is a couple years younger and a better blocker.

Joe Klopfenstein Height: 6-6 Weight: 245 College: Colorado Draft: 2006/2 (46) Born: 9-Nov-1983 Age: 24 Risk: Red

Year	Team	G	Rec	Pass	Yds	C%	Yd/C	TD	YAC	Rk	DVOA	Rk	DPAR	Rk	PAR	Short	Mid	Deep	Bomb
2006	STL	16	20	34	226	59%	11.3	1	4.0	12	2.0%	24	2.5	27	2.7	52%	23%	26%	0%
2007	STL		23		309		13.4	2											

In 2005 the Rams threw to their tight ends less frequently than any other team in the league (5.4 percent of pass attempts compared to a league average of 19 percent). That had a lot to do with Mike Martz's presence as the 2005 Rams, true to the Mad Martz style, led the league in four wide sets. Under new head coach Scott Linehan in 2006, tight ends were a factor once more, both as blockers and receivers, and the Rams threw to their tight ends 17 percent of the time last year (league average, 19.1 percent). Klopfenstein caught 20 passes for 226 yards in his rookie season. An improving blocker with a great work ethic, he will compete for catches with Randy McMichael, who played under Linehan when the latter was Miami's offensive coordinator.

Donald Lee Height: 6-3 Weight: 255 College: Mississippi State Draft: 2003/5 (156) Born: 31-Aug-1980 Age: 27 Risk: Red

Year	Team	G	Rec	Pass	Yds	C%	Yd/C	TD	YAC	Rk	DVOA	Rk	DPAR	Rk	PAR	Short	Mid	Deep	Bomb
2004	MIA	16	13	20	110	65%	8.5	1	—	—	-28.1%	—	-2.2	—	-3.7	—	—	—	—
2005	GB	15	33	55	294	60%	8.9	2	4.9	15	-4.4%	27	2.5	26	-0.1	67%	18%	11%	4%
2006	GB	15	10	21	150	48%	15.0	0	9.6	—	-11.8%	—	0.1	—	0.0	37%	47%	16%	0%
2007	GB		·21		233		11.0	2											

Lee is a solid blocker, and, with the Packers possibly releasing Bubba Franks before the season starts, he may be featured more prominently in the passing game this year—in pass *protection*, that is. As Lee showed in 2005, pass receiving is not his forte.

Marcedes Lewis Height: 6-6 Weight: 255 College: UCLA Draft: 2006/1 (28) Born: 19-May-1984 Age: 23 Risk: Yellow

Year	Team	G	Rec	Pass	Yds	C%	Yd/C	TD	YAC	Rk	DVOA	Rk	DPAR	Rk	PAR	Short	Mid	Deep	Bomb
2006	JAC	14	13	21	126	62%	9.7	1	4.4	—	-1.5%	—	1.4	—	0.7	44%	39%	11%	6%
2007	JAC		37		420		11.3	4											

Much like fellow rookie first-rounder Vernon Davis, Lewis had his introduction to the NFL slowed by injury. In Lewis's case, a high ankle sprain suffered in training camp bothered him for the first two months of the season. Eleven of Lewis's 13 receptions came during Weeks 9–17. The Jaguars are going to be getting more out of Lewis in 2007, but don't expect him to

(continued next page)

Marcedes Lewis (*continued*)

explode onto the league just because he isn't a rookie anymore. First-round tight ends from 1990 to 2005, leaving out players who lost a season to injury, averaged 27 catches, 293 yards, and two touchdowns. In their sophomore years, these players averaged 34 catches, 399 yards, and four touchdowns. First-round tight ends are rarely busts, but they don't develop immediately either.

John Madsen
Height: 6-5 Weight: 220 College: Utah Draft: 2006/FA Born: 9-May-1983 Age: 24 Risk: Red

Year	Team	G	Rec	Pass	Yds	C%	Yd/C	TD	YAC	Rk	DVOA	Rk	DPAR	Rk	PAR	Short	Mid	Deep	Bomb
2006	OAK	15	11	19	146	58%	13.3	1	3.0	—	-14.0%	—	-0.1	—	0.4	24%	53%	6%	18%
2007	OAK		23		219		9.6	2											

Madsen is a solid possession receiver and was one of the few players on the Oakland offense who actually looked like he was trying last year. The Raiders moved him to tight end, and, depending on how Lane Kiffin uses him in the red zone, the 6-foot-5 Utah product could be a sleeper pick to catch a lot of jump-ball touchdown passes. On the other hand, given the large number of wide receivers, tight ends, and running backs who are going to training camp with the Raiders, he could just as easily be playing somewhere else in 2007.

Kris Mangum
Height: 6-4 Weight: 249 College: Mississippi Draft: 1997/7 (228) Born: 15-Aug-1973 Age: 34 Risk: NA

Year	Team	G	Rec	Pass	Yds	C%	Yd/C	TD	YAC	Rk	DVOA	Rk	DPAR	Rk	PAR	Short	Mid	Deep	Bomb
2004	CAR	15	34	58	323	59%	9.5	3	—	—	-10.7%	29	1.0	29	3.1	—	—	—	—
2005	CAR	14	23	35	202	66%	8.8	2	3.1	37	4.3%	20	3.7	23	3.1	34%	59%	6%	0%
2006	CAR	14	21	33	170	64%	8.1	1	3.8	31	-18.2%	35	-1.1	35	-0.3	61%	35%	3%	0%

Mangum retired in February, ending a long and sometimes productive career in Carolina.

Brandon Manumaleuna
Height: 6-2 Weight: 288 College: Arizona Draft: 2001/4 (129) Born: 4-Jan-1980 Age: 27 Risk: Yellow

Year	Team	G	Rec	Pass	Yds	C%	Yd/C	TD	YAC	Rk	DVOA	Rk	DPAR	Rk	PAR	Short	Mid	Deep	Bomb
2004	STL	16	15	21	174	71%	11.6	1	—	—	15.5%	—	3.7	—	3.4	—	—	—	—
2005	STL	14	13	20	129	65%	9.9	1	6.8	—	-47.2%	—	-4.7	—	-4.5	56%	31%	6%	6%
2006	SD	16	14	17	91	82%	6.5	3	4.7	—	31.5%	—	4.3	—	3.9	82%	18%	0%	0%
2007	SD		20		144		7.3	2											

Because of Manumaleuna's size—and the fact that he's not Antonio Gates—TV announcers refer to him as a "blocking tight end" all the time, but away from the Mike Martz offense that fit him like a leotard on Warren Sapp, Manumaleuna proved to be a useful possession receiver on short-yardage plays. Over the last two seasons, he's caught nine of ten passes in the red zone, with four touchdowns. *Manumaleuna, homem gol. Manumaleuna, homem gol.*

David Martin
Height: 6-4 Weight: 260 College: Tennessee Draft: 2001/6 (198) Born: 13-Mar-1979 Age: 28 Risk: Red

Year	Team	G	Rec	Pass	Yds	C%	Yd/C	TD	YAC	Rk	DVOA	Rk	DPAR	Rk	PAR	Short	Mid	Deep	Bomb
2004	GB	9	5	12	88	42%	17.6	0	—	—	-3.9%	—	0.7	—	1.7	—	—	—	—
2005	GB	12	27	39	224	69%	8.3	3	3.0	41	13.5%	10	6.2	18	4.5	46%	38%	11%	5%
2006	GB	11	21	36	198	58%	9.4	2	3.5	34	5.3%	19	3.9	23	2.3	47%	28%	17%	8%
2007	MIA		27		230		8.6	2											

Martin's tenure in Green Bay will always be remembered for its unfulfilled promise. The athletic tight end never developed as a competent blocker and failed to emerge as a consistent receiver. Now he heads to Miami, where he'll take over for Randy McMichael and be expected to use the space created by Chris Chambers and Ted Ginn to his advantage.

Randy McMichael
Height: 6-3 Weight: 250 College: Georgia Draft: 2002/4 (114) Born: 28-Jun-1979 Age: 28 Risk: Red

Year	Team	G	Rec	Pass	Yds	C%	Yd/C	TD	YAC	Rk	DVOA	Rk	DPAR	Rk	PAR	Short	Mid	Deep	Bomb
2004	MIA	16	73	118	791	62%	10.8	4	—	—	3.9%	22	11.1	11	4.5	—	—	—	—
2005	MIA	16	60	104	582	58%	9.7	5	4.9	14	-20.3%	38	-4.7	42	-2.7	61%	30%	8%	1%
2006	MIA	16	62	96	640	65%	10.3	3	4.9	11	11.1%	10	13.9	8	11.2	52%	34%	13%	1%
2007	STL		45		503		11.3	3											

No Rams tight end has caught more than 50 passes in a season since Pete Holohan in 1989. Ernie Conwell caught his share of checkdown and red zone passes in the late 1990s, but tight ends generally had bit parts in The Greatest Show on Turf. McMichael gives Marc Bulger a new type of target: a big seam splitter who will occupy safeties, freeing Torry Holt and Isaac Bruce for more aerial thrills and providing a few of his own. McMichael won't be targeted 100 times on a team with two excellent receivers, but he'll make the most of the passes that do come his way.

Itula Mili   Height: 6-4   Weight: 260   College: BYU   Draft: 1997/6 (174)   Born: 20-Apr-1973   Age: 34   Risk: NA

Year	Team	G	Rec	Pass	Yds	C%	Yd/C	TD	YAC	Rk	DVOA	Rk	DPAR	Rk	PAR	Short	Mid	Deep	Bomb
2004	SEA	15	23	36	240	64%	10.4	1	—	—	3.8%	23	3.9	24	3.5	—	—	—	—
2006	SEA	10	10	18	69	56%	6.9	0	3.2	—	-38.5%	—	-3.1	—	-2.9	65%	24%	0%	12%

Released by Seattle in January and now retired, Mili had struggled with various ailments (including a blocked intestine) over the last two seasons. He holds the Seattle single-season record for receptions by a tight end with 46 in 2003.

Billy Miller   Height: 6-3   Weight: 230   College: USC   Draft: 1999/7 (218)   Born: 24-Apr-1977   Age: 30   Risk: Red

Year	Team	G	Rec	Pass	Yds	C%	Yd/C	TD	YAC	Rk	DVOA	Rk	DPAR	Rk	PAR	Short	Mid	Deep	Bomb
2004	HOU	16	17	34	178	50%	10.5	1	—	—	-20.9%	32	-1.7	31	-1.8	—	—	—	—
2006	NO	10	14	22	129	64%	9.2	0	2.5	—	-31.2%	—	-2.4	—	-1.1	56%	31%	13%	0%
2007	NO		14		193		14.0	2											

A sit-in-the-zone receiving tight end, Miller took over Ernie Conwell's role in the Saints' offense when Conwell got hurt. Eric Johnson is a better receiver, and Mark Campbell is a better blocker, so Miller will have a hard time making the team.

Heath Miller   Height: 6-5   Weight: 256   College: Virginia   Draft: 2005/1 (30)   Born: 22-Oct-1982   Age: 25   Risk: Red

Year	Team	G	Rec	Pass	Yds	C%	Yd/C	TD	YAC	Rk	DVOA	Rk	DPAR	Rk	PAR	Short	Mid	Deep	Bomb
2005	PIT	16	39	52	459	75%	11.8	6	4.7	19	29.3%	5	14.1	9	14.3	41%	43%	13%	2%
2006	PIT	16	34	55	393	62%	11.6	5	5.3	4	9.0%	14	7.5	16	7.3	46%	37%	17%	0%
2007	PIT		36		466		12.8	3											

Playing tight end for the Steelers under Bill Cowher always meant trying to make the most of limited opportunities. That could change under Mike Tomlin. If so, Miller could be poised for a breakout year. Despite the Steelers' throwing the ball much more in 2006, Miller had five fewer catches than in his rookie season of 2005. It wasn't his fault: Only six teams directed a lower percentage of passes at their tight ends.

Zach Miller   Height: 6-4   Weight: 256   College: Arizona State   Draft: 2007/2 (38)   Born: 12-Nov-1985   Age: 22   Risk: Red

Year	Team	G	Rec	Pass	Yds	C%	Yd/C	TD	YAC	Rk	DVOA	Rk	DPAR	Rk	PAR	Short	Mid	Deep	Bomb
2007	OAK		27		344		13.0	1											

Miller, who replaced Todd Heap at Arizona State, was the second-ranked tight end on most draft boards. He's in a bind, though. He could use a little more weight to improve his blocking, but he's done growing, and any added weight is going to take away from his already borderline speed. He's also already had some shoulder and ankle injuries. Miller will never be an elite tight end on the NFL level, but he has excellent hands and runs good routes, which means he's a safe pick and likely to be competent tight end as soon as this year.

Ryan Neufeld   Height: 6-4   Weight: 250   College: UCLA   Draft: 1999/FA   Born: 22-Nov-1975   Age: 32   Risk: Red

Year	Team	G	Rec	Pass	Yds	C%	Yd/C	TD	YAC	Rk	DVOA	Rk	DPAR	Rk	PAR	Short	Mid	Deep	Bomb
2004	BUF	16	6	14	61	43%	10.2	0	—	—	-25.8%	—	-1.3	—	-1.9	—	—	—	—
2005	BUF	13	1	4	9	25%	9.0	0	4.0	—	-57.2%	—	-1.0	—	-1.0	25%	75%	0%	0%
2007	BUF		16		106		6.6	1											

One of the Bills' interchangeable tight ends, Neufeld is the ultimate zero-sum player. Over the last two seasons, he's had two catches for 13 yards and three kick returns for 39 yards, a total of 52 yards of progress. Over those same two seasons, he dropped a seven-yard pass, made two special-team penalties costing a total of 33 return yards, and was flagged for a penalty on offense that wiped out a 13-yard Anthony Thomas gain. That's a loss of 53 yards. Neufeld also ended each of the last two seasons on injured reserve. Neufeld is the summer starter at H-Back, but he has limited fantasy value.

Greg Olsen Height: 6-6 Weight: 254 College: Miami   Draft: 2007/1 (31) Born: 11-Mar-1985 Age: 22   Risk: Red

Year	Team	G	Rec	Pass	Yds	C%	Yd/C	TD	YAC	Rk	DVOA	Rk	DPAR	Rk	PAR	Short	Mid	Deep	Bomb
2007	CHI		24		279		11.5	2											

As a freshman at Miami, Olsen and some friends calling themselves "The 7th Floor Crew" recorded a raunchy gangsta rap song in which Olsen (a.k.a. G-Reg) boasts about his sexual prowess to the tune of an Aaliyah song. While the song had been discussed when it was initially released in 2004, it came up again hours after the draft (and a few days after Don Imus discovered that female college athletes don't like to be insulted on national broadcasts). Despite being a first-round pick, G-Reg was suddenly front-page news for all the wrong reasons. The whole affair turned into a ludicrous media feeding frenzy that ended with one of those over-the-top apologies that made you think Olsen was guilty of international terror-ism, not amateur musical aspirations. There's a lesson to be learned here: Never, ever refer to yourself as G-Reg on video. You are just asking for trouble.

Olsen isn't quite a prospect in the Jeremy Shockey class. He became a first-round pick in a tight end–weak draft, but he's more of a developmental player in the Kevin Everett mold.

Justin Peelle Height: 6-4 Weight: 255 College: Oregon   Draft: 2002/4 (103) Born: 15-Mar-1979 Age: 28   Risk: Red

Year	Team	G	Rec	Pass	Yds	C%	Yd/C	TD	YAC	Rk	DVOA	Rk	DPAR	Rk	PAR	Short	Mid	Deep	Bomb
2004	SD	16	10	20	84	50%	8.4	2	—	—	-48.4%	—	-4.1	—	-4.1	—	—	—	—
2005	SD	16	11	20	38	55%	3.5	1	3.5	—	-61.8%	—	-6.1	—	-5.5	65%	29%	6%	0%
2006	MIA	15	16	18	116	89%	7.3	1	3.9	—	3.6%	—	1.8	—	1.2	72%	22%	6%	0%
2007	MIA		19		105		5.6	0											

After five years, what you see is what you get: 10 to 15 catches per year in the flat and decent blocking. Peelle once looked like he could be a Jason Witten–caliber contributor, but he never developed as a receiver.

Marcus Pollard Height: 6-3 Weight: 247 College: Bradley   Draft: 1995/FA Born: 8-Feb-1972 Age: 35   Risk: Red

Year	Team	G	Rec	Pass	Yds	C%	Yd/C	TD	YAC	Rk	DVOA	Rk	DPAR	Rk	PAR	Short	Mid	Deep	Bomb
2004	IND	13	29	41	309	71%	10.7	6	—	—	27.1%	6	10.6	12	11.8	—	—	—	—
2005	DET	16	46	78	516	59%	11.2	3	4.7	20	-11.9%	34	0.6	33	1.9	41%	39%	20%	0%
2006	DET	15	12	17	100	71%	8.3	0	4.7	—	-17.3%	—	-0.6	—	-0.8	76%	24%	0%	0%
2007	SEA		18		176		9.6	1											

Maybe the Lions should avoid signing Colts free agents. Rick DeMulling was a disaster, and Pollard was not a lot better. He gradually lost his starting job over the course of the 2006 season and did not have a reception in the last six games. Now he is off to Seattle to finish what has been a very solid career, but if the Seahawks actually plan on putting him in the starting lineup, they might want to note that they've signed a 35-year-old tight end who relies on his speed. Here is the entire list of all 35-year-old tight ends with at least ten receptions in a season since 1978:

Shannon Sharpe	2003 Broncos	(62 catches, 770 yards, 8 TD)
Wesley Walls	2001 Panthers	(43 catches, 452 yards, 5 TD)
Pete Metzelaars	1995 Panthers	(20 catches, 171 yards, 3 TD)
Jimmie Giles	1989 Eagles	(16 catches, 225 yards, 2 TD)
Bob Tucker	1980 Vikings	(15 catches, 173 yards, 1 TD)
Russ Francis	1988 Patriots	(11 catches, 161 yards, 0 TD)

Not a long list, is it?

Leonard Pope Height: 6-8 Weight: 250 College: Georgia   Draft: 2006/3 (72) Born: 9-Sep-1983 Age: 24   Risk: Red

Year	Team	G	Rec	Pass	Yds	C%	Yd/C	TD	YAC	Rk	DVOA	Rk	DPAR	Rk	PAR	Short	Mid	Deep	Bomb
2006	ARI	16	16	23	161	70%	10.1	0	4.8	—	-6.6%	—	1.0	—	1.9	67%	29%	5%	0%
2007	ARI		23		213		9.2	2											

A raw prospect with great physical potential, Pope needs development (especially in blocking), but is worth keeping an eye on over time, especially as the Whisenhunt regime places a new emphasis on coaching and conditioning that wasn't always seen on Dennis Green's watch.

Jeb Putzier Height: 6-4 Weight: 256 College: Boise State   Draft: 2002/6 (191) Born: 20-Jan-1979 Age: 28 Risk: Red

Year	Team	G	Rec	Pass	Yds	C%	Yd/C	TD	YAC	Rk	DVOA	Rk	DPAR	Rk	PAR	Short	Mid	Deep	Bomb
2004	DEN	16	36	54	572	67%	15.9	2	—	—	35.9%	4	16.8	6	19.6	—	—	—	—
2005	DEN	16	37	58	481	64%	13.0	0	5.9	5	13.0%	11	9.7	12	10.1	43%	37%	19%	2%
2006	HOU	14	13	22	125	59%	9.6	0	5.6	—	-9.6%	—	0.4	—	0.2	53%	42%	5%	0%
2007	HOU		23		229		10.0	2											

Gary Kubiak brought Jeb Putzier along with him from Denver, then buried him on the depth chart behind rookie Owen Daniels, which certainly surprised any fantasy football owner who thought Putzier was a reasonable late-draft alternative at tight end. The Cincinnati police department blocks more linebackers in a week than Putzier does in a year, and he's never been a goal-line threat, so you have to wonder how much longer he'll have a role in Houston. Nevertheless, he's not yet toast at age 28 and could still help another team that needs a receiving-first tight end.

Dante Rosario Height: 6-4 Weight: 250 College: Oregon   Draft: 2007/5 (155) Born: 25-Oct-1984 Age: 23 Risk: Red

Year	Team	G	Rec	Pass	Yds	C%	Yd/C	TD	YAC	Rk	DVOA	Rk	DPAR	Rk	PAR	Short	Mid	Deep	Bomb
2007	CAR		12		130		11.0	0											

Rosario started his college career at fullback, then moved to tight end when Oregon switched to a spread offense. He excelled as an underneath receiver and projects as a pass-catching H-back in the NFL. The Panthers need a player like Rosario to complement Michael Gaines, the blocking-oriented starter at tight end.

Robert Royal Height: 6-4 Weight: 257 College: LSU   Draft: 2002/5 (160) Born: 15-May-1979 Age: 28 Risk: Red

Year	Team	G	Rec	Pass	Yds	C%	Yd/C	TD	YAC	Rk	DVOA	Rk	DPAR	Rk	PAR	Short	Mid	Deep	Bomb
2004	WAS	14	8	15	70	53%	8.8	4	—	—	10.4%	—	2.1	—	2.5	—	—	—	—
2005	WAS	15	18	35	131	51%	7.3	1	6.9	4	-35.1%	43	-5.1	43	-5.6	81%	13%	6%	0%
2006	BUF	16	23	39	233	59%	10.1	3	4.4	16	4.7%	20	4.2	22	3.9	51%	30%	14%	5%
2007	BUF		17		180		10.5	2											

In his first season with Buffalo, Royal showed a wide variety of drive-killing abilities. He drew two flags in the red zone. His four blown blocks leading to sacks trailed only linemen Jason Peters (5) and Mike Gandy (9) on the Bills. He also dropped three passes, including two that would have given the team first downs, matching the total of dropped first downs by the rest of the Buffalo receiving corps. Drops are nothing new for Royal; in 2005 we charted 11 incomplete passes to Royal, ten of which were drops.

Sean Ryan Height: 6-4 Weight: 264 College: Boston College   Draft: 2004/5 (144) Born: 27-Mar-1980 Age: 27 Risk: Red

Year	Team	G	Rec	Pass	Yds	C%	Yd/C	TD	YAC	Rk	DVOA	Rk	DPAR	Rk	PAR	Short	Mid	Deep	Bomb
2006	NYJ	16	6	9	44	67%	7.3	0	3.3	—	-57.5%	—	-2.4	—	-2.6	75%	25%	0%	0%
2007	NYJ		7		39		5.8	0											

Ryan played defensive end for a season at Boston College, then went on to be an All-Big East tight end. He doesn't have the speed or athleticism to be a starter in the NFL, but he's useful to the Jets on special teams and as a blocker in two-tight-end sets.

Bo Scaife Height: 6-2 Weight: 249 College: Texas   Draft: 2005/6 (179) Born: 6-Jan-1981 Age: 26 Risk: Red

Year	Team	G	Rec	Pass	Yds	C%	Yd/C	TD	YAC	Rk	DVOA	Rk	DPAR	Rk	PAR	Short	Mid	Deep	Bomb
2005	TEN	16	37	55	273	67%	7.4	2	4.3	24	-10.3%	33	0.7	32	-0.8	79%	17%	4%	0%
2006	TEN	14	29	56	370	52%	12.8	2	5.0	9	-8.4%	30	1.5	30	1.9	50%	31%	17%	2%
2007	TEN		34		405		12.0	3											

Best random and essentially meaningless stat of the year: Scaife led all tight ends in rushing yards, and was the first tight end to score a rushing touchdown in the NFL since the days when the big guys occasionally got the ball on reverses. Scaife's 13-yard rushing touchdown came against the Ravens when Vince Young lateralled to his former college teammate to escape a sack. Scaife's raw numbers look good because Vince Young trusts him and throws to him a lot, but he is really an H-back type who shouldn't have a huge role in the offense if Ben Troupe is healthy and effective. There's no truth to the rumor that Young got Scaife a 97 rating in *Madden 08* as part of his cover deal.

Tony Scheffler   Height: 6-6   Weight: 260   College: Western Michigan   Draft: 2006/2 (61)   Born: 15-Feb-1983   Age: 24   Risk: Yellow

Year	Team	G	Rec	Pass	Yds	C%	Yd/C	TD	YAC	Rk	DVOA	Rk	DPAR	Rk	PAR	Short	Mid	Deep	Bomb
2006	DEN	13	18	37	286	49%	15.9	4	3.8	29	8.6%	15	5.4	21	7.3	18%	46%	28%	8%
2007	DEN		31		355		11.4	4											

The big, athletic Scheffler was a revelation as a rookie out of Western Michigan. Having Scheffler's short game to complement the deep speed of Javon Walker and Brandon Marshall will give the Broncos a good passing game if Jay Cutler delivers. Scheffler's role will be reduced some by Daniel Graham's arrival and the need to justify Graham's salary with some statistics. Scheffler broke his foot at the beginning of May and may be slowed at the beginning of the season.

Matt Schobel   Height: 6-5   Weight: 257   College: TCU   Draft: 2002/3 (67)   Born: 4-Nov-1978   Age: 29   Risk: Red

Year	Team	G	Rec	Pass	Yds	C%	Yd/C	TD	YAC	Rk	DVOA	Rk	DPAR	Rk	PAR	Short	Mid	Deep	Bomb
2004	CIN	16	21	33	201	64%	9.6	4	—	—	11.2%	17	3.9	23	0.8	—	—	—	—
2005	CIN	16	18	25	193	72%	10.7	1	3.5	33	6.3%	18	2.5	25	2.4	37%	47%	16%	0%
2006	PHI	16	14	22	214	64%	15.3	2	8.4	—	9.3%	—	3.3	—	4.0	52%	29%	14%	5%
2007	PHI		17		199		11.7	2											

Portrait of an Eagles backup tight end. Week 3: Schobel hauls in a dump-off pass and rumbles 60 yards to set up a garbage-time touchdown against the Niners. Week 4: Schobel catches an 11-yard pass from punter David Akers on one of the dumbest fake kicks in history. The play occurs at the Eagles 36-yard line in the closing seconds of the first half, and half the Packers roster appears ready for the fake. Week 6: Schobel splits the seam for a 40-yard catch against the Saints, but Reggie Brown holds while blocking on the play. The penalty knocks the Eagles out of field goal range. Weeks 10–15: Schobel disappears from the gameplan as the Eagles adjust their scheme to emphasize the run. Weeks 16–17: Schobel resurfaces and catches touchdown passes from Jeff Garcia and A. J. Feeley. Schobel has a skillset similar to starter L. J. Smith, and the Eagles like to put both tight ends on the field and see who gets covered by the slower linebacker. Schobel's effective in his role, but there are only so many balls to go around in Philly.

Mike Sellers   Height: 6-3   Weight: 260   College: Walla Walla CC   Draft: 1998/FA   Born: 21-Jul-1975   Age: 32   Risk: Red

Year	Team	G	Rec	Pass	Yds	C%	Yd/C	TD	YAC	Rk	DVOA	Rk	DPAR	Rk	PAR	Short	Mid	Deep	Bomb
2004	WAS	16	1	2	14	50%	14.0	0	—	—	29.5%	—	0.4	—	0.4	—	—	—	—
2005	WAS	15	12	16	72	75%	6.0	7	4.8	—	50.2%	—	6.9	—	7.2	83%	17%	0%	0%
2006	WAS	16	18	22	105	82%	5.8	1	5.0	—	-28.2%	—	-2.2	—	-1.6	100%	0%	0%	0%
2007	WAS		26		155		6.0	2											

Sellers might be the most underrated player in head coach Joe Gibbs's offense. The 6-foot-3, 277-pound H-back registered a dozen carries and 18 receptions in 2006, but his real strength is as a blocker. In 14 games last season, Sellers helped running back Ladell Betts rush for over 1,000 yards for the first time in his career.

Visanthe Shiancoe   Height: 6-4   Weight: 250   College: Morgan State   Draft: 2003/3 (91)   Born: 18-Jun-1980   Age: 27   Risk: Red

Year	Team	G	Rec	Pass	Yds	C%	Yd/C	TD	YAC	Rk	DVOA	Rk	DPAR	Rk	PAR	Short	Mid	Deep	Bomb
2004	NYG	16	5	7	25	71%	5.0	1	—	—	3.3%	—	0.8	—	1.1	—	—	—	—
2005	NYG	16	8	17	91	47%	11.4	0	3.4	—	-13.2%	—	-0.2	—	-0.6	57%	29%	14%	0%
2006	NYG	16	12	14	81	86%	6.8	0	3.3	—	-13.9%	—	-0.2	—	-0.7	83%	17%	0%	0%
2007	MIN		13		106		8.5	0											

Shiancoe spent four seasons in New York and showed flashes of big-play potential, but never caught more than 12 passes in a season. His DPAR has been below replacement level in three of four seasons. The Giants were interested in re-signing him this offseason, but the Vikings offered Shiancoe an absurd amount of money to come to Minnesota (the deal included $8.2 million in guarantees). Nope, doesn't make sense to us either.

Jeremy Shockey   Height: 6-5   Weight: 253   College: Miami   Draft: 2002/1 (14)   Born: 18-Aug-1980   Age: 27   Risk: Green

Year	Team	G	Rec	Pass	Yds	C%	Yd/C	TD	YAC	Rk	DVOA	Rk	DPAR	Rk	PAR	Short	Mid	Deep	Bomb
2004	NYG	15	61	97	666	63%	10.9	6	—	—	10.9%	19	14.6	8	13.2	—	—	—	—
2005	NYG	15	65	122	891	53%	13.7	7	4.9	13	5.2%	19	14.2	8	17.5	29%	51%	12%	8%
2006	NYG	15	66	115	623	57%	9.4	7	2.9	38	-2.1%	25	7.9	14	11.8	36%	49%	14%	1%
2007	NYG		63		709		11.2	6											

Despite struggling with a balky ankle for parts of the season, Shockey started 15 games in 2006. Although Tiki Barber was often cited as an outspoken critic of head coach Tom Coughlin, Shockey also got in a few shots. After an embarrassing early season loss to the Seahawks, the sixth-year tight end announced that the Giants were "outplayed and outcoached." Of course, if we pointed out every player who doesn't like Tom Coughlin, this book would be a foot thick. Shockey finished outside the top ten in DPAR for the first time in three seasons, but was second on the team in pass receptions with 66, the second-highest total of his career.

Alex Smith

Height: 6-4 Weight: 258 College: Stanford   Draft: 2005/3 (71) Born: 22-May-1982 Age: 25   Risk: Red

Year	Team	G	Rec	Pass	Yds	C%	Yd/C	TD	YAC	Rk	DVOA	Rk	DPAR	Rk	PAR	Short	Mid	Deep	Bomb
2005	TB	16	41	60	367	68%	9.0	2	4.1	30	-1.1%	24	4.8	21	7.6	67%	24%	8%	2%
2006	TB	14	35	53	250	66%	7.1	3	3.4	36	-22.7%	38	-3.6	41	-4.9	73%	16%	10%	2%
2007	TB		27		296		10.8	2											

Smith looked great in Week 3, catching four passes for 72 yards against the Panthers, breaking tackles, and displaying impressive speed in the open field. Once Chris Simms got hurt and Bruce Gradkowski took over, Smith's production sagged. He dropped some passes, wasn't targeted as often, and saw his touches limited to two- or three-yard pass plays into the flat. Smith is capable of putting up L. J. Smith/Ben Watson–type numbers and may get better opportunities now that Simms or Jeff Garcia (a real tightendophile) is throwing him the ball.

L. J. Smith

Height: 6-3 Weight: 258 College: Rutgers   Draft: 2003/2 (61) Born: 13-May-1980 Age: 27   Risk: Green

Year	Team	G	Rec	Pass	Yds	C%	Yd/C	TD	YAC	Rk	DVOA	Rk	DPAR	Rk	PAR	Short	Mid	Deep	Bomb
2004	PHI	16	34	54	377	63%	11.1	5	—	—	10.9%	18	8.4	15	9.3	—	—	—	—
2005	PHI	16	61	114	682	59%	11.2	3	4.8	17	-8.2%	30	3.6	24	5.3	53%	35%	12%	0%
2006	PHI	16	50	80	611	63%	12.2	5	5.2	6	3.3%	21	8.6	13	10.7	50%	42%	5%	3%
2007	PHI		45		591		13.2	5											

If he's honest with himself, L. J. Smith looks at Billy Miller and says, "There but for the grace of God go I." An average tight end doesn't normally get to see this many passes, but Smith has had the good fortune of playing for four years with a great quarterback (when he's healthy) on a team with a dearth of standout receivers. With the Eagles showing signs of coming out of their wide receiver dark ages, however, Smith could see a drastic drop-off in his opportunities. Some people in the Philadelphia gripeosphere will see that as the Eagles' trying to depress the value of a potential free agent in a contract year, but it will really be what it usually is with the Eagles: good business.

Matt Spaeth

Height: 6-7 Weight: 270 College: Minnesota   Draft: 2007/3 (77) Born: 24-Nov-1983 Age: 24   Risk: Red

Year	Team	G	Rec	Pass	Yds	C%	Yd/C	TD	YAC	Rk	DVOA	Rk	DPAR	Rk	PAR	Short	Mid	Deep	Bomb
2007	PIT		8		78		9.6	0											

Spaeth is big enough to act as an extra tackle on the end of the line of scrimmage and also presents an intriguing downfield target. He should see the field plenty in the two-tight-end sets that new Pittsburgh offensive coordinator Bruce Arians promises to deploy.

Jerramy Stevens

Height: 6-7 Weight: 260 College: Washington   Draft: 2002/1 (28) Born: 13-Nov-1979 Age: 28   Risk: Red

Year	Team	G	Rec	Pass	Yds	C%	Yd/C	TD	YAC	Rk	DVOA	Rk	DPAR	Rk	PAR	Short	Mid	Deep	Bomb
2004	SEA	16	31	47	349	66%	11.3	3	—	—	14.3%	13	8.5	14	9.7	—	—	—	—
2005	SEA	16	45	68	554	66%	12.3	5	2.9	42	23.9%	7	16.6	5	16.9	25%	63%	11%	2%
2006	SEA	11	22	48	231	46%	10.5	4	2.7	41	-20.9%	37	-2.1	37	-0.1	28%	63%	8%	3%
2007	TB		25		281		11.1	2											

If the game itself didn't settle it, we can now call a winner in the pre–Super Bowl XL Joey Porter–Jerramy Stevens feud. Porter is enjoying a new Dolphins contract with $20 million in guaranteed money (though he's blown the whole "what happens in Vegas, stays in Vegas" thing), and Stevens followed up his XL dropfest with a season in which he missed five games and started only six after suffering a torn meniscus in his surgically repaired left knee. Among tight ends with at least 25 passes, only Ben Troupe had a lower Catch Rate last year. Though he caught two touchdown passes in the Seahawks' playoff win over Dallas, Stevens's career in Seattle ended with his mid-March arrest in Arizona for drunk driving and marijuana possession. Tampa Bay signed him on April 29, the headline hidden in a deluge of draft coverage. Stevens missed out on the most lucrative offseason for free agents in league history—and it was nobody's fault but his.

Tony Stewart   Height: 6-5   Weight: 260 College: Penn State   Draft: 2001/5 (147) Born: 9-Aug-1979   Age: 28   Risk: Red

Year	Team	G	Rec	Pass	Yds	C%	Yd/C	TD	YAC	Rk	DVOA	Rk	DPAR	Rk	PAR	Short	Mid	Deep	Bomb
2004	CIN	16	10	25	48	40%	4.8	1	—	—	-50.3%	39	-6.4	37	-8.1	—	—	—	—
2005	CIN	14	4	6	26	67%	6.5	0	1.5	—	-46.3%	—	-1.3	—	-1.1	100%	0%	0%	0%
2006	CIN	16	14	18	120	78%	8.6	1	3.7	—	17.9%	—	3.2	—	2.6	75%	13%	0%	13%
2007	OAK		13		70		5.6	0											

Tony Stewart is basically a carbon copy of Cincinnati's other tight end, Reggie Kelly. He signed with Oakland, where he'll compete with rookie tight end Zach Miller and incumbents Courtney Anderson, John Madsen, and Randal Williams for the right to get throws from an inaccurate rookie quarterback playing behind a woeful offensive line. It's not all fun and games in pro football, you know.

Quinn Sypniewski   Height: 6-7   Weight: 265 College: Colorado   Draft: 2006/5 (166) Born: 14-Apr-1982   Age: 25   Risk: Red

Year	Team	G	Rec	Pass	Yds	C%	Yd/C	TD	YAC	Rk	DVOA	Rk	DPAR	Rk	PAR	Short	Mid	Deep	Bomb
2006	BAL	16	2	2	15	100%	7.5	0	2.5	—	60.3%	—	0.9	—	0.7	50%	50%	0%	0%
2007	BAL		10		78		7.8	1											

The "Unfrozen Caveman Tight End" is a monster blocker, so he'll always have a home in a run-oriented offense. His hands? Those are another story, but they aren't much of a concern on a team that employs Todd Heap.

David Thomas   Height: 6-3   Weight: 245 College: Texas   Draft: 2006/3 (86) Born: 5-Jul-1983   Age: 24   Risk: Yellow

Year	Team	G	Rec	Pass	Yds	C%	Yd/C	TD	YAC	Rk	DVOA	Rk	DPAR	Rk	PAR	Short	Mid	Deep	Bomb
2006	NE	15	11	16	159	69%	14.5	1	8.3	—	46.1%	—	5.7	—	5.8	56%	38%	6%	0%
2007	NE		27		336		12.6	4											

Thomas's role will expand this year with the departure of Daniel Graham. Thomas is a poor man's Chris Cooley, a move blocker with a great feel for zones who can blow through some tackles in the open field. He probably won't have a more spectacular-looking catch in his life than the diving grab he made against Jacksonville for a touchdown in Week 16, but neither will 99.999 percent of the population, either.

Ben Troupe   Height: 6-4   Weight: 262 College: Florida   Draft: 2004/2 (40) Born: 1-Sep-1982   Age: 25   Risk: Red

Year	Team	G	Rec	Pass	Yds	C%	Yd/C	TD	YAC	Rk	DVOA	Rk	DPAR	Rk	PAR	Short	Mid	Deep	Bomb
2004	TEN	14	33	54	329	61%	10.0	1	—	—	-29.9%	36	-5.4	35	-3.4	—	—	—	—
2005	TEN	15	55	80	530	69%	9.6	4	5.2	10	-4.0%	26	4.8	20	7.4	67%	24%	9%	0%
2006	TEN	10	13	29	150	45%	11.5	2	7.3	2	-14.8%	33	-0.5	33	-1.2	54%	42%	4%	0%
2007	TEN		32		342		10.7	3											

Troupe was a potted plant in the Titans offense for the first ten games of the year, catching no passes in two games and just one pass in five others. He then broke his ankle and watched Vince Young and Bo Scaife give each other the secret "Hook 'Em" handshake as Scaife solidified his role as the go-to tight end. Troupe was a productive receiver in 2005, but that was when Steve McNair was throwing the ball, and McNair loved dishing it to tight ends in the flat. There's room in Tennessee's offense for two pass-catching tight ends, but Ben Hartsock is also in the mix, and Norm Chow will eventually want to open up things and get the receivers involved. Troupe needs a strong camp to get his career back on track.

Ben Utecht   Height: 6-6   Weight: 249 College: Minnesota   Draft: 2004/FA Born: 30-Jun-1981   Age: 26   Risk: Green

Year	Team	G	Rec	Pass	Yds	C%	Yd/C	TD	YAC	Rk	DVOA	Rk	DPAR	Rk	PAR	Short	Mid	Deep	Bomb
2005	IND	12	3	12	59	25%	19.7	2	0.0	0	-11.1%	—	0.1	—	-0.3	0%	71%	14%	14%
2006	IND	14	37	53	377	70%	10.2	0	4.9	10	10.1%	11	7.3	17	7.4	45%	47%	8%	0%
2007	IND		23		211		9.1	3											

See "Bryan Fletcher." Utecht was thrown more passes than Fletcher and caught about the same percentage of those passes, but Fletcher did more with them in more crucial situations. Utecht is a solid blocker and adequate receiver, but his DVOA and DPAR are residue of the Colts' offense, not indicators that he could go elsewhere and catch 50 passes.

Delanie Walker Height: 6-2 Weight: 215 College: Central Missouri Draft: 2006/6 (175) Born: 12-Aug-1984 Age: 23 Risk: N/A

Year	Team	G	Rec	Pass	Yds	C%	Yd/C	TD	YAC	Rk	DVOA	Rk	DPAR	Rk	PAR	Short	Mid	Deep	Bomb
2006	SF	7	2	4	30	50%	15.0	0	15.5	—	-4.3%	—	0.2	—	-0.4	50%	50%	0%	0%
2007	SF		14		138		9.9	0											

A converted college wideout, Walker had a disappointing rookie season last year. After suffering a separated shoulder in San Francisco's final exhibition game, he played a bit and had offseason surgery in January. Coming out of college, he had a rep for dropping too many balls due to poor concentration, but the 49ers liked him enough to let Eric Johnson leave. If healthy, he'll be "the guy who is not Vernon Davis" when the Niners run two-tight-end sets.

Ben Watson Height: 6-3 Weight: 253 College: Georgia Draft: 2004/1 (32) Born: 18-Dec-1980 Age: 26 Risk: Green

Year	Team	G	Rec	Pass	Yds	C%	Yd/C	TD	YAC	Rk	DVOA	Rk	DPAR	Rk	PAR	Short	Mid	Deep	Bomb
2004	NE	1	2	4	16	50%	8.0	0	—	—	-49.4%	—	-0.7	—	-0.4	—	—	—	—
2005	NE	15	29	54	441	54%	15.2	4	4.9	12	11.7%	13	8.4	15	8.9	35%	33%	29%	2%
2006	NE	13	49	91	643	54%	13.1	3	4.1	21	-2.2%	26	5.7	20	2.7	37%	36%	16%	11%
2007	NE		45		552		12.3	5											

Watson was the only tight end in the league targeted for more than six bombs. He was among the most effective third-down targets in the league, with a DVOA of 41.4 percent on 27 passes. As effective as Watson was, the Patriots want their wide receivers to pick up more of the slack on deep routes and third downs. With Donte' Stallworth, Wes Welker, and Kelley Washington joining the incumbents at wideout this year, Watson should play a more traditional Dallas Clark–type role as an underneath target, and he will excel.

Jermaine Wiggins Height: 6-2 Weight: 255 College: Georgia Draft: 2000/FA Born: 18-Jan-1975 Age: 32 Risk: Yellow

Year	Team	G	Rec	Pass	Yds	C%	Yd/C	TD	YAC	Rk	DVOA	Rk	DPAR	Rk	PAR	Short	Mid	Deep	Bomb
2004	MIN	14	71	92	705	77%	9.9	4	—	—	14.9%	12	16.0	7	16.5	—	—	—	—
2005	MIN	16	69	90	560	76%	8.2	1	3.6	32	11.0%	14	12.5	10	7.7	60%	35%	5%	0%
2006	MIN	16	46	67	386	69%	8.4	1	2.6	42	-8.2%	29	1.8	29	0.9	59%	34%	7%	0%
2007	JAC		25		292		11.9	2											

A poor fit for Brad Childress's West Coast offense, Wiggins rarely started and saw less and less time on the field as the season progressed. He has good hands, but cannot stretch a defense and is a mediocre blocker. He signed with Jacksonville, where he'll be responsible from keeping junk food away from Marcedes Lewis. Never the most athletic player, Wiggins could be heading for a sharp decline at age 32.

Daniel Wilcox Height: 6-1 Weight: 245 College: Appalachian State Draft: 2001/FA Born: 23-Mar-1977 Age: 30 Risk: Red

Year	Team	G	Rec	Pass	Yds	C%	Yd/C	TD	YAC	Rk	DVOA	Rk	DPAR	Rk	PAR	Short	Mid	Deep	Bomb
2004	BAL	16	25	35	219	71%	8.8	1	—	—	10.7%	20	4.6	21	1.9	—	—	—	—
2005	BAL	13	20	28	154	71%	7.7	1	5.5	8	-10.2%	32	0.4	34	0.0	68%	29%	4%	0%
2006	BAL	14	20	27	166	74%	8.3	3	3.6	33	-16.9%	34	-0.6	34	0.3	73%	23%	4%	0%
2007	BAL		20		189		9.6	1											

Wilcox shows decent pass-catching skills and managed three touchdowns on just 20 receptions last year, with an excellent Catch Rate. Still, he's 30 and, on a team with Todd Heap, he is never going to be more than the second tight end in two-tight-end sets, and he comes out in favor of Quinn Sypniewski when it's time for the second tight end to block.

Randal Williams Height: 6-3 Weight: 220 College: New Hampshire Draft: 2001/FA Born: 21-May-1978 Age: 29 Risk: Red

Year	Team	G	Rec	Pass	Yds	C%	Yd/C	TD	YAC	Rk	DVOA	Rk	DPAR	Rk	PAR	Short	Mid	Deep	Bomb
2004	DAL	2	1	3	14	33%	14.0	0	—	—	-35.1%	—	-0.4	—	-0.5	—	—	—	—
2005	OAK	16	13	26	164	50%	12.6	0	5.4	9	0.9%	22	2.0	28	0.6	33%	33%	28%	6%
2006	OAK	16	28	57	293	49%	10.5	0	2.3	43	-23.4%	39	-3.9	42	-7.1	28%	54%	12%	6%
2007	OAK		20		272		13.5	1											

It's time for another sign that you may be clueless. If you take a replacement-level H-back and special-teamer, start him ten times, and throw him 57 passes, eight of them in the red zone, then you just might be clueless. We recommend a long vacation at an Idaho bed and breakfast.

Kris Wilson Height: 6-2 Weight: 251 College: Pittsburgh Draft: 2004/2 (61) Born: 22-Aug-1981 Age: 26 Risk: Red

Year	Team	G	Rec	Pass	Yds	C%	Yd/C	TD	YAC	Rk	DVOA	Rk	DPAR	Rk	PAR	Short	Mid	Deep	Bomb
2005	KC	14	3	5	33	60%	11.0	0	6.7	—	23.4%	—	1.2	—	0.9	60%	20%	20%	0%
2006	KC	16	15	24	132	63%	8.8	3	5.2	—	21.1%	—	4.3	—	4.0	74%	17%	9%	0%
2007	KC		19		109		5.8	1											

Some people thought Wilson would become the heir apparent to Tony Gonzalez, but the Chiefs changed his position listing on their official depth chart from tight end to fullback last year. Your fantasy league may still list him as a tight end, but he's a good blocker and nothing special as a receiver.

Kellen Winslow Height: 6-4 Weight: 243 College: Miami Draft: 2004/1 (6) Born: 21-Jul-1983 Age: 24 Risk: Yellow

Year	Team	G	Rec	Pass	Yds	C%	Yd/C	TD	YAC	Rk	DVOA	Rk	DPAR	Rk	PAR	Short	Mid	Deep	Bomb
2004	CLE	2	5	11	50	45%	10.0	0	—	—	-28.4%	—	-1.0	—	-0.6	—	—	—	—
2006	CLE	16	89	120	875	74%	9.8	3	3.7	32	6.6%	18	14.7	6	14.6	52%	36%	9%	3%
2007	CLE		63		774		12.2	3											

Give Winslow a lot of credit, after missing almost all of his rookie year with a broken leg and almost all of his second season after he tore up his knee playing Evel Knievel, he was outstanding when he finally got on the field last year. His numbers don't tell the whole story. Remember, the Browns' offense was terrible, and the opposing defense knew he was the focal point of the passing game. Unfortunately, that knee continues to bother Winslow, and we'll probably never see him run the way he did in college at Miami. Still, Winslow is one of the league's top tight ends.

Jason Witten Height: 6-5 Weight: 257 College: Tennessee Draft: 2003/3 (69) Born: 6-May-1982 Age: 25 Risk: Yellow

Year	Team	G	Rec	Pass	Yds	C%	Yd/C	TD	YAC	Rk	DVOA	Rk	DPAR	Rk	PAR	Short	Mid	Deep	Bomb
2004	DAL	16	87	122	980	71%	11.3	6	—	—	20.5%	7	25.1	3	24.2	—	—	—	—
2005	DAL	16	66	94	757	73%	11.5	6	4.2	26	32.3%	3	25.9	2	25.6	41%	49%	11%	0%
2006	DAL	16	64	91	754	70%	11.8	1	4.0	26	20.1%	7	18.2	3	21.6	32%	50%	12%	6%
2007	DAL		60		672		11.1	4											

Witten's 2006 season was nearly a statistical clone of his 2005 with roughly the same number of passes, catches, and yards per catch. Still, Witten's touchdown total and DPAR dipped because he wasn't as effective in the red zone; he caught nine of 12 red zone passes for 63 yards and five touchdowns in 2005 but just 4 of 10 for 23 yards and one touchdown in 2006. That decrease isn't very significant, statistically. Witten is positive clubhouse influence on a team that needs a few locker room leaders, and he has carved out a niche as a productive player in the shadow of two temperamental superstar receivers. He could churn out 65-catch, 750-yard seasons for the rest of the decade.

George Wrighster Height: 6-3 Weight: 260 College: Oregon Draft: 2002/4 (104) Born: 1-Apr-1981 Age: 26 Risk: Red

Year	Team	G	Rec	Pass	Yds	C%	Yd/C	TD	YAC	Rk	DVOA	Rk	DPAR	Rk	PAR	Short	Mid	Deep	Bomb
2004	JAC	4	10	14	69	71%	6.9	1	—	—	-38.9%	—	-1.9	—	-2.0	—	—	—	—
2005	JAC	16	13	23	120	57%	9.2	2	5.1	—	-21.7%	—	-1.3	—	-1.5	55%	20%	20%	5%
2006	JAC	16	39	63	353	62%	9.1	3	2.7	40	-6.5%	28	2.5	26	2.2	45%	38%	15%	2%
2007	JAC		16		193		11.9	1											

We always say the tight end is an even bigger target in the red zone—this precept has been drilled into the heads of anyone who plays *Madden* with the sound on —but with Wrighster, it's even more true than usual. Last year, Wrighster caught eight of ten passes in the red zone for 66 yards. Since 2004 his DVOA in the red zone is 64.0 percent—and, remember, that's compared to other tight ends, not to other players in general.

Going Deep

Michael Allan, KC: Allan caught 53 passes for 1,109 yards at Division III Whitworth College, then performed well at the Combine and became a seventh-round pick. He's a good athlete with a basketball background, but he needs to get into NFL shape and learn how to get open against real competition

Billy Bajema, SF: Bajema, a seventh-round pick in 2005, didn't get on the field much after the 49ers took Vernon Davis with the sixth-overall pick in 2006. With Eric Johnson gone, however, Bajema will get more playing time. He doesn't have anything close to Davis's upside, but 49ers observers have very positive things to say about him. Either Bajema or Delanie Walker could catch 25 passes as the second tight end in an offense struggling for targets.

Eric Beverly, FA: A college tight end who started at center and guard for several seasons with the Lions, Beverly has enjoyed a strange second career as a blocking tight end. He caught the first pass of his ten-year career in the season finale against the Eagles last year, but, since the Falcons cut him right afterward, it may have also been his last.

Troy Bienemann, ARI: Bienemann, an undrafted free agent who spent last year on New Orleans's practice squad, struggled with injury throughout his career at Washington State. He's got ideal size and good hands, but his best chance of an NFL career is using his long-snapping skills.

Kevin Boss, NYG: A fifth-round pick from Western Oregon, Boss fills Visanthe Shiancoe's role on the Giants as the developmental backup tight end with good measurables, but little else to contribute.

John Bronson, ARI: Bronson is the fourth tight end on a team that doesn't have one good one. General rule of thumb: If your team asks you to show up at the official team draft party, and you need the money so badly or feel the need to suck up to the team so badly that you actually go, chances are that you'll be hanging out while the team picks players who will be taking your roster spot, Keyshawn-style. Don't go to the draft party. Say you're busy lifting or something.

Dominique Byrd, STL: A speedy, athletic tight end with a rep as a trash talker at USC, Byrd spent his rookie season as the Rams' third tight end while fellow rookie Joe Klopfenstein started and veteran Aaron Walker backed up. Byrd had two catches for 39 yards, although one was a touchdown (109.4 percent DVOA, 2.4 DPAR). In April, Byrd pleaded guilty to DUI charges, and the Rams, who had already signed free-agent tight end Randy McMichael, quickly re-signed Walker. Byrd is probably not going to be on the Rams much longer.

Brett Celek, PHI: Philadelphia's fifth-round pick out of Cincinnati, Celek stood out at the Shrine Game and has some potential as a receiver. He's a poor man's L. J. Smith.

Brad Cieslak, BUF: Talk about depth: Each of the last two years, Ryan Neufeld went down with injury, and the Buffalo Bills had Cieslak available on the practice squad to plug into the "backup tight end with odd vowel combination" role. As long as Cieslak's around, former Cowboy David LaFleur can stay retired, and someone else can draft Minnesota's Matt Spaeth. Two of Cieslak's first four catches went for first downs, but his big moment in the sun was the pass that bounced off his hands and into the arms of Tennessee's Chris Hope. Oops.

Casey Cramer, TEN: Cramer is Sean Morey's evil twin from the mirror universe of Dartmouth: He doesn't play a role on offense, but he's a useful special-teams guy.

Tim Day, CIN: This Oregon product spent 2006 on the Bears' and Eagles' practice squads, but made his way to a better situation in Cincinnati. He's an excellent athlete, but he's lazy on and off the field. If there ever was a time for him to hunker down and impress, it would be now.

Darnell Dinkins, CLE: As Kellen Winslow's replacement in short-yardage situations, Dinkins is a solid blocker. He shows up on special teams, and the Browns pass to him a couple times a year just to keep the opposing defenses honest. He caught two passes for 14 yards and a touchdown in 2006 (51.9 percent DVOA, 1.3 DPAR).

Jason Dunn, KC: When healthy, Dunn is one of the league's best blocking tight ends and a nice complement to Tony Gonzalez in the two-tight-end formation, but he is rarely involved as a receiver. He caught four of ten passes for 40 yards last year (–13.4 percent DVOA, –0.1 DPAR).

Tyler Ecker, WAS: Ecker is a 25-year-old rookie seventh-round pick who only caught 57 passes in his career at Michigan. He has some potential as a blocker and fits the Redskins' multi-tight-end system, but he's a poor prospect as a receiver.

Kevin Everett, BUF: Like Willis McGahee once upon a time, Everett was a Buffalo first-day draft pick out of Miami who missed his entire rookie year with a knee injury. Unlike McGahee, this 2005 third-rounder didn't do anything when he got back on the field. Everett seems to have been tagged as one of the old Mike Mularkey regime's "guys," and that, along with his three penalties in limited time, has earned him a permanent spot in the doghouse.

Christian Fauria, FA: The Redskins signed Fauria a year ago because of his blocking ability, but he suffered through most of the 2006 season with a foot injury and ended the year on injured reserve. He caught two passes for 17 yards in 2006 (–12.1 percent DVOA, 0.0 DPAR) and is now probably retired, with a future in television.

Daniel Fells, ATL: The 6-foot-4 Fells is quickly becoming a coach's favorite for his work ethic, versatility, and blocking skills. The Falcons cut Eric Beverly to ensure that Fells would have a roster spot, so expect to see a lot of Fells as an H-back and a tight end in 2007.

Ronnie Ghent, CIN: This Louisville product spent 2006 on the practice squad, then "upgraded" to injured reserve when he broke his foot. The Bengals need a second tight end, and it'll either be Ghent or Tim Day.

John Gilmore, CHI: Gilmore was only a part-time starter at Penn State and entered the 2002 draft class with just a handful of catches on his résumé, a 40-time of 4.95, and a reputation as a soft blocker. It's a testament to his tenacity that he was playing in the Super Bowl five years later as a backup tight end and special-teams ace. Gilmore had six catches on 12 passes last year, with 38 yards and two touchdowns (–12.6 percent DVOA, 0.0 DPAR), but, with Greg Olsen in town, he'll be concentrating on the special-teams part of his job.

Roy Hall, IND: Hall backed up Ted Ginn Jr. and Anthony Gonzalez as a wide receiver at Ohio State. He's 6-foot-3, weighs 240 pounds, and runs a 4.41 40, so the Colts will probably give him a tryout as a tight end/H-back after taking him in the fifth round. He's a system player who may be in the right system in Indy. He could replace Ben Utecht or Dallas Clark if they leave in the offseason, but he'll have to learn the offense first.

Clark Harris, GB: Harris is a good-hands, no-block H-back type from Rutgers with some long-snapping ability. The Packers drafted him with the 243rd overall pick near the end of the seventh round.

Tony Humphrey, GB: The Packers signed Humphrey as an undrafted free agent out of Central Michigan back in 2005, and, while he's never spent much time on the active roster, that's likely to change this year. With the Packers thinking about releasing Bubba Franks, Humphrey could move up to second-string behind Donald Lee.

Nate Jackson, DEN: Jackson has managed a five-year NFL career after a college career at the little-known Menlo College. He can play both tight end and wide receiver, although he doesn't do either particularly well. Jackson caught five of six passes in 2006 for 49 yards (0.2 percent DVOA, 0.5 DPAR).

Bennie Joppru, SEA: Incredibly, 2006 was the first season in Joppru's four-year career in which he wasn't placed on injured reserve. He played special teams down the stretch, and is part of Seattle's bid to field the least exciting collection of tight ends in NFL history.

Brian Kozlowski, FA: I block, therefore I am. Kozlowski has been known to square up pan handlers, priests, cardboard cutouts, compact cars, Bob's Big Boy, those big blue mailboxes, and anything else that looks like it might try to get past him and head toward his quarterback/family/item of value. He is probably done, though.

Nate Lawrie, FA: Lawrie followed Eric Johnson at Yale, which sadly is not yet known as "Tight End U." He was crowded out by a deep group of tight ends in New Orleans, and will need to move elsewhere to see playing time.

Martrez Milner, ATL: Atlanta's fourth-round pick, Milner caught 30 passes for Georgia last season, but suffered through an early season case of the dropsies and had an awful game against Florida, in which he dropped a pass and appeared to quit on a goal-line seam route late in the game with Gators safety Reggie Nelson closing in for the kill. He's a top athlete with a basketball background, but he needs to improve his concentration in the pros.

Dave Moore, FA: Moore is a veteran long-snapper who seems to catch one pass every year in some three-tight-end, short-yardage set. How veteran is he? Moore played on the 1992 Buccaneers with Steve DeBerg and Vinny Testaverde. Reggie Cobb was the running back, Mark Carrier the top wideout, and Eddie Murray the kicker. That team went 5–11 under Sam Wyche. Moore left the Bucs for Buffalo in 2002 and 2003, so he missed the Super Bowl season. Life can be so cruel.

Chad Mustard, DEN: The 277-pound Mustard would probably have a better NFL career if he gained 30 pounds and moved to the offensive line. As is, his role as a blocking tight end has just about disappeared following the acquisition of Daniel Graham.

Legedu Naanee, SD: Some quick facts: (1) Naanee started his Boise State career at quarterback and served as a quarterback/wide receiver/tight end in 2004. (2) He set several school weightlifting records and has a 40-inch vertical leap. (3) On the second day of May minicamp, Norv Turner moved Naanee from wide receiver to tight end. "We're going to move him around and see what all he can do," Turner said. San Diego's fifth-round pick will start his career as Antonio Gates's understudy. There's no telling where he will end up.

Joe Newton, SEA: Newton never got drafted during the second-day rush on tight ends, but he could stick as an undrafted free agent on a Seattle team that has blocking specialist Will Heller, injured reserve frequent-flyer Bennie Joppru, and 35-year-old warhorse Marcus Pollard on the roster.

John Owens, NO: This former Notre Dame lineman is currently the Saints' fourth-string tight end. A switch back to the offensive line would probably give him a better shot at playing time at this point.

Richard Owens, MIN: It seems as though every team has a Richard Owens. You're not quite sure what he provides that is special, but he hangs around for a number of years on special teams and in the nether regions of the depth chart. Owens has started two games in his three years in the league, and he caught six of nine passes for 45 yards and a touchdown in 2006 (–24.3 percent DVOA, –0.7 DPAR).

Ben Patrick, ARI: Not to be confused with onetime Colorado and San Diego catcher Ben Petrick, this former Duke and Delaware tight end was a seventh-round pick by Arizona. He has good hands and is agile for his size (252 pounds), but he lacks speed and separation ability. With Arizona's tight end cupboard mostly bare, Patrick will likely stick as a backup and play on special teams.

Gabe Reid, FA: Those who do it would likely not have it any other way, but the Mormon mission definitely hurts a player's NFL career. Reid struggled to make a team after college, then lost a year to injury. He finally worked himself onto a roster as a contributor last year, and caught four of ten passes for 37 yards (–58.6 percent DVOA, –2.7 DPAR). Reid turned 30 over the offseason, so the Bears decided not to re-sign him. Sadly, he may forever be best known for fumbling a squib kick in Super Bowl XLI.

Mike Seidman, IND: The former Panthers third-rounder has torn his ACL twice in three pro seasons. He's buried deep on the depth chart, but Dallas Clark and Ben Utecht are both injury-prone, and, if they go down, Seidman has the hands to be a worthwhile receiver.

Jerame Tuman, PIT: Tuman's role continues to be that of blocking tight end, although he caught all seven of the passes he was thrown in 2006 for 73 yards and a touchdown (63.4 percent DVOA, 3.6 DPAR). He was one of the Steelers who was impersonated in an attempt to pick up girls in the Pittsburgh area; one day, we will calibrate replacement-level to "...can get you laid on name and occupation alone."

Fred Wakefield, OAK: Wakefield signed with the Raiders, where he probably won't be playing tight end anymore. He could move back to his former spot on the defensive line (he's still listed at 318 pounds), or move over to tackle. Could he really be that much worse than Robert Gallery?

Aaron Walker, STL: Cut by the 49ers in the 2005 preseason, Walker was signed by St. Louis that December and played in all 16 games for the Rams in 2006. Though he played mostly on special teams, he did catch a pass in each of the Rams' final four games last year totaling five passes for 68 yards (89.3 percent DVOA, 3.4 DPAR). St. Louis re-signed him to a one-year deal in the offseason, but with Randy McMichael and Joe Klopfenstein taking the reps at tight end, Walker will continue to be more of a special-teams player than an offensive one.

Cooper Wallace, TEN: Wallace spent most of the season on the Titans' practice squad, joining the active roster when Bo Scaife went down and catching one pass for six yards (–7.1 percent DVOA, 0.0 DPAR). His role in 2007 is likely to be "Graduate Assistant."

Todd Yoder, WAS: While it's true that the Redskins lack depth at a lot of positions, Yoder's a very useful blocker, and, while he needs to work on his routes to get more playing time, he's one of the few guys on the Redskins' bench worth his salt. He caught one pass for four yards in 2006 (–18.0 percent DVOA, –0.1 DPAR).

Tearing Down the Rookie Wall

Bill Barnwell and Mike Tanier

He carried your fantasy team, and his NFL team, at the start of the season: the hotshot rookie who left the gate at full gallop, gaining hundreds of yards and racking up fantasy points. But by midseason, the young thoroughbred became a plow horse, chewing up turf at 2.3 yards per carry or cooling his hooves on the bench. He hit the rookie wall, the point at which nagging injuries, exhaustion, and inexperience catch up with young players.

We've all heard of the rookie wall. But is it real? And if it is, when do first-year players hit it? To find the answers, we performed a ten-year study of rookie skill position players. We started with every rookie who attempted 200 passes, rushed 100 times, or caught 30 balls in his first season. We then weeded out the "late start" guys, players who got all of their playing time in the second half of the year (and consequently were in no position to "hit the wall.") If the rookie didn't have 40 carries, 40 attempts, or ten catches after his team's fourth game, he was out of the study. That left rookies who made some sort of early-season splash. Could they carry that September success into December?

For the most part, they could. At most positions, the rookie wall is little more than a soft barricade, one that good young players have little trouble blasting through. In fact, rookie production usually improves late in the season.

Quarterbacks

There's no appreciable or significant difference between quarterbacks in any particular subset of the season (table 1). The sample size of 13 quarterbacks results in one player's performance influencing the results slightly more than normal—so while it looks like quarterbacks really struggle with interceptions at the beginning of the season, that's actually only one quarterback throwing a significant amount of passes. That obviously in-over-his-head bust of a quarterback who threw 11 interceptions in his first four games would ride his laser-accurate rocket arm to a 2006 Super Bowl championship; but in the first half of 1998, Peyton Manning was fantasy poison, and his numbers skew the results in the table.

On the other hand, Vince Young is an extreme example of how a quarterback can improve over the course of a season. His completion percentage through his first eight games was a ghastly 46 percent, a figure that is near-impossible to win with. In the second half, Young completed just under 56 percent of his passes, an incredible improvement. The game in which he turned it all around? Week 12 against the Giants, when he followed an 8-for-22 day against the Eagles by going 24-for-35 for 268 yards with two scores and no picks. From there, Young played at a high level until struggling against the Patriots in Week 17.

Running Backs

The 36 rookie running backs in our study didn't really hit a wall; it was more of a Halloween hurdle (table 2). Running backs that start the season strong often turn into pumpkins halfway through the season, but they bounce back in December, just in time for the fantasy playoffs (if you make them).

Cadillac Williams's 2005 season was a fine example of this slump 'n' surge trend. He started the season hot: 434 yards and two rushing touchdowns in his first three games. Then he got banged up and endured a six-week stretch in which he missed two games and carried 45 times for 82

Table 1. Quarterbacks

Games	Comp	Att	C%	Yds	Yd/Att	TD	INT
Games 1–8	14.9	27.4	54.2%	166	6.1	0.8	1.1
Games 9–16	14.3	26.4	53.9%	160	6.1	0.9	0.9
Games 1–4	13.7	25.9	52.3%	149	5.8	0.6	1.3
Games 5–8	15.9	29.3	55.0%	179	6.2	1.0	1.0
Games 9–12	14.8	27.3	53.4%	161	5.8	0.9	0.9
Games 13–16	13.6	25.1	57.6%	168	6.6	0.7	0.9

Table 2. Running Backs

	Runs	Yds	Yd/Att	TD
Games 1–8	15.9	60.9	3.83	0.5
Games 9–17	16.2	68.0	4.20	0.6
Games 1–4	16.3	64.1	3.93	0.6
Games 5–8	15.6	57.6	3.69	0.5
Games 9–12	15.8	66.7	4.22	0.7
Games 13–16	17.1	71.3	4.17	0.8

yards when he did play. But he finished the season strong, averaging 95 yards per game and 4.2 yards per carry over his final seven games.

Many rookie runners of the past decade have battled this Cadillac Syndrome, a sudden midseason slump that lasts several weeks. In his first three games as a featured back in 2001, Anthony Thomas carried 80 times for 411 yards (5.1) and three touchdowns. He then gained 157 yards in one five-game stretch, only to finish the season with two 150+ yard performances in the final five weeks. Jamal Lewis carried 34 times for 192 yards in his first two starts in 2000, then spent a month posting 17-carry, 44-yard stat lines before racking up 927 yards in his final eight games. Fred Taylor, Eddie George, Warrick Dunn, Mike Anderson, LaDainian Tomlinson, Laurence Maroney, and others followed a more-or-less similar pattern.

One of the exceptions to this rule was Colts running back Joseph Addai, whose numbers rose with the team's confidence in him. In his first four games, the Colts gave Addai 46 carries as he learned the team's offense and blocking schemes. Addai averaged 4.5 yards per carry—a solid figure for most teams, but not the Colts. Addai's workload increased to 59 carries in his next four games, then to 66 carries in Games 9–12, during which he hit his peak of 5.4 yards per carry. During his final four games, the Colts pushed Addai back to 63 carries to rest him for the playoffs. That worked out well.

Remember that all of the running backs in the study had to have early-season success, so there are no late bloomers arriving in the final weeks to pump up the numbers. The running backs in the study produced 22 100-yard games in the first four games of the season, 16 in the next four games, 15 in the next four, and 28 in the final games. There were a total of 29 games in which a back gained over 130 yards in the study. Eight of those big games occurred in the first five games of the season, just three occurred in the next six weeks, and 18 occurred in the final five weeks.

Our rookies bottomed out in their team's ninth games, and while several backs never recovered from their midseason slump, the best players worked their way back into the lineup. Eight rookie running backs in the last decade posted at least two 100-yard rushing efforts in their teams' first four games. All of them (including Cadillac) had at least one more 100-yard game in the final four weeks of the season.

Wide Receivers and Tight Ends

Wide receivers display a pattern similar to running backs. Their numbers slowly decrease over the course of the season,

bottoming out in games 9–12. But as the season ends, rookie wide receivers return to form, saving their gaudiest statistics for the last four games of the regular season (table 3).

The worst week for rookie receivers, by far, is Week 12; if you were to just measure Weeks 9–11, rookie receivers averaged 3.7 catches per game, which is slightly more in line with the rest of the season's reception rates. There's nothing special about Week 12; the data set isn't large enough to weed out random fluctuations. But it's still hard to find any evidence of a late-season slump.

Many rookie receivers find more balls heading their way late in the season. The three players who raised their game most in the final weeks were Marvin Harrison (1996), Torry Holt (1999), and Lee Evans (2004). Each of these three receivers was targeted at least two more times per game in the final four weeks of the season compared to the previous twelve. Evans, in particular, became a focal point of the offense; 38 percent of his total targets came during the final four weeks of the season (26 of 69). But even when these three players are removed from the study, there's an upward trend in wideouts' late-season numbers.

The rookie wide receiver of note in 2006, Marques Colston, did not follow this pattern. Instead, Colston got off to a good start and then got hotter as the season went on, with the climax being a three-game stretch against Baltimore, Tampa Bay, and Pittsburgh in Weeks 9–11 where he caught 27 balls for 452 yards and three touchdowns. An injury towards the end of the season hampered Colston's performance, which otherwise might rank up with the top rookie performances any wide receiver has ever posted.

Tight ends, meanwhile, shrug in the face of the alleged rookie wall (table 4). Both receptions and yards by rookie tight ends increase as the season goes on, and yardage totals for the big guys are appreciably better in the second half of the season, as the table below shows. Rookie tight ends are rarely worth starting in fantasy leagues, but their improved performance in the second half may allow you to find waiver-wire bargains in midseason. Mediocre first-

Table 3. Wide Receivers

	Rec	Yds	TD
Games 1–8	3.3	45.1	0.3
Games 9–17	3.3	44.6	0.5
Games 1–4	3.3	45.4	0.5
Games 5–8	3.3	44.9	0.4
Games 9–12	3.1	41.8	0.5
Games 13–16	3.4	48.3	0.7

Table 4. Tight Ends

	Rec	Yds	TD
Games 1–8	2.7	28.3	0.3
Games 9–17	3.2	35.8	0.3
Games 1–4	2.3	24.4	0.4
Games 5–8	3.0	32.2	0.5
Games 9–12	3.1	34.2	0.3
Games 13–16	3.1	29.4	0.8

year prospects such as Stephen Alexander, Cameron Cleeland, and Alex Smith all upped their game dramatically over the season's final quarter, averaging over four catches and around 40 yards a game.

Conclusion

Forget about the rookie wall. That rookie running back, receiver, or tight end is actually more likely to help you at the end of the season than he was in October (and if you are counting on a rookie quarterback late in the year). Just remember that rookie performance is generally more volatile than veteran performance; these guys are often one fumble, missed block, or blown route from a benching, but the best rookies bounce back, and the patient fantasy owner can plug the youngster back in the lineup at playoff time, with big dividends.

Opposition: When Is Alex Smith Better than Carson Palmer?

Bill Barnwell

PFP Staff League: Week 1, 2007

Carnevale's Cacaphony	Pos	Barnwell's Blitzkreig
Carson Palmer, CIN	QB	Alex Smith, SF
Rudi Johnson, CIN	RB	DeShaun Foster, CAR
Warrick Dunn, ATL	RB	Lawrence Maroney, NE
Lee Evans, BUF	WR	Jerry Porter, OAK
Roy Williams, DET	WR	Eddie Kennison, KC

The question posed in the title of this essay has several answers. One might be "When the Bengals are on a bye." Another might be "When Carson Palmer is sitting next to Jerome Bettis on NBC in 2014 and Alex Smith is still chucking passes in San Francisco." The answer we were looking for, however, is "Week 1 of the 2007 season."

Consider the two teams presented above. Comparing them position-by-position, it's easy to see that Alex Carnevale's team far surpasses my own, which looks like it was selected by auto-pick after I failed to show up for the draft. In a head-to-head matchup, Alex's team would win going away most weeks. In Week 1 of 2007, however, not only does my team have a shot, I'd say it is the clear favorite.

The reason why is a detail left out of the table—the opposition each player is up against. Alex's team is full of awful Week 1 matchups: Warrick Dunn faces an excellent run defense (Minnesota), Evans and Williams face excellent pass defenses (Denver and Oakland, respectively), and Palmer and Johnson face an excellent-at-everything defense (Baltimore). On the other hand, my team faces some of the weakest defenses in the league, including Arizona (Smith), St. Louis (Foster), the Jets (Maroney), Detroit (Porter), and Houston (Kennison).

Every good fantasy player pays attention to the matchups when trying to decide who to sit and who to start each week, but how many are actually willing to bench elite players such as Johnson and Dunn for second-tier players such as Foster when the matchups favor the latter? Understanding the matchups each week and the effects of a defense on player performance can provide you with a competitive advantage, even in the toughest leagues.

Let's take a look at how the strength of the opposing defense can affect player performance at each of the three major fantasy skill positions.

Running Backs

To measure the effect of the opposing defense on an offensive player's performance, we first split the 32 NFL defenses into these five categories:

Replacement-level	+13.3% DVOA or worse
Poor	+4.5% to +13.3% DVOA
Average	+4.4% to −4.4% DVOA
Good	−4.5 % to −13.3% DVOA
Great	−13.3% DVOA or better

Table 1 shows how the average running back performed against each of these five categories over the past eleven seasons (1996–2006). As you can see, against a replacement-level rush defense, the average running back becomes an effective fantasy starter gaining 4.63 yards per carry, scoring more than a touchdown per game, and averaging 17.8 fantasy points.[1] As the defenses get better, however, those numbers all get steadily worse until that same running back is gaining only 3.44 yards per carry, scoring less than 60 percent as many touchdowns, and averaging only 11.6 fantasy points. This idea may seem like a tautology—offensive performance decreases against a better defense—but table 1 proves that theories about how teams attack good rush defenses (with a short passing attack or by using different types of running plays) are untrue. In general, teams who play great run defenses run the ball about as often, just not as well.

---

1. Our generic fantasy scoring system gives one point for every 20 yards passing, 10 yards rushing, and 20 yards receiving, with four points for a passing touchdown, six for a rushing or receiving touchdown, and −2 points for an interception. All data in this essay is from 1996–2006.

Table 1. Average RB Performance Split By Defensive Pass DVOA

Defensive Rush DVOA	Runs	Yds	Yd/R	RecYd	TD	FP
Replacement	21.8	100.5	4.63	19.2	1.13	17.8
Poor	20.7	91.3	4.41	20.0	0.97	15.9
Average	20.7	87.1	4.18	18.1	0.82	14.6
Good	20.3	76.7	3.76	18.0	0.74	13.0
Great	20.0	68.8	3.44	17.2	0.65	11.6
Total	20.7	84.9	4.08	18.5	0.86	14.6

Table 3. Average WR Performance Split By Defensive Pass DVOA

Defensive Pass DVOA	REC	YDS	AVG	TD	FP
Replacement	4.6	64.0	14.0	0.59	11.4
Poor	4.4	60.2	13.8	0.56	10.8
Average	4.5	58.7	13.1	0.48	10.3
Good	4.3	57.6	13.5	0.51	10.2
Great	4.2	56.1	13.2	0.45	9.8
Total	4.1	59.3	13.5	0.52	10.5

Having seen how the quality of the opposing defense affects the average running back, the question then becomes, how do opposing defenses impact the performance of elite running backs, and is there a point at which it makes sense to sit an elite back who is facing a great defense in favor of a lesser back facing a lesser defense.

We ranked every back who had at least one game with 15 or more carries over the last eleven years by their total number of 15-carry games, then split those rankings into six tiers from the elite top-20 backs (1–20) to the replacement level (100+) (table 2). We used 15-carry games rather than DPAR or DVOA to rank the backs so that our rankings would more closely resemble existing fantasy rankings, which are compiled on raw numbers and familiarity and don't account for context like DPAR and DVOA.

What table 2 shows us is that, on average, the best running backs lose as much of their fantasy value (6.4 fantasy points, or about 37 percent) when facing a great rush defense as the worst starting running backs (5.0 points, also 37 percent) do. Even more surprising, when facing replacement-level run defenses, the worst starting running backs perform, on average, slightly better than the best running backs do against great rush defenses. Indeed, last year, Houston's Ron Dayne racked up 27 fantasy points against the league-worst Indianapolis run defense in Week

16, while LaDanian Tomlinson scored just nine points against Baltimore in Week 4, and only four against Pittsburgh in Week 5. Of course, there will be games in which a great running back will put up 25 fantasy points against a good defense, while a mediocre back will only score three against an awful one, but such games are the exception, not the rule.

Table 3 also shows that these trends are consistent, as running back performance slowly decreases as defensive quality increases, while the superior backs generally outperform their lower-ranked brethren against defenses of equal quality. One notable exception is the noticeable jump for backs ranked 81–100 against "poor" defenses (rush DVOA of 4.5% to 13.4%). That blip in the data is thanks to several huge performances, including Lee Suggs, who put up a 186-yard day against Cincinnati in 2003, Troy Hambrick, who gained 189 yards against Washington the same year, and Greg Hill's 158 yards against Buffalo in 1998.

Wide Receivers

Our wide receiver rankings are according to the total number of games in which a receiver caught three or more passes. What we see in table 3 is that the effect of the defense on wide receiver performance is far less than it is on running back performance. That said, there is still some effect, and the 1.6-point drop in the average receiver's performance against the best defenses represents about 15 percent of his production against a replacement-level defense.

The data in table 4 shows that, unlike with running backs, an excellent wide receiver against a great defense remains a better bet than even a mediocre receiver against an awful one (table 4). These numbers suggest that it's good to stick with your elite wideout unless he's facing a particularly poor matchup; for example, if he's going to play Denver, where he'll get to say hello to Champ Bailey.

While the data is similar for tight ends (they lose 1.46 points of value when playing a great defense as opposed to a bad one), total pass defense DVOA does not necessarily give the whole story about defense against tight ends. Often, excellent pass defenses will struggle against tight

Table 2. Average RB Fantasy Points, Split by RB Rank and Defensive Rush DVOA

Defensive Rush DVOA	RB Rank 1996–2006						Average
	1–20	21–40	41–60	61–80	81–100	101+	
Replacement	18.4	16.7	18.6	15.8	11.2	13.6	15.74
Poor	17.5	15.5	15.5	13.4	15.1	13.1	15.02
Average	16.0	14.4	14.7	13.4	12.3	13.0	13.96
Good	14.5	12.4	12.8	12.2	11.2	11.2	12.38
Great	12.1	12.0	11.2	10.0	8.9	8.6	10.46
Average	15.7	14.2	14.6	13.0	11.7	11.9	13.51
Difference*	6.4	4.7	7.5	5.8	2.3	5.0	5.28

NOTE: RBs ranked by games played with 15+ carries, 1996–2006.

*Difference is between average fantasy points against the worst rush defenses (+13.4% DVOA) and the best (−13.4% DVOA).

Table 4. Average WR Fantasy Points, Split by WR Rank and Defensive Pass DVOA

Defensive Pass DVOA	WR Rank 1996–2006						Average
	1–20	21–40	41–60	61–80	81–100	101+	
Replacement	13.3	12.7	12.2	11.2	11.5	9.5	11.7
Poor	12.6	11.6	11.2	10.2	11.1	9.1	11.0
Average	12.1	11.9	12.0	10.0	10.3	8.3	10.8
Good	11.8	10.7	10.5	10.3	9.5	8.2	10.2
Great	11.4	10.5	9.9	9.8	8.9	8.1	9.8
Average	**12.2**	**11.5**	**11.2**	**10.3**	**10.3**	**8.6**	**10.7**
Difference*	**1.9**	**2.2**	**2.4**	**1.4**	**2.6**	**1.4**	**2.0**

NOTE: WRs ranked by games played with 3 or more receptions, 1996–2006.

*Difference is between average fantasy points against the worst pass defenses (+13.4% DVOA) and the best (−13.4% DVOA).

ends, but do well against all other receivers. Jacksonville was a good example last season. The opposite is true as well—the Jets shut down tight ends, but not really much else. One option is to check out the rankings on the Football Outsiders site for DVOA vs. specific types of receivers, which are updated during the season at the bottom of the team defense page (www.footballoutsiders.com/stats/teamdef.php). In general, however, playing matchups with wide receivers and tight ends is far less helpful than it is with running backs.

Quarterbacks

Given the mythology that surrounds field generals and their abilities to overwhelm even the best defenses with their clutch godliness, quarterback would seem to be the position most likely to avoid the effects of good defenses. After all, Peyton Manning showed up against the Bears and Patriots last year, right? Actually, Manning's regular season performances were pretty typical. The best pass defense he faced was the third-ranked Jaguars', and he put up 13 and 14 fantasy points against them in their two meetings. He scored 15 against the sixth-ranked pass defense of Buf-

Table 5. Average QB Performance Split By Defensive Pass DVOA

Defensive Pass DVOA	Att	Comp	C%	Yds	Yd/At	TD	INT	FP
Replacement	29.5	17.5	59.2%	205.2	6.95	1.4	0.9	14.2
Poor	27.8	16.1	58.0%	186.0	6.70	1.2	0.9	12.3
Average	28.6	16.3	57.0%	183.2	6.41	1.2	1.1	11.7
Good	27.7	15.4	55.5%	174.4	6.30	1.1	1.2	10.8
Great	27.2	14.7	54.0%	163.1	6.00	0.9	1.4	9.1
Total	**28.2**	**16.0**	**56.7%**	**182.4**	**6.47**	**1.2**	**1.1**	**11.6**

falo, and 11 against eighth-ranked Philadelphia. Those performances were plenty competent, but none were spectacular. Meanwhile, he scored 29 against the worst pass defense in football, the Redskins, and 32 and 22 against the Texans, who were second-worst. In fact, Manning was not only not a model of consistency, but a player who suffered larger swings than the average quarterback, mainly because he was so dominant against replacement-level defenses (sorry, Texans).

The Manning issue is similar with other quarterbacks of his caliber (our quarterback rankings are according to total games with 15 or more pass attempts). Per table 6, the top 20 quarterbacks lose, on average, 5.3 fantasy points per game when they play the best defenses as opposed to the worst, while the worst starting quarterbacks of the last 11 years lost an average of 4.9. As a percentage of their total value, the worst quarterbacks do indeed see a sharper decline (44 percent value lost vs. 30 percent for the top-20 QBs), but the net value lost is actually greater for the elite signal callers.

Unlike with wide receivers, it does make sense to play the matchups with your fantasy quarterbacks, no matter how good they are. Even the quarterbacks ranked 80–100 in table 6 outperformed the top-20 QBs when the former were facing replacement-level pass defenses and the latter were facing the league's best.

Getting back to our title question, Week 1 presents an excellent example of this matchup quandary. Carson Palmer goes up against a Baltimore pass defense that was the best in football last year (−25.2% DVOA) and against which he averaged 12 fantasy points in two games last year. Meanwhile, Alex Smith and the 49ers will play Arizona and its poor pass defense (18.1% DVOA, 29th in the league). Smith averaged 12.5 fantasy points against the Cardinals last year. While that half-point difference might not seem like

Table 6. Average QB Fantasy Points, Split by QB Rank and Defensive Pass DVOA

Defensive Pass DVOA	QB Rank 1996–2006						Average
	1–20	21–40	41–60	61–80	81–100	101+	
Replacement	17.4	16.3	16.0	13.5	12.6	11.2	14.5
Poor	15.4	14.2	14.7	11.1	11.2	10.0	12.8
Average	14.2	13.4	13.1	11.1	11.8	9.0	12.1
Good	14.1	12.1	13.2	9.7	9.5	7.9	11.1
Great	12.1	11.4	10.6	8.2	9.0	6.2	9.6
Average	**14.6**	**13.5**	**13.5**	**10.7**	**10.8**	**8.8**	**12.0**
Difference*	**5.3**	**4.9**	**5.4**	**5.2**	**3.6**	**4.9**	**4.9**

Note: QBs ranked by games played with 15+ pass attempts, 1996–2006.

*Difference is between average fantasy points against the worst pass defenses (+13.4% DVOA) and the best (−13.4% DVOA).

that much, Smith had 18 points in his Week 1 game against Arizona last year. He only had seven in his second game against the Cardinals, but he also didn't have left tackle Jonas Jennings or his best wide receiver, Antonio Bryant, available for the game. With the return of Jennings, the new wide receivers in Smith's arsenal, and the suspension of Bengals slot receiver Chris Henry, it seems a rather safe bet that Smith will outperform Palmer in Week 1 this year.

As we've seen, the impact of defense on fantasy performance is quantifiable and real, but the decision to sit or start your first-round player isn't as simple as plugging in a value. That being said, here are two fundamental matchup concepts that can help guide your sit/start decisions: (1) Quarterbacks and running backs lose about a third of their value against the best defenses in the league as opposed to the worst, while the effect is about half as strong for wide receivers. (2) The effect described in (1) is roughly the same for all players at a given position, regardless of how good they are.

Remember that all the numbers provided above are averages. Other factors, such as weather, injuries, or playing surface might help swing your decision one way or another. Much like all of the Football Outsiders stats, these splits are designed to be used in tandem with scouting and other research, not as a catch-all. Nevertheless, if you do manage to get a friend to bet on Alex's team instead of mine in Week 1, remember to cut me in on the deal.

Fantasy Risers and Fallers

Alex Carnevale

The top fantasy football draft picks change on an annual basis. Peyton Manning and Tom Brady will be safe picks for the next five years, but it's hard to say the same about anyone else, especially when it comes to running backs. This makes keeper strategy in fantasy football especially precarious. KUBIAK is here to sort out the real studs from the pretenders, and it starts at the running back position, where two of the three top choices from a year ago now ride our fantasy-fallers charts, while two of last year's rookies ascend to become top picks.

Players are listed along with their rank at their position based on fantasy points, using a simple scoring system of one point for ten yards rushing or receiving, one point for 20 yards passing, four points for a passing touchdown, six points for a rushing touchdown, and minus two points for an interception.

Don't forget that you can follow the fantasy football season Football Outsiders-style with our weekly fantasy column, "Scramble for the Ball."

Top 10 Fantasy Risers

Frank Gore   RB   San Francisco

2006: 312 carries	1,695 rushing yards	61 receptions	485 receiving yards	9 TD	Rank: 4
2007: 347 carries	1,627 rushing yards	47 receptions	355 receiving yards	17 TD	Rank: 1

Coming into 2006, Gore's emergence in the feature back role pegged him as a fantasy sleeper. Despite a propensity to fumble, he made good on that promise, averaging 5.4 yards per carry. That gaudy performance has KUBIAK frothing at the mouth. Despite the likelihood that Gore won't match his total yardage from last season, an improved San Francisco offense will enhance his value by giving him more opportunities in the red zone.

Joseph Addai   RB   Indianapolis

2006: 226 carries	1,081 rushing yards	40 receptions	325 receiving yards	8 TD	Rank: 11
2007: 330 carries	1,430 rushing yards	57 receptions	453 receiving yards	12 TD	Rank: 4

Addai does everything Edgerrin James used to do in the Colts' offense, except he doesn't fumble the ball away at the goal line. He led the league in Success Rate and shows the same pass-catching ability Edge had in his early years with the Colts. With Dominic Rhodes out of the picture, Addai gets the feature back role all to himself. He exploded for 122 yards and a score in the Colts' first-round playoff game against Kansas City, but he was even more impressive in a red zone sequence at the end of the AFC Championship Game against the Patriots. Addai is certainly in the right offense to have a big year, and there are not many backs we'd rather have in 2007. Well, there is always that guy who scores touchdowns in bunches for San Diego—his name escapes us for the moment.

Laurence Maroney   RB   New England

2006: 175 carries	745 rushing yards	22 receptions	194 receiving yards	7 TD	Rank: 29
2007: 304 carries	1,411 rushing yards	43 receptions	351 receiving yards	13 TD	Rank: 6

The key to Maroney's season will be the coaching staff's willingness to use him late in games to run out the clock. Maroney wore down late last year, which means Belichick & Co. may prefer to flip the script and stick with the passing game in the fourth quarter to keep Maroney fresh. After all, the Patriots are likely more intent on having Maroney healthy in the post-season than on riding him to get there. Using another back to run out the clock is the right decision for the Patriots, but it would be the wrong one for Maroney's prospective fantasy owners, as it could significantly decrease his total yardage. Is Maroney worth the sixth pick in your draft? That's debatable, but he's an enormous asset for a team with championship aspirations, and there are much worse options.

Willis McGahee   RB   Baltimore

| **2006:** 259 carries | 990 rushing yards | 18 receptions | 156 receiving yards | 6 TD | Rank: 24 |
| **2007:** 311 carries | 1,290 rushing yards | 31 receptions | 257 receiving yards | 10 TD | Rank: 9 |

McGahee's reputation has far outstripped his production since he began playing for the Bills, but his move to Baltimore is good news for fantasy owners. Brian Billick loves to ride one workhorse running back, and Willis McGahee gets to be it. Jamal Lewis had nine touchdowns behind the Ravens' offensive line last year, and McGahee could easily get more, since Todd Heap is really the Ravens' only reliable receiver in the red zone. Although McGahee's injury history will always be worrisome, and the Ravens don't have the easiest of schedules, he's almost guaranteed to deliver plenty of fantasy points.

Vince Young   QB   Tennessee

| **2006:** 2,199 passing yards | 12 passing TD | 13 INT | 552 rushing yards | 7 rushing TD | Rank: 12 |
| **2007:** 3,336 passing yards | 20 passing TD | 16 INT | 634 rushing yards | 5 rushing TD | Rank: 4 |

Yes, the Titans have the *Madden 2007* coverboy, but relax—they don't have much to worry about when it comes to their franchise quarterback. Even if your league doesn't recognize Young's proclivity for making plays with his feet, that passing projection should excite you. The Titans' receiving corps hardly got the Tom Brady treatment over the offseason, but Young managed in 2006, and as he continues to learn how to use his incredible physical tools . . . watch out. If you can get all the value that Young provides the Titans, in the air and on the ground, you're looking at one of the most valuable commodities in both fantasy and real football over the short- and long-term. Just remember that Young has less value in a league in which passing touchdowns count for six points instead of four, because that reduces his rushing advantage over other quarterbacks.

Rex Grossman   QB   Chicago

| **2006:** 3,193 passing yards | 23 TD | 20 INT | Rank: 13 |
| **2007:** 3,598 passing yards | 23 TD | 16 INT | Rank: 15 |

How can Rex Grossman be a "riser" if his projected rank is lower than his rank in 2006? The answer has to do with Grossman's perceived value, which dropped through the floor after a largely unspectacular postseason that climaxed in a Super Bowl he had no prayer of winning. Rex Grossman has a solid projection. He showed plenty of fantasy potential at times during his Jekyll and Hyde 2006 season—those good weeks explain why he ranked 13th despite his struggles—and he is a very good quarterback to play week-to-week matchups with because the Bears are in such a weak division. For example, Grossman threw five touchdowns and no picks against the Lions in two games last year, and he'll face that 30th-ranked pass defense twice this year before his Week 9 bye. He's still a risky pick, but it's a manageable risk.

Larry Fitzgerald   WR   Arizona

| **2006:** 69 receptions | 946 receiving yards | 6 TD | Rank: 24 |
| **2007:** 76 receptions | 1,069 receiving yards | 7 TD | Rank: 8 |

Last year we predicted that Fitzgerald would have the better season than his talented counterpart, the self-proclaimed best basketball player in the NFL, Anquan Boldin. Boldin had a nice year, but, despite missing time with an injury, Fitzgerald justified our faith, nearing 1,000 yards despite battling hamstring problems. Sure, hamstring injuries can come back, but his upside when it comes to touchdowns is even greater than KUBIAK thinks. He is still the best bet on an improved Arizona team.

Vincent Jackson   WR   San Diego

| **2006:** 27 receptions | 453 receiving yards | 6 TD | Rank: 53 |
| **2007:** 48 receptions | 758 receiving yards | 5 TD | Rank: 36 |

This 6-foot-5 wideout's physical tools have never been in doubt, and his success in the end zone in an emerging passing attack is likely to continue as he and Chargers quarterback Philip Rivers develop better chemistry. Jackson's more prominent role in the offense makes him the best bet of an inexperienced core of receivers. A two-TD, 97-yard game against the Seahawks in Week 16 hints at what he may be able to do in 2007.

D. J. Hackett   WR   Seattle

| **2006:** 37 receptions | 309 receiving yards | 2 TD | Rank: 51 |
| **2007:** 59 receptions | 852 receiving yards | 6 TD | Rank: 24 |

Hackett's performance in 2006 made Darrell Jackson expendable. Seattle runs up against a string of poor pass defenses, and Hackett lining up at split end when healthy gives Seattle a capable, speedy receiver who could become an increasingly popular red zone option as the season wears on. Watch the training camp competition between Hackett and Nate Burleson—if Hackett wins out, as he should, fantasy owners should be delighted with him as their number three receiver.

Stephen Gostkowski K   New England

2006: 20-26 FG	43 XP	103 Points	Rank: 19
2007: 31-36 FG	48 XP	141 Points	Rank: 1

The Patriots' organizational philosophy doesn't favor the use of the field goal, but being a talented kicker on one of the top teams in the league is almost always a recipe for success. Indeed, Gostkowski is our top-rated kicker, and for good reason. He put away the jitters early in his rookie year, vindicating the Patriots' decision to draft him instead of retaining Super Bowl hero Adam Vinatieri, and field-goal kickers almost always improve between their first and second seasons. He's about as close to a lock for 30 field goals as you can get in the chaotic fantasy kicking game, and he'll score plenty of extra points, too.

Top Ten Fantasy Fallers

Larry Johnson   RB   Kansas City

2006: 416 carries	1,789 rushing yards	41 receptions	410 receiving yards	17 TD	Rank: 2
2007: 342 carries	1200 rushing yards	33 receptions	257 receiving yards	14 TD	Rank: 7

Coming off his 416-carry season, Johnson is about the worst bet for a premium back imaginable—he depends on running through people, his offensive line lost a key cog, his team doesn't have a quarterback or a coach of any note, and it's not as though he was coming off that great a season. His 4.3 yards per carry in 2006 were well short of Gore's 5.4. Johnson's real drop off in productivity may not come until 2008, but there will be much better options at the very top of the first round this year, even though Johnson will still likely go in the first three picks.

Shaun Alexander   RB   Seattle

2006: 252 carries	896 rushing yards	12 receptions	48 receiving yards	7 TD	Rank: 28
2007: 250 carries	945 rushing yards	14 receptions	56 receiving yards	6 TD	Rank: 33

After he was beset by a broken foot a year ago, the Seahawks had no reason to play Alexander before he was completely healthy. The same will be true in 2007. Even if he does start and stay healthy, he doesn't do nearly as much for your fantasy team if your league isn't heavily weighted towards touchdowns, even if he gets the red zone chances the Seahawks like to set up for him. The larger picture is far bleaker. There's a lot of tread on those tires, the Seahawks have a plethora of pathetic pass defenses on their schedule that will lure them away from the run, and KUBIAK's not optimistic. We're projecting Alexander to put up stats over a full season that aren't much different from the stats he put up last year in just ten games.

Deuce McAllister   RB   New Orleans

2006: 244 carries	1,057 rushing yards	30 receptions	198 receiving yards	10 TD	Rank: 13
2007: 225 carries	936 rushing yards	37 receptions	260 receiving yards	6 TD	Rank: 26

Don't get caught paying for past performance when it comes to McAllister. A time-sharing arrangement worked out well last year, but he'll have fourth-round pick Antonio Pittman pushing him for goal-line carries, and somebody named Bush in the backfield the rest of the time. Bush improved markedly in the second half of the season, and his increased role in the offense heading into 2007 is only a minus for McAllister's fantasy owners. McAllister's injury history doesn't help matters.

Warrick Dunn   RB   Atlanta

2006: 286 carries	1,140 rushing yards	22 receptions	170 receiving yards	5 TD	Rank: 24
2007: 201 carries	823 rushing yards	19 receptions	152 receiving yards	7 TD	Rank: 32

He's been a fixture with the Falcons since he signed with the team in 2002 as a free agent, but Dunn is now 32 years old. His role in the Atlanta offense may not change much, but his effectiveness is likely to decline, as it did last season. With their win projection, the Falcons are going to spend a lot of time behind in games, which means more emphasis on the passing game. A shoulder injury early in minicamp isn't helping Dunn's cause.

Jeff Garcia   QB   Tampa Bay

2006: 1,309 passing yards	10 TD	2 INT	Rank (Weeks 12–17): 3
2007: 2,640 passing yards	18 TD	21 INT	Rank: 32

After Donovan McNabb went down with another season-ending injury in a Week 11 loss to the Titans, there was a mad rush to pluck Jeff Garcia off the waiver wire, a strange occurrence given that Garcia had previously been such a dismal failure. Reunited with his former offensive coordinator from San Francisco, Marty Mornhinweg, Garcia rewarded those waiver claims with a nice little run. Garcia had the perfect complement of players and system in Philadelphia, but he moves to a far worse situation in Tampa Bay. He does beat having nothing and no one at the most important position on the field, but he's unlikely to throw more touchdowns than interceptions again in his career. Of course, Garcia may not win the job over Chris Simms, but if he does, other owners in your league may expect a return trip to the fountain of youth. You should not.

Tony Romo   QB   Dallas

2006: 2,903 passing yards   19 TD   13 INT   Rank (Weeks 9–17): 10
2007: 3,567 passing yards   21 TD   19 INT   Rank: 18

Fantasy players and Cowboys fans cooled their Romo love after his play deteriorated following his Pro Bowl selection, so he probably won't be going too high in drafts. Still, there's reason to think he won't be an asset no matter when he is taken. You'll get the same value out of Denver's Jay Cutler, without the Jessica Simpson rumors and "I Was a Pro Bowler" knit sweaters.

Robbie Gould   K   Chicago

2006: 32–36 FG   47 XP   143 points   Rank: 1
2007: 22–28 FG   35 XP   101 points   Rank: 23

Gould had an extraordinary year during the Bears' Super Bowl run, but it's not as though he was showing off a particularly strong leg; he didn't even attempt a field goal over fifty yards. With a weak NFC and a weaker division, Gould may seem like a strong bet in 2007, but you can't count on kickers to be consistent from year to year, and he may never get near 47 extra points again. He's still not a bad kicker by any means, he's just not a top-five kicker, be it in your fantasy league or the National Football League.

Terrell Owens   WR   Dallas

2006: 85 receptions   1,180 receiving yards   13 TD   Rank: 2
2007: 71 receptions   938 receiving yards   8 TD   Rank: 14

Terrell Owens scored a touchdown once every 6.5 receptions in 2006, and touchdowns are not as consistent from year to year as receptions and yardage. The top 30 wide receivers in fantasy football scored a touchdown once every 10.5 receptions, and T.O.'s ratio of yards to touchdowns is likely to be more similar to that number in 2007. On top of that, we're projecting a general decline from the Cowboys offense, Owens is now 34 years old, and the man is a wacko. Even if he stays on the field, even if he keeps up his level of performance, even if he plays if Dallas is out of the playoff race, do you still want to bet a top pick on T.O.?

Isaac Bruce   WR   St. Louis

2006: 74 receptions   1,098 receiving yards   3 TD   Rank: 25
2007: 66 receptions   813 receiving yards   4 TD   Rank: 39

Bruce is another old receiver on a team that's going nowhere fast. It would be one thing if you could count on the Rams to be so far behind in games that they would have to resort to the passing game more often than not, but their division schedule is soft, so it may be Steven Jackson who gets the benefit of the other team's defensive approach.

Desmond Clark   TE   Chicago

2006: 45 receptions   626 receiving yards   6 TD   Rank: 8
2007: 33 receptions   399 receiving yards   3 TD   Rank: 20

Basketball's resident statistical guru, John Hollinger, invented a concept for the NBA called the Fluke Rule. In an attempt to find the players most likely to regress, Hollinger looked at players 28 years old or older who performed markedly better than they had the previous season. Basketball players generally don't sustain improvements in performance at that age, and the same is true of 30-year-old tight ends. Clark beat up on bad teams to pad his stats as the Bears rolled to an NFC title, but you don't want Clark anywhere near your tight end spot in 2007 unless he plays Detroit or Minnesota and your starter is on a bye week. NFL teams have a way of spotting these faux improvements better than NBA teams, and the selection of first-round tight end Greg Olsen in this year's draft proves the Chicago Bears organization is smarter than whoever signed Mark Blount.

Kicker and Defense Projections

Kickers

Listed in table 1 are the 2007 KUBIAK projections for kickers. For reasons discussed in the Arizona chapter, kickers are projected almost entirely based on team forecasts. Individual factors play a role in these projections in only three ways:

- More experience leads to a slightly higher field-goal percentage in general, with the biggest jump between a kicker's rookie and sophomore seasons.

- Kickers with a better career field-goal percentage tend to get more attempts, although they are not necessarily more accurate.

- Field-goal percentage on kicks over 40 yards tends to regress to the mean.

The statistics in the table below are, from left to right following the kicker's name and team: field goals made and attempted (**FG**), field goal percentage (**Pct**), extra points made (**XP**), total points (**PTS**), and fantasy **Risk** of Green, Yellow, or Red. The fantasy risk system is explained in the introduction to the section on quarterbacks.

After the 32 projected starters, we also give projections for six kickers who will be competing with established starters in training camp.

Table 1. 2007 KUBIAK Projections for Kickers

Kicker	Team	FG	Pct	XP	PTS	Risk	Kicker	Team	FG	Pct	XP	PTS	Risk
Stephen Gostkowski	NE	31–36	86%	48	141	Yellow	Matt Bryant	TB	23–29	79%	34	103	Red
Josh Scobee	JAC	29–34	85%	48	135	Red	Shaun Suisham	WAS	23–30	77%	32	101	Red
Jason Elam	DEN	30–34	88%	41	131	Green	Olindo Mare	NO	21–25	84%	38	101	Red
David Akers	PHI	26–30	87%	49	127	Green	Robbie Gould	CHI	22–28	79%	35	101	Red
Adam Vinatieri	IND	23–28	82%	49	118	Yellow	Jeff Wilkins	STL	23–29	79%	31	100	Red
Jeff Reed	PIT	27–31	87%	35	116	Yellow	Jason Hanson	DET	23–29	79%	30	99	Red
Ryan Longwell	MIN	29–33	88%	29	116	Red	Rian Lindell	BUF	22–27	81%	32	98	Green
Shayne Graham	CIN	23–28	82%	46	115	Green	Kris Brown	HOU	22–27	81%	31	97	Yellow
Josh Brown	SEA	27–32	84%	33	114	Yellow	Neil Rackers	ARI	23–29	79%	26	95	Yellow
Matt Stover	BAL	25–30	83%	39	114	Yellow	Justin Medlock	KC	20–28	71%	31	91	Yellow
Nate Kaeding	SD	22–27	81%	47	113	Red	Sebastian Janikowski	OAK	20–25	80%	26	86	Red
Dave Rayner	GB	26–31	84%	35	113	Yellow	Jay Feely	MIA	19–25	76%	23	80	Red
Joe Nedney	SF	25–31	81%	37	112	Red	**Possible Alternatives**						
Mike Nugent	NYJ	24–30	80%	38	110	Yellow	Aaron Elling	ATL	24–29	83%	38	110	Red
Phil Dawson	CLE	26–31	84%	30	108	Green	Mason Crosby	GB	24–31	77%	34	106	Yellow
Bill Cundiff	ATL	23–28	82%	38	107	Red	John Vaughn	TEN	19–26	73%	36	93	Yellow
John Kasay	CAR	24–29	83%	34	106	Red	Josh Huston	NYG	19–27	70%	34	91	Red
Rob Bironas	TEN	23–29	79%	35	104	Yellow	Nick Folk	DAL	18–26	69%	34	88	Red
Martin Gramatica	DAL	23–29	79%	35	104	Red	Jesse Ainsworth	CLE	18–25	72%	28	82	Yellow
Lawrence Tynes	NYG	23–30	77%	34	103	Red							

Defenses

Listed in table 2 are the 2007 KUBIAK projections for fantasy defenses, along with a Risk assessment of Green, Yellow, or Red. Our generic fantasy scoring formula is based on one point for a sack, two points for a fumble recovery, safety, or interception, and six points for a touchdown.

The method for projecting defensive points is discussed in an essay in *Pro Football Prospectus 2006,* the key conclusions of which were:

- Schedule strength is very important for projecting fantasy defense.

- Categories used for scoring in fantasy defense have no consistency from year-to-year whatsoever, with the exception of sacks and interceptions.

Fumble recoveries, safeties, and defensive touchdowns are forecast solely based on the projected sacks and interceptions, rather than the team's totals in these categories from a year ago. This is why the 2007 projections will look very different from the fantasy defense values from the 2006 season. Fantasy defense also measures very specific categories, not a team's actual ability to stop its opponents, which is why some of the defenses we project to play well in 2007 (Jacksonville, New England, Baltimore) are not projected with many fantasy points.

Table 2. 2007 KUBIAK Projections for Defense

Team	Pts	Risk	Team	Pts	Risk	Team	Pts	Risk	Team	Pts	Risk	Team	Pts	Risk
PIT	139	Green	PHI	125	Yellow	TB	110	Red	STL	101	Red	MIA	91	Red
OAK	137	Red	SF	123	Red	DAL	109	Yellow	JAC	101	Yellow	TEN	87	Yellow
GB	136	Green	WAS	123	Red	DET	109	Red	NO	99	Red	HOU	86	Yellow
CAR	133	Yellow	DEN	122	Yellow	BAL	106	Yellow	CIN	98	Red	IND	84	Yellow
ATL	129	Yellow	CHI	120	Green	CLE	106	Yellow	SD	98	Red			
MIN	127	Green	ARI	115	Red	NE	105	Yellow	KC	95	Red			
BUF	125	Yellow	SEA	113	Red	NYG	102	Red	NYJ	91	Red			

Beyond Sacks

Aaron Schatz

For the Indianapolis Colts, defensive success starts with a strong pass rush. The Tampa-2 defensive style generally depends on the front four to provide pressure so the other seven players can remain in coverage. The Colts fit this design to a T. With a defense built around two undersized speed-rushers on the outside, Dwight Freeney and Robert Mathis, the Colts had 46 sacks in 2005, tied for fifth in the NFL.

So it was a bit of a surprise when, halfway through the 2006 season, the Colts had only sacked opposing quarterbacks 11 times. Four of those sacks came against the pitiful Texans, and three came against a Jets line starting two rookies with three weeks of NFL experience. Dwight Freeney, after four straight years with double-digit sacks, had just a measly half-sack to his name.

The Colts picked things up in the second half, but they still ended up with just 25 sacks. Only Washington had fewer. Yet, if you watched the Colts play, it sure didn't look like their pass rush had disappeared. Sure, the run defense was horrible, but Freeney and Mathis were still wreaking havoc with opposing linemen and frustrating quarterbacks.

Watch any NFL telecast, and you'll see numbers pop up on the screen for "hits" and "hurries." Go searching the Internet, however, and you won't find these numbers, because they are not official NFL statistics. After a telecast is over, these numbers get metaphorically tossed in the trash, gone forever.

Or, maybe not. In 2006, as part of an expansion of the data kept in the official play-by-play, NFL scorers began to record quarterback hits. The Football Outsiders game charting project tried to record quarterback hurries. Neither of these efforts was entirely successful, as there's a lot of noise in the data, but, like a rural football fan in the days before cable, we're willing to put up with some static to get what we want, and hits and hurries give us a bigger antenna.

Adjusted Sack Rate

The first step in improving pass rush statistics is to consider opportunity, and the 2006 Colts had less than any other team. The Colts' opponents dropped back to pass only 437 times last year, the lowest total in the league.[1]

That's a mind-boggling statistic for a 12–4 division champion. Winning teams almost always face a high number of pass attempts because opponents have to abandon the run in the second half, but the Colts had the worst run defense in the NFL last year. Nobody is going to abandon the run when it is getting 5.3 yards per carry.

The Colts were still below the league average when we measure sacks per pass attempt, but by a much smaller margin. NFL quarterbacks were sacked once every 15 pass attempts in 2006. The Colts defense sacked the quarterback once every 17.6 pass attempts.

That gives us Sack Rate, but there's a reason why the stat in *Pro Football Prospectus* is called Adjusted Sack Rate. When it comes to sack opportunity, not all pass attempts are created equal. Defenses sacked the quarterback once every 17.5 pass attempts on first or second down, but once every 11.4 pass attempts on third or fourth down. The Colts faced fewer third-down pass attempts than any other team; again, this is what happens when you give up more than five yards per carry.

There are two other tweaks in Adjusted Sack Rate. It considers strength of schedule, and it includes both sacks and intentional grounding. Longtime *PFP* readers will notice that the second change is new for 2007, but the cause and effect for intentional grounding and for sacks are the same. The pass rush and coverage combine to cause both events, and both events result in a loss of yardage. The only difference is the amount of pain felt by the quarterback afterwards.

For the most part, the addition of intentional grounding doesn't change the numbers much, but there is one huge exception: Philadelphia's defense forced *seven* intentional grounding calls in 2006. No other defense forced more than two. Those intentional grounding calls pushed the Eagles into first place in Adjusted Sack Rate, while the Colts, tied for 30th in total sacks, now rank 21st (table 1).

The Hit Parade

The NFL added several pieces of data to the official play-by-play in 2006, and among that new data was quarterback hits. In the play-by-play notation, defenders knocking the quarterback to the ground after the pass were marked with

---

1. The official total is 440, but Football Outsiders numbers exclude clock-killing spikes.

Table 1. Sacks and Adjusted Sack Rate, 2006

Rank	Team	Sack	Pass	Sack%	Adj Sack%
1	PHI	40	561	7.1%	9.3%
2	BAL	60	568	10.6%	9.3%
3	SD	61	594	10.3%	9.0%
4	MIA	47	544	8.6%	8.4%
5	GB	46	558	8.2%	8.1%
6	BUF	40	551	7.3%	8.1%
7	CAR	41	539	7.6%	8.0%
8	ATL	38	551	6.9%	7.8%
9	NO	38	510	7.5%	7.8%
10	NE	44	560	7.9%	7.8%
Average	NFL	36	546	6.7%	6.8%
21	IND	25	437	5.7%	6.1%

brackets, which distinguished them from tackles marked with parentheses. Simple contact wasn't marked; the quarterback actually had to hit the ground for a "hit" to be recorded. While the hits statistic doesn't actually appear anywhere on NFL.com, the data is there in the play-by-play, waiting to be analyzed.

When counting quarterback hits, we included every play, including those cancelled by penalties. After all, if the quarterback gets knocked down on a pass called back for holding, it doesn't hurt any less.

Unfortunately, figuring out quarterback hits is not as simple as just totaling the numbers and running a table. When we do that, we find that New England led the league with 72 quarterback hits. The Patriots have a good pass rush, so that doesn't seem strange ... until you see that no other defense had more than 58, and the league average was 40. This became even more suspicious when we noticed that several teams that had recorded a high number of quarterback hits on defense also had a high number of quarterback hits on offense, including not only New England (72 on defense/49 on offense) but also Baltimore (58/53), Cleveland (56/54), Cincinnati (50/57), and Tampa Bay (49/62).

What's the problem? Well, although they appear in the official play-by-play, quarterback hits are an "unofficial" stat, just like passes defensed. That means that official scorers varied widely in their interpretation of what constituted a hit, and, more importantly, in their diligence in recording them.

Our Football Outsiders game charters were asked to mark when a quarterback hit was missing from the official gamebook, so we noticed this problem early on. Some examples: many defenders were not listed with a hit by the NFL when they were called for roughing the passer; five hits on Chris Simms during the game in which he ruptured his spleen were not captured in the original play-by-play; the hit on which Seattle quarterback Matt Hasselbeck tore his MCL was not listed in the original play-by-play. Thanks

to a contact between Football Outsiders and NFL.com, the league added a number of quarterback hits listed by our charters into the official play-by-play (including on the plays I just mentioned) but discrepancies still exist. If we understand those discrepancies, however, we can still get plenty of information from quarterback hits.

The most obvious spike in the data occurs in two games from Week 3. That week, the Broncos and Patriots combined for 30 hits in Foxboro, and the Ravens and Browns combined for 28 hits in Cleveland. Each of the four teams recorded at least 12 hits in these two games. There were only five other games all season in which both teams *combined* had more than 12 hits, and no other game in which both combined to have more than 16. We don't know why these games ended up as outliers, but it's pretty safe to assume that something was amiss.

Looking over the entire season, we can see which official scorers marked the most hits (table 2). As you might have suspected, the official scorers in New England and Cleveland recorded the highest number of hits, but those numbers are high even without considering the two Week 3 games. At the bottom of the list, the official scorers in Pittsburgh, Detroit, and Oakland were either more strict or less diligent when it came to recording hits. The 21 hits from Pittsburgh zone blitzes and 21 hits against Pittsburgh's struggling offensive line recorded in the Steelers' road games certainly sound more realistic than the seven and six recorded at Heinz Field.

The solution from here might be to weight the numbers based on how often an official scorer recorded a hit, but that's not always the issue either. Minnesota had a lot of hits both home and away, for example, while Houston had very few hits both home and away. (This seems ridiculous given the Texans' poor offensive line, but there doesn't seem to be any Houston scorer bias.)

Did the Colts have four times as many hits at home because the gamebooks were home-cooked? Indianapolis fans would argue that the fast RCA Dome turf favors the speed-rushing techniques of Freeney and Mathis—and the evidence supports this argument, because there's an equal discrepancy in sacks. The Colts had 33 hits and 20 sacks at home, but only eight hits and six sacks on the road. (For what it's worth, Peyton Manning was sacked more often at home as well.)

As you can see, it's hard to generalize about just where the hit totals go awry, so other than those two Week 3 games, the best solution is to just look at the standard totals, but to do so bearing in mind our knowledge of which scorers preferred the hit statistic. To analyze which defenses were putting the hurt on quarterbacks, we add both hits and sacks, including plays cancelled by penalty, to get **Knockdowns.** Not all sacks knock the quarterback to

Table 2. Quarterback Hits, Home and Away, 2006

Team	Defensive Hits		Offensive Hits		Total Hits		Diff
	Home	Away	Home	Away	Home	Away	
NE	53	19	33	16	86	35	51
CLE	44	12	35	19	79	31	48
CIN	34	16	37	20	71	36	35
NO	33	23	31	9	64	32	32
TEN	30	9	17	16	47	23	22
IND	33	8	14	18	47	26	21
TB	34	15	31	31	65	46	19
SEA	22	11	21	14	43	25	18
NYG	28	18	18	12	46	30	16
SF	25	10	21	22	46	32	14
KC	21	11	13	13	34	24	10
STL	21	20	13	7	34	27	7
MIN	24	15	27	30	51	45	6
HOU	21	11	10	15	31	26	5
WAS	23	11	22	31	45	42	3
BUF	26	12	12	24	38	36	2
ARI	20	18	21	23	41	41	0
MIA	14	14	24	24	38	38	0
DAL	15	16	18	18	33	34	−1
CAR	19	24	15	20	34	44	−10
GB	24	32	21	26	45	58	−13
CHI	28	24	13	33	41	57	−16
OAK	8	13	11	23	19	36	−17
JAC	14	15	19	36	33	51	−18
PHI	14	26	15	25	29	51	−22
SD	11	18	10	26	21	44	−23
NYJ	4	21	10	21	14	42	−28
ATL	12	27	9	23	21	50	−29
PIT	7	21	6	21	13	42	−29
DET	11	24	8	25	19	49	−30
DEN	10	32	13	25	23	57	−34
BAL	23	35	13	40	36	75	−39

NOTE: The Giants and Jets share a stadium but have different official scorers.

Table 3. Defensive Knockdown Rate, 2006

Defense	Hits	Sacks	Knockdowns	Rate
BAL	52*	60	112	18.8%
NE	66*	45	111	18.6%
NO	56	40	96	18.0%
GB	56	47	103	17.5%
STL	41	35	76	14.9%
CHI	52	43	95	14.8%
IND	41	26	67	14.7%
CAR	43	40	83	14.7%
SD	29	61	90	14.5%
TB	49	25	74	14.1%
CIN	50	35	85	14.0%
CLE	48*	28	76	13.8%
BUF	38	39	77	13.6%
PHI	40	41	81	13.6%
ARI	38	39	77	13.2%
ATL	39	38	77	13.2%
MIA	28	46	74	13.1%
SEA	33	40	73	12.8%
NYG	46	32	78	12.7%
OAK	21	35	56	12.2%
SF	35	35	70	12.2%
DAL	31	36	67	11.8%
KC	32	33	65	11.6%
PIT	28	39	67	11.6%
DEN	34*	34	68	11.6%
DET	35	29	64	11.4%
JAC	29	37	66	11.3%
TEN	39	25	64	11.0%
MIN	39	31	70	10.7%
HOU	32	28	60	10.7%
NYJ	25	35	60	10.4%
WAS	34	19	53	9.9%

* Only half credit for hits in Week 3.

the ground, but while the play-by-play does not specify strip-sacks, it does specify the quarterback running out of bounds behind the line of scrimmage, so those sacks are not included in the total for Knockdowns. We've also adjusted for the two Week 3 games by only giving those hits half credit. Then we divide Knockdowns by all passes, including those cancelled by penalty, to get **Knockdown Rate** (table 3).

When it comes to knocking down the quarterback, the most impressive defense in 2006 probably belongs to the Green Bay Packers. Unlike the three teams above them in Knockdown Rate, the Packers had more hits scored on the road than at home, and, unlike the three teams above them, the Packers were usually not playing with a lead that would force the opposition into an obvious passing situation.

A major reason why the Packers were so good at hitting the quarterback is that they had the player who was best in the league at hitting the quarterback: defensive end Aaron Kampman. Kampman had 18 hits, plus 14 sacks and three half-sacks, giving him 35 total knockdowns (table 4).

Second behind Kampman is Leonard Little of the Rams, which explains why St. Louis's otherwise pedestrian pass rush was fifth in the league in knockdown rate. Four other Packers had at least four hits, led by Kabeer Gbaja-Biamila with 13, but Little was the only member of the Rams defense with more than three quarterback hits, and the only one with more than six sacks.

NFL sack leader Shawne Merriman is eighth because he had only five quarterback hits to go with his 17 sacks. Merriman is not the only prolific sack artist who rarely

Table 4. Top 10 Defenders in Knockdowns, 2006

Player	Team	Hits	Full Sk	Half Sk	Knockdowns
Aaron Kampman	GB	18	14	3	35
Leonard Little	STL	17	14	0	31
Rosevelt Colvin	NE	19*	8	2	29
Kamerion Wimbley	CLE	15.5*	10	2	27.5
Kyle Vanden Bosch	TEN	19	7	1	27
DeMarcus Ware	DAL	11	13	1	25
Aaron Schobel	BUF	10	12	3	25
Shawne Merriman	SD	5	17	2	24
Trevor Pryce	BAL	9.5*	11	3	23.5
Jason Taylor	MIA	9	13	1	23

* Week 3 hits only given half credit.

knocked the quarterback down otherwise. Bears rookie Mark Anderson had 12 sacks but only one quarterback hit. Anderson can't blame the official scorer in Chicago, because his teammate Brian Urlacher had ten hits, by far the highest number of hits among players who had no sacks in 2006.

When your franchise quarterback is returning from a horrible knee injury, the last thing you want is for him to get knocked to the ground over and over by opposing defenses. Nonetheless, thanks in part to a series of injuries on the Cincinnati offensive line, this is exactly what happened to Carson Palmer. Palmer was knocked to the ground 56 times, more than any other quarterback in the league. He did not lead the league in knockdowns, however, because Jon Kitna of Detroit was hit 33 times and sacked 61 times, for a total of 94 knockdowns (table 5). The offense that allowed the most quarterback knockdowns per pass attempt was—no surprise here—the Oakland Raiders. It's no coincidence that three of the four worst offenses in knockdown rate, Oakland, Cleveland, and Jacksonville, had to use multiple quarterbacks in 2006 because of injuries (table 6).

Table 5. Top 10 Quarterbacks in Knockdowns, 2006

Player	Team	Hits	Sacks	Knockdowns
Jon Kitna	DET	33	61	94
Carson Palmer	CIN	56	35	91
Charlie Frye	CLE	44*	46	90
J. P. Losman	BUF	36	48	84
Alex Smith	SF	43	36	79
Brad Johnson	MIN	47	30	77
Michael Vick	ATL	31	44	75
Ben Roethlisberger	PIT	24	47	71
Marc Bulger	STL	20	51	71
Tom Brady	NE	40.5*	27	67.5

* Only half credit for hits in Week 3.

Table 6. Offensive Knockdown Rate, 2006

Offense	Hits	Sacks	Knockdowns	Rate
OAK	34	73	107	18.3%
CLE	48*	56	104	17.6%
BUF	36	48	84	17.0%
JAC	55	28	83	16.8%
MIN	57	44	101	16.6%
ATL	32	46	78	16.1%
TB	62	32	94	16.0%
CIN	57	35	92	15.9%
SF	43	36	79	15.8%
SEA	35	49	84	14.5%
WAS	53	21	74	14.4%
MIA	48	41	89	13.8%
ARI	44	38	82	13.7%
DET	33	61	94	13.7%
KC	26	41	67	13.2%
PIT	27	49	76	12.9%
SD	36	29	65	12.8%
HOU	25	44	69	12.7%
TEN	33	29	62	12.7%
DEN	31.5*	32	63.5	12.6%
DAL	36	37	73	12.6%
CHI	46	25	71	12.6%
NE	40.5*	30	70.5	12.2%
NYJ	31	35	66	12.1%
CAR	35	32	67	11.3%
PHI	40	27	67	11.3%
BAL	45*	16	61	10.9%
STL	20	51	71	10.6%
NO	40	25	65	10.5%
GB	47	24	71	10.4%
NYG	30	27	57	10.0%
IND	32	15	47	8.0%

* Only half credit for hits in Week 3.

Hurries

What is the definition of a hurry? Is it just a good pass rush? Does it have to clearly interfere with the quarterback's throwing motion? When a defender forces the quarterback from the pocket, is that a hurry, even if the quarterback has time to set his feet and throw after scrambling? What about a defender who forces the quarterback into the position where a different defender gets a sack?

We gave the volunteers of the Football Outsiders game charting project the following definition: Mark a hurry if the quarterback clearly has to rush his motion, or leaves the pocket after originally setting up in the pocket to throw. If the quarterback stood tall and delivered the pass with defenders in his face, this was not a hurry. Obviously there is a bit of selection bias in these numbers—the defensive pressure that will get Tony Romo out of the pocket won't cause Tom Brady to move at all—but if certain quarterbacks, such as Romo's predecessor Drew Bledsoe, take more sacks because of their personal style, it makes sense that certain quarterbacks would also be easier to hurry. Charters could also attribute a hurry to "Overall Pressure" or list a play as a "Coverage Scramble" when the quarterback wasn't under pressure but ran because there were no open receivers. (The former is counted in the team numbers for hurries on both offense and defense, the latter is not.)

The league was able to give its official scorers a strict definition of a quarterback hit, but different official scorers still marked the stat at widely varying rates. So as you might imagine, the scoring for hurries by our unofficial game charters was also inconsistent. However, it wasn't that much more inconsistent than the official scoring for hits. 22 of the 32 official scorers fell within one standard deviation of the league average for hits per pass play. Looking at the 32 game charters who charted the most pass attempts, 21 were within one standard deviation of the league average for hurries per pass play, including eight of the top ten.

After analyzing the numbers, we developed a system of weights, to adjust the hurries marked by the few specific charters who deviated significantly from the rest of the group. Adjusting for charters who were overcounting or undercounting hurries was much easier than trying to adjust for official scorers who did not correctly mark hits, because our game charters worked games involving a variety of teams in a variety of stadiums. Of course, some charters marked a lot of hurries because they actually saw a lot of hurries, even by the strictest possible definition. This usually involved the Arizona Cardinals. The result of this work was Adjusted Hurry Percentage: hurries per charted pass attempt or scramble, adjusted for the charter's personal habits.

As befits a team that likes to blitz six or seven defenders, Philadelphia had the highest Adjusted Hurry Percentage (18.9 percent) (table 7). No other team was above 16.4 percent, but this doesn't seem to be an issue related to the game charters themselves (no one person charted more than six Philadelphia halves). At the bottom of the list is Denver, the only team below 10 percent. Some Denver fans have argued that the Broncos' low sack total doesn't do justice to the team's pass rush, which harasses the quarterback in other ways. Based on our research, that's not true. Denver is near the bottom of the league in sacks, hurries, and hits.

Which individual player did the most to harass the quarterback without actually taking him down? Well, if you are looking for where Dwight Freeney made the biggest impact in 2006, you've finally come to the right place. Freeney led the league with 33 hurries, which works out to one every 14.5 charted passes (table 8). Robert Mathis had

Table 7. Defenses by Adjusted Hurry Percentage, 2006

Team	Charted Pass/ Scram	Hurries	Adj Hur Pct
PHI	605	112	18.9%
CAR	522	78	16.4%
NE	586	105	16.3%
DAL	570	95	16.3%
CHI	628	108	16.2%
GB	564	90	15.5%
BAL	595	94	15.2%
MIN	604	81	14.8%
JAC	562	80	14.6%
TEN	584	85	14.1%
IND	479	66	14.1%
KC	515	66	13.9%
BUF	582	88	13.9%
NYJ	586	93	13.9%
ATL	576	84	13.6%
TB	553	74	13.4%
NO	525	69	13.2%
SEA	566	79	13.1%
WAS	532	68	13.1%
CIN	593	73	12.6%
MIA	570	76	12.5%
STL	500	54	12.4%
HOU	561	70	11.9%
SF	549	65	11.3%
DET	580	65	11.3%
PIT	595	70	11.2%
OAK	463	55	11.2%
CLE	559	62	11.2%
SD	631	76	11.1%
ARI	592	71	10.9%
NYG	620	43	10.5%
DEN	588	61	9.5%

15 hurries, and together the two starting ends for the Indianapolis Colts were in the quarterback's face on 10 percent of all charted passes or scrambles—in other words, more often than the entire Denver Broncos defense combined. (This does not count the previous evening, when Champ Bailey appears in the quarterback's nightmares.)

For the most part, the players with the most hurries are the same players near the top of the league in sacks and hits. The player suspiciously missing from the top of the list is league sack champion Shawne Merriman. He only had 12 hurries, tied for 39th in the NFL with four players including Cincinnati veteran Bryan Robinson (who only had three sacks).

What about the other side of the ball, the offenses? In last year's book, we joked that Buffalo quarterback J. P. Losman went to an elementary school where kids only

Table 8. Top 10 Defenders in Hurries, 2006

Player	Team	Hurries
Dwight Freeney	IND	33
Julius Peppers	CAR	32
Kyle Vanden Bosch	TEN	29
Leonard Little	STL	26
Aaron Schobel	BUF	26
DeMarcus Ware	DAL	25
Aaron Kampman	GB	24
Charles Grant	NO	21
Jason Taylor	MIA	21
Rosevelt Colvin	NE	20

NOTE: Individual hurries are also adjusted, both for the tendencies of the game charter and to make up for the handful of games left uncharted.

Table 9. Offenses by Adjusted Hurry Percentage, 2006

Team	Charted Pass/ Scram	Hurries	Adj Hur Pct
BUF	508	106	18.7%
CHI	550	99	18.5%
SF	493	93	18.4%
ARI	602	118	17.2%
JAC	480	83	16.8%
TB	604	96	16.7%
PHI	610	105	16.5%
DAL	553	88	15.7%
WAS	491	78	15.6%
ATL	582	87	14.7%
MIN	595	83	14.5%
PIT	595	88	14.3%
TEN	550	77	13.9%
BAL	539	78	13.7%
HOU	563	77	13.6%
NYG	548	49	13.2%
DET	684	88	13.1%
CLE	612	81	13.0%
SEA	586	82	12.8%
CAR	541	63	12.5%
GB	624	76	12.2%
OAK	582	73	12.1%
SD	516	64	12.0%
NO	585	71	11.9%
MIA	643	78	11.4%
NE	579	72	11.2%
CIN	563	58	10.4%
DEN	516	60	10.2%
NYJ	552	63	10.1%
IND	580	53	10.0%
KC	479	40	9.3%
STL	630	29	5.7%

counted to "one Mississippi" at recess, because he ditched the pocket at the slightest hint of pass pressure. Losman was much improved overall in 2006, but he still was hurried on many of his passes, the highest percentage in the league according to our game charters (table 9). Oddly enough, as noted in his comment in the Quarterbacks chapter, Losman got better when the defense blitzed—his problem was getting hurried when the defense came with the normal four pass rushers.

The offenses with the highest Adjusted Hurry Percentages fit nicely with conventional wisdom. The top four were Buffalo, Chicago, San Francisco, and Arizona, each of which featured a young, inexperienced quarterback. In Arizona, interestingly, veteran Kurt Warner was hurried more often than the rookie Matt Leinart. Even more interesting was the team that ranked fifth, Jacksonville, where the mobile David Garrard and the less mobile Byron Leftwich were hurried at the exact same rate. Jacksonville's offensive line really gelled in 2006 when it came to run-blocking, but numbers for both hits and hurries would seem to indicate that the Jaguars may still have a ways to go when it comes to pass-blocking.

The offenses hurried the least were St. Louis, Kansas City, and Indianapolis. However, St. Louis is so far below the rest of the league, even after our attempt to adjust for the inconsistencies of our game charters, that it is reasonable to assume that their rating is not quite accurate.

What Hits and Hurries Mean for the Offense

Did hits and hurries have any effect?

Quarterback hits were based on knocking the quarterback down after the pass, so they don't necessarily represent harassment of the quarterback before the pass, as they often resulted from a pass rusher coming up from behind while the quarterback was unaware of their charge. Nonetheless, most hits seemed to show the pass rush was having an effect on the play. Quarterbacks completed just 37.7 percent of passes when they were knocked down either during the throw or afterwards.

Hurries had an even stronger effect on the passing game, leaving quarterbacks with a completion percentage of just 34.0 percent. One out of every 20 hurries turned into an interception, and the overall DVOA of all plays with a hurry was −66.5%.

On the other hand, many hurries led to scrambles, and those scrambles led to positive yardage and a DVOA of 33.6%. One out of every three scrambles caused by a hurry ended in a touchdown or first down. Take out the scrambles, and the passing DVOA when hurried is even worse, −76.4%.

There's a possibility for bias here—if a pass looks bad, it might influence the charter to believe that the pressure "hurried" the quarterback—but there's no way bias alone is responsible for numbers this strong.

Even with scrambles included, only seven of the 45 quarterbacks with at least 100 pass attempts in 2006 had positive DVOA ratings when they were hurried by the defense (table 10). Dallas switched to Tony Romo at midseason specifically because he could handle the pass rush better than Drew Bledsoe, and Romo's DVOA of 42.2% when hurried was the second-highest in the league. Ben Roethlisberger, known for being able to throw on the run, is third. Peyton Manning, who is great at everything, is fourth. The two mobile Philadelphia quarterbacks, Donovan McNabb and Jeff Garcia, rank sixth and seventh.

However, the identity of the quarterback who had the highest DVOA when hurried is a complete shock: Seattle backup Seneca Wallace. On the 85 percent of passes on which our game charters did not record a hurry, Wallace had a −43.8% DVOA. That would have made him the worst quarterback in the league last year—except that in the 15 percent of passes on which we *did* record a hurry, Wallace had a mind-boggling 79.8% DVOA. He averaged 7.9 yards per pass when he was hurried, but only 6.4 yards per pass when he was not. That doesn't even count scrambles. Wallace scrambled on three hurried pass attempts for a total of 57 rushing yards, which gives him a total DVOA when hurried of 107.6%.

Wallace, of course, is a mobile, somewhat short quarterback who was replacing an injured starter behind an injury-rattled offensive line, so it makes sense that he was out of the pocket frequently. He certainly created some of his own pass pressure by running around trying to make something happen instead of just finding a receiver or throwing the ball away. The same is true for players such as Michael Vick, Vince Young, and David Garrard, and they certainly did not have a positive DVOA when hurried. Garrard was 12th, Vick 25th, and Young 30th—even with scrambles included.

Other than the few exceptions given above, even the best quarterbacks had trouble when the pass rush was in their face. Carson Palmer had a −35.4% DVOA when hurried and Tom Brady and Marc Bulger were even worse. Eight quarterbacks had a DVOA below −100% when hurried, primarily those known for being mistake-prone under pressure such as Drew Bledsoe, Rex Grossman, and Jake Delhomme. Tampa Bay's Chris Simms was the worst quarterback when hurried, with a horrible −256.9% DVOA and 1.6 yards per pass, although there certainly were extenuating circumstances considering that many of these pass attempts came in the Week 3 game against Carolina in which he ruptured his spleen.

Table 10. Quarterback DVOA when Hurried, 2006

Player	Team	Pass DVOA	Yd/P	Scram	Yd/Scr	Tot DVOA
S. Wallace	SEA	79.8%	7.9	3	19.0	107.6%
T. Romo	DAL	47.5%	7.0	9	7.0	42.2%
B. Roethlisberger	PIT	17.6%	6.6	7	7.7	23.9%
P. Manning	IND	23.0%	5.1	1	10.0	23.4%
D. Huard	KC	7.6%	5.1	0	0.0	11.7%
D. McNabb	PHI	−16.9%	6.0	6	8.3	11.3%
J. Garcia	PHI	−10.2%	4.3	4	9.8	8.0%
K. Warner	ARI	−5.4%	4.7	2	5.0	−3.2%
S. McNair	BAL	−31.2%	4.1	5	10.0	−14.1%
T. Rattay	TB	−15.1%	3.5	0	0.0	−15.1%
D. Brees	NO	−19.7%	6.0	4	5.8	−17.6%
D. Garrard	JAC	−25.1%	4.8	2	5.5	−25.6%
A. Smith	SF	−38.3%	2.7	13	6.0	−29.8%
T. Green	KC	−87.7%	1.6	6	6.0	−31.5%
B. Gradkowski	TB	−45.7%	3.1	14	4.8	−33.4%
A. Walter	OAK	−35.0%	3.2	0	0.0	−35.0%
C. Palmer	CIN	−41.2%	5.0	3	6.0	−35.4%
J. Losman	BUF	−50.5%	5.6	10	7.4	−36.3%
E. Manning	NYG	−38.0%	4.6	1	2.0	−38.8%
A. Brooks	OAK	−56.6%	3.5	4	9.0	−40.7%
B. Favre	GB	−40.9%	3.6	0	0.0	−40.9%
T. Brady	NE	−41.9%	3.9	2	5.5	−41.9%
J. Kitna	DET	−59.5%	4.1	9	8.3	−43.4%
M. Leinart	ARI	−52.1%	3.6	6	5.3	−49.7%
M. Vick	ATL	−65.0%	3.1	16	5.9	−52.3%
J. Campbell	WAS	−70.9%	6.0	7	4.1	−53.6%
B. Leftwich	JAC	−76.0%	3.6	4	3.8	−56.2%
D. Carr	HOU	−58.3%	2.4	10	5.6	−56.5%
M. Bulger	STL	−57.1%	2.5	0	0.0	−57.1%
V. Young	TEN	−87.1%	3.4	9	11.8	−57.3%
M. Hasselbeck	SEA	−78.6%	2.9	4	8.3	−61.3%
P. Rivers	SD	−62.1%	2.4	0	0.0	−62.1%
C. Frye	CLE	−108.7%	2.0	14	6.6	−72.5%
C. Pennington	NYJ	−73.2%	6.2	5	3.8	−72.7%
J. Harrington	MIA	−83.6%	3.8	3	3.0	−74.2%
J. Plummer	DEN	−112.4%	1.5	4	6.0	−80.7%
B. Johnson	MIN	−122.4%	2.3	6	4.8	−98.4%
D. Culpepper	MIA	−110.8%	5.1	1	7.0	−104.1%
D. Bledsoe	DAL	−134.9%	1.3	3	6.3	−114.6%
J. Delhomme	CAR	−115.3%	1.9	0	0.0	−115.3%
R. Grossman	CHI	−116.6%	2.9	0	0.0	−116.6%
M. Brunell	WAS	−136.8%	0.6	2	5.0	−125.4%
D. Anderson	CLE	−158.5%	0.3	0	0.0	−158.5%
J. Cutler	DEN	−216.8%	4.9	2	1.5	−199.1%
C. Simms	TB	−256.9%	1.6	0	0.0	−256.9%

NOTE: These numbers do not include sacks.

Conclusion

The best evidence that these measures of hits and hurries are on the right track is the fact that, for the most part, they agree with conventional wisdom. Players who are considered strong pass-rushers come out with a high number of hits and hurries, even if they did not have a high number of sacks during the 2006 season. The offensive lines that gave up the most hits and hurries were generally poor: Buffalo, Arizona, and Oakland, to give three examples. The numbers support Bill Parcells's decision to bench Drew Bledsoe for Tony Romo based specifically on the issue of grace under (pass) pressure. They also allowed us to find Dwight Freeney's missing ability to get to the quarterback during last year's regular season.

Our compatriots at Baseball Prospectus have discovered that doubles and home runs are often products of the same skill, hitting for power, and that a high count of doubles often forecasts a future increase in home runs. Just as power-hitting is a specific baseball skill, pass-rushing is a specific football skill, and its products are sacks, hits, and hurries. Shawne Merriman led the league with 17 sacks, but only had five hits and 12 hurries. Dwight Freeney had just 5.5 sacks, but nine hits and 33 hurries. Do those numbers forecast that Merriman's sack total will decrease in 2007, while Freeney's sack total will increase?

The fact that our hit and hurry statistics match conventional wisdom when it comes to most players and teams makes the areas where they *don't* agree with conventional wisdom even more interesting. Is Seneca Wallace's wizardry on the run simply an issue of sample size? Does the Jacksonville offensive line have trouble with pass protection? Does Tom Brady feel the pass rush as well as everyone believes? If Leonard Little is so good at harassing quarterbacks, just how awful is the St. Louis secondary?

Given two and three years of this data, we'll be able to answer some of these questions by analyzing which of these statistics are most consistent from year-to-year, and how their effects change. One thing is for sure: there is more to a pass rush than just sacks. When it comes to quarterback performance, hits and hurries matter.

Bend But Don't Break Defenses

Ned Macey and Jim Armstrong

Seemingly every Sunday during the NFL season, some team marches the ball up and down the field but keeps settling for field goals, while its opponent puts two or three touchdown drives together and escapes with a win. When this happens, the post-game coverage unfailingly focuses on how the winning team's defense "bent but didn't break." Nearly every team has racked up a win in this fashion, but what does the term "bend but don't break" actually mean? And, if this phenomenon exists, is it repeatable from year to year?

One thing our research has shown in the past is that there's a direct relationship between the number of yards a defense allows and the number of points it allows. With that in mind, a "bend but don't break" defense would be one that allows fewer points than would normally be expected given the number of yards it allows, as that would indicate that it "bent" (gave up yards), but "didn't break" (prevented the opposition from scoring the expected number of points).

The first step in learning anything about the nature of these alleged Bend But Don't Break defense then is to assemble a real life list of such teams. For that we turned to our drive stats, which include the average yards per drive and points per drive that a given team allows. To create our list of Bend But Don't Break defenses, we simply subtracted actual points allowed per drive from the expected points per drive to gives us a statistic we've named Points Prevented per drive (PP/d).

We calculated PP/d figures for the 283 team seasons played between 1998 and 2006, producing results that ranged from the 2001 Bears at .589 PP/d to the 1999 Bengals at −.514 PP/d. Remember our statistic is Points *Prevented*, so a positive number indicates a defense that didn't break, while a negative number indicates a defense that was especially brittle. The standard deviation from the average of zero was .184, leaving 41 teams performing more than one standard deviation worse than expected (-.184 or below) and 44 teams performing more than one standard deviation better. Those 44 teams are our Bend But Don't Break defenses (table 1).

Having created our list we've already learned one thing about the nature of Bend But Don't Break defenses as 15 percent of the teams in our 283-team sample were either above or below one standard deviation. That is a higher percentage than would be expected in a normal distribution, suggesting there is indeed skill involved in creating this type of defense.

If it is a skill, however, a closer look suggests that it's a skill that doesn't usually remain consistent from season to season. The correlation coefficient of PP/d from one year to the next is .09, which is extremely weak.[1]

Then again, a weak correlation for the whole population does not mean that no single team proved capable of repeating a successful Bend But Don't Break strategy. Looking at our list of 44 Bend But Don't Break teams, we see representatives of 20 different franchises, six of which made the list in consecutive years. Overall, the teams in our sample had consecutive seasons with a PP/d more than one standard deviation above average eight times. So

Table 1. Top 44 Teams in Points Prevented per Drive, 1998–2006

Year	Team	PP/d	Year	Team	PP/d	Year	Team	PP/d	Year	Team	PP/d	Year	Team	PP/d
2001	CHI	0.589	2004	PHI	0.313	1998	MIN	0.261	2006	NYJ	0.229	1999	DAL	0.200
2001	NE	0.510	2000	BAL	0.308	2003	HOU	0.252	2003	NE	0.226	2005	SEA	0.197
2004	JAC	0.475	2005	IND	0.298	2005	CHI	0.250	2005	DEN	0.225	2003	KC	0.193
2006	NE	0.443	2001	PHI	0.296	2003	MIA	0.247	1998	SEA	0.224	2000	IND	0.193
1999	MIN	0.365	2000	MIA	0.290	2001	GB	0.243	2006	BAL	0.216	2000	WAS	0.188
2000	CAR	0.363	2002	PHI	0.281	2004	NYJ	0.240	2006	PHI	0.210	2006	JAC	0.187
2004	NE	0.356	2000	PHI	0.270	2004	IND	0.236	2001	NYJ	0.208	1999	CHI	0.187
2003	NYJ	0.329	2002	SEA	0.268	2001	PIT	0.229	2002	NYJ	0.204	2004	BAL	0.184
1998	DAL	0.313	2001	SF	0.264	2004	SD	0.229	1999	STL	0.201			

---

1. Correlation coefficient is explained in "Statistical Toolbox" near the beginning of the book.

not only is there skill involved in Bending But Not Breaking, but that skill can be repeated from season to season, even if it's uncommon for a team to do so.

The most interesting of the teams that fielded Bend But Don't Break defenses in consecutive years are the Patriots, Eagles, and Jets, who together were responsible for 13 of the 44 teams on our list. Bill Belichick arrived in New England in 2000 and has had four Bend But Don't Break defenses in seven years. Jim Johnson took over as defensive coordinator in Philadelphia in 1999 and has had five BBDB defenses in eight years. The year before he joined the Eagles, Johnson was a defensive assistant on the 1998 Seahawks, another team on this list. Herm Edwards was head coach of the Jets from 2001 to 2005 and had four BBDB defenses in his five years in New York. Including Johnson's final year in Seattle, those three coaches account for 32 percent of our Bend But Don't Break list.

Now that we know that certain teams and, even more compellingly, certain coaches are able to produce Bend But Don't Break defenses with a certain regularity, the question becomes, what qualities influence a team's ability to bend without breaking, and how those qualities manifested themselves on teams coached by Belichick, Johnson, and Edwards.

The Components of Points Prevented

The first step in understanding what allows a defense to bend without breaking is to identify those factors that correlate with our Points Prevented per drive metric. Those factors are listed in table 2. Notice that points per drive, scores per drive, and touchdowns per drive are strongly correlated (negatively, of course), but field goals on their own are not. In our example at the top of this essay, our prototypical Bend But Don't Break defense actually gave

Table 2. Correlation of Points Prevented per Down to Other Measures, 1998–2006

Opponent's Average Initial Line of Scrimmage	−0.64
Points/Drive	−0.57
TD/Drive	−0.56
Scores/Drive	−0.55
Red Zone DVOA	−0.47
Turnovers/Drive	0.45
Red Zone Passing DVOA	−0.40
Interceptions/Drive	0.37
Front Zone DVOA	−0.32
Goal to Go DVOA	−0.32
Total DVOA	−0.31
Fumbles	0.24
Field Goals	−0.21

up a fair number of field goals. In fact, some would consider allowing a field goal a typical Bend But Don't Break result. Then again, field goals still count as points. Since points have a strong negative correlation, it makes sense that allowing a field goal, which might otherwise have a strong positive correlation, would ultimately have a weak correlation, as it is worse than allowing nothing but better than allowing a touchdown.

That overall defensive quality (as measured by Total DVOA) is correlated with Bending But Not Breaking might appear troubling at first as it might suggest that all we've done is sort out the best defenses in the league. Looking at the average defensive DVOA of our 44 defenses, however, this is clearly not the case. The average defensive DVOA of the teams on table 1 was a decent but hardly overwhelming −7.1%, which would have been good for 10th in the league in 2006. More than a quarter of the teams on the list actually had below-average defenses, all the way down to the 2003 Jets with a defensive DVOA of 12.3%. In fact, the correlation with Total DVOA is among the weakest in table 2. (Note that since defensive DVOA is better when negative, a negative correlation is actually a direct correlation. As PP/d go up, a team's defensive DVOA is likely to be more negative, and thus better.) What's more, some correlation should occur as DVOA is context-driven. Turning touchdowns into field goals is extremely valuable, and it would be problematic if DVOA did not pick up this difference.

On the other hand, the strongest correlation to PP/d is the opponent's average initial line of scrimmage, which is troubling. Sure, it makes sense; poor opponent's field position (meaning poor from the opponent's perspective) allows a defense to give up a significant number of yards before the offense is within scoring range, but opponent's field position is in part a function of offense and special teams, so we should be uncomfortable with its impact on a defensive measurement. Still, a defense has a substantial impact on the field position of its opponents as well. A bad defense gets poor field position for its own offense which results in good field position for the opponent. The relationship between the opponent's average line of scrimmage and overall defensive DVOA is small but not meaningless at .21.

More good news is that the teams in table 1 have largely not benefited from good field position. That group has an average line of scrimmage only 1.5 yards better than our entire 283-team sample. This minor difference is likely only determinative at the margins, and, for now, we will just keep it in the back of our mind when analyzing individual teams. Also, within just the teams in table 1, the correlation between opponent's initial line of scrimmage and PP/d is almost non-existent. The impact is much stronger on those teams with poor PP/d. Among the subset of teams more than one standard deviation worse than the mean, the correlation is a fairly strong –.36. This suggests that opponent's field position is more effective in preventing BBDB defenses by eating up the territory in which they can bend, than it is in creating BBDB defenses by providing extra room to bend.

Next, turnovers, particularly interceptions, correlate strongly with PP/d. Theoretically, this makes sense because a drive that ends in a turnover can't produce a score. What's more, Bend But Don't Break defenses will require their opponents to make more plays, leading to an increase in both the likelihood of and opportunities to create turnovers. The turnover phenomenon is more pronounced than the general increase in plays would indicate, however. Teams in table 1 faced two percent more plays per drive than our larger sample did as a whole, but 15 percent more turnovers. Perhaps because of the somewhat random nature of fumble recovery, PP/d correlates more strongly with interceptions (.37) than fumbles (.24).

Finally, in checking the correlations between PP/d and various DVOA splits, two sets of numbers stand out: Red Zone DVOA and, to a lesser extent, the "Front Zone" DVOA (the latter referring to performance in the twenty yards before the red zone, between the defense's 20- and 40-yard lines). The reason for this is obvious enough. Success in the front zone will lead to long field goal tries or short punts, while success in the red zone will prevent touchdowns, and force field goals, or, even better, the occasional turnover.

Note that performance in the red zone as a whole has a better correlation than just performance on goal-to-go situations. This may seem counterintuitive, but it actually supports the findings of a study that appeared in *Pro Football Prospectus 2005* that dubbed the outer ten yards of the red zone between the 10- and 20-yard lines "The Most Important Real Estate in Football."

Teams with a Bend But Don't Break Tendency

Now that we know what aspects of performance tend to correlate generally with a Bend But Don't Break defense, we can look to see what typifies those teams that are able to sustain it. As mentioned above, our Bend But Don't Break defenses were not necessarily the best defenses from our 283-team sample. In fact, the list includes teams that did a great deal of bending (the 2002 Seahawks allowed the sixth most yards per drive in the sample) and very little (the 2000 Ravens allowed the fifth fewest). The common denominator is that they "broke" less than teams that gave up a similar number of yards. On average, our 44 Bend But Don't Break defenses allowed only .06 yards per drive less than our 283-team sample as a whole, but allowed .28 fewer points per drive. Using the Chargers' 2006 total of 182 drives, that translates to 51 fewer points than expected. To put that in context, the San Diego Chargers allowed 303 points last year, good for sev-

enth in the league. Had they allowed 51 more points, they would have ranked 22nd. We can turn to Pythagorean record to put that in terms of wins. Increasing the Chargers' points allowed by 51 points would give them 10.5 Pythagorean wins compared to their actual 12.1 Pythagorean wins. In theory, our BBDB teams gained at least a full win over what their yards per drive would have indicated.

If we return now to the areas of correlation for the whole sample, we can search for the unique strengths of our subset of consistent Bend But Don't Break teams—those coached by Belichick, Edwards, and Johnson. Among the table 1 teams, the difference between touchdowns and field goals is even more pronounced. The correlation between PP/d and field goals per drive for the teams in table 1 is only –.05, while the correlation between PP/d and touchdowns is –.24. As that split between touchdowns and field goal might suggest, this subset of teams is particularly strong in the red zone, where they have an average defensive DVOA of –25.5% compared with –7% overall, and only six of the 44 teams were below average in the red zone. These teams were even stronger against the pass in the red zone, with a red zone pass defense DVOA of –46.0% and only four teams below average. Prior research has shown that strong red zone performance is at least moderately repeatable, thus red zone defense and red zone pass defense in particular would appear to be keys to building a consistent Bend But Don't Break defense.

A strong red zone defense is always a good thing, but two other indicators that these Bend But Don't Break defenses share raise concerns about each team going forward. In general, our BBDB teams struggle in the "deep" zone (the opposite of the red zone, i.e. between the offense's 20-yard line and its own goal line), and benefit from good luck thanks to the poor performance of opposing field-goal kickers.

The correlation between PP/d and deep zone DVOA is positive, meaning that as defensive DVOA gets higher (i.e. worse), the team's Points Prevented per drive increase. This finding is consistent with the theory that Bend But Don't Break defenses tend to give up yardage on the far side of the field (bend), but not give up many points (don't break).

The problem is that poor performance in the deep zone does not appear to be consistent from season to season, making it not only a poor indicator for Bend But Don't Break consistency, but a decent indicator that a team will *not* have a repeat BBDB season. The Jets, for example, were abysmal in the deep zone in 2003 and 2004, but they were fifth-best in the entire 283-team sample in 2001 and above average in 2002 (as well as 2005, a season not included on our BBDB list). Between 1998 and 2005, 14 teams in table 1 have had a deep zone DVOA at least 20 percentage points worse than their overall DVOA. Of those 14 teams, only one, the 2000 Eagles, saw an improved PP/d the next season. On average, those 14 teams had .31 PP/d in the season with the deep zone discrepancy but –.01 PP/d in the following season. Over the league average of 184 drives, that translates to 60 more points allowed if the same yardage is allowed.

Missed field goals are an even worse predictor of Bend But Don't Break consistency because not only does the ability of the defense in question have absolutely nothing to do with field goals being missed by its opponents, but, as per the essay in the Arizona chapter, not even field goal kickers themselves have much control over their success rates from year to year. Rather than explore the correlation here, the preferable solution is to factor field goal misses out entirely. We can calculate how many points a team saved on missed field goals by figuring out how many of the attempts made against that team should have been successful based on the league average success rate at the given distance, then subtracting the actual number of successful field goals made against that team and multiplying by three. Over the course of a season, these numbers can add up. On the extreme, the 2001 Steelers were saved 18.7 points thanks to the windy conditions at then newly-opened Heinz Field.

If we add those missing points back onto each team's overall points allowed and recalculate their PP/d, we find that ten teams in table 1 were saved at least .03 points per drive. That's admittedly relatively minor, but it's enough to knock those 2001 Steelers as well as the 2000 Colts, 2006 Jaguars, and 1999 Bears off our BBDB list. At the same time, several teams that just missed our list due to an unusually high opponent's field goal success rate would join the list, including the 2004 Saints, 1999 Seahawks, and 2004 Redskins.

The Eagles and the Curious Case of Red Zone Defense

As the above correlations indicate, the best indicator of Bend But Don't Break consistency is a strong red zone defense. A perfect example of this is the performance of the Philadelphia Eagles under coordinator Jim Johnson. The Eagles have had an above average red zone defense in every year of Johnson's tenure except for their injury-plagued 2005 season, and have had an a PP/d of .165 or more every year except 2005. Even more impressive is that their red zone pass defense has had a DVOA of –19.0% or better each season, again with one huge exception. In 2005, the Eagles defense was decimated by injuries and their red zone pass defense was 56.3%, one of the 15 worst in the entire 283-team sample.

The Eagles also dominated the red zone in 1999, Johnson's first season with the team, but their opponent's excellent starting field position, nearly the 35-yard line, meant the Eagles gave up fewer yards before clamping down

inside the 20, and therefore their ratio of yards to points allowed was closer to normal. As a result, that 1999 team is not in table 1 despite having tendencies similar to the other Johnson defenses.

It is not completely satisfying to say that the Eagles simply have a good red zone defense without addressing why. The obvious answer to any Jim Johnson question is that he loves to blitz. The blitz is especially effective when a defense is backed up against its own goal line because the secondary has less ground to cover. Official data on blitzing is hard to find, but our game charting project has tracked pass rushers for two seasons. On average, a team rushes more than four linemen 34 percent of the time in the red zone. The Eagles only did so 28 percent of the time in 2006, but that does not mean that Eagles do not blitz; they just rarely blitz five. The average team sent six or more rushers 15 percent of the time, while the Eagles did so 26 percent of the time. Although the Eagles' personnel was worse in 2005, the philosophy was the same; the Eagles were one of the top three teams in bringing six-man blitzes.

This connection between the blitz, a strong red zone defense, and Bend But Don't Break tendencies brings us to the last of our three consistent BBDB teams, the Patriots. The Pats have shown pronounced Bend But Don't Break tendencies in 2001, 2003, 2004, and 2006 and had a red zone pass defense DVOA of –57.1% or better in 2003, 2004, and 2006. (Like the Eagles, they had major injury issues in 2005.) The 2006 data shows that the Patriots also blitz frequently, albeit differently from the Eagles. The Patriots sent at least five rushers 67 percent of the time in the red zone, rushing exactly five an amazing 49 percent of the time. This difference is likely largely attributable to the Pats' 3-4 defense compared with the Eagles' 4-3. The Eagles rarely send one extra rusher, as he is easily picked up, thus their tendency to rush six men. For the Patriots, five rushers are two extra men. Again, like the Eagles, the Patriots were one of the top three blitzing teams in 2005. (For those curious, Denver was the third.) As for the 2001 Patriots, their Bend But Don't Break tendencies that season were driven by excellent performance in the front zone, leading to the fourth highest ratio of field goals to touchdowns in the whole sample.

It's important to note that red zone DVOA is not highly correlated from year to year for most teams, which further emphasizes how unsustainable Bend But Don't Break defenses are. The Eagles and Patriots are notable for their ability to consistently perform at a high level in the red zone, but they are the exceptions, not the rule. In fact, while we are comfortable writing 2005 off as injury aberrations for both teams, it is worth noting that both teams also struggled immensely in the red zone that season.

This information is still valuable because it gives us another way to identify overachieving teams. If a team has a high PP/d but not a particularly high turnover rate or strong red zone defense, it is likely to experience a big fall in the win-loss column the following season. The 2007 Jets, for instance, scream regression for a number of reasons outside the scope of this article, but these metrics do not provide any encouragement. The 2006 Jets were below average in turnovers per drive and had a red zone defense worse than their overall defense. Meanwhile, they were terrible in the deep zone and protected their defense with good field position. Color us extremely skeptical that they will allow only 295 points again next season.

Another Approach Suggests Another Bend But Don't Break Coach

The Points Prevented approach is valuable for determining which teams gave up fewer points than expected, but the poor correlation from year to year highlights some lack of descriptiveness. Most troubling is the impact of the opponent's initial line of scrimmage on the larger data set. Another way of approaching the problem is through Drive Success Rate, a metric we introduced in *Pro Football Prospectus 2005*. DSR measures the success rate of each series of downs such that only a first down or touchdown (but not a field goal) is considered a success. For defense, therefore, a lower number is better.

To look for Bend But Don't Break defenses, we compared the DSR during each team's first two series of downs in a drive (the bend portion) and with its DSR for all of the remaining sets of downs in that drive (the break). Adjustments were made for touchdowns scored on the first or second set of downs, since an 80-yard bomb takes the whole issue of bending out of the equation.

Not surprisingly, this ratio of bend to break (BTB) correlates somewhat substantially with PP/d, with a correlation coefficient of .44. However, the two systems do not seem to identify similar teams as possessing Bend But Don't Break defenses. Only three teams are in the top 20 in both lists, the 2006 Patriots, 1999 Vikings, and 2002 Seahawks, and only 18 are in both top 50s, including four Patriots teams, but only two Eagles and two Jets teams.

The team that appears most often among the top 50 teams in BTB ratio is the Seahawks, who appear five times, including four consecutive years from 1999 through 2002. Mike Holmgren came to the Seahawks in 1999, but he is usually thought of as an offensive coach. Still, this BTB performance persisted despite a revolving door of defensive coordinators that included Fritz Shurmur, Steve Sidwell, Ray Rhodes, and John Marshall.

The performance by Holmgren's Seahawks in PP/d is not far behind their performance in BTB ratio. The 2002

and 2005 teams rank high on both lists, and the 1999 to 2003 Seahawks all rank in the top 100 in PP/d. The difference between these seasons highlights a key difference between the two methodologies. The 1999 and 2002 squads, which both rank relatively high in PP/d, both forced a significantly higher number of turnovers than the other relevant squads. The 2005 team appears to be a different beast altogether, achieving notoriety thanks to an amazing .68 ratio of touchdowns to field goals, the best in our entire 283-team sample. That TD/FG ratio was the result of comparatively better play in the front and red zones despite a comparative lack of turnovers. The points scored on those field goals are the difference between the 2005 Seahawks' merely good performance in PP/d (which, as a point-based system, rewards turnovers, but punishes field goals) and their dominant performance in BTB ratio (which treats turnovers and field goals equally as failed sets of downs).

One common thread is that, like PP/d, the BTB methodology shows little year-to-year consistency, with almost no correlation from one year to the next. This finding provides further evidence that, except in unique circumstances, a Bend But Don't Break defense is most often a one-game or, at best, one-year phenomenon.

Final Conclusions

The Bend But Don't Break phenomenon is real as we rather easily identified a substantial list of teams that showed a pronounced ability to Bend But Don't Break during a given season. Those teams were, as a result, more successful in preventing their opponents from scoring (not breaking) than their underlying yardage allowed per drive (bending) would suggest. In most instances, however, that ability is not repeated from year to year, making a "bend but don't break" defense a good indicator for decline the following season.

Exceptions to that year-to-year variation were found in teams coached by Bill Belichick, Jim Johnson, Herm Edwards, and Mike Holmgren. Finding a consistent rationale for Edwards's tendencies proved difficult, but Holmgren has had a string of defenses adept at keeping the opposition out of the end zone due to a strong front zone performance and the ability to force turnovers. The success of Belichick and Johnson seems particularly instructive. Those two coaches are associated with two of the league's most successful franchises, teams on the cutting edge of statistical research. Their teams generally have superior red zone defenses due to a tendency to blitz inside the red zone, suggesting a strategy that other coaches could use to develop more consistent Bend But Don't Break defenses of their own.

The Disappearing Two-Point Conversion

Jim Armstrong

Week 9 featured one of the more exciting football games of the season when the Cowboys visited the Redskins in a matchup of longtime divisional rivals, each with playoff aspirations in the wide-open NFC East. The game had plenty of excitement throughout, starting with a safety on the Cowboys' first offensive play. Yellow flags flew early and often, resulting in nearly 200 yards of penalty yardage. Moreover, the antics of Dallas receiver Terrell Owens were on full display. Following a touchdown reception, T.O. pretended to take a nap by using the football as a pillow, yet later in the game he dropped another potential touchdown pass after getting open deep behind the Washington defense. The drama was building toward a crazy finish with the score tied 19–19 in the fourth quarter. After the Redskins' Nick Novak missed a 49-yard field goal attempt that would have broken the tie with 31 seconds remaining, Mike Vanderjagt of the Cowboys had a potential game-winning field goal of his own blocked as time expired. During the return of the blocked kick, Dallas was flagged for a facemask. The penalty resulted in a rare un-timed down at the end of regulation, and placed the ball on the Cowboys' 29-yard line, giving Novak a chance to redeemed himself in the form of a 47-yard field goal attempt, which he nailed, lifting the Redskins to a 22–19 victory.

Among the most crucial and controversial plays leading up to that wild ending was Dallas head coach Bill Parcells's decision to attempt a two-point conversion early in the second quarter after scoring a touchdown to take a 6–5 lead. On the conversion try, Tony Romo's pass intended for Patrick Crayton fell incomplete, and Parcells was second-guessed for passing up a near-certain extra point that might have made the difference in the game's outcome. If it seemed like an unusual situation to go for two, it was; in fact, it was the only two-point conversion attempt in the entire 2006 NFL season that was called for by a coach during the first half of a game. It stood out for another reason as well: the two-point conversion is slowly disappearing from the NFL.

The NFL added the two-point conversion to its rulebook in 1994. Teams were initially fascinated by it, but, in recent years, they have been gradually avoiding it. Nearly

Table 1. Total Two-Point Conversion Attempts

Season	2pt Att	Suc Rate
1998	98	41%
1999	77	39%
2000	78	45%
2001	84	48%
2002	93	51%
2003	62	47%
2004	77	50%
2005	50	54%
2006	35	60%

100 two-point conversions were attempted in the NFL in 1998; last season teams attempted only 35 (table 1). From 1998 to 2006, NFL teams attempted two-point conversions after about six percent of all regular season touchdowns, but on an annual basis that figure has gradually declined from nine percent in 1998 to just three percent last season. Before examining what has changed, we first need to understand in exactly which situations NFL coaches have historically gone for two.

To do this, we first assembled scoring summary data from all regular season games from the last nine years. Next, we grouped all touchdowns in our data set by the game score differential immediately following the score, but prior to the extra point, and then computed the rate at which teams attempted two-point conversions at each score differential (table 2). The results were fairly predictable. There are a few specific point differentials at which teams usually go for two and a handful of others at which they sometimes go for two, but, in most situations, they almost never leave their place-kicker on the sidelines. Besides the current score, the other major factor coaches consider in making their extra point decisions is the time remaining in the game. Teams are much more likely to attempt the two-point conversion later in the game (table 3).

In order to determine what has changed in recent years, we examined the two-point conversion attempt rate by situation, season by season, and found several situations in which NFL teams used to go for two much more

Table 2. Two-Point Conversion Attempts by Score

Trail by	TD	2pt Att	Rate	Trail by	TD	2pt Att	Rate
21+	187	36	19%	6	59	2	3%
20	8	2	25%	5	204	102	50%
19	28	7	25%	2	104	85	82%
18	59	28	48%	**Lead by**	**TD**	**2pt Att**	**Rate**
17	30	14	47%	1	83	69	83%
16	19	12	63%	4	63	29	46%
15	123	5	4%	5	129	66	51%
13	30	17	57%	8	66	1	2%
12	101	27	27%	12	162	45	28%
11	183	4	2%	14	86	3	4%
10	55	45	82%	19	108	19	18%
9	56	10	18%				

NOTE: On all other scores, the rate of two-point conversion attempts is one percent or less.

Table 3. Two-Point Conversion Attempts by Quarter

Qtr	TD	2pt Att	Rate
1	2140	2	<1%
2	3128	55	2%
3	2270	128	6%
4	3057	466	15%

Table 5. Sample Two-Point Conversion Chart

Lead by	Go for	Trail by	Go for	Lead by	Go for	Trail by	Go for
1	2 PT	1	XP	11	XP	11	2 PT
2	XP	2	2 PT	12	2 PT	12	2 PT
3	XP	3	XP	13	XP	13	XP
4	2 PT	4	Either	14	XP	14	XP
5	2 PT	5	2 PT	15	2 PT	15	XP
6	XP	6	XP	16	XP	16	2 PT
7	XP	7	XP	17	XP	17	XP
8	XP	8	XP	18	XP	18	XP
9	XP	9	2 PT	19	2 PT	19	2 PT
10	XP	10	XP	20	XP	20	XP

SOURCE: NFL.com

Table 4. Changes in Two-Point Conversion Strategy, 1998–2006

Season	Q3	Trail by 5	Lead by 5	Trail by 16+
1998	7%	57%	75%	35%
1999	10%	58%	53%	34%
2000	8%	47%	86%	38%
2001	9%	74%	73%	31%
2002	7%	61%	48%	43%
2003	3%	40%	40%	24%
2004	4%	50%	50%	25%
2005	3%	25%	36%	20%
2006	<1%	33%	31%	12%

frequently than they have the last few years. Coaches have all but eliminated the two-point conversion attempt in the third quarter of the game. The specific point differentials that have been most affected are trailing or leading by five points, and trailing by 16 or more points (table 4).

How do coaches make their extra point decisions during a game? When Bill Parcells was asked after the game why he went for two during the Cowboys' loss to the Redskins, his response was simple and to the point: "I go by the chart." The chart he was referring to is a table all coaches have on their laminated play sheet indicating the preferred extra point decision based on the current score differential (table 5). As the story goes, the chart was created in 1970 by UCLA head football coach Tommy Prothro and his assistant Dick Vermeil and has been passed around from coach to coach ever since. But as Steve Mariucci noted on the NFL Network last season, different coaches have slightly different versions of the chart, which he discovered during research he did while coaching in the league. As Mariucci explained, since the chart typically doesn't consider the time remaining, coaches must use their own intuition in deciding how early in the game to use the chart.

In the early stages of a football game, coaches typically select the mix of plays that is likely to score the most points. After all, scoring more points than your opponent is the object of the game. However, because football is a timed game—60 minutes in regulation—and because points are scored in non-continuous increments (2, 3, 6, 7, 8 points) of varying likelihoods, attempting to score as many points as possible is not always the best strategy. With regards to extra points, coaches seem to believe that the increased risk involved in going for two means that kicking the extra point is not only the safer choice, but will also score more points, on average. At some point in every game, each team usually decides to deviate from its point-maximizing play-calling to a strategy that increases its chances of winning the game. This may include more conservative plays for the leading team and more risky plays for the trailing team. This change in a team's strategic approach most often occurs in third or fourth quarter, depending on the exact score. Likewise, teams also change their usual approach to extra points later in the game when scoring the maximum number of points is no longer the primary objective. When the coach has a better idea of how close the game will be, that's when he becomes more reliant on his chart.

It isn't clear why NFL coaches have abandoned the two-point conversion so dramatically, since there's been no obvious consensus among football analysts that they should do so. In *Pro Football Prospectus 2006*, we examined the decisions NFL coaches make on fourth downs and cited several published research articles concluding that coaches should be much more aggressive in going for the first down. The near-unanimous parade continued this past season with new web sites and even bestselling author Michael Lewis joining the chorus of critics labeling football coaches as cowards for being too conservative on fourth downs. Yet, despite the abundance of evidence, NFL coaches have not become noticeably bolder on fourth downs over the past ten years.

In contrast, on the subject of extra point decisions, the research has been sparse and the conclusions mixed. Several years ago, Rutgers statistics professor Harold Sackrowitz published an article in the statistical journal *Chance* analyzing extra point decisions. His research was featured in the *New York Times* and other media outlets through which he criticized coaches for being too quick to go for two in some situations. Conversely, on his website footballcommentary.com, William Krasker encourages coaches to go for two more often, based on the results of his own statistical model. Another possible influence on the frequency of two-point conversion attempts is author Gregg Easterbrook, whose popular "Tuesday Morning Quarterback" column has long featured an "immutable law" he dubs Take One Till the Fourth, which discourages coaches from going for two until the fourth quarter. One common link among these experts' opinions is that they all cite a two-point conversion success rate of about 40 percent, which they weigh against the virtual certainty of an extra point kick as the basis for their analysis. At Football Outsiders, we have reason to believe that the true probability of converting a two-point try is significantly higher.

Since 1998, about 98 percent of extra point kick attempts have been converted. In fact, that success rate has held remarkably steady over the past decade, so we can be fairly confident that it represents an accurate estimation of the chance of a successful kick. However, determining the true probability of converting a two-point attempt is a trickier exercise.

Although the NFL doesn't publish two-point conversion success rates as an official statistic, the numbers are often reported during television broadcasts or posted on various web sites. However, these rates can be misleading because they usually include kick attempts on which the snap or hold is botched. These plays technically become two-point conversion attempts when the holder or kicker picks up the ball and makes a mad dash for the end zone or perhaps launches a desperation heave toward the vicinity of a teammate. But these attempts aren't *planned* two-point plays as dictated by the coach. More importantly, these attempts almost always fail, since no player on the kicking team is expecting to block for a run or receive a

pass. There are usually about five to ten of these failed unintentional two-point conversion attempts in the league each regular season.

We have re-categorized these as failed one-point attempts and then calculated the two-point conversion success rates considering only planned attempts. The overall success rate in the NFL since 1998 is 47 percent, but it has been steadily increasing in recent years (table 1). Since 2002, the league-wide success rate is 51 percent, and last season it was a whopping 60 percent! If the extra point kick success rate is 98 percent, two-point conversions need to be successful at least 49 percent of the time to produce more points on average than kick attempts. The increasing success rate of the two-point conversion in recent years should be enough to convince coaches to start thinking about going for two more often early in the game.

Another trend can be observed when examining the types of plays called on two-point conversion attempts. Teams have been calling passing plays increasingly often compared to running plays, yet the conversion rate on passing plays is just 44 percent since 1998. However, the success rate on running plays over that same period is 54 percent and jumps to 63 percent during the past four seasons (table 6). This shouldn't be a surprise to anyone who has studied the Football Outsiders stats on power situations. The conversion rate on 4th-and-2 plays is 58 percent on the ground and just 42 percent in the air. Since the ball is spotted at the two-yard line for the two-point try after a touchdown, coaches should be looking toward their rushing game more often, just as they do in other short-yardage situations. Although a team probably shouldn't expect to score on 60 percent of its two-point conversion attempts, a more aggressive approach to extra point decisions with greater emphasis on running the ball could be beneficial.

Of course, there are many other factors for coaches to consider when making their extra point decisions—for example, the weather conditions, injuries to key players, and the strengths of the offensive and defensive units

Table 6. Success Rate for Two-Point Conversions: Run vs. Pass, 1998–2006

Season	Run Pct	Run Suc Rate	Pass Suc Rate
1998	28%	44%	39%
1999	30%	48%	35%
2000	41%	53%	39%
2001	29%	67%	40%
2002	39%	44%	54%
2003	27%	53%	44%
2004	22%	69%	45%
2005	26%	69%	49%
2006	17%	67%	59%

involved. However, it doesn't appear that the two-point conversion success rate has risen simply because teams are picking on the worst defenses. With only about two conversion attempts per team per season, it's difficult to say with much confidence that any particular team is much better or worse than the league average at converting the two-point try.

It's also possible that the decreasing number of two-point conversion attempts is leading to a higher success rate. As attempts become rarer, defenses become less prepared to stop them, but if attempts became more common again, perhaps defenses would adjust accordingly and the success rate would fall. This may be particularly true for rushing attempts, as defenses don't usually line up for the two-point try expecting a power run, but could easily change if they notice that more of their opponents have been attempting to run the ball in that situation. Even so, until defenses do adjust, there appears to be an opportunity for offenses to increase their point-scoring potential by using the two-point conversion more liberally.

Perhaps the most puzzling aspect of the trend away from the two-point conversion is the increasing reluctance of coaches to attempt it when trailing by more than two touchdowns. At a time when teams are forced to take more risks by passing the ball frequently and running a hurry-up offense in an effort to catch up, it seems odd that they would play it safe on the extra point. Perhaps coaches have simply become too reliant upon their charts.

As for the decision Parcells made to go for two in the second quarter of last year's game against the Redskins, leading by one is actually the point margin at which coaches are the most likely to go for two; it just rarely occurs so early in the game. Although the failed pass attempt ended up costing the Cowboys a nearly certain extra point that might have provided the winning margin, given the increasing success rate of the two-point conversion in the NFL, it's hard to fault Parcells for using the chart so early in the game. We do have one quibble with his decision, though: he should have run the ball.

Optimal Play-Action Strategy

Bill Barnwell and Aaron Schatz

The importance and effectiveness of the play-action pass is taken for granted in football. Like many things, when it works, game announcers drill it into your head; when it doesn't, it's quickly forgotten. At Football Outsiders, "take for granted" isn't in our vocabulary. Using our 2006 game charting data, we set out to see whether the play-action pass was effective, and, if so, in which situations it works, and what teams run it best. The short answer is that play-action passes are effective in the right situations, but can also be awful in the wrong ones, and it is surprising to see which teams excel at play-action passing, and even more surprising to see which teams do not.

Down and Distance

Play-action passes are most effective on first down, and still generally effective on second down, but worse than non-play action plays in most third and fourth down situations (table 1). While passes on first and second down are more successful than running plays in general, as Andy Reid will tell you, play-action passes are still significantly more effective than regular passes on both. The average play-action pass attempt on first down gains 7.6 yards, while the average standard pass attempt gains only 6.2 yards.

A surprising fact is that play-action passes work better with seven or more yards to go than they do for shorter distances, which nullifies the idea that 2nd-and-2 and 3rd-and-1 play-action passes are good ideas. This makes some sense when you consider that pass plays in short-yardage situations are generally more risky than runs because the

former can lead to a sack or interception, which is significantly worse than a running back getting stuffed at the line. Lest you think that the numbers in table 1 are due to those seven-plus yard plays picking up meaningless yardage short of the first down, remember that DVOA is based upon achieving successful chunks of yardage as opposed to meaningless ones; on third down, for example, the only way a play can be measured a success is if it picks up the required yardage for a first down.

Inside the Ten-Yard Line

Inside their opponent's ten-yard line, offenses employ the play-action pass to create holes for their running game on subsequent downs as well as punch it in with passes to obscure targets such as third-string tight ends, attention-starved tackles, and Mike Vrabel. The space issues and resulting shift in defensive schemes within the ten change the rules for how an offense operates, affecting our look at the play-action pass.

From the one-foot line to the six-yard line, the play-action pass is better than a regular pass, and about as good as the average non-play action play, regardless of whether it's a pass or a run (figure 1). Outside the six, though, play-action passes are significantly worse than either play, with regular passes becoming much more effective. What we

Table 1. Play-Action Passes vs. Other Plays by Down and Distance, 2006

Situation	DVOA Advantage	Yardage Advantage
All 1st Downs	22.1%	1.4
2nd-and-1-2	−6.7%	−1.5
2nd-and-3-6	−1.3%	−0.1
2nd-and-7+	15.9%	1.2
All 2nd Downs	14.2%	0.7
3rd/4th-and-1-2	−10.4%	0.4
3rd/4th-and-3-6	−17.6%	−1.5
3rd/4th-and-7+	15.7%	0.4
All 3rd/4th Downs	−9.9%	−0.3

Figure 1. Play-Action DVOA Inside 10-Yard Line

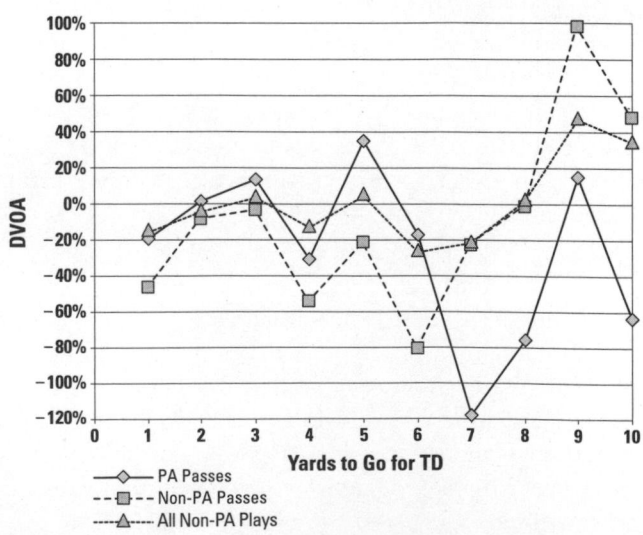

can infer, then, is that the spacing concerns about offensive and defensive schemes come into play starting on the six.

Overuse of Play Fakes

Like a lot of strategy in football, the play-action fake is based on deception. It thus stands to reason that the more a team uses it, the less effective it becomes, because the defense stops being fooled. For example, when we researched the effectiveness of blitzing in *Pro Football Prospectus 2006*, we discovered that blitzing six or more pass-rushers becomes counterproductive if a team does it nine or more times per game.

Is there a similar trend with the play-action fake? In 2006, the answer was no. Whether it was the first play-fake or the tenth play-fake by that offense in that game, offensive DVOA on play-action passes was usually positive. There was no trend that showed play-action becoming more or less effective the more it was used until the 13th play-fake of the game, at which point DVOA began to drop significantly. However, there were so few teams that used play-action that much that those numbers are ultimately meaningless. Less than two percent of all play-action passes came after the attempting team had already made at least 12 previous play-action attempts in that game.

Getting It Right

Now that we've established when and where the play-action pass is successful, we can ascertain how it's done best and which teams employ those best practices.

An effective running game seems like an obvious prerequisite for a successful play-action pass. That statement is very true, but the emphasis needs to be placed on "effective." There's a very strong correlation between a team's DVOA on play-action passes and both rushing DVOA (.47) and rushing DVOA in the first half (.51). There is no correlation between the number of times a team runs the ball and their play-action pass DVOA, which proves that defenses simply don't respect the play-action fake when the offense has a mediocre ground game.

In general, teams that have a successful passing attack also are successful at the play-action pass. A strong correlation (.48) exists between DVOA on non-play-action passes and DVOA on play-action passes.

The Best Actors

As we said, the list of teams at either end of the play-action spectrum might surprise you. The best teams (table 2) are teams that are generally excellent at passing the ball (notably Indianapolis and Cincinnati, who were first and second in standard passing DVOA in 2006). The only below-average passing team with excellent play fakes was Jacksonville.

The worst play-action teams struggled with mediocre quarterbacks and/or position battles. Miami, in particular, was absolutely atrocious on play-action passes. Some of that may have to do with Chris Chambers's struggles to catch the ball, but a more likely indicator is that the Dolphins had the third-worst first-half rushing DVOA in the NFL in 2006. Atlanta's failures on play-action come with an asterisk. If we included scrambles on play-action passes in the play-action pass DVOA, Atlanta's figure would go from −28.4% to a respectable 8.7%, which is evidence of Michael Vick's running ability.

We're not looking for the best or worst passing teams, though; we're looking for the teams that are good or bad at the play-action pass. To do that, let's look at the difference between passing DVOA on play-action and non-play action plays (table 3). These lists of teams result in some strange bedfellows. While the high-powered Cincinnati attack remains, the baby steps of Houston and the multi-headed quarterback hydra of Washington show up. This suggests that play-action is a team-based skill, not a quarterback-based one. Indeed, the strength of Washington's running game surely played a part in their success with the play-action pass.

The list of the worst play-action teams, when compared to overall passing DVOA, is even more bizarre. Why would Kansas City, a team with a dominant rushing attack and a veteran quarterback (well, two of them) struggle on play-action passes? It seems strange, but, despite Larry Johnson's big year, Kansas City's rushing in the first-half of games was poor (−11.9% DVOA), and, as we've seen, positive rushing DVOA in the first half is the leading indicator of play-action

Table 2. Best and Worst Play-Action Pass DVOA

Best		Worst	
CIN	61.9%	MIA	−56.1%
IND	50.4%	CAR	−38.1%
PIT	49.0%	ATL	−28.4%
JAC	47.5%	MIN	−26.9%
STL	45.0%	ARI	−21.6%

Table 3. Difference in DVOA between Play-Action and Other Passes

Best		Worst	
JAC	64.9%	MIA	−52.4%
PIT	39.7%	CAR	−35.7%
HOU	38.4%	NE	−29.5%
CIN	36.7%	KC	−24.7%
WAS	36.4%	ARI	−21.9%

success. Perhaps even stranger is the presence of New England, as Tom Brady is famed for being the quarterback who does all the little things right *and* the Patriots' running game was above-average in the first half. We don't have an answer for that one, but we will certainly be keeping a close eye on the Patriots' play action in this year's game charting in the hope of revisiting their performance with an additional year of data.

Defending the Play Action

Something not often discussed is how successful teams are at defending the play-action pass, and why. Since we are tracking how offenses fare when employing play action, we might as well take a look at how defenses do against it. What we found was that the correlations between stopping the play-action pass and defensive performance were relatively weak, except for one: a defense that faced many first half runs, *regardless of their quality,* had a moderately strong correlation (.35) to play-action pass DVOA (remember, defensive DVOA is supposed to be negative, so a positive correlation is a bad thing). This raises questions about the correlation we saw on offense between a specifically successful rushing attack and successful play-action passing.

Making the same comparison between a team's pass defense DVOAs on play action and non-play action plays that we discussed on the offensive side again reveals oddities (table 4). There's no real discernible trend amongst the best play-action defenders; some were good at stopping the pass altogether, some only succeeded against the run, and some were just terrible. New England has veteran linebackers who would theoretically be able to identify fakes well, but Houston has a young group of linebackers who would theoretically bite more often, and an even younger

secondary behind them. There are no real similarities between the worst teams, either, which doesn't mean that there's no rhyme or reason to defending play action, just that the data hasn't revealed obvious causation as of yet.

There are many interesting questions from this study that will influence the way we observe the 2007 season. Is Tom Brady really that bad at the play-action fake? Can Miami's play-action passing actually get worse if Trent Green's issues with play-action follow him there? Is Jacksonville really that incredible on the play-action pass, and if so, why? On a larger scale, the issue of a team having more to do with a successful play-action than a quarterback seems strange when you think about the way in which some quarterbacks seem to treat it as an afterthought while others employ elaborate tomfoolery to sell the fake. Then again, a fake that takes out the hard cam doesn't do a quarterback any good if he still winds up taking a sack because his offensive line caves or his receivers can't get open. One thing we do know: When it comes to offenses running the play-action, the run truly does set up the pass—as long as the run is actually effective.

Table 4. Difference in DVOA between Play-Action and Other Passes, Defense

Best		Worst	
NYJ	−45.8%	PHI	57.5%
STL	−31.2%	KC	54.4%
NE	−27.5%	ATL	53.2%
HOU	−24.4%	GB	51.0%
NYG	−19.0%	IND	41.4%

Post-Concussion Fallout

Will Carroll

There is a concussion epidemic in American sports. The cause is simple and known, but until the recent development of tools to measure their force and frequency, we were unaware of just how often players take dangerous blows to the head. Changes in equipment, diagnosis, and treatment have all been made in response to this new knowledge and to the new imperative felt in the medical arena. As we go to press, NFL Commissioner Roger Goodell has called for a league-wide "concussion summit," saying that "at no time should competitive issues override medical issues." That is all well and good for the Commissioner, but his job isn't decided by wins and losses. Missing a snap won't cost Goodell or his staff their jobs.

Of course, coming on the heels of a damning report from ESPN's Peter Keating in the middle of last season, one could see this new imperative as reactionary ass-covering. Nevertheless, concussions have been perceived as a growing problem, not just in the NFL but across all levels of football and even in other sports. In the past year, four baseball players have had significant post-concussive syndrome. Mike Matheny, a catcher for the St. Louis Cardinals and San Francisco Giants, retired due to the lingering effects of years of home-plate collisions and foul tips off his mask. Hockey star Brendan Shanahan missed a month after a severe concussion and created a controversy by coming back so quickly. At the college, high school, and even youth level, the problem is drawing increased attention as well, with reporting of such injuries increasing across the board. One top researcher called last year's 350,000 reported concussions a "gross under-representation." The problem is serious enough that doctors and scientists have tried to move away from the term "concussion" to one that has more—no pun intended—impact. Calling a concussion a "concussive brain trauma" might add a few syllables, but hearing the words "brain" and "trauma" together will make anyone sit up and notice—unless they've been knocked unconscious.

Prompted by this hysteria, a recent study was performed that sought to determine the actual level of concussion risk present in college football. Using a system of accelerometers in the helmets of players, Virginia Tech team physicians analyzed each play and had a computer alert them when a player took a hit that should have created a concussive brain trauma. Their findings were astounding.

The system was set at a level that alerted medical staff after the helmet received an impact with a force of 98g, a force equivalent to that of a driver hitting a golf ball or, perhaps more meaningfully, an impact level that would cause a passenger car to fail frontal impact levels because "the occupant would die." The 98g mark was used based on information published by the NFL's former concussion guru, Dr. Elliott Pellman. After four years of testing at Virginia Tech, Brown, and Dartmouth, it was found that symptomatic concussions occurred at both lower levels (as little as 60g) and at higher levels (one recorded at 180g.) The study noted most emphatically that big hits, the ones above the Pellman threshold, occurred far more frequently than expected. Of 250,000 recorded impacts, 3,000 were found to be above this threshold, a full 12 percent. Amazingly, only 11 concussions occurred during these recordings.

Given the findings of the Virginia Tech study, it is safe to assume that almost every player experiences significant blows to the head during a game. What's shocking is the infrequency with which those blows resulted in concussions. Certainly some of the impact of those blows is absorbed by a player's equipment, and some new equipment, such as the Riddell Revolution helmet widely adopted in the NFL, has been shown in studies to reduce concussive brain traumas by two percent. The larger difference, however, is not the quality of the helmet, but the quality of what is inside. Simply put, it appears that football players can take a hit to the head better than the average person. This physical advantage might in large part explain why concussive brain trauma statistics decrease at each successive level. (To be fair, there are far more high school athletes than professional players, but then, it is safe to assume that the pros are taking the harder blows.) Just as lesser athletic abilities are deselected as players progress from level to level—a wide receiver who runs a 4.8 40 can get by in college, but won't make it in the pros—so too are the players most likely to become symptomatic from a concussive-level hit deselected. Having a hard head could be just as important to a budding NFL career as being fast, strong, or agile.

This does not mean, however, that football players can afford to shrug off concussion risk. If the average person is more susceptible to brain trauma than the average football player, the logical next step is that some football players are more susceptible than others. Some quarterbacks take a hit, "shake it off," and lead the offense down the field. Others start making suboptimal decisions. The same is likely true of players at other positions, though it is harder to see the impact of their play from the sidelines. While efforts to reduce impact to the brain have helped, incidence of such trauma has not been reduced. It is at the very nature of the game. In many cases it appears that the groups of symptoms we are seeing are the result of cumulative traumas exacerbated by an acute event, meaning that even the hits that a player appears to have absorbed without harm are actually causing lasting damage. Such cumulative traumas, which result in post-concussive symptoms, pose more danger for players than single events.

With new tools such as Functional MRI, which creates a 3D map of the brain and allows doctors to note which functions (such as memory or sight) might have been affected by a concussive brain trauma, or Diffusion Tensor Imaging (DTI), which allows doctors the chance to find and diagnose micro-bleeding inside the brain, one would think that the solution to this problem is being found in new diagnostic techniques. Unfortunately, these tools are only useful once symptoms have occurred. It's reaction, not action, and sadly ill-positioned to improve the game or the health of its players.

The biggest risk is that we aren't seeing these delayed-onset results until well after players are out of the public eye. Just as Muhammad Ali has gone from the fast-talking, baddest man in the world to a shuffling shell of his former self due to the blows he absorbed in the ring, we've also seen football players end up in similar situations. Andre Watters, a former NFL player, killed himself after experiencing what was described as Alzheimer's-like symptoms and profound depression. Ted Johnson, the former Patriots linebacker, attacked the culture of the sport that demanded that he put his future at risk by returning. That culture, however, isn't changing. Player agent Leigh Steinberg attended a concussive brain trauma summit held at the University of Pittsburgh Medical Center, one of the leading concussive brain trauma research centers, and told the Associated Press that "most athletes are in a state of denial. They're taught to ignore pain."

Dan Morgan of the Carolina Panthers has had five documented concussions during his playing career, yet he was cleared to return in 2007 when testing showed that he had no deficits in his memory or motor skills compared to the league-mandated baselines. For the first time, all 32 teams will be required to test every player on these baseline skills, making a post-injury comparison possible. Research being done at the University of Buffalo shows that there is hope for even those athletes that haven't been

as fortunate as Morgan. A new rehabilitation program, one that is extremely gradual, is being plotted there that would place players under close medical supervision. This use of slow-paced rehab is leading to increasing calls for a Rugby Union-style rule. Under this rule, Rugby players diagnosed with the symptoms of a concussion are subject to a three-week "standdown." Unfortunately, the result of this rule is not better management or care, but an underreporting of symptoms so as not to place a team at disadvantage. We can hardly expect such a rule to have a different impact in the highly competitive NFL.

The culture isn't changing, but perhaps our attitude should be. If players are, in fact, self-selecting for quicker recovery from brain trauma through the same Darwinian ecology that weeds out the slower and weaker players, then the focus moves from prevention of brain injury to preservation of brain function. While I am not suggesting that the efforts to prevent and reduce concussive brain trauma be slowed or stopped, we must acknowledge that when players that are already self-selected for quick recovery from such events are injured beyond their innate abilities to recover, it has to be treated differently. When a player is finally hit so hard or so many times that he begins to suffer from the same consequences and symptoms as a "normal person," he is in fact way beyond normal human tolerance. For every Ron Jaworski, who states that he had over 30 concussions in his NFL career without loss of function today, there's another player who'll be facing serious, life-changing symptoms long after the cheers have stopped.

Balancing a player's long-term best interest with the competitive needs of the team is difficult for any team's medical staff. Add in that the player is often going to be the biggest advocate for a quick return and the job gets harder. Shifting the focus from mere protection to aggressive care upon diagnosis of symptoms will result in a difficult short term situation, but will ultimately best serve the player. Of course, this strategy is proven to cause under- or misreporting. That leaves only one solution: the NFL itself must take over the monitoring of concussive brain traumas, taking it out of the hands of the teams, whose interests are conflicted, while providing a level playing field for all 32 teams. A neutral monitor and non-affiliated physicians should treat and assess head injuries and not allow a return to activity until that athlete returns to his previous baseline.

It's a bold plan, but one that truly has the best interests of the game in mind. The NFL has always prided itself on being at the forefront of sports. This is an opportunity for it to reaffirm that position by setting an example that should help this national epidemic be taken seriously at every level. Mr. Goodell, there's time to act before one more player has his brain permanently damaged.

Looking Back at the Class of '96

Aaron Schatz

It is not hyperbole to call the wide receiver class of 1996 the greatest draft class in NFL history at a single position. Wide receivers from the 1996 draft have combined for more than 7,600 receptions and 105,000 yards through 2006. That's more than 1,000 receptions and 10,000 yards more than any other wide receiver class since 1967, and the gap will continue to grow (table 1). Ten wide receivers from the Class of '96 were still active last season, and three of them—Terry Glenn and Terrell Owens, of the Cowboys, and Marvin Harrison, of the Colts—had 1,000-yards seasons.

By comparison, the wide receiver class of 1998 currently has just 54,120 receiving yards. Using nonnormalized numbers, this ranks the 1998 group 11th among all draft classes since 1967. Although these players are two years younger, only six of the receivers from the 1998 draft were still active last year, and out of those six, only Hines Ward had at least 600 yards.

Conveniently, 1996 was also the first year that the NFL made play-by-play available on the Internet, which means that we've been able to compile DVOA and DPAR ratings that cover the full careers of the Class of '96 receivers. With those ratings we go back and take a more detailed look at these great players from their rookie season through today.

The Class of '96 certainly didn't burst out of the gate, not by Football Outsiders standards. Out of the 81 receivers with

at least 50 passes in 1997, players from the 1996 draft ranked 71st in DPAR (Eddie Kennison), 74th (Bobby Engram), 77th (Eric Moulds), 78th (Muhsin Muhammad), and 81st (Charlie Jones). Only Terrell Owens (seventh) and Marvin Harrison (16th) ranked in the top 20. When the Class of '98 was in its second year, four receivers ranked in the top 20 (Randy Moss fifth, Tim Dwight 14th, Az Hakim 16th, and Germaine Crowell 17th) and only one ranked in the bottom 20 (Corey Bradford, 71st). When the Class of '96 was in its third year in the league, however, Muhammad and Engram moved into the top 20 in DPAR, and Moulds shot all the way up to number one, just ahead of his classmate Terrell Owens, who ranked second.

The Class of '96 put up great numbers in their twenties, but where they really dominate other classes of wide receivers is in their thirties. Historically, wide receivers begin to decline around age 30. Three years ago, we actually wrote an article on our website suggesting that the Class of '96 receivers were going to decline in 2004, when they would be 30 or 31 years old.[1]

Instead, the top ten receivers from the Class of '96 collectively had their best year ever in 2004. Six of them reached 1,000 yards, with Keyshawn Johnson just missing at 976, and four of them had double-digit touchdowns. Since turning 30, players from the Class of '96 have combined for

Table 1. Top WR Draft Classes, 1967–2006

Year	Rec	Yds	Norm Rec*	Norm Yds*	Top Players
1996	7,646	105,866	7,472	102,071	Marvin Harrison, Terrell Owens, Keyshawn Johnson
1985	6,256	90,713	6,846	91,419	Jerry Rice, Andre Reed, Eric Martin
1988	6,373	92,908	6,568	91,808	Tim Brown, Michael Irvin, Anthony Miller
1991	6,452	91,979	6,411	89,298	Keenan McCardell, Herman Moore, Jeff Graham
1976	3,932	63,190	5,631	76,010	Steve Largent, Pat Tilley, Henry Marshall
1971	3,007	48,682	4,806	64,945	Harold Carmichael, Bob Chandler, Frank Lewis
1974	3,344	52,297	4,651	60,802	John Stallworth, Lynn Swann, "White Shoes" Johnson
1983	3,619	59,506	4,189	61,052	Henry Ellard, Mark Clayton, Anthony Carter
1984	3,680	55,877	4,139	56,774	Irving Fryar, Gary Clark, Ricky Sanders
1994	4,179	60,250	4,097	57,907	Isaac Bruce, Johnnie Morton, Derrick Alexander

* Each season normalized to 16 games in 2006 offensive environment; see Washington chapter.

1. http://www.footballoutsiders.com/2004/07/08/ramblings/stat-analysis/228/

17 1,000-yard seasons, ten seasons with double-digit touchdowns—and, for good measure, two Super Bowl championships and five conference championships.

Despite all this dominance, only two receivers from the Class of '96 have spent their entire careers with a single team: Marvin Harrison and Amani Toomer. It's not strange for veteran receivers in the modern NFL to play for multiple teams. What's strange is *why* these receivers have played for multiple teams. Nearly every one of the star receivers from 1996 has been discarded by his team at some point, and not even for salary cap-related reasons. Always whining about his contract, Glenn was dumped by the Patriots for two fourth-round picks, and then by the Packers for a single seventh-round pick. The Bucs and Eagles cut Johnson and Owens, respectively, in the middle of productive seasons because they caused so much locker room turmoil. Eddie Kennison turned the tables and just up and quit on the Denver Broncos in the middle of the 2001 season.

In part for that reason, Marvin Harrison stands as the most highly regarded member of the Class of '96. Of course, there's more to his standing than his lack of off-field headlines. Whether you judge by standard stats or our advanced metrics, Harrison is the most productive member of this class. He has the most catches, yards, and touchdowns, and the highest DVOA and DPAR. Beyond the scope of his classmates, Harrison currently ranks sixth all-time in receiving yards, and third in receiving touchdowns. But is Harrison truly the greatest receiver from the 1996 draft, or does that honor belong to Owens? Where do we rank players such as Joe Horn, Muhsin Muhammad, and Eric Moulds? Does Harrison have an unfair advantage because of his partnership with Peyton Manning, one of the top ten quarterbacks in NFL history? What about the influence of the Colts' other starting wideout, Reggie Wayne, who would be the number-one receiver on many other teams? Harrison sure seems to be getting a lot of help out there. DPAR compares a receiver to replacement level, and DVOA compares him to league average, but what if his teammates are better than the league average, or worse than replacement level, all the way down at Kyle Orton level?

To try to account for this, we ran numbers comparing each member of the class of '96 in each season to all the other wide receivers and tight ends on his team that year. For example, Harrison averaged .299 DPAR per pass last year. The rest of the Colts' receivers and tight ends averaged .233 DPAR per pass. The difference between those two figures, multiplied by Harrison's 148 passes, gives us his Value Over Team: 9.9 points. That number pales in comparison to his 44.3 Defense-adjusted Points Above Replacement, but it is still the highest figure for last year among the ten remaining Class of '96 receivers.

Does this number punish a player for having talented teammates? That's a problem, of course. There's no doubt that Harrison helps to contribute to his teammates' success by drawing the attention of the defense, but that works both ways. Harrison also sees less double coverage because teams have to account for Wayne, or deal with Joseph Addai and the stretch play-fake. Sometimes Harrison is going deep to clear room for Dallas Clark underneath, but sometimes Clark is the one going deep to clear room for Harrison.

Below, we present the ten receivers from the Class of '96 who were active through the 2006 season in reverse order of career Value Over Team. We've also added an 11th receiver, one who was among the top players of this class early on, then faded away long before the rest, but still ranks eighth in his class in career Value Over Team.

Each player is listed with his original team and draft position, followed by his career statistics and his best and worst seasons according to Value Over Team. We're not going to shorten that to VOT, because we have enough acronyms in our alphabet soup. On the tables below, it's simply called "Value." Also note that "Pass" is the total number of passes directed toward that receiver, whether they were complete or incomplete.

Eddie Kennison

Rams: Round 1, Pick 18 (Louisiana State)

		DPAR	DVOA	Pass	Yds	TD	C%	Value
Career		128.2	5.2%	1011	8223	44	53%	−3.8
Best	2005	30.6	27.2%	108	1104	5	63%	14.0
Worst	1999	0.3	−14.6%	129	835	6	47%	−20.0

Is Eddie Kennison at the bottom of our list because we used tight ends as part of our team comparison? Not at all. Kennison's four worst seasons are his first four, before he ever played alongside Tony Gonzalez.

Kennison is a classic example of a player whose high workload gave him reasonable standard statistics, but whose miserable Catch Rate made him a serious problem. Kennison's rookie year was great—900 yards, nine touchdowns, and a 47 percent Catch Rate—but over the next two years, he had just 638 yards with one touchdown and a 37 percent Catch Rate. The frustrated Rams let him go as a free agent, and, if you look up Kennison in your imaginary copy of *Pro Football Prospectus 1999*, you will find us belittling New Orleans for signing a troublesome speedster with no idea how to catch the ball.

Kennison was replacement level in 1999, but not when you compare him to his teammates. The quarterbacks for the 3–13 Saints were the interception-happy Billy Joe twins (Hobert and Tolliver) and an unknown, undrafted rookie named Jake Delhomme. Somehow, Andre Hastings and Keith Poole managed to rank 11th and 16th in DVOA catching passes from these guys. Kennison was 66th. The Saints let Kennison go and replaced him with another guy from the Class of '96, but we'll get to him later.

Chicago got a reasonable year out of Kennison, but they didn't want him either, so he went to Denver. For reasons that have never been explained, Kennison abruptly retired in the middle of the 2001 season, then un-retired a week later to sign with Denver's archrivals in Kansas City. The Broncos received no compensation whatsoever, and Kennison went on to have the five most productive years of his career with the Chiefs—by standard numbers, at least. Kennison's only two seasons with a Value Over Team above 5.0 were 2002 and 2005. The other nine members of the Class of '96 who were active through 2006 each have at least four.

Terry Glenn

Patriots: Round 1, Pick 7 (Ohio State)

		DPAR	DVOA	Pass	Yds	TD	C%	Value
Career		133.6	3.4%	1085	8784	45	55%	2.4
Best	1999	22.7	14.5%	116	1147	4	59%	7.6
Worst	2000	9.7	−5.4%	163	947	7	48%	−10.7

Based on Value Over Team, Glenn has been the most consistent member of the Class of '96. Other than that career-worst year in 2000, Glenn has had a Value Over Team between 8.0 and −8.0 in each of the ten remaining seasons of his career. Glenn was once a loud and controversial figure when catching Drew Bledsoe passes under the tutelage of Bill Parcells in New England, but he developed into a quietly productive and surprisingly team-oriented player while catching Drew Bledsoe passes under the tutelage of Bill Parcells in Dallas.

In between came fights with Bill Belichick and Glenn's lost 2002 season in Green Bay. The latter was like that year Reggie Jackson spent in Baltimore; unless you see a picture of him in that uniform, you forget it ever happened.

Glenn's best and worst seasons in Value Over Team give an example of how much more we learn about a receiver by considering incomplete passes. Looking at the traditional stats, his 2000 doesn't look much worse than his 1999. Glenn had fewer yards in the former, but also more catches and touchdowns. Of course, he had more catches because he had more passes. Lots and lots more passes. This wasn't a issue with a new offensive coordinator sending Glenn on more low-percentage deep routes. Glenn's yards per catch dropped by more than four yards per reception that year.

Glenn is the rare player who seems to be getting less injury-prone as he gets older. He's played 16 games in three of his four Dallas seasons, but he only played a full 16-game season once before that.

Eric Moulds

Bills: Round 1, Pick 24 (Mississippi State)

		DPAR	DVOA	Pass	Yds	TD	C%	Value
Career		125.0	−0.1%	1282	9676	50	57%	5.6
Best	1998	40.7	38.8%	116	1368	9	58%	25.9
Worst	2002	8.5	−8.5%	179	1283	10	55%	−21.0

You can try to filter out the quality of the quarterback by comparing the receiver to the other receivers on his team, but you are never going to filter out the mind meld Moulds had with Doug Flutie. In the three seasons he spent catching passes from Flutie, 1998 to 2000, Moulds totaled 87.7 DPAR and 45.2 Value Over Team. In his other eight seasons combined, Moulds has 38.3 DPAR and −39.6 Value Over Team. After Flutie left Buffalo, Moulds ranked 54th or lower in DVOA for five straight seasons, finally having another above-average year for Houston in 2006.

Moulds's entire reputation is built off those three seasons with Flutie, and he simply hasn't been very good otherwise. Sure, he finished fourth in receptions and touchdowns in 2002, but that's because Drew Bledsoe threw him the ball 179 times. Moulds's 2002 season actually has the lowest Value Over Team of any season by any player from this class. Moulds had a DVOA of −8.5% that year. The next lowest DVOA by a wide receiver or tight end for the 2002 Bills was 5.6% by Dave Moore, whose primary responsibility was to long snap.

Jermaine Lewis

Ravens: Round 5, Pick 153 (Maryland)

		DPAR	DVOA	Pass	Yds	TD	C%	Value
Career		30.1	2.8%	269	2135	17	53%	18.9
Best	1997	16.9	21.7%	70	648	6	60%	14.7
Worst	1999	−6.1	−31.0%	58	281	2	43%	−4.5

Now here's the guy that nobody expected to see, the one major receiver from the Class of '96 who wasn't still in the league ten years later. Most people now remember Lewis as the kick returner for the Super Bowl champion Ravens, but for his first couple years, it looked like he would be the second-day steal of the 1996 receiver class.

As a rookie, Lewis played primarily on special teams. The Ravens began to use him more on offense in his second year, and he gained 648 yards and six touchdowns as a slot receiver. Then, in 1998, he moved into the starting lineup and led the Ravens with 787 yards and six touchdowns. Had Football Outsiders been around at the time, we would have raved about Lewis, who had a DVOA of 21.7% in 1997 for a Ravens team that was 20th in passing offense, and a DVOA of 7.0% in 1998 for a Ravens team that was 24th in passing offense.

Lewis remained a dangerous return man until he retired, but his flameout as a receiver was quite remarkable.

In 1999, he just plain forgot how to catch the ball. Brian Billick pulled him from the starting lineup by Week 7, and his DVOA of −31.0% ranked 79th out of 82 receivers for the year. Lewis had 35 passes in Baltimore's Super Bowl season and just five the year after. He spent a year in Houston and one in Jacksonville, but by then, he was nothing more than a short-term hired gun for the return game.

Bobby Engram
Bears: Round 2, Pick 52 (Penn State)

		DPAR	DVOA	Pass	Yds	TD	C%	Value
Career		100.1	4.6%	805	6055	29	63%	29.2
Best	1998	19.5	10.9%	114	987	5	56%	15.2
Worst	1997	−3.1	−20.9%	75	399	2	60%	−7.7

In 1994, Engram won the first-ever Biletnikoff Award as the best receiver in college football. (Glenn, incidentally, won the next year.) He alternated good and bad years in Chicago and was primarily known for kick and punt returns until he tore his ACL early in the 2000 season. The Bears cut him before the 2001 season, and he signed a one-year make-good contract with Seattle and has made good on it for six years now as the man we call "The First Down Machine." Unlike most of his classmates, Engram hasn't had a complex or controversial career. He's quiet, he's consistent, and he's one of our favorite players. He's also clearly not cut out to be a starter. Engram's only negative Value Over Team since joining the Seahawks was in their Super Bowl season, when injuries forced him into the starting lineup for large stretches of time.

Muhsin Muhammad
Panthers: Round 2, Pick 43 (Michigan State)

		DPAR	DVOA	Pass	Yds	TD	C%	Value
Career		132.3	0.9%	1245	9419	55	57%	33.5
Best	2004	41.5	23.8%	160	1407	16	58%	34.4
Worst	1997	−4.4	−25.9%	62	417	0	44%	−11.6

Muhammad's Value Over Team alternated between negative and positive every year from 1997 to 2004. The pattern would have continued through 2006, but he eked out a Value of 1.0 during his first year in Chicago in 2005. Look at traditional statistics, and Muhammad's 2004 career year sticks out like a sore thumb. Look at *these* numbers, and that year sticks out like a sore thumb that's been nailed to a two-by-four. With Steve Smith injured, Muhammad somehow lifted his game into the stratosphere. That year, Smith had a positive DVOA on nine passes before breaking his leg, and tight end Mike Seidman had a positive DVOA on 13 passes. Every other wide receiver and tight end on the 2004 Panthers was below average.

Keyshawn Johnson
Jets: Round 1, Pick 1 (USC)

		DPAR	DVOA	Pass	Yds	TD	C%	Value
Career		185.9	5.1%	1449	10604	64	56%	48.2
Best	1999	27.5	12.2%	147	1170	8	61%	24.8
Other	1998	26.9	12.1%	149	1131	10	56%	−1.7
Worst	2005	10.9	−0.9%	123	839	6	58%	−15.4

Why "Other"? To show how Keyshawn's 1998 and 1999 seasons are virtually identical in all respects, except for Value Over Team. The other difference is Catch Rate, but that difference is entirely based on his performance on first downs and represents very little yardage. In 1998, Johnson caught 52 percent of passes on first down, but gained 6.5 yards per pass. In 1999, he caught 60 percent of passes on first down, but only gained 6.1 yards per pass, so the higher Catch Rate did not lead to more production.

The difference in Value Over Team demonstrates the difficulty of separating a receiver's performance from the context of the team surrounding him. In 1998, Wayne Chrebet was fabulous and Dedric Ward was average. In 1999, Chrebet was average and Ward was awful. Did Chrebet and Ward decline in 1999, or was the difference having Vinny Testaverde at quarterback in 1998 and Ray Lucas and Rick Mirer at quarterback in 1999? If the latter, how was Johnson able to stay consistent both years despite the drop-off in play at the quarterback position?

Not every first-overall pick is going to end up as the best player in his class, and Johnson enjoyed a pretty good career before he retired this past offseason. The acrimonious split with Tampa Bay in 2003 came in the middle of what otherwise would have been his best season. In the final rankings for 2003, Johnson was sixth among receivers in DVOA (48.4%) and eighth in DPAR (23.5) even though he missed six games. He also earned 18.6 Value Over Team, but clearly Keyshawn valued himself over the team by a lot more than that. Our stats can't measure the negative value of annoying your coach so much that he sends you home.

Amani Toomer
Giants: Round 2, Pick 34 (Michigan)

		DPAR	DVOA	Pass	Yds	TD	C%	Value
Career		149.5	7.4%	1054	8146	47	53%	81.7
Best	2000	44.5	45.5%	124	1094	7	63%	37.3
Worst	1996	−4.4	−80.7%	10	12	0	10%	−4.7

After two seasons, if you wanted to look for draft busts from this class, you headed straight for New York.

The problem wasn't Keyshawn Johnson, but the Jets' first pick in the second round, Alex Van Dyke. Van Dyke had the lowest DVOA (−51.1%) and DPAR (−10.3) of any receiver with at least 25 passes in 1996, but you didn't need advanced stats to see that he was awful. He caught 17 passes for 118 yards, an average of 6.9 yards per catch. That's the lowest average in modern NFL history for a receiver with more than a dozen receptions. Van Dyke had just three catches in 1997 and none in 1998.

The other New York team took a receiver three picks later, and, early on, he looked just as bad. The Giants threw ten passes to rookie Amani Toomer in 1996 and he managed to catch one of them before blowing out his knee at midseason. In 1997, he caught 16 of 37 passes, and Neil Best of *Newsday* wrote in December that "coaches and some teammates privately shake their heads over the mistakes Toomer makes running routes or dropping balls and wonder whether he ever will develop into an elite receiver."

By 1998, Toomer's Catch Rate was over 50 percent, and he had five touchdowns. He seemed to be coming around, but "seems to be coming around" is not what a team wants from a 34th overall pick with three years of experience.

Then, without warning, Toomer exploded on the league in 1999. All of a sudden he was in the starting lineup, catching 79 passes and gaining more yardage than anyone from his draft class except for Marvin Harrison. The next year, he ranked third in the NFL in both receiving DPAR and receiving DVOA and was the leading offensive weapon on a team that won the NFC Championship. Two years later, he had another big year, ranking second among receivers with 40.0 DPAR and third with a 31.4% DVOA.

If someone had told you in 1998 that Amani Toomer would still be starting in the NFL eight years later, while Jermaine Lewis would catch just ten passes after 2000, you would have laughed at them. If they told you that Lewis and Toomer would meet in the Super Bowl just two years later, you would have laughed a little more and then asked when Lewis was getting traded out of Baltimore. Giants fans should feel free to mention this to anyone who asks about Sinorice Moss.

Marvin Harrison

Colts: Round 1, Pick 19 (Syracuse)

		DPAR	DVOA	Pass	Yds	TD	C%	Value
Career		347.8	17.4%	1651	13694	124	62%	101.0
Best	2001	51.4	31.2%	164	1524	17	66%	39.6
Worst	2004	28.6	14.6%	139	1113	15	62%	−15.4

Harrison dominated the league at his peak thanks to a partnership with one of the greatest quarterbacks who ever played. He ranked in the top ten in receiving DPAR for five straight seasons, from 1999 to 2003, and led the league in both 2001 and 2002. His 2001 season has the highest receiving DPAR ever, or at least until we get our hands on play-by-play from Jerry Rice's 1,848-yard season in 1995. It also has the highest Value Over Team of any season in this article. His 2002 season has a Value Over Team of 33.9.

Most years, however, Marvin Harrison has been only slightly better than the Indianapolis passing game as a whole. This was true even before Reggie Wayne entered the picture. In 2000, Harrison had 1,413 yards, 14 touchdowns, and a 18.7% DVOA. That DVOA ranked fourth out of the top five most active receivers on the team. Terrence Wilkins had a DVOA of 26.1%, and Jerome Pathon had a DVOA of 15.2%. Tight end Ken Dilger was at 32.6%, and backup Marcus Pollard had an insane DVOA of 85.0% on 42 passes. (How insane? The second-highest tight end DVOA of the past decade, minimum 25 passes, was 62.2% by Tony McGee in 1998.)

What about life before Manning? In 1997, when the Colts used three different quarterbacks (Jim Harbaugh, Paul Justin, and Kelly Holcomb), Harrison had a DVOA of 12.0%. The combined DVOA of the Colts' other wide receivers and tight ends that year was 7.8%, almost the same.

The idea that there was something wrong with Harrison's 2004 season seems ridiculous, but look closer. That season was the most offense-friendly year in NFL history. Harrison's quarterback was having a season which we rated two years ago as the second-best since 1960, even after correcting for league-wide offensive levels. Yet Harrison had his lowest Catch Rate since 2000 and his lowest yardage total since 1998. Brandon Stokley and Reggie Wayne finished first and second in the league in receiving DVOA. Harrison finished 32nd, and had the lowest receiving DVOA of any Indianapolis player with at least three passes, including the tight ends and running backs.

That's not to say that Harrison isn't one of the greatest receivers who ever played the game. It's just ironic that the one year he was completely surrounded by greatness, he was merely good.

Joe Horn

Chiefs: Round 5, Pick 135 (Itawamba Community College)

		DPAR	DVOA	Pass	Yds	TD	C%	Value
Career		197.4	16.5%	1002	8497	58	58%	121.0
Best	2004	41.6	25.8%	153	1399	11	61%	36.3
Worst	2005	−0.5	−15.7%	103	656	1	48%	−12.3

Horn played special teams for two years in Kansas City. He got a little playing time at receiver in 1998, and a lot more in 1999. That last year he was far superior to teammates such as Andre Rison and Derrick Alexander, with 586 yards, six touchdowns, and a DVOA of 35.1%, third in the league for players with over 50 passes.

When the legendary Joel Buchsbaum ranked the top 101 free agents of the 2000 offseason in *Pro Football Weekly,* he included receivers such as Az Hakim, James McKnight, and Donald Hayes. Horn was not on the list. Conventional wisdom said that Horn was a small-time receiver with a big-time ego. The Saints signed him anyway, and stuck him in the starting lineup in place of the departed Eddie Kennison.

Horn talked the talk, but he also walked the walk. Beginning with his final year in Kansas City, he had Value Over Team of at least 12.0 for six straight years. He did this with a constantly revolving cast of receiving partners and an inconsistent young quarterback. Who would you rather have throwing you passes: Peyton Manning or Aaron Brooks?

In 2002, Horn finished fifth overall in receiving DPAR. The other Saints starter, ironically, was Marvin Harrison's old teammate, Jerome Pathon. Pathon ranked 64th. Peyton Manning made Jerome Pathon play like Marvin Harrison. Aaron Brooks made Jerome Pathon play like Jerome Pathon.

Horn's problem is that he got a later start than the other receivers from this draft class. He got a later start in the NFL because he sat on the bench for two years, but he also got a later start playing football in general. Horn didn't come straight from community college. He actually played for the CFL's Memphis Mad Dogs in 1995, during the Canadian Football League's short-lived American experiment, and that's what brought him to the NFL's attention.

By the time he was drafted, Horn was already 24 years old. He's the oldest member of the Class of '96: six months older than Johnson, seven months older than Harrison, and at least a year older than everyone else. Thus it's no surprise that he felt the effects of age first. Horn has been dealing with nagging injuries for two seasons, and there's no reason to believe he'll be fully healthy for the Falcons in 2007.

That's too bad, because if there was ever a team to test the idea that Joe Horn will put up big numbers no matter who throws the ball or stands in the other receiver positions, it's the Atlanta Falcons.

Terrell Owens

49ers: Round 3, Pick 89 (Tennessee-Chattanooga)

		DPAR	DVOA	Pass	Yds	TD	C%	Value
Career		277.1	16.5%	1335	11716	117	60%	147.1
Best	2001	36.8	19.0%	154	1412	18	60%	35.2
Worst	2006	27.3	12.1%	152	1180	13	56%	−4.5

You think Marvin Harrison is hurt by this system because he's being compared to Reggie Wayne? Terrell Owens spent four of his first five years playing alongside the greatest receiver in NFL history. From 1998 through 2000, Owens had much better numbers than Jerry Rice every year. Owens finished third, 39th, and sixth in receiving DPAR in those three seasons. Rice finished 27th, 60th, and 45th. In 1999, when the 49ers went 4–12 in Jeff Garcia's first NFL season, Owens was the only wide receiver or tight end on the team with a positive DVOA. We're not comparing Owens to Rice at his peak, of course, but Rice wasn't a doddering old man either. In 2001, at the age of 39, Rice signed with Oakland as a free agent and ranked second in the NFL in DPAR.

Terrell Owens has never had a negative DVOA. Even Harrison had a negative DVOA once, in Peyton Manning's rookie season. Owens has ranked in the top ten for DPAR seven times, Harrison only six.

Owens is the only player from the Class of '96 whose worst year was last year, at least when it comes to Value Over Team. The other starting wideout in Dallas, classmate Terry Glenn, also had a good year, Jason Witten was even better, and slot receiver Patrick Crayton caught 75 percent of his passes. Given those performances from his teammates, and the fact that he played much of the season with a broken hand, Owens's Value Over Team of −4.5 is not so bad.

When you consider his quarterbacks and teammates, Terrell Owens has been the best receiver from the Class of '96—on the field. Still, there's more to football than just performance on the field. Marvin Harrison, unlike Terrell Owens and Joe Horn, has never caused a problem in the clubhouse. Marvin Harrison, unlike Terrell Owens and Joe Horn, hasn't felt the effects of age with nagging injuries over the past couple of seasons.

Harrison is the number one receiver of the Class of '96 by nearly every measure. He leads the class in both traditional and advanced individual stats, in team wins, in durability, and in being a nice guy who doesn't cause trouble. He's not number one in Value Over Team right now, but if he keeps going when his classmates start to slow down, he'll end up number one in that statistic too.

Addendum: Wide receiver rankings for 1996, according to the Palmer-Hughes Draft Guide:

1. Keyshawn Johnson
2. Eric Moulds
3. Marvin Harrison
4. Bobby Engram
5. Amani Toomer
6. Dietrich Jells, Pittsburgh
7. Patrick Jeffers, Virginia
8. Kevin Jordan, UCLA
9. Gregory Spann, Jackson State
10. Toderick Malone, Alabama
13. Jermaine Lewis
15. Terrell Owens
26. Muhsin Muhammad

Kennison and Glenn were not included because they were juniors who came out early; Horn was unlisted.

Class of '96 Trivia

- Carolina and Indianapolis have the most total seasons from Class of '96 receivers. The Panthers have employed Muhsin Muhammad, Patrick Jeffers, Iheanyi Uwaezuoke, and Keyshawn Johnson; the Colts have 11 years of Marvin Harrison and two of Chris Doering.

- Five franchises have never employed a member of the Class of '96: Arizona, Cleveland, Minnesota, Oakland, and Tennessee. Atlanta has just half a year of Bryan Still, but Horn should change that in 2007 if he's healthy enough to stay on the field.

- Seven receivers drafted in 1996 never played in the NFL, led by Tampa Bay sixth-rounder Nilo Silvan,

Quarterbacks: Career Progression

David Lewin

Understanding how players change as they age and accumulate experience is crucial to evaluating them. There are certain points in a player's career at which he is most likely to break out or drop off. Looking at the general career progression of recent quarterbacks suggests several likely breakout players for the 2007 season.

When creating the college quarterback projection system a year ago, I faced a number of obstacles. One of the biggest was that I was dealing with quarterbacks who were at many different stages in their careers. Some, such as Alex Smith, were just starting out their careers, while others, such as Jake Plummer, were winding down. In order to accurately compare the NFL success of these players it was necessary to first put them on a level playing field.

To create a better measure of overall NFL performance, I decided to adjust my DPAR per game metric by controlling for the year of player's career in which a given performance occurred. Year one was treated differently from year two, which was treated differently from year three, and so on. Players were rated not on how well they performed, but based on how well they performed relative to the expected performance of someone with their number of years of NFL experience.

Below I detail what I found out about the effects of age and years spent in the NFL on quarterback passing performance. In the future I hope to study the effect of actual game experience, but to date this has proven infeasible. I also hope to add scrambling value to this study at a later date. The values in all tables in the study come from a sample of 333 quarterback-seasons by the 72 quarterbacks who were drafted after 1990 and played significantly in multiple seasons during the period 1997 to 2006.

Years in NFL

If we look at the development of quarterbacks as they gain more NFL experience, the results are pretty much as expected (table 1). Quarterbacks make a significant jump from year one to year two, then gradually increase toward their prime in year eight, then begin to decline. The value for year nine is based on only 19 quarterback-seasons, so it is unclear exactly how much of a drop-off occurs at that point.

This progression is not as smooth as one might expect, with declines in performance in years four and seven, but this is likely simply random variation. The only two year-to-year changes that are statistically significant are the change from year one to year two and the change from year four to year five. There is no statistically significant difference between years two, three and four. There is also no statistically significant difference between years five, six, seven, eight, and nine.

This tells us that the average quarterback's career has four stages. Stage one is a player's first year in the NFL. Everyone struggles in his rookie year—even Peyton Manning, who ranked 18th in DPAR for 1998, right below Charlie Batch and just ahead of Eric Kramer and Billy Joe Tolliver. Luckily stage two, years two through four, comes soon. Performance rises to a plateau of about 2.0 DPAR per game better than rookie level, but still about 1.5 below peak level.

Stage three is a player's prime, starting in year five. This is the year many players make the leap to stardom. Examples include Marc Bulger, Matt Hasselbeck, and Tom Brady. This plateau lasts through year eight, typically the best year of a player's career.

Stage four is the gradual decline beginning in year nine. DPAR does not yet date far enough back to describe this phase with any real specificity, but a decline clearly occurs. Hopefully over the next couple of years more data will clarify this progression further, but the available data provide a good indication of its general shape.

Table 1. Average Improvement in Passing DPAR per Game

From	To	Single Year	Cumulative
Year 1	Year 2	1.99	1.99
Year 2	Year 3	0.06	2.05
Year 3	Year 4	−0.25	1.80
Year 4	Year 5	1.26	3.06
Year 5	Year 6	0.30	3.36
Year 6	Year 7	−0.14	3.22
Year 7	Year 8	0.37	3.60
Year 8	Year 9	−1.24	2.35

Effects of Age

It is very difficult to separate the effects of experience from age, since most players enter the league at either age 22 or 23. Average improvement based on age does not look much different from average improvement based on experience (table 2). There is clearly a lot of noise (i.e. random variation) in the data based on age, and the only statistically significant differences seem to be from age 21 to 22, and from age 24 to 25. (Given the boundaries of the sample, there is not enough data on quarterbacks between age 30 and 31 to classify the large drop in the numbers as statistically significant.) These differences echo the improvements we saw in years two and five above.

Table 2. Average Improvement in Passing DPAR per Game

From	To	Single Year	Cumulative
Age 21	Age 22	3.75	3.75
Age 22	Age 23	0.90	4.65
Age 23	Age 24	−0.16	4.49
Age 24	Age 25	1.28	5.78
Age 25	Age 26	−0.03	5.75
Age 26	Age 27	0.92	6.66
Age 27	Age 28	−0.60	6.07
Age 28	Age 29	0.76	6.82
Age 29	Age 30	−0.36	6.46
Age 30	Age 31	−2.57	3.89

Combining Age and Experience

Although it might not be possible to entirely separate the effects of age and experience, it is useful to know the overall effect. Table 3 separates out those who entered the league at age 22 and at age 23. These values show more noise than the overall values because of the smaller sample size, but they are more accurate for the included players. These are the two most common ages for quarterbacks entering the league, and the only two for which there is sufficient data to create a specific progression.

As you can see, those who enter at age 23 experience a much smaller year one-to-year two jump than those who enter at age 22. Also, those who begin their careers at age 23 on average achieve a peak value only 3.0 DPAR per game above their rookie year performance, while those who begin their careers at age 22 achieve a peak value more than 4.0 DPAR per game better than their rookie year performance. It is reasonable to conclude from this that players entering the league at a younger age have more potential, but this does not mean that drafting younger quarterbacks is necessarily wiser. A younger quarterback might improve more from his rookie year, but if his rookie year

was really bad (such as, say, Alex Smith's) then even a significant improvement may not get them up to the desired performance level.

Generalized Model

Table 4 shows the results of a model that includes both NFL experience and age as variables. Including both in the model isolates the effect of one when the other is constant, but that can be tricky because, in reality, a player's age increases with each subsequent year in the league. The data suggest that after age 22 players enter a physical decline. This decline is more than offset by increasing NFL experience through year seven or eight, ages 28 to 30, but after this point the effect of age outweighs the value of increased experience, and performance declines.

Using one or more of the included tables, we can predict future player performance. Let's take Donovan McNabb for instance. In 2006, his eighth year in the league, McNabb was 29 years old and posted a DPAR of 57 in ten games. Because he is entering his ninth year in the league we can expect his DPAR per game to increase by .68. McNabb is also turning 30, which means his DPAR per game should decrease by 1.40. This sums to a total decrease in DPAR per game of .72. This is relatively close to the expected decrease of .52 suggested by table 3 (McNabb entered the league at age 22), the expected decrease of .36 suggested by table 2, and the expected decrease of 1.24 suggested by table 1. Based on these numbers, it is likely that McNabb's DPAR per game in 2007 will fall somewhere between 4.5 and 5.5.

Table 3. Average Change in Passing DPAR/G; Entered the League at Age 22 or 23

From		To		Single Year	Cumulative
Age 22					
Year 1	Age 22	Year 2	Age 23	2.31	2.31
Year 2	Age 23	Year 3	Age 24	−1.09	1.21
Year 3	Age 24	Year 4	Age 25	1.00	2.21
Year 4	Age 25	Year 5	Age 26	0.83	3.04
Year 5	Age 26	Year 6	Age 27	1.29	4.33
Year 6	Age 27	Year 7	Age 28	−0.70	3.63
Year 7	Age 28	Year 8	Age 29	0.75	4.38
Year 8	Age 29	Year 9	Age 30	−0.52	3.86
Age 23					
Year 1	Age 23	Year 2	Age 24	1.12	1.12
Year 2	Age 24	Year 3	Age 25	1.43	2.56
Year 3	Age 25	Year 4	Age 26	−0.93	1.62
Year 4	Age 26	Year 5	Age 27	1.35	2.97
Year 5	Age 27	Year 6	Age 28	−1.16	1.82
Year 6	Age 28	Year 7	Age 29	1.21	3.02
Year 7	Age 29	Year 8	Age 30	−0.22	2.80

Table 4. Expected Year to Year DPAR/G Changes

From	To	Change	Cumulative
Holding Age Constant			
Year 1	Year 2	3.61	3.61
Year 2	Year 3	1.28	4.89
Year 3	Year 4	0.81	5.70
Year 4	Year 5	2.64	8.35
Year 5	Year 6	1.87	10.22
Year 6	Year 7	1.53	11.75
Year 7	Year 8	1.56	13.31
Year 8	Year 9	0.68	13.99
Holding Experience Constant			
Age 22	Age 23	−1.76	−1.76
Age 23	Age 24	−2.21	−3.97
Age 24	Age 25	−0.07	−4.05
Age 25	Age 26	−1.69	−5.73
Age 26	Age 27	−1.22	−6.95
Age 27	Age 28	−2.30	−9.25
Age 28	Age 29	−0.74	−9.99
Age 29	Age 30	−1.40	−11.39

The biggest problem with this generalized model is that because of the colinearity between NFL experience and age, the coefficients are very rough estimates. Tables 1–3 are fairly accurate and the values in them are often statistically significant. Table 4, on other hand, is included mostly for entertainment purposes. Because of the intense colinearity, no values in either case are statistically significant. Players who entered the league at abnormal ages carry a great deal of weight because there are so few observations available to differentiate the effects of age from those of experience.

My current data set features the rookie seasons of only three players who entered the league at an age younger than 22: Drew Bledsoe, Brett Favre, and Michael Vick. Chris Weinke is the only player in the data who was drafted at an age older than 24. These four players proved to be excessively influential in determining how to distribute the credit between age and experience, which is what makes this particular table somewhat unreliable. Undrafted players, such as Kurt Warner, were also excluded from my data set, as their career progressions are too irregular and would only create noise in the results.

Breakout Players for 2007

The point of all these tables is to predict which players are likely to have breakout seasons in 2007. The most likely candidates are the second-year players: Matt Leinart, Jay Cutler, and Vince Young. Any way you slice it, quarterbacks generally make a huge jump from their first year to their second year. (These players are discussed further in the essay "Projecting Rookie Quarterbacks, Revisited").

The more interesting—and less obvious—likely breakout players are the quarterbacks from the class of 2003: Carson Palmer, Bryon Leftwich, Kyle Boller, Rex Grossman, and Chris Simms. Palmer, Leftwich, Grossman, and Simms are entering their fifth year at age 27. Boller is entering his fifth year at age 26. Table 1 shows that quarterbacks in their fifth year generally take a large step forward, more than one point of DPAR per game on average. This is especially true for quarterbacks at age 27.

For Carson Palmer, this means that he has a good shot at reaching the 8.0 DPAR per game level previously attained only three times over a full 16-game season (by Peyton Manning in 2004 and 2006, and by Daunte Culpepper in 2004). For Leftwich and Grossman, this means that it is now or never to get their erratic careers on track. Leftwich is a good bet to realize the Pro Bowl potential he flashed in 2004 and 2005, as long as Jack Del Rio doesn't screw with him too much. Grossman is not nearly as good as Leftwich, but he is likely to show enough improvement to be considered at least a mediocre starter. If you flip to the player comments section of the book, you'll notice that our KUBIAK fantasy football projection system makes a similar forecast for both players.

Boller and Simms are somewhat less likely to break out, in large part because neither one is guaranteed to see the field in 2007. If Simms can beat out Jeff Garcia for the Tampa Bay starting job, his improvement should pick up where it left off back at the end of the 2005 season. Boller still has a chance to be a decent player. He showed improvement down the stretch in 2005 and was pretty solid in limited action in 2006. If Steve McNair goes down this year, Boller will surprise people by not being terrible.

The player for whom this research might be most relevant is Dolphins second-round pick John Beck. He will be 26 years old by the start of the 2007 season and is older than Ben Roethlisberger and Philip Rivers, among others. He is only three months younger than the four-year veteran Boller. This does not mean that Beck cannot be successful, but it does mean that he needs to do it soon. If Beck is not a good passer by his second year, it is not going to happen. JaMarcus Russell and Brady Quinn will both be 22 at the start of the 2007 season. Kevin Kolb and Drew Stanton will be 23. These are the most common ages for quarterbacks to enter the league. It is very likely that Beck will follow a much different career development path than his fellow rookie quarterbacks.

Conclusions

This study constitutes a starting point for understanding the effects of age and experience on passing performance by NFL quarterbacks. The largest problem with this study is a lack of data. My data set is quite large, but because of the significant inherent colinearity issues with age and experience and the high amount of variability in quarterback performance, an even greater amount of data is needed to reach statistically significant conclusions. One possible way to solve this issue would be to incorporate more data by using the statistically approximated DPAR values introduced in *PFP 2005*'s article on the best quarterback seasons of all time.

There were a couple of reasons why I chose not to do this. One is that I have found that older quarterbacks generally have a higher actual DPAR than their statistical approximation based solely on conventional statistics, while younger players show the opposite trend. This could very well be the impact of experience, which is one of the variables I'm attempting to test for, but without actual DPAR figures I lose the variability in the data that could reveal that impact. I am working on ways to get around this, and I hope that next year I may be able to look at a somewhat larger sample of players to get a more reliable, precise estimate of age and experience effects. I am also somewhat wary of going back too far with this study, because, as training techniques, rules, and equipment change, the typical career arc should be expected to

change as well. By limiting the data to the DPAR era (1996 to present) I avoid these complications.

Another minor confounding factor is the need for a cutoff for player age, which in this case is September 1 (not the *PFP* standard of January 1). Using a hard cutoff date is a bit unfair, as, for instance, Quinn is ten months older than Russell, but is classified as being the same age, while Kolb is only two months older than Quinn but gets classified as a year older because of where their birthdays fall relative to the cutoff. This problem would occur no matter which date was chosen for the cutoff, but, for the purposes of this study, it was easier to just draw the line somewhere than to make the variable continuous and deal with fractional years.

Hopefully we can now better understand what to expect from players as they age. Next year, with another season of data available, it should be possible to start mapping the decline part of a quarterback's career. Similar research for running backs, done in the Atlanta chapter of last year's book, accurately forecasted the decline of Warrick Dunn and Edgerrin James. This research suggests that the best candidates for breakout years are second and fifth year quarterbacks, which should come as good news to several teams, in particular Arizona, Denver, Jacksonville, and Chicago.

A Year in the Life of the Competition Committee

Doug Farrar

> Pass the rule, whatever you want, but make sure you know how you're going to officiate it and make sure the officials do it. The more objectivity you give to the officials, the more problems you're going to have.
>
> — BILL PARCELLS

The Competition Committee was founded in 1970 as part of the NFL-AFL merger, and as a more focused offshoot of the old Rules Committee. It has been chaired by some of the brightest minds the game has ever seen. From former Cowboys president and general manager Tex Schramm to ex-Saints GM Jim Finks to the current co-chairs, Titans coach Jeff Fisher and Falcons president Rich McKay, those who serve on this Committee have been charged with administering the future of the game within the game—from overtime to officiating to player safety to the scope of the rulebook itself.

Specifically, the Competition Committee is responsible for the rules alterations which affect the game on the field, and endeavors to keep new developments in check with the best interests of the game's future. If they see uncalled hand-checks on receivers by intrepid defensive backs, they'll implement a more stringent version of the illegal contact rule. When they felt that more accurate rulings on the field were required prior to the 1986 season, the Committee implemented instant replay. When the replay system proved to be ineffective and bogged down by embryonic technology, the Committee abolished it just five years after its invention. However, once the technology caught up with the concept in the late 1990s and the perception shifted once again to the belief that replay could help the game (influenced in no small part by back judge Phil Luckett's infamous inability to tell the difference between Vinny Testaverde's helmet and a football), the Committee reinstated it. If there's a questionable call in a major game, or a series of calls in minor games, which alters the playing field to an unacceptable degree, it is the Competition Committee that is responsible for making sure that doesn't happen again.

Two of the Committee's more notable reactions to on-field incidents in recent memory were the modifications to the illegal contact rule for 2004 after the 2003 AFC Championship game between the Patriots and Colts, and the creation for 2005 of The Horse-Collar Tackle Rule, Version 1.0. The latter was called the "Roy Williams Rule" in response to the Dallas safety, who had injured several players, most notably then-Philadelphia receiver Terrell Owens, by grabbing them by the back of their jersey collar and shoulder pads and dragging them down from behind.

What was interesting in those cases was how these two rule changes each had a different degree of impact upon the play on the field. The illegal contact rules not only caused an explosion in passing offense—2004 saw 5,169 more passing yards, 78 more touchdowns, and 14 fewer interceptions—but forever blurred the line between contact and defensive pass interference in the minds of many officials. The rule had a dramatic effect right away.

The horse-collar rule, on the other hand, took much longer to make its impact felt on the field of play, as the results from its first year of implementation revealed the need for some refinement in the rule. In 2005, the penalty was only called once, on Green Bay tight end David Martin after he tackled Carolina cornerback Ken Lucas during an interception return. The Competition Committee next conferred at the 2006 Owner's Meetings. According to co-chairman Rich McKay, who spoke extensively about the proposed points of emphasis in a media conference call, the rule's scope wasn't appropriate. "We also are going to propose and talk about the broadening of the horse-collar tackle rule to include the inside of the jersey beyond just the shoulder pad. [There were] only a few calls this year and a few fines, and yet, when we watched the tape, we were not comfortable with a number of plays that were made and the number of tackles and the effectiveness of those tackles, and [we] seek to potentially broaden that rule."

"I don't know that it went uncalled, because the way we wrote the language last year was so narrow that you really had to see the hand inside the shoulder pad and inside the collar of the shoulder pad, and we knew that was going to be difficult. We saw a lot more tackles done this way, both in college football and in pro football, and it concerned us. So all we're proposing for discussion and trying to see if we can get past is the jersey now be included in the description, not just the shoulder pad. And we'll see, and I know that we'll hear from some of the defensive coaches with respect to that expansion. But it was very concerning. When you watch the tape and you watch the manner in which these players are tackled when they're tackled from behind up near the shoulder pad or the jersey and pulled immediately to the ground, it was not a good-looking sight. It looks like it's the potential for a lot of injuries, so that's why we're suggesting it."

It was a nice thought, but, early on, the infraction itself was the only thing that "broadened." In a Week 2 contest between the Seahawks and Cardinals, two Arizona defenders—cornerback Antrel Rolle and defensive tackle Darnell Dockett—dragged Seattle running back Shaun Alexander down by the back of his jersey on two separate plays. On both occasions, the violations were obvious and occurred outside the tackle box, but the officials in place to throw the flags, side judge Carl Cheffers and umpire Undrey Walsh, did not do so. Both Rolle and Dockett were fined by the league after the plays were reviewed. Eventually, the new focus took hold, and 14 horse-collars were flagged during the 2006 season.

The expansion of the horse-collar rule was but one reform discussed during the 2006 Owner's Meetings. Here are four others, along with a look at how they affected the way the game was played in the 2006 season.

Player Safety

Action: On October 11, 2005, the Steelers and San Diego Chargers faced off in an eventual 24–22 Pittsburgh victory. In the fourth quarter of that game, Chargers defensive tackle Luis Castillo tackled Pittsburgh quarterback Ben Roethlisberger low. Roethlisberger's left knee bent back awkwardly after being hit by Castillo's helmet. Fortunately, Roethlisberger suffered only a hyperextension and a bone bruise, and played two weeks later in a win over the Bengals.

In the 2005 AFC Wild Card Game between the Bengals and Steelers, Pittsburgh defensive tackle Kimo von Oelhoffen rolled into Cincinnati quarterback Carson Palmer's lower leg, tearing the ACL and MCL in Palmer's left knee. Although Palmer's career was thought to be in question, he rebounded to start the Bengals' season opener eight months later. In fact, he started all 16 games in 2006.

Reaction: "We always focus on player safety, but I think this year we've got a number of rules that are all directed at player safety," McKay said. "The first one and the one that

I'm sure will get the most talk will be about the quarterback, low hits on quarterbacks, putting a little more burden in the proposed rule on the defensive player.

"I don't know that the Palmer play was the driving force, but it was certainly a force. We look at a tape that virtually looks at every major injury at every position. We definitely spent a lot of time looking at the quarterback tape and the quarterback injuries. We tried to look at how they occurred, and came to the conclusion that we should at least try because the quarterback position is a defenseless position when his feet are on the ground and he's throwing the football. We have to find ways to try to protect him. In this proposal that we're making, we're going to put a little more onus on the defensive player when the defensive player has an opportunity to avoid, he must take that opportunity to avoid."

Result: It was a year marked by a few ridiculously touchy roughing calls, so you might be surprised to learn that roughing the passer was actually called fewer times in 2006 (100) than in 2005 (122). In Week 12, New York Giants rookie defensive end Matthias Kiwanuka brought the penalty to light on a play in which it wasn't called. Kiwanuka had Tennessee Titans rookie quarterback Vince Young in a bear hug on a fourth-down, game-clinching play, when he simply let go. Young ran for 19 yards and a first down, and the Titans went on to win the game. Kiwanuka later said that he was hyper-conscious of picking up a roughing penalty, because he thought Young had thrown the ball.

In a conference call before the 2007 Owner's Meetings, McKay addressed the roughing-the-passer calls in 2006. "Because of a few unique plays, it was not as consistently called as it should have been," he said. "So, we watched a lot of tape, and we'll make some recommendations with respect to certain interpretations of the rule. We hope to continue to clarify it and make it as consistent as it can be from an officiating standpoint and from a player understanding standpoint."

Officiating Consistency

Action: The league became concerned that some crews are calling far more penalties than others.

Reaction: "That's something that I know is important to [Vice President of Officiating] Mike Pereira and [Director of Officiating Operations] Larry Upson, because what we're trying to do is create consistency," McKay said. "When you get the swings that you get in some of the crews, I think what Mike's focused on is trying to make sure that, during the season, we're paying attention to those trends, and that we're communicating with those crews in understanding what they're seeing and why they're calling it and seeing if

Table 1. Penalties per Game, 2004–2006

Crew Chief	2004	2005	2006	Average
Bernie Kukar	19.5	17.3	—	18.4
Larry Nemmers	18.7	20.6	15.1	18.1
Tom White	18.5	17.7	—	18.1
Ron Winter	19	18.5	15.7	17.7
Ed Hochuli	17.7	19.1	15.3	17.4
Terry McAulay	16.9	18.6	15.9	17.1
Tony Corrente	16.8	15.7	16.1	16.2
Jeff Triplette	15.5	18.1	14.7	16.1
Mike Carey	16.7	17.7	13.5	16.0
Johnny Grier	15.5	—	—	15.5
Bill Carollo	16.7	17.4	12.4	15.5
Walt Coleman	17.1	18.5	10.4	15.3
Gene Steratore	—	—	15.3	15.3
Jerome Boger	—	—	15.3	15.3
Scott Green	16.7	16.6	12.5	15.3
Pete Morelli	16.9	16.8	10.9	14.9
Walt Anderson	15.4	15.3	12.9	14.5
Gerry Austin	14.4	15.3	13.8	14.5
Bill Leavy	15.7	16.4	10.9	14.3
Bill Vinovich	16.1	12.3	13.9	14.1

we're all on the same page. I think we always have to strive to bring those numbers closer. They'll never be the same, and they'll never be within five percent, but we'd certainly like them to be closer than they are."

Result: The most flag-friendly crew called penalties 35 percent more often than the least flag-friendly crew in 2004, 67 percent more often in 2005, and 55 percent more often in 2006 (table 1). Those numbers suggest that we're still far from real consistency, though 2005 seems to have been an anomaly in many ways. The swing from crew to crew on the most frequently-called infractions, such as false starts and offensive holding, can be mind-boggling. In 2006, the variance on holding calls ranged from the 44 called by Walt Anderson's crew, to the 11 by Bill Carollo's bunch. How this can be changed in the future, and how much teams actually "scout" upcoming crews and their tendencies, remain interesting topics of research and debate.

Offensive Holding

Action: Early in the fourth quarter of Super Bowl XL, the Seattle Seahawks, down 14–10, were driving down the field. Matt Hasselbeck threw an 18-yard pass to tight end Jerramy Stevens which would have given the Seahawks 1st-and-goal on the one-yard line. However, a holding call on right tackle Sean Locklear negated the play, forcing Seattle back to the Pittsburgh 29-yard line. Hasselbeck threw an interception three plays later. When explaining the call two weeks later on the NFL Network, Director of Officiating

Mike Pereira said that Locklear's play contained the "ingredients of a hold," implying that the hold was not actually seen, and that the cause of the flag was the fact that Steelers linebacker Clark Haggans had been brought to the ground by Locklear.

Reaction: "We've got a big section in our book that will be on blocking clarifications and dealing with holding, really, and really just rewriting the rule, not changing the way it's officiated, but rewriting the rule so everybody has a clear understanding as we tried to do with defensive pass interference a number of years ago," McKay said. "One of the things we emphasized in there was seeing the entire foul. If you do not see the entire foul, you cannot call holding. That's specifically applied when players go to the ground. Because what often happens is you see a player, a defensive player on the ground, the offensive player is on the ground and you see a flag, foul it. If you don't see the entire action, you cannot assume that it was holding that caused that player to go to the ground."

Asked to clarify that the idea was to simply make sure that the infraction was called correctly, McKay concurred. "Not [the] go-to-the-ground penalty, which is basically a flag that you see a lot of times when two guys end up on the ground, it's offensive holding—what we said is we want the officials to see the entire action, to make sure that they saw the holding and the restriction that caused the player to go to the ground."

McKay, a longtime friend and associate of Seahawks president Tim Ruskell, was then asked if he thought the official responsible saw the whole play before throwing the flag on Locklear. "You know, that's one call," he said. "I'm not going to be the one to—I leave that to Mike Pereira."

Result: Offensive holding calls plummeted in 2006 by an astonishing 33 percent, from 868 in the 2005 regular season (including declined and offsetting penalties) to just 570 last year. Seahawks center Robbie Tobeck led the NFL in 2005 with ten holds, and Cleveland tackle Kevin Shaffer was 2006's top man with only seven. However, sacks did not increase to any significant degree (1,163 in 2005, 1,181 in 2006), which would lead your average observer to assume that holding itself really didn't change that much.

As we have seen, holding is also a prime example of how different crews call specific penalties at markedly different rates.

False Starts

Action: The NFL became concerned that game momentum was affected by too many false start calls, which rose from a total of 795 in 2003, to 818 in 2004, to 846 in 2005. In 2005, nine of the 17 crews called over 50 false starts, with Larry Nemmers's crew topping the list at 73.

Reaction: "With respect to false starts, the penalty is becoming extremely high, penalty meaning in total number of fouls," McKay said. "We're trying to find ways to limit that. One of the things we will propose is allowing eligible receivers to reset so instead of killing the play, the receiver will be given the opportunity to replay and there will be no stoppage. That would not apply if the receiver took a step and had a complete false start, then they'd have to shut the play down. We think this is the way to cut the number of fouls significantly if we deal with that area in false starts."

"When you look at the numbers, I think false starts total were in excess of 800 [in 2005]. We believe a lot of those are the flinches. We became uncomfortable in trying to expand it at this time to the offensive line, although we've talked about potentially this year expanding that to the offensive line in NFL Europe and trying to experiment over there and seeing how it would be officiated and seeing how players would play if we modified the rules. We've looked at the outside receivers and said we've got a number of calls and a number of plays shut down where literally nothing happens other than a slight flinch, a couple-second delay and then the ball is snapped, but we shut the play down because we've told the officials it's a false start. We don't want to predict the number of fouls, but we think it is a big number that we think we can save some time and save some shutdown of the game for a penalty that does not have any effect on the game. We'll see the true numbers, but, as I say, we don't break it down by flinch and then true false start . . ."

McKay's suggestion was that officials allow receivers to reset themselves rather than automatically whistling a play dead if a receiver flinches but the defense doesn't react.

"Now, if the defender immediately reacts, it's on the offense. I mean, it's not a free pass. If you've got, for instance, a slot receiver and the slot receiver literally wiggles his back and nobody reacts and the quarterback snaps the ball, two seconds later, no foul, and the play moves on. So that's all we're trying to talk about. We're trying to inch our way into trying to limit false starts."

Result: Though the number of false starts did decline in 2006—down to a four-year low of 723, which was 85 percent of the 2005 total—the number of false starts called on wide receivers and tight ends was reduced only 11 percent, from 204 to 182. As with holding, the implementation of this call seemed more general than specific. Oakland's Randy Moss led the NFL in false starts by receivers and tight ends with seven in 2005. Dallas tight end Jason Witten led the league last year with the same number. As noted in the St. Louis chapter, false starts don't just affect game momentum. No penalty has a stronger correlation with losing games.

What to Expect in 2007

McKay's 2007 Competition Committee conference call had much less to do with in-game rules and how play might be affected than the 2006 version, with the exception of a continued focus on taunting and post-play celebration. The owners did finally vote to make instant replay permanent after nearly a decade of study, a move which will have all teams installing high-definition equipment for official review. McKay expressed happiness at the fact that average game time was down almost three minutes from 2005, which might mean that the 2006 trend of fewer called penalties will hold in the long term. Instead, the emphasis this season looks to be on the further maintenance of a system which still suffers from a great deal of inconsistency, and making sure that the checks and balances on the field reflect what's been established in the meeting rooms.

Show Me the Money: The Business of the NFL

Maury Brown

The 2006–2007 offseason brought several changes that will impact the NFL for many years to come, not the least of which were the passing of the torch to a new commissioner and the signing of a new labor agreement that enacted changes in revenue sharing and the salary cap. If that weren't enough, the league also did legal battle over the way in which NFL Sunday Ticket and the NFL Network will be made available to television viewers and expanded its efforts to build shiny new stadiums. Peeling back the pigskin, let's take a look at some of the key events that happened outside the hash marks in the lead-up to the 2007 NFL season, the effects of which may linger longer than a helmet-to-helmet hit from Rodney Harrison.

Tagliabue Retires but Not Before Wrapping Up Television Deals and a Labor Agreement

Paul Tagliabue decided to go out on top. In March of 2006, he announced that he would retire as Commissioner of the NFL in July after a 16-year tenure that can be best described as harmonious and prosperous. During his commissionership, the man who had the tall task of following in Pete Rozelle's footsteps had seen the league's gross revenues grow from $1.1 billion in 1990 to $5.8 billion in 2006. When accounting for inflation, the gross revenues for the NFL grew a staggering 256 percent during Tagliabue's reign.

Tagliabue's last orders of business before retirement were to wrap up an expansive television contract that encompassed agreements with four networks (CBS, FOX, NBC, and ESPN), and finalize a new labor agreement with the Players Association.

Collectively, the television deals pull in an impressive total in excess of $3.7 billion annually:

- CBS: $622.5 million per year for the AFC, 2006–2011
- FOX: $712.5 million per year for the NFC, 2006–2011
- NBC: $650 million per year for *Sunday Night Football,* 2006–2012
- ESPN: $1.1 billion per year for *Monday Night Football,* 2006–2014

When adding in the 5-year, $3.5-billion extension reached with DirecTV to show NFL Sunday Ticket and the NFL Network ($400 million annually in 2004 and 2005, increasing to $700 million annually from 2006 to 2010), the total revenues from these various agreements could be as high as $23.91 billion. That means that nearly a quarter of a trillion dollars will have flooded into the NFL's coffers through television deals alone.

The final order of business for Tagliabue was a new Collective Bargaining Agreement, which was reached twelve days before he announced his intent to retire. The most difficult labor agreement to negotiate since the league and player's union agreed to free agency and a salary cap in 1992, this CBA may wind up being less about owners vs. players, and more about high-revenue teams, such as the Redskins and Cowboys, vs. low-revenue teams, such as the Bills and Bengals.

The new CBA brings about a significant shift in how revenues are dispersed between the high- and low-revenue teams. Whereas, in prior labor agreements, centralized revenues from television and ticket sales made up the majority of the revenues paid out to the players, the new deal adds in all team revenues, everything from sponsorships and naming rights to parking, concessions, and merchandising.

With the expansion of revenues pulled in by the players, the salary cap was restructured. In 2006, the cap was increased to $102 million, a jump of $7.5 million from what it had been under the previous agreement. For 2007, the cap will be $109 million. After that, the cap will be determined by revenue. The owners' collective contribution to salary pool starts at just under 60 percent of the league's total revenues. The deal shifts an additional $850 million to $900 million to the players over the life of the contract, as long as the owners do not opt out of it in 2008.

The new deal is structured for revenue sharing, as only the 15 teams that pull in the highest revenues have to contribute to the player pool. The top five teams pay the most, the second five pay less, and the third five pay less still. The

17 teams that pull in the lowest revenues do not contribute to the salary pool at all.

For the better part of two years, Tagliabue had dealt with owners scrapping over how to structure revenue sharing. Even with this agreement, there are matters that remain unresolved, but, by reaching this new agreement, the owners avoided having 2007 as an uncapped year, which it would have been under the prior CBA. That alone will keep the disparity between the higher- and lower-revenue franchises somewhat in check.

The man some simply referred to as "Tags" did not part from the NFL entirely in July of 2006. His voice was an important part of the selection process for his successor, and he will remain as a consultant through 2008. In the end, Tagliabue's tenure marked incredible growth in the NFL. The stability of labor peace, the increased visibility through television, and America's continued addiction to the NFL saw the league grow from 28 to 32 teams during his tenure (adding Carolina, Jacksonville, Cleveland, and Houston). The aforementioned cash glut from television revenues and a total of 17 new stadiums helped add to the bottom line. Tagliabue decided to get out while the getting was good, but, given the health and well-being of the league at the time of his departure, it should have come as no surprise that his successor came from close to home.

Meet the New Boss: Roger Goodell Selected as Next NFL Commissioner

The work to find the fifth commissioner of the NFL began the moment Paul Tagliabue announced his intent to retire. An eight-man search committee was quickly assembled with Pittsburgh Steelers chairman Dan Rooney and Carolina Panthers owner Jerry Richardson providing direction as co-chairmen Richardson and Rooney pulled together a short list of candidates. NFL outside counsel Gregg Levy, Cleveland-based attorney Frederick Nance, Fidelity Investments Vice Chairman and Chief Operating Officer Robert Reynolds, and Constellation Energy Chairman, President, and CEO Mayo Shattuck were on the list, but, truth be told, there was already an heir apparent waiting in the wings. Given how well Tagliabue's tenure had gone, looking closely within the NFL was certain to yield a solid candidate and, from the outset, Tagliabue's right-hand man, NFL COO Roger Goodell, was the clear favorite to win the position. Short of Goodell falling on his own sword, the position seemed to be all but his.

Goodell had a near-storybook climb to the top of the NFL. Goodell's first job in football was as an intern with the New York Jets' public relations department, where he spent his time copying and clipping stories out of newspapers for the front office. By 1984, Goodell had become a public relations assistant in the NFL office, and, by 1987, he had

become assistant to Kansas City Chiefs owner and then-AFC President Lamar Hunt, a position he held until 1990.

Over the next decade, Goodell rose rapidly through the ranks of the NFL to become a key figure and sounding board within the league and ownership ranks. His list of titles over those ten years is astonishing: director of international development and club administration; vice president of operations; vice president of business development; senior vice president of league and football development; executive vice president of business and football development; and executive vice president of business, properties and club services. Through his experience in these positions, Goodell came to absorb nearly every facet of how the NFL operated.

In 2001, Goodell was selected as executive vice president and chief operating officer of the league and started to work closely with Tagliabue on everything from expansion and new stadium construction, to the contract with the NFL Referees Association, to the launch of the NFL Network and negotiations for the NFL's television agreements. As New York Giants co-owner John Mara said, "He's been at the forefront of every major decision the league has made over the past dozen years."

Given this background, when the time came on August 8th to announce the selection, it came as no surprise that the 47-year-old Goodell had been selected unanimously over fellow finalist Gregg Levy.

Much as Tagliabue remained active right up until his retirement, Goodell almost immediately had to deal with a series of issues that confronted the NFL, not the least of which were the unfinished aspects of the new CBA, which the owners have the ability to opt out of in 2008.

Goodell's first order of business, however, was a crackdown on player discipline. Given that there had been more than 50 NFL players arrested since the beginning of 2006, the league's image had started to come under heavy scrutiny. In early April of 2007, Goodell handed down a one-year suspension to Titans cornerback Adam "Pacman" Jones for his conduct in ten separate off-the-field incidents, including a fight and shooting at a strip club in Las Vegas that left a man paralyzed during the NBA All-Star weekend and an eight-game suspension to Cincinnati Bengals receiver Chris Henry, who was arrested four times in a 14-month span. Not minutes later, the new commissioner announced a "zero tolerance" discipline policy in the NFL. The policy will surely define Goodell early in his tenure. "It is important that the NFL be represented consistently by outstanding people as well as great football players, coaches, and staff," Goodell said at the announcement of the discipline policy. "We hold ourselves to higher standards of responsible conduct because of what it means to be part of the National Football League. We have long had policies and programs designed to encourage responsible behavior, and this policy is a further step in ensuring that everyone who is part of the NFL meets that standard. We will continue to review the policy and modify it as warranted."

While player conduct will surely grab the headlines throughout 2007, it may be what Goodell confronts behind the scenes over the course of his first year in office that will determine the headlines for the NFL in 2008.

Spreading the Wealth: The New Revenue Sharing System, and Will Owners Opt out of the CBA?

While Tagliabue will be remembered for having a tenure that revolved around labor peace, he did, nonetheless, leave his successor holding the bag with regard to the new Collective Bargaining Agreement. While a CBA was reached in 2006 under Tagliabue's watch, the method of how revenues would be shared among the owners under that agreement was not fully defined. That heavy lifting would have to come from Roger Goodell.

Over the last year, 13 separate committee meetings were held to address how revenue sharing would be handled. On March 26, 2007 an agreement was reached by the owners (a 30–2 vote with the Bengals and Jaguars opposing), but to say that even all 30 who voted in favor of it were "happy" about its provisions would be stretching the limits of the truth.

The agreement takes a $430 million pool pulled from the 15 top-grossing teams and distributes it over four years to as many as 15 lower-revenue teams per season. The agreement was retroactive to 2006, the first year of the new CBA, with a pool of $100 million; each year from 2007 through 2009, the pool will be $110 million. This agreement instantly raised the salary cap by $7.5 million. To qualify to receive revenue sharing funds, franchises must meet the following obligations and restrictions:

- At least 65 percent of revenues must be spent on player payroll.

- Gate receipts must be at least 90 percent of the league average.

- The franchise must not have been sold between 2006 and 2009.

- If the franchise moves into a new or renovated facility, with costs of at least $150 million, it does not qualify for the funds for the first five years.

- The franchise will stop receiving revenue-sharing once it reaches the threshold of 65 percent of total revenues on player payroll during the duration of the agreement.

The revenue-sharing system does not touch any of the revenues from the league's various television agreements, which are evenly distributed among all 32 teams. Those obligations and restrictions highlight the increased tension between the lower-revenue franchises and those at the upper end of the revenue scale that may terminate the agreement in its current form before 2009 arrives. The owners will have to decide by November 8, 2008 whether to extend the agreement or to opt out of it. The odds seem particularly high that the latter will be the case, since only nine owners need to vote to opt out to kill the deal. With that, 2007 and 2008 are likely to see a lot of positioning by the owners on this topic, particularly as that November date draws closer.

The Eye in the Sky—NFL Sunday Ticket and the DirecTV Monopoly

The broadcast rights to the NFL have become an incredible source of revenue for the league. While the agreements with CBS, FOX, NBC, CBS, and ESPN have come with the normal rancor that accompanies deals in the millions or billions of dollars, it's the status of the NFL Network and NFL Sunday Ticket that has created the most controversy.

In the case of NFL Sunday Ticket, the package that allows fans to watch their favorite team (or any other) out-of-market, the issue is one of monopoly. Since its inception in 1994, NFL Sunday Ticket has only been available through the DirecTV satellite service. At its inception, its total household and business reach was estimated at approximately 1.8 million subscribers. Since then, members of Congress have looked into whether the NFL's antitrust exemption with regard to broadcasting, which is based on the Sports Broadcasting Act of 1961, should be narrowed or lifted. That Act allows the NFL to negotiate the broadcast rights collectively for all of its 32 teams. The FCC ruled in 1994, when DirecTV first procured exclusive rights to NFL Sunday Ticket, and again in 1997, that the NFL's television policies were consistent with the 1961 Act and that no action was needed to prevent the monopoly with DirecTV, much to the consternation of the cable operators.

Senator Arlen Specter (R-PA) threatened to introduce a bill in 2006 that would have repealed that aspect of the Act and set up a scenario in which teams would negotiate their television deals separately, a potential blow to the NFL's ability to share those funds centrally across all 32 teams. Specter said in a hearing last December, "As I look at what the NFL is doing today with the NFL channel with the DirecTV... a lot of people, including myself, would like to be able to have that ticket."

Specter's comments came against the backdrop of Major League Baseball's plans to move MLB Extra Innings exclusively to DirecTV (the baseball package had previously been available on cable and DISH Network). Baseball's controversy brought the NFL's monopoly further into the spotlight. While Senator Specter's actions may have come as a final bit of grandstanding before leaving his position as Chairman of the Senate Judiciary Committee, it seems only a matter of time before the antitrust aspects of NFL Sunday Ticket are raised again.

There's Nothing "Basic" about the NFL Network

What do you do when you have a product that is so hot that millions will follow it year round? Create your own channel. Control your content. If you're the National Football League, you create the NFL Network, a 24-hour cable station (with an accompanying on-demand service) which carries live preseason games, replays of regular-season games, a nightly football news show, programming from NFL Films, and—most importantly—eight live regular-season NFL games not offered to any other cable or broadcast network (although they are simulcast on over-the-air stations in the local markets of the two teams in each game).

The NFL Network was started in 2003, with all 32 teams collectively kicking in $100 million, but has since become the subject of a legal battle between the league and the cable carriers over exactly how the channel will be made available to cable subscribers. At the heart of the dispute is the NFL Network's effort to negotiate a monthly rate of $0.70 per household for cable companies to carry the channel on what is called the basic tier—the smallest, least expensive channel package, which, correspondingly, has the highest distribution. Carriers who wish to add the channel see the cost as exorbitant, claiming that they would have to pass that extra cost onto their subscribers, many of whom, at the basic tier level, are not interested in paying extra for an all-football channel. The larger carriers, such as Time Warner and Comcast, want to place the channel on a sports tier which already carries an additional cost. Under that plan, only those subscribers who choose to pay for additional sports programming will incur the extra charge. The problem from the NFL's perspective is that doing so would greatly reduce the number of households that receive the channel.

For two solid months during 2006, Time Warner and the NFL Network were actively engaged in negotiations, but the two sides couldn't come to an agreement over the subscriber rate. In the meantime, Time Warner Cable purchased Adelphia Communications in a bankruptcy sale and pulled the NFL Network off of the newly-acquired provider altogether. That prompted the NFL to appeal to the FCC.

On August 7, the FCC ruled that Time Warner Cable violated its contract with its consumers by not giving them 30 days' notice that the channel was going to be pulled. The lights (and, supposedly, the negotiations) were back on for the NFL Network with the nation's second-largest carrier, with the FCC giving the two sides until September 15 to see if a compromise could be reached. When the deadline came, however, Time Warner once again dropped the network, reviving its acrimonious relationship with the NFL.

In the midst of all of this, competing cable provider Comcast, which had recently purchased some of Time Warner's regional systems, such as Time Warner-Houston, quietly inked a deal to carry the NFL Network on its digital tier, which has less than one-third of the total subscribers of Comcast's basic tier. Signed in mid-September, this new agreement was in addition to, but separate from, another deal Comcast had made with the NFL Network back in 2004. As part of the 2004 agreement, Comcast had the option to move the NFL Network from the basic tier to the sports tier if the company was unable to reach an agreement with the NFL over two issues: the ability to carry eight late-season NFL games on Comcast's own Versus network, and the ability to offer NFL Sunday Ticket to Comcast subscribers, ending DirecTV's exclusive rights to the package. Neither the deal for Versus nor the access to Sunday Ticket transpired, and, in October of 2006, Comcast announced that it was indeed going to move the NFL Network to its sports tier, much to the consternation of NFL. The move would make the channel available to only 750,000 subscribers, as opposed to the 7 million subscribers on the digital tier, or the 23 million-plus subscribers the NFL Network had hoped to tap into at the basic tier level. Unsurprisingly, the NFL Network sued Comcast over the matter. On May 10, 2007, a Manhattan Supreme Court justice ruled in favor of Comcast.

"The final word on this issue is most likely to come from the appellate courts," said Seth Palansky, a spokesman for the NFL Network, at the time of the court ruling. In the meantime, subscribers will get whiplash looking for the channel as it does a dance across providers, tiers, and channel guides that would have made Ickey Woods proud.

That New Stadium Smell

One thing that persists no matter the commissioner or the television arrangements is the endless search by NFL owners for new stadiums. The Arizona Cardinals finally got into their new digs last season (a year later than planned) when the 63,000-seat (expandable to 73,000) University of Phoenix Stadium opened in Glendale. The HOK-designed stadium's cost is reported to be $455 million, a considerable jump from the projected price tag of $355.3 million set in 2003. Then again, $455 million is nothing compared to where stadium costs are headed.

The Colts Strike Oil—In late 2004, the Colts and the City of Indianapolis reached a deal for a new 63,000-seat stadium (expandable to 70,000) now called Lucas Oil Stadium.

Ground was broken on the retractable-roof stadium in September of 2005 right next door to the RCA Dome, which will have its date with the wrecking ball when Lucas Oil Stadium is completed. Costs are estimated at $675 million for the Colts' new facility, with the franchise kicking in $100 million. With Lucas Oil paying $121.5 million over 20 years for the naming rights, the outlay by the Colts is completely offset, and then some.

On the public funding side of the ledger, there is a new one-percent tax on prepared food in nine of the ten counties that surround Indianapolis. Marion County will add an additional one-percent tax to the original one percent it already pays for the RCA Dome. In addition, there is already a funding gap looming for the stadium before one game is played in it.

The city's Capital Improvement Board estimates that the new stadium could cost the city $10 million more a year to operate than the RCA Dome. With nearly all revenues for the stadium going to ownership, this gap has yet to be resolved. As you may have guessed, talk is focusing on some form of taxation to fill the hole.

Jerry's World—In September of 2005, Jerry Jones got a shovel in the dirt for a new stadium for the Dallas Cowboys that will have a basic seating arrangement of 80,000 (expandable to 100,000), 200 suites, 15,000 club seats, and, yes, a retractable roof that will "allow God to watch his favorite team." As with many other stadium projects, the initial cost estimate was less than what the actual total will be. The original projected cost for the yet-unnamed stadium was $650 million, but it is now projected to be in excess of $1 billion, making it, for now, the most expensive stadium in the United States.

The new HKS Design stadium is scheduled to open for the 2009 season, with the City of Arlington covering $325 million of the cost through a voter-approved increase in the city's sales tax by one-half percent, the hotel occupancy tax by two percent, and car rental tax by five percent. Jones is on the hook for any cost overruns.

Niners Look to Get in a TIF—The San Francisco 49ers are looking to remove the "San Francisco" from their name and move to Santa Clara after efforts to build a new stadium and mixed development of housing and retail at Candlestick Point bottomed out.

The location selected for the 49ers' new 68,000-seat stadium would be near the Great America amusement park in Santa Clara, and, like other stadiums currently on the cusp or being constructed, costs are expected to run close to a billion dollars.

In April of 2007, the Niners laid out their financial plan for an $854-million stadium, a price that could increase dramatically depending on inflation. The public would kick in $160 million, plus $20–$30 million to move an existing electric substation that is on the proposed stadium site. The team is also asking the city to move a parking garage it had planned to build next to the city's convention center, which might add $40 million to the overall cost.

Without mentioning where the public funds would come from, sources close to the team said that 11 acres of land could be developed to the Niners' benefit. The city could tap a reserve fund for Santa Clara's electric utility or use Tax Increment Financing (a TIF) as in Arlington and Indianapolis. As for the rest of the funding, a government-run sports authority would pay for $330 million using in-stadium revenue streams such as ticket taxes, personal seat licenses, naming rights, and taxes on concessions. $363 million more would come through contributions from the NFL and the 49ers, but exactly when that would happen (up front, or over time) has not been determined.

What does Santa Clara get? Half of all revenues from non-NFL events at the stadium, which could translate to as much as $3 million a year in general fund revenues.

Gettin' Zygi with It—Not to be outdone by the Cowboys (or possibly the Minnesota Twins), Vikings owner Zygi Wilf wants to build a $2-billion complex in Minneapolis' Downtown East district that would put a new $954-million retractable-roof stadium for the Vikings on the site of the Metrodome and dedicate an additional $1 billion to refurbishing the surrounding area. How much are Wilf and the Vikings willing to pitch in? Approximately $250 million, or one-third the cost of the stadium. What's ironic is that Wilf pledged $280 million toward construction of a new stadium in Blaine, a plan which fell of deaf ears in Anoka County, yet he's pledged to kick in $80 million less for the new proposed project.

Give Zygi credit: he's a visionary. At the time he announced his grand plan in early May of 2007, there was no direction given on where to find the vast sums of money to make up for the difference after the Vikings' investment—three-quarters of a billion dollars.

Wilf will most likely find it difficult to get his massive project off the ground given Hennepin County's hangover from passing funding for a new ballpark for the Twins.

The Chargers Go House Hunting—It seems like the Chargers have been working the public relations front in an attempt to get a new stadium in San Diego forever, but in reality, they've only been working seriously since 2002. In 1995, the Chargers and the City of San Diego signed a deal for the use of Jack Murphy Stadium (now Qualcomm) that was due to run through 2020, but a clause in the agreement allowed the Chargers to opt out if certain revenue thresholds were not met. In 2003, the team exercised that opt-out, but the next year the Chargers and the city reached a supplemental deal that reads, in part, that, prior to January 1, 2007, the Chargers or any other affiliate of the Chargers would not engage in any "discussions, communications, negotiations, preliminary or otherwise, over terms and conditions of a Chargers' relocation to any stadium or facility not in the City, including, but not limited to, stadium financing, lease or other proposed transaction terms."

The San Diego City Council granted the Chargers the right to negotiate with other cities in San Diego County in May of 2006 in an effort to keep the Chargers in the area. Since then, the team fielded calls and potential offers from three bidders in the San Diego area: Chula Vista, National City, plus what is currently a less serious offer from Oceanside. In the end, however, it may be only Chula Vista that has a substantive offer.

HomeFed Corp., a residential real estate developer out of Carlsbad, has said it is interested in developing a stadium in Chula Vista. The company controls several parcels of land including ones of 494 acres, 320 acres, and 268 acres, all of which might be used for a development project in which profits from the development of the housing units around the stadium would be used to help offset the actual stadium costs. The Chargers had originally looked in the Mission Valley area, where 6,000 condos on roughly 60 acres would have helped construct a $450 million facility. That price tag has ballooned to over $1 billion and will escalate over time as the Chargers continue to try to reach a deal for a facility.

National City was exploring bay-front property along with a location near Interstate 5. That deal seemed tenuous from the outset, however, as the Port Authority owns the bay-front land (32 of the 52 acres) on which the stadium might have been situated. There was a litany of infrastructure concerns around transportation and the relocation of businesses in the area, which would have added approximately $50 million to the deal. In mid-May of 2007, National City pulled out of the relocation derby for the Chargers. "From Day One, I knew it would be an uphill battle because I've worked with local governments for a long time," National City Mayor Ron Morrison said. "This is a very fast process, and local government isn't used to moving very fast."

Regardless of where the Chargers might end up, they are on the hook to pay off the remaining debt on Qualcomm Stadium when they move out. That debt is likely to be in the tens of millions when, or if, moving day arrives. Given the complexities of a deal for the Chargers, any relocation talk will probably continue into 2008.

New Orleans Remains Saintly Till at Least 2010

The resurgent New Orleans Saints were the feel-good story of last season. The team going 10–6, winning the NFC South, and reaching the NFC Championship Game in the wake of Hurricane Katrina, was something to behold. With that incredible run—they became the first team ever to go to the NFC Championship after losing 13 or more games in the previous season—the team became a symbol of a city rising in the face of adversity.

With the City of New Orleans dealing with the Herculean effort to rebuild after Katrina hit in late August of 2005, owner Tom Benson's attempts to relocate the Saints—which had been occurring since 2001—came extraordinarily close to succeeding. With the Superdome deemed unsafe for public use and being considered for demolition, the Saints played their 2005 home games in San Antonio's Alamodome and at Louisiana State University's Tiger Stadium. In the midst of the catastrophe, Benson played relocation talks up to the hilt. At one point, San Antonio mayor Phil Hardberger said that Benson had agreed to meet with the NFL and San Antonio officials about relocating the team there permanently.

Then, on November 4, 2005, Benson and Louisiana Governor Kathleen Blanco reached an agreement that postponed two critical deadlines for either side to void the team's lease of the Superdome, which Benson seemed very close to doing. With the postponement, Benson agreed to postpone any discussions of voiding the lease till 2007.

Now that 2007 is here, the Saints are riding high on the field and off. The Superdome has undergone an incredible rebuilding process, and support from fans, both locally and around the nation, has resulted in a waiting list of 25,000 for season tickets. The Saints have sold out all of their luxury suites for the upcoming season, and Saints merchandise is one of the hottest selling properties in the NFL.

As for those talks of relocation, the State of Louisiana and the Saints reached an agreement in late March of 2007 that will keep the team in New Orleans through at least 2010. The agreement removed a provision that would have allowed the Saints to relocate by reimbursing the state approximately $70 million in inducements. "For the foreseeable future, Louisiana's team will keep marching to victory right here," Gov. Blanco said at the time of the announcements.

Talks seeking to reach a long-term agreement to extend the lease for the Saints through at least 2025 are underway, and Blanco, in her final term as governor, has vowed to work on the extended agreement until she leaves office and to work with her replacement to make sure that the long-term deal is reached.

"We will work very hard to keep them here permanently," said Doug Thornton, the regional vice president of SMG, the company that manages the Superdome.

Overtime: A 17th Regular-Season Game

During this past offseason, league officials began to discuss the possible addition of a 17th regular-season game. The extra game would take place in neutral cities, with the primary goal of promoting the game overseas by having meaningful games in Europe, although games could also be held in Mexico or in American cities that don't currently have teams, such as Los Angeles and San Antonio. To allow for the addition of this 17th game, a preseason game would be removed from the schedule.

"It is preliminary, but we certainly are putting resources into pulling that together," Mark Waller, NFL senior vice president international, told the Associated Press in early May of 2007. "For now, we have the one game per season or two per season outside of the U.S., but we know it can be tough on home fans since we're taking a game away.

"So we have asked how do we create more inventory without taking games away from fans? That idea came up in internal conversations and we now have an international committee of owners and we talked it through with them, and they asked us to do some groundwork."

The game won't be on the schedule by 2008, but 2009 or 2010 has been discussed as a possibility. That leaves you plenty of time to kick up your feet and wait to see if the owners opt out of the CBA, when the new stadiums get built, whether teams relocate, and if you'll be able to get the NFL Network in your home, and watch all the other fun and games that take place outside the hashmarks.

How Medical Personnel Impact the Draft

Will Carroll

The show is on. It's too bad that the NFL Draft and the Westminster Dog Show no longer take place in the same building, because the two events are actually quite similar. Everyone likes to watch, but no one really knows how the judging works. For football fans around the country, Draft Day has become a giant holiday of hope, as they wait for their team to grab that one piece that will push them to the next championship.

In truth, few NFL personnel think the draft has the impact that the public does. This is not to say that they don't think a good draft, or in some cases simply avoiding a bust, is not of paramount importance. It's just that, for the teams, it's not about hope, it's about parameters, results, careful study, and science. In what looks like a dog show, the actual selection process is now down to micrometer standards.

While the due diligence process on prospects begins at the start of each college season and even before, it is the few weeks between the end of the college season and the NFL Combine in early February when the bulk of the work is done. Despite the continuing trend for top tier players to pass on performing certain activities at the Combine or even during their Pro Day, the process is remarkably transparent and shared among teams. In fact, hiding information is counterproductive for prospects. "They're going to find it," one top player agent told me. "You get it out there, you address it on your terms. I know it before they do, so at least for a while, I have more info."

Team doctors say the same thing. "It's better to get it out and on the table," said Dr. Neil ElAttrache, former team physician for the Rams and now Director of Sports Medicine at the world-renowned Kerlan-Jobe Orthopedic Clinic in Los Angeles. "The players come in, they know they're facing a comprehensive process. We have their medical records and the ability to both examine them and conduct more tests if needed." Despite the competition between teams on the field and on Draft Day, each player's information is shared equally. The National Scouting service, one of two services that runs the Combine, distributes a med-ical summary to each team. The full record is kept sepa-rately, due to privacy and security concerns, but is available for review by team medical staffs.

"By the time the players reach the Combine," ElAttrache said, "you know what you're looking for." The medical summary highlights the obvious red flags, things such as previous surgeries, missed games, and even missed practices are noted and, when possible, explained. "For a guy who had knee surgery," ElAttrache continued, "you know what to look for. Did he come back? Do I know the doctor that did it? Do I need to look at the knee?" Most will be just this straightforward. Why then do some teams see a certain injury as a problem when another is okay with it? "We're all different," ElAttrache said of his colleagues. "I might think something's a bit loose while another doctor thinks it's within his normal range. A lot of times we'll hear when someone disagrees and discuss it." In other words, there are up to 32 chances for a team to weed out injury information.

This process gets harder with complex cases. ElAttrache explained that "it comes down to the team. If I see a guy who has a chronic problem, I'll bring that up. It's up to the [player personnel staff] to decide what they're willing to accept." Often, the front office will ask their doctors and trainers to make the call—will this player hold up or not? "It's judgment," ElAttrache told me. Teams show biases, often having more to do with the recent injury history of their team than any other factor. Media scrutiny also comes up at this stage, often reducing the risk a team is willing to accept with their higher picks. "You can get away with a gamble on a second-day guy," one team official told me at the Combine.

One complex case was this year's seventh-overall pick, Adrian Peterson. The former Oklahoma running back ended his college career with a collarbone injury that set off red flags around the league. After he re-injured the collarbone during the Fiesta Bowl, news of Peterson's injury began to spread as a rumor prior to the Combine. While it was sure to be noted in any physical, Peterson's agent, Ben Dogra, sent his athlete to Dr. James Andrews, one of the top orthopedists in sports, to check the collarbone prior to the Combine. "If the doctors have any questions," said one source, "they know they're going to have to disagree with Andrews." While several physicians I spoke to refused to comment on whether the Andrews opinion would change their opinion, they all acknowledged that this kind of move was a smart tactic. Instead of hiding the injury, Peterson's management tackled the situation head-on, saving Peterson from falling further and losing money.

The doctors' involvement doesn't end with the physicals. "We watch the workouts too," ElAttrache said, a fact echoed by several team officials. "It's more for guys that are top picks as well as the ones we have some questions about." By watching the athlete in action, doctors and trainers can see if there are any biomechanical signs of injury compensation. Someone with a leg injury might limp. A quarterback with shoulder problems might lack arm strength or change his throwing motion. Back injuries can often manifest themselves in certain movement patterns during agility drills. "They may have designed the lineman drills to check foot speed," said one team executive, "but it's more useful to us to see which of these big uglies has back problems."

The NFL Combine has become less and less secretive over the years. More media is there, the workouts are televised on the NFL Network, and Mel Kiper Jr. is no voice in the wilderness. While the physicals will likely never be a part of the television package, there's very little need for secrecy. The process might happen in a back room, but the up-front and transparent nature of the exams makes them another tool in a team's arsenal rather than a secret weapon.

Projecting Rookie Quarterbacks, Revisited

David Lewin

In *Pro Football Prospectus 2006,* I introduced a college statistics–based projection system for rookie quarterbacks. This system was designed solely to forecast quarterbacks chosen in the first two rounds of the NFL Draft, and it primarily used just two numbers: college completion percentage and college games started.

Although the formula was simplistic, it made some remarkably accurate predictions about what we could expect from a number of young passers, including Philip Rivers, Matt Leinart, Jay Cutler, Vince Young, and Jason Campbell. Still, there were many questions left unanswered: Can we predict quarterbacks chosen after the second round? Why does starting a lot of games in college indicate likely NFL success? Is there really no difference in NFL success between first- and second-round picks? The following will address these questions and give projections for this year's crop of young signal callers.

Projecting Later-Round Quarterbacks

The most popular question after the initial study was "What about quarterbacks drafted after the second round?"

I limited my initial study to the top two rounds for two main reasons: (1) Every quarterback drafted in the top two rounds gets a chance to play. This is not the case later in the draft and simplifies things significantly. (2) Every quarterback drafted in the top two rounds has been certified by scouts as having the talent to succeed in the NFL. Moving out of the top two rounds and leaving these helpful assumptions behind can be problematic. As of the end of the 2006 season, only 35 of the 79 quarterbacks drafted after the second round between 1997 and 2005 ever attempted an NFL pass, and, of those 35, 11 had attempted 100 or fewer passes. This raises the question of what to do with those guys who never got to play. It seems unfair to assume that the reason they did not play was because they weren't good enough, yet if they are excluded we risk biasing the study.

Ultimately this lack of data was prohibitive. I was not able to create a formula to predict the NFL success of those drafted after the first two rounds. However, I did find some interesting trends.

The most important, although not at all unexpected, trend I found was that, as you get later in the draft, players get less predictable. In the first round, players are very predictable, in the second a little less so, in the third significantly less so, and on down. This is because the predictive power of college games started disappears after the top two rounds, and the predictive power of completion percentage declines steadily. No matter the round, you are still better off taking the player with the higher completion percentage if everything else is equal, but, once you get out of the first two rounds, it's mostly a crapshoot.

Picks 1–16 vs. Picks 17–64

Last year I used a model that treated all players drafted in the first two rounds equally. This was appropriate because where a player was drafted in the first two rounds appeared to have no effect on NFL performance. After adding more data this year, it has become clear that there are differences between players picked in the top half of the first round and those picked numbers 17 to 64.

The differences align quite nicely with the overall trends I found in my original study. Games started is much less significant for those quarterbacks drafted after pick 16, while completion percentage maintains approximately the same level of significance, but gains greater relative importance due to the decreased influence of games started. Overall, the predictive power of the general model declines from 70 percent for those in the top 16 to 54 percent for those picked 17 to 64. Because of these differences, this year I am using different projection models for the two groups. I believe this will increase the accuracy of the projections, especially for those drafted after the top half of the first round.

Why Games Started?

Games started is by far the most important predictor of NFL success among those drafted in the top 16 picks, and is about equal to completion percentage in importance for those picked 17 to 64. There are many possible reasons why games started has this predictive power. If a player is good, then, all else being equal, he will start more games in college, hence, games started in college signals that the player is good. Additionally, the experience of starting games might make one better. Perhaps more importantly, the more games a player starts, the more chances scouts have to watch the player in person or on film.

I suspect that this third reason is the most important. Scouts more accurately evaluate players on whom they have more information (i.e. more games). The fewer games a top prospect has started in college, the more scouts will need to add information from off-field workouts and the NFL scouting combine to make their evaluations. This is a poor substitute for reviewing actual game performance, and often leads to mistaken evaluations of players whose physical gifts may not necessarily translate to better quarterback performance.

It makes sense that games started would decline in importance as you get deeper in the draft. For top picks, multiple scouts watch every bit of available film. The more available film, the more accurate the scouting report. As you go deeper in the draft, teams devote fewer scout-hours to each player. A greater number of games on film is irrelevant if scouts aren't watching it. If teams are going to have a couple of scouts watch a couple of games each, then it doesn't matter if a player started 20 games or 50, scouts will get an equally accurate read on each. Hence, after the first two rounds, when that scenario comes into play, games started lose their importance. Even within the first two rounds, the greater attention devoted to high picks leads to the greater relative importance of games started for top-16 picks.

With these findings in mind, let's take a look at the young quarterbacks from the last four drafts, starting with this year's rookie signal callers. Each player is listed along with their relevant college stats: completion percentage and games started. I then list each player with their projection for 2007 as well as something I call their career age-adjusted DPAR per game projection, which utilizes the research presented in my quarterback projection article in this book to project the player's average level of performance during his peak seasons (his fifth through ninth years in the league). To simplify things, I've multiplied this per-game figure by 16 to produce an annual average which I'm calling their "peak projection." The number in parentheses is where that DPAR total would have ranked among the 45 quarterbacks who had at least 100 pass attempts in 2006. Quarterbacks who have already started more than a couple of games in the NFL are also listed with their actual 2006 passing DPAR and rank.

One last important note regarding these projections: unlike the KUBIAK projection system, the college quarterback projection system does not consider the quality of the rest of the team. This obviously has an important effect in

any given season, but it tends to balance out over the course of a player's career (or not, in the case of David Carr).

The Class of 2007

JaMarcus Russell (61.8%, 29 GS)

Peak Projection: 33.9 DPAR (15)
2007 Projection: −23.7 DPAR (44)

I cannot help but be a bit worried about the number-one overall pick. Anyone who has seen him play can recognize his enormous talent; he already has, hands down, the best arm of any player in the league. However, almost equally obvious is his lack of understanding of the game. Russell's career at LSU was marred by boneheaded mistakes which came at the worst possible times. He played well enough to win most of the time, but the team was stacked, and, if not for some early-season brain cramps on Russell's part LSU would have been in the thick of the national title race.

Russell reminds me somewhat of another former number-one pick with a golden arm: Jeff George. While they are not physically similar, both are players who tantalize with their talent, and at times justify the hype, but ultimately leave you disappointed. George had some decent years in Atlanta, Oakland, and Minnesota but is generally regarded as a bust. Russell's projection is not very good because he only started 29 games in college, although his completion rate was solid. His college numbers are not that far from what Vince Young's were, though Young did have two more starts. Young has been a mediocre passer so far, but still made an impact as a rookie because he is a dynamic runner in a way that Russell is not.

If Russell plays this year, I expect him to struggle as almost all rookie quarterbacks do. Down the road, I think he'll have an up and down career with some "did you see that!" throws and plenty of "what the heck was he thinking!" moments. Russell will likely prove to be no better than the third-best quarterback to come out of this draft.

Brady Quinn (58.0%, 46 GS)

Peak Projection: 71.2 DPAR (7)
2007 Projection: 13.6 DPAR (24)

Quinn's slide was the biggest story of the 2007 NFL draft. It was the same story we saw in 2005 with Aaron Rodgers; only a few teams were in the market for a quarterback, and, once they passed, Quinn was in free fall. I don't think this reflects too poorly on Quinn. The general consensus is that he is a good, but not great, prospect. He has all the tools and great experience, but he has consistently displayed less than stellar accuracy.

Quinn's statistical profile backs up this scouting report. He started 46 games at Notre Dame, which means that, in all likelihood, he is who we thought he was. Scouts rarely miss on guys with that many starts, the only exceptions being when they undervalue the importance of accuracy (for example, Kyle Boller who had 40 starts, but a mere 48 percent completion rate, at the University of California). Quinn's career completion percentage of 58 percent is adequate and in the neighborhood of success stories such as Carson Palmer (59 percent), Donovan McNabb (58 percent), and Jay Cutler (57 percent). On the other hand, Quinn's completion percentage was significantly lower before offensive guru Charlie Weis arrived at Notre Dame and installed his quarterback-friendly offense.

Of course, the lessons Weis taught Tom Brady when he was quarterback coach and offensive coordinator in New England seem to be sticking despite Weis moving on, so the Weis effect may be somewhat overrated. Some observers felt that, given Weis's past relationship and constant communication with Browns head coach Romeo Crennel, the Browns would not have initially passed on Quinn if Weis truly felt the quarterback was going to be good in the NFL. The idea is a bit absurd; choosing tackle Joe Thomas ahead of Quinn is a statement only about the relative value the Browns placed on those two players, not the team's overall opinion of Quinn.

Indeed, the Browns clearly think Quinn will be very good, or they would not have traded away next year's first-round pick to draft him. Most people have overlooked the cap savings the Browns will gain by moving up 14 spots and getting Quinn late in the first round. Not only do the Browns get their franchise quarterback a year early, but they also get him at roughly half the price of what Brian Brohm or some other quarterback would cost them in the top five picks of 2008.

Quinn will develop into a solid NFL passer. He has not shown the accuracy to play consistently at the elite level of Peyton Manning and Tom Brady, but he has the tools to put himself comfortably in the second tier. He should certainly be good enough to prove his myriad of doubters wrong, though not in 2007. Rookie quarterbacks almost always struggle, and, playing for the Browns, Quinn will be no exception.

Kevin Kolb (61.6%, 50 GS)

Peak Projection: 96.3 DPAR (5)
2007 Projection: 38.9 DPAR (15)

Donovan McNabb's future with the Eagles should be one of the most interesting subplots of the 2007 NFL season, and it is discussed at length in the Philadelphia chapter of this book. Regardless of how he plays, McNabb will soon be looking over his shoulder, because Kevin Kolb is going to be good. Very good. Kolb started 50 games in college and completed 61.6 percent of his passes. At 6-foot-3 and 220 pounds, Kolb has good size, above-average arm strength,

and a quick release. Kolb is also a good runner and is adept at avoiding the rush. He compares favorably to Drew Brees, who was drafted in a similar position, The biggest difference between the two is the level of competition they faced, but Kolb addressed this concern to some degree with his 386-yard, three-touchdown performance in the Liberty Bowl against a South Carolina team from the consensus best conference in the nation (SEC).

For some reason, Mel Kiper Jr. spent the last day and a half of ESPN's draft coverage talking about how Kolb reminds him of Baltimore quarterback Kyle Boller. If you read last year's essay introducing the quarterback projection system, you know how absurd this statement truly is. At Cal, Boller had a completion percentage of under 48 percent. Over the past decade, he is the only quarterback chosen in the first two rounds of the draft who completed fewer than 50 percent of his passes in college. Statistics aside, Boller was drafted high because he allegedly had great arm strength, while some feel that Kolb is unspectacular in that area. The comparison is puzzling to say the least.

Many experts have questioned the validity of Kolb's numbers because of the spread offense he ran at Houston. Scouts are still haunted by the spectres of Dave Klingler and Andre Ware, who were first-round busts in the NFL after putting up huge numbers when Houston used the Run 'n' Shoot during the early 1990s. Kolb is the first Houston quarterback to put up big numbers since Klingler and Ware, but he did it in a completely different system, a spread offense based on the system Mike Leach runs at Texas Tech. By now, scouts should be familiar with the effects of this offense—you can thank Tim Couch for that—and be able to accurately tell how much it affected Kolb's performance. In the ten years before Kolb played at Houston, the average completion percentage for the school's starting quarterbacks was 56 percent. When grading Kolb, scouts will take into account the somewhat easier competition of a non-BCS conference, but Kolb rose far above the level of performance established by previous Houston quarterbacks who played under similar conditions.

Kolb's selection was a complete surprise, but it will end up being a very pleasant one. Kolb is probably not going to be ready to play this year, but McNabb will be on the hot seat in 2008. As stated above, the projections have slightly less accuracy for second-rounders, but Kolb would have to deviate from his projection by more than any quarterback has ever done previously in order to be anything less than a Pro Bowl–caliber player.

John Beck (62.4%, 38 GS)

Peak Projection: 72.0 DPAR (7)
2007 Projection: 14.4 DPAR (24)

With the Dolphins' quarterback situation unsettled at best, Beck has an excellent chance to make an impact this year. While 14.4 DPAR seems fairly modest, it is better than what the Dolphins got out of their starting quarterbacks last year. It is possible that Daunte Culpepper will turn things around, Cleo Lemon will build on his strong play in limited action last year, or the Dolphins will get a revitalized Trent Green. However, if none of those things happen, the cerebral Beck should be ready to step in and play.

Beck better be ready to play soon, because he'll be 26 by the time he takes the field in a Dolphins uniform. Beck's projection is slightly higher than Quinn's, but don't conclude that Miami made the right decision passing on Quinn just yet. Other than Chris Weinke, there isn't much of a precedent on which to base the projection for a quarterback Beck's age, but I suspect Beck will fall a bit short of what his college stats suggest. He will be 30 years old by his fifth year in the league, the year in which most quarterbacks enter their prime. His age won't necessarily prevent him from being successful, but if he hasn't made it by his second year in the league, he probably never will.

Drew Stanton (64.2%, 29 GS)

Peak Projection: 58.9 DPAR (7)
2007 Projection: 0.1 DPAR (37)

At Michigan State, Drew Stanton was consistently inconsistent. Like the Spartans as a whole, sometimes he would look great, other times he was an abomination.

At 6 foot 3, 230 pounds with a strong arm and superb athleticism it is easy to see why Stanton appealed to Mike Martz. At Michigan State, he was an accurate passer, completing better than 60 percent of his passes each year and 64 percent overall. That high completion percentage means that Stanton made his reads and completed his assignments on a regular basis. Stanton was occasionally erratic, but the Spartans did not win games because his teammates and coaches were far more erratic. Stanton also rushed for over 1,500 yards in his collegiate career. He is nothing if not a competitor, almost to a fault, as his desire to gain every last yard opens him up to a lot of big hits.

Stanton's competitiveness carries over to throwing the ball, as he will often force throws into tough situations. He is also inconsistent at throwing a spiral because he presses and over-grips the ball. If Stanton had to play this year, he would most likely be a disaster. Luckily, he has the opportunity to sit behind Jon Kitna and learn from Martz. By the time Stanton gets his chance two to three years down the road, he will likely have developed into a solid player, and will have the advantage of throwing to the half-dozen first-round wide receivers that Matt Millen will have accumulated by then.

The Class of 2006

Vince Young (61.8%, 32 GS)

2006 Season: 7.7 DPAR (27)
Peak Projection: 51.8 DPAR (10)
2007 Projection: 26.2 DPAR (19)

Young exceeded his rookie passing projection by a small amount, although he wasn't nearly as good as the press made him out to be. Young produced about equal value running and passing in 2006, and I expect that to be true again in 2007. (Remember, the statistics above include passing only, not rushing.) The success that Young experienced last year may ultimately hurt his development. He still has a long way to go as a passer, and, if he believes otherwise, his development could stall, a la Mike Vick. Young should have a productive sophomore year, but it will be mostly due to his running ability. I think many in the media will be disappointed with his development as a passer.

Matt Leinart (64.8%, 39 GS)

2006 Season: 28.3 DPAR (16)
Peak Projection: 77.1 DPAR (6)
2007 Projection: 51.5 DPAR (10)

He didn't receive nearly as much attention as Young, but Leinart had a much better rookie season. His standard statistics don't fully show how well he played because of the situational issues that DPAR filters out: the poor Arizona defense and return game put Leinart in bad field position, the offensive line did not provide adequate protection, and the struggling running game, exacerbated by that poor offensive line, constantly forced Leinart to convert second- or third-and-long. As long as the rest of the team can improve under new head coach Ken Whisenhunt, Leinart will entrench himself in the upper echelon of NFL quarterbacks over the next two or three years. Arizona's other problems explain the conservative KUBIAK projection for Leinart in 2007, but his upside makes him a great late-round fantasy flier.

Jay Cutler (57.2%, 45 GS)

2006 Season: 3.6 DPAR (33)
Peak Projection: 69.3 DPAR (7)
2007 Projection: 43.7 DPAR (14)

Mike Shanahan's decision to replace Jake Plummer with Cutler late last season was a real head-scratcher. Cutler is destined to be a much better player than Plummer, but the Broncos were in the midst of a playoff race, and it is extremely rare for a quarterback to play well in his rookie season. On the other hand, if Denver's aging offensive line can stay healthy in 2007, Cutler has a great chance to emerge as an efficient, effective passer.

Kellen Clemens (61.0%, 32 GS)

Peak Projection: 51.8 DPAR (10)
2007 Projection: 26.2 DPAR (19)

Clemens only threw one pass last year because of the remarkable resurgence of Chad Pennington. Before the shoulder injuries, Pennington was one of the most promising young quarterbacks in the league, with excellent decision-making skills and a good touch on intermediate-range passes. He no longer has the arm strength to be an elite quarterback, but, hamstrung last year by the lack of any semblance of a running game, Pennington still managed to rank ninth in passing DPAR. This year, expect Pennington, another year removed from the injury, to continue to play at a high level. Barring an injury to Pennington, Clemens is not likely to get a chance to show what he can do anytime soon. When he does get a chance, he'll be a slightly above-average NFL starter.

Clemens missed several games with injuries while at Oregon, and his projection would be nearly a point of DPAR per game higher if he had started those games. Last year, it was suggested that missing games due to injury might be better than missing games because you are sitting on the bench. If this were the case, Clemens would likely outperform his projection. However, based on further research, it looks as though that is not the case, and Clemens's projection should be taken at face value. Analyst Ron Jaworski has always been sky-high on Clemens, however, and the Football Outsiders crew is generally sky high on Jaws, so Clemens may surprise when he gets a chance.

Tarvaris Jackson (54.7%, 36 GS)

Peak Projection: 31.8 DPAR (15)
2007 Projection: 6.1 DPAR (29)

I go to school in Minnesota, so I am subjected to a greater than average amount of Vikings-related optimism. Somehow people have convinced themselves that a guy who was a 55 percent passer in Division I-AA can be successful in the NFL. I am skeptical. Jackson played very little last year, but when he did he played very poorly (–3.97 DPAR per game). Still, the Vikings probably won't regret passing on Brady Quinn that much because Jackson's putrid play will put them in great position to take Brian Brohm with the number-one overall pick next year.

The Class of 2005

Alex Smith (66.3%, 22 GS)

2006 Season: 1.5 DPAR (35)
Peak Projection: 27.0 DPAR (19)
2007 Projection: 2.4 DPAR (34)

Given the quality of the team around him, it's hard to pass judgment on Smith's abysmal rookie season. Last year, he made significant strides as a professional, but Florida's run to the national title without him suggests that Smith's collegiate excellence probably had more to do with Gators coach Urban Meyer than Smith himself.

Smith should continue to develop, and, since he entered the league at the very young age of 21, he may surpass his projection by a bit. The 49ers have given him some weapons, but their best bet is still to hand the rock to über-stud tailback Frank Gore.

Aaron Rodgers (63.8%, 22 GS)

Peak Projection: 40.6 DPAR (15)
2007 Projection: 16.0 DPAR (22)

With Brett Favre's return, the Packers have delayed for at least one more season finding out whether Aaron Rodgers can actually play. All reports out of Green Bay indicate that the Packers are not in love with what they have seen from Rodgers, but they don't want to draft another young quarterback until they see what he can do. This is good news for Rodgers, because it means that he will get a chance to prove himself eventually, and that, when his chance finally comes, he will have mastered the offense and be close to his prime. Even under these ideal conditions, Rodgers shouldn't be more than an average player, and, if his limited performances so far (–12.8 DPAR in two games) are any indication, he might be far worse than average.

Jason Campbell (64.6%, 39 GS)

2006 Season: 14.8 DPAR (23)
Peak Projection: 84.2 DPAR (6)
2007 Projection: 59.4 DPAR (7)

Campbell took over from Mark Brunell at mid-season and played decently. This year he is ready to make the leap to Pro Bowl–level performance, firmly establishing himself as the best quarterback to come out the 2005 draft. The Redskins are a bit of a mess overall, but a breakout year from Campbell could cure a lot of ills. Like Leinart, Campbell makes an excellent late-round fantasy pick despite a conservative KUBIAK projection.

The Class of 2004

Eli Manning (60.8%, 37 GS)

2006 Season: 28.0 DPAR (33)
Peak Projection: 56.3 DPAR (8)
2007 Projection: 27.5 DPAR (19)

Eli Manning took a step backwards in 2006, but the problem has never been with Manning himself. The problem has always been about expectation. Eli Manning is, always has been, and always will be an average to slightly above-average NFL passer. The Giants made a colossal mistake trading Philip Rivers and a bunch of picks for him, but you can't go back in time, so Giants fans have to accept Manning for what he is. He won't carry the team, but you can win with him.

Philip Rivers (63.5%, 51 GS)

2006 Season: 85.1 DPAR (5)

Peak Projection: 111.5 DPAR (2)

2007 Projection: 82.7 DPAR (6)

With a huge performance in his first year as an NFL starter, Philip Rivers did a lot to prove the legitimacy of the quarterback projection system. It was no fluke. Rivers may have tailed off a bit towards the end of the season, but, as we point out in the Chicago chapter, a small second-half decline in passing numbers is meaningless in the long run. Philip Rivers is here to stay.

Ben Roethlisberger (65.5%, 38 GS)

2006 Season: 42.6 DPAR (14)

Peak Projection: 76.3 DPAR (6)

2007 Projection: 47.5 DPAR (13)

Ben Roethlisberger surpassed his peak projection in his very first season with 75.3 DPAR in just 14 games back in 2004. That works out to 5.4 DPAR per game, compared to his peak projection of 4.8 per game. Roethlisberger took a small step back in his second year, and a huge one in his third. It's impossible to know how much his motorcycle accident played a role in this performance, but even taking that into account, his 2006 season was a huge disappointment. Roethlisberger tossed a league leading 23 interceptions last year. Clearly, spending his first two years in an offense that only required him to throw 22 times per game masked some significant deficiencies. Assuming Roethlisberger can overcome the maturity issues he battled in 2006, he should bounce back and play well, but he may never recapture the greatness of his first two years.

J. P. Losman (57.8%, 27 GS)

2006 Season: 21.2 DPAR (20)

Peak Projection: 25.8 DPAR (19)

2007 Projection: −3.0 DPAR (37)

Many Bills fans objected to my comment in last year's book that the Bills would regret passing on Matt Leinart. The perception is that Losman has exceeded his projection. Losman did exceed his projection for 2006. However, that is only one of Losman's two seasons as Buffalo's starting quarterback, and Losman's 2005 performance (−31.3 DPAR) was far, far below his projection. Still, we expect young quarterbacks to improve, so there is a reasonable possibility that Losman will again exceed his projection for the upcoming season. On average, quarterbacks actually decline from their third to fourth seasons, but Losman's strong play in the second half of the 2006 season is good reason to believe he may buck this trend. If Losman continues on the path he started in 2006 then he is projected

to reach a prime level of 45.9 DPAR, better than his projection of 25.8 but hardly spectacular.

All reports say that Losman is a very hard worker who takes coaching well, and that could help him make another jump in 2007. He has the potential to be an above-average player, but Losman has a long way to go if he wants to prove me wrong about Matt Leinart.

2008 Prospects

The 2008 draft should offer one of the strongest quarterback classes in recent memory. Brian Brohm of Louisville, Erik Ainge of Tennessee, Chad Henne of Michigan, John David Booty of USC, Colt Brennan of Hawaii, Andre Woodson of Kentucky, and even Matt Ryan of Boston College have a chance of being picked in the first two rounds. Right now, Brohm is the presumptive number one pick. Ainge, Booty, and Woodson all have the talent to challenge him if they post strong seasons.

Brohm and Brennan both seriously considered entering the 2007 NFL draft and likely would have been the third and fourth quarterbacks taken, respectively, if they had. Brohm and Brennan would not have had enough games started to justify a first-round pick, but their high completion percentages would have made them good second-round prospects (table 1). By returning to school, both have an excellent chance of being rated highly by the system next year, assuming they stay healthy, maintain their completion percentages, and continue to be rated as good prospects, but will Brohm and Brennan really be much better NFL prospects next year? Does one year of college really change a player's ability by a large amount? I think the answer is no. I am sure another year of college football will improve the skills of both, but I don't think that fully accounts for the large expected change in their projections.

More likely, the reason why the projection system will hold them in much higher regard next year is because of risk. Given 13 more games to scout each player, we will know a lot more about Brennan and Brohm. If they continue to perform at a high level, then we will be even more

Table 1. Top QB Prospects for 2008 NFL Draft

Player	School	GS	C%
Colt Brennan	Hawaii	24	70.4%
Brian Brohm	Louisville	21	66.3%
John David Booty	USC	13	61.6%
Andre Woodson	Kentucky	25	61.1%
Matt Ryan	Boston College	18	60.5%
Chad Henne	Michigan	37	60.1%
Eric Ainge	Tennessee	23	59.0%

NOTE: Stats through 2006 season.

confident that they belong at the top of the draft. If they get exposed, as Brady Quinn did a little this year, then they may fall out of the top two rounds.

This is a key point of the projection system: staying in college through senior year is important for scouting because any quarterback with a hot junior season who is destined to be an NFL bust is likely to be exposed in his senior year. This could be because of a drop in performance, because of the emergence of flaws (Quinn's ability to handle pressure, for example) or because they get injured. If JaMarcus Russell had returned to school, one of two things would have occurred.

1. He would have had a poor senior season, demonstrating that he would have been a bust if picked first overall in the 2007 draft, or

2. He would have maintained his draft status and completion percentage while starting 13 more games.

The latter would have made Russell a less risky prospect, and his peak projection would have increased from 2.1 to 4.8 DPAR per game. That is huge, roughly the difference between Drew Brees and Kyle Boller.

The implications of this theory are profound. First of all, Russell made a great decision to go pro now. He avoided having to go back to a quarterback competition at LSU, risking injury, and having to deal with the scrutiny that Brady Quinn dealt with all year. He avoided giving scouts another opportunity to watch him make infuriating mistakes and think, "Hmm, maybe I don't want this guy on my team after all."

By that same measure, Brohm and Brennan may have made a mistake. Although they are not as likely to lose ground due to their return to school as Russell, they are still exposing themselves to significant risk. Brennan is coming off, statistically speaking at least, the best season a college quarterback has ever had. He threw for 5,549 yards and 58 touchdowns while completing an absurd 72.6 percent of his passes. Regression to the mean suggests that Brennan is extremely unlikely to duplicate that level of success this year.

The last quarterback to have a season of similar magnitude was Omar Jacobs of Bowling Green, who threw for 4,002 yards, 41 touchdowns, and 4 interceptions and completed 67 percent of his passes as a sophomore in 2004. As he was not eligible for the draft, Jacobs returned to school. His junior season numbers (2,591 yards, 26 touchdowns, seven interceptions, and 61 percent completions) were good, but not nearly as good his previous season, and his stock dropped into the third round. Looking a little further back, we find the man whose touchdown record Brennan broke this year, David Klingler. As a junior in 1990, Klingler threw for 5,140 yards and 54 touchdowns. Klingler, too, stayed in

school and was not nearly as successful the following year, with only 29 TD passes and 3,388 yards. Klingler was still a top ten pick, but cost himself a shot at being number one.

Brennan needs to maintain his absurd level of production because scouts know that Hawaii's spread offense makes it easy to put up big numbers. A good senior year will not cut it; by returning to school, Brennan has put a tremendous amount of pressure on himself to be great. We'll see if he rises to the occasion.

Brohm's situation is a little different. There are no questions about his talent. He was an All-American in high school, and his older brother Jeff, currently Louisville's quarterbacks coach, played in the NFL. However, Brian has struggled with injuries the last two years, including a torn ACL. By returning to school, he has risked further injury problems which could aversely affect his draft stock. Brohm also faces the challenge of learning a new offensive system with coach Bobby Petrino now babysitting Ron Mexico. Louisville's new head coach, Steve Kragthorpe, is an excellent offensive mind, but it's not uncommon for quarterbacks to struggle in their first year in a new system. I think Brohm will maintain his draft stock, but the fact that he would have a somewhat low projection were he in the draft this year reflects the significant risks currently associated with him.

The rest of the 2008 class did not give serious thought to coming out early. The 6-foot-6 Ainge (nephew of Boston Celtics general manager Danny Ainge), who has started off and on since his freshman year, has all the tools to be an elite prospect if he can recover from a torn meniscus suffered this spring. He also has to perform more consistently against a tough SEC schedule.

Andre Woodson is perhaps the only quarterback in this class with more raw talent than Ainge. At 6-foot-5, 230 pounds, Woodson possesses excellent athleticism and a rifle arm that has scouts drooling, though he was not on anybody's radar before his 2006 season in which he lit up the SEC for 3,515 yards and 31 touchdowns. Woodson actually had a better junior year than JaMarcus Russell, especially when you take into account that Russell was throwing to (at least) three NFL-caliber receivers for LSU and Woodson was fighting the uphill battle that is Kentucky football. Against common opponents (Mississippi, Mississippi State, Tennessee, and Florida), Russell was 86 for 133, for 1,028 yards, ten touchdowns, and six interceptions. Woodson was 93 for 138, for 1,069 yards, eight touchdowns and one interception. It makes you wonder whether Russell might have been a bit overhyped. Of course, Woodson would have been as poor a prospect as Russell had he come out in 2007, for many of the same reasons. If he duplicates the success of his junior season, however, Woodson will have shown he is worth a high pick in 2008.

John David Booty probably has the inside track at the Heisman for 2007. He has big-time talent and plays for USC, aka the Heisman factory. A fifth-year senior, Booty seems to have been in college forever. This is because he graduated high school a full year early in order to try to win the starting quarterback job left vacant by Carson Palmer in 2003. Unfortunately, he lost a three-way battle to some guy named Matt Leinart (the third guy was current Patriots backup quarterback Matt Cassel). After sitting behind Leinart for three years, Booty finally got his chance last year and excelled as expected. If he has a great year in 2007, his big-time talent will be hard for teams picking at the top of the draft to ignore. Unfortunately, no matter what he does this year, the projection system will not like him because he only started for two years. This is one place where the projection system may be off; just because Booty got stuck behind Matt Leinart does not mean he isn't good. We would be more sure about his skill level if he had started a greater number of games, but he could still be very successful in the NFL

Michigan's Chad Henne reminds me a bit of Carson Palmer at the same stage in his career. As a four-year starter at a powerhouse school, Henne has had an up and down career. If he can put it all together in 2007, there will be a lot of teams interested in the strong-armed passer.

Conclusion

The 2006 season was a good year for the projection system. Most of its predictions were pretty much on target. The assumptions upon which it is based appeared to hold true. With that in mind, I'm confident about its predictions for the 2007 season, but there are some signs that teams are beginning to catch on in ways that will require re-evaluation of this method.

As discussed in last year's article, the projection only deals with players chosen in the first two rounds of the draft. That means that all the players considered have a high grade from scouts. Consequently, the system focuses on the college statistics that predict NFL success, but are undervalued by NFL teams. Over the past ten years, games started and completion percentage have both been undervalued.

Recently it seems as though there has been a slight but real shift towards favoring players who displayed accuracy in college. This contributed significantly to Brady Quinn's slide. If this is in fact the case, then completion percentage's predictive power should decline because teams now value it properly and thus the quarterbacks chosen in the first round of the draft will display less variety in completion percentage. Players with sub-par accuracy who previously would have gone in the second round might slide to the third. Meanwhile, less talented prospects with good accuracy move up from the third round into the second, which some believed happened with Kolb. If these trends continue, the quarterback projection system will have to change to account for them. The 2007 draft class should provide significant information on any shifts in the NFL's current quarterback scouting paradigm.

The NFL Fan's Guide to the 2007 College Football Season

Russell Levine and Vin Gauri

What follows is our third-annual NFL fan's guide to the coming college football season. Whether or not you love the college game, following it provides some early foresight into the next generation of NFL stars. The games listed below highlight some of the top names you'll hear called in the next few NFL drafts while also serving as a guide to many of the upcoming season's biggest games.

NOTE: All players listed are seniors eligible for the 2008 NFL Draft except those denoted by the following:
* juniors who are eligible for the 2008 and 2009 Drafts,
** sophomores who are eligible for the 2009 and 2010 Drafts.

September 1

Tennessee at California—A Cal season with high hopes got off to a rough start in a nationally televised rout in Knoxville last season. Coach Jeff Tedford's Golden Bears look to even the score back on their home turf this year. The Bears lost tailback Marshawn Lynch to the NFL, but still have one of the game's most explosive players in return man and **WR DeSean Jackson***, a threat to score every time he touches the ball. The junior has already returned five kicks for touchdowns in his first two seasons. Cal **QB Nate Longshore*** took a while to bounce back from an awful performance against the Vols last season, but he has the talent to be the next Tedford product to reach the NFL. Tennessee counters with **QB Erik Ainge,** back for his senior season after making huge strides as a junior under the tutelage of offensive coordinator David Cutcliffe. Ainge has prototypical NFL size, and another year of improvement could make him a first-day pick.

September 3

Florida State at Clemson—Labor Day evening has been the exclusive property of Florida State-Miami in recent seasons, but, after some recent snoozers, ABC and ACC executives have decided to change things up in favor of the annual Bowden Bowl. Clemson and coach Tommy Bowden have had the better of this rivalry recently, winning three of the last four matchups. The Clemson offense features a pair of big-play **RBs, James Davis*** and **C. J. Spiller****, both of whom could play on Sundays. The elusive Spiller is the more intriguing prospect, as he possesses the extra gear to separate from defenders in the open field. Whoever is toting the rock for Clemson will be sure to follow in the path of **OT Barry Richardson,** one of the nation's best at his position and the only experienced member of the Clemson line. Florida State has slipped a bit in recent years, mostly due to struggles on offense (where former offensive coordinator Jeff Bowden is the official fall guy), but the Seminoles still churn out NFL defenders with regularity. The latest such prospect is **DT Andre Fluellen,** who could be a first-rounder in April.

September 8

Oregon at Michigan—The talent level at Michigan, which slipped a bit in the early part of the decade, is back up. The 2007 draft saw four Wolverine defenders taken in the first two rounds. In 2008, it will be the offense's turn. Scouts are mixed on **QB Chad Henne,** who could go anywhere in the first four rounds. A big senior season, however, could push the rifle-armed Henne into the middle of round one. His prime target will be **WR Mario Manningham*,** who was having an explosive sophomore 2006 season (nine touchdowns in his first six games) before being derailed by a knee injury. The Wolverines also still have **RB Mike Hart,** who is too strong, sure-handed, and elusive not to play in the NFL, but who lacks the top-end speed and prototypical size to be a high-round pick. The real star of the Michigan offense is **OT Jake Long,** who could have been a top-ten pick after his junior season. He could go much higher—possibly first overall—if he has a dominating senior season. For Oregon, **RB Jonathan Stewart*** is the player to watch. Stewart could be the best back in the Pac-10 and he's also a premier kick returner. Another player to keep an eye on for the Ducks: **DE Dexter Manley II.**

Virginia Tech at LSU—This interconference matchup is one of the premier games of the non-conference season. LSU has produced as much NFL talent as any school in the country the last five seasons, a trend that should continue this season. The Tigers' defensive line features a pair of terrors in **DT Glenn Dorsey** and **DE Tyson Jackson.** Dorsey is a bit undersized for a tackle, but has the power and quickness that NFL teams covet and could be the first interior defensive lineman selected. Jackson is tackle-sized, but has the quickness to play end. Virginia Tech is not without some defensive talent of its own. Hokies' **LBs Vince Hall** and **Xavier Adibi** are excellent NFL prospects. Adibi gets more publicity, but we prefer Hall, who has the versatility to play inside or outside.

September 15

Texas A&M at Miami—Much like its in-state rival Florida State, Miami has been sunk of late by weak offenses, but, just like the Seminoles, the Hurricanes are still turning out defensive studs. This year's crop includes **DE Calais Campbell*,** a terror off the edge (10.5 sacks, 20.5 tackles for loss in 2006). The secondary features **S Kenny Phillips.** Both will have their hands full with a Texas A&M attack led by efficient **QB Stephen McGee*** and bruising, plus-sized **RB Jorvorskie Lane*.** The Aggies' best pro prospect may be **TE Martellus Bennett*,** a 6-foot-7 target who grabbed 37 passes for 491 yards as a sophomore in 2006.

USC at Nebraska—NFL Draft prospects aside, this game should be mandatory viewing for all college football fans, if for no other reason than to reward the Trojans for being about the last team willing to schedule a tough non-conference slate. Despite all the pro talent the program has turned out in recent seasons, the Trojans are loaded once again. **OT Sam Baker** will be in a season-long battle with Michigan's Jake Long to become the first lineman selected. He'll guard the blind side for **QB John David Booty*.** The defense is no slouch either, not with **DE Lawrence Jackson** and **DT Sedrick Ellis** terrorizing quarterbacks. But the best prospect on the Trojans' defense may be weak-side **LB Keith Rivers,** a possible first-round pick. For Nebraska, **ILB Steve Octavien** and **S Zack Bowman**—the latter a top prospect before a pair of knee injuries—lead the latest edition of the Blackshirt defense.

September 22

Penn State at Michigan—Penn State, known as "Linebacker U," has another great prospect at the position in **LB Dan Connor,** who may be a better all-around player than 2006 second-rounder Paul Posluszny. Nittany Lions **QB Anthony Morelli** was a prized recruit who has had a rocky career at State College, but came on towards the end of last season. A big senior year could earn him an NFL paycheck. A good start would be earning Penn State's first victory over the Maize and Blue since 1996. Wolverines **OLB Shawn Crable** is no longer surrounded by last year's star-studded defense, and could emerge as the star of this year's unit.

September 29

Auburn at Florida—Graduation and the NFL Draft robbed the defending national champions of many of last year's key players, especially on defense, but the cupboard is hardly bare in Gainesville. **DE Derrick Harvey*** has first-round talent, while **S Tony Joiner** is no longer in the shadow of the departed Reggie Nelson. On offense, **QB Tim Tebow**** played the role of fullback-under-center on running downs last season, but this year he'll be running the entire offense and free to display the talents that made him such a sought-after recruit. He'll throw it plenty to **WR Andre Caldwell,** younger brother of NFL veteran Reche. Keep an eye on all-purpose **RB Percy Harvin**,** who is as fast and shifty as any player in college football. Auburn **DE Quentin Groves** is one of the best edge rushers in the SEC (9.5 sacks in 2006).

October 4

Kentucky at South Carolina—Coach Rich Brooks breathed some life into a moribund Kentucky program last season by unleashing a pass-happy offense that scored points in bunches. The key to the attack is the trigger man, **QB Andre' Woodson** (31 touchdowns, seven interceptions in 2006), who has the size (6-foot-5, 235 pounds) to be more than just a system quarterback. Woodson could play himself into the first round with another big year as a senior. Woodson's favorite mark is **WR Keenan Burton,** a big target with the speed to get deep. **TE Jacob Tamme** also has the skills to play in the NFL. Steve Spurrier has ruffled some SEC feathers since returning to the college game at South Carolina, but he has yet to make a big splash. If that's to change this year, it will be on the strength of a defense led by **ILB Jasper Brinkley,** one of the best in college football.

October 6

Virginia Tech at Clemson—Gaines Adams, who was selected fourth in the 2007 draft by Tampa Bay, dominated the headlines for the Clemson defense last season, but he was outplayed at times by his counterpart on the other side, **DE Phillip Merling*.** The Clemson defense also features another standout in **OLB Nick Watkins.** The Virginia Tech offense is paced by **RB Brandon Ore*,** who could come out early if he has a big junior season. Hokies **WR Eddie Royal** could be a solid mid-round pick.

October 13

Georgia at Vanderbilt—Georgia's defense features an outstanding secondary led by **CB Paul Oliver,** who will be in the mix to be the first defensive back selected. He has the size (six-foot, 205 pounds) that NFL scouts covet, and made a name for himself by shutting down Calvin Johnson last season. Versatile **DB Kelin Johnson** can play corner or safety, and should also hear his name called next April. For Vanderbilt, keep your eyes on **ILB Jonathan Goff.** He should be hard to miss—he'll be the one making plays all over the field.

October 20

USC at Notre Dame—Charlie Weis has restored expectations in South Bend, but Notre Dame came up small in big games in 2006. Weis is starting over on offense, but he can count on **C John Sullivan** and athletic **TE John Carlson** (634 receiving yards, four touchdowns in 2006). Carlson, who has logged time with the Irish hoops team, can stretch the field on the vertical route. **S Tom Zbikowski** leads a Notre Dame defense looking to lose the laughingstock label under new defensive coordinator Corwin Brown. Irish fans hope Brown, an advocate of the 3-4 defense from the Parcells/Belichick coaching tree, can take some heat off an oft-skewered secondary. On the flip side, Pete Carroll is still grinning and clapping thanks in part to **ILB Ray Maualuga*** and hulking **S Taylor Mays**.**

October 27

Indiana at Wisconsin—Wisconsin returns 16 starters, the two best of which are **CB Jack Ikegwuonu*** and **TE Travis Beckum*.** **RB P. J. Hill**** had an outstanding freshman season (1,569 yards, 15 TDs) a year ago. Hill had drawn comparisons to Ron Dayne, but dropped weight in the offseason along with having rotator cuff surgery. The Hoosiers should have a very potent offense, led by lanky **WR James Hardy*** and **QB Kellen Lewis**.** Hardy has Calvin Johnson's size (he may even be an inch taller), but isn't quite as explosive. **RB Marcus Thigpen*** isn't assured of a starting spot in the backfield, but has proven himself on special teams (three touchdowns on kickoff returns in 2006)

Nebraska at Texas—Texas **WR Limas Sweed** is the best jump-ball threat in the college game. He has developed some chemistry with **QB Colt McCoy**,** who has shown great mobility to complement a strong arm. **DT Frank Okam** is another member of a great defensive tackle pool for the 2008 Draft. The Longhorns will have to replace a pair of defensive backs who were first-round picks in April

as well as defensive coordinator Gene Chizik, who is now the head coach at Iowa State. Nebraska coach Bill Callahan is no longer content settling for the Big XII North crown. He has a quarterback derby on his hands between Arizona State transfer **Sam Keller** and **Joe Ganz*.** WRs **Maurice Purify** and **Terrence Nunn** lead a strong receiving corps for the Cornhuskers. Nebraska will have four new starters on the defensive line in 2007.

November 3

San Jose State at Boise State—QB Chris Peterson may own the greatest audition tape ever assembled for a head coach: the Broncos' awe-inspiring 2007 Fiesta Bowl victory over Oklahoma. It will be tough to duplicate the success of his 13–0 rookie campaign, but he'll have another veteran offensive line led by standout **OT Ryan Clady*.** **RB Ian Johnson*** will also be hard-pressed for an encore of 2006. Not only because of his 25 touchdowns, but because he scored the clinching points in overtime of the Fiesta on an improbable Statue of Liberty play, then promptly proposed to his girlfriend, a Broncos cheerleader, in the end zone. (Thanks for blowing the surprise, Chris Myers.) San Jose State is also looking to replicate last season's success (9–4 and its first bowl win since 1990). Old war horse Dick Tomey has 15 starters returning, including **CB Dwight Lowery** (9 interceptions in 2006), **LB Matt Costelo** and **QB Adam Tafralis.**

November 8

West Virginia at Louisville—The Big East title should hang in the balance again in this matchup. Louisville **QB Brian Brohm** is the top-rated quarterback on the 2008 draft board. He has the size, arm, and head (if not great mobility) to be an NFL star. Most importantly, Brohm has proven accuracy (completing 66.3% of his career passes) and experience (21 starts). If he stays healthy, Brohm should be a top-five pick. For West Virginia, **RB Steve Slaton*** (7.0 yards per carry, 16 touchdowns in 2006) and **QB Pat White*** (7.4 yards per carry, 18 TDs), college football's biggest home run threats, return to Morgantown. Slaton is a blink faster than White, but must prove he can hold onto the ball. Against Louisville last year, Slaton lost two fumbles in a 44–34 loss. White vastly improved his passing in 2006, doubling his passing yards from his redshirt freshman season. Another Mountaineer to watch is **DT Keilen Dykes.**

November 10

Virginia at Miami—Some great defensive talent will be on display here, including Virginia **DE Chris Long** (Howie's son). Long has faced frequent double-teams in his career, but should be a first-day pick. The Cavs have two productive

TEs in **Tom Santi** and **Jonathan Stupar.** Without consistent quarterback play, Miami's offense will rely on speedy **RBs Javarris James**** and **Graig Cooper***.**

November 17

Ohio State at Michigan—Ohio State coach Jim Tressel has owned Michigan's Lloyd Carr to the tune of a 5–1 record since taking over in Columbus. Still, the Buckeyes may have to rely on their defense with so many offensive stars from last season landing in the NFL. Ohio State **LB James Laurinaitis*** and undersized (but freakishly strong) **DE Vernon Gholston*** may jump to the NFL after 2007. Laurinaitis is great in pursuit, but could do a better job of shedding blocks in the run game. Expect Buckeye **RB Chris "Beanie" Wells**** to emerge as a star. Wolverines **DT Terrance Taylor*** and **P Zoltan Mesko*** are other players to watch.

November 23

Arkansas at LSU—No one had a more tumultuous off-season than Arkansas coach Houston Nutt. Fortunately, he has **RB Darren "Humanity Advanced" McFadden*** returning to his "Wildcat" formation with **RB Felix Jones*** (1,176 rushing yards, 7.6 yards per carry in 2006). McFadden ran (1,647 rushing yards, 14 rushing touchdowns, one kickoff return TD) and threw (three passing TDs) the Hogs all the way to the SEC title game a year ago. Many think he'll be the first running back selected if he opts for the 2008 draft, and he's another candidate for the first selection overall. Gangly **WR Marcus Monk** hauled in 962 receiving yards and 11 TDs despite Arkansas's struggles at the quarterback position. **WR Early Doucett** (772 receiving yards in 2006) will be the primary downfield threat for the Tigers.

Boise State at Hawaii—One of the particular treats that college football has to offer is late-night (mainland time) kickoffs from Honolulu. It helps that the Warriors have been pretty entertaining to watch ever since head coach June Jones returned to rescue the program in 1999. Record-setting **QB Colt Brennan** opted to return for his senior season after throwing for a ridiculous 58 touchdowns and 5,549 yards in 2006. More importantly in scouts' eyes, he threw just 12 interceptions on 559 pass attempts while completing 72.6 percent of his passes. Brennan has NFL size at 6-foot-3, but a somewhat unorthodox throwing motion. He will also have to combat the notion that he is a system quarterback, but he is one of the more intriguing prospects in the 2008 draft.

November 24

Oklahoma State at Oklahoma—Some of the better receivers in the nation will be on the field in this year's edition of the Bedlam Series: Oklahoma State **WR Adarius Bowman** and Oklahoma's **Malcom Kelly*, Juaquin Iglesias*** and **Manuel Johnson*.** Sooners **RB Allen Patrick** spelled departed star Adrian Peterson for stretches last season and had a big game in Stillwater. Cowboys **DEs Marque Fountain** and **Nate Peterson** are prospects worth watching.

November 29

Rutgers at Louisville—Rutgers's win over Louisville last season was the most momentous event in Piscataway since the first official college football game was played there in 1869. The Scarlet Knights' **RB Ray Rice*** (1,794 rushing yards and 20 touchdowns in 2006) returns for at least one more season. With the versatile Brian Leonard in the NFL, Rice will draw even more attention from defenses this year. The two best place-kickers in the country, or at least east of Corvallis (hello, Alex Serna), are featured in this matchup. Rutgers' **K Jeremy "Judge" Ito** nailed the kick to beat the Cardinals last season, while Louisville **K Art Carmody** (please, don't tell Chris Berman about him) has the 2006 Lou Groza Award on his mantle.

Top 25 Prospects

Michael David Smith

Since our first edition of *Pro Football Prospectus* two years ago, one of the most common questions from readers has been, "Why doesn't *Pro Football Prospectus* write about up-and-coming prospects, the way *Baseball Prospectus* does?"

The answer is obvious, when you think about it. The men who will be NFL stars in 2010 are not hidden away in the Florida State League, playing every night to 2,000 fans. You can see them every Saturday on regional or national television, playing big-time college football. There are hundreds of websites devoted to these players: sites with mock NFL drafts for three years hence, sites for fans of each individual college, even sites that follow the high school recruiting process. You don't need *Pro Football Prospectus* to tell you that Brian Brohm can throw the ball.

On the other hand, what happens to these college stars after draft day? If they don't start immediately, players who started every game in the ACC or Big Ten disappear as role players on NFL rosters. Hardcore fans know every player on their favorite team, but not necessarily every player around the league. Meanwhile, the obsessive subculture of NFL draftniks has moved on to the next crop of 21-year-olds.

That's the gap our first-ever Top Prospects list is meant to fill. Instead of writing about the same top college players that Mel Kiper Jr. has already discussed ad infinitum, we tried to identify 25 young, up-and-coming players who are already in the NFL, but haven't yet reached stardom or even the starting lineup. Some of these players may never make it, but we believe many of these players will become significantly more important—and significantly more well-known—in seasons to come.

To be considered for our top prospects list, players had to meet the following criteria:

- Drafted or signed between 2004 and 2006

- Drafted in rounds three through seven, or undrafted

- Less than five career games started.

Without any further ado, we present our first annual list of the *Pro Football Prospectus* Top 25 Prospects:

1. Jerious Norwood, RB, Falcons

A third-round pick out of Mississippi State last year, Norwood was nothing short of outstanding as a rookie. He averaged 6.4 yards per carry, and that's not the result of just one or two big runs. Norwood also ranked eighth in success rate, third in rushing DVOA, and 15th in rushing DPAR despite not even reaching 100 carries. He can run, he can catch, he can block, and he's eight years younger than Warrick Dunn. That all adds up to indicate that Dunn's days as the number-one back in the Atlanta attack are over. Norwood is a significantly better player than Dunn right now and should carry the load in Bobby Petrino's offense.

2. Michael Turner, RB, Chargers

In all three of his NFL seasons, Turner has had a higher DVOA than LaDainian Tomlinson. That doesn't mean he's a better player than Tomlinson—Turner hasn't proven that he can perform at that level for over 350 carries a season—but it does mean that he's extremely talented. In terms of straight-line speed, Turner is one of the fastest backs in the NFL, and he's more powerful in short yardage than you might think.

3. Mark Anderson, DE, Bears

As long as Chicago has Alex Brown and Adewale Ogunleye, Anderson will be a backup, but he's a phenomenal talent and a very smart player for a rookie. Watch the tape of any of his 12 professional sacks and you'll see that he uses his brains as well as his speed, often faking out much more experienced offensive linemen by taking a sharp step to the inside before making his move to the outside. So few people thought highly of Anderson a year ago that, to the extent he was discussed at all in the weeks leading up to the 2006 draft, analysts were suggesting that he should move to linebacker. No matter what position scouts saw the 6-foot-4, 258-pound Anderson playing, it's hard to believe that he lasted until the fifth round after a good college career as a three-year starter at Alabama.

4. Matt Schaub, QB, Texans

It's possible that we're going overboard about Schaub. After all, he still has very, very little actual NFL experience. When he does get on the field, however, he looks like a classic drop-back passer and a marvelous fit for Gary Kubiak's offense, which is similar to what Kubiak ran both at Virginia and with the Falcons. Perhaps most importantly, Schaub looks like he has an understanding of how to read blitzes and a natural feel for when the pass rush is getting to him, both of which David Carr lacked.

5. Elvis Dumervil, DE, Broncos

The 5-foot-10 Dumervil doesn't look like a defensive end, but when the Broncos took him out of Louisville in the fourth round of last year's draft, they added the player who might have the quickest first step of any defensive lineman in the NFL. Last year, the 23-year-old Dumervil led the Broncos with 8.5 sacks despite never starting a game. This year, new assistant head coach for defense Jim Bates is likely to give him more playing time, and Dumervil is likely to respond with more sacks.

6. Ronnie Prude, CB, Ravens

Prude is one of those guys who makes you scratch your head and question how in the world all the NFL scouts overlooked him. He's a good all-around athlete who was a high school quarterback before switching to defensive back at LSU, where he started 21 games. The Ravens were given a gift when Prude arrived as an undrafted rookie last year. Prude played in 15 games and showed very early that he belonged in the NFL by picking off a pass and returning it 54 yards for a touchdown in the second game of the season. He had a limited sample of 16 passes in our game charting, but allowed just 4.2 yards per pass with a Success Rate of 83 percent. He could push Samari Rolle out of a starting job very soon.

7. Wesley Britt, OT, Patriots

A fifth-round draft choice by the Chargers in 2005, Britt was waived, and then spent the year on the Patriots' practice squad. In 2006, he made the active roster, playing in ten games and starting one. He backs up Nick Kaczur and Matt Light, so he'll have a hard time winning a job in a training camp battle, but he sure looked like a phenomenal talent in his one start last year. Playing right tackle, Britt helped the Patriots run for 238 yards against the Bengals, their highest one-game total since 1993. Also, Tom Brady was not sacked in that game. A four-year starter at Alabama, the 6-foot-8, 320-pound Britt looks like he could be a Pro Bowl player as soon as he gets the chance.

8. Marion Barber, RB, Cowboys

The Cowboys' fourth-round pick out of Minnesota in 2004, Barber has started just three games in his career, but there's no doubt that he's one of the league's elite young runners. Last year, Barber ranked second in rushing DVOA and fourth in Success Rate, while starter Julius Jones was 28th in rushing DVOA and 30th in Success Rate. Bill Parcells apparently preferred Jones because he has better straight-line speed than Barber and a better understanding of the running back's role in blitz pickup, but Barber is so superior at finding holes and breaking tackles that it's hard not to expect the new coaching staff in Dallas to give Barber at least half the carries.

9. Brandon Jacobs, RB, Giants

Buried behind Ronnie Brown and Cadillac Williams on the depth chart at Auburn, Jacobs had two options: Switch to tight end or transfer. He chose the latter, leaving for Southern Illinois, and the Giants were impressed enough with what he did there to make him their fourth-round pick in 2004. He still hasn't started a game in his NFL career, but that will change now that Tiki Barber is spending his mornings chatting with Matt Lauer. Even with the signing of Reuben Droughns, Jacobs should get at least half the carries for the Giants, and we already know that Tom Coughlin loves giving Jacobs the ball in goal-to-go situations.

10. Stacy Andrews, OT, Bengals

When Andrews entered the NFL draft in 2004, scouts salivated. Guys who are 6-foot-7 and 350 pounds like Andrews are simply not supposed to be as agile as he is. So why did he last until the fourth round of the draft? Because his senior season at Ole Miss was the first year in his life that he played organized football. While his brother, Eagles lineman Shawn Andrews, was playing football, Stacy preferred to focus on the shot put. However, an Ole Miss coach pointed out that there are a lot more jobs available for professional football players than there are for professional shot putters, and that convinced Andrews to give football a try. Andrews's playing time has gradually increased from hardly any at all in his rookie year to a good bit off the bench his second year. In 2006, his third year, he played in 16 games and made three starts. Now he's getting ready for his fourth year and looking like he'll become a very good NFL offensive lineman. It's been an unusual route to that destination, but the Bengals are glad he made the trip.

11. Brad Smith, WR, Jets

A converted quarterback from Missouri, Smith had 18 rushes for 103 yards and nine catches for 61 yards as a rookie in 2006. Those numbers don't sound great, but the Jets' regular-season finale against the Raiders may have shown us the impact he'll have in 2007. Smith got the ball only twice against Oakland, but both plays were the type that keep opposing defensive coordinators up late at night. The first was an end-around handoff on which Smith's pure speed allowed him to turn the corner and gain 20 yards. The second was a quarterback sneak on which Smith lined up at wide receiver, went in motion in front of quarterback Chad Pennington, took the snap from center and dove forward for a three-yard gain on 3rd-and-2. Smith, who passed for more than 8,000 yards and ran for more than 4,000 in college, has such a unique set of skills that it's hard to envision a scenario in which he doesn't develop into a very good player.

12. Freddie Keiaho, LB, Colts

A late third-round pick in 2006 from San Diego State, Keiaho is the likely replacement for the departed free agent Cato June. Although Keiaho was an inside linebacker in college who only started one season with the Aztecs, he seems like an ideal fit in Tony Dungy's defense, and he is probably a better tackler than June. Keiaho got increased playing time in the playoffs and was one reason (though obviously a less important reason than Bob Sanders) that the Colts' defense got better in January.

13. Brandon Marshall, WR, Broncos

A fourth-round pick last year out of Central Florida, Marshall only looked so-so as a rookie, but so-so in last year's Denver passing game was actually fairly good. Marshall has good speed for a 6-foot-4, 230-pounder, and the best reason to think he'll keep getting better is that he's still learning the position; he played defensive back at Central Florida until switching to receiver for his senior season. Marshall needs to learn to be more aggressive in going to get the ball—he sometimes looks like he's just waiting for the ball to hit him in the numbers rather than reaching out and grabbing it with his hands—but if he does learn, he could be a dynamic player for several years.

14. Cortland Finnegan, CB, Titans

With Pacman Jones unavailable, the Titans are desperately hoping Finnegan will develop into a high-quality corner. Based on his rookie year, he looks like he has the talent to do just that. A Division I-AA All-American at Samford, Finnegan was the Titans' seventh-round pick last year and played in all 16 games. He showed great versatility both in coverage and on blitzes, on which he recorded two sacks. Although you have to take his game charting numbers with a grain of salt—he barely made it over the 40-pass minimum to be ranked—Finnegan ranked third out of 85 cornerbacks in Success Rate and 15th in yards allowed per pass. Finnegan returned kicks in college, so he may be able to fill in for Jones on special teams as well.

15. David Anderson, WR, Texans

Yes, he had just one catch his rookie year, and, yes, he was a little-known seventh-round pick out of Colorado State in 2006, but now that David Carr isn't holding back the Texans' offense anymore, Gary Kubiak will try to turn the Houston attack into something similar to the one he ran in Denver, and Anderson should get a chance to show what he can do. Kubiak has always loved receivers who are good blockers (going back to his days coaching Rod Smith), and Anderson qualifies there.

16. Charlie Johnson, OT, Colts

A sixth-round rookie from Oklahoma State, Johnson hardly played last year, starting just one game, but when he was forced to enter the lineup in the middle of the Super Bowl, he stepped right in and played very well against the ferocious Bears defense. Colts general manager Bill Polian believes in building an offensive line with late-round picks, and he seems to have found another good one in Johnson.

17. Stephen Tulloch, LB, Titans

From looking at him, you'd never believe that Tulloch is an NFL linebacker. Generously listed as 5-foot-11 and 230 pounds, he looks like a safety, maybe, but linebacker? That's what the personnel guys in the war rooms were no doubt saying when they passed on him until the fourth round of last year's draft, but as a rookie out of North Carolina State, Tulloch played in all 16 games for the Titans, starting three, and he looked like a fast and fierce player who's going to get better every year for the foreseeable future.

18. Jonathan Lewis, DT, Cardinals

Much like Dumervil, Lewis is a defensive lineman who would have gone a few rounds higher if he were a few inches taller. At Virginia Tech, Lewis and Darryl Tapp were both part of an excellent defensive line, but, while Tapp was drafted in the second round by the Seahawks last year, Lewis lasted until the sixth. The 6-foot-1, 310-pound Lewis doesn't look big enough to be a disruptive presence in the middle of the line, but in the limited playing time he got with the Cardinals last season, he looked like a good one-gap tackle who could surprise given the new coaching staff's emphasis on toughness and technique.

19. Ruvell Martin, WR, Packers

If you're one of the few people who actually watched the Week 17 Packers-Bears game on New Year's Eve, you saw what Martin is capable of. Yes, it was meaningless as far as the Bears were concerned, but, even in a meaningless game, Martin's seven catches for 118 yards were impressive. An undrafted rookie out of Saginaw Valley State, Martin was invited to camp by the San Diego Chargers, who then told him he ought to give NFL Europe a try. He did. In 2005, he led that league with 679 receiving yards and twelve touchdowns, and his Amsterdam Admirals won the World Bowl. In 2007, he should finally get some playing time in a game bigger than a Week 17 snoozer or a World Bowl, and he should make the most of it.

20. Leonard Weaver, FB, Seahawks

Weaver played tight end for Division II powerhouse Carson-Newman. The Seahawks signed him after he wasn't picked in the 2005 draft and moved him to fullback. He played in all 16 games as a rookie, demonstrating that he can be a devastating blocker and a good runner when he gets the opportunity. Weaver spent the 2006 season on injured reserve with a high ankle sprain, but the Seattle coaches love what he can do. He is surprisingly agile for his size (251 pounds), and he should be required to register his stiff-arm as a lethal weapon. He could be a factor in 2007, especially if Mack Strong's blocking continues to deteriorate.

21. Scott Starks, CB, Jaguars

Jacksonville took Starks out of Wisconsin late in the third round of the 2005 draft. He hasn't played a lot yet, but our game charting numbers show that he plays well when he gets on the field. His 63 percent Success Rate last year was the highest on the team, although we should note that it came on just 16 passes, many of them against the Titans' sub-par receivers. College fans remember Starks for picking up a Kyle Orton fumble and running it in for a touchdown, single-handedly ending talk that the Purdue quarterback was a Heisman Trophy candidate.

22. Michael Robinson, RB, 49ers

Entering the 2006 draft, NFL scouts were lukewarm on Robinson. They knew they wanted him to switch from quarterback, which he played at Penn State, to some other position, but they weren't sure which position (receiver? running back? safety?). Robinson didn't help matters much by declining to participate in any workouts at the scouting combine. Still, the 49ers took him in the fourth round, and he made an instant impact, ranking second on the team in special teams tackles. He still hasn't found his niche on offense, but as he learns to run better routes and get tougher in short-yardage situations, he should be a valuable player.

23. Zach Strief, OG, Saints

Last year's seventh-round pick out of Northwestern, Strief is a colossal offensive lineman, but not a good athlete. He's a project, for sure, but at Northwestern the 6-foot-7, 349-pounder looked like a guy who could turn into a stud if he had the right coaching, and Saints offensive line coach Doug Marrone (who doubles as the offensive coordinator)

showed last year with the Jets that he's more than capable of developing solid players.

24. Junior Glymph, DE/OLB, Cowboys

Look, it's another undrafted free agent from Carson-Newman, this one from the class of 2004. Glymph looked absolutely dominant in the 1996 preseason, like a proto-typical 6-foot-6, 275-pound pass rusher. He then played in just two games in the regular season. It's a bit dangerous to get too excited about preseason warriors such as Glymph, who has spent one year in Atlanta and two in Dallas, but has played in only eight games, but he looks like he'd be an excellent fit in the Wade Phillips defense, and this could finally be the year he gets a chance at some sustained playing time.

25. Marques Hagans, WR/KR, Rams

A two-year starter at quarterback at Virginia (he took over after Schaub left), Hagans also saw time at wide receiver, returner, and tailback in college. Although he spent the entire 2006 season on the practice squad, his ability and versatility will have him competing for a receiver/return spot this season. Torry Holt is 31 and Isaac Bruce is 34. They won't be around forever, and Hagans is a good bet to pick up some of the slack.

Honorable mention:

Miles Austin, WR, Cowboys

Mike Bell, RB, Broncos

Jerome Harrison, RB, Browns

Rob Sims, OG, Seahawks

Mike Wright, DT, Patriots

Statistical Appendix

Fantasy Projections

Table 1 shows the top-200 players according to the KUBIAK projection system, ranked by projected fantasy value (**FANT**) in 2007. We've used the following generic scoring system:

- 1 point for each 10 yards rushing, 10 yards receiving, or 20 yards passing
- 6 points for each rushing or receiving TD, 4 points for each passing TD
- −2 points for each interception
- 1 point for each extra point, 3 points for each field goal
- Team defense: 2 points for a fumble recovery, interception, or safety, 1 point for a sack, and 6 points for a touchdown.

Note that the fantasy totals in table 1 may not match these calculations exactly because each touchdown projection is not necessarily a round number. (For example, a quarterback listed with 2 rushing touchdowns may actually be projected with 2.4 rushing touchdowns, which will add 14 fantasy points to the player's total rather than 12.) Fantasy value does not include adjustments for week-to-week consistency, but we have listed each player's **Risk** for 2007, based on the likelihood that the player will fail to meet his projection for any reason, including injury or decline. The risk colors are:

- Red: Standard risk
- Yellow: Less than usual risk
- Green: Least amount of risk
- Blue: Peyton Manning

Players are ranked in order based on the marginal value of each player, the idea being that you draft based on how many more points a player will score than the worst starting player at his position, not how many points he will score overall. The ranks in this table are based on a league that starts 1 QB, 2 RB, 3 WR, 1 TE, 1 K, and 1 DEF. The rankings also include half value for the first running back on the bench, and reduce the value of kickers and defenses to reflect the general drafting habits of fantasy football players.

The columns from left to right are player name and team, the week of the season on which that team has a bye, the player's position, passing yards and touchdowns, interceptions, runs, running yards and touchdowns, receptions, receiving yards and touchdowns, field goals, extra points, fantasy rank, and risk. The final two columns list each player's value in a league that adds one point per reception (**PPR**) as well as draft value rank (**Rk**) for a 12-team PPR league.

A customizable spreadsheet featuring these projections will be available at FootballOutsiders.com for a nominal fee. This spreadsheet will include updates based on injuries and changing forecasts of playing time during the preseason.

Table 1. 2007 KUBIAK Projections for Top 200 Players

Player	Team	Bye	Pos	PaYd	PaTD	INT	Ru	RuYd	RuTD	Rec	RcYd	RcTD	FG	XP	Fant	Risk	PPR	Rk
Frank Gore	SF	6	RB	0	0	0	347	1627	16	47	355	1	0	0	303	Green	350	2
LaDainian Tomlinson	SD	7	RB	25	1	0	327	1443	17	44	305	3	0	0	300	Yellow	344	3
Brian Westbrook	PHI	5	RB	0	0	0	266	1329	10	73	620	4	0	0	278	Yellow	351	1
Joseph Addai	IND	6	RB	0	0	0	330	1430	11	57	453	1	0	0	264	Green	321	5
Steven Jackson	STL	9	RB	0	0	0	312	1372	7	78	719	2	0	0	260	Yellow	338	4
Laurence Maroney	NE	10	RB	0	0	0	304	1411	12	43	351	1	0	0	256	Green	299	8
Marvin Harrison	IND	6	WR	0	0	0	0	0	0	90	1272	10	0	0	190	Green	280	7
Antonio Gates	SD	7	TE	0	0	0	0	0	0	79	970	9	0	0	153	Green	232	9
Donovan McNabb	PHI	5	QB	4221	28	14	64	242	3	0	0	0	0	0	340	Yellow	340	13
Larry Johnson	KC	8	RB	0	0	0	342	1200	13	33	257	1	0	0	227	Red	260	17
Maurice Jones-Drew	JAC	4	RB	0	0	0	239	1161	11	44	347	2	0	0	227	Yellow	271	12

(continued next page)

Table 1. 2007 KUBIAK Projections for Top 200 Players (continued)

Player	Team	Bye	Pos	PaYd	PaTD	INT	Ru	RuYd	RuTD	Rec	RcYd	RcTD	FG	XP	Fant	Risk	PPR	Rk
Steve Smith	CAR	7	WR	0	0	0	10	70	0	88	1241	7	0	0	175	Yellow	263	10
Willis McGahee	BAL	8	RB	0	0	0	311	1290	10	31	257	0	0	0	216	Yellow	247	25
Chad Johnson	CIN	5	WR	0	0	0	0	0	0	82	1258	8	0	0	174	Green	256	11
Rudi Johnson	CIN	5	RB	0	0	0	314	1281	12	21	104	0	0	0	214	Yellow	235	35
Reggie Bush	NO	4	RB	0	0	0	148	698	5	93	859	5	0	0	213	Yellow	306	6
Peyton Manning	IND	6	QB	4263	31	13	18	35	1	0	0	0	0	0	322	Blue	322	23
Willie Parker	PIT	6	RB	0	0	0	316	1298	9	37	212	1	0	0	208	Green	245	26
Donald Driver	GB	7	WR	0	0	0	0	0	0	81	1195	7	0	0	162	Yellow	244	14
Marques Colston	NO	4	WR	0	0	0	0	0	0	82	1172	7	0	0	160	Yellow	242	15
Tom Brady	NE	10	QB	3994	30	10	37	94	1	0	0	0	0	0	312	Green	312	30
Cedric Benson	CHI	9	RB	0	0	0	287	1164	7	43	368	1	0	0	199	Green	242	29
Reggie Wayne	IND	6	WR	0	0	0	0	0	0	79	1082	8	0	0	156	Green	234	18
Vince Young	TEN	4	QB	3336	20	16	96	634	5	0	0	0	0	0	307	Green	307	34
Alge Crumpler	ATL	8	TE	0	0	0	0	0	0	64	811	6	0	0	119	Green	183	28
Ronnie Brown	MIA	9	RB	0	0	0	310	1187	7	46	332	0	0	0	195	Yellow	241	31
Lee Evans	BUF	6	WR	0	0	0	0	0	0	77	1089	7	0	0	152	Yellow	229	20
Larry Fitzgerald	ARI	8	WR	0	0	0	0	0	0	79	1066	7	0	0	151	Green	230	19
Torry Holt	STL	9	WR	0	0	0	0	0	0	89	1114	7	0	0	151	Yellow	239	16
Michael Vick	ATL	8	QB	2550	16	10	141	892	7	0	0	0	0	0	304	Green	304	38
T. J. Houshmandzadeh	CIN	5	WR	0	0	0	0	0	0	77	1082	7	0	0	150	Green	227	21
Travis Henry	DEN	6	RB	0	0	0	283	1254	8	21	144	0	0	0	191	Yellow	212	52
Ladell Betts	WAS	4	RB	0	0	0	239	1065	6	45	428	1	0	0	190	Yellow	235	36
Anquan Boldin	ARI	8	WR	0	0	0	5	30	0	79	1073	6	0	0	148	Yellow	227	22
Jamal Lewis	CLE	7	RB	0	0	0	315	1219	10	20	80	0	0	0	190	Yellow	210	53
Carson Palmer	CIN	5	QB	4146	29	14	20	39	0	0	0	0	0	0	300	Green	300	41
Roy Williams	DET	6	WR	0	0	0	0	0	0	80	1069	6	0	0	145	Yellow	225	24
Chris Cooley	WAS	4	TE	0	0	0	0	0	0	62	745	6	0	0	108	Green	170	39
Hines Ward	PIT	6	WR	0	0	0	0	0	0	76	1029	6	0	0	142	Yellow	218	27
Jeremy Shockey	NYG	9	TE	0	0	0	0	0	0	63	709	6	0	0	106	Green	170	42
Terrell Owens	DAL	8	WR	0	0	0	0	0	0	71	938	8	0	0	141	Green	212	33
Javon Walker	DEN	6	WR	0	0	0	8	50	0	69	964	6	0	0	139	Yellow	209	37
Thomas Jones	NYJ	10	RB	0	0	0	299	1130	9	27	109	0	0	0	181	Green	208	55
Donte Stallworth	NE	10	WR	0	0	0	0	0	0	63	975	7	0	0	137	Yellow	200	43
Laveranues Coles	NYJ	10	WR	0	0	0	0	0	0	78	1020	6	0	0	137	Yellow	215	32
Muhsin Muhammad	CHI	9	WR	0	0	0	0	0	0	69	985	6	0	0	135	Yellow	204	40
Brandon Jacobs	NYG	9	RB	0	0	0	236	973	9	10	158	1	0	0	176	Yellow	186	76
Tony Gonzalez	KC	8	TE	0	0	0	0	0	0	61	705	5	0	0	98	Yellow	158	46
Drew Brees	NO	4	QB	4091	26	16	25	51	0	0	0	0	0	0	284	Green	284	49
Randy Moss	NE	10	WR	0	0	0	0	0	0	61	911	7	0	0	130	Yellow	191	48
Mark Clayton	BAL	8	WR	0	0	0	5	30	0	64	976	5	0	0	130	Red	193	45
Kellen Winslow	CLE	7	TE	0	0	0	0	0	0	63	774	3	0	0	94	Yellow	157	47
Reggie Brown	PHI	5	WR	0	0	0	0	0	0	52	926	6	0	0	129	Yellow	181	59
Cadillac Williams	TB	10	RB	0	0	0	284	1207	6	25	99	0	0	0	170	Yellow	195	65
Todd Heap	BAL	8	TE	0	0	0	0	0	0	60	645	5	0	0	93	Green	153	51
Santana Moss	WAS	4	WR	0	0	0	10	70	0	60	864	6	0	0	128	Green	188	50
Byron Leftwich	JAC	4	QB	3780	23	10	39	94	1	0	0	0	0	0	279	Red	279	56
Marshawn Lynch	BUF	6	RB	0	0	0	245	1040	6	28	209	1	0	0	167	Yellow	196	64
Edgerrin James	ARI	8	RB	0	0	0	269	1054	6	37	260	0	0	0	167	Red	204	61
Deion Branch	SEA	8	WR	0	0	0	0	0	0	59	877	6	0	0	124	Green	183	54
Vernon Davis	SF	6	TE	0	0	0	0	0	0	49	604	5	0	0	89	Yellow	138	73
Jason Witten	DAL	8	TE	0	0	0	0	0	0	60	672	4	0	0	88	Yellow	149	57
Ahman Green	HOU	10	RB	0	0	0	250	971	6	35	287	0	0	0	165	Yellow	200	62

Player	Team	Bye	Pos	PaYd	PaTD	INT	Ru	RuYd	RuTD	Rec	RcYd	RcTD	FG	XP	Fant	Risk	PPR	Rk
L. J. Smith	PHI	5	TE	0	0	0	0	0	0	45	591	5	0	0	87	Green	132	91
Ben Watson	NE	10	TE	0	0	0	0	0	0	45	552	5	0	0	86	Green	130	95
D. J. Hackett	SEA	8	WR	0	0	0	0	0	0	59	852	6	0	0	121	Yellow	179	60
Stephen Gostkowski	NE	10	K	0	0	0	0	0	0	0	0	0	31	48	141	Yellow	141	66
Joey Galloway	TB	10	WR	0	0	0	0	0	0	53	823	6	0	0	119	Yellow	172	74
Santonio Holmes	PIT	6	WR	0	0	0	0	0	0	59	925	4	0	0	118	Red	177	63
Chris Chambers	MIA	9	WR	0	0	0	8	50	0	64	847	5	0	0	118	Yellow	182	58
Philip Rivers	SD	7	QB	3748	27	16	24	55	1	0	0	0	0	0	271	Green	271	69
Marion Barber	DAL	8	RB	0	0	0	172	756	9	34	274	1	0	0	160	Yellow	193	68
Braylon Edwards	CLE	7	WR	0	0	0	0	0	0	52	951	4	0	0	118	Red	170	80
Josh Scobee	JAC	4	K	0	0	0	0	0	0	0	0	0	29	48	135	Red	135	71
Matt Hasselbeck	SEA	8	QB	3822	21	16	47	156	1	0	0	0	0	0	268	Green	268	75
Jason Elam	DEN	6	K	0	0	0	0	0	0	0	0	0	30	41	131	Green	131	77
Greg Jennings	GB	7	WR	0	0	0	0	0	0	55	831	5	0	0	113	Red	168	86
Jerricho Cotchery	NYJ	10	WR	0	0	0	5	25	0	63	820	5	0	0	113	Red	176	67
Bernard Berrian	CHI	9	WR	0	0	0	0	0	0	51	820	5	0	0	113	Red	164	98
Steelers	PIT	6	DEF	0	0	0	0	0	0	0	0	0	0	0	139	Green	139	81
David Akers	PHI	5	K	0	0	0	0	0	0	0	0	0	26	49	127	Green	127	82
Andre Johnson	HOU	10	WR	0	0	0	0	0	0	82	842	5	0	0	112	Yellow	193	44
Jerious Norwood	ATL	8	RB	0	0	0	205	922	6	25	232	1	0	0	154	Yellow	179	85
Deuce McAllister	NO	4	RB	0	0	0	225	936	6	35	227	1	0	0	154	Red	189	70
Raiders	OAK	5	DEF	0	0	0	0	0	0	0	0	0	0	0	137	Green	137	84
Terry Glenn	DAL	8	WR	0	0	0	0	0	0	59	834	5	0	0	111	Yellow	170	79
Packers	GB	7	DEF	0	0	0	0	0	0	0	0	0	0	0	136	Green	136	87
Clinton Portis	WAS	4	RB	0	0	0	234	980	4	27	277	0	0	0	153	Red	180	83
Tarvaris Jackson	MIN	5	QB	3363	16	16	101	607	0	0	0	0	0	0	263	Red	263	88
Julius Jones	DAL	8	RB	0	0	0	227	975	6	14	172	0	0	0	151	Red	165	112
Darrell Jackson	SF	6	WR	0	0	0	0	0	0	56	791	5	0	0	110	Green	166	92
Panthers	CAR	7	DEF	0	0	0	0	0	0	0	0	0	0	0	133	Yellow	133	90
Plaxico Burress	NYG	9	WR	0	0	0	0	0	0	52	754	6	0	0	109	Green	162	110
Adam Vinatieri	IND	6	K	0	0	0	0	0	0	0	0	0	23	49	118	Yellow	118	94
Falcons	ATL	8	DEF	0	0	0	0	0	0	0	0	0	0	0	129	Yellow	129	96
Vincent Jackson	SD	7	WR	0	0	0	0	0	0	48	758	5	0	0	107	Yellow	155	126
Brett Favre	GB	7	QB	4031	23	21	19	35	1	0	0	0	0	0	260	Green	260	99
Dallas Clark	IND	6	TE	0	0	0	0	0	0	38	434	5	0	0	72	Green	110	162
Vikings	MIN	5	DEF	0	0	0	0	0	0	0	0	0	0	0	127	Green	127	101
Jeff Reed	PIT	6	K	0	0	0	0	0	0	0	0	0	27	35	116	Yellow	116	102
Ryan Longwell	MIN	5	K	0	0	0	0	0	0	0	0	0	29	29	116	Red	116	103
Shayne Graham	CIN	5	K	0	0	0	0	0	0	0	0	0	23	46	115	Green	115	104
Fred Taylor	JAC	4	RB	0	0	0	190	784	8	17	124	0	0	0	142	Yellow	159	121
Vernand Morency	GB	7	RB	0	0	0	185	818	6	28	219	1	0	0	142	Red	171	100
Ronald Curry	OAK	5	WR	0	0	0	0	0	0	67	844	3	0	0	105	Yellow	172	72
Kevin Curtis	PHI	5	WR	0	0	0	0	0	0	47	761	5	0	0	105	Yellow	152	131
Bills	BUF	6	DEF	0	0	0	0	0	0	0	0	0	0	0	125	Yellow	125	105
Josh Brown	SEA	8	K	0	0	0	0	0	0	0	0	0	27	33	114	Yellow	114	106
Matt Stover	BAL	8	K	0	0	0	0	0	0	0	0	0	25	39	114	Yellow	114	107
Eagles	PHI	5	DEF	0	0	0	0	0	0	0	0	0	0	0	125	Yellow	125	108
LenDale White	TEN	4	RB	0	0	0	214	903	3	33	254	1	0	0	141	Red	173	93
Marc Bulger	STL	9	QB	3980	20	14	21	53	0	0	0	0	0	0	258	Yellow	258	109
Nate Kaeding	SD	7	K	0	0	0	0	0	0	0	0	0	22	47	113	Red	113	111
Isaac Bruce	STL	9	WR	0	0	0	0	0	0	66	813	4	0	0	104	Yellow	170	78
Matt Jones	JAC	4	WR	0	0	0	0	0	0	46	765	5	0	0	104	Green	150	142
Devery Henderson	NO	4	WR	0	0	0	4	30	0	47	749	4	0	0	104	Yellow	151	140

(continued next page)

Table 1. 2007 KUBIAK Projections for Top 200 Players (continued)

Player	Team	Bye	Pos	PaYd	PaTD	INT	Ru	RuYd	RuTD	Rec	RcYd	RcTD	FG	XP	Fant	Risk	PPR	Rk
Warrick Dunn	ATL	8	RB	0	0	0	201	823	6	19	152	1	0	0	139	Green	157	123
Dave Rayner	GB	7	K	0	0	0	0	0	0	0	0	0	26	35	113	Yellow	113	113
49ers	SF	6	DEF	0	0	0	0	0	0	0	0	0	0	0	123	Red	123	114
Shaun Alexander	SEA	8	RB	0	0	0	250	945	6	14	56	1	0	0	138	Red	152	128
Redskins	WAS	4	DEF	0	0	0	0	0	0	0	0	0	0	0	123	Red	123	115
Joe Nedney	SF	6	K	0	0	0	0	0	0	0	0	0	25	37	112	Red	112	116
Heath Miller	PIT	6	TE	0	0	0	0	0	0	36	466	3	0	0	67	Red	103	176
DeAngelo Williams	CAR	7	RB	0	0	0	165	714	5	37	312	1	0	0	135	Yellow	171	97
Broncos	DEN	6	DEF	0	0	0	0	0	0	0	0	0	0	0	122	Yellow	122	118
Ben Roethlisberger	PIT	6	QB	3768	19	15	40	114	2	0	0	0	0	0	254	Green	254	119
Mike Nugent	NYJ	10	K	0	0	0	0	0	0	0	0	0	24	38	110	Yellow	110	122
Randy McMichael	STL	9	TE	0	0	0	0	0	0	45	503	3	0	0	66	Red	110	160
Tatum Bell	DET	6	RB	0	0	0	180	684	5	44	255	1	0	0	132	Red	177	89
Bears	CHI	9	DEF	0	0	0	0	0	0	0	0	0	0	0	120	Green	120	124
Phil Dawson	CLE	7	K	0	0	0	0	0	0	0	0	0	26	30	108	Green	108	125
Antwaan Randle El	WAS	4	WR	40	1	0	15	100	0	42	638	3	0	0	99	Yellow	140	169
Marcedes Lewis	JAC	4	TE	0	0	0	0	0	0	37	420	4	0	0	64	Yellow	101	181
Chester Taylor	MIN	5	RB	0	0	0	173	718	3	35	292	1	0	0	126	Red	162	117
Adrian Peterson	MIN	5	RB	0	0	0	192	833	4	20	142	1	0	0	126	Red	146	135
Bill Cundiff	ATL	8	K	0	0	0	0	0	0	0	0	0	23	38	107	Red	107	127
LaMont Jordan	OAK	5	RB	0	0	0	189	793	4	25	178	0	0	0	125	Red	150	130
John Kasay	CAR	7	K	0	0	0	0	0	0	0	0	0	24	34	106	Red	106	129
Wes Welker	NE	10	WR	0	0	0	0	0	0	51	684	5	0	0	97	Yellow	148	149
Bo Scaife	TEN	4	TE	0	0	0	0	0	0	34	405	3	0	0	61	Red	95	191
Mike Furrey	DET	6	WR	0	0	0	0	0	0	62	761	3	0	0	96	Red	158	120
Bobby Engram	SEA	8	WR	0	0	0	0	0	0	48	705	4	0	0	95	Yellow	143	163
Cardinals	ARI	8	DEF	0	0	0	0	0	0	0	0	0	0	0	115	Red	115	132
Rob Bironas	TEN	4	K	0	0	0	0	0	0	0	0	0	23	35	104	Yellow	104	133
Martin Gramatica	DAL	8	K	0	0	0	0	0	0	0	0	0	23	35	104	Red	104	134
Rex Grossman	CHI	9	QB	3598	23	16	25	45	0	0	0	0	0	0	247	Yellow	247	136
Mike Bell	DEN	6	RB	0	0	0	143	648	5	25	214	0	0	0	119	Yellow	144	141
Lawrence Tynes	NYG	9	K	0	0	0	0	0	0	0	0	0	23	34	103	Red	103	137
Jon Kitna	DET	6	QB	3743	18	20	47	165	2	0	0	0	0	0	247	Green	247	138
Matt Bryant	TB	10	K	0	0	0	0	0	0	0	0	0	23	34	103	Red	103	139
Tony Scheffler	DEN	6	TE	0	0	0	0	0	0	31	355	4	0	0	58	Yellow	90	199
Eric Parker	SD	7	WR	0	0	0	0	0	0	50	767	3	0	0	93	Red	143	164
Seahawks	SEA	8	DEF	0	0	0	0	0	0	0	0	0	0	0	113	Red	113	143
Steve McNair	BAL	8	QB	3444	21	16	39	124	1	0	0	0	0	0	246	Yellow	246	144
Shaun Suisham	WAS	4	K	0	0	0	0	0	0	0	0	0	23	32	101	Red	101	145
Owen Daniels	HOU	10	TE	0	0	0	0	0	0	33	388	3	0	0	57	Red	90	198
Olindo Mare	NO	4	K	0	0	0	0	0	0	0	0	0	21	38	101	Red	101	147
Robbie Gould	CHI	9	K	0	0	0	0	0	0	0	0	0	22	35	101	Red	101	148
Desmond Clark	CHI	9	TE	0	0	0	0	0	0	33	399	3	0	0	57	Red	90	197
Joe Horn	ATL	8	WR	0	0	0	0	0	0	52	687	4	0	0	92	Yellow	144	161
Derrick Mason	BAL	8	WR	0	0	0	0	0	0	56	719	3	0	0	91	Red	147	151
Jeff Wilkins	STL	9	K	0	0	0	0	0	0	0	0	0	23	31	100	Red	100	150
Dwayne Jarrett	CAR	7	WR	0	0	0	0	0	0	41	614	5	0	0	90	Red	132	188
Troy Williamson	MIN	5	WR	0	0	0	0	0	0	43	680	4	0	0	90	Yellow	134	184
Jason Hanson	DET	6	K	0	0	0	0	0	0	0	0	0	23	30	99	Red	99	152
Jerry Porter	OAK	5	WR	0	0	0	0	0	0	49	671	4	0	0	90	Yellow	139	172
Bucs	TB	10	DEF	0	0	0	0	0	0	0	0	0	0	0	110	Red	110	153
Rian Lindell	BUF	6	K	0	0	0	0	0	0	0	0	0	22	32	98	Green	98	154

Player	Team	Bye	Pos	PaYd	PaTD	INT	Ru	RuYd	RuTD	Rec	RcYd	RcTD	FG	XP	Fant	Risk	PPR	Rk
Cowboys	DAL	8	DEF	0	0	0	0	0	0	0	0	0	0	0	109	Yellow	109	155
DeShaun Foster	CAR	7	RB	0	0	0	173	696	3	32	217	0	0	0	109	Red	142	146
Tony Romo	DAL	8	QB	3567	21	19	41	139	1	0	0	0	0	0	242	Red	242	156
Lions	DET	6	DEF	0	0	0	0	0	0	0	0	0	0	0	109	Red	109	157
Reggie Williams	JAC	4	WR	0	0	0	4	20	0	46	632	4	0	0	89	Green	135	183
Reuben Droughns	NYG	9	RB	0	0	0	161	662	3	26	186	0	0	0	107	Red	134	158
Kris Brown	HOU	10	K	0	0	0	0	0	0	0	0	0	22	31	97	Yellow	97	159
Calvin Johnson	DET	6	WR	0	0	0	0	0	0	40	641	4	0	0	87	Red	127	194
Ernest Wilford	JAC	4	WR	0	0	0	0	0	0	41	588	5	0	0	86	Green	128	193
Ravens	BAL	8	DEF	0	0	0	0	0	0	0	0	0	0	0	106	Yellow	106	165
Neil Rackers	ARI	8	K	0	0	0	0	0	0	0	0	0	23	26	95	Yellow	95	166
Browns	CLE	7	DEF	0	0	0	0	0	0	0	0	0	0	0	106	Yellow	106	167
Ruvell Martin	GB	7	WR	0	0	0	0	0	0	41	647	3	0	0	85	Yellow	126	195
Patriots	NE	10	DEF	0	0	0	0	0	0	0	0	0	0	0	105	Yellow	105	168
Joe Jurevicius	CLE	7	WR	0	0	0	0	0	0	43	600	4	0	0	83	Green	126	196
Justin Medlock	KC	8	K	0	0	0	0	0	0	0	0	0	20	31	91	Yellow	91	170
Giants	NYG	9	DEF	0	0	0	0	0	0	0	0	0	0	0	102	Red	102	171
Chris Henry	TEN	4	RB	0	0	0	140	562	4	17	127	1	0	0	96	Red	113	180
Brandon Marshall	DEN	6	WR	0	0	0	0	0	0	41	559	4	0	0	82	Green	123	200
Matt Leinart	ARI	8	QB	3626	18	18	31	85	1	0	0	0	0	0	234	Yellow	234	173
Rams	STL	9	DEF	0	0	0	0	0	0	0	0	0	0	0	101	Red	101	174
Brandon Jackson	GB	7	RB	0	0	0	146	563	3	23	158	1	0	0	93	Red	116	178
Jaguars	JAC	4	DEF	0	0	0	0	0	0	0	0	0	0	0	101	Yellow	101	175
Jay Cutler	DEN	6	QB	3174	25	17	30	66	1	0	0	0	0	0	232	Green	232	177
Saints	NO	4	DEF	0	0	0	0	0	0	0	0	0	0	0	99	Red	99	179
Brandon Jones	TEN	4	WR	0	0	0	0	0	0	50	569	4	0	0	79	Red	129	190
Eddie Kennison	KC	8	WR	0	0	0	0	0	0	52	595	3	0	0	78	Yellow	130	189
Dominic Rhodes	OAK	5	RB	0	0	0	113	446	3	24	189	0	0	0	85	Red	100	185
Kevin Jones	DET	6	RB	0	0	0	83	345	3	31	271	0	0	0	81	Red	112	182
Chris Simms	TB	10	QB	3414	18	12	27	50	1	0	0	0	0	0	228	Red	228	186
Chad Pennington	NYJ	10	QB	3192	20	14	36	106	1	0	0	0	0	0	228	Yellow	228	187
Jason Campbell	WAS	4	QB	3204	18	18	51	185	1	0	0	0	0	0	224	Green	224	192

The Greatest Running Back Seasons of All Time

From the essay "The Greatest Running Back Seasons of All Time," located in the front of this book, here are the top-100 running back seasons between 1957 and 2006. Table 2 gives actual stats, while table 3 gives the numbers adjusted to modern running back usage patterns and the current offensive environment.

Each table lists rank (**Rk**), the player's **Name**, **Year**, and **Team**, **Runs**, rushing yards (**RuYd**), rushing touchdowns (**RuTD**), yards per rush (**Yd/R**), receptions (**Rec**), receiving

Table 2. Top 100 RB Seasons: Actual Numbers

Rk	Name	Year	Team	G	Runs	RuYd	RuTD	Yd/R	Rec	RcYd	RcTD	Fum	%Tm	Tm RuFD
1	O. J. Simpson	1975	BUF	14	329	1817	16	5.5	28	426	7	7	56%	162
2	Marshall Faulk	1999	STL	16	253	1381	7	5.5	87	1048	5	2	59%	102
3	Barry Sanders	1997	DET	16	335	2053	11	6.1	33	305	3	3	75%	120
4	Earl Campbell	1980	HOU	15	373	1934	13	5.2	11	47	0	4	65%	155
5	Thurman Thomas	1991	BUF	15	288	1407	7	4.9	62	631	5	5	57%	128
6	Leroy Kelly	1968	CLE	14	248	1239	16	5.0	22	297	4	6	55%	104
7	Barry Sanders	1994	DET	16	331	1883	7	5.7	44	283	1	0	82%	94
8	Terrell Davis	1998	DEN	16	392	2008	21	5.1	25	217	2	2	75%	135
9	Jim Brown	1963	CLE	14	291	1863	12	6.4	24	268	3	7	63%	135
10	Larry Csonka	1971	MIA	14	195	1051	7	5.4	13	113	1	0	40%	121
11	O. J. Simpson	1973	BUF	14	332	2003	12	6.0	6	70	0	7	55%	152
12	Larry Johnson	2005	KC	16	336	1750	20	5.2	33	343	1	5	65%	138
13	William Andrews	1983	ATL	16	331	1567	7	4.7	59	609	4	6	67%	118
14	Jim Brown	1965	CLE	14	289	1544	17	5.3	34	328	4	6	61%	133
15	Emmitt Smith	1995	DAL	16	377	1773	25	4.7	62	375	0	7	76%	141
16	James Brooks	1986	CIN	16	205	1087	5	5.3	54	686	4	2	39%	134
17	Jim Taylor	1962	GB	14	272	1474	19	5.4	22	106	0	5	53%	145
18	Barry Sanders	1995	DET	16	314	1500	11	4.8	48	398	1	3	81%	91
19	Billy Sims	1981	DET	14	296	1437	13	4.9	28	451	2	9	50%	167
20	Priest Holmes	2003	KC	16	320	1420	27	4.4	74	690	0	1	72%	120
21	Walter Payton	1977	CHI	14	339	1852	14	5.5	27	269	2	11	57%	141
22	Marshall Faulk	2000	STL	14	253	1359	18	5.4	81	830	8	0	66%	112
23	Otis Armstrong	1974	DEN	14	263	1407	9	5.3	38	405	3	6	54%	120
24	Tom Matte	1969	BAL	14	235	909	11	3.9	43	513	2	4	56%	99
25	Priest Holmes	2002	KC	14	313	1615	21	5.2	70	672	3	1	68%	140
26	Barry Sanders	1990	DET	16	255	1304	13	5.1	36	480	3	4	70%	112
27	Jim Taylor	1964	GB	13	235	1169	12	5.0	38	354	3	6	47%	133
28	Clem Daniels	1963	OAK	14	215	1099	3	5.1	30	685	5	8	60%	85
29	Garrison Hearst	1998	SF	16	310	1570	7	5.1	39	535	2	4	63%	129
30	Roger Craig	1985	SF	16	214	1050	9	4.9	92	1016	6	5	45%	137
31	O. J. Simpson	1976	BUF	14	290	1503	8	5.2	22	259	1	6	53%	135
32	Lorenzo White	1992	HOU	16	265	1226	7	4.6	57	641	1	2	75%	101
33	LaDainian Tomlinson	2006	SD	16	348	1815	28	5.2	56	508	3	2	67%	137
34	Wilbert Montgomery	1981	PHI	15	286	1402	8	4.9	49	521	2	3	51%	157
35	Earl Campbell	1979	HOU	16	368	1697	19	4.6	16	94	0	8	60%	149
36	Jim Taylor	1961	GB	14	243	1307	15	5.4	25	175	1	2	51%	142
37	Steve Owens	1971	DET	14	246	1035	8	4.2	32	350	2	5	46%	131
38	Jim Brown	1960	CLE	12	215	1257	9	5.8	19	204	2	9	56%	107
39	Emmitt Smith	1994	DAL	15	368	1484	21	4.0	50	341	1	1	67%	136
40	Marshall Faulk	2001	STL	14	260	1382	12	5.3	83	765	9	3	63%	104
41	Charlie Garner	2002	OAK	16	180	959	7	5.3	91	941	4	0	43%	113
42	Joe Morrison	1969	NYG	14	107	387	4	3.6	44	647	7	0	27%	91
43	Gale Sayers	1965	CHI	14	166	867	14	5.2	29	507	6	9	35%	132
44	Terrell Davis	1997	DEN	15	369	1750	15	4.7	42	287	0	4	71%	138
45	Jim Brown	1964	CLE	14	280	1446	7	5.2	36	340	2	6	64%	119
46	Freeman McNeil	1982	NYJ	9	151	786	6	5.2	16	187	1	7	50%	87

(continued on page 508)

yards (**RcYd**), receiving touchdowns (**RcTD**), fumbles (**Fum**), the player's share of total team carries (**%Tm**), and the team's total of rushing first downs (**Tm RuFD**). The table with actual numbers also gives games played (**G**). The table with adjusted numbers also gives the player's Z-score (**Z**), as explained in the essay, and the impact of defensive opponents (**Def**). This represents the difference in the given Z-score and the Z-score without adjusting for schedule, with negative numbers representing easier schedules and positive numbers representing harder schedules.

Table 3. Top 100 RB Seasons: Adjusted Numbers

Rk	Name	Year	Team	Runs	RuYd	RuTD	Yd/R	Rec	RcYd	RcTD	Fum	%Tm	Tm RuFD	Z	Def
1	O. J. Simpson	1975	BUF	337	1841	21	5.7	33	427	4	4	63%	138	3.35	−0.19
2	Marshall Faulk	1999	STL	265	1498	8	5.8	90	1005	3	2	62%	117	3.33	−0.51
3	Barry Sanders	1997	DET	345	2134	13	6.4	43	394	2	3	77%	126	3.32	0.02
4	Earl Campbell	1980	HOU	396	2194	19	5.4	11	40	0	2	79%	136	3.09	0.18
5	Thurman Thomas	1991	BUF	347	1766	8	5.1	73	734	5	5	70%	135	3.06	−0.53
6	Leroy Kelly	1968	CLE	335	1717	24	5.1	32	349	3	5	73%	112	3.04	0.06
7	Barry Sanders	1994	DET	372	2298	9	6.3	49	303	1	0	86%	104	3.02	0.15
8	Terrell Davis	1998	DEN	365	1975	22	5.3	29	219	1	2	73%	144	2.89	0.09
9	Jim Brown	1963	CLE	368	2358	19	6.5	39	298	1	5	79%	134	2.88	−0.27
10	Larry Csonka	1971	MIA	246	1361	12	5.5	21	162	1	0	52%	127	2.83	0.13
11	O. J. Simpson	1973	BUF	310	1811	18	6.1	8	77	0	6	59%	162	2.75	−0.67
12	Larry Johnson	2005	KC	338	1829	19	5.4	40	430	1	6	65%	138	2.74	0.28
13	William Andrews	1983	ATL	313	1497	8	4.8	61	529	2	4	70%	102	2.70	0.24
14	Jim Brown	1965	CLE	384	2154	27	5.6	47	319	2	4	79%	127	2.69	−0.23
15	Emmitt Smith	1995	DAL	382	1843	23	4.9	64	384	0	6	76%	148	2.64	−0.16
16	James Brooks	1986	CIN	222	1257	6	5.6	62	711	3	1	46%	126	2.63	0.18
17	Jim Taylor	1962	GB	342	1041	18	5.5	31	109	0	3	66%	129	2.62	0.05
18	Barry Sanders	1995	DET	339	1729	12	5.0	49	407	1	3	81%	96	2.61	0.21
19	Billy Sims	1981	DET	264	1345	13	5.0	26	354	1	6	51%	143	2.58	0.15
20	Priest Holmes	2003	KC	302	1302	25	4.4	69	675	0	1	70%	121	2.55	0.21
21	Walter Payton	1977	CHI	310	1791	20	5.8	36	299	1	7	63%	151	2.55	−0.39
22	Marshall Faulk	2000	STL	266	1406	18	5.4	76	687	5	0	66%	114	2.53	−0.35
23	Otis Armstrong	1974	DEN	307	1701	14	5.7	46	407	2	4	67%	115	2.48	−0.26
24	Tom Matte	1969	BAL	331	1331	19	4.0	62	567	1	4	75%	108	2.40	0.74
25	Priest Holmes	2002	KC	328	1645	18	5.1	58	542	2	1	69%	131	2.37	−0.09
26	Barry Sanders	1990	DET	331	1704	18	5.2	51	553	2	3	88%	112	2.35	0.12
27	Jim Taylor	1964	GB	315	1648	23	5.1	45	324	1	4	61%	129	2.32	0.12
28	Clem Daniels	1963	OAK	276	1425	5	5.2	49	763	2	5	75%	84	2.31	0.12
29	Garrison Hearst	1998	SF	300	1549	8	5.3	46	540	1	4	82%	130	2.30	0.25
30	Roger Craig	1985	SF	214	1055	11	4.9	93	866	4	3	47%	117	2.30	0.10
31	O. J. Simpson	1976	BUF	289	1458	13	5.2	32	290	1	4	60%	123	2.29	−0.24
32	Lorenzo White	1992	HOU	292	1395	9	4.7	61	637	1	2	82%	115	2.26	−0.02
33	LaDainian Tomlinson	2006	SD	334	1719	28	5.2	54	486	5	3	66%	139	2.25	−0.18
34	Wilbert Montgomery	1981	PHI	253	1251	9	5.0	45	409	1	2	53%	134	2.21	−0.17
35	Earl Campbell	1979	HOU	356	1690	21	4.8	18	94	0	4	68%	116	2.20	0.09
36	Jim Taylor	1961	GB	335	1695	19	5.3	37	185	0	1	69%	131	2.19	−0.29
37	Steve Owens	1971	DET	312	1398	17	4.3	51	501	1	5	60%	138	2.19	0.31
38	Jim Brown	1960	CLE	351	2101	16	5.9	33	259	1	8	81%	117	2.19	0.23
39	Emmitt Smith	1994	DAL	377	1727	25	4.5	56	365	1	1	70%	151	2.18	0.11
40	Marshall Faulk	2001	STL	274	1426	15	5.4	79	705	6	3	65%	119	2.18	−0.36
41	Charlie Garner	2002	OAK	193	983	6	5.2	76	759	3	0	44%	106	2.18	−0.25
42	Joe Morrison	1969	NYG	151	560	6	3.7	63	715	5	0	36%	100	2.14	−0.02
43	Gale Sayers	1965	CHI	230	1277	24	5.5	40	493	3	7	45%	127	2.14	0.13
44	Terrell Davis	1997	DEN	373	1882	21	4.9	54	371	0	4	73%	145	2.14	0.29
45	Jim Brown	1964	CLE	365	1942	12	5.3	43	311	1	4	82%	116	2.12	−0.01
46	Freeman McNeil	1982	NYJ	262	1441	15	5.6	27	262	1	7	56%	142	2.12	0.24

(continued on page 509)

Table 2. Top 100 RB Seasons: Actual Numbers (continued from page 506)

Rk	Name	Year	Team	G	Runs	RuYd	RuTD	Yd/R	Rec	RcYd	RcTD	Fum	%Tm	Tm RuFD
47	William Andrews	1982	ATL	9	139	573	5	4.1	42	503	2	1	45%	79
48	Eric Dickerson	1988	IND	16	388	1659	14	4.3	36	377	1	5	71%	153
49	Leroy Kelly	1966	CLE	14	209	1141	15	5.5	32	366	1	1	50%	117
50	Marcus Allen	1984	OAK	16	275	1168	13	4.2	64	758	5	8	53%	114
51	Priest Holmes	2001	KC	16	327	1555	8	4.8	62	614	2	4	73%	119
52	Curtis Martin	2004	NYJ	16	371	1697	12	4.6	41	245	2	2	70%	135
53	Leroy Kelly	1967	CLE	14	235	1205	11	5.1	20	282	2	7	53%	119
54	Tiki Barber	2005	NYG	16	357	1860	9	5.2	54	530	2	5	76%	106
55	Herschel Walker	1987	DAL	12	209	891	7	4.3	60	715	1	4	45%	93
56	Walter Payton	1979	CHI	16	369	1610	14	4.4	31	313	2	7	59%	140
57	Chuck Foreman	1976	MIN	14	278	1155	13	4.2	55	567	1	7	51%	125
58	Barry Sanders	1996	DET	16	307	1553	11	5.1	24	147	0	4	79%	105
59	Edgerrin James	1999	IND	16	369	1553	13	4.2	62	586	4	9	88%	89
60	Walter Payton	1978	CHI	16	333	1395	11	4.2	50	480	0	5	53%	136
61	Lenny Moore	1959	BAL	12	91	422	2	4.6	47	846	6	4	21%	95
62	Hoyle Granger	1967	HOU	14	236	1194	6	5.1	31	300	3	1	50%	111
63	Terrell Davis	1996	DEN	16	345	1538	13	4.5	36	310	2	5	66%	134
64	MacArthur Lane	1970	STL	14	206	977	11	4.7	32	365	2	2	48%	110
65	Edgerrin James	2004	IND	16	334	1548	9	4.6	51	483	0	6	78%	94
66	Edgerrin James	2000	IND	16	387	1709	13	4.4	63	594	5	5	89%	111
67	Lenny Moore	1961	BAL	13	92	648	7	7.0	49	728	8	1	20%	124
68	James Brooks	1989	CIN	16	221	1239	7	5.6	37	306	2	9	42%	136
69	Neal Anderson	1989	CHI	16	274	1275	11	4.7	50	434	4	5	53%	136
70	Abner Haynes	1962	DTEX	14	221	1049	13	4.7	39	573	6	4	46%	119
71	Gerald Riggs	1985	ATL	16	397	1719	10	4.3	33	267	0	0	71%	149
72	Lenny Moore	1960	BAL	12	91	374	4	4.1	45	936	9	3	26%	64
73	Gale Sayers	1966	CHI	14	229	1231	8	5.4	34	447	2	2	49%	96
74	Lenny Moore	1957	BAL	12	98	488	3	5.0	40	687	7	6	23%	91
75	Albert Bentley	1987	IND	12	142	631	7	4.4	34	447	2	3	29%	122
76	Ron Johnson	1972	NYG	14	298	1182	9	4.0	45	451	5	3	57%	120
77	Curt Warner	1986	SEA	16	319	1481	13	4.6	41	342	0	6	62%	123
78	Walter Payton	1984	CHI	16	381	1684	11	4.4	45	368	0	5	57%	164
79	Larry Brown	1970	WAS	13	237	1125	5	4.7	37	341	2	6	53%	122
80	Jerome Bettis	1993	LARM	16	294	1429	7	4.9	26	244	0	4	65%	95
81	Tony Dorsett	1977	DAL	14	208	1007	12	4.8	29	273	1	7	37%	118
82	Shaun Alexander	2005	SEA	16	370	1880	27	5.1	15	78	1	5	71%	142
83	Emmitt Smith	1993	DAL	14	283	1486	9	5.3	57	414	1	4	58%	91
84	Lenny Moore	1958	BAL	12	82	598	7	7.3	50	938	7	5	18%	117
85	Eric Dickerson	1984	LARM	16	379	2105	14	5.6	21	139	0	14	70%	140
86	LaDainian Tomlinson	2003	SD	16	313	1645	13	5.3	100	725	4	2	75%	117
87	Corey Dillon	1997	CIN	16	233	1129	10	4.8	27	259	0	1	52%	104
88	Thurman Thomas	1990	BUF	16	271	1297	11	4.8	49	532	2	6	57%	123
89	Jim Brown	1961	CLE	14	305	1408	8	4.6	46	459	2	6	64%	116
90	Barry Sanders	1989	DET	15	280	1470	14	5.3	24	282	0	10	67%	117
91	Clinton Portis	2002	DEN	16	273	1508	15	5.5	33	364	2	5	60%	125
92	Tony Reed	1978	KC	16	206	1053	5	5.1	48	483	1	6	31%	160
93	Shaun Alexander	2004	SEA	16	353	1696	16	4.8	23	170	4	4	75%	110
94	Herschel Walker	1986	DAL	16	151	737	12	4.9	76	837	2	5	34%	98
95	Corey Dillon	2004	NE	15	345	1635	12	4.7	15	103	1	5	66%	120
96	Stephen Davis	1999	WAS	14	290	1405	17	4.8	23	111	0	4	63%	121
97	John David Crow	1960	STL	12	183	1071	6	5.9	25	462	3	11	38%	127
98	Walter Payton	1983	CHI	16	314	1421	6	4.5	53	607	2	5	54%	154
99	Abner Haynes	1964	KC	14	139	697	4	5.0	38	562	3	0	33%	90
100	Thurman Thomas	1989	BUF	16	298	1244	6	4.2	60	669	6	7	56%	136

Table 3. Top 100 RB Seasons: Adjusted Numbers *(continued from page 507)*

Rk	Name	Year	Team	Runs	RuYd	RuTD	Yd/R	Rec	RcYd	RcTD	Fum	%Tm	Tm RuFD	Z	Def
47	William Andrews	1982	ATL	254	1174	11	4.5	71	704	2	1	50%	129	2.10	0.00
48	Eric Dickerson	1988	IND	402	1762	16	4.4	41	397	1	3	84%	136	2.10	−0.33
49	Leroy Kelly	1966	CLE	279	1605	20	5.8	41	333	0	1	63%	118	2.07	0.00
50	Marcus Allen	1984	OAK	258	1145	14	4.4	63	697	3	5	55%	105	2.06	−0.02
51	Priest Holmes	2001	KC	347	1723	11	4.8	59	566	1	4	76%	136	2.05	0.18
52	Curtis Martin	2004	NYJ	377	1740	13	4.6	46	266	2	2	72%	140	2.04	0.34
53	Leroy Kelly	1967	CLE	321	1739	17	5.4	26	306	1	6	69%	117	2.01	−0.02
54	Tiki Barber	2005	NYG	364	1963	9	5.4	65	664	2	6	76%	106	2.00	0.08
55	Herschel Walker	1987	DAL	266	1182	10	4.5	91	996	1	4	62%	97	1.99	−0.10
56	Walter Payton	1979	CHI	336	1533	15	4.5	35	313	1	4	67%	109	1.99	0.05
57	Chuck Foreman	1976	MIN	274	1180	21	4.2	79	634	1	4	59%	114	1.99	0.27
58	Barry Sanders	1996	DET	321	1706	12	5.4	31	202	0	4	81%	117	1.98	0.08
59	Edgerrin James	1999	IND	388	1803	17	4.5	64	562	2	9	93%	103	1.98	0.50
60	Walter Payton	1978	CHI	297	1335	15	4.4	53	464	0	3	61%	113	1.97	0.16
61	Lenny Moore	1959	BAL	167	757	2	4.5	92	1345	5	5	36%	97	1.96	−0.07
62	Hoyle Granger	1967	HOU	319	1687	9	5.3	41	326	2	1	65%	109	1.96	−0.10
63	Terrell Davis	1996	DEN	349	1651	14	4.8	47	426	2	5	68%	149	1.95	−0.17
64	MacArthur Lane	1970	STL	284	1377	18	5.1	44	395	1	2	65%	132	1.94	−0.31
65	Edgerrin James	2004	IND	354	1637	10	4.6	58	524	0	5	80%	98	1.93	−0.13
66	Edgerrin James	2000	IND	388	1764	15	4.5	59	492	3	5	88%	113	1.93	0.12
67	Lenny Moore	1961	BAL	126	855	10	6.9	73	770	3	1	27%	114	1.92	−0.16
68	James Brooks	1989	CIN	240	1410	7	5.9	46	318	2	6	48%	132	1.90	0.11
69	Neal Anderson	1989	CHI	313	1535	12	4.9	62	450	3	4	61%	132	1.87	0.38
70	Abner Haynes	1962	DTEX	281	1328	13	4.8	55	589	3	3	58%	105	1.87	−0.11
71	Gerald Riggs	1985	ATL	397	1766	14	4.4	33	228	0	0	75%	127	1.83	0.32
72	Lenny Moore	1960	BAL	154	634	7	4.2	79	1190	5	3	38%	70	1.80	−0.02
73	Gale Sayers	1966	CHI	209	1725	12	5.7	44	407	1	2	62%	97	1.78	0.06
74	Lenny Moore	1957	BAL	197	1018	6	5.3	105	1166	5	8	43%	93	1.78	−0.18
75	Albert Bentley	1987	IND	182	842	11	4.7	52	623	2	3	40%	128	1.78	−0.08
76	Ron Johnson	1972	NYG	329	1327	15	4.0	64	473	3	3	65%	116	1.76	0.10
77	Curt Warner	1986	SEA	364	1795	14	4.9	47	355	0	4	73%	116	1.76	0.17
78	Walter Payton	1984	CHI	346	1510	11	4.5	44	338	0	3	58%	151	1.75	−0.49
79	Larry Brown	1970	WAS	333	1667	11	5.1	51	369	1	6	72%	146	1.74	0.12
80	Jerome Bettis	1993	LARM	354	1777	15	5.2	31	271	0	4	78%	118	1.74	0.15
81	Tony Dorsett	1977	DAL	198	1066	20	5.2	39	304	1	4	41%	127	1.73	0.27
82	Shaun Alexander	2005	SEA	369	1866	24	5.2	18	98	1	6	71%	142	1.73	−0.38
83	Emmitt Smith	1993	DAL	334	1787	16	5.6	68	460	1	4	69%	113	1.72	−0.12
84	Lenny Moore	1958	DAL	176	1208	9	7.1	109	1335	5	7	34%	108	1.70	−0.12
85	Eric Dickerson	1984	LARM	366	2014	14	5.7	21	128	0	8	72%	129	1.70	−0.27
86	LaDainian Tomlinson	2003	SD	305	1548	12	5.2	93	710	4	2	73%	118	1.70	−0.13
87	Corey Dillon	1997	CIN	239	1236	13	5.0	35	335	0	1	53%	110	1.68	0.13
88	Thurman Thomas	1990	BUF	336	1562	12	4.8	70	612	2	4	72%	123	1.67	−0.45
89	Jim Brown	1961	CLE	400	1881	14	4.5	68	485	1	4	86%	107	1.67	0.14
90	Barry Sanders	1989	DET	308	1645	14	5.5	30	293	0	7	76%	114	1.66	−0.20
91	Clinton Portis	2002	DEN	284	1503	13	5.4	28	294	1	5	60%	117	1.65	−0.30
92	Tony Reed	1978	KC	186	970	7	5.3	51	467	1	3	36%	133	1.64	−0.07
93	Shaun Alexander	2004	SEA	353	1666	15	4.8	26	184	4	4	78%	114	1.60	−0.20
94	Herschel Walker	1986	DAL	173	889	15	5.1	87	868	2	3	40%	92	1.60	0.23
95	Corey Dillon	2004	NE	346	1641	12	4.7	17	112	1	5	68%	125	1.59	0.16
96	Stephen Davis	1999	WAS	307	1605	22	5.1	24	106	0	4	66%	139	1.58	0.00
97	John David Crow	1960	STL	291	1715	10	5.9	44	588	2	10	55%	138	1.58	−0.14
98	Walter Payton	1983	CHI	271	1218	6	4.6	55	527	1	3	56%	133	1.57	−0.34
99	Abner Haynes	1964	KC	185	975	7	5.2	45	514	1	0	43%	88	1.57	0.09
100	Thurman Thomas	1989	BUF	322	1368	6	4.4	74	694	5	5	64%	132	1.57	−0.43

Drive Stats

The stats in tables 4, 5, and 6 are computed from the NFL drive charts and are not adjusted for strength of schedule or situation. The numbers include total drives (**Tot**), yards per drive (**Yd/Dr**), points per drive (**Pts/Dr**), touchdowns per drive (**TD/Dr**), punts per drive (**Punt/Dr**), turnovers per drive (**TO/Dr**), percentage of drives that went three-and-out (**3Out%**), average starting field position based on the line of scrimmage on the first play of a drive (**LOS/Dr**), and Drive Success Rate (**DSR**) along with the team's league **Rank** in each category. DSR, introduced in *Pro Football Prospectus 2005*, measures the percentage of time that the offense converted a set of downs for a first down or touchdown. Kneeldowns at the end of a half are discarded from this data. The net values in the third table are simply offense minus defense.

Table 4. 2006 Offensive Drive Stats

Team	Tot	Yd/Dr	Rank	Pts/Dr	Rank	TD/Dr	Rank	Punt/Dr	Rank	TO/Dr	Rank	3Out%	Rank	LOS/Dr	Rank	DSR	Rank
IND	148	41.0	1	2.80	1	0.32	1	0.32	1	0.115	5	15%	1	28.7	27	79%	1
DAL	173	33.1	4	2.25	3	0.27	3	0.32	2	0.156	22	16%	2	31.9	6	73%	2
SD	179	32.3	6	2.63	2	0.31	2	0.39	6	0.073	1	23%	14	31.6	7	72%	3
NE	178	30.8	8	2.11	5	0.25	5	0.39	7	0.146	18	20%	3	32.5	3	71%	4
NO	183	34.0	2	2.17	4	0.26	4	0.42	13	0.126	9	25%	20	29.2	25	71%	5
PIT	177	33.2	3	1.88	11	0.22	9	0.37	4	0.192	29	22%	8	27.9	29	70%	6
STL	181	32.2	7	1.96	9	0.20	11	0.41	12	0.088	2	22%	9	28.1	28	70%	7
PHI	180	33.0	5	2.01	7	0.24	6	0.43	19	0.117	6	25%	19	29.9	20	70%	8
CIN	182	30.2	9	2.03	6	0.23	7	0.42	14	0.126	10	23%	15	31.1	13	69%	9
KC	177	28.9	14	1.79	13	0.20	13	0.41	10	0.130	13	23%	17	31.3	9	69%	10
JAC	179	29.6	10	2.00	8	0.22	8	0.40	8	0.117	7	21%	5	32.5	2	68%	11
NYJ	171	29.2	13	1.73	14	0.19	14	0.43	16	0.140	16	23%	18	30.8	15	68%	12
HOU	164	26.8	20	1.50	23	0.17	21	0.46	26	0.140	15	27%	25	27.9	30	67%	13
WAS	175	29.4	11	1.66	17	0.18	15	0.46	25	0.097	3	28%	27	29.5	24	67%	14
ARI	174	28.3	15	1.65	18	0.17	20	0.38	5	0.155	21	21%	6	30.1	19	67%	15
NYG	187	26.8	21	1.83	12	0.21	10	0.41	11	0.139	14	26%	22	32.3	4	67%	16
CHI	191	28.0	16	1.90	10	0.20	12	0.40	9	0.168	27	23%	12	32.2	5	66%	17
SEA	195	25.8	25	1.61	20	0.17	18	0.44	22	0.174	28	23%	16	31.2	10	66%	18
ATL	179	29.4	12	1.56	21	0.17	19	0.43	15	0.112	4	22%	11	30.1	17	66%	19
BAL	180	27.1	19	1.71	15	0.18	16	0.48	27	0.122	8	22%	10	32.9	1	66%	20
DEN	182	28.0	17	1.68	16	0.18	17	0.44	21	0.154	20	23%	13	26.5	32	66%	21
DET	183	26.4	24	1.62	19	0.16	22	0.36	3	0.213	30	20%	4	29.9	21	66%	22
GB	194	27.9	18	1.38	26	0.14	26	0.43	18	0.165	25	25%	21	29.8	22	64%	23
MIA	185	26.5	22	1.29	28	0.12	29	0.46	24	0.130	12	22%	7	31.0	14	63%	24
TEN	183	26.5	23	1.43	25	0.15	24	0.48	28	0.142	17	27%	26	29.6	23	63%	25
CAR	193	25.4	27	1.32	27	0.14	27	0.51	32	0.130	11	29%	28	27.1	31	63%	26
MIN	193	25.4	28	1.27	29	0.14	28	0.49	29	0.161	24	29%	29	30.1	16	62%	27
SF	185	25.8	26	1.53	22	0.15	25	0.44	20	0.157	23	30%	30	30.1	18	61%	28
CLE	185	22.1	31	1.17	30	0.12	30	0.45	23	0.216	31	27%	24	31.5	8	61%	29
BUF	183	23.1	29	1.45	24	0.15	23	0.50	31	0.148	19	32%	32	31.1	11	60%	30
OAK	178	20.8	32	0.78	32	0.07	32	0.43	17	0.253	32	26%	23	31.1	12	59%	31
TB	187	22.7	30	1.02	31	0.11	31	0.50	30	0.166	26	32%	31	28.9	26	59%	32

Table 5. 2006 Defensive Drive Stats

Team	Tot	Yd/Dr	Rank	Pts/Dr	Rank	TD/Dr	Rank	Punt/Dr	Rank	TO/Dr	Rank	3Out%	Rank	LOS/Dr	Rank	DSR	Rank
BAL	189	22.7	2	1.05	1	0.11	1	0.46	10	0.206	1	29%	4	28.2	1	59%	1
CHI	205	22.5	1	1.12	2	0.12	3	0.49	4	0.200	2	28%	8	29.4	11	59%	2
JAC	182	25.1	4	1.28	4	0.14	5	0.48	5	0.132	24	28%	9	28.5	4	62%	3
MIN	186	25.4	6	1.45	5	0.13	4	0.43	17	0.172	6	28%	7	30.7	22	63%	4
NE	178	27.1	13	1.20	3	0.12	2	0.44	13	0.185	4	20%	26	28.8	5	63%	5
CAR	187	25.4	7	1.58	11	0.17	10	0.52	1	0.112	29	33%	1	29.8	15	63%	6
MIA	184	25.4	8	1.46	6	0.16	7	0.50	3	0.130	25	30%	3	29.6	14	63%	7
OAK	181	25.0	3	1.75	19	0.18	13	0.38	27	0.122	27	24%	18	35.0	32	64%	8
PIT	181	26.1	9	1.55	8	0.17	11	0.47	6	0.160	9	25%	13	32.7	30	64%	9
NO	182	26.3	10	1.62	13	0.20	20	0.52	2	0.093	31	31%	2	29.0	8	64%	10
SEA	189	26.8	12	1.66	15	0.19	15	0.47	8	0.122	26	29%	5	29.9	17	64%	11
SD	190	25.2	5	1.54	7	0.17	9	0.46	9	0.137	21	29%	6	28.4	2	64%	12
DEN	181	27.7	14	1.57	9	0.14	6	0.41	21	0.149	16	24%	17	33.5	31	65%	13
GB	193	26.7	11	1.78	21	0.20	19	0.43	16	0.171	7	27%	10	30.1	18	65%	14
BUF	182	28.2	15	1.59	12	0.18	12	0.47	7	0.121	28	26%	12	29.5	12	67%	15
CLE	182	30.4	22	1.74	17	0.19	16	0.42	18	0.148	17	23%	19	29.9	16	67%	16
PHI	182	28.9	18	1.58	10	0.17	8	0.45	11	0.154	12	25%	14	28.9	6	67%	17
TB	183	28.6	16	1.78	20	0.20	21	0.44	14	0.104	30	25%	15	31.6	26	67%	18
KC	176	29.3	20	1.72	16	0.18	14	0.42	20	0.153	13	19%	27	29.6	13	67%	19
DAL	179	29.2	19	1.82	22	0.21	22	0.40	23	0.156	11	23%	20	30.3	19	67%	20
NYG	185	28.7	17	1.87	24	0.22	24	0.37	28	0.151	14	22%	22	31.8	27	68%	21
NYJ	175	29.7	21	1.63	14	0.19	17	0.42	19	0.143	19	19%	28	29.2	10	69%	22
ATL	176	30.4	23	1.74	18	0.19	18	0.44	15	0.136	22	24%	16	28.5	3	69%	23
WAS	172	33.1	31	2.11	30	0.23	27	0.45	12	0.058	32	27%	11	29.0	7	69%	24
DET	177	31.3	25	2.09	29	0.23	26	0.38	26	0.158	10	19%	30	30.7	21	70%	25
ARI	176	31.4	27	2.00	25	0.21	23	0.33	31	0.188	3	19%	29	31.8	29	70%	26
TEN	182	32.3	29	2.14	31	0.24	31	0.37	29	0.137	20	20%	25	31.1	24	70%	27
STL	172	32.4	30	2.04	26	0.24	32	0.39	25	0.174	5	23%	21	30.5	20	71%	28
CIN	179	31.3	26	1.83	23	0.22	25	0.40	22	0.151	15	21%	23	29.0	9	71%	29
SF	178	31.1	24	2.20	32	0.24	30	0.37	30	0.146	18	17%	31	31.8	28	71%	30
HOU	165	32.1	28	2.07	27	0.23	28	0.39	24	0.133	23	21%	24	31.6	25	71%	31
IND	155	33.8	32	2.09	28	0.23	29	0.30	32	0.168	8	15%	32	30.8	23	73%	32

Table 6. 2006 Net Drive Stats

Team	Yd/Dr	Rank	Pts/Dr	Rank	TD/Dr	Rank	Punt/Dr	Rank	TO/Dr	Rank	3Out%	Rank	LOS/Dr	Rank	DSR	Rank
NE	3.7	10	0.91	2	0.14	2	−0.06	7	−0.039	5	−0.6%	15	3.7	3	8.5%	1
SD	7.0	4	1.08	1	0.14	1	−0.08	6	−0.064	3	−6.0%	5	3.2	4	8.0%	2
CHI	5.5	5	0.78	3	0.08	6	−0.09	3	−0.032	7	−5.3%	8	2.8	5	7.3%	3
BAL	4.5	7	0.66	6	0.07	7	0.02	20	−0.084	2	−6.9%	3	4.7	1	7.2%	4
NO	7.7	1	0.56	7	0.06	9	−0.10	2	0.032	26	−5.6%	7	0.2	18	6.6%	5
PIT	7.1	3	0.33	10	0.05	10	−0.10	1	0.032	25	−2.8%	10	−4.7	31	6.1%	6
IND	7.3	2	0.71	5	0.09	3	0.01	17	−0.053	4	0.0%	16	−2.1	25	5.8%	7
JAC	4.5	6	0.72	4	0.08	4	−0.08	4	−0.015	12	−6.8%	4	4.0	2	5.4%	8
DAL	3.9	9	0.43	8	0.07	8	−0.08	5	0.000	18	−7.3%	2	1.6	10	5.3%	9
PHI	4.1	8	0.43	9	0.08	5	−0.02	11	−0.037	6	0.3%	17	1.0	15	2.3%	10
SEA	−1.0	19	−0.06	16	−0.01	17	−0.03	9	0.053	28	−6.0%	6	1.3	14	1.7%	11
KC	−0.4	17	0.08	14	0.02	12	−0.01	14	−0.023	11	3.8%	25	1.7	7	1.2%	12
DEN	0.3	13	0.11	12	0.03	11	0.03	23	0.005	19	−1.2%	13	−7.0	32	0.3%	13
MIA	1.1	12	−0.17	19	−0.03	20	−0.04	8	−0.001	17	−8.3%	1	1.4	13	0.1%	14
MIN	0.0	14	−0.18	20	0.01	14	0.06	29	−0.011	14	1.1%	18	−0.6	20	−0.6%	15
CAR	0.0	15	−0.27	22	−0.04	21	−0.01	13	0.017	23	−3.6%	9	−2.7	27	−0.8%	16
GB	1.2	11	−0.41	24	−0.06	25	0.00	15	−0.006	15	−1.7%	11	−0.3	19	−0.9%	17
STL	−0.2	16	−0.08	17	−0.04	22	0.03	21	−0.086	1	−0.6%	14	−2.3	26	−1.0%	18
NYG	−1.9	22	−0.04	15	−0.01	16	0.04	25	−0.012	13	4.0%	26	0.5	17	−1.1%	19
NYJ	−0.5	18	0.10	13	0.00	15	0.00	16	−0.003	16	4.5%	27	1.6	12	−1.2%	20
CIN	−1.0	21	0.20	11	0.01	13	0.02	19	−0.024	10	2.4%	22	2.1	6	−1.5%	21
WAS	−3.7	24	−0.45	25	−0.04	24	0.02	18	0.039	27	1.3%	19	0.5	16	−2.0%	22
ATL	−1.0	20	−0.19	21	−0.03	19	−0.01	12	−0.025	9	−1.5%	12	1.6	9	−3.0%	23
ARI	−3.0	23	−0.35	23	−0.04	23	0.05	26	−0.032	8	1.9%	21	−1.8	24	−3.1%	24
HOU	−5.3	28	−0.57	28	−0.07	27	0.07	30	0.007	21	6.2%	29	−3.7	29	−3.8%	25
DET	−4.8	26	−0.47	26	−0.06	26	−0.02	10	0.055	29	1.6%	20	−0.8	21	−4.5%	26
OAK	−4.1	25	−0.98	32	−0.11	32	0.06	28	0.131	32	2.6%	23	−3.9	30	−4.8%	27
BUF	−5.1	27	−0.15	18	−0.02	18	0.04	24	0.027	24	5.9%	28	1.6	11	−6.3%	28
CLE	−8.3	32	−0.56	27	−0.07	28	0.03	22	0.068	31	3.4%	24	1.7	8	−6.7%	29
TEN	−5.9	30	−0.71	30	−0.09	29	0.11	32	0.005	20	7.0%	31	−1.5	22	−7.7%	30
TB	−5.9	31	−0.75	31	−0.10	31	0.06	27	0.062	30	7.0%	30	−2.7	28	−8.6%	31
SF	−5.3	29	−0.67	29	−0.09	30	0.07	31	0.011	22	12.3%	32	−1.7	23	−9.9%	32

Author Biographies

Lead Writer and Statistician

Aaron Schatz is the creator of FootballOutsiders.com and the proprietary statistics within *Pro Football Prospectus*. During the season, he is a regular contributor to FOXS ports.com and *ESPN the Magazine,* and covers the NFL for the *New York Sun*. He has also written for *The New York Times, The Boston Globe,* The New Republic Online, and Slate.com, and has done custom research for a number of NFL teams. Before creating FootballOutsiders.com, he was a radio disc jockey and spent three years tracking search trends online as the writer and producer of the Internet column "The Lycos 50." He has a BA in Economics from Brown University and lives in Framingham, Massachusetts with his wife Kathryn and daughter Mirinae.

Football Outsiders Staff

Bill Barnwell is a recent graduate of Northeastern University; having settled in Boston, he currently enjoys the post-collegiate lull of short-term employment, buying overly-expensive beer, post-punk non-sequiturs, and waiting for online poker to be legalized again. He should snap out of this sometime around 2009.

Alex Carnevale is a writer living in New York. A graduate of Brown University, his work has appeared on SI.com and BaseballProspectus.com, and in the pages of *n + 1* magazine. He compiles the regular "The Week in Quotes" feature for both BaseballProspectus.com and FootballOutsiders.com.

Will Carroll is the pre-eminent injury analyst in sports, continuing his Bo Jackson routine as a football and baseball injury expert. His weekly column on football injuries has been lauded by industry insiders as "our worst f#@!ing nightmare," which he takes as a compliment. He's been published pretty much everywhere and hangs out with models. (We don't get it either.) Will also writes the "Under the Knife" column at BaseballProspectus.com and worked at ESPN during the 2006 NFL season, which ended just as he predicted, with the Colts winning the Super Bowl. He's calling for a repeat.

Doug Farrar was born in Milan, Italy, and grew up with the first wave of Broncomania in Denver. He now holds true allegiance to Seattle and her ever-beleaguered Seahawks, having resided in the Emerald City since 1985. He is Editor-in-Chief of Seahawks.net and contributed to the 2005 and 2006 Scout.com fantasy football annuals as well as the 2007 Rotoworld fantasy football annual. He joined Football Outsiders in September 2006, writing the weekend wrap-up column "Manic Monday" for FOXSports.com during football season.

Like many of the Outsiders, Tim Gerheim attended Brown University. He is currently a student at The University of Texas School of Law and has interned at the NFL Players Association. He is assistant editor for FootballOutsiders.com and, during the season, fills the important role of deputy grammar police.

Football is not just a Sunday passion for Web producer Russell Levine, who covers college football for the *New York Sun* and in the weekly Football Outsiders column "Confessions of a Football Junkie." He also co-writes the weekly college picks column "Seventh Day Adventure" with Chicago lawyer and fellow Michigan grad Vinny Gauri, who contributed to the college preview article in this book. Russell lives in West Orange, New Jersey with his very understanding wife, Susan, and their two children, Trevor and Lindsay, who can already do a mean duet on "Hail to the Victors."

Indianapolis native Ned Macey is still celebrating the Colts' first Super Bowl championship since the Mayflower trucks delivered them to his hometown. Thanks to NFL Sunday Ticket, Ned could follow the Colts for every week of the glorious 2006 season while studying for his law degree at the University of Michigan. Sadly, for the purposes of this book, he was also forced to endure a season of Lions' futility despite this wonder of modern technology. During the season his column "Any Given Sunday" analyzes the biggest upset of the week, Football Outsiders-style. He lives in suburban Detroit with his wife, Melanie.

Boston native Bill Moore graduated from Babson College and is currently a hedge fund portfolio manager in New York City when he is not coordinating the activities of over two dozen volunteers each week for the Football Outsiders Game Charting Project. Although his probation period of ten years has expired, his wife has still not completely forgiven him for kicking a hole in their couch during Super Bowl XXXI.

Michael David Smith's weekly feature, "Every Play Counts," was described by the *Wall Street Journal*'s Daily Fix as "packing more game analysis into a single column than many beat writers display over a full season." He has written about football for *The New York Times, New York Sun, Orange County Register,* FOXSports.com, Deadspin.com, The New Republic Online, and *ESPN the Magazine.* He is a regular guest on WSCR sports radio in Chicago and a contributor to both AOL FanHouse and ProFootballTalk.com. Contrary to popular belief, he never appears on *Around the Horn;* that's a different Michael Smith. Our Michael lives in Chicago with his wife Sarah, a lawyer.

Mike Tanier teaches math at Audubon High School and writes numerous features for Football Outsiders and FOX Sports.com. His work has also appeared in *ESPN the Magazine,* the Rotoworld Fantasy Football Guide, the *Philadelphia Inquirer,* the *New York Sun,* and other publications. He lives in South Jersey with his wife Karen, sons C. J. and Michael, and pit bull Rosie.

Ryan Wilson was raised in North Carolina but went to school in Pittsburgh, where he became a maniacal Steelers fan. On game days, he sports a homemade reversible Steelers jersey honoring either Troy Polamalu or Casey Hampton, depending on his mood. Ryan is the main man behind the Football Outsiders weblog, Extra Points, and lives in the Washington, D. C. area with his wife, Audrey.

Special Contributors

Dr. Benjamin Alamar is the founding editor of the *Journal of Quantitative Analysis in Sports* and has consulted for various NFL and NBA franchises. He holds a doctorate in economics from the University of California at Santa Barbara.

Jim Armstrong is a software developer by day and a Packers fan by birthright. His work has appeared in *ESPN the Magazine* as well as on FootballOutsiders.com and in previous editions of *Pro Football Prospectus.* He lives in the Boston area with his wife, Lynne, and their daughter, Carrie.

Maury Brown is the creator of BizofBaseball.com as well as the new Business of Sports network. He has covered sports business for both *The Hardball Times* and Baseball Prospectus, in print and online, and lives in Portland, Oregon with his loving and patient wife, Glenna, and sons Tyler and Travis.

Shawn Krest left a lucrative career building fraud models for a top-three credit card company so he could write about football. His NFL coverage for Buffalo's *Sports & Leisure Magazine* has been honored by the Pro Football Writers Association in their annual writing awards. He lives in western New York with his wife, five daughters, two dogs, a cat, and a parrot.

David Lewin, originally from Wayland, Massachusetts, is a 20-year-old junior at Macalester College in St. Paul, Minnesota. During the season, he plays for the Macalester football team. In the offseason, in addition to contributing to Football Outsiders, he works as a statistical analyst for an NBA franchise.

Jason McKinley is a former scientist, current social worker, and (he hopes) future actuary. He lives in St. Louis with his wife, Laura, and roots for the Rams.

Acknowledgments

As always, we would like to start by thanking Gregg Easterbrook, whose support and friendship helped Football Outsiders to blossom back in 2003. We are also grateful for the support of Prospectus Entertainment Ventures, Inc., particularly Nate Silver, Christina Kahrl, Steven Goldman, and Joe Sheehan. They have made it possible for us to write three books—and not just by giving us the title. We also want to thank Cliff Corcoran for shepherding this third book along, as well as Don Rodgers for layout, and Mary Pomponio for promotion.

We cannot express enough gratitude to all the volunteers who have participated in the Football Outsiders game charting project over the last two years. There are too many contributors to name everyone, but we do want to mention those charters who have done the most to build the data. They include Sergio Becerril Lopez, Bill Benetti, David Blevins, Cory Cook, Dave DuPlantis, Tom Gower, Tom Massimo, Louis Mazza, Sean McCormick, Brian McIntyre, Scott Metcalf, Nate Richards, Vince Rocchi, Bryan Tang, and Vince Verhei, as well as a number of writers in this book. Thanks to Michael Mulvihill, Theo Westgeest, and Mark Kamal for providing game telecasts that we needed for the charting project. Thanks also to the San Francisco 49ers and Carolina Panthers for providing missing gamebooks from 1996.

Some of the ideas in this book, or portions of the essays, originally appeared as part of our work at FOXSports.com or in the *New York Sun.* We would like to thank Ed Bunnell and Jim Reineking at FOXSports.com, as well as Matt Oshinsky and Geoff Foster at the *Sun.* Thanks also to Bob Goetz, who gave us the chance to write for *The New York Times;* Scott Burton and Chad Millman, who gave us a shot at *ESPN The Magazine;* Jamie Mottram from AOL Fanhouse; Will Leitch from Deadspin, who invited us to help cover the NFL draft; and Mike Florio from ProFootball Talk.com.

We want to acknowledge the support of many other folks, including Bruce Allen, Matt Burke, Greg Cosell, Gabriel Desjardins, Doug Drinen, Eddie Epstein, Michael Epstein from ESPNews, Stefan Fatsis, Mike Frazier, Bob Ganley, Jascha Hoffman, John Hollinger, Chris Holtege and

Steve Alic at the NFL, Sam Hudson and Steve Deutsch at Foley-Hoag, Ron Jaworski, K. C. Joyner, Richard Just, King Kaufman, Bill Kent and everybody at Sports Management Worldwide (visit SMWW.com), Peter King, Sydelle Kramer, William Krasker, Russ Lande, David Leonhardt, Oleg Lyubner, Jeff Ma, Paraag Marathe, Jeff Merron, Daryl Morey, Meyer Freeman and Drew Mahlic of the Oregon Sports Authority, Rob Neyer (who gave us the idea for the Cam Cameron essay), Dean Oliver, Kevin Pelton, Mike Reiss, Richard Rosen, Gregg Rosenthal, David Schoenfeld, Jim Schwartz, Tom Seeley, Michael "not David" Smith, all the people from Scout.com, the brothers of Zeta Delta Xi at Brown University, and anybody who has written about us anywhere at any time.

A special thank you to Roland Beech of TwoMinute Warning.com and 82games.com for the original ideas that spawned our individual defense statistics, and to Mike Sando of the *Tacoma News-Tribune* for some very specific advice.

Thanks to all the readers of Football Outsiders, particularly everyone who participates in the online discussions. Thanks to the interns who helped compile data for this book: Daniel Haverkamp, Jeremiah Methven, Darrel Michaud, Ryan Restivo, Alex Rubin, Jake Schumaker, and John Zerebynsky. Thanks to the folks from Football Outsiders whose work you won't see in this book, particularly designer Benjy Rose, cartoonist Jason Beattie, programmers Pat Laverty and Sean McCall, and departed writers Al Bogdan, Ian Dembsky, and Vivek Ramgopal. Thanks to Eliot Horowitz and Dennis Doughty, who wrote the data parser, John Argentiero, who writes all the stat compilers, and Chris Povirk, who has done a little bit of everything. Thanks to Jeff Bathurst for help covering the league this offseason while we were busy writing the book. Thanks to anyone we mistakenly forgot.

Finally, thanks to all our wives and children, as well as three people in particular whose help allowed us to complete the extensive amount of writing in this book: Steve Ireland, the greatest student teacher in all of South Jersey, and Aaron's mother and stepfather, Paula and Roy Klein, who are the best grandparents that any little girl could have—especially when the little girl's mother is writing a graduate school thesis and her father is writing a 500-page book, and the deadlines are within a week of each other.